Oxford
Color German
Dictionary Plus

Revised second edition

GERMAN–ENGLISH
ENGLISH–GERMAN

DEUTSCH–ENGLISCH
ENGLISCH–DEUTSCH

OXFORD
UNIVERSITY PRESS

OXFORD
UNIVERSITY PRESS

Great Clarendon Street, Oxford OX2 6DP

Oxford University Press is a department of the University of Oxford.
It furthers the University's objective of excellence in research, scholarship,
and education by publishing worldwide in

Oxford New York

Auckland Bangkok Buenos Aires Cape Town Chennai
Dar es Salaam Delhi Hong Kong Istanbul Karachi Kolkata
Kuala Lumpur Madrid Melbourne Mexico City Mumbai Nairobi
São Paulo Shanghai Taipei Tokyo Toronto

Oxford is a registered trade mark of Oxford University Press
in the UK and in certain other countries

British Library Cataloguing in Publication Data

Data available

Library of Congress Cataloging in Publication Data

Data available
ISBN 0-19-860901-9
ISBN 0-19-860899-3 (US edition)

10 9 8 7 6 5 4 3 2

Typeset by Morton
Word Processing Ltd
Printed in China

Contents

Preface

The *Oxford Color German Dictionary Plus* is a dictionary designed primarily for students of German. Its clear presentation and use of color headwords make it easily accessible. It contains completely new sections, not found in the *Oxford Color German Dictionary*, on German life and culture, letter-writing, and German grammar, making it even more useful for students up to intermediate level.

List of contributors

Revised Second Edition

Editor:
Gunhild Prowe

Second Edition

Editors:
Roswitha Morris
Robin Sawers

Supplementary Material:
Robin Sawers
Neil and Roswitha Morris
Valerie Grundy
Eva Vennebusch

Data Capture:
Susan Wilkin
Anne McConnell
Anna Cotgreave

Proof-reading:
Andrew Hodgson

First Edition

Editors:
Gunhild Prowe
Jill Schneider

Introduction

The text of this dictionary reflects recent changes to the spelling of German ratified in July 1996. The symbol * has been introduced to refer from the old spelling to the new, preferred one:

> **As*** *nt* -ses, -se *s.* **Ass**
> **dasein*** *vi sep (sein)* **da sein,** *s.* **da**
> **Schiffahrt*** *f s.* **Schifffahrt**

Where both the old and new forms are valid, an equals sign = is used to refer to the preferred form:

> **aufwändig** *a* = **aufwendig**
> **Tunfisch** *m* = **Thunfisch**

When such forms follow each other alphabetically, they are given with commas, with the preferred form in first place:

> **Panther, Panter** *m* -s, -
> panther

In phrases, *od* (oder) is used:

> …**deine(r,s)** *poss pron* yours;
> **die D~en** *od* **d~en** *pl* your family *sg*

On the English–German side, only the preferred German form is given.

- A swung dash ~ represents the headword or that part of the headword preceding a vertical bar |. The initial letter of a German headword is given to show whether or not it is a capital.

- The vertical bar | follows the part of the headword which is not repeated in compounds or derivatives.

- Square brackets [ ] are used for optional material.

- Angled brackets < > are used after a verb translation to indicate the object; before a verb translation to indicate the subject; before an adjective to indicate a typical noun which it qualifies.

- Round brackets ( ) are used for field or style labels (see list on pages xxiii–xxv), and for explanatory matter.

- A box □ indicates a new part of speech within an entry.

- *od* (oder) and *or* denote that words or portions of a phrase are synonymous. An oblique stroke / is used where there is a difference in usage or meaning.

- ≈ is used where no exact equivalent exists in the other language.

- A dagger † indicates that a German verb is irregular and that the parts can be found in the verb table on pages 601–606. Compound verbs are not listed there as they follow the pattern of the basic verb.

- The stressed vowel is marked in a German headword by ‗ (long) or . (short). A phonetic transcription is only given for words which do not follow the normal rules of pronunciation. These rules can be found on page xi.

- German headword nouns are followed by the gender and, with the exception of compound nouns, by the genitive and plural. These are only given at compound nouns if they present some difficulty. Otherwise the user should refer to the final element.

- Nouns that decline like adjectives are entered as follows: **-e(r)** *m/f*, **-e(s)** *nt*.

- Adjectives which have no undeclined form are entered in the feminine form with the masculine and neuter in brackets **-e(r,s)**.

- The reflexive pronoun **sich** is accusative unless marked (*dat*).

Proprietary terms

This dictionary includes some words which are, or are asserted to be, proprietary names or trademarks. Their inclusion does not imply that they have acquired for legal purposes a non-proprietary or general significance, nor is any other judgement implied concerning their legal status. In cases where the editor has some evidence that a word is used as a proprietary name or trademark this is indicated by the letter (P), but no judgement concerning the legal status of such words is made or implied thereby.

Phonetic symbols used for German words

a	Hand	hant	ŋ	lang	laŋ
a:	Bahn	ba:n	o	Moral	mo'ra:l
ɐ	Ober	'o:bɐ	o:	Boot	bo:t
ɐ̯	Uhr	u:ɐ̯	ǫ	loyal	lǫa'ja:l
ã	Conférencier	kõferã'sɪ̯e:	õ	Konkurs	kõ'kʊrs
ã:	Abonnement	abɔnə'mã:	õ:	Ballon	ba'lõ:
aɪ̯	weit	vaɪ̯t	ɔ	Post	pɔst
aʊ̯	Haut	haʊ̯t	ø	Ökonom	øko'no:m
b	Ball	bal	ø:	Öl	ø:l
ç	ich	ɪç	œ	göttlich	'gœtlɪç
d	dann	dan	ɔy	heute	'hɔytə
dʒ	Gin	dʒɪn	p	Pakt	pakt
e	Metall	me'tal	r	Rast	rast
e:	Beet	be:t	s	Hast	hast
ɛ	mästen	'mɛstən	ʃ	Schal	ʃa:l
ɛ:	wählen	'vɛ:lən	t	Tal	ta:l
ɛ̃	Cousin	ku'zɛ̃:	ts	Zahl	tsa:l
ə	Nase	'na:zə	tʃ	Couch	kaʊ̯tʃ
f	Faß	fas	u	Kupon	ku'põ:
g	Gast	gast	u:	Hut	hu:t
h	haben	'ha:bən	ụ	aktuell	ak'tụɛl
i	Rivale	ri'va:lə	ʊ	Pult	pʊlt
i:	viel	fi:l	v	was	vas
ị	Aktion	ak'tsi̯o:n	x	Bach	bax
ɪ	Birke	'bɪrkə	y	Physik	fy'zi:k
j	ja	ja:	y:	Rübe	'ry:bə
k	kalt	kalt	ỹ	Nuance	'nỹã:sə
l	Last	last	ʏ	Fülle	'fʏlə
m	Mast	mast	z	Nase	'na:zə
n	Naht	na:t	ʒ	Regime	re'ʒi:m

ʔ Glottal stop, e.g. Koordination / koʔɔrdina'tsion /.

: length sign after a vowel, e.g. Chrom / kro:m /.

' Stress mark before stressed syllable, e.g. Balkon / bal'kõ:/.

Guide to German pronunciation

Consonants

Produced as in English with the following exceptions:

b	as	p	
d	as	t	*at the end of a word or syllable*
g	as	k	

ch	as in Scottish lo<u>ch</u>		*after a, o, u, au*
	like an exaggerated h as in <u>h</u>uge		*after i, e, ä, ö, ü, eu, ei*
-chs	as	x	(as in bo<u>x</u>)
-ig	as	-ich / ıç /	*when a suffix*
j	as	y	(as in <u>y</u>es)
ps			the p is pronounced
pn			
qu	as	k + v	
s	as	z	(as in <u>z</u>ero) *at the beginning of a word*
	as	s	(as in bu<u>s</u>) *at the end of a word or syllable, before a consonant, or when doubled*
sch	as	sh	
sp	as	shp	*at the beginning of a word*
st	as	sht	*at the beginning of a word*
v	as	f	(as in <u>f</u>or)
	as	v	(as in <u>v</u>ery) *within a word*
w	as	v	(as in <u>v</u>ery)
z	as	ts	

Vowels

Approximately as follows:

a	short	as	u	(as in b<u>u</u>t)
	long	as	a	(as in c<u>a</u>r)
e	short	as	e	(as in p<u>e</u>n)
	long	as	a	(as in p<u>a</u>per)
i	short	as	i	(as in b<u>i</u>t)
	long	as	ee	(as in qu<u>ee</u>n)
o	short	as	o	(as in h<u>o</u>t)
	long	as	o	(as in p<u>o</u>pe)
u	short	as	oo	(as in f<u>oo</u>t)
	long	as	oo	(as in b<u>oo</u>t)

Vowels are always short before a double consonant, and long when followed by an h or when double

ie	is pronounced	ee	(as in k<u>ee</u>p)

Diphthongs

au	as	ow	(as in h<u>ow</u>)
ei ai	as	y	(as in m<u>y</u>)
eu äu	as	oy	(as in b<u>oy</u>)

Pronunciation of the alphabet

English/Englisch		German/Deutsch
eɪ	a	aː
biː	b	beː
siː	c	͟tseː
diː	d	deː
iː	e	eː
ef	f	ɛf
dʒiː	g	geː
eɪtʃ	h	haː
aɪ	i	iː
dʒeɪ	j	jɔt
keɪ	k	kaː
el	l	ɛl
em	m	ɛm
en	n	ɛn
əʊ	o	oː
piː	p	peː
kjuː	q	kuː
aː(r)	r	ɛr
es	s	ɛs
tiː	t	teː
juː	u	uː
viː	v	faŭ
'dʌbljuː	w	veː
eks	x	ɪks
waɪ	y	'ʏpsilɔn
zed	z	͟tsɛt
eɪ umlaut	ä	ɛː
əʊ umlaut	ö	øː
juː umlaut	ü	yː
es'zed	ß	ɛs'͟tsɛt

Glossary of grammatical terms

Abbreviation A shortened form of a word or phrase: **etc.** = **usw.**

Accusative The case of a direct object; some German prepositions take the accusative

Active In the active form the subject of the verb performs the action: **he asked** = **er hat gefragt**

Adjective A word describing a noun: **a** *red* **pencil** = **ein** *roter* **Stift**

Adverb A word that describes or changes the meaning of a verb, an adjective, or another adverb: **she sings** *beautifully* = **sie singt** *schön*

Article The definite article, **the** = **der/die/das**, and indefinite article, **a/an** = **ein/eine/ein**, used in front of a noun

Attributive An adjective or noun is attributive when it is used directly before a noun: **the** *black* **dog** = **der** *schwarze* **Hund**; *farewell* **speech** = **Abschiedsrede**

Auxiliary verb One of the verbs – as German **haben, sein, werden** – used to form the perfect or future tense: **I will help** = **ich** *werde* **helfen**

Cardinal number A whole number representing a quantity: **one/two/three** = **eins/zwei/drei**

Case The form of a noun, pronoun, adjective, or article that shows the part it plays in a sentence; there are four cases in German – nominative, accusative, genitive, and dative

Clause A self-contained section of a sentence that contains a subject and a verb

Collective noun A noun that is singular in form but refers to a group of individual persons or things, e.g. **royalty, grain**

Collocate A word that regularly occurs with another; in German, **Buch** is a typical collocate of the verb **lesen**

Comparative The form of an adjective or adverb that makes it "more": **smaller** = **kleiner**, **more clearly** = **klarer**

Compound adjective An adjective formed from two or more separate words: **selbstbewusst (selbst + bewusst)** = **self-confident**

Compound noun A noun formed from two or more separate words: **der Flughafen (Flug + Hafen)** = **airport**

Compound verb A verb formed by adding a prefix to a simple verb; in German, some compound verbs are separable **(an|fangen)**, and some are inseparable **(verlassen)**

Conditional tense A tense of a verb that expresses what would happen if something else occurred: **he would go** = **er würde gehen**

Conjugation Variation of the form of a verb to show tense, person, mood, etc.

Conjunction A word used to join clauses together: **and = und, because = weil**

Dative The case of an indirect object; many German prepositions take the dative

Declension The form of a noun, pronoun, or adjective that corresponds to a particular case, number, or gender; some German nouns decline like adjectives, e.g. **Beamte, Taube**

Definite article: the = der/die/das

Demonstrative pronoun A pronoun indicating the person or thing referred to; *this* is my bicycle = *das* ist mein Fahrrad

Direct object The noun or pronoun directly affected by the verb: he caught *the ball* = er fing *den Ball*

Direct speech A speaker's actual words or the use of these in writing

Ending Letters added to the stem of verbs, as well as to nouns and adjectives, according to tense, case, etc.

Feminine One of the three noun genders in German: **die Frau = the woman**

Future tense The tense of a verb that refers to something that will happen in the future: I will go = ich werde gehen

Gender One of the three groups of nouns in German: masculine, feminine, or neuter

Genitive The case that shows possession; some prepositions in German take the genitive

Imperative A form of a verb that expresses a command: **go away! = geh weg!**

Imperfect tense The tense of a verb that refers to an uncompleted or a habitual action in the past: I went there every Friday = ich ging jeden Freitag dorthin

Impersonal verb A verb in English used only with 'it', and in German only with 'es': it is raining = es regnet

Indeclinable adjective An adjective that has no inflected forms, as German **klasse, Moskauer**

Indefinite article: a/an = ein/eine/ein

Indefinite pronoun A pronoun that does not identify a specific person or object: **one = man, something = etwas**

Indicative form The form of a verb used when making a statement of fact or asking questions of fact: he is just coming = er kommt gleich

Indirect object The noun or pronoun indirectly affected by the verb, at which the direct object is aimed: I gave *him* the book = ich gab *ihm* das Buch

Indirect speech A report of what someone has said which does not reproduce the exact words

Infinitive The basic part of a verb: **to play = spielen**

Inflect To change the ending

or form of a word to show its tense or its grammatical relation to other words: **gehe** and **gehst** are inflected forms of the verb **gehen**

Inseparable verb A verb with a prefix that can never be separated from it: **verstehen, ich verstehe**

Interjection A sound, word, or remark expressing a strong feeling such as anger, fear, or joy: **oh!** = **ach!**

Interrogative pronoun A pronoun that asks a question: **who?** = **wer?**

Intransitive verb A verb that does not have a direct object: **he died suddenly** = **er ist plötzlich gestorben**

Irregular verb A verb that does not follow one of the set patterns and has its own individual forms

Masculine One of the three noun genders in German: **der Mann** = **the man**, **der Stuhl** = **the chair**

Modal verb A verb that is used with another verb (not a model) to express permission, obligation, possibility, etc., as German **können, sollen,** English **might, should**

Negative expressing refusal or denial; **there aren't any** = **es gibt keine**

Neuter One of the three noun genders in German: **das Buch** = **the book**, **das Kind** = **the child**

Nominative The case of the subject of a sentence; in sentences with **sein** and **werden** the noun after the verb is in the nominative: **that is my car** = **das ist mein Auto**

Noun A word that names a person or a thing

Number The state of being either singular or plural

Object The word or words naming the person or thing acted upon by a verb or preposition, as '**Buch**' in **er las das Buch** or '**ihm**' in **ich traue ihm**

Ordinal number A number that shows a person's or thing's position in a series: **the *twenty-first* century** = **das *einundzwanzigste* Jahrhundert**, **the *second* door on the left** = **die *zweite* Tür links**

Part of speech A grammatical term for the function of a word; noun, verb, adjective, etc., are parts of speech.

Passive In the passive form the subject of the verb experiences the action rather than performs it: **he was asked** = **er wurde gefragt**

Past participle The part of a verb used to form past tenses: **she had *gone*, er hat *gelogen***

Perfect tense The tense of a verb that refers to a completed action in the past or an action that started in the past and is still going on: **I have already eaten** = **ich habe schon gegessen; I have been reading all day** = **ich habe den ganzen Tag gelesen**

Person Any of the three groups of personal pronouns

and forms taken by verbs; the **first person** (e.g. **I/ich**) refers to the person(s) speaking, the **second person** (e.g. **you/du**) refers to the person(s) spoken to; the **third person** (e.g. **he/er**) refers to the persons spoken about

Personal pronoun A pronoun that refers to a person or thing: **he/she/it = er/sie/es**

Phrasal verb A verb in English combined with a preposition or an adverb to have a particular meaning: **run away = weglaufen**

Phrase A self-contained section of a sentence that does not contain a full verb

Pluperfect tense The tense of a verb that refers to something that happened before a particular point in the past: **als ich ankam, *war* er schon *losgefahren* = when I arrived, he *had* already *left***

Plural Of nouns etc., referring to more than one: **the trees = die Bäume**

Possessive adjective An adjective that shows possession, belonging to someone or something; **my = mein/meine/mein**

Possessive pronoun A pronoun that shows possession, belonging to someone or something: **mine = meiner/meine/meins**

Predicate The part of a sentence that says something about the **subject**, e.g. **went home** in **John went home**

Predicative An adjective is predicative when it comes after a verb such as **be** or **become** in English, or after **sein** or **werden** in German: **she is beautiful = sie ist schön**

Prefix A letter or group of letters added to the beginning of a word to change its meaning; in German, the prefix can move from separable verbs (**an|fangen**), but stays fixed to inseparable verbs (**verlassen**)

Preposition A word that stands in front of a noun or pronoun, relating it to the rest of the sentence; in German prepositions are always followed by a particular case, usually either the accusative or dative, but occasionally the genitive: **with = mit (+ dative)**, **for = für (+ accusative)**, **because of = wegen (+ genitive)**

Present participle The part of a verb that in English ends in –**ing**, and in German adds –**d** to the infinitive: **asking = fragend**

Present tense The tense of a verb that refers to something happening now: **I make = ich mache**

Pronoun A word that stands instead of a noun: **he = er, she = sie, mine = meiner/meine/meins**

Proper noun A name of a person, place, institution, etc., in English written with a capital letter at the start; **Germany**, the **Atlantic**, **Karl**, **Europa** are all proper nouns

Reflexive pronoun A pronoun that goes with a

reflexive verb: in German **mich, dich, sich, uns, euch, sich**

Reflexive verb A verb whose object is the same as its subject; in German, it is used with a reflexive pronoun: **du sollst dich waschen = you should wash yourself**

Regular verb A verb that follows a set pattern in its different forms

Relative pronoun A pronoun that introduces a subordinate clause, relating to a person or thing mentioned in the main clause: **the man *who* visited us = der Mann, *der* uns besucht hat**

Reported Speech Another name for **Indirect speech**

Sentence A sequence of words, with a subject and a verb, that can stand on their own to make a statement, ask a question, or give a command

Separable verb A verb with a prefix that can be separated from it in some tenses: **anfangen, anzufangen, angefangen**, but **ich fange an, du fingst an**

Singular Of nouns etc., referring to just one: **the tree = der Baum**

Stem The part of a verb to which endings are added; **fahr-** is the stem of **fahren**

Subject In a clause or sentence, the noun or pronoun that causes the action of the verb: ***he* caught the ball = *er* fing den Ball**

Subjunctive A verb form that is used to express doubt or unlikelihood: **if I were to tell you that ... = wenn ich dir sagen würde, dass ...**

Subordinate clause A clause which adds information to the main clause of a sentence but cannot be used as a sentence by itself

Suffix A letter or group of letters joined to the end of a word to make another word, as **–heit** in **Schönheit**

Superlative The form of an adjective or adverb that makes it "most": **the *smallest* house = das *kleinste* Haus, most clearly = am klarsten**

Tense The form of a verb that tells when the action takes place: present, future, imperfect, perfect, pluperfect

Transitive verb A verb that is used with a direct object: **she read the book = sie las das Buch**

Verb A word or group of words that describes an action: **the children *are playing* = die Kinder *spielen***

Abbreviations/Abkürzungen

English	Abbr	German
adjective	*a*	Adjektiv
abbreviation	*abbr*	Abkürzung
accusative	*acc*	Akkusativ
Administration	*Admin*	Administration
adverb	*adv*	Adverb
American	*Amer*	amerikanisch
Anatomy	*Anat*	Anatomie
Archaeology	*Archaeol*	Archäologie
Architecture	*Archit*	Architektur
Astronomy	*Astr*	Astronomie
attributive	*attrib*	attributiv
Austrian	*Aust*	österreichisch
Motor vehicles	*Auto*	Automobil
Aviation	*Aviat*	Luftfahrt
Biology	*Biol*	Biologie
Botany	*Bot*	Botanik
Chemistry	*Chem*	Chemie
collective	*coll*	Kollektivum
Commerce	*Comm*	Handel
conjunction	*conj*	Konjunktion
Cookery	*Culin*	Kochkunst
dative	*dat*	Dativ
definite article	*def art*	bestimmter Artikel
demonstrative	*dem*	Demonstrativ-
dialect	*dial*	Dialekt
Electricity	*Electr*	Elektrizität
something	*etw*	etwas
feminine	*f*	Femininum
figurative	*fig*	figurativ
genitive	*gen*	Genitiv
Geography	*Geog*	Geographie
Geology	*Geol*	Geologie
Geometry	*Geom*	Geometrie
Grammar	*Gram*	Grammatik
Horticulture	*Hort*	Gartenbau
impersonal	*impers*	unpersönlich
indefinite article	*indef art*	unbestimmter Artikel
indefinite pronoun	*indef pron*	unbestimmtes Pronomen
infinitive	*inf*	Infinitiv

inseparable	*insep*	untrennbar
interjection	*int*	Interjektion
invariable	*inv*	unveränderlich
irregular	*irreg*	unregelmäßig
someone	*jd*	jemand
someone	*jdm*	jemandem
someone	*jdn*	jemanden
someone's	*jds*	jemandes
Journalism	*Journ*	Journalismus
Law	*Jur*	Jura
Language	*Lang*	Sprache
literary	*liter*	dichterisch
masculine	*m*	Maskulinum
Mathematics	*Math*	Mathematik
Medicine	*Med*	Medizin
Meteorology	*Meteorol*	Meteorologie
Military	*Mil*	Militär
Mineralogy	*Miner*	Mineralogie
Music	*Mus*	Musik
noun	*n*	Substantiv
Nautical	*Naut*	nautisch
North German	*N Ger*	Norddeutsch
nominative	*nom*	Nominativ
neuter	*nt*	Neutrum
or	*od*	oder
Proprietary term	*P*	Warenzeichen
pejorative	*pej*	abwertend
Photography	*Phot*	Fotografie
Physics	*Phys*	Physik
plural	*pl*	Plural
Politics	*Pol*	Politik
possessive	*poss*	Possessiv-
past participle	*pp*	zweites Partizip
predicative	*pred*	prädikativ
prefix	*pref*	Präfix
preposition	*prep*	Präposition
present	*pres*	Präsens
present participle	*pres p*	erstes Partizip
pronoun	*pron*	Pronomen
Psychology	*Psych*	Psychologie
past tense	*pt*	Präteritum
Railway	*Rail*	Eisenbahn
reflexive	*refl*	reflexiv
regular	*reg*	regelmäßig
relative	*rel*	Relativ-
Religion	*Relig*	Religion

see	*s.*	siehe
School	*Sch*	Schule
separable	*sep*	trennbar
singular	*sg*	Singular
South German	*S Ger*	Süddeutsch
someone	*s.o.*	jemand
something	*sth*	etwas
Technical	*Techn*	Technik
Telephone	*Teleph*	Telefon
Textiles	*Tex*	Textilien
Theatre	*Theat*	Theater
Television	*TV*	Fernsehen
Typography	*Typ*	Typographie
University	*Univ*	Universität
auxiliary verb	*v aux*	Hilfsverb
intransitive verb	*vi*	intransitives Verb
reflexive verb	*vr*	reflexives Verb
transitive verb	*vt*	transitives Verb
vulgar	*vulg*	vulgär
Zoology	*Zool*	Zoologie
familiar	!	familiär
slang	✖	Slang
old spelling	*	alte Schreibung

German–English Dictionary

Aal *m* -[e]s, -e eel

Aas *nt* -es carrion; swine

ab *prep* (+ *dat*) from ● *adv* off; (*weg*) away; (*auf Fahrplan*) departs; **ab und zu** now and then; **auf und ab** up and down

abändern *vt sep* alter; (*abwandeln*) modify

Abbau *m* dismantling; (*Kohlen-*) mining. **a~en** *vt sep* dismantle; mine <*Kohle*>

abbeißen† *vt sep* bite off

abbeizen *vt sep* strip

abberufen† *vt sep* recall

abbestellen *vt sep* cancel; **jdn a~** put s.o. off

abbiegen† *vi sep* (*sein*) turn off; **[nach] links a~** turn left

Abbildung *f* -, -en illustration

abblättern *vi sep* (*sein*) flake off

abblend|en *vt/i sep* (*haben*) **[die Scheinwerfer] a~en** dip one's headlights. **A~licht** *nt* dipped headlights *pl*

abbrechen† *v sep* ● *vt* break off; (*abreißen*) demolish; (*Computer*) cancel ● *vi* (*sein/haben*) break off

abbrennen† *v sep* ● *vt* burn off; (*niederbrennen*) burn down ● *vi* (*sein*) burn down

abbringen† *vt sep* dissuade (**von** from)

Abbruch *m* demolition; (*Beenden*) breaking off

abbuchen *vt sep* debit

abbürsten *vt sep* brush down; (*entfernen*) brush off

abdanken *vi sep* (*haben*) resign; <*Herrscher:*> abdicate

abdecken *vt sep* uncover; (*abnehmen*) take off; (*zudecken*) cover; **den Tisch a~** clear the table

abdichten *vt sep* seal

abdrehen *vt sep* turn off

Abdruck *m* (*pl* -̈e) impression. **a~en** *vt sep* print

abdrücken *vt/i sep* (*haben*) fire; **sich a~** leave an impression

Abend *m* -s, -e evening; **am A~** in the evening; **heute A~** this evening, tonight; **gestern A~** yesterday evening, last night. **A~brot** *nt* supper. **A~essen** *nt* dinner; (*einfacher*) supper. **A~mahl** *nt* (*Relig*) [Holy] Communion. **a~s** *adv* in the evening

Abenteuer *nt* -s,- adventure; (*Liebes-*) affair. **a~lich** *a* fantastic

aber *conj* but; **oder a~** or else ● *adv* (*wirklich*) really

Aber|glaube *m* superstition. **a~gläubisch** *a* superstitious

abfahr|en *v sep* ● *vi* (*sein*) leave; <*Auto:*> drive off ● *vt* take away; (*entlangfahren*) drive along; use <*Fahrkarte*>; **abgefahrene Reifen** worn tyres. **A~t** *f* departure; (*Talfahrt*) descent; (*Piste*) run; (*Ausfahrt*) exit

Abfall *m* refuse, rubbish; (*auf der Straße*) litter; (*Industrie-*) waste

abfallen† *vi sep* (*sein*) drop, fall; (*übrig bleiben*) be left (**für** for); (*sich neigen*) slope away. **a~d** *a* sloping

Abfallhaufen *m* rubbish-dump

abfällig *a* disparaging

abfangen† *vt sep* intercept

abfärben *vi sep* (*haben*) <*Farbe:*> run; <*Stoff:*> not be colour-fast

abfassen *vt sep* draft

abfertigen *vt sep* attend to; (*zollamtlich*) clear; **jdn kurz a~** give s.o. short shrift

abfeuern *vt sep* fire

abfind|en† *vt sep* pay off; (*entschädigen*) compensate; **sich a~en mit** come to terms with. **A~ung** *f* -, **-en** compensation

abfliegen† *vi sep* (*sein*) fly off; (*Aviat*) take off

abfließen† *vi sep* (*sein*) drain *or* run away

Abflug *m* (*Aviat*) departure

Abfluss *m* drainage; (*Öffnung*) drain. **A~rohr** *nt* drain-pipe

abfragen *vt sep* **jdn** *od* **jdm Vokabeln a~** test s.o. on vocabulary

Abfuhr *f* - removal; (*fig*) rebuff

abführ|en *vt sep* take *or* lead away. **A~mittel** *nt* laxative

abfüllen *vt sep* **auf** *od* **in Flaschen a~** bottle

Abgase *ntpl* exhaust fumes

abgeben† *vt sep* hand in; (*abliefern*) deliver; (*verkaufen*) sell; (*zur Aufbewahrung*) leave; (*Fußball*) pass; (*ausströmen*) give off; (*abfeuern*) fire; (*verlauten lassen*) give; cast <*Stimme*>; **jdm etw a~** give s.o. a share of sth

abgehen† *v sep* ● *vi* (*sein*) leave; (*Theat*) exit; (*sich lösen*) come off; (*abgezogen werden*) be deducted ● *vt* walk along

abgehetzt *a* harassed. **abgelegen** *a* remote. **abgeneigt** *a* **etw** (*dat*) **nicht abgeneigt sein** not be averse to sth. **abgenutzt** *a* worn. **Abgeordnete(r)** *m/f* deputy; (*Pol*) Member of Parliament. **abgepackt** *a* pre-packed

abgeschieden *a* secluded

abgeschlossen *a* (*fig*) complete; <*Wohnung*> self-contained. **abgesehen** *prep* apart (from **von**). **abgespannt** *a* exhausted. **abgestanden** *a* stale. **abgestorben** *a* dead; <*Glied*> numb. **abgetragen** *a* worn. **abgewetzt** *a* threadbare

abgewinnen† *vt sep* win (**jdm** from s.o.); **etw** (*dat*) **Geschmack a~** get a taste for sth

abgewöhnen *vt sep* **jdm/sich das Rauchen a~** cure s.o. of/ give up smoking

abgießen† *vt sep* pour off; drain <*Gemüse*>

Abgott *m* idol

abgöttisch *adv* **a~ lieben** idolize

abgrenz|en *vt sep* divide off; (*fig*) define. **A~ung** *f* - demarcation

Abgrund *m* abyss; (*fig*) depths *pl*

abgucken *vt sep* Ⓘ copy

Abguss *m* cast

abhacken *vt sep* chop off

abhaken *vt sep* tick off

abhalten† *vt sep* keep off; (*hindern*) keep, prevent (**von** from); (*veranstalten*) hold

abhanden *adv* **a~ kommen** get lost

Abhandlung *f* treatise

Abhang *m* slope

abhängen¹ *vt sep* (*reg*) take down; (*abkuppeln*) uncouple

abhäng|en²† *vi sep* (*haben*) depend (**von** on). **a~ig** *a* dependent (**von** on). **A~igkeit** *f* - dependence

abhärten *vt sep* toughen up

abheben† *v sep* ● *vt* take off; (*vom Konto*) withdraw; **sich a~** stand out (**gegen** against) ● *vi* (*haben*) (*Cards*) cut [the cards]; (*Aviat*) take off; <*Rakete:*> lift off

abheften *vt sep* file

Abhilfe *f* remedy

abholen *vt sep* collect

abhör|en *vt sep* listen to; (*überwachen*) tap; **jdn** *od* **jdm Vokabeln a~en** test s.o. on vocabulary. **A~gerät** *nt* bugging device

Abitur *nt* **-s** ≈ A levels *pl*

abkaufen *vt sep* buy (*dat* from)

abklingen† *vi sep* (*sein*) die away; (*nachlassen*) subside

abkochen *vt sep* boil

abkommen† vi sep (sein) a~ von stray from; (aufgeben) give up. A~ nt -s,- agreement

Abkömmling m -s, -e descendant

abkratzen vt sep scrape off

abkühlen vt/i sep (sein) cool; sich a~ cool [down]

Abkunft f - origin

abkuppeln vt sep uncouple

abkürzen† vt sep shorten; abbreviate <Wort>. A~ung f short cut; (Wort) abbreviation

abladen† vt sep unload

Ablage f shelf; (für Akten) tray

ablagern vt sep deposit. A~ung f -, -en deposit

ablassen† vt sep drain [off]; let off <Dampf>

Ablauf m drain; (Verlauf) course; (Ende) end; (einer Frist) expiry. a~en† v sep ● vi (sein) run or drain off; (verlaufen) go off; (enden) expire; <Zeit:> run out; <Uhrwerk:> run down ● vt walk along; (absuchen) scour (nach for)

ablegen v sep ● vt put down; discard <Karte>; (abheften) file; (ausziehen) take off; sit, take <Prüfung>; abgelegte Kleidung cast-offs pl ● vi (haben) take off one's coat; (Naut) cast off. A~er m -s,- (Bot) cutting; (Schössling) shoot

ablehnen vt sep refuse; (missbilligen) reject. A~ung f -, -en refusal; rejection

ableiten vt sep divert; sich a~en be derived (von/aus from). A~ung f derivation; (Wort) derivative

ablenken vt sep deflect; divert <Aufmerksamkeit>. A~ung f -, -en distraction

ablesen† vt sep read

ablichten vt sep photocopy. A~ung f photocopy

abliefern vt sep deliver

ablösen vt sep detach; (abwechseln) relieve; sich a~en come off; (sich abwechseln) take turns. A~ung f relief

abmachen vt sep remove; (ausmachen) arrange; (vereinbaren) agree. A~ung f -, -en agreement

abmagern vi sep (sein) lose weight. A~ungskur f slimming diet

abmelden vt sep cancel; sich a~ (im Hotel) check out; (Computer) log off

abmessen† vt sep measure

abmühen (sich) vr sep struggle

Abnäher m -s,- dart

abnehmen† v sep ● vt take off, remove; pick up <Hörer>; jdm etw a~en take/(kaufen) buy sth from s.o. ● vi (haben) decrease; (nachlassen) decline; <Person:> lose weight; <Mond:> wane. A~er m -s,- buyer

Abneigung f dislike (gegen of)

abnorm a abnormal

abnutzen vt sep wear out. A~ung f - wear [and tear]

Abonnement /abɔnəˈmãː/ nt -s, -s subscription. A~nent m -en, -en subscriber. a~nieren vt take out a subscription to

abpassen vt sep wait for; gut a~ time well

abraten† vi sep (haben) jdm von etw a~ advise s.o. against sth

abräumen vt sep (haben) clear away

abrechnen v sep ● vt deduct ● vi (haben) settle up. A~ung f settlement; (Rechnung) account

Abreise f departure. a~n vi sep (sein) leave

abreißen† v sep ● vt tear off; (demolieren) pull down ● vi (sein) come off

abrichten vt sep train

Abriss m demolition; (Übersicht) summary

abrufen† *vt sep* call away;
(*Computer*) retrieve
abrunden *vt sep* round off
abrüst|en *vi sep* (*haben*) disarm.
A~ung *f* disarmament
abrutschen *vi sep* (*sein*) slip
Absage *f* -, -n cancellation;
(*Ablehnung*) refusal. **a~n** *v sep*
● *vt* cancel ● *vi* (*haben*) **[jdm] a~n**
cancel an appointment [with
s.o.]; (*auf Einladung*) refuse
[s.o.'s invitation]
Absatz *m* heel; (*Abschnitt*)
paragraph; (*Verkauf*) sale
abschaffen *vt sep* abolish; get rid
of <*Auto, Hund*>
abschalten *vt/i sep* (*haben*)
switch off
Abscheu *m* - revulsion
abscheulich *a* revolting
abschicken *vt sep* send off
Abschied *m* -[e]s, -e farewell;
(*Trennung*) parting; **A~ nehmen**
say goodbye (**von** to)
abschießen† *vt sep* shoot down;
(*abfeuern*) fire; launch <*Rakete*>
abschirmen *vt sep* shield
abschlagen† *vt sep* knock off;
(*verweigern*) refuse
Abschlepp|dienst *m* breakdown
service. **a~en** *vt sep* tow away.
A~seil *nt* tow-rope
abschließen† *v sep* ● *vt* lock;
(*beenden, abmachen*) conclude;
make <*Wette*>; balance <*Bücher*>
● *vi* (*haben*) lock up; (*enden*) end.
a~d *adv* in conclusion
Abschluss *m* conclusion.
A~zeugnis *nt* diploma
abschmecken *vt sep* season
abschmieren *vt sep* lubricate
abschneiden† *v sep* ● *vt* cut off
● *vi* (*haben*) **gut/schlecht a~** do
well/badly
Abschnitt *m* section; (*Stadium*)
stage; (*Absatz*) paragraph
abschöpfen *vt sep* skim off
abschrauben *vt sep* unscrew

abschreck|en *vt sep* deter;
(*Culin*) put in cold water <*Ei*>.
a~end *a* repulsive.
A~ungsmittel *nt* deterrent
abschreib|en† *v sep* ● *vt* copy;
(*Comm & fig*) write off ● *vi*
(*haben*) copy. **A~ung** *f* (*Comm*)
depreciation
Abschrift *f* copy
Abschuss *m* shooting down;
(*Abfeuern*) firing; (*Raketen-*)
launch
abschüssig *a* sloping; (*steil*)
steep
abschwellen† *vi sep* (*sein*) go
down
abseh|bar *a* **in a~barer Zeit** in the
foreseeable future. **a~en**† *vt/i*
sep (*haben*); (*voraussehen*)
foresee; **a~en von** disregard;
(*aufgeben*) refrain from
abseits *adv* apart; (*Sport*) offside
● *prep* (+ *gen*) away from. **A~** *nt*
- (*Sport*) offside
absend|en† *vt sep* send off. **A~er**
m sender
absetzen *v sep* ● *vt* put *or* set
down; (*ablagern*) deposit;
(*abnehmen*) take off; (*abbrechen*)
stop; (*entlassen*) dismiss;
(*verkaufen*) sell; (*abziehen*)
deduct ● *vi* (*haben*) pause
Absicht *f* -, -en intention; **mit A~**
intentionally, on purpose
absichtlich *a* intentional
absitzen† *v sep* ● *vi* (*sein*)
dismount ● *vt* 🔢 serve <*Strafe*>
absolut *a* absolute
absolvieren *vt* complete;
(*bestehen*) pass
absonder|n *vt sep* separate;
(*ausscheiden*) secrete. **A~ung** *f* -,
-en secretion
absorbieren *vt* absorb
abspeisen *vt sep* fob off (**mit**
with)
absperr|en *vt sep* cordon off;
(*abstellen*) turn off; (*SGer*) lock.
A~ung *f* -, -en barrier

abspielen vt sep play; (Fußball) pass; **sich a~** take place

Absprache f agreement

absprechen† vt sep arrange; **sich a~** agree

abspringen† vi sep (sein) jump off; (mit Fallschirm) parachute; (abgehen) come off

Absprung m jump

abspülen vt sep rinse

abstamm|en vi sep (haben) be descended (**von** from). **A~ung** f - descent

Abstand m distance; (zeitlich) interval; **A~ halten** keep one's distance

abstatten vt sep **jdm einen Besuch a~** pay s.o. a visit

Abstecher m **-s,-** detour

abstehen† vi sep (haben) stick out

absteigen† vi sep (sein) dismount; (niedersteigen) descend; (Fußball) be relegated

abstell|en vt sep put down; (lagern) store; (parken) park; (abschalten) turn off. **A~gleis** nt siding. **A~raum** m box-room

absterben† vi sep (sein) die; (gefühllos werden) go numb

Abstieg m **-[e]s, -e** descent; (Fußball) relegation

abstimm|en v sep ●vi (haben) vote (**über** + acc on) ●vt coordinate (**auf** + acc with). **A~ung** f vote

Abstinenzler m **-s, -** teetotaller

abstoßen† vt sep knock off; (verkaufen) sell; (fig: ekeln) repel. **a~d** a repulsive

abstreiten† vt sep deny

Abstrich m (Med) smear

abstufen vt sep grade

Absturz m fall; (Aviat) crash

abstürzen vi sep (sein) fall; (Aviat) crash

absuchen vt sep search

absurd a absurd

Abszess m **-es, -e** abscess

Abt m **-[e]s,-̈e** abbot

abtasten vt sep feel; (Techn) scan

abtauen vt/i sep (sein) thaw; (entfrosten) defrost

Abtei f **-, -en** abbey

Abteil nt compartment

Abteilung f **-, -en** section; (Admin, Comm) department

abtragen† vt sep clear; (einebnen) level; (abnutzen) wear out

abträglich a detrimental (dat to)

abtreib|en† vt sep (Naut) drive off course; **ein Kind a~en** have an abortion. **A~ung** f **-, -en** abortion

abtrennen vt sep detach; (abteilen) divide off

Abtreter m **-s,-** doormat

abtrocknen vt/i sep (haben) dry; **sich a~** dry oneself

abtropfen vi sep (sein) drain

abtun† vt sep (fig) dismiss

abwägen† vt sep (fig) weigh

abwandeln vt sep modify

abwarten v sep ●vt wait for ●vi (haben) wait [and see]

abwärts adv down[wards]

Abwasch m **-[e]s** washing-up; (Geschirr) dirty dishes pl. **a~en†** v sep ●vt wash; wash up <Geschirr>; (entfernen) wash off ●vi (haben) wash up. **A~lappen** m dishcloth

Abwasser nt **-s,-̈** sewage. **A~kanal** m sewer

abwechseln vi/r sep (haben) [sich] **a~** alternate; <Personen:> take turns. **a~d** a alternate

Abwechslung f **-, -en** change; **zur A~** for a change

abwegig a absurd

Abwehr f - defence; (Widerstand) resistance; (Pol) counter-espionage. **a~en** vt sep ward off. **A~system** nt immune system

abweich|en† vi sep (sein) deviate/(von Regel) depart (**von** from); (sich unterscheiden) differ (**von** from). **a~end** a divergent;

(*verschieden*) different. **A~ung** *f*
-, **-en** deviation

abweis|en† *vt sep* turn down;
turn away <*Person*>. **a~end** *a*
unfriendly. **A~ung** *f* rejection

abwenden† *vt sep* turn away;
(*verhindern*) avert

abwerfen† *vt sep* throw off;
throw <*Reiter*>; (*Aviat*) drop;
(*Kartenspiel*) discard; shed
<*Haut, Blätter*>; yield <*Gewinn*>

abwert|en *vt sep* devalue. **A~ung**
f -, **-en** devaluation

Abwesenheit *f* - absence;
absent-mindedness

abwickeln *vt sep* unwind;
(*erledigen*) settle

abwischen *vt sep* wipe

abzahlen *vt sep* pay off

abzählen *vt sep* count

Abzahlung *f* instalment

Abzeichen *nt* badge

abzeichnen *vt sep* copy

Abzieh|bild *nt* transfer. **a~en**† *v*
sep ● *vt* pull off; take off
<*Laken*>; strip <*Bett*>; (*häuten*)
skin; (*Phot*) print; run off
<*Kopien*>; (*zurückziehen*)
withdraw; (*abrechnen*) deduct
● *vi* (*sein*) go away, <*Rauch:*>
escape

Abzug *m* withdrawal;
(*Abrechnung*) deduction; (*Phot*)
print (*Korrektur-*) proof; (*am*
Gewehr) trigger; (*A~söffnung*)
vent; **A~e** *pl* deductions

abzüglich *prep* (+ *gen*) less

Abzugshaube *f* [cooker] hood

abzweig|en *v sep* ● *vi* (*sein*)
branch off ● *vt* divert. **A~ung** *f* -,
-en junction; (*Gabelung*) fork

ach *int* oh; **a~ je!** oh dear! **a~ so** I
see

Achse *f* -, **-n** axis; (*Rad-*) axle

Achsel *f* -, **-n** shoulder. **A~höhle** *f*
armpit. **A~zucken** *nt* **-s** shrug

acht *inv a*, **A~** *f* -, **-en** eight

Acht *f* **A~ geben** be careful; **A~**
geben auf (+ *acc*) look after; **außer**

A~ lassen disregard; **sich in A~**
nehmen be careful

acht|e(r,s) *a* eighth. **a~eckig** *a*
octagonal. **A~el** *nt* **-s,-** eighth.

achten *vt* respect ● *vi* (*haben*) **a~**
auf (+ *acc*) pay attention to;
(*aufpassen*) look after

Achterbahn *f* roller-coaster

achtlos *a* careless

achtsam *a* careful

Achtung *f* - respect (**vor** + *dat*
for); **A~!** look out!

acht|zehn *inv a* eighteen.
a~zehnte(r,s) *a* eighteenth.
a~zig *a inv* eighty. **a~zigste(r,s)**
a eightieth

Acker *m* **-s,-̈** field. **A~bau** *m*
agriculture. **A~land** *nt* arable
land

addieren *vt/i* (*haben*) add

Addition /-'tsio:n/ *f* -, **-en** addition

ade *int* goodbye

Adel *m* **-s** nobility

Ader *f* -, **-n** vein

Adjektiv *nt* **-s, -e** adjective

Adler *m* **-s,-** eagle

adlig *a* noble. **A~e(r)** *m*
nobleman

Administration /-'tsio:n/ *f* -
administration

Admiral *m* **-s,-̈e** admiral

adop|tieren *vt* adopt. **A~tion**
/-'tsio:n/ *f* -, **-en** adoption.
A~tiveltern *pl* adoptive parents.
A~tivkind *nt* adopted child

Adrenalin *nt* **-s** adrenalin

Adres|se *f* -, **-n** address. **a~sieren**
vt address

Adria *f* - Adriatic

Adverb *nt* **-s, -ien** /-iən/ adverb

Affäre *f* -, **-n** affair

Affe *m* **-n, -n** monkey; (*Menschen-*)
ape

affektiert *a* affected

affig *a* affected; (*eitel*) vain

Afrika *nt* **-s** Africa

Afrikan|er(in) *m* **-s,-** (*f* -, **-nen**)
African. **a~isch** *a* African

After *m* **-s,-** anus

Agen|t(in) *m* -en, -en (*f* -, -nen) agent. **A~tur** *f* -, -en agency

Aggres|sion *f* -, -en aggression. **a~siv** *a* aggressive

Agnostiker *m* -s,- agnostic

Ägypten /ɛˈɡʏptən/ *nt* -s Egypt. **Ä~er(in)** *m* -s,- (*f* -, -nen) Egyptian. **ä~isch** *a* Egyptian

ähneln *vi* (*haben*) (+ *dat*) resemble; **sich ä~** be alike

ahnen *vt* have a presentiment of; (*vermuten*) suspect

Ahnen *mpl* ancestors. **A~forschung** *f* genealogy

ähnlich *a* similar; **jdm ä~ sehen** resemble s.o. **Ä~keit** *f* -, -en similarity; resemblance

Ahnung *f* -, -en premonition; (*Vermutung*) idea, hunch

Ähre *f* -, -n ear [of corn]

Aids /eːts/ *nt* - Aids

Airbag /ˈɛːɐbɛk/ *m* -s, -s (*Auto*) air bag

Akademie *f* -, -n academy

Akadem|iker(in) *m* -s,- (*f* -, -nen) university graduate. **a~isch** *a* academic

akklimatisieren (sich) *vr* become acclimatized

Akkord *m* -[e]s, -e (*Mus*) chord. **A~arbeit** *f* piece-work

Akkordeon *nt* -s, -s accordion

Akkumulator *m* -s, -en /-ˈtoːrən/ (*Electr*) accumulator

Akkusativ *m* -s, -e accusative. **A~objekt** *nt* direct object

Akrobat|(in) *m* -en, -en (*f* -, -nen) acrobat. **a~isch** *a* acrobatic

Akt *m* -[e]s, -e act; (*Kunst*) nude

Akte *f* -, -n file; **A~n** documents. **A~ntasche** *f* briefcase

Aktie /ˈaktsiə/ *f* -, -n (*Comm*) share. **A~ngesellschaft** *f* joint-stock company

Aktion /akˈtsioːn/ *f* -, -en action. **A~är** *m* -s, -e shareholder

aktiv *a* active

aktuell *a* topical; (*gegenwärtig*) current

Akupunktur *f* - acupuncture

Akustik *f* - acoustics *pl*

akut *a* acute

Akzent *m* -[e]s, -e accent

akzept|abel *a* acceptable. **a~ieren** *vt* accept

Alarm *m* -s alarm; (*Mil*) alert. **a~ieren** *vt* alert; (*beunruhigen*) alarm

Albdruck *m* nightmare

albern *a* silly ● *vi* (*haben*) play the fool

Albtraum *m* nightmare

Album *nt* -s, -ben album

Algebra *f* - algebra

Algen *fpl* algae

Algerien /-iən/ *nt* -s Algeria

Alibi *nt* -s, -s alibi

Alkohol *m* -s alcohol. **a~frei** *a* non-alcoholic

Alkohol|iker(in) *m* -s,- (*f* -, -nen) alcoholic. **a~isch** *a* alcoholic

all *inv pron* **all das/mein Geld** all the/my money; **all dies** all this

All *nt* -s universe

alle *pred a* finished

all|e(r,s) *pron* all; (*jeder*) every; **a~es** everything; (*alle Leute*) everyone; **a~e** *pl* all; **a~es Geld** all the money; **a~e beide** both [of them/us]; **a~e Tage** every day; **a~e drei Jahre** every three years; **ohne a~en Grund** without any reason; **vor a~em** above all; **a~es in a~em** all in all; **a~es aussteigen!** all change!

Allee *f* -, -n avenue

allein *adv* alone; (*nur*) only; **a~ stehend** single; **a~ der Gedanke** the mere thought; **von a~[e]** of its/<*Person*> one's own accord; (*automatisch*) automatically ● *conj* but. **A~erziehende(r)** *m/f* single parent. **a~ig** *a* sole. **A~stehende** *pl* single people

allemal *adv* every time; (*gewiss*) certainly

allenfalls *adv* at most; (*eventuell*) possibly

aller|beste(r,s) *a* very best; **am a~besten** best of all. **a~dings** *adv* indeed; (*zwar*) admittedly. **a~erste(r,s)** *a* very first

Allergie *f* -, -n allergy

allergisch *a* allergic (**gegen** to)

Aller|heiligen *nt* -s All Saints Day. **a~höchstens** *adv* at the very most. **a~lei** *inv a* all sorts of ● *pron* all sorts of things. **a~letzte(r,s)** *a* very last. **a~liebste(r,s)** *a* favourite ● *adv* **am a~liebsten** for preference; **a~liebsten haben** like best of all. **a~meiste(r,s)** *a* most ● *adv* **am a~meisten** most of all. **A~seelen** *nt* -s All Souls Day. **a~wenigste(r,s)** *a* very least ● *adv* **am a~wenigsten** least of all

allgemein *a* general, *adv* -ly; **im A~en (a~en)** in general. **A~heit** *f* - community; (*Öffentlichkeit*) general public

Allianz *f* -, -en alliance

Alligator *m* -s, -en /-'to:rən/ alligator

alliiert *a* allied; **die A~en** *pl* the Allies

all|jährlich *a* annual. **a~mählich** *a* gradual

Alltag *m* working day; **der A~** (*fig*) everyday life

alltäglich *a* daily; (*gewöhnlich*) everyday; <*Mensch*> ordinary

alltags *adv* on weekdays

allzu *adv* [far] too; **a~ oft** all too often; **a~ vorsichtig** over-cautious

Alm *f* -, -en alpine pasture

Almosen *ntpl* alms

Alpdruck *m* = **Albdruck**

Alpen *pl* Alps

Alphabet *nt* -[e]s, -e alphabet. **a~isch** *a* alphabetical, *adv* -ly

Alptraum *m* = **Albtraum**

als *conj* as; (*zeitlich*) when; (*mit Komparativ*) than; **nichts als** nothing but; **als ob** as if *or* though

also *adv & conj* so; **a~ gut** all right then; **na a~!** there you are!

alt *a* old; (*gebraucht*) second-hand; (*ehemalig*) former; **alt werden** grow old

Alt *m* -s (*Mus*) contralto

Altar *m* -s, ̈-e altar

Alt|e(r) *m/f* old man/woman; **die A~en** old people. **A~eisen** *nt* scrap iron. **A~enheim** *nt* old people's home

Alter *nt* -s,- age; (*Bejahrtheit*) old age; **im A~ von** at the age of

älter *a* older; **mein ä~er Bruder** my elder brother

altern *vi* (*sein*) age

Alternative *f* -, -n alternative

Alters|grenze *f* age limit. **A~heim** *nt* old people's home. **A~rente** *f* old-age pension. **a~schwach** *a* old and infirm

Alter|tum *nt* -s, ̈-er antiquity. **a~tümlich** *a* old; (*altmodisch*) old-fashioned

altklug *a* precocious

alt|modisch *a* old-fashioned. **A~papier** *nt* waste paper. **A~warenhändler** *m* second-hand dealer

Alufolie *f* [aluminium] foil

Aluminium *nt* -s aluminium, (*Amer*) aluminum

am *prep* = **an dem**; **am Montag** on Monday; **am Morgen** in the morning; **am besten** [the] best

Amateur /-'tø:ɐ̯/ *m* -s, -e amateur

Ambition /-'tsi̯o:n/ *f* -, -en ambition

Amboss *m* -es, -e anvil

ambulan|t *a* out-patient ... ● *adv* **a~t behandeln** treat as an out-patient. **A~z** *f* -, -en out-patients' department

Ameise *f* -, -n ant

amen *int*, **A~** *nt* -s amen

Amerika *nt* -s America

Amerikan|er(in) *m* -s,- (*f* -, -nen) American. **a~isch** *a* American

Ammoniak *nt* -s ammonia

Amnestie f -, -n amnesty

amoralisch a amoral

Ampel f -, -n traffic lights pl

Amphitheater nt amphitheatre

Amput|ation /-'tsio:n/ f -, -en amputation. **a∼ieren** vt amputate

Amsel f -, -n blackbird

Amt nt -[e]s,∹er office; (Aufgabe) task; (Teleph) exchange. **a∼lich** a official. **A∼szeichen** nt dialling tone

Amulett nt -[e]s, -e [lucky] charm

amüs|ant a amusing. **a∼ieren** vt amuse; **sich a∼ieren** be amused (über + acc at); (sich vergnügen) enjoy oneself

an
● preposition (+ dative)
❗ Note that **an** plus **dem** can become **am**
····▶ (räumlich) on; (Gebäude, Ort) at. **an der Wand** on the wall. **Frankfurt an der Oder** Frankfurt on [the] Oder. **an der Ecke** at the corner. **am Bahnhof** at the station. **an ... vorbei** past
····▶ (zeitlich) on. **am Montag** on Monday. **an jedem Sonntag** every Sunday. **am 24. Mai** on May 24th
····▶ (sonstige Verwendungen) **arm/reich an Vitaminen** low/rich in vitamins. **jdn an etw erkennen** recognize s.o. by sth. **an etw leiden** suffer from sth. **an einer Krankheit sterben** die of a disease. **an [und für] sich** actually
● preposition (+ accusative)
❗ Note that **an** plus **das** can become **ans**
····▶ to. **schicke es an deinen Bruder** send it to your brother. **er ging ans Fenster** he went to the window
····▶ (auf, gegen) on. **etw an die Wand hängen** to hang sth on the wall. **lehne es an den Baum** lean it on or against the tree

····▶ (sonstige Verwendungen) **an etw/jdn glauben** believe in sth/ s.o. **an etw denken** think of sth. **sich an etw erinnern** remember sth
● adverb
····▶ (auf Fahrplan) **Köln an: 9.15** arriving Cologne 09.15
····▶ (angeschaltet) on. **die Waschmaschine/der Fernseher/das Licht/das Gas ist an** the washing machine/television/light/gas is on
····▶ (ungefähr) around; about. **an [die] 20 000 DM** around or about 20,000 DM
····▶ (in die Zukunft) **von heute an** from today (onwards)

analog a analogous; (Computer) analog. **A∼ie** f -, -n analogy

Analphabet m -en, -en illiterate person. **A∼entum** nt -s illiteracy

Analy|se f -, -n analysis. **a∼sieren** vt analyse. **A∼tiker** m -s,- analyst. **a∼tisch** a analytical

Anämie f - anaemia

Ananas f -, -[se] pineapple

Anatomie f - anatomy

Anbau m cultivation; (Gebäude) extension. **a∼en** vt sep build on; (anpflanzen) cultivate, grow

anbei adv enclosed

anbeißen† v sep ● vt take a bite of ● vi (haben) <Fisch:> bite

anbeten vt sep worship

Anbetracht m **in A∼** (+ gen) in view of

anbieten† vt sep offer; **sich a∼** offer (zu to)

anbinden† vt sep tie up

Anblick m sight. **a∼en** vt sep look at

anbrechen† v sep ● vt start on; break into <Vorräte> ● vi (sein) begin; <Tag:> break; <Nacht:> fall

anbrennen† v sep ● vt light ● vi (sein) burn

anbringen† *vt sep* bring [along]; *(befestigen)* fix

Anbruch *m (fig)* dawn; **bei A~ des Tages/der Nacht** at daybreak/nightfall

Andacht *f* -, **-en** reverence; *(Gottesdienst)* prayers *pl*

andächtig *a* reverent; *(fig)* rapt

andauern *vi sep (haben)* last; *(anhalten)* continue. **a~d** *a* persistent; *(ständig)* constant

Andenken *nt* **-s,-** memory; *(Souvenir)* souvenir

ander|e(r,s) *a* other; *(verschieden)* different; *(nächste)* next; **ein a~er, eine a~e** another ● *pron* **der a~e/die a~en** the other/others; **ein a~er** another [one]; *(Person)* someone else; **kein a~er** no one else; **einer nach dem a~en** one after the other; **alles a~e/nichts a~es** everything/nothing else; **unter a~em** among other things. **a~enfalls** *adv* otherwise. **a~erseits** *adv* on the other hand. **a~mal** *adv* **ein a~mal** another time

ändern *vt* alter; *(wechseln)* change; **sich ä~** change

andernfalls *adv* otherwise

anders *pred a* different; **a~ werden** change ● *adv* differently; *<riechen, schmecken>* different; *(sonst)* else; **jemand a~** someone else

anderseits *adv* on the other hand

andersherum *adv* the other way round

anderthalb *inv a* one and a half; **a~ Stunden** an hour and a half

Änderung *f* -, **-en** alteration; *(Wechsel)* change

andeut|en *vt sep* indicate; *(anspielen)* hint at. **A~ung** *f* -, **-en** indication; hint

Andrang *m* rush *(nach* for); *(Gedränge)* crush

androhen *vt sep* **jdm etw a~** threaten s.o. with sth

aneignen *vt sep* **sich** *(dat)* **a~** appropriate; *(lernen)* learn

aneinander *adv & pref* together; *<denken>* of one another; **a~ vorbei** past one another; **a~ geraten** quarrel

Anekdote *f* -, **-n** anecdote

anerkannt *a* acknowledged

anerkenn|en† *vt sep* acknowledge, recognize; *(würdigen)* appreciate. **a~end** *a* approving. **A~ung** *f* - acknowledgement, recognition; appreciation

anfahren† *v sep* ● *vt* deliver; *(streifen)* hit ● *vi (sein)* start

Anfall *m* fit, attack. **a~en**† *v sep* ● *vt* attack ● *vi (sein)* arise; *<Zinsen:>* accrue

anfällig *a* susceptible *(für* to); *(zart)* delicate

Anfang *m* **-s,¨e** beginning, start; **zu od am A~** at the beginning; *(anfangs)* at first. **a~en**† *vt/i sep (haben)* begin, start; *(tun)* do

Anfänger(in) *m* **-s,-** (*f* -, **-nen**) beginner

anfangs *adv* at first. **A~buchstabe** *m* initial letter. **A~gehalt** *nt* starting salary

anfassen *vt sep* touch; *(behandeln)* treat; tackle *<Arbeit>*; **sich a~** hold hands

anfechten† *vt sep* contest

anfertigen *vt sep* make

anfeuchten *vt sep* moisten

anflehen *vt sep* implore, beg

Anflug *m (Avia)* approach

anforder|n *vt sep* demand; *(Comm)* order. **A~ung** *f* demand

Anfrage *f* enquiry. **a~n** *vi sep (haben)* enquire, ask

anfreunden (sich) *vr sep* make friends *(mit* with)

anfügen *vt sep* add

anfühlen *vt sep* feel; **sich weich a~** feel soft

anführ|en *vt sep* lead; *(zitieren)* quote; *(angeben)* give. **A~er** *m* leader. **A~ungszeichen** ntpl quotation marks

Angabe f statement; (*Anweisung*) instruction; (*Tennis*) service; **nähere A~n** particulars

angeb|en† v sep ● vt state; give <*Namen, Grund*>; (*anzeigen*) indicate; set <*Tempo*> ● vi (*haben*) (*Tennis*) serve; (🗓 *protzen*) show off. **A~er(in)** m -s,- (f -, -nen) 🗓 show-off. **A~erei** f - 🗓 showing-off

angeblich a alleged

angeboren a innate; (*Med*) congenital

Angebot nt offer; (*Auswahl*) range; **A~ und Nachfrage** supply and demand

angebracht a appropriate

angeheiratet a <*Onkel, Tante*> by marriage

angeheitert a 🗓 tipsy

angehen† v sep ● vi (*sein*) begin, start; <*Licht, Radio:*> come on; (*anwachsen*) take root; **a~ gegen** fight ● vt attack; tackle <*Arbeit*>; (*bitten*) ask (**um** for); (*betreffen*) concern

angehör|en vi sep (*haben*) (+ *dat*) belong to. **A~ige(r)** m/f relative

Angeklagte(r) m/f accused

Angel f -, -n fishing-rod; (*Tür-*) hinge

Angelegenheit f matter

Angel|haken m fish-hook. **a~n** vi (*haben*) fish (**nach** for); **a~n gehen** go fishing ● vt (*fangen*) catch. **A~rute** f fishing-rod

angelsächsisch a Anglo-Saxon

angemessen a commensurate (*dat* with); (*passend*) appropriate

angenehm a pleasant; (*bei Vorstellung*) **a~!** delighted to meet you!

angeregt a animated

angesehen a respected; <*Firma*> reputable

angesichts prep (+ *gen*) in view of

angespannt a intent; <*Lage*> tense

Angestellte(r) m/f employee

angewandt a applied

angewiesen a dependent (**auf** + acc on); **auf sich selbst a~** on one's own

angewöhnen vt sep **jdm etw a~** get s.o. used to sth; **sich** (*dat*) **etw a~** get into the habit of doing sth

Angewohnheit f habit

Angina f - tonsillitis

angleichen† vt sep adjust (*dat* to)

anglikanisch a Anglican

Anglistik f - English [language and literature]

Angorakatze f Persian cat

angreif|en† vt sep attack; tackle <*Arbeit*>; (*schädigen*) damage. **A~er** m -s,- attacker; (*Pol*) aggressor

angrenzen vi sep (*haben*) adjoin (**an etw** acc sth). **a~d** a adjoining

Angriff m attack; **in A~ nehmen** tackle. **a~slustig** a aggressive

Angst f -,-̈e fear; (*Psych*) anxiety; (*Sorge*) worry (**um** about); **A~ haben** be afraid (**vor** + *dat* of); (*sich sorgen*) be worried (**um** about); **jdm A~ machen** frighten s.o.

ängstigen vt frighten; (*Sorge machen*) worry; **sich ä~** be frightened; be worried (**um** about)

ängstlich a nervous; (*scheu*) timid; (*verängstigt*) frightened, scared; (*besorgt*) anxious

angucken vt sep 🗓 look at

angurten (sich) vr sep fasten one's seat-belt

anhaben† vt sep have on; **er/es kann mir nichts a~** (*fig*) he/it cannot hurt me

anhalt|en† v sep ● vt stop; hold <*Atem*>; **jdn zur Arbeit a~en** urge s.o. to work ● vi (*haben*) stop; (*andauern*) continue. **a~end** a persistent. **A~er(in)** m -s,- (f -,

-nen) hitchhiker; **per A~er fahren** hitchhike. **A~spunkt** m clue

anhand prep (+ gen) with the aid of

Anhang m appendix

anhängen¹ vt sep (reg) hang up; (befestigen) attach

anhäng|en²† vi (haben) be a follower of. **A~er** m **-s,-** follower; (Auto) trailer; (Schild) [tie-on] label; (Schmuck) pendant. **A~erin** f **-, -nen** follower. **a~lich** a affectionate

anhäufen vt sep pile up

Anhieb m **auf A~** straight away

Anhöhe f hill

anhören vt sep listen to; **sich gut a~** sound good

animieren vt encourage (**zu** to)

Anis m **-es** aniseed

Anker m **-s,-** anchor; **vor A~ gehen** drop anchor. **a~n** vi (haben) anchor; (liegen) be anchored

anketten vt sep chain up

Anklage f accusation; (Jur) charge; (Ankläger) prosecution. **A~bank** f dock. **a~n** vt sep accuse (gen of); (Jur) charge (gen with)

Ankläger m accuser; (Jur) prosecutor

anklammern vt sep clip on; **sich a~** cling (**an** + acc to)

ankleben v sep ● vt stick on ● vi (sein) stick (**an** + dat to)

anklicken vt sep click on

anklopfen vi sep (haben) knock

anknipsen vt sep 🔲 switch on

ankommen† vi sep (sein) arrive; (sich nähern) approach; **gut a~** arrive safely; (fig) go down well (**bei** with); **nicht a~ gegen** (fig) be no match for; **a~ auf** (+ acc) depend on; **das kommt darauf an** it [all] depends

ankreuzen vt sep mark with a cross

ankündig|en vt sep announce. **A~ung** f announcement

Ankunft f **-** arrival

ankurbeln vt sep (fig) boost

anlächeln vt sep smile at

anlachen vt sep smile at

Anlage f **-, -n** installation; (Industrie-) plant; (Komplex) complex; (Geld-) investment; (Plan) layout; (Beilage) enclosure; (Veranlagung) aptitude; (Neigung) predisposition; **[öffentliche] A~n** [public] gardens; **als A~** enclosed

Anlass m **-es,:-e** reason; (Gelegenheit) occasion; **A~ geben zu** give cause for

anlass|en† vt sep (Auto) start; 🔲 leave on <Licht>; keep on <Mantel>. **A~er** m **-s,-** starter

anlässlich prep (+ gen) on the occasion of

Anlauf m (Sport) run-up; (fig) attempt. **a~en†** v sep ● vi (sein) start; (beschlagen) mist up; <Metall:> tarnish; **rot a~en** blush

anlegen v sep ● vt put (**an** + acc against); put on <Kleidung, Verband>; lay back <Ohren>; aim <Gewehr>; (investieren) invest; (ausgeben) spend (**für** on); draw up <Liste>; **es darauf a~** (fig) aim (**zu** to) ● vi (haben) <Schiff:> moor; **a~ auf** (+ acc) aim at

anlehnen vt sep lean (**an** + acc against); **sich a~** lean (**an** + acc on)

Anleihe f **-, -n** loan

anleit|en vt sep instruct. **A~ung** f instructions pl

anlernen vt sep train

Anliegen nt **-s,-** request; (Wunsch) desire

anlieg|en† vi sep (haben) [eng] **a~en** fit closely; **[eng] a~end** close-fitting. **A~er** mpl residents; **'A~er frei'** 'access for residents only'

anlügen† vt sep lie to

anmachen vt sep 🔲 fix; (anschalten) turn on; dress <Salat>

anmalen vt sep paint

Anmarsch m (Mil) approach

anmeld|en vt sep announce; (Admin) register; **sich a~en** say that one is coming; (Admin) register; (Sch) enrol; (im Hotel) check in; (beim Arzt) make an appointment; (Computer) log on. **A~ung** f announcement; (Admin) registration; (Sch) enrolment

anmerk|en vt sep mark; **sich** (dat) **etw a~en lassen** show sth. **A~ung** f -, -en note

Anmut f - grace; (Charme) charm

anmutig a graceful

annähen vt sep sew on

annäher|nd a approximate. **A~ungsversuche** mpl advances

Annahme f -, -n acceptance; (Adoption) adoption; (Vermutung) assumption

annehm|bar a acceptable. **a~en†** vt sep accept; (adoptieren) adopt; acquire <Gewohnheit>; (sich zulegen, vermuten) assume; **angenommen, dass** assuming that. **A~lichkeiten** fpl comforts

Anno adv **A~ 1920** in the year 1920

Annon|ce /a'nõ:sə/ f -, -n advertisement. **a~cieren** /-'si:-/ vt/i (haben) advertise

annullieren vt annul; cancel

Anomalie f -, -n anomaly

anonym a anonymous

Anorak m -s, -s anorak

anordn|en vt sep arrange; (befehlen) order. **A~ung** f arrangement; order

anorganisch a inorganic

anormal a abnormal

anpass|en vt sep try on; (angleichen) adapt (dat to); **sich a~** adapt (dat to). **A~ung** f - adaptation. **a~ungsfähig** a adaptable. **A~ungsfähigkeit** f adaptability

Anpfiff m (Sport) kick-off

Anprall m -[e]s impact. **a~en** vi sep (sein) strike (**an etw** acc sth)

anpreisen† vt sep commend

Anprob|e f fitting. **a~ieren** vt sep try on

anrechnen vt sep count (**als** as); (berechnen) charge for; (verrechnen) allow <Summe>

Anrecht nt right (**auf** + acc to)

Anrede f [form of] address. **a~n** vt sep address; speak to

anreg|en vt sep stimulate; (ermuntern) encourage (**zu** to); (vorschlagen) suggest. **a~end** a stimulating. **A~ung** f stimulation; (Vorschlag) suggestion

Anreise f journey; (Ankunft) arrival. **a~n** vi sep (sein) arrive

Anreiz m incentive

Anrichte f -, -n sideboard. **a~n** vt sep (Culin) prepare; (garnieren) garnish (**mit** with); (verursachen) cause

anrüchig a disreputable

Anruf m call. **A~beantworter** m -s,- answering machine. **a~en†** v sep ● vt call to; (bitten) call on (**um** for); (Teleph) ring ● vi (haben) ring (**bei jdm** s.o.)

anrühren vt sep touch; (verrühren) mix

ans prep = **an das**

Ansage f announcement. **a~n** vt sep announce

ansamm|eln vt sep collect; (anhäufen) accumulate; **sich a~eln** collect; (sich häufen) accumulate; <Leute:> gather. **A~lung** f collection; (Menschen-) crowd

ansässig a resident

Ansatz m beginning; (Versuch) attempt

anschaffen vt sep [**sich** dat] **etw a~** acquire/(kaufen) buy sth

anschalten vt sep switch on

anschauen vt sep look at. **a~lich** a vivid, adv -ly. **A~ung** f -, -en (fig) view

Anschein m appearance. **a~end** adv apparently

anschirren vt sep harness

Anschlag m notice; (Vor-) estimate; (Überfall) attack (auf + acc on); (Mus) touch; (Techn) stop. **a~en†** v sep ● vt put up <Aushang>; strike <Note, Taste>; cast on <Masche>; (beschädigen) chip ● vi (haben) strike/(stoßen) knock (an + acc against); (wirken) be effective ● vi (sein) knock (an + acc against)

anschließen† v sep ● vt connect (an + acc to); (zufügen) add; **sich a~ an** (+ acc) (anstoßen) adjoin; (folgen) follow; (sich anfreunden) become friendly with; **sich jdm a~** join s.o. ● vi (haben) **a~ an** (+ acc) adjoin; (folgen) follow. **a~d** a adjoining; (zeitlich) following ● adv afterwards

Anschluss m connection; (Kontakt) contact; **A~ finden** make friends; **im A~ an** (+ acc) after

anschmiegsam a affectionate

anschmieren vt sep smear

anschnallen vt sep strap on; **sich a~** fasten one's seat-belt

anschneiden† vt sep cut into; broach <Thema>

anschreiben† vt sep write (an + acc on); (Comm) put on s.o.'s account; (sich wenden) write to

Anschrift f address

anschuldig|en vt sep accuse. **A~ung** f -, -en accusation

anschwellen† vi sep (sein) swell

ansehen† vt sep look at; (einschätzen) regard (als as); [**sich** dat] **etw a~** look at sth; (TV) watch sth. **A~** nt -s respect; (Ruf) reputation

ansehnlich a considerable

ansetzen v sep ● vt join (an + acc to); (veranschlagen) estimate ● vi (haben) (anbrennen) burn; **zum Sprung a~** get ready to jump

Ansicht f view; **meiner A~ nach** in my view; **zur A~** (Comm) on approval. **A~s[post]karte** f picture postcard. **A~ssache** f matter of opinion

ansiedeln (sich) vr sep settle

ansonsten adv apart from that

anspannen vt sep hitch up; (anstrengen) strain; tense <Muskel>

Anspielung f -, -en allusion; hint

Anspitzer m -s,- pencil-sharpener

Ansprache f address

ansprechen† v sep ● vt speak to; (fig) appeal to ● vi (haben) respond (auf + acc to)

anspringen† v sep ● vt jump at ● vi (sein) (Auto) start

Anspruch m claim/(Recht) right (auf + acc to); **A~ haben** be entitled (auf + acc to); **in A~ nehmen** make use of; (erfordern) demand; take up <Zeit>; occupy <Person>; **hohe A~e stellen** be very demanding. **a~slos** a undemanding. **a~svoll** a demanding; (kritisch) discriminating; (vornehm) up-market

anstacheln vt sep (fig) spur on

Anstalt f -, -en institution

Anstand m decency; (Benehmen) [good] manners pl

anständig a decent; (ehrbar) respectable; (richtig) proper

anstandslos adv without any trouble

anstarren vt sep stare at

anstatt conj & prep (+ gen) instead of

ansteck|en v sep ● vt pin (an + acc to/on); put on <Ring>; (anzünden) light; (in Brand stecken) set fire to; (Med) infect; **sich a~en** catch an infection (bei

from) ●*vi* (*haben*) be infectious.
a~end *a* infectious. **A~ung** *f* -,
-en infection

anstehen† *vi sep* (*haben*) queue

anstelle *prep* (+ *gen*) instead of

anstellen *vt sep* put, stand (**an** +
acc against); (*einstellen*) employ;
(*anschalten*) turn on; (*tun*) do;
sich a~en queue [up]. **A~ung** *f*
employment; (*Stelle*) job

Anstieg *m* -[e]s, -e climb; (*fig*) rise

anstiften *vt sep* cause; (*anzetteln*)
instigate

Anstoß *m* (*Anregung*) impetus;
(*Stoß*) knock; (*Fußball*) kick-off;
A~ erregen give offence (**an** + *dat*
at). **a~en** *v sep* ●*vt* knock; (*mit
dem Ellbogen*) nudge ●*vi* (*sein*)
knock (**an** + *acc* against) ●*vi*
(*haben*) adjoin (**an etw** *acc* sth);
a~en auf (+ *acc*) drink to; **mit der
Zunge a~en** lisp

anstößig *a* offensive

anstrahlen *vt sep* floodlight

anstreichen† *vt sep* paint;
(*anmerken*) mark

anstreng|en *vt sep* strain;
(*ermüden*) tire; **sich a~en** exert
oneself; (*sich bemühen*) make an
effort (**zu** to). **a~end** *a* strenuous;
(*ermüdend*) tiring. **A~ung** *f* -, -en
strain; (*Mühe*) effort

Anstrich *m* coat [of paint]

Ansturm *m* rush; (*Mil*) assault

Ansuchen *nt* -s,- request

Antarktis *f* - Antarctic

Anteil *m* share; **A~ nehmen** take
an interest (**an** + *dat* in).
A~nahme *f* - interest (**an** + *dat*
in); (*Mitgefühl*) sympathy

Antenne *f* -, -n aerial

Anthologie *f* -, -n anthology

Anthrax *m* - anthrax

Anthropologie *f* - anthropology

Anti|alkoholiker *m* teetotaller.
A~biotikum *nt* -s, -ka antibiotic

antik *a* antique. **A~e** *f* -
[classical] antiquity

Antikörper *m* antibody

Antilope *f* -, -n antelope

Antiquariat *nt* -[e]s, -e antiquarian
bookshop

Antiquitäten *fpl* antiques.
A~händler *m* antique dealer

Antrag *m* -[e]s,⸚e proposal; (*Pol*)
motion; (*Gesuch*) application.
A~steller *m* -s,- applicant

antreffen† *vt sep* find

antreten† *v sep* ●*vt* start; take up
<*Amt*> ●*vi* (*sein*) line up

Antrieb *m* urge; (*Techn*) drive;
aus eigenem A~ of one's own
accord

Antritt *m* start; **bei A~ eines Amtes**
when taking office

antun† *vt sep* **jdm etw a~** do sth
to s.o.; **sich** (*dat*) **etwas a~** take
one's own life

Antwort *f* -, -en answer, reply (**auf**
+ *acc* to). **a~en** *vt/i* (*haben*)
answer (**jdm** s.o.)

anvertrauen *vt sep* entrust/
(*mitteilen*) confide (**jdm** to s.o.)

Anwalt *m* -[e]s,⸚e, **Anwältin** *f* -,
-nen lawyer; (*vor Gericht*) counsel

Anwandlung *f* -, -en fit (**von** of)

Anwärter(in) *m(f)* candidate

anweis|en† *vt sep* assign (*dat* to);
(*beauftragen*) instruct. **A~ung** *f*
instruction; (*Geld-*) money order

anwend|en *vt sep* apply (**auf** + *acc*
to); (*gebrauchen*) use. **A~ung** *f*
application; use

anwerben† *vt sep* recruit

Anwesen *nt* -s,- property

anwesen|d *a* present (**bei** at); **die
A~den** those present. **A~heit** *f* -
presence

anwidern *vt sep* disgust

Anwohner *mpl* residents

Anzahl *f* number

anzahl|en *vt sep* pay a deposit on.
A~ung *f* deposit

anzapfen *vt sep* tap

Anzeichen *nt* sign

Anzeige *f* -, -n announcement;
(*Inserat*) advertisement; **A~
erstatten gegen jdn** report s.o. to

the police. **a~n** vt sep announce; (*inserieren*) advertise; (*melden*) report [to the police]; (*angeben*) indicate

anzieh|en† vt sep ● vt attract; (*festziehen*) tighten; put on <*Kleider, Bremse*>; (*ankleiden*) dress; **sich a~en** get dressed. **a~end** a attractive. **A~ungskraft** f attraction; (*Phys*) gravity

Anzug m suit

anzüglich a suggestive

anzünden vt sep light; (*in Brand stecken*) set fire to

anzweifeln vt sep question

apart a striking

Apathie f - apathy

apathisch a apathetic

Aperitif m -s, -s aperitif

Apfel m -s,- apple

Apfelsine f -, -n orange

Apostel m -s,- apostle

Apostroph m -s, -e apostrophe

Apotheke f -, -n pharmacy. **A~er(in)** m -s, - (f -, -nen) pharmacist, [dispensing] chemist

Apparat m -[e]s, -e device; (*Phot*) camera; (*Radio, TV*) set; (*Teleph*) telephone; **am A~!** speaking!

Appell m -s, -e appeal; (*Mil*) roll-call. **a~ieren** vi (*haben*) appeal (**an** + acc to)

Appetit m -s appetite; **guten A~!** enjoy your meal! **a~lich** a appetizing

Applaus m -es applause

Aprikose f -, -n apricot

April m -[s] April

Aquarell nt -s, -e water-colour

Aquarium nt -s, -ien aquarium

Äquator m -s equator

Ära f - era

Araber(in) m -s,- (f -, -nen) Arab

arabisch a Arab; (*Geog*) Arabian; <*Ziffer*> Arabic

Arbeit f -, -en work; (*Anstellung*) employment, job; (*Aufgabe*) task; (*Sch*) [written] test; (*Abhandlung*) treatise; (*Qualität*) workmanship;

sich an die A~ machen set to work; **sich** (*dat*) **viel A~ machen** go to a lot of trouble. **a~en** v sep ● vi (*haben*) work (**an** + dat on) ● vt make. **A~er(in)** m -s,- (f -, -nen) worker; (*Land-, Hilfs-*) labourer. **A~erklasse** f working class

Arbeit|geber m -s,- employer. **A~nehmer** m -s,- employee

Arbeits|amt nt employment exchange. **A~erlaubnis**, **A~genehmigung** f work permit. **A~kraft** f worker. **a~los** a unemployed; **~los sein** be out of work. **A~lose(r)** m/f unemployed person; **die A~losen** the unemployed pl. **A~losenunterstützung** f unemployment benefit. **A~losigkeit** f - unemployment

arbeitsparend a labour-saving

Arbeitsplatz m job

Archäo|loge m -n, -n archaeologist. **A~logie** f - archaeology

Arche f - **die A~** Noah Noah's Ark

Architekt(in) m -en, -en (f -, -nen) architect. **a~tonisch** a architectural. **A~tur** f - architecture

Archiv nt -s, -e archives pl

Arena f -, -nen arena

arg a bad; (*groß*) terrible

Argentin|ien /-iən/ nt -s Argentina. **a~isch** a Argentinian

Ärger m -s annoyance; (*Unannehmlichkeit*) trouble. **ä~lich** a annoyed; (*leidig*) annoying; **ä~lich sein** be annoyed. **ä~n** vt annoy; (*necken*) tease; **sich ä~n** get annoyed (**über** jdn/etw with s.o./ about sth). **Ä~nis** nt -ses, -se annoyance; **öffentliches Ä~nis** public nuisance

Arglist f - malice

arglos a unsuspecting

Argument nt -[e]s, -e argument.
a~ieren vi (haben) argue (**dass**
that)
Arie /'a:riə/ f -, -n aria
Aristo|krat m -en, -en aristocrat.
A~kratie f - aristocracy.
a~kratisch a aristocratic
Arkt|is f - Arctic. a~isch a Arctic
arm a poor
Arm m -[e]s, -e arm; **jdn auf den
Arm nehmen** 🛈 pull s.o.'s leg
Armaturenbrett nt instrument
panel; (Auto) dashboard
Armband nt (pl -bänder) bracelet;
(Uhr-) watch-strap. A~uhr f
wrist-watch
Arm|e(r) m/f poor man/woman;
die A~en the poor pl
Armee f -, -n army
Ärmel m -s,- sleeve. Ä~kanal m
[English] Channel. ä~los a
sleeveless
Arm|lehne f arm. A~leuchter m
candelabra
ärmlich a poor; (elend) miserable
armselig a miserable
Armut f - poverty
Arran|gement /arãʒə'mã:/ nt -s, -s
arrangement. a~gieren /-'ʒi:rən/
vt arrange
arrogant a arrogant
Arsch m -[e]s,¨e (vulg) arse
Arsen nt -s arsenic
Art f -, -en manner; (Weise) way;
(Natur) nature; (Sorte) kind;
(Biol) species; **auf diese Art** in this
way
Arterie /-iə/ f -, -n artery
Arthritis f - arthritis
artig a well-behaved
Artikel m -s,- article
Artillerie f - artillery
Artischocke f -, -n artichoke
Arznei f -, -en medicine
Arzt m -[e]s,¨e doctor
Ärzt|in f -, -nen [woman] doctor.
ä~lich a medical
As* nt -ses, -se s. **Ass**
Asbest m -[e]s asbestos

Asche f - ash. A~nbecher m
ashtray. A~rmittwoch m Ash
Wednesday
Asiat|(in) m -en, -en (f -, -nen)
Asian. a~isch a Asian
Asien /'a:ziən/ nt -s Asia
asozial a antisocial
Aspekt m -[e]s, -e aspect
Asphalt m -[e]s asphalt. a~ieren
vt asphalt
Ass nt -es, -e ace
Assistent(in) m -en, -en (f -, -nen)
assistant
Ast m -[e]s,¨e branch
asthetisch a aesthetic
Asth|ma nt -s asthma. a~matisch
a asthmatic
Astro|loge m -n, -n astrologer.
A~logie f - astrology. A~naut m
-en, -en astronaut. A~nomie f -
astronomy
Asyl nt -s, -e home; (Pol) asylum.
A~ant m -en, -en asylum-seeker
Atelier /-'lie:/ nt -s studio
Atem m -s breath. a~los a
breathless. A~zug m breath
Atheist m -en, -en atheist
Äther m -s ether
Äthiopien /-iən/ nt -s Ethiopia
Athlet|(in) m -en, -en (f -, -nen)
athlete. a~isch a athletic
Atlant|ik m -s Atlantic. a~isch a
Atlantic; **der A~ische Ozean** the
Atlantic Ocean
Atlas m -lasses, -lanten atlas
atmen vt/i (haben) breathe
Atmosphäre f -, -n atmosphere
Atmung f - breathing
Atom nt -s, -e atom. A~bombe f
atom bomb. A~krieg m nuclear
war
Atten|tat nt -[e]s, -e assassination
attempt. A~täter m assassin
Attest nt -[e]s, -e certificate
Attrak|tion /-'tsio:n/ f -, -en
attraction. a~tiv a attractive
Attribut nt -[e]s, -e attribute

ätzen vt corrode; (Med) cauterize; (Kunst) etch. ä~d a corrosive; <Spott> caustic

au int ouch; **au fein!** oh good!

Aubergine /oberˈʒiːnə/ f -, -n aubergine

auch adv & conj also, too; (außerdem) what's more; (selbst) even; **a~ wenn** even if; **sie weiß es a~ nicht** she doesn't know either; **wer/wie/was a~ immer** whoever/however/whatever

Audienz f -, -en audience

audiovisuell a audio-visual

Auditorium nt -s, -ien (Univ) lecture hall

auf
● preposition (+ dative)
····➤ (nicht unter) on. **auf dem Tisch** on the table. **auf Deck** on deck. **auf der Erde** on earth. **auf der Welt** in the world. **auf der Straße** in the street
····➤ (bei Institution, Veranstaltung usw.) at; (bei Gebäude, Zimmer) in. **auf der Schule/Uni** at school/university. **auf einer Party/Hochzeit** at a party/wedding. **Geld auf der Bank haben** have money in the bank. **sie ist auf ihrem Zimmer** she's in her room. **auf Urlaub** on holiday
● preposition (+ accusative)
····➤ (nicht unter) on[to]. **er legte das Buch auf den Tisch** he laid the book on the table. **auf eine Mauer steigen** climb onto a wall. **auf die Straße gehen** go [out] into the street
····➤ (bei Institution, Veranstaltung usw.) to. **auf eine Party/die Toilette gehen** go to a party/the toilet. **auf die Schule/Uni gehen** go to school/university. **auf Urlaub schicken** send on holiday
····➤ (bei Entfernung) **auf 10 km [Entfernung] zu sehen/hören** visible/audible for [a distance of] 10 km
····➤ (zeitlich) (wie lange) for; (bis) until; (wann) on. **auf Jahre [hinaus]** for years [to come]. **auf ein paar Tage** for a few days. **etw auf nächsten Mittwoch verschieben** postpone sth until next Wednesday. **das fällt auf einen Montag** it falls on a Monday
····➤ (Art und Weise) in. **auf diese [Art und] Weise** in this way. **auf Deutsch/Englisch** in German/English
····➤ (aufgrund) **auf Wunsch** on request. **auf meine Bitte** on or at my request. **auf Befehl** on command
····➤ (Proportion) to. **ein Teelöffel auf einen Liter Wasser** one teaspoon to one litre of water. **auf die Sekunde/den Millimeter [genau]** [precise] to the nearest second/millimetre
····➤ (Toast) **auf deine Gesundheit!** your health!
● adverb
····➤ (aufgerichtet, aufgestanden) up. **auf!** (steh auf!) up you get! **auf und ab** (hin und her) up and down
····➤ (aufsetzen) **Helm/Hut/Brille auf!** helmet/hat/glasses on!
····➤ (geöffnet, offen) open. **Fenster/Mund auf!** open the window/your mouth!

aufatmen vi sep (haben) heave a sigh of relief

aufbahren vt sep lay out

Aufbau m construction; (Struktur) structure. **a~en** v sep ● vt construct, build; (errichten) erect; (schaffen) build up; (arrangieren) arrange; **sich a~en** (fig) be based (auf + dat on) ● vi (haben) be based (auf + dat on)

aufbauschen vt sep puff out; (fig) exaggerate

aufbekommen† vt sep get open; (Sch) be given [as homework]

aufbessern vt sep improve; (erhöhen) increase

aufbewahr|en vt sep keep; (lagern) store. **A~ung** f - safe keeping; storage; (Gepäck-) left-luggage office

aufblas|bar a inflatable. **a~en†** vt sep inflate

aufbleiben† vi sep (sein) stay open; <Person:> stay up

aufblenden vt/i sep (haben) (Auto) switch to full beam

aufblühen vi sep (sein) flower

aufbocken vt sep jack up

aufbrauchen vt sep use up

aufbrechen† v sep ●vt break open ●vi (sein) <Knospe:> open; (sich aufmachen) set out, start

aufbringen† vt sep raise <Geld>; find <Kraft>

Aufbruch m start, departure

aufbrühen vt sep make <Tee>

aufbürden vt sep **jdm etw a~** (fig) burden s.o. with sth

aufdecken vt sep (auflegen) put on; (abdecken) uncover; (fig) expose

aufdrehen vt sep turn on

aufdringlich a persistent

aufeinander adv one on top of the other; <schießen> at each other; <warten> for each other; **a~ folgend** successive; <Tage> consecutive.

Aufenthalt m stay; **10 Minuten A~ haben** <Zug:> stop for 10 minutes. **A~serlaubnis, A~sgenehmigung** f residence permit. **A~sraum** m recreation room; (im Hotel) lounge

Auferstehung f - resurrection

aufessen† vt sep eat up

auffahr|en† vi sep (sein) drive up; (aufprallen) crash, run (**auf** + acc into). **A~t** f drive; (Autobahn-) access road, slip road; (Bergfahrt) ascent

auffallen† vi sep (sein) be conspicuous; **unangenehm a~** make a bad impression

auffällig a conspicuous

auffangen† vt sep catch; pick up

auffass|en vt sep understand; (deuten) take. **A~ung** f understanding; (Ansicht) view

aufforder|n vt sep ask; (einladen) invite. **A~ung** f request; invitation

auffrischen v sep ●vt freshen up; revive <Erinnerung>; **seine Englischkenntnisse a~** brush up one's English

aufführ|en vt sep perform; (angeben) list; **sich a~en** behave. **A~ung** f performance

auffüllen vt sep fill up

Aufgabe f task; (Rechen-) problem; (Verzicht) giving up; **A~n** (Sch) homework sg

Aufgang m way up; (Treppe) stairs pl; (Astr) rise

aufgeben† v sep ●vt give up; post <Brief>; send <Telegramm>; place <Bestellung>; register <Gepäck>; put in the paper <Annonce>; **jdm eine Aufgabe a~** set s.o. a task; **jdm Suppe a~** serve s.o. with soup ●vi (haben) give up

Aufgebot nt contingent (**an** + dat of); (Relig) banns pl

aufgedunsen a bloated

aufgehen† vi sep (sein) open; (sich lösen) come undone; <Teig, Sonne:> rise; <Saat:> come up; (Math) come out exactly; **in Flammen a~** go up in flames

aufgelegt a **gut/schlecht a~ sein** be in a good/bad mood

aufgeregt a excited; (erregt) agitated

aufgeschlossen a (fig) openminded

aufgeweckt a (fig) bright

aufgießen† vt sep pour on; (aufbrühen) make <Tee>

aufgreifen† *vt sep* pick up; take up <*Vorschlag, Thema*>

aufgrund *prep* (+ *gen*) on the strength of

Aufguss *m* infusion

aufhaben† *v sep* ● *vt* have on; **den Mund a~** have one's mouth open; **viel a~** (*Sch*) have a lot of homework ● *vi* (*haben*) be open

aufhalten† *vt sep* hold up; (*anhalten*) stop; (*abhalten*) keep; (*offenhalten*) hold open; hold out <*Hand*>; **sich a~** stay; (*sich befassen*) spend one's time (**mit** on)

aufhäng|en *vt/i sep* (*haben*) hang up; (*henken*) hang; **sich a~en** hang oneself. **A~er** *m* **-s,-** loop

aufheben† *vt sep* pick up; (*hochheben*) raise; (*aufbewahren*) keep; (*beenden*) end; (*rückgängig machen*) lift; (*abschaffen*) abolish; (*Jur*) quash <*Urteil*>; repeal <*Gesetz*>; (*ausgleichen*) cancel out; **gut aufgehoben sein** be well looked after

aufheitern *vt sep* cheer up; **sich a~** <*Wetter:*> brighten up

aufhellen *vt sep* lighten; **sich a~** <*Himmel:*> brighten

aufhetzen *vt sep* incite

aufholen *v sep* ● *vt* make up ● *vi* (*haben*) catch up; (*zeitlich*) make up time

aufhören *vi sep* (*haben*) stop

aufklappen *vt/i sep* (*sein*) open

aufklär|en *vt sep* solve; **jdn a~en** enlighten; **sich a~en** be solved; <*Wetter:*> clear up. **A~ung** *f* solution; enlightenment; (*Mil*) reconnaissance; **sexuelle A~ung** sex education

aufkleb|en *vt sep* stick on. **A~er** *m* **-s,-** sticker

aufknöpfen *vt sep* unbutton

aufkochen *v sep* ● *vt* bring to the boil ● *vi* (*sein*) come to the boil

aufkommen† *vi sep* (*sein*) start; <*Wind:*> spring up; <*Mode:*> come in

aufkrempeln *vt sep* roll up

aufladen† *vt sep* load; (*Electr*) charge

Auflage *f* impression; (*Ausgabe*) edition; (*Zeitungs-*) circulation

auflassen† *vt sep* leave open; leave on <*Hut*>

Auflauf *m* crowd; (*Culin*) ≈ soufflé

auflegen *v sep* ● *vt* apply (**auf** + *acc* to); put down <*Hörer*>; **neu a~** reprint ● *vi* (*haben*) ring off

auflehn|en (sich) *vr sep* (*fig*) rebel. **A~ung** *f* - rebellion

auflesen† *vt sep* pick up

aufleuchten *vi sep* (*haben*) light up

auflös|en *vt sep* dissolve; close <*Konto*>; **sich a~en** dissolve; <*Nebel:*> clear. **A~ung** *f* dissolution; (*Lösung*) solution

aufmach|en *v sep* ● *vt* open; (*lösen*) undo; **sich a~en** set out (**nach** for) ● *vi* (*haben*) open; **jdm a~en** open the door to s.o. **A~ung** *f* **-, -en** get-up

aufmerksam *a* attentive; **a~ werden auf** (+ *acc*) notice; **jdn a~ machen auf** (+ *acc*) draw s.o.'s attention to. **A~keit** *f* **-, -en** attention; (*Höflichkeit*) courtesy

aufmuntern *vt sep* cheer up

Aufnahme *f* **-, -n** acceptance; (*Empfang*) reception; (*in Klub, Krankenhaus*) admission; (*Einbeziehung*) inclusion; (*Beginn*) start; (*Foto*) photograph; (*Film-*) shot; (*Mus*) recording; (*Band-*) tape recording. **a~fähig** *a* receptive. **A~prüfung** *f* entrance examination

aufnehmen† *vt sep* pick up; (*absorbieren*) absorb; take <*Nahrung, Foto*>; (*fassen*) hold; (*annehmen*) accept; (*leihen*) borrow; (*empfangen*) receive; (*in

Klub, Krankenhaus) admit;
(beherbergen, geistig erfassen)
take in; *(einbeziehen)* include;
(beginnen) take up;
(niederschreiben) take down;
(filmen) film, shoot; *(Mus)* record;
auf Band a~ tape[-record]
aufopfer|n vt sep sacrifice; **sich
a~n** sacrifice oneself. **A~ung** f
self-sacrifice
aufpassen vi sep *(haben)* pay
attention; *(sich vorsehen)* take
care; **a~ auf** (+ *acc*) look after
Aufprall m -[e]s impact. **a~en** vi
sep *(sein)* **a~en auf** (+ *acc*) hit
aufpumpen vt sep pump up,
inflate
aufputsch|en vt sep incite.
A~mittel nt stimulant
aufquellen† vi sep *(sein)* swell
aufraffen vt sep pick up; **sich a~**
pick oneself up; *(fig)* pull oneself
together
aufragen vi sep *(sein)* rise [up]
aufräumen vt/i sep *(haben)* tidy
up; *(wegräumen)* put away
aufrecht a & adv upright.
a~erhalten† vt sep *(fig)* maintain
aufreg|en vt excite; *(beunruhigen)*
upset; *(ärgern)* annoy; **sich a~en**
get excited; *(sich erregen)* get
worked up. **a~end** a exciting.
A~ung f excitement
aufreiben† vt sep chafe; *(fig)*
wear down. **a~d** a trying
aufreißen† v sep ● vt tear open;
dig up *<Straße>*; open wide
<Augen, Mund> ● vi *(sein)* split
open
aufrichtig a sincere. **A~keit** f -
sincerity
aufrollen vt sep roll up;
(entrollen) unroll
aufrücken vi sep *(sein)* move up;
(fig) be promoted
Aufruf m appeal (**an** + *dat* to).
a~en† vt sep call out *<Namen>*;
jdn a~en call s.o.'s name

Aufruhr m -s, -e turmoil;
(Empörung) revolt
aufrühr|en vt sep stir up. **A~er** m
-s,- rebel. **a~erisch** a
inflammatory; *(rebellisch)*
rebellious
aufrunden vt sep round up
aufrüsten vi sep *(haben)* arm
aufsagen vt sep recite
aufsässig a rebellious
Aufsatz m top; *(Sch)* essay
aufsaugen† vt sep soak up
aufschauen vi sep *(haben)* look
up (**zu** at/*(fig)* to)
aufschichten vt sep stack up
aufschieben† vt sep slide open;
(verschieben) put off, postpone
Aufschlag m impact; *(Tennis)*
service; *(Hosen-)* turn-up;
(Ärmel-) upturned cuff; *(Revers)*
lapel; *(Comm)* surcharge. **a~en†**
v sep ● vt open; crack *<Ei>*;
(hochschlagen) turn up;
(errichten) put up; *(erhöhen)*
increase; cast on *<Masche>*; **sich**
(dat) **das Knie a~en** cut [open]
one's knee ● vi *(haben)* hit (**auf
etw** *acc/dat* sth); *(Tennis)* serve;
(teurer werden) go up
aufschließen† v sep ● vt unlock
● vi *(haben)* unlock the door
aufschlussreich a revealing;
(lehrreich) informative
aufschneiden† v sep ● vt cut
open; *(in Scheiben)* slice ● vi
(haben) 🅸 exaggerate
Aufschnitt m sliced sausage, cold
meat [and cheese]
aufschrauben vt sep screw on;
(abschrauben) unscrew
Aufschrei m [sudden] cry
aufschreiben† vt sep write down;
jdn a~ *<Polizist:>* book s.o.
Aufschrift f inscription; *(Etikett)*
label
Aufschub m delay; *(Frist)* grace
aufschürfen vt sep **sich** *(dat)* **das
Knie a~** graze one's knee

aufschwingen† (sich) *vr sep* find the energy (**zu** for)

Aufschwung *m* (*fig*) upturn

aufsehen† *vi sep* (*haben*) look up (**zu** at/(*fig*) to). **A~** *nt* -s **A~ erregen** cause a sensation; **A~erregend** sensational

Aufseher(in) *m* -s,- (*f* -, -nen) supervisor; (*Gefängnis-*) warder

aufsetzen *vt sep* put on; (*verfassen*) draw up; (*entwerfen*) draft; **sich a~** sit up

Aufsicht *f* supervision; (*Person*) supervisor. **A~srat** *m* board of directors

aufsperren *vt sep* open wide

aufspielen *v sep* ● *vi* (*haben*) play ● *vr* **sich a~** show off

aufspießen *vt sep* spear

aufspringen† *vi sep* (*sein*) jump up; (*aufprallen*) bounce; (*sich öffnen*) burst open

aufspüren *vt sep* track down

aufstacheln *vt sep* incite

Aufstand *m* uprising, rebellion

aufständisch *a* rebellious

aufstehen† *vi sep* (*sein*) get up; (*offen sein*) be open; (*fig*) rise up

aufsteigen† *vi sep* (*sein*) get on; <*Reiter:*> mount; <*Bergsteiger:*> climb up; (*hochsteigen*) rise [up]; (*fig: befördert werden*) rise (**zu** to); (*Sport*) be promoted

aufstell|en *vt sep* put up; (*Culin*) put on; (*postieren*) post; (*in einer Reihe*) line up; (*nominieren*) nominate; (*Sport*) select <*Mannschaft*>; make out <*Liste*>; lay down <*Regel*>; make <*Behauptung*>; set up <*Rekord*>. **A~ung** *f* nomination; (*Liste*) list

Aufstieg *m* -[e]s, -e ascent; (*fig*) rise; (*Sport*) promotion

Aufstoßen *nt* -s burping

aufstrebend *a* (*fig*) ambitious

Aufstrich *m* [sandwich] spread

aufstützen *vt sep* rest (**auf** + *acc* on); **sich a~** lean (**auf** + *acc* on)

Auftakt *m* (*fig*) start

auftauchen *vi sep* (*sein*) emerge; (*fig*) turn up; <*Frage:*> crop up

auftauen *vt/i sep* (*sein*) thaw

aufteil|en *vt sep* divide [up]. **A~ung** *f* division

auftischen *vt sep* serve [up]

Auftrag *m* -[e]s,"e task; (*Kunst*) commission; (*Comm*) order; **im A~** (+ *gen*) on behalf of. **a~en†** *vt sep* apply; (*servieren*) serve; (*abtragen*) wear out; **jdm a~en** instruct s.o. (**zu** to). **A~geber** *m* -s,- client

auftrennen *vt sep* unpick, undo

auftreten† *vi sep* (*sein*) tread; (*sich benehmen*) behave, act; (*Theat*) appear; (*die Bühne betreten*) enter; (*vorkommen*) occur

Auftrieb *m* buoyancy; (*fig*) boost

Auftritt *m* (*Theat*) appearance; (*auf die Bühne*) entrance; (*Szene*) scene

aufwachen *vi sep* (*sein*) wake up

aufwachsen† *vi sep* (*sein*) grow up

Aufwand *m* -[e]s expenditure; (*Luxus*) extravagance; (*Mühe*) trouble; **A~ treiben** be extravagant

aufwändig *a* = **aufwendig**

aufwärmen *vt sep* heat up; (*fig*) rake up; **sich a~** warm oneself; (*Sport*) warm up

Aufwartefrau *f* cleaner

aufwärts *adv* upwards; (*bergauf*) uphill; **es geht a~ mit jdm/etw** s.o./sth is improving

Aufwartung *f* - cleaner

aufwecken *vt sep* wake up

aufweichen *v sep* ● *vt* soften ● *vi* (*sein*) become soft

aufweisen† *vt sep* have, show

aufwend|en† *vt sep* spend; **Mühe a~en** take pains. **a~ig** *a* lavish; (*teuer*) expensive

aufwert|en *vt sep* revalue. **A~ung** *f* revaluation

aufwickeln vt sep roll up; (auswickeln) unwrap
Aufwiegler m -s,- agitator
aufwisch|en vt sep wipe up; wash <Fußboden>. **A~lappen** m floorcloth
aufwühlen vt sep churn up
aufzähl|en vt sep enumerate, list. **A~ung** f list
aufzeichn|en vt sep record; (zeichnen) draw. **A~ung** f recording; **A~ungen** notes
aufziehen† v sep ● vt pull up; hoist <Segel>; (öffnen) open; draw <Vorhang>; (großziehen) bring up; rear <Tier>; mount <Bild>; thread <Perlen>; wind up <Uhr>; (🗊 necken) tease ● vi (sein) approach
Aufzug m hoist; (Fahrstuhl) lift, (Amer) elevator; (Prozession) procession; (Theat) act
Augapfel m eyeball
Auge nt -s, -n eye; (Punkt) spot; **vier A~n werfen** throw a four; **gute A~n** good eyesight; **unter vier A~n** in private; **im A~ behalten** keep in sight; (fig) bear in mind
Augenblick m moment; **A~!** just a moment! **a~lich** a immediate; (derzeitig) present ● adv immediately; (derzeit) at present
Augen|braue f eyebrow. **A~-höhle** f eye socket. **A~licht** nt sight. **A~lid** nt eyelid
August m -[s] August
Auktion /-'tsjo:n/ f -, -en auction
Aula f -, -len (Sch) [assembly] hall
Au-pair-Mädchen /o'pε:r-/ nt aupair
aus prep (+ dat) out of; (von) from; (bestehend) [made] of; **aus Angst** from or out of fear; **aus Spaß** for fun ● adv out; <Licht, Radio> off; **aus sein auf** (+ acc) be after; **aus und ein** in and out; **von sich aus** of one's own accord; **von mir aus** as far as I'm concerned
ausarbeiten vt sep work out

ausarten vi sep (sein) degenerate (in + acc into)
ausatmen vt/i sep (haben) breathe out
ausbauen vt sep remove; (vergrößern) extend; (fig) expand
ausbedingen† vt sep sich (dat) **a~** insist on; (zur Bedingung machen) stipulate
ausbesser|n vt sep mend, repair. **A~ung** f repair
ausbeulen vt sep remove the dents from; (dehnen) make baggy
ausbild|en vt sep train; (formen) form; (entwickeln) develop; sich **a~en** train (als/zu as); (entstehen) develop. **A~ung** f training; (Sch) education
ausbitten† vt sep sich (dat) **a~** ask for; (verlangen) insist on
ausblasen† vt sep blow out
ausbleiben† vi sep (sein) fail to appear; <Erfolg:> materialize; (nicht heimkommen) stay out
Ausblick m view
ausbrech|en† vi sep (sein) break out; <Vulkan:> erupt; (fliehen) escape; **in Tränen a~en** burst into tears. **A~er** m runaway
ausbreit|en vt sep spread [out]. **A~ung** f spread
Ausbruch m outbreak; (Vulkan-) eruption; (Wut-) outburst; (Flucht) escape, break-out
ausbrüten vt sep hatch
Ausdauer f perseverance; (körperlich) stamina. **a~nd** a persevering; (unermüdlich) untiring
ausdehnen vt sep stretch; (fig) extend; sich **a~** stretch; (Phys & fig) expand; (dauern) last
ausdenken† vt sep sich (dat) **a~** think up; (sich vorstellen) imagine
Ausdruck m expression; (Fach-) term; (Computer) printout. **a~en** vt sep print

ausdrücken vt sep squeeze out;
squeeze <Zitrone>; stub out
<Zigarette>; (äußern) express
ausdrucks|los a expressionless.
a~**voll** a expressive
auseinander adv apart; (entzwei)
in pieces; a~ **falten** unfold; a~
gehen part; <Linien, Meinungen:>
diverge; <Ehe:> break up; a~
halten tell apart; a~ **nehmen** take
apart or to pieces; a~ **setzen**
explain (jdm to s.o.); **sich a~**
setzen sit apart; (sich
aussprechen) have it out (mit jdm
with s.o.); come to grips (mit
einem Problem with a problem).
A~**setzung** f -, -en discussion;
(Streit) argument
auserlesen a select, choice
Ausfahrt f drive; (Autobahn-,
Garagen-) exit
Ausfall m failure; (Absage)
cancellation; (Comm) loss. a~**en†**
vi sep (sein) fall out; (versagen)
fail; (abgesagt werden) be
cancelled; **gut/schlecht a~en** turn
out to be good/poor
ausfallend, ausfällig a abusive
ausfertig|en vt sep make out.
A~**ung** f -, -en **in doppelter A~ung**
in duplicate
ausfindig a a~ **machen** find
Ausflug m excursion, outing
Ausflügler m -s,- [day-]tripper
Ausfluss m outlet; (Abfluss)
drain; (Med) discharge
ausfragen vt sep question
Ausfuhr f -, -en (Comm) export
ausführ|en vt sep take out;
(Comm) export; (erklären)
explain. a~**lich** a detailed ●adv
in detail. A~**ung** f execution;
(Comm) version; (äußere) finish;
(Qualität) workmanship;
(Erklärung) explanation
Ausgabe f issue; (Buch-) edition;
(Comm) version
Ausgang m way out, exit;
(Flugsteig) gate; (Ende) end;
(Ergebnis) outcome. A~**spunkt** m
starting-point. A~**ssperre** f
curfew
ausgeben† vt sep hand out; issue
<Fahrkarten>; spend <Geld>; **sich**
a~ **als** pretend to be
ausgebildet a trained
ausgebucht a fully booked;
<Vorstellung> sold out
ausgefallen a unusual
ausgefranst a frayed
ausgeglichen a [well-]balanced
ausgeh|en† vi sep (sein) go out;
<Haare:> fall out; <Vorräte,
Geld:> run out; (verblassen) fade;
gut/schlecht a~en end well/badly;
davon a~en, dass assume that.
A~**verbot** nt curfew
ausgelassen a high-spirited
ausgemacht a agreed
ausgenommen conj except; a~
wenn unless
ausgeprägt a marked
ausgeschlossen pred a out of
the question
ausgeschnitten a low-cut
ausgesprochen a marked ●adv
decidedly
ausgestorben a extinct; [wie] a~
<Straße:> deserted
Ausgestoßene(r) m/f outcast
ausgezeichnet a excellent
ausgiebig a extensive;
(ausgedehnt) long; a~ **Gebrauch**
machen von make full use of
ausgießen† vt sep pour out
Ausgleich m -[e]s balance;
(Entschädigung) compensation.
a~**en†** v sep ●vt balance; even
out <Höhe>; (wettmachen)
compensate for; **sich a~en**
balance out ●vi (haben) (Sport)
equalize. A~**streffer** m equalizer
ausgrab|en† vt sep dig up;
(Archaeol) excavate. A~**ung** f -,
-en excavation
Ausguss m [kitchen] sink
aushaben† vt sep have finished
<Buch>

aushalten† vt sep bear, stand; hold <Note>; (Unterhalt zahlen für) keep; **nicht auszuhalten, nicht zum A~** unbearable

aushändigen vt sep hand over

aushängen¹ vt sep (reg) display; take off its hinges <Tür>

aushäng|en² vi sep (haben) be displayed. **A~eschild** nt sign

ausheben† vt sep excavate

aushecken vt sep (fig) hatch

aushelfen† vi sep (haben) help out (jdm s.o.)

Aushilf|e f [temporary] assistant; **zur A~e** to help out. **A~skraft** f temporary worker. **a~sweise** adv temporarily

aushöhlen vt sep hollow out

auskennen† (sich) vr sep know one's way around; **sich mit/in etw** (dat) **a~** know all about sth

auskommen† vi sep (sein) manage (mit/ohne with/without); (sich vertragen) get on (gut well)

auskugeln vt sep **sich** (dat) **den Arm a~** dislocate one's shoulder

auskühlen vt/i sep (sein) cool

auskundschaften vt sep spy out

Auskunft f -,¨e information; (A~sstelle) information desk/ (Büro) bureau; (Teleph) enquiries pl; **eine A~** a piece of information

auslachen vt sep laugh at

Auslage f [window] display; **A~n** expenses

Ausland nt **im/ins A~** abroad

Ausländ|er(in) m -s,- (f -, -nen) foreigner. **a~isch** a foreign

Auslandsgespräch nt international call

auslass|en† vt sep let out; let down <Saum>; (weglassen) leave out; (versäumen) miss; (Culin) melt; (fig) vent <Ärger> (an + dat on). **A~ungszeichen** nt apostrophe

Auslauf m run. **a~en**† vi sep (sein) run out; <Farbe:> run;

(Naut) put to sea; <Modell:> be discontinued

ausleeren vt sep empty [out]

auslegen vt sep lay out; display <Waren>; (auskleiden) line (mit with); (bezahlen) pay; (deuten) interpret. **A~ung** f -, -en interpretation

ausleihen† vt sep lend; **sich** (dat) **a~** borrow

Auslese f - selection; (fig) pick; (Elite) elite

ausliefer|n vt sep hand over; extradite. **A~ung** f handing over; (Jur) extradition; (Comm) distribution

ausloggen vi sep log off or out

auslosen vt sep draw lots for

auslös|en vt sep set off, trigger; (fig) cause; arouse <Begeisterung>; (einlösen) redeem; pay a ransom for <Gefangene>. **A~er** m -s,- trigger; (Phot) shutter release

Auslosung f draw

auslüften vt/i sep (haben) air

ausmachen vt sep put out; (abschalten) turn off; (abmachen) arrange; (erkennen) make out; (betragen) amount to; (wichtig sein) matter

Ausmaß nt extent; **A~e** dimensions

Ausnahm|e f -, -n exception. **A~ezustand** m state of emergency. **a~slos** adv without exception. **a~sweise** adv as an exception

ausnehmen† vt sep take out; gut <Fisch>; **sich gut a~** look good. **a~d** adv exceptionally

ausnutz|en, ausnutz|en vt sep exploit. **A~ung** f exploitation

auspacken vt sep unpack; (auswickeln) unwrap

ausplaudern vt sep let out, blab

ausprobieren vt sep try out

Auspuff *m* **-s** exhaust [system].
 A~gase *ntpl* exhaust fumes.
 A~rohr *nt* exhaust pipe
auspusten *vt sep* blow out
ausradieren *vt sep* rub out
ausrauben *vt sep* rob
ausräuchern *vt sep* smoke out;
 fumigate *<Zimmer>*
ausräumen *vt sep* clear out
ausrechnen *vt sep* work out
Ausrede *f* excuse. **a~n** *v sep* ● *vi*
 (haben) finish speaking ● *vt* **jdm
 etw a~n** talk s.o. out of sth
ausreichen *vi sep (haben)* be
 enough. **a~d** *a* adequate
Ausreise *f* departure. **a~n** *vi sep*
 (sein) leave the country.
 A~visum *nt* exit visa
ausreißen† *v sep* ● *vt* pull *or* tear
 out ● *vi (sein)* 🔟 run away
ausrenken *vt sep* dislocate
ausrichten *vt sep* align;
 (bestellen) deliver; *(erreichen)*
 achieve; **jdm a~** tell s.o. **(dass**
 that); **ich soll Ihnen Grüße von X
 a~** X sends [you] his regards
ausrotten *vt sep* exterminate;
 (fig) eradicate
Ausruf *m* exclamation. **a~en**† *vt
 sep* exclaim; call out *<Namen>*;
 (verkünden) proclaim; **jdn a~en
 lassen** have s.o. paged.
 A~ezeichen *nt* exclamation mark
ausruhen *vt/i sep (haben)* rest;
 sich a~ have a rest
ausrüst|en *vt sep* equip. **A~ung** *f*
 equipment; *(Mil)* kit
ausrutschen *vi sep (sein)* slip
Aussage *f* **-, -n** statement; *(Jur)*
 testimony, evidence; *(Gram)*
 predicate. **a~n** *vt/i sep (haben)*
 state; *(Jur)* give evidence, testify
ausschalten *vt sep* switch off
Ausschank *m* sale of alcoholic
 drinks; *(Bar)* bar
Ausschau *f* **- A~ halten nach** look
 out for

ausscheiden† *vi sep (sein)* leave;
 (Sport) drop out; *(nicht in Frage
 kommen)* be excluded
ausschenken *vt sep* pour out
ausscheren *vi sep (sein) (Auto)*
 pull out
ausschildern *vt sep* signpost
ausschimpfen *vt sep* tell off
ausschlafen† *vi/r sep (haben)*
 [sich] a~ get enough sleep;
 (morgens) sleep late
Ausschlag *m (Med)* rash; **den A~
 geben** *(fig)* tip the balance.
 a~gebend *a* decisive
ausschließ|en† *vt sep* lock out;
 (fig) exclude; *(entfernen)* expel.
 a~lich *a* exclusive
ausschlüpfen *vi sep (sein)* hatch
Ausschluss *m* exclusion;
 expulsion; **unter A~ der
 Öffentlichkeit** in camera
ausschneiden† *vt sep* cut out
Ausschnitt *m* excerpt, extract;
 (Zeitungs-) cutting; *(Hals-)*
 neckline
ausschöpfen *vt sep* ladle out;
 (Naut) bail out; exhaust
 <Möglichkeiten>
ausschreiben† *vt sep* write out;
 (ausstellen) make out;
 (bekanntgeben) announce; put
 out to tender *<Auftrag>*
Ausschreitungen *fpl* riots;
 (Exzesse) excesses
Ausschuss *m* committee; *(Comm)*
 rejects *pl*
ausschütten *vt sep* tip out;
 (verschütten) spill; *(leeren)* empty
aussehen† *vi sep (haben)* look;
 wie sieht er/es aus? what does
 he/it look like? **A~** *nt* **-s**
 appearance
außen *adv* [on the] outside; **nach
 a~** outwards. **A~bordmotor** *m*
 outboard motor. **A~handel** *m*
 foreign trade. **A~minister** *m*
 Foreign Minister. **A~politik** *f*
 foreign policy. **A~seite** *f* outside.
 A~seiter *m* **-s,-** outsider; *(fig)*

misfit. **A~stände** *mpl* outstanding debts

außer *prep* (+ *dat*) except [for], apart from; (*außerhalb*) out of; **a~ sich** (*fig*) beside oneself ● *conj* except; **a~ wenn** unless. **a~dem** *adv* in addition, as well ● *conj* moreover

äußer|e(r,s) *a* external; <*Teil, Schicht*> outer. **Ä~e(s)** *nt* exterior; (*Aussehen*) appearance

außer|ehelich *a* extramarital. **a~gewöhnlich** *a* exceptional. **a~halb** *prep* (+ *gen*) outside ● *adv* **a~halb wohnen** live outside town

äußer|lich *a* external; (*fig*) outward. **ä~n** *vt* express; **sich ä~n** comment; (*sich zeigen*) manifest itself

außerordentlich *a* extraordinary

äußerst *adv* extremely

äußerste|(r,s) *a* outermost; (*weiteste*) furthest; (*höchste*) utmost, extreme; (*letzte*) last; (*schlimmste*) worst. **Ä~(s)** *nt* **das Ä~** the limit; (*Schlimmste*) the worst; **sein Ä~s tun** do one's utmost; **aufs Ä~** extremely

Äußerung *f* -, **-en** comment; (*Bemerkung*) remark

aussetzen *v sep* ● *vt* expose (*dat* to); abandon <*Kind*>; launch <*Boot*>; offer <*Belohnung*>; **etwas auszusetzen haben an** (+ *dat*) find fault with ● *vi* (*haben*) stop; <*Motor*:> cut out

Aussicht *f* -, **-en** view/(*fig*) prospect (**auf** + *acc* of); **weitere A~en** (*Meteorol*) further outlook *sg*. **a~slos** *a* hopeless

ausspannen *v sep* ● *vt* spread out; unhitch <*Pferd*> ● *vi* (*haben*) rest

aussperren *vt sep* lock out

ausspielen *v sep* ● *vt* play <*Karte*>; (*fig*) play off (**gegen** against) ● *vi* (*haben*) (*Kartenspiel*) lead

Aussprache *f* pronunciation; (*Gespräch*) talk

aussprechen† *vt sep* pronounce; (*äußern*) express; **sich a~** talk; come out (**für/gegen** in favour of/against)

Ausspruch *m* saying

ausspucken *v sep* ● *vt* spit out ● *vi* (*haben*) spit

ausspülen *vt sep* rinse out

ausstatt|en *vt sep* equip. **A~ung** *f* -, **-en** equipment; (*Innen-*) furnishings *pl*; (*Theat*) scenery and costumes *pl*

ausstehen† *v sep* ● *vt* suffer; **Angst a~** be frightened; **ich kann sie nicht a~** I can't stand her ● *vi* (*haben*) be outstanding

aussteigen† *vi sep* (*sein*) get out; (*aus Bus, Zug*) get off; **alles a~!** all change!

ausstell|en *vt sep* exhibit; (*Comm*) display; (*ausfertigen*) make out; issue <*Pass*>. **A~ung** *f* exhibition; (*Comm*) display

aussterben† *vi sep* (*sein*) die out; (*Biol*) become extinct

Aussteuer *f* trousseau

Ausstieg *m* **-[e]s, -e** exit

ausstopfen *vt sep* stuff

ausstoßen† *vt sep* emit; utter <*Fluch*>; heave <*Seufzer*>; (*ausschließen*) expel

ausstrahl|en *vt/i sep* (*sein*) radiate, emit; (*Radio, TV*) broadcast. **A~ung** *f* radiation

ausstrecken *vt sep* stretch out; put out <*Hand*>

ausstreichen† *vt sep* cross out

ausströmen *v sep* ● *vi* (*sein*) pour out; (*entweichen*) escape ● *vt* emit; (*ausstrahlen*) radiate

aussuchen *vt sep* pick, choose

Austausch *m* exchange. **a~bar** *a* interchangeable. **a~en** *vt sep* exchange; (*auswechseln*) replace

austeilen *vt sep* distribute

Auster *f* -, **-n** oyster

austragen† *vt sep* deliver; hold
<Wettkampf>; play *<Spiel>*
Austral|ien /-iən/ *nt* -s Australia.
A~ier(in) *m* -s,- (*f* -, -nen)
Australian. **a~isch** *a* Australian
austreiben† *vt sep* drive out;
(*Relig*) exorcize
austreten† *v sep* ● *vt* stamp out;
(*abnutzen*) wear down ● *vi* (*sein*)
come out; (*ausscheiden*) leave
(**aus etw** sth); [mal] **a~** 🔢 go to
the loo
austrinken† *vt/i sep* (*haben*)
drink up; (*leeren*) drain
Austritt *m* resignation
austrocknen *vt/i sep* (*sein*) dry
out
ausüben *vt sep* practise; carry on
<Handwerk>; exercise *<Recht>*;
exert *<Druck, Einfluss>*
Ausverkauf *m* [clearance] sale.
a~t *a* sold out
Auswahl *f* choice, selection;
(*Comm*) range; (*Sport*) team
auswählen *vt sep* choose, select
Auswander|er *m* emigrant. **a~n**
vi sep (*sein*) emigrate. **A~ung** *f*
emigration
auswärt|ig *a* non-local;
(*ausländisch*) foreign. **a~s** *adv*
outwards; (*Sport*) away. **A~sspiel**
nt away game
auswaschen† *vt sep* wash out
auswechseln *vt sep* change;
(*ersetzen*) replace; (*Sport*)
substitute
Ausweg *m* (*fig*) way out
ausweichen† *vi sep* (*sein*) get out
of the way; **jdm/etw a~en** avoid/
(*sich entziehen*) evade s.o./sth
Ausweis *m* -es, -e pass;
(*Mitglieds-, Studenten-*) card.
a~en† *vt sep* deport; **sich a~en**
prove one's identity. **A~papiere**
ntpl identification papers. **A~ung**
f deportation
auswendig *adv* by heart
auswerten *vt sep* evaluate
auswickeln *vt sep* unwrap

auswirk|en (sich) *vr sep* have an
effect (**auf** + *acc* on). **A~ung** *f*
effect; (*Folge*) consequence
auswringen *vt sep* wring out
auszahlen *vt sep* pay out;
(*entlohnen*) pay off; (*abfinden*)
buy out; **sich a~** (*fig*) pay off
auszählen *vt sep* count; (*Boxen*)
count out
Auszahlung *f* payment
auszeichn|en *vt sep* (*Comm*)
price; (*ehren*) honour; (*mit einem
Preis*) award a prize to; (*Mil*)
decorate; **sich a~en** distinguish
oneself. **A~ung** *f* honour; (*Preis*)
award; (*Mil*) decoration; (*Sch*)
distinction
ausziehen† *v sep* ● *vt* pull out;
(*auskleiden*) undress; take off
<Mantel, Schuhe> ● *vi* (*sein*)
move out; (*sich aufmachen*) set
out
Auszug *m* departure; (*Umzug*)
move; (*Ausschnitt*) extract;
(*Bank-*) statement
Auto *nt* -s, -s car; **A~ fahren** drive;
(*mitfahren*) go in the car.
A~bahn *f* motorway
Autobiographie *f* autobiography
Auto|bus *m* bus. **A~fahrer(in)**
m(f) driver, motorist. **A~fahrt** *f*
drive
Autogramm *nt* -s, -e autograph
Automat *m* -en, -en automatic
device; (*Münz-*) slot-machine;
(*Verkaufs-*) vending-machine;
(*Fahrkarten-*) machine; (*Techn*)
robot. **A~ik** *f* - automatic
mechanism; (*Auto*) automatic
transmission
automatisch *a* automatic
Autonummer *f* registration
number
Autopsie *f* -, -n autopsy
Autor *m* -s, -en /-'to:rən/ author
Auto|reisezug *m* Motorail.
A~rennen *nt* motor race
Autorin *f* -, -nen author[ess]

B

Autori|sation /-'tsio:n/ f - authorization. **A~tät** f -, -en authority

Auto|schlosser m motor mechanic. **A~skooter** /-sku:tɐ/ m -s, -s dodgem. **A~stopp** m -s per **A~stopp fahren** hitch-hike. **A~verleih** m car hire [firm]. **A~waschanlage** f car wash

autsch int ouch

Axt f -,-̈e axe

B, b /be:/ nt - (Mus) B flat
Baby /'be:bi/ nt -s, -s baby. **B~ausstattung** f layette. **B~sitter** /-sɪtɐ/ m -s, - babysitter
Bach m -[e]s,-̈e stream
Backbord nt -[e]s port [side]
Backe f -, -n cheek
backen vt/i† (haben) bake; (braten) fry
Backenzahn m molar
Bäcker m -s,- baker. **B~ei** f -, -en, **B~laden** m baker's shop
Back|obst nt dried fruit. **B~ofen** m oven. **B~pfeife** f 🗌 slap in the face. **B~pflaume** f prune. **B~pulver** nt baking-powder. **B~stein** m brick
Bad nt -[e]s,-̈er bath; (Zimmer) bathroom; (Schwimm-) pool; (Ort) spa
Bade|anstalt f swimming baths pl. **B~anzug** m swim-suit. **B~hose** f swimming trunks pl. **B~kappe** f bathing-cap. **B~mantel** m bathrobe. **b~n** vi (haben) have a bath; (im Meer) bathe ● vt bath; (waschen) bathe. **B~ort** m seaside resort.

B~wanne f bath. **B~zimmer** nt bathroom
Bagger m -s,- excavator; (Nass-) dredger. **B~see** m flooded gravel-pit
Bahn f -, -en path; (Astr) orbit; (Sport) track; (einzelne) lane; (Rodel-) run; (Stoff-) width; (Eisen-) railway; (Zug) train; (Straßen-) tram. **b~brechend** a (fig) pioneering. **B~hof** m [railway] station. **B~steig** m -[e]s, -e platform. **B~übergang** m level crossing
Bahre f -, -n stretcher
Baiser /bɛ'ze:/ nt -s, -s meringue
Bake f -, -n (Naut, Aviat) beacon
Bakterien /-iən/ fpl bacteria
Balanc|e /ba'lā:sə/ f - balance. **b~ieren** vt/i (haben/sein) balance
bald adv soon; (fast) almost
Baldachin /-xi:n/ m -s, -e canopy
bald|ig a early; <Besserung> speedy. **b~möglichst** adv as soon as possible
Balg nt & m -[e]s,-̈er 🗌 brat
Balkan m -s Balkans pl
Balken m -s,- beam
Balkon /bal'kõ:/ m -s, -s balcony; (Theat) circle
Ball¹ m -[e]s,-̈e ball
Ball² m -[e]s,-̈e (Tanz) ball
Ballade f -, -n ballad
Ballast m -[e]s ballast. **B~stoffe** mpl roughage sg
Ballen m -s,- bale; (Anat) ball of the hand/(Fuß-) foot; (Med) bunion
Ballerina f -, -nen ballerina
Ballett nt -s, -e ballet
Ballon /ba'lõ:/ m -s, -s balloon
Balsam m -s balm
Balt|ikum nt -s Baltic States pl. **b~isch** a Baltic
Bambus m -ses, -se bamboo
banal a banal
Banane f -, -n banana
Banause m -n, -n philistine

Band¹ *nt* **-[e]s,¨er** ribbon; (*Naht-, Ton-, Ziel-*) tape; **am laufenden B~** ⚏ non-stop

Band² *m* **-[e]s,¨e** volume

Band³ *nt* **-[e]s, -e** (*fig*) bond

Band⁴ /bɛnt/ *f* **-, -s** [jazz] band

Bandag|e /ban'da:ʒə/ *f* **-, -n** bandage. **b~ieren** *vt* bandage

Bande *f* **-, -n** gang

bändigen *vt* control, restrain; (*zähmen*) tame

Bandit *m* **-en, -en** bandit

Band|maß *nt* tape-measure. **B~scheibe** *f* (*Anat*) disc. **B~wurm** *m* tapeworm

Bang|e *f* **B~e haben** be afraid; **jdm B~e machen** frighten s.o. **b~en** *vi* (*haben*) fear (**um** for)

Banjo *nt* **-s, -s** banjo

Bank¹ *f* **-,¨e** bench

Bank² *f* **-, -en** (*Comm*) bank. **B~einzug** *m* direct debit

Bankett *nt* **-s, -e** banquet

Bankier /baŋ'kje:/ *m* **-s, -s** banker

Bankkonto *nt* bank account

Bankrott *m* **-s, -s** bankruptcy. **b~** *a* bankrupt

Bankwesen *nt* banking

Bann *m* **-[e]s, -e** (*fig*) spell. **b~en** *vt* exorcize; (*abwenden*) avert; **[wie] gebannt** spellbound

Banner *nt* **-s,-** banner

bar *a* (*rein*) sheer; <*Gold*> pure; **b~es Geld** cash; **[in] bar bezahlen** pay cash

Bar *f* **-, -s** bar

Bär *m* **-en, -en** bear

Baracke *f* **-, -n** (*Mil*) hut

Barb|ar *m* **-en, -en** barbarian. **b~arisch** *a* barbaric

bar|fuß *adv* barefoot. **B~geld** *nt* cash

barmherzig *a* merciful

barock *a* baroque. **B~** *nt & m* **-[s]** baroque

Barometer *nt* **-s,-** barometer

Baron *m* **-s, -e** baron. **B~in** *f* **-, -nen** baroness

Barren *m* **-s,-** (*Gold-*) bar, ingot; (*Sport*) parallel bars *pl*. **B~gold** *nt* gold bullion

Barriere *f* **-, -n** barrier

Barrikade *f* **-, -n** barricade

barsch *a* gruff

Barsch *m* **-[e]s, -e** (*Zool*) perch

Bart *m* **-[e]s,¨e** beard; (*der Katze*) whiskers *pl*

bärtig *a* bearded

Barzahlung *f* cash payment

Basar *m* **-s, -e** bazaar

Base¹ *f* **-, -n** [female] cousin

Base² *f* **-, -n** (*Chem*) alkali, base

Basel *nt* **-s** Basle

basieren *vi* (*haben*) be based (**auf** + *dat* on)

Basilikum *nt* **-s** basil

Basis *f* **-,Basen** base; (*fig*) basis

basisch *a* (*Chem*) alkaline

Bask|enmütze *f* beret. **b~isch** *a* Basque

Bass *m* **-es,¨e** bass

Bassin /ba'sɛ̃:/ *nt* **-s, -s** pond; (*Brunnen-*) basin; (*Schwimm-*) pool

Bassist *m* **-en, -en** bass player; (*Sänger*) bass

Bast *m* **-[e]s** raffia

basteln *vt* make ● *vi* (*haben*) do handicrafts

Batterie *f* **-, -n** battery

Bau¹ *m* **-[e]s, -e** burrow; (*Fuchs-*) earth

Bau² *m* **-[e]s, -ten** construction; (*Gebäude*) building; (*Auf-*) structure; (*Körper-*) build; (*B~stelle*) building site. **B~arbeiten** *fpl* building work *sg*; (*Straßen-*) road-works

Bauch *m* **-[e]s, Bäuche** abdomen, belly; (*Magen*) stomach; (*Bauchung*) bulge. **b~ig** *a* bulbous. **B~nabel** *m* navel. **B~redner** *m* ventriloquist. **B~schmerzen** *mpl* stomach-ache *sg*. **B~speicheldrüse** *f* pancreas

bauen *vt* build; (*konstruieren*) construct ● *vi* (*haben*) build (**an**

B

etw *dat* sth); **b~ auf** (+ *acc*) (*fig*) rely on

Bauer¹ *m* **-s, -n** farmer; (*Schach*) pawn

Bauer² *nt* **-s,-** [bird]cage

bäuerlich *a* rustic

Bauern|haus *nt* farmhouse. **B~hof** *m* farm

bau|fällig *a* dilapidated. **B~genehmigung** *f* planning permission. **B~gerüst** *nt* scaffolding. **B~jahr** *nt* year of construction. **B~kunst** *f* architecture. **b~lich** *a* structural

Baum *m* **-[e]s, Bäume** tree

baumeln *vi* (*haben*) dangle

bäumen (sich) *vr* rear [up]

Baum|schule *f* [tree] nursery. **B~wolle** *f* cotton

Bausch *m* **-[e]s, Bäusche** wad; **in B~ und Bogen** (*fig*) wholesale. **b~en** *vt* puff out

Bau|sparkasse *f* building society. **B~stein** *m* building brick. **B~stelle** *f* building site; (*Straßen-*) roadworks *pl*. **B~unternehmer** *m* building contractor

Bayer|(in) *m* **-s, -n** (*f* **-, -nen**) Bavarian. **B~n** *nt* **-s** Bavaria

bay[e]risch *a* Bavarian

Bazillus *m* **-,** **-llen** bacillus

beabsichtig|en *vt* intend. **b~t** *a* intended; intentional

beacht|en *vt* take notice of; (*einhalten*) observe; (*folgen*) follow; **nicht b~en** ignore. **b~lich** *a* considerable. **B~ung** *f* - observance; **etw** (*dat*) **keine B~ung schenken** take no notice of sth

Beamte(r) *m*, **Beamtin** *f* **-, -nen** official; (*Staats-*) civil servant; (*Schalter-*) clerk

beanspruchen *vt* claim; (*erfordern*) demand

beanstand|en *vt* find fault with; (*Comm*) make a complaint about. **B~ung** *f* **-, -en** complaint

beantragen *vt* apply for

beantworten *vt* answer

bearbeiten *vt* work; (*weiter-*) process; (*behandeln*) treat (**mit** with); (*Admin*) deal with; (*redigieren*) edit; (*Theat*) adapt; (*Mus*) arrange

Beatmungsgerät *nt* ventilator

beaufsichtig|en *vt* supervise. **B~ung** *f* **-** supervision

beauftragen *vt* instruct; commission <*Künstler*>

bebauen *vt* build on; (*bestellen*) cultivate

beben *vi* (*haben*) tremble

Becher *m* **-s,-** beaker; (*Henkel-*) mug; (*Joghurt-, Sahne-*) carton

Becken *nt* **-s,-** basin; pool; (*Mus*) cymbals *pl*; (*Anat*) pelvis

bedacht *a* careful; **darauf b~** anxious (**zu** to)

bedächtig *a* careful; slow

bedanken (sich) *vr* thank (**bei jdm** s.o.)

Bedarf *m* **-s** need/(*Comm*) demand (**an** + *dat* for); **bei B~** if required. **B~shaltestelle** *f* request stop

bedauer|lich *a* regrettable. **b~licherweise** *adv* unfortunately. **b~n** *vt* regret; (*bemitleiden*) feel sorry for; **bedaure!** sorry! **b~nswert** *a* pitiful; (*bedauerlich*) regrettable

bedeckt *a* covered; <*Himmel*> overcast

bedenken† *vt* consider; (*überlegen*) think over. **B~** *pl* misgivings; **ohne B~** without hesitation

bedenklich *a* doubtful; (*verdächtig*) dubious; (*ernst*) serious

bedeut|en *vi* (*haben*) mean. **b~end** *a* important; (*beträchtlich*) considerable. **B~ung** *f* **-, -en** meaning; (*Wichtigkeit*) importance. **b~ungslos** *a* meaningless; (*unwichtig*) unimportant. **b~ungsvoll** *a* significant; (*vielsagend*) meaningful

bedien|en *vt* serve; (*betätigen*) operate; **sich [selbst] b~en** help oneself. **B~ung** *f* -, **-en** service; (*Betätigung*) operation; (*Kellner*) waiter; (*Kellnerin*) *f* waitress. **B~ungsgeld** *nt* service charge

Bedingung *f* -, **-en** condition; **B~en** conditions; (*Comm*) terms. **b~slos** *a* unconditional

bedroh|en *vt* threaten. **b~lich** *a* threatening. **B~ung** *f* threat

bedrücken *vt* depress

bedruckt *a* printed

bedürf|en† *vi* (*haben*) (+ *gen*) need. **B~nis** *nt* **-ses, -se** need

Beefsteak /'bi:fste:k/ *nt* **-s, -s** steak; **deutsches B~** hamburger

beeilen (sich) *vr* hurry; hasten (**zu** to)

beeindrucken *vt* impress

beeinflussen *vt* influence

beeinträchtigen *vt* mar; (*schädigen*) impair

beengen *vt* restrict

beerdig|en *vt* bury. **B~ung** *f* -, **-en** funeral

Beere *f* -, **-n** berry

Beet *nt* **-[e]s, -e** (*Hort*) bed

Beete *f* -, **-n rote B~** beetroot

befähig|en *vt* enable; (*qualifizieren*) qualify. **B~ung** *f* - qualification; (*Fähigkeit*) ability

befahrbar *a* passable

befallen† *vt* attack; <*Angst:*> seize

befangen *a* shy; (*gehemmt*) self-conscious; (*Jur*) biased. **B~heit** *f* - shyness; self-consciousness; bias

befassen (sich) *vr* concern oneself/(*behandeln*) deal (**mit** with)

Befehl *m* **-[e]s, -e** order; (*Leitung*) command (**über** + *acc* of). **b~en†** *vt* **jdm etw b~en** order s.o. to do sth ● *vi* (*haben*) give the orders.

B~sform *f* (*Gram*) imperative. **B~shaber** *m* **-s,-** commander

befestigen *vt* fasten (**an** + *dat* to); (*Mil*) fortify

befeuchten *vt* moisten

befind|en (sich) *vr* be. **B~** *nt* **-s** [state of] health

beflecken *vt* stain

befolgen *vt* follow

beförder|n *vt* transport; (*im Rang*) promote. **B~ung** *f* -, **-en** transport; promotion

befragen *vt* question

befrei|en *vt* free; (*räumen*) clear (**von** of); (*freistellen*) exempt (**von** from); **sich b~en** free oneself. **B~er** *m* **-s,-** liberator. **B~ung** *f* - liberation; exemption

befreunden (sich) *vr* make friends; **befreundet sein** be friends

befriedig|en *vt* satisfy. **b~end** *a* satisfying; (*zufrieden stellend*) satisfactory. **B~ung** *f* - satisfaction

befrucht|en *vt* fertilize. **B~ung** *f* - fertilization; **künstliche B~ung** artificial insemination

Befugnis *f* -, **-se** authority

Befund *m* result

befürcht|en *vt* fear. **B~ung** *f* -, **-en** fear

befürworten *vt* support

begab|t *a* gifted. **B~ung** *f* -, **-en** gift, talent

begeben† (sich) *vr* go; **sich in Gefahr b~** expose oneself to danger

begegn|en *vi* (*sein*) **jdm/etw b~en** meet s.o./sth. **B~ung** *f* -, **-en** meeting

begehr|en *vt* desire. **b~t** *a* sought-after

begeister|n *vt* **jdn b~n** arouse s.o.'s enthusiasm. **b~t** *a* enthusiastic; (*eifrig*) keen. **B~ung** *f* - enthusiasm

Begierde *f* -, **-n** desire

Beginn *m* **-s** beginning. **b~en†** *vt/i* (*haben*) start, begin

B

beglaubigen vt authenticate
begleichen† vt settle
begleit|en vt accompany. **B~er** m
-s, - companion; (Mus)
accompanist. **B~ung** f **-, -en**
company; (Mus) accompaniment
beglück|en vt make happy.
b~wünschen vt congratulate (zu
on)
begnadig|en vt (Jur) pardon.
B~ung f **-, -en** (Jur) pardon
begraben† vt bury
Begräbnis n **-ses, -se** burial;
(Feier) funeral
begreif|en† vt understand; **nicht
zu b~en** incomprehensible.
b~lich a understandable
begrenz|en vt form the boundary
of; (beschränken) restrict. **b~t** a
limited. **B~ung** f **-, -en** restriction;
(Grenze) boundary
Begriff m **-[e]s, -e** concept;
(Ausdruck) term; (Vorstellung)
idea
begründ|en vt give one's reason
for. **b~et** a justified. **B~ung** f **-,
-en** reason
begrüß|en vt greet; (billigen)
welcome. **b~enswert** a welcome.
B~ung f **-** greeting; welcome
begünstigen vt favour
begütert a wealthy
behaart a hairy
behäbig a portly
behag|en vi (haben) please (jdm
s.o.). **B~en** nt **-s** contentment;
(Genuss) enjoyment. **b~lich** a
comfortable. **B~lichkeit** f **-**
comfort
behalten† vt keep; (sich merken)
remember
Behälter m **-s,-** container
behand|eln vt treat; (sich
befassen) deal with. **B~lung** f
treatment
beharr|en vi (haben) persist (auf +
dat in). **b~lich** a persistent
behaupt|en vt maintain;
(vorgeben) claim; (sagen) say;

(bewahren) retain; **sich b~en** hold
one's own. **B~ung** f **-, -en**
assertion; claim; (Äußerung)
statement
beheben† vt remedy
behelf|en† (sich) vr make do (mit
with). **b~smäßig** a make-shift
● adv provisionally
beherbergen vt put up
beherrsch|en vt rule over;
(dominieren) dominate; (meistern,
zügeln) control; (können) know.
b~t a self-controlled. **B~ung** f **-**
control
beherzigen vt heed
behilflich a **jdm b~ sein** help s.o.
behinder|n vt hinder; (blockieren)
obstruct. **b~t** a handicapped;
(schwer) disabled. **B~te(r)** m/f
handicapped/disabled person.
B~ung f **-, -en** obstruction; (Med)
handicap; disability
Behörde f **-, -n** [public] authority
behüte|n vt protect. **b~t** a
sheltered
behutsam a careful; (zart) gentle

bei
● preposition (+ dative)
❗ Note that bei plus dem can
become **beim**
····▸ (nahe) near; (dicht an, neben)
by; (als Begleitung) with. **wer
steht da bei ihm?** who is standing
there next to or with him? **etw
bei sich haben** have sth with or
on one. **bleiben Sie beim Gepäck/
bei den Kindern** stay with the
luggage/the children. **war heute
ein Brief für mich bei der Post?**
was there a letter for me in the
post today?
····▸ (an) by. **jdn bei der Hand
nehmen** take s.o. by the hand
····▸ (in der Wohnung von) at …'s
home or house/flat. **bei mir [zu
Hause]** at my home or 🇬🇧 place.
bei seinen Eltern leben live with
one's parents. **wir sind bei Ulrike**

eingeladen we have been invited to Ulrike's. **bei Schmidt** at the Schmidts'; (*Geschäft*) at Schmidts'; (*auf Briefen*) c/o Schmidt. **bei jdm/einer Firma arbeiten** work for s.o./a firm. **bei uns tut man das nicht** we don't do that where I come from.

····▶ (*gegenwärtig*) at; (*verwickelt*) in. **bei einer Hochzeit/einem Empfang** at a wedding/reception. **bei einem Unfall** in an accident

····▶ (*im Falle von*) in the case of, with; (*bei Wetter*) in. **wie bei den Römern** as with the Romans. **bei Nebel** in fog, if there is fog. **bei dieser Hitze** in this heat

····▶ (*angesichts*) with; (*trotz*) in spite of. **bei deinen guten Augen** with your good eyesight. **bei all seinen Bemühungen** in spite of *or* despite all his efforts

····▶ (*Zeitpunkt*) at, on. **bei diesen Worten errötete er** he blushed at this *or* on hearing this. **bei seiner Ankunft** on his arrival. **bei Tag/ Nacht** by day/night.

····▶ (*Gleichzeitigkeit, mit Verbalsubstantiv*) **beim …en** while *or* when …ing. **beim Spazierengehen im Walde** while walking in the woods. **beim Überqueren der Straße** when crossing the road. **sie war beim Lesen** she was reading. **wir waren beim Frühstück** we were having breakfast

beibehalten† *vt sep* keep

beibringen† *vt sep* **jdm etw b~** teach s.o. sth; (*mitteilen*) break sth to s.o.; (*zufügen*) inflict sth on s.o.

Beicht|e *f* -, -n confession. **b~en** *vt/i* (*haben*) confess. **B~stuhl** *m* confessional

beide *a & pron* both; **b~s** both; **dreißig b~** (*Tennis*) thirty all.

b~rseitig *a* mutual. **b~rseits** *adv & prep* (+ *gen*) on both sides (of)

beeinander *adv* together

Beifahrer(in) *m(f)* [front-seat] passenger; (*Motorrad*) pillion passenger

Beifall *m* -[e]s applause; (*Billigung*) approval; **B~ klatschen** applaud

beifügen *vt sep* add; (*beilegen*) enclose

beige /bɛːʒ/ *inv a* beige

beigeben† *vt sep* add

Beihilfe *f* financial aid; (*Studien-*) grant; (*Jur*) aiding and abetting

Beil *nt* -[e]s, -e hatchet, axe

Beilage *f* supplement; (*Gemüse*) vegetable

beiläufig *a* casual

beilegen *vt sep* enclose; (*schlichten*) settle

Beileid *nt* condolences *pl*. **B~sbrief** *m* letter of condolence

beiliegend *a* enclosed

beim *prep* = **bei dem**; **b~ Militär** in the army; **b~ Frühstück** at breakfast

beimessen† *vt sep* (*fig*) attach (*dat* to)

Bein *nt* -[e]s, -e leg; **jdm ein B~ stellen** trip s.o. up

beinah[e] *adv* nearly, almost

Beiname *m* epithet

beipflichten *vi sep* (*haben*) agree (*dat* with)

Beirat *m* advisory committee

beisammen *adv* together; **b~ sein** be together

Beisein *nt* presence

beiseite *adv* aside; (*abseits*) apart; **b~ legen** put aside; (*sparen*) put by

beisetz|en *vt sep* bury. **B~ung** *f* -, -en funeral

Beispiel *nt* example; **zum B~** for example. **b~sweise** *adv* for example

beißen† vt/i (haben) bite; (brennen) sting; (sich b∼ <Farben:> clash
Bei|stand m -[e]s help. **b∼stehen**† vi sep (haben) jdm b∼stehen help s.o.
beistimmen vi sep (haben) agree
Beistrich m comma
Beitrag m -[e]s,¨e contribution; (Mitglieds-) subscription; (Versicherungs-) premium; (Zeitungs-) article. **b∼en**† vt/i sep (haben) contribute
bei|treten† vi sep (sein) (+ dat) join. **B∼tritt** m joining
Beize f -, -n (Holz-) stain
beizeiten adv in good time
beizen vt stain <Holz>
bejahen vt answer in the affirmative; (billigen) approve of
bejahrt a aged, old
bekämpf|en vt fight. **B∼ung** f fight (gen against)
bekannt a well-known; (vertraut) familiar; **jdn b∼ machen** introduce s.o.; **etw b∼ machen** od **geben** announce sth; **b∼ werden** become known. **B∼e(r)** m/f acquaintance; (Freund) friend. **B∼gabe** f announcement. **b∼lich** adv as is well known. **B∼machung** f -, -en announcement; (Anschlag) notice. **B∼schaft** f - acquaintance; (Leute) acquaintances pl; (Freunde) friends pl
bekehr|en vt convert. **B∼ung** f -, -en conversion
bekenn|en† vt confess, profess <Glauben>; **sich [für] schuldig b∼en** admit one's guilt. **B∼tnis** nt -ses, -se confession; (Konfession) denomination
beklag|en vt lament; (bedauern) deplore; **sich b∼en** complain. **b∼enswert** a unfortunate. **B∼te(r)** m/f (Jur) defendant
bekleid|en vt hold <Amt>. **B∼ung** f clothing

Beklemmung f -, -en feeling of oppression
bekommen† vt get; have <Baby>; catch <Erkältung> ● vi (sein) jdm gut b∼ do s.o. good; <Essen:> agree with s.o.
beköstig|en vt feed. **B∼ung** f - board; (Essen) food
bekräftigen vt reaffirm
bekreuzigen (sich) vr cross oneself
bekümmert a troubled; (besorgt) worried
bekunden vt show
Belag m -[e]s,¨e coating; (Fußboden-) covering; (Brot-) topping; (Zahn-) tartar; (Brems-) lining
belager|n vt besiege. **B∼ung** f -, -en siege
Belang m **von B∼** of importance; **B∼e** pl interests. **b∼los** a irrelevant; (unwichtig) trivial
belassen† vt leave; **es dabei b∼** leave it at that
belasten vt load; (fig) burden; (beanspruchen) put a strain on; (Comm) debit; (Jur) incriminate
belästigen vt bother; (bedrängen) pester; (unsittlich) molest
Belastung f -, -en load; (fig) strain; (Comm) debit. **B∼smaterial** nt incriminating evidence. **B∼szeuge** m prosecution witness
belaufen† **(sich)** vr amount (auf + acc to)
belauschen vt eavesdrop on
beleb|en vt (fig) revive; (lebhaft machen) enliven. **b∼t** a lively; <Straße> busy
Beleg m -[e]s, -e evidence; (Beispiel) instance (für of); (Quittung) receipt. **b∼en** vt cover/(garnieren) garnish (mit with); (besetzen) reserve; (Univ) enrol for; (nachweisen) provide evidence for; **den ersten Platz b∼en** (Sport) take first place.

B~schaft f -, -en work-force. **b~t** a occupied; <Zunge> coated; <Stimme> husky; **b~te Brote** open sandwiches

belehren vt instruct

beleidig|en vt offend; (absichtlich) insult. **B~ung** f -, -en insult

belesen a well-read

beleucht|en vt light; (anleuchten) illuminate. **B~ung** f -, -en illumination

Belg|ien /-jən/ nt -s Belgium. **B~ier(in)** m -s,- (f -, -nen) Belgian. **b~isch** a Belgian

belicht|en vt (Phot) expose. **B~ung** f - exposure

Belieb|en nt -s nach **B~en** [just] as one likes. **b~ig** a eine **b~ige Zahl** any number you like ●adv **b~ig oft** as often as one likes. **b~t** a popular

bellen vi (haben) bark

belohn|en vt reward. **B~ung** f -, -en reward

belustig|en vt amuse. **B~ung** f -, -en amusement

bemalen vt paint

bemängeln vt criticize

bemannt a manned

bemerk|bar a sich **b~bar machen** attract attention. **b~en** vt notice; (äußern) remark. **b~enswert** a remarkable. **B~ung** f -, -en remark

bemitleiden vt pity

bemüh|en vt trouble; sich **b~en** try (zu to; um etw to get sth); (sich kümmern) attend (um to); **b~t sein** endeavour (zu to). **B~ung** f -, -en effort

benachbart a neighbouring

benachrichtig|en vt inform; (amtlich) notify. **B~ung** f -, -en notification

benachteiligen vt discriminate against; (ungerecht sein) treat unfairly

benehmen† (sich) vr behave. **B~ nt** -s behaviour

beneiden vt envy (um etw sth)

Bengel m -s,- boy; (Rüpel) lout

benötigen vt need

benutz|en, (SGer) **benütz|en** vt use; take <Bahn>. **B~ung** f use

Benzin nt -s petrol

beobacht|en vt observe. **B~er** m -s,- observer. **B~ung** f -, -en observation

bequem a comfortable; (mühelos) easy; (faul) lazy. **b~en** (sich) vr deign (zu to). **B~lichkeit** f -, -en comfort; (Faulheit) laziness

berat|en† vt advise; (überlegen) discuss; sich **b~en** confer ●vi (haben) discuss (über etw acc sth); (beratschlagen) confer. **B~er(in)** m -s,- (f -, -nen) adviser. **B~ung** f -, -en guidance; (Rat) advice; (Besprechung) discussion; (Med, Jur) consultation

berechn|en vt calculate; (anrechnen) charge for; (abfordern) charge. **B~ung** f calculation

berechtig|en vt entitle; (befugen) authorize; (fig) justify. **b~t** a justified, justifiable. **B~ung** f -, -en authorization; (Recht) right; (Rechtmäßigkeit) justification

bered|en vt talk about; sich **b~en** talk. **B~samkeit** f - eloquence

beredt a eloquent

Bereich m -[e]s, -e area; (fig) realm; (Fach-) field

bereichern vi enrich

bereit a ready. **b~en** vt prepare; (verursachen) cause; give <Überraschung>. **b~halten†** vt sep have/(ständig) keep ready. **b~legen** vt sep put out [ready]. **b~machen** vt sep get ready. **b~s** adv already

Bereitschaft f -, -en readiness; (Einheit) squad. **B~sdienst** m **B~sdienst haben** (Mil) be on

stand-by; <*Arzt*:> be on call.
B~spolizei f riot police
bereit|stehen† vi sep (haben) be
ready. **b~stellen** vt sep put out
ready; (verfügbar machen) make
available. **B~ung** f - preparation.
b~willig a willing
bereuen vt regret
Berg m -[e]s, -e mountain;
(Anhöhe) hill; **in den B~en** in the
mountains. **b~ab** adv downhill.
B~arbeiter m miner. **b~auf** adv
uphill. **B~bau** m -[e]s mining
bergen† vt recover; (Naut)
salvage; (retten) rescue
Berg|führer m mountain guide.
b~ig a mountainous. **B~kette** f
mountain range. **B~mann** m (pl
-leute) miner. **B~steiger(in)** m -s,-
(f -, -nen) mountaineer, climber
Bergung f - recovery; (Naut)
salvage; (Rettung) rescue
Berg|wacht f mountain rescue
service. **B~werk** nt mine
Bericht m -[e]s, -e report; (Reise-)
account. **b~en** vt/i (haben)
report; (erzählen) tell (von of).
B~erstatter(in) m -s,- (f -, -nen)
reporter
berichtigen vt correct
berieseln vt irrigate.
B~ungsanlage f sprinkler
system
Berlin nt -s Berlin. **B~er** m -s,-
Berliner
Bernhardiner m -s,- St Bernard
Bernstein m amber
berüchtigt a notorious
berücksichtig|en vt take into
consideration. **B~ung** f -
consideration
Beruf m profession; (Tätigkeit)
occupation; (Handwerk) trade.
b~en† vt appoint; **sich b~en**
refer (auf + acc to); (vorgeben)
plead (auf etw acc sth); ● a
competent; **b~en sein** be
destined (zu to). **b~lich** a
professional; <Ausbildung>

vocational ● adv professionally;
b~lich tätig sein work, have a job.
B~sberatung f vocational
guidance. **b~smäßig** adv
professionally. **B~sschule** f
vocational school. **B~ssoldat** m
regular soldier. **b~stätig** a
working; **b~stätig sein** work, have
a job. **B~stätige(r)** m/f working
man/woman. **B~ung** f -, -en
appointment; (Bestimmung)
vocation; (Jur) appeal; **B~ung
einlegen** appeal. **B~ungsgericht**
nt appeal court
beruhen vi (haben) be based (auf
+ dat on)
beruhig|en vt calm [down];
(zuversichtlich machen) reassure.
b~end a calming; (tröstend)
reassuring; (Med) sedative.
B~ung f - calming; reassurance;
(Med) sedation. **B~ungsmittel** nt
sedative; (bei Psychosen)
tranquillizer
berühmt a famous. **B~heit** f -, -en
fame; (Person) celebrity
berühr|en vt touch; (erwähnen)
touch on. **B~ung** f -, -en touch;
(Kontakt) contact
besänftigen vt soothe
Besatz m -es,¨e trimming
Besatzung f -, -en crew; (Mil)
occupying force
beschädig|en vt damage. **B~ung**
f -, -en damage
beschaffen vt obtain, get ● a **so
b~ sein, dass** be such that.
B~heit f - consistency
beschäftig|en vt occupy;
<Arbeitgeber:> employ; **sich b~en**
occupy oneself. **b~t** a busy;
(angestellt) employed (bei at).
B~ung f -, -en occupation;
(Anstellung) employment
beschämt a ashamed; (verlegen)
embarrassed
beschatten vt shade;
(überwachen) shadow

Bescheid m -[e]s information; **jdm B~ sagen** od **geben** let s.o. know; **B~ wissen** know

bescheiden a modest. **B~heit** f - modesty

bescheinen† vt shine on; **von der Sonne beschienen** sunlit

bescheinig|en vt certify. **B~ung** f -, -en [written] confirmation; (Schein) certificate

beschenken vt give a present/ presents to

Bescherung f -, -en distribution of Christmas presents

beschildern vt signpost

beschimpf|en vt abuse, swear at. **B~ung** f -, -en abuse

beschirmen vt protect

Beschlag m in **B~ nehmen** monopolize. **b~en**† vt shoe ● vi (sein) steam or mist up ● a steamed or misted up. **B~nahme** f -, -n confiscation; (Jur) seizure. **b~nahmen** vt confiscate; (Jur) seize

beschleunig|en vt hasten; (schneller machen) speed up <Schritt> ● vi (haben) accelerate. **B~ung** f - acceleration

beschließen† vt decide; (beenden) end ● vi (haben) decide (**über** + acc about)

Beschluss m decision

beschmutzen vt make dirty

beschneid|en† vt trim; (Hort) prune; (Relig) circumcise. **B~ung** f - circumcision

beschnüffeln vt sniff at

beschönigen vt (fig) gloss over

beschränken vt limit, restrict; **sich b~ auf** (+ acc) confine oneself to

beschrankt a <Bahnübergang> with barrier[s]

beschränk|t a limited; (geistig) dull-witted. **B~ung** f -, -en limitation, restriction

beschreib|en† vt describe. **B~ung** f -, -en description

beschuldig|en vt accuse. **B~ung** f -, -en accusation

beschummeln vt ① cheat

Beschuss m (Mil) fire; (Artillerie-) shelling

beschütz|en vt protect. **B~er** m -s,- protector

Beschwer|de f -, -n complaint; **B~den** (Med) trouble sg. **b~en** vt weight down; **sich b~en** complain. **b~lich** a difficult

beschwindeln vt cheat (um out of); (belügen) lie to

beschwipst a ① tipsy

beseitig|en vt remove. **B~ung** f - removal

Besen m -s,- broom

besessen a obsessed (**von** by)

besetz|en vt occupy; fill <Posten>; (Theat) cast <Rolle>; (verzieren) trim (**mit** with). **b~t** a occupied; <Toilette, Leitung> engaged; <Zug, Bus> full up; **der Platz ist b~t** this seat is taken. **B~tzeichen** nt engaged tone. **B~ung** f -, -en occupation; (Theat) cast

besichtig|en vt look round <Stadt>; (prüfen) inspect; (besuchen) visit. **B~ung** f -, -en visit; (Prüfung) inspection; (Stadt-) sightseeing

besiedelt a **dünn/dicht b~** sparsely/densely populated

besiegen vt defeat

besinn|en† (sich) vr think, reflect; (sich erinnern) remember (**auf** jdn/etw s.o./sth). **B~ung** f - reflection; (Bewusstsein) consciousness; **bei/ohne B~ung** conscious/unconscious. **b~ungslos** a unconscious

Besitz m possession; (Eigentum, Land-) property; (Gut) estate. **b~en**† vt own, possess; (haben) have. **B~er(in)** m -s,- (f -, -nen) owner; (Comm) proprietor

besoffen a ⊠ drunken; **b~ sein** be drunk

B

besonder|e(r,s) *a* special; (*bestimmt*) particular; (*gesondert*) separate. **b~s** *adv* [e]specially, particularly; (*gesondert*) separately

besonnen *a* calm

besorg|en *vt* get; (*kaufen*) buy; (*erledigen*) attend to; (*versorgen*) look after. **b~t** *a* worried/ (*bedacht*) concerned (**um** about). **B~ung** *f* -, -en errand; **B~ungen machen** do shopping

bespitzeln *vt* spy on

besprech|en† *vt* discuss; (*rezensieren*) review. **B~ung** *f* -, -en discussion; review; (*Konferenz*) meeting

besser *a & adv* better. **b~n** *vt* improve; **sich b~n** get better. **B~ung** *f* - improvement; **gute B~ung!** get well soon!

Bestand *m* -[e]s,ᵉe existence; (*Vorrat*) stock (**an** + *dat* of)

beständig *a* constant; <*Wetter*> settled; **b~ gegen** resistant to

Bestand|saufnahme *f* stocktaking. **B~teil** *m* part

bestätig|en *vt* confirm; acknowledge <*Empfang*>; **sich b~en** prove to be true. **B~ung** *f* -, -en confirmation

bestatt|en *vt* bury. **B~ung** *f* -, -en funeral

Bestäubung *f* - pollination

bestaunen *vt* gaze at in amazement; (*bewundern*) admire

best|e(r,s) *a* best; **b~en Dank!** many thanks! **B~e(r,s)** *m*/*f*/*nt* best; **sein B~es tun** do one's best

bestech|en† *vt* bribe; (*bezaubern*) captivate. **b~end** *a* captivating. **b~lich** *a* corruptible. **B~ung** *f* - bribery. **B~ungsgeld** *nt* bribe

Besteck *nt* -[e]s, -e [set of] knife, fork and spoon; (*coll*) cutlery

bestehen† *vi* (*haben*) exist; (*fortdauern*) last; (*bei Prüfung*) pass; **~ aus** consist/(*gemacht*

sein) be made of; **~ auf** (+ *dat*) insist on **●** *vt pass* <*Prüfung*>

besteig|en† *vt* climb; (*aufsteigen*) mount; ascend <*Thron*>. **B~ung** *f* ascent

bestell|en *vt* order; (*vor-*) book; (*ernennen*) appoint; (*bebauen*) cultivate; (*ausrichten*) tell; **zu sich b~en** send for; **b~t sein** have an appointment; **kann ich etwas b~en?** can I take a message? **B~schein** *m* order form. **B~ung** *f* order; (*Botschaft*) message; (*Bebauung*) cultivation

besteuer|n *vt* tax. **B~ung** *f* - taxation

Bestie /ˈbɛstiə/ *f* -, -n beast

bestimm|en *vt* fix; (*entscheiden*) decide; (*vorsehen*) intend; (*ernennen*) appoint; (*ermitteln*) determine; (*definieren*) define; (*Gram*) qualify **●** *vi* (*haben*) be in charge (**über** + *acc* of). **b~t** *a* definite; (*gewiss*) certain; (*fest*) firm,. **B~ung** *f* fixing; (*Vorschrift*) regulation; (*Ermittlung*) determination; (*Definition*) definition; (*Zweck*) purpose; (*Schicksal*) destiny. **B~ungsort** *m* destination

Bestleistung *f* (*Sport*) record

bestraf|en *vt* punish. **B~ung** *f* -, -en punishment

Bestrahlung *f* radiotherapy

Bestreb|en *nt* -s endeavour; (*Absicht*) aim. **B~ung** *f* -, -en effort

bestreiten† *vt* dispute; (*leugnen*) deny; (*bezahlen*) pay for

bestürz|t *a* dismayed; (*erschüttert*) stunned. **B~ung** *f* - dismay, consternation

Bestzeit *f* (*Sport*) record [time]

Besuch *m* -[e]s, -e visit; (*kurz*) call; (*Schul-*) attendance; (*Gast*) visitor; (*Gäste*) visitors *pl*; **B~ haben** have a visitor/visitors; **bei jdm zu** *od* **auf B~ sein** be staying with s.o. **b~en** *vt* visit; (*kurz*) call

on; *(teilnehmen)* attend; go to
<*Schule, Ausstellung*>. **B~er(in)**
m **-s,-** *(f* -, **-nen)** visitor; caller.
B~szeit *f* visiting hours *pl*

betagt *a* aged, old

betätig|en *vt* operate; **sich b~en**
work **(als** as). **B~ung** *f* -, **-en**
operation; *(Tätigkeit)* activity

betäub|en *vt* stun; <*Lärm:*>
deafen; *(Med)* anaesthetize;
(lindern) ease; deaden
<*Schmerz*>; **wie b~t** dazed.
B~ung *f* - daze; *(Med)*
anaesthesia. **B~ungsmittel** *nt*
anaesthetic

Bete *f* -, **-n Rote B~** beetroot

beteilig|en *vt* give a share to; **sich
b~en** take part **(an** + *dat* in);
(beitragen) contribute **(an** + *dat*
to). **b~t** *a* **b~t sein** take part/*(an
Unfall)* be involved/*(Comm)* have
a share **(an** + *dat* in); **alle B~ten**
all those involved. **B~ung** *f* -, **-en**
participation; involvement;
(Anteil) share

beten *vi (haben)* pray

Beton /be'tɔŋ/ *m* **-s** concrete

betonen *vt* stressed, emphasize

beton|t *a* stressed; *(fig)* pointed.
B~ung *f* -, **-en** stress

Betracht *m* **in B~ ziehen** consider;
außer B~ lassen disregard; **nicht
in B~ kommen** be out of the
question. **b~en** *vt* look at; *(fig)*
regard **(als** as)

beträchtlich *a* considerable

Betrachtung *f* -, **-en**
contemplation; *(Überlegung)*
reflection

Betrag *m* **-[e]s,:̈e** amount. **b~en†**
vt amount to; **sich b~en** behave.
B~en *nt* **-s** behaviour; *(Sch)*
conduct

betreff|en† *vt* affect; *(angehen)*
concern. **b~end** *a* relevant. **b~s**
prep (+ *gen)* concerning

betreiben† *vt (leiten)* run;
(ausüben) carry on

betreten† *vt* step on; *(eintreten)*
enter; '**B~ verboten**' 'no entry';
(bei Rasen) 'keep off [the grass]'

betreu|en *vt* look after. **B~er(in)**
m **-s,-** *(f* -, **-nen)** helper;
(Kranken-) nurse. **B~ung** *f* - care

Betrieb *m* business; *(Firma)* firm;
(Treiben) activity; *(Verkehr)*
traffic; **außer B~** not in use;
(defekt) out of order

**Betriebs|anleitung,
B~anweisung** *f* operating
instructions *pl.* **B~ferien** *pl*
firm's holiday. **B~leitung** *f*
management. **B~rat** *m* works
committee. **B~störung** *f*
breakdown

betrinken† (sich) *vr* get drunk

betroffen *a* disconcerted; **b~ sein**
be affected **(von** by)

betrüb|en *vt* sadden. **b~t** *a* sad

Betrug *m* **-[e]s** deception; *(Jur)*
fraud

betrüg|en† *vt* cheat, swindle;
(Jur) defraud; *(in der Ehe)* be
unfaithful to. **B~er(in)** *m* **-s,-** *(f* -,
-nen) swindler. **B~erei** *f* -, **-en**
fraud

betrunken *a* drunken; **b~ sein** be
drunk. **B~e(r)** *m* drunk

Bett *nt* **-[e]s, -en** bed. **B~couch** *f*
sofa-bed. **B~decke** *f* blanket;
(Tages-) bedspread

Bettel|ei *f* - begging. **b~n** *vi*
(haben) beg

Bettler(in) *m* **-s,-** *(f* -, **-nen)** beggar

Bettpfanne *f* bedpan

Betttuch (Bettuch) *nt* sheet

Bett|wäsche *f* bed linen. **B~zeug**
nt bedding

betupfen *vt* dab **(mit** with)

beug|en *vt* bend; *(Gram)* decline;
conjugate <*Verb*>; **sich b~en**
bend; *(lehnen)* lean; *(sich fügen)*
submit *(dat* to). **B~ung** *f* -, **-en**
(Gram) declension; conjugation

Beule *f* -, **-n** bump; *(Delle)* dent

beunruhig|en *vt* worry; **sich b~en**
worry. **B~ung** *f* - worry

B

beurlauben vt give leave to
beurteil|en vt judge. **B~ung** f -,
-en judgement; (Ansicht) opinion
Beute f - booty, haul; (Jagd-) bag;
(eines Raubtiers) prey
Beutel m -s,- bag; (Tabak- & Zool)
pouch. **B~tier** nt marsupial
Bevölkerung f -, -en population
bevollmächtigen vt authorize
bevor conj before; **b~ nicht** until
bevormunden vt treat like a child
bevorstehen† vi sep (haben)
approach; (unmittelbar) be
imminent. **b~d** a approaching,
forthcoming; **unmittelbar b~d**
imminent
bevorzug|en vt prefer;
(begünstigen) favour. **b~t** a
privileged; <Behandlung>
preferential
bewachen vt guard
Bewachung f - guard; **unter B~**
under guard
bewaffn|en vt arm. **b~et** a
armed. **B~ung** f - armament;
(Waffen) arms pl
bewahren vt protect (vor + dat
from); (behalten) keep; **die Ruhe**
b~ keep calm
bewähren (sich) vr prove one's/
<Ding:> its worth; (erfolgreich
sein) prove a success
bewähr|t a reliable; (erprobt)
proven. **B~ung** f - (Jur)
probation. **B~ungsfrist** f [period
of] probation. **B~ungsprobe** f
(fig) test
bewältigen vt cope with;
(überwinden) overcome
bewässer|n vt irrigate. **B~ung** f -
irrigation
bewegen¹ vt (reg) move; **sich b~**
move; (körperlich) take exercise
bewegen²† vt **jdn dazu b~, etw zu**
tun induce s.o. to do sth
Beweg|grund m motive. **b~lich** a
movable, mobile; (wendig) agile.
B~lichkeit f - mobility; agility.
B~ung f -, -en movement; (Phys)

motion; (Rührung) emotion;
(Gruppe) movement; **körperliche**
B~ung physical exercise.
b~ungslos a motionless
Beweis m -es, -e proof; (Zeichen)
token; **B~e** evidence sg. **b~en†**
vt prove; (zeigen) show; **sich**
b~en prove oneself/<Ding:>
itself. **B~material** nt evidence
bewerb|en (sich) vr apply (**um**
for; **bei** to). **B~er(in)** m -s,- (f -,
-nen) applicant. **B~ung** f -, -en
application
bewerten vt value; (einschätzen)
rate; (Sch) mark, grade
bewilligen vt grant
bewirken vt cause; (herbeiführen)
bring about
bewirt|en vt entertain. **B~ung** f -
hospitality
bewohn|bar a habitable. **b~en** vt
inhabit, live in. **B~er(in)** m -s,- (f
-, -nen) resident, occupant;
(Einwohner) inhabitant
bewölk|en (sich) vr cloud over;
b~t cloudy. **B~ung** f - clouds pl
bewunder|n vt admire. **b~nswert**
a admirable. **B~ung** f -
admiration
bewusst a conscious (gen of);
(absichtlich) deliberate. **b~los** a
unconscious. **B~losigkeit** f -
unconsciousness; **B~sein** nt -s
consciousness; (Gewissheit)
awareness; **bei B~sein** conscious
bezahl|en vt/i (haben) pay; pay
for <Ware, Essen>. **B~ung** f -
payment; (Lohn) pay.
B~fernsehen nt pay television;
pay TV
bezaubern vt enchant
bezeichn|en vt mark; (bedeuten)
denote; (beschreiben, nennen)
describe (**als** as). **b~end** a
typical. **B~ung** f marking;
(Beschreibung) description (**als**
as); (Ausdruck) term; (Name)
name
bezeugen vt testify to

bezichtigen vt accuse (gen of)
bezieh|en† vt cover; (einziehen) move into; (beschaffen) obtain; (erhalten) get; (in Verbindung bringen) relate (auf + acc to); **sich b~en** (bewölken) cloud over; **sich b~en auf** (+ acc) refer to; **das Bett frisch b~en** put clean sheets on the bed. **B~ung** f -, -en relation; (Verhältnis) relationship; (Bezug) respect; **B~ungen haben** have connections. **b~ungsweise** adv respectively; (vielmehr) or rather
Bezirk m -[e]s, -e district
Bezug m cover; (Kissen-) case; (Beschaffung) obtaining; (Kauf) purchase; (Zusammenhang) reference; **B~ë** pl earnings; **B~ nehmen** refer (auf + acc to); **in B~ auf** (+ acc) regarding
bezüglich prep (+ gen) regarding ● a relating (auf + acc to)
bezwecken vt (fig) aim at
bezweifeln vt doubt
BH /beːˈhaː/ m -[s], -[s] bra
Bibel f -, -n Bible
Biber m -s,- beaver
Biblio|thek f -, -en library. **B~thekar(in)** m -s,- (f -, -nen) librarian
biblisch a biblical
bieg|en† vt bend; **sich b~en** bend ● vi (sein) curve (nach to); **um die Ecke b~en** turn the corner. **b~sam** a flexible, supple. **B~ung** f -, -en bend
Biene f -, -n bee. **B~nstock** m beehive. **B~nwabe** f honey-comb
Bier nt -s, -e beer. **B~deckel** m beer-mat. **B~krug** m beer-mug
bieten† vt offer; (bei Auktion) bid
Bifokalbrille f bifocals pl
Bigamie f - bigamy
Bikini m -s, -s bikini
Bilanz f -, -en balance sheet; (fig) result; **die B~ ziehen** (fig) draw conclusions (aus from)

bilden vt form; (sein) be; (erziehen) educate
Bild|erbuch nt picture-book. **B~fläche** f screen. **B~hauer** m -s,- sculptor. **b~lich** a pictorial; (figurativ) figurative. **B~nis** nt -ses, -se portrait. **B~schirm** m (TV) screen. **B~schirmgerät** nt visual display unit, VDU. **b~schön** a very beautiful. **B~telefon** nt videophone
Bildung f - formation; (Erziehung) education; (Kultur) culture
Billard /ˈbɪljart/ nt -s billiards sg. **B~tisch** m billiard table
Billett /bɪlˈjɛt/ nt -[e]s, -e & -s ticket
Billiarde f -, -n thousand million million
billig a cheap; (dürftig) poor; **recht und b~** right and proper. **b~en** vt approve. **B~ung** f - approval
Billion /bɪlioːn/ f -, -en million million, billion
Bimsstein m pumice stone
Binde f -, -n band; (Verband) bandage; (Damen-) sanitary towel. **B~hautentzündung** f conjunctivitis. **b~n†** vt tie (an + acc to); make <Strauß>; bind <Buch>; (fesseln) tie up; (Culin) thicken; **sich b~n** commit oneself. **B~strich** m hyphen. **B~wort** nt (pl -wörter) (Gram) conjunction
Bind|faden m string. **B~ung** f -, -en (fig) tie; (Beziehung) relationship; (Verpflichtung) commitment; (Ski-) binding; (Tex) weave
binnen prep (+ dat) within. **B~handel** m home trade
Bio- pref organic
Bio|chemie f biochemistry. **b~dynamisch** m organic. **B~graphie, B~grafie** f -, -n biography
Bio|hof m organic farm. **B~laden** m health-food store

Biolog|e *m* -n, -n biologist. **B~ie** *f* - biology. **b~isch** *a* biological; **b~ischer Anbau** organic farming; **b~isch angebaut** organically grown

Bioterrorismus *m* bioterrorism

Birke *f* -, -n birch [tree]

Birm|a *nt* -s Burma. **b~anisch** *a* Burmese

Birn|baum *m* pear-tree. **B~e** *f* -, -n pear; (*Electr*) bulb

bis *prep* (+ *acc*) as far as, [up] to; (*zeitlich*) until, till; (*spätestens*) by; **bis zu** up to; **bis auf** (+ *acc*) (*einschließlich*) [down] to; (*ausgenommen*) except [for]; **drei bis vier Minuten** three to four minutes; **bis morgen!** see you tomorrow! ● *conj* until

Bischof *m* -s,⸚e bishop

bisher *adv* so far, up to now

Biskuit|rolle /bɪsˈkviːt-/ *f* Swiss roll. **B~teig** *m* sponge mixture

Biss *m* -es, -e bite

bisschen *inv pron* **ein b~** a bit, a little; **kein b~** not a bit

Biss|en *m* -s,- bite, mouthful. **b~ig** *a* vicious; (*fig*) caustic

bisweilen *adv* from time to time

bitt|e *adv* please; (*nach Klopfen*) come in; (*als Antwort auf 'danke'*) don't mention it, you're welcome; **wie b~e?** pardon? **B~e** *f* -, -n request/(*dringend*) plea (**um** for). **b~en†** *vt/i* (*haben*) ask/ (*dringend*) beg (**um** for); (*einladen*) invite, ask

bitter *a* bitter. **B~keit** *f* - bitterness. **b~lich** *adv* bitterly

Bittschrift *f* petition

bizarr *a* bizarre

bläh|en *vt* swell; <*Vorhang, Segel:*> billow ● *vi* (*haben*) cause flatulence. **B~ungen** *fpl* flatulence *sg*, 🛈 wind *sg*

Blamage /blaˈmaːʒə/ *f* -, -n humiliation; (*Schande*) disgrace

blamieren *vt* disgrace; **sich b~** disgrace oneself; (*sich lächerlich machen*) make a fool of oneself

blanchieren /blãˈʃiːrən/ *vt* (*Culin*) blanch

blank *a* shiny. **B~oscheck** *m* blank cheque

Blase *f* -, -n bubble; (*Med*) blister; (*Anat*) bladder. **b~n†** *vt/i* (*haben*) blow; play <*Flöte*>. **B~nentzündung** *f* cystitis

Blas|instrument *nt* wind instrument. **B~kapelle** *f* brass band

blass *a* pale; (*schwach*) faint

Blässe *f* - pallor

Blatt *nt* -[e]s,⸚er (*Bot*) leaf; (*Papier*) sheet; (*Zeitung*) paper

Blattlaus *f* greenfly

blau *a*, **B~** *nt* -s,- blue; **b~er Fleck** bruise; **b~es Auge** black eye; **b~ sein** 🛈 be tight; **Fahrt ins B~e** mystery tour. **B~beere** *f* bilberry. **B~licht** *nt* blue flashing light

Blech *nt* -[e]s, -e sheet metal; (*Weiß-*) tin; (*Platte*) metal sheet; (*Back-*) baking sheet; (*Mus*) brass; (🛈 *Unsinn*) rubbish. **B~schaden** *m* (*Auto*) damage to the bodywork

Blei *nt* -[e]s lead

Bleibe *f* - place to stay. **b~n†** *vi* (*sein*) remain, stay; (*übrig-*) be left; **ruhig b~n** keep calm; **bei etw b~n** (*fig*) stick to sth; **b~n Sie am Apparat** hold the line; **etw b~n lassen** not to do sth. **b~nd** *a* permanent; (*anhaltend*) lasting

bleich *a* pale. **b~en†** *vi* (*sein*) bleach; (*ver-*) fade ● *vt* (*reg*) bleach. **B~mittel** *nt* bleach

blei|ern *a* leaden. **b~frei** *a* unleaded. **B~stift** *m* pencil. **B~stiftabsatz** *m* stiletto heel. **B~stiftspitzer** *m* -s,- pencil sharpener

Blende *f* -, -n shade, shield; (*Sonnen-*) [sun] visor; (*Phot*)

diaphragm; (*Öffnung*) aperture; (*an Kleid*) facing. **b~n** vt dazzle, blind

Blick m -[e]s, -e look; (*kurz*) glance; (*Aussicht*) view; **auf den ersten B~** at first sight. **b~en** vi (*haben*) look/(*kurz*) glance (**auf** + acc at). **B~punkt** m (*fig*) point of view

blind a blind; (*trübe*) dull; **b~er Alarm** false alarm; **b~er Passagier** stowaway. **B~darm** m appendix. **B~darmentzündung** f appendicitis. **B~e(r)** m/f blind man/woman; **die B~en** the blind pl. **B~enhund** m guidedog. **B~enschrift** f braille. **B~gänger** m -s,- (*Mil*) dud. **B~heit** f - blindness

blink|en vi (*haben*) flash; (*funkeln*) gleam; (*Auto*) indicate. **B~er** m -s,- (*Auto*) indicator. **B~licht** nt flashing light

blinzeln vi (*haben*) blink

Blitz m -es, -e [flash of] lightning; (*Phot*) flash. **B~ableiter** m lightning-conductor. **b~artig** a lightning … ● adv like lightning. **b~en** vi (*haben*) flash; (*funkeln*) sparkle; **es hat geblitzt** there was a flash of lightning. **B~licht** nt (*Phot*) flash. **b~sauber** a spick and span. **b~schnell** a lightning … ● adv like lightning

Block m -[e]s,ːe block ● -[e]s, -s & ːe pad; (*Häuser-*) block

Blockade f -, -n blockade

Blockflöte f recorder

blockieren vt block; (*Mil*) blockade

Blockschrift f block letters pl

blöd[e] a feeble-minded; (*dumm*) stupid

Blödsinn m -[e]s idiocy; (*Unsinn*) nonsense

blöken vi (*haben*) bleat

blond a fair-haired; <*Haar*> fair

bloß a bare; (*alleinig*) mere ● adv only, just

bloß|legen vt sep uncover. **b~stellen** vt sep compromise

Bluff m -s, -s bluff. **b~en** vt/i (*haben*) bluff

blühen vi (*haben*) flower; (*fig*) flourish. **b~d** a flowering; (*fig*) flourishing, thriving

Blume f -, -n flower; (*vom Wein*) bouquet. **B~nbeet** nt flower-bed. **B~ngeschäft** nt flower-shop, florist's. **B~nkohl** m cauliflower. **B~nmuster** nt floral design. **B~nstrauß** m bunch of flowers. **B~ntopf** m flowerpot; (*Pflanze*) pot plant. **B~nzwiebel** f bulb

blumig a (*fig*) flowery

Bluse f -, -n blouse

Blut nt -[e]s blood. **b~arm** a anaemic. **B~bahn** f bloodstream. **B~bild** nt blood count. **B~druck** m blood pressure. **b~dürstig** a bloodthirsty

Blüte f -, -n flower, bloom; (*vom Baum*) blossom; (*B~zeit*) flowering period; (*Baum-*) blossom time; (*Höhepunkt*) peak, prime

Blut|egel m -s,- leech. **b~en** vi (*haben*) bleed

Blüten|blatt nt petal. **B~staub** m pollen

Blut|er m -s,- haemophiliac. **B~erguss** m bruise. **B~gefäß** nt blood-vessel. **B~gruppe** f blood group. **b~ig** a bloody. **B~körperchen** nt -s,- corpuscle. **B~probe** f blood test. **b~rünstig** a (*fig*) bloody, gory. **B~schande** f incest. **B~spender** m blood donor. **B~sturz** m haemorrhage. **B~transfusion, B~übertragung** f blood transfusion. **B~ung** f -, -en bleeding; (*Med*) haemorrhage; (*Regel-*) period. **b~unterlaufen** a bruised; <*Auge*> bloodshot. **B~vergiftung** f blood-poisoning. **B~wurst** f black pudding

Bö f -, -en gust; (*Regen-*) squall

Bob m -s, -s bob[-sleigh]

Bock m -[e]s,⸚e buck; (*Ziege*) billy goat; (*Schaf*) ram; (*Gestell*) support. **b~ig** a ⒤ stubborn. **B~springen** nt leap-frog

Boden m -s,⸚ ground; (*Erde*) soil; (*Fuß-*) floor; (*Grundfläche*) bottom; (*Dach-*) loft, attic. **B~satz** m sediment. **B~schätze** mpl mineral deposits. **B~see** (der) Lake Constance

Bogen m -s,- & ⸚ curve; (*Geom*) arc; (*beim Skilauf*) turn; (*Archit*) arch; (*Waffe, Geigen-*) bow; (*Papier*) sheet; **einen großen B~ um jdn/etw machen** ⒤ give s.o./sth a wide berth. **B~schießen** nt archery

Bohle f -, -n [thick] plank

Böhm|en nt -s Bohemia. **b~isch** a Bohemian

Bohne f -, -n bean; **grüne B~n** French beans

bohner|n vt polish. **B~wachs** nt floor-polish

bohr|en vt/i (*haben*) drill (**nach** for); drive <*Tunnel*>; sink <*Brunnen*>; <*Insekt:*> bore. **B~er** m -s,- drill. **B~insel** f [offshore] drilling rig. **B~turm** m derrick

Boje f -, -n buoy

Bolzen m -s,- bolt; (*Stift*) pin

bombardieren vt bomb; (*fig*) bombard (**mit** with)

Bombe f -, -n bomb. **B~nangriff** m bombing raid. **B~nerfolg** m huge success

Bon /bɔŋ/ m -s, -s voucher; (*Kassen-*) receipt

Bonbon /bɔŋˈbɔŋ/ m & nt -s, -s sweet

Bonus m -[sses], -[sse] bonus

Boot nt -[e]s, -e boat. **B~ssteg** m landing-stage

Bord¹ nt -[e]s, -e shelf

Bord² m (*Naut*) **an B~** aboard, on board; **über B~** overboard. **B~buch** nt log[-book]

Bordell nt -s, -e brothel

Bordkarte f boarding-pass

borgen vt borrow; **jdm etw b~** lend s.o. sth

Börse f -, -n purse; (*Comm*) stock exchange. **B~nmakler** m stockbroker

Borste f -, -n bristle. **b~ig** a bristly

Borte f -, -n braid

Böschung f -, -en embankment

böse a wicked, evil; (*unartig*) naughty; (*schlimm*) bad; (*zornig*) cross; **jdm** od **auf jdn b~ sein** be cross with s.o.

bos|haft a malicious, spiteful. **B~heit** f -, -en malice; spite; (*Handlung*) spiteful act/ (*Bemerkung*) remark

böswillig a malicious

Botani|k f - botany. **B~ker(in)** m -s,- (f -, -nen) botanist

Bot|e m -n, -n messenger. **B~engang** m errand. **B~schaft** f -, -en message; (*Pol*) embassy. **B~schafter** m -s,- ambassador

Bouillon /buˈljɔŋ/ f -, -s clear soup. **B~würfel** m stock cube

Bowle /ˈboːlə/ f -, -n punch

Box f -, -en box; (*Pferde-*) loose box; (*Lautsprecher-*) speaker; (*Autorennen*) pit

box|en vi (*haben*) box ● vt punch. **B~en** nt -s boxing. **B~er** m -s,- boxer

brachliegen† vi sep (*haben*) lie fallow

Branche /ˈbrɑ̃:ʃə/ f -, -n [line of] business. **B~nverzeichnis** nt (*Teleph*) classified directory

Brand m -[e]s,⸚e fire; (*Med*) gangrene; (*Bot*) blight; **in B~ geraten** catch fire; **in B~ setzen** od **stecken** set on fire. **B~bombe** f incendiary bomb

Brand|stifter m arsonist. **B~stiftung** f arson

Brandung f - surf

Brand|wunde f burn. **B~zeichen** nt brand

Branntwein m spirit; (*coll*) spirits pl. **B~brennerei** f distillery

bras|ilianisch *a* Brazilian. **B~ilien** /-iən/ *nt* **-s** Brazil

Brat|apfel *m* baked apple. **b~en†** *vt/i* (*haben*) roast; (*in der Pfanne*) fry. **B~en** *m* **-s,-** roast; (*B~stück*) joint. **B~e** *f* -, **-n** width; breadth; (*Geog*) latitude. **b~en** *vt* spread ready. **B~hähnchen** *nt* roasting chicken. **B~kartoffeln** *fpl* fried potatoes. **B~pfanne** *f* frying-pan

Bratsche *f* -, **-n** (*Mus*) viola

Bratspieß *m* spit

Brauch *m* **-[e]s,Bräuche** custom. **b~bar** *a* usable; (*nützlich*) useful. **b~en** *vt* need; (*ge-, verbrauchen*) use; take (*Zeit*); **er b~t es nur zu sagen** he only has to say

Braue *f* -, **-n** eyebrow

brau|en *vt* brew. **B~er** *m* **-s,-** brewer. **B~erei** *f* -, **-en** brewery

braun *a*, **B~** *nt* **-s,-** brown; **b~ werden** (*Person:*) get a tan; **b~ [gebrannt] sein** be [sun-]tanned

Bräune *f* - [sun-]tan. **b~n** *vt/i* (*haben*) brown; (*in der Sonne*) tan

Braunschweig *nt* **-s** Brunswick

Brause *f* -, **-n** (*Dusche*) shower; (*an Gießkanne*) rose; (*B~limonade*) fizzy drink

Braut *f* -,¨-e bride; (*Verlobte*) fiancée

Bräutigam *m* **-s,** **-e** bridegroom; (*Verlobte*) fiancé

Brautkleid *nt* wedding dress

Brautpaar *nt* bridal couple; (*Verlobte*) engaged couple

brav *a* good; (*redlich*) honest ● *adv* dutifully; (*redlich*) honestly

bravo *int* bravo!

BRD *abbr* (**Bundesrepublik Deutschland**) FRG

Brech|eisen *nt* jemmy; (*B~stange*) crowbar. **b~en†** *vt* break; (*Phys*) refract (*Licht*); (*erbrechen*) vomit; **sich b~en** (*Wellen:*) break; (*Licht:*) be refracted; **sich** (*dat*) **den Arm b~en** break one's arm ● *vi* (*sein*) break ● *vi* (*haben*) vomit, be sick.

B~reiz *m* nausea. **B~stange** *f* crowbar

Brei *m* **-[e]s, -e** paste; (*Culin*) purée; (*Hafer-*) porridge

breit *a* wide; (*Schultern, Grinsen*) broad. **B~e** *f* -, **-n** width; breadth; (*Geog*) latitude. **b~en** *vt* spread (**über** + *acc* over). **B~engrad** *m* [degree of] latitude. **B~enkreis** *m* parallel

Bremse¹ *f* -, **-n** horsefly

Bremse² *f* -, **-n** brake. **b~n** *vt* slow down; (*fig*) restrain ● *vi* (*haben*) brake

Bremslicht *nt* brake-light

brenn|bar *a* combustible; **leicht b~bar** highly [in]flammable. **b~en†** *vi* (*haben*) burn; (*Licht:*) be on; (*Zigarette:*) be alight; (*weh tun*) smart, sting ● *vt* burn; (*rösten*) roast; (*im Brennofen*) fire; (*destillieren*) distil. **b~end** *a* burning; (*angezündet*) lighted; (*fig*) fervent **B~erei** *f* -, **-en** distillery

Brennnessel* *f s.* **Brennnessel**

Brenn|holz *nt* firewood. **B~ofen** *m* kiln. **B~nessel** *f* stinging nettle. **B~punkt** *m* (*Phys*) focus. **B~spiritus** *m* methylated spirits. **B~stoff** *m* fuel

Bretagne /brε'tanjə/ (**die**) - Brittany

Brett *nt* **-[e]s, -er** board; (*im Regal*) shelf; **schwarzes B~** notice board. **B~spiel** *nt* board game

Brezel *f* -, **-n** pretzel

Bridge /brɪtʃ/ *nt* - (*Spiel*) bridge

Brief *m* **-[e]s, -e** letter. **B~beschwerer** *m* **-s,-** paperweight. **B~freund(in)** *m(f)* pen-friend. **B~kasten** *m* letter-box. **B~kopf** *m* letter-head. **b~lich** *a & adv* by letter. **B~marke** *f* [postage] stamp. **B~öffner** *m* paper-knife. **B~papier** *nt* notepaper. **B~tasche** *f* wallet. **B~träger** *m* postman. **B~umschlag** *m*

envelope. **B~wahl** f postal vote.
B~wechsel m correspondence
Brikett nt -s, -s briquette
Brillant m -en, -en [cut] diamond
Brille f -, -n glasses pl, spectacles
pl; (Schutz-) goggles pl; (Klosett-)
toilet seat
bringen† vt bring; (fort-) take;
(ein-) yield; (veröffentlichen)
publish; (im Radio) broadcast;
show <Film>; **ins Bett b~** put to
bed; **jdn nach Hause b~** take/
(begleiten) see s.o. home; **um etw
b~** deprive of sth; **jdn dazu b~,
etw zu tun** get s.o. to do sth; **es
weit b~** (fig) go far
Brise f -, -n breeze
Brit|e m -n, -n, **B~in** f -, -nen
Briton. **b~isch** a British
Bröck|chen nt -s,- (Culin)
crouton. **b~elig** a crumbly;
<Gestein:> friable. **b~eln** vt/i
(haben/sein) crumble
Brocken m -s,- chunk; (Erde,
Kohle) lump
Brokat m -[e]s, -e brocade
Brokkoli pl broccoli sg
Brombeere f blackberry
Bronchitis f - bronchitis
Bronze /'brõ:sə/ f -, -n bronze
Brosch|e f -, -n brooch. **b~iert** a
paperback. **B~üre** f -, -n
brochure; (Heft) booklet
Brösel mpl (Culin) breadcrumbs
Brot n -[e]s, -e bread; **ein B~** a loaf
[of bread]; (Scheibe) a slice of
bread
Brötchen nt -s,- [bread] roll
Brotkrümel m breadcrumb
Bruch m -[e]s,-̈e break; (Brechen)
breaking; (Rohr-) burst; (Med)
fracture; (Eingeweide-) rupture,
hernia; (Math) fraction; (fig)
breach; (in Beziehung) break-up
brüchig a brittle
Bruch|landung f crash-landing.
B~rechnung f fractions pl.
B~stück nt fragment. **B~teil** m
fraction

Brücke f -, -n bridge; (Teppich)
rug
Bruder m -s,-̈ brother
brüderlich a brotherly, fraternal
Brügge nt -s Bruges
Brüh|e f -, -n broth, stock.
B~würfel m stock cube
brüllen vt/i (haben) roar
brumm|eln vt/i (haben) mumble.
b~en vi (haben) <Insekt:> buzz;
<Bär:> growl; <Motor:> hum;
(murren) grumble **B~er** m -s,- 🅸
bluebottle. **b~ig** a 🅸 grumpy
brünett a dark-haired
Brunnen m -s,- well; (Spring-)
fountain; (Heil-) spa water
brüsk a brusque
Brüssel nt -s Brussels
Brust f -,-̈e chest; (weibliche,
Culin: B~stück) breast. **B~bein**
nt breastbone
brüsten (sich) vr boast
Brustschwimmen nt breaststroke
Brüstung f -, -en parapet
Brustwarze f nipple
Brut f -, -en incubation
brutal a brutal
brüten vi (haben) sit (on eggs);
(fig) ponder (über + dat over)
Brutkasten m (Med) incubator
brutto adv, **B~-** pref gross
BSE f - BSE
Bub m -en, -en (SGer) boy. **B~e** m
-n, -n (Karte) jack, knave
Buch nt -[e]s,-̈er book; **B~ führen**
keep a record (über + acc of); **die
B~er führen** keep the accounts
Buche f -, -n beech
buchen vt book; (Comm) enter
Bücher|ei f -, -en library. **B~regal**
nt bookcase, bookshelves pl.
B~schrank m bookcase
Buchfink m chaffinch
Buch|führung f bookkeeping.
B~halter(in) m -s,- (f -, -nen)
bookkeeper, accountant.
B~haltung f bookkeeping,
accountancy; (Abteilung)

accounts department.
B~handlung f bookshop

Büchse f -, -n box; (*Konserven-*) tin, can

Buch|stabe m -n, -n letter.
b~stabieren vt spell [out].
b~stäblich adv literally

Bucht f -, -en (*Geog*) bay

Buchung f -, -en booking, reservation; (*Comm*) entry

Buckel m -s,- hump; (*Beule*) bump; (*Hügel*) hillock

bücken (sich) vr bend down

bucklig a hunchbacked

Bückling m -s, -e smoked herring

Buddhis|mus m - Buddhism.
B~t(in) m -en, -en (f -, -nen) Buddhist. **b~tisch** a Buddhist

Bude f -, -n hut; (*Kiosk*) kiosk; (*Markt-*) stall; (I *Zimmer*) room

Budget /by'dʒe:/ nt -s, -s budget

Büfett nt -[e]s, -e sideboard; (*Theke*) bar; **kaltes B~** cold buffet

Büffel m -s,- buffalo

Bügel m -s,- frame; (*Kleider-*) coathanger; (*Steig-*) stirrup; (*Brillen-*) sidepiece. **B~brett** nt ironing-board. **B~eisen** nt iron. **B~falte** f crease. **b~frei** a non-iron. **b~n** vt/i (*haben*) iron

Bühne f -, -n stage. **B~nbild** nt set. **B~neingang** m stage door

Buhrufe mpl boos

Bukett nt -[e]s, -e bouquet

Bulgarien /-iən/ nt -s Bulgaria

Bull|auge nt (*Naut*) porthole.
B~dogge f bulldog. **B~dozer** /-do:zɐ/ m -s,- bulldozer. **B~e** m -n, -n bull; (✖ *Polizist*) cop

Bummel m -s,- I stroll. **B~lei** f - I dawdling

bummel|ig a I slow; (*nachlässig*) careless. **b~n** vi (*sein*) I stroll ● vi (*haben*) I dawdle. **B~streik** m go-slow. **B~zug** m I slow train

Bums m -es, -e I bump, thump

Bund¹ nt -[e]s, -e bunch

Bund² m -[e]s,ˉe association; (*Bündnis*) alliance; (*Pol*) federation; (*Rock-, Hosen-*) waistband; **der B~** the Federal Government

Bündel nt -s,- bundle. **b~n** vt bundle [up]

Bundes|- pref Federal.
B~genosse m ally. **B~kanzler** m Federal Chancellor. **B~land** nt [federal] state; (*Aust*) province. **B~liga** f German national league. **B~rat** m Upper House of Parliament. **B~regierung** f Federal Government. **B~republik** f **die B~republik Deutschland** the Federal Republic of Germany. **B~tag** m Lower House of Parliament. **B~wehr** f [Federal German] Army

bünd|ig a & adv **kurz und b~ig** short and to the point. **B~nis** nt -sses, -sse alliance

Bunker m -s,- bunker; (*Luftschutz-*) shelter

bunt a coloured; (*farbenfroh*) colourful; (*grell*) gaudy; (*gemischt*) varied; (*wirr*) confused; **b~e Platte** assorted cold meats. **B~stift** m crayon

Bürde f -, -n (*fig*) burden

Burg f -, -en castle

Bürge m -n, -n guarantor. **b~n** vi (*haben*) **b~n für** vouch for; (*fig*) guarantee

Bürger|(in) m -s,- (f -, -nen) citizen. **B~krieg** m civil war. **b~lich** a civil; <*Pflicht*> civic; (*mittelständisch*) middle-class. **B~liche(r)** m/f commoner. **B~meister** m mayor. **B~rechte** npl civil rights. **B~steig** m -[e]s, -e pavement

Bürgschaft f -, -en surety

Burgunder m -s,- (*Wein*) Burgundy

Büro nt -s, -s office.
B~angestellte(r) m/f office-worker. **B~klammer** f paper-clip.

B∼kratie *f* -, -n bureaucracy.
b∼kratisch *a* bureaucratic
Bursche *m* -n, -n lad, youth
Bürste *f* -, -n brush. b∼n *vt* brush.
B∼nschnitt *m* crew cut
Bus *m* -ses, -se bus; (*Reise-*) coach
Busch *m* -[e]s,¨e bush
Büschel *nt* -s,- tuft
buschig *a* bushy
Busen *m* -s,- bosom
Buße *f* -, -n penance; (*Jur*) fine
Bußgeld *nt* (*Jur*) fine
Büste *f* -, -n bust; (*Schneider-*)
dummy. B∼nhalter *m* -s,- bra
Butter *f* - butter. B∼blume *f*
buttercup. B∼brot *nt* slice of
bread and butter. B∼milch *f*
buttermilk. b∼n *vt* butter
b.w. *abbr* (**bitte wenden**) P.T.O.

Café /ka'fe:/ *nt* -s, -s café
Camcorder /'kamkɔrdɐ/ *m* -s, -
camcorder
camp|en /'kɛmpən/ *vi* (*haben*) go
camping. C∼ing *nt* -s camping.
C∼ingplatz *m* campsite
Caravan /'ka[:]ravan/ *m* -s, -s
(*Auto*) caravan; (*Kombi*) estate
car
CD /tse:'de:/ *f* -, -s compact disc,
CD. **CD-ROM** /tse:de:'rɔm/ *f* -,-(s)
CD-ROM
Cell|ist(in) /tʃɛ'lɪst(ɪn)/ *m* -en, -en
(*f* -, -nen) cellist. C∼o /'tʃɛlo/ *nt* -,
-los & -li cello
Celsius /'tsɛlziʊs/ *inv* Celsius,
centigrade
Cent /tsɛnt/ *m* -[s], -[s] cent
Champagner /ʃam'panjɐ/ *m* -s
champagne

Champignon /'ʃampɪnjɔn/ *m* -s, -s
[field] mushroom
Chance /'ʃã:s[ə]/ *f* -, -n chance
Chaos /'ka:ɔs/ *nt* - chaos
Charakter /ka'raktɐ/ *m* -s, -e
/-'te:rə/ character. c∼isieren *vt*
characterize. c∼istisch *a*
characteristic (**für** of)
charm|ant /ʃar'mant/ *a* charming.
C∼e /ʃarm/ *m* -s charm
Charter|flug /'tʃ-, 'ʃartɐ-/ *m*
charter flight. c∼n *vt* charter
Chassis /ʃa'si:/ *nt* -,- /-'si:[s], -'si:s/
chassis
Chauffeur /ʃɔ'fø:ɐ/ *m* -s, -e
chauffeur; (*Taxi-*) driver
Chauvinist /ʃovi'nɪst/ *m* -en, -en
chauvinist
Chef /ʃɛf/ *m* -s, -s head; 🛈 boss
Chemie /çe'mi:/ *f* - chemistry
Chem|iker(in) /'çe:-/ *m* -s,- (*f* -,
-nen) chemist. c∼isch *a*
chemical; c∼ische Reinigung
dry-cleaning; (*Geschäft*) dry-
cleaner's
Chicorée /'ʃɪkore/ *m* -s chicory
Chiffre /'ʃɪfɐ, 'ʃɪfrə/ *f* -, -n cipher
Chile /'çi:le/ *nt* -s Chile
Chin|a /'çi:na/ *nt* -s China. C∼ese
m -n, -n, C∼esin *f* -, -nen Chinese.
c∼esisch *a* Chinese. C∼esisch
nt -[s] (*Lang*) Chinese
Chip /tʃɪp/ *m* -s, -s [micro]chip.
C∼s *pl* crisps
Chirurg /çi'rʊrk/ *m* -en, -en
surgeon. C∼ie /-'gi:/ *f* - surgery
Chlor /klo:ɐ/ *nt* -s chlorine
Choke /tʃo:k/ *m* -s, -s (*Auto*)
choke
Cholera /'ko:lera/ *f* - cholera
cholerisch /ko'le:rɪʃ/ *a* irascible
Cholesterin /ço-, kolɛste'ri:n/ *nt* -s
cholesterol
Chor /ko:ɐ/ *m* -[e]s,¨e choir
Choreographie, Choreografie
/koreogra'fi:/ *f* -, -n choreography
Christ /krɪst/ *m* -en, -en Christian.
C∼baum *m* Christmas tree.

C~entum nt -s Christianity
c~lich a Christian
Christus /'krɪstʊs/ m -ti Christ
Chrom /kro:m/ nt -s chromium
Chromosom /kromo'zo:m/ nt -s,
-en chromosome
Chronik /'kro:nɪk/ f -, -en
chronicle
chronisch /'kro:nɪʃ/ a chronic
Chrysantheme /kryzan'te:mə/ f -,
-n chrysanthemum
Clique /'klɪkə/ f -, -n clique
Clown /klaun/ m -s, -s clown
Club /klʊp/ m -s, -s club
Cocktail /'kɔkte:l/ m -s, -s cocktail
Code /'ko:t/ m -s, -s code
Comic-Heft /'kɔmɪk-/ nt comic
Computer /kɔm'pju:tɐ/ m -s,-
computer. **c~isieren** vt
computerize. **C~spiel** nt
computer game
Conférencier /kõ'ferã'sie:/ m -s,-
compère
Cord /kɔrt/ m -s, **C~samt** m
corduroy
Couch /kautʃ/ f -, -es settee
Cousin /ku'zɛ̃:/ m -s, -s [male]
cousin. **C~e** /-'zi:nə/ f -, -n
[female] cousin
Creme /kre:m/ f -s, -s cream;
(Speise) cream dessert
Curry /'kari, 'kœri/ nt & m -s curry
powder ● nt -s, -s (Gericht) curry
Cursor /'kœːɐsə/ m -s, - cursor
Cyberspace /'sajbəspe:s/ m -
cyberspace

da adv there; (hier) here; (zeitlich)
then; (in dem Fall) in that case;
von da an from then on; **da sein**

be there/(hier) here; (existieren)
exist; **wieder da sein** be back
● conj as, since
dabei (emphatic: **dabei**) adv
nearby; (daran) with it;
(eingeschlossen) included;
(hinsichtlich) about it;
(währenddem) during this;
(gleichzeitig) at the same time;
(doch) and yet; **dicht d~** close by;
d~ sein be present; (mitmachen)
be involved; **d~ sein, etw zu tun**
be just doing sth
Dach nt -[e]s,-̈er roof. **D~boden** m
loft. **D~luke** f skylight. **D~rinne** f
gutter
Dachs m -es, -e badger
Dachsparren m -s,- rafter
Dackel m -s,- dachshund
dadurch (emphatic: **dadurch**) adv
through it/them; (Ursache) by it;
(deshalb) because of that; **d~,**
dass because
dafür (emphatic: **dafür**) adv for it/
them; (anstatt) instead; (als
Ausgleich) but [on the other
hand]; **d~, dass** considering that;
ich kann nichts dafür it's not my
fault
dagegen (emphatic: **dagegen**) adv
against it/them; (Mittel, Tausch)
for it; (verglichen damit) by
comparison; (jedoch) however;
hast du was d~? do you mind?
daheim adv at home
daher (emphatic: **daher**) adv from
there; (deshalb) for that reason;
das kommt d~, weil that's because
● conj that is why
dahin (emphatic: **dahin**) adv there;
bis d~ up to there; (bis dann)
until/(Zukunft) by then; **jdn**
d~bringen, dass er etw tut get s.o.
to do sth
dahinten adv back there
dahinter (emphatic: **dahinter**) adv
behind it/them; **d~ kommen** (fig)
get to the bottom of it
Dahlie /-iə/ f -, -n dahlia

dalassen† *vt sep* leave there

daliegen† *vi sep* (*haben*) lie there

damalig *a* at that time; **der d~e Minister** the then minister

damals *adv* at that time

Damast *m* -es, -e damask

Dame *f* -, -n lady; (*Karte, Schach*) queen; (*D~spiel*) draughts *sg.* **d~nhaft** *a* ladylike

damit (*emphatic:* **damit**) *adv* with it/them; (*dadurch*) by it; **hör auf d~!** stop it! ● *conj* so that

Damm *m* -[e]s,⁓e

dämmerig *a* dim. **D~licht** *nt* twilight. **d~n** *vi* (*haben*) <*Morgen:*> dawn; **es d~t** it is getting light/(*abends*) dark. **D~ung** *f* dawn; (*Abend-*) dusk

Dämon *m* -s, -en /-'mo:nən/ demon

Dampf *m* -es,⁓e steam; (*Chem*) vapour. **d~en** *vi* (*haben*) steam

dämpfen *vt* (*Culin*) steam; (*fig*) muffle <*Ton*>; lower <*Stimme*>

Dampf|er *m* -s,- steamer. **D~kochtopf** *m* pressure-cooker. **D~maschine** *f* steam engine. **D~walze** *f* steamroller

danach (*emphatic:* **danach**) *adv* after it/them; <*suchen*> for it/them; <*riechen*> of it; (*später*) afterwards; (*entsprechend*) accordingly; **es sieht d~ aus** it looks like it

Däne *m* -n, -n Dane

daneben (*emphatic:* **daneben**) *adv* beside it/them; (*außerdem*) in addition; (*verglichen damit*) by comparison

Dän|emark *nt* -s Denmark. **D~in** *f* -, -nen Dane. **d~isch** *a* Danish

Dank *m* -es thanks *pl*; **vielen D~!** thank you very much! **d~** *prep* (+ *dat or gen*) thanks to. **d~bar** *a* grateful; (*erleichtert*) thankful; (*lohnend*) rewarding. **D~barkeit** *f* - gratitude. **d~e** *adv* **d~e [schön od sehr]!** thank you [very much]! **d~en** *vi* (*haben*) thank (**jdm** s.o.);

(*ablehnen*) decline; **nichts zu d~en!** don't mention it!

dann *adv* then; **selbst d~, wenn** even if

daran (*emphatic:* **daran**) *adv* on it/them; at it/them; <*denken*> of it; **nahe d~** on the point (**etw zu tun** of doing sth). **d~setzen** *vt sep* **alles d~setzen** do one's utmost (**zu** to)

darauf (*emphatic:* **darauf**) *adv* on it/them; <*warten*> for it; <*antworten*> to it; (*danach*) after that; (*d~hin*) as a result. **d~hin** *adv* as a result

daraus (*emphatic:* **daraus**) *adv* out of *or* from it/them; **er macht sich nichts d~** he doesn't care for it

darlegen *vt sep* expound; (*erklären*) explain

Darlehen *nt* -s,- loan

Darm *m* -[e]s,⁓e intestine

darstell|en *vt sep* represent; (*bildlich*) portray; (*Theat*) interpret; (*spielen*) play; (*schildern*) describe. **D~er** *m* -s,- actor. **D~erin** *f* -, -nen actress. **D~ung** *f* representation; interpretation; description

darüber (*emphatic:* **darüber**) *adv* over it/them; (*höher*) above it/them; <*sprechen, lachen, sich freuen*> about it; (*mehr*) more; **d~ hinaus** beyond [it]; (*dazu*) on top of that

darum (*emphatic:* **darum**) *adv* round it/them; <*bitten, kämpfen*> for it; (*deshalb*) that is why; **d~, weil** because

darunter (*emphatic:* **darunter**) *adv* under it/them; (*tiefer*) below it/them; (*weniger*) less; (*dazwischen*) among them

das *def art & pron s.* **der**

dasein* *vi sep* (*sein*) da sein, *s.* **da**. **D~** *nt* -s existence

dass *conj* that

dasselbe *pron s.* **derselbe**

Daten|sichtgerät nt visual display unit, VDU. **D~verarbeitung** f data processing

datieren vt/i (haben) date

Dativ m -s, -e dative. **D~objekt** nt indirect object

Dattel f -, -n date

Datum nt s, -ten date; **Daten** dates; (Angaben) data

Dauer f - duration, length; (Jur) term; **auf die D~** in the long run. **D~auftrag** m standing order. **d~haft** a lasting, enduring; (fest) durable. **D~karte** f season ticket. **d~n** vi (haben) last; **lange d~n** take a long time. **d~nd** a lasting; (ständig) constant. **D~welle** f perm

Daumen m -s,- thumb; **jdm den D~ drücken** od **halten** keep one's fingers crossed for s.o.

Daunen fpl down sg. **D~decke** f [down-filled] duvet

davon (emphatic: **davon**) adv from it/them; (dadurch) by it; (damit) with it/them; (darüber) about it; (Menge) of it/them; **das kommt d~!** it serves you right! **d~kommen†** vi sep (sein) escape (mit dem Leben with one's life). **d~laufen†** vi sep (sein) run away. **d~machen (sich)** vr sep ⓘ make off. **d~tragen†** vt sep carry off; (erleiden) suffer; (gewinnen) win

davor (emphatic: **davor**) adv in front of it/them; <sich fürchten> of it; (zeitlich) before it/them

dazu (emphatic: **dazu**) adv to it/them; (damit) with it/them; (dafür) for it; **noch d~** in addition to that; **jdn d~ bringen, etw zu tun** get s.o. to do sth; **ich kam nicht d~** I didn't get round to [doing] it. **d~kommen†** vi sep (sein) arrive [on the scene]; (hinzukommen) be added. **d~rechnen** vt sep add to it/them

dazwischen (emphatic: **dazwischen**) adv between them; in between; (darunter) among them. **d~kommen†** vi sep (sein) (fig) crop up; **wenn nichts d~kommt** if all goes well

Debat|te f -, -n debate; **zur D~te stehen** be at issue. **d~tieren** vt/i (haben) debate

Debüt /de'by:/ nt -s, -s début

Deck nt -[e]s, -s (Naut) deck; **an D~** on deck. **D~bett** nt duvet

Decke f -, -n cover; (Tisch-) table-cloth; (Bett-) blanket; (Reise-) rug; (Zimmer-) ceiling; **unter einer D~stecken** ⓘ be in league

Deckel m -s,- lid; (Flaschen-) top; (Buch-) cover

decken vt cover; tile <Dach>; lay <Tisch>; (schützen) shield; (Sport) mark; meet <Bedarf>; **jdn d~** (fig) cover up for s.o.; **sich d~** (fig) cover oneself (**gegen** against); (übereinstimmen) coincide

Deckname m pseudonym

Deckung f - (Mil) cover; (Sport) defence; (Mann-) marking; (Boxen) guard; (Sicherheit) security; **in D~ gehen** take cover

defin|ieren vt define. **D~ition** /-'tsio:n/ f -, -en definition

Defizit nt -s, -e deficit

deformiert a deformed

deftig a ⓘ <Mahlzeit> hearty; <Witz> coarse

Degen m -s,- sword; (Fecht-) épée

degeneriert a (fig) degenerate

degradieren vt (Mil) demote; (fig) degrade

dehn|bar a elastic. **d~en** vt stretch; lengthen <Vokal>; **sich d~en** stretch

Deich m -[e]s, -e dike

dein poss pron your. **d~e(r,s)** poss pron yours; **die D~en** od **d~en** pl your family sg. **d~erseits** adv for your part.

d~etwegen *adv* for your sake; (*wegen dir*) because of you, on your account. **d~etwillen** *adv* um **d~etwillen** for your sake. **d~ige** *poss pron* der/die/das **d~ige** yours. **d~s** *poss pron* yours

Dekan *m* **-s, -e** dean

Deklin|ation /-'tsio:n/ *f* **-, -en** declension. **d~ieren** *vt* decline

Dekolleté, Dekolletee /dekɔl'te:/ *nt* **-s, -s** low neckline

Dekor *m & nt* **-s** decoration. **D~ateur** /-'tø:ɐ/ *m* **-s, -e** interior decorator; (*Schaufenster-*) window-dresser. **D~ation** /-'tsio:n/ *f* **-, -en** decoration; (*Schaufenster-*) window-dressing; (*Auslage*) display. **d~ativ** *a* decorative. **d~ieren** *vt* decorate; dress <*Schaufenster*>

Deleg|ation /-'tsio:n/ *f* **-, -en** delegation. **D~ierte(r)** *m/f* delegate

delikat *a* delicate; (*lecker*) delicious; (*taktvoll*) tactful. **D~essengeschäft** *nt* delicatessen

Delikt *nt* **-[e]s, -e** offence

Delinquent *m* **-en, -en** offender

Delle *f* **-, -n** dent

Delphin *m* **-s, -e** dolphin

Delta *nt* **-s, -s** delta

dem *def art & pron s.* der

dementieren *vt* deny

dem|entsprechend *a* corresponding; (*passend*) appropriate ● *adv* accordingly; (*passend*) appropriately. **d~nächst** *adv* soon; (*in Kürze*) shortly

Demokrat *m* **-en, -en** democrat. **D~ie** *f* **-, -n** democracy. **d~isch** *a* democratic

demolieren *vt* wreck

Demonstr|ant *m* **-en, -en** demonstrator. **D~ation** /-'tsio:n/ *f* **-, -en** demonstration. **d~ieren** *vt/i* (*haben*) demonstrate

demontieren *vt* dismantle

Demoskopie *f* **-** opinion research

Demut *f* **-** humility

den *def art & pron s.* der. **d~en** *pron s.* der

denk|bar *a* conceivable. **d~en†** *vt/i* (*haben*) think (**an** + *acc* of); (*sich erinnern*) remember (**an etw** *acc* sth); **das kann ich mir d~en** I can imagine [that]; **ich d~e nicht daran** I have no intention of doing it. **D~mal** *nt* memorial; (*Monument*) monument. **d~würdig** *a* memorable

denn *conj* for; besser/mehr **d~** je better/more than ever ● *adv* wie/ wo **d~?** but how/where? warum **d~** nicht? why ever not? es sei **d~** [, dass] unless

dennoch *adv* nevertheless

Denunz|iant *m* **-en, -en** informer. **d~ieren** *vt* denounce

Deodorant *nt* **-s, -s** deodorant

deplaciert, deplatziert /-'tsi:ɐt/ *a* (*fig*) out of place

Deponie *f* **-, -n** dump. **d~ren** *vt* deposit

deportieren *vt* deport

Depot /de'po:/ *nt* **-s, -s** depot; (*Lager*) warehouse; (*Bank-*) safe deposit

Depression *f* **-, -en** depression

deprimieren *vt* depress

....

der, die, das, *pl* **die**
● *definite article*
   (*acc* **den, die, das,** *pl* **die;** *gen* **des, der, des,** *pl* **der;** *dat* **dem, der, dem,** *pl* **den**)
····▸ the. **der Mensch** the person; (*als abstrakter Begriff*) man. **die Natur** nature. **das Leben** life. **das Lesen/Tanzen** reading/dancing. **sich** (*dat*) **das Gesicht/die Hände waschen** wash one's face/hands. **3 Euro das Pfund** 3 euros a pound
● *pronoun*
   (*acc* **den, die, das,** *pl* **die;** *gen* **dessen, deren, dessen,** *pl*

deren; *dat* **dem, der, dem**, *pl* **denen**)

● *demonstrative pronoun*

····▶ that; (*pl*) those

····▶ (*attributiv*) **der Mann war es** it was 'that man

····▶ (*substantivisch*) he, she, it; (*pl*) they. **der war es** it was 'him. **die da** (*person*) that woman/girl; (*thing*) that one

● *relative pronoun*

····▶ (*Person*) who. **der Mann, der/ dessen Sohn hier arbeitet** the man who/whose son works here. **die Frau, mit der ich Tennis spiele** the woman with whom I play tennis, the woman I play tennis with. **das Mädchen, das ich gestern sah** the girl I saw yesterday

····▶ (*Ding*) which, that. **ich sah ein Buch, das mich interessierte** I saw a book that interested me. **die CD, die ich mir anhöre** the CD I am listening to. **das Auto, mit dem wir nach Deutschland fahren** the car we are going to Germany in *or* in which we are going to Germany

derb *a* tough; (*kräftig*) strong; (*grob*) coarse; (*unsanft*) rough

deren *pron s.* **der**

dergleichen *inv a* such ● *pron* such a thing/such things

der-/die-/dasselbe, *pl* **dieselben** *pron* the same; **ein- und dasselbe** one and the same thing

derzeit *adv* at present

des *def art s.* **der**

Desert|eur /-'tø:ɐ̯/ *m* **-s, -e** deserter. **d~ieren** *vi* (*sein/haben*) desert

desgleichen *adv* likewise ● *pron* the like

deshalb *adv* for this reason; (*also*) therefore

Designer(in) /di'zaɪnɐ, -nərɪn/ *m* **-s,-** (*f,* **-, -nen**) designer

Desin|fektion /dɛs?ɪnfɛk'tsi̯o:n/ *f* disinfecting. **D~fektionsmittel** *nt* disinfectant. **d~fizieren** *vt* disinfect

dessen *pron s.* **der**

Destill|ation /-'tsi̯o:n/ *f* - distillation. **d~ieren** *vt* distil

desto *adv* **je mehr d~ besser** the more the better

deswegen *adv* = **deshalb**

Detektiv *m* **-s, -e** detective

Deton|ation /-'tsi̯o:n/ *f* -, **-en** explosion. **d~ieren** *vi* (*sein*) explode

deut|en *vt* interpret; predict <*Zukunft*> ● *vi* (*haben*) point (**auf** + *acc* at/(*fig*) to). **d~lich** *a* clear; (*eindeutig*) plain

deutsch *a* German. **D~** *nt* **-[s]** (*Lang*) German; **auf D~** in German. **D~e(r)** *m/f* German. **D~land** *nt* **-s** Germany

Deutung *f* -, **-en** interpretation

Devise *f* -, **-n** motto. **D~n** *pl* foreign currency *or* exchange *sg*

Dezember *m* **-s,-** December

dezent *a* unobtrusive; (*diskret*) discreet

Dezernat *nt* **-[e]s, -e** department

Dezimalzahl *f* decimal

d.h. *abbr* (*das heißt*) i.e.

Dia *nt* **-s, -s** (*Phot*) slide

Diabet|es *m* - diabetes. **D~iker** *m* **-s,-** diabetic

Diadem *nt* **-s, -e** tiara

Diagnose *f* -, **-n** diagnosis

diagonal *a* diagonal. **D~e** *f* -, **-n** diagonal

Diagramm *nt* **-s, -e** diagram; (*Kurven-*) graph

Diakon *m* **-s, -e** deacon

Dialekt *m* **-[e]s, -e** dialect

Dialog *m* **-[e]s, -e** dialogue

Diamant *m* **-en, -en** diamond

Diapositiv *nt* **-s, -e** (*Phot*) slide

Diaprojektor *m* slide projector

Diät *f* -, **-en** (*Med*) diet; **D~ leben** be on a diet

MMMMMMMMMMMMMMMMMMMMMMMMMMMMMMMMMMMMMM

Dirndl nt -s,- dirndl [dress]

Diskette f -, -n floppy disc

Disko f -, -s 🗓 disco. **D~thek** f -, -en discothèque

diskret a discreet

Diskus m -, -se & **Disken** discus

Disku|ssion f -, -en discussion. **d~tieren** vt/i (haben) discuss

disponieren vi (haben) make arrangements; **d~ [können] über** (+ acc) have at one's disposal

Disqualifi|kation /-'tsio:n/ f disqualification. **d~zieren** vt disqualify

Dissertation /-'tsio:n/ f -, -en dissertation

Dissident m -en, -en dissident

Distanz f -, -en distance. **d~ieren (sich)** vr dissociate oneself (von from). **d~iert** a aloof

Distel f -, -n thistle

Disziplin f -, -en discipline. **d~arisch** a disciplinary. **d~iert** a disciplined

dito adv ditto

diverse attrib a pl various

Divid|ende f -, -en dividend. **d~ieren** vt divide (durch by)

Division f -, -en division

DJH abbr (**Deutsche Jugendherberge**) [German] youth hostel

DM abbr (**Deutsche Mark**) DM

doch conj & adv but; (dennoch) yet; (trotzdem) after all; **wenn d~ ...!** if only ...! **nicht d~!** don't!

Docht m -[e]s, -e wick

Dock nt -s, -s dock. **d~en** vt/i (haben) dock

Dogge f -, -n Great Dane

Dogm|a nt -s, -men dogma. **d~atisch** a dogmatic

Doktor m -s, -en /-'to:rən/ doctor. **D~arbeit** f [doctoral] thesis

Dokument nt -[e]s, -e document. **D~arbericht** m documentary. **D~arfilm** m documentary film

Dolch m -[e]s, -e dagger

Dollar m -s,- dollar

dolmetsch|en vt/i (haben) interpret. **D~er(in)** m -s,- (f -, -nen) interpreter

Dom m -[e]s, -e cathedral

Domino nt -s, -s dominoes sg. **D~stein** m domino

Dompfaff m -en, -en bullfinch

Donau f - Danube

Donner m -s thunder. **d~n** vi (haben) thunder

Donnerstag m Thursday. **d~s** adv on Thursdays

doof a 🗓 stupid

Doppel nt -s,- duplicate; (Tennis) doubles pl. **D~bett** nt double bed. **D~decker** m -s,-doubledecker [bus]. **d~deutig** a ambiguous. **D~gänger** m -s,-double. **D~kinn** nt double chin. **d~klicken** vi (haben) double-click (auf + acc on). **D~name** m double-barrelled name. **D~punkt** m (Gram) colon. **D~stecker** m two-way adaptor. **d~t** a double; <Boden> false; **die d~te Menge** twice the amount ● adv doubly; (zweimal) twice; **d~t so viel** twice as much. **D~zimmer** nt double room

Dorf nt -[e]s,̈er village. **D~bewohner** m villager

dörflich a rural

Dorn m -[e]s, -en thorn. **d~ig** a thorny

Dorsch m -[e]s, -e cod

dort adv there. **d~ig** a local

Dose f -, -n tin, can

dösen vi (haben) doze

Dosen|milch f evaporated milk. **D~öffner** m tin or can opener

dosieren vt measure out

Dosis f -, Dosen dose

Dot-com-Firma f dot-com (company)

Dotter m & nt -s,- [egg] yolk

Dozent(in) m -en, -en (f -, -nen) (Univ) lecturer

Dr. abbr (**Doktor**) Dr

Drache m -n, -n dragon. **D~n** m -s,- kite. **D~nfliegen** nt hang-gliding

Draht m -[e]s,"e wire; **auf D~** 🛈 on the ball. **D~seilbahn** f cable railway

Dram|a nt -s, -men drama. **D~atik** f - drama. **D~atiker** m -s,- dramatist. **d~atisch** a dramatic

dran adv 🛈 = **daran; gut/schlecht d~ sein** be well off/in a bad way; **ich bin d~** it's my turn

Drang m -[e]s urge; (*Druck*) pressure

dräng|eln vt/i (*haben*) push; (*bedrängen*) pester. **d~en** vt push; (*bedrängen*) urge; **sich d~en** crowd (**um** round) ● vi (*haben*) push; (*eilen*) be urgent; **d~en auf** (+ acc) press for

dran|halten (**sich**) vr sep hurry. **d~kommen**† vi sep (*sein*) have one's turn

drauf adv 🛈 = **darauf; d~ und dran sein** be on the point (**etw zu tun** of doing sth). **D~gänger** m -s,- daredevil

draußen adv outside; (*im Freien*) out of doors

drechseln vt (*Techn*) turn

Dreck m -s dirt; (*Morast*) mud

Dreh m -s 🛈 knack; **den D~ herausbaben** have got the hang of it. **D~bank** f lathe. **D~bleistift** m propelling pencil. **D~buch** nt screenplay, script. **d~en** vt turn; (*im Kreis*) rotate; (*verschlingen*) twist; roll <*Zigarette*>; shoot <*Film*>; lauter/leiser **d~en** turn up/down; **sich d~en** turn; (*im Kreis*) rotate; (*schnell*) spin; <*Wind:*> change; **sich d~en um** revolve around; (*sich handeln*) be about ● vi (*haben*) turn; <*Wind:*> change; **an etw** (*dat*) **d~en** turn sth. **D~stuhl** m swivel chair. **D~tür** f revolving door. **D~ung** f -, -en turn; (*im Kreis*) rotation. **D~zahl** f number of revolutions

drei inv a, **D~** f -, -en three; (*Sch*) ≈ pass. **D~eck** nt -[e]s, -e triangle. **d~eckig** a triangular. **d~erlei** inv a three kinds of ● pron three things. **d~fach** a triple. **d~mal** adv three times. **D~rad** nt tricycle

dreißig inv a thirty. **d~ste(r,s)** a thirtieth

dreiviertel* inv a **drei viertel**, s. **viertel. D~stunde** f three-quarters of an hour

dreizehn inv a thirteen **d~te(r,s)** a thirteenth

dreschen† vt thresh

dress|ieren vt train. **D~ur** f - training

dribbeln vi (*haben*) dribble

Drill m -[e]s (*Mil*) drill. **d~en** vt drill

Drillinge mpl triplets

dringlich a urgent

Drink m -[s], -s [alcoholic] drink

drinnen adv inside

dritt adv **zu d~** in threes; **wir waren zu d~** there were three of us. **d~e(r,s)** a third; **ein D~er** a third person. **d~el** nt -s,- third. **d~ens** adv thirdly. **d~rangig** a third-rate

Drog|e f -, -n drug. **D~enabhängige(r)** m/f drug addict. **D~erie** f -, -n chemist's shop. **D~ist** m -en, -en chemist

drohen vi (*haben*) threaten (**jdm** s.o.)

dröhnen vi (*haben*) resound; (*tönen*) boom

Drohung f -, -en threat

drollig a funny; (*seltsam*) odd

Drops m -,- [fruit] drop

Drossel f -, -n thrush

drosseln vt (*Techn*) throttle; (*fig*) cut back

drüben adv over there

Druck[1] m -[e]s,"e pressure; **unter D~ setzen** (*fig*) pressurize

Druck² *m* -[e]s, -e printing; (*Schrift, Reproduktion*) print. **D~buchstabe** *m* block letter
drucken *vt* print
drücken *vt/i* (*haben*) press; (*aus-*) squeeze; <*Schuh:*> pinch; (*umarmen*) hug; **Preise d~** force down prices; (*an Tür*) **d~** push; **sich d~** 🚹 make oneself scarce; **sich d~ vor** (+ *dat*) 🚹 shirk. **d~d** *a* heavy; (*schwül*) oppressive
Drucker *m* -s,- printer
Druckerei *f* -, -en printing works
Druck|fehler *m* misprint. **D~knopf** *m* press-stud. **D~luft** *f* compressed air. **D~sache** *f* printed matter. **D~schrift** *f* type; (*Veröffentlichung*) publication; **in D~schrift** in block letters *pl*
Druckstelle *f* bruise
Drüse *f* -, -n (*Anat*) gland
Dschungel *m* -s,- jungle
du *pron* (*familiar address*) you; **auf Du und Du** on familiar terms
Dübel *m* -s,- plug
Dudelsack *m* bagpipes *pl*
Duell *nt* -s, -e duel
Duett *nt* -s, -e [vocal] duet
Duft *m* -[e]s, ̈e fragrance, scent; (*Aroma*) aroma. **d~en** *vi* (*haben*) smell (*nach* of)
dulden *vt* tolerate; (*erleiden*) suffer ● *vi* (*haben*) suffer
dumm *a* stupid; (*unklug*) foolish; (🚹 *lästig*) awkward; **wie d~!**. **d~erweise** *adv* stupidly; (*leider*) unfortunately. **D~heit** *f* -, -en stupidity; (*Torheit*) foolishness; (*Handlung*) folly. **D~kopf** *m* 🚹 fool.
dumpf *a* dull
Düne *f* -, -n dune
Dung *m* -s manure
Düng|emittel *nt* fertilizer. **d~en** *vt* fertilize. **D~er** *m* -s,- fertilizer
dunk|el *a* dark; (*vage*) vague; (*fragwürdig*) shady; **d~les Bier** brown ale; **im D~eln** in the dark

Dunkel|heit *f* - darkness. **D~kammer** *f* dark-room. **d~n** *vi* (*haben*) get dark
dünn *a* thin; <*Buch*> slim; (*spärlich*) sparse; (*schwach*) weak
Dunst *m* -es, ̈e mist, haze; (*Dampf*) vapour
dünsten *vt* steam
dunstig *a* misty, hazy
Duo *nt* -s, -s [instrumental] duet
Duplikat *nt* -[e]s, -e duplicate
Dur *nt* - (*Mus*) major [key]
durch *prep* (+ *acc*) through; (*mittels*) by; [*geteilt*] **d~** (*Math*) divided by ● *adv* **die Nacht d~** throughout the night; **d~ und d~** nass wet through
durchaus *adv* absolutely; **d~ nicht** by no means
durchblättern *vt sep* leaf through
durchblicken *vi sep* (*haben*) look through; **d~ lassen** (*fig*) hint at
Durchblutung *f* circulation
durchbohren *vt insep* pierce
durchbrechen¹† *vt/i sep* (*haben*) break [in two]
durchbrechen²† *vt insep* break through; break <*Schallmauer*>
durchbrennen† *vi sep* (*sein*) burn through; <*Sicherung:*> blow
Durchbruch *m* breakthrough
durchdrehen *v sep* ● *vt* mince ● *vi* (*haben/sein*) 🚹 go crazy
durchdringen† *vi sep* (*sein*) penetrate; (*sich durchsetzen*) get one's way. **d~d** *a* penetrating; <*Schrei*> piercing
durcheinander *adv* in a muddle; <*Person*> confused; **d~ bringen** muddle [up]; confuse <*Person*>; **d~ geraten** get mixed up; **d~ reden** all talk at once. **D~** *nt* -s muddle
durchfahren *vi sep* (*sein*) drive through; <*Zug:*> go through
Durchfahrt *f* journey/drive through; **auf der D~** passing through; **'D~ verboten'** 'no thoroughfare'

Durchfall *m* diarrhoea. **d~en†** *vi sep* (*sein*) fall through; (ⓘ *versagen*) flop; (*bei Prüfung*) fail

Durchfuhr *f* - (*Comm*) transit

durchführ|bar *a* feasible. **d~en** *vt sep* carry out

Durchgang *m* passage; (*Sport*) round; 'D~ verboten' 'no entry'. **D~sverkehr** *m* through traffic

durchgeben† *vt sep* pass through; (*übermitteln*) transmit; (*Radio, TV*) broadcast

durchgebraten *a* **gut d~** well done

durchgehen† *vi sep* (*sein*) go through; (*davonlaufen*) run away; <*Pferd:*> bolt; **jdm etw d~ lassen** let s.o. get away with sth. **d~d** *a* continuous; **d~d geöffnet** open all day; **d~der Zug** through train

durchgreifen† *vi sep* (*haben*) reach through; (*vorgehen*) take drastic action. **d~d** *a* drastic

durchhalte|n† *v sep* (*fig*) ● *vi* (*haben*) hold out ● *vt* keep up. **D~vermögen** *nt* stamina

durchkommen† *vi sep* (*sein*) come through; (*gelangen, am Telefon*) get through

durchlassen† *vt sep* let through

durchlässig *a* permeable; (*undicht*) leaky

Durchlauferhitzer *m* -s,- geyser

durchlesen† *vt sep* read through

durchleuchten *vt insep* X-ray

durchlöchert *a* riddled with holes

durchmachen *vt sep* go through; (*erleiden*) undergo

Durchmesser *m* -s,- diameter

durchnässt *a* wet through

durchnehmen† *vt sep* (*Sch*) do

durchnummeriert *a* numbered consecutively

durchpausen *vt sep* trace

durchqueren *vt insep* cross

Durchreiche *f* -, -n hatch

Durchreise *f* journey through; **auf der D~** passing through. **d~n** *vi sep* (*sein*) pass through

durchreißen† *vt/i sep* (*sein*) tear

Durchsage *f* -, -n announcement. **d~n** *vt sep* announce

Durchschlag *m* carbon copy; (*Culin*) colander. **d~en†** *v sep* ● *vt* (*Culin*) rub through a sieve; **sich d~en** (*fig*) struggle through ● *vi* (*sein*) <*Sicherung:*> blow

durchschlagend *a* (*fig*) effective; <*Erfolg:*> resounding

durchschneiden† *vt sep* cut

Durchschnitt *m* average; **im D~** on average. **d~lich** *a* average ● *adv* on average. **D~s-** *pref* average

Durchschrift *f* carbon copy

durchsehen† *v sep* ● *vi* (*haben*) see through ● *vt* look through

durchseihen *vt sep* strain

durchsetzen *vt sep* force through; **sich d~** assert oneself; <*Mode:*> catch on

Durchsicht *f* check

durchsichtig *a* transparent

durchsickern *vi sep* (*sein*) seep through; <*Neuigkeit:*> leak out

durchstehen† *vt sep* (*fig*) come through

durchstreichen† *vt sep* cross out

durchsuch|en *vt insep* search. **D~ung** *f* -, -en search

durchwachsen *a* <*Speck*> streaky; (ⓘ *gemischt*) mixed

durchwählen *vi sep* (*haben*) (*Teleph*) dial direct

durchweg *adv* without exception

durchwühlen *vt insep* rummage through; ransack <*Haus*>

Durchzug *m* through draught

dürfen†
● *transitive & auxiliary verb*
····▸ (*Erlaubnis haben zu*) be allowed; may, can. **etw [tun] dürfen** be allowed to do sth. **darf ich das tun?** may *or* can I do

that? **nein, das darfst du nicht** no you may not *or* cannot [do that]. **er sagte mir, ich dürfte sofort gehen** he told me I could go at once. **hier darf man nicht rauchen** smoking is prohibited here. **sie darf/durfte es nicht sehen** she must not/was not allowed to see it.

┈┈➤ (*in Höflichkeitsformeln*) may. **darf ich rauchen?** may I smoke? **darf/dürfte ich um diesen Tanz bitten?** may/might I have the pleasure of this dance?

┈┈➤ **dürfte** (*sollte*) should, ought. **jetzt dürften sie dort angekommen sein** they should *or* ought to be there by now. **das dürfte nicht allzu schwer sein** that should not be too difficult. **ich hätte es nicht tun/sagen dürfen** I ought not to have done/said it

● *intransitive verb*

┈┈➤ (*irgendwohin gehen dürfen*) be allowed to go; may go; can go. **darf ich nach Hause?** may *or* can I go home? **sie durfte nicht ins Theater** she was not allowed to go to the theatre

dürftig *a* poor; <*Mahlzeit*> scanty
dürr *a* dry; <*Boden*> arid; (*mager*) skinny. **D∼e** *f* -, -n drought
Durst *m* -[e]s thirst; **D∼ haben** be thirsty. **d∼ig** *a* thirsty
Dusche *f* -, -n shower. **d∼n** *vi/r* (*haben*) [sich] **d∼n** have a shower
Düse *f* -, -n nozzle. **D∼nflugzeug** *nt* jet
Dutzend *nt* -s, -e dozen
duzen *vt* **jdn d∼** call s.o. 'du'
DVD *f* -, -s DVD
Dynam|ik *f* - dynamics *sg*; (*fig*) dynamism. **d∼isch** *a* dynamic; <*Rente*> index-linked
Dynamit *nt* -es dynamite
Dynamo *m* -s, -s dynamo
Dynastie *f* -, -n dynasty
D-Zug /'de:-/ *m* express [train]

Ebbe *f* -, -n low tide
eben *a* level; (*glatt*) smooth; **zu e∼er Erde** on the ground floor
● *adv* just; (*genau*) exactly; **e∼ noch** only just; (*gerade vorhin*) just now; **das ist es e∼!** that's just it! **E∼bild** *nt* image
Ebene *f* -, -n (*Geog*) plain; (*Geom*) plane; (*fig: Niveau*) level
eben|falls *adv* also; **danke, e∼falls** thank you, [the] same to you. **E∼holz** *nt* ebony. **e∼so** *adv* just the same; (*ebenso sehr*) just as much; **e∼so gut** just as good; *adv* just as well; **e∼so sehr** just as much; **e∼so viel** just as much/ many; **e∼so wenig** just as little/ few; (*noch*) no more
Eber *m* -s,- boar
ebnen *vt* level; (*fig*) smooth
Echo *nt* -s, -s echo
echt *a* genuine, real; authentic
● *adv* Ⓕ really; typically. **E∼heit** *f* - authenticity
Eck|ball *m* (*Sport*) corner. **E∼e** *f* -, -n corner; **um die E∼e bringen** Ⓕ bump off. **e∼ig** *a* angular; <*Klammern*> square; (*unbeholfen*) awkward. **E∼zahn** *m* canine tooth
Ecu, ECU /e'ky:/ *m* -[s], -[s] ecu
edel *a* noble; (*wertvoll*) precious; (*fein*) fine. **e∼mütig** *a* magnanimous. **E∼stahl** *m* stainless steel. **E∼stein** *m* precious stone
Efeu *m* -s ivy
Effekt *m* -[e]s, -e effect. **E∼en** *pl* securities. **e∼iv** *a* actual, *adv* -ly; (*wirksam*) effective
EG *f* - *abbr* (**Europäische Gemeinschaft**) EC

egal a das ist mir e∼ 🆑 it's all the same to me ● adv e∼ wie/wo no matter how/where

Egge f -, -n harrow

Ego|ismus m - selfishness. **E∼ist(in)** m -en, -en (f -, -nen) egoist. **e∼istisch** a selfish

eh adv (Aust, fam) anyway

ehe conj before; **ehe nicht** until

Ehe f -, -n marriage. **E∼bett** nt double bed. **E∼bruch** m adultery. **E∼frau** f wife. **e∼lich** a marital; <Recht> conjugal; <Kind> legitimate

ehemalig a former. **e∼s** adv formerly

Ehe|mann m (pl -männer) husband. **E∼paar** nt married couple

eher adv earlier, sooner; (lieber, vielmehr) rather; (mehr) more

Ehering m wedding ring

Ehr|e f -, -n honour. **e∼en** vt honour. **e∼enamtlich** a honorary ● adv in an honorary capacity. **E∼engast** m guest of honour. **e∼enhaft** a honourable. **E∼ensache** f point of honour. **E∼enwort** nt word of honour. **e∼erbietig** a deferential. **E∼furcht** f reverence; (Scheu) awe. **e∼fürchtig** a reverent. **E∼gefühl** nt sense of honour. **E∼geiz** m ambition. **e∼geizig** a ambitious. **e∼lich** a honest; **e∼lich gesagt** to be honest. **E∼lichkeit** f - honesty. **e∼los** a dishonourable. **e-würdig** a venerable; (als Anrede) Reverend

Ei nt -[e]s, -er egg

Eibe f -, -n yew

Eiche f -, -n oak. **E∼l** f -, -n acorn

eichen vt standardize

Eichhörnchen nt -s, - squirrel

Eid m -[e]s, -e oath

Eidechse f -, -n lizard

eidlich a sworn ● adv on oath

Eidotter m & nt egg yolk

Eier|becher m egg-cup. **E∼kuchen** m pancake; (Omelett) omelette. **E∼schale** f eggshell. **E∼schnee** m beaten egg-white. **E∼stock** m ovary

Eifer m -s eagerness. **E∼sucht** f jealousy. **e∼süchtig** a jealous

eifrig a eager

Eigelb nt -[e]s, -e [egg] yolk

eigen a own; (typisch) characteristic (dat of); (seltsam) odd; (genau) particular. **E∼art** f peculiarity. **e∼artig** a peculiar. **e∼händig** a personal; <Unterschrift> own. **E∼heit** f -, -en peculiarity. **E∼name** m proper name. **e∼nützig** a selfish. **e∼s** adv specially. **E∼schaft** f -, -en quality; (Phys) property; (Merkmal) characteristic; (Funktion) capacity. **E∼schaftswort** nt (pl -wörter) adjective. **E∼sinn** m obstinacy. **e∼sinnig** a obstinate

eigentlich a actual, real; (wahr) true ● adv actually, really; (streng genommen) strictly speaking

Eigen|tor nt own goal. **E∼tum** nt -s property. **E∼tümer(in)** m -s,- (f -, -nen) owner. **E∼tumswohnung** f freehold flat. **e∼willig** a self-willed; <Stil> highly individual

Eil|brief m express letter. **E∼e** f - hurry; **E∼e haben** be in a hurry; <Sache:> be urgent. **e∼en** vi (sein) hurry ● (haben) (drängen) be urgent. **e∼ig** a hurried; (dringend) urgent; **es e∼ig haben** be in a hurry. **E∼zug** m semi-fast train

Eimer m -s,- bucket; (Abfall-) bin

ein
● indefinite article
····▸ a, (vor Vokal) an. **ein Kleid/ Apfel/Hotel/Mensch** a dress/an apple/a[n] hotel/a human being.

so ein such a. **was für ein …** (*Frage*) what kind of a …? (*Ausruf*) what a …!
● *adjective*
····▸ (*Ziffer*) one. **eine Minute** one minute. **wir haben nur eine Stunde** we only have an/(*betont*) one hour. **eines Tages/Abends** one day/evening
····▸ (*derselbe*) the same. **einer Meinung sein** be of the same opinion. **mit jdm in einem Zimmer schlafen** sleep in the same room as s.o.

einander *pron* one another
Einäscherung *f* -, -en cremation
einatmen *vt/i sep* (*haben*) inhale, breathe in
Einbahnstraße *f* one-way street
einbalsamieren *vt sep* embalm
Einband *m* binding
Einbau *m* installation; (*Montage*) fitting. **e∼en** *vt sep* install; (*montieren*) fit. **E∼küche** *f* fitted kitchen
einbegriffen *pred a* included
Einberufung *f* call-up
Einbettzimmer *nt* single room
einbeulen *vt sep* dent
einbeziehen† *vt sep* [mit] **e∼** include; (*berücksichtigen*) take into account
einbiegen† *vi sep* (*sein*) turn
einbild|en *vt sep* **sich** (*dat*) **etw e∼en** imagine sth; **sich** (*dat*) **viel e∼en** be conceited. **E∼ung** *f* imagination; (*Dünkel*) conceit. **E∼ungskraft** *f* imagination
einblenden *vt sep* fade in
Einblick *m* insight
einbrech|en† *vi sep* (*haben/sein*) break in; **bei uns ist eingebrochen worden** we have been burgled. **E∼er** *m* burglar
einbringen† *vt sep* get in; bring in <*Geld*>
Einbruch *m* burglary; **bei E∼ der Nacht** at nightfall

einbürger|n *vt sep* naturalize. **E∼ung** *f* - naturalization
einchecken /-tʃɛkən/ *vt/i sep* (*haben*) check in
eindecken (sich) *vr sep* stock up
eindeutig *a* unambiguous; (*deutlich*) clear
eindicken *vt sep* (*Culin*) thicken
eindringen† *vi sep* (*sein*) **e∼en in** (+ *acc*) penetrate into; (*mit Gewalt*) <*Wasser:*> its way into; (*Mil*) invade
Eindruck *m* impression
eindrücken *vt sep* crush
eindrucksvoll *a* impressive
ein|e(r,s) *pron* one; (*jemand*) someone; (*man*) one, you
einebnen *vt sep* level
eineiig *a* <*Zwillinge*> identical
eineinhalb *inv a* one and a half; **e∼ Stunden** an hour and a half
Einelternfamilie *f* one-parent family
einengen *vt sep* restrict
Einer *m* -s,- (*Math*) unit. **e∼** *pron s.* **eine(r,s). e∼lei** *inv a* ● *attrib a* one kind of; (*eintönig, einheitlich*) the same ● *pred a* 🄸 immaterial; **es ist mir e∼lei** it's all the same to me. **e∼seits** *adv* on the one hand
einfach *a* simple; <*Essen*> plain; <*Faden, Fahrt*> single; **e∼er Soldat** private. **E∼heit** *f* - simplicity
einfädeln *vt sep* thread; (*fig; arrangieren*) arrange
einfahr|en† *v sep* ● *vi* (*sein*) arrive; <*Zug:*> pull in ● *vt* (*Auto*) run in. **E∼t** *f* arrival; (*Eingang*) entrance, way in; (*Auffahrt*) drive; (*Autobahn-*) access road; **keine E∼t** no entry
Einfall *m* idea; (*Mil*) invasion. **e∼en**† *vi sep* (*sein*) collapse; (*eindringen*) invade; **jdm e∼en** occur to s.o.; **was fällt ihm ein!** what does he think he is doing!
Einfalt *f* - naïvety

E

einfarbig *a* of one colour; <*Stoff, Kleid*> plain

einfass|en *vt sep* edge; set <*Edelstein*>. **E~ung** *f* border, edging

einfetten *vt sep* grease

Einfluss *m* influence. **e~reich** *a* influential

einförmig *a* monotonous. **E~keit** *f* - monotony

einfrieren† *vt/i sep* (*sein*) freeze

einfügen *vt sep* insert; (*einschieben*) interpolate; **sich e~** fit in

einfühlsam *a* sensitive

Einfuhr *f* -, -en import

einführ|en *vt sep* introduce; (*einstecken*) insert; (*einweisen*) initiate; (*Comm*) import. **e~end** *a* introductory. **E~ung** *f* introduction; (*Einweisung*) initiation

Eingabe *f* petition; (*Computer*) input

Eingang *m* entrance, way in; (*Ankunft*) arrival

eingebaut *a* built-in; <*Schrank*> fitted

eingeben† *vt sep* hand in; (*Computer*) feed in

eingebildet *a* imaginary; (*überheblich*) conceited

Eingeborene(r) *m/f* native

eingehen† *v sep* ● *vi* (*sein*) come in; (*ankommen*) arrive; (*einlaufen*) shrink; (*sterben*) die; <*Zeitung, Firma*:> fold; **auf etw** (*acc*) **e~** go into sth; (*annehmen*) agree to sth ● *vt* enter into; contract <*Ehe*>; make <*Wette*>; take <*Risiko*>

eingemacht *a* (*Culin*) bottled

eingenommen *pred a* (*fig*) taken (*von* with); prejudiced (*gegen* against)

eingeschneit *a* snowbound

eingeschrieben *a* registered

Einge|ständnis *nt* admission. **e~stehen†** *vt sep* admit

eingetragen *a* registered

Eingeweide *pl* bowels, entrails

eingewöhnen (sich) *vr sep* settle in

eingießen† *vt sep* pour in; (*einschenken*) pour

eingleisig *a* single-track

eingliedern *vt sep* integrate. **E~ung** *f* integration

eingravieren *vt sep* engrave

eingreifen† *vi sep* (*haben*) intervene. **E~** *nt* **-s** intervention

Eingriff *m* intervention; (*Med*) operation

einhaken *vt/r sep* **jdn e~** *od* **sich bei jdm e~** take s.o.'s arm

einhalten† *v sep* ● *vt* keep; (*befolgen*) observe ● *vi* (*haben*) stop

einhändigen *vt sep* hand in

einhängen *vt sep* hang; put down <*Hörer*>

einheimisch *a* local; (*eines Landes*) native; (*Comm*) homeproduced. **E~e(r)** *m/f* local, native

Einheit *f* -, -en unity; (*Maß-, Mil*) unit. **e~lich** *a* uniform. **E~spreis** *m* standard price; (*Fahrpreis*) flat fare

einholen *vt sep* catch up with; (*aufholen*) make up for; (*erbitten*) seek; (*einkaufen*) buy

einhüllen *vt sep* wrap

einhundert *inv a* one hundred

einig *a* united; [**sich** (*dat*)] **e~ sein** be in agreement

einig|e(r,s) *pron* some; (*ziemlich viel*) quite a lot of; (*substantivisch*) **e~e** *pl* some; (*mehrere*) several; (*ziemlich viele*) quite a lot; **e~es** *sg* some things; **vor e~er Zeit** some time ago

einigen *vt* unite; unify <*Land*>; **sich e~** come to an agreement

einigermaßen *adv* to some extent; (*ziemlich*) fairly; (*ziemlich gut*) fairly well

Einigkeit *f* - unity; (*Übereinstimmung*) agreement

einjährig *a* one-year-old; **e~e Pflanze** annual

einkalkulieren *vt sep* take into account

einkassieren *vt sep* collect

Einkauf *m* purchase; (*Einkaufen*) shopping; **Einkäufe machen** do some shopping. **e~en** *vt sep* buy; **e~en gehen** go shopping. **E~swagen** *m* shopping trolley

einklammern *vt sep* bracket

Einklang *m* harmony; **in E~ stehen** be in accord (**mit** with)

einkleben *vt sep* stick in

einkleiden *vt sep* fit out

einklemmen *vt sep* clamp

einkochen *v sep* ● *vi* (*sein*) boil down ● *vt* preserve, bottle

Einkommen *nt* **-s** income. **E~[s]steuer** *f* income tax

Einkünfte *pl* income *sg*; (*Einnahmen*) revenue *sg*

einlad|en† *vt sep* load; (*auffordern*) invite; (*bezahlen für*) treat. **E~ung** *f* invitation

Einlage *f* enclosure; (*Schuh-*) arch support; (*Programm-*) interlude; (*Comm*) investment; (*Bank-*) deposit; **Suppe mit E~** soup with noodles/dumplings

Ein|lass *m* **-es** admittance. **e~lassen†** *vt sep* let in; run <*Bad, Wasser*>; **sich auf etw** (*acc*) **e~lassen** get involved in sth

einleben (sich) *vr sep* settle in

Einlege|arbeit *f* inlaid work. **e~n** *vt sep* put in; lay in <*Vorrat*>; lodge <*Protest*>; (*einfügen*) insert; (*Auto*) engage <*Gang*>; (*Culin*) pickle; (*marinieren*) marinade; **eine Pause e~n** have a break. **E~sohle** *f* insole

einleit|en *vt sep* initiate; (*eröffnen*) begin. **E~ung** *f* introduction

einleuchten *vi sep* (*haben*) be clear (*dat* to). **e~d** *a* convincing

einliefer|n *vt sep* take (**ins Krankenhaus** to hospital). **E~ung** *f* admission

einlösen *vt sep* cash <*Scheck*>; redeem <*Pfand*>; (*fig*) keep

einmachen *vt sep* preserve

einmal *adv* once; (*eines Tages*) one *or* some day; **noch/schon e~** again/before; **noch e~ so teuer** twice as expensive; **auf e~** at the same time; (*plötzlich*) suddenly; **nicht e~** not even. **E~eins** *nt* - [multiplication] tables *pl*. **e~ig** *a* (*einzigartig*) unique; (☐ *großartig*) fantastic

einmarschieren *vi sep* (*sein*) march in

einmisch|en (sich) *vr sep* interfere. **E~ung** *f* interference

Einnahme *f* -, -n taking; (*Mil*) capture; **E~n** *pl* income *sg*; (*Einkünfte*) revenue *sg*; (*Comm*) receipts; (*eines Ladens*) takings

einnehmen† *vt sep* take; have <*Mahlzeit*>; (*Mil*) capture; take up <*Platz*>

einordnen *vt sep* put in its proper place; (*klassifizieren*) classify; **sich e~** fit in; (*Auto*) get in lane

einpacken *vt sep* pack

einparken *vt sep* park

einpflanzen *vt sep* plant; implant <*Organ*>

einplanen *vt sep* allow for

einprägen *vt sep* impress (**jdm** [up]on s.o.); **sich** (*dat*) **etw e~en** memorize sth

einrahmen *vt sep* frame

einrasten *vi sep* (*sein*) engage

einräumen *vt sep* put away; (*zugeben*) admit; (*zugestehen*) grant

einrechnen *vt sep* include

einreden *v sep* ● *vt* **jdm/sich** (*dat*) **etw e~** persuade s.o./oneself of sth.

einreiben† *vt sep* rub (**mit** with)

einreichen *vt sep* submit; **die Scheidung e~** file for divorce

E

Einreih|er *m* -s,- single-breasted suit. **e~ig** *a* single-breasted
Einreise *f* entry. **e~n** *vi sep* (*sein*) enter (**nach Irland** Ireland)
einrenken *vt sep* (*Med*) set
einricht|en *vt sep* fit out; (*möblieren*) furnish; (*anordnen*) arrange; (*Med*) set <*Bruch*>; (*eröffnen*) set up; **sich e~en** furnish one's home; (*sich einschränken*) economize; (*sich vorbereiten*) prepare (**auf** + *acc* for). **E~ung** *f* furnishing; (*Möbel*) furnishings *pl*; (*Techn*) equipment; (*Vorrichtung*) device; (*Eröffnung*) setting up; (*Institution*) institution; (*Gewohnheit*) practice
einrosten *vi sep* (*sein*) rust; (*fig*) get rusty
eins *inv a & pron* one; **noch e~** one other thing; **mir ist alles e~** 🔢 it's all the same to me. **E~** *f* -, **-en** one; (*Sch*) ≈ A
einsam *a* lonely; (*allein*) solitary; (*abgelegen*) isolated. **E~keit** *f* - loneliness; solitude; isolation
einsammeln *vt sep* collect
Einsatz *m* use; (*Mil*) mission; (*Wett-*) stake; (*E~teil*) insert; **im E~** in action
einschalt|en *vt sep* switch on; (*einschieben*) interpolate; (*fig: beteiligen*) call in; **sich e~en** (*fig*) intervene. **E~quote** *f* (*TV*) viewing figures *pl*; ≈ ratings *pl*
einschätzen *vt sep* assess; (*bewerten*) rate
einschenken *vt sep* pour
einscheren *vi sep* (*sein*) pull in
einschicken *vt sep* send in
einschieben† *vt sep* push in; (*einfügen*) insert
einschiff|en (sich) *vr sep* embark. **E~ung** *f* - embarkation
einschlafen† *vi sep* (*sein*) go to sleep; (*aufhören*) peter out

einschläfern *vt sep* lull to sleep; (*betäuben*) put out; (*töten*) put to sleep. **e~d** *a* soporific
Einschlag *m* impact. **e~en†** *v sep* ● *vt* knock in; (*zerschlagen*) smash; (*drehen*) turn; take <*Weg*>; take up <*Laufbahn*> ● *vi* (*haben*) hit/<*Blitz*:> strike (**in etw** *acc* sth); (*Erfolg haben*) be a hit
einschleusen *vt sep* infiltrate
einschließ|en† *vt sep* lock in; (*umgeben*) enclose; (*einkreisen*) surround; (*einbeziehen*) include; **sich e~en** lock oneself in; **Bedienung eingeschlossen** service included. **e~lich** *adv* inclusive ● *prep* (+ *gen*) including
einschneiden† *vt/i sep* (*haben*) **[in] etw** *acc* **e~** cut into sth. **e~d** *a* (*fig*) drastic
Einschnitt *m* cut; (*Med*) incision; (*Lücke*) gap; (*fig*) decisive event
einschränk|en *vt sep* restrict; (*reduzieren*) cut back; **sich e~en** economize. **E~ung** *f* -, -en restriction; (*Reduzierung*) reduction; (*Vorbehalt*) reservation
Einschreib|[e]brief *m* registered letter. **e~en†** *vt sep* enter; register <*Brief*>; **sich e~en** put one's name down; (*sich anmelden*) enrol. **E~en** *nt* registered letter/packet; **als** *od* **per E~en** by registered post
einschüchtern *vt sep* intimidate
Einsegnung *f* -, -en confirmation
einsehen† *vt sep* inspect; (*lesen*) consult; (*begreifen*) see
einseitig *a* one-sided; (*Pol*) unilateral ● *adv* on one side; (*fig*) one-sidedly; (*Pol*) unilaterally
einsenden† *vt sep* send in
einsetzen *v sep* ● *vt* put in; (*einfügen*) insert; (*verwenden*) use; put on <*Zug*>; call out <*Truppen*>; (*Mil*) deploy; (*ernennen*) appoint; (*wetten*) stake; (*riskieren*) risk ● *vi*

(*haben*) start; <*Winter, Regen:*> set in

Einsicht *f* insight; (*Verständnis*) understanding; (*Vernunft*) reason. **e~ig** *a* understanding

Einsiedler *m* hermit

einsinken† *vi sep* (*sein*) sink in

einspannen *vt sep* harness; **jdn e~** 🗉 rope s.o. in

einsparen *vt sep* save

einsperren *vt sep* shut/(*im Gefängnis*) lock up

einsprachig *a* monolingual

einspritzen *vt sep* inject

Einspruch *m* objection; **E~ erheben** object; (*Jur*) appeal

einspurig *a* single-track; (*Auto*) single-lane

einst *adv* once; (*Zukunft*) one day

Einstand *m* (*Tennis*) deuce

einstecken *vt sep* put in; post <*Brief*>; (*Electr*) plug in; (🗉 *behalten*) pocket; (🗉 *hinnehmen*) take; suffer <*Niederlage*>; **etw e~** put sth in one's pocket

einsteigen† *vi sep* (*sein*) get in; (*in Bus/Zug*) get on

einstell|en *vt sep* put in; (*anstellen*) employ; (*aufhören*) stop; (*regulieren*) adjust, set; (*Optik*) focus; tune <*Motor, Zündung*>; tune to <*Sender*>; **sich e~en** turn up; <*Schwierigkeiten:*> arise; **sich e~en auf** (+ *acc*) adjust to; (*sich vorbereiten*) prepare for. **E~ung** *f* employment; (*Regulierung*) adjustment; (*TV, Auto*) tuning; (*Haltung*) attitude

einstig *a* former

einstimmig *a* unanimous. **E~keit** *f* - unanimity

einstöckig *a* single-storey

einstudieren *vt sep* rehearse

einstufen *vt sep* classify

Ein|sturz *m* collapse. **e~stürzen** *vi sep* (*sein*) collapse

einstweilen *adv* for the time being; (*inzwischen*) meanwhile

eintasten *vt sep* key in

eintauchen *vt/i sep* (*sein*) dip in

eintauschen *vt sep* exchange

eintausend *inv a* one thousand

einteil|en *vt sep* divide (**in** + *acc* into); (*Biol*) classify; **sich** (*dat*) **seine Zeit gut e~en** organize one's time well. **e~ig** *a* one piece. **E~ung** *f* division

eintönig *a* monotonous. **E~keit** *f* - monotony

Eintopf *m*, **E~gericht** *nt* stew

Eintracht *f* - harmony

Eintrag *m* **-[e]s,⸚e** entry. **e~en†** *vt sep* enter; (*Admin*) register; **sich e~en** put one's name down

einträglich *a* profitable

Eintragung *f* **-, -en** registration

eintreffen† *vi sep* (*sein*) arrive; (*fig*) come true

eintreiben† *vt sep* drive in; (*einziehen*) collect

eintreten† *v sep* ● *vi* (*sein*) enter; (*geschehen*) occur; **in einen Klub e~** join a club; **e~ für** (*fig*) stand up for ● *vt* kick in

Eintritt *m* entrance; (*zu Veranstaltung*) admission; (*Beitritt*) joining; (*Beginn*) beginning. **E~skarte** *f* [admission] ticket

einüben *vt sep* practise

einundachtzig *inv a* eighty-one

Einvernehmen *nt* **-s** understanding; (*Übereinstimmung*) agreement

einverstanden *a* **e~ sein** agree

Einverständnis *nt* agreement; (*Zustimmung*) consent

Einwand *m* **-[e]s,⸚e** objection

Einwander|er *m* immigrant. **e~n** *vi sep* (*sein*) immigrate. **E~ung** *f* immigration

einwandfrei *a* perfect

einwärts *adv* inwards

einwechseln *vt sep* change

einwecken *vt sep* preserve, bottle

Einweg- *pref* non-returnable

einweichen *vt sep* soak

E

einweih|en vt sep inaugurate; (Relig) consecrate; (einführen) initiate; **in ein Geheimnis e~en** let into a secret. **E~ung** f -, -en inauguration; consecration; initiation

einweisen† vt sep direct; (einführen) initiate; **ins Krankenhaus e~** send to hospital

einwerfen† vt sep insert; post <Brief>; (Sport) throw in

einwickeln vt sep wrap [up]

einwillig|en vi sep (haben) consent, agree (in + acc to). **E~ung** f - consent

Einwohner|(in) m -s,- (f -, -nen) inhabitant. **E~zahl** f population

Einwurf m interjection; (Einwand) objection; (Sport) throw-in; (Münz-) slot

Einzahl f (Gram) singular

einzahl|en vt sep pay in. **E~ung** f payment; (Einlage) deposit

einzäunen vt sep fence in

Einzel nt -s,- (Tennis) singles pl. **E~bett** nt single bed. **E~gänger** m -s,- loner. **E~haft** f solitary confinement. **E~handel** m retail trade. **E~händler** m retailer. **E~haus** nt detached house. **E~heit** f -, -en detail. **E~karte** f single ticket. **E~kind** nt only child

einzeln a single; (individuell) individual; (gesondert) separate; odd <Handschuh, Socken>; **e~e Fälle** some cases. **E~e(r,s)** pron der/die **E~e** the individual; **E~e** pl some; **im E~en** in detail

Einzel|teil nt [component] part. **E~zimmer** nt single room

einziehen† v sep ● vt pull in; draw in <Atem, Krallen>; (Zool, Techn) retract; indent <Zeile>; (aus dem Verkehr ziehen) withdraw; (beschlagnahmen) confiscate; (eintreiben) collect; make <Erkundigungen>; (Mil) call

up ● vi (sein) enter; (umziehen) move in; (eindringen) penetrate

einzig a only; (einmalig) unique; **eine e~e Frage** a single question ● adv only; **e~ und allein** solely. **E~e(r,s)** pron der/die/das **E~e** the only one; **ein/kein E~er** a/not a single one; **das E~e, was mich stört** the only thing that bothers me

Eis nt -es ice; (Speise-) ice-cream; **Eis am Stiel** ice lolly; **Eis laufen** skate. **E~bahn** f ice rink. **E~bär** m polar bear. **E~becher** m ice-cream sundae. **E~berg** m iceberg. **E~diele** f ice-cream parlour

Eisen nt -s,- iron. **E~bahn** f railway

eisern a iron; (fest) resolute; **e~er Vorhang** (Theat) safety curtain; (Pol) Iron Curtain

Eis|fach nt freezer compartment. **e~gekühlt** a chilled. **e~ig** a icy. **E~kaffee** m iced coffee. **E~lauf** m skating. **E~läufer(in)** m(f) skater. **E~pickel** m ice-axe. **E~scholle** f ice-floe. **E~vogel** m kingfisher. **E~würfel** m icecube. **E~zapfen** m icicle. **E~zeit** f ice age

eitel a vain; (rein) pure. **E~keit** f - vanity

Eiter m -s pus. **e~n** vi (haben) discharge pus

Eiweiß nt -es, -e egg-white

Ekel m -s disgust; (Widerwille) revulsion. **e~haft** a nauseating; (widerlich) repulsive. **e~n** vt/i (haben) **mich** od **mir e~t [es] davor** it makes me feel sick ● vr **sich e~n vor** (+ dat) find repulsive

eklig a disgusting, repulsive

Ekzem nt -s, -e eczema

elastisch a elastic; (federnd) springy; (fig) flexible

Elch m -[e]s, -e elk

Elefant m -en, -en elephant

elegan|t *a* elegant. **E~z** *f* -elegance
Elektri|ker *m* -s,- electrician. **e~sch** *a* electric
Elektrizität *f* - electricity. **E~swerk** *nt* power station
Elektr|oartikel *mpl* electrical appliances. **E~ode** *f* -, -n electrode. **E~onik** *f* - electronics *sg.* **e~onisch** *a* electronic
Elend *nt* -s misery; (*Armut*) poverty. **e~** *a* miserable; (*krank*) poorly; (*gemein*) contemptible. **E~sviertel** *nt* slum
elf *inv a,* **E~** *f* -, -en eleven
Elfe *f* -, -n fairy
Elfenbein *nt* ivory
Elfmeter *m* (*Fußball*) penalty
elfte(r,s) *a* eleventh
Ell[en]bogen *m* elbow
Ellip|se *f* -, -n ellipse. **e~tisch** *a* elliptical
Elsass *nt* - Alsace
elsässisch *a* Alsatian
Elster *f* -, -n magpie
elter|lich *a* parental. **E~n** *pl* parents. **e~nlos** *a* orphaned. **E~nteil** *m* parent
Email /e'maj/ *nt* -s, -s, **E~le** /e'maljə/ *f* -, -n enamel
E-Mail /'iːmeːl/ *f* -, -s e-mail; e-mail message
Emanzi|pation /-'tsjoːn/ *f* -emancipation. **e~piert** *a* emancipated
Embargo *nt* -s, -s embargo
Embryo *m* -s, -s embryo
Emigr|ant(in) *m* -en, -en (*f* -, -nen) emigrant. **E~ation** /-'tsjoːn/ *f* -emigration. **e~ieren** *vi* (*sein*) emigrate
Empfang *m* -[e]s,ˆe reception; (*Erhalt*) receipt; **in E~ nehmen** receive; (*annehmen*) accept. **e~en†** *vt* receive; (*Biol*) conceive
Empfäng|er *m* -s,- recipient; (*Post-*) addressee; (*Zahlungs-*) payee; (*Radio, TV*) receiver. **E~nis** *f* - (*Biol*) conception

Empfängnisverhütung *f* contraception. **E~smittel** *nt* contraceptive
Empfangs|bestätigung *f* receipt. **E~dame** *f* receptionist. **E~halle** *f* [hotel] foyer
empfehl|en† *vt* recommend. **E~ung** *f* -, -en recommendation; (*Gruß*) regards *pl*
empfind|en† *vt* feel. **e~lich** *a* sensitive (**gegen** to); (*zart*) delicate. **E~lichkeit** *f* -sensitivity; delicacy; tenderness; touchiness. **E~ung** *f* -, -en sensation; (*Regung*) feeling
empor *adv* (*liter*) up[wards]
empören *vt* incense; **sich e~** be indignant; (*sich auflehnen*) rebel
Emporkömmling *m* -s, -e upstart
empör|t *a* indignant. **E~ung** *f* -indignation; (*Auflehnung*) rebellion
Ende *nt* -s, -n end; (*eines Films, Romans*) ending; (Ⓘ *Stück*) bit; **zu E~ sein** be finished; **etw zu E~ schreiben** finish writing sth; **am E~** at the end; (*schließlich*) in the end; (Ⓘ *vielleicht*) perhaps; (Ⓘ *erschöpft*) at the end of one's tether
end|en *vi* (*haben*) end. **e~gültig** *a* final; (*bestimmt*) definite
Endivie /-iə/ *f* -, -n endive
end|lich *adv* at last, finally; (*schließlich*) in the end. **e~los** *a* endless. **E~station** *f* terminus. **E~ung** *f* -, -en (*Gram*) ending
Energie *f* - energy
energisch *a* resolute; (*nachdrücklich*) vigorous
eng *a* narrow; (*beengt*) cramped; (*anliegend*) tight; (*nah*) close; **e~ anliegend** tight-fitting
Engagement /ãɡaʒə'mãː/ *nt* -s, -s (*Theat*) engagement; (*fig*) commitment
Engel *m* -s,- angel
England *nt* -s England

Engländer m -s,- Englishman;
(Techn) monkey-wrench; **die E~**
the English pl. **E~in** f -, -nen
Englishwoman
englisch a English. **E~** nt -[s]
(Lang) English; **auf E~** in English
Engpass m (fig) bottle-neck
en gros /ã'gro:/ adv wholesale
Enkel m -s,- grandson; **E~** pl
grandchildren. **E~in** f -, -nen
granddaughter. **E~kind** nt
grandchild. **E~sohn** m grandson.
E~tochter f granddaughter
Ensemble /ã'sã:bəl/ nt -s, -s
ensemble; (Theat) company
entart|en vi (sein) degenerate.
e~et a degenerate
entbehren vt do without;
(vermissen) miss
entbind|en† vt release (von from);
(Med) deliver (von of) ● vi
(haben) give birth. **E~ung** f
delivery. **E~ungsstation** f
maternity ward
entdeck|en vt discover. **E~er** m
-s,- discoverer; (Forscher)
explorer. **E~ung** f -, -en discovery
Ente f -, -n duck
entehren vt dishonour
enteignen vt dispossess;
expropriate <Eigentum>
enterben vt disinherit
Enterich m -s, -e drake
entfallen† vi (sein) not apply; **auf
jdn e~** be s.o.'s share
entfern|en vt remove; **sich e~en**
leave. **e~t** a distant; (schwach)
vague; **2 Kilometer e~t** 2
kilometres away; **e~t verwandt**
distantly related. **E~ung** f -, -en
removal; (Abstand) distance;
(Reichweite) range
entfliehen† vi (sein) escape
entfremden vt alienate
entfrosten vt defrost
entführ|en vt abduct, kidnap;
hijack <Flugzeug>. **E~er** m
abductor, kidnapper; hijacker.

E~ung f abduction,
hijacking
entgegen adv towards ● p[...]
dat) contrary to. **e~gehen†** v[...]
(sein) (+ dat) go to meet; (fig) be
heading for. **e~gesetzt** a
opposite; (gegensätzlich)
opposing. **e~kommen†** vi sep
(sein) (+ dat) come to meet;
(zukommen auf) come towards;
(fig) oblige. **E~kommen** nt -s
helpfulness; (Zugeständnis)
concession. **e~kommend** a
approaching; <Verkehr>
oncoming; (fig) obliging.
e~nehmen† vt sep accept.
e~wirken vi sep (haben) (+ dat)
counteract; (fig) oppose
entgegn|en vt reply (auf + acc to).
E~ung f -, -en reply
entgehen† vi sep (sein) (+ dat)
escape; **jdm e~** (unbemerkt
bleiben) escape s.o.'s notice; **sich**
(dat) etw e~ **lassen** miss sth
Entgelt nt -[e]s payment; **gegen
E~** for money
entgleis|en vi (sein) be derailed;
(fig) make a gaffe. **E~ung** f -, -en
derailment; (fig) gaffe
entgräten vt fillet, bone
Enthaarungsmittel nt depilatory
enthalt|en† vt contain; **in etw** (dat)
e~en sein be contained/
(eingeschlossen) included in sth;
sich der Stimme e~en (Pol)
abstain. **e~sam** a abstemious.
E~ung f (Pol) abstention
enthaupten vt behead
entheben† vt **jdn seines Amtes e~**
relieve s.o. of his post
Enthüllung f -, -en revelation
Enthusias|mus m - enthusiast.
E~t m -en, -en enthusiast
entkernen vt stone; core <Apfel>
entkleiden vt undress; **sich e~en**
undress
entkommen† vi (sein) escape
entkorken vt uncork

...eceding
...ng; **die**
...ad; **an etw**
~fahren† *vi*
...ng. **e~gehen†**
vi se ...long
entlarven ...ask
entlass|en† *vt* ...smiss; (*aus
Krankenhaus*) discharge; (*aus der
Haft*) release. **E~ung** *f* -, -en
dismissal; discharge; release
entlast|en *vt* relieve the strain
on; ease <*Gewissen, Verkehr*>;
relieve (**von** of); (*Jur*) exonerate.
E~ung *f* - relief; exoneration
entlaufen† *vi* (*sein*) run away
entleeren *vt* empty
entlegen *a* remote
entlohnen *vt* pay
entlüft|en *vt* ventilate. **E~er** *m* -s,-
extractor fan. **E~ung** *f*
ventilation
entmündigen *vt* declare
incapable of managing his own
affairs
entmutigen *vt* discourage
entnehmen† *vt* take (*dat* from);
(*schließen*) gather (*dat* from)
entpuppen (sich) *vr* (*fig*) turn out
(**als etw** to be sth)
entrahmt *a* skimmed
entrichten *vt* pay
entrinnen† *vi* (*sein*) escape
entrüst|en *vt* fill with indignation;
sich e~en be indignant (**über** +
acc at). **e~et** *a* indignant. **E~ung**
f - indignation
entsaft|en *vt* extract the juice
from. **E~er** *m* -s,- juice extractor
entsagen *vi* (*haben*) (+ *dat*)
renounce
entschädig|en *vt* compensate.
E~ung *f* -, -en compensation
entschärfen *vt* defuse

entscheid|en† *vt/i* (*haben*)
decide; **sich e~en** decide;
<*Sache:*> be decided. **e~end** *a*
decisive; (*kritisch*) crucial.
E~ung *f* decision
entschließen† (sich) *vr* decide,
make up one's mind; **sich anders
e~** change one's mind
entschlossen *a* determined;
(*energisch*) resolute; **kurz e~**
without hesitation. **E~heit** *f* -
determination
Entschluss *m* decision
entschlüsseln *vt* decode
entschuld|bar *a* excusable.
e~igen *vt* excuse; **sich e~igen**
apologize (**bei** to); **e~igen Sie
[bitte]!** sorry! (*bei Frage*) excuse
me. **E~igung** *f* -, -en apology;
(*Ausrede*) excuse; **um E~igung
bitten** apologize
entsetz|en *vt* horrify. **E~en** *nt* -s
horror. **e~lich** *a* horrible;
(*schrecklich*) terrible
Entsorgung *f* - waste disposal
entspann|en *vt* relax; **sich e~en**
relax; <*Lage:*> ease. **E~ung** *f* -
relaxation; easing; (*Pol*) détente
entsprech|en† *vi* (*haben*) (+ *dat*)
correspond to; (*übereinstimmen*)
agree with. **e~end** *a*
corresponding; (*angemessen*)
appropriate; (*zuständig*) relevant
● *adv* correspondingly;
appropriately; (*demgemäß*)
accordingly ● *prep* (+ *dat*) in
accordance with
entspringen† *vi* (*sein*) <*Fluss:*>
rise; (*fig*) arise, spring (*dat* from)
entstammen *vi* (*sein*) come/
(*abstammen*) be descended (*dat*
from)
entsteh|en† *vi* (*sein*) come into
being; (*sich bilden*) form; (*sich
entwickeln*) develop; <*Brand:*>
start; (*stammen*) originate.
E~ung *f* - origin; formation;
development

entstell|en vt disfigure; (verzerren) distort. **E~ung** f disfigurement; distortion

entstört a (Electr) suppressed

enttäusch|en vt disappoint. **E~ung** f disappointment

entwaffnen vt disarm

entwässer|n vt drain. **E~ung** f - drainage

entweder conj & adv either

entwerfen† vt design; (aufsetzen) draft; (skizzieren) sketch

entwert|en vt devalue; (ungültig machen) cancel. **E~er** m -s,- ticket-cancelling machine. **E~ung** f devaluation; cancelling

entwick|eln vt develop; **sich e~eln** develop. **E~lung** f -, -en development; (Biol) evolution. **E~lungsland** nt developing country

entwöhnen vt wean (gen from); cure <Süchtige>

entwürdigend a degrading

Entwurf m design; (Konzept) draft; (Skizze) sketch

entwurzeln vt uproot

entzie|hen† vt take away (dat from); **jdm den Führerschein e~hen** disqualify s.o. from driving; **sich e~hen** (+ dat) withdraw from. **E~hungskur** f treatment for drug/alcohol addiction

entziffern vt decipher

Entzug m withdrawal; (Vorenthaltung) deprivation

entzünd|en vt ignite; (anstecken) light; (fig: erregen) inflame; **sich e~en** ignite; (Med) become inflamed. **e~et** a (Med) inflamed. **e~lich** a inflammable. **E~ung** f (Med) inflammation

entzwei a broken

Enzian m -s, -e gentian

Enzyklo|pädie f -, -en encyclopaedia. **e~pädisch** a encyclopaedic

Enzym nt -s, -e enzyme

Epidemie f -, -n epidemic

Epi|lepsie f - epilepsy. **E~leptiker(in)** m -s,- (f -, -nen) epileptic. **e~leptisch** a epileptic

Epilog m -s, -e epilogue

Episode f -, -n episode

Epoche f -, -n epoch

Epos nt -/Epen epic

er pron he; (Ding, Tier) it

erachten vt consider (für nötig necessary). **E~** nt -s meines E~s in my opinion

erbarmen (sich) vr have pity/ <Gott:> mercy (gen on). **E~** nt -s pity; mercy

erbärmlich a wretched

erbauen vt build; (fig) edify; **nicht erbaut von** 🖬 not pleased about

Erbe¹ m -n, -n heir

Erbe² nt -s inheritance; (fig) heritage. **e~n** vt inherit

erbeuten vt get; (Mil) capture

Erbfolge f (Jur) succession

erbieten† (sich) vr offer (zu to)

Erbin f -, -nen heiress

erbitten† vt ask for

erbittert a bitter; (heftig) fierce

erblassen vi (sein) turn pale

erblich a hereditary

erblicken vt catch sight of

erblinden vi (sein) go blind

erbrechen† vt vomit ● vi/r [sich] **e~** vomit. **E~** nt -s vomiting

Erbschaft f -, -en inheritance

Erbse f -, -n pea

Erb|stück nt heirloom. **E~teil** nt inheritance

Erd|apfel m (Aust) potato. **E~beben** nt -s,- earthquake. **E~beere** f strawberry

Erde f -, -n earth; (Erdboden) ground; (Fußboden) floor. **e~n** vt (Electr) earth

erdenklich a imaginable

Erd|gas nt natural gas. **E~geschoss** nt ground floor. **E~kugel** f globe. **E~kunde** f geography. **E~nuss** f peanut. **E~öl** nt [mineral] oil

erdrosseln vt strangle
erdrücken vt crush to death
Erd|rutsch m landslide. **E~teil** m continent
erdulden vt endure
ereignen (sich) vr happen
Ereignis nt -ses, -se event. **e~los** a uneventful. **e~reich** a eventful
Eremit m -en, -en hermit
erfahr|en† vt learn, hear; (erleben) experience ● a experienced. **E~ung** f -, -en experience; **in E~ung bringen** find out
erfassen vt seize; (begreifen) grasp; (einbeziehen) include; (aufzeichnen) record
erfind|en† vt invent. **E~er** m -s,- inventor. **e~erisch** a inventive. **E~ung** f -, -en invention
Erfolg m -[e]s, -e success; (Folge) result; **E~ haben** be successful. **e~en** vi (sein) take place; (geschehen) happen. **e~los** a unsuccessful. **e~reich** a successful
erforder|lich a required, necessary. **e~n** vt require, demand
erforsch|en vt explore; (untersuchen) investigate. **E~ung** f exploration; investigation
erfreu|en vt please. **e~lich** a pleasing. **e~licherweise** adv happily. **e~t** a pleased
erfrier|en† vi (sein) freeze to death; <Glied:> become frostbitten; <Pflanze:> be killed by the frost. **E~ung** f -, -en frostbite
erfrisch|en vt refresh. **E~ung** f -, -en refreshment
erfüll|en vt fill; (nachkommen) fulfil; serve <Zweck>; discharge <Pflicht:> **sich e~en** come true. **E~ung** f fulfilment
erfunden a invented
ergänz|en vt complement; (hinzufügen) add. **E~ung** f complement; supplement; (Zusatz) addition

ergeben† vt produce; (zeigen) show, establish; **sich e~en** result; <Schwierigkeit:> arise; (kapitulieren) surrender; (sich fügen) submit ● a devoted; (resigniert) resigned
Ergebnis nt -ses, -se result. **e~los** a fruitless
ergiebig a productive; (fig) rich
ergreifen† vt seize; take <Maßnahme, Gelegenheit>; take up <Beruf>; (rühren) move; **die Flucht e~** flee. **e~d** a moving
ergriffen a deeply moved. **E~heit** f - emotion
ergründen vt (fig) get to the bottom of
erhaben a raised; (fig) sublime
Erhalt m -[e]s receipt. **e~en†** vt receive, get; (gewinnen) obtain; (bewahren) preserve, keep; (instand halten) maintain; (unterhalten) support; **am Leben e~en** keep alive ● a **gut/schlecht e~en** in good/bad condition; **e~en bleiben** survive
erhältlich a obtainable
Erhaltung f - preservation; maintenance
erhängen (sich) vr hang oneself
erheb|en† vt raise; levy <Steuer>; charge <Gebühr>; **Anspruch e~en** lay claim (**auf** + acc to); **Protest e~en** protest; **sich e~en** rise; <Frage:> arise. **e~lich** a considerable. **E~ung** f -, -en elevation; (Anhöhe) rise; (Aufstand) uprising; (Ermittlung) survey
erheiter|n vt amuse. **E~ung** f - amusement
erhitzen vt heat
erhöh|en vt raise; (fig) increase; **sich e~en** rise, increase. **E~ung** f -, -en increase
erhol|en (sich) vr recover (**von** from); (nach Krankheit)

convalesce; (*sich ausruhen*) have
a rest. **e~sam** *a* restful. **E~ung** *f*
- recovery; (*Ruhe*) rest

erinner|n *vt* remind (**an** + *acc* of);
sich e~n remember (**an jdn/etw**
s.o./sth). **E~ung** *f* -, -en memory;
(*Andenken*) souvenir

erkält|en (sich) *vr* catch a cold;
e~et sein have a cold. **E~ung** *f* -,
-en cold

erkenn|bar *a* recognizable;
(*sichtbar*) visible. **e~en†** *vt*
recognize; (*wahrnehmen*)
distinguish. **E~tnis** *f* -, -se
recognition; realization; (*Wissen*)
knowledge; **die neuesten E~tnisse**
the latest findings

Erker *m* -s,- bay

erklär|en *vt* declare; (*erläutern*)
explain; **sich bereit e~en** agree
(**zu** to). **e~end** *a* explanatory.
e~lich *a* explicable;
(*verständlich*) understandable.
e~licherweise *adv*
understandably. **E~ung** *f* -, -en
declaration; explanation;
öffentliche E~ung public
statement

erkrank|en *vi* (*sein*) fall ill; be
taken ill (**an** + *dat* with). **E~ung** *f*
-, -en illness

erkundig|en (sich) *vr* enquire
(**nach jdm/etw** after s.o./about
sth). **E~ung** *f* -, -en enquiry

erlangen *vt* attain, get

Erlass *m* -es,⸚e (*Admin*) decree;
(*Befreiung*) exemption; (*Straf-*)
remission

erlassen† *vt* (*Admin*) issue; **jdm
etw e~** exempt s.o. from sth; let
s.o. off <*Strafe*>

erlauben *vt* allow, permit; **ich
kann es mir nicht e~** I can't afford
it

Erlaubnis *f* - permission.
E~schein *m* permit

erläutern *vt* explain

Erle *f* -, -n alder

erleb|en *vt* experience; (*mit-*) see;
have <*Überraschung*>. **E~nis** *nt*
-ses, -se experience

erledigen *vt* do; (*sich befassen
mit*) deal with; (*beenden*) finish;
(*entscheiden*) settle; (*töten*) kill

erleichter|n *vt* lighten;
(*vereinfachen*) make easier;
(*befreien*) relieve; (*lindern*) ease.
e~t *a* relieved. **E~ung** *f* - relief

erleiden† *vt* suffer

erleuchten *vt* illuminate; **hell
erleuchtet** brightly lit

erlogen *a* untrue, false

Erlös *m* -es proceeds *pl*

erlöschen† *vi* (*sein*) go out;
(*vergehen*) die; (*aussterben*) die
out; (*ungültig werden*) expire;
erloschener Vulkan extinct volcano

erlös|en *vt* save; (*befreien*)
release (**von** from); (*Relig*)
redeem. **e~t** *a* relieved. **E~ung** *f*
release; (*Erleichterung*) relief;
(*Relig*) redemption

ermächtig|en *vt* authorize.
E~ung *f* -, -en authorization

Ermahnung *f* exhortation;
admonition

ermäßig|en *vt* reduce. **E~ung** *f* -,
-en reduction

ermessen† *vt* judge; (*begreifen*)
appreciate. **E~** *nt* -s discretion;
(*Urteil*) judgement; **nach eigenem
E~** at one's own discretion

ermitt|eln *vt* establish;
(*herausfinden*) find out ● *vi*
(*haben*) investigate (**gegen jdn**
s.o.). **E~lungen** *fpl*
investigations. **E~lungsverfahren**
nt (*Jur*) preliminary inquiry

ermöglichen *vt* make possible

ermord|en *vt* murder. **E~ung** *f* -,
-en murder

ermüd|en *vt* tire ● *vi* (*sein*) get
tired. **E~ung** *f* - tiredness

ermutigen *vt* encourage. **e~d** *a*
encouraging

ernähr|en *vt* feed; (*unterhalten*)
support, keep; **sich e~en von**

live/<*Tier*:> feed on. **E~er** *m* **-s,-**
breadwinner. **E~ung** *f* -
nourishment; nutrition; (*Kost*)
diet

ernenn|en† *vt* appoint. **E~ung** *f* **-,**
-en appointment

erneu|ern *vt* renew;
(*auswechseln*) replace; change
<*Verband*>; (*renovieren*)
renovate. **E~erung** *f* renewal;
replacement; renovation. **e~t** *a*
renewed; (*neu*) new ● *adv* again

ernst *a* serious; **e~ nehmen** take
seriously. **E~** *m* **-es** seriousness;
im E~ seriously; **mit einer Drohung**
E~ machen carry out a threat; **ist**
das dein E~? are you serious?
e~haft *a* serious. **e~lich** *a*
serious

Ernte *f* **-, -n** harvest; (*Ertrag*) crop.
E~dankfest *nt* harvest festival.
e~n *vt* harvest; (*fig*) reap, win

ernüchter|n *vt* sober up; (*fig*)
bring down to earth. **e~nd** *a* (*fig*)
sobering

Erober|er *m* **-s,-** conqueror. **e~n**
vt conquer. **E~ung** *f* **-, -en**
conquest

eröffn|en *vt* open; **jdm etw e~en**
announce sth to s.o. **E~ung** *f*
opening; (*Mitteilung*)
announcement

erörter|n *vt* discuss. **E~ung** *f* **-,**
-en discussion

Erot|ik *f* **-** eroticism. **e~isch** *a*
erotic

Erpel *m* **-s,-** drake

erpicht *a* **e~auf** (+ *acc*) keen on

erpress|en *vt* extort; blackmail
<*Person*>. **E~er** *m* **-s,-**
blackmailer. **E~ung** *f* **-** extortion;
blackmail

erprob|en *vt* test. **e~t** *a* proven

erraten† *vt* guess

erreg|bar *a* excitable. **e~en** *vt*
excite; (*hervorrufen*) arouse; **sich**
e~en get worked up. **e~end** *a*
exciting. **E~er** *m* **-s,-** (*Med*) germ.

e~t *a* agitated; (*hitzig*) heated.
E~ung *f* **-** excitement

erreich|bar *a* within reach; <*Ziel*>
attainable; <*Person*> available.
e~en *vt* reach; catch <*Zug*>; live
to <*Alter*>; (*durchsetzen*) achieve

errichten *vt* erect

erringen† *vt* gain, win

erröten *vi* (*sein*) blush

Errungenschaft *f* **-, -en**
achievement; (🎚 *Anschaffung*)
acquisition

Ersatz *m* **-es** replacement,
substitute; (*Entschädigung*)
compensation. **E~reifen** *m* spare
tyre. **E~teil** *nt* spare part

erschaffen† *vt* create

erschein|en† *vi* (*sein*) appear;
<*Buch*:> be published. **E~ung** *f* **-,**
-en appearance; (*Person*) figure;
(*Phänomen*) phenomenon;
(*Symptom*) symptom; (*Geist*)
apparition

erschieß|en† *vt* shoot [dead].
E~ungskommando *nt* firing
squad

erschlaffen *vi* (*sein*) go limp

erschlagen† *vt* beat to death;
(*tödlich treffen*) strike dead; **vom**
Blitz e~ werden be killed by
lightning

erschließen† *vt* develop

erschöpf|en *vt* exhaust. **e~t** *a*
exhausted. **E~ung** *f* **-** exhaustion

erschrecken† *vi* (*sein*) get a
fright ● *vt* (*reg*) startle;
(*beunruhigen*) alarm; **du hast mich**
erschreckt you gave me a fright

erschrocken *a* frightened;
(*erschreckt*) startled

erschütter|n *vt* shake; (*ergreifen*)
upset deeply. **E~ung** *f* **-, -en**
shock

erschwinglich *a* affordable

ersehen† *vt* (*fig*) see (**aus** from)

ersetzen *vt* replace; make good
<*Schaden*>; refund <*Kosten*>; **jdm**
etw e~ compensate s.o. for sth

ersichtlich *a* obvious, apparent

erspar|en vt save. **E~nis** f -, -se saving; **E~nisse** savings

erst adv (zuerst) first; (noch nicht mehr als) only; (nicht vor) not until; **e~ dann** only then; **eben e~** [only] just

erstarren vi (sein) solidify; (gefrieren) freeze; (steif werden) go stiff; (vor Schreck) be paralysed

erstatten vt (zurück-) refund; **Bericht e~** report (jdm to s.o.)

Erstaufführung f first performance, première

erstaun|en vt amaze, astonish. **E~en** nt amazement, astonishment. **e~lich** a amazing

Erst|ausgabe f first edition. **e~e(r,s)** a first; (beste) best; **e~e Hilfe** first aid. **E~e(r)** m/f first; (Beste) best; **fürs E~e** for the time being; **als E~es** first of all; **er kam als E~er** he arrived first

erstechen† vt stab to death

ersteigern vt buy at an auction

erstens adv firstly, in the first place. **e~ere(r,s)** a the former; **der/die/das E~ere** the former

ersticken vt suffocate; smother <Flammen> ● vi (sein) suffocate. **E~** nt -s suffocation; **zum E~** stifling

erstklassig a first-class

ersuchen vt ask, request. **E~** nt -s request

ertappen vt Ⓘ catch

erteilen vt give (jdm s.o.)

ertönen vi (sein) sound; (erschallen) ring out

Ertrag m -[e]s,⸚e yield. **e~en†** vt bear

erträglich a bearable; (leidlich) tolerable

ertränken vt drown

ertrinken† vi (sein) drown

erübrigen (sich) vr be unnecessary

erwachsen a grown-up. **E~e(r)** m/f adult, grown-up

erwäg|en† vt consider. **E~ung** f -, -en consideration; **in E~ung ziehen** consider

erwähn|en vt mention. **E~ung** f -, -en mention

erwärmen vt warm; **sich e~** warm up; (fig) warm (für to)

erwart|en vt expect; (warten auf) wait for. **E~ung** f -, -en expectation

erweisen† vt prove; (bezeigen) do <Gefallen, Dienst, Ehre>; **sich e~ als** prove to be

erweitern vt widen; dilate <Pupille>; (fig) extend, expand

Erwerb m -[e]s acquisition; (Kauf) purchase; (Brot-) livelihood; (Verdienst) earnings pl. **e~en†** vt acquire; (kaufen) purchase. **e~slos** a unemployed. **e~stätig** a employed

erwider|n vt reply; return <Besuch, Gruß>. **E~ung** f -, -en reply

erwirken vt obtain

erwürgen vt strangle

Erz nt -es, -e ore

erzähl|en vt tell (jdm s.o.) ● vi (haben) talk (von about). **E~er** m -s,- narrator. **E~ung** f -, -en story, tale

Erzbischof m archbishop

erzeug|en vt produce; (Electr) generate. **E~er** m -s,- producer. **E~nis** nt -ses, -se product; **landwirtschaftliche E~nisse** farm produce sg.

erzieh|en† vt bring up; (Sch) educate. **E~er** m -s,- [private] tutor. **E~erin** f -, -nen governess. **E~ung** f - upbringing; education

erzielen vt achieve; score <Tor>

erzogen a **gut/schlecht e~** well/badly brought up

es
● pronoun
····▶ (Sache) it; (weibliche Person) she/her; (männliche Person)

he/him. **ich bin es** it's me. **wir sind traurig, ihr seid es auch** we are sad, and so are you. **er ist es, der ...** he is the one who .... **es sind Studenten** they are students
····▶ (*impers*) it. **es hat geklopft** there was a knock. **es klingelt** someone is ringing. **es wird schöner** the weather is improving. **es geht ihm gut/ schlecht** he is well/unwell. **es lässt sich aushalten** it is bearable. **es gibt** there is *or* (*pl*)
····▶ (*als formales Objekt*) **er hat es gut** he has it made; he's well off. **er meinte es gut** he meant well. **ich hoffe/glaube es** I hope/think so

Esche f -, -n ash
Esel m -s,- donkey; (🡒 *Person*) ass
Eskimo m -[s], -[s] Eskimo
Eskort|e f -, -n (*Mil*) escort. **e~ieren** vt escort
essbar a edible
essen† vt/i (*haben*) eat; **zu Mittag Abend e~** have lunch/supper; **e~ gehen** eat out. **E~** nt -s,- food; (*Mahl*) meal; (*festlich*) dinner
Esser(in) m -s,- (f -, -nen) eater
Essig m -s vinegar. **E~gurke** f [pickled] gherkin
Esslöffel m ≈ dessertspoon. **Essstäbchen** ntpl chopsticks. **Esstisch** m dining-table. **Esswaren** fpl food sg; (*Vorräte*) provisions. **Esszimmer** nt dining-room
Estland nt -s Estonia
Estragon m -s tarragon
etablieren (sich) vr establish oneself/<Geschäft:> itself
Etage /e'ta:ʒə/ f -, -n storey. **E~nbett** nt bunk-beds pl. **E~nwohnung** f flat
Etappe f -, -n stage
Etat /e'ta:/ m -s, -s budget

Eth|ik f - ethic; (*Sittenlehre*) ethics sg. **e~isch** a ethical
ethnisch a ethnic; **e~e Säuberung** ethnic cleansing
Etikett nt -[e]s, -e[n] label; (*Preis-*) tag. **e~ieren** vt label
Etui /e'tvi:/ nt -s, -s case
etwa adv (*ungefähr*) about; (*zum Beispiel*) for instance; (*womöglich*) perhaps; **nicht e~, dass ...** not that ...; **denkt nicht e~ ...** don't imagine ...
etwas pron something; (*fragend/ verneint*) anything; (*ein bisschen*) some, a little; **sonst noch e~?** anything else? **so e~ Ärgerliches!** what a nuisance! ● adv a bit
Etymologie f - etymology
euch pron (*acc* of **ihr** pl) you; (*dat*) [to] you; (*refl*) yourselves; (*einander*) each other
euer poss pron pl your. **e~e, e~t- s.** **eure, euret-**
Eule f -, -n owl
Euphorie f - euphoria
eur|e poss pron pl your. **e~e(r,s)** poss pron yours. **e~etwegen** adv for your sake; (*wegen euch*) because of you, on your account. **e~etwillen** adv um **e~etwillen** for your sake. **e~ige** poss pron **der/ die/das e~ige** yours
Euro m -[s], -[s] euro. **E~-** pref Euro-
Europa nt -s Europe. **E~-** pref European
Europä|er(in) m -s,- (f -, -nen) European. **e~isch** a European
Euter nt -s,- udder
evakuier|en vt evacuate. **E~ung** f - evacuation
evan|gelisch a Protestant. **E~gelium** nt -s, -ien gospel
eventuell a possible ● adv possibly; (*vielleicht*) perhaps
Evolution /-'tsio:n/ f - evolution
ewig a eternal; (*endlos*) never-ending; **e~ dauern** 🡒 take ages. **E~keit** f - eternity

Examen *nt* -s,- & -mina (*Sch*) examination

Exemplar *nt* -s, -e specimen; (*Buch*) copy. **e~isch** *a* exemplary

exerzieren *vt/i* (*haben*) (*Mil*) drill; (*üben*) practise

exhumieren *vt* exhume

Exil *nt* -s exile

Existenz *f* -, -en existence; (*Lebensgrundlage*) livelihood

existieren *vi* (*haben*) exist

exklusiv *a* exclusive. **e~e** *prep* (+ *gen*) excluding

exkommunizieren *vt* excommunicate

Exkremente *npl* excrement *sg*

Expedition /-'tsio:n/ *f* -, -en expedition

Experiment *nt* -[e]s, -e experiment. **e~ieren** *vi* (*haben*) experiment

Experte *m* -n, -n expert

explo|dieren *vi* (*sein*) explode. **E~sion** *f* -, -en explosion

Expor|t *m* -[e]s, -e export. **E~teur** /-'tø:ɐ/ *m* -s, -e exporter. **e~tieren** *vt* export

extra *adv* separately; (*zusätzlich*) extra; (*eigens*) specially; (🛈 *absichtlich*) on purpose

extravagan|t *a* flamboyant; (*übertrieben*) extravagant

extravertiert *a* extrovert

extrem *a* extreme. **E~ist** *m* -en, -en extremist

Exzellenz *f* - (*title*) Excellency

Exzentr|iker *m* -s,- eccentric. **e~isch** *a* eccentric

Fabel *f* -, -n fable. **f~haft** *a* 🛈 fantastic

Fabrik *f* -, -en factory. **F~ant** *m* -en, -en manufacturer. **F~at** *nt* -[e]s, -e product; (*Marke*) make. **F~ation** /-'tsio:n/ *f* - manufacture

Fach *nt* -[e]s,-̈er compartment; (*Schub-*) drawer; (*Gebiet*) field; (*Sch*) subject. **F~arbeiter** *m* skilled worker. **F~arzt** *m*, **F~ärztin** *f* specialist. **F~ausdruck** *m* technical term

Fächer *m* -s,- fan

Fach|gebiet *nt* field. **f~kundig** *a* expert. **f~lich** *a* technical; (*beruflich*) professional. **F~mann** *m* (*pl* -leute) expert. **f~männisch** *a* expert. **F~schule** *f* technical college. **F~werkhaus** *nt* half-timbered house. **F~wort** *nt* (*pl* -wörter) technical term

Fackel *f* -, -n torch

fade *a* insipid; (*langweilig*) dull

Faden *m* -s,-̈ thread; (*Bohnen-*) string; (*Naut*) fathom

Fagott *nt* -[e]s, -e bassoon

fähig *a* capable (*zu/gen* of); (*tüchtig*) able, competent. **F~keit** *f* -, -en ability; competence

fahl *a* pale

fahnd|en *vi* (*haben*) search (**nach** for). **F~ung** *f* -, -en search

Fahne *f* -, -n flag; (*Druck-*) galley [proof]; **eine F~ haben** 🛈 reek of alcohol. **F~nflucht** *f* desertion

Fahr|ausweis *m* ticket. **F~bahn** *f* carriageway; (*Straße*) road. **f~bar** *a* mobile

Fähre *f* -, -n ferry

fahr|en† *vi* (*sein*) go, travel; <*Fahrer:*> drive; <*Radfahrer:*> ride; (*verkehren*) run, (*ab-*) leave;

<Schiff:> sail; **mit dem Auto/Zug f~en** go by car/train; **was ist in ihn gefahren?** I what has got into him? ● *vt* drive; ride *<Fahrrad>*; take *<Kurve>*. **f~end** *a* moving; *(f~bar)* mobile; *(nicht sesshaft)* travelling. **F~er** *m* **-s,-** driver. **F~erflucht** *f* failure to stop after an accident. **F~erhaus** *nt* driver's cab. **F~erin** *f* **-, -nen** woman driver. **F~gast** *m* passenger. **F~geld** *nt* fare. **F~gestell** *nt* chassis; *(Aviat)* undercarriage. **F~karte** *f* ticket. **F~kartenschalter** *m* ticket office. **f~lässig** *a* negligent. **F~lässigkeit** *f* - negligence. **F~lehrer** *m* driving instructor. **F~plan** *m* timetable. **f~planmäßig** *a* scheduled ● *adv* according to/*(pünktlich)* on schedule. **F~preis** *m* fare. **F~prüfung** *f* driving test. **F~rad** *nt* bicycle. **F~schein** *m* ticket. **F~schule** *f* driving school. **F~schüler(in)** *m(f)* learner driver. **F~stuhl** *m* lift

Fahrt *f* **-, -en** journey; *(Auto)* drive; *(Ausflug)* trip; *(Tempo)* speed

Fährte *f* **-, -n** track; *(Witterung)* scent

Fahr|tkosten *pl* travelling expenses. **F~werk** *nt* undercarriage. **F~zeug** *nt* **-[e]s, -e** vehicle; *(Wasser-)* craft, vessel

fair /fɛːɐ/ *a* fair

Fakultät *f* **-, -en** faculty

Falke *m* **-n, -n** falcon

Fall *m* **-[e]s,¨e** fall; *(Jur, Med, Gram)* case; **im F~[e]** in case *(gen* of); **auf jeden F~** in any case; *(bestimmt)* definitely; **für alle F~¨e** just in case; **auf keinen F~** on no account

Falle *f* **-, -n** trap

fallen† *vi* *(sein)* fall; *(sinken)* go down; **[im Krieg] f~** be killed in

the war; **f~ lassen** drop *<etw, fig: Plan, jdn>*; make *<Bemerkung>*

fällen *vt* fell; *(fig)* pass *<Urteil>*

fällig *a* due; *<Wechsel>* mature; **längst f~** long overdue. **F~keit** *f* - *(Comm)* maturity

falls *conj* in case; *(wenn)* if

Fallschirm *m* parachute. **F~jäger** *m* paratrooper. **F~springer** *m* parachutist

Falltür *f* trapdoor

falsch *a* wrong; *(nicht echt, unaufrichtig)* false; *(gefälscht)* forged; *<Geld>* counterfeit; *<Schmuck>* fake ● *adv* wrongly; falsely; *<singen>* out of tune; **f~ gehen** *<Uhr:>* be wrong

fälschen *vt* forge, fake

Falschgeld *nt* counterfeit money

fälschlich *a* wrong; *(irrtümlich)* mistaken

Falsch|meldung *f* false report; *(absichtlich)* hoax report. **F~münzer** *m* **-s,-** counterfeiter

Fälschung *f* **-, -en** forgery, fake

Falte *f* **-, -n** fold; *(Rock-)* pleat; *(Knitter-)* crease; *(im Gesicht)* line; wrinkle

falten *vt* fold

Falter *m* **-s,-** butterfly; moth

faltig *a* creased; *<Gesicht>* lined; wrinkled

familiär *a* family …; *(vertraut, zudringlich)* familiar; *(zwanglos)* informal

Familie /-iə/ *f* **-, -n** family. **F~nforschung** *f* genealogy. **F~nname** *m* surname. **F~nplanung** *f* family planning. **F~nstand** *m* marital status

Fan /fɛn/ *m* **-s, -s** fan

Fana|tiker *m* **-s,-** fanatic. **f~tisch** *a* fanatical

Fanfare *f* **-, -n** trumpet; *(Signal)* fanfare

Fang *m* **-[e]s,¨e** capture; *(Beute)* catch; **F~¨e** *(Krallen)* talons; *(Zähne)* fangs. **F~arm** *m* tentacle. **f~en†** *vt* catch; *(ein-)* capture;

gefangen nehmen take prisoner.
F~en *nt* **-s F~en spielen** play tag.
F~frage *f* catch question
Fantasie *f* -, -n = **Phantasie**
Farb|aufnahme *f* colour
photograph. **F~band** *nt* (*pl*
-bänder) typewriter ribbon. **F~e** *f*
-, -n colour; (*Maler-*) paint; (*zum*
Färben) dye; (*Karten*) suit.
f~echt *a* colour-fast
färben *vt* colour; dye <*Textilien,*
Haare> ● *vi* (*haben*) not be
colour-fast
farb|enblind *a* colour-blind.
f~enfroh *a* colourful. **F~film** *m*
colour film. **f~ig** *a* coloured
● *adv* in colour. **F~ige(r)** *m/f*
coloured man/woman. **F~kasten**
m box of paints. **f~los** *a*
colourless. **F~stift** *m* crayon.
F~stoff *m* dye; (*Lebensmittel-*)
colouring. **F~ton** *m* shade
Färbung *f* -, -en colouring
Farn *m* -[e]s, -e fern
Färse *f* -, -n heifer
Fasan *m* -[e]s, -e[n] pheasant
Faschierte(s) *nt* (*Aust*) mince
Fasching *m* -s (*SGer*) carnival
Faschis|mus *m* - fascism. **F~t** *m*
-en, -en fascist. **f~tisch** *a* fascist
Faser *f* -, -n fibre
Fass *nt* -es, ̈er barrel, cask; **Bier**
vom F~ draught beer
Fassade *f* -, -n façade
fassbar *a* comprehensible;
(*greifbar*) tangible
fassen *vt* take [hold of], grasp;
(*ergreifen*) seize; (*fangen*) catch;
(*ein-*) set; (*enthalten*) hold; (*fig:*
begreifen) take in, grasp;
conceive <*Plan*>; make
<*Entschluss*>; **sich f~** compose
oneself; **sich kurz f~** be brief;
nicht zu f~ (*fig*) unbelievable ● *vi*
(*haben*) **f~ an** (+ *acc*) touch
Fassung *f* -, -en mount;
(*Edelstein-*) setting; (*Electr*)
socket; (*Version*) version;
(*Beherrschung*) composure; **aus**

der F~ bringen disconcert. **f~slos**
a shaken; (*erstaunt*)
flabbergasted. **F~svermögen** *nt*
capacity
fast *adv* almost, nearly; **f~ nie**
hardly ever
fast|en *vi* (*haben*) fast. **F~enzeit** *f*
Lent. **F~nacht** *f* Shrovetide;
(*Karneval*) carnival.
F~nachtsdienstag *m* Shrove
Tuesday
fatal *a* fatal; (*peinlich*)
embarrassing
Fata Morgana *f* - -/- -nen mirage
fauchen *vi* (*haben*) spit, hiss ● *vt*
snarl
faul *a* lazy; (*verdorben*) rotten,
bad; <*Ausrede*> lame
faul|en *vi* (*sein*) rot; <*Zahn:*>
decay; (*verwesen*) putrefy.
f~enzen *vi* (*haben*) be lazy.
F~enzer *m* -s,- lazy-bones *sg*.
F~heit *f* - laziness
Fäulnis *f* - decay
Fauna *f* - fauna
Faust *f* -,Fäuste fist; **auf eigene F~**
(*fig*) off one's own bat.
F~handschuh *m* mitten.
F~schlag *m* punch
Fauxpas /fo'pa/ *m* -,- /-[s], -s/
gaffe
Favorit(in) /favo'ri:t(ɪn)/ *m* -en, -en
(*f* -, -nen) (*Sport*) favourite
Fax *nt* -, -[e] fax. **f~en** *vt* fax
Faxen *fpl* Ⓘ antics; **F~ machen**
fool about
Faxgerät *nt* fax machine
Februar *m* -s, -e February
fecht|en† *vi* (*haben*) fence. **F~er**
m -s,- fencer
Feder *f* -, -n feather; (*Schreib-*)
pen; (*Spitze*) nib; (*Techn*) spring.
F~ball *m* shuttlecock; (*Spiel*)
badminton. **F~busch** *m* plume.
f~leicht *a* as light as a feather.
f~n *vi* (*haben*) be springy;
(*nachgeben*) give; (*hoch-*) bounce.
f~nd *a* springy; (*elastisch*)

F

elastic. F~ung f - (Techn) springs
pl; (Auto) suspension
Fee f -, -n fairy
Fegefeuer nt purgatory
fegen vt sweep
Fehde f -, -n feud
fehl a f~ am Platze out of place.
F~betrag m deficit. f~en vi
(haben) be missing/(Sch) absent;
(mangeln) be lacking; mir f~t die
Zeit I haven't got the time; was
f~t ihm? what's the matter with
him? das hat uns noch gefehlt!
that's all we need! f~end a
missing; (Sch) absent
Fehler m -s,- mistake, error;
(Sport & fig) fault; (Makel) flaw.
f~frei a faultless. f~haft a faulty.
f~los a flawless
Fehl|geburt f miscarriage. F~griff
m mistake. F~kalkulation f
miscalculation. F~schlag m
failure. f~schlagen† vi sep (sein)
fail. F~start m (Sport) false start.
F~zündung f (Auto) misfire
Feier f -, -n celebration;
(Zeremonie) ceremony; (Party)
party. F~abend m end of the
working day; F~abend machen
stop work. f~lich a solemn;
(förmlich) formal. f~n vt
celebrate; hold <Fest> ● vi
(haben) celebrate. F~tag m
[public] holiday; (kirchlicher)
feast-day; erster/zweiter F~tag
Christmas Day / Boxing Day.
f~tags adv on public holidays
feige a cowardly; f~ sein be a
coward ● adv in a cowardly way
Feige f -, -n fig
Feig|heit f - cowardice. F~ling m
-s, -e coward
Feile f -, -n file. f~n vt/i (haben)
file
feilschen vi (haben) haggle
fein a fine; (zart) delicate;
<Strümpfe> sheer; <Unterschied>
subtle; (scharf) keen; (vornehm)
refined; (prima) great; sich f~

machen dress up. F~arbeit f
precision work
Feind(in) m -es, -e (f -, -nen)
enemy. f~lich a enemy; (f~selig)
hostile. F~schaft f -, -en enmity
fein|fühlig a sensitive. F~gefühl
nt sensitivity; (Takt) delicacy.
F~heit f -, -en fineness; delicacy;
subtlety; refinement; F~heiten
subtleties. F~kostgeschäft nt
delicatessen [shop]
feist a fat
Feld nt -[e]s, -er field; (Fläche)
ground; (Sport) pitch; (Schach-)
square; (auf Formular) box.
F~bett nt camp-bed.
F~forschung f fieldwork. F~herr
m commander. F~stecher m -s,-
field-glasses pl. F~webel m -s,-
(Mil) sergeant. F~zug m
campaign
Felge f -, -n [wheel] rim
Fell nt -[e]s, -e (Zool) coat; (Pelz)
fur; (abgezogen) skin, pelt
Fels m -en, -en rock. F~block m
boulder. F~en m -s,- rock
Femininum nt -s, -na (Gram)
feminine
Feminist|(in) m -en, -en (f -, -nen)
feminist. f~isch a feminist
Fenchel m -s fennel
Fenster nt -s,- window. F~brett nt
window-sill. F~scheibe f
[window-]pane
Ferien /'fe:riən/ pl holidays;
(Univ) vacation sg; F~ haben be
on holiday. F~ort m holiday
resort
Ferkel nt -s,- piglet
fern a distant; der F~e Osten the
Far East; sich f~ halten keep
away ● adv far away; von f~
from a distance ● prep (+ dat) far
[away] from. F~bedienung f
remote control. F~e f - distance;
in weiter F~e far away; (zeitlich)
in the distant future. f~er a
further ● adv (außerdem)
furthermore; (in Zukunft) in

future. **f~gelenkt** *a* remote-controlled; <*Rakete*> guided. **F~gespräch** *nt* long-distance call. **F~glas** *nt* binoculars *pl*. **F~kurs[us]** *m* correspondence course. **F~licht** *nt* (*Auto*) full beam. **F~meldewesen** *nt* telecommunications *pl*. **F~rohr** *nt* telescope. **F~schreiben** *nt* telex

Fernseh|apparat *m* television set. **f~en**† *vi sep* (*haben*) watch television. **F~en** *nt* **-s** television. **F~er** *m* **-s,-** [television] viewer; (*Gerät*) television set
Fernsprech|amt *nt* telephone exchange. **F~er** *m* telephone
Fernsteuerung *f* remote control
Ferse *f* **-, -n** heel
fertig *a* finished; (*bereit*) ready; (*Comm*) ready-made; <*Gericht*> ready-to-serve; **f~ werden mit** finish; (*bewältigen*) cope with; **f~ sein** have finished; (*fig*) be through (**mit jdm** with s.o.); (⚠ *erschöpft*) be all in/(*seelisch*) shattered; **etw f~ bringen** manage to do sth; (*beenden*) finish sth; **etw/jdn f~ machen** finish sth; (*bereitmachen*) get sth/s.o. ready; (⚠ *erschöpfen*) wear s.o. out; (*seelisch*) shatter s.o.; **sich f~ machen** get ready; **etw f~ stellen** complete ● *adv* **f~ essen/lesen** finish eating/reading. **F~bau** *m* (*pl* **-bauten**) prefabricated building. **f~en** *vt* make. **F~gericht** *nt* ready-to-serve meal. **F~haus** *nt* prefabricated house. **F~keit** *f* **-, -en** skill. **F~stellung** *f* completion. **F~ung** *f* **-** manufacture
fesch *a* ⚠ attractive
Fessel *f* **-, -n** ankle
fesseln *vt* tie up; tie (**an** + *acc* to); (*fig*) fascinate
fest *a* firm; (*nicht flüssig*) solid; (*erstarrt*) set; (*haltbar*) strong;

(*nicht locker*) tight; (*feststehend*) fixed; (*ständig*) steady; <*Anstellung*> permanent; <*Schlaf*> sound; <*Blick, Stimme*> steady; **f~ werden** harden; <*Gelee:*> set; **f~e Nahrung** solids *pl* ● *adv* firmly; tightly; steadily; soundly; (*kräftig, tüchtig*) hard; **f~ schlafen** be fast asleep; **f~ angestellt** permanent
Fest *nt* **-[e]s, -e** celebration; (*Party*) party; (*Relig*) festival; **frohes F~!** happy Christmas!
fest|binden† *vt sep* tie (**an** + *dat* to). **f~bleiben**† *vi sep* (*sein*) (*fig*) remain firm. **f~halten**† *v sep* ● *vt* hold on to; (*aufzeichnen*) record; **sich f~halten** hold on ● *vi* (*haben*) **f~halten an** (+ *dat*) (*fig*) stick to; cling to <*Tradition*>. **f~igen** *vt* strengthen. **F~iger** *m* **-s,-** styling lotion/(*Schaum-*) mousse. **F~igkeit** *f* **-** firmness; solidity; strength; steadiness. **F~land** *nt* mainland; (*Kontinent*) continent. **f~legen** *vt sep* (*fig*) fix, settle; lay down <*Regeln*>; tie up <*Geld*>; **sich f~legen** commit oneself
festlich *a* festive **F~keiten** *fpl* festivities
fest|liegen† *vi sep* (*haben*) be fixed, settled. **f~machen** *v sep* ● *vt* fasten/(*binden*) tie (**an** + *dat* to); (*f~legen*) fix, settle ● *vi* (*haben*) (*Naut*) moor. **F~mahl** *nt* feast. **F~nahme** *f* **-, -n** arrest. **f~nehmen**† *vt sep* arrest. **f~setzen** *vt sep* fix, settle; (*inhaftieren*) gaol; **sich f~setzen** collect. **f~sitzen**† *vi sep* (*haben*) be firm/<*Schraube:*> tight; (*haften*) stick; (*nicht weiterkommen*) be stuck. **F~spiele** *npl* festival *sg*. **f~stehen**† *vi sep* (*haben*) be certain. **f~stellen** *vt sep* fix; (*ermitteln*) establish; (*bemerken*) notice; (*sagen*) state. **F~tag** *m* special day

Festung f -, -en fortress
Festzug m [grand] procession
Fete /ˈfeːtə, ˈfɛːtə/ f -, -n party
fett a fat; fatty; (fettig) greasy; (üppig) rich; <Druck> bold. **F~** nt -[e]s, -e fat; (flüssig) grease. **f~arm** a low-fat. **F~en** vt grease ● vi (haben) be greasy. **F~fleck** m grease mark. **f~ig** a greasy
Fetzen m -s,- scrap; (Stoff) rag
feucht a damp, moist; <Luft> humid. **F~igkeit** f - dampness; (Nässe) moisture; (Luft-) humidity. **F~igkeitscreme** f moisturizer
Feuer nt -s,- fire; (für Zigarette) light; (Begeisterung) passion; **F~machen** light a fire. **F~alarm** m fire alarm. **f~gefährlich** a [in]flammable. **F~leiter** f fire-escape. **F~löscher** m -s,- fire extinguisher. **F~melder** m -s,- fire alarm. **f~n** vi (haben) fire (auf + acc on). **F~probe** f (fig) test. **f~rot** a crimson. **F~stein** m flint. **F~stelle** f hearth. **F~treppe** f fire-escape. **F~wache** f fire station. **F~waffe** f firearm. **F~wehr** f -, -en fire brigade. **F~wehrauto** nt fire-engine. **F~wehrmann** m (pl -männer & -leute) fireman. **F~werk** nt firework display, fireworks pl. **F~zeug** nt lighter
feurig a fiery; (fig) passionate
Fiaker m -s,- (Aust) horse-drawn cab
Fichte f -, -n spruce
Fieber nt -s [raised] temperature; **F~ haben** have a temperature. **f~n** vi (haben) be feverish. **F~thermometer** nt thermometer
fiebrig a feverish
Figur f -, -en figure; (Roman-, Film-) character; (Schach-) piece
Filet /fiˈleː/ nt -s, -s fillet
Filiale f -, -n (Comm) branch
Filigran nt -s filigree

Film m -[e]s, -e film; (Kino-) film; (Schicht) coating. **f~en** vt/i (haben) film. **F~kamera** f cine/(für Kinofilm) film camera
Filt|er m & (Techn) nt -s,- filter; (Zigaretten-) filter-tip. **f~ern** vt filter. **F~erzigarette** f filter-tipped cigarette. **f~rieren** vt filter
Filz m -es felt. **F~stift** m felt-tipped pen
Fimmel m -s,- 🆀 obsession
Finale nt -s,- (Mus) finale; (Sport) final
Finanz f -, -en finance. **F~amt** nt tax office. **f~iell** a financial. **f~ieren** vt finance. **F~minister** m minister of finance
find|en† vt find; (meinen) think; **den Tod f~en** meet one's death; **wie f~est du das?** what do you think of that? **es wird sich f~en** it'll turn up; (fig) it'll be all right ● vi (haben) find one's way. **F~er** m -s,- finder. **F~erlohn** m reward. **f~ig** a resourceful
Finesse f -, -n (Kniff) trick; **F~n** (Techn) refinements
Finger m -s,- finger; **die F~ lassen von** 🆀 leave alone. **F~abdruck** m finger-mark; (Admin) fingerprint. **F~hut** m thimble. **F~nagel** m finger-nail. **F~spitze** f finger-tip. **F~zeig** m -[e]s, -e hint
Fink m -en, -en finch
Finn|e m -n, -n, **F~in** f -, -nen Finn. **f~isch** a Finnish. **F~land** nt -s Finland
finster a dark; (düster) gloomy; (unheildrohend) sinister. **F~nis** f - darkness; (Astr) eclipse
Firma f -, -men firm, company
Firmen|wagen m company car. **F~zeichen** nt trade mark, logo
Firmung f -, -en (Relig) confirmation
Firnis m -ses, -se varnish. **f~sen** vt varnish
First m -[e]s, -e [roof] ridge

Fisch *m* -[e]s, -e fish; **F~e** (*Astr*) Pisces. **F~dampfer** *m* trawler. **f~en** *vt/i* (*haben*) fish. **F~er** *m* -s,- fisherman. **F~erei** *f* - fishing. **F~händler** *m* fishmonger. **F~reiher** *m* heron

Fiskus *m* - der F~ the Treasury

fit *a* fit. **Fitness** *f* - fitness

fix *a* 🔢 quick; (*geistig*) bright; **f~e Idee** obsession; **fix und fertig** all finished; (*bereit*) all ready; (🔢 *erschöpft*) shattered. **F~er** *m* -s,- 🔲 junkie

fixieren *vt* stare at; (*Phot*) fix

Fjord *m* -[e]s, -e fiord

flach *a* flat; (*eben*) level; (*niedrig*) low; (*nicht tief*) shallow

Fläche *f* -, -n area; (*Ober-*) surface; (*Seite*) face. **F~nmaß** *nt* square measure

Flachs *m* -es flax. **f~blond** *a* flaxen-haired; <*Haar*> flaxen

flackern *vi* (*haben*) flicker

Flagge *f* -, -n flag

Flair /flɛːɐ̯/ *nt* -s air, aura

Flak *f* -, -[s] anti-aircraft artillery/ (*Geschütz*) gun

flämisch *a* Flemish

Flamme *f* -, -n flame; (*Koch-*) burner

Flanell *m* -s (*Tex*) flannel

Flanke *f* -, -n flank. **f~ieren** *vt* flank

Flasche *f* -, -n bottle. **F~nbier** *nt* bottled beer. **F~nöffner** *m* bottle-opener

flatter|haft *a* fickle. **f~n** *vi* (*sein/ haben*) flutter; <*Segel:*> flap

flau *a* (*schwach*) faint; (*Comm*) slack

Flaum *m* -[e]s down. **f~ig** *a* downy; **f~ig rühren** (*Aust Culin*) cream

flauschig *a* fleecy; <*Spielzeug*> fluffy

Flausen *fpl* 🔢 silly ideas

Flaute *f* -, -n (*Naut*) calm; (*Comm*) slack period; (*Schwäche*) low

fläzen (sich) *vr* 🔢 sprawl

Flechte *f* -, -n (*Med*) eczema; (*Bot*) lichen; (*Zopf*) plait. **f~n†** *vt* plait; weave <*Korb*>

Fleck *m* -[e]s, -e[n] spot; (*größer*) patch; (*Schmutz-*) stain, mark; **blauer F~** bruise. **f~en** *vi* (*haben*) stain. **f~enlos** *a* spotless. **F~entferner** *m* -s,- stain remover. **f~ig** *a* stained

Fledermaus *f* bat

Flegel *m* -s,- lout. **f~haft** *a* loutish

flehen *vi* (*haben*) beg (**um** for)

Fleisch *nt* -[e]s flesh; (*Culin*) meat; (*Frucht-*) pulp; **F~ fressend** carnivorous. **F~er** *m* -s,- butcher. **F~fresser** *m* -s,- carnivore. **f~ig** *a* fleshy. **f~lich** *a* carnal. **F~wolf** *m* mincer

Fleiß *m* -es diligence; **mit F~** diligently; (*absichtlich*) on purpose. **f~ig** *a* diligent; (*arbeitsam*) industrious

fletschen *vt* **die Zähne f~** <*Tier:*> bare its teeth

flex|ibel *a* flexible; <*Einband*> limp. **F~ibilität** *f* - flexibility

flicken *vt* mend; (*mit Flicken*) patch. **F~ m** -s,- patch

Flieder *m* -s lilac

Fliege *f* -, -n fly; (*Schleife*) bow-tie. **f~n†** *vi* (*sein*) fly; (*geworfen werden*) be thrown; (🔢 *fallen*) fall; (🔢 *entlassen werden*) be fired/(*von der Schule*) expelled; **in die Luft f~n** blow up ●*vt* fly. **f~nd** *a* flying. **F~r** *m* -s,- airman; (*Pilot*) pilot; (🔢 *Flugzeug*) plane. **F~rangriff** *m* air raid

flieh|en *vi* (*sein*) flee (**vor** + *dat* from); (*entweichen*) escape ●*vt* shun. **f~end** *a* fleeing; <*Kinn, Stirn*> receding

Fliese *f* -, -n tile

Fließ|band *nt* assembly line. **f~en†** *vi* (*sein*) flow; (*aus Wasserhahn*) run. **f~end** *a* flowing; <*Wasser*> running; <*Verkehr*> moving; (*geläufig*) fluent

flimmern vi (haben) shimmer; (TV) flicker

flink a nimble; (schnell) quick

Flinte f -, -n shotgun

Flirt /flœrt/ m -s, -s flirtation. **f~en** vi (haben) flirt

Flitter m -s sequins pl. **F~wochen** fpl honeymoon sg

flitzen vi (sein) 🅸 dash

Flock|e f -, -n flake; (Wolle) tuft. **f~ig** a fluffy

Floh m -[e]s,-̈e flea. **F~spiel** nt tiddly-winks sg

Flora f - flora

Florett nt -[e]s, -e foil

florieren vi (haben) flourish

Floskel f -, -n [empty] phrase

Floß nt -es,-̈e raft

Flosse f -, -n fin; (Seehund-, Gummi-) flipper; (🅇 Hand) paw

Flöt|e f -, -n flute; (Block-) recorder. **f~en** vi (haben) play the flute/recorder; (🅸 pfeifen) whistle ● vt play on the flute/recorder. **F~ist(in)** m -en, -en (f -, -nen) flautist

flott a quick; (lebhaft) lively; (schick) smart

Flotte f -, -n fleet

flottmachen vt sep wieder f~ (Naut) refloat; get going again <Auto>; put back on its feet <Unternehmen>

Flöz nt -es, -e [coal] seam

Fluch m -[e]s,-̈e curse. **f~en** vi (haben) curse, swear

Flucht f - flight; (Entweichen) escape; **die F~ ergreifen** take flight. **f~artig** a hasty

flücht|en vi (sein) flee (vor + dat from); (entweichen) escape ● vr sich f~en take refuge. **f~ig** a fugitive; (kurz) brief; <Blick> fleeting; <Bekanntschaft> passing; (oberflächlich) cursory; (nicht sorgfältig) careless. **f~ig kennen** know slightly. **F~igkeitsfehler** m slip. **F~ling** m -s, -e fugitive; (Pol) refugee

Fluchwort nt (pl -wörter) swear-word

Flug m -[e]s,-̈e flight. **F~abwehr** f anti-aircraft defence

Flügel m -s,- wing; (Fenster-) casement; (Mus) grand piano

Fluggast m [air] passenger

flügge a fully-fledged

Flug|gesellschaft f airline. **F~hafen** m airport. **F~lotse** m air-traffic controller. **F~platz** m airport; (klein) airfield. **F~preis** m air fare. **F~schein** m air ticket. **F~schneise** f flight path. **F~schreiber** m -s,- flight recorder. **F~schrift** f pamphlet. **F~steig** m -[e]s, -e gate. **F~zeug** nt -[e]s, -e aircraft, plane

Flunder f -, -n flounder

flunkern vi (haben) 🅸 tell fibs

Flur m -[e]s, -e [entrance] hall; (Gang) corridor

Fluss m -es,-̈e river; (Fließen) flow; **im F~** (fig) in a state of flux. **f~abwärts** adv down-stream. **f~aufwärts** adv up-stream

flüssig a liquid; <Lava> molten; (fließend) fluent; <Verkehr> freely moving. **F~keit** f -, -en liquid; (Anat) fluid

Flusspferd nt hippopotamus

flüstern vt/i (haben) whisper

Flut f -, -en high tide; (fig) flood

Föderation /-'tsio:n/ f -, -en federation

Fohlen nt -s,- foal

Föhn m -s föhn [wind]; (Haartrockner) hair-drier. **f~en** vt [blow-]dry

Folg|e f -, -n consequence; (Reihe) succession; (Fortsetzung) instalment; (Teil) part. **f~en** vi (sein) follow (jdm/etw s.o./sth); (zuhören) listen (dat to); **wie f~t** as follows ● (haben) (gehorchen) obey (jdm s.o.). **f~end** a following; **F~endes** the following

folgern vt conclude (**aus** from).
F~ung f -, -en conclusion
folglich adv consequently.
f~sam a obedient
Folie /'fo:liə/ f -, -n foil; (Plastik-)
film
Folklore f - folklore
Folter f -, -n torture. f~n vt
torture
Fön (P) m -s, -e hair-drier
Fonds /fõ:/ m -,- /-[s], -s/ fund
fönen* vt s. föhnen
Förder|band nt (pl -bänder)
conveyor belt. f~lich a beneficial
fordern vt demand;
(beanspruchen) claim; (zum
Kampf) challenge
fördern vt promote; (unterstützen)
encourage; (finanziell) sponsor;
(gewinnen) extract
Forderung f -, -en demand;
(Anspruch) claim
Förderung f - promotion;
encouragement; (Techn)
production
Forelle f -, -n trout
Form f -, -en form; (Gestalt) shape;
(Culin, Techn) mould; (Back-) tin;
[gut] in F~ in good form
Formalität f -, -en formality
Format nt -[e]s, -e format; (Größe)
size; (fig: Bedeutung) stature
formatieren vt format
Formel f -, -n formula
formen vt shape, mould; (bilden)
form; sich f~ take shape
förmlich a formal
form|los a shapeless; (zwanglos)
informal. F~sache f formality
Formular nt -s, -e [printed] form
formulier|en vt formulate, word.
F~ung f -, -en wording
forsch|en vi (haben) search (nach
for). f~end a searching. F~er m
-s,- research scientist; (Reisender)
explorer. F~ung f -, -en research
Forst m -[e]s, -e forest
Förster m -s,- forester
Forstwirtschaft f forestry

Fort nt -s, -s (Mil) fort

fort adv away; f~ sein be away;
(gegangen/verschwunden) have
gone; und so f~ and so on; in
einem f~ continuously.
F~bewegung f locomotion.
F~bildung f further education/
training. f~bleiben† vi sep (sein)
stay away. f~bringen† vt sep
take away. f~fahren† vi sep
(sein) go away ● (haben/sein)
continue (zu to). f~fallen† vi sep
(sein) be dropped/(ausgelassen)
omitted; (entfallen) no longer
apply; (aufhören) cease. f~führen
vt sep continue. f~gehen† vi sep
(sein) leave, go away; (ausgehen)
go out; (andauern) go on.
f~geschritten a advanced; (spät)
late. F~geschrittene(r) m/f
advanced student. f~lassen† vt
sep let go; (auslassen) omit.
f~laufen† vi sep (sein) run away;
(sich f~setzen) continue.
f~laufend a consecutive.
f~pflanzen (sich) vr sep
reproduce; <Ton, Licht:> travel.
F~pflanzung f - reproduction.
F~pflanzungsorgan nt
reproductive organ. f~schicken
vt sep send away; (abschicken)
send off. f~schreiten† vi sep
(sein) continue; (Fortschritte
machen) progress, advance.
f~schreitend a progressive;
<Alter> advancing. F~schritt m
progress; F~schritte machen make
progress. f~schrittlich a
progressive. f~setzen vt sep
continue; sich f~setzen continue.
F~setzung f -, -en continuation;
(Folge) instalment; F~setzung
folgt to be continued.
F~setzungsroman m serialized
novel, serial. f~während a
constant. f~ziehen† v sep ● vt
pull away ● vi (sein) move away

Fossil nt -, -ien /-iən/ fossil

Foto nt -s, -s photo. **F~apparat** m camera. **F~gen** a photogenic

Fotograf|(in) m -en, -en (f -, -nen) photographer. **F~ie** f -, -n photography; (Bild) photograph. **f~ieren** vt take a photo[graph] of ● vi (haben) take photographs. **f~isch** a photographic

Fotokopie f photocopy. **f~ren** vt photocopy. **F~rgerät** nt photocopier

Fötus m -, -ten foetus

Foul /faul/ nt -s, -s (Sport) foul. **f~en** vt foul

Fracht f -, -en freight. **F~er** m -s,- freighter. **F~gut** nt freight. **F~schiff** nt cargo boat

Frack m -[e]s,̈e & -s tailcoat

Frage f -, -n question; **nicht in F~ kommen** s. infrage. **F~bogen** m questionnaire. **f~n** vt (haben) ask; **sich f~n** wonder (**ob** whether). **f~nd** a questioning. **F~zeichen** nt question mark

frag|lich a doubtful; <Person, Sache> in question. **f~los** adv undoubtedly

Fragment nt -[e]s, -e fragment

fragwürdig a questionable; (verdächtig) dubious

Fraktion /-'tsi̯o:n/ f -, -en parliamentary party

Franken¹ m -s,- (Swiss) franc

Franken² nt -s Franconia

frankieren vt stamp, frank

Frankreich nt -s France

Fransen fpl fringe sg

Franz|ose m -n, -n Frenchman; **die F~osen** the French pl. **F~ösin** f -, -nen Frenchwoman. **f~ösisch** a French. **F~ösisch** nt -[s] French

Fraß m -es feed; (pej: Essen) muck

Fratze f -, -n grotesque face; (Grimasse) grimace

Frau f -, -en woman; (Ehe-) wife; **F~Thomas** Mrs Thomas; **Unsere Liebe F~** (Relig) Our Lady

Frauen|arzt m, **F~ärztin** f gynaecologist. **F~rechtlerin** f -, -nen feminist

Fräulein nt -s,- single woman; (jung) young lady; (Anrede) Miss

frech a cheeky; (unverschämt) impudent. **F~heit** f -, -en cheekiness; impudence; (Äußerung) impertinence

frei a free; (freischaffend) freelance; <Künstler> independent; (nicht besetzt) vacant; (offen) open; (bloß) bare; **f~er Tag** day off; **sich** (dat) **f~ nehmen** take time off; **f~ machen** (räumen) clear; vacate <Platz>; (befreien) liberate; **f~ lassen** leave free; **ist dieser Platz f~?** is this seat taken? 'Zimmer f~' 'vacancies' ● adv freely; (ohne Notizen) without notes; (umsonst) free

Frei|bad nt open-air swimming pool. **f~beruflich** a & adv freelance. **F~e** nt im **F~en** in the open air, out of doors. **F~gabe** f release. **f~geben†** v sep ● vt release; (eröffnen) open; **jdm einen Tag f~geben** give s.o. a day off ● vi (haben) **jdm** give s.o. time off. **f~gebig** a generous. **F~gebigkeit** f - generosity. **f~haben†** v sep ● vt **eine Stunde f~haben** have an hour off; (Sch) have a free period ● vi (haben) be off work/(Sch) school; (beurlaubt sein) have time off. **f~händig** adv without holding on

Freiheit f -, -en freedom, liberty. **F~sstrafe** f prison sentence

Frei|herr m baron. **F~körperkultur** f naturism. **F~lassung** f - release. **F~lauf** m free-wheel. **f~legen** vt sep expose. **f~lich** adv admittedly; (natürlich) of course. **F~lichttheater** nt open-air theatre. **f~machen** vt sep (frankieren) frank; (entkleiden)

bare; **einen Tag f~machen** take a day off. **f~maurer** m Freemason. **f~schaffend** a freelance. **f~schwimmen† (sich)** v sep pass one's swimming test. **F~sprecheinrichtung** f hands-free kit. **f~sprechen†** vt sep acquit. **F~spruch** m acquittal. **f~stehen†** vi (haben) stand empty; **es steht ihm f~** (fig) he is free (**zu** to). **f~stellen** vt sep exempt (**von** from); **jdm etw f~stellen** leave sth up to s.o. **F~stil** m freestyle. **F~stoß** m free kick

Freitag m Friday. **f~s** adv on Fridays

Frei|tod m suicide. **F~umschlag** m stamped envelope. **f~weg** adv freely; (offen) openly. **f~willig** a voluntary. **F~willige(r)** m/f volunteer. **F~zeichen** nt ringing tone; (Rufzeichen) dialling tone. **F~zeit** f free or spare time; (Muße) leisure. **F~zeit-** pref leisure ... **F~zeitbekleidung** f casual wear. **f~zügig** a unrestricted; (großzügig) liberal

fremd a foreign; (unbekannt) strange; (nicht das eigene) other people's; **in f~er Mann** a stranger; **f~e Leute** strangers; **unter f~em Namen** under an assumed name; **ich bin hier f~** I'm a stranger here. **F~e** f - in der F~e away from home; (im Ausland) in a foreign country. **F~e(r)** m/f stranger; (Ausländer) foreigner; (Tourist) tourist. **F~enführer** m [tourist] guide. **F~enverkehr** m tourism. **F~enzimmer** nt room [to let]; (Gäste-) guest room. **f~gehen†** vi sep (sein) 🔲 be unfaithful. **F~sprache** f foreign language. **F~wort** nt (pl -wörter) foreign word

Freske f -,-n, **Fresko** nt -s,-ken fresco
Fresse f -,-n 🔲 (Mund) gob; (Gesicht) mug. **f~n†** vt/i (haben)

eat. **F~n** nt -s feed; (🔲 Essen) grub

Freud|e f -,-n pleasure; (innere) joy; **mit F~en** with pleasure; **jdm eine F~e machen** please s.o. **f~ig** a joyful

freuen vt please; **sich f~** be pleased (**über** + acc about); **sich f~ auf** (+ acc) look forward to; **es freut mich** I'm glad (**dass** that)

Freund m -es, -e friend; (Verehrer) boyfriend. **F~in** f -, -nen friend; (Liebste) girlfriend. **f~lich** a kind; (umgänglich) friendly; (angenehm) pleasant. **f~licherweise** adv kindly. **F~lichkeit** f -, -en kindness; friendliness; pleasantness

Freund|schaft f -, -en friendship; **F~schaft schließen** become friends. **f~lich** a friendly

Frieden m -s peace; **F~ schließen** make peace; **im F~** in peacetime; **lass mich in F~!** leave me alone! **F~svertrag** m peace treaty

Fried|hof m cemetery. **f~lich** a peaceful

frieren† vi (haben) <Person:> be cold; impers **es friert/hat gefroren** it is freezing/there has been a frost; **frierst du?** are you cold? ● (sein) (gefrieren) freeze

Fries m -es, -e frieze

frisch a fresh; (sauber) clean; (leuchtend) bright; (munter) lively; (rüstig) fit; **sich f~ machen** freshen up ● adv freshly, newly; **ein Bett f~ beziehen** put clean sheets on a bed; **f~ gestrichen!** wet paint! **F~e** f - freshness; brightness; liveliness; fitness. **F~haltepackung** f vacuum pack

Fri|seur /friˈzøːɐ/ m -s, -e hairdresser; (Herren-) barber. **F~seursalon** m hairdressing salon. **F~seuse** /-ˈzøːzə/ f -, -n hairdresser

frisier|en vt jdn/sich f~en do s.o.'s/one's hair; **die Bilanz/einen Motor f~en** 🔢 fiddle the accounts/soup up an engine
Frisör m -s, -e = Friseur
Frist f -, -en period; (Termin) deadline; (Aufschub) time; **drei Tage F~** three days' grace. **f~los** a frivolous
Frisur f -, -en hairstyle
frittieren vt deep-fry
frivol /fri'vo:l/ a frivolous
froh a happy; (freudig) joyful; (erleichtert) glad
fröhlich a cheerful; (vergnügt) merry. **F~keit** f - cheerfulness; merriment
fromm a devout; (gutartig) docile
Frömmigkeit f - devoutness
Fronleichnam m Corpus Christi
Front f -, -en front. **f~al** a frontal; <Zusammenstoß> head-on ● adv from the front; <zusammenstoßen> head-on. **F~alzusammenstoß** m head-on collision
Frosch m -[e]s,¨e frog. **F~laich** m frog-spawn. **F~mann** m (pl -männer) frogman
Frost m -[e]s,¨e frost. **F~beule** f chilblain
frösteln vi (haben) shiver
frost|ig a frosty. **F~schutzmittel** nt antifreeze
Frottee nt & m -s towelling
frottier|en vt rub down. **F~[hand]tuch** nt terry towel
Frucht f -,¨e fruit; **F~ tragen** bear fruit. **f~bar** a fertile; (fig) fruitful. **F~barkeit** f - fertility
früh a early ● adv early; (morgens) in the morning; **heute f~** this morning; **von f~ an** od **auf** from an early age. **F~aufsteher** m -s,- early riser. **F~e** f - in aller **F~e** bright and early; **in der F~e** (SGer) in the morning. **f~er** adv earlier; (eher) sooner; (ehemals) formerly; (vor langer Zeit) in the

old days; **f~er oder später** sooner or later; **ich wohnte f~er in X** I used to live in X. **f~ere(r,s)** a earlier; (ehemalig) former; (vorige) previous; **in f~eren Zeiten** in former times. **f~estens** adv at the earliest. **F~geburt** f premature birth/(Kind) baby. **F~jahr** nt spring. **F~ling** m -s, -e spring. **f~morgens** adv early in the morning. **f~reif** a precocious
Frühstück nt breakfast. **f~en** vi (haben) have breakfast
frühzeitig a & adv early; (vorzeitig) premature
Frustr|ation /-'tsio:n/ f -, -en frustration. **f~ieren** vt frustrate
Fuchs m -es,¨e fox; (Pferd) chestnut. **f~en** vt 🔢 annoy
Füchsin f -, -nen vixen
Fuge¹ f -, -n joint
Fuge² f -, -n (Mus) fugue
füg|en vt fit (in + acc into); (an-) join (an + acc on to); (dazu-) add (zu to); sich f~en fit (in + acc into); adjoin/(folgen) follow (an etw acc sth); (fig: gehorchen) submit (dat to). **f~sam** a obedient. **F~ung** f -, -en eine **F~ung des Schicksals** a stroke of fate
fühl|bar a noticeable. **f~en** vt/i (haben) feel; **sich f~en** feel (krank/einsam ill/lonely); (🔢 stolz sein) fancy oneself. **F~er** m -s,- feeler. **F~ung** f - contact
Fuhre f -, -n load
führ|en vt lead; guide <Tourist>; (geleiten) take; (leiten) run; (befehligen) command; (verkaufen) stock; bear <Namen>; keep <Liste, Bücher>; **bei** od **mit sich f~en** carry ● vi (haben) lead; (verlaufen) go, run; **zu etw f~en** lead to sth. **f~end** a leading. **F~er** m -s,- leader; (Fremden-) guide; (Buch) guide[book]. **F~erhaus** nt driver's cab. **F~erschein** m driving licence;

F

den **F~erschein machen** take one's driving test. **F~erscheinentzug** m disqualification from driving. **F~ung** f -, -en leadership; (*Leitung*) management; (*Mil*) command; (*Betragen*) conduct; (*Besichtigung*) guided tour; (*Vorsprung*) lead; **in F~ung gehen** go into the lead

Fuhr|unternehmer m haulage contractor. **F~werk** nt cart

Fülle f -, -n abundance, wealth (**an** + dat of); (*Körper-*) plumpness. **f~n** vt fill; (*Culin*) stuff

Füllen nt -s, - foal

Füll|er m -s, -, **🔲**, **F~federhalter** m fountain pen. **F~ung** f -, -en filling; (*Braten-*) stuffing

fummeln vi (*haben*) fumble (**an** + dat with)

Fund m -[e]s, -e find

Fundament nt -[e]s, -e foundations pl. **f~al** a fundamental

Fundbüro nt lost-property office

fünf inv a, **F~** f -, -en five; (*Sch*) ≈ fail mark. **F~linge** mpl quintuplets. **f~te(r,s)** a fifth. **f~zehn** inv a fifteen. **f~zehnte(r,s)** a fifteenth. **f~zig** inv a fifty. **f~zigste(r,s)** a fiftieth

fungieren vi (*haben*) act (**als** as)

Funk m -s radio. **F~e** m -n, -n spark. **f~eln** vi (*haben*) sparkle; <*Stern:*> twinkle. **F~en** m -s, - spark. **f~en** vt radio. **F~sprechgerät** nt walkie-talkie. **F~spruch** m radio message. **F~streife** f [police] radio patrol

Funktion /-'tsɪo:n/ f -, -en function; (*Stellung*) position; (*Funktionieren*) working; **außer F~** out of action. **F~är** m -s, -e official. **f~ieren** vi (*haben*) work

für prep (+ acc) for; **Schritt für Schritt** step by step; **was für [ein]** what [a]! (*fragend*) what sort of [a]? **Für** nt **das Für und Wider** the pros and cons pl

Furche f -, -n furrow

Furcht f - fear (**vor** + dat of); **F~ erregend** terrifying. **f~bar** a terrible

fürcht|en vt/i (*haben*) fear; **sich f~en** be afraid (**vor** + dat of). **f~erlich** a dreadful

füreinander adv for each other

Furnier nt -s, -e veneer. **f~t** a veneered

Fürsorg|e f care; (*Admin*) welfare; (**🔲** *Geld*) ≈ social security. **F~er(in)** m -s, - (f -, -nen) social worker. **f~lich** a solicitous

Fürst m -en, -en prince. **F~entum** nt -s, -̈er principality. **F~in** f -, -nen princess

Furt f -, -en ford

Furunkel m -s, - (*Med*) boil

Fürwort nt (pl -wörter) pronoun

Furz m -es, -e (*vulg*) fart

Fusion f -, -en fusion; (*Comm*) merger

Fuß m -es,-̈e foot; (*Aust: Bein*) leg; (*Lampen-*) base; (*von Weinglas*) stem; **zu Fuß** on foot; **zu Fuß gehen** walk; **auf freiem Fuß** free. **F~abdruck** m footprint. **F~abtreter** m -s, - doormat. **F~ball** m football. **F~ballspieler** m footballer. **F~balltoto** nt football pools pl. **F~bank** f footstool. **F~boden** m floor

Fussel f -, -n & m -s, -[n] piece of fluff; **F~n** fluff sg. **f~n** vi (*haben*) shed fluff

fußen vi (*haben*) be based (**auf** + dat on)

Fußgänger|(in) m -s, - (f -, -nen) pedestrian. **F~brücke** f footbridge. **F~zone** f pedestrian precinct

Fuß|geher m -s, - (*Aust*) = **F~gänger**. **F~gelenk** nt ankle. **F~hebel** m pedal. **F~nagel** m toenail. **F~note** f footnote. **F~pflege** f chiropody. **F~rücken** m instep. **F~sohle** f sole of the foot. **F~tritt** m kick. **F~weg** m

footpath; **eine Stunde F~weg** an
hour's walk
futsch *pred a* 🔟 gone
Futter¹ *nt* **-s** feed; *(Trocken-)*
fodder
Futter² *nt* **-s,-** *(Kleider-)* lining
Futteral *nt* **-s, -e** case
füttern¹ *vt* feed
füttern² *vt* line
Futur *nt* **-s** *(Gram)* future

Gabe *f* **-, -n** gift; *(Dosis)* dose
Gabel *f* **-, -n** fork. **g~n (sich)** *vr*
fork. **G~stapler** *m* **-s,-** fork-lift
truck. **G~ung** *f* **-, -en** fork
gackern *vi (haben)* cackle
gaffen *vi (haben)* gape, stare
Gage /'ga:ʒə/ *f* **-, -n** *(Theat)* fee
gähnen *vi (haben)* yawn
Gala *f* - ceremonial dress
Galavorstellung *f* gala
performance
Galerie *f* **-, -n** gallery
Galgen *m* **-s,-** gallows *sg.* **G~frist**
f 🔟 reprieve
Galionsfigur *f* figurehead
Galle *f* - bile; *(G~nblase)* gall-
bladder. **G~nblase** *f* gall-
bladder. **G~nstein** *m* gallstone
Galopp *m* **-s** gallop; **im G~** at a
gallop. **g~ieren** *vi (sein)* gallop
gammeln *vi (haben)* 🔟 loaf
around. **G~ler(in)** *m* **-s,-** (*f* **-, -nen**)
drop-out
Gams *f* **-, -en** *(Aust)* chamois
Gämse *f* **-, -n** chamois
Gang *m* **-[e]s,ṡe** walk; *(G~art)*
gait; *(Boten-)* errand;
(Funktionieren) running;
(Verlauf, Culin) course; *(Durch-)*

passage; *(Korridor)* corridor;
(zwischen Sitzreihen) aisle,
gangway; *(Anat)* duct; *(Auto)*
gear; **in G~ bringen** get going; **im
G~e sein** be in progress; **Essen
mit vier G~en** four-course meal
gängig *a* common; *(Comm)*
popular
Gangschaltung *f* gear change
Gangster /'gɛŋstɐ/ *m* **-s,-** gangster
Ganove *m* **-n, -n** 🔟 crook
Gans *f* -,ṡe goose
Gänse|blümchen *nt* **-s,-** daisy.
G~füßchen *ntpl* inverted
commas. **G~haut** *f* goose-
pimples *pl.* **G~rich** *m* **-s, -e**
gander
ganz *a* whole, entire; *(vollständig)*
complete; *(🔟 heil)* undamaged,
intact; **die g~e Zeit** all the time,
the whole time; **eine g~e Weile/
Menge** quite a while/lot; *inv* **g~
Deutschland** the whole of
Germany; **wieder g~ machen** 🔟
mend; **im Großen und G~en** on
the whole ● *adv* quite; *(völlig)*
completely, entirely; *(sehr)* very;
nicht g~ not quite; **g~ allein** all
on one's own; **g~ und gar**
completely, totally; **g~ und gar
nicht** not at all. **G~e(s)** *nt* whole.
g~jährig *adv* all the year round.
g~tägig *a & adv* full-time;
<geöffnet> all day. **g~tags** *adv* all
day; *<arbeiten>* full-time
gar¹ *a* done, cooked
gar² *adv* **gar nicht/nichts/niemand**
not/nothing/no one at all
Garage /ga'ra:ʒə/ *f* **-, -n** garage
Garantie *f* **-, -n** guarantee. **g~ren**
vt/i (haben) **[für] etw g~ren**
guarantee sth. **G~schein** *m*
guarantee
Garderobe *f* **-, -n** *(Kleider)*
wardrobe; *(Ablage)* cloakroom;
(Künstler-) dressing-room.
G~nfrau *f* cloakroom attendant
Gardine *f* **-, -n** curtain
garen *vt/i (haben)* cook

gären† vi (haben) ferment; (fig) seethe

Garn nt -[e]s, -e yarn; (Näh-) cotton

Garnele f -, -n shrimp; prawn

garnieren vt decorate; (Culin) garnish

Garnison f -, -en garrison

Garnitur f -, -en set; (Möbel-) suite

Garten m -s, "- garden. **G~arbeit** f gardening. **G~bau** m horticulture. **G~haus** nt, **G~laube** f summerhouse. **G~schere** f secateurs pl

Gärtner|(in) m -s, - (f -, -nen) gardener. **G~ei** f -, -en nursery

Gärung f - fermentation

Gas nt -es, -e gas; **Gas geben** 🅸 accelerate. **G~maske** f gas mask. **G~pedal** nt (Auto) accelerator

Gasse f -, -n alley; (Aust) street

Gast m -[e]s, "-e guest; (Hotel-) visitor; (im Lokal) patron; **zum Mittag G~e haben** have people to lunch; **bei jdm zu G~ sein** be staying with s.o. **G~arbeiter** m foreign worker. **G~bett** nt spare bed

Gäste|bett nt spare bed. **G~buch** nt visitors' book. **G~zimmer** nt [hotel] room; (privat) spare room

gast|freundlich a hospitable. **G~freundschaft** f hospitality. **G~geber** m -s, - host. **G~geberin** f -, -nen hostess. **G~haus** nt, **G~hof** m inn, hotel

gastlich a hospitable

Gastronomie f - gastronomy

Gast|spiel nt guest performance. **G~spielreise** f (Theat) tour. **G~stätte** f restaurant. **G~wirt** m landlord. **G~wirtin** f landlady. **G~wirtschaft** f restaurant

Gas|werk nt gasworks sg. **G~zähler** m gas-meter

Gatte m -n, -n husband

Gattin f -, -nen wife

Gattung f -, -en kind; (Biol) genus; (Kunst) genre

Gaudi f - (Aust, fam) fun

Gaumen m -s, - palate

Gauner m -s, - crook, swindler. **G~ei** f -, -en swindle

Gaze /'ga:zə/ f - gauze

Gazelle f -, -n gazelle

Gebäck nt -s [cakes and] pastries pl; (Kekse) biscuits pl

Gebälk nt -s timbers pl

geballt a <Faust> clenched

Gebärde f -, -n gesture

gebär|en† vt give birth to, bear; **geboren werden** be born. **G~mutter** f womb, uterus

Gebäude nt -s, - building

Gebeine ntpl [mortal] remains

Gebell nt -s barking

geben† vt give; (tun, bringen) put; (Karten) deal; (aufführen) perform; (unterrichten) teach; **etw verloren g~** give sth up as lost; **viel/wenig g~ auf** (+ acc) set great/little store by; **sich g~** (nachlassen) wear off; (besser werden) get better; (sich verhalten) behave ● impers **es gibt** there is/are; **was gibt es Neues/zum Mittag/im Kino?** what's the news/for lunch/on at the cinema? **es wird Regen g~** it's going to rain ● vi (haben) (Karten) deal

Gebet nt -[e]s, -e prayer

Gebiet nt -[e]s, -e area; (Hoheits-) territory; (Sach-) field

gebieten† vt command; (erfordern) demand ● vi (haben) rule

Gebilde nt -s, - structure

gebildet a educated; (kultiviert) cultured

Gebirg|e nt -s, - mountains pl. **g~ig** a mountainous

Gebiss nt -es, -e teeth pl; (künstliches) false teeth pl; dentures pl, (des Zaumes) bit

geblümt a floral, flowered

gebogen a curved

G

geboren *a* born; **g~er Deutscher** German by birth; **Frau X, g~e Y** Mrs X, née Y
Gebot *nt* -[e]s, -e rule
gebraten *a* fried
Gebrauch *m* use; (*Sprach-*) usage; **Gebräuche** customs; **in G~** in use; **G~ machen von** make use of. **g~en** *vt* use; **zu nichts zu g~en** useless
gebräuchlich *a* common; <*Wort*> in common use
Gebrauch|sanleitung, G~sanweisung *f* directions *pl* for use. **g~t** *a* used; (*Comm*) secondhand. **G~twagen** *m* used car
gebrechlich *a* frail, infirm
gebrochen *a* broken ● *adv* **g~ Englisch sprechen** speak broken English
Gebrüll *nt* -s roaring
Gebühr *f* -, -en charge, fee; **über G~** excessively. **g~end** *a* due; (*geziemend*) proper. **g~enfrei** *a* free ● *adv* free of charge. **g~enpflichtig** *a & adv* subject to a charge; **g~enpflichtige Straße** toll road
Geburt *f* -, -en birth; **von G~** by birth. **G~enkontrolle, G~enregelung** *f* birth-control. **G~enziffer** *f* birth-rate
gebürtig *a* native (**aus** of); **g~er Deutscher** German by birth
Geburts|datum *nt* date of birth. **G~helfer** *m* obstetrician. **G~hilfe** *f* obstetrics *sg*. **G~ort** *m* place of birth. **G~tag** *m* birthday. **G~urkunde** *f* birth certificate
Gebüsch *nt* -[e]s, -e bushes *pl*
Gedächtnis *nt* -ses memory; **aus dem G~** from memory
Gedanke *m* -ns, -n thought (**an** + *acc* of); (*Idee*) idea; **sich** (*dat*) **G~n machen worry** (**über** + *acc* about). **g~nlos** *a* thoughtless; (*zerstreut*) absent-minded. **G~nstrich** *m* dash

Gedärme *ntpl* intestines; (*Tier-*) entrails
Gedeck *nt* -[e]s, -e place setting; (*auf Speisekarte*) set meal
gedeihen† *vi* (*sein*) thrive, flourish
gedenken† *vi* (*haben*) propose (**etw zu tun** to do sth); **jds g~** remember s.o. **G~** *nt* -s memory
Gedenk|feier *f* commemoration. **G~gottesdienst** *m* memorial service
Gedicht *nt* -[e]s, -e poem
Gedräng|e *nt* -s crush, crowd. **g~t** *a* (*knapp*) concise ● *adv* **g~t voll** packed
Geduld *f* - patience; **G~ haben** be patient. **g~en** (**sich**) *vr* be patient. **g~ig** *a* patient.
G~[s]spiel *nt* puzzle
gedunsen *a* bloated
geehrt *a* honoured; **Sehr g~er Herr X** Dear Mr X
geeignet *a* suitable; **im g~en Moment** at the right moment
Gefahr *f* -, -en danger; **in G~** in danger; **auf eigene G~** at one's own risk; **G~ laufen** run the risk (**etw zu tun** of doing sth)
gefähr|den *vt* endanger; (*fig*) jeopardize. **g~lich** *a* dangerous
gefahrlos *a* safe
Gefährt *nt* -[e]s, -e vehicle
Gefährte *m* -n, -n, **Gefährtin** *f* -, -nen companion
gefahrvoll *a* dangerous, perilous
Gefälle *nt* -s,- slope; (*Straßen-*) gradient
gefallen† *vi* (*haben*) **jdm g~** please s.o.; **er/es gefällt mir** I like him/it; **sich** (*dat*) **etw g~ lassen** put up with sth
Gefallen[1] *m* -s,- favour
Gefallen[2] *nt* -s pleasure (**an** + *dat* in); **dir zu G~** to please you
Gefallene(r) *m* soldier killed in the war
gefällig *a* pleasing; (*hübsch*) attractive; (*hilfsbereit*) obliging;

noch etwas g~? will there be anything else? **G~keit** f -, -en favour; (*Freundlichkeit*) kindness

Gefangen|e(r) m/f prisoner. **G~nahme** f - capture. **g~nehmen*** vt sep **g~ nehmen**, s. fangen. **G~schaft** f - captivity

Gefängnis nt -ses, -se prison; (*Strafe*) imprisonment. **G~strafe** f imprisonment; (*Urteil*) prison sentence. **G~wärter** m [prison] warder

Gefäß nt -es, -e container; (*Blut-*) vessel

gefasst a composed; (*ruhig*) calm; **g~ sein auf** (+ acc) be prepared for

gefedert a sprung

gefeiert a celebrated

Gefieder nt -s plumage

gefleckt a spotted

Geflügel nt -s poultry. **G~klein** nt -s giblets pl. **g~t** a winged

Geflüster nt -s whispering

Gefolge nt -s retinue, entourage

gefragt a popular

Gefreite(r) m lance-corporal

gefrier|en† vi (sein) freeze. **G~fach** nt freezer compartment. **G~punkt** m freezing point. **G~schrank** m upright freezer. **G~truhe** f chest freezer

gefroren a frozen

gefügig a compliant; (*gehorsam*) obedient

Gefühl nt -[e]s, -e feeling; (*Empfindung*) sensation; (*G~sregung*) emotion; **im G~ haben** know instinctively. **g~los** a insensitive; (*herzlos*) unfeeling; (*taub*) numb. **g~smäßig** a emotional; (*instinktiv*) instinctive. **G~sregung** f emotion. **g~voll** a sensitive; (*sentimental*) sentimental

gefüllt a filled; (*voll*) full

gefürchtet a feared, dreaded

gefüttert a lined

gegeben a given; (*bestehend*) present; (*passend*) appropriate. **g~enfalls** adv if need be

gegen prep (+ acc) against; (*Sport*) versus; (*g~über*) to[-wards]; (*Vergleich*) compared with; (*Richtung, Zeit*) towards; (*ungefähr*) around; **ein Mittel g~** a remedy for ● adv **g~ 100 Leute** about 100 people. **G~angriff** m counter-attack

Gegend f -, -en area, region; (*Umgebung*) neighbourhood

gegeneinander adv against/ (*gegenüber*) towards one another

Gegen|fahrbahn f opposite carriageway. **G~gift** nt antidote. **G~maßnahme** f countermeasure. **G~satz** m contrast; (*Widerspruch*) contradiction; (*G~teil*) opposite; **im G~satz zu** unlike. **g~seitig** a mutual; **sich g~seitig hassen** hate one another. **G~stand** m object; (*Gram, Gesprächs-*) subject. **G~stück** nt counterpart; (*G~teil*) opposite. **G~teil** nt opposite, contrary; **im G~teil** on the contrary. **g~teilig** a opposite

gegenüber prep (+ dat) opposite; (*Vergleich*) compared with; **jdm g~ höflich sein** be polite to s.o. ● adv opposite. **G~** nt -s person opposite. **g~liegend** a opposite. **g~stehen†** vi sep (haben) (+ dat) face; **feindlich g~stehen** (+ dat) be hostile to. **g~stellen** vt sep confront; (*vergleichen*) compare

Gegen|verkehr m oncoming traffic. **G~vorschlag** m counter-proposal. **G~wart** f - present; (*Anwesenheit*) presence. **g~wärtig** a present ● adv at present. **G~wehr** f - resistance. **G~wert** m equivalent. **G~wind** m head wind. **g~zeichnen** vt sep countersign

geglückt a successful

Gegner|(in) m -s,- (f -, -nen) opponent. **g~isch** a opposing
Gehabe nt -s affected behaviour
Gehackte(s) nt mince
Gehalt nt -[e]s,:̈er salary. **G~serhöhung** f rise
gehässig a spiteful
gehäuft a heaped
Gehäuse nt -s,- case; (TV, Radio) cabinet; (Schnecken-) shell
Gehege nt -s,- enclosure
geheim a secret; **g~ halten** keep secret; **im G~en** secretly. **G~dienst** m Secret Service. **G~nis** nt -ses, -se secret. **g~nisvoll** a mysterious
gehemmt a (fig) inhibited

gehen†
● intransitive verb (sein)
····▶ (sich irgendwohin begeben) go; (zu Fuß) walk. **tanzen/ schwimmen/einkaufen gehen** go dancing/swimming/shopping. **schlafen gehen** go to bed. **zum Arzt gehen** go to the doctor's. **in die Schule gehen** go to school. **auf und ab gehen** walk up and down. **über die Straße gehen** cross the street
····▶ (weggehen; fam: abfahren) go; leave. **ich muss bald gehen** I must go soon. **Sie können gehen** you may go. **der Zug geht um zehn Uhr** 🔢 the train leaves or goes at ten o'clock
····▶ (funktionieren) work. **der Computer geht wieder/nicht mehr** the computer is working again/ has stopped working. **meine Uhr geht falsch/richtig** my watch is wrong/right
····▶ (möglich sein) be possible. **ja, das geht** yes, I or we can manage it. **das geht nicht** that can't be done; (🔢 ist nicht akzeptabel) it's not good enough, it's not on 🔢. **es geht einfach nicht, dass du so spät

nach Hause kommst** it simply won't do for you to come home so late
····▶ (🔢 gerade noch angehen) **es geht [so]** it is all right. **Wie war die Party? — Es ging so** How was the party? — Not bad or So-so
····▶ (sich entwickeln) do; go. **der Laden geht gut** the shop is doing well. **es geht alles nach Wunsch** everything is going to plan
····▶ (impers) **wie geht es Ihnen?** how are you? **es geht ihm gut/ schlecht** (gesundheitlich) he is well/not well; (geschäftlich) he is doing well/badly; **ein gut g~des Geschäft** a thriving business
····▶ (impers; sich um etw handeln) **es geht um** it concerns. **worum geht es hier?** what is this all about? **es geht ihr nur ums Geld** she is only interested in money

Geheul nt -s howling
Gehilfe m -n, -n, **Gehilfin** f -, -nen trainee; (Helfer) assistant
Gehirn nt -s brain; (Verstand) brains pl **G~erschütterung** f concussion. **G~hautentzündung** f meningitis. **G~wäsche** f brainwashing
gehoben a (fig) superior
Gehöft nt -[e]s, -e farm
Gehör nt -s hearing
gehorchen vi (haben) (+ dat) obey
gehören vi (haben) belong (dat to); **dazu gehört Mut** that takes courage; **es gehört sich nicht** it isn't done
gehörlos a deaf
Gehörn nt -s, -e horns pl; (Geweih) antlers pl
gehorsam a obedient. **G~** m -s obedience
Geh|steig m -[e]s, -e pavement. **G~weg** m = Gehsteig; (Fußweg) footpath

Geier m -s,- vulture

Geig|e f -, -n violin. **g~en** vi
(haben) play the violin ●vt play
on the violin. **G~er(in)** m -s,- (f -,
-nen) violinist

geil a lecherous; randy; (ℹ toll)
great

Geisel f -, -n hostage

Geiß f -, -en (SGer) [nanny-]goat.
G~blatt nt honeysuckle

Geist m -[e]s, -er mind; (Witz) wit;
(Gesinnung) spirit; (Gespenst)
ghost; **der Heilige G~** the Holy
Ghost or Spirit

geistes|abwesend a absent-
minded. **G~blitz** m brainwave.
g~gegenwärtig adv with great
presence of mind. **g~gestört** a
[mentally] deranged. **g~krank** a
mentally ill. **G~krankheit** f
mental illness.
G~wissenschaften fpl arts.
G~zustand m mental state

geist|ig a mental; (intellektuell)
intellectual. **g~lich** a spiritual;
(religiös) religious; <Musik>
sacred; <Tracht> clerical.
G~liche(r) m clergyman.
G~lichkeit f - clergy. **g~reich** a
clever; (witzig) witty

Geiz m -es meanness. **g~en** vi
(haben) be mean (**mit** with).
G~hals m ℹ miser. **g~ig** a
mean, miserly. **G~kragen** m ℹ
miser

Gekicher nt -s giggling

geknickt a ℹ dejected

gekonnt a accomplished ●adv
expertly

gekränkt a offended, hurt

Gekritzel nt -s scribble

Gelächter nt -s laughter

geladen a loaded

gelähmt a paralysed

Geländer nt -s,- railings pl;
(Treppen-) banisters

gelangen vi (sein) reach/(fig)
attain (**zu etw/an etw** acc sth)

gelassen a composed; (ruhig)
calm. **G~heit** f - equanimity;
(Fassung) composure

Gelatine /ʒela-/ f - gelatine

geläufig a common, current;
(fließend) fluent; **jdm g~ sein** be
familiar to s.o.

gelaunt a **gut/schlecht g~ sein** be
in a good/bad mood

gelb a yellow; (bei Ampel) amber;
das G~e vom Ei the yolk of the
egg. **G~** nt -s,- yellow. **g~lich** a
yellowish. **G~sucht** f jaundice

Geld nt -es, -er money; **öffentliche
G~er** public funds. **G~automat**
m cashpoint machine. **G~beutel**
m, **G~börse** f purse. **G~geber** m
-s,- backer. **g~lich** a financial.
G~mittel ntpl funds. **G~schein**
m banknote. **G~schrank** m safe.
G~strafe f fine. **G~stück** nt coin

Gelee /ʒe'le:/ nt -s, -s jelly

gelegen a situated; (passend)
convenient

Gelegenheit f -, -en opportunity,
chance; (Anlass) occasion;
(Comm) bargain; **bei G~** some
time. **G~sarbeit** f casual work.
G~skauf m bargain

gelegentlich a occasional ●adv
occasionally; (bei Gelegenheit)
some time

Gelehrte(r) m/f scholar

Geleit nt -[e]s escort; **freies G~**
safe conduct. **g~en** vt escort

Gelenk nt -[e]s, -e joint. **g~ig** a
supple; (Techn) flexible

gelernt a skilled

Geliebte(r) m/f lover

gelingen† vi (sein) succeed, be
successful. **G~** nt -s success

gellend a shrill

geloben vt promise [solemnly];
das Gelobte Land the Promised
Land

gelöst a (fig) relaxed

gelten† vi (haben) be valid;
<Regel:> apply; **g~ als** be
regarded as; **etw nicht g~ lassen**

G

not accept sth; **wenig/viel g~** be worth/(*fig*) count for little/a lot; **jdm g~** be meant for s.o.; **das gilt nicht** that doesn't count. **g~d** *a* valid; <*Preise*> current; <*Meinung*> prevailing

Geltung *f* - validity; (*Ansehen*) prestige; **zur G~ bringen** set off

gelungen *a* successful

Gelüst *nt* -[e]s, -e desire

gemächlich *a* leisurely ● *adv* in a leisurely manner

Gemahl *m* -s, -e husband. **G~in** *f* -, -nen wife

Gemälde *nt* -s,- painting. **G~galerie** *f* picture gallery

gemäß *prep* (+ *dat*) in accordance with

gemäßigt *a* moderate; <*Klima*> temperate

gemein *a* common; (*unanständig*) vulgar; (*niederträchtig*) mean; **g~er Soldat** private

Gemeinde *f* -, -n [local] community; (*Admin*) borough; (*Pfarr-*) parish; (*bei Gottesdienst*) congregation. **G~rat** *m* local council/(*Person*) councillor. **G~wahlen** *fpl* local elections

gemein|gefährlich *a* dangerous. **G~heit** *f* -, -en commonness; vulgarity; meanness; (*Bemerkung, Handlung*) mean thing [to say/do]; **so eine G~heit!** how mean! **G~kosten** *pl* overheads. **g~nützig** *a* charitable. **g~sam** *a* common ● *adv* together

Gemeinschaft *f* -, -en community. **g~lich** *a* joint; <*Besitz*> communal ● *adv* jointly; (*zusammen*) together. **G~sarbeit** *f* teamwork

Gemenge *nt* -s,- mixture

Gemisch *nt* -[e]s, -e mixture. **g~t** *a* mixed

Gemme *f* -, -n engraved gem

Gemse* *f* -, -n s.**Gämse**

Gemurmel *nt* -s murmuring

Gemüse *nt* -s,- vegetable; (*coll*) vegetables *pl*. **G~händler** *m* greengrocer

gemustert *a* patterned

Gemüt *nt* -[e]s, -er nature, disposition; (*Gefühl*) feelings *pl*

gemütlich *a* cosy; (*gemächlich*) leisurely; (*zwanglos*) informal; <*Person*> genial; **es sich** (*dat*) **g~ machen** make oneself comfortable. **G~keit** *f* - cosiness

Gen *nt* -s, -e gene

genau *a* exact, precise; <*Waage, Messung*> accurate; (*sorgfältig*) meticulous; (*ausführlich*) detailed; **nichts G~es wissen** not know any details; **g~ genommen** strictly speaking; **g~!** exactly! **G~igkeit** *f* - exactitude; precision; accuracy; meticulousness

genauso *adv* just the same; (*g~sehr*) just as much; **g~ teuer** just as expensive; **g~ gut** just as good; *adv* just as well; **g~ sehr** just as much; **g~ viel** just as much/many; **g~ wenig** just as little/few; (*noch*) no more

Gendarm /ʒã'darm/ *m* -en, -en (*Aust*) policeman

Genealogie *f* - genealogy

genehmig|en *vt* grant; approve <*Plan*>. **G~ung** *f* -, -en permission; (*Schein*) permit

geneigt *a* sloping, inclined; (*fig*) well-disposed (*dat* towards)

General *m* -s,ͤe general. **G~direktor** *m* managing director. **G~probe** *f* dress rehearsal. **G~streik** *m* general strike

Generation /-'tsi̯oːn/ *f* -, -en generation

Generator *m* -s, -en /-'toːrən/ generator

generell *a* general

genes|en† *vi* (*sein*) recover. **G~ung** *f* - recovery; (*Erholung*) convalescence

Genetik *f* - genetics *sg*

genetisch *a* genetic

Genf *nt* -s Geneva. **G~er** *a* Geneva ...; **G~er See** Lake Geneva

genial *a* brilliant. **G~ität** *f* genius

Genick *nt* -s, -e [back of the] neck; **sich** (*dat*) **das G~ brechen** break one's neck

Genie /ʒe'ni:/ *nt* -s, -s genius

genieren /ʒe'ni:rən/ *vt* embarrass; **sich g~** feel *or* be embarrassed

genieß|bar *a* fit to eat/drink. **g~en†** *vt* enjoy; (*verzehren*) eat/drink

Genitiv *m* -s, -e genitive

genmanipuliert *a* genetically modified

Genom *nt* -s, -e genome

Genosse *m* -n, -n (*Pol*) comrade. **G~nschaft** *f* -, -en cooperative

Gentechnologie *f* genetic engineering

genug *inv a & adv* enough

Genüge *f* **zur G~** sufficiently. **g~n** *vi* (*haben*) be enough. **g~nd** *inv a* sufficient, enough; (*Sch*) fair ● *adv* sufficiently, enough

Genuss *m* -es,̈-e enjoyment; (*Vergnügen*) pleasure; (*Verzehr*) consumption

geöffnet *a* open

Geo|graphie, G~grafie *f* - geography. **g~graphisch, g~grafisch** *a* geographical. **G~logie** *f* - geology. **g~logisch** *a* geological. **G~meter** *m* -s,- surveyor. **G~metrie** *f* - geometry. **g~metrisch** *a* geometric[al]

geordnet *a* well-ordered; (*stabil*) stable; **alphabetisch g~** in alphabetical order

Gepäck *nt* -s luggage, baggage. **G~ablage** *f* luggage-rack. **G~aufbewahrung** *f* left-luggage office. **G~schein** *m* left-luggage ticket; (*Aviat*) baggage check. **G~träger** *m* porter; (*Fahrrad-*) luggage carrier; (*Dach-*) roof-rack

gepflegt *a* well-kept; <*Person*> well-groomed; <*Hotel*> first-class

gepunktet *a* spotted

gerade *a* straight; (*direkt*) direct; (*aufrecht*) upright; (*aufrichtig*) straightforward; <*Zahl*> even ● *adv* straight; directly; (*eben*) just; (*genau*) exactly; (*besonders*) especially; **g~ sitzen/stehen** sit/stand [up] straight; **g~ erst** only just. **G~ f** -, -n straight line. **g~aus** *adv* straight ahead/on. **g~heraus** *adv* (*fig*) straight out. **g~so** *adv* just the same; **g~so gut** just as good; *adv* just as well. **g~stehen†** *vi sep* (*haben*) (*fig*) accept responsibility (**für** for). **g~zu** *adv* virtually; (*wirklich*) absolutely

Geranie /-iə/ *f* -, -n geranium

Gerät *nt* -[e]s, -e tool; (*Acker-*) implement; (*Küchen-*) utensil; (*Elektro-*) appliance; (*Radio-, Fernseh-*) set; (*Turn-*) piece of apparatus; (*coll*) equipment

geraten† *vi* (*sein*) get; **in Brand g~** catch fire; **in Wut g~** get angry; **gut g~** turn out well

Geratewohl *nt* **aufs G~** at random

geräuchert *a* smoked

geräumig *a* spacious, roomy

Geräusch *nt* -[e]s, -e noise. **g~los** *a* noiseless

gerben *vt* tan

gerecht *a* just; (*fair*) fair. **g~fertigt** *a* justified. **G~igkeit** *f* - justice; fairness

Gerede *nt* -s talk

geregelt *a* regular

gereizt *a* irritable

Geriatrie *f* - geriatrics *sg*

Gericht¹ *nt* -[e]s, -e (*Culin*) dish

Gericht² *nt* -[e]s, -e court [of law]; **vor G~** in court; **das Jüngste G~** the Last Judgement. **g~lich** *a* judicial; <*Verfahren*> legal ● *adv* **g~lich vorgehen** take legal action. **G~shof** *m* court of justice.

G~smedizin f forensic medicine.
G~ssaal m court-room.
G~svollzieher m -s,- bailiff
gerieben a grated; (🔲 schlau) crafty
gering a small; (niedrig) low; (g~fügig) slight. **g~fügig** a slight. **g~schätzig** a contemptuous; <Bemerkung> disparaging. **g~ste(r,s)** a least; **nicht im G~sten** not in the least
gerinnen† vi (sein) curdle; <Blut:> clot
Gerippe nt -s,- skeleton; (fig) framework
gerissen a 🔲 crafty
Germ m -[e]s & (Aust) f - yeast
German|e m -n, -n [ancient] German. **g~isch** a Germanic. **G~istik** f - German [language and literature]
gern[e] adv gladly; **g~ haben** like; (lieben) be fond of; **ich tanze g~** I like dancing; **willst du mit?—g~!** do you want to come?—I'd love to!
Gerste f - barley. **G~nkorn** nt (Med) stye
Geruch m -[e]s,⸚e smell (von/nach of). **g~los** a odourless. **G~ssinn** m sense of smell
Gerücht nt -[e]s, -e rumour
gerührt a (fig) moved, touched
Gerümpel nt -s lumber, junk
Gerüst nt -[e]s, -e scaffolding; (fig) framework
gesammelt a collected; (gefasst) composed
gesamt a entire, whole.
G~ausgabe f complete edition.
G~eindruck m overall impression. **G~heit** f - whole.
G~schule f comprehensive school. **G~summe** f total
Gesandte(r) m/f envoy
Gesang m -[e]s,⸚e singing; (Lied) song; (Kirchen-) hymn. **G~verein** m choral society
Gesäß nt -es buttocks pl

Geschäft nt -[e]s, -e business; (Laden) shop, store; (Transaktion) deal; **schmutzige G~e** shady dealings; **ein gutes G~machen** do very well (**mit** out of). **g~ig** a busy; <Treiben> bustling. **G~igkeit** f - activity. **g~lich** a business ... ●adv on business
Geschäfts|brief m business letter. **G~führer** m manager; (Vereins-) secretary. **G~mann** m (pl -leute) businessman. **G~stelle** f office; (Zweigstelle) branch. **g~tüchtig** a **g~tüchtig sein** be a good businessman/-woman. **G~zeiten** fpl hours of business
geschehen† vi (sein) happen (dat to); **das geschieht dir recht!** it serves you right! **gern g~!** you're welcome! **G~** nt -s events pl
gescheit a clever
Geschenk nt -[e]s, -e present, gift
Geschicht|e f -, -n history; (Erzählung) story; (🔲 Sache) business. **g~lich** a historical
Geschick nt -[e]s fate; (Talent) skill. **G~lichkeit** f - skilfulness, skill. **g~t** a skilful; (klug) clever
geschieden a divorced
Geschirr nt -s, -e (coll) crockery; (Porzellan) china; (Service) service; (Pferde-) harness; **schmutziges G~** dirty dishes pl. **G~spülmaschine** f dishwasher. **G~tuch** nt tea-towel
Geschlecht nt -[e]s, -er sex; (Gram) gender; (Generation) generation. **g~lich** a sexual. **G~skrankheit** f venereal disease. **G~steile** ntpl genitals. **G~sverkehr** m sexual intercourse. **G~swort** nt (pl -wörter) article
geschliffen a (fig) polished
Geschmack m -[e]s,⸚e taste; (Aroma) flavour; (G~ssinn) sense of taste; **einen guten G~ haben** (fig) have good taste.

g~los *a* tasteless; **g~los sein** (*fig*) be in bad taste. **g~voll** *a* (*fig*) tasteful

Geschoss *nt* **-es, -e** missile; (*Stockwerk*) storey, floor

Geschrei *nt* **-s** screaming; (*fig*) fuss

Geschütz *nt* **-es, -e** gun, cannon

geschützt *a* protected; <*Stelle*> sheltered

Geschwader *nt* **-s,-** squadron

Geschwätz *nt* **-es** talk

geschweige *conj* **g~ denn** let alone

Geschwindigkeit *f* **-, -en** speed; (*Phys*) velocity. **G~sbegrenzung, G~sbeschränkung** *f* speed limit

Geschwister *pl* brother[s] and sister[s]; siblings

geschwollen *a* swollen; (*fig*) pompous

Geschworene|(r) *m*/*f* juror; **die G~n** the jury *sg*

Geschwulst *f* **-,-̈e** swelling; (*Tumor*) tumour

geschwungen *a* curved

Geschwür *nt* **-s, -e** ulcer

gesellig *a* sociable; (*Zool*) gregarious; (*unterhaltsam*) convivial; **g~er Abend** social evening

Gesellschaft *f* **-, -en** company; (*Veranstaltung*) party; **die G~** society; **jdm G~ leisten** keep s.o. company. **g~lich** *a* social. **G~sspiel** *nt* party game

Gesetz *nt* **-es, -e** law. **G~entwurf** *m* bill. **g~gebend** *a* legislative. **G~gebung** *f* - legislation. **g~lich** *a* legal. **g~mäßig** *a* lawful; (*gesetzlich*) legal. **g~widrig** *a* illegal

gesichert *a* secure

Gesicht *nt* **-[e]s, -er** face; (*Aussehen*) appearance. **G~sfarbe** *f* complexion. **G~spunkt** *m* point of view. **G~szüge** *mpl* features

Gesindel *nt* **-s** riff-raff

Gesinnung *f* **-, -en** mind; (*Einstellung*) attitude

gesondert *a* separate

Gespann *nt* **-[e]s, -e** team; (*Wagen*) horse and cart/carriage

gespannt *a* taut; (*fig*) tense; <*Beziehungen*> strained; (*neugierig*) eager; (*erwartungsvoll*) expectant; **g~ sein, ob** wonder whether; **auf etw g~ sein** look forward eagerly to sth

Gespenst *nt* **-[e]s, -er** ghost. **g~isch** *a* ghostly; (*unheimlich*) eerie

Gespött *nt* **-[e]s** mockery; **zum G~ werden** become a laughing-stock

Gespräch *nt* **-[e]s-e** conversation; (*Telefon-*) call; **ins G~ kommen** get talking; **im G~ sein** be under discussion. **g~ig** *a* talkative. **G~sthema** *nt* topic of conversation

Gestalt *f* **-, -en** figure; (*Form*) shape, form; **G~ annehmen** (*fig*) take shape. **g~en** *vt* shape; (*organisieren*) arrange; (*schaffen*) create; (*entwerfen*) design; **sich g~en** turn out

Geständnis *nt* **-ses, -se** confession

Gestank *m* **-s** stench, [bad] smell

gestatten *vt* allow, permit; **nicht gestattet** prohibited; **g~ Sie?** may I?

Geste /'gɛ-, 'geːstə/ *f* **-, -n** gesture

Gesteck *nt* **-[e]s, -e** flower arrangement

gestehen† *vt*/*i* (*haben*) confess; confess to <*Verbrechen*>

Gestein *nt* **-[e]s, -e** rock

Gestell *nt* **-[e]s, -e** stand; (*Flaschen-*) rack; (*Rahmen*) frame

gesteppt *a* quilted

gestern *adv* yesterday; **g~ Nacht** last night

gestrandet *a* stranded

gestreift *a* striped

gestrichelt *a* <*Linie*> dotted

gestrichen *a* **g~er Teelöffel** level teaspoon[ful]

G

gestrig /'gɛstrɪç/ a yesterday's; **am g~en Tag** yesterday

Gestrüpp nt -s, -e undergrowth

Gestüt nt -[e]s, -e stud [farm]

Gesuch nt -[e]s, -e request; (Admin) application. **g~t** a sought-after

gesund a healthy; **g~ sein** be in good health; <Sport, Getränk:> be good for one; **wieder g~ werden** get well again

Gesundheit f - health; **G~!** (bei Niesen) bless you! **g~lich** a health ...; **g~licher Zustand** state of health ● adv **es geht ihm g~lich gut/schlecht** he is in good/poor health. **g~sschädlich** a harmful

getäfelt a panelled

Getöse nt -s racket, din

Getränk nt -[e]s, -e drink. **G~ekarte** f wine-list

getrauen vt sich (dat) etw g~ dare [to] do sth; **sich g~** dare

Getreide nt -s (coll) grain

getrennt a separate; **g~ leben** live apart; **g~ schreiben** write as two words

getreu a faithful ● prep (+ dat) true to. **g~lich** adv faithfully

Getriebe nt -s,- bustle; (Techn) gear; (Auto) transmission; (Gehäuse) gearbox

getrost adv with confidence

Getto nt -s, -s ghetto

Getue nt -s [!] fuss

Getümmel nt -s tumult

geübt a skilled

Gewächs nt -es, -e plant

gewachsen a jdm g~ sein be a match for s.o.

Gewächshaus nt greenhouse

gewagt a daring

gewählt a refined

gewahr a g~ werden become aware (acc/gen of)

Gewähr f - guarantee

gewähr|en vt grant; (geben) offer. **g~leisten** vt guarantee

Gewahrsam m -s safekeeping; (Haft) custody

Gewalt f -, -en power; (Kraft) force; (Brutalität) violence; **mit G~** by force. **G~herrschaft** f tyranny. **g~ig** a powerful; (🔲 groß) enormous; (stark) tremendous. **g~sam** a forcible; <Tod> violent. **g~tätig** a violent. **G~tätigkeit** f -, -en violence; (Handlung) act of violence

Gewand nt -[e]s,-̈er robe

gewandt a skilful. **G~heit** f - skill

Gewebe nt -s,- fabric; (Anat) tissue

Gewehr nt -s, -e rifle, gun

Geweih nt -[e]s, -e antlers pl

Gewerb|e nt -s,- trade. **g~lich** a commercial. **g~smäßig** a professional

Gewerkschaft f -, -en trade union. **G~ler(in)** m -s,- (f -, -nen) trade unionist

Gewicht nt -[e]s, -e weight; (Bedeutung) importance. **G~heben** nt -s weight-lifting

Gewinde nt -s,- [screw] thread

Gewinn m -[e]s, -e profit; (fig) gain, benefit; (beim Spiel) winnings pl; (Preis) prize; (Los) winning ticket. **G~beteiligung** f profit-sharing. **g~en†** vt win; (erlangen) gain; (fördern) extract ● vi (haben) win; **g~en an** (+ dat) gain in. **g~end** a engaging. **G~er(in)** m -s,- (f -, -nen) winner

Gewirr nt -s, -e tangle; (Straßen-) maze

gewiss a certain

Gewissen nt -s,- conscience. **g~haft** a conscientious. **g~los** a unscrupulous. **G~sbisse** mpl pangs of conscience

gewissermaßen adv to a certain extent; (sozusagen) as it were

Gewissheit f - certainty

Gewitt|er nt -s,- thunderstorm. **g~rig** a thundery

gewogen a (fig) well-disposed (dat towards)

gewöhnen vt jdn/sich g~ an (+ acc) get s.o. used to/get used to; [an] jdn/etw gewöhnt sein be used to s.o./sth

Gewohnheit f -, -en habit. **G~recht** nt common law

gewöhnlich a ordinary; (üblich) usual; (ordinär) common

gewohnt a customary; (vertraut) familiar; (üblich) usual; **etw** (acc) **g~ sein** be used to sth

Gewölbe nt -s,- vault

Gewühl nt -[e]s crush

gewunden a winding

Gewürz nt -es, -e spice. **G~nelke** f clove

gezackt a serrated

gezähnt a serrated; <Säge> toothed

Gezeiten fpl tides

gezielt a specific; <Frage> pointed

geziert a affected

gezwungen a forced. **g~ermaßen** adv of necessity

Gicht f - gout

Giebel m -s,- gable

Gier f - greed (**nach** for). **g~ig** a greedy

gieß|en† vt pour; water <Blumen, Garten>; (Techn) cast ● v impers **es g~t** it is pouring [with rain]. **G~kanne** f watering-can

Gift nt -[e]s, -e poison; (Schlangen-) venom; (Biol, Med) toxin. **g~ig** a poisonous; <Schlange> venomous; (Med, Chem) toxic; (fig) spiteful. **G~müll** m toxic waste. **G~pilz** m toadstool

Gilde f -, -n guild

Gin /dʒɪn/ m -s gin

Ginster m -s (Bot) broom

Gipfel m -s,- summit, top; (fig) peak. **G~konferenz** f summit conference. **g~n** vi (haben) culminate (**in** + dat in)

Gips m -es plaster. **G~verband** m (Med) plaster cast

Giraffe f -, -n giraffe

Girlande f -, -n garland

Girokonto /'ʒiːro-/ nt current account

Gischt m -[e]s & f - spray

Gitar|re f -, -n guitar. **G~rist(in)** m -en, -en (f -, -nen) guitarist

Gitter nt -s,- bars pl; (Rost) gratting, grid; (Geländer, Zaun) railings pl; (Fenster-) grille; (Draht-) wire screen

Glanz m -es shine; (von Farbe, Papier) gloss; (Seiden-) sheen; (Politur) polish; (fig) brilliance; (Pracht) splendour

glänzen vi (haben) shine. **g~d** a shining, bright; <Papier> glossy; (fig) brilliant

glanz|los a dull. **G~stück** nt masterpiece

Glas nt -es,̈er glass; (Brillen-) lens; (Fern-) binoculars pl; (Marmeladen-) [glass] jar. **G~er** m -s,- glazier

glasieren vt glaze; ice <Kuchen>

glas|ig a glassy; (durchsichtig) transparent. **G~scheibe** f pane

Glasur f -, -en glaze; (Culin) icing

glatt a smooth; (eben) even; <Haar> straight; (rutschig) slippery; (einfach) straightforward; <Absage> flat; **g~ streichen** smooth out; **g~ rasiert** clean-shaven; **g~ gehen** go off smoothly; **das ist g~ gelogen** it's a downright lie

Glätte f - smoothness; (Rutschigkeit) slipperiness

Glatt|eis nt [black] ice. **g~weg** adv Ⅰ outright

Glatz|e f -, -n bald patch; (Voll-) bald head; **eine G~e bekommen** go bald. **g~köpfig** a bald

Glaube m -ns belief (**an** + acc in); (Relig) faith; **G~n schenken** (+ dat) believe. **g~n** vt/i (haben) believe (**an** + acc in); (vermuten)

think; **jdm g~n** believe s.o.; **nicht zu g~n** unbelievable, incredible. **G~nbekenntnis** *nt* creed
gläubig *a* religious; (*vertrauend*) trusting. **G~e(r)** *m/f* (*Relig*) believer; **die G~en** the faithful. **G~er** *m* -s,- (*Comm*) creditor
glaub|lich *a* **kaum g~lich** scarcely believable. **g~würdig** *a* credible; <*Person*> reliable
gleich *a* same; (*identisch*) identical; (*g~wertig*) equal; **g~ bleibend** constant; **2 mal 5 [ist] g~ 10** two times 5 equals 10; **das ist mir g~** it's all the same to me; **ganz g~, wo/wer** no matter where/who ●*adv* equally; (*übereinstimmend*) identically, the same; (*sofort*) immediately; (*in Kürze*) in a minute; (*fast*) nearly; (*direkt*) right. **g~altrig** *a* [of] the same age. **g~bedeutend** *a* synonymous. **g~berechtigt** *a* equal. **G~berechtigung** *f* equality
gleichen† *vi* (*haben*) **jdm/etw g~** be like *or* resemble s.o./sth
gleich|ermaßen *adv* equally. **g~falls** *adv* also, likewise; **danke g~falls** thank you, the same to you. **G~gewicht** *nt* balance; (*Phys & fig*) equilibrium. **g~gültig** *a* indifferent; (*unwichtig*) unimportant. **G~gültigkeit** *f* indifference. **g~machen** *vt sep* make equal; **dem Erdboden g~machen** raze to the ground. **g~mäßig** *a* even, regular; (*beständig*) constant. **G~mäßigkeit** *f* - regularity
Gleichnis *nt* -ses, -se parable
Gleich|schritt *m* **im G~schritt** in step. **g~setzen** *vt sep* equate/ (*g~stellen*) place on a par (*dat/ mit* with). **g~stellen** *vt sep* place on a par (*dat* with). **G~strom** *m* direct current
Gleichung *f* -, -en equation
gleichwertig *adv* of equal value. **g~zeitig** *a* simultaneous

Gleis *nt* -es, -e track; (*Bahnsteig*) platform; **G~ 5** platform 5
gleiten† *vi* (*sein*) glide; (*rutschen*) slide. **g~d** *a* sliding; **g~de Arbeitszeit** flexitime
Gleitzeit *f* flexitime
Gletscher *m* -s,- glacier
Glied *nt* -[e]s, -er limb; (*Teil*) part; (*Ketten-*) link; (*Mitglied*) member; (*Mil*) rank. **g~ern** *vt* arrange; (*einteilen*) divide. **G~maßen** *fpl* limbs
glitschig *a* slippery
glitzern *vi* (*haben*) glitter
globalisier|en *vt* globalize. **G~ung** *f* -, -en globalization
Globus *m* - & -busses, -ben & -busse globe
Glocke *f* -, -n bell. **G~nturm** *m* bell-tower, belfry
glorreich *a* glorious
Glossar *nt* -s, -e glossary
Glosse *f* -, -n comment
glotzen *vi* (*haben*) stare
Glück *nt* -[e]s [good] luck; (*Zufriedenheit*) happiness; **G~ bringend** lucky; **G~/kein G~ haben** be lucky/unlucky; **zum G~** luckily, fortunately; **auf gut G~** on the off chance; (*wahllos*) at random. **g~en** *vi* (*sein*) succeed
glücklich *a* lucky, fortunate; (*zufrieden*) happy; (*sicher*) safe ●*adv* happily; safely. **g~erweise** *adv* luckily, fortunately
Glücksspiel *nt* game of chance; (*Spielen*) gambling
Glückwunsch *m* good wishes *pl*; (*Gratulation*) congratulations *pl*; **herzlichen G~!** congratulations! (*zum Geburtstag*) happy birthday! **G~karte** *f* greetings card
Glüh|birne *f* light-bulb. **g~en** *vi* (*haben*) glow. **g~end** *a* glowing; (*rot-*) red-hot; <*Hitze*> scorching; (*leidenschaftlich*) fervent. **G~faden** *m* filament. **G~wein** *m*

mulled wine. **G~würmchen** nt
-s,- glow-worm

Glukose f - glucose

Glut f - embers pl; (Röte) glow;
(Hitze) heat; (fig) ardour

Glyzinie /-iə/ f -, -n wisteria

GmbH abbr (Gesellschaft mit
beschränkter Haftung) ≈ plc

Gnade f - mercy; (Gunst) favour;
(Relig) grace. **G~nfrist** f reprieve

gnädig a gracious; (mild) lenient;
g~e Frau Madam

Gnom m -en, -en gnome

Gobelin /gobəˈlɛ̃/ m -s, -s tapestry

Gold nt -[e]s gold. **g~en** a gold ...;
(g~farben) golden. **G~fisch** m
goldfish. **g~ig** a sweet, lovely.
G~lack m wallflower. **G~regen**
m laburnum. **G~schmied** m
goldsmith

Golf[1] m -[e]s, -e (Geog) gulf

Golf[2] nt -s golf. **G~platz** m golf-
course. **G~schläger** m golf-club.
G~spieler(in) m(f) golfer

Gondel f -, -n gondola; (Kabine)
cabin

gönnen vt jdm etw g~ not
begrudge s.o. sth; **jdm etw nicht
g~** begrudge s.o. sth

Gör nt -s, -en, **Göre** f -, -n 🔲 kid

Gorilla m -s, -s gorilla

Gosse f -, -n gutter

Got|ik f - Gothic. **g~isch** a Gothic

Gott m -[e]s,¨er God; (Myth) god

Götterspeise f jelly

Gottes|dienst m service.
G~lästerung f blasphemy

Gottheit f -, -en deity

Göttin f -, -nen goddess

göttlich a divine

gottlos a ungodly; (atheistisch)
godless

Grab nt -[e]s,¨er grave

graben† vi (haben) dig

Graben m -s,¨ ditch; (Mil) trench

Grab|mal nt tomb. **G~stein** m
gravestone, tombstone

Grad m -[e]s, -e degree

Graf m -en, -en count

Grafik f -, -en graphics sg; (Kunst)
graphic arts pl; (Druck) print

Gräfin f -, -nen countess

grafisch a graphic; **g~e
Darstellung** diagram

Grafschaft f -, -en county

Gram m -s grief

grämen (sich) vr grieve

Gramm nt -s, -e gram

Gram|matik f -, -en grammar.
g~matikalisch a grammatical

Granat m -[e]s, -e (Miner) garnet.
G~e f -, -n shell; (Hand-) grenade

Granit m -s, -e granite

Gras nt -es,¨er grass. **g~en** vi
(haben) graze. **G~hüpfer** m -s,-
grasshopper

grässlich a dreadful

Grat m -[e]s, -e [mountain] ridge

Gräte f -, -n fishbone

Gratifikation /-ˈtsi̯oːn/ f -, -en
bonus

gratis adv free [of charge].
G~probe f free sample

Gratu|lant(in) m -en, -en (f -, -nen)
well-wisher. **G~lation** /-ˈtsi̯oːn/ f
-, -en congratulations pl;
(Glückwünsche) best wishes pl.
g~lieren vi (haben) jdm g~lieren
congratulate s.o. (zu on); (zum
Geburtstag) wish s.o. happy
birthday

grau a, **G~** nt -s,- grey

Gräuel m -s,- horror

grauen v impers mir graut [es]
davor I dread it. **G~** nt -s dread.
g~haft a gruesome; (grässlich)
horrible

gräulich a horrible

grausam a cruel. **G~keit** f -, -en
cruelty

graus|en v impers mir graust davor
I dread it. **G~en** nt -s horror,
dread. **g~ig** a gruesome

gravieren vt engrave. **g~d** a (fig)
serious

graziös a graceful

greifen† vt take hold of; (*fangen*) catch ●vi (*haben*) reach (**nach** for); **um sich g~** (*fig*) spread

Greis m -es, -e old man. **G~in** f -, -nen old woman

grell a glaring; <*Farbe*> garish; (*schrill*) shrill

Gremium nt -s, -ien committee

Grenz|e f -, -n border; (*Staats-*) frontier; (*Grundstücks-*) boundary; (*fig*) limit. **g~en** vi (*haben*) border (**an** + *acc* on). **g~enlos** a boundless; (*maßlos*) infinite

Griech|e m -n, -n Greek. **G~enland** nt -s Greece. **G~in** f -, -nen Greek woman. **g~isch** a Greek. **G~isch** nt -[s] (*Lang*) Greek

Grieß m -es semolina

Griff m -[e]s, -e grasp, hold; (*Hand-*) movement of the hand; (*Tür-, Messer-*) handle; (*Schwert-*) hilt. **g~bereit** a handy

Grill m -s, -s grill; (*Garten-*) barbecue

Grille f -, -n (*Zool*) cricket

grill|en vt grill; (*im Freien*) barbecue ●vi (*haben*) have a barbecue. **G~fest** nt barbecue

Grimasse f -, -n grimace; **G~n schneiden** pull faces

grimmig a furious; <*Kälte*> bitter

grinsen vi (*haben*) grin

Grippe f -, -n influenza, **Ⅰ** flu

grob a coarse; (*unsanft, ungefähr*) rough; (*unhöflich*) rude; (*schwer*) gross; <*Fehler*> bad; **g~ geschätzt** roughly. **G~ian** m -s, -e brute

Groll m -[e]s resentment. **g~en** vi (*haben*) be angry (*dat* with); <*Donner:*> rumble

Grönland nt -s Greenland

Gros nt -ses,- (*Maß*) gross

Groschen m -s,- (*Aust*) groschen; **Ⅰ** ten-pfennig piece

groß a big; <*Anzahl, Summe*> large; (*bedeutend, stark*) great; (*g~artig*) grand; <*Buchstabe*> capital; **g~e Ferien** summer holidays; **der größte Teil** the majority *or* bulk; **g~ werden** <*Person:*> grow up; **g~ in etw** (*dat*) **sein** be good at sth; **G~ und Klein** young and old; **im G~en und Ganzen** on the whole ●adv <*feiern*> in style; (**Ⅰ** *viel*) much

groß|artig a magnificent. **G~aufnahme** f close-up. **G~britannien** nt -s Great Britain. **G~buchstabe** m capital letter. **G~e(r)** m/f unser **G~er** our eldest; **die G~en** the grown-ups; (*fig*) the great *pl*

Größe f -, -n size; (*Ausmaß*) extent; (*Körper-*) height; (*Bedeutsamkeit*) greatness; (*Math*) quantity; (*Person*) great figure

Großeltern pl grandparents

Groß|handel m wholesale trade. **G~händler** m wholesaler. **G~macht** f superpower. **g~mütig** a magnanimous. **G~mutter** f grandmother. **G~schreibung** f capitalization. **g~spurig** a pompous; (*überheblich*) arrogant. **G~stadt** f [large] city. **g~städtisch** a city … **G~teil** m large proportion; (*Hauptteil*) bulk

größtenteils adv for the most part

groß|tun† (sich) vr sep brag. **G~vater** m grandfather. **g~ziehen†** vt sep bring up; rear <*Tier*>. **g~zügig** a generous. **G~zügigkeit** f - generosity

Grotte f -, -n grotto

Grübchen nt -s,- dimple

Grube f -, -n pit

grübeln vi (*haben*) brood

Gruft f -,ˑe [burial] vault

grün a green; **im G~en** out in the country; **die G~en** the Greens

Grund m -[e]s,ˑe ground; (*Boden*) bottom; (*Hinter-*) background; (*Ursache*) reason; **aus diesem**

G~e for this reason; **im G~e [genommen]** basically; **auf G~ laufen** (*Naut*) run aground; **zu G~e richten/gehen** *s.* zugrunde. **G~begriffe** *mpl* basics. **G~besitzer** *m* landowner

gründ|en *vt* found, set up; start <*Familie*>; (*fig*) base (**auf** + *acc* on); **sich g~en** be based (**auf** + *acc* on). **G~er(in)** *m* -s,- (*f* -, -nen) founder

Grund|farbe *f* primary colour. **G~form** *f* (*Gram*) infinitive. **G~gesetz** *nt* (*Pol*) constitution. **G~lage** *f* basis, foundation

gründlich *a* thorough. **G~keit** *f* - thoroughness

Gründonnerstag *m* Maundy Thursday

Grund|regel *f* basic rule. **G~riss** *m* ground-plan; (*fig*) outline. **G~satz** *m* principle. **g~sätzlich** *a* fundamental; (*im Allgemeinen*) in principle; (*prinzipiell*) on principle; **G~schule** *f* primary school. **G~stück** *nt* plot [of land]

Gründung *f* -, -en foundation

Grün|span *m* verdigris. **G~streifen** *m* grass verge; (*Mittel-*) central reservation

grunzen *vi* (*haben*) grunt

Gruppe *f* -, -n group; (*Reise-*) party

gruppieren *vt* group

Grusel|geschichte *f* horror story. **g~ig** *a* creepy

Gruß *m* -es,¨e greeting; (*Mil*) salute; **einen schönen G~ an X** give my regards to X; **viele/ herzliche G~e** regards; **Mit freundlichen G~en** Yours sincerely/faithfully

grüßen *vt/i* (*haben*) say hallo (**jdn** to s.o.); (*Mil*) salute; **g~Sie X von mir** give my regards to X; **grüß Gott!** (*SGer, Aust*) good morning/afternoon/evening!

gucken *vi* (*haben*) 🔢 look

Guerilla /geˈrɪlja/ *f* - guerrilla warfare. **G~kämpfer** *m* guerrilla

Gulasch *nt & m* -[e]s goulash

gültig *a* valid

Gummi *m & nt* -s, -[s] rubber; (*Harz*) gum. **G~band** *nt* (*pl* -bänder) elastic *or* rubber band

gummiert *a* gummed

Gummi|knüppel *m* truncheon. **G~stiefel** *m* gumboot, wellington. **G~zug** *m* elastic

Gunst *f* - favour

günstig *a* favourable; (*passend*) convenient

Gurgel *f* -, -n throat. **g~n** *vi* (*haben*) gargle

Gurke *f* -, -n cucumber; (*Essig-*) gherkin

Gurt *m* -[e]s, -e strap; (*Gürtel*) belt; (*Auto*) safety-belt. **G~band** *nt* (*pl* -bänder) waistband

Gürtel *m* -s,- belt. **G~linie** *f* waistline. **G~rose** *f* shingles *sg*

Guss *m* -es,¨e (*Techn*) casting; (*Strom*) stream; (*Regen-*) downpour; (*Torten-*) icing. **G~eisen** *nt* cast iron

gut *a* good; <*Gewissen*> clear; (*gütig*) kind (**zu** to); **jdm gut sein** be fond of s.o.; **im G~en** amicably; **schon gut** that's all right ● *adv* well; <*schmecken, riechen*> good; (*leicht*) easily; **gut zu sehen** clearly visible; **gut drei Stunden** a good three hours

Gut *nt* -[e]s,¨er possession, property; (*Land-*) estate; **Gut und Böse** good and evil; **Güter** (*Comm*) goods

Gutacht|en *nt* -s,- expert's report. **G~er** *m* -s,- expert

gutartig *a* good-natured; (*Med*) benign

Gute|(s) *nt* **etwas/nichts G~s** something/nothing good; **G~s tun** do good; **alles G~!** all the best!

Güte *f* -, -n goodness, kindness; (*Qualität*) quality

Güterzug *m* goods train

gut|gehen* *vi sep* (*sein*) gut
gehen, *s.* gehen. **g~gehend*** *a* gut
gehend, *s.* gehen. **g~gläubig** *a*
trusting. **g~haben†** *vt sep* **fünfzig
Euro g~haben** have fifty euros
credit (**bei with**). **G~haben** *nt* **-s,-**
[credit] balance; (*Kredit*) credit
gut|machen *vt sep* make up for;
make good *<Schaden>*. **g~mütig**
a good-natured. **G~mütigkeit** *f* -
good nature. **G~schein** *m* credit
note; (*Bon*) voucher; (*Geschenk-*)
gift token. **g~schreiben†** *vt sep*
credit. **G~schrift** *f* credit
Guts|haus *nt* manor house
gut|tun* *vi sep* (*haben*) gut tun, *s.*
tun. **g~willig** *a* willing
Gymnasium *nt* **-s, -ien** ≈ grammar
school
Gymnastik *f* - [keep-fit] exercises
pl; (*Turnen*) gymnastics *sg*
Gynäko|loge *m* **-n, -n**
gynaecologist. **G~logie** *f* -
gynaecology

H, h /ha:/ *nt*, **-,-** (*Mus*) B, b
Haar *nt* **-[e]s, -e** hair; **sich** (*dat*) **die
Haare** *od* **das H~ waschen** wash
one's hair; **um ein H~** 🗓 very
nearly. **H~bürste** *f* hairbrush.
h~en *vi* (*haben*) shed hairs;
<Tier:> moult ●*vr* **sich h~en**
moult. **h~ig** *a* hairy; 🗓 tricky.
H~klemme *f* hair-grip.
H~nadelkurve *f* hairpin bend.
H~schnitt *m* haircut. **H~spange**
f slide. **H~waschmittel** *nt*
shampoo
Habe *f* - possessions *pl*

haben†
● *transitive verb*
····▸ have; (*im Präsens*) have got
🗓. **er hat kein Geld** he has no
money *or* 🗓 he hasn't got any
money. **ich habe/hatte die Grippe**
I've got flu/had flu. **was haben
Sie da?** what have you got
there? **wenn ich die Zeit hätte** if I
had the time
····▸ (*empfinden*) **Angst/Hunger/
Durst haben** be frightened/
hungry/thirsty. **was hat er?**
what's wrong with him?
····▸ (+ *Adj., es*) **es gut/schlecht
haben** be well/badly off. **es
schwer haben** be having a
difficult time
····▸ (+ *zu*) (*müssen*) **du hast zu
gehorchen** you must obey
● *auxiliary verb*
····▸ have. **ich habe/hatte ihn eben
gesehen** I have *or* I've/I had *or*
I'd just seen him. **er hat es
gewusst** he knew it. **er hätte ihr
geholfen** he would have helped
her
● *reflexive verb*
····▸ (🗓 *sich aufregen*) make a
fuss. **hab dich nicht so!** don't
make such a fuss!

Habgier *f* greed. **h~ig** *a* greedy
Habicht *m* **-[e]s, -e** hawk
Hachse *f* -, **-n** (*Culin*) knuckle
Hacke¹ *f* -, **-n** hoe; (*Spitz-*) pick
Hacke² *f* -, **-n**, **Hacken** *m* **-s,-** heel
hack|en *vt* hoe; (*schlagen,
zerkleinern*) chop; *<Vogel:>* peck.
H~fleisch *nt* mince
Hafen *m* **-s,-̈** harbour; (*See-*) port.
H~arbeiter *m* docker. **H~stadt** *f*
port
Hafer *m* **-s** oats *pl*. **H~flocken** *fpl*
[rolled] oats

Haft f - (Jur) custody; (H~strafe) imprisonment. **h~bar** a (Jur) liable. **H~befehl** m warrant

haften vi (haben) cling; (kleben) stick; (bürgen) vouch/(Jur) be liable (für for)

Häftling m -s, -e detainee

Haftpflicht f (Jur) liability. **H~versicherung** f (Auto) third-party insurance

Haftung f - (Jur) liability

Hagebutte f -, -n rose-hip

Hagel m -s hail. **h~n** vi (haben) hail

hager a gaunt

Hahn m -[e]s, -̈e cock; (Techn) tap

Hähnchen nt -s, - (Culin) chicken

Hai[fisch] m -[e]s, -e shark

Häkchen nt -s, - tick

häkel|n vt/i (haben) crochet. **H~nadel** f crochet-hook

Haken m -s, - hook; (Häkchen) tick; (𝔦 Schwierigkeit) snag. **h~** vt hook (an + acc to). **H~kreuz** nt swastika

halb a half; **auf h~em Weg** halfway ● adv half; **h~drei** half past two; **fünf [Minuten] vor/nach h~vier** twenty-five [minutes] past three/to four. **H~e(r,s)** f/m/nt half [a litre]

halber prep (+ gen) for the sake of; **Geschäfte h~** on business

Halbfinale nt semifinal

halbieren vt halve, divide in half; (Geom) bisect

Halb|insel f peninsula. **H~kreis** m semicircle. **H~kugel** f hemisphere. **h~laut** a low ● adv in an undertone. **h~mast** adv at half-mast. **H~mond** m half moon. **H~pension** f half-board. **h~rund** a semicircular. **H~schuh** m [flat] shoe. **H~tags** adv [for] half a day; **h~tags arbeiten** ≈ work part-time. **H~ton** m semitone. **h~wegs** adv half-way; (ziemlich) more or less. **h~wüchsig** a adolescent. **H~zeit**

f (Sport) half-time; (Spielzeit) half

Halde f -, -n dump, tip

Hälfte f -, -n half; **zur H~** half

Halfter f -, -n & nt -s, - holster

Halle f -, -n hall; (Hotel-) lobby; (Bahnhofs-) station concourse

hallen vi (haben) resound; (wider-) echo

Hallen- pref indoor

hallo int hallo

Halluzination /-'tsio:n/ f -, -en hallucination

Halm m -[e]s, -e stalk; (Gras-) blade

Hals m -es, -̈e neck; (Kehle) throat; **aus vollem H~e** at the top of one's voice; <lachen> out loud. **H~band** nt (pl -bänder) collar. **H~schmerzen** mpl sore throat sg

halt int stop! (Mil) halt! 𝔦 wait a minute!

Halt m -[e]s, -e hold; (Stütze) support; (innerer) stability; (Anhalten) stop; **H~ machen** stop. **h~bar** a durable; (Tex) hard-wearing; (fig) tenable; **h~bar bis … (Comm)** use by …

halten† vt hold; make <Rede>; give <Vortrag>; (einhalten, bewahren) keep; **[sich** (dat)**] etw h~** keep <Hund>; take <Zeitung>; **h~ für** regard as; **viel h~ von** think highly of; **sich links h~** keep left; **sich h~ an** (+ acc) (fig) keep to ● vi (haben) hold; (haltbar sein, bestehen bleiben) keep; <Freundschaft, Blumen:> last; (Halt machen) stop; **auf sich** (acc) **h~** take pride in oneself; **zu jdm h~** be loyal to s.o.

Halte|stelle f stop. **H~verbot** nt waiting restriction; **'H~verbot'** 'no waiting'

Haltung f -, -en (Körper-) posture; (Verhalten) manner; (Einstellung) attitude; (Fassung) composure; (Halten) keeping

H

Hạmmel *m* -s,- ram; (*Culin*)
mutton. **H~fleisch** *nt* mutton
Hạmmer *m* -s,⸚ hammer
hạmmern *vt/i* (*haben*) hammer
Hạmster *m* -s,- hamster. **h~n** *vt/i*
🔟 hoard
Hạnd *f* -,⸚e hand; **jdm die H~ geben**
shake hands with s.o.; **rechter/
linker H~** on the right/left; **zweiter
H~** second-hand; **unter der H~**
unofficially; (*geheim*) secretly;
H~ und Fuß haben (*fig*) be sound.
H~arbeit *f* manual work;
(*handwerklich*) handicraft;
(*Nadelarbeit*) needlework;
(*Gegenstand*) hand-made article.
H~ball *m* [German] handball.
H~bewegung *f* gesture.
H~bremse *f* handbrake. **H~buch**
nt handbook, manual
Hạndedruck *m* handshake
Hạndel *m* -s trade, commerce;
(*Unternehmen*) business;
(*Geschäft*) deal; **H~ treiben** trade.
h~n *vi* (*haben*) act; (*Handel
treiben*) trade (**mit** in); **von etw** *od*
über etw (*acc*) **h~n** deal with sth;
sich h~n um be about, concern.
H~smarine *f* merchant navy.
H~sschiff *nt* merchant vessel.
H~sschule *f* commercial college.
H~sware *f* merchandise
Hạnd|feger *m* -s,- brush.
H~fläche *f* palm. **H~gelenk** *nt*
wrist. **H~gemenge** *nt* -s,- scuffle.
H~gepäck *nt* hand-luggage.
h~geschrieben *a* hand-written.
h~greiflich *a* tangible; **h~greiflich
werden** become violent. **H~griff**
m handle
handhaben *vt insep* (*reg*) handle
Handikap /'hɛndikɛp/ *nt* -s, -s
handicap
Hạndkuss *m* kiss on the hand
Hạndler *m* -s,- dealer, trader
hạndlich *a* handy
Hạndlung *f* -, -en act; (*Handeln*)
action; (*Roman-*) plot; (*Geschäft*)
shop. **H~sweise** *f* conduct

Hạnd|schellen *fpl* handcuffs.
H~schlag *m* handshake.
H~schrift *f* handwriting; (*Text*)
manuscript. **H~schuh** *m* glove.
H~stand *m* handstand.
H~tasche *f* handbag. **H~tuch** *nt*
towel
Hạndwerk *nt* craft, trade. **H~er** *m*
-s,- craftsman; (*Arbeiter*)
workman
Handy /'hɛndi/ *nt* -s, -s mobile
phone
Hạnf *m* -[e]s hemp
Hạng *m* -[e]s,⸚e slope; (*fig*)
inclination
Hạnge|brücke *f* suspension
bridge. **H~matte** *f* hammock
hạngen[1] *vt* (*reg*) hang
hạngen[2]† *vi* (*haben*) hang; **h~ an**
(+ *dat*) (*fig*) be attached to; **h~
lassen** leave
Hannover *nt* -s Hanover
hạnseln *vt* tease
hantieren *vi* (*haben*) busy oneself
Hạppen *m* -s,- mouthful; **einen H~
essen** have a bite to eat
Hạrfe *f* -, -n harp
Hạrke *f* -, -n rake. **h~n** *vt/i*
(*haben*) rake
hạrmlos *a* harmless; (*arglos*)
innocent
Harmonie *f* -, -n harmony
Harmonika *f* -, -s accordion;
(*Mund-*) mouth-organ
harmonisch *a* harmonious
Hạrn *m* -[e]s urine. **H~blase** *f*
bladder
Harpune *f* -, -n harpoon
hạrt *a* hard; (*heftig*) violent;
(*streng*) harsh
Hạrte *f* -, -n hardness; (*Strenge*)
harshness; (*Not*) hardship. **h~n**
vt harden
Hạrt|faserplatte *f* hardboard.
h~näckig *a* stubborn;
(*ausdauernd*) persistent.
H~näckigkeit *f* - stubbornness;
persistence
Hạrz *nt* -es, -e resin

Haschee nt -s, -s (Culin) hash
Haschisch nt & m -[s] hashish
Hase m -n, -n hare
Hasel f -, -n hazel. **H~maus** f
  dormouse. **H~nuss** f hazel-nut
Hass m -es hatred
hassen vt hate
hässlich a ugly; (unfreundlich)
  nasty. **H~keit** f - ugliness;
  nastiness
Hast f - haste. **h~ig** a hasty,
  hurried
hast, hat, hatte, hätte s. haben
Haube f -, -n cap; (Trocken-)
  drier; (Kühler-) bonnet
Hauch m -[e]s breath; (Luft-)
  breeze; (Duft) whiff; (Spur) tinge.
  h~dünn a very thin
Haue f -, -n pick; (⊞ Prügel)
  beating. **h~n†** vt beat; (hämmern)
  knock; (meißeln) hew; **sich h~n**
  fight; **übers Ohr h~n** ⊞ cheat ● vi
  (haben) bang (**auf** + acc on); **jdm
  ins Gesicht h~n** hit s.o. in the
  face
Haufen m -s,- heap, pile; (Leute)
  crowd
häufen vt heap or pile [up]; **sich
  h~** pile up; (zunehmen) increase
häufig a frequent
Haupt nt -[e]s, **Häupter** head.
  H~bahnhof m main station.
  H~fach nt main subject.
  H~gericht nt main course
Häuptling m -s, -e chief
Haupt|mahlzeit f main meal
  H~mann m (pl -leute) captain.
  H~post f main post office.
  H~quartier nt headquarters pl.
  H~rolle f lead; (fig) leading role.
  H~sache f main thing; **in der
  H~sache** in the main.
  h~sächlich a main. **H~satz** m
  main clause. **H~stadt** f capital.
  H~verkehrsstraße f main road.
  H~verkehrszeit f rush-hour.
  H~wort nt (pl -wörter) noun
Haus nt -es, **Häuser** house;
  (Gebäude) building; (Schnecken-)

shell; **zu H~e** at home; **nach H~e**
  home. **H~arbeit** f housework;
  (Sch) homework. **H~arzt** m
  family doctor. **H~aufgaben** fpl
  homework sg. **H~besetzer** m -s,-
  squatter
hausen vi (haben) live; (wüten)
  wreak havoc
Haus|frau f housewife.
  h~gemacht a home-made.
  H~halt m -[e]s, -e household;
  (Pol) budget. **h~halten†** vi sep
  (haben) **h~halten mit** manage
  carefully; conserve <Kraft>.
  H~hälterin f -, -nen housekeeper.
  H~haltsgeld nt housekeeping
  [money]. **H~haltsplan** m budget.
  H~herr m head of the
  household; (Gastgeber) host
Hausierer m -s,- hawker
Hauslehrer m [private] tutor.
  H~in f governess
häuslich a domestic, <Person>
  domesticated
Haus|meister m caretaker.
  H~ordnung f house rules pl.
  H~putz m cleaning. **H~rat** m
  -[e]s household effects pl.
  H~schlüssel m front-door key.
  H~schuh m slipper. **H~suchung**
  f [police] search.
  H~suchungsbefehl m search-
  warrant. **H~tier** nt domestic
  animal; (Hund, Katze) pet. **H~tür**
  f front door. **H~wirt** m landlord.
  H~wirtin f landlady
Haut f -,Häute skin; (Tier-) hide.
  H~arzt m dermatologist
häuten vt skin; **sich h~** moult
haut|eng a skin-tight. **H~farbe** f
  colour; (Teint) complexion
Hebamme f -, -n midwife
Hebel m -s,- lever
heben† vt lift; (hoch-, steigern)
  raise; **sich h~** rise; <Nebel:> lift;
  (sich verbessern) improve
hebräisch a Hebrew
hecheln vi (haben) pant
Hecht m -[e]s, -e pike

Heck nt -s, -s (Naut) stern; (Aviat) tail; (Auto) rear
Hecke f -, -n hedge
Heck|fenster nt rear window. **H~tür** f hatchback
Heer nt -[e]s, -e army
Hefe f - yeast
Heft nt -[e]s, -e booklet; (Sch) exercise book; (Zeitschrift) issue. **h~en** vt (nähen) tack; (stecken) pin/(klammern) clip/(mit Heftmaschine) staple (an + acc to). **H~er** m -s,- file
heftig a fierce, violent; <Regen> heavy; <Schmerz, Gefühl> intense
Heft|klammer f staple; (Büro-) paper-clip. **H~maschine** f stapler. **H~zwecke** f -, -n drawing-pin
Heide[1] m -n, -n heathen
Heide[2] f -, -n heath; (Bot) heather. **H~kraut** nt heather
Heidelbeere f bilberry
Heidin f -, -nen heathen
heikel a difficult, tricky
heil a undamaged, intact; <Person> unhurt; **mit h~er Haut** 🔟 unscathed
Heil nt -s salvation
Heiland m -s (Relig) Saviour
Heil|anstalt f sanatorium; (Nerven-) mental hospital. **H~bad** nt spa. **h~bar** a curable
Heilbutt m -[e]s, -e halibut
heilen vt cure; heal <Wunde> ● vi (sein) heal
Heilgymnastik f physiotherapy
heilig a holy; (geweiht) sacred; **der H~e Abend** Christmas Eve; **die h~e Anna** Saint Anne; **h~ sprechen** canonize. **H~abend** m Christmas Eve. **H~e(r)** m/f saint. **H~enschein** m halo. **H~keit** f - sanctity, holiness. **H~tum** nt -s,-̈er shrine
heil|kräftig a medicinal. **H~kräuter** ntpl medicinal herbs. **H~mittel** nt remedy. **H~praktiker** m -s,- practitioner of

alternative medicine. **H~sarmee** f Salvation Army. **H~ung** f - cure
Heim nt -[e]s, -e home; (Studenten-) hostel. **h~** adv home
Heimat f -, -en home; (Land) native land. **H~stadt** f home town
heim|begleiten vt sep see home. **H~computer** m home computer. **h~fahren**† v sep ● vi (sein) go/ drive home ● vt take/drive home. **H~fahrt** f way home. **h~gehen**† vi sep (sein) go home
heimisch a native, indigenous; (Pol) domestic
Heim|kehr f - return [home]. **h~kehren** vi sep (sein) return home. **h~kommen**† vi sep (sein) come home
heimlich a secret; **etw h~ tun** do sth secretly. **H~keit** f -, -en secrecy; **H~keiten** secrets
Heim|reise f journey home. **H~spiel** nt home game. **h~suchen** vt sep afflict. **h~tückisch** a treacherous; <Krankheit> insidious. **h~wärts** adv home. **H~weg** m way home. **H~weh** nt -s homesickness. **H~weh haben** be homesick. **H~werker** m -s,- [home] handyman. **h~zahlen** vt sep jdm etw h~zahlen (fig) pay s.o. back for sth
Heirat f -, -en marriage. **h~en** vt/i (haben) marry. **H~santrag** m proposal; **jdm einen H~santrag machen** propose to s.o.
heiser a hoarse. **H~keit** f - hoarseness
heiß a hot; (hitzig) heated; (leidenschaftlich) fervent
heißen† vi (haben) be called; (bedeuten) mean; **ich heiße ...** my name is ...; **wie h~ Sie?** what is your name? **wie heißt ... auf Englisch?** what's the English for ...? ● vt call; **jdn etw tun h~** tell s.o. to do sth

heiter a cheerful; <*Wetter*> bright; (*amüsant*) amusing; **aus h~em Himmel** (*fig*) out of the blue

Heiz|anlage f heating; (*Auto*) heater. **H~decke** f electric blanket. **H~en** vt heat; light <*Ofen*> ● vi (*haben*) put the heating on; <*Ofen:*> give out heat. **H~gerät** nt heater. **H~kessel** m boiler. **H~körper** m radiator. **H~lüfter** m -s,- fan heater. **H~material** nt fuel. **H~ung** f -, -en heating; (*Heizkörper*) radiator

Hektar nt & m -s,- hectare

Held m -en, -en hero. **h~enhaft** a heroic. **H~entum** nt -s heroism. **H~in** f -, -nen heroine

helf|en† vi (*haben*) help (**jdm** s.o.); (*nützen*) be effective; **sich** (*dat*) **nicht zu h~en wissen** not know what to do; **es hilft nichts** it's no use. **H~er(in)** m -s,- (f -, -nen) helper, assistant

hell a light; (*Licht ausstrahlend, klug*) bright; <*Stimme*> clear; (🗌 *völlig*) utter; **h~es Bier** ≈ lager ● adv brightly

Hell|igkeit f - brightness. **H~seher(in)** m -s,- (f -, -nen) clairvoyant

Helm m -[e]s, -e helmet

Hemd nt -[e]s, -en vest; (*Ober-*) shirt

Hemisphäre f -, -n hemisphere

hemm|en vt check; (*verzögern*) impede; (*fig*) inhibit. **H~ung** f -, -en (*fig*) inhibition; (*Skrupel*) scruple; **H~ungen haben** be inhibited. **h~ungslos** a unrestrained

Hendl nt -s, -[n] (*Aust*) chicken

Hengst m -[e]s, -e stallion

Henkel m -s,- handle

Henne f -, -n hen

her adv here; (*zeitlich*) ago; **her mit ...!** give me ...! **von Norden/weit her** from the north/far away; **vom Thema her** as far as the subject is

concerned; **her sein** come (**von** from); **es ist schon lange her** it was a long time ago

herab adv down [here]; **von oben h~** from above; (*fig*) condescending

herab|lassen† vt sep let down; **sich h~** condescend (**zu** to)

herab|sehen† vi sep (*haben*) look down (**auf** + acc on). **h~setzen** vt sep reduce, cut; (*fig*) belittle

Heraldik f - heraldry

heran adv near; **[bis] h~ an** (+ acc) up to. **h~kommen†** vi sep (*sein*) approach; **h~kommen an** (+ acc) come up to; (*erreichen*) get at; (*fig*) measure up to. **h~machen (sich)** vr sep **sich h~machen an** (+ acc) approach; get down to <*Arbeit*>. **h~wachsen†** vi sep (*sein*) grow up. **h~ziehen†** v sep ● vt pull up (**an** + acc to); (*züchten*) train; (*h~bilden*) train; (*hinzuziehen*) call in ● vi (*sein*) approach

herauf adv up [here]; **die Treppe h~** up the stairs. **h~setzen** vt sep raise, increase

heraus adv out (**aus** of); **h~ damit** od **mit der Sprache!** out with it! **h~bekommen†** vt sep get out; (*ausfindig machen*) find out; (*lösen*) solve; **Geld h~bekommen** get change. **h~finden†** v sep ● vt find out ● vi (*haben*) find one's way out. **h~fordern** vt sep provoke; challenge <*Person*>. **H~forderung** f provocation; challenge. **H~gabe** f handing over; (*Admin*) issue; (*Veröffentlichung*) publication. **h~geben†** vt sep hand over; (*Admin*) issue; (*veröffentlichen*) publish; edit <*Zeitschrift*>; **jdm Geld h~geben** give s.o. change ● vi (*haben*) give change (**auf** + acc for). **H~geber** m -s,- publisher; editor. **h~halten† (sich)** vr sep (*fig*) keep out (**aus**

of). **h~kommen**† *vi sep* (*sein*) come out; (*aus Schwierigkeit, Takt*) get out; **auf eins** *od* **dasselbe h~kommen** 🅸 come to the same thing. **h~lassen**† *vt sep* let out. **h~nehmen**† *vt sep* take out; **sich zu viel h~nehmen** (*fig*) take liberties. **h~reden (sich)** *vr sep* make excuses. **h~rücken** *v sep* ● *vt* move out; (*hergeben*) hand over ● *vi* (*sein*) **h~rücken mit** hand over; (*fig: sagen*) come out with. **h~schlagen**† *vt sep* knock out; (*fig*) gain. **h~stellen** *vt sep* put out; **sich h~stellen** turn out (**als** to be; **dass** that). **h~ziehen**† *vt sep* pull out

herb *a* sharp; <*Wein*> dry; (*fig*) harsh

herbei *adv* here. **h~führen** *vt sep* (*fig*) bring about. **h~schaffen** *vt sep* get. **h~sehnen** *vt sep* long for

Herberg|e *f* -, -n [youth] hostel; (*Unterkunft*) lodging. **H~svater** *m* warden

herbestellen *vt sep* summon

herbitten† *vt sep* ask to come

herbringen† *vt sep* bring [here]

Herbst *m* -[e]s, -e autumn. **h~lich** *a* autumnal

Herd *m* -[e]s, -e stove, cooker

Herde *f* -, -n herd; (*Schaf-*) flock

herein *adv* in [here]; **h~!** come in! **h~bitten**† *vt sep* ask in. **h~fallen**† *vi sep* (*sein*) 🅸 be taken in (**auf** + *acc* by). **h~kommen**† *vi sep* (*sein*) come in. **h~lassen**† *vt sep* let in. **h~legen** *vt sep* 🅸 take for a ride

Herfahrt *f* journey/drive here

herfallen† *vi sep* (*sein*) **~ über** (+ *acc*) attack; fall upon <*Essen*>

hergeben† *vt sep* hand over; (*fig*) give up

hergehen† *vi sep* (*sein*) **h~ vor** (+ *dat*) walk along in front of; **es ging lustig her** 🅸 there was a lot of merriment

herholen *vt sep* fetch; **weit hergeholt** (*fig*) far-fetched

Hering *m* -s, -e herring; (*Zeltpflock*) tent-peg

her|kommen† *vi sep* (*sein*) come here; **wo kommt das her?** where does it come from? **h~kömmlich** *a* traditional. **H~kunft** *f* - origin

herleiten *vt sep* derive

hermachen *vt sep* **viel/wenig h~** be impressive/unimpressive; (*wichtig nehmen*) make a lot of/ little fuss (**von** of); **sich h~ über** (+ *acc*) fall upon; tackle <*Arbeit*>

Hermelin[1] *nt* -s, -e (*Zool*) stoat

Hermelin[2] *m* -s, -e (*Pelz*) ermine

Hernie /ˈhɛrniə/ *f* -, -n hernia

Heroin *nt* -s heroin

heroisch *a* heroic

Herr *m* -n, -en gentleman; (*Gebieter*) master (**über** + *acc* of); [Gott,] **der H~** the Lord [God]; **H~ Meier** Mr Meier; **Sehr geehrte H~en** Dear Sirs. **H~enhaus** *nt* manor [house]. **h~enlos** *a* ownerless; <*Tier*> stray

Herrgott *m* **der H~** the Lord

herrichten *vt sep* prepare; **wieder h~** renovate

Herrin *f* -, -nen mistress

herrlich *a* marvellous; (*großartig*) magnificent

Herrschaft *f* -, -en rule; (*Macht*) power; (*Kontrolle*) control; **meine H~en!** ladies and gentlemen!

herrsch|en *vi* (*haben*) rule; (*verbreitet sein*) prevail; **es h~te Stille** there was silence. **H~er(in)** *m* -s,- (*f* -, -nen) ruler

herrühren *vi sep* (*haben*) stem (**von** from)

herstammen *vi sep* (*haben*) come (**aus/von** from)

herstell|en *vt sep* establish; (*Comm*) manufacture, make. **H~er** *m* -s,- manufacturer, maker. **H~ung** *f* - establishment; manufacture

herüber *adv* over [here]

herum adv im Kreis h~ [round] in a circle; **falsch h~** the wrong way round; **um ... h~** round ...; (ungefähr) [round] about ...; **h~ sein** be over. **h~drehen** vt sep turn round/(wenden) over; turn <Schlüssel>. **h~gehen†** vi sep (sein) walk around; <Zeit:> pass; **h~gehen um** go round. **h~kommen†** vi sep (sein) get about; **h~kommen um** get round; come round <Ecke>; **um etw [nicht] h~kommen** (fig) [not] get out of sth. **h~sitzen†** vi sep (haben) sit around; **h~sitzen um** sit round. **h~sprechen† (sich)** vr sep <Gerücht:> get about. **h~treiben† (sich)** vr sep hang around. **h~ziehen†** vi sep (sein) move around; (ziellos) wander about

herunter adv down [here]; **die Treppe h~** down the stairs. **h~fallen†** vi fall off. **h~gekommen** a (fig) run-down; <Gebäude:> dilapidated; <Person> down-at-heel. **h~kommen†** vi sep (sein) come down; (fig) go to rack and ruin; <Firma, Person:> go downhill; (gesundheitlich) get run down. **h~lassen†** vt sep let down, lower. **h~machen** vt sep ⊡ reprimand; (herabsetzen) run down. **h~spielen** vt sep (fig) play down

hervor adv out (aus of). **h~bringen†** vt sep produce; utter <Wort>. **h~gehen†** vi sep (sein) come/(sich ergeben) emerge/ (folgen) follow (aus from). **h~heben†** vt sep (fig) stress, emphasize. **h~ragen** vi sep (haben) jut out; (fig) stand out. **h~ragend** a (fig) outstanding. **h~rufen†** vt sep (fig) cause. **h~stehen†** vi sep (haben) protrude. **h~treten†** vi sep (sein) protrude, bulge; (fig) stand out. **h~tun† (sich)** vr sep (fig)

distinguish oneself; (angeben) show off

Herweg m way here
Herz nt -ens, -en heart; (Kartenspiel) hearts pl; **sich** (dat) **ein H~ fassen** pluck up courage. **H~anfall** m heart attack. **herzhaft** a hearty; (würzig) savoury

herziehen† v sep ● vt **hinter sich** (dat) **h~** pull along [behind one] ● vi (sein) **hinter jdm h~** follow along behind s.o.; **über jdn h~** ⊡ run s.o. down

herz|ig a sweet, adorable. **H~infarkt** m heart attack. **H~klopfen** nt -s palpitations pl. **herzlich** a cordial; (warm) warm; (aufrichtig) sincere; **h~en Dank!** many thanks! **h~e Grüße** kind regards

herzlos a heartless
Herzog m -s,-̈e duke. **H~in** f -, -nen duchess. **H~tum** nt -s,-̈er duchy

Herzschlag m heartbeat; (Med) heart failure
Hessen nt -s Hesse
heterosexuell a heterosexual
Hetze f - rush; (Kampagne) virulent campaign (**gegen** against). **h~n** vt chase; **sich h~n** hurry

Heu nt -s hay
Heuchelei f - hypocrisy
heuch|eln vt feign ● vi (haben) pretend. **H~ler(in)** m -s,- (f -, -nen) hypocrite. **h~lerisch** a hypocritical

heuer adv (Aust) this year
heulen vi (haben) howl; (⊡ weinen) cry
Heu|schnupfen m hay fever. **H~schober** m -s,- haystack. **H~schrecke** f -,-n grasshopper
heut|e adv today; (heutzutage) nowadays; **h~e früh** od **Morgen** this morning; **von h~e auf morgen** from one day to the next. **h~ig** a

today's ...; (*gegenwärtig*) present;
der h~ige Tag today. **h~zutage**
adv nowadays
Hexe *f* -, -n witch. **h~n** *vi* (*haben*)
work magic. **H~nschuss** *m*
lumbago
Hieb *m* -[e]s, -e blow; (*Peitschen-*)
lash; **H~e** hiding *sg*
hier *adv* here; **h~ sein/bleiben/**
lassen/behalten be/stay/leave/
keep here; **h~ und da** here and
there; (*zeitlich*) now and again
hier|auf *adv* on this/these;
(*antworten*) to this; (*zeitlich*) after
this. **h~aus** *adv* out of or from
this/these. **h~durch** *adv* through
this/these; (*Ursache*) as a result
of this. **h~her** *adv* here. **h~hin**
adv here. **h~in** *adv* in this/these.
h~mit *adv* with this/these;
(*Comm*) herewith; (*Admin*)
hereby. **h~nach** *adv* after this/
these; (*demgemäß*) according to
this/these. **h~über** *adv* over/
(*höher*) above this/these;
<*sprechen, streiten*> about this/
these. **h~von** *adv* from this/
these; (*h~über*) about this/these;
(*Menge*) of this/these. **h~zu** *adv*
to this/these; (*h~für*) for this/
these. **h~zulande** *adv* here
hiesig *a* local. **h~e(r)** *m/f* local
Hilf|e *f* -, -n help, aid; **um H~e**
rufen call for help. **h~los** *a*
helpless. **H~losigkeit** *f* -
helplessness. **h~reich** *a* helpful
Hilfs|arbeiter *m* unskilled
labourer. **h~bedürftig** *a* needy;
h~bedürftig sein be in need of
help. **h~bereit** *a* helpful.
H~kraft *f* helper. **H~mittel** *nt*
aid. **H~verb** *nt* auxiliary verb
Himbeere *f* raspberry
Himmel *m* -s, - sky; (*Relig & fig*)
heaven; (*Bett-*) canopy; **unter**
freiem H~ in the open air.
H~bett *nt* four-poster [bed].
H~fahrt *f* Ascension
himmlisch *a* heavenly

hin *adv* there; **hin und her** to and
fro; **hin und zurück** there and
back; (*Rail*) return; **hin und wieder**
now and again; **an** (+ *dat*) ... **hin**
along; **auf** (+ *acc*) ... **hin** in reply
to <*Brief, Anzeige*>; on <*jds Rat*>;
zu *od* **nach ... hin** towards; **hin sein**
🔟 be gone; **es ist noch lange hin**
it's a long time yet
hinauf *adv* up [there]. **h~gehen†**
vi sep (*sein*) go up. **h~setzen** *vt*
sep raise
hinaus *adv* out [there]; (*nach*
draußen) outside; **zur Tür h~** out
of the door; **auf Jahre h~** for
years to come; **über etw** (*acc*) **h~**
beyond sth; (*Menge*) [over and]
above sth; **über etw** (*acc*) **h~ sein**
(*fig*) be past sth. **h~gehen†** *vi*
sep (*sein*) go out; <*Zimmer:*> face
(**nach Norden** north); **h~gehen**
über (+ *acc*) go beyond, exceed.
h~laufen† *vi sep* (*sein*) run out;
h~laufen auf (+ *acc*) (*fig*) amount
to. **h~lehnen (sich)** *vr sep* lean
out. **h~schieben†** *vt sep* push
out; (*fig*) put off. **h~werfen†** *vt*
sep throw out; (🔟 *entlassen*) fire.
h~wollen† *vi sep* (*haben*) want to
go out; **h~wollen auf** (+ *acc*) (*fig*)
aim at. **h~ziehen†** *v sep* ●*vt* pull
out; (*in die Länge ziehen*) drag
out; (*verzögern*) delay; **sich**
h~ziehen drag on; be delayed
●*vi* (*sein*) move out. **h~zögern** *vt*
delay; **sich h~zögern** be delayed
Hinblick *m* **im H~ auf** (+ *acc*) in
view of; (*hinsichtlich*) regarding
hinder|lich *a* awkward; **jdm h~lich**
sein hamper s.o. **h~n** *vt* hamper;
(*verhindern*) prevent. **H~nis** *nt*
-ses, -se obstacle. **H~nisrennen**
nt steeplechase
Hindu *m* -s, -s Hindu. **H~ismus** *m*
- Hinduism
hindurch *adv* through it/them
hinein *adv* in [there]; (*nach*
drinnen) inside; **h~ in** (+ *acc*)
into. **h~fallen†** *vi sep* (*sein*) fall

in. **h~gehen**† vi sep (sein) go in;
h~gehen in (+ acc) go into.
h~reden vi sep (haben) **jdm**
h~reden interrupt s.o.; (sich
einmischen) interfere in s.o.'s
affairs. **h~versetzen (sich)** vr sep
sich in jds Lage h~versetzen put
oneself in s.o.'s position.
h~ziehen† vt sep pull in;
h~ziehen in (+ acc) pull into; **in**
etw (acc) **h~gezogen werden** (fig)
become involved in sth
hin|fahren† v sep vi (sein) go/
drive there ● vt take/drive there.
H~fahrt f journey/drive there;
(Rail) outward journey.
h~fallen† vi sep (sein) fall.
h~fliegen† v sep ● vi (sein) fly
there; 🛈 fall ● vt fly there.
H~flug m flight there; (Admin)
outward flight
Hingeb|ung f - devotion.
h~ungsvoll a devoted
hingehen† vi sep (sein) go/(zu
Fuß) walk there; (vergehen) pass;
h~ zu go up to; **wo gehst du hin?**
where are you going?
hingerissen a rapt; **h~ sein** be
carried away (**von** by)
hinhalten† vt sep hold out;
(warten lassen) keep waiting
hinken vi (haben/sein) limp
hin|knien (sich) vr sep kneel
down. **h~kommen**† vi sep (sein)
get there; (h~gehören) belong,
go; (🛈 auskommen) manage (**mit**
with); (🛈 stimmen) be right.
h~laufen† vi sep (sein) run/
(gehen) walk there. **h~legen** vt
sep lay or put down; **sich h~legen**
lie down. **h~nehmen**† vt sep (fig)
accept
hinreichen v sep ● vt hand (dat
to) ● vi (haben) extend (**bis** to);
(ausreichen) be adequate. **h~d** a
adequate
Hinreise f journey there; (Rail)
outward journey

hinreißen† vt sep (fig) carry
away; **sich h~ lassen** get carried
away. **h~d** a ravishing
hinricht|en vt sep execute.
H~ung f execution
hinschreiben† vt sep write there;
(aufschreiben) write down
hinsehen† vi sep (haben) look
hinsetzen vt sep put down; **sich**
h~ sit down
Hinsicht f - **in dieser H~** in this
respect; **in finanzieller H~**
financially. **h~lich** prep (+ gen)
regarding
hinstellen vt sep put or set down;
park <Auto>
hinstrecken vt sep hold out; **sich**
h~ extend
hinten adv at the back; **dort h~**
back there; **nach/von h~** to the
back/from behind. **h~herum** adv
round the back; 🛈 by devious
means
hinter prep (+ dat/acc) behind;
(nach) after; **h~ jdm/etw herlaufen**
run after s.o./sth; **h~ etw** (dat)
stecken (fig) be behind sth; **h~**
etw (acc) **kommen** (fig) get to the
bottom of sth; **etw h~ sich** (acc)
bringen get sth over [and done]
with
Hinterbliebene pl (Admin)
surviving dependants; **die H~n**
the bereaved family sg
hintere|(r,s) a back, rear; **h~s**
Ende far end
hintereinander adv one behind/
(zeitlich) after the other; **dreimal**
h~ three times in succession
Hintergedanke m ulterior motive
hintergehen† vt deceive
Hinter|grund m background.
H~halt m -[e]s, -e ambush.
h~hältig a underhand
hinterher adv behind, after;
(zeitlich) afterwards
Hinter|hof m back yard. **H~kopf**
m back of the head

hinterlassen† vt leave [behind]; (Jur) leave, bequeath (dat to). **H~schaft** f -, -en (Jur) estate
hinterlegen vt deposit
Hinter|leib m (Zool) abdomen. **H~list** f deceit. **h~listig** a deceitful. **H~n** m -s,- 🔲 bottom, backside. **H~rad** nt rear or back wheel. **h~rücks** adv from behind. **h~ste(r,s)** a last; **h~ste Reihe** back row. **H~teil** nt 🔲 behind. **H~treppe** f back stairs pl
hinterziehen† vt (Admin) evade
hinüber adv over or across [there]; **h~** sein (🔲 unbrauchbar, tot) have had it. **h~gehen†** vi sep (sein) go over or across; **h~gehen über** (+ acc) cross
hinunter adv down [there]. **h~gehen†** vi sep (sein) go down. **h~schlucken** vt sep swallow
Hinweg m way there
hinweg adv away, off; **h~ über** (+ acc) over; **über eine Zeit h~** over a period. **h~kommen†** vt sep (sein) **h~kommen über** (+ acc) (fig) get over. **h~sehen†** vi sep (haben) **h~sehen über** (+ acc) see over; (fig) overlook. **h~setzen** (sich) vr sep **sich h~setzen über** (+ acc) ignore
Hinweis m -es, -e reference; (Andeutung) hint; (Anzeichen) indication; **unter H~ auf** (+ acc) with reference to. **h~en†** ● vi (haben) point (**auf** + acc to) ● vt **jdn auf etw** (acc) **h~en** point sth out to s.o.
hinwieder adv on the other hand
hin|zeigen vi sep (haben) point (**auf** + acc to). **h~ziehen†** vt sep pull; (fig: in die Länge ziehen) drag out; (verzögern) delay; **sich h~ziehen** drag on
hinzu adv in addition. **h~fügen** vt sep add. **h~kommen†** vt sep (sein) be added; (ankommen) arrive [on the scene]; join (**zu jdm** s.o.). **h~ziehen†** vt sep call in

Hiobsbotschaft f bad news sg
Hirn nt -s brain; (Culin) brains pl. **H~hautentzündung** f meningitis
Hirsch m -[e]s, -e deer; (männlich) stag; (Culin) venison
Hirse f - millet
Hirt m -en, -en, **Hirte** m -n, -n shepherd
hissen vt hoist
Histor|iker m -s,- historian. **h~isch** a historical; (bedeutend) historic
Hitz|e f - heat. **h~ig** a (fig) heated; <Person> hot-headed; (jähzornig) hot-tempered. **H~schlag** m heat-stroke
H-Milch /'ha:-/ f long-life milk
Hobby nt -s, -s hobby
Hobel m -s,- (Techn) plane; (Culin) slicer. **h~n** vt/i (haben) plane. **H~späne** mpl shavings
hoch a (attrib **hohe(r,s)**) high; <Baum, Mast> tall; <Offizier> high-ranking; <Alter> great; <Summe> large; <Strafe> heavy; **hohe Schuhe** ankle boots ● adv high; (sehr) highly; **h~ gewachsen** tall; **h~ begabt** highly gifted; **h~ gestellte Persönlichkeit** important person; **die Treppe h~** up the stairs; **sechs Mann h~** six of us/them. **H~** nt -s, -s cheer; (Meteorol) high
Hoch|achtung f high esteem. **H~achtungsvoll** adv Yours faithfully. **H~betrieb** m great activity; **in den Geschäften herrscht H~betrieb** the shops are terribly busy. **H~deutsch** nt High German. **H~druck** m high pressure. **H~ebene** f plateau. **h~fahren†** vi sep (sein) go up; (auffahren) start up; (aufbrausen) flare up. **h~gehen†** vi sep (sein) go up; (explodieren) blow up; (aufbrausen) flare up. **h~gestellt** attrib a <Zahl> superior; (fig) *h~gestellt, s. hoch. **H~glanz** m high gloss. **h~gradig** a extreme.

h~hackig a high-heeled.
h~halten† vt sep hold up; (fig)
uphold. **H~haus** nt high-rise
building. **h~heben†** vt sep lift
up; raise <Hand>. **h~kant** adv on
end. **h~kommen†** vi sep (sein)
come up; (aufstehen) get up; (fig)
get on [in the world].
H~konjunktur f boom.
h~krempeln vt sep roll up.
h~leben vi sep (haben) **h~leben**
lassen give three cheers for;
H~mut m pride, arrogance.
h~näsig a ① snooty. **H~ofen** m
blast-furnace. **h~ragen** vi sep
rise [up]; <Turm:> soar. **H~ruf** m
cheer. **H~saison** f high season.
h~schlagen† vt sep turn up
<Kragen>. **H~schule** f university;
(Musik-, Kunst-) academy.
H~sommer m midsummer.
H~spannung f high/(fig) great
tension. **h~spielen** vt sep (fig)
magnify. **H~sprung** m high jump
höchst adv extremely, most
Hochstapler m -s,- confidence
trickster
höchst|e(r,s) a highest; <Baum,
Turm> tallest; (oberste, größte)
top; **es ist h~e Zeit** it is high time.
h~ens adv at most; (es sei denn)
except perhaps.
H~geschwindigkeit f top or
maximum speed. **H~maß** nt
maximum. **h~persönlich** adv in
person. **H~preis** m top price.
H~temperatur f maximum
temperature
Hoch|verrat m high treason.
H~wasser nt high tide;
(Überschwemmung) floods pl.
H~würden m -s Reverend;
(Anrede) Father
Hochzeit f -, -en wedding.
H~skleid nt wedding dress.
H~sreise f honeymoon [trip].
H~stag m wedding day/
(Jahrestag) anniversary

Hocke f - **in der H~sitzen** squat.
h~n vi (haben) squat ● vr **sich**
h~n squat down
Hocker m -s,- stool
Höcker m -s,- bump; (Kamel-)
hump
Hockey /hɔki/ nt -s hockey
Hode f -, -n, **Hoden** m -s,- testicle
Hof m -[e]s,ːe [court]yard;
(Bauern-) farm; (Königs-) court;
(Schul-) playground; (Astr) halo
hoffen vt/i (haben) hope (auf +
acc for). **h~tlich** adv I hope, let
us hope
Hoffnung f -, -en hope. **h~slos** a
hopeless. **h~svoll** a hopeful
höflich a polite. **H~keit** f -, -en
politeness, courtesy
hohe(r,s) a s. hoch
Höhe f -, -n height; (Aviat, Geog)
altitude; (Niveau) level; (einer
Summe) size; (An-) hill
Hoheit f -, -en (Staats-)
sovereignty; (Titel) Highness.
H~sgebiet nt [sovereign]
territory. **H~szeichen** nt national
emblem
Höhe|nlinie f contour line.
H~nsonne f sun-lamp. **H~punkt**
m (fig) climax, peak. **h~r** a & adv
higher; **h~re Schule** secondary
school
hohl a hollow; (leer) empty
Höhle f -, -n cave; (Tier-) den;
(Hohlraum) cavity; (Augen-)
socket
Hohl|maß nt measure of capacity.
H~raum m cavity
Hohn m -s scorn, derision
höhnen vt deride
holen vt fetch, get; (kaufen) buy;
(nehmen) take (aus from)
Holland nt -s Holland
Holländ|er m -s,- Dutchman; **die**
H~er the Dutch pl. **H~erin** f -,
-nen Dutchwoman. **h~isch** a
Dutch
Höll|e f - hell. **h~isch** a infernal;
(schrecklich) terrible

Holunder m -s (Bot) elder
Holz nt -es,⁻er wood; (Nutz-) timber. **H~blasinstrument** nt woodwind instrument
hölzern a wooden
Holz|hammer m mallet. **h~ig** a woody. **H~kohle** f charcoal. **H~schnitt** m woodcut. **H~wolle** f wood shavings pl
Homöopathie f - homoeopathy
homosexuell a homosexual. **H~e(r)** m/f homosexual
Honig m -s honey. **H~wabe** f honeycomb
Hono|rar nt -s, -e fee. **h~rieren** vt remunerate; (fig) reward
Hopfen m -s hops pl; (Bot) hop
hopsen vi (sein) jump
horchen vi (haben) listen (auf + acc to); (heimlich) eavesdrop
hören vt hear; (an-) listen to ● vi (haben) hear; (horchen) listen; (gehorchen) obey; **h~ auf** (+ acc) listen to
Hör|er m -s,- listener; (Teleph) receiver. **H~funk** m radio. **H~gerät** nt hearing-aid
Horizon|t m -[e]s horizon. **h~tal** a horizontal
Hormon nt -s, -e hormone
Horn nt -s,⁻er horn. **H~haut** f hard skin; (Augen-) cornea
Hornisse f -, -n hornet
Horoskop nt -[e]s, -e horoscope
Horrorfilm m horror film
Hör|saal m (Univ) lecture hall. **H~spiel** nt radio play
Hort m -[e]s, -e (Schatz) hoard; (fig) refuge. **h~en** vt hoard
Hortensie /-iə/ f -, -n hydrangea
Hose f -, -n, **Hosen** pl trousers pl. **H~nrock** m culottes pl. **H~nschlitz** m fly, flies pl. **H~nträger** mpl braces
Hostess f -, -tessen hostess; (Aviat) air hostess
Hostie /'hɔstiə/ f -, -n (Relig) host
Hotel nt -s, -s hotel
hübsch a pretty; (nett) nice

Hubschrauber m -s,- helicopter
Huf m -[e]s, -e hoof. **H~eisen** nt horseshoe
Hüft|e f -, -n hip. **H~gürtel** m -s,- girdle
Hügel m -s,- hill. **h~ig** a hilly
Huhn nt -s,⁻er chicken; (Henne) hen
Hühn|chen nt -s,- chicken. **H~erauge** nt corn **H~erstall** m henhouse
Hülle f -, -n cover; (Verpackung) wrapping; (Platten-) sleeve. **h~n** vt wrap
Hülse f -, -n (Bot) pod; (Etui) case. **H~nfrüchte** fpl pulses
human a humane. **H~ität** f - humanity
Hummel f -, -n bumble-bee
Hummer m -s,- lobster
Hum|or m -s humour; **H~or haben** have a sense of humour. **h~orvoll** a humorous
humpeln vi (sein/haben) hobble
Humpen m -s,- tankard
Hund m -[e]s, -e dog; (Jagd-) hound. **H~ehütte** f kennel
hundert inv a one/a hundred. **H~** nt -s, -e hundred; **H~e** od **h~e von** hundreds of. **H~jahrfeier** f centenary. **h~prozentig** a & adv one hundred per cent. **h~ste(r,s)** a hundredth. **H~stel** nt -s,- hundredth
Hündin f -, -nen bitch
Hüne m -n, -n giant
Hunger m -s hunger; **H~ haben** be hungry. **h~n** vi (haben) starve. **H~snot** f famine
hungrig a hungry
Hupe f -, -n (Auto) horn. **h~n** vi (haben) sound one's horn
hüpfen vi (sein) skip; <Frosch:> hop; <Grashüpfer:> jump
Hürde f -, -n (Sport & fig) hurdle; (Schaf-) pen, fold
Hure f -, -n whore
hurra int hurray

husten vi (haben) cough. **H~** m -s
cough. **H~saft** m cough mixture
Hut[1] m -[e]s,¨e hat; (Pilz-) cap
Hut[2] f - auf der **H~sein** be on one's
guard (vor + dat against)
hüten vt watch over; tend
<Tiere>; (aufpassen) look after;
das Bett h~ müssen be confined
to bed; **sich h~** be on one's guard
(vor + dat against); **sich h~, etw
zu tun** take care not to do sth
Hütte f -, -n hut; (Hunde-) kennel;
(Techn) iron and steel works.
H~nkäse m cottage cheese.
H~nkunde f metallurgy
Hyäne f -, -n hyena
hydraulisch a hydraulic
Hygien|e /hy'gie:nə/ f - hygiene.
h~isch a hygienic
Hypno|se f - hypnosis. **h~tisch** a
hypnotic. **H~tiseur** /-'zø:ɐ/ m -s,
-e hypnotist. **h~tisieren** vt
hypnotize
Hypochonder /hypo'xɔndɐ/ m -s,-
hypochondriac
Hypothek f -, -en mortgage
Hypothese f -, -n hypothesis
Hys|terie f - hysteria. **h~terisch** a
hysterical

ich pron I; **ich bins** it's me. **Ich** nt
-[s], -[s] self; (Psych) ego
IC-Zug /i'tse:-/ m inter-city train
ideal a ideal. **I~** nt -s, -e ideal.
I~ismus m - idealism. **I~ist(in)** m
-en, -en (f -, -nen) idealist.
i~istisch a idealistic
Idee f -, -n idea; **fixe I~** obsession
identifizieren vt identify
identisch a identical

Ideo|logie f -, -n ideology.
i~logisch a ideological
idiomatisch a idiomatic
Idiot m -en, -en idiot. **i~isch** a
idiotic
idyllisch /i'dylɪʃ/ a idyllic
Igel m -s,- hedgehog
ihm pron (dat of er, es) [to] him;
(Ding, Tier) [to] it
ihn pron (acc of er) him; (Ding,
Tier) it. **i~en** pron (dat of sie pl)
[to] them. **I~en** pron (dat of Sie)
[to] you
ihr pron (2nd pers pl) you ● (dat
of sie sg) [to] her; (Ding, Tier)
[to] it ● poss pron her; (Ding,
Tier) its; (pl) their. **Ihr** poss pron
your. **i~e(r,s)** poss pron hers; (pl)
theirs. **I~e(r,s)** poss pron yours.
i~erseits adv for her/(pl) their
part. **I~erseits** adv on your part.
i~etwegen adv for her/(Ding,
Tier) its/(pl) their sake; (wegen)
because of her/it/them, on her/
its/their account. **I~etwegen** adv
for your sake; (wegen) because of
you, on your account. **i~ige** poss
pron der/die/das **i~ige** hers; (pl)
theirs. **I~ige** poss pron der/die/
das **I~ige** yours. **i~s** poss pron
hers; (pl) theirs. **I~s** poss pron
yours
Ikone f -, -n icon
illegal a illegal
Illus|ion f -, -en illusion. **i~orisch**
a illusory
Illustr|ation /-'tsio:n/ f -, -en
illustration. **i~ieren** vt illustrate.
I~ierte f -n, -[n] [illustrated]
magazine
Iltis m -ses, -se polecat
im prep = in dem
Imbiss m snack. **I~stube** f
snack-bar
Imit|ation /-'tsio:n/ f -, -en
imitation. **i~ieren** vt imitate
Imker m -s,- bee-keeper

Immatrikul|ation /-'tsio:n/ *f* -
(*Univ*) enrolment. **i~ieren** *vt*
(*Univ*) enrol; **sich i~ieren** enrol
immer *adv* always; **für i~** for ever;
(*endgültig*) for good; **i~ noch** still;
i~ mehr more and more; **was i~**
whatever. **i~hin** *adv* (*wenigstens*)
at least; (*trotzdem*) all the same;
(*schließlich*) after all. **i~zu** *adv* all
the time
Immobilien /-iən/ *pl* real estate
sg. **I~makler** *m* estate agent
immun *a* immune (**gegen** to)
Imperialismus *m* - imperialism
impf|en *vt* vaccinate, inoculate.
I~stoff *m* vaccine. **I~ung** *f* -, -en
vaccination, inoculation
imponieren *vi* (*haben*) impress
(**jdm** s.o.)
Impor|t *m* -[e]s, -e import. **I~teur**
/-'tø:ɐ̯/ *m* -s, -e importer. **i~tieren**
vt import
impoten|t *a* (*Med*) impotent. **I~z** *f*
- (*Med*) impotence
imprägnieren *vt* waterproof
Impressionismus *m* -
impressionism
improvisieren *vt/i* (*haben*)
improvise
imstande *pred a* able (**zu** to);
capable (**etw zu tun** of doing sth)
in *prep* (+ *dat*) in; (+ *acc*) into, in;
(*bei Bus, Zug*) on; **in der Schule** at
school; **in die Schule** to school ●
a **in sein** be in
Inbegriff *m* embodiment
indem *conj* (*während*) while;
(*dadurch*) by (+ -ing)
Inder(in) *m* -s,- (*f* -, -nen) Indian
indessen *conj* while ●*adv*
(*unterdessen*) meanwhile
Indian|er(in) *m* -s,- (*f* -, -nen)
(American) Indian. **i~isch** *a*
Indian
Indien /'ɪndiən/ *nt* -s India
indirekt *a* indirect
indisch *a* Indian
indiskret *a* indiscreet

indiskutabel *a* out of the
question
Individu|alist *m* -en, -en
individualist. **I~alität** *f* -
individuality. **i~ell** *a* individual
Indizienbeweis /ɪn'di:tsiən-/ *m*
circumstantial evidence
industrialisiert *a* industrialized.
I~ie *f* -, -n industry. **i~iell** *a*
industrial
ineinander *adv* in/into one
another
Infanterie *f* - infantry
Infektion /-'tsio:n/ *f* -, -en
infection. **I~skrankheit** *f*
infectious disease
infizieren *vt* infect; **sich i~**
become/ <*Person.*> be infected
Inflation /-'tsio:n/ *f* - inflation.
i~är *a* inflationary
infolge *prep* (+ *gen*) as a result of.
i~dessen *adv* consequently
Inform|atik *f* - information
science. **I~ation** /-'tsio:n/ *f* -, -en
information; **I~ationen**
information *sg*. **i~ieren** *vt*
inform; **sich i~ieren** find out (**über**
+ *acc* about)
infrage *adv* **etw i~ stellen** question
sth; (*ungewiss machen*) make sth
doubtful; **nicht i~ kommen** be out
of the question
infrarot *a* infra-red
Ingenieur /ɪnʒe'niø:ɐ̯/ *m* -s, -e
engineer
Ingwer *m* -s ginger
Inhaber(in) *m* -s,- (*f* -, -nen)
holder; (*Besitzer*) proprietor;
(*Scheck-*) bearer
inhaftieren *vt* take into custody
inhalieren *vt/i* (*haben*) inhale
Inhalt *m* -[e]s, -e contents *pl*;
(*Bedeutung, Gehalt*) content;
(*Geschichte*) story. **I~sangabe** *f*
summary. **I~sverzeichnis** *nt*
list/(*in Buch*) table of contents
Initiative /initsia'ti:və/ *f* -, -n
initiative

inklusive prep (+ gen) including ● adv inclusive

inkonsequent a inconsistent

inkorrekt a incorrect

Inkubationszeit /-'tsio:ns-/ f (Med) incubation period

Inland nt -[e]s home country; (Binnenland) interior. **I~sgespräch** nt inland call

inmitten prep (+ gen) in the middle of; (unter) amongst

innen adv inside; **nach i~** inwards. **I~architekt(in)** m(f) interior designer. **I~minister** m Minister of the Interior; (in UK) Home Secretary. **I~politik** f domestic policy. **I~stadt** f town centre

inner|e(r,s) a inner; (Med, Pol) internal. **I~e(s)** nt interior; (Mitte) centre; (fig: Seele) inner being. **I~eien** fpl (Culin) offal sg. **i~halb** prep (+ gen) inside; (zeitlich & fig) within; (während) during ● adv **i~halb von** within. **i~lich** a internal

innig a sincere

innovativ a innovative

Innung f -, -en guild

ins prep = **in das**

Insasse m -n, -n inmate; (im Auto) occupant; (Passagier) passenger

insbesondere adv especially

Inschrift f inscription

Insekt nt -[e]s, -en insect. **I~envertilgungsmittel** nt insecticide

Insel f -, -n island

Inser|at nt -[e]s, -e [newspaper] advertisement. **i~ieren** vt/i (haben) advertise

insge|heim adv secretly. **i~samt** adv [all] in all

insofern, insoweit adv /-'zo:-/ in this respect; **i~ als** in as much as

Insp|ektion /ɪnspɛk'tsio:n/ f -, -en inspection. **I~ektor** m -en, -en /-'to:rən/ inspector

Install|ateur /ɪnstala'tø:ʀ/ m -s, -e fitter; (Klempner) plumber. **i~ieren** vt install

instand adv **i~ halten** maintain; (pflegen) look after. **I~haltung** f -maintenance, upkeep

Instandsetzung f - repair

Instanz /-st-/ f -, -en authority

Instinkt /-st-/ m -[e]s, -e instinct. **i~iv** a instinctive

Institut /-st-/ nt -[e]s, -e institute

Instrument /-st-/ nt -[e]s, -e instrument. **I~almusik** f instrumental music

Insulin nt -s insulin

inszenier|en vt (Theat) produce. **I~ung** f -, -en production

Integr|ation /-'tsio:n/ f - integration. **i~ieren** vt integrate; **sich i~ieren** integrate

Intellekt m -[e]s intellect. **i~uell** a intellectual

intelligen|t a intelligent. **I~z** f - intelligence

Intendant m -en, -en director

Intensivstation f intensive-care unit

interaktiv a interactive

inter|essant a interesting. **I~esse** nt -s, -n interest; **I~esse haben** be interested (**an** + dat in). **I~essengruppe** f pressure group. **I~essent** m -en, -en interested party; (Käufer) prospective buyer. **i~essieren** vt interest; **sich i~essieren** be interested (**für** in)

Inter|nat nt -[e]s, -e boarding school. **i~national** a international. **I~nist** m -en, -en specialist in internal diseases. **I~pretation** /-'tsio:n/ f -, -en interpretation. **i~pretieren** vt interpret. **I~vall** nt -s, -e interval. **I~vention** /-'tsio:n/ f -, -en intervention

Internet nt -s, -s Internet; **im I~** on the Internet

Interview /'ɪntɐvju:/ *nt* **-s, -s**
interview. **i~en** /-'vju:ən/ *vt*
interview
intim *a* intimate
intoleran|t *a* intolerant. **l~z** *f* -
intolerance
intravenös *a* intravenous
Intrige *f* -, -n intrigue
introvertiert *a* introverted
Invalidenrente *f* disability
pension
Invasion *f* -, -en invasion
Inven|tar *nt* **-s, -e** furnishings and
fittings *pl*; (*Techn*) equipment;
(*Bestand*) stock; (*Liste*) inventory.
l~tur *f* -, -en stock-taking
investieren *vt* invest
inwie|fern *adv* in what way.
i~weit *adv* how far, to what
extent
Inzest *m* **-[e]s** incest
inzwischen *adv* in the meantime
Irak (der) **-[s]** Iraq. **i~isch** *a* Iraqi
Iran (der) **-[s]** Iran. **i~isch** *a*
Iranian
irdisch *a* earthly
Ire *m* **-n, -n** Irishman; **die l~n** the
Irish *pl*
irgend *adv* **wenn i~ möglich** if at
all possible. **i~ein** *indef art*
some/any; **i~ein anderer**
someone/anyone else. **i~eine(r,s)**
pron any one; (*jemand*)
someone/anyone. **i~etwas** *pron*
something; anything. **i~jemand**
pron someone; anyone. **i~wann**
pron at some time [or other]/at
any time. **i~was** *pron* 🔲
something [or other]/anything.
i~welche(r,s) *pron* any. **i~wer**
pron someone/anyone. **i~wie** *adv*
somehow [or other]. **i~wo** *adv*
somewhere/anywhere
Irin *f* -, -nen Irishwoman
irisch *a* Irish
Irland *nt* **-s** Ireland
Ironie *f* - irony
ironisch *a* ironic

irre *a* mad, crazy; (🔲 *gewaltig*)
incredible. **l~(r)** *m/f* lunatic.
i~führen *vt sep* (*fig*) mislead
irre|machen *vt sep* confuse. **i~n**
vi/r (*haben*) **[sich] i~n** be
mistaken ● *vi* (*sein*) wander.
l~nanstalt *f*, **l~nhaus** *nt* lunatic
asylum. **i~werden†** *vi sep* (*sein*)
get confused
Irrgarten *m* maze
irritieren *vt* irritate
Irr|sinn *m* madness, lunacy.
i~sinnig *a* mad; (🔲 *gewaltig*)
incredible. **l~tum** *m* **-s,-̈er**
mistake
Ischias *m & nt* - sciatica
Islam (der) **-[s]** Islam. **islamisch** *a*
Islamic
Island *nt* **-s** Iceland
Isolier|band *nt* insulating tape.
i~en *vt* isolate; (*Phys, Electr*)
insulate; (*gegen Schall*)
soundproof. **l~ung** *f* - isolation;
insulation; soundproofing
Israel /'ɪsraeːl/ *nt* **-s** Israel. **l~eli**
m **-[s], -s &** *f* **-, -[s]** Israeli.
i~elisch *a* Israeli
ist *s.* **sein; er ist** he is
Ital|ien /-iən/ *nt* **-s** Italy.
l~iener(in) *m* **-s,-** (*f* -, -nen)
Italian. **i~ienisch** *a* Italian.
l~ienisch *nt* **-[s]** (*Lang*) Italian

ja *adv*, **Ja** *nt* **-[s]** yes; **ich glaube ja** I
think so; **ja nicht!** not on any
account! **da seid ihr ja!** there you
are!
Jacht *f* -, -en yacht
Jacke *f* -, -n jacket; (*Strick-*)
cardigan

Jackett /ʒaˈkɛt/ nt -s, -s jacket
Jade m -[s] & f -jade
Jagd f -, -en hunt; (Schießen)
shoot; (Jagen) hunting; shooting;
(fig) pursuit (nach of); auf die J~
gehen go hunting/shooting.
J~gewehr nt sporting gun.
J~hund m gun-dog: (Hetzhund)
hound
jagen vt hunt; (schießen) shoot;
(verfolgen, wegjagen) chase;
(treiben) drive; sich j~ chase
each other; in die Luft j~ blow up
● vi (haben) hunt, go hunting/
shooting; (fig) chase (nach after)
● vi (sein) race, dash
Jäger m -s,- hunter
Jahr nt -[e]s, -e year. **j~elang** adv
for years. **J~eszahl** f year.
J~eszeit f season. **J~gang** m
year; (Wein) vintage. **J~hundert**
nt century
jährlich a annual, yearly
Jahr|markt m fair. **J~tausend** nt
millennium. **J~zehnt** nt -[e]s, -e
decade
Jähzorn m violent temper. **j~ig** a
hot-tempered
Jalousie /ʒaluˈziː/ f -, -n venetian
blind
Jammer m -s misery
jämmerlich a miserable; (Mitleid
erregend) pitiful
jammern vi (haben) lament ● vt
jdn j~n arouse s.o.'s pity
Jänner m -s,- (Aust) January
Januar m -s, -e January
Jap|an nt -s Japan. **J~aner(in)** m
-s,- (f -, -nen) Japanese. **j~anisch**
a Japanese. **J~anisch** nt -[s]
(Lang) Japanese
jäten vt/i (haben) weed
jaulen vi (haben) yelp
Jause f -, -n (Aust) snack
jawohl adv yes
Jazz /jats, dʒɛs/ m - jazz
je adv (jemals) ever; (jeweils)
each; (pro) per; je nach according
to; seit eh und je always ● conj je

mehr, desto besser the more the
better ● prep (+ acc) per
Jeans /dʒiːns/ pl jeans
jed|e(r,s) pron every; (j~er
Einzelne) each; (j~er Beliebige)
any; (substantivisch) everyone;
each one; anyone; ohne j~en
Grund without any reason.
j~enfalls adv in any case;
(wenigstens) at least. **j~ermann**
pron everyone. **j~erzeit** adv at
any time. **j~esmal** adv every
time
jedoch adv & conj however
jemals adv ever
jemand pron someone,
somebody; (fragend, verneint)
anyone, anybody
jen|e(r,s) pron that; (pl) those;
(substantivisch) that one; (pl)
those. **j~seits** prep (+ gen) [on]
the other side of
jetzt adv now
jiddisch a, **J~** nt -[s] Yiddish
Job /dʒɔp/ m -s, -s job. **j~ben** vi
(haben) Ⓘ work
Joch nt -[e]s, -e yoke
Jockei, Jockey /ˈdʒɔki/ m -s, -s
jockey
Jod nt -[e]s iodine
jodeln vi (haben) yodel
Joga m & nt -[s] yoga
joggen /ˈdʒɔɡən/ vi (haben/sein)
jog
Joghurt, Jogurt m & nt -[s]
yoghurt
Johannisbeere f redcurrant
Joker m -s,- (Karte) joker
Jolle f -, -n dinghy
Jongleur /ʒõˈɡløːɐ̯/ m -s, -e juggler
Jordanien /-iən/ nt -s Jordan
Journalis|mus /ʒʊrnaˈlɪsmʊs/ m -
journalism. **J~t(in)** m -en, -en (f -,
-nen) journalist
Jubel m -s rejoicing, jubilation.
j~n vi (haben) rejoice
Jubiläum nt -s,-äen jubilee;
(Jahrestag) anniversary

J

jucken vi (haben) itch; **sich j~en**
scratch; **es j~t mich** I have an
itch

Jude m -n, -n Jew. **J~ntum** nt -s
Judaism; (Juden) Jewry

Jüd|in f -, -nen Jewess. **j~isch** a
Jewish

Judo nt -[s] judo

Jugend f - youth; (junge Leute)
young people pl. **J~herberge** f
youth hostel. **J~kriminalität** f
juvenile delinquency. **j~lich** a
youthful. **J~liche(r)** m/f young
man/woman. **J~liche** pl young
people. **J~stil** m art nouveau

Jugoslaw|ien /-iən/ nt -s
Yugoslavia. **j~isch** a Yugoslav

Juli m -[s], -s July

jung a young; <Wein> new ● pron
J~ und Alt young and old. **J~e** m
-n, -n boy. **J~e(s)** nt young
animal/bird; (Katzen-) kitten;
(Bären-) cub; (Hunde-) pup; **die
J~en** the young pl

Jünger m -s,- disciple

Jung|frau f virgin; (Astr) Virgo.
J~geselle m bachelor

Jüngling m -s, -e youth

jüngst|e(r,s) a youngest; (neueste)
latest; **in j~er Zeit** recently

Juni m -[s], -s June

Jura pl law sg

Jurist|(in) m -en, -en (f -, -nen)
lawyer. **j~isch** a legal

Jury /ʒy'ri:/ f -, -s jury; (Sport)
judges pl

Justiz f - die **J~** justice

Juwel nt -s, -en & (fig) -e jewel.
J~ier m -es, -e jeweller

Jux m -es, -e ⚠ joke; **aus Jux** for
fun

Kabarett nt -s, -s & -e cabaret
Kabel nt -s,- cable. **K~fernsehen**
nt cable television
Kabeljau m -s, -e & -s cod
Kabine f -, -n cabin; (Umkleide-)
cubicle; (Telefon-) booth; (einer
K~nbahn) car. **K~nbahn** f
cable-car
Kabinett nt -s, -e (Pol) Cabinet
Kabriolett nt -s, -s convertible
Kachel f -, -n tile. **k~n** vt tile
Kadenz f -, -en (Mus) cadence
Käfer m -s,- beetle
Kaffee /'kafe:, ka'fe:/ m -s, -s
coffee. **K~kanne** f coffee-pot.
K~maschine f coffee-maker.
K~mühle f coffee-grinder
Käfig m -s, -e cage
kahl a bare; (haarlos) bald; **k~
geschoren** shaven
Kahn m -s,¨e boat; (Last-) barge
Kai m -s, -s quay
Kaiser m -s,- emperor. **K~in** f -,
-nen empress. **k~lich** a imperial.
K~reich nt empire. **K~schnitt** m
Caesarean [section]
Kajüte f -, -n (Naut) cabin
Kakao /ka'kaṷ/ m -s cocoa
Kakerlak m -s & -en, -en
cockroach
Kaktus m -, -teen /-'te:ən/ cactus
Kalb nt -[e]s,¨er calf. **K~fleisch** nt
veal
Kalender m -s,- calendar;
(Termin-) diary
Kaliber nt -s,- calibre; (Gewehr-)
bore
Kalium nt -s potassium
Kalk m -[e]s, -e lime; (Kalzium)
calcium. **k~en** vt whitewash.
K~stein m limestone

Kalkul|ation /-'tsi̯o:n/ *f* -, -en calculation. **k~ieren** *vt/i (haben)* calculate

Kalorie *f* -, -n calorie

kalt *a* cold; **mir ist k~** I am cold

Kälte *f* - cold; *(Gefühls-)* coldness; **10 Grad K~** 10 degrees below zero

Kalzium *nt* -s calcium

Kamel *nt* -s, -e camel

Kamera *f* -, -s camera

Kamerad(in) *m* -en, -en *(f* -, -nen) companion; *(Freund)* mate; *(Mil, Pol)* comrade

Kameramann *m (pl* **-männer &** **-leute)** cameraman

Kamille *f* - camomile

Kamin *m* -s, -e fireplace; *(SGer: Schornstein)* chimney

Kamm *m* -[e]s, ¨e comb; *(Berg-)* ridge; *(Zool, Wellen-)* crest

kämmen *vt* comb; **jdn/sich k~** comb s.o.'s/one's hair

Kammer *f* -, -n small room; *(Techn, Biol, Pol)* chamber. **K~musik** *f* chamber music

Kammgarn *nt (Tex)* worsted

Kampagne /kam'panjə/ *f* -, -n *(Pol, Comm)* campaign

Kampf *m* -es, ¨e fight; *(Schlacht)* battle; *(Wett-)* contest; *(fig)* struggle

kämpf|en *vi (haben)* fight; **sich k~en durch** fight one's way through. **K~er(in)** *m* -s, - *(f* -, -nen) fighter

Kampfrichter *m (Sport)* judge

Kanada *nt* -s Canada

Kanad|ier(in) /-iɐ, -iɐrn/ *m* -s, - *(f* -, -nen) Canadian. **k~isch** *a* Canadian

Kanal *m* -s, ¨e canal; *(Abfluss-)* drain, sewer; *(Radio, TV)* channel; **der K~** the [English] Channel

Kanalisation /-'tsi̯o:n/ *f* - sewerage system, drains *pl*

Kanarienvogel /-iən-/ *m* canary

Kanarisch *a* **K~e Inseln** Canaries

Kandidat(in) *m* -en, -en *(f* -, -nen) candidate

kandiert *a* candied

Känguru *nt* -s, -s kangaroo

Kaninchen *nt* -s, - rabbit

Kanister *m* -s, - canister; *(Benzin-)* can

Kännchen *nt* -s, - [small] jug; *(Kaffee-)* pot

Kanne *f* -, -n jug; *(Tee-)* pot; *(Öl-)* can; *(große Milch-)* churn

Kannibal|e *m* -n, -n cannibal. **K~ismus** *m* - cannibalism

Kanon *m* -s, -s canon; *(Lied)* round

Kanone *f* -, -n cannon, gun

kanonisieren *vt* canonize

Kantate *f* -, -n cantata

Kante *f* -, -n edge

Kanten *m* -s, - crust [of bread]

Kanter *m* -s, - canter

kantig *a* angular

Kantine *f* -, -n canteen

Kanton *m* -s, -e *(Swiss)* canton

Kanu *nt* -s, -s canoe

Kanzel *f* -, -n pulpit; *(Aviat)* cockpit

Kanzler *m* -s, - chancellor

Kap *nt* -s, -s *(Geog)* cape

Kapazität *f* -, -en capacity

Kapelle *f* -, -n chapel; *(Mus)* band

kapern *vt (Naut)* seize

kapieren *vt* 🛈 understand

Kapital *nt* -s capital. **K~ismus** *m* - capitalism. **K~ist** *m* -en, -en capitalist. **K~istisch** *a* capitalist

Kapitän *m* -s, -e captain

Kapitel *nt* -s, - chapter

Kaplan *m* -s, ¨e curate

Kappe *f* -, -n cap

Kapsel *f* -, -n capsule; *(Flaschen-)* top

kaputt *a* 🛈 broken; *(zerrissen)* torn; *(defekt)* out of order; *(ruiniert)* ruined; *(erschöpft)* worn out. **k~gehen†** *vi sep (sein)* 🛈 break; *(zerreißen)* tear; *(defekt werden)* pack up; <*Ehe, Freundschaft:*> break up.

K

k∼lachen (sich) vr sep 🖫 be in stitches. **k∼machen** vt sep 🖫 break; (zerreißen) tear; (defekt machen) put out of order; (erschöpfen) wear out; **sich k∼machen** wear oneself out

Kapuze f -, -n hood

Kapuzinerkresse f nasturtium

Karaffe f -, -n carafe; (mit Stöpsel) decanter

Karamell m -s caramel. **K∼bonbon** m & nt ≈ toffee

Karat nt -[e]s, -e carat

Karawane f -, -n caravan

Kardinal m -s, ̈e cardinal. **K∼zahl** f cardinal number

Karfreitag m Good Friday

karg a meagre; (frugal) frugal; (spärlich) sparse; (unfruchtbar) barren; (gering) scant

Karibik f - Caribbean

kariert a check[ed]; <Papier> squared; **schottisch k∼** tartan

Karik|atur f -, -en caricature; (Journ) cartoon. **k∼ieren** vt caricature

Karneval m -s, -e & -s carnival

Kärnten nt -s Carinthia

Karo nt -s, -s (Raute) diamond; (Viereck) square; (Muster) check (Kartenspiel) diamonds pl

Karosserie f -, -n bodywork

Karotte f -, -n carrot

Karpfen m -s, - carp

Karren m -s, - cart; (Hand-) barrow. **k∼** vt cart

Karriere /ka'rie̯:rə/ f -, -n career; **K∼ machen** get to the top

Karte f -, -n card; (Eintritts-, Fahr-) ticket; (Speise-) menu; (Land-) map

Kartei f -, -en card index

Karten|spiel nt card-game; (Spielkarten) pack of cards. **K∼vorverkauf** m advance booking

Kartoffel f -, -n potato. **K∼brei** m nt mashed potatoes

Karton /kar'tɔŋ/ m -s, -s cardboard; (Schachtel) carton

Karussell nt -s, -s & -e roundabout

Käse m -s, - cheese

Kaserne f -, -n barracks pl

Kasino nt -s, -s casino

Kasperle nt & m -s, - Punch. **K∼theater** nt Punch and Judy show

Kasse f -, -n till; (Registrier-) cash register; (Zahlstelle) cash desk; (im Supermarkt) check-out; (Theater-) box-office; (Geld) pool [of money], 🖫 kitty; (Kranken-) health insurance scheme; **knapp bei K∼ sein** 🖫 be short of cash. **K∼nwart** m -[e]s, -e treasurer. **K∼nzettel** m receipt

Kasserolle f -, -n saucepan

Kassette f -, -n cassette; (Film-, Farbband-) cartridge. **K∼nrekorder** /-rəkɔrdɐ/ m -s, - cassette recorder

kassier|en vt (haben) collect the money/(im Bus) the fares ●vt collect. **K∼er(in)** m -s, - (f -, -nen) cashier

Kastanie /kas'ta:niə̯/ f -, -n [horse] chestnut, 🖫 conker

Kasten m -s, ̈ box; (Brot-) bin; (Flaschen-) crate; (Brief-) letter-box; (Aust: Schrank) cupboard

kastrieren vt castrate; neuter

Katalog m -[e]s, -e catalogue

Katalysator m -s, -en /-'to:rən/ catalyst; (Auto) catalytic converter

Katapult nt -[e]s, -e catapult

Katarrh, Katarr m -s, -e catarrh

Katastrophe f -, -n catastrophe

Katechismus m - catechism

Kategorie f -, -n category

Kater m -s, - tom-cat; (🖫 Katzenjammer) hangover

Kathedrale f -, -n cathedral

Kath|olik(in) m -en, -en (f -, -nen) Catholic. **k∼olisch** a Catholic. **K∼olizismus** m - Catholicism

Kätzchen nt -s,- kitten; (Bot) catkin

Katze f -, -n cat. **K~njammer** m 🔢 hangover. **K~nsprung** m ein **K~nsprung** 🔢 a stone's throw

Kauderwelsch nt -[s] gibberish

kauen vt/i (haben) chew; bite <Nägel>

Kauf m -[e]s, Käufe purchase; **guter K~** bargain; **in K~nehmen** (fig) put up with. **k~en** vt/i (haben) buy; **k~en bei** shop at

Käufer(in) m -s,- (f -, -nen) buyer; (im Geschäft) shopper

Kauf|haus nt department store. **K~laden** m shop

käuflich a saleable; (bestechlich) corruptible; **k~ erwerben** buy

Kauf|mann m (pl -leute) businessman; (Händler) dealer; (dial) grocer. **K~preis** m purchase price

Kaugummi m chewing-gum

Kaulquappe f -, -n tadpole

kaum adv hardly

Kaution /-'tsio:n/ f -, -en surety; (Jur) bail; (Miet-) deposit

Kautschuk m -s rubber

Kauz m -es, Käuze owl

Kavalier m -s, -e gentleman

Kavallerie f - cavalry

Kaviar m -s caviare

keck a bold; cheeky

Kegel m -s,- skittle; (Geom) cone. **K~bahn** f skittle-alley. **k~n** vi (haben) play skittles

Kehl|e f -, -n throat; **aus voller K~e** at the top of one's voice. **K~kopf** m larynx. **K~kopfentzündung** f laryngitis

Kehr|e f -, -n [hairpin] bend. **k~en** vi (haben) (fegen) sweep ● vt sweep; (wenden) turn; **sich nicht k~en an** (+ acc) not care about. **K~icht** m -[e]s sweepings pl. **K~reim** m refrain. **K~seite** f (fig) drawback. **k~tmachen** vi sep (haben) turn back; (sich umdrehen) turn round

Keil m -[e]s, -e wedge

Keilriemen m fan belt

Keim m -[e]s, -e (Bot) sprout; (Med) germ. **k~en** vi (haben) germinate; (austreiben) sprout. **k~frei** a sterile

kein pron no; not a; **k~e fünf Minuten** less than five minutes. **k~e(r,s)** pron no one, nobody; (Ding) none, not one. **k~esfalls** adv on no account. **k~eswegs** adv by no means. **k~mal** adv not once. **k~s** pron none, not one

Keks m -[es], -[e] biscuit

Kelch m -[e]s, -e goblet, cup; (Relig) chalice; (Bot) calyx

Kelle f -, -n ladle; (Maurer) trowel

Keller m -s,- cellar. **K~ei** f -, -en winery. **K~wohnung** f basement flat

Kellner m -s,- waiter. **K~in** f -, -nen waitress

keltern vt press

keltisch a Celtic

Kenia nt -s Kenya

kenn|en† vt know; **k~en lernen** get to know; (treffen) meet; **sich k~en lernen** meet; (näher) get to know one another. **K~er** m -s,-, **K~erin** f -, -nen connoisseur; (Experte) expert. **k~tlich** a recognizable; **k~tlich machen** mark. **K~tnis** f -, -se knowledge; **zur K~tnis nehmen** take note of; **in K~tnis setzen** inform (von of). **K~wort** nt (pl -wörter) reference; (geheimes) password. **K~zeichen** nt distinguishing mark or feature; (Merkmal) characteristic, (Markierung) marking; (Auto) registration. **k~zeichnen** vt distinguish; (markieren) mark

kentern vi (sein) capsize

Keramik f -, -en pottery

Kerbe f -, -n notch

Kerker m -s,- dungeon; (Gefängnis) prison

Kerl m -s, -e & -s 🔢 fellow, bloke

K

Kern m -s, -e pip; (*Kirsch-*) stone; (*Nuss-*) kernel; (*Techn*) core; (*Atom-, Zell- & fig*) nucleus; (*Stadt-*) centre; (*einer Sache*) heart. **K~energie** f nuclear energy. **K~gehäuse** nt core. **k~los** a seedless. **K~physik** f nuclear physics sg

Kerze f -, -n candle. **K~nhalter** m -s,- candlestick

kess a pert

Kessel m -s,- kettle

Kette f -, -n chain; (*Hals-*) necklace. **k~n** vt chain (**an** + acc to). **K~nladen** m chain store

Ketze|r(in) m -s,- (f -, -nen) heretic. **K~rei** f - heresy

keuch|en vi (*haben*) pant. **K~husten** m whooping cough

Keule f -, -n club; (*Culin*) leg; (*Hühner-*) drumstick

keusch a chaste

Khaki nt - khaki

kichern vi (*haben*) giggle

Kiefer[1] f -, -n pine[-tree]

Kiefer[2] m -s,- jaw

Kiel m -s, -e (*Naut*) keel

Kiemen fpl gills

Kies m -es gravel. **K~el** m -s,-, **K~elstein** m pebble

Kilo nt -s, -[s] kilo. **K~gramm** nt kilogram. **K~hertz** nt kilohertz. **K~meter** m kilometre. **K~meterstand** m ≈ mileage. **K~watt** nt kilowatt

Kind nt -es, -er child; von K~ auf from childhood

Kinder|arzt m, **K~ärztin** f paediatrician. **K~bett** nt child's cot. **K~garten** m nursery school. **K~geld** nt child benefit. **K~lähmung** f polio. **k~leicht** a very easy. **k~los** a childless. **K~mädchen** nt nanny. **K~reim** m nursery rhyme. **K~spiel** nt children's game. **K~tagesstätte** f day nursery. **K~teller** m children's menu. **K~wagen** m pram. **K~zimmer** nt child's/

children's room; (*für Baby*) nursery

Kind|heit f - childhood. **k~isch** a childish. **k~lich** a childlike

kinetisch a kinetic

Kinn nt -[e]s, -e chin. **K~lade** f jaw

Kino nt -s, -s cinema

Kiosk m -[e]s, -e kiosk

Kippe f -, -n (*Müll-*) dump; (Ⓘ *Zigaretten-*) fag-end. **k~n** vt tilt; (*schütten*) tip (**in** + acc into) ● vi (*sein*) topple

Kirch|e f -, -n church. **K~enbank** f pew. **K~endiener** m verger. **K~enlied** nt hymn. **K~enschiff** nt nave. **K~hof** m churchyard. **k~lich** a church ... ● adv **k~lich getraut werden** be married in church. **K~turm** m church tower, steeple. **K~weih** f -, -en [village] fair

Kirmes f -, -sen = Kirchweih

Kirsche f -, -n cherry

Kissen nt -s,- cushion; (*Kopf-*) pillow

Kiste f -, -n crate; (*Zigarren-*) box

Kitsch m -es sentimental rubbish; (*Kunst*) kitsch

Kitt m -s [adhesive] cement; (*Fenster-*) putty

Kittel m -s,- overall, smock

Kitz nt -es, -e (*Zool*) kid

Kitz|el m -s,- tickle; (*Nerven-*) thrill. **k~eln** vt/i (*haben*) tickle. **k~lig** a ticklish

kläffen vi (*haben*) yap

Klage f -, -n lament; (*Beschwerde*) complaint; (*Jur*) action. **k~n** vi (*haben*) lament; (*sich beklagen*) complaint; (*Jur*) sue

Kläger(in) m -s,- (f -, -nen) (*Jur*) plaintiff

klamm a cold and damp; (*steif*) stiff. **K~** f -, -en (*Geog*) gorge

Klammer f -, -n (*Wäsche-*) peg; (*Büro-*) paper-clip; (*Heft-*) staple; (*Haar-*) grip; (*für Zähne*) brace;

(*Techn*) clamp; (*Typ*) bracket.
k~n (sich) *vr* cling (**an** + *acc* to)
Klang *m* **-[e]s,⁔e** sound; (*K~farbe*)
tone

Klapp|e *f* **-, -n** flap; (I *Mund*)
trap. **k~en** *vt* fold; (*hoch-*) tip up
● *vi* (*haben*) I work out
Klapper *f* **-, -n** rattle. **k~n** *vi*
(*haben*) rattle. **K~schlange** *f*
rattlesnake
klapp|rig *a* rickety; (*schwach*)
decrepit. **K~stuhl** *m* folding
chair
Klaps *m* **-es, -e** pat, smack
klar *a* clear; **sich** (*dat*) **k~ werden**
make up one's mind; (*erkennen*)
realize (**dass** that); **sich** (*dat*) **k~**
od **im K~en sein** realize (**dass**
that) ● *adv* clearly; (I *natürlich*)
of course
klären *vt* clarify; **sich k~** clear;
(*fig: sich lösen*) resolve itself
Klarheit *f* **-,-** clarity
Klarinette *f* **-, -n** clarinet
klar|machen *vt sep* make clear
(*dat* to); **sich** (*dat*) **etw k~machen**
understand sth. **k~stellen** *vt sep*
clarify
Klärung *f* **-** clarification
Klasse *f* **-, -n** class; (*Sch*) class,
form; (*Zimmer*) classroom. **k~**
inv a I super. **K~narbeit** *f*
[written] test. **K~nzimmer** *nt*
classroom
Klass|ik *f* **-** classicism; (*Epoche*)
classical period. **K~iker** *m* **-s,-**
classical author/(*Mus*) composer.
k~isch *a* classical; (*typisch*)
classic
Klatsch *m* **-[e]s** gossip. **K~base** *f*
I gossip. **k~en** *vt* slap; **Beifall**
k~en applaud ● *vi* (*haben*) make
a slapping sound; (*im Wasser*)
splash; (*tratschen*) gossip;
(*applaudieren*) clap. **k~nass** *a* I
soaking wet
klauen *vt/i* (*haben*) I steal
Klausel *f* **-, -n** clause

Klaustrophobie *f* **-**
claustrophobia
Klausur *f* **-, -en** (*Univ*) paper
Klavier *nt* **-s, -e** piano.
K~spieler(in) *m(f)* pianist
kleb|en *vt* stick/(*mit Klebstoff*)
glue (**an** + *acc* to) ● *vi* (*haben*)
stick (**an** + *dat* to). **k~rig** *a* sticky.
K~stoff *m* adhesive, glue.
K~streifen *m* adhesive tape
Klecks *m* **-es, -e** stain; (*Tinten-*)
blot; (*kleine Menge*) dab. **k~en** *vi*
(*haben*) make a mess
Klee *m* **-s** clover
Kleid *nt* **-[e]s, -er** dress; **K~er**
dresses; (*Kleidung*) clothes. **k~en**
vt dress; (*gut stehen*) suit.
K~erbügel *m* coat-hanger.
K~erbürste *f* clothes-brush.
K~erhaken *m* coat-hook.
K~erschrank *m* wardrobe.
K~sam *a* becoming. **K~ung** *f* **-**
clothes *pl*, clothing.
K~ungsstück *nt* garment
Kleie *f* **-** bran
klein *a* small, little; (*von kleinem
Wuchs*) short; **k~ schneiden** cut
up small. **von k~ auf** from
childhood. **K~arbeit** *f*
painstaking work. **K~e(r,s)** *m/f/*
nt little one. **K~geld** *nt* [small]
change. **K~handel** *m* retail trade.
K~heit *f* **-** smallness; (*Wuchs*)
short stature. **K~holz** *nt*
firewood. **K~igkeit** *f* **-, -en** trifle;
(*Mahl*) snack. **K~kind** *nt* infant.
k~laut *a* subdued. **k~lich** *a* petty
klein|schreiben† *vt sep* write
with a small [initial] letter.
K~stadt *f* small town.
k~städtisch *a* provincial
Kleister *m* **-s** paste. **k~n** *vt* paste
Klemme *f* **-, -n** [hair-]grip. **k~n** *vt*
jam; **sich** (*dat*) **den Finger k~n** get
one's finger caught ● *vi* (*haben*)
jam, stick
Klempner *m* **-s,-** plumber
Klerus (der) **-** the clergy
Klette *f* **-, -n** burr

K

kletter|n vi (sein) climb. **K~pflanze** f climber
Klettverschluss m Velcro (P) fastening
klicken vi (haben) click
Klient(in) /kli'ɛnt(m)/ m -en, -en (f -, -nen) (Jur) client
Kliff nt -[e]s, -e cliff
Klima nt -s climate. **K~anlage** f air-conditioning
klimat|isch a climatic. **k~isiert** a air-conditioned
klimpern vi (haben) jingle; **k~ auf** (+ dat) tinkle on <Klavier>; strum <Gitarre>
Klinge f -, -n blade
Klingel f -, -n bell. **k~n** vi (haben) ring; **es k~t** there's a ring at the door
klingen† vi (haben) sound
Klinik f -, -en clinic
Klinke f -, -n [door] handle
Klippe f -, -n [submerged] rock
Klips m -es, -e clip; (Ohr-) clip-on ear-ring
klirren vi (haben) rattle <Glas:> chink
Klo nt -s, -s 🆄 loo
Klon m -s, -e clone. **k~en** vt clone
klopfen vi (haben) knock; (leicht) tap; <Herz:> pound; **es k~te** there was a knock at the door
Klops m -es, -e meatball
Klosett nt -s, -s lavatory
Kloß m -es, ̈-e dumpling
Kloster nt -s, ̈- monastery; (Nonnen-) convent
klösterlich a monastic
Klotz m -es, ̈-e block
Klub m -s, -s club
Kluft f -, ̈-e cleft; (fig: Gegensatz) gulf
klug a intelligent; (schlau) clever. **K~heit** f - cleverness
Klumpen| m -s,- lump
knabbern vt/i (haben) nibble
Knabe m -n, -n boy. **k~nhaft** a boyish
Knäckebrot nt crispbread

knack|en vt/i (haben) crack. **K~s** m -es, -e crack
Knall m -[e]s, -e bang. **K~bonbon** m cracker. **k~en** vi (haben) go bang; <Peitsche:> crack ● vt (🆄 werfen) chuck; **jdm eine k~en** 🆄 clout s.o. **k~ig** a 🆄 gaudy
knapp a (gering) scant; (kurz) short; (mangelnd) scarce; (gerade ausreichend) bare; (eng) tight. **K~heit** f - scarcity
knarren vi (haben) creak
Knast m -[e]s 🆄 prison
knattern vi (haben) crackle; <Gewehr:> stutter
Knäuel m & nt -s,- ball
Knauf m -[e]s, Knäufe knob
knauserig a 🆄 stingy
knautschen vt 🆄 crumple ● vi (haben) crease
Knebel m -s,- gag. **k~n** vt gag
Knecht m -[e]s, -e farm-hand; (fig) slave
kneifen† vt pinch ● vi (haben) pinch; (🆄 sich drücken) chicken out. **K~zange** f pincers pl
Kneipe f -, -n 🆄 pub
knet|en vt knead; (formen) mould. **K~masse** f Plasticine(P)
Knick m -[e]s, -e bend; (Kniff) crease. **k~en** vt bend; (kniffen) fold; **geknickt sein** 🆄 be dejected
Knicks m -es, -e curtsy. **k~en** vi (haben) curtsy
Knie nt -s,- /'kni:ə/ knee
knien /'kni:ən/ vi (haben) kneel ● vr **sich k~** kneel [down]
Kniescheibe f kneecap
Kniff m -[e]s, -e pinch; (Falte) crease; (🆄 Trick) trick. **k~en** vt fold
knipsen vt (lochen) punch; (Phot) photograph ● vi (haben) take a photograph/photographs
Knirps m -es, -e 🆄 little chap; (P) (Schirm) telescopic umbrella
knirschen vi (haben) grate; <Schnee, Kies:> crunch

knistern vi (haben) crackle;
⟨Papier:⟩ rustle
Knitter|falte f crease. **k~frei** a
crease-resistant. **k~n** vi (haben)
crease
knobeln vi (haben) toss (um for)
Knoblauch m -s garlic
Knöchel m -s,- ankle; (Finger-)
knuckle
Knochen m -s,- bone. **K~mark** nt
bone marrow
knochig a bony
Knödel m -s,- (SGer) dumpling
Knolle f -, -n tuber
Knopf m -[e]s,ˆe button; (Griff)
knob
knöpfen vt button
Knopfloch nt buttonhole
Knorpel m -s gristle; (Anat)
cartilage
Knospe f bud
Knoten m -s,- knot; (Med) lump;
(Haar-) bun, chignon. **k~** vt
knot. **K~punkt** m junction
knüll|en vt crumple ● vi (haben)
crease. **K~er** m -s,- 🛈 sensation
knüpfen vt knot; (verbinden)
attach (an + acc to)
Knüppel m -s,- club; (Gummi-)
truncheon
knurren vi (haben) growl;
⟨Magen:⟩ rumble
knusprig a crunchy, crisp
knutschen vi (haben) 🛈 smooch
k.o. /kaˈʔoː/ a **k.o. schlagen** knock
out; **k.o. sein** 🛈 be worn out
Koalition /koaliˈtsi̯oːn/ f -, -en
coalition
Kobold m -[e]s, -e goblin, imp
Koch m -[e]s,ˆe cook; (im
Restaurant) chef. **K~buch** nt
cookery book. **k~en** vt cook;
(sieden) boil; make ⟨Kaffee, Tee⟩;
hart gekochtes Ei hard-boiled egg
● vi (haben) cook; (sieden) boil;
🛈 seethe (vor + dat with). **K~en**
nt -s cooking; (Sieden) boiling.
k~end a boiling. **K~herd** m
cooker, stove

Köchin f -, -nen [woman] cook
Koch|löffel m wooden spoon.
K~nische f kitchenette.
K~platte f hotplate. **K~topf** m
saucepan
Köder m -s,- bait
Koffein /kɔfeˈiːn/ nt -s caffeine.
k~frei a decaffeinated
Koffer m -s,- suitcase. **K~kuli** m
luggage trolley. **K~raum** m
(Auto) boot
Kognak /ˈkɔnjak/ m -s, -s brandy
Kohl m -[e]s cabbage
Kohle f -, -n coal. **K~[n]hydrat** nt
-[e]s, -e carbohydrate.
K~nbergwerk nt coal-mine,
colliery. **K~ndioxid** nt carbon
dioxide. **K~nsäure** f carbon
dioxide. **K~nstoff** m carbon
Koje f -, -n (Naut) bunk
Kokain /kokaˈiːn/ nt -s cocaine
kokett a flirtatious. **k~ieren** vi
(haben) flirt
Kokon /koˈkõː/ m -s, -s cocoon
Kokosnuss (f) coconut
Koks m -es coke
Kolben m -s,- (Gewehr-) butt;
(Mais-) cob; (Techn) piston;
(Chem) flask
Kolibri m -s, -s humming-bird
Kolik f -, -en colic
Kollaborateur /-ˈtøːɐ̯/ m -s, -e
collaborator
Kolleg nt -s, -s & -ien /-i̯ən/ (Univ)
course of lectures
Kolleg|e m -n, -n, **K~in** f -, -nen
colleague. **K~ium** nt -s, -ien staff
Kollekte f -, -n (Relig) collection.
K~tion /-ˈtsi̯oːn/ f -, -en collection
Köln nt -s Cologne.
K~ischwasser, K~isch Wasser
nt eau-de-Cologne
Kolonie f -, -n colony
Kolonne f -, -n column; (Mil)
convoy
Koloss m -es, -e giant
Koma nt -s, -s coma
Kombi m -s, -s = **K~wagen**.
K~nation /-ˈtsi̯oːn/ f -, -en

combination; (*Folgerung*) deduction; (*Kleidung*) co-ordinating outfit. **k~nieren** *vt* combine; (*fig*) reason; (*folgern*) deduce. **K~wagen** *m* estate car

Kombüse *f* -, -n (*Naut*) galley

Komet *m* -en, -en comet

Komfort /kɔm'foːɐ̯/ *m* -s comfort; (*Luxus*) luxury

Komik *f* - humour. **K~er** *m* -s,- comic, comedian

komisch *a* funny; <*Oper*> comic; (*sonderbar*) odd, funny. **k~erweise** *adv* funnily enough

Komitee *nt* -s, -s committee

Komma *nt* -s, -s & -ta comma; (*Dezimal-*) decimal point; **drei K~ fünf** three point five

Kommando *nt* -s, -s order; (*Befehlsgewalt*) command; (*Einheit*) detachment. **K~brücke** *f* bridge

kommen† *vi* (*sein*) come; (*eintreffen*) arrive; (*gelangen*) get (**nach** to); **k~ lassen** send for; **auf/hinter etw** (*acc*) **k~** think of/ find out about sth; **um/zu etw k~** lose/acquire sth; **wieder zu sich k~** come round; **wie kommt das?** why is that? **k~d** *a* coming; **k~den Montag** next Monday

Kommen|tar *m* -s, -e commentary; (*Bemerkung*) comment. **k~tieren** *vt* comment on

kommerziell *a* commercial

Kommissar *m* -s, -e commissioner; (*Polizei-*) superintendent

Kommission *f* -, -en commission; (*Gremium*) committee

Kommode *f* -, -en chest of drawers

Kommunalwahlen *fpl* local elections

Kommunion *f* -, -en [Holy] Communion

Kommun|ismus *m* - Communism. **K~ist(in)** *m* -en, -en (*f* -, -nen)

Communist. **k~istisch** *a* Communist

kommunizieren *vi* (*haben*) receive [Holy] Communion

Komödie /ko'møːdiə/ *f* -, -n comedy

Kompagnon /'kɔmpanjõː/ *m* -s, -s (*Comm*) partner

Kompanie *f* -, -n (*Mil*) company

Komparse *m* -n, -n (*Theat*) extra

Kompass *m* -es, -e compass

komplett *a* complete

Komplex *m* -es, -e complex

Komplikation /-'tsioːn/ *f* -, -en complication

Kompliment *nt* -[e]s, -e compliment

Komplize *m* -n, -n accomplice

komplizier|en *vt* complicate. **k~t** *a* complicated

Komplott *nt* -[e]s, -e plot

kompo|nieren *vt/i* (*haben*) compose. **K~nist** *m* -en, -en composer

Kompost *m* -[e]s compost

Kompott *nt* -[e]s, -e stewed fruit

Kompromiss *m* -es, -e compromise; **einen K~ schließen** compromise. **k~los** *a* uncompromising

Konden|sation /-'tsioːn/ *f* - condensation. **k~sieren** *vt* condense

Kondensmilch *f* evaporated/ (*gesüßt*) condensed milk

Kondition /-'tsioːn/ *f* - (*Sport*) fitness; **in K~** in form

Konditor *m* -s, -en /-'toːrən/ confectioner. **K~ei** *f* -, -en patisserie

Kondo|lenzbrief *m* letter of condolence. **k~lieren** *vi* (*haben*) express one's condolences

Kondom *nt* & *m* -s, -e condom

Konfekt *nt* -[e]s confectionery; (*Pralinen*) chocolates *pl*

Konfektion /-'tsioːn/ *f* - ready-to-wear clothes *pl*

Konferenz f -, -en conference; (*Besprechung*) meeting
Konfession f -, -en [religious] denomination. **k~ell** a denominational
Konfetti nt -s confetti
Konfirm|and(in) m -en, -en (f -, -nen) candidate for confirmation. **K~ation** /-'tsi̯o:n/ f -, -en (*Relig*) confirmation. **k~ieren** vt (*Relig*) confirm
Konfitüre f -, -n jam
Konflikt m -[e]s, -e conflict
Konföderation /-'tsi̯o:n/ f confederation
konfus a confused
Kongress m -es, -e congress
König m -s, -e king. **K~in** f -, -nen queen. **k~lich** a royal; (*hoheitsvoll*) regal; (*großzügig*) handsome. **K~reich** nt kingdom
Konjunktiv m -s, -e subjunctive
Konjunktur f - economic situation; (*Hoch-*) boom
konkret a concrete
Konkurren|t(in) m -en, -en (f -, -nen) competitor, rival. **K~z** f - competition; **jdm K~z machen** compete with s.o. **K~zkampf** m competition, rivalry
konkurrieren vi (*haben*) compete
Konkurs m -es, -e bankruptcy

können†
● *auxiliary verb*
····▸ (*vermögen*) be able to; (*Präsens*) can; (*Vergangenheit, Konditional*) could. **ich kann nicht schlafen** I cannot or can't sleep. **kann ich Ihnen helfen?** can I help you? **kann/könnte das explodieren?** can/could it explode? **es kann sein, dass er kommt** he may come
! Distinguish **konnte** and **könnte** (both can be 'could'): **er konnte sie nicht retten** he couldn't or was unable to rescue her. **er konnte sie**

noch retten he was able to rescue them. **er könnte sie noch retten, wenn ...** he could still rescue them if ...
····▸ (*dürfen*) can, may. **kann ich gehen?** can or may I go? **können wir mit[kommen]?** can or may we come too?
● *transitive verb*
····▸ (*beherrschen*) know <language>; be able to play <game>. **können Sie Deutsch?** do you know any German? **sie kann das [gut]** she can do that [well]. **ich kann nichts dafür** I can't help that, I'm not to blame
● *intransitive verb*
····▸ (*fähig sein*) **ich kann [heute] nicht** I can't [today]. **er kann nicht anders** there's nothing else he can do; (*es ist seine Art*) he can't help it. **er kann nicht mehr** Ⓘ he can't go on; (*nicht mehr essen*) he can't eat any more
····▸ (*irgendwohin gehen können*) be able to go; can. **ich kann nicht ins Kino** I can't go to the cinema. **er konnte endlich nach Florenz** at last he was able to go to Florence

konsequen|t a consistent; (*logisch*) logical. **K~z** f -, -en consequence
konservativ a conservative
Konserv|en fpl tinned or canned food sg. **K~endose** f tin, can. **K~ierungsmittel** nt preservative
Konsonant m -en, -en consonant
Konstitution /-'tsi̯o:n/ f -, -en constitution. **k~ell** a constitutional
konstruieren vt construct; (*entwerfen*) design
Konstruk|tion /-'tsi̯o:n/ f -, -en construction; (*Entwurf*) design. **k~tiv** a constructive
Konsul m -s, -n consul. **K~at** nt -[e]s, -e consulate

Konsum *m* -s consumption.
 K~güter *npl* consumer goods
Kontakt *m* -[e]s, -e contact.
 K~linsen *fpl* contact lenses.
 K~person *f* contact
kontern *vt/i* (*haben*) counter
Kontinent /'kɔn-, kɔnti'nɛnt/ *m*
 -[e]s, -e continent
Konto *nt* -s, -s account. **K~auszug**
 m [bank] statement. **K~nummer**
 f account number. **K~stand** *m*
 [bank] balance
Kontrabass *m* double-bass
Kontroll|abschnitt *m* counterfoil.
 K~e *f* -, -n control; (*Prüfung*)
 check. **K~eur** /-'løːɐ̯/ *m* -s, -e
 [ticket] inspector. **k~ieren** *vt*
 check; inspect <*Fahrkarten*>;
 (*beherrschen*) control
Kontroverse *f* -, -n controversy
Kontur *f* -, -en contour
konventionell *a* conventional
Konversationslexikon *nt*
 encyclopaedia
konvert|ieren *vi* (*haben*) (*Relig*)
 convert. **K~it** *m* -en, -en convert
Konzentration /-'tsi̯oːn/ *f* -, -en
 concentration. **K~slager** *nt*
 concentration camp
konzentrieren *vt* concentrate;
 sich k~ concentrate (**auf** + *acc*
 on)
Konzept *nt* -[e]s, -e [rough] draft;
 jdn aus dem K~bringen put s.o. off
 his stroke
Konzern *m* -s, -e (*Comm*) group
 [of companies]
Konzert *nt* -[e]s, -e concert;
 (*Klavier*-) concerto
Konzession *f* -, -en licence;
 (*Zugeständnis*) concession
Konzil *nt* -s, -e (*Relig*) council
Kooperation /ko°opera'tsi̯oːn/ *f*
 co-operation
Koordin|ation /ko°ɔrdina'tsi̯oːn/ *f*
 - co-ordination. **k~ieren** *vt* co-
 ordinate
Kopf *m* -[e]s, ̈e head; **ein K~ Kohl**/
 Salat a cabbage/lettuce; **aus dem**

K~ from memory; (*auswendig*)
 by heart; **auf dem K~** (*verkehrt*)
 upside down; **K~ stehen** stand on
 one's head; **sich** (*dat*) **den K~**
 waschen wash one's hair; **sich**
 (*dat*) **den K~ zerbrechen** rack
 one's brains. **K~ball** *m* header
köpfen *vt* behead; (*Fußball*) head
Kopf|ende *nt* head. **K~haut** *f*
 scalp. **K~hörer** *m* headphones *pl*.
 K~kissen *nt* pillow. **k~los** *a*
 panic-stricken. **K~rechnen** *nt*
 mental arithmetic. **K~salat** *m*
 lettuce. **K~schmerzen** *mpl*
 headache *sg*. **K~sprung** *m*
 header, dive. **K~stand** *m*
 headstand. **K~steinpflaster** *nt*
 cobble-stones *pl*. **K~tuch** *nt*
 headscarf. **k~über** *adv* head first;
 (*fig*) headlong. **K~wäsche** *f*
 shampoo. **K~weh** *nt* headache
Kopie *f* -, -n copy. **k~ren** *vt* copy
Koppel[1] *f* -, -n enclosure; (*Pferde*-)
 paddock
Koppel[2] *nt* -s,- (*Mil*) belt. **k~n** *vt*
 couple
Koralle *f* -, -n coral
Korb *m* -[e]s, ̈e basket; **jdm einen**
 K~ geben (*fig*) turn s.o. down.
 K~ball *m* [kind of] netball
Kord *m* -s (*Tex*) corduroy
Kordel *f* -, -n cord
Korinthe *f* -, -n currant
Kork *m* -s,- cork. **K~en** *m* -s,-
 cork. **K~enzieher** *m* -s,-
 corkscrew
Korn *nt* -[e]s, ̈er grain, (*Samen*-)
 seed; (*am Visier*) front sight
Körn|chen *nt* -s,- granule. **k~ig** *a*
 granular
Körper *m* -s,- body; (*Geom*) solid.
 K~bau *m* build, physique.
 k~behindert *a* physically
 disabled. **k~lich** *a* physical;
 <*Strafe*> corporal. **K~pflege** *f*
 personal hygiene. **K~schaft** *f* -,
 -en corporation, body
korrekt *a* correct. **K~or** *m* -s, -en
 /-'toːrən/ proof-reader. **K~ur** *f* -,

-en correction. **K~urabzug** m proof

Korrespon|dent(in) m -en, -en (f -, -nen) correspondent. **K~denz** f -, -en correspondence

Korridor m -s, -e corridor

korrigieren vt correct

Korrosion f - corrosion

korrup|t a corrupt. **K~tion** /-'tsio:n/ f - corruption

Korsett nt -[e]s, -e corset

koscher a kosher

Kosename m pet name

Kosmet|ik f - beauty culture. **K~ika** ntpl cosmetics. **K~ikerin** f -, -nen beautician. **k~isch** a cosmetic; <Chirurgie> plastic

kosm|isch a cosmic. **K~onaut(in)** m -en, -en (f -, -nen) cosmonaut

Kosmos m - cosmos

Kost f - food; (Ernährung) diet; (Verpflegung) board

kostbar a precious. **K~keit** f -, -en treasure

kosten[1] vt/i (haben) [von] etw k~ taste sth

kosten[2] vt cost; (brauchen) take; **wie viel kostet es?** how much is it? **K~** pl expense sg, cost sg; (Jur) costs; **auf meine K~** at my expense. **K~[vor]anschlag** m estimate. **k~los** a free ● adv free [of charge]

köstlich a delicious; (entzückend) delightful

Kostprobe f taste; (fig) sample

Kostüm nt -s, -e (Theat) costume; (Verkleidung) fancy dress; (Schneider-) suit. **k~iert** a k~iert sein be in fancy dress

Kot m -[e]s excrement

Kotelett /kɔt'lɛt/ nt -s, -s chop, cutlet. **K~en** pl sideburns

Köter m -s,- (pej) dog

Kotflügel m (Auto) wing

kotzen vi (haben) ⊠ throw up

Krabbe f -, -n crab, shrimp

krabbeln vi (sein) crawl

Krach m -[e]s,·̈e din, racket; (Knall) crash; (⊡ Streit) row; (⊡ Ruin) crash. **k~en** vi (haben) crash; **es hat gekracht** there was a bang/(⊡ Unfall) a crash ● (sein) break, crack; (auftreffen) crash (gegen into)

krächzen vi (haben) croak

Kraft f -,·̈e strength; (Gewalt) force; (Arbeits-) worker; **in/außer K~** in/no longer in force. **K~fahrer** m driver. **K~fahrzeug** nt motor vehicle.

K~fahrzeugbrief m [vehicle] registration document

kräftig a strong; (gut entwickelt) sturdy; (nahrhaft) nutritious; (heftig) hard

kraft|los a weak. **K~probe** f trial of strength. **K~stoff** m (Auto) fuel. **K~wagen** m motor car. **K~werk** nt power station

Kragen m -s,- collar

Krähe f -, -n crow

krähen vi (haben) crow

Kralle f -, -n claw

Kram m -s ⊡ things pl, ⊡ stuff; (Angelegenheiten) business. **k~en** vi (haben) rummage about (in + dat in; nach for)

Krampf m -[e]s,·̈e cramp. **K~adern** fpl varicose veins. **k~haft** a convulsive; (verbissen) desperate

Kran m -[e]s,·̈e (Techn) crane

Kranich m -s, -e (Zool) crane

krank a sick; <Knie, Herz> bad; **k~ sein/werden** be/fall ill. **K~e(r)** m/f sick man/woman, invalid; **die K~en** the sick pl

kränken vt offend, hurt

Kranken|bett nt sick-bed. **K~geld** nt sickness benefit. **K~gymnast(in)** m -en, -en (f -, -nen) physiotherapist. **K~gymnastik** f physiotherapy. **K~haus** nt hospital. **K~kasse** f health insurance scheme/(Amt) office. **K~pflege** f nursing.

K

K~saal m [hospital] ward.
K~schein m certificate of
entitlement to medical treatment.
K~schwester f nurse.
K~versicherung f health
insurance. K~wagen m
ambulance
Krankheit f -, -en illness, disease
kränklich a sickly
krank|melden vt sep jdn
k~melden report s.o. sick; sich
k~melden report sick
Kranz m -es,ˉe wreath
Krapfen m -s,- doughnut
Krater m -s,- crater
kratzen vt/i (haben) scratch.
K~er m -s,- scratch
Kraul nt -s (Sport) crawl. k~en¹ vi
(haben/sein) (Sport) do the crawl
kraulen² vt tickle; sich am Kopf k~
scratch one's head
kraus a wrinkled; <Haar> frizzy;
(verworren) muddled. K~e f -, -n
frill
kräuseln vt wrinkle; frizz <Haar-
>; gather <Stoff>; sich k~
wrinkle; (sich kringeln) curl;
<Haar:> go frizzy
Kraut nt -[e]s, Kräuter herb; (SGer)
cabbage; (Sauer-) sauerkraut
Krawall m -s, -e riot; (Lärm) row
Krawatte f -, -n [neck]tie
krea|tiv /krea'ti:f/ a creative.
K~tur f -, -en creature
Krebs m -es, -e crayfish; (Med)
cancer; (Astr) Cancer
Kredit m -s, -e credit; (Darlehen)
loan; auf K~ on credit. K~karte f
credit card
Kreide f - chalk. k~ig a chalky
kreieren /kre'i:rən/ vt create
Kreis m -es, -e circle; (Admin)
district
kreischen vt/i (haben) screech;
(schreien) shriek
Kreisel m -s,- [spinning] top
kreis|en vi (haben) circle; revolve
(um around). k~förmig a
circular. K~lauf m cycle; (Med)

circulation. K~säge f circular
saw. K~verkehr m [traffic]
roundabout
Krem f -, -s & m -s, -e cream
Krematorium nt -s, -ien
crematorium
Krempe f -, -n [hat] brim
krempeln vt turn (nach oben up)
Krepp m -s, -s & -e crêpe
Kreppapier nt crêpe paper
Kresse f -, -n cress; (Kapuziner-)
nasturtium
Kreta nt -s Crete
Kreuz nt -es, -e cross; (Kreuzung)
intersection; (Mus) sharp;
(Kartenspiel) clubs pl; (Anat)
small of the back; über K~
crosswise; das K~ schlagen cross
oneself. k~en vt cross; sich k~en
cross; <Straßen:> intersect;
<Meinungen:> clash ●vi (haben/
sein) cruise. K~fahrt f (Naut)
cruise. K~gang m cloister
kreuzig|en vt crucify. K~ung f -,
-en crucifixion
Kreuz|otter f adder, common
viper. K~ung f -, -en intersection;
(Straßen-) crossroads sg.
K~verhör nt cross-examination.
k~weise adv crosswise.
K~worträtsel nt crossword
[puzzle]. K~zug m crusade
kribbel|ig a edgy. k~n vi
(haben) tingle; (kitzeln) tickle
kriech|en† vi (sein) crawl; (fig)
grovel (vor + dat to). K~spur f
(Auto) crawler lane. K~tier nt
reptile
Krieg m -[e]s, -e war
kriegen vt get; ein Kind k~
have a baby
kriegs|beschädigt a war-
disabled. K~dienstverweigerer
m -s,- conscientious objector.
K~gefangene(r) m prisoner of
war. K~gefangenschaft f
captivity. K~gericht nt court
martial. K~list f stratagem.

K~rat m council of war. **K~recht** nt martial law

Krimi m **-s, -s** 🎬 crime story/film. **K~nalität** f - crime; (*Vorkommen*) crime rate. **K~nalpolizei** f criminal investigation department. **K~nalroman** m crime novel. **k~nell** a criminal

Krippe f -, -n manger; (*Weihnachts-*) crib; (*Kinder-*) crèche. **K~nspiel** nt Nativity play

Krise f -, -n crisis

Kristall nt -s crystal; (*geschliffen*) cut glass

Kritik f -, -en criticism; (*Rezension*) review; **unter aller K~** 🎬 abysmal

Kriti|ker m -s, - critic; (*Rezensent*) reviewer. **k~sch** a critical. **k~sieren** vt criticize; review

kritzeln vt/i (*haben*) scribble

Krokodil nt -s, -e crocodile

Krokus m -, -[se] crocus

Krone f -, -n crown; (*Baum-*) top

krönen vt crown

Kronleuchter m chandelier

Krönung f -, -en coronation; (*fig: Höhepunkt*) crowning event

Kropf m -[e]s,-e (*Zool*) crop; (*Med*) goitre

Kröte f -, -n toad

Krücke f -, -n crutch

Krug m -[e]s,-e jug; (*Bier-*) tankard

Krümel m -s,- crumb. **k~ig** a crumbly. **k~n** vt crumble ● vi (*haben*) be crumbly

krumm a crooked; (*gebogen*) curved; (*verbogen*) bent

krümmen vt bend; crook <*Finger*>; **sich k~** bend; (*sich winden*) writhe; (*vor Lachen*) double up

Krümmung f -, -en bend, curve

Krüppel m -s,- cripple

Kruste f -, -n crust; (*Schorf*) scab

Kruzifix nt -es, -e crucifix

Kub|a nt -s Cuba. **k~anisch** a Cuban

Kübel m -s,- tub; (*Eimer*) bucket; (*Techn*) skip

Küche f -, -n kitchen; (*Kochkunst*) cooking; **kalte/warme K~** cold/hot food

Kuchen m -s,- cake

Küchen|herd m cooker, stove. **K~maschine** f food processor, mixer. **K~schabe** f -, -n cockroach

Kuckuck m -s, -e cuckoo

Kufe f -, -n [sledge] runner

Kugel f -, -n ball; (*Geom*) sphere; (*Gewehr-*) bullet; (*Sport*) shot. **k~förmig** a spherical. **K~lager** nt ball-bearing. **k~n** vt/i (*haben*) roll; **sich k~n** (*vor Lachen*) fall about. **K~schreiber** m -s,-, ballpoint [pen]. **k~sicher** a bullet-proof. **K~stoßen** nt -s shot-putting

Kuh f -,-e cow

kühl a cool; (*kalt*) chilly. **K~box** f -, -en cool-box. **K~e** f - coolness; chilliness. **k~en** vt cool; refrigerate <*Lebensmittel*>; chill <*Wein*>. **K~er** m -s,-; (*Auto*) radiator. **K~erhaube** f bonnet. **K~fach** nt frozen-food compartment. **K~raum** m cold store. **K~schrank** m refrigerator. **K~truhe** f freezer. **K~wasser** nt [radiator] water

kühn a bold

Kuhstall m cowshed

Küken nt -s,- chick; (*Enten-*) duckling

Kulissen fpl (*Theat*) scenery sg; (*seitlich*) wings; **hinter den K~** (*fig*) behind the scenes

Kult m -[e]s, -e cult

kultivier|en vt cultivate. **k~t** a cultured

Kultur f -, -en culture. **K~beutel** m toiletbag. **k~ell** a cultural. **K~film** m documentary film

Kultusminister m Minister of Education and Arts

Kümmel *m* -s caraway; (*Getränk*) kümmel

Kummer *m* -s sorrow, grief; (*Sorge*) worry; (*Ärger*) trouble

kümmer|lich *a* puny; (*dürftig*) meagre; (*armselig*) wretched. **k~n** *vt* concern; **sich k~n um** look after; (*sich befassen*) concern oneself with; (*beachten*) take notice of

kummervoll *a* sorrowful

Kumpel *m* -s,- 🗓 mate

Kunde *m* -n, -n customer. **K~ndienst** *m* [after-sales] service

Kundgebung *f* -, -en (*Pol*) rally

kündig|en *vt* cancel <*Vertrag*>; give notice of withdrawal for <*Geld*>; give notice to quit <*Wohnung*>; **seine Stellung k~en** give [in one's] notice ● *vi* (*haben*) give [in one's] notice; **jdm k~en** give s.o. notice. **K~ung** *f* -, -en cancellation; notice [of withdrawal/dismissal/to quit]; (*Entlassung*) dismissal. **K~ungsfrist** *f* period of notice

Kund|in *f* -, -nen [woman] customer. **K~schaft** *f* - clientele, customers *pl*

künftig *a* future ● *adv* in future

Kunst *f* -,̈e art; (*Können*) skill. **K~faser** *f* synthetic fibre. **K~galerie** *f* art gallery. **K~geschichte** *f* history of art. **K~gewerbe** *nt* arts and crafts *pl*. **K~griff** *m* trick

Künstler *m* -s,- artist; (*Könner*) master. **K~in** *f* -, -nen [woman] artist. **k~isch** *a* artistic

künstlich *a* artificial

Kunst|stoff *m* plastic. **K~stück** *nt* trick; (*große Leistung*) feat. **k~voll** *a* artistic; (*geschickt*) skilful

kunterbunt *a* multicoloured; (*gemischt*) mixed

Kupfer *nt* -s copper

Kupon /ku'põ:/ *m* -s, -s voucher; (*Zins-*) coupon; (*Stoff-*) length

Kuppe *f* -, -n [rounded] top

Kuppel *f* -, -n dome

kupp|eln *vt* couple (**an** + *acc* to) ● *vi* (*haben*) (*Auto*) operate the clutch. **K~lung** *f* -, -en coupling; (*Auto*) clutch

Kur *f* -, -en course of treatment, cure

Kür *f* -, -en (*Sport*) free exercise; (*Eislauf*) free programme

Kurbel *f* -, -n crank. **K~welle** *f* crankshaft

Kürbis *m* -ses, -se pumpkin

Kurier *m* -s, -e courier

kurieren *vt* cure

kurios *a* curious, odd. **K~ität** *f* -, -en oddness; (*Objekt*) curiosity

Kurort *m* health resort; (*Badeort*) spa

Kurs *m* -es, -e course; (*Aktien-*) price. **K~buch** *nt* timetable

kursieren *vi* (*haben*) circulate

kursiv *a* italic ● *adv* in italics. **K~schrift** *f* italics *pl*

Kursus *m* -,**Kurse** course

Kurswagen *m* through carriage

Kurtaxe *f* visitors' tax

Kurve *f* -, -n curve; (*Straßen-*) bend

kurz *a* short; (*knapp*) brief; (*rasch*) quick; (*schroff*) curt; **k~e Hosen** shorts; **vor k~em** a short time ago; **seit k~em** lately; **den Kürzeren ziehen** get the worst of it; **k~ vor** shortly before; **sich k~ fassen** be brief; **k~ und gut** in short; **zu k~ kommen** get less than one's fair share. **k~ärmelig** *a* short-sleeved. **k~atmig** *a* **k~atmig sein** be short of breath

Kürze *f* - shortness; (*Knappheit*) brevity; **in K~** shortly. **k~n** *vt* shorten; (*verringern*) cut

kurzfristig *a* short-term ● *adv* at short notice

kürzlich *adv* recently

Kurz|meldung f newsflash.
K~schluss m short circuit.
K~schrift f shorthand. **k~sichtig**
a short-sighted. **K~sichtigkeit** f -
short-sightedness.
K~streckenrakete f short-range
missile
Kürzung f -, -en shortening;
(*Verringerung*) cut (*gen* in)
Kurz|waren fpl haberdashery sg.
K~welle f short wave
kuscheln (sich) vr snuggle (**an** +
acc up to)
Kusine f -, -n [female] cousin
Kuss m -es,⸚e kiss
küssen vt/i (*haben*) kiss; **sich k~**
kiss
Küste f -, -n coast
Küster m -s,- verger
Kutsch|e f -, -n [horse-drawn]
carriage/(*geschlossen*) coach.
K~er m -s,- coachman, driver
Kutte f -, -n (*Relig*) habit
Kutter m -s,- (*Naut*) cutter
Kuvert /ku'veːɐ̯/ nt -s, -s envelope

Labor nt -s, -s & -e laboratory.
L~ant(in) m -en, -en (f -, -nen)
laboratory assistant
Labyrinth nt -[e]s, -e maze,
labyrinth
Lache f -, -n puddle; (*Blut-*) pool
lächeln vi (*haben*) smile. **L~** nt -s
smile. **l~d** a smiling
lachen vi (*haben*) laugh. **L~** nt -s
laugh; (*Gelächter*) laughter
lächerlich a ridiculous; **sich l~**
machen make a fool of oneself.
L~keit f -, -en ridiculousness;
(*Kleinigkeit*) triviality

Lachs m -es, -e salmon
Lack m -[e]s, -e varnish; (*Japan-*)
lacquer; (*Auto*) paint. **l~en** vt
varnish. **l~ieren** vt varnish;
(*spritzen*) spray. **L~schuhe** mpl
patent-leather shoes
laden† vt load; (*Electr*) charge;
(*Jur: vor-*) summon
Laden m -s,⸚ shop; (*Fenster-*)
shutter. **L~dieb** m shop-lifter.
L~schluss m [shop] closing-
time. **L~tisch** m counter
Laderaum m (*Naut*) hold
lädieren vt damage
Ladung f -, -en load; (*Naut, Aviat*)
cargo; (*elektrische*) charge
Lage f -, -n position, situation;
(*Schicht*) layer; **nicht in der L~**
sein not be in a position (**zu** to)
Lager nt -s,- camp; (*L~haus*)
warehouse; (*Vorrat*) stock;
(*Techn*) bearing; (*Erz-, Ruhe-*)
bed; (*eines Tieres*) lair; **[nicht] auf**
L~ [not] in stock. **L~haus** nt
warehouse. **l~n** vt store; (*legen*)
lay; **sich l~n** settle. **L~raum** m
store-room. **L~ung** f - storage
Lagune f -, -n lagoon
lahm a lame. **l~en** vi (*haben*) be
lame
lähmen vt paralyse
Lähmung f -, -en paralysis
Laib m -[e]s, -e loaf
Laich m -[e]s (*Zool*) spawn
Laie m -n, -n layman; (*Theat*)
amateur. **l~nhaft** a amateurish
Laken nt -s,- sheet
Lakritze f - liquorice
lallen vt/i (*haben*) mumble;
<*Baby:*> babble
Lametta nt -s tinsel
Lamm nt -[e]s,⸚er lamb
Lampe f -, -n lamp; (*Decken-,*
Wand-) light; (*Glüh-*) bulb.
L~nfieber nt stage fright
Lampion /lam'piɔŋ/ m -s, -s
Chinese lantern
Land nt -[e]s,⸚er country; (*Fest-*)
land; (*Bundes-*) state, Land;

(*Aust*) province; **auf dem L~e** in the country; **an L~ gehen** (*Naut*) go ashore. **L~arbeiter** *m* agricultural worker. **L~ebahn** *f* runway. **l~en** *vt/i* (*sein*) land; (🔲 *gelangen*) end up

Ländereien *pl* estates

Länderspiel *nt* international

Landesverrat *m* treason

Landkarte *f* map

ländlich *a* rural

Land|schaft *f* -, -en scenery; (*Geog, Kunst*) landscape; (*Gegend*) country[side]. **l~schaftlich** *a* scenic; (*regional*) regional. **L~streicher** *m* -s,- tramp. **L~tag** *m* state/(*Aust*) provincial parliament

Landung *f* -, -en landing

Land|vermesser *m* -s,- surveyor. **L~weg** *m* country lane; **auf dem L~weg** overland. **L~wirt** *m* farmer. **L~wirtschaft** *f* agriculture; (*Hof*) farm. **l~wirtschaftlich** *a* agricultural

lang[1] *adv & prep* (+ *preceding acc or preceding* an + *dat*) along; **den od am Fluss l~** along the river

lang[2] *a* long; (*groß*) tall; **seit l~em** for a long time ● *adv* **eine Stunde l~** for an hour; **mein Leben l~** all my life. **l~ärmelig** *a* long-sleeved. **l~atmig** *a* long-winded. **l~e** *adv* a long time; <*schlafen*> late; **schon l~e** [for] a long time; (*zurückliegend*) a long time ago; **l~e nicht** not for a long time; (*bei weitem nicht*) nowhere near

Länge *f* -, -n length; (*Geog*) longitude; **der L~nach** lengthways

Läng|engrad *m* degree of longitude. **l~er** *a & adv* longer; (*längere Zeit*) [for] some time

Langeweile *f* - boredom; **L~ haben** be bored

lang|fristig *a* long-term; <*Vorhersage*> long-range. **l~jährig** *a* long-standing; <*Erfahrung*> long

länglich *a* oblong; **l~ rund** oval

längs *adv & prep* (+ *gen/dat*) along; (*der Länge nach*) lengthways

lang|sam *a* slow. **L~samkeit** *f* - slowness

längst *adv* [**schon**] **l~** for a long time; (*zurückliegend*) a long time ago; **l~ nicht** nowhere near

Lang|strecken- *pref* long-distance; (*Mil, Aviat*) long-range. **l~weilen** *vt* bore; **sich l~weilen** be bored. **l~weilig** *a* boring

Lanze *f* -, -n lance

Lappalie /la'pa:liə/ *f* -, -n trifle

Lappen *m* -s,- cloth; (*Anat*) lobe

Lärche *f* -, -n larch

Lärm *m* -s noise. **l~end** *a* noisy

Larve /'larfə/ *f* -, -n larva; (*Maske*) mask

lasch *a* listless; (*schlaff*) limp

Lasche *f* -, -n tab, flap

Laser /'le:-, 'la:zɐ/ *m* -s,- laser

lassen†
● *transitive verb*
····▸ (+ *inf: veranlassen*) **etw tun lassen** have *or* get sth done. **jdn etw tun lassen** make s.o. do sth.; get s.o. to do sth. **sich** *dat* **die Haare schneiden lassen** have *or* get one's hair cut. **jdn warten lassen** make *or* let s.o. wait; keep s.o. waiting. **jdn grüßen lassen** send one's regards to s.o. **jdn kommen/rufen lassen** send for s.o.
····▸ (+ *inf: erlauben*) let; allow; (*hineinlassen/herauslassen*) let *or* allow (**in** + *acc* into, **aus** + *dat* out of). **jdn etw tun lassen** let s.o. do sth; allow s.o. to do sth. **er ließ mich nicht ausreden** he didn't let me finish [what I was saying]
····▸ (*belassen, bleiben lassen*) leave. **jdn in Frieden lassen** leave s.o. in peace. **etw ungesagt lassen** leave sth unsaid

----> (*unterlassen*) stop. **das Rauchen lassen** stop smoking. **er kann es nicht lassen, sie zu quälen** he can't stop *or* he is forever tormenting her

----> (*überlassen*) **jdm etw lassen** let s.o. have sth

----> (*als Aufforderung*) **lass/lasst uns gehen/fahren!** let's go!

● *reflexive verb*

----> **das lässt sich machen** that can be done. **das lässt sich nicht beweisen** it can't be proved. **die Tür lässt sich leicht öffnen** the door opens easily

● *intransitive verb*

----> ⚠ **Lass mal. Ich mache das schon** Leave it. I'll do it

lässig *a* casual. **L~keit** *f* - casualness

Lasso *nt* **-s, -s** lasso

Last *f* -, **-en** load; (*Gewicht*) weight; (*fig*) burden; **L~en** charges; (*Steuern*) taxes. **L~auto** *nt* lorry. **l~en** *vi* (*haben*) weigh heavily/(*liegen*) rest (**auf** + *dat* on)

Laster¹ *m* **-s, -** ⚠ lorry

Laster² *nt* **-s, -** vice

läster|n *vt* blaspheme ● *vi* (*haben*) make disparaging remarks (**über** + *acc* about). **L~ung** *f* -, **-en** blasphemy

lästig *a* troublesome; **l~ sein/werden** be/become a nuisance

Last|kahn *m* barge. **L~[kraft]wagen** *m* lorry

Latein *nt* **-[s]** Latin. **L~amerika** *nt* Latin America. **l~isch** *a* Latin

Laterne *f* -, **-n** lantern; (*Straßen-*) street lamp. **L~npfahl** *m* lamppost

latschen *vi* (*sein*) ⚠ traipse

Latte *f* -, **-n** slat; (*Tor-, Hochsprung-*) bar

Latz *m* **-es, ̈e** bib

Lätzchen *nt* **-s, -** [baby's] bib

Latzhose *f* dungarees *pl*

Laub *nt* **-[e]s** leaves *pl*; (*L~werk*) foliage. **L~baum** *m* deciduous tree

Laube *f* -, **-n** summer-house

Laub|säge *f* fretsaw. **L~wald** *m* deciduous forest

Lauch *m* **-[e]s** leeks *pl*

Lauer *f* **auf der L~ liegen** lie in wait. **l~n** *vi* (*haben*) lurk; **l~n auf** (+ *acc*) lie in wait for

Lauf *m* **-[e]s, Läufe** run; (*Laufen*) running; (*Verlauf*) course; (*Wett-*) race; (*Sport: Durchgang*) heat; (*Gewehr-*) barrel; **im L~[e]** (+ *gen*) in the course of. **L~bahn** *f* career. **l~en†** *vi* (*sein*) run; (*zu Fuß gehen*) walk; (*gelten*) be valid; **Ski/Schlittschuh l~en** ski/skate. **l~end** *a* running; (*gegenwärtig*) current; (*regelmäßig*) regular; **auf dem L~enden sein** be up to date ● *adv* continually

Läufer *m* **-s, -** (*Person, Teppich*) runner; (*Schach*) bishop

Lauf|gitter *nt* play-pen. **L~masche** *f* ladder. **L~zettel** *m* circular

Lauge *f* -, **-n** soapy water

Laun|e *f* -, **-n** mood; (*Einfall*) whim; **guter L~e sein, gute L~e haben** be in a good mood. **l~isch** *a* moody

Laus *f* -, **Läuse** louse; (*Blatt-*) greenfly

lauschen *vi* (*haben*) listen

laut *a* loud; (*geräuschvoll*) noisy; **l~ lesen** read aloud; **l~er stellen** turn up ● *prep* (+ *gen/dat*) according to. **L~ m** **-es, -e** sound

Laute *f* -, **-n** (*Mus*) lute

lauten *vi* (*haben*) <*Text:*> run, read

läuten *vt/i* (*haben*) ring

lauter *a* pure; (*ehrlich*) honest; <*Wahrheit*> plain ● *a inv* sheer; (*nichts als*) nothing but

laut|hals *adv* at the top of one's voice, <*lachen*> out loud. **l~los** *a*

silent, *<Stille>* hushed. **L~schrift**
f phonetics *pl.* **L~sprecher** *m*
loudspeaker. **L~stärke** *f* volume

lauwarm *a* lukewarm

Lava *f* -, **-ven** lava

Lavendel *m* **-s** lavender

lavieren *vi* (*haben*) manœuvre

Lawine *f* -, **-n** avalanche

Lazarett *nt* **-[e]s, -e** military
hospital

leasen /'liːsən/ *vt* rent

Lebehoch *nt* cheer

leben *vt/i* (*haben*) live (**von** on);
leb wohl! farewell! **L~** *nt* **-s,-** life,
(*Treiben*) bustle; **am L~** alive.
l~d *a* living

lebendig *a* live; (*lebhaft*) lively;
(*anschaulich*) vivid; **l~ sein** be
alive. **L~keit** *f* - liveliness;
vividness

Lebens|abend *m* old age. **L~alter**
nt age. **l~fähig** *a* viable.
L~gefahr *f* mortal danger; **in**
L~gefahr in mortal danger;
<Patient> critically ill.
l~gefährlich *a* extremely
dangerous; *<Verletzung>* critical.
L~haltungskosten *pl* cost of
living *sg*. **l~länglich** *a* life ...
● *adv* for life. **L~lauf** *m*
curriculum vitae. **L~mittel** *ntpl*
food *sg*. **L~mittelgeschäft** *nt*
food shop. **L~mittelhändler** *m*
grocer. **L~retter** *m* rescuer; (*beim*
Schwimmen) life-guard.
L~unterhalt *m* livelihood; **seinen**
L~unterhalt verdienen earn one's
living. **L~versicherung** *f* life
assurance. **L~wandel** *m* conduct.
l~wichtig *a* vital. **L~zeit** *f* **auf**
L~zeit for life

Leber *f* -, **-n** liver. **L~fleck** *m* mole

Lebe|wesen *nt* living being.
L~wohl *nt* **-s, -s &** **-e** farewell

leb|haft *a* lively; *<Farbe>* vivid.
L~kuchen *m* gingerbread. **l~los**
a lifeless. **L~zeiten** *fpl* **zu jds**
L~zeiten in s.o.'s lifetime

leck *a* leaking. **L~** *nt* **-s, -s** leak.
l~en¹ *vi* (*haben*) leak

lecken² *vi* (*haben*) lick

lecker *a* tasty. **L~ bissen** *m*
delicacy

Leder *nt* **-s,-** leather

ledig *a* single

leer *a* empty; (*unbesetzt*) vacant;
l~ laufen (*Auto*) idle. **l~en** *vt*
empty; **sich l~en** empty. **L~lauf**
m (*Auto*) neutral. **L~ung** *f* -, **-en**
(*Post*) collection

legal *a* legal. **l~isieren** *vt* legalize.
L~ität *f* - legality

Legasthenie *f* - dyslexia
L~theniker *m* **-s,-** dyslexic

legen *vt* put; (*hin-, ver-*) lay; set
<Haare>; **sich l~** lie down;
(*nachlassen*) subside

Legende *f* -, **-n** legend

leger /le'ʒeːɐ̯/ *a* casual

Legierung *f* -, **-en** alloy

Legion *f* -, **-en** legion

Legislative *f* - legislature

legitim *a* legitimate. **L~ität** *f* -
legitimacy

Lehm *m* **-s** clay

Lehn|e *f* -, **-n** (*Rücken-*) back;
(*Arm-*) arm. **l~en** *vt* lean (**an** +
acc **against**); **sich l~en** lean (**an** +
acc **against**) ● *vi* (*haben*) be
leaning (**an** + *acc* **against**)

Lehr|buch *nt* textbook. **L~e** *f* -, **-n**
apprenticeship; (*Anschauung*)
doctrine; (*Theorie*) theory;
(*Wissenschaft*) science;
(*Erfahrung*) lesson. **l~en** *vt/i*
(*haben*) teach. **L~er** *m* **-s,-**
teacher; (*Fahr-*) instructor.
L~erin *f* -, **-nen** teacher.
L~erzimmer *nt* staff-room.
L~fach *nt* (*Sch*) subject. **L~gang**
m course. **L~kraft** *f* teacher.
L~ling *m* **-s, -e** apprentice;
(*Auszubildender*) trainee. **L~plan**
m syllabus. **l~reich** *a* instructive.
L~stelle *f* apprenticeship.
L~stuhl *m* (*Univ*) chair. **L~zeit** *f*
apprenticeship

Leib m -es, -er body; (*Bauch*) belly. **L~eserziehung** f (*Sch*) physical education. **L~gericht** nt favourite dish. **l~lich** a physical; (*blutsverwandt*) real, natural. **L~wächter** m bodyguard.

Leiche f -, -n [dead] body; corpse. **L~nbestatter** m -s,- undertaker. **L~nhalle** f mortuary. **L~nwagen** m hearse. **L~nzug** m funeral procession, cortège

Leichnam m -s, -e [dead] body

leicht a light; <*Stoff*> lightweight; (*gering*) slight; (*mühelos*) easy; **jdm l~ fallen** be easy for s.o.; **etw l~ machen** make sth easy (**dat** for); **es sich** (*dat*) **l~ machen** take the easy way out; **etw l~ nehmen** (*fig*) take sth lightly. **L~athletik** f [track and field] athletics sg. **L~gewicht** nt (*Boxen*) lightweight. **l~gläubig** a gullible. **l~hin** adv casually. **L~igkeit** f - lightness; (*Mühelosigkeit*) ease; (*L~sein*) easiness; **mit L~igkeit** with ease. **L~sinn** m carelessness; recklessness; (*Frivolität*) frivolity. **l~sinnig** a careless; (*unvorsichtig*) reckless

Leid nt -[e]s sorrow, grief; (*Böses*) harm; **es tut mir L~** I am sorry; **er tut mir L~** I feel sorry for him. **l~** a **jdn/etw l~ sein/werden** be/get tired of s.o./sth

Leide|form f passive. **l~n†** vt/i (*haben*) suffer (**an +** dat from); **jdn/etw nicht l~n können** dislike s.o./sth. **L~n** nt -s,- suffering; (*Med*) complaint; (*Krankheit*) disease. **l~nd** a suffering. **L~nschaft** f -, -en passion. **l~nschaftlich** a passionate

leider adv unfortunately; **l~ er ja/nicht** I'm afraid so/not

Leier|kasten m barrel-organ. **l~n** vt/i (*haben*) wind; (*herunter-*) drone out

Leih|e f -, -n loan. **l~en†** vt lend; **sich** (*dat*) **etw l~en** borrow sth.

L~gabe f loan. **L~gebühr** f rental; lending charge. **L~haus** nt pawnshop. **L~wagen** m hire-car. **l~weise** adv on loan

Leim m -s glue. **l~en** vt glue

Leine f -, -n rope; (*Wäsche-*) line; (*Hunde-*) lead, leash

Lein|en nt -s linen. **L~wand** f linen; (*Kunst*) canvas; (*Film-*) screen

leise a quiet; <*Stimme, Berührung*> soft; (*schwach*) faint; (*leicht*) light; **l~r stellen** turn down

Leiste f -, -n strip; (*Holz-*) batten; (*Anat*) groin

leist|en vt achieve, accomplish; **sich** (*dat*) **etw l~en** treat oneself to sth; (𝕀 *anstellen*) get up to sth; **ich kann es mir nicht l~en** I can't afford it. **L~ung** f -, -en achievement; (*Sport, Techn*) performance; (*Produktion*) output; (*Zahlung*) payment

Leit|artikel m leader, editorial. **l~en** vt run, manage; (*an-/hinführen*) lead; (*Mus, Techn, Phys*) conduct; (*lenken, schicken*) direct. **l~end** a leading; <*Posten*> executive

Leiter[1] f -, -n ladder

Leit|er[2] m -s,- director; (*Comm*) manager; (*Führer*) leader; (*Mus, Phys*) conductor. **L~erin** f -, -nen director; manageress; leader. **L~planke** f crash barrier. **L~spruch** m motto. **L~ung** f -, -en (*Führung*) direction; (*Comm*) management; (*Aufsicht*) control; (*Electr: Schnur*) lead, flex; (*Kabel*) cable; (*Telefon-*) line; (*Rohr-*) pipe; (*Haupt-*) main. **L~ungswasser** nt tap water

Lektion /-'tsio:n/ f -, -en lesson

Lektor m -s, -en /-'to:rən/, **Lektorin** f -, -nen (*Univ*) assistant lecturer; (*Verlags-*) editor. **L~üre** f -, -n reading matter

Lende f -, -n loin

L

lenk|en vt guide; (steuern) steer; (regeln) control; **jds Aufmerksamkeit auf sich** (acc) **l~en** attract s.o.'s attention. **L~rad** nt steering-wheel. **L~stange** f handlebars pl. **L~ung** f - steering
Leopard m -en, -en leopard
Lepra f - leprosy
Lerche f -, -n lark
lernen vt/i (haben) learn; (für die Schule) study
Lesb|ierin /'lɛsbjərɪn/ f -, -nen lesbian. **l~isch** a lesbian
les|en† vt/i (haben) read; (Univ) lecture ● vt pick, gather. **L~en** nt -s reading. **L~er(in)** m -s,- (f -, -nen) reader. **l~erlich** a legible. **L~ezeichen** nt bookmark
lethargisch a lethargic
Lettland nt -s Latvia
letzt|e(r,s) a last; (neueste) latest; **in l~er Zeit** recently; **l~en Endes** in the end. **l~ens** adv recently; (zuletzt) lastly. **l~ere(r,s)** a the latter; **die/der/das L~ere** the latter
Leucht|e f -, -n light. **l~en** vi (haben) shine. **l~end** a shining. **L~er** m -s,- candlestick. **L~feuer** nt beacon. **L~rakete** f flare. **L~reklame** f neon sign. **L~röhre** f fluorescent tube. **L~turm** m lighthouse
leugnen vt deny
Leukämie f - leukaemia
Leumund m -s reputation
Leute pl people; (Mil) men; (Arbeiter) workers
Leutnant m -s, -s second lieutenant
Lexikon nt -s, -ka encyclopaedia; (Wörterbuch) dictionary
Libanon (der) -s Lebanon
Libelle f -, -n dragonfly
liberal a (Pol) Liberal
Libyen nt -s Libya
Licht nt -[e]s, -er light; (Kerze) candle; **L~ machen** turn on the light. **l~** a bright; (Med) lucid; (spärlich) sparse. **L~bild** nt

[passport] photograph; (Dia) slide. **L~blick** m (fig) ray of hope. **l~en** vt thin out; **den Anker l~en** (Naut) weigh anchor; **sich l~en** become less dense; thin.
L~hupe f headlight flasher; **die L~hupe betätigen** flash one's headlights. **L~maschine** f dynamo. **L~ung** f -, -en clearing
Lid nt -[e]s, -er [eye]lid. **L~schatten** m eye-shadow
lieb a dear; (nett) nice; (artig) good; **jdn l~ haben** be fond of s.o.; (lieben) love s.o.; **es wäre mir l~er** I should prefer it (wenn if)
Liebe f -, -n love. **l~n** vt love; (mögen) like; **sich l~n** love each other; (körperlich) make love. **l~nd** a loving. **l~nswert** a lovable. **l~nswürdig** a kind. **l~nswürdigerweise** adv very kindly
lieber adv rather; (besser) better; **l~ mögen** like better; **ich trinke l~ Tee** I prefer tea
Liebes|brief m love letter. **L~dienst** m favour. **L~kummer** m heartache. **L~paar** nt [pair of] lovers pl
lieb|evoll a loving, affectionate. **L~haber** m -s,- lover; (Sammler) collector. **L~haberei** f -, -en hobby. **L~kosung** f -, -en caress. **l~lich** a lovely; (sanft) gentle; (süß) sweet. **L~ling** m -s, -e darling; (Bevorzugte) favourite. **L~lings-** pref favourite. **l~los** a loveless; **<Eltern>** uncaring; (unfreundlich) unkind. **L~schaft** f -, -en [love] affair. **l~ste(r,s)** a dearest; (bevorzugt) favourite ● adv **am l~sten** best [of all]; **jdn/ etw am l~sten mögen** like s.o./sth best [of all]. **L~ste(r)** m/f beloved; (Schatz) sweetheart
Lied nt -[e]s, -er song
liederlich a slovenly; (unordentlich) untidy. **L~keit** f - slovenliness; untidiness

Lieferant *m* -en, -en supplier
liefer|bar *a* (*Comm*) available.
  l~n *vt* supply; (*zustellen*) deliver;
  (*hervorbringen*) yield. **L~ung** *f* -,
  -en delivery; (*Sendung*)
  consignment
Liege *f* -, -n couch. l~n† *vi*
  (*haben*) lie; (*gelegen sein*) be
  situated; l~n **bleiben** remain lying
  [there]; (*im Bett*) stay in bed;
  <*Ding:*> be left; <*Schnee:*> settle;
  <*Arbeit:*> remain undone;
  (*zurückgelassen werden*) be left
  behind; l~n **lassen** leave;
  (*zurücklassen*) leave behind;
  (*nicht fortführen*) leave undone;
  l~n **an** (+ *dat*) (*fig*) be due to;
  (*abhängen*) depend on; **jdm** [**nicht**]
  l~n suit s.o.; **mir liegt viel**
  daran it is very important to me.
  L~stuhl *m* deck-chair. **L~stütz**
  m -es, -e press-up, (*Amer*) push-
  up. **L~wagen** *m* couchette car
Lift *m* -[e]s, -e & -s lift
Liga *f* -, -gen league
Likör *m* -s, -e liqueur
lila *inv a* mauve; (*dunkel*) purple
Lilie /'li:liə/ *f* -, -n lily
Liliutaner(in) *m* -s,- (*f* -, -nen)
  dwarf
Limo *f* -, -[s] 🄸, **L~nade** *f* -, -n
  fizzy drink; lemonade
Limousine /limu'zi:nə/ *f* -, -n
  saloon
lind *a* mild
Linde *f* -, -n lime tree
linder|n *vt* relieve, ease. **L~ung** *f* -
  relief
Lineal *nt* -s, -e ruler
Linie /-iə/ *f* -, -n line; (*Zweig*)
  branch; (*Bus-*) route; **L~ 4**
  number 4 [bus/tram]; **in erster L~**
  primarily. **L~nflug** *m* scheduled
  flight. **L~nrichter** *m* linesman
lin[i]iert *a* lined, ruled
Link|e *f* -n, -n left side; (*Hand*) left
  hand; (*Boxen*) left; **die L~e** (*Pol*)
  the left. l~e(r,s) *a* left; (*Pol*)
  leftwing; l~e **Masche** purl

links *adv* on the left; (*bei Stoff*) on
  the wrong side; (*verkehrt*) inside
  out; l~ **stricken** purl.
  L~händer(in) *m* -s,- (*f* -, -nen)
  lefthander. l~händig *a* & *adv*
  lefthanded
Linoleum /-leʊm/ *nt* -s lino,
  linoleum
Linse *f* -, -n lens; (*Bot*) lentil
Lippe *f* -, -n lip. **L~nstift** *m*
  lipstick
Liquid|ation /-'tsio:n/ *f* -, -en
  liquidation. l~ieren *vt* liquidate
lispeln *vt/i* (*haben*) lisp
List *f* -, -en trick, ruse
Liste *f* -, -n list
listig *a* cunning, crafty
Litanei *f* -, -en litany
Litauen *nt* -s Lithuania
Liter *m* & *nt* -s,- litre
Literatur *f* - literature
Liturgie *f* -, -n liturgy
Litze *f* -, -n braid
Lizenz *f* -, -en licence
Lob *nt* -[e]s praise
Lobby /'lɔbi/ *f* - (*Pol*) lobby
loben *vt* praise
löblich *a* praiseworthy
Lobrede *f* eulogy
Loch *nt* -[e]s,¨er hole. l~en *vt*
  punch a hole/holes in; punch
  <*Fahrkarte:*>. **L~er** *m* -s,- punch
löcherig *a* full of holes
Locke *f* -, -n curl. l~n¹ *vt* curl; **sich**
  l~n curl
locken² *vt* lure, entice; (*reizen*)
  tempt. l~d *a* tempting
Lockenwickler *m* -s,- curler;
  (*Rolle*) roller
locker *a* loose; <*Seil*> slack;
  <*Erde*> light; (*zwanglos*) casual;
  (*zu frei*) lax. l~n *vt* loosen;
  slacken <*Seil*>; break up
  <*Boden*>; relax <*Griff*>; **sich** l~n
  become loose; <*Seil:*> slacken;
  (*sich entspannen*) relax
lockig *a* curly
Lockmittel *nt* bait
Loden *m* -s (*Tex*) loden

L

Löffel m -s,- spoon; (L∼ voll) spoonful. l∼n vt spoon up

Logarithmus m -, -men logarithm

Logbuch nt (Naut) log-book

Loge /ˈloːʒə/ f -, -n lodge; (Theat) box

Log|ik f - logic. l∼isch a logical

Logo nt -s, -s logo

Lohn m -[e]s,ˀe wages pl, pay; (fig) reward. L∼empfänger m wage-earner. l∼en vi|r (haben) [sich] l∼en be worth it or worth while ● vt be worth. l∼end a worthwhile; (befriedigend) rewarding. L∼erhöhung f [pay] rise. L∼steuer f income tax

Lok f -, -s 🔲 = Lokomotive

Lokal nt -s, -e restaurant; (Trink-) bar

Lokomotiv|e f -, -n engine, locomotive. L∼führer m engine driver

London nt -s London. L∼er a London ... ● m -s,- Londoner

Lorbeer m -s, -en laurel. L∼blatt nt (Culin) bay-leaf

Lore f -, -n (Rail) truck

Los nt -es, -e lot; (Lotterie-) ticket; (Schicksal) fate

los pred a los sein be loose; jdn/etw los sein be rid of s.o./sth; was ist [mit ihm] los? what's the matter [with him]? ● adv los! go on! Achtung, fertig, los! ready, steady, go!

lösbar a soluble

losbinden† vt sep untie

Lösch|blatt nt sheet of blotting-paper. l∼en vt put out, extinguish; quench <Durst>; blot <Tinte>; (tilgen) cancel; (streichen) delete

Löschfahrzeug nt fire-engine

lose a loose

Lösegeld nt ransom

losen vt (haben) draw lots (um for)

lösen vt undo; (lockern) loosen; (entfernen) detach; (klären) solve; (auflösen) dissolve; cancel <Vertrag>; break off <Beziehung>; (kaufen) buy; sich l∼ come off; (sich trennen) detach oneself/itself; (lose werden) come undone; (sich klären) resolve itself; (sich auflösen) dissolve

los|fahren† vi sep (sein) start; <Auto:> drive off; l∼fahren auf (+ acc) head for. l∼gehen† vi sep (sein) set off; (🔲 anfangen) start; <Bombe:> go off; l∼gehen auf (+ acc) head for; (fig: angreifen) go for. l∼kommen† vi sep (sein) get away (von from). l∼lassen† vt sep let go of; (freilassen) release

löslich a soluble

los|lösen vt sep detach; sich l∼lösen become detached; (fig) break away (von from). l∼machen† vt sep detach; untie. l∼reißen† vt sep tear off; sich l∼reißen break free; (fig) tear oneself away. l∼schicken vt sep send off. l∼sprechen† vt sep absolve (von from)

Losung f -, -en (Pol) slogan; (Mil) password

Lösung f -, -en solution. L∼smittel nt solvent

loswerden† vt sep get rid of

Lot nt -[e]s, -e perpendicular; (Blei-) plumb[-bob]. l∼en vt plumb

löt|en vt solder. L∼lampe f blow-lamp

lotrecht a perpendicular

Lotse m -n, -n (Naut) pilot. l∼n vt (Naut) pilot; (fig) guide

Lotterie f -, -n lottery

Lotto nt -s, -s lotto; (Lotterie) lottery

Löw|e m -n, -n lion; (Astr) Leo. L∼enzahn m (Bot) dandelion. L∼in f -, -nen lioness

loyal /loaˈjaːl/ a loyal. L∼ität f - loyalty

Luchs m -es, -e lynx

Lücke f -, -n gap. **l~nhaft** a incomplete; <Wissen> patchy. **l~nlos** a complete; <Folge> unbroken

Luder nt -s,- ⊠ (Frau) bitch

Luft f -,⁻e air; **tief L~ holen** take a deep breath; **in die L~ gehen** explode. **L~angriff** m air raid. **L~aufnahme** f aerial photograph. **L~ballon** m balloon. **L~blase** f air bubble. **L~druck** m atmospheric pressure

lüften vt air; raise <Hut>; reveal <Geheimnis>

Luft|fahrt f aviation. **L~fahrtgesellschaft** f airline. **L~gewehr** nt airgun. **l~ig** a airy; <Kleid> light. **L~kissenfahrzeug** nt hovercraft. **L~krieg** m aerial warfare. **l~leer** a **l~leerer Raum** vacuum. **L~linie** f **100 km L~linie** 100 km as the crow flies. **L~matratze** f air-bed, inflatable mattress. **L~pirat** m hijacker. **L~post** f airmail. **L~röhre** f windpipe. **L~schiff** nt airship. **L~schlange** f [paper] streamer. **L~schutzbunker** m air-raid shelter

Lüftung f - ventilation

Luft|veränderung f change of air. **L~waffe** f air force. **L~zug** m draught

Lüg|e f -, -n lie. **l~en†** vt/i (haben) lie. **L~ner(in)** m -s,- (f -, -nen) liar. **l~nerisch** a untrue; <Person> untruthful

Luke f -, -n hatch; (Dach-) skylight

Lümmel m -s,- lout

Lump m -en, -en scoundrel. **L~en** m -s,- rag; **in L~en** in rags. **L~enpack** nt riff-raff. **L~ensammler** m rag-and-bone man. **l~ig** a mean, shabby

Lunge f -, -n lungs pl; (L~nflügel) lung. **L~nentzündung** f pneumonia

Lupe f -, -n magnifying glass

Lurch m -[e]s, -e amphibian

Lust f -,⁻e pleasure; (Verlangen) desire; (sinnliche Begierde) lust; **L~ haben** feel like (auf etw acc sth); **ich habe keine L~** I don't feel like it; (will nicht) I don't want to

lustig a jolly; (komisch) funny; **sich l~ machen über** (+ acc) make fun of

Lüstling m -s, -e lecher

lust|los a listless. **L~mörder** m sex killer. **L~spiel** nt comedy

lutsch|en vt/i (haben) suck. **L~er** m -s,- lollipop

Lüttich nt -s Liège

Luv f & nt - **nach Luv** (Naut) to windward

luxuriös a luxurious

Luxus m - luxury

Lymph|drüse /'lymf-/ f, **L~knoten** m lymph gland

lynchen /'lynçən/ vt lynch

Lyr|ik f - lyric poetry. **L~iker** m -s,- lyric poet. **l~isch** a lyrical

Machart f style

machen

● transitive verb

····▸ (herstellen, zubereiten) make <money, beds, music, exception, etc>. **aus Plastik/Holz gemacht** made of plastic/wood. **sich** (dat) **etw machen lassen** have sth made. **etw aus jdm machen** make s.o. into sth. **jdn zum Präsidenten machen** make s.o. president. **er machte sich** (dat) **viele Freunde/Feinde** he made a lot of friends/enemies. **jdm/sich** (dat) **[einen]**

Kaffee machen make [some] coffee for s.o./oneself. **ein Foto machen** take a photo
••••➤ (*verursachen*) make, cause <*difficulties*>; cause <*pain, anxiety*>. **jdm Arbeit machen** make [extra] work for s.o., cause s.o. extra work. **jdm Mut/ Hoffnung machen** give s.o. courage/hope. **das macht Hunger/Durst** this makes you hungry/thirsty. **das macht das Wetter** that's [because of] the weather
••••➤ (*ausführen, ordnen*) do <*job, repair* 🔢: *room, washing, etc.*>; take <*walk, trip, exam, course*>. **sie machte mir die Haare** 🔢 she did my hair for me. **einen Besuch [bei jdm] machen** pay [s.o.] a visit
••••➤ (*tun*) do <*nothing, everything*>. **was machst du [da]?** what are you doing? **so etwas macht man nicht** that [just] isn't done
••••➤ **was macht ...?** (*wie ist es um ... bestellt?*) how is ...? **was macht die Gesundheit/Arbeit?** how are you keeping/how is the job [getting on]?
••••➤ (*Math: ergeben*) be. **zwei mal zwei macht vier** two times two is four. **das macht 6 Euro [zusammen]** that's *or* that comes to six euros [altogether]
••••➤ (*schaden*) **was macht das schon?** what does it matter? **[das] macht nichts!** 🔢 it doesn't matter
••••➤ **machs gut!** 🔢 look after yourself!; (*auf Wiedersehen*) so long!
● *reflexive verb*
••••➤ **sich machen** 🔢 do well
••••➤ **sich an etw** (*acc*) **machen** get down to sth. **sie machte sich an die Arbeit** she got down to work
● *intransitive verb*

••••➤ **das macht hungrig/durstig** it makes you hungry/thirsty. **das macht dick** it's fattening

Macht *f* -,-̈e power. **M∼haber** *m* -s,- ruler
mächtig *a* powerful ●*adv* 🔢 terribly
machtlos *a* powerless
Mädchen *nt* -s,- girl; (*Dienst-*) maid. **m∼haft** *a* girlish. **M∼name** *m* girl's name; (*vor der Ehe*) maiden name
Made *f* -, -n maggot
madig *a* maggoty
Madonna *f* -, -nen madonna
Magazin *nt* -s, -e magazine; (*Lager*) warehouse; store-room
Magd *f* -,-̈e maid
Magen *m* -s,-̈ stomach. **M∼verstimmung** *f* stomach upset
mager *a* thin; <*Fleisch*> lean; <*Boden*> poor; (*dürftig*) meagre. **M∼keit** *f* - thinness; leanness. **M∼sucht** *f* anorexia
Magie *f* - magic
Magier /'ma:giɐ/ *m* -s,- magician. **m∼isch** *a* magic
Magistrat *m* -s, -e city council
Magnet *m* -en & -[e]s, -e magnet. **m∼isch** *a* magnetic
Mahagoni *nt* -s mahogany
Mäh|drescher *m* -s,- combine harvester. **m∼en** *vt/i* (*haben*) mow
Mahl *nt* -[e]s,-̈er & -e meal
mahlen† *vt* grind
Mahlzeit *f* meal; **M∼!** enjoy your meal!
Mähne *f* -, -n mane
mahn|en *vt/i* (*haben*) remind (**wegen** about); (*ermahnen*) admonish; (*auffordern*) urge (**zu** to). **M∼ung** *f* -, -en reminder; admonition
Mai *m* -[e]s, -e May; **der Erste Mai** May Day. **M∼glöckchen** *nt* -s,- lily of the valley
Mailand *nt* -s Milan

Mais m -es maize; (*Culin*) sweet corn

Majestät f -, -en majesty. **m~isch** a majestic

Major m -s, -e major

Majoran m -s marjoram

makaber a macabre

Makel m -s,- blemish; (*Defekt*) flaw

Makkaroni pl macaroni sg

Makler m -s,- (*Comm*) broker

Makrele f -, -n mackerel

Makrone f -, -n macaroon

mal adv (*Math*) times; (*bei Maßen*) by; (🔲 *einmal*) once; (*eines Tages*) one day; **nicht mal** not even

Mal nt -[e]s, -e time; **zum ersten/ letzten Mal** for the first/last time; **ein für alle Mal** once and for all; **jedes Mal** every time; **jedes Mal, wenn** whenever

Mal|buch nt colouring book. **m~en** vt/i (*haben*) paint. **M~er** m -s,- painter. **M~erei** f -, -en painting. **M~erin** f -, -nen painter. **m~erisch** a picturesque

Mallorca /maˈlɔrka, -ˈjɔrka/ nt -s Majorca

malnehmen† vt sep multiply (**mit** by)

Malz nt -es malt

Mama /ˈmama, maˈmaː/ f -s, -s mummy

Mammut nt -s, -e & -s mammoth

mampfen vt 🔲 munch

man pron one, you; (*die Leute*) people, they; **man sagt** they say, it is said

manch|e(r,s) pron many a; **[so] m~es Mal** many a time; **m~e Leute** some people
● (*substantivisch*) **m~er/m~e** many a man/woman; **m~e** pl some; (*Leute*) some people; (*viele*) many [people]; **m~es** some things; (*vieles*) many things. **m~erlei** inv a various
● pron various things

manchmal adv sometimes

Mandant(in) m -en, -en (f -, -nen) (*Jur*) client

Mandarine f -, -n mandarin

Mandat nt -[e]s, -e mandate; (*Jur*) brief; (*Pol*) seat

Mandel f -, -n almond; (*Anat*) tonsil. **M~entzündung** f tonsillitis

Manege /maˈneːʒə/ f -, -n ring; (*Reit-*) arena

Mangel¹ m -s,- lack; (*Knappheit*) shortage; (*Med*) deficiency; (*Fehler*) defect

Mangel² f -, -n mangle

mangel|haft a faulty, defective; (*Sch*) unsatisfactory. **m~n¹** vi (*haben*) **es m~t an** (+ *dat*) there is a lack/(*Knappheit*) shortage of

mangeln² vt put through the mangle

Manie f -, -n mania

Manier f -, -en manner; **M~en** manners. **m~lich** a well-mannered ● adv properly

Manifest nt -[e]s, -e manifesto

Maniküre f -, -n manicure; (*Person*) manicurist. **M~n** vt manicure

Manko nt -s, -s disadvantage; (*Fehlbetrag*) deficit

Mann m -[e]s,-er man; (*Ehe-*) husband

Männchen nt -s,- little man; (*Zool*) male

Mannequin /ˈmanəkɛ̃/ nt -s, -s model

männlich a male; (*Gram & fig*) masculine; (*mannhaft*) manly; <*Frau*> mannish. **M~keit** f - masculinity; (*fig*) manhood

Mannschaft f -, -en team; (*Naut*) crew

Manöv|er nt -s,- manœuvre; (*Winkelzug*) trick. **m~rieren** vt/i (*haben*) manœuvre

Mansarde f -, -n attic room; (*Wohnung*) attic flat

Manschette f -, -n cuff. **M~nknopf** m cuff-link

M

Mantel m -s,⸚ coat; overcoat
Manuskript nt -[e]s, -e manuscript
Mappe f - folder; (Akten-) briefcase; (Schul-) bag
Märchen nt -s,- fairy-tales
Margarine f - margarine
Marienkäfer /maˈriːən-/ m ladybird
Marihuana nt -s marijuana
Marine f marine; (Kriegs-) navy. m~blau a navy [blue]
marinieren vt marinade
Marionette f -, -n puppet, marionette
Mark¹ f -,- (alte Währung) mark; **drei M~** three marks
Mark² nt -[e]s (Knochen-) marrow (Bot)pith; (Frucht-) pulp
markant a striking
Marke f -, -n token; (rund) disc; (Erkennungs-) tag; (Brief-) stamp; (Lebensmittel-) coupon; (Spiel-) counter; (Markierung) mark; (Fabrikat) make; (Tabak-) brand. M~nartikel m branded article
markieren vt mark; (🖪 vortäuschen) fake
Markise f -, -n awning
Markstück nt one-mark piece
Markt m -[e]s,⸚e market; (M~-platz) market-place. M~forschung f market research
Marmelade f -, -n jam; (Orangen-) marmalade
Marmor m -s marble
Marokko nt -s Morocco
Marone f -, -n [sweet] chestnut
Marsch m -[e]s,⸚e march. m~ int (Mil) march!
Marschall m -s,⸚e marshal
marschieren vi (sein) march
Marter f -, -n torture. m~n vt torture
Märtyrer(in) m -s,- (f -, -nen) martyr
Marxismus m - Marxism
März m -, -e March
Marzipan nt -s marzipan

Masche f -, -n stitch; (im Netz) mesh; (🖪 Trick) dodge. M~ndraht m wire netting
Maschin|e f -, -n machine; (Flugzeug) plane; (Schreib-) typewriter; M~e schreiben type. m~egeschrieben a typewritten, typed. m~ell a machine … ● adv by machine. M~enbau m mechanical engineering. M~engewehr nt machine-gun. M~ist m -en, -en machinist; (Naut) engineer
Masern pl measles sg
Maserung f -, -en [wood] grain
Maske f -, -n mask; (Theat) make-up
maskieren vt mask; sich m~ dress up (als as)
maskulin a masculine
Masochist m -en, -en masochist
Maß¹ nt -es, -e measure; (Abmessung) measurement; (Grad) degree; (Mäßigung) moderation; in hohem Maße to a high degree
Maß² f -,- (SGer) litre [of beer]
Massage /maˈsaːʒə/ f -, -n massage
Massaker nt -s,- massacre
Maßband nt (pl -bänder) tape-measure
Masse f -, -n mass; (Culin) mixture; (Menschen-) crowd; eine M~ Arbeit 🖪 masses of work. m~nhaft adv in huge quantities. M~nproduktion f mass production. m~nweise adv in huge numbers
Masseu|r /maˈsøːɐ̯/ m -s, -e masseur. M~se /-ˈsøːzə/ f -, -n masseuse
maß|gebend a authoritative; (einflussreich) influential. m~geblich a decisive. m~geschneidert a made-to-measure
massieren vt massage
massig a massive

mäßig a moderate; (*mittelmäßig*) indifferent. **m~en** vt moderate; **sich m~en** moderate; (*sich beherrschen*) restrain oneself. **M~ung** f - moderation

massiv a solid; (*stark*) heavy

Maß|krug m beer mug. **m~los** a excessive; (*grenzenlos*) boundless; (*äußerst*) extreme. **M~nahme** f -, -n measure

Maßstab m scale; (*Norm & fig*) standard. **m~sgerecht, m~sgetreu** a scale … ● adv to scale

Mast¹ m -[e]s, -en pole; (*Überland-*) pylon; (*Naut*) mast

Mast² f - fattening

mästen vt fatten

masturbieren vi (*haben*) masturbate

Material nt -s, -ien /-iən/ material; (*coll*) materials pl. **M~ismus** m - materialism. **m~istisch** a materialistic

Mathe f - 🆒 maths sg

Mathe|matik f - mathematics sg. **M~matiker** m -s,- mathematician. **m~matisch** a mathematical

Matinee f -, -n (*Theat*) morning performance

Matratze f -, -n mattress

Matrose m -n, -n sailor

Matsch m -[e]s mud; (*Schnee-*) slush

matt a weak; (*gedämpft*) dim; (*glanzlos*) dull; <*Politur, Farbe*> matt. **M~** nt -s (*Schach*) mate

Matte f -, -n mat

Mattglas nt frosted glass

Matura f - (*Aust*) ≈ A levels pl

Mauer f -, -n wall. **M~werk** nt masonry

Maul nt -[e]s, Mäuler (*Zool*) mouth; **halts M~!** 🆒 shut up! **M~- und Klauenseuche** f foot-and-mouth disease. **M~korb** m muzzle. **M~tier** nt mule. **M~wurf** m mole

Maurer m -s,- bricklayer

Maus f -, Mäuse mouse

Maut f -, -en (*Aust*) toll. **M~straße** f toll road

maximal a maximum

Maximum nt -s, -ma maximum

Mayonnaise /majo'nɛ:zə/ f -, -n mayonnaise

Mechan|ik /me'ça:nɪk/ f - mechanics sg; (*Mechanismus*) mechanism. **M~iker** m -s,- mechanic. **m~isch** a mechanical. **m~isieren** vt mechanize. **M~ismus** m -, -men mechanism

meckern vi (*haben*) bleat; (🆒 *nörgeln*) grumble

Medaill|e /me'daljə/ f -, -n medal. **M~on** /-'jõ:/ nt -s, -s medallion; (*Schmuck*) locket

Medikament nt -[e]s, -e medicine

Medit|ation /-'tsio:n/ f -, -en meditation. **m~ieren** vi (*haben*) meditate

Medium nt -s, -ien medium; **die Medien** the media

Medizin f -, -en medicine. **M~er** m -s,- doctor; (*Student*) medical student. **m~isch** a medical; (*heilkräftig*) medicinal

Meer nt -[e]s, -e sea. **M~enge** f strait. **M~esspiegel** m sea-level. **M~jungfrau** f mermaid. **M~rettich** m horseradish. **M~schweinchen** nt -s,- guinea-pig

Mehl nt -[e]s flour. **M~schwitze** f (*Culin*) roux

mehr pron & adv more; **nicht m~** no more; (*zeitlich*) no longer; **nichts m~** no more; (*nichtsweiter*) nothing else; **nie m~** never again. **m~eres** pron several things pl. **m~fach** a multiple; (*mehrmalig*) repeated ● adv several times. **M~fahrtenkarte** f book of tickets. **M~heit** f -, -en majority. **m~malig** a repeated. **m~mals** adv several times. **m~sprachig** a multilingual. **M~wertsteuer** f value-added tax, VAT. **M~zahl** f

majority; (*Gram*) plural.
M~zweck- *pref* multi-purpose
meiden† *vt* avoid, shun
Meile *f* -, -n mile. m~nweit *adv*
[for] miles
mein *poss pron* my. m~e(r,s)
poss pron mine; **die M~en** *od*
m~en *pl* my family *sg*
Meineid *m* perjury
meinen *vt* mean; (*glauben*) think;
(*sagen*) say
mein|erseits *adv* for my part.
m~etwegen *adv* for my sake;
(*wegen mir*) because of me; (**!**
von mir aus) as far as I'm
concerned
Meinung *f* -, -en opinion; **jdm die
M~ sagen** give s.o. a piece of
one's mind. **M~sumfrage** *f*
opinion poll
Meise *f* -, -n (*Zool*) tit
Meißel *m* -s,- chisel. m~n *vt/i*
(*haben*) chisel
meist *adv* mostly; (*gewöhnlich*)
usually. m~e *a* der/die/das m~e
most; **die m~en Leute** most
people; **am m~en** [the] most
● *pron* **das m~e** most [of it]; **die
m~en** most. m~ens *adv* mostly;
(*gewöhnlich*) usually
Meister *m* -s,- master craftsman;
(*Könner*) master; (*Sport*)
champion. m~n *vt* master.
M~schaft *f* -, -en mastery; (*Sport*)
championship
meld|en *vt* report; (*anmelden*)
register; (*ankündigen*) announce;
sich m~en report (**bei** to); (*zum
Militär*) enlist; (*freiwillig*)
volunteer; (*Teleph*) answer; (*Sch*)
put up one's hand; (*von sich
hören lassen*) get in touch (**bei**
with). **M~ung** *f* -, -en report;
(*Anmeldung*) registration
melken† *vt* milk
Melodie *f* -, -n tune, melody
melodisch *a* melodic; melodious
Melone *f* -, -n melon

Memoiren /me'moa:rən/ *pl*
memoirs
Menge *f* -, -n amount, quantity;
(*Menschen-*) crowd; (*Math*) set;
eine M~ Geld a lot of money.
m~n *vt* mix
Mensa *f* -, -sen (*Univ*) refectory
Mensch *m* -en, -en human being;
der M~ man; **die M~en** people;
jeder/kein M~ everybody/nobody.
M~enaffe *m* ape. m~enfeindlich
a antisocial. **M~enfresser** *m* -s,-
cannibal; (*Zool*) man-eater.
m~enfreundlich *a* philanthropic.
M~enleben *nt* human life;
(*Lebenszeit*) lifetime. m~enleer *a*
deserted. **M~enmenge** *f* crowd.
M~enraub *m* kidnapping.
M~enrechte *ntpl* human rights.
m~enscheu *a* unsociable.
m~enwürdig *a* humane. **M~heit**
f - **die M~heit** mankind,
humanity. m~lich *a* human;
(*human*) humane. **M~lichkeit** *f* -
humanity
Menstru|ation /-'tsio:n/ *f* -
menstruation. m~ieren *vi*
(*haben*) menstruate
Mentalität *f* -, -en mentality
Menü *nt* -s, -s menu; (*festes M~*)
set meal
Meridian *m* -s, -e meridian
merk|bar *a* noticeable. **M~blatt** *nt*
[explanatory] leaflet. m~en *vt*
notice; **sich** (*dat*) **etw m~en**
remember sth. **M~mal** *nt* feature
merkwürdig *a* odd, strange
Messe[1] *f* -, -n (*Relig*) mass;
(*Comm*) [trade] fair
Messe[2] *f* -, -n (*Mil*) mess
messen† *vt/i* (*haben*) measure;
(*ansehen*) look at; **[bei jdm] Fieber
m~** take s.o.'s temperature; **sich
mit jdm m~ können** be a match
for s.o.
Messer *nt* -s,- knife
Messias *m* - Messiah
Messing *nt* -s brass
Messung *f* -, -en measurement

Metabolismus m - metabolism
Metall nt -s, -e metal. **m~isch** a metallic
Metamorphose f -, -n metamorphosis
metaphorisch a metaphorical
Meteor m -s, -e meteor. **M~ologie** f - meteorology
Meter m & nt -s,- metre. **M~maß** nt tape-measure
Method|e f -, -n method. **m~isch** a methodical
Metropole f -, -n metropolis
Metzger m -s,- butcher. **M~ei** f -, -en butcher's shop
Meuterei f -, -en mutiny
meutern vi (haben) mutiny; (🆒 schimpfen) grumble
Mexikan|er(in) m -s,- (f -, -nen) Mexican. **m~isch** a Mexican
Mexiko nt -s Mexico
miauen vi (haben) mew, miaow
mich pron (acc of **ich**) me; (refl) myself
Mieder nt -s,- bodice
Miene f -, -n expression
mies a 🆒 lousy
Miet|e f -, -n rent; (Mietgebühr) hire charge; **zur M~e wohnen** live in rented accommodation. **m~en** vt rent <Haus, Zimmer>; hire <Auto, Boot>. **M~er(in)** m -s,- (f -, -nen) tenant. **m~frei** a & adv rent-free. **M~shaus** nt block of rented flats. **M~vertrag** m lease. **M~wagen** m hire-car. **M~wohnung** f rented flat; (zu vermieten) flat to let
Migräne f -, -n migraine
Mikro|chip m microchip. **M~computer** m microcomputer. **M~film** m microfilm
Mikro|fon, M~phon nt -s, -e microphone. **M~skop** nt -s, -e microscope. **m~skopisch** a microscopic
Mikrowelle f microwave. **M~nherd** m microwave oven
Milbe f -, -n mite

Milch f - milk. **M~glas** nt opal glass. **m~ig** a milky. **M~mann** m (pl -männer) milkman. **M~straße** f Milky Way
mild a mild; (nachsichtig) lenient. **M~e** f - mildness; leniency. **m~ern** vt make milder; (mäßigen) moderate; (lindern) ease; **sich m~ern** become milder; (sich mäßigen) moderate; <Schmerz:> ease; **m~ernde Umstände** mitigating circumstances
Milieu /mi'liø:/ nt -s, -s [social] environment
Militär nt -s army; (Soldaten) troops pl; **beim M~** in the army. **m~isch** a military
Miliz f -, -en militia
Milliarde /mɪ'liardə/ f -, -n thousand million, billion
Milli|gramm nt milligram. **M~meter** m & nt millimetre. **M~meterpapier** nt graph paper
Million /mɪ'lioːn/ f -, -en million. **M~är** m -s, -e millionaire
Milz f - (Anat) spleen. **~brand** m anthrax
mimen vt (🆒 vortäuschen) act
Minderheit f -, -en minority
minderjährig a (Jur) under-age. **M~e(r)** m/f (Jur) minor
mindern vt diminish; decrease
minderwertig a inferior. **M~keit** f - inferiority. **M~keitskomplex** m inferiority complex
Mindest- pref minimum. **m~e** a & pron **der/die/das M~e** od **m~e** the least; **nicht im M~en** not in the least. **m~ens** adv at least. **M~lohn** m minimum wage. **M~maß** nt minimum
Mine f -, -n mine; (Bleistift-) lead; (Kugelschreiber-) refill. **M~nräumboot** nt minesweeper
Mineral nt -s, -e & -ien /-iən/ mineral. **m~isch** a mineral. **M~wasser** nt mineral water
Miniatur f -, -en miniature

M

Minigolf nt miniature golf
minimal a minimal
Minimum nt -s, -ma minimum
Mini|ster m, -s,- minister.
m~steriell a ministerial.
M~sterium nt -s, -ien ministry
minus conj, adv & prep (+ gen)
minus. **M~** nt - deficit; (Nachteil)
disadvantage. **M~zeichen** nt
minus [sign]
Minute f -, -n minute
mir pron (dat of ich) [to] me; (refl)
myself
Misch|ehe f mixed marriage.
m~en vt mix; blend <Tee,
Kaffee>; toss <Salat>; shuffle
<Karten>; **sich m~en** mix;
<Person;> mingle (unter + acc
with); **sich m~en in** (+ acc) join in
<Gespräch>; meddle in
<Angelegenheit> ● vi (haben)
shuffle the cards. **M~ling** m -s, -e
half-caste. **M~ung** f -, -en
mixture; blend
miserabel a abominable
missachten vt disregard
Miss|achtung f disregard.
M~bildung f deformity
missbilligen vt disapprove of
Miss|billigung f disapproval.
M~brauch m abuse.
missbrauchen vt abuse;
(vergewaltigen) rape
Misserfolg m failure
Misse|tat f misdeed. **M~täter** m
🖪 culprit
missfallen† vi (haben) displease
(jdm s.o.)
Miss|fallen nt -s displeasure;
(Missbilligung) disapproval.
M~geburt f freak; (fig)
monstrosity. **M~geschick** nt
mishap; (Unglück) misfortune
miss|glücken vi (sein) fail.
m~gönnen vt begrudge
misshandeln vt ill-treat
Misshandlung f ill-treatment
Mission f -, -en mission

Missionar(in) m -s, -e (f -, -nen)
missionary
Missklang m discord
misslingen† vi (sein) fail; **es
misslang ihr** she failed. **M~** nt -s
failure
Missmut m ill humour. **m~ig** a
morose
missraten† vi (sein) turn out
badly
Miss|stand m abuse; (Zustand)
undesirable state of affairs.
M~stimmung f discord; (Laune)
bad mood
misstrauen vi (haben) jdm/etw
m~ mistrust s.o./sth; (Argwohn
hegen) distrust s.o./sth
Misstrau|en nt -s mistrust;
(Argwohn) distrust. **M~ensvotum**
nt vote of no confidence. **m~isch**
a distrustful; (argwöhnisch)
suspicious
Miss|verständnis nt
misunderstanding.
m~verstehen† vt misunderstand.
M~wirtschaft f mismanagement
Mist m -[e]s manure; 🖪 rubbish
Mistel f -, -n mistletoe
Misthaufen m dungheap
mit prep (+ dat) with; <sprechen>
to; (mittels) by; (inklusive)
including; (bei) at; **mit Bleistift** in
pencil; **mit lauter Stimme** in a loud
voice; **mit drei Jahren** at the age of
three ● adv (auch) as well; **mit
anfassen** (fig) lend a hand
Mitarbeit f collaboration. **m~en**
vi sep collaborate (an + dat on).
M~er(in) m(f) collaborator;
(Kollege) colleague; employee
Mitbestimmung f
co-determination
mitbringen† vt sep bring [along]
miteinander adv with each other
Mitesser m (Med) blackhead
mitfahren† vi sep (sein) go/come
along; **mit jdm m~** go with s.o.;
(mitgenommen werden) be given
a lift by s.o.

mitfühlen *vi sep* (haben) sympathize

mitgeben† *vt sep* jdm etw m~ give s.o. sth to take with him

Mitgefühl *nt* sympathy

mitgehen† *vi sep* (sein) mit jdm m~ go with s.o.

Mitgift *f* -, -en dowry

Mitglied *nt* member. **M~schaft** *f* - membership

mithilfe *prep* (+ gen) with the aid of

Mithilfe *f* assistance

mitkommen† *vi sep* (sein) come [along] too; (fig: folgen können) keep up; (verstehen) follow

Mitlaut *m* consonant

Mitleid *nt* pity, compassion; **M~erregend** pitiful. **m~ig** *a* pitying; (mitfühlend) compassionate. **m~slos** *a* pitiless

mitmachen *v sep* ● *vt* take part in; (erleben) go through ● *vi* (haben) join in

Mitmensch *m* fellow man

mitnehmen† *vt sep* take along; (mitfahren lassen) give a lift to; (fig: schädigen) affect badly; (erschöpfen) exhaust; **'zum M~'** 'to take away'

mitreden *vi sep* (haben) join in [the conversation]; (mit entscheiden) have a say (bei in)

mitreißen† *vt sep* sweep along; (fig: begeistern) carry away; **m~d** rousing

mitsamt *prep* (+ dat) together with

mitschreiben† *vt sep* (haben) take down

Mitschuld *f* partial blame. **m~ig** *a* **m~ig sein** be partly to blame

Mitschüler(in) *m(f)* fellow pupil

mitspielen *vi sep* (haben) join in; (Theat) be in the cast; (beitragen) play a part

Mittag *m* midday, noon; (Mahlzeit) lunch; (Pause) lunch-break; **heute/gestern M~** at

lunch-time today/yesterday; **[zu] M~ essen** have lunch. **M~essen** *nt* lunch. **m~s** *adv* at noon; (als Mahlzeit) for lunch; **um 12 Uhr m~s** at noon. **M~spause** *f* lunch-hour; (Pause) lunch-break. **M~sschlaf** *m* after-lunch nap

Mittäter|(in) *m(f)* accomplice. **M~schaft** *f* - complicity

Mitte *f* -, -n middle; (Zentrum) centre; **die goldene M~** the golden mean; **M~ Mai** in mid-May; **in unserer M~** in our midst

mitteil|en *vt sep* jdm etw m~en tell s.o. sth; (amtlich) inform s.o. of sth. **M~ung** *f* -, -en communication; (Nachricht) piece of news

Mittel *nt* -s,- means *sg*; (Heil) remedy; (Medikament) medicine; (M~wert) mean; (Durchschnitt) average; **M~** *pl* (Geld-) funds, resources. **m~** *pred a* medium; (m~mäßig) middling. **M~alter** *nt* Middle Ages *pl*. **m~alterlich** *a* medieval. **M~ding** *nt* (fig) cross. **m~europäisch** *a* Central European. **M~finger** *m* middle finger. **m~los** *a* destitute. **m~mäßig** *a* middling; [nur] **m~mäßig** mediocre. **M~meer** *nt* Mediterranean. **M~punkt** *m* centre; (fig) centre of attention

mittels *prep* (+ gen) by means of

Mittel|schule *f* = Realschule. **M~smann** *m* (pl -männer) intermediary, go-between. **M~stand** *m* middle class. **m~ste(r,s)** *a* middle. **M~streifen** *m* (Auto) central reservation. **M~stürmer** *m* centre-forward. **M~welle** *f* medium wave. **M~wort** *nt* (pl -wörter) participle

mitten *adv* **m~ in/auf** (dat/acc) in the middle of. **m~durch** *adv* [right] through the middle

Mitternacht *f* midnight

mittler|e(r,s) *a* middle; <Größe, Qualität> medium;

(*durchschnittlich*) mean, average.
m~**weile** *adv* meanwhile;
(*seitdem*) by now
Mittwoch *m* -s, -e Wednesday.
m~s *adv* on Wednesdays
mitunter *adv* now and again
mitwirk|en *vi sep* (*haben*) take
part; (*helfen*) contribute. M~**ung**
f participation
mix|en *vt* mix. M~**er** *m* -s,- (*Culin*)
liquidizer, blender
Möbel *pl* furniture *sg.* M~**stück**
nt piece of furniture. M~**wagen**
m removal van
Mobiliar *nt* -s furniture
mobilisier|en *vt* mobilize. M~**ung**
f - mobilization
Mobil|machung *f* - mobilization.
M~**telefon** *nt* mobile phone
möblier|en *vt* furnish; m~**tes**
Zimmer furnished room
mochte, möchte *s.* mögen
Mode *f* -, -n fashion; M~ **sein** be
fashionable
Modell *nt* -s, -e model. m~**ieren** *vt*
model
Modenschau *f* fashion show
Modera|tor *m* -s, -en /-'to:rən/,
M~**torin** *f* -, -nen (*TV*) presenter
modern *a* modern; (*modisch*)
fashionable. m~**isieren** *vt*
modernize
Mode|schmuck *m* costume
jewellery. M~**schöpfer** *m* fashion
designer
modisch *a* fashionable
Modistin *f* -, -nen milliner
modrig *a* musty
modulieren *vt* modulate
Mofa *nt* -s, -s moped
mogeln *vi* (*haben*) 🄸 cheat

mögen†
● *transitive verb*
····▸ like. **sie mag ihn sehr [gern]**
she likes him very much.
möchten Sie ein Glas Wein? would
you like a glass of wine? **lieber**

mögen prefer. **ich möchte lieber
Tee** I would prefer tea
● *auxiliary verb*
····▸ (*wollen*) want to. **sie mochte
nicht länger bleiben** she didn't
want to stay any longer. **ich
möchte ihn [gerne] sprechen** I'd
like to speak to him. **möchtest du
nach Hause?** do you want to go
home? *or* would you like to go
home?
····▸ (*Vermutung, Möglichkeit*)
may. **ich mag mich irren** I may be
wrong. **wer/was mag das sein?**
whoever/whatever can it be?
[das] mag sein that may well be.
mag kommen, was da will come
what may

möglich *a* possible; **alle** m~**en** all
sorts of; **über alles** M~**e sprechen**
talk about all sorts of things.
m~**erweise** *adv* possibly. M~**keit**
f -, -en possibility. M~**keitsform** *f*
subjunctive. m~**st** *adv* if
possible; m~**st viel** as much as
possible
Mohammedan|er(in) *m* -s,- (*f* -,
-nen) Muslim. m~**isch** *a* Muslim
Mohn *m* -s poppy
Möhre, Mohrrübe *f* -, -n carrot
Mokka *m* -s mocha; (*Geschmack*)
coffee
Molch *m* -[e]s, -e newt
Mole *f* -, -n (*Naut*) mole
Molekül *nt* -s, -e molecule
Molkerei *f* -, -en dairy
Moll *nt* - (*Mus*) minor
mollig *a* cosy; (*warm*) warm;
(*rundlich*) plump
Moment *m* -s, -e moment;
M~**[mal]!** just a moment! m~**an** *a*
momentary; (*gegenwärtig*) at the
moment
Monarch *m* -en, -en monarch.
M~**ie** *f* -, -n monarchy
Monat *m* -s, -e month. m~**elang**
adv for months. m~**lich** *a & adv*
monthly

Mönch m -[e]s, -e monk

Mond m -[e]s, -e moon

mondän a fashionable

Mond|finsternis f lunar eclipse. **m~hell** a moonlit. **M~sichel** f crescent moon. **M~schein** m moonlight

monieren vt criticize

Monitor m -s, -en /-'to:rən/ (Techn) monitor

Monogramm nt -s, -e monogram

Mono|log m -s, -e monologue. **M~pol** nt -s, -e monopoly. **m~ton** a monotonous

Monster nt -s,- monster

Monstrum nt -s, -stren monster

Monsun m -s, -e monsoon

Montag m Monday

Montage /mɔn'ta:ʒə/ f -, -n fitting; (Zusammenbau) assembly; (Film-) editing; (Kunst) montage

montags adv on Mondays

Montanindustrie f coal and steel industry

Monteur /mɔn'tø:ɐ̯/ m -s, -e fitter. **M~anzug** m overalls pl

montieren vt fit; (zusammenbauen) assemble

Monument nt -[e]s, -e monument. **m~al** a monumental

Moor nt -[e]s, -e bog; (Heide-) moor

Moos nt es, -e moss **m~ig** a mossy

Moped nt -s, -s moped

Mopp m -s, -s mop

Moral f - morals pl, (Selbstvertrauen) morale; (Lehre) moral. **m~isch** a moral

Mord m -[e]s, -e murder, (Pol) assassination. **M~anschlag** m murder/assassination attempt. **m~en** vt/i (haben) murder, kill

Mörder m -s,- murderer, (Pol) assassin. **M~in** f -, -nen murderess. **m~isch** a murderous; (🔟 schlimm) dreadful

morgen adv tomorrow; **m~ Abend** tomorrow evening

Morgen m -s,- morning; (Maß) ≈ acre; **am M~** in the morning; **heute/Montag M~** this/Monday morning. **M~dämmerung** f dawn. **M~rock** m dressing-gown. **M~rot** nt red sky in the morning. **m~s** a in the morning

morgig a tomorrow's; **der m~e Tag** tomorrow

Morphium nt -s morphine

morsch a rotten

Morsealphabet nt Morse code

Mörtel m -s mortar

Mosaik /moza'i:k/ nt -s, -e[n] mosaic

Moschee f -, -n mosque

Mosel f - Moselle

Moskau nt -s Moscow

Moskito m -s, -s mosquito

Moslem m -s, -s Muslim

Motiv nt -s, -e motive; (Kunst) motif

Motor /'mo:tɔr, mo'to:ɐ̯/ m -s, -en /-'to:rən/ engine; (Elektro-) motor. **M~boot** nt motor boat

motorisieren vt motorize

Motor|rad nt motor cycle. **M~roller** m motor scooter

Motte f -, -n moth. **M~nkugel** f mothball

Motto nt -s, -s motto

Möwe f -, -n gull

Mücke f -, -n gnat; (kleine) midge; (Stech-) mosquito

müd|e a tired; **es m~e sein** be tired (**etw zu tun** of doing sth). **M~igkeit** f - tiredness

muffig a musty; (🔟 mürrisch) grumpy

Mühe f -, -n effort; (Aufwand) trouble; **sich** (dat) **M~ geben** make an effort; (sich bemühen) try; **nicht der M~ wert** not worth while; **mit M~ und Not** with great difficulty; (gerade noch) only just. **m~los** a effortless

muhen vi (haben) moo

Mühl|e f -, -n mill; (Kaffee-) grinder. **M~stein** m millstone
Müh|sal f -, -e (liter) toil; (Mühe) trouble. **m~sam** a laborious; (beschwerlich) difficult
Mulde f -, -n hollow
Müll m -s refuse. **M~abfuhr** f refuse collection
Mullbinde f gauze bandage
Mülleimer m waste bin; (Mülltonne) dustbin
Müller m -s,- miller
Müll|halde f [rubbish] dump. **M~schlucker** m refuse chute. **M~tonne** f dustbin
multi|national a multinational. **M~plikation** /-'tsio:n/ f -, -en multiplication. **m~plizieren** vt multiply
Mumie /'mu:miə/ f -, -n mummy
Mumm m -s Ⓘ energy
Mumps m - mumps
Mund m -[e]s,¨er mouth; ein M~ voll Suppe a mouthful of soup; halt den M~! ⊠ shut up! **M~art** f dialect. **m~artlich** a dialect
Mündel nt & m -s,- (Jur) ward. **m~sicher** a gilt-edged
münden vi (sein) flow/<Straße:> lead (in + acc into)
Mundharmonika f mouth-organ
mündig a **m~ sein/werden** (Jur) be/come of age. **M~keit** f - (Jur) majority
mündlich a verbal; **m~e Prüfung** oral
Mündung f -, -en (Fluss-) mouth; (Gewehr-) muzzle
Mundwinkel m corner of the mouth
Munition /-'tsio:n/ f - ammunition
munkeln vt/i (haben) talk (von of); **es wird gemunkelt** rumour has it (dass that)
Münster nt -s,- cathedral
munter a lively; (heiter) merry; **m~ sein** (wach) be wide awake ; **gesund und m~** fit and well

Münz|e f -, -n coin; (M~stätte) mint. **M~fernsprecher** m payphone
mürbe a crumbly; <Obst> mellow; <Fleisch> tender. **M~teig** m short pastry
Murmel f -, -n marble
murmeln vt/i (haben) murmur; (undeutlich) mumble
Murmeltier nt marmot
murren vt/i (haben) grumble
mürrisch a surly
Mus nt -es purée
Muschel f -, -n mussel; [sea] shell
Museum /mu'ze:ʊm/ nt -s, -seen /-'ze:ən/ museum
Musik f - music. **m~alisch** a musical
Musiker(in) m -s,- (f -, -nen) musician
Musik|instrument nt musical instrument. **M~kapelle** f band. **M~pavillon** m bandstand
musisch a artistic
musizieren vi (haben) make music
Muskat m -[e]s nutmeg
Muskel m -s, -n muscle. **M~kater** m stiff and aching muscles pl
muskulös a muscular
muss s. **müssen**
Muße f - leisure

---

müssen†
● auxiliary verb
····▸ (gezwungen/verpflichtet/ notwendig sein) have to; must. **er muss es tun** he must or has to do it; Ⓘ he's got to do it. **ich musste schnell fahren** I had to drive fast. **das muss 1968 gewesen sein** it must have been in 1968. **er muss gleich hier sein** he must be here at any moment
····▸ (in negativen Sätzen; ungezwungen) **sie muss es nicht tun** she does not have to or Ⓘ she hasn't got to do it. **es musste**

nicht so sein it didn't have to be like that

····➤ **es müsste** (*sollte*) **doch möglich sein** it ought to or should be possible. **du müsstest es mal versuchen** you ought to or should try it

● *intransitive verb*

····➤ (*irgendwohin gehen müssen*) have to or must go. **ich muss nach Hause/zum Arzt** I have to or must go home/to the doctor. **ich musste mal [aufs Klo]** I had to go [to the loo]

müßig *a* idle

musste, müsste *s.* **müssen**

Muster *nt* -s,- pattern; (*Probe*) sample; (*Vorbild*) model. **M~beispiel** *nt* typical example; (*Vorbild*) perfect example. **m~gültig, m~haft** *a* exemplary. **m~n** *vt* eye; (*inspizieren*) inspect. **M~ung** *f* -, -en inspection; (*Mil*) medical; (*Muster*) pattern

Mut *m* -[e]s courage; **jdm Mut machen** encourage s.o.; **zu M~e sein** = **zumute sein**, *s.* **zumute**

mut|ig *a* courageous. **m~los** *a* despondent

mutmaßen *vt* presume; (*Vermutungen anstellen*) speculate

Mutprobe *f* test of courage

Mutter¹ *f* -,-̈ mother

Mutter² *f* -, -n (*Techn*) nut

Muttergottes *f* -,- madonna

Mutterland *nt* motherland

mütterlich *a* maternal; (*fürsorglich*) motherly. **m~erseits** *adv* on one's/the mother's side

Mutter|mal *nt* birthmark; (*dunkel*) mole. **M~schaft** *f* - motherhood. **m~seelenallein** *a & adv* all alone. **M~sprache** *f* mother tongue. **M~tag** *m* Mother's Day

Mütze *f* -, -n cap; **wollene M~** woolly hat

MwSt. *abbr* (**Mehrwertsteuer**) VAT

mysteriös *a* mysterious

Mystik /'mʏstɪk/ *f* - mysticism

myth|isch *a* mythical. **M~ologie** *f* - mythology

na *int* well; **na gut** all right then

Nabel *m* -s,- navel. **N~schnur** *f* umbilical cord

nach

● *preposition* (+ *dative*)

····➤ (*räumlich*) to. **nach London fahren** go to London. **der Zug nach München** the train to Munich; (*noch nicht abgefahren*) the train for Munich; the Munich train. **nach Hause gehen** go home. **nach Osten [zu]** eastwards; towards the east

····➤ (*zeitlich*) after; (*Uhrzeit*) past. **nach fünf Minuten/dem Frühstück** after five minutes/breakfast. **zehn [Minuten] nach zwei** ten [minutes] past two

····➤ (*[räumliche und zeitliche] Reihenfolge*) after. **nach Ihnen/dir!** after you!

····➤ (*mit bestimmten Verben*) for. **greifen/streben/schicken nach** grasp/strive/send for

····➤ (*gemäß*) according to. **nach der neuesten Mode gekleidet** dressed in [accordance with] the latest fashion. **dem Gesetz nach** in accordance with the law; by law. **nach meiner Ansicht** *od* **Meinung, meiner Ansicht** *od* **Meinung nach** in my view or

opinion. **nach etwas schmecken/ riechen** taste/smell of sth
● *adverb*
····► (*zeitlich*) **nach und nach** little by little; gradually. **nach wie vor** still

nachahm|en vt sep imitate. **N~ung** f -, -en imitation.

Nachbar|(in) m -n, -n (f -, -nen) neighbour. **N~haus** nt house next door. **n~lich** a neighbourly; (*Nachbar-*) neighbouring. **N~schaft** f - neighbourhood

nachbestell|en vt sep reorder. **N~ung** f repeat order

nachbild|en vt sep copy, reproduce. **N~ung** f copy, reproduction

nachdatieren vt sep backdate

nachdem conj after; **je n~** it depends

nachdenk|en† vi sep (haben) think (**über** + acc about). **n~lich** a thoughtful

nachdrücklich a emphatic

nacheinander adv one after the other

Nachfahre m -n, -n descendant

Nachfolg|e f succession. **N~er(in)** m -s,- (f -, -nen) successor

nachforsch|en vi sep (haben) make enquiries. **N~ung** f enquiry

Nachfrage f (Comm) demand. **n~n** vi sep (haben) enquire

nachfüllen vt sep refill

nachgeben† v sep ● vi (haben) give way: (*sich fügen*) give in, yield ● vt **jdm Suppe n~** give s.o. more soup

Nachgebühr f surcharge

nachgehen† vi sep (sein) <Uhr:> be slow; **jdm/etw n~** follow s.o./ sth; follow up <Spur, Angelegenheit>; pursue <Angelegenheit>

Nachgeschmack m after-taste

nachgiebig a indulgent; (*gefällig*) compliant. **N~keit** f - indulgence; compliance

nachgrübeln vi sep (haben) ponder (**über** + acc on)

nachhaltig a lasting

nachhelfen† vi sep (haben) help

nachher adv later; (*danach*) afterwards; **bis n~!** see you later!

Nachhilfeunterricht m coaching

Nachhinein adv **im N~** afterwards

nachhinken vi sep (sein) (*fig*) lag behind

nachholen vt sep (*später holen*) fetch later; (*mehr holen*) get more; (*später machen*) do later; (*aufholen*) catch up on

Nachkomme m -n, -n descendant. **n~n†** vi sep (sein) follow [later], come later; **etw** (dat) **n~n** (*fig*) comply with <Bitte>; carry out <Pflicht>. **N~nschaft** f - descendants pl, progeny

Nachkriegszeit f post-war period

Nachlass m -es,ˉe discount; (Jur) [deceased's] estate

nachlassen† v sep ● vi (haben) decrease; <Regen, Hitze:> let up; <Schmerz:> ease; <Sturm:> abate; <Augen, Leistungen:> deteriorate ● vt **etw vom Preis n~** take sth off the price

nachlässig a careless; (*leger*) casual; (*unordentlich*) sloppy. **N~keit** f - carelessness; sloppiness

nachlesen† vt sep look up

nachlöse|n vi sep (haben) pay one's fare on the train/on arrival. **N~schalter** m excess-fare office

nachmachen vt sep (*später machen*) do later; (*imitieren*) imitate, copy; (*fälschen*) forge

Nachmittag m afternoon; **heute/ gestern N~** this/yesterday afternoon. **n~s** adv in the afternoon

Nachnahme f etw per N~ schicken
send sth cash on delivery or
COD

Nachname m surname

Nachporto nt excess postage

nachprüfen vt sep check, verify

Nachricht f -, -en [piece of] news
sg; N~en news sg; eine N~
hinterlassen leave a message; jdm
N~ geben inform s.o. N~endienst
m (Mil) intelligence service

nachrücken vi sep (sein) move
up

Nachruf m obituary

nachsagen vt sep repeat (jdm
after s.o.); jdm Schlechtes/Gutes
n~ speak ill/well of s.o.

Nachsaison f late season

nachschicken vt sep (später
schicken) send later; (hinterher-)
send after (jdm to s.o.); send on
<Post> (jdm to s.o.)

nachschlagen† v sep ●vt look
up ●vi (haben) in einem
Wörterbuch n~en consult a
dictionary; jdm n~en take after
s.o.

Nachschrift f transcript;
(Nachsatz) postscript

Nachschub m (Mil) supplies pl

nachsehen† v sep ●vt (prüfen)
check; (nachschlagen) look up;
(hinwegsehen über) overlook ●vi
(haben) have a look; (prüfen)
check; im Wörterbuch n~ consult
a dictionary

nachsenden† vt sep forward
<Post> (jdm to s.o.); 'bitte n~'
'please forward'

nachsichtig a forbearing; lenient;
indulgent

Nachsilbe f suffix

nachsitzen† vi sep (haben) n~
müssen be kept in [after school];
jdn n~ lassen give s.o. detention.
N~ nt -s (Sch) detention

Nachspeise f dessert, sweet

nachsprechen† vt sep repeat
(jdm after s.o.)

nachspülen vt sep rinse

nächst /-çst/ prep (+ dat) next to.
n~beste(r,s) a first [available];
(zweitbeste) next best. n~e(r,s) a
next; (nächstgelegene) nearest;
<Verwandte> closest; in n~er
Nähe close by; am n~en sein be
nearest or closest ●pron der/die/
das N~e the next; der N~e bitte
next please; als N~es next; fürs
N~e for the time being. N~e(r)
m fellow man

nachstehend a following ●adv
below

Nächst|enliebe f charity. n~ens
adv shortly. n~gelegen a nearest

nachsuchen vi sep (haben)
search; n~ um request

Nacht f -, ⸚e night; über/bei N~
overnight/at night; morgen N~
tomorrow night; heute N~
tonight; (letzte Nacht) last night;
gestern N~ last night; (vorletzte
Nacht) the night before last.
N~dienst m night duty

Nachteil m disadvantage; zum N~
to the detriment (gen of)

Nacht|falter m moth. N~hemd nt
night-dress; (Männer-) night-
shirt

Nachtigall f -, -en nightingale

Nachtisch m dessert

Nachtklub m night-club

nächtlich a nocturnal, night ...

Nacht|lokal nt night-club.
N~mahl nt (Aust) supper

Nachtrag m postscript;
(Ergänzung) supplement. n~en†
vt sep add; jdm etw n~en (fig)
bear a grudge against s.o. for sth.
n~end a vindictive; n~end sein
bear grudges

nachträglich a subsequent, later;
(verspätet) belated ●adv later;
(nachher) afterwards; (verspätet)
belatedly

Nacht|ruhe f night's rest;
angenehme N~ruhe! sleep well!
n~s adv at night; 2 Uhr n~s 2

o'clock in the morning.
N~schicht f night-shift. **N~tisch** m bedside table. **N~tischlampe** f bedside lamp. **N~topf** m chamber-pot. **N~wächter** m night-watchman. **N~zeit** f night-time
Nachuntersuchung f check-up
Nachwahl f by-election
Nachweis m -es, -e proof. **n~bar** a demonstrable. **n~en†** vt sep prove; (aufzeigen) show; (vermitteln) give details of; **jdm nichts n~en können** have no proof against s.o.
Nachwelt f posterity
Nachwirkung f after-effect
Nachwuchs m new generation; (🛈 Kinder) offspring. **N~spieler** m young player
nachzahlen vt/i sep (haben) pay extra; (später zahlen) pay later; **Steuern n~** pay tax arrears
nachzählen vt/i sep (haben) count again; (prüfen) check
Nachzahlung f extra/later payment; (Gehalts-) back-payment
nachzeichnen vt sep copy
Nachzügler m -s,- late-comer; (Zurückgebliebener) straggler
Nacken m -s,- nape or back of the neck
nackt a naked; (bloß, kahl) bare; <Wahrheit> plain. **N~heit** f - nakedness, nudity. **N~kultur** f nudism. **N~schnecke** f slug
Nadel f -, -n needle; (Häkel-) hook; (Schmuck-, Hut-) pin. **N~arbeit** f needlework. **N~baum** m conifer. **N~stich** m stitch; (fig) pinprick. **N~wald** m coniferous forest
Nagel m -s,- nail. **N~haut** f cuticle. **N~lack** m nail varnish. **n~n** vt nail. **n~neu** a brand-new
nagen vt/i (haben) gnaw (an + dat at); **n~d** (fig) nagging
Nagetier nt rodent

nah a, adv & prep = nahe
Näharbeit f sewing
Nahaufnahme f close-up
nahe a nearby; (zeitlich) imminent; (eng) close; **der N~ Osten** the Middle East; **in n~r Zukunft** in the near future; **von n~m** [from] close to; **n~ sein** be close (dat to) ● adv near, close; <verwandt> closely; **n~ an** (+ acc/dat) near [to], close to; **n~ daran sein, etw zu tun** nearly do sth; **n~ liegen** be close; (fig) be highly likely; **n~ legen** (fig) recommend (dat to); **jdm n~ legen, etw zu tun** urge s.o. to do sth; **jdm n~ gehen** (fig) affect s.o. deeply; **jdm zu n~ treten** (fig) offend s.o. ● prep (+ dat) near [to], close to
Nähe f - nearness, proximity; **aus der N~** [from] close to; **in der N~** near or close by
nahe|gehen* vi sep (sein) n~ gehen, s. nahe. **n~legen*** vt sep n~ legen, s. nahe. **n~liegen*** vi sep (haben) n~ liegen, s. nahe
nähen vt/i (haben) sew; (anfertigen) make; (Med) stitch [up]
näher a closer; <Weg> shorter; <Einzelheiten> further ● adv closer; (genauer) more closely; **n~ kommen** come closer; (fig) get closer (dat to); **sich n~ erkundigen** make further enquiries; **n~ an** (+ acc/dat) nearer [to], closer to ● prep (+ dat) nearer [to], closer to. **N~e[s]** nt [further] details pl. **n~n (sich)** vr approach
nahezu adv almost
Nähgarn nt [sewing] cotton
Nahkampf m close combat
Näh|maschine f sewing machine. **N~nadel** f sewing-needle
nähren vt feed; (fig) nurture
nahrhaft a nutritious
Nährstoff m nutrient

Nahrung f - food, nourishment. **N~smittel** nt food

Nährwert m nutritional value

Naht f -,⸚e seam; (*Med*) suture. **n~los** a seamless

Nahverkehr m local service

Nähzeug nt sewing; (*Zubehör*) sewing kit

naiv /naˈiːf/ a naïve. **N~ität** /-viˈtɛːt/ f - naïvety

Name m -ns, -n name; im N~n (+ gen) in the name of; <handeln> on behalf of. **n~nlos** a nameless; (*unbekannt*) unknown, anonymous. **N~nstag** m name-day. **N~nsvetter** m namesake. **N~nszug** m signature. **n~ntlich** adv by name; (*besonders*) especially

namhaft a noted; (*ansehnlich*) considerable; n~ machen name

nämlich adv why (und zwar) namely; (*denn*) because

nanu int hallo

Napf m -[e]s,⸚e bowl

Narbe f -, -n scar

Narkose f -, -n general anaesthetic. **N~arzt** m anaesthetist. **N~mittel** nt anaesthetic

Narr m -en, -en fool; zum N~en halten make a fool of. **n~en** vt fool

Närr|in f -, -nen fool. **n~isch** a foolish; (**Ⅰ** verrückt) crazy (auf + acc about)

Narzisse f -, -n narcissus

naschen vt/i (*haben*) nibble (an + dat at)

Nase f -, -n nose

näseln vi (*haben*) speak through one's nose; n~d nasal

Nasen|bluten nt -s nosebleed. **N~loch** nt nostril

Nashorn nt rhinoceros

nass a wet

Nässe f - wet; wetness. **n~n** vt wet

Nation /naˈtsi̯oːn/ f -, -en nation. **n~al** a national. **N~alhymne** f national anthem. **N~alismus** m - nationalism. **N~alität** f -, -en nationality. **N~alspieler** m international

Natrium nt -s sodium

Natron nt -s doppeltkohlensaures N~ bicarbonate of soda

Natter f -, -n snake; (*Gift-*) viper

Natur f -, -en nature; von N~ aus by nature. **n~alisieren** vt naturalize. **N~alisierung** f -, -en naturalization

Naturell nt -s, -e disposition

Natur|erscheinung f natural phenomenon. **N~forscher** m naturalist. **N~kunde** f natural history

natürlich a natural ● adv naturally; (*selbstverständlich*) of course. **N~keit** f - naturalness

natur|rein a pure. **N~schutz** m nature conservation; unter N~schutz stehen be protected. **N~schutzgebiet** nt nature reserve. **N~wissenschaft** f [natural] science. **N~wissenschaftler** m scientist

nautisch a nautical

Navigation /-ˈtsi̯oːn/ f - navigation

Nazi m -s, -s Nazi

n.Chr. abbr (nach Christus) AD

Nebel m -s,- fog; (*leicht*) mist

neben prep (+ dat/acc) next to, beside; (+ dat) (*außer*) apart from. **n~an** adv next door

Neben|anschluss m (*Teleph*) extension. **N~ausgaben** fpl incidental expenses

nebenbei adv in addition; (*beiläufig*) casually

Neben|bemerkung f passing remark. **N~beruf** m second job

nebeneinander adv next to each other, side by side

N

Neben|eingang m side entrance.
N~fach nt (Univ) subsidiary
subject. **N~fluss** m tributary
nebenher adv in addition
nebenhin adv casually
Neben|höhle f sinus. **N~kosten**
pl additional costs. **N~produkt** nt
by-product. **N~rolle** f supporting
role; (Kleine) minor role.
N~sache f unimportant matter.
n~sächlich a unimportant.
N~satz m subordinate clause.
N~straße f minor road; (Seiten-)
side street. **N~wirkung** f side-
effect. **N~zimmer** nt room next
door
neblig a foggy; (leicht) misty
neck|en vt tease. **N~erei** f -
teasing. **n~isch** a teasing
Neffe m -n, -n nephew
negativ a negative. **N~** nt -s, -e
(Phot) negative
Neger m -s,- Negro
nehmen† vt take (dat from); **sich**
(dat) **etw n~** take sth; help
oneself to <Essen>
Neid m -[e]s envy, jealousy.
n~isch a envious, jealous (**auf +**
acc of); **auf jdn n~isch sein** envy
s.o.
neig|en vt incline; (zur Seite) tilt;
(beugen) bend; **sich n~en** incline;
<Boden:> slope; <Person:> bend
(**über +** acc over) ● vi (haben)
n~en zu (fig) have a tendency
towards; be prone to
<Krankheit>; incline towards
<Ansicht>; **dazu n~en, etw zu tun**
tend to do sth. **N~ung** f -, -en
inclination; (Gefälle) slope; (fig)
tendency
nein adv, **N~** nt -s no
Nektar m -s nectar
Nelke f -, -n carnation; (Culin)
clove
nenn|en† vt call; (taufen) name;
(angeben) give; (erwähnen)
mention; **sich n~en** call oneself.
n~enswert a significant

Neon nt -s neon. **N~beleuchtung**
f fluorescent lighting
Nerv m -s, -en /-fan/ nerve; **die**
N~en verlieren lose control of
oneself. **n~en** vt **jdn n~en** 🗵 get
on s.o.'s nerves. **N~enarzt** m
neurologist. **n~enaufreibend** a
nerve-racking. **N~enkitzel** m 🔟
thrill. **N~ensystem** nt nervous
system. **N~enzusammenbruch** m
nervous breakdown
nervös a nervy, edgy; (Med)
nervous; **n~ sein** be on edge
Nervosität f - nerviness, edginess
Nerz m -es, -e mink
Nessel f -, -n nettle
Nest nt -[e]s, -er nest; (🔟 Ort)
small place
nett a nice; (freundlich) kind
netto adv net
Netz nt -es, -e net; (Einkaufs-)
string bag; (Spinnen-) web; (auf
Landkarte) grid; (System)
network; (Electr) mains pl.
N~haut f retina. **N~karte** f area
season ticket. **N~werk** nt
network
neu a new; (modern) modern; **wie**
neu as good as new; **das ist mir**
neu it's news to me; **von n~em** all
over again ● adv newly; (gerade
erst) only just; (erneut) again; **etw**
neu schreiben rewrite sth; **neu**
vermähltes Paar newly-weds pl.
N~auflage f new edition;
(unverändert) reprint. **N~bau** m
(pl -ten) new house/building
Neu|e(r) m/f new person,
newcomer; (Schüler) new boy/
girl. **N~e(s)** nt **das N~e** the new;
etwas N~es something new;
(Neuigkeit) a piece of news; **was**
gibts N~es? what's the news?
neuerdings adv [just] recently
neuest|e(r,s) a newest; (letzte)
latest; **seit n~em** just recently.
N~e nt **das N~e** the latest thing;
(Neuigkeit) the latest news sg
neugeboren a newborn

Neugier, Neugierde f - curiosity;
(Wissbegierde) inquisitiveness
neugierig a curious (**auf** + acc
about); (wissbegierig) inquisitive
Neuheit f -, -en novelty; newness
Neuigkeit f -, -en piece of news;
N~en news sg
Neujahr nt New Year's Day; **über**
N~ over the New Year
neulich adv the other day
Neumond m new moon
neun inv a, N~ f -, -en nine.
n~te(r,s) a ninth. n~zehn inv a
nineteen. n~zehnte(r,s) a
nineteenth. n~zig inv a ninety.
n~zigste(r,s) a ninetieth
Neuralgie f -, -n neuralgia
neureich a nouveau riche
Neurologe m -n, -n neurologist
Neurose f -, -n neurosis
Neuschnee m fresh snow
Neuseeland nt -s New Zealand
neuste(r,s) a = neueste(r,s)
neutral a neutral. N~ität f -
neutrality
Neutrum nt -s, -tra neuter noun
neu|vermählt* a n~ vermählt, s.
neu. N~zeit f modern times pl
nicht adv not; **ich kann n~**
cannot or can't; **er ist n~**
gekommen he hasn't come; **bitte
n~!** please don't! n~ **berühren!** do
not touch! **du kennst ihn doch,
n~?** you know him, don't you?
Nichte f -, -n niece
Nichtraucher m non-smoker
nichts pron & a nothing; n~ **mehr**
no more; n~ **ahnend**
unsuspecting; n~ **sagend**
meaningless; (uninteressant)
nondescript. N~ nt -
nothingness; (fig: Leere) void
Nichtschwimmer m non-
swimmer
nichts|nutzig a good-for-nothing;
(🛈 unartig) naughty. n~**sagend***
a n~ sagend, s. nichts. N~**tun** nt
-s idleness
Nickel nt -s nickel

nicken vi (haben) nod
Nickerchen nt -s,- 🛈 nap
nie adv never
nieder a low ● adv down.
n~**brennen†** vt/i sep (sein) burn
down. N~**deutsch** nt Low
German. N~**gang** m (fig) decline.
n~**gedrückt** a (fig) depressed.
n~**geschlagen** a dejected,
despondent. N~**kunft** f -,-̈e
confinement. N~**lage** f defeat
Niederlande (die) pl the
Netherlands
Niederländ|er m -s,- Dutchman;
die N~er the Dutch pl. **N~erin** f -,
-nen Dutchwoman. n~**isch** a
Dutch
nieder|lassen† vt sep let down;
sich n~lassen settle; (sich setzen)
sit down. N~**lassung** f -, -en
settlement; (Zweigstelle) branch.
n~**legen** vt sep put or lay down;
resign <Amt>; **die Arbeit n~legen**
go on strike. n~**metzeln** vt sep
massacre. N~**sachsen** nt Lower
Saxony. N~**schlag** m
precipitation; (Regen) rainfall;
(radioaktiver) fallout.
n~**schlagen†** vt sep knock down;
lower <Augen>; (unterdrücken)
crush. n~**schmettern** vt sep (fig)
shatter. n~**setzen** vt sep put or
set down; **sich n~setzen** sit down.
n~**strecken** vt sep fell; (durch
Schuss) gun down. n~**trächtig** a
base, vile. n~**walzen** vt sep
flatten
niedlich a pretty; sweet
niedrig a low; (fig: gemein) base
● adv low
niemals adv never
niemand pron nobody, no one
Niere f -, -n kidney; **künstliche N~**
kidney machine
nieseln vi (haben) drizzle.
N~**regen** m drizzle
niesen vi (haben) sneeze. N~ nt
-s sneezing; (Nieser) sneeze
Niete¹ f -, -n rivet; (an Jeans) stud

N

Niete² *f* -, -n blank; 🔟 failure
nieten *vt* rivet
Nikotin *nt* -s nicotine
Nil *m* -[s] Nile. **N~pferd** *nt* hippopotamus
nimmer *adv* (*SGer*) not any more; **nie und n~** never
nirgend|s, n~wo *adv* nowhere
Nische *f* -, -n recess, niche
nisten *vi* (*haben*) nest
Nitrat *nt* -[e]s, -e nitrate
Niveau /ni'vo:/ *nt* -s, -s level; (*geistig, künstlerisch*) standard
nix *adv* 🔟 nothing
Nixe *f* -, -n mermaid
nobel *a* noble; (🔟 *luxuriös*) luxurious; (🔟 *großzügig*) generous
noch *adv* still; (*zusätzlich*) as well; (*mit Komparativ*) even; **n~ nicht** not yet; **gerade n~** only just; **n~ immer** *od* **immer n~** still; **n~ letzte Woche** only last week; **wer n~?** who else? **n~ etwas** something else; (*Frage*) anything else? **n~ einmal** again; **n~ ein Bier** another beer; **n~ größer** even bigger; **n~ so sehr** however much ● *conj* **weder ... n~** neither ... nor
nochmals *adv* again
Nomad|e *m* -n, -n nomad. **n~isch** *a* nomadic
nominier|en *vt* nominate. **N~ung** *f* -, -en nomination
Nonne *f* -, -n nun. **N~nkloster** *nt* convent
Nonstopflug *m* direct flight
Nord *m* -[e]s north. **N~amerika** *nt* North America
Norden *m* -s north
nordisch *a* Nordic
nördlich *a* northern; <*Richtung*> northerly ● *adv & prep* (+ *gen*) **n~ [von] der Stadt** [to the] north of the town
Nordosten *m* north-east
Nord|pol *m* North Pole. **N~see** *f* - North Sea. **N~westen** *m* north-west

Nörgelei *f* -, -en grumbling
nörgeln *vi* (*haben*) grumble
Norm *f* -, -en norm; (*Techn*) standard; (*Soll*) quota
normal *a* normal. **n~erweise** *adv* normally
normen *vt* standardize
Norwe|gen *nt* -s Norway. **N~ger(in)** *m* -s,- (*f* -, -nen) Norwegian. **n~gisch** *a* Norwegian
Nost|algie *f* - nostalgia. **n~algisch** *a* nostalgic
Not *f* -,:e need; (*Notwendigkeit*) necessity; (*Entbehrung*) hardship; (*seelisch*) trouble; **Not leiden** be in need, suffer hardship; **Not leidende Menschen** needy people; **zur Not** if need be; (*äußerstenfalls*) at a pinch
Notar *m* -s, -e notary public
Not|arzt *m* emergency doctor. **N~ausgang** *m* emergency exit. **N~behelf** *m* -[e]s, -e makeshift. **N~bremse** *f* emergency brake. **N~dienst** *m* **N~dienst haben** be on call
Note *f* -, -n note; (*Zensur*) mark; **ganze/halbe N~** (*Mus*) semibreve/minim; **N~n lesen** read music; **persönliche N~** personal touch. **N~nblatt** *nt* sheet of music. **N~nschlüssel** *m* clef
Notfall *m* emergency; **für den N~** just in case. **n~s** *adv* if need be
notieren *vt* note down; (*Comm*) quote; **sich** (*dat*) **etw n~** make a note of sth
nötig *a* necessary; **n~ haben** need; **das N~ste** the essentials *pl* ● *adv* urgently. **n~enfalls** *adv* if need be. **N~ung** *f* - coercion
Notiz *f* -, -en note; (*Zeitungs-*) item; **[keine] N~ nehmen von** take [no] notice of. **N~buch** *nt* notebook. **N~kalender** *m* diary
Not|lage *f* plight. **n~landen** *vi* (*sein*) make a forced landing. **N~landung** *f* forced landing.

n~leidend* a **Not leidend**, s. **Not**.
N~lösung f stopgap
Not|ruf m emergency call; (*Naut, Aviat*) distress call; (*Nummer*) emergency services number. **N~signal** nt distress signal. **N~stand** m state of emergency. **N~unterkunft** f emergency accommodation. **N~wehr** f - (*Jur*) self-defence
notwendig a necessary; essential ● adv urgently. **N~keit** f -, -en necessity
Notzucht f - (*Jur*) rape
Nougat /'nu:gat/ m & nt -s nougat
Novelle f -, -n novella; (*Pol*) amendment
November m -s,- November
Novize m -n, -n, **Novizin** f -, -nen (*Relig*) novice
Nu m in ein **Nu** ▯ in a flash
nüchtern a sober; (*sachlich*) matter-of-fact; (*schmucklos*) bare; (*ohne Würze*) bland; **auf n~en Magen** on an empty stomach
Nudel f -, -n piece of pasta; **N~n** pasta sg; (*Band-*) noodles. **N~holz** nt rolling-pin
Nudist m -en, -en nudist
nuklear a nuclear
null inv a zero, nought; (*Teleph*) O; (*Sport*) nil; (*Tennis*) love; **n~ Fehler** no mistakes; **n~ und nichtig** (*Jur*) null and void. **N~** f -, -en nought, zero; (*fig: Person*) nonentity. **N~punkt** m zero
numerieren* vt s. **nummerieren**
Nummer f -, -n number; (*Ausgabe*) issue; (*Darbietung*) item; (*Zirkus-*) act; (*Größe*) size. **n~ieren** vt number. **N~nschild** nt number-plate
nun adv now; (*na*) well; (*halt*) just; **nun gut!** very well then!
nur adv only, just; **wo kann sie nur sein?** wherever can she be? **er soll es nur versuchen!** just let him try!

Nürnberg nt -s Nuremberg
nuscheln vt/i (*haben*) mumble
Nuss f -,̈-e nut. **N~knacker** m -s,- nutcrackers pl
Nüstern fpl nostrils
Nut f -, -en, **Nute** f -, -n groove
Nutte f -, -n ▯ tart ▯
nutz|bar a usable; **n~bar machen** utilize; cultivate <*Boden*>. **n~bringend** a profitable
nutzen vt use, utilize; (*aus-*) take advantage of ● vi (*haben*) = **nützen**. **N~** m -s benefit; (*Comm*) profit; **N~ ziehen aus** benefit from; **von N~ sein** be useful
nützen vi (*haben*) be useful or of use (*dat* to); <*Mittel:*> be effective; **nichts n~** be useless or no use; **was nützt mir das?** what good is that to me? ● vt = **nutzen**
nützlich a useful. **N~keit** f - usefulness
nutz|los a useless; (*vergeblich*) vain. **N~losigkeit** f - uselessness. **N~ung** f - use, utilization
Nylon /'nailon/ nt -s nylon
Nymphe /'nymfə/ f -, -n nymph

o int **o ja/nein!** oh yes/no!
Oase f -, -n oasis
ob conj whether; **ob reich, ob arm** rich or poor; **und ob!** ▯ you bet!
Obacht f **O~ geben** pay attention; **O~!** look out!
Obdach nt -[e]s shelter. **o~los** a homeless. **O~lose(r)** m/f homeless person; **die O~losen** the homeless pl
Obduktion /-'tsi̯o:n/ f -, -en post-mortem

O-Beine ntpl 🔟 bow-legs, bandy legs

oben adv at the top; (auf der Oberseite) on top; (eine Treppe hoch) upstairs; (im Text) above; **da o~** up there; **o~ im Norden** up in the north; **siehe o~** see above; **o~ auf** (+ acc/dat) on top of; **nach o~** up[wards]; (die Treppe hinauf) upstairs; **von o~** from above/upstairs; **von o~ bis unten** from top to bottom/<Person> to toe; **jdn von o~ bis unten mustern** look s.o. up and down; **o~ erwähnt** od **genannt** above-mentioned. **o~drein** adv on top of that

Ober m -s,- waiter

Ober|arm m upper arm. **O~arzt** m ≈ senior registrar. **O~deck** nt upper deck. **o~e(r,s)** a upper; (höhere) higher. **O~fläche** f surface. **o~flächlich** a superficial. **O~geschoss** nt upper storey. **o~halb** adv & prep (+ gen) above. **O~haupt** nt (fig) head. **O~haus** nt (Pol) upper house; (in UK) House of Lords. **O~hemd** nt [man's] shirt. **o~irdisch** a surface ... ● adv above ground. **O~kiefer** m upper jaw. **O~körper** m upper part of the body. **O~leutnant** m lieutenant. **O~lippe** f upper lip

Obers nt - (Aust) cream

Ober|schenkel m thigh. **O~schule** f grammar school. **O~seite** f upper/(rechte Seite) right side

Oberst m -en & -s, -en colonel

oberste(r,s) a top; (höchste) highest; <Befehlshaber, Gerichtshof> supreme; (wichtigste) first

Ober|stimme f treble. **O~teil** nt top. **O~weite** f chest/(der Frau) bust size

obgleich conj although

Obhut f - care

obig a above

Objekt nt -[e]s, -e object; (Haus, Grundstück) property

Objektiv nt -s, -e lens. **o~** a objective. **O~ität** f - objectivity

Oblate f -, -n (Relig) wafer

Obmann m (pl -männer) [jury] foreman; (Sport) referee

Oboe /o'bo:ə/ f -, -n oboe

Obrigkeit f - authorities pl

obschon conj although

Observatorium nt -s, -ien observatory

obskur a obscure; dubious

Obst nt -es (coll) fruit. **O~baum** m fruit-tree. **O~garten** m orchard. **O~händler** m fruiterer

obszön a obscene

O-Bus m trolley bus

obwohl conj although

Ochse m -n, -n ox

öde a desolate; (unfruchtbar) barren; (langweilig) dull. **Öde** f - desolation; barrenness; dullness

oder conj or; (du kennst ihn doch, o~)? you know him, don't you?

Ofen m -s,∸ stove; (Heiz-) heater; (Back-) oven; (Techn) furnace

offen a open; <Haar> loose; <Flamme> naked; (o~herzig) frank; (o~ gezeigt) overt; (unentschieden) unsettled; **o~e Stelle** vacancy; **Wein o~ verkaufen** sell wine by the glass; **o~ bleiben** remain open; **o~ halten** hold open <Tür>; keep open <Mund, Augen>; **o~ lassen** leave open; leave vacant <Stelle>; **o~ stehen** be open; <Rechnung:> be outstanding; **jdm o~ stehen** (fig) be open to s.o.; adv **o~ gesagt** od **gestanden** to be honest. **o~bar** a obvious ● adv apparently. **o~baren** vt reveal. **O~barung** f -, -en revelation. **O~heit** f - frankness, openness. **o~sichtlich** a obvious

offenstehen* vi sep (haben) **offen stehen**, s. **offen**

öffentlich a public. **Ö~keit** f - public; **in aller Ö~keit** in public, publicly

Offerte f -, -n (Comm) offer

offiziell a official

Offizier m -s, -e (Mil) officer

öffn|en vt/i (haben) open; **sich ö~en** open. **Ö~er** m -s,- opener. **Ö~ung** f -, -en opening. **Ö~ungszeiten** fpl opening hours

oft adv often

öfter adv quite often. **ö~e(r,s)** a frequent; **des Ö~en** frequently. **ö~s** adv Ⅱ quite often

oh int oh!

ohne prep (+ acc) without; **o~ mich!** count me out! **oben o~** topless ●conj **o~ zu überlegen** without thinking; **o~ dass ich es merkte** without my noticing it. **o~dies** adv anyway. **o~gleichen** pred a unparalleled. **o~hin** adv anyway

Ohn|macht f -, -en faint; (fig) powerlessness; **in O~macht fallen** faint. **o~mächtig** a unconscious; (fig) powerless; **o~mächtig werden** faint

Ohr nt -[e]s, -en ear

Öhr nt -[e]s, -e eye

Ohrenschmalz nt ear-wax. **O~schmerzen** mpl earache sg

Ohrfeige f slap in the face. **o~n** vt jdn **o~n** slap s.o.'s face

Ohr|läppchen nt -s,- ear-lobe. **O~ring** m ear-ring. **O~wurm** m earwig

oje int oh dear!

okay /o'ke:/ a & adv Ⅱ OK

Öko|logie f - ecology. **ö~logisch** a ecological. **Ö~nomie** f - economy; (Wissenschaft) economics sg. **ö~nomisch** a economic; (sparsam) economical

Oktave f -, -n octave

Oktober m -s,- October

ökumenisch a ecumenical

Öl nt -[e]s, -e oil; **in Öl malen** paint in oils. **Ölbaum** m olivetree. **ölen**

vt oil. **Ölfarbe** f oil-paint. **Ölfeld** nt oilfield. **Ölgemälde** nt oil-painting. **ölig** a oily

Oliv|e f -, -n olive. **O~enöl** nt olive oil

Ölmessstab m dip-stick. **Ölsardinen** fpl sardines in oil. **Ölstand** m oil-level. **Öltanker** m oil-tanker. **Ölteppich** m oil-slick

Olympiade f -, -n Olympic Games pl, Olympics pl

Olymp|iasieger(in) /o'lympia-/ m(f) Olympic champion. **o~isch** a Olympic; **O~ische Spiele** Olympic Games

Ölzeug nt oilskins pl

Oma f -, -s Ⅱ granny

Omnibus m bus; (Reise-) coach

onanieren vi (haben) masturbate

Onkel m -s,- uncle

Opa m -s, -s Ⅱ grandad

Opal m -s, -e opal

Oper f -, -n opera

Operation /-'tsio:n/ f -, -en operation. **O~ssaal** m operating theatre

Operette f -, -n operetta

operieren vt operate on <Patient, Herz>; **sich o~ lassen** have an operation ●vi (haben) operate

Opernglas nt opera-glasses pl

Opfer nt -s,- sacrifice; (eines Unglücks) victim; **ein O~ bringen** make a sacrifice; **jdm/etw zum O~ fallen** fall victim to s.o./sth. **o~n** vt sacrifice

Opium nt -s opium

Opposition /-'tsio:n/ f - opposition. **O~spartei** f opposition party

Optik f - optics sg, (Ⅱ Objektiv) lens. **O~er** m -s,- optician

optimal a optimum

Optimis|mus m - optimism. **O~t** m -en, -en optimist. **o~tisch** a optimistic

optisch a optical; <Eindruck> visual

Orakel nt -s,- oracle

O

Orange /oˈrãːʒə/ f -, -n orange. **o~** *inv a* orange. **O~ade** /orãˈʒaːdə/ f -, -n orangeade. **O~nmarmelade** f [orange] marmalade

Oratorium *nt* -s, -ien oratorio

Orchester /ɔrˈkɛstɐ/ *nt* -s,- orchestra

Orchidee /ɔrçiˈdeːə/ f -, -n orchid

Orden *m* -s,- (Ritter-, Kloster-) order; (Auszeichnung) medal, decoration

ordentlich *a* neat. tidy; (anständig) respectable; (ordnungsgemäß ▣: richtig) proper; <Mitglied, Versammlung> ordinary; (▣ gut) decent; (▣ gehörig) good

ordinär *a* common

Order f -, -s & -n order

Ordination /-ˈtsi̯oːn/ f -, -en (Relig) ordination; (Aust) surgery

ordn|en *vt* put in order; tidy; (an-) arrange. **O~er** *m* -s,- steward; (Akten-) file

Ordnung f - order; **O~ machen** tidy up; **in O~ bringen** put in order; (aufräumen) tidy; (reparieren) mend; (fig) put right; **in O~ sein** be in order; (ordentlich sein) be tidy; (fig) be all right; **[geht] in O~!** OK! **o~sgemäß** *a* proper. **O~sstrafe** f (Jur) fine. **o~swidrig** *a* improper

Ordonnanz, Ordonanz f -, -en (Mil) orderly

Organ *nt* -s, -e organ; voice

Organisation /-ˈtsi̯oːn/ f -, -en organization

organisch *a* organic

organisieren *vt* organize; (▣ beschaffen) get [hold of]

Organismus *m* -, -men organism; (System) system

Organspenderkarte f donor card

Orgasmus *m* -, -men orgasm

Orgel f -, -n (Mus) organ. **O~pfeife** f organ-pipe

Orgie /ˈɔrgi̯ə/ f -, -n orgy

Orien|t /ˈoːri̯ɛnt/ *m* -s Orient. **o~talisch** *a* Oriental

orientier|en /ori̯ɛnˈtiːrən/ *vt* inform (über + acc about); **sich o~en** get one's bearings, orientate oneself; (unterrichten) inform oneself (über + acc about). **O~ung** f - orientation; **die O~ung verlieren** lose one's bearings

original *a* original. **O~** *nt* -s, -e original. **O~übertragung** f live transmission

originell *a* original; (eigenartig) unusual

Orkan *m* -s, -e hurricane

Ornament *nt* -[e]s, -e ornament

Ort *m* -[e]s, -e place; (Ortschaft) [small] town; **am Ort** locally; **am Ort des Verbrechens** at the scene of the crime

ortho|dox *a* orthodox. **O~graphie, O~grafie** f - spelling. **O~päde** *m* -n, -n orthopaedic specialist

örtlich *a* local

Ortschaft f -, -en [small] town; (Dorf) village; **geschlossene O~** (Auto) built-up area

Orts|gespräch *nt* (Teleph) local call. **O~verkehr** *m* local traffic. **O~zeit** f local time

Öse f -, -n eyelet; (Schlinge) loop; **Haken und Öse** hook and eye

Ost *m* -[e]s east

Osten *m* -s east; **nach O~** east

ostentativ *a* pointed

Osteopath *m* -en, -en osteopath

Oster|ei /ˈoːstɐʔai̯/ *nt* Easter egg. **O~fest** *nt* Easter. **O~glocke** f daffodil. **O~n** *nt* -,- Easter; **frohe O~n!** happy Easter!

Österreich *nt* -s Austria. **Ö~er** *m*, -s,-, **Ö~erin** f -, -nen Austrian. **ö~isch** *a* Austrian

östlich *a* eastern; <Richtung> easterly ●*adv & prep* (+ gen) **ö~ [von] der Stadt** [to the] east of the town

Ostsee f Baltic [Sea]

Otter¹ *m* -s,- otter
Otter² *f* -, -n adder
Ouverture /uvɛr'ty:rə/ *f* -, -n
overture
oval *a* oval. **O~** *nt* -s, -e oval
Oxid, Oxyd *nt* -[e]s, -e oxide
Ozean *m* -s, -e ocean
Ozon *nt* -s ozone. **O~loch** *nt* hole
in the ozone layer. **O~schicht** *f*
ozone layer

paar *pron inv* **ein p~** a few; **ein p~**
Mal a few times; **alle p~ Tage**
every few days. **P~** *nt* -[e]s, -e
pair; (*Ehe-, Liebes-*) couple.
p~en *vt* mate; (*verbinden*)
combine; **sich p~en** mate. **P~ung**
f -, -en mating. **p~weise** *adv* in
pairs, in twos
Pacht *f* -, -en lease; (*P~summe*)
rent. **p~en** *vt* lease
Pächter *m* -s,- lessee; (*eines*
Hofes) tenant
Pachtvertrag *m* lease
Päckchen *nt* -s,- package, small
packet
pack|en *vt/i* (*haben*) pack;
(*ergreifen*) seize; (*fig: fesseln*)
grip. **P~en** *m* -s,- bundle. **p~end**
a (*fig*) gripping. **P~papier** *nt*
[strong] wrapping paper. **P~ung**
f -, -en packet; (*Med*) pack
Pädagog|e *m* -n, -n educationalist;
(*Lehrer*) teacher. **P~ik** *f* -
educational science
Paddel *nt* -s,- paddle. **P~boot** *nt*
canoe. **p~n** *vt/i* (*haben/sein*)
paddle. **P~sport** *m* canoeing
Page /'pa:ʒə/ *m* -n, -n page
Paillette /paj'jɛtə/ *f* -, -n sequin

Paket *nt* -[e]s, -e packet; (*Post-*)
parcel
Pakist|an *nt* -s Pakistan.
P~aner(in) *m* -s,- (*f* -, -nen)
Pakistani. **p~anisch** *a* Pakistani
Palast *m* -[e]s,"-e palace
Paläst|ina *nt* -s Palestine.
P~inenser(in) *m* -s,- (*f* -, -nen)
Palestinian. **p~inensisch** *a*
Palestinian
Palette *f* -, -n palette
Palme *f* -, -n palm[-tree]
Pampelmuse *f* -, -n grapefruit
Panier|mehl *nt* (*Culin*)
breadcrumbs *pl*. **p~t** *a* (*Culin*)
breaded
Panik *f* - panic
Panne *f* -, -n breakdown; (*Reifen-*)
flat tyre; (*Missgeschick*) mishap
Panther, Panter *m* -s,- panther
Pantine *f* -, -n [wooden] clog
Pantoffel *m* -s, -n slipper; mule
Pantomime¹ *f* -, -n mime
Pantomime² *m* -n, -n mime artist
Panzer *m* -s,- armour; (*Mil*) tank;
(*Zool*) shell. **p~n** *vt* armourplate.
P~schrank *m* safe
Papa /'papa, pa'pa:/ *m* -s, -s daddy
Papagei *m* -s & -en, -en parrot
Papier *nt* -[e]s, -e paper. **P~korb**
m waste-paper basket.
P~schlange *f* streamer.
P~waren *fpl* stationery *sg*
Pappe *f* - cardboard
Pappel *f* -, -n poplar
pappig *a* Ⓘ sticky
Papp|karton *m*, **P~schachtel** *f*
cardboard box
Paprika *m* -s, -[s] [sweet] pepper;
(*Gewürz*) paprika
Papst *m* -[e]s,"-e pope
päpstlich *a* papal
Parade *f* -, -n parade
Paradies *nt* -es, -e paradise
Paraffin *nt* -s paraffin
Paragraph, Paragraf *m* -en, -en
section
parallel *a & adv* parallel. **P~e** *f* -,
-n parallel

P

Paranuss f Brazil nut
Parasit m -en, -en parasite
parat a ready
Parcours /par'ku:ɐ̯/ m -,- /-[s], -s/ (Sport) course
Pardon /par'dõ:/ int sorry!
Parfüm nt -s, -e & -s perfume, scent. **p~iert** a perfumed, scented
parieren vi (haben) ⊡ obey
Park m -s, -s park. **p~en** vt/i (haben) park. **P~en** nt -s parking; 'P~en verboten' 'no parking'
Parkett nt -[e]s, -e parquet floor; (Theat) stalls pl
Park|haus nt multi-storey car park. **P~kralle** f wheel clamp. **P~lücke** f parking space. **P~platz** m car park; parking space. **P~scheibe** f parking-disc. **P~schein** m car-park ticket. **P~uhr** f parking-meter. **P~verbot** nt parking ban; 'P~verbot' 'no parking'
Parlament nt -[e]s, -e parliament. **p~arisch** a parliamentary
Parodie f -, -n parody
Parole f -, -n slogan; (Mil) password
Partei f -, -en (Pol, Jur) party; (Miet-) tenant; **für jdn P~ ergreifen** take s.o.'s part. **p~isch** a biased
Parterre /par'tɛr/ nt -s, -s ground floor; (Theat) rear stalls pl
Partie f -, -n part; (Tennis, Schach) game; (Golf) round; (Comm) batch
Partikel nt -s,- particle
Partitur f -, -en (Mus) full score
Partizip nt -s, -ien /-iən/ participle
Partner|(in) m -s,- (f -, -nen) partner. **P~schaft** f -, -en partnership. **P~stadt** f twin town
Party /'pa:ɐ̯ti/ f -, -s party
Parzelle f -, -n plot [of ground]
Pass m -es, ̈-e passport; (Geog, Sport) pass

Passage /pa'sa:ʒə/ f -, -n passage; (Einkaufs-) shopping arcade
Passagier /pasa'ʒi:ɐ̯/ m -s, -e passenger
Passant(in) m -en, -en (f -, -nen) passer-by
Passe f -, -n yoke
passen vi (haben) fit; (geeignet sein) be right (für for); (Sport) pass the ball; (aufgeben) pass; **p~ zu** go [well] with; (übereinstimmen) match; **jdm p~** fit s.o.; (gelegen sein) suit s.o.; **[ich] passe** pass. **p~d** a suitable; (angemessen) appropriate; (günstig) convenient; (übereinstimmend) matching
passier|en vt pass; cross <Grenze>; (Culin) rub through a sieve ● vi (sein) happen (jdm to s.o.); **es ist ein Unglück p~t** there has been an accident. **P~schein** m pass
Passiv nt -s, -e (Gram) passive
Passstraße f pass
Paste f -, -n paste
Pastell nt -[e]s, -e pastel
Pastete f -, -n pie; (Gänseleber-) pâté
pasteurisieren /pastøri'zi:rən/ vt pasteurize
Pastor m -s, -en /-'to:rən/ pastor
Pate m -n, -n godfather; (fig) sponsor; **P~n** godparents. **P~nkind** nt godchild
Patent nt -[e]s, -e patent; (Offiziers-) commission. **p~** a ⊡ clever; <Person> resourceful. **p~ieren** vt patent
Pater m -s,- (Relig) Father
Patholog|e m -n, -n pathologist. **p~isch** a pathological
Patience /pa'siã:s/ f -, -n patience
Patient(in) /pa'tsiɛnt(m)/ m -en, -en (f -, -nen) patient
Patin f -, -nen godmother
Patriot|(in) m -en, -en (f -, -nen) patriot. **p~isch** a patriotic. **P~ismus** m - patriotism

Patrone f -, -n cartridge

Patrouille /pa'trʊljə/ f -, -n patrol

Patsch|e f in der P~e sitzen 🛈 be in a jam. **p~nass** a 🛈 soaking wet

Patt nt -s stalemate

Patz|er m -s,- 🛈 slip. **p~ig** a 🛈 insolent

Pauk|e f -, -n kettledrum; auf die P~e hauen 🛈 have a good time; (prahlen) boast. **p~en** vt/i (haben) 🛈 swot

pauschal a all-inclusive; (einheitlich) flat-rate; (fig) sweeping <Urteil>; **p~e Summe** lump sum. **P~e** f -, -n lump sum. **P~reise** f package tour. **P~summe** f lump sum

Pause¹ f -, -n break; (beim Sprechen) pause; (Theat) interval; (im Kino) intermission; (Mus) rest; **P~ machen** have a break

Pause² f -, -n tracing. **p~n** vt trace

pausenlos a incessant

pausieren vi (haben) have a break; (ausruhen) rest

Pauspapier nt tracing-paper

Pavian m -s, -e baboon

Pavillon /'pavɪljõ/ m -s, -s pavilion

Pazifi|k m -s Pacific [Ocean]. **p~sch** a Pacific

Pazifist m -en, -en pacifist

Pech nt -s pitch; (Unglück) bad luck; **P~ haben** be unlucky

Pedal nt -s, -e pedal

Pedant m -en, -en pedant

Pediküre f -, -n pedicure

Pegel m -s,- level; (Gerät) water-level indicator. **P~stand** m [water] level

peilen vt take a bearing on

peinigen vt torment

peinlich a embarrassing, awkward; (genau) scrupulous; **es war mir sehr p~** I was very embarrassed

Peitsche f -, -n whip. **p~n** vt whip; (fig) lash ●vi (sein) lash

(an + acc against). **P~nhieb** m lash

Pelikan m -s, -e pelican

Pell|e f -, -n skin. **p~en** vt peel; shell <Ei>; **sich p~en** peel

Pelz m -es, -e fur

Pendel nt -s,- pendulum. **p~n** vi (haben) swing ●vi (sein) commute. **P~verkehr** m shuttle-service; (für Pendler) commuter traffic

Pendler m -s,- commuter

penetrant a penetrating; (fig) obtrusive

Penis m -, -se penis

Penne f -, -n 🛈 school

Pension /pã'zio:n/ f -, -en pension; (Hotel) guest-house; **bei voller/ halber P~** with full/half board. **P~är(in)** m -s, -e (f -, -nen) pensioner. **P~at** nt -[e]s, -e boarding-school. **p~ieren** vt retire. **P~ierung** f - retirement

Pensum nt -s [allotted] work

Peperoni f -,- chilli

per prep (+ acc) by

Perfekt nt -s (Gram) perfect

Perfektion /-'tsio:n/ f - perfection

perforiert a perforated

Pergament nt -[e]s, -e parchment. **P~papier** nt grease-proof paper

Period|e f -, -n period. **p~isch** a periodic

Perl|e f -, -n pearl; (Glas-, Holz-) bead; (Sekt-) bubble. **P~mutt** nt -s mother-of-pearl

Pers|ien /-iən/ nt -s Persia. **p~isch** a Persian

Person f -, -en person; (Theat) character; **für vier P~en** for four people

Personal nt -s personnel, staff. **P~ausweis** m identity card. **P~chef** m personnel manager. **P~ien** /-iən/ pl personal particulars. **P~mangel** m staff shortage

persönlich a personal ● adv
personally, in person. **P~keit** f -,
-en personality
Perücke f -, -n wig
pervers a [sexually] perverted.
P~ion f -, -en perversion
Pessimis|mus m - pessimism.
P~t m -en, -en pessimist. **p~tisch**
a pessimistic
Pest f - plague
Petersilie /-iə/ f - parsley
Petroleum /-leum/ nt -s paraffin
Petze f -, -n ⓘ sneak. **p~n** vi
(haben) ⓘ sneak
Pfad m -[e]s, -e path. **P~finder** m
-s, - [Boy] Scout. **P~finderin** f -,
-nen [Girl] Guide
Pfahl m -[e]s,¨e stake, post
Pfalz (die) - the Palatinate
Pfand nt -[e]s,¨er pledge; (beim
Spiel) forfeit; (Flaschen-) deposit
pfänd|en vt (Jur) seize. **P~erspiel**
nt game of forfeits
Pfandleiher m -s,- pawnbroker
Pfändung f -, -en (Jur) seizure
Pfann|e f -, -n (frying-)pan.
P~kuchen m pancake
Pfarr|er m -s,- vicar, parson;
(katholischer) priest. **P~haus** nt
vicarage
Pfau m -s, -en peacock
Pfeffer m -s pepper. **P~kuchen** m
gingerbread. **P~minze** f - (Bot)
peppermint. **p~n** vt pepper; (ⓘ
schmeißen) chuck. **P~streuer** m
-s,- pepperpot
Pfeif|e f -, -n whistle; (Tabak-,
Orgel-) pipe. **p~en†** vt/i (haben)
whistle; (als Signal) blow the
whistle
Pfeil m -[e]s, -e arrow
Pfeiler m -s,- pillar; (Brücken-)
pier
Pfennig m -s, -e pfennig
Pferch m -[e]s, -e [sheep] pen
Pferd nt -es, -e horse; **zu P~e** on
horseback. **P~erennen** nt
horse-race; (als Sport) [horse-]
racing. **P~eschwanz** m horse's

tail; (Frisur) pony-tail. **P~estall**
m stable. **P~estärke** f
horsepower
Pfiff m -[e]s, -e whistle
Pfifferling m -s, -e chanterelle
pfiffig a smart
Pfingst|en nt -s Whitsun. **P~rose**
f peony
Pfirsich m -s, -e peach
Pflanz|e f -, -n plant. **p~en** vt
plant. **P~enfett** nt vegetable fat.
p~lich a vegetable
Pflaster nt -s,- pavement; (Heft-)
plaster. **p~n** vt pave
Pflaume f -, -n plum
Pflege f - care; (Kranken-)
nursing; **in P~ nehmen** look after;
(Admin) foster <Kind>.
p~bedürftig a in need of care.
P~eltern pl foster-parents.
P~kind nt foster-child. **p~leicht**
a easy-care. **p~n** vt look after,
care for; nurse <Kranke>;
cultivate <Künste, Freundschaft>.
P~r(in) m -s,- (f -, -nen) nurse;
(Tier-) keeper
Pflicht f -, -en duty; (Sport)
compulsory exercise/routine.
p~bewusst a conscientious.
P~gefühl nt sense of duty
pflücken vt pick
Pflug m -[e]s,¨e plough
pflügen vt/i (haben) plough
Pforte f -, -n gate
Pförtner m -s,- porter
Pfosten m -s,- post
Pfote f -, -n paw
Pfropfen m -s,- stopper; (Korken-)
cork. **p~** vt graft (auf + acc on
[to]); (ⓘ pressen) cram (in + acc
into)
pfui int ugh
Pfund nt -[e]s, -e & - pound
Pfusch|arbeit f ⓘ shoddy work.
p~en vi (haben) ⓘ botch one's
work. **P~erei** f -, -en ⓘ botch-up
Pfütze f -, -n puddle
Phantasie f -, -n imagination; **P~n**
fantasies; (Fieber-)

hallucinations. **p~los** a
unimaginative. **p~ren** vi (haben)
fantasize; (im Fieber) be
delirious. **p~voll** a imaginative
phantastisch a fantastic
pharma|zeutisch a
pharmaceutical. **P~zie** f -
pharmacy
Phase f -, -n phase
Philologie f - [study of] language
and literature
Philosoph m -en, -en philosopher.
P~ie f -, -n philosophy
philosophisch a philosophical
Phobie f -, -n phobia
Phonet|ik f - phonetics sg.
p~isch a phonetic
Phosphor m -s phosphorus
Photo nt, **Photo-** = **Foto**, **Foto-**
Phrase f -, -n empty phrase
Physik f - physics sg. **p~alisch** a
physical
Physiker(in) m -s,- (f -, -nen)
physicist
Physiologie f - physiology
physisch a physical
Pianist(in) m -en, -en (f -, -nen)
pianist
Pickel m -s,- pimple, spot;
(Spitzhacke) pick. **p~ig** a spotty
Picknick nt -s, -s picnic
piep[s]|en vi (haben) <Vogel:>
cheep; <Maus:> squeak; (Techn)
bleep. **P~er** m -s,- bleeper
Pier m -s, -e [harbour] pier
Pietät /piɛ'tɛːt/ f - reverence.
p~los a irreverent
Pigment nt -[e]s, -e pigment.
P~ierung f - pigmentation
Pik nt -s, -s (Karten) spades pl
pikant a piquant; (gewagt) racy
piken vt 🔲 prick
pikiert a offended, hurt
Pilger|(in) m -s,- (f -, -nen) pilgrim.
P~fahrt f pilgrimage. **p~n** vi
(sein) make a pilgrimage
Pille f -, -n pill
Pilot m -en, -en pilot

Pilz m -es, -e fungus; (essbarer)
mushroom
pingelig a 🔲 fussy
Pinguin m -s, -e penguin
Pinie /-iə/ f -, -n stone-pine
pinkeln vi (haben) 🔲 pee
Pinsel m -s,- [paint]brush
Pinzette f -, -n tweezers pl
Pionier m -s, -e (Mil) sapper; (fig)
pioneer
Pirat m -en, -en pirate
Piste f -, -n (Ski-) run, piste;
(Renn-) track; (Aviat) runway
Pistole f -, -n pistol
pitschnass a 🔲 soaking wet
pittoresk a picturesque
Pizza f -, -s pizza
Pkw /'peːkaveː/ m -s, -s car
plädieren vi (haben) plead (für
for); **auf Freispruch p~** (Jur) ask
for an acquittal
Plädoyer /plɛdoa'jeː/ nt -s, -s (Jur)
closing speech; (fig) plea
Plage f -, -n [hard] labour; (Mühe)
trouble; (Belästigung) nuisance.
p~n vt torment, plague;
(bedrängen) pester; **sich p~n**
struggle
Plakat nt -[e]s, -e poster
Plakette f -, -n badge
Plan m -[e]s,⸚e plan
Plane f -, -n tarpaulin; (Boden-)
groundsheet
planen vt/i (haben) plan
Planet m -en, -en planet
planier|en vt level. **P~raupe** f
bulldozer
Planke f -, -n plank
plan|los a unsystematic.
p~mäßig a systematic;
<Ankunft> scheduled
Plansch|becken nt paddling
pool. **p~en** vi (haben) splash
about
Plantage /plan'taːʒə/ f -, -n
plantation
Planung f - planning
plappern vi (haben) chatter ● vt
talk <Unsinn>

P

plärren vi (haben) bawl

Plasma nt -s plasma

Plastik¹ f -, -en sculpture

Plast|ik² nt -s plastic. **p~isch** a three-dimensional; (formbar) plastic; (anschaulich) graphic

Plateau /pla'to:/ nt -s, -s plateau

Platin nt -s platinum

platonisch a platonic

plätschern vi (haben) splash; <Bach:> babble ● vi (sein) <Bach:> babble along

platt a & adv flat. **P~** nt -[s] (Lang) Low German

Plättbrett nt ironing-board

Platte f -, -n slab; (Druck-) plate; (Metall-, Glas-) sheet; (Fliese) tile; (Koch-) hotplate; (Tisch-) top; (Schall-) record, disc; (zum Servieren) [flat] dish, platter; **kalte P~** assorted cold meats and cheeses pl

Plätt|eisen nt iron. **p~en** vt/i (haben) iron

Plattenspieler m record-player

Platt|form f -, -en platform. **P~füße** mpl flat feet

Platz m -es, ̈-e place; (von Häusern umgeben) square; (Sitz-) seat; (Sport-) ground; (Fußball-) pitch; (Tennis-) court; (Golf-) course; (freier Raum) room, space; **P~ nehmen** take a seat; **P~ machen** make room; **vom P~ stellen** (Sport) send off. **P~anweiserin** f -, -nen usherette

Plätzchen nt -s,- spot; (Culin) biscuit

platzen vi (sein) burst; (auf-) split; (⊞ scheitern) fall through; <Verlobung:> be off

Platz|karte f seat reservation ticket. **P~mangel** m lack of space. **P~patrone** f blank. **P~verweis** m (Sport) sending off. **P~wunde** f laceration

Plauderei f -, -en chat

plaudern vi (haben) chat

plausibel a plausible

pleite a ⊞ **p~ sein** be broke: <Firma:> be bankrupt. **P~** f -, -n ⊞ bankruptcy; (Misserfolg) flop; **P~ gehen** od **machen** go bankrupt▮

plissiert a [finely] pleated

Plomb|e f -, -n seal; (Zahn-) filling. **p~ieren** vt seal; fill <Zahn>

plötzlich a sudden

plump a plump; clumsy

plumpsen vi (sein) ⊞ fall

plündern vt/i (haben) loot

Plünderstück nt Danish pastry

Plural m -s, -e plural

plus adv, conj & prep (+ dat) plus. **P~** nt - surplus; (Gewinn) profit (Vorteil) advantage, plus. **P~punkt** m (Sport) point; (fig) plus

Po m -s, -s ⊞ bottom

Pöbel m -s mob, rabble. **p~haft** a loutish

pochen vi (haben) knock, <Herz:> pound; **p~ auf** (+ acc) (fig) insist on

pochieren /pɔ'ʃi:rən/ vt poach

Pocken pl smallpox sg

Podest nt -[e]s, -e rostrum

Podium nt -s, -ien /-iən/ platform; (Podest) rostrum

Poesie /poe'zi:/ f - poetry

poetisch a poetic

Pointe /'poɛ̃:tə/ f -, -n point (of a joke)

Pokal m -s, -e goblet; (Sport) cup

pökeln vt (Culin) salt

Poker nt -s poker

Pol m -s, -e pole. **p~ar** a polar

Polarstern m pole-star

Pole m, -n, -n Pole. **P~n** nt -s Poland

Police /po'li:sə/ f -, -n policy

Polier m -s, -e foreman

polieren vt polish

Polin f -, -nen Pole

Politesse f -, -n [woman] traffic warden

Politik f - politics sg; (Vorgehen, Maßnahme) policy

Polit|iker(in) m -s,- (f, -, -nen) politician. **p~isch** a political

Politur f -, -en polish

Polizei f - police pl. **p~lich** a police ... ● adv by the police; <sich anmelden> with the police. **P~streife** f police patrol. **P~stunde** f closing time. **P~wache** f police station

Polizist m -en, -en policeman. **P~in** f -, -nen policewoman

Pollen m - pollen

polnisch a Polish

Polster nt -s,- pad; (Kissen) cushion; (Möbel-) upholstery. **p~n** vt pad; upholster <Möbel>. **P~ung** f - padding; upholstery

Polter|abend m wedding-eve party. **p~n** vi (haben) thump bang

Polyäthylen nt -s polythene

Polyester m -s polyester

Polyp m -en, -en polyp. **P~en** adenoids pl

Pommes frites /pɔm'fri:t/ pl chips; (dünner) French fries

Pomp m -s pomp

Pompon /põ'põ:/ m -s, -s pompon

pompös a ostentatious

Pony¹ nt -s, -s pony

Pony² m -s, -s fringe

Pop m -[s] pop

Popo m -s, -s Ⓘ bottom

populär a popular

Pore f -, -n pore

Porno|graphie, Pornografie f - pornography. **p~graphisch, p~grafisch** a pornographic

Porree m -s leeks pl

Portal nt -s, -e portal

Portemonnaie /pɔrtmɔ'ne:/ nt -s, -s purse

Portier /pɔr'tje:/ m -s, -s doorman, porter

Portion /-'tsio:n/ f -, -en helping, portion

Portmonee nt -s, -s = **Portemonnaie**

Porto nt -s postage. **p~frei** adv post free, post paid

Porträ|t /pɔr'trɛ:/ nt -s, -s portrait. **p~tieren** vt paint a portrait of

Portugal nt -s Portugal

Portugies|e m -n, -n, **P~in** f -, -nen Portuguese. **p~isch** a Portuguese

Portwein m port

Porzellan nt -s china, porcelain

Posaune f -, -n trombone

Position /-'tsio:n/ f -, -en position

positiv a positive. **P~** nt -s, -e (Phot) positive

Post f - post office; (Briefe) mail, post; **mit der P~** by post

postalisch a postal

Post|amt nt post office. **P~anweisung** f postal money order. **P~bote** m postman

Posten m -s,- post; (Wache) sentry; (Waren-) batch; (Rechnungs-) item, entry

Poster nt & m -s,- poster

Postfach nt post-office or PO box

Post|karte f postcard. **p~lagernd** adv poste restante. **P~leitzahl** f postcode. **P~scheckkonto** nt ≈ National Girobank account. **P~stempel** m postmark

postum a posthumous

post|wendend adv by return of post. **P~wertzeichen** nt [postage] stamp

Potenz f -, -en potency; (Math & fig) power

Pracht f - magnificence, splendour

prächtig a magnificent; splendid

prachtvoll a magnificent

Prädikat nt -[e]s, -e rating; (Comm) grade; (Gram) predicate

prägen vt stamp (auf + acc on); emboss <Leder>; mint <Münze>; coin <Wort>; (fig) shape

prägnant a succinct

prähistorisch a prehistoric

prahl|en vi (haben) boast, brag (mit about)

P

Prakti|k f -, -en practice.
P~kant(in) m -en, -en (f -, -nen)
trainee
Prakti|kum nt -s, -ka practical
training. p~sch a practical;
(nützlich) handy; (tatsächlich)
virtual; p~scher Arzt general
practitioner ● adv practically;
virtually; (in der Praxis) in
practice. p~zieren vt/i (haben)
practise; (anwenden) put into
practice; (🔲 bekommen) get
Praline f -, -n chocolate
prall a bulging; (dick) plump;
<Sonne> blazing ● adv p~ gefüllt
full to bursting. p~en vi (sein)
p~ auf (+ acc)/gegen collide with,
hit; <Sonne:> blaze down on
Prämie /-ie/ f -, -n premium;
(Preis) award
präm[i]ieren vt award a prize to
Pranger m -s,- pillory
Pranke f -, -n paw
Präparat nt -[e]s, -e preparation
Präsens nt - (Gram) present
präsentieren vt present
Präsenz f - presence
Präservativ nt -s, -e condom
Präsident|(in) m -en, -en (f -, -nen)
president. P~schaft f -
presidency
Präsidium nt -s presidency;
(Gremium) executive committee;
(Polizei-) headquarters pl
prasseln vi (haben) <Regen:> beat
down; <Feuer:> crackle
Präteritum nt -s imperfect
Praxis f -, -xen practice;
(Erfahrung) practical experience;
(Arzt-) surgery; in der P~ in
practice
Präzedenzfall m precedent
präzis[e] a precise
predig|en vt/i (haben) preach.
P~t f -, -en sermon
Preis m -es, -e price; (Belohnung)
prize. P~ausschreiben nt
competition

Preiselbeere f (Bot) cowberry;
(Culin) ≈ cranberry
preisen† vt praise
preisgeben† vt sep abandon (dat
to); reveal <Geheimnis>
preis|gekrönt a award-winning.
p~günstig a reasonably priced
● adv at a reasonable price.
P~lage f price range. p~lich a
price ... ● adv in price. P~richter
m judge. P~schild nt price-tag.
P~träger(in) m(f) prize-winner.
p~wert a reasonable
Prell|bock m buffers pl. p~en vt
bounce; (verletzen) bruise; (🔲
betrügen) cheat. P~ung f -, -en
bruise
Premiere /prə'mie:rə/ f -, -n
première
Premierminister(in) /prə'mie:-/
m(f) Prime Minister
Presse f -, -n press. p~n vt press
Pressluftbohrer m pneumatic
drill
Preuß|en nt -s Prussia. p~isch a
Prussian
prickeln vi (haben) tingle
Priester m -s,- priest
prima inv a first-class, first-rate;
(🔲 toll) fantastic
primär a primary
Primel f -, -n primula
primitiv a primitive
Prinz m -en, -en prince. P~essin f
-, -nen princess
Prinzip nt -s, -ien /-iən/ principle.
p~iell a <Frage> of principle
● adv on principle
Prise f -, -n P~ Salz pinch of salt
Prisma nt -s, -men prism
privat a private, personal.
P~adresse f home address.
p~isieren vt privatize
Privileg nt -[e]s, -ien /-iən/
privilege. p~iert a privileged
pro prep (+ dat) per. **Pro** nt - das
Pro und Kontra the pros and cons
pl

Probe f -, -n test, trial; (*Menge, Muster*) sample; (*Theat*) rehearsal; **auf die P~ stellen** put to the test; **ein Auto P~ fahren** test-drive a car. **p~n** vt/i (*haben*) (*Theat*) rehearse. **p~weise** adv on a trial basis. **P~zeit** f probationary period

probieren vt/i (*haben*) try; (*kosten*) taste; (*proben*) rehearse

Problem nt -s, -e problem. **p~atisch** a problematic

problemlos a problem-free ● adv without any problems

Produkt nt -[e]s, -e product

Produk|tion /-'tsio:n/ f -, -en production. **p~tiv** a productive

Produ|zent m -en, -en producer. **p~zieren** vt produce

Professor m -s, -en /-'so:rən/ professor

Profi m -s, -s (*Sport*) professional

Profil nt -s, -e profile; (*Reifen-*) tread; (*fig*) image

Profit m -[e]s, -e profit. **p~ieren** vi (*haben*) profit (**von** from)

Prognose f -, -n forecast; (*Med*) prognosis

Programm nt -s, -e programme; (*Computer-*) program; (*TV*) channel; (*Comm: Sortiment*) range. **p~ieren** vt/i (*haben*) (*Computer*) program. **P~ierer(in)** m -s,- (f -, -nen) [computer] programmer

Projekt nt -[e]s, -e project

Projektor m -s, -en /-'to:rən/ projector

Prolet m -en, -en boor. **P~ariat** nt -[e]s proletariat

Prolog m -s, -e prologue

Promenade f -, -n promenade

Promille pl 🔟 alcohol level *sg* in the blood; **zu viel P~ haben** 🔟 be over the limit

Prominenz f - prominent figures *pl*

Promiskuität f - promiscuity

promovieren vi (*haben*) obtain one's doctorate

prompt a prompt

Pronomen nt -s,- pronoun

Propaganda f - propaganda; (*Reklame*) publicity

Propeller m -s,- propeller

Prophet m -en, -en prophet

prophezei|en vt prophesy. **P~ung** f -, -en prophecy

Proportion /-'tsio:n/ f -, -en proportion

Prosa f - prose

prosit int cheers!

Prospekt m -[e]s, -e brochure; (*Comm*) prospectus

prost int cheers!

Prostitu|ierte f -n, -n prostitute. **P~tion** /-'tsio:n/ f - prostitution

Protest m -[e]s, -e protest

Protestant|(in) m -en, -en (f -, -nen) (*Relig*) Protestant. **p~isch** a (*Relig*) Protestant

protestieren vi (*haben*) protest

Prothese f -, -n artificial limb; (*Zahn-*) denture

Protokoll nt -s, -e record; (*Sitzungs-*) minutes *pl*; (*diplomatisches*) protocol

protz|en vi (*haben*) show off (**mit etw** sth). **p~ig** a ostentatious

Proviant m -s provisions *pl*

Provinz f -, -en province

Provision f -, -en (*Comm*) commission

provisorisch a provisional, temporary

Provokation /-'tsio:n/ f -, -en provocation

provozieren vt provoke

Prozedur f -, -en [lengthy] business

Prozent nt -[e]s, -e & - per cent; 5 **P~** 5 per cent. **P~satz** m percentage. **p~ual** a percentage ...

Prozess m -es, -e process; (*Jur*) lawsuit; (*Kriminal-*) trial

Prozession f -, -en procession

P

prüde *a* prudish

prüf|en *vt* test/(*über-*) check (**auf** + *acc* for); audit <*Bücher*>; (*Sch*) examine; **p~ender Blick** searching look. **P~er** *m* **-s,-** inspector; (*Buch-*) auditor; (*Sch*) examiner. **P~ling** *m* **-s, -e** examination candidate. **P~ung** *f* **-, -en** examination; (*Test*) test; (*Bücher-*) audit; (*fig*) trial

Prügel *m* **-s,-** cudgel; **P~** *pl* hiding *sg*, beating *sg*. **P~ei** *f* **-, -en** brawl, fight. **p~n** *vt* beat, thrash

Prunk *m* **-[e]s** magnificence, splendour

Psalm *m* **-s, -en** psalm

Pseudonym *nt* **-s, -e** pseudonym

pst *int* shush!

Psychi|ater *m* **-s,-** psychiatrist. **P~atrie** *f* **-** psychiatry. **p~atrisch** *a* psychiatric

psychisch *a* psychological

Psycho|analyse *f* psychoanalysis. **P~loge** *m* **-n, -n** psychologist. **P~logie** *f* **-** psychology. **p~logisch** *a* psychological

Pubertät *f* **-** puberty

Publi|kum *nt* **-s** public; (*Zuhörer*) audience; (*Zuschauer*) spectators *pl*. **p~zieren** *vt* publish

Pudding *m* **-s, -s** blancmange; (*im Wasserbad gekocht*) pudding

Pudel *m* **-s,-** poodle

Puder *m* & 🔲 *nt* **-s,-** powder. **P~dose** *f* [powder] compact. **p~n** *vt* powder. **P~zucker** *m* icing sugar

Puff *m* & *nt* **-s, -s** ✖ brothel

Puffer *m* **-s,-** (*Rail*) buffer; (*Culin*) pancake. **P~zone** *f* buffer zone

Pull|i *m* **-s, -s** jumper. **P~over** *m* **-s,-** jumper; (*Herren-*) pullover

Puls *m* **-es** pulse. **P~ader** *f* artery

Pult *nt* **-[e]s, -e** desk

Pulver *nt* **-s,-** powder. **p~ig** *a* powdery

Pulverkaffee *m* instant coffee

pummelig *a* 🔲 chubby

Pumpe *f* **-, -n** pump. **p~n** *vt/i* (*haben*) pump; (🔲 *leihen*) lend; [**sich** (*dat*)] **etw p~n** (🔲 *borgen*) borrow sth

Pumps /pœmps/ *pl* court shoes

Punkt *m* **-[e]s, -e** dot; (*Tex*) spot; (*Geom, Sport & fig*) point; (*Gram*) full stop, period; **P~ sechs Uhr** at six o'clock sharp

pünktlich *a* punctual. **P~keit** *f* **-** punctuality

Pupille *f* **-, -n** (*Anat*) pupil

Puppe *f* **-, -n** doll; (*Marionette*) puppet; (*Schaufenster-, Schneider-*) dummy; (*Zool*) chrysalis

pur *a* pure; (🔲 *bloß*) sheer

Püree *nt* **-s, -s** purée; (*Kartoffel-*) mashed potatoes *pl*

purpurrot *a* crimson

Purzel|baum *m* 🔲 somersault. **p~n** *vi* (*sein*) 🔲 tumble

Puste *f* **-** 🔲 breath. **p~n** *vt/i* (*haben*) 🔲 blow

Pute *f* **-, -n** turkey

Putsch *m* **-[e]s, -e** coup

Putz *m* **-es** plaster; (*Staat*) finery. **p~en** *vt* clean; (*Aust*) dry-clean; (*zieren*) adorn; **sich p~en** dress up; **sich** (*dat*) **die Zähne/Nase p~en** clean one's teeth/blow one's nose. **P~frau** *f* cleaner, charwoman. **p~ig** *a* 🔲 amusing, cute; (*seltsam*) odd

Puzzlespiel /'pazl-/ *nt* jigsaw

Pyramide *f* **-, -n** pyramid

Quacksalber *m* **-s,-** quack

Quadrat *nt* **-[e]s, -e** square. **q~isch** *a* square

quaken vi (haben) quack; <Frosch:> croak
Quäker(in) m -s,- (f -, -nen) Quaker
Qual f -, -en torment; (Schmerz) agony
quälen vt torment; (foltern) torture; (bedrängen) pester; **sich q~** torment oneself; (leiden) suffer; (sich mühen) struggle
Quälerei f -, -en torture
Qualifi|kation /-'tsio:n/ f -, -en qualification. **q~zieren** vt qualify. **q~ziert** a qualified; (fähig) competent; (Arbeit) skilled
Qualität f -, -en quality
Qualle f -, -n jellyfish
Qualm m -s [thick] smoke
qualvoll a agonizing
Quantum nt -s, -ten quantity; (Anteil) share, quota
Quarantäne f - quarantine
Quark m -s quark, ≈ curd cheese
Quartal nt -s, -e quarter
Quartett nt -[e]s, -e quartet
Quartier nt -s, -e accommodation; (Mil) quarters pl
Quarz m -es quartz
quasseln vi (haben) 🄻 jabber
Quaste f -, -n tassel
Quatsch m -[e]s 🄻 nonsense, rubbish. **Q~ machen** (Unfug machen) fool around; (etw falsch machen) do a silly thing. **q~en** 🄻 vi (haben) talk; <Wasser, Schlamm:> squelch ● vt talk
Quecksilber nt mercury
Quelle f -, -n spring; (Fluss- & fig) source
quengeln vi 🄻 whine
quer adv across, crosswise; (schräg) diagonally; **q~ gestreift** horizontally striped
Quere f - der **Q~ nach** across, crosswise; **jdm in die Q~ kommen** get in s.o.'s way
Quer|latte f crossbar. **Q~schiff** nt transept. **Q~schnitt** m cross-section. **q~schnittsgelähmt** a

paraplegic. **Q~straße** f side-street. **Q~verweis** m cross-reference
quetschen vt squash; (drücken) squeeze; (zerdrücken) crush; (Culin) mash; **sich q~ in** (+ acc) squeeze into
Queue /kø:/ nt -s, -s cue
quieken vi (haben) squeal; <Maus:> squeak
quietschen vi (haben) squeal; <Tür, Dielen:> creak
Quintett nt -[e]s, -e quintet
quirlen vt mix
Quitte f -, -n quince
quittieren vt receipt <Rechnung>; sign for <Geldsumme, Sendung>; **den Dienst q~** resign
Quittung f -, -en receipt
Quiz /kvɪs/ nt -, quiz
Quote f -, -n proportion

Rabatt m -[e]s, -e discount
Rabatte f -, -n (Hort) border
Rabattmarke f trading stamp
Rabbiner m -s,- rabbi
Rabe m -n, -n raven
Rache f - revenge, vengeance
Rachen m -s,- pharynx
rächen vt avenge; **sich r~** take revenge (an + dat on); <Fehler:> cost s.o. dear
Rad nt -[e]s,̈er wheel; (Fahr-) bicycle, 🄻 bike; **Rad fahren** cycle
Radar m & nt -s radar
Radau m -s 🄻 din, racket
radeln vi (sein) 🄻 cycle
Rädelsführer m ringleader

radfahr|en* vi sep (sein) Rad
fahren, s. Rad. **R~er(in)** m(f) -s,- (f
-, -nen) cyclist
radier|en vt/i (haben) rub out;
(Kunst) etch. **R~gummi** m eraser,
rubber. **R~ung** f -, -en etching
Radieschen /-'di:sçən/ nt -s,-
radish
radikal a radical, drastic
Radio nt -s, -s radio
radioaktiv a radioactive. **R~ität** f
- radioactivity
Radius m -, -ien /-iən/ radius
Rad|kappe f hub-cap. **R~ler** m
-s,- cyclist; (Getränk) shandy
raffen vt grab; (kräuseln) gather;
(kürzen) condense
Raffin|ade f - refined sugar.
R~erie f -, -n refinery. **R~esse** f
-, -n refinement; (Schlauheit)
cunning. **r~iert** a ingenious;
(durchtrieben) crafty
ragen vi (haben) rise [up]
Rahm m -s (SGer) cream
rahmen vt frame. **R~** m -s,-
frame; (fig) framework; (Grenze)
limits pl; (einer Feier) setting
Rakete f -, -n rocket; (Mil) missile
Rallye /'rali/ nt -s, -s rally
rammen vt ram
Rampe f -, -n ramp; (Theat) front
of the stage
Ramsch m -[e]s junk
ran adv = heran
Rand m -[e]s,¨er edge; (Teller-,
Gläser-, Brillen-) rim; (Zier-)
border, edging; (Brief-) margin;
(Stadt-) outskirts pl; (Ring) ring
randalieren vi (haben) rampage
Randstreifen m (Auto) hard
shoulder
Rang m -[e]s,¨e rank; (Theat) tier;
erster/zweiter **R~** (Theat) dress/
upper circle; ersten **R~es** first-
class
rangieren /raŋ'ʒi:rən/ vt shunt
● vi (haben) rank (vor + dat
before)

Rangordnung f order of
importance; (Hierarchie)
hierarchy
Ranke f -, -n tendril; (Trieb) shoot
ranken (sich) vr (Bot) trail; (in die
Höhe) climb
Ranzen m -s,- (Sch) satchel
ranzig a rancid
Rappe m -n, -n black horse
Raps m -es (Bot) rape
rar a rare; er macht sich rar [T] we
don't see much of him. **R~ität** f
-, -en rarity
rasant a fast; (schnittig, schick)
stylish
rasch a quick
rascheln vi (haben) rustle
Rasen m -s,- lawn
rasen vi (sein) tear [along];
<Puls:> race; <Zeit:> fly; gegen
eine Mauer r~ career into a wall
● vi (haben) rave; <Sturm:> rage.
r~d a furious; (tobend) raving;
<Sturm, Durst:> raging;
<Schmerz> excruciating;
<Beifall> tumultuous
Rasenmäher m lawn-mower
Rasier|apparat m razor. **r~en** vt
shave; sich **r~en** shave. **R~klinge**
f razor blade. **R~wasser** nt
aftershave [lotion]
Raspel f -, -n rasp; (Culin) grater.
r~n vt grate
Rasse f -, -n race. **R~hund** m
pedigree dog
Rassel f -, -n rattle. **r~n** vi
(haben) rattle; <Schlüssel:>
jangle; <Kette:> clank
Rassendiskriminierung f racial
discrimination
Rassepferd nt thoroughbred.
rassisch a racial
Rassis|mus m - racism. **r~tisch** a
racist
Rast f -, -en rest. **R~platz** m
picnic area. **R~stätte** f motorway
restaurant [and services]
Rasur f -, -en shave

Rat m -[e]s [piece of] advice; **sich**
(dat) **keinen Rat wissen** not know
what to do; **zu Rat[e] ziehen** =
zurate ziehen, s. **zurate**

Rate f -, -n instalment

raten† vt guess; (empfehlen)
advise ● vi (haben) guess; **jdm r~**
advise s.o.

Ratenzahlung f payment by
instalments

Rat|geber m -s,- adviser; (Buch)
guide. **R~haus** nt town hall

ratifizier|en vt ratify. **R~ung** f -,
-en ratification

Ration /ra'tsĭo:n/ f -, -en ration.
r~ell a efficient. **r~ieren** vt
ration

rat|los a helpless; **r~los sein** not
know what to do. **r~sam** pred a
advisable; prudent. **R~schlag** m
piece of advice; **R~schläge** advice
sg

Rätsel nt -s,- riddle; (Kreuzwort-)
puzzle; (Geheimnis) mystery.
r~haft a puzzling, mysterious.
r~n vi (haben) puzzle

Ratte f -, -n rat

rau a rough; (unfreundlich) gruff;
<Klima:> harsh, raw; (heiser)
husky; <Hals:> sore

Raub m -[e]s robbery;
(Menschen-) abduction; (Beute)
loot, booty. **r~en** vt steal; abduct
<Menschen>

Räuber m -s,- robber

Raub|mord m robbery with
murder. **R~tier** nt predator.
R~vogel m bird of prey

Rauch m -[e]s smoke. **r~en** vt/i
(haben) smoke. **R~en** nt -s
smoking. 'R~en verboten' 'no
smoking'. **R~er** m -s, -smoker

Räucher|lachs m smoked
salmon. **r~n** vt (Culin) smoke

rauf adv = herauf, hinauf

rauf|en vt pull ● vr/i (haben)
[sich] **r~en** fight. **R~erei** f -,-en
fight

rauh* a s. rau

Raum m -[e]s, Räume room;
(Gebiet) area; (Welt-) space

räumen vt clear; vacate
<Wohnung>; evacuate <Gebäude,
Gebiet, (Mil) Stellung>; (bringen)
put (in/auf + acc into/on); (holen)
get (aus out of)

Raum|fahrer m astronaut.
R~fahrt f space travel. **R~inhalt**
m volume

räumlich a spatial

Raum|pflegerin f cleaner.
R~schiff nt spaceship

Räumung f - clearing; vacating;
evacuation. **R~sverkauf** m
clearance/closing-down sale

Raupe f -, -n caterpillar

raus adv = heraus, hinaus

Rausch m -[e]s, Räusche
intoxication; (fig) exhilaration;
einen R~haben be drunk

rauschen vi (haben) <Wasser,
Wind:> rush; <Bäume Blätter:>
rustle ● vi (sein) rush [along]

Rauschgift nt [narcotic] drug;
(coll) drugs pl. **R~süchtige(r)** m/f
drug addict

räuspern (sich) vr clear one's
throat

rausschmeißen† vt sep Ⅰ throw
out; (entlassen) sack

Raute f -, -n diamond

Razzia f -, -ien /-iən/ [police] raid

Reagenzglas nt test-tube

reagieren vi (haben) react (auf +
acc to)

Reaktion /-'tsĭo:n/ f -, -en reaction.
r~är a reactionary

Reaktor m -s, -en /-'to:rən/ reactor

realisieren vt realize

Realis|mus m - realism. **R~t** m
-en, -en realist. **r~tisch** a realistic

Realität f -, -en reality

Realschule f ≈ secondary
modern school

Rebe f -, -n vine

Rebell m -en, -en rebel. **r~ieren** vi
(haben) rebel. **R~ion** f -, -en
rebellion

R

rebellisch a rebellious

Rebhuhn nt partridge

Rebstock m vine

Rechen m -s- rake

Rechen|aufgabe f arithmetical problem; (Sch) sum. **R~maschine** f calculator

recherchieren /reʃɛr'ʃiːrən/ vt/i (haben) investigate; (Journ) research

rechnen vi (haben) do arithmetic; (schätzen) reckon; (zählen) count (**zu** among; **auf** + acc on); **r~ mit** reckon with; (erwarten) expect ● vt calculate, work out; (fig) count (**zu** among). **R~nt-s** arithmetic

Rechner m -s,- calculator; (Computer) computer

Rechnung f -, -en bill; (Comm) invoice; (Berechnung) calculation; **R~ führen über** (+ acc) keep account of. **R~sjahr** nt financial year. **R~sprüfer** m auditor

Recht nt -[e]s, -e law; (Berechtigung) right (**auf** + acc to); **im R~ sein** be in the right; **R~ haben/behalten** be right; **jdm R~ geben** agree with s.o.; **mit** od **zu R~** rightly

recht a right; (wirklich) real; **ich habe keine r~e Lust** I don't really feel like it; **es jdm r~ machen** please s.o.; **jdm r~ sein** be all right with s.o. **r~ vielen Dank** many thanks

Recht|e f -n, -[n] right side; (Hand) right hand; (Boxen) right; **die R~e** (Pol) the right; **zu meiner R~en** on my right. **r~e(r,s)** a right; (Pol) right-wing; **r~e Masche** plain stitch. **R~e(r)** m/f **der/die R~e** the right man/woman; **R~e(s)** nt **das R~e** the right thing; **etwas R~es lernen** learn something useful; **nach dem R~en sehen** see that everything is all right

Rechteck nt -[e]s, -e rectangle. **r~ig** a rectangular

rechtfertigen vt justify; **sich r~en** justify oneself

recht|haberisch a opinionated. **r~lich** a legal. **r~mäßig** a legitimate

rechts adv on the right; (bei Stoff) on the right side; **von/nach r~** from/to the right; **zwei r~, zwei links stricken** knit two, purl two. **R~anwalt** m, **R~anwältin** f lawyer

Rechtschreib|programm nt spell checker. **R~ung** f - spelling

Rechts|händer(in) m -s,- (f -, -nen) right-hander. **r~händig** a & adv right-handed. **r~kräftig** a legal. **R~streit** m law suit. **R~verkehr** m driving on the right. **R~widrig** a illegal. **R~wissenschaft** f jurisprudence

rechtzeitig a & adv in time

Reck nt -[e]s, -e horizontal bar

recken vt stretch

Redakteur /redak'tøːɐ/ m -s, -e editor; (Radio, TV) producer

Redaktion /-'tsioːn/ f -, -en editing; (Radio, TV) production; (Abteilung) editorial/production department

Rede f -, -n speech; **zur R~ stellen** demand an explanation from; **nicht der R~ wert** not worth mentioning

reden vi (haben) talk (**von** about; **mit** to); (eine Rede halten) speak ● vt talk; speak <Wahrheit>. **R~sart** f saying

Redewendung f idiom

redigieren vt edit

Redner m -s,- speaker

reduzieren vt reduce

Reeder m -s,- shipowner. **R~ei** f -, -en shipping company

Refer|at nt -[e]s, -e report; (Abhandlung) paper; (Abteilung) section. **R~ent(in)** m -en, -en (f -, -nen) speaker; (Sachbearbeiter) expert. **R~enz** f -, -en reference

Reflex m -es, -e reflex; (*Widerschein*) reflection. **R~ion** f -, -en reflection. **r~iv** a reflexive

Reform f -, -en reform. **R~ation** /-'tsio:n/ f - (*Relig*) Reformation

Reform|haus nt health-food shop. **r~ieren** vt reform

Refrain /rə'frɛ̃:/ m -s, -s refrain

Regal nt -s, -e [set of] shelves pl

Regatta f -, -ten regatta

rege a active; (*lebhaft*) lively; (*geistig*) alert; <*Handel*> brisk

Regel f -, -n rule; (*Monats-*) period. **r~mäßig** a regular. **r~n** vt regulate; direct <*Verkehr*>; (*erledigen*) settle. **r~recht** a real, proper ●adv really. **R~ung** f -, -en regulation; settlement

regen vt move; **sich r~** move; (*wach werden*) stir

Regen m -s,- rain. **R~bogen** m rainbow. **R~bogenhaut** f iris

Regener|ation /-'tsio:n/ f - regeneration. **r~ieren** vt regenerate

Regen|mantel m raincoat. **R~schirm** m umbrella. **R~tag** m rainy day. **R~wetter** nt wet weather. **R~wurm** m earthworm

Regie /re'ʒi:/ f - direction; **R~ führen** direct

regier|en vt/i (*haben*) govern, rule; <*Monarch:*> reign [over]; (*Gram*) take. **R~ung** f -, -en government; (*Herrschaft*) rule; (*eines Monarchen*) reign

Regiment nt -[e]s, -er regiment

Region f -, -en region. **r~al** a regional

Regisseur /reʒɪ'søːɐ̯/ m -s, -e director

Register nt -s,- register; (*Inhaltsverzeichnis*) index; (*Orgel-*) stop

Regler m -s,- regulator

reglos a & adv motionless

regn|en vi (*haben*) rain; **es r~et** it is raining. **r~erisch** a rainy

regul|är a normal; (*rechtmäßig*) legitimate. **r~ieren** vt regulate

Regung f -, -en movement; (*Gefühls-*) emotion. **r~slos** a & adv motionless

Reh nt -[e]s, -e roe-deer; (*Culin*) venison

Rehbock m roebuck

reib|en† vt rub; (*Culin*) grate ●vi (*haben*) rub. **R~ung** f - friction. **r~ungslos** a (*fig*) smooth

reich a rich (**an** + dat in)

Reich nt -[e]s, -e empire; (*König-*) kingdom; (*Bereich*) realm

Reiche(r) m/f rich man/woman; **die R~en** the rich pl

reichen vt hand; (*anbieten*) offer ●vi (*haben*) be enough; (*in der Länge*) be long enough; **r~ bis zu** reach [up to]; (*sich erstrecken*) extend to; **mit dem Geld r~** have enough money

reich|haltig a extensive, large <*Mahlzeit*> substantial. **r~lich** a ample: <*Vorrat*> abundant. **R~tum** m -s, -tümer wealth (**an** + dat of); **R~tümer** riches. **R~weite** f reach; (*Techn, Mil*) range

Reif m -[e]s [hoar-]frost

reif a ripe; (*fig*) mature; **r~ für** ready for. **r~en** vi (*sein*) ripen; <*Wein, Käse & fig*> mature

Reifen m -s,- hoop; (*Arm-*) bangle; (*Auto-*) tyre. **R~druck** m tyre pressure. **R~panne** f puncture, flat tyre

reiflich a careful

Reihe f -, -n row; (*Anzahl & Math*) series; **der R~ nach** in turn; **wer ist an der R~?** whose turn is it? **r~n (sich)** vr sich r~n an (+ acc) follow. **R~nfolge** f order. **R~nhaus** nt terraced house

Reiher m -s,- heron

Reim m -[e]s, -e rhyme. **r~en** vt rhyme; **sich r~en** rhyme

rein¹ a pure; (*sauber*) clean; <*Unsinn, Dummheit*> sheer; **ins**

R~e schreiben make a fair copy of

rein² *adv* = **herein, hinein**

Reineclaude /rɛːnəˈkloːdə/ *f* -, -n greengage

Reinfall *m* ⓵ let-down; (*Misserfolg*) flop

Rein|gewinn *m* net profit. R~heit *f* - purity

reinig|en *vt* clean; (*chemisch*) dry-clean. R~ung *f* -, -en cleaning; (*chemische*) dry-cleaning; (*Geschäft*) dry cleaner's

reinlegen *vt sep* put in; ⓵ dupe; (*betrügen*) take for a ride

reinlich *a* clean. R~keit *f* - cleanliness

Reis *m* -es rice

Reise *f* -, -n journey; (*See-*) voyage; (*Urlaubs-, Geschäfts-*) trip. R~andenken *nt* souvenir. R~büro *nt* travel agency. R~bus *m* coach. R~führer *m* tourist guide; (*Buch*) guide. R~gesellschaft *f* tourist group. R~leiter(in) *m(f)* courier. r~n *vi* (*sein*) travel. R~nde(r) *m/f* traveller. R~pass *m* passport. R~scheck *m* traveller's cheque. R~veranstalter *m* -s,- tour operator. R~ziel *nt* destination

Reisig *nt* -s brushwood

Reißaus *m* R~ nehmen ⓵ run away

Reißbrett *nt* drawing-board

reißen† *vt* tear; (*weg-*) snatch; (*töten*) kill; Witze r~ crack jokes; an sich (*acc*) r~snatch; seize <*Macht*>; sich r~ um ⓵ fight for ● *vi* (*sein*) tear; <*Seil, Faden:*> break ● *vi* (*haben*) r~ an (+ *dat*) pull at

Reißer *m* -s,- ⓵ thriller; (*Erfolg*) big hit

Reiß|nagel *m* = R~zwecke. R~verschluss *m* zip [fastener]. R~wolf *m* shredder. R~zwecke *f* ⓵ drawing-pin

reit|en† *vt/i* (*sein*) ride. R~er(in) *m* -s,- (*f* -, -nen) rider. R~hose *f* riding breeches *pl.* R~pferd *nt* saddle-horse. R~weg *m* bridle-path

Reiz *m* -es, -e stimulus; (*Anziehungskraft*) attraction, appeal; (*Charme*) charm. r~bar *a* irritable. R~barkeit *f* - irritability. r~en *vt* provoke; (*Med*) irritate; (*interessieren, locken*) appeal to, attract; arouse <*Neugier*>; (*beim Kartenspiel*) bid. R~ung *f* -, -en (*Med*) irritation. r~voll *a* attractive

rekeln (sich) *vr* stretch

Reklamation /-ˈtsiːoːn/ *f* -, -en (*Comm*) complaint

Reklam|e *f* -, -n advertising, publicity; (*Anzeige*) advertisement; (*TV, Radio*) commercial; R~e machen advertise (**für etw** sth). r~ieren *vt* complain about; (*fordern*) claim ● *vi* (*haben*) complain

Rekord *m* -[e]s, -e record

Rekrut *m* -en, -en recruit

Rek|tor *m* -s, -en /-ˈtoːrən/ (*Sch*) head[master]; (*Univ*) vice-chancellor. R~torin *f* -, -nen head, headmistress; vice-chancellor

Relais /rəˈlɛː/ *nt* -,- /-ˈs, -s/ (*Electr*) relay

relativ *a* relative

Religi|on *f* -, -en religion; (*Sch*) religious education. r~ös *a* religious

Reling *f* -, -s (*Naut*) rail

Reliquie /reˈliːkviə/ *f* -, -n relic

rempeln *vt* jostle; (*stoßen*) push

Reneklode *f* -, -n greengage

Renn|bahn *f* race-track; (*Pferde-*) racecourse. R~boot *nt* speed-boat. r~en† *vt/i* (*sein*) run; um die Wette r~en have a race. R~en *nt* -s,- race. R~pferd *nt* racehorse. R~sport *m* racing. R~wagen *m* racing car

renommiert *a* renowned; *<Hotel, Firma>* of repute

renovier|en *vt* renovate; redecorate *<Zimmer>*. **R~ung** *f* - renovation; redecoration

rentabel *a* profitable

Rente *f* -, -n pension; **in R~ gehen** 🛈 retire. **R~nversicherung** *f* pension scheme

Rentier *nt* reindeer

rentieren (sich) *vr* be profitable; *(sich lohnen)* be worth while

Rentner(in) *m* -s,- *(f* -, -nen) [oldage] pensioner

Reparatur *f* -, -en repair. **R~werkstatt** *f* repair workshop; *(Auto)* garage

reparieren *vt* repair, mend

Reportage /-'taːʒə/ *f* -, -n report

Reporter(in) *m* -s,- *(f* -, -nen) reporter

repräsentativ *a* representative *(für* of); *(eindrucksvoll)* imposing

Reprodu|ktion /-'tsi̯oːn/ *f* -, -en reproduction. **r~zieren** *vt* reproduce

Reptil *nt* -s, -ien /-i̯ən/ reptile

Republik *f* -, -en republic. **r~anisch** *a* republican

Requisiten *pl (Theat)* properties, 🛈 props

Reservat *nt* -[e]s, -e reservation

Reserve *f* -, -n reserve; *(Mil, Sport)* reserves *pl*. **R~rad** *nt* spare wheel

reservier|en *vt* reserve; **r~en lassen** book. **r~t** *a* reserved. **R~ung** *f* -, -en reservation

Reservoir /rezɛr'voaːɐ̯/ *nt* -s, -s reservoir

Residenz *f* -, -en residence

Resign|ation /-'tsi̯oːn/ *f* - resignation. **r~ieren** *vi (haben) (fig)* give up. **r~iert** *a* resigned

resolut *a* resolute

Resonanz *f* -, -en resonanance

Respekt /-sp-, -ʃp-/ *m* -[e]s respect *(vor + dat* for). **r~ieren** *vt* respect

respektlos *a* disrespectful

Ressort /rɛ'soːɐ̯/ *nt* -s, -s department

Rest *m* -[e]s, -e remainder, rest; **R~e** remains; *(Essens-)* leftovers

Restaurant /rɛsto'rãː/ *nt* -s, -s restaurant

Restaur|ation /rɛstau̯ra'tsi̯oːn/ *f* - restoration. **r~ieren** *vt* restore

Rest|betrag *m* balance. **r~lich** *a* remaining

Resultat *nt* -[e]s, -e result

rett|en *vt* save (**vor** + *dat* from); *(aus Gefahr befreien)* rescue; **sich r~en** save oneself; *(flüchten)* escape. **R~er** *m* -s,- rescuer; *(fig)* saviour

Rettich *m* -s, -e white radish

Rettung *f* -, -en rescue; *(fig)* salvation; **jds letzte R~** s.o.'s last hope. **R~sboot** *nt* lifeboat. **R~sdienst** *m* rescue service. **R~sgürtel** *m* lifebelt. **r~slos** *adv* hopelessly. **R~sring** *m* lifebelt. **R~swagen** *m* ambulance

retuschieren *vt (Phot)* retouch

Reue *f* - remorse; *(Relig)* repentance

Revanch|e /re'vãːʃə/ *f* -, -n revenge; **R~e fordern** *(Sport)* ask for a return match. **r~ieren (sich)** *vr* take revenge; *(sich erkenntlich zeigen)* reciprocate (**mit** with)

Revers /re've:ɐ̯/ *nt* -,- /-[s], -s/ lapel

Revier *nt* -s, -e district; *(Zool & fig)* territory; *(Polizei-)* [police] station

Revision *f* -, -en revision; *(Prüfung)* check; *(Jur)* appeal

Revolution /-'tsi̯oːn/ *f* -, -en revolution. **r~är** *a* revolutionary. **r~ieren** *vt* revolutionize

Revolver *m* -s,- revolver

rezen|sieren *vt* review. **R~sion** *f* -, -en review

Rezept *nt* -[e]s, -e prescription; *(Culin)* recipe

Rezession *f* -, -en recession

R

R-Gespräch nt reverse-charge call

Rhabarber m -s rhubarb

Rhein m -s Rhine. **R~land** nt -s Rhineland. **R~wein** m hock

Rhetorik f - rhetoric

Rheum|a nt -s, **R~atismus** m - rheumatism

Rhinozeros nt -[ses], -se rhinoceros

rhyth|misch /'ryt-/ a rhythmic[al]. **R~mus** m -, -men rhythm

richten vt direct (**auf** + acc at); address <*Frage*> (**an** + acc to); aim <*Waffe*> (**auf** + acc at); (*einstellen*) set; (*vorbereiten*) prepare; (*reparieren*) mend; **in die Höhe r~** raise [up]; **sich r~** be directed (**auf** + acc; **gegen** against); <*Blick:*> turn (**auf** + acc on); **sich r~ nach** comply with <*Vorschrift*>; fit in with <*jds Plänen*>; (*abhängen*) depend on ● vi (*haben*) **r~ über** (+ acc) judge

Richter m -s,- judge

richtig a right, correct; (*wirklich, echt*) real; **das R~e** the right thing ● adv correctly; really; **r~ stellen** put right <*Uhr*>; (*fig*) correct <*Irrtum*>; **die Uhr geht r~** the clock is right

Richtlinien fpl guidelines

Richtung f -, -en direction

riechen† vt/i (*haben*) smell (**nach** of; **an etw** dat sth)

Riegel m -s,- bolt; (*Seife*) bar

Riemen m -s,- strap; (*Ruder*) oar

Riese m -n, -n giant

rieseln vi (*sein*) trickle; <*Schnee:*> fall lightly

riesengroß a huge, enormous

riesig a huge; (*gewaltig*) enormous ● adv 𝕀 terribly

Riff nt -[e]s, -e reef

Rille f -, -n groove

Rind nt -es, -er ox; (*Kuh*) cow; (..er) bull; (*R~fleisch*) beef; ..er cattle pl

Rinde f -, -n bark; (*Käse-*) rind; (*Brot-*) crust

Rinder|braten m roast beef. **R~wahnsinn** m 𝕀 mad cow disease

Rindfleisch nt beef

Ring m -[e]s, -e ring

ringeln (sich) vr curl

ring|en† vi (*haben*) wrestle; (*fig*) struggle (**um/nach** for) ● vt wring <*Hände*>. **R~er** m -s,- wrestler. **R~kampf** m wrestling match; (*als Sport*) wrestling

rings|herum, r~um adv all around

Rinn|e f -, -n channel; (*Dach-*) gutter. **r~en†** vi (*sein*) run; <*Sand:*> trickle. **R~stein** m gutter

Rippe f -, -n rib

Risiko nt -s, -s & -ken risk

risk|ant a risky. **r~ieren** vt risk

Riss m -es, -e tear; (*Mauer-*) crack; (*fig*) rift

rissig a cracked; <*Haut*> chapped

Rist m -[e]s, -e instep

Ritt m -[e]s, -e ride

Ritter m -s,- knight

Ritual nt -s, -e ritual

Ritz m -es, -e scratch. **R~e** f -, -n crack; (*Fels-*) cleft; (*zwischen Betten, Vorhängen*) gap. **r~en** vt scratch

Rival|e m -n, -n, **R~in** f -, -nen rival. **R~ität** f -, -en rivalry

Robbe f -, -n seal

Robe f -, -n gown; (*Talar*) robe

Roboter m -s,- robot

robust a robust

röcheln vi (*haben*) breathe stertorously

Rock¹ m -[e]s,ᵉ skirt; (*Jacke*) jacket

Rock² m -[s] (*Mus*) rock

rodel|n vi (*sein/haben*) toboggan. **R~schlitten** m toboggan

roden vt clear <*Land*>; grub up <*Stumpf*>

Roggen m -s rye

roh a rough; (*ungekocht*) raw; <*Holz*> bare; (*brutal*) brutal. **R~bau** m -[e]s, -ten shell. **R~kost** f raw [vegetarian] food. **R~ling** m -s, -e brute. **R~öl** nt crude oil

Rohr nt -[e]s, -e pipe; (*Geschütz-*) barrel; (*Bot*) reed; (*Zucker-, Bambus-*) cane

Röhre f -, -n tube; (*Radio-*) valve; (*Back-*) oven

Rohstoff m raw material

Rokoko nt -s rococo

Roll|bahn f taxiway; (*Start-/Landebahn*) runway. **R~balken** m scroll bar

Rolle f -, -n roll; (*Garn-*) reel; (*Draht-*) coil; (*Techn*) roller; (*Seil-*) pulley; (*Lauf-*) castor; (*Theat*) part, role; **das spielt keine R~** (*fig*) that doesn't matter. **r~n** vt roll; (*auf-*) roll up; (*Computer*) scroll; **sich r~n** roll ●vi (*sein*) roll; <*Flugzeug:*> taxi. **R~r** m -s,- scooter. **R~rblades (P)** /-ble:ds/ mpl Rollerblades (P)

Roll|feld nt airfield. **R~kragen** m polo-neck. **R~mops** m rollmop[s] sg

Rollo nt -s, -s [roller] blind

Roll|schuh m roller-skate; **R~schuh laufen** roller-skate. **R~stuhl** m wheelchair. **R~treppe** f escalator

Rom nt -s Rome

Roman m -s, -e novel. **r~isch** a Romanesque; <*Sprache*> Romance

Romant|ik f - romanticism. **r~isch** a romantic

Röm|er(in) m -s,- (f -, -nen) Roman. **r~isch** a Roman

Rommé, Rommee /'rɔme:/ nt -s rummy

röntgen vt X-ray. **R~aufnahme** f, **R~bild** nt X-ray. **R~strahlen** mpl X-rays

rosa inv a, **R~** nt -[s],- pink

Rose f -, -n rose. **R~nkohl** m [Brussels] sprouts pl. **R~nkranz** m (*Relig*) rosary

Rosine f -, -n raisin

Rosmarin m -s rosemary

Ross nt -es,¨er horse

Rost¹ m -[e]s, -e grating; (*Kamin-*) grate; (*Brat-*) grill

Rost² m -[e]s rust. **r~en** vi (*haben*) rust

rösten vt roast; toast <*Brot*>

rostfrei a stainless

rostig a rusty

rot a, **Rot** nt -s,- red; **rot werden** turn red; (*erröten*) go red, blush

Röte f - redness; (*Scham-*) blush

Röteln pl German measles sg

röten vt redden; **sich r~** turn red

rothaarig a red-haired

rotieren vi (*haben*) rotate

Rot|kehlchen nt -s,- robin. **R~kohl** m red cabbage

rötlich a reddish

Rotwein m red wine

Rou|lade /ru'la:də/ f -, -n beef olive. **R~leau** /-'lo:/ nt -s, -s [roller] blind

Routin|e /ru'ti:nə/ f -, -n routine; (*Erfahrung*) experience. **r~emäßig** a routine … ●adv routinely. **r~iert** a experienced

Rowdy /'raudi/ m -s, -s hooligan

Rübe f -, -n beet; **rote R~** beetroot

Rubin m -s, -e ruby

Ruck m -[e]s, -e jerk

ruckartig a jerky

rück|bezüglich a (*Gram*) reflexive. **R~blende** f flashback. **R~blick** m (*fig*) review (**auf** + acc of). **r~blickend** adv in retrospect. **r~datieren** vt (*inf & pp only*) backdate

Rücken m -s,- back; (*Buch-*) spine; (*Berg-*) ridge. **R~lehne** f back. **R~mark** nt spinal cord. **R~schwimmen** nt backstroke. **R~wind** m following wind; (*Aviat*) tail wind

rückerstatten vt (*inf & pp only*) refund

Rückfahr|karte f return ticket. **R~t** f return journey

R

Rück|fall m relapse. **R~flug** m return flight. **R~frage** f [further] query. **r~fragen** vi (haben) (inf & pp only) check (bei with). **R~gabe** f return. **r~gängig** a **r~gängig machen** cancel; break off <Verlobung>. **R~grat** nt -[e]s, -e spine, backbone. **R~hand** f backhand. **R~kehr** f return. **R~lagen** fpl reserves. **R~licht** nt rear-light. **R~reise** f return journey

Rucksack m rucksack

Rück|schau f review. **R~schlag** m (Sport) return; (fig) set-back. **r~schrittlich** a retrograde. **R~seite** f back; (einer Münze) reverse

Rücksicht f -, -en consideration. **R~nahme** f - consideration. **r~slos** a inconsiderate; (schonungslos) ruthless. **r~svoll** a considerate

Rück|sitz m back seat; (Sozius) pillion. **R~spiegel** m rear-view mirror. **R~spiel** nt return match. **R~stand** m (Chem) residue; (Arbeits-) backlog; **im R~stand sein** be behind. **r~ständig** a (fig) backward. **R~stau** m (Auto) tailback. **R~strahler** m -s,- reflector. **R~tritt** m resignation; (Fahrrad) back pedalling

rückwärt|ig a back ..., rear ... **r~s** adv backwards. **R~sgang** m reverse [gear]

Rückweg m way back

rück|wirkend a retrospective. **R~wirkung** f retrospective force; **mit R~wirkung vom** backdated to. **R~zahlung** f repayment

Rüde m -n, -n [male] dog

Rudel nt -s,- herd; (Wolfs-) pack; (Löwen-) pride

Ruder nt -s,- oar; (Steuer-) rudder; ~m R~ (Naut & fig) at the helm. ~oot nt rowing boat. **r~n** vt/i ~en/sein) row

Ruf m -[e]s, -e call; (laut) shout; (Telefon) telephone number; (Ansehen) reputation. **r~en†** vt/i (haben) call (nach for); **r~en lassen** send for

Ruf|name m forename by which one is known. **R~nummer** f telephone number. **R~zeichen** nt dialling tone

Rüge f -, -n reprimand. **r~n** vt reprimand; (kritisieren) criticize

Ruhe f - rest; (Stille) quiet; (Frieden) peace; (innere) calm; (Gelassenheit) composure; **R~ [da]!** quiet! **r~los** a restless. **r~n** vi (haben) rest (auf + dat on); <Arbeit, Verkehr:> have stopped. **R~pause** f rest, break. **R~stand** m retirement; **im R~stand** retired. **R~störung** f disturbance of the peace. **R~tag** m day of rest; 'Montag R~tag' 'closed on Mondays'

ruhig a quiet; (erholsam) restful; (friedlich) peaceful; (unbewegt, gelassen) calm; **man kann r~ darüber sprechen** there's no harm in talking about it

Ruhm m -[e]s fame; (Ehre) glory

rühmen vt praise

ruhmreich a glorious

Ruhr f - (Med) dysentery

Rühr|ei nt scrambled eggs pl. **r~en** vt move; (Culin) stir; **sich r~en** move ●vi (haben) stir; **r~en an** (+ acc) touch; (fig) touch on. **r~end** a touching

Rührung f - emotion

Ruin m -s ruin. **R~e** f -, -n ruin; ruins pl (gen of). **r~ieren** vt ruin

rülpsen vi (haben) Ⓣ belch

Rum m -s rum

Rumän|ien /-iən/ nt -s Romania. **r~isch** a Romanian

Rummel m -s Ⓣ hustle and bustle; (Jahrmarkt) funfair

Rumpelkammer f junk-room

Rumpf m -[e]s,ˮe body, trunk; (Schiffs-) hull; (Aviat) fuselage

rund *a* round ● *adv* approximately; **r~ um** [a]round. **R~blick** *m* panoramic view. **R~brief** *m* circular [letter]

Runde *f* -, -n round; (*Kreis*) circle; (*eines Polizisten*) beat; (*beim Rennen*) lap; **eine R~ Bier** a round of beer

Rund|fahrt *f* tour. **R~frage** *f* poll

Rundfunk *m* radio; **im R~** on the radio. **R~gerät** *nt* radio [set]

Rund|gang *m* round; (*Spaziergang*) walk (**durch** round). **r~heraus** *adv* straight out. **r~herum** *adv* all around. **r~lich** *a* rounded; (*mollig*) plump. **R~reise** *f* [circular] tour. **R~schreiben** *nt* circular. **r~um** *adv* all round. **R~ung** *f* -, -en curve

Runzel *f* -, -n wrinkle

runzlig *a* wrinkled

Rüpel *m* -s,- 🆒 lout

rupfen *vt* pull out; pluck <*Geflügel*>

Rüsche *f* -, -n frill

Ruß *m* -es soot

Russe *m* -n, -n Russian

Rüssel *m* -s,- (*Zool*) trunk

Russ|in *f* -, -nen Russian. **r~isch** *a* Russian. **R~isch** *nt* -[s] (*Lang*) Russian

Russland *nt* -s Russia

rüsten *vi* (*haben*) prepare (**zu/für** for) ● *vr* **sich r~** get ready

rüstig *a* sprightly

rustikal *a* rustic

Rüstung *f* -, -en armament; (*Harnisch*) armour. **R~skontrolle** *f* arms control

Rute *f* -, -n twig; (*Angel-, Wünschel-*) rod; (*zur Züchtigung*) birch; (*Schwanz*) tail

Rutsch *m* -[e]s, -e slide. **R~bahn** *f* slide. **R~e** *f* -, -n chute. **r~en** *vt* slide; (*rücken*) move ● *vi* (*sein*) slide; (*aus-, ab-*) slip; (*Auto*) skid. **r~ig** *a* slippery

rütteln *vt* shake ● *vi* (*haben*) **r~ an** (+ *dat*) rattle

Saal *m* -[e]s, **Säle** hall; (*Theat*) auditorium; (*Kranken-*) ward

Saat *f* -, -en seed; (*Säen*) sowing; (*Gesätes*) crop

sabbern *vi* (*haben*) 🆒 slobber; <*Baby:*> dribble; (*reden*) jabber

Säbel *m* -s,- sabre

Sabo|tage /zabo'ta:ʒə/ *f* - sabotage. **S~teur** /-'tø:ɐ̯/ *m* -s, -e saboteur. **s~tieren** *vt* sabotage

Sach|bearbeiter *m* expert. **S~buch** *nt* non-fiction book

Sache *f* -, -n matter, business; (*Ding*) thing; (*fig*) cause

Sach|gebiet *nt* (*fig*) area, field. **s~kundig** *a* expert. **s~lich** *a* factual; (*nüchtern*) matter-of-fact

sächlich *a* (*Gram*) neuter

Sachse *m* -n, -n Saxon. **S~n** *nt* -s Saxony

sächsisch *a* Saxon

Sach|verhalt *m* -[e]s facts *pl*. **S~verständige(r)** *m/f* expert

Sack *m* -[e]s,¨e sack

Sack|gasse *f* cul-de-sac; (*fig*) impasse. **S~leinen** *nt* sacking

Sadis|mus *m* - sadism. **S~t** *m* -en, -en sadist

säen *vt/i* (*haben*) sow

Safe /ze:f/ *m* -s, -s safe

Saft *m* -[e]s,¨e juice; (*Bot*) sap. **s~ig** *a* juicy

Sage *f* -, -n legend

Säge *f* -, -n saw. **S~mehl** *nt* sawdust

sagen *vt* say; (*mitteilen*) tell; (*bedeuten*) mean

sägen vt/i (haben) saw
sagenhaft a legendary
Säge|späne mpl wood shavings. **S~werk** nt sawmill
Sahn|e f - cream. **S~ebonbon** m & nt ≈ toffee. **s~ig** a creamy
Saison /zɛˈzõ:/ f -, -s season
Saite f -, -n (Mus, Sport) string. **S~ninstrument** nt stringed instrument
Sakko m & nt -s, -s sports jacket
Sakrament nt -[e]s, -e sacrament
Sakristei f -, -en vestry
Salat m -[e]s, -e salad. **S~soße** f salad-dressing
Salbe f -, -n ointment
Salbei m -s & f - sage
salben vt anoint
Saldo m -s, -dos & -den balance
Salon /zaˈlõ:/ m -s, -s salon
salopp a casual; <Benehmen> informal
Salto m -s, -s somersault
Salut m -[e]s, -e salute. **s~ieren** vi (haben) salute
Salve f -, -n volley; (Geschütz-) salvo, (von Gelächter) burst
Salz nt -es, -e salt. **s~en†** vt salt. **S~fass** nt salt-cellar. **s~ig** a salty. **S~kartoffeln** fpl boiled potatoes. **S~säure** f hydrochloric acid
Samen m -s,- seed; (Anat) semen, sperm
Sammel|becken nt reservoir. **s~n** vt/i (haben) collect; (suchen, versammeln) gather; **sich s~n** collect; (sich versammeln) gather; (sich fassen) collect oneself. **S~name** m collective noun
Samm|ler(in) m -s,- (f -, -nen) collector. **S~lung** f -, -en collection; (innere) composure
Samstag m -s, -e Saturday. **s~s** adv on Saturdays
⎣ prep (+ dat) together with
⎣ m -[e]s velvet

sämtlich indef pron inv all. **s~e(r,s)** indef pron all the; **s~e Werke** complete works
Sanatorium nt -s, -ien sanatorium
Sand m -[e]s sand
Sandale f -, -n sandal
Sand|bank f sandbank. **S~kasten** m sand-pit. **S~papier** nt sandpaper
sanft a gentle
Sänger(in) m -s,- (f -, -nen) singer
sanieren vt clean up; redevelop <Gebiet>; (modernisieren) modernize; make profitable <Industrie, Firma>; **sich s~** become profitable
sanitär a sanitary
Sanität|er m -s,- first-aid man; (Fahrer) ambulance man; (Mil) medical orderly. **S~swagen** m ambulance
Sanktion /zaŋkˈtsi̯o:n/ f -, -en sanction. **s~ieren** vt sanction
Saphir m -s, -e sapphire
Sardelle f -, -n anchovy
Sardine f -, -n sardine
Sarg m -[e]s, ̈-e coffin
Sarkasmus m - sarcasm
Satan m -s Satan; (🔟 Teufel) devil
Satellit m -en, -en satellite. **S~enfernsehen** nt satellite television. **S~enschüssel** f satellite dish
Satin /zaˈtɛŋ/ m -s satin
Satire f -, -n satire
satt a full; <Farbe> rich; **s~ sein** have had enough [to eat]; **etw s~ haben** 🔟 be fed up with sth
Sattel m -s, ̈- saddle. **s~n** vt saddle. **S~zug** m articulated lorry
sättigen vt satisfy; (Chem & fig) saturate ● vi (haben) be filling
Satz m -es, ̈-e sentence; (Teil-) clause; (These) proposition; (Math) theorem; (Mus) movement; (Tennis, Zusammengehöriges) set;

(*Boden-*) sediment; (*Kaffee-*) grounds *pl*; (*Steuer-, Zins-*) rate; (*Druck-*) setting; (*Schrift-*) type; (*Sprung*) leap, bound.
S~aussage *f* predicate.
S~gegenstand *m* subject.
S~zeichen *nt* punctuation mark
Sau *f* -,**Säue** sow
sauber *a* clean; (*ordentlich*) neat; (*anständig*) decent; **s~ machen** clean. **S~keit** *f* - cleanliness; neatness
säuberlich *a* neat
Sauce /'zo:sə/ *f* -, -n sauce; (*Braten-*) gravy
Saudi-Arabien /-iən/ *nt* -s Saudi Arabia
sauer *a* sour; (*Chem*) acid; (*eingelegt*) pickled; (*schwer*) hard; **saurer Regen** acid rain
Sauerkraut *nt* sauerkraut
säuerlich *a* slightly sour
Sauerstoff *m* oxygen
saufen† *vt/i* (*haben*) drink; ⊠ booze
Säufer *m* -s,- ⊠ boozer
saugen† *vt/i* (*haben*) suck; (*staub-*) vacuum, hoover; **sich voll Wasser s~** soak up water
säugen *vt* suckle
Säugetier *nt* mammal
saugfähig *a* absorbent
Säugling *m* -s, -e infant
Säule *f* -, -n column
Saum *m* -[e]s,**Säume** hem; (*Rand*) edge
säumen *vt* hem; (*fig*) line
Sauna *f* -, -nas & -nen sauna
Säure *f* -, -n acidity; (*Chem*) acid
sausen *vi* (*haben*) rush; <*Ohren:*> buzz ●*vi* (*sein*) rush [along]
Saxophon, Saxofon *nt* -s, -e saxophone
S-Bahn *f* city and suburban railway
Scanner *m* -s,- scanner
sch *int* shush! (*fort*) shoo!
Schabe *f* -, -n cockroach
schaben *vt/i* (*haben*) scrape

schäbig *a* shabby
Schablone *f* -, -n stencil; (*Muster*) pattern; (*fig*) stereotype
Schach *nt* -s chess; **S~!** check!
S~brett *nt* chessboard
Schachfigur *f* chess-man
schachmatt *a* **s~ setzen** checkmate; **s~!** checkmate!
Schachspiel *nt* game of chess
Schacht *m* -[e]s,-̈e shaft
Schachtel *f* -, -n box; (*Zigaretten-*) packet
Schachzug *m* move
schade *a* **s~ sein** be a pity or shame: **zu s~ für** too good for
Schädel *m* -s, skull. **S~bruch** *m* fractured skull
schaden *vi* (*haben*) (+ *dat*) damage; (*nachteilig sein*) hurt.
S~ *m* -s,-̈ damage; (*Defekt*) defect; (*Nachteil*) disadvantage.
S~ersatz *m* damages *pl.*
S~freude *f* malicious glee.
s~froh *a* gloating
schädig|en *vt* damage, harm.
S~ung *f* -, -en damage
schädlich *a* harmful
Schädling *m* -s, -e pest.
S~sbekämpfungsmittel *nt* pesticide
Schaf *nt* -[e]s, -e sheep. **S~bock** *m* ram
Schäfer *m* -s,- shepherd. **S~hund** *m* sheepdog; **Deutscher S~hund** alsatian
schaffen¹† *vt* create; (*herstellen*) establish; make ●<*Platz*>
schaffen² *v* (*reg*) ●*vt* manage [to do]; pass <*Prüfung*>; catch <*Zug*>; (*bringen*) take
Schaffner *m* -s,- conductor; (*Zug-*) ticket-inspector
Schaffung *f* - creation
Schaft *m* -[e]s,-̈e shaft; (*Gewehr-*) stock; (*Stiefel-*) leg
Schal *m* -s, -s scarf
Schale *f* -, -n skin; (*abgeschält*) peel; (*Eier-, Nuss-, Muschel-*) shell; (*Schüssel*) dish

S

schälen vt peel; **sich s~** peel
Schall m -[e]s sound. **S~dämpfer** m silencer. **s~dicht** a soundproof. **s~en** vi (haben) ring out: (nachhallen) resound.
S~mauer f sound barrier.
S~platte f record, disc
schalt|en vt switch ● vi (haben) switch/<Ampel:> turn (**auf** + acc to); (Auto) change gear; (🄸 begreifen) catch on. **S~er** m -s,- switch; (Post-, Bank-) counter; (Fahrkarten-) ticket window.
S~hebel m switch; (Auto) gear lever. **S~jahr** nt leap year.
S~ung f -, -en circuit: (Auto) gear change
Scham f - shame; (Anat) private parts pl
schämen (sich) vr be ashamed
scham|haft a modest. **s~los** a shameless
Schampon nt -s shampoo.
s~ieren vt shampoo
Schande f - disgrace, shame
schändlich a disgraceful
Schanktisch m bar
Schanze f, -, -n [ski-]jump
Schar f -, -en crowd; (Vogel-) flock
Scharade f -, -n charade
scharen vt **um sich s~** gather round one; **sich s~ um** flock round. **s~weise** adv in droves
scharf a sharp; (stark) strong; (stark gewürzt) hot; <Geruch> pungent; <Wind, Augen, Verstand> keen; (streng) harsh; <Galopp> hard; <Munition> live; <Hund> fierce; **s~ einstellen** (Phot) focus; **s~ sein** (Phot) be in focus; **s~ sein auf** (+ acc) 🄸 be keen on
Schärfe f sharpness; strength; hotness; pungency; keenness; harshness. **s~n** vt sharpen
Scharf|richter m executioner.
S~schütze m marksman. **S~sinn** m tutenes
rlach m -s scarlet fever

Scharlatan m -s, -e charlatan
Scharnier nt -s, -e hinge
Schärpe f -, -n sash
scharren vi (haben) scrape; <Huhn> scratch ● vt scrape
Schaschlik m & nt -s, -s kebab
Schatten m -s,- shadow; (schattige Stelle) shade. **S~riss** m silhouette. **S~seite** f shady side; (fig) disadvantage
schattier|en vt shade. **S~ung** f -, -en shading
schattig a shady
Schatz m -es,¨e treasure; (Freund, Freundin) sweetheart
schätzen vt estimate; (taxieren) value; (achten) esteem; (würdigen) appreciate
Schätzung f -, -en estimate; (Taxierung) valuation
Schau f -, -en show. **S~ bild** nt diagram
Schauder m -s shiver; (vor Abscheu) shudder. **s~ haft** a dreadful. **s~n** vi (haben) shiver; (vor Abscheu) shudder
schauen vi (haben) (SGer, Aust) look; **s~, dass** make sure that
Schauer m -s,- shower; (Schauder) shiver. **S~geschichte** f horror story. **s~lich** a ghastly
Schaufel f -, -n shovel; (Kehr-) dustpan. **s~n** vt shovel; (graben) dig
Schaufenster nt shop-window.
S~puppe f dummy
Schaukel f -, -n swing. **s~n** vt rock ● vi (haben) rock; (auf einer Schaukel) swing; (schwanken) sway. **S~pferd** nt rocking-horse.
S~stuhl m rocking-chair
Schaum m -[e]s foam; (Seifen-) lather; (auf Bier) froth; (als Frisier-, Rasiermittel) mousse
schäumen vi (haben) foam, froth; <Seife:> lather
Schaum|gummi m foam rubber.
s~ig a frothy; **s~ig rühren** (Culin)

cream. **S~stoff** m [synthetic] foam. **S~wein** m sparkling wine
Schauplatz m scene
schaurig a dreadful; (*unheimlich*) eerie
Schauspiel nt play; (*Anblick*) spectacle. **S~er** m actor. **S~erin** f actress
Scheck m -s, -s cheque. **S~buch**, **S~heft** nt cheque-book. **S~karte** f cheque card
Scheibe f -, -n disc; (*Schieß-*) target; (*Glas-*) pane; (*Brot-, Wurst-*) slice. **S~nwischer** m -s,- windscreen-wiper
Scheich m -s, -e & -s sheikh
Scheide f -, -n sheath; (*Anat*) vagina
scheid|en† vt separate; (*unterscheiden*) distinguish; dissolve <*Ehe*> vi **sich s~en lassen** get divorced ● vi (*sein*) leave; (*voneinander*) part. **S~ung** f -, -en divorce
Schein m -[e]s, -e light; (*Anschein*) appearance; (*Bescheinigung*) certificate; (*Geld-*) note. **s~bar** a apparent. **s~en†** vi (*haben*) shine; (*den Anschein haben*) seem, appear
scheinheilig a hypocritical
Scheinwerfer m -s,- floodlight; (*Such-*) searchlight; (*Auto*) headlight; (*Theat*) spotlight
Scheiße f -, (*vulg*) shit. **s~n†** vi (*haben*) (*vulg*) shit
Scheit nt -[e]s, -e log
Scheitel m -s,- parting
scheitern vi (*sein*) fail
Schelle f -, -n bell. **s~n** vi (*haben*) ring
Schellfisch m haddock
Schelm m -s, -e rogue
Schelte f - scolding
Schema nt -s, -mata model, pattern; (*Skizze*) diagram
Schemel m -s,- stool
Schenke f -, -n tavern
Schenkel m -s,- thigh

schenken vt give [as a present]; **jdm Vertrauen s~** trust s.o.
Scherbe f -, -n [broken] piece
Schere f -, -n scissors pl; (*Techn*) shears pl; (*Hummer-*) claw. **s~n¹** vt shear; crop <*Haar*>
scheren² vt (*reg*) Ⓘ bother; **sich nicht s~ um** not care about
Scherenschnitt m silhouette
Scherereien fpl Ⓘ trouble sg
Scherz m -es, -e joke; **im/zum S~** as a joke. **s~en** vi (*haben*) joke
scheu a shy; <*Tier*> timid; **s~ werden** <*Pferd:*> shy
scheuchen vt shoo
scheuen vt be afraid of; (*meiden*) shun; **keine Mühe/Kosten s~** spare no effort/expense; **sich s~** be afraid (**vor** + dat of); shrink (**etw zu tun** from doing sth)
scheuern vt scrub; (*reiben*) rub; **[wund] s~n** chafe ● vi (*haben*) rub, chafe
Scheuklappen fpl blinkers
Scheune f -, -n barn
Scheusal nt -s, -e monster
scheußlich a horrible
Schi m -s, -er ski; **S~ fahren** od **laufen** ski
Schicht f -, -en layer; (*Geol*) stratum; (*Gesellschafts-*) class; (*Arbeits-*) shift. **S~arbeit** f shift work. **s~en** vt stack [up]
schick a stylish; <*Frau*> chic. **S~** m -[e]s style
schicken vt/i (*haben*) send; **s~ nach** send for
Schicksal nt -s, -e fate. **S~sschlag** m misfortune
Schieb|edach nt (*Auto*) sun-roof. **s~en†** vt push; (*gleitend*) slide; (Ⓘ *handeln mit*) traffic in; **etw s~en auf** (+ acc) (*fig*) put sth down to; shift <*Schuld*> on to ● vi (*haben*) push. **S~etür** f sliding door. **S~ung** f -, -en Ⓘ illicit deal; (*Betrug*) rigging, fixing

S

Schieds|gericht nt panel of judges; (*Jur*) arbitration tribunal. **S~richter** m referee; (*Tennis*) umpire; (*Jur*) arbitrator

schief a crooked; (*unsymmetrisch*) lopsided; (*geneigt*) slanting, sloping; (*nicht senkrecht*) leaning; <*Winkel*> oblique; (*fig*) false; suspicious ● *adv* not straight; **s~ gehen** ⏍ go wrong

Schiefer m -s slate

schielen vi (*haben*) squint

Schienbein nt shin

Schiene f -, -n rail; (*Gleit-*) runner; (*Med*) splint. **s~n** vt (*Med*) put in a splint

Schieß|bude f shooting-gallery. **s~en†** vt shoot; fire <*Kugel*>; score <*Tor*> ● vi (*haben*) shoot, fire (**auf** + *acc* at). **S~scheibe** f target. **S~stand** m shooting-range

Schifahr|en nt skiing. **S~er(in)** m(f) skier

Schiff nt -[e]s, -e ship; (*Kirchen-*) nave; (*Seiten-*) aisle

Schiffahrt* f s. **Schifffahrt**

schiff|bar a navigable. **S~bruch** m shipwreck. **s~brüchig** a shipwrecked. **S~fahrt** f shipping

Schikan|e f -, -n harassment; **mit allen S~en** ⏍ with every refinement. **s~ieren** vt harass

Schi|laufen nt -s skiing. **S~läufer(in)** m(f) -s,- (f -, -nen) skier

Schild¹ m -[e]s, -e shield

Schild² nt -[e]s, -er sign; (*Nummern-*) plate; (*Mützen-*) badge; (*Etikett*) label

Schilddrüse f thyroid [gland]

schilder|n vt describe. **S~ung** f -, -en description

Schild|kröte f tortoise; (*See-*) turtle. **S~patt** nt -[e]s tortoiseshell

Schilf nt -[e]s reeds pl

schillern vi (*haben*) shimmer

Schimmel m -s,- mould; (*Pferd*) white horse. **s~n** vi (*haben/sein*) go mouldy

schimmern vi (*haben*) gleam

Schimpanse m -n, -n chimpanzee

schimpf|en vi (*haben*) grumble (**mit** at; **über** + *acc* about); scold (**mit jdm** s.o.) ● vt call. **S~wort** nt (*pl* -wörter) swear-word

Schinken m -s,- ham. **S~speck** m bacon

Schippe f -, -n shovel. **s~n** vt shovel

Schirm m -[e]s, -e umbrella; (*Sonnen-*) sunshade; (*Lampen-*) shade; (*Augen-*) visor; (*Mützen-*) peak; (*Ofen-, Bild-*) screen; (*fig: Schutz*) shield. **S~herrschaft** f patronage. **S~mütze** f peaked cap

schizophren a schizophrenic. **S~ie** f - schizophrenia

Schlacht f -, -en battle

schlachten vt slaughter, kill

Schlacht|feld nt battlefield. **S~hof** m abattoir

Schlacke f -, -n slag

Schlaf m -[e]s sleep; **im S~** in one's sleep. **S~anzug** m pyjamas pl

Schläfe f -, -n (*Anat*) temple

schlafen† vi (*haben*) sleep; **s~ gehen** go to bed; **er schläft noch** he is still asleep

schlaff a limp; <*Seil*> slack; <*Muskel*> flabby

Schlaf|lied nt lullaby. **s~los** a sleepless. **S~losigkeit** f - insomnia. **S~mittel** nt sleeping drug

schläfrig a sleepy

Schlaf|saal m dormitory. **S~sack** m sleeping-bag. **S~tablette** f sleeping-pill. **S~wagen** m sleeping-car, sleeper. **s~wandeln** vi (*haben/sein*) sleep-walk. **S~zimmer** nt bedroom

Schlag *m* -[e]s,⸚e blow; (*Faust*-) punch; (*Herz-, Puls-, Trommel-*) beat; (*einer Uhr*) chime; (*Glocken-, Gong- & Med*) stroke; (*elektrischer*) shock; (*Art*) type; **S~e bekommen** get a beating; **S~ auf S~** in rapid succession. **S~ader** *f* artery. **S~anfall** *m* stroke. **S~baum** *m* barrier

schlagen† *vt* hit, strike; (*fällen*) fell; knock <*Loch, Nagel*> (in + *acc* into); (*prügeln, besiegen*) beat; (*Culin*) whisk <*Eiweiß*>; whip <*Sahne*>; (*legen*) throw; (*wickeln*) wrap; **sich s~** fight ● *vi* (*haben*) beat; <*Tür:*> bang; <*Uhr:*> strike; (*melodisch*) chime; **mit den Flügeln s~** flap its wings ● *vi* (*sein*) **in etw** (*acc*) **s~** <*Blitz, Kugel:*> strike sth; **nach jdm s~** (*fig*) take after s.o.

Schlager *m* -s,- popular song; (*Erfolg*) hit

Schläger *m* -s,- racket; (*Tischtennis*-) bat; (*Golf*-) club; (*Hockey*-) stick. **S~ei** *f* -, -en fight, brawl

schlagfertig *a* quick-witted. **S~loch** *nt* pot-hole. **S~sahne** *f* whipped cream; (*ungeschlagen*) whipping cream. **S~seite** *f* (*Naut*) list. **S~stock** *m* truncheon. **S~wort** *nt* (*pl* -worte) slogan. **S~zeile** *f* headline. **S~zeug** *nt* (*Mus*) percussion. **S~zeuger** *m* -s,- percussionist; (*in Band*) drummer

Schlamm *m* -[e]s mud. **s~ig** *a* muddy

Schlampe|e *f* -, -n 🛈 slut. **s~en** *vi* (*haben*) 🛈 be sloppy (**bei** in). **s~ig** *a* slovenly; <*Arbeit:*> sloppy

Schlange *f* -, -n snake; (*Menschen-, Auto-*) queue; **S~ stehen** queue

schlängeln (sich) *vr* wind; <*Person:*> weave (**durch** through)

schlank *a* slim. **S~heitskur** *f* slimming diet

schlapp *a* tired; (*schlaff*) limp

schlau *a* clever; (*gerissen*) crafty; **ich werde nicht s~ daraus** I can't make head or tail of it

Schlauch *m* -[e]s,Schläuche tube; (*Wasser*-) hose[pipe]. **S~boot** *nt* rubber dinghy

Schlaufe *f* -, -n loop

schlecht *a* bad; (*böse*) wicked; (*unzulänglich*) poor; **s~ werden** go bad; <*Wetter:*> turn bad; **mir ist s~** I feel sick; **s~ machen** 🛈 run down. **s~gehen*** *vi sep* (*sein*) **s~ gehen, s. gehen**

schlecken *vt/i* (*haben*) lick (**an etw** *dat* sth); (*auf*-) lap up

Schlegel *m* -s,- (*SGer: Keule*) leg; (*Hühner*-) drumstick

schleichen† *vi* (*sein*) creep; (*langsam gehen/fahren*) crawl ● *vr* **sich s~** creep. **s~d** *a* creeping

Schleier *m* -s,- veil; (*fig*) haze

Schleife *f* -, -n bow; (*Fliege*) bowtie; (*Biegung*) loop

schleifen¹ *v* (*reg*) ● *vt* drag ● *vi* (*haben*) trail, drag

schleifen²† *vt* grind; (*schärfen*) sharpen; cut <*Edelstein, Glas*>

Schleim *m* -[e]s slime; (*Anat*) mucus; (*Med*) phlegm. **s~ig** *a* slimy

schlendern *vi* (*sein*) stroll

schlenkern *vt/i* (*haben*) swing; **s~ mit** swing; dangle <*Beine*>

Schlepp|dampfer *m* tug. **S~e** *f* -, -n train. **s~en** *vt* drag; (*tragen*) carry; (*ziehen*) tow; **sich s~en** drag oneself; (*sich hinziehen*) drag on; **sich s~en mit** carry. **S~er** *m* -s,- tug; (*Traktor*) tractor. **S~kahn** *m* barge. **S~lift** *m* T-bar lift. **S~tau** *nt* tow-rope; **ins S~tau nehmen** take in tow

Schleuder *f* -, -n catapult; (*Wäsche*-) spin-drier. **s~n** *vt* hurl; spin <*Wäsche*> ● *vi* (*sein*) skid; **ins S~n geraten** skid. **S~sitz** *m* ejector seat

S

Schleuse f -, -n lock; (Sperre) sluice[-gate]. **s~n** vt steer

schliche pl tricks

schlicht a plain; simple

Schlichtung f - settlement; (Jur) arbitration

Schließe f -, -n clasp; buckle

schließen† vt close (ab-) lock; fasten <Kleid, Verschluss>; (stilllegen) close down; (beenden, folgern) conclude; enter into <Vertrag>; **sich s~** close; **etw s~ an** (+ acc) connect sth to; **sich s~ an** (+ acc) follow ● vi (haben) close, (den Betrieb einstellen) close down; (den Schlüssel drehen) turn the key; (enden, folgern) conclude

Schließ|fach nt locker. **s~lich** adv finally, in the end; (immerhin) after all. **S~ung** f -, -en closure

Schliff m -[e]s cut; (Schleifen) cutting; (fig) polish

schlimm a bad

Schlinge f -, -n loop; (Henkers-) noose; (Med) sling; (Falle) snare

Schlingel m -s,- ☐ rascal

schlingen† vt wind, wrap; tie <Knoten> ● vi (haben) bolt one's food

Schlips m -es, -e tie

Schlitten m -s,- sledge; (Rodel-) toboggan; (Pferde-) sleigh; **S~ fahren** toboggan

schlittern vi (haben/ sein) slide

Schlittschuh m skate; **S~ laufen** skate. **S~läufer(in)** m(f) -s,- (f -, -nen) skater

Schlitz m -es, -e slit; (für Münze) slot; (Jacken-) vent; (Hosen-) flies pl. **s~en** vt slit

Schloss nt -es,¨er lock; (Vorhänge-) padlock; (Verschluss) clasp; (Gebäude) castle; palace

Schlosser m -s,- locksmith; (Auto-) mechanic

Schlucht f -, -en ravine, gorge

schluchzen vi (haben) sob

Schluck m -[e]s, -e mouthful; (klein) sip

Schluckauf m -s hiccups pl

schlucken vt/i (haben) swallow

Schlummer m -s slumber

Schlund m -[e]s [back of the] throat; (fig) mouth

schlüpf|en vi (sein) slip; [aus dem Ei] **s~en** hatch. **S~er** m -s,- knickers pl. **s~rig** a slippery

schlürfen vt/i (haben) slurp

Schluss m -es,¨e end; (S~folgerung) conclusion; **zum S~** finally; **S~ machen** stop (mit etw sth); finish (mit jdm with s.o.)

Schlüssel m -s,- key; (Schrauben-) spanner; (Geheim-) code; (Mus) clef. **S~bein** nt collar-bone. **S~bund** m & nt bunch of keys. **S~loch** nt keyhole

Schlussfolgerung f conclusion

schlüssig a conclusive

Schluss|licht nt rear-light. **S~verkauf** m sale

schmächtig a slight

schmackhaft a tasty

schmal a narrow; (dünn) thin; (schlank) slender; (karg) meagre

schmälern vt diminish; (herabsetzen) belittle

Schmalz¹ nt -es lard; (Ohren-) wax

Schmalz² m -es ☐ schmaltz

Schmarotzer m -s,- parasite; (Person) sponger

schmatzen vi (haben) eat noisily

schmausen vi (haben) feast

schmecken vi (haben) taste (nach of); [gut] **s~** taste good ● vt taste

Schmeichelei f -, -en flattery; (Kompliment) compliment

schmeichel|haft a complimentary, flattering. **s~n** vi (haben) (+ dat) flatter

schmeißen† vt/i (haben) **s~** [mit] ☐ chuck

Schmeißfliege f bluebottle

schmelz|en† *vt/i* (*sein*) melt; smelt <*Erze*>. **S~wasser** *nt* melted snow and ice

Schmerbauch *m* 🔟 paunch

Schmerz *m* **-es, -en** pain; (*Kummer*) grief; **S~en haben** be in pain. **s~en** *vt* hurt; (*fig*) grieve ● *vi* (*haben*) hurt, be painful. **S~ensgeld** *nt* compensation for pain and suffering. **s~haft** *a* painful. **s~los** *a* painless **s~stillend** *a* pain-killing; **s~stillendes Mittel** analgesic, pain-killer. **S~tablette** *f* pain-killer

Schmetterball *m* (*Tennis*) smash

Schmetterling *m* **-s, -e** butterfly

schmettern *vt* hurl; (*Tennis*) smash; (*singen*) sing ● *vi* (*haben*) sound

Schmied *m* **-[e]s, -e** blacksmith

Schmiede *f* **-, -n** forge. **S~eisen** *nt* wrought iron. **s~n** *vt* forge

Schmier|e *f* **-, -n** grease; (*Schmutz*) mess. **s~en** *vt* lubricate; (*streichen*) spread; (*schlecht schreiben*) scrawl ● *vi* (*haben*) smudge; (*schreiben*) scrawl. **S~geld** *nt* 🔟 bribe. **s~ig** *a* greasy; (*schmutzig*) grubby. **S~mittel** *nt* lubricant

Schminke *f* **-, -n** make-up. **s~n** *vt* make up; **sich s~n** put on make-up; **sich** (*dat*) **die Lippen s~n** put on lipstick

schmirgel|n *vt* sand down. **S~papier** *nt* emery-paper

schmollen *vi* (*haben*) sulk

schmor|en *vt/i* (*haben*) braise. **S~topf** *m* casserole

Schmuck *m* **-[e]s** jewellery; (*Verzierung*) ornament, decoration

schmücken *vt* decorate, adorn

schmuck|los *a* plain. **S~stück** *nt* piece of jewellery

Schmuggel *m* **-s** smuggling. **s~n** *vt* smuggle. **S~ware** *f* contraband

Schmuggler *m* **-s,-** smuggler

schmunzeln *vi* (*haben*) smile

schmusen *vi* (*haben*) cuddle

Schmutz *m* **-es** dirt. **s~en** *vi* (*haben*) get dirty. **s~ig** *a* dirty

Schnabel *m* **-s,⸚** beak, bill; (*eines Kruges*) lip; (*Tülle*) spout

Schnalle *f* **-, -n** buckle. **s~n** *vt* strap; (*zu-*) buckle

schnalzen *vi* (*haben*) **mit der Zunge s~** click one's tongue

schnapp|en *vi* (*haben*) **s~en nach** snap at; gasp for <*Luft*> ● *vt* snatch, grab; (🔟 *festnehmen*) nab. **S~schloss** *nt* spring lock. **S~schuss** *m* snapshot

Schnaps *m* **-es,⸚e** schnapps

schnarchen *vi* (*haben*) snore

schnaufen *vi* (*haben*) puff, pant

Schnauze *f* **-, -n** muzzle; (*eines Kruges*) lip; (*Tülle*) spout

schnäuzen (sich) *vr* blow one's nose

Schnecke *f* **-, -n** snail; (*Nackt-*) slug; (*Spirale*) scroll. **S~nhaus** *nt* snail-shell

Schnee *m* **-s** snow; (*Eier-*) beaten egg-white. **S~besen** *m* whisk. **S~brille** *f* snow-goggles *pl*. **S~fall** *m* snow-fall. **S~flocke** *f* snowflake. **S~glöckchen** *nt* **-s,-** snowdrop. **S~kette** *f* snow chain. **S~mann** *m* (*pl* -männer) snowman. **S~pflug** *m* snowplough. **S~schläger** *m* whisk. **S~sturm** *m* snowstorm, blizzard. **S~wehe** *f* **-, -n** snowdrift

Schneide *f* **-, -n** [cutting] edge; (*Klinge*) blade

schneiden† *vt* cut; (*in Scheiben*) slice; (*kreuzen*) cross; (*nicht beachten*) cut dead; **Gesichter s~** pull faces; **sich s~** cut oneself; (*über-*) intersect

Schneider *m* **-s,-** tailor. **S~in** *f* **-, -nen** dressmaker. **s~n** *vt* make <*Anzug, Kostüm*>

Schneidezahn *m* incisor

schneien *vi* (*haben*) snow; **es schneit** it is snowing

S

Schneise f -, -n path
schnell a quick; <*Auto, Tempo*>
fast ●adv quickly; (*in s~em
Tempo*) fast; (*bald*) soon; **mach
s~!** hurry up! **S~igkeit** f -
rapidity; (*Tempo*) speed.
S~kochtopf m pressure-cooker.
s~stens adv as quickly as
possible. **S~zug** m express
[train]
schnetzeln vt cut into thin strips
Schnipsel m & nt -s,- scrap
Schnitt m -[e]s, -e cut; (*Film-*)
cutting; (*S~muster*) [paper]
pattern; **im S~** (*durchschnittlich*)
on average
Schnitte f -, -n slice [of bread]
schnittig a stylish;
(*stromlinienförmig*) streamlined
Schnitt|lauch m chives pl.
S~muster nt [paper] pattern.
S~punkt m [point of]
intersection. **S~wunde** f cut
Schnitzel nt -s,- scrap; (*Culin*)
escalope. **s~n** vt shred
schnitzen vt/i (*haben*) carve
schnodderig a Ⅰ brash
Schnorchel m -s,- snorkel
Schnörkel m -s,- flourish; (*Kunst*)
scroll. **s~ig** a ornate
schnüffeln vi (*haben*) sniff (**an
etw** dat sth); (Ⅰ *spionieren*)
snoop [around]
Schnuller m -s,- [baby's] dummy
Schnupf|en m -s,- [head] cold.
S~tabak m snuff
schnuppern vt/i (*haben*) sniff (**an
etw** dat sth)
Schnur f -, -̈e string; (*Kordel*) cord;
(*Electr*) flex
schnüren vt tie; lace [up]
<*Schuhe*>
Schnurr|bart m moustache. **s~en**
vi (*haben*) hum; <*Katze:*> purr
Schnürsenkel m [shoe-]lace
Schock m -[e]s, -s shock. **s~en** vt
Ⅰ shock. **s~ieren** vt shock
Schöffe m -n, -n lay judge
Schokolade f - chocolate

Scholle f -, -n clod [of earth];
(*Eis-*) [ice-]floe; (*Fisch*) plaice
schon adv already; (*allein*) just;
(*sogar*) even; (*ohnehin*) anyway;
s~ einmal before; (*jemals*) ever;
s~ immer/oft/wieder always/
often/again; **s~ deshalb** for that
reason alone; **das ist s~ möglich**
that's quite possible; **ja s~, aber**
well yes, but
schön a beautiful; <*Wetter*> fine;
(*angenehm, nett*) nice; (*gut*) good;
(Ⅰ *beträchtlich*) pretty; **s~en
Dank!** thank you very much!
schonen vt spare; (*gut behandeln*)
look after. **s~d** a gentle
Schönheit f -, -en beauty.
S~sfehler m blemish.
S~skonkurrenz f beauty contest
Schonung f -, -en gentle care;
(*nach Krankheit*) rest; (*Baum-*)
plantation. **s~slos** a ruthless
Schonzeit f close season
schöpf|en vt scoop [up]; ladle
<*Suppe*>; **Mut s~en** take heart.
s~erisch a creative. **S~kelle** f.
S~löffel m ladle. **S~ung** f -, -en
creation
Schoppen m -s,- (*SGer*) ≈ pint
Schorf m -[e]s scab
Schornstein m chimney. **S~fege**
m -s,- chimney-sweep
Schoß m -es, -̈e lap; (*Frack-*) tail
Schössling m -s, -e (*Bot*) shoot
Schote f -, -n pod; (*Erbse*) pea
Schotte m -n, -n Scot, Scotsman
Schotter m -s gravel
schott|isch a Scottish, Scots.
S~land nt -s Scotland
schraffieren vt hatch
schräg a diagonal; (*geneigt*)
sloping; **s~ halten** tilt. **S~strich**
m oblique stroke
Schramme f -, -n scratch
Schrank m -[e]s, -̈e cupboard;
(*Kleider-*) wardrobe; (*Akten-,
Glas-*) cabinet
Schranke f -, -n barrier

Schraube f -, -n screw; (Schiffs-) propeller. **s~n** vt screw; (ab-) unscrew; (drehen) turn. **S~nschlüssel** m spanner. **S~nzieher** m -s,- screwdriver
Schraubstock m vice
Schreck m -[e]s, -e fright. **S~en** m -s,- fright; (Entsetzen) horror
Schreck|gespenst nt spectre. **s~haft** a easily frightened; (nervös) jumpy. **s~lich** a terrible. **S~schuss** m warning shot
Schrei m -[e]s, -e cry, shout; (gellend) scream; der letzte **S~** 𝕀 the latest thing
schreib|en† vt/i (haben) write; (auf der Maschine) type; **richtig/ falsch s~en** spell right/wrong; **sich s~en** <Wort:> be spelt; (korrespondieren) correspond. **S~en** nt -s,- writing; (Brief) letter. **S~fehler** m spelling mistake. **S~heft** nt exercise book. **S~kraft** f clerical assistant; (für Maschineschreiben) typist. **S~maschine** f typewriter. **S~tisch** m desk. **S~ung** f -, -en spelling. **S~waren** fpl stationery sg.
schreien† vt/i (haben) cry; (gellend) scream; (rufen, laut sprechen) shout
Schreiner m -s,- joiner
schreiten† vi (sein) walk
Schrift f -, -en writing; (Druck-) type; (Abhandlung) paper; die **Heilige S~** the Scriptures pl. **S~führer** m secretary. **s~lich** a written ● adv in writing. **S~sprache** f written language. **S~steller(in)** m -s,- (f -, -nen) writer. **S~stück** nt document. **S~zeichen** nt character
schrill a shrill
Schritt m -[e]s, -e step; (Entfernung) pace; (Gangart) walk; (der Hose) crotch. **S~macher** m -s,- pace-maker. **s~weise** adv step by step

schroff a precipitous; (abweisend) brusque; (unvermittelt) abrupt; <Gegensatz> stark
Schrot m & nt -[e]s coarse meal; (Blei-) small shot. **S~flinte** f shotgun
Schrott m -[e]s scrap[-metal]; **zu S~ fahren** 𝕀 write off. **S~platz** m scrap-yard
schrubben vt/i (haben) scrub
Schrull|e f -, -n whim; **alte S~e** 𝕀 old crone. **s~ig** a cranky
schrumpfen vi (sein) shrink
schrump[e]lig a wrinkled
Schub m -[e]s,¨e (Phys) thrust; (S~fach) drawer; (Menge) batch. **S~fach** nt drawer. **S~karre** f, **S~karren** m wheelbarrow. **S~lade** f drawer
Schubs m -es, -e push, shove **s~en** vt push, shove
schüchtern a shy. **S~heit** f - shyness
Schuft m -[e]s, -e (pej) swine
Schuh m -[e]s, -e shoe. **S~anzieher** m -s,- shoehorn. **S~band** nt (pl -bänder) shoe-lace. **S~creme** f shoe-polish. **S~löffel** m shoehorn. **S~macher** m -s,- shoemaker
Schul|abgänger m -s,- schoolleaver. **S~arbeiten, S~aufgaben** fpl homework sg.
Schuld f -, -en guilt; (Verantwortung) blame; (Geld-) debt; **S~en machen** get into debt; **S~ haben** be to blame (an + dat for); **jdm S~ geben** blame s.o. ● **s~ sein** be to blame (an + dat for). **s~en** vt owe
schuldig a guilty (gen of); (gebührend) due; **jdm etw s~ sein** owe s.o. sth. **S~keit** f - duty
schuld|los a innocent. **S~ner** m -s,- debtor. **S~spruch** m guilty verdict
Schule f -, -n school; **in der/die S~** at/to school. **s~n** vt train
Schüler(in) m -s,- (f -, -nen) pupil

schul|frei *a* s∼freier Tag day without school; **wir haben morgen s∼frei** there's no school tomorrow. **S∼hof** *m* [school] playground. **S∼jahr** *nt* school year; (*Klasse*) form. **S∼kind** *nt* schoolchild. **S∼stunde** *f* lesson

Schulter *f* -, -n shoulder. **S∼blatt** *nt* shoulder-blade

Schulung *f* - training

schummeln *vi* (*haben*) 🔲 cheat

Schund *m* -[e]s trash

Schuppe *f* -, -n scale; **S∼n** *pl* dandruff *sg*. s∼n (sich) *vr* flake [off]

Schuppen *m* -s,- shed

schürf|en *vt* mine; **sich** (*dat*) **das Knie s∼en** graze one's knee ● *vi* (*haben*) **s∼en nach** prospect for. **S∼wunde** *f* abrasion, graze

Schürhaken *m* poker

Schurke *m* -n, -n villain

Schürze *f* -, -n apron

Schuss *m* -es,̈e shot; (*kleine Menge*) dash

Schüssel *f* -, -n bowl; (*TV*) dish

Schuss|fahrt *f* (*Ski*) schuss. **S∼waffe** *f* firearm

Schuster *m* -s,- = Schuhmacher

Schutt *m* -[e]s rubble. **S∼abladeplatz** *m* rubbish dump

Schüttel|frost *m* shivering fit. **s∼n** *vt* shake; **sich s∼n** shake oneself/itself; (*vor Ekel*) shudder; **jdm die Hand s∼n** shake s.o.'s hand

schütten *vt* pour; (*kippen*) tip; (*ver-*) spill ● *vi* (*haben*) **es schüttet** it is pouring [with rain]

Schutz *m* -es protection; (*Zuflucht*) shelter; (*Techn*) guard; **S∼ suchen** take refuge. **S∼anzug** *m* protective suit. **S∼blech** *nt* mudguard. **S∼brille** *f* goggles *pl*

Schütze *m* -n, -n marksman; (*Tor-*) scorer; (*Astr*) Sagittarius

schützen *vt* protect/(*Zuflucht gewähren*) shelter (**vor** + *dat* from) ● *vi* (*haben*) give

protection/shelter (**vor** + *dat* from)

Schutz|engel *m* guardian angel. **S∼heilige(r)** *m/f* patron saint

Schützling *m* -s, -e charge

schutz|los *a* defenceless, helpless. **S∼mann** *m* (*pl* **-männer** & **-leute**) policeman. **S∼umschlag** *m* dust-jacket

Schwaben *nt* -s Swabia

schwäbisch *a* Swabian

schwach *a* weak; (*nicht gut; gering*) poor; (*leicht*) faint

Schwäche *f* -, -n weakness. s∼n *vt* weaken

schwäch|lich *a* delicate. **S∼ling** *m* -s, -e weakling

Schwachsinn *m* mental deficiency. **s∼ig** *a* mentally deficient; 🔲 idiotic

Schwager *m* -s,̈ brother-in-law

Schwägerin *f* -, -nen sister-in-law

Schwalbe *f* -, -n swallow

Schwall *m* -[e]s torrent

Schwamm *m* -[e]s,̈e sponge; (*SGer: Pilz*) fungus; (*essbar*) mushroom. s∼ig *a* spongy

Schwan *m* -[e]s,̈e swan

schwanger *a* pregnant

Schwangerschaft *f* -, -en pregnancy

Schwank *m* -[e]s,̈e (*Theat*) farce

schwank|en *vi* (*haben*) sway; <*Boot:*> rock; (*sich ändern*) fluctuate; (*unentschieden sein*) be undecided ● (*sein*) stagger. **S∼ung** *f* -, -en fluctuation

Schwanz *m* -es,̈e tail

schwänzen *vt* 🔲 skip; **die Schule s∼** play truant

Schwarm *m* -[e]s,̈e swarm; (*Fisch-*) shoal; (🔲 *Liebe*) idol

schwärmen *vi* (*haben*) swarm; **s∼ für** 🔲 adore; (*verliebt sein*) have a crush on

Schwarte *f* -, -n (*Speck-*) rind

schwarz *a* black; (🔲 *illegal*) illegal; s∼er Markt black market; s∼ gekleidet dressed in black; s∼

auf weiß in black and white; **s~ sehen** (*fig*) be pessimistic; **ins S~e treffen** score a bull's-eye. **S~ nt -[e]s,-** black. **S~arbeit** *f* moonlighting. **s~arbeiten** *vi sep* (*haben*) moonlight. **S~e(r)** *m/f* black

Schwärze *f* - blackness. **s~n** *vt* blacken

Schwarz|fahrer *m* fare-dodger. **S~handel** *m* black market (**mit** in). **S~händler** *m* black marketeer. **S~markt** *m* black market. **S~wald** *m* Black Forest. **s~weiß** *a* black and white

schwätzen, (SGer) schwätzen *vi* (*haben*) chat; (*klatschen*) gossip; (*Sch*) talk [in class] ● *vt* talk

Schwebe *f* - **in der S~** (*fig*) undecided. **S~bahn** *f* cable railway. **s~n** *vi* (*haben*) float; (*fig*) be undecided; <*Verfahren:*> be pending; **in Gefahr s~n** be in danger ● (*sein*) float

Schwed|e *m* -n, -n Swede. **S~en** *nt* -s Sweden. **S~in** *f* -, -nen Swede. **s~isch** *a* Swedish

Schwefel *m* -s sulphur

schweigen† *vi* (*haben*) be silent; **ganz zu s~ von** let alone. **S~** *nt* -s silence; **zum S~ bringen** silence. **schweigsam** *a* silent; (*wortkarg*) taciturn

Schwein *nt* -[e]s, -e pig; (*Culin*) pork; (🗙 *Schuft*) swine; **S~ haben** 🔟 be lucky. **S~ebraten** *m* roast pork. **S~efleisch** *nt* pork. **S~erei** *f* -, -en 🗙 [dirty] mess; (*Gemeinheit*) dirty trick. **S~estall** *m* pigsty. **S~sleder** *nt* pigskin

Schweiß *m* -es sweat

schweißen† *vt* weld

Schweiz (die) - Switzerland. **S~er** *a & m* -s,-, **S~erin** *f* -, -nen Swiss. **s~erisch** *a* Swiss

Schwelle *f* -, -n threshold; (*Eisenbahn-*) sleeper

schwell|en† *vi* (*sein*) swell. **S~ung** *f* -, -en swelling

schwer *a* heavy; (*schwierig*) difficult; (*mühsam*) hard; (*ernst*) serious; (*schlimm*) bad; **3 Pfund s~ sein** weigh 3 pounds ● *adv* heavily; with difficulty; (*mühsam*) hard; (*schlimm, sehr*) badly, seriously; **s~ krank/verletzt** seriously ill/injured; **s~ hören** be hard of hearing; **etw s~ nehmen** take sth seriously; **jdm s~ fallen** be hard for s.o.; **es jdm s~ machen** make it *or* things difficult for s.o.; **sich s~ tun** have difficulty (**mit** with); **s~ zu sagen** difficult *or* hard to say

Schwere *f* - heaviness; (*Gewicht*) weight; (*Schwierigkeit*) difficulty; (*Ernst*) gravity. **S~losigkeit** *f* - weightlessness

schwer|fällig *a* ponderous, clumsy. **S~gewicht** *nt* heavyweight. **s~hörig** *a* **s~hörig sein** be hard of hearing. **S~kraft** *f* (*Phys*) gravity. **s~mütig** *a* melancholic. **S~punkt** *m* centre of gravity; (*fig*) emphasis

Schwert *nt* -[e]s, -er sword. **S~lilie** *f* iris

Schwer|verbrecher *m* serious offender. **s~wiegend** *a* weighty

Schwester *f* -, -n sister; (*Kranken-*) nurse. **s~lich** *a* sisterly

Schwieger|eltern *pl* parents-in-law. **S~mutter** *f* mother-in-law. **S~sohn** *m* son-in-law. **S~tochter** *f* daughter-in-law. **S~vater** *m* father-in-law

schwierig *a* difficult. **S~keit** *f* -, -en difficulty

Schwimm|bad *nt* swimming-baths *pl*. **S~becken** *nt* swimming-pool. **s~en†** *vt/i* (*sein/haben*) swim; (*auf dem Wasser treiben*) float. **S~weste** *f* life-jacket

Schwindel *m* -s dizziness, vertigo; (🔟 *Betrug*) fraud; (*Lüge*) lie. **S~anfall** *m* dizzy spell. **s~frei** *a*

S

s~frei sein have a good head for heights. **s~n** vi (*haben*) lie

Schwindl|er m -s,- liar; (*Betrüger*) fraud, con-man. **s~ig** a dizzy; **mir ist** od **wird s~ig** I feel dizzy

schwing|en† vi (*haben*) swing; (*Phys*) oscillate; (*vibrieren*) vibrate ●vt swing; wave <*Fahne*>; (*drohend*) brandish. **S~ung** f -, -en oscillation; vibration

Schwips m -es, -e **einen S~ haben** 🔢 be tipsy

schwitzen vi (*haben*) sweat; **ich schwitze** I am hot

schwören† vt/i (*haben*) swear (**auf** + *acc* by)

schwul a (🔢 *homosexuell*) gay

schwül a close. **S~e** f - closeness

Schwung m -[e]s, ̈e swing; (*Bogen*) sweep; (*Schnelligkeit*) momentum; (*Kraft*) vigour. **s~los** a dull. **s~voll** a vigorous; <*Bogen, Linie*> sweeping; (*mitreißend*) spirited

Schwur m -[e]s, ̈e vow; (*Eid*) oath. **S~gericht** nt jury [court]

sechs inv a, **S~** f -, -en six; (*Sch*) ≈ fail mark. **s~eckig** a hexagonal. **s~te(r,s)** a sixth

sech|zehn inv a sixteen. **s~zehnte(r,s)** a sixteenth. **s~zig** inv a sixty. **s~zigste(r,s)** a sixtieth

See¹ m -s, -n /'ze:ən/ lake

See² f - sea; **an die/der See** to/at the seaside; **auf See** at sea. **S~fahrt** f [sea] voyage; (*Schifffahrt*) navigation. **S~gang** m **schwerer S~gang** rough sea. **S~hund** m seal. **s~krank** a seasick

Seele f -, -n soul

seelisch a psychological; (*geistig*) mental

See|macht f maritime power. **S~mann** m (pl -**leute**) seaman, sailor. **S~not** f **in S~not** in distress. **S~räuber** m pirate.

S~reise f [sea] voyage. **S~rose** f water-lily. **S~sack** m kitbag. **S~stern** m starfish. **S~tang** m seaweed. **s~tüchtig** a seaworthy. **S~zunge** f sole

Segel nt -s,- sail. **S~boot** nt sailing-boat. **S~flugzeug** nt glider. **s~n** vt/i (*sein/haben*) sail. **S~schiff** nt sailing-ship. **S~sport** m sailing. **S~tuch** nt canvas

Segen m -s blessing

Segler m -s,- yachtsman

segnen vt bless

sehen† vt see; watch <*Fernsehsendung*>; **jdn/etw wieder s~** see s.o./sth again; **sich s~ lassen** show oneself ●vi (*haben*) see; (*blicken*) look (**auf** + *acc* at); (*ragen*) show (**aus** above); **gut/ schlecht s~** have good/bad eyesight; **vom S~ kennen** know by sight; **s~ nach** keep an eye on; (*betreuen*) look after; (*suchen*) look for. **s~swert, s~swürdig** a worth seeing. **S~swürdigkeit** f -, -en sight

Sehne f -, -n tendon; (*eines Bogens*) string

sehnen (sich) vr long (**nach** for)

Sehn|sucht f - longing (**nach** for). **s~süchtig** a longing; <*Wunsch*> dearest

sehr adv very; (*mit Verb*) very much; **so s~, dass** so much that

seicht a shallow

seid s. **sein¹**

Seide f -, -n silk

Seidel nt -s,- beer-mug

seiden a silk … **S~papier** nt tissue paper. **S~raupe** f silk-worm

seidig a silky

Seife f -, -n soap. **S~npulver** nt soap powder. **S~nschaum** m lather

Seil nt -[e]s, -e rope; (*Draht*-) cable. **S~bahn** f cable railway. **s~springen†** vi (*sein*) (*inf & pp*)

only). skip. **S~tänzer(in)** *m(f)* tightrope walker

sein†¹
● *intransitive verb* (*sein*)
····▸ be. **ich bin glücklich** I am happy. **er ist Lehrer/Schwede** he is a teacher/Swedish. **bist du es?** is that you? **sei still!** be quiet! **sie waren in Paris** they were in Paris. **morgen bin ich zu Hause** I shall be at home tomorrow. **er ist aus Berlin** he is *or* comes from Berlin
····▸ (*impers + dat*) **mir ist kalt/besser** I am cold/better. **ihr ist schlecht** she feels sick
····▸ (*existieren*) be. **es ist/sind ...** there is/are .... **es ist keine Hoffnung mehr** there is no more hope. **es sind vier davon** there are four of them. **es war einmal ein Prinz** once upon a time there was a prince
● *auxiliary verb*
····▸ (*zur Perfektumschreibung*) have. **er ist gestorben** he has died. **sie sind angekommen** they have arrived. **sie war dort gewesen** she had been there. **ich wäre gefallen** I would have fallen
····▸ (*zur Bildung des Passivs*) be. **wir sind gerettet worden/wir waren gerettet** we were saved
····▸ (+ *zu + Infinitiv*) be to be. **es war niemand zu sehen** there was no one to be seen. **das war zu erwarten** that was to be expected. **er ist zu bemitleiden** he is to be pitied. **die Richtlinien sind strengstens zu beachten** the guidelines are to be strictly followed

sein² *poss pron* his; (*Ding, Tier*) its; (*nach man*) one's; **sein Glück versuchen** try one's luck. **s~e(r,s)** *poss pron* his; (*nach man*) one's own; **das S~e tun** do one's share.

s~erseits *adv* for his part. **s~erzeit** *adv* in those days. **s~etwegen** *adv* for his sake; (*wegen ihm*) because of him, on his account. **s~ige** *poss pron* **der/die/das s~ige** his

seins *poss pron* his; (*nach man*) one's own

seit *conj & prep* (+ *dat*) since; **s~ einiger Zeit** for some time [past]; **ich wohne s~ zehn Jahren hier** I've lived here for ten years. **s~dem** *conj* since ● *adv* since then

Seite *f* **-, -n** side; (*Buch-*) page; **zur S~ treten** step aside; **auf der einen/anderen S~** (*fig*) on the one/other hand

seitens *prep* (+ *gen*) on the part of

Seiten|schiff *nt* [side] aisle. **S~sprung** *m* infidelity. **S~stechen** *nt* **-s** (*Med*) stitch. **S~straße** *f* side-street. **S~streifen** *m* verge; (*Autobahn-*) hard shoulder

seither *adv* since then

seit|lich *a* side ... ● *adv* at/on the side; **s~lich von** to one side of ● *prep* (+ *gen*) to one side of. **s~wärts** *adv* on/to one side; (*zur Seite*) sideways

Sekret|är *m* **-s, -e** secretary; (*Schrank*) bureau. **S~ariat** *nt* **-[e]s, -e** secretary's office. **S~ärin** *f* **-, -nen** secretary

Sekt *m* **-[e]s** [German] sparkling wine

Sekte *f* **-, -n** sect

Sektor *m* **-s, -en** /-'to:rən/ sector

Sekunde *f* **-, -n** second

selber *pron* Ⅰ = **selbst**

selbst *pron* oneself; **ich/du/er/sie s~** I myself /you yourself/ he himself/she herself; **wir/ihr/sie s~** we ourselves/you yourselves/ they themselves; **ich schneide mein Haar s~** I cut my own hair; **von s~** of one's own accord;

S

(*automatisch*) automatically; **s~
gemacht** home-made ● *adv* even
selbständig *a* = selbstständig.
S~keit *f* - = Selbstständigkeit
Selbst|bedienung *f* self-service.
S~befriedigung *f* masturbation.
s~bewusst *a* self-confident.
S~bewusstsein *nt* self-
confidence. **S~bildnis** *nt* self-
portrait. **S~erhaltung** *f* self-
preservation. **s~gemacht*** *a* **s~
gemacht**, *s.* selbst. **s~haftend** *a*
self-adhesive. **S~hilfe** *f* self-
help. **s~klebend** *a* self-adhesive.
S~kostenpreis *m* cost price.
S~laut *m* vowel. **s~los** *a*
selfless. **S~mord** *m* suicide.
S~mörder(in) *m(f)* suicide.
s~mörderisch *a* suicidal.
S~porträt *nt* self-portrait.
s~sicher *a* self-assured.
s~ständig *a* independent; self-
employed <*Handwerker*>; **s~
ständig machen** set up on one's
own. **S~ständigkeit** *f* -
independence. **s~süchtig** *a*
selfish. **S~tanken** *nt* self-service
(*for petrol*). **s~tätig** *a* automatic.
S~versorgung *f* self-catering.
s~verständlich *a* natural; **etw für
s~ halten** take sth for granted;
das ist s~ that goes without
saying; **s~!** of course!
S~verteidigung*f* self-defence.
S~vertrauen *nt* self-confidence.
S~verwaltung *f* self-government
selig *a* blissfully happy; (*Relig*)
blessed; (*verstorben*) late. **S~keit**
f - bliss
Sellerie *m* -s, -s & *f* -,- celeriac;
(*Stangen-*) celery
selten *a* rare ● *adv* rarely,
seldom; (*besonders*)
exceptionally. **S~heit** *f* -, -en
rarity
seltsam *a* odd, strange.
s~erweise *adv* oddly
Semester *nt* -s,- (*Univ*) semester
Semikolon *nt* -s, -s semicolon

Seminar *nt* -s, -e seminar;
(*Institut*) department; (*Priester-*)
seminary
Semmel *f* -, -n [bread] roll.
S~brösel *pl* breadcrumbs
Senat *m* -[e]s, -e senate. **S~or** *m*
-s, -en /-'to:rən/ senator
senden[1]† *vt* send
sende|n[2] *vt* (*reg*) broadcast; (*über
Funk*) transmit, send. **S~r** *m* -s,-
[broadcasting] station; (*Anlage*)
transmitter. **S~reihe** *f* series
Sendung *f* -, -en consignment,
shipment; (*TV*) programme
Senf *m* -s mustard
senil *a* senile. **S~ität** *f* - senility
Senior *m* -s, -en /-'o:rən/ senior;
S~en senior citizens. **S~enheim**
nt old people's home
senken *vt* lower; bring down
<*Fieber, Preise*>; bow <*Kopf*>;
sich s~ come down, fall;
(*absinken*) subside
senkrecht *a* vertical. **S~e** *f* -n, -n
perpendicular
Sensation /-'tsio:n/ *f* -, -en
sensation. **s~êll** *a* sensational
Sense *f* -, -n scythe
sensibel *a* sensitive
sentimental *a* sentimental
September *m* -s,- September
Serie /'ze:riə/ *f* -, -n series;
(*Briefmarken*) set; (*Comm*) range
S~nnummer *f* serial number
seriös *a* respectable; (*zuverlässig*)
reliable
Serpentine *f* -, -n winding road;
(*Kehre*) hairpin bend
Serum *nt* -s,Sera serum
Service[1] /zɛr'vi:s/ *nt* -[s],-
/-'vi:s[əs], -'vi:sə/ service, set
Service[2] /'zœːɐvɪs/ *m & nt* -s
/-vɪs[əs]/ (*Comm, Tennis*) service
servier|en *vt/i* (*haben*) serve.
S~erin *f* -, -nen waitress
Serviette *f* -, -n napkin, serviette
Servus *int* (*Aust*) cheerio;
(*Begrüßung*) hallo

Sessel m -s,- armchair. **S~bahn** f,
S~lift m chair-lift
sesshaft a settled
Set /zɛt/ nt & m -[s], -s set;
(Deckchen) place-mat
setz|en vt put; (abstellen) set
down; (hin-) sit down <Kind>;
move <Spielstein>; (pflanzen)
plant; (schreiben, wetten) put;
sich s~en sit down; (sinken)
settle ● vi (sein) leap ● vi (haben)
s~en auf (+ acc) back
Seuche f -, -n epidemic
seufz|en vi (haben) sigh. **S~er** m
-s,- sigh
Sex /zɛks/ m -[es] sex
Sexualität f - sexuality. **s~ell** a
sexual
sezieren vt dissect
Shampoo /ʃam'puː/, **Shampoon**
/ʃam'poːn/ nt -s shampoo
siamesisch a Siamese
sich refl pron oneself; (mit er/
sie/es) himself/herself/itself; (mit
sie pl) themselves; (mit Sie)
yourself; (pl) yourselves;
(einander) each other; **s~ kennen**
know oneself/(einander) each
other; **s~ waschen** have a wash;
s~ (dat) **die Haare kämmen** comb
one's hair; **s~ wundern** be
surprised; **s~ gut verkaufen** sell
well; **von s~ aus** of one's own
accord
Sichel f -, -n sickle
sicher a safe; (gesichert) secure;
(gewiss) certain; (zuverlässig)
reliable; sure <Urteil>; steady
<Hand>; (selbstbewusst) self-
confident; **bist du s~?** are you
sure? ● adv safely; securely;
certainly; reliably; self-
confidently; (wahrscheinlich)
most probably; **s~!** certainly!
s~gehen† vi sep (sein) (fig) be
sure
Sicherheit f - safety; (Pol, Psych,
Comm) security; (Gewissheit)
certainty; (Zuverlässigkeit)

reliability; (des Urteils) surety;
(Selbstbewusstsein) self-
confidence. **S~sgurt** m safety-
belt; (Auto) seat-belt. **S~snadel** f
safety-pin
sicherlich adv certainly;
(wahrscheinlich) most probably
sicher|n vt secure; (garantieren)
safeguard; (schützen) protect; put
the safety-catch on <Pistole>.
S~ung f -, -en safeguard,
protection; (Gewehr-) safety-
catch; (Electr) fuse
Sicht f - view; (S~weite) visibility;
auf lange S~ in the long term.
s~bar a visible. **S~vermerk** m
visa. **S~weite** f visibility; **außer**
S~weite out of sight
sie pron (nom) (sg) she; (Ding,
Tier) it; (pl) they; (acc) (sg) her;
(Ding, Tier) it; (pl) them
Sie pron you; **gehen/warten Sie!**
go/wait!
Sieb nt -[e]s, -e sieve; (Tee-)
strainer. **s~en¹** vt sieve, sift
sieben² inv a, **S~** f -, -en seven.
S~sachen fpl 🔲 belongings.
s~te(r,s) a seventh
sieb|te(r,s) a seventh. **s~zehn** inv
a seventeen. **s~zehnte(r,s)** a
seventeenth. **s~zig** inv a
seventy. **s~zigste(r,s)** a
seventieth
siede|n† vt/i (haben) boil.
S~punkt m boiling point
Siedlung f -, -en [housing] estate;
(Niederlassung) settlement
Sieg m -[e]s, -e victory
Siegel nt -s,- seal. **S~ring** m
signet-ring
sieg|en vi (haben) win. **S~er(in)**
m -s,- (f -, -nen) winner. **s~reich**
a victorious
siezen vt jdn s~ call s.o. 'Sie'
Signal nt -s, -e signal
Silbe f -, -n syllable
Silber nt -s silver. **s~n** a silver
Silhouette /zɪˈlu̯ɛtə/ f -, -n
silhouette

S

Silizium nt -s silicon
Silo m & nt -s, -s silo
Silvester nt -s New Year's Eve
Sims m & nt -es, -e ledge
simultan a simultaneous
sind s. **sein**[1]
Sinfonie f -, -n symphony
singen† vt/i (haben) sing
Singvogel m songbird
sinken† vi (sein) sink; (nieder-) drop; (niedriger werden) go down, fall
Sinn m -[e]s, -e sense; (Denken) mind; (Zweck) point; **in gewissem S~e** in a sense; **es hat keinen S~** it is pointless. **S~bild** nt symbol
sinnlich a sensory; (sexuell) sensual; <Genüsse> sensuous. **S~keit** f - sensuality; sensuousness
sinn|los a senseless; (zwecklos) pointless. **s~voll** a meaningful; (vernünftig) sensible
Sintflut f flood
Siphon /'zi:fõ/ m -s, -s siphon
Sippe f -, -n clan
Sirene f -, -n siren
Sirup m -s, -e syrup; treacle
Sitte f -, -n custom; **S~n** manners
sittlich a moral. **S~keit** f - morality. **S~keitsverbrecher** m sex offender
sittsam a well-behaved; (züchtig) demure
Situa|tion /-'tsio:n/ f -, -en situation. **s~iert** a **gut/schlecht s~iert** well/badly off
Sitz m -es, -e seat; (Passform) fit
sitzen† vi (haben) sit; (sich befinden) be; (passen) fit; (🖪 treffen) hit home; **[im Gefängnis] s~** 🖪 be in jail; **s~ bleiben** remain seated; 🖪 (Sch) stay or be kept down; (nicht heiraten) be left on the shelf; **s~ bleiben auf** (+ dat) be left with
Sitz|gelegenheit f seat. **S~platz** m seat. **S~ung** f -, -en session
Sizilien /-iən/ nt -s Sicily
Skala f -, -len scale; (Reihe) range

Skalpell nt -s, -e scalpel
skalpieren vt scalp
Skandal m -s, -e scandal. **s~ös** a scandalous
Skandinav|ien /-iən/ nt -s Scandinavia. **s~isch** a Scandinavian
Skat m -s skat
Skateboard /'ske:tbo:ɐt/ nt -s, -s skateboard
Skelett nt -[e]s, -e skeleton
Skep|sis f - scepticism. **s~tisch** a sceptical
Ski /ʃi:/ m -s, -er ski; **Ski fahren** od **laufen** ski. **S~fahrer(in)**, **S~läufer(in)** m(f) -s,- (f -, -nen) skier. **S~sport** m skiing
Skizz|e f -, -n sketch. **s~ieren** vt sketch
Sklav|e m -n, -n slave. **S~erei** f - slavery. **S~in** f -, -nen slave
Skorpion m -s, -e scorpion; (Astr) Scorpio
Skrupel m -s,- scruple. **s~los** a unscrupulous
Skulptur f -, -en sculpture
Slalom m -s, -s slalom
Slaw|e m -n, -n, **S~in** f -, -nen Slav. **s~isch** a Slav; (Lang) Slavonic
Slip m -s, -s briefs pl
Smaragd m -[e]s, -e emerald
Smoking m -s, -s dinner jacket
Snob m -s, -s snob. **S~ismus** m - snobbery **s~istisch** a snobbish
so adv so; (so sehr) so much; (auf diese Weise) like this/that; (solch) such; (🖪 sowieso) anyway; (🖪 umsonst) free; (🖪 ungefähr) about; **so viel** so much; **so gut/ bald wie** as good/soon as; **so ein** Zufall! what a coincidence! **mir ist so, als ob** I feel as if; **so oder so** in any case; **so um zehn Euro** 🖪 about ten euros; **so?** really? ● conj (also) so; (dann) then; **so dass = sodass**
sobald conj as soon as
Söckchen nt -s,- [ankle] sock

Socke _f_ -, -n sock
Sockel _m_ -s,- plinth, pedestal
Socken _m_ -s,- sock
sodass _conj_ so that
Sodawasser _nt_ soda water
Sodbrennen _nt_ -s heartburn
soeben _adv_ just [now]
Sofa _nt_ -s, -s settee, sofa
sofern _adv_ provided [that]
sofort _adv_ at once, immediately;
  (_auf der Stelle_) instantly
Software /ˈzɔftvɛːɐ̯/ _f_ - software
sogar _adv_ even
sogenannt _a_ so-called
sogleich _adv_ at once
Sohle _f_ -, -n sole; (_Tal-_) bottom
Sohn _m_ -[e]s,ᵉe son
Sojabohne _f_ soya bean
solange _conj_ as long as
solch _inv pron_ such; s∼ ein(e)
  such a; s∼ einer/eine/eins one/
  (_Person_) someone like that.
  s∼e(r,s) _pron_ such
  ● (_substantivisch_) ein s∼er/eine
  s∼e/ein s∼es one/(_Person_)
  someone like that; s∼e _pl_ those;
  (_Leute_) people like that
Soldat _m_ -en, -en soldier
Söldner _m_ -s,- mercenary
Solidarität _f_ - solidarity
solide _a_ solid; (_haltbar_) sturdy;
  (_sicher_) sound; (_anständig_)
  respectable
Solist(in) _m_ -en, -en (_f_ -, -nen)
  soloist
Soll _nt_ -s (_Comm_) debit;
  (_Produktions-_) quota

sollen†
● _auxiliary verb_
⋯▸ (_Verpflichtung_) be [supposed
  _or_ meant] to. **er soll morgen zum
  Arzt gehen** he is [supposed] to
  go to the doctor tomorrow. **die
  beiden Flächen sollen fluchten** the
  two surfaces are meant to _or_
  should be in alignment. **du
  solltest ihn anrufen** you were

meant to phone him _or_ should
have phoned him
⋯▸ (_Befehl_) **du sollst sofort damit
aufhören** you're to stop that at
once. **er soll hereinkommen** he is
to come in; (_sagen Sie es ihm_)
tell him to come in
⋯▸ **sollte** (_subjunctive_) should;
ought to. **wir sollten früher
aufstehen** we ought to _or_ should
get up earlier. **das hätte er nicht
tun/sagen sollen** he shouldn't
have done/said that
⋯▸ (_Zukunft, Geplantes_) be to. **ich
soll die Abteilung übernehmen** I
am to take over the department.
**du sollst dein Geld
zurückbekommen** you are to _or_
shall get your money back. **es
soll nicht wieder vorkommen** it
won't happen again. **sie sollten
ihr Reiseziel nie erreichen** they
were never to reach their
destination
⋯▸ (_Ratlosigkeit_) be to; shall. **was
soll man nur machen?** what is
one to do?; what shall I/we do?
ich weiß nicht, was ich machen soll
I don't know what I should do
_or_ what to do
⋯▸ (_nach Bericht_) be supposed
to. **er soll sehr reich sein** he is
supposed _or_ is said to be very
rich. **sie soll geheiratet haben** they
say _or_ I gather she has got
married
⋯▸ (_Absicht_) be meant _or_
supposed to. **was soll dieses Bild
darstellen?** what is this picture
supposed to represent? **das
sollte ein Witz sein** that was
meant _or_ supposed to be a joke
⋯▸ (_in Bedingungssätzen_) should.
sollte er anrufen, falls _od_ **wenn er
anrufen sollte** should he _or_ if he
should telephone
● _intransitive verb_
⋯▸ (_irgendwohin gehen sollen_) be
[supposed] to go. **er soll morgen**

S

zum Arzt/nach Berlin he is [supposed] to go to the doctor/ to Berlin tomorrow. **ich sollte ins Theater** I was supposed to go to the theatre

···▶ (*sonstige Wendungen*) **soll er doch!** let him! **was soll das?** what's that in aid of? ⓘ

Solo *nt* -s, -los & -li solo

somit *adv* therefore, so

Sommer *m* -s,- summer. **s~lich** *a* summery; (*Sommer-*) summer ... ● *adv* **s~lich warm** as warm as summer. **S~sprossen** *fpl* freckles

Sonate *f* -, -n sonata

Sonde *f* -, -n probe

Sonder|angebot *nt* special offer. **s~bar** *a* odd. **S~fahrt** *f* special excursion. **S~fall** *m* special case. **s~gleichen** *adv* **eine Gemeinheit s~gleichen** unparalleled meanness. **S~ling** *m* -s, -e crank. **S~marke** *f* special stamp

sondern *conj* but; **nicht nur ... s~ auch** not only ... but also

Sonder|preis *m* special price. **S~schule** *f* special school

Sonett *nt* -[e]s, -e sonnet

Sonnabend *m* -s, -e Saturday. **s~s** *adv* on Saturdays

Sonne *f* -, -n sun. **s~n (sich)** *vr* sun oneself

Sonnen|aufgang *m* sunrise. **s~baden** *vi* (*haben*) sunbathe. **S~bank** *f* sun-bed. **S~blume** *f* sunflower. **S~brand** *m* sun-burn. **S~brille** *f* sun-glasses *pl*. **S~energie** *f* solar energy. **S~finsternis** *f* solar eclipse. **S~milch** *f* sun-tan lotion. **S~öl** *nt* sun-tan oil. **S~schein** *m* sunshine. **S~schirm** *m* sunshade. **S~stich** *m* sunstroke. **S~uhr** *f* sundial. **S~untergang** *m* sunset. **S~wende** *f* solstice

sonnig *a* sunny

Sonntag *m* -s, -e Sunday. **s~s** *adv* on Sundays

sonst *adv* (*gewöhnlich*) usually; (*im Übrigen*) apart from that; (*andernfalls*) otherwise, or [else]; **wer/was/wie/wo s~?** who/what/ how/where else? **s~ niemand** no one else; **s~ noch etwas?** anything else? **s~ noch Fragen?** any more questions? **s~ jemand** *od* **wer** someone/(*fragend, verneint*) anyone else; (*irgendjemand*) [just] anyone; **s~ wo** somewhere/(*fragend, verneint*) anywhere else; (*irgendwo*) [just] anywhere. **s~ig** *a* other

sooft *conj* whenever

Sopran *m* -s, -e soprano

Sorge *f* -, -n worry (**um** about); (*Fürsorge*) care; **sich** (*dat*) **S~n machen** worry. **s~n** *vi* (*haben*) **s~n für** look after, care for; (*vorsorgen*) provide for; (*sich kümmern*) see to; **dafür s~n, dass** see *or* make sure that ● *vr* **sich s~n** worry. **s~nfrei** *a* carefree. **s~nvoll** *a* worried. **S~recht** *nt* (*Jur*) custody

Sorg|falt *f* - care. **s~fältig** *a* careful

Sorte *f* -, -n kind, sort; (*Comm*) brand

sort|ieren *vt* sort [out]; (*Comm*) grade. **S~iment** *nt* -[e]s, -e range

sosehr *conj* however much

Soße *f* -, -n sauce; (*Braten-*) gravy; (*Salat-*) dressing

Souvenir /zuvəˈniːɐ̯/ *nt* -s, -s souvenir

souverän /zuvəˈrɛːn/ *a* sovereign

soviel *conj* however much; **s~ ich weiß** as far as I know ● *adv* *so viel, s.* **viel**

soweit *conj* as far as; (*insoweit*) [in] so far as ● *adv* *so weit, s.* **weit**

sowenig *conj* however little ● *adv* *so wenig, s.* **wenig**

sowie *conj* as well as; (*sobald*) as soon as

sowieso *adv* anyway, in any case
sowjet|isch *a* Soviet. **S~union** *f* - Soviet Union
sowohl *adv* **s~ ... als** *od* **wie auch ... ...** as well as ...
sozial *a* social; *<Einstellung, Beruf>* caring. **S~arbeit** *f* social work. **S~demokrat** *m* social democrat. **S~hilfe** *f* social security
Sozialis|mus *m* - socialism. **S~t** *m* -en, -en socialist
Sozial|versicherung *f* National Insurance. **S~wohnung** *f* ≈ council flat
Soziologie *f* - sociology
Sozius *m* -, -se *(Comm)* partner; *(Beifahrersitz)* pillion
Spachtel *m* -s,- & *f* -, -n spatula
Spagat *m* -[e]s, -e *(Aust)* string; **S~ machen** do the splits *pl*
Spaghetti, Spagetti *pl* spaghetti *sg*
Spalier *nt* -s, -e trellis
Spalt|e *f* -, -n crack; *(Gletscher-)* crevasse; *(Druck-)* column; *(Orangen-)* segment. **s~en†** *vt* split. **S~ung** *f* -, -en splitting; *(Kluft)* split; *(Phys)* fission
Span *m* -[e]s,ːe [wood] chip
Spange *f* -, -n clasp; *(Haar-)* slide; *(Zahn-)* brace
Span|ien /-iən/ *nt* -s Spain. **S~ier** *m* -s,-, **S~ierin** *f* -, -nen Spaniard. **s~isch** *a* Spanish. **S~isch** *nt* -[s] *(Lang)* Spanish
Spann *m* -[e]s instep
Spanne *f* -, -n span; *(Zeit-)* space; *(Comm)* margin
spann|en *vt* stretch; put up *<Leine>*; *(straffen)* tighten; *(an-)* harness **(an** + *acc* to); **sich s~en** tighten ● *vi (haben)* be too tight. **s~end** *a* exciting. **S~ung** *f* -, -en tension; *(Erwartung)* suspense; *(Electr)* voltage
Spar|buch *nt* savings book. **S~büchse** *f* money-box. **s~en** *vt/i (haben)* save; *(sparsam sein)*

economize **(mit/an** + *dat* on). **S~er** *m* -s,- saver
Spargel *m* -s,- asparagus
Spar|kasse *f* savings bank. **S~konto** *nt* deposit account
sparsam *a* economical; *<Person>* thrifty. **S~keit** *f* - economy; thrift
Sparschwein *nt* piggy bank
Sparte *f* -, -n branch; *(Zeitungs-)* section; *(Rubrik)* column
Spaß *m* -es,ːe fun; *(Scherz)* joke; **im/aus/zum S~** for fun; **S~ machen** be fun; *<Person:>* be joking; **viel S~!** have a good time! **s~en** *vi (haben)* joke. **S~vogel** *m* joker
Spastiker *m* -s,- spastic
spät *a* & *adv* late; **wie s~ ist es?** what time is it? **zu s~ kommen** be late
Spaten *m* -s,- spade
später *a* later; *(zukünftig)* future ● *adv* later
spätestens *adv* at the latest
Spatz *m* -en, -en sparrow
Spätzle *pl (Culin)* noodles
spazieren *vi (sein)* stroll; **s~ gehen** go for a walk
Spazier|gang *m* walk; **einen S~gang machen** go for a walk. **S~gänger(in)** *m* -s,- *(f* -, -nen) walker. **S~stock** *m* walking-stick
Specht *m* -[e]s, -e woodpecker
Speck *m* -s bacon. **s~ig** *a* greasy
Spedi|teur /ʃpedi'tøːɐ̯/ *m* -s, -e haulage/*(für Umzüge)* removals contractor. **S~tion** /-'tsi̯oːn/ *f* -, -en carriage, haulage; *(Firma)* haulage/*(für Umzüge)* removals firm
Speer *m* -[e]s, -e spear; *(Sport)* javelin
Speiche *f* -, -n spoke
Speichel *m* -s saliva
Speicher *m* -s,- warehouse; *(dial: Dachboden)* attic; *(Computer)* memory. **s~n** *vt* store
Speise *f* -, -n food; *(Gericht)* dish; *(Pudding)* blancmange. **S~eis** *nt*

ice-cream. S~**kammer** f larder.
S~**karte** f menu. s~**n** vi (haben)
eat ● vt feed. S~**röhre** f
oesophagus. S~**saal** m dining-
room. S~**wagen** m dining-car
Spektrum nt -s, -tra spectrum
Spekul|ant m -en, -en speculator.
s~**ieren** vi (haben) speculate;
s~**ieren auf** (+ acc) [!] hope to get
Spelze f -, -n husk
spendabel a generous
Spende f -, -n vt donation. s~**n** vt
donate; give <Blut, Schatten>;
Beifall s~**n** applaud. S~**r** m -s,-
donor; (Behälter) dispenser
spendieren vt pay for
Sperling m -s, -e sparrow
Sperre f -, -n barrier; (Verbot)
ban; (Comm) embargo. s~**n** vt
close; (ver-) block; (verbieten)
ban; cut off <Strom, Telefon>;
stop <Scheck, Kredit>; s~**n in** (+
acc) put in <Gefängnis, Käfig>
Sperr|holz nt plywood. S~**müll** m
bulky refuse. S~**stunde** f closing
time
Spesen pl expenses
spezial|isieren (sich) vr
specialize (auf + acc in). S~**ist** m
-en, -en specialist. S~**ität** f -, -en
speciality
spicken vt (Culin) lard; **gespickt
mit** (fig) full of
Spiegel m -s,- mirror; (Wasser-,
Alkohol-) level. S~**bild** nt
reflection. S~**ei** nt fried egg. s~**n**
vt reflect; **sich** s~**n** be reflected
● vi (haben) reflect [the light];
(glänzen) gleam. S~**ung** f -, -en
reflection
Spiel nt -[e]s, -e game; (Spielen)
playing; (Glücks-) gambling;
(Schau-) play; (Satz) set; **auf dem
S~ stehen** be at stake; **aufs S~
setzen** risk. S~**automat** m fruit
machine. S~**bank** f casino.
S~**dose** f musical box. s~**en** vt/i
(haben) play; (im Glücksspiel)
gamble; (vortäuschen) act;

<Roman:> be set (in + dat in);
s~**en mit** (fig) toy with
Spieler(in) m -s,- (f -, -nen) player;
(Glücks-) gambler
Spiel|feld nt field, pitch.
~**konsole** f games console.
S~**marke** f chip. S~**plan** m
programme. S~**platz** m
playground. S~**raum** m (fig)
scope; (Techn) clearance.
S~**regeln** fpl rules [of the game].
S~**sachen** fpl toys. S~**verderber**
m -s,- spoilsport. S~**waren** fpl
toys. S~**warengeschäft** nt
toyshop. S~**zeug** nt toy;
(S~sachen) toys pl
Spieß m -es, -e spear; (Brat-) spit;
skewer; (Fleisch-) kebab. S~**er** m
-s,- [petit] bourgeois. s~**ig** a
bourgeois
Spike[s]reifen /ˈʃpaɪk[s]-/ m
studded tyre
Spinat m -s spinach
Spindel f -, -n spindle
Spinne f -, -n spider
spinn|en† vt/i (haben) spin; **er
spinnt** [!] he's crazy.
S~**[en]gewebe** nt, S~**webe** f -, -n
cobweb
Spion m -s, -e spy
Spionage /ʃpioˈnaːʒə/ f -
espionage, spying. S~**abwehr** f
counter-espionage
spionieren vi (haben) spy
Spionin f -, -nen [woman] spy
Spiral|e f -, -n spiral. s~**ig** a spiral
Spirituosen pl spirits
Spiritus m - alcohol; (Brenn-)
methylated spirits pl. S~**kocher**
m spirit stove
spitz a pointed; (scharf) sharp;
(schrill) shrill; (Winkel) acute.
S~**bube** m scoundrel
Spitze f -, -n point; (oberer Teil)
top; (vorderer Teil) front; (Pfeil-,
Finger-, Nasen-) tip; (Schuh-,
Strumpf-) toe; (Zigarren-,
Zigaretten-) holder;
(Höchstleistung) maximum; (Tex)

lace; (⚄ *Anspielung*) dig; **an der S∼ liegen** be in the lead

Spitzel *m* **-s,-** informer

spitzen *vt* sharpen; purse <*Lippen*>; prick up <*Ohren*>. **S∼geschwindigkeit** *f* top speed

Spitzname *m* nickname

Spleen /ʃpliːn/ *m* **-s, -e** obsession

Splitter *m* **-s,-** splinter. **s∼n** *vi* (*sein*) shatter

sponsern *vt* sponsor

Spore *f* **-, -n** (*Biol*) spore

Sporn *m* **-[e]s, Sporen** spur

Sport *m* **-[e]s** sport; (*Hobby*) hobby. **S∼art** *f* sport. **S∼ler** *m* **-s,-** sportsman. **S∼lerin** *f* **-, -nen** sportswoman. **s∼lich** *a* sports ...; (*fair*) sporting; (*schlank*) sporty. **S∼platz** *m* sports ground. **S∼verein** *m* sports club. **S∼wagen** *m* sports car; (*Kinder-*) push-chair, (*Amer*) stroller

Spott *m* **-[e]s** mockery

spotten *vi* (*haben*) mock; **s∼ über** (+ *acc*) make fun of; (*höhnend*) ridicule

spöttisch *a* mocking

Sprach|e *f* **-, -n** language; (*Sprechfähigkeit*) speech; **zur S∼e bringen** bring up. **S∼fehler** *m* speech defect. **S∼labor** *nt* language laboratory. **s∼lich** *a* linguistic. **s∼los** *a* speechless

Spray /ʃpreː/ *nt & m* **-s, -s** spray. **S∼dose** *f* aerosol [can]

Sprechanlage *f* intercom

sprechen† *vi* (*haben*) speak/(*sich unterhalten*) talk (**über** + *acc*/**von** about/of); **Deutsch s∼** speak German ● *vt* speak; (*sagen*) say; pronounce <*Urteil*>; **schuldig s∼** find guilty; **Herr X ist nicht zu s∼** Mr X is not available

Sprecher(in) *m* **-s,-** (*f* **-, -nen**) speaker; (*Radio, TV*) announcer; (*Wortführer*) spokesman, *f* spokeswoman

Sprechstunde *f* consulting hours *pl*; (*Med*) surgery. **S∼nhilfe** *f* (*Med*) receptionist

Sprechzimmer *nt* consulting room

spreizen *vt* spread

spreng|en *vt* blow up; blast <*Felsen*>; (*fig*) burst; (*begießen*) water; (*mit Sprenger*) sprinkle; dampen <*Wäsche*>. **S∼er** *m* **-s,-** sprinkler. **S∼kopf** *m* warhead. **S∼körper** *m* explosive device. **S∼stoff** *m* explosive

Spreu *f* **-** chaff

Sprich|wort *nt* (*pl* **-wörter**) proverb. **s∼wörtlich** *a* proverbial

Springbrunnen *m* fountain

spring|en† *vi* (*sein*) jump; (*Schwimmsport*) dive; <*Ball:*> bounce; (*spritzen*) spurt; (*zer-*) break; (*rissig werden*) crack; (*SGer: laufen*) run. **S∼er** *m* **-s,-** jumper; (*Kunst-*) diver; (*Schach*) knight. **S∼reiten** *nt* show-jumping

Sprint *m* **-s, -s** sprint

Spritz|e *f* **-, -n** syringe; (*Injektion*) injection; (*Feuer-*) hose. **s∼en** *vt* spray; (*be-, ver-*) splash; (*Culin*) pipe; (*Med*) inject ● *vi* (*haben*) splash; <*Fett:*> spit ● *vi* (*sein*) splash; (*hervor-*) spurt. **S∼er** *m* **-s,-** splash; (*Schuss*) dash

spröde *a* brittle; (*trocken*) dry

Sprosse *f* **-, -n** rung

Sprotte *f* **-, -n** sprat

Spruch *m* **-[e]s,⸚e** saying; (*Denk-*) motto; (*Zitat*) quotation. **S∼band** *nt* (*pl* **-bänder**) banner

Sprudel *m* **-s,-** sparkling mineral water. **s∼n** *vi* (*haben/sein*) bubble

Sprüh|dose *f* aerosol [can]. **s∼en** *vt* spray ● *vi* (*sein*) <*Funken:*> fly; (*fig*) sparkle

Sprung *m* **-[e]s,⸚e** jump, leap; (*Schwimmsport*) dive; (⚄ *Katzen-*) stone's throw; (*Riss*) crack. **S∼brett** *nt* springboard.

S

S∼**schanze** f ski-jump. S∼**seil** nt skipping-rope

Spucke f - spit. s∼**n** vt/i (haben) spit; (sich übergeben) be sick

Spuk m -[e]s, -e [ghostly] apparition. s∼**en** vi (haben) <Geist:> walk; **in diesem Haus s∼t es** this house is haunted

Spülbecken nt sink

Spule f -, -n spool

Spüle f -, -n sink

spulen vt spool

spül|en vt rinse; (schwemmen) wash; **Geschirr s∼en** wash up ●vi (haben) flush [the toilet]. S∼**kasten** m cistern. S∼**mittel** nt washing-up liquid

Spur f -, -en track; (Fahr-) lane; (Fährte) trail; (Anzeichen) trace; (Hinweis) lead

spürbar a noticeable

spür|en vt feel; (seelisch) sense. S∼**hund** m tracker dog

spurlos adv without trace

spurten vi (sein) put on a spurt

sputen (sich) vr hurry

Staat m -[e]s, -en state; (Land) country; (Putz) finery. s∼**lich** a state … ●adv by the state

Staatsangehörig|e(r) m/f national. S∼**keit** f - nationality

Staats|anwalt m state prosecutor. S∼**beamte(r)** m civil servant. S∼**besuch** m state visit. S∼**bürger(in)** m(f) national. S∼**mann** m (pl -männer) statesman. S∼**streich** m coup

Stab m -[e]s, "e rod; (Gitter-) bar (Sport) baton; (Mil) staff

Stäbchen ntpl chopsticks

Stabhochsprung m pole-vault

stabil a stable; (gesund) robust; (solide) sturdy

Stachel m -s,- spine; (Gift-) sting; (Spitze) spike. S∼**beere** f gooseberry. S∼**draht** m barbed wire. S∼**schwein** nt porcupine

Stadion nt -s, -ien stadium

Stadium nt -s, -ien stage

Stadt f -, "e town; (Groß-) city

städtisch a urban; (kommunal) municipal

Stadt|mitte f town centre. S∼**plan** m street map. S∼**teil** m district

Staffel f -, -n team; (S∼lauf) relay; (Mil) squadron

Staffelei f -, -en easel

Staffel|lauf m relay race. s∼**n** vt stagger; (abstufen) grade

Stahl m -s steel. S∼**beton** m reinforced concrete

Stall m -[e]s, "e stable; (Kuh-) shed; (Schweine-) sty; (Hühner-) coop; (Kaninchen-) hutch

Stamm m -[e]s-"e trunk; (Sippe) tribe; (Wort-) stem. S∼**baum** m family tree; (eines Tieres) pedigree

stammeln vt/i (haben) stammer

stammen vi (haben) come/ (zeitlich) date (von/aus from)

stämmig a sturdy

Stamm|kundschaft f regulars pl. S∼**lokal** nt favourite pub

stampfen vi (haben) stamp; <Maschine:> pound ●vi (sein) tramp ●vt pound; mash <Kartoffeln>

Stand m -[e]s, "e standing position; (Zustand) state; (Spiel-) score; (Höhe) level; (gesellschaftlich) class; (Verkaufs-) stall; (Messe-) stand; (Taxi-) rank; **auf den neuesten S∼ bringen** up-date

Standard m -s, -s standard

Standbild nt statue

Ständer m -s,- stand; (Geschirr-) rack; (Kerzen-) holder

Standes|amt nt registry office. S∼**beamte(r)** m registrar

standhaft a steadfast

ständig a constant; (fest) permanent

Stand|licht nt sidelights pl. S∼**ort** m position; (Firmen-) location; (Mil) garrison. S∼**punkt** m point of view. **S~uhr** *f* grandfather clock

Stange *f* -, -n bar; (*Holz-*) pole; (*Gardinen-*) rail; (*Hühner-*) perch; (*Zimt-*) stick; **von der S~** 🇮 off the peg

Stängel *m* -s,- stalk, stem

Stangenbohne *f* runner bean

Stanniol *nt* -s tin foil. **S~papier** *nt* silver paper

stanzen *vt* stamp; punch <*Loch*>

Stapel *m* -s,- stack, pile. **S~lauf** *m* launch[ing]. **s~n** *vt* stack *or* pile up

Star[1] *m* -[e]s, -e starling

Star[2] *m* -[e]s (*Med*) [**grauer**] **S~** cataract; **grüner S~** glaucoma

Star[3] *m* -s, -s (*Theat, Sport*) star

stark *a* strong; <*Motor*> powerful; <*Verkehr, Regen*> heavy; <*Hitze, Kälte*> severe; (*groß*) big; (*schlimm*) bad; (*dick*) thick; (*korpulent*) stout ● *adv* (*sehr*) very much

Stärk|e *f* -, -n strength; power; thickness; stoutness; (*Größe*) size; (*Mais-, Wäsche-*) starch. **S~emehl** *nt* cornflour. **s~en** *vt* strengthen; starch <*Wäsche*>; **sich s~en** fortify oneself. **S~ung** *f* -, -en strengthening; (*Erfrischung*) refreshment

starr *a* rigid; (*steif*) stiff

starren *vi* (*haben*) stare

Starr|sinn *m* obstinacy. **s~sinnig** *a* obstinate

Start *m* -s, -s start; (*Aviat*) take-off. **S~bahn** *f* runway. **s~en** *vi* (*sein*) start; (*Aviat*) take off ● *vt* start; (*fig*) launch

Station /-'tsio:n/ *f* -, -en station; (*Haltestelle*) stop; (*Abschnitt*) stage; (*Med*) ward; **S~ machen** break one's journey. **s~är** *adv* as an inpatient. **s~ieren** *vt* station

statisch *a* static

Statist(in) *m* -en, -en (*f* -, -nen) (*Theat*) extra

Statisti|k *f* -, -en statistics *sg*; (*Aufstellung*) statistics *pl*. **s~sch** *a* statistical

Stativ *nt* -s, -e (*Phot*) tripod

statt *prep* (+ *gen*) instead of; **an seiner s~** in his place; **an Kindes s~ annehmen** adopt ● *conj* **s~ etw zu tun** instead of doing sth. **s~dessen** *adv* instead

statt|finden† *vi sep* (*haben*) take place. **s~haft** *a* permitted

Statue /'ʃta:tuə/ *f* -, -n statue

Statur *f* - build, stature

Status *m* - status. **S~symbol** *nt* status symbol

Statut *nt* -[e]s, -en statute

Stau *m* -[e]s, -s congestion; (*Auto*) [traffic] jam; (*Rück-*) tailback

Staub *m* -[e]s dust; **S~ wischen** dust; **S~ saugen** vacuum, hoover

Staubecken *nt* reservoir

staub|ig *a* dusty. **s~saugen** *vt/i* (*haben*) vacuum, hoover. **S~sauger** *m* vacuum cleaner, Hoover (P)

Staudamm *m* dam

stauen *vt* dam up; **sich s~** accumulate; <*Autos:*> form a tailback

staunen *vi* (*haben*) be amazed *or* astonished

Stau|see *m* reservoir. **S~ung** *f* -, -en congestion; (*Auto*) [traffic] jam

Steak /ʃte:k, ste:k/ *nt* -s, -s steak

stechen† *vt* stick (**in** + *acc* in); (*verletzen*) prick; (*mit Messer*) stab; <*Insekt:*> sting; <*Mücke:*> bite ● *vi* (*haben*) prick; <*Insekt:*> sting; <*Mücke:*> bite; (*mit Stechuhr*) clock in/out; **in See s~** put to sea

Stech|ginster *m* gorse. **S~kahn** *m* punt. **S~palme** *f* holly. **S~uhr** *f* time clock

Steck|brief *m* 'wanted' poster. **S~dose** *f* socket. **s~en** *vt* put; (*mit Nadel, Reißzwecke*) pin; (*pflanzen*) plant ● *vi* (*haben*) be;

S

(*fest-*) be stuck; **s~ bleiben** get stuck; **den Schlüssel s~ lassen** leave the key in the lock
Steckenpferd *nt* hobby-horse
Steck|er *m* -s,- (*Electr*) plug. **S~nadel** *f* pin
Steg *m* -[e]s, -e foot-bridge; (*Boots-*) landing-stage; (*Brillen-*) bridge
stehen† *vi* (*haben*) stand; (*sich befinden*) be; (*still-*) be stationary; <*Maschine, Uhr:*> have stopped; **s~ bleiben** remain standing; <*Gebäude:*> be left standing; (*anhalten*) stop; <*Motor:*> stall; <*Zeit:*> stand still; **vor dem Ruin s~** face ruin; **zu jdm/etw s~** (*fig*) stand by s.o./sth; **jdm [gut] s~** suit s.o.; **sich gut s~** be on good terms; **es steht 3 zu 1** the score is 3–1. **s~d** *a* standing; (*sich nicht bewegend*) stationary; <*Gewässer:*> stagnant
Stehlampe *f* standard lamp
stehlen† *vt/i* (*haben*) steal; **sich s~** steal, creep
Steh|platz *m* standing place. **S~vermögen** *nt* stamina, staying-power
steif *a* stiff
Steig|bügel *m* stirrup. **S~eisen** *nt* crampon
steigen† *vi* (*sein*) climb; (*hochgehen*) rise, go up; <*Schulden, Spannung:*> mount; **s~ auf** (+ *acc*) climb on [to] <*Stuhl*>; climb <*Berg, Leiter*>; get on <*Pferd, Fahrrad*>; **s~ in** (+ *acc*) climb into; get in <*Auto*>; get on <*Bus, Zug*>; **s~ aus** climb out of; get out of <*Bett, Auto*>; get off <*Bus, Zug*>; **s~de Preise** rising prices
steiger|n *vt* increase; **sich s~n** increase; (*sich verbessern*) improve. **S~ung** *f* -, -en increase; improvement; (*Gram*) comparison
steil *a* steep. **S~küste** *f* cliffs *pl*

Stein *m* -[e]s, -e stone; (*Ziegel-*) brick; (*Spiel-*) piece. **S~bock** *m* ibex; (*Astr*) Capricorn. **S~bruch** *m* quarry. **S~garten** *m* rockery. **S~gut** *nt* earthenware. **s~ig** *a* stony. **s~igen** *vt* stone. **S~kohle** *f* [hard] coal. **S~schlag** *m* rock fall
Stelle *f* -, -n place; (*Fleck*) spot; (*Abschnitt*) passage; (*Stellung*) job, post; (*Behörde*) authority; **auf der S~** immediately
stellen *vt* put; (*aufrecht*) stand; set <*Wecker, Aufgabe*>; ask <*Frage*>; make <*Antrag, Forderung, Diagnose*>; **zur Verfügung s~** provide; **lauter/leiser s~** turn up/down; **kalt/warm s~** chill/keep hot; **sich s~** [go and] stand; give oneself up (**der Polizei** to the police); **sich tot s~** pretend to be dead; **gut gestellt sein** be well off
Stellen|anzeige *f* job advertisement. **S~vermittlung** *f* employment agency. **s~weise** *adv* in places
Stellung *f* -, -en position; (*Arbeit*) job; **S~ nehmen** make a statement (**zu** on). **S~suche** *f* job-hunting
Stellvertreter *m* deputy
Stelzen *fpl* stilts. **S~** *vi* (*sein*) stalk
stemmen *vt* press; lift <*Gewicht*>
Stempel *m* -s,- stamp; (*Post-*) post-mark; (*Präge-*) die; (*Feingehalts-*) hallmark. **s~n** *vt* stamp; hallmark <*Silber*>; cancel <*Marke*>
Stengel* *m* -s,- *s*. **Stängel**
Steno *f* - 🔲 shorthand
Steno|gramm *nt* -[e]s, -e shorthand text. **S~grafie** *f* - shorthand. **s~grafieren** *vt* take down in shorthand ● *vi* (*haben*) do shorthand
Steppdecke *f* quilt
Steppe *f* -, -n steppe

Stepptanz m tap-dance
sterben† vi (sein) die (**an** + dat
of); **im S~ liegen** be dying
sterblich a mortal. **S~keit** f -
mortality
stereo adv in stereo. **S~anlage** f
stereo [system]
steril a sterile. **s~isieren** vt
sterilize. **S~ität** f - sterility
Stern m -[e]s, -e star. **S~bild** nt
constellation. **S~chen** nt -s,-
asterisk. **S~kunde** f astronomy.
S~schnuppe f -, -n shooting star.
S~warte f -, -n observatory
stets adv always
Steuer[1] nt -s, - steering-wheel;
(Naut) helm; **am S~** at the wheel
Steuer[2] f -, -n tax
Steuer|bord nt -[e]s starboard
[side]. **S~erklärung** f tax return.
s~frei a & adv tax-free. **S~mann**
m (pl -leute) helmsman; (beim
Rudern) cox. **s~n** vt steer; (Aviat)
pilot; (Techn) control ● vi (haben)
be at the wheel/(Naut) helm.
s~pflichtig a taxable. **S~rad** nt
steering-wheel. **S~ruder** nt
helm. **S~ung** f - steering; (Techn)
controls pl. **S~zahler** m -s,-
taxpayer
Stewardess /'stju:ɐdɛs/ f -, -en air
hostess, stewardess
Stich m -[e]s, -e prick; (Messer-)
stab; (S~wunde) stab wound;
(Bienen-) sting; (Mücken-) bite;
(Schmerz) stabbing pain; (Näh-)
stitch; (Kupfer-) engraving;
(Kartenspiel) trick
stick|en vt/i (haben) embroider.
S~erei f - embroidery
Stickstoff m nitrogen
Stiefel m -s,- boot
Stief|kind nt stepchild. **S~mutter**
f stepmother. **S~mütterchen** nt
-s,- pansy. **S~sohn** m stepson.
S~tochter f stepdaughter.
S~vater m stepfather
Stiege f -, -n stairs pl

Stiel m -[e]s, -e handle; (Blumen-,
Gläser-) stem; (Blatt-) stalk
Stier m -[e]s, -e bull; (Astr) Taurus
Stierkampf m bullfight
Stift[1] m -[e]s, -e pin; (Nagel) tack;
(Blei-) pencil; (Farb-) crayon
Stift[2] nt -[e]s, -e [endowed]
foundation. **s~en** vt endow;
(spenden) donate; create <Unheil,
Verwirrung>; bring about
<Frieden>. **S~ung** f -, -en
foundation; (Spende) donation
Stil m -[e]s, -e style
still a quiet; (reglos, ohne
Kohlensäure) still; (heimlich)
secret; **der S~e Ozean** the Pacific;
im S~en secretly. **S~e** f - quiet;
(Schweigen) silence
Stilleben* nt s. Stillleben
stillen vt satisfy; quench <Durst>;
stop <Schmerzen, Blutung>;
breast-feed <Kind>
still|halten† vi sep (haben) keep
still. **S~leben** nt still life.
s~legen vt sep close down.
S~schweigen nt silence.
S~stand m standstill; **zum
S~stand bringen/kommen** stop.
s~stehen† vi sep (haben) stand
still; (anhalten) stop; <Verkehr:>
be at a standstill
Stimm|bänder ntpl vocal cords.
s~berechtigt a entitled to vote.
S~bruch m **er ist im S~bruch** his
voice is breaking
Stimme f -, -n voice; (Wahl-) vote
stimmen† vi (haben) be right;
(wählen) vote ● vt tune
Stimmung f -, -en mood;
(Atmosphäre) atmosphere
Stimmzettel m ballot-paper
stink|en† vi (haben) smell/(stark)
stink (nach of). **S~tier** nt skunk
Stipendium nt -s, -ien scholarship;
(Beihilfe) grant
Stirn f -, -en forehead
stochern vi (haben) **s~ in** (+ dat)
poke <Feuer>; pick at <Essen>

S

Stock[1] m -[e]s,¨e stick; (Ski-) pole; (Bienen-) hive; (Rosen-) bush; (Reb-) vine

Stock[2] m -[e]s,- storey, floor. **S~bett** nt bunk-beds pl.

stock|en vi (haben) stop; <Verkehr:> come to a standstill; <Person:> falter. **S~ung** f -, -en hold-up

Stockwerk nt storey, floor

Stoff m -[e]s, -e substance; (Tex) fabric, material; (Thema) subject [matter]; (Gesprächs-) topic. **S~wechsel** m metabolism

stöhnen vi (haben) groan, moan

Stola f -, -len stole

Stollen m -s,- gallery; (Kuchen) stollen

stolpern vi (sein) stumble; **s~ über** (+ acc) trip over

stolz a proud (auf + acc of). **S~** m -es pride

stopfen vt stuff; (stecken) put; (ausbessern) darn ● vi (haben) be constipating

Stopp m -s, -s stop. **s~** int stop!

stoppelig a stubbly

stopp|en vt stop; (Sport) time ● vi (haben) stop. **S~uhr** f stop-watch

Stöpsel m -s,- plug; (Flaschen-) stopper

Storch m -[e]s,¨e stork

Store /ʃtoːɐ/ m -s, -s net curtain

stören vt disturb; disrupt <Rede>; jam <Sender>; (missfallen) bother ● vi (haben) be a nuisance

stornieren vt cancel

störrisch a stubborn

Störung f -, -en disturbance; disruption; (Med) trouble; (Radio) interference; **technische S~** technical fault

Stoß m -es,¨e push, knock; (mit Ellbogen) dig; (Hörner-) butt; (mit Waffe) thrust; (Schwimm-) stroke; (Ruck) jolt; (Erd-) shock; (Stapel) stack, pile. **S~dämpfer** m -s,- shock absorber

stoßen† vt push, knock; (mit Füßen) kick; (mit Kopf) butt; (an-) poke, nudge; (treiben) thrust; **sich s~** knock oneself; **sich (dat) den Kopf s~** hit one's head ● vi (haben) push; **s~ an** (+ acc) knock against; (angrenzen) adjoin ● vi (sein) **s~ gegen** knock against; bump into <Tür>; **s~ auf** (+ acc) bump into; (entdecken) come across; strike <Öl>

Stoß|stange f bumper. **S~verkehr** m rush-hour traffic. **S~zahn** m tusk. **S~zeit** f rush-hour

stottern vt/i (haben) stutter, stammer

Str. abbr (Straße) St

Strafanstalt f prison

Strafe f -, -n punishment; (Jur & fig) penalty; (Geld-) fine; (Freiheits-) sentence. **s~n** vt punish

Strafgesetz nt criminal law

sträf|lich a criminal. **S~ling** m -s, -e prisoner

Straf|mandat nt (Auto) [parking/speeding] ticket. **S~porto** nt excess postage. **S~raum** m penalty area. **S~stoß** m penalty. **S~tat** f crime

Strahl m -[e]s, -en ray; (einer Taschenlampe) beam; (Wasser-) jet. **s~en** vi (haben) shine; (funkeln) sparkle; (lächeln) beam. **S~enbehandlung** f radiotherapy. **S~ung** f - radiation

Strähne f -, -n strand

stramm a tight

Strampel|höschen /-sç-/ nt -s,- rompers pl. **s~n** vi (haben) <Baby:> kick

Strand m -[e]s,¨e beach. **s~en** vi (sein) run aground

Strang m -[e]s,¨e rope

Strapaz|e f -, -n strain. **s~ieren** vt be hard on; tax <Nerven>

Strass m - & -es paste
Straße f -, -n road; (in der Stadt auch) street; (Meeres-) strait. **S~nbahn** f tram. **S~nkarte** f road-map. **S~nsperre** f road-block
Strat|egie f -, -n strategy. **s~egisch** a strategic
Strauch m -[e]s, Sträucher bush
Strauß¹ m -es, Sträuße bunch [of flowers]; (Bukett) bouquet
Strauß² m -es, -e ostrich
streben vi (haben) strive (nach for) ● vi (sein) head (nach/zu for)
Streber m -s,- pushy person
Strecke f -, -n stretch, section; (Entfernung) distance; (Rail) line; (Route) route
strecken vt stretch; (aus-) stretch out; (gerade machen) straighten; (Culin) thin down; **den Kopf aus dem Fenster s~** put one's head out of the window
Streich m -[e]s, -e prank, trick
streicheln vt stroke
streichen† vt spread; (weg-) smooth; (an-) paint; (aus-) delete; (kürzen) cut ● vi (haben) **s~ über** (+ acc) stroke
Streichholz nt match
Streich|instrument nt stringed instrument. **S~käse** m cheese spread. **S~orchester** nt string orchestra. **S~ung** f -, -en deletion; (Kürzung) cut
Streife f -, -n patrol
streifen vt brush against; (berühren) touch; (verletzen) graze; (fig) touch on <Thema>
Streifen m -s,- stripe; (Licht-) streak; (auf der Fahrbahn) line; (schmales Stück) strip
Streifenwagen m patrol car
Streik m -s, -s strike; **in den S~ treten** go on strike. **S~brecher** m strike-breaker, (pej) scab. **s~en** vi (haben) strike; 🔢 refuse; (versagen) pack up

Streit m -[e]s, -e quarrel; (Auseinandersetzung) dispute. **s~en**† vr/i (haben) [sich] s~en quarrel. **S~igkeiten** fpl quarrels. **S~kräfte** fpl armed forces
streng a strict; <Blick, Ton> stern; (rau, nüchtern) severe; <Geschmack> sharp; **s~ genommen** strictly speaking. **S~e** f - strictness; sternness; severity
Stress m -es, -e stress
streuen vt spread; (ver-) scatter; sprinkle <Zucker, Salz>; **die Straßen s~** grit the roads
streunen vi (sein) roam
Strich m -[e]s, -e line; (Feder-, Pinsel-) stroke; (Morse-, Gedanken-) dash. **S~kode** m bar code. **S~punkt** m semicolon
Strick m -[e]s, -e cord; (Seil) rope
strick|en vt/i (haben) knit. **S~jacke** f cardigan. **S~leiter** f rope-ladder. **S~nadel** f knitting-needle. **S~waren** fpl knitwear sg. **S~zeug** nt knitting
striegeln vt groom
strittig a contentious
Stroh nt -[e]s straw. **S~blumen** fpl everlasting flowers. **S~dach** nt thatched roof. **S~halm** m straw
Strolch m -[e]s, -e 🔢 rascal
Strom m -[e]s, ̈-e river; (Menschen-, Auto-, Blut-) stream; (Tränen-) flood; (Schwall) torrent; (Electr) current, power; **gegen den S~** (fig) against the tide. **s~abwärts** adv downstream. **s~aufwärts** adv upstream
strömen vi (sein) flow; <Menschen, Blut:> stream, pour
Strom|kreis m circuit. **s~linienförmig** a streamlined. **S~sperre** f power cut
Strömung f -, -en current
Strophe f -, -n verse
Strudel m -s,- whirlpool; (SGer Culin) strudel
Strumpf m -[e]s, ̈-e stocking; (Knie-) sock. **S~band** nt (pl

-bänder) suspender. **S~hose** f
tights pl
struppig a shaggy
Stube f -, -n room. **s~nrein** a
house-trained
Stuck m -s stucco
Stück nt -[e]s, -e piece; (Zucker-)
lump; (Seife) tablet; (Theater-)
play; (Gegenstand) item;
(Exemplar) specimen; **ein S~**
(Entfernung) some way. **S~chen**
nt -s,- [little] bit
Student|(in) m -en, -en (f -, -nen)
student. **s~isch** a student ...
Studie /-iə/ f -, -n study
studieren vt/i (haben) study
Studio nt -s, -s studio
Studium nt -s, -ien studies pl
Stufe f -, -n step; (Treppen-)
stair; (Raketen-) stage; (Niveau)
level. **s~n** vt terrace; (staffeln) grade
Stuhl m -[e]s,-e chair; (Med) stools
pl. **S~gang** m bowel movement
stülpen vt put (über + acc over)
stumm a dumb; (schweigsam)
silent
Stummel m -s,- stump;
(Zigaretten-) butt; (Bleistift-) stub
Stümper m -s,- bungler
stumpf a blunt; <Winkel> obtuse;
(glanzlos) dull; (fig) apathetic.
S~ m -[e]s,-e stump
Stumpfsinn m apathy; tedium
Stunde f -, -n hour; (Sch) lesson
stunden vt jdm eine Schuld s~
give s.o. time to pay a debt
Stunden|kilometer mpl
kilometres per hour. **s~lang** adv
for hours. **S~lohn** m hourly rate.
S~plan m timetable. **s~weise**
adv by the hour
stündlich a & adv hourly
stur a pigheaded
Sturm m -[e]s,-e gale; storm; (Mil)
assault
stürm|en vi (haben) <Wind:> blow
hard ●vi (sein) rush ●vt storm;
(bedrängen) besiege. **S~er** m -s,-

forward. **s~isch** a stormy;
<Überfahrt> rough
Sturz m -es,-e [heavy] fall;
(Preis-) sharp drop; (Pol)
overthrow
stürzen vi (sein) fall [heavily]; (in
die Tiefe) plunge; <Preise:> drop
sharply; <Regierung:> fall; (eilen)
rush ●vt throw; (umkippen) turn
upside down; turn out <Speise,
Kuchen>; (Pol) overthrow, topple;
sich s~ throw oneself (aus/in +
acc out of/into)
Sturzhelm m crash-helmet
Stute f -, -n mare
Stütze f -, -n support
stützen vt support; (auf-) rest;
sich s~ auf (+ acc) lean on
stutzig a puzzled; (misstrauisch)
suspicious
Stützpunkt m (Mil) base
Substantiv nt -s, -e noun
Substanz f -, -en substance
Subvention /-'tsio:n/ f -, -en
subsidy. **s~ieren** vt subsidize
Such|e f - search; **auf der S~e
nach** looking for. **s~en** vt look
for; (intensiv) search for; seek
<Hilfe, Rat>; 'Zimmer gesucht'
'room wanted' ●vi (haben) look,
search (nach for). **S~er** m -s,-
(Phot) viewfinder. **S~maschine** f
search engine
Sucht f -,-e addiction; (fig) mania
süchtig a addicted. **S~e(r)** m/f
addict
Süd m -[e]s south. **S~afrika** nt
South Africa. **S~amerika** nt
South America. **s~deutsch** a
South German
Süden m -s south; **nach S~** south
Süd|frucht f tropical fruit. **s~lich**
a southern; <Richtung> southerly
●adv & prep (+ gen) **s~lich der
Stadt** south of the town. **S~pol** m
South Pole. **s~wärts** adv
southwards
Sühne f -, -n atonement; (Strafe)
penalty. **s~n** vt atone for

Sultanine *f* -, -n sultana
Sülze *f* -, -n [meat] jelly
Summe *f* -, -n sum
summen *vi* (*haben*) hum;
  <*Biene:*> buzz ● *vt* hum
summieren (sich) *vr* add up
Sumpf *m* -[e]s,̈e marsh, swamp
Sünd|e *f* -, -n sin. **S~enbock** *m*
  scapegoat. **S~er(in)** *m* -s,- (*f* -,
  -nen) sinner. **s~igen** *vi* (*haben*)
  sin
super *inv a* 🔲 great. **S~markt** *m*
  supermarket
Suppe *f* -, -n soup. **S~nlöffel** *m*
  soup-spoon. **S~nteller** *m* soup-
  plate. **S~nwürfel** *m* stock cube
Surf|brett /'sø:ɐ̯f-/ *nt* surfboard.
  s~en *vi* (*haben*) surf. **S~en** *nt* -s
  surfing
surren *vi* (*haben*) whirr
süß *a* sweet. **S~e** *f* - sweetness.
  s~en *vt* sweeten. **S~igkeit** *f* -, -en
  sweet. **s~lich** *a* sweetish; (*fig*)
  sugary. **S~speise** *f* sweet.
  S~stoff *m* sweetener. **S~waren**
  fpl confectionery *sg*, sweets *pl*.
  S~wasser- *pref* freshwater …
Sylvester *nt* -s = Silvester
Symbol *nt* -s, -e symbol. **S~ik** *f* -
  symbolism. **s~isch** *a* symbolic
Sym|metrie *f* - symmetry.
  s~metrisch *a* symmetrical
Sympathie *f* - sympathy
sympathisch *a* agreeable;
  <*Person*> likeable
Symptom *nt* -s, -e symptom.
  s~atisch *a* symptomatic
Synagoge *f* -, -n synagogue
synchronisieren /zynkroni'zi:rən/
  vt synchronize; dub <*Film*>
Syndikat *nt* -[e]s, -e syndicate
Syndrom *nt* -s, -e syndrome
synonym *a* synonymous
Synthese *f* -, -n synthesis
Syrien /-iən/ *nt* -s Syria
System *nt* -s, -e system. **s~atisch**
  a systematic
Szene *f* -, -n scene

Tabak *m* -s, -e tobacco
Tabelle *f* -, -n table; (*Sport*)
  league table
Tablett *nt* -[e]s, -s tray
Tablette *f* -, -n tablet
tabu *a* taboo. **T~** *nt* -s, -s taboo
Tacho *m* -s, -s, **Tachometer** *m* &
  nt speedometer
Tadel *m* -s,- reprimand; (*Kritik*)
  censure; (*Sch*) black mark. **t~los**
  a impeccable. **t~n** *vt* reprimand;
  censure
Tafel *f* -, -n (*Tisch, Tabelle*) table;
  (*Platte*) slab; (*Anschlag-,
  Hinweis-*) board; (*Gedenk-*)
  plaque; (*Schiefer-*) slate; (*Wand-*)
  blackboard; (*Bild-*) plate;
  (*Schokolade*) bar
Täfelung *f* - panelling
Tag *m* -[e]s, -e day; **unter T~e**
  underground; **es wird Tag** it is
  getting light; **guten Tag!** good
  morning/afternoon!
Tage|buch *nt* diary. **t~lang** *adv*
  for days
Tages|anbruch *m* daybreak.
  T~ausflug *m* day trip. **T~decke** *f*
  bedspread. **T~karte** *f* day ticket;
  (*Speise-*) menu of the day.
  T~licht *nt* daylight. **T~mutter** *f*
  child-minder. **T~ordnung** *f*
  agenda. **T~rückfahrkarte** *f* day
  return [ticket]. **T~zeit** *f* time of
  the day. **T~zeitung** *f* daily
  [news]paper
täglich *a* & *adv* daily; **zweimal t~**
  twice a day
tags *adv* by day; **t~ zuvor/darauf**
  the day before/after
tagsüber *adv* during the day

tag|täglich *a* daily ● *adv* every single day. **T~ung** *f* -, -en meeting; conference
Taill|e /'taljə/ *f* -, -n waist. **t~iert** /ta'jiːɛt/ *a* fitted
Takt *m* -[e]s, -e tact; (*Mus*) bar; (*Tempo*) time; (*Rhythmus*) rhythm; **im T~** in time
Taktik *f* - tactics *pl*.
takt|los *a* tactless. **T~losigkeit** *f* - tactlessness. **T~stock** *m* baton. **t~voll** *a* tactful
Tal *nt* -[e]s, -ä valley
Talar *m* -s, -e robe; (*Univ*) gown
Talent *nt* -[e]s, -e talent. **t~iert** *a* talented
Talg *m* -s tallow; (*Culin*) suet
Talsperre *f* dam
Tampon /tam'põː/ *m* -s, -s tampon
Tank *m* -s, -s tank. **t~en** *vt* fill up with <*Benzin*> ● *vi* (*haben*) fill up with petrol; (*Aviat*) refuel. **T~er** *m* -s,- tanker. **T~stelle** *f* petrol station. **T~wart** *m* -[e]s, -e petrol-pump attendant
Tanne *f* -, -n fir [tree]. **T~nbaum** *m* fir tree; (*Weihnachtsbaum*) Christmas tree. **T~nzapfen** *m* fir cone
Tante *f* -, -n aunt
Tantiemen /tan'tieːmən/ *pl* royalties
Tanz *m* -es, -ä dance. **t~en** *vt/i* (*haben*) dance
Tänzer(in) *m* -s,- (*f* -, -nen) dancer
Tapete *f* -, -n wallpaper
tapezieren *vt* paper
tapfer *a* brave. **T~keit** *f* - bravery
Tarif *m* -s, -e rate; (*Verzeichnis*) tariff
tarn|en *vt* disguise; (*Mil*) camouflage. **T~ung** *f* - disguise; camouflage
Tasche *f* -, -n bag; (*Hosen-, Mantel-*) pocket. **T~nbuch** *nt* paper-back. **T~ndieb** *m* pickpocket. **T~ngeld** *nt* pocket-money. **T~nlampe** *f* torch.

T~nmesser *nt* penknife.
T~ntuch *nt* handkerchief
Tasse *f* -, -n cup
Tastatur *f* -, -en keyboard
Tast|e *f* -, -n key; (*Druck-*) push-button. **t~en** *vi* (*haben*) feel, grope (*nach* for) ● *vt* key in <*Daten*>; **sich t~en** feel one's way (*zu* to)
Tat *f* -, -en action; (*Helden-*) deed; (*Straf-*) crime; **auf frischer Tat ertappt** caught in the act
Täter(in) *m* -s,- (*f* -, -nen) culprit; (*Jur*) offender
tätig *a* active; **t~ sein** work. **T~keit** *f* -, -en activity; (*Arbeit*) work, job
Tatkraft *f* energy
Tatort *m* scene of the crime
tätowier|en *vt* tattoo. **T~ung** *f* -, -en tattooing; (*Bild*) tattoo
Tatsache *f* fact. **T~nbericht** *m* documentary
tatsächlich *a* actual
Tatze *f* -, -n paw
Tau¹ *m* -[e]s dew
Tau² *nt* -[e]s, -e rope
taub *a* deaf; (*gefühllos*) numb
Taube *f* -, -n pigeon; dove. **T~nschlag** *m* pigeon-loft
Taub|heit *f* - deafness. **t~stumm** *a* deaf and dumb
tauch|en *vt* dip, plunge; (*unter-*) duck ● *vi* (*haben/sein*) dive/(*ein-*) plunge (*in* + *acc* into); (*auf-*) appear (*aus* out of). **T~er** *m* -s,- diver. **T~eranzug** *m* diving-suit
tauen *vi* (*sein*) melt, thaw ● *impers* **es taut** it is thawing
Tauf|becken *nt* font. **T~e** *f* -, -n christening, baptism. **t~en** *vt* christen, baptize. **T~pate** *m* godfather
taugen *vi* (*haben*) **etwas/nichts t~n** be good/no good
tauglich *a* suitable; (*Mil*) fit
Tausch *m* -[e]s, -e exchange, 🔲 swap. **t~en** *vt* exchange/ (*handeln*) barter (*gegen* for) ● *vi*

(haben) swap (**mit etw** sth; **mit jdm** with s.o.)

täuschen vt deceive, fool; betray <*Vertrauen*>; **sich t~** delude oneself; *(sich irren)* be mistaken ●vi *(haben)* be deceptive. **t~d** a deceptive; <*Ähnlichkeit*> striking

Täuschung f -, -en deception; *(Irrtum)* mistake; *(Illusion)* delusion

tausend inv a one/a thousand. **T~** m -s, -e thousand. **T~füßler** m -s,- centipede. **t~ste(r, s)** a thousandth. **T~stel** nt -s,- thousandth

Tau|tropfen m dewdrop. **T~wetter** nt thaw

Taxe f -, -n charge; *(Kur-)* tax; *(Taxi)* taxi

Taxi nt -s, -s taxi, cab

Taxi|fahrer m taxi driver. **T~stand** m taxi rank

Teakholz /'ti:k-/ nt teak

Team /ti:m/ nt -s, -s team

Techni|k f -, -en technology; *(Methode)* technique. **T~ker** m -s,- technician. **t~sch** a technical; *(technologisch)* technological; **T~sche Hochschule** Technical University

Techno|logie f -, -n technology. **t~logisch** a technological

Teddybär m teddy bear

Tee m -s, -s tea. **T~beutel** m teabag. **T~kanne** f teapot. **T~löffel** m teaspoon

Teer m -s tar. **t~en** vt tar

Tee|sieb nt tea-strainer. **T~wagen** m [tea] trolley

Teich m -[e]s, -e pond

Teig m -[e]s, -e pastry; *(Knet-)* dough; *(Rühr-)* mixture; *(Pfannkuchen-)* batter. **T~rolle** f rolling-pin. **T~waren** fpl pasta sg

Teil m -[e]s, -e part; *(Bestand-)* component; *(Jur)* party; **zum T~** partly; **zum großen/größten T~** for the most part ●m & nt -[e]s *(Anteil)* share; **ich für mein[en] T~**

for my part ●nt -[e]s, -e part; *(Ersatz-)* spare part; *(Anbau-)* unit

teil|bar a divisible. **T~chen** nt -s,- particle. **t~en** vt divide; *(auf-)* share out; *(gemeinsam haben)* share; *(Pol)* partition <*Land*>; **sich** *(dat)* **etw t~en** share sth; **sich t~en** divide; <*Meinungen:*> differ ●vi *(haben)* share

Teilhaber m -s,- *(Comm)* partner

Teilnahme f - participation; *(innere)* interest; *(Mitgefühl)* sympathy

teilnehm|en† vi sep *(haben)* **t~en an** (+ dat) take part in; *(mitfühlen)* share [in]. **T~er(in)** m -s,- *(f -, -nen)* participant; *(an Wettbewerb)* competitor

teil|s adv partly. **T~ung** f -, -en division; *(Pol)* partition. **t~weise** a partial ●adv partially, partly. **T~zahlung** f part-payment; *(Rate)* instalment. **T~zeitbeschäftigung** f part-time job

Teint /tɛ̃:/ m -s, -s complexion

Telearbeit f teleworking

Telefax nt fax

Telefon nt -s, -e [tele]phone. **T~anruf** m, **T~at** nt -[e]s, -e [tele]phone call. **T~buch** nt [tele]phone book. **t~ieren** vi *(haben)* [tele]phone

telefon|isch a [tele]phone … ●adv by [tele]phone. **T~ist(in)** m -en, -en *(f -, -nen)* telephonist. **T~karte** f phone card. **T~nummer** f [tele]phone number. **T~zelle** f [tele]phone box

Telegraf m -en, -en telegraph. **T~enmast** m telegraph pole. **t~ieren** vi *(haben)* send a telegram. **t~isch** a telegraphic ●adv by telegram

Telegramm nt -s, -e telegram

Teleobjektiv nt telephoto lens

Telepathie f - telepathy

T

Teleskop nt -s, -e telescope
Telex nt -, -[e] telex. **t~en** vt telex
Teller m -s,- plate
Tempel m -s,- temple
Temperament nt -s, -e temperament; (*Lebhaftigkeit*) vivacity
Temperatur f -, -en temperature
Tempo nt -s, -s speed; **T~** [**T~**]! hurry up!
Tendenz f -, -en trend; (*Neigung*) tendency
Tennis nt - tennis. **T~platz** m tennis-court. **T~schläger** m tennis-racket
Teppich m -s,e carpet. **T~boden** m fitted carpet
Termin m -s, -e date; (*Arzt-*) appointment. **T~kalender** m [appointments] diary
Terrasse f -, -n terrace
Terrier /'tɛriə/ m -s,- terrier
Terrine f -, -n tureen
Territorium nt -s, -ien territory
Terror m -s terror. **t~isieren** vt terrorize. **T~ismus** m - terrorism. **T~ist** m -en, -en terrorist
Tesafilm (P) m ≈ Sellotape (P)
Test m -[e]s, -s & -e test
Testament nt -[e]s, -e will; Altes/Neues T~ Old/New Testament. **T~svollstrecker** m -s,- executor
testen vt test
Tetanus m - tetanus
teuer a expensive; (*lieb*) dear; wie t~? how much?
Teufel m -s,- devil. **T~skreis** m vicious circle
teuflisch a fiendish
Text m -[e]s, -e text; (*Passage*) passage; (*Bild-*) caption; (*Lied-*) lyrics pl. **T~er** m -s,- copy-writer; (*Schlager-*) lyricist
Textilien /-iən/ pl textiles; (*Textilwaren*) textile goods
Text|nachricht f text message. **T~verarbeitungssystem** nt word processor

Theater nt -s,- theatre; (**ⓘ** *Getue*) fuss. **T~kasse** f box-office. **T~stück** nt play
Theke f -, -n bar; (*Ladentisch*) counter
Thema nt -s, -men subject
Themse f - Thames
Theolo|ge m -n, -n theologian. **T~gie** f - theology
theor|etisch a theoretical. **T~ie** f -, -n theory
Therapeut(in) m -en, -en (f -, -nen) therapist
Therapie f -, -n therapy
Thermalbad nt thermal bath
Thermometer nt -s,- thermometer
Thermosflasche (P) f Thermos flask (P)
Thermostat m -[e]s, -e thermostat
These f -, -n thesis
Thrombose f -, -n thrombosis
Thron m -[e]s, -e throne. **t~en** vi (*haben*) sit [in state]. **T~folge** f succession. **T~folger** m -s,- heir to the throne
Thunfisch m tuna
Thymian m -s thyme
ticken vi (*haben*) tick
tief a deep; (*t~ liegend, niedrig*) low; (*t~gründig*) profound; **t~er Teller** soup-plate ●adv deep; low; (*sehr*) deeply, profoundly; <*schlafen*> soundly. **T~** nt -s, -s (*Meteorol*) depression. **T~bau** m civil engineering. **T~e** f -, -n depth. **T~garage** f underground car park. **t~gekühlt** a [deep-] frozen
Tiefkühl|fach nt freezer compartment. **T~kost** f frozen food. **T~truhe** f deep-freeze
Tiefsttemperatur f minimum temperature
Tier nt -[e]s, -e animal. **T~arzt** m, **T~ärztin** f vet, veterinary surgeon. **T~garten** m zoo. **T~kreis** m zodiac. **T~kunde** f zoology. **T~quälerei** f cruelty to animals

Tiger m -s,- tiger
tilgen vt pay off <Schuld>; (streichen) delete; (fig: auslöschen) wipe out
Tinte f -, -n ink. **T~nfisch** m squid
Tipp m -s, -s 🄸 tip
tipp|en vt 🄸 type ●vi (haben) (berühren) touch (**auf/an etw** acc sth); (🄸 Maschine schreiben) type; **t~en auf** (+ acc) (🄸 wetten) bet on. **T~schein** m pools/lottery coupon
tipptopp a 🄸 immaculate
Tirol nt -s [the] Tyrol
Tisch m -[e]s, -e table; (Schreib-) desk; **nach T~** after the meal. **T~decke** f table-cloth. **T~gebet** nt grace. **T~ler** m -s,- joiner; (Möbel-) cabinet-maker. **T~rede** f after-dinner speech. **T~tennis** nt table tennis
Titel m -s,- title
Toast /to:st/ m -[e]s, -e toast; (Scheibe) piece of toast. **T~er** m -s,- toaster
toben vi (haben) rave; <Sturm:> rage; <Kinder:> play boisterously
Tochter f -,: daughter. **T~gesellschaft** f subsidiary
Tod m -es death
Todes|angst f mortal fear. **T~anzeige** f death announcement; (Zeitungs-) obituary. **T~fall** m death. **T~opfer** nt fatality, casualty. **T~strafe** f death penalty. **T~urteil** nt death sentence
todkrank a dangerously ill
tödlich a fatal; <Gefahr> mortal
Toilette /toa'lɛtə/ f -, -n toilet. **T~npapier** nt toilet paper
toler|ant a tolerant. **T~anz** f - tolerance. **t~ieren** vt tolerate
toll a crazy, mad; (🄸 prima) fantastic; (schlimm) awful ●adv (sehr) very; (schlimm) badly. **t~kühn** a foolhardy. **T~wut** f rabies. **t~wütig** a rabid
Tölpel m -s,- fool

Tomate f -, -n tomato. **T~nmark** nt tomato purée
Tombola f -, -s raffle
Ton¹ m -[e]s clay
Ton² m -[e]s,:e tone; (Klang) sound; (Note) note; (Betonung) stress; (Farb-) shade; **der gute Ton** (fig) good form. **T~abnehmer** m -s,- pick-up. **t~angebend** a (fig) leading. **T~art** f tone [of voice]; (Mus) key. **T~band** nt (pl -bänder) tape. **T~bandgerät** nt tape recorder
tönen vi (haben) sound ●vt tint
Tonleiter f scale
Tonne f -, -n barrel, cask: (Müll-) bin; (Maß) tonne, metric ton
Topf m -[e]s,:e pot; (Koch-) pan
Topfen m -s (Aust) ≈ curd cheese
Töpferei f -, -en pottery
Topf|lappen m oven-cloth. **T~pflanze** f potted plant
Tor nt -[e]s, -e gate; (Einfahrt) gateway; (Sport) goal
Torf m -s peat
torkeln vi (sein/habe) stagger
Tornister m -s,- knapsack; (Sch) satchel
Torpedo m -s, -s torpedo
Torpfosten m goal-post
Torte f -, -n gateau; (Obst-) flan
Tortur f -, -en torture
Torwart m -s, -e goalkeeper
tot a dead; **tot geboren** stillborn; **sich tot stellen** pretend to be dead
total a total. **T~schaden** m ≈ write-off
Tote|(r) m/f dead man/woman; (Todesopfer) fatality; **die T~n** the dead pl
töten vt kill
Toten|gräber m -s,- grave-digger. **T~kopf** m skull. **T~schein** m death certificate
totfahren† vt sep run over and kill
Toto nt & m -s football pools pl. **T~schein** m pools coupon

T

tot|schießen† vt sep shoot dead. **T~schlag** m (Jur) manslaughter. **t~schlagen†** vt sep kill

Tötung f -, -en killing; **fahrlässige T~** (Jur) manslaughter

Toup|et /tu'pe:/ nt -s, -s toupee. **t~ieren** vt back-comb

Tour /tu:ɐ/ f -, -en tour; (Ausflug) trip; (Auto-) drive; (Rad-) ride; (Strecke) distance; (Techn) revolution; (Ⅱ Weise) way

Touris|mus /tu'rɪsmʊs/ m - tourism. **T~t** m -en, -en tourist

Tournee /tʊr'ne:/ f -, -n tour

Trab m -[e]s trot

Trabant m -en, -en satellite

traben vi (haben/sein) trot

Tracht f -, -en [national] costume

Tradition /-'tsio:n/ f -, -en tradition. **t~ell** a traditional

Trag|bahre f stretcher. **t~bar** a portable; <Kleidung> wearable

tragen† vt carry; (an-/ aufhaben) wear; (fig) bear ●vi (haben) carry; **gut t~** <Baum:> produce a good crop

Träger m -s,- porter; (Inhaber) bearer; (eines Ordens) holder; (Bau-) beam; (Stahl-) girder; (Achsel-) [shoulder] strap. **T~kleid** nt pinafore dress

Trag|etasche f carrier bag. **T~flächenboot, T~flügelboot** nt hydrofoil

Trägheit f - sluggishness; (Faulheit) laziness; (Phys) inertia

Trag|ik f - tragedy. **t~isch** a tragic

Tragödie /-iə/ f -, -n tragedy

Train|er /'trɛ:nɐ/ m -s,- trainer; (Tennis-) coach. **t~ieren** vt/i (haben) train

Training /'trɛ:nɪŋ/ nt -s training. **T~sanzug** m tracksuit. **T~s-schuhe** mpl trainers

Traktor m -s, -en /-'to:rən/ tractor

trampeln vi (haben) stamp one's feet ●vi (sein) trample (auf + acc on) ●vt trample

trampen /'trɛmpən/ vi (sein) ⅡＩ hitch-hike

Tranchiermesser /trã'ʃi:ɐ-/ nt carving-knife

Träne f -, -n tear. **t~n** vi (haben) water. **T~ngas** nt tear-gas

Tränke f -, -n watering-place; (Trog) drinking-trough. **t~n** vt water <Pferd>; (nässen) soak (mit with)

Trans|formator m -s, -en /-'to:rən/ transformer. **T~fusion** f -, -en [blood] transfusion

Transit /tran'zi:t/ m -s transit

transparent nt -[e]s, -e banner; (Bild) transparency

transpirieren vi (haben) perspire

Transport m -[e]s, -e transport; (Güter-) consignment. **t~ieren** vt transport

Trapez nt -es, -e trapeze

Tratte f -, -n (Comm) draft

Traube f -, -n bunch of grapes; (Beere) grape; (fig) cluster. **T~nzucker** m glucose

trauen vi (haben) (+ dat) trust ●vt marry; **sich t~** dare (etw zu tun [to] do sth); venture (in + acc/aus into/out of)

Trauer f - mourning; (Schmerz) grief (um for); **T~ tragen** be [dressed] in mourning. **T~fall** m bereavement. **T~feier** f funeral service. **t~n** vi (haben) grieve; **t~n um** mourn [for]. **T~spiel** nt tragedy. **T~weide** f weeping willow

Traum m -[e]s, Träume dream

Trauma nt -s, -men trauma

träumen vt/i (haben) dream

traumhaft a dreamlike; (schön) fabulous

traurig a sad; (erbärmlich) sorry. **T~keit** f - sadness

Trau|ring m wedding-ring. **T~schein** m marriage certificate. **T~ung** f -, -en wedding [ceremony]

Treff nt -s, -s (Karten) spades pl

treff|en† vt hit; <Blitz:> strike; (fig: verletzen) hurt; (zusammenkommen mit) meet; take <Maßnahme>; **sich t~en** meet (mit jdm s.o.); **sich gut t~en** be convenient; **es gut/schlecht t~en** be lucky/unlucky ● vi (haben) hit the target; **t~en auf** (+ acc) meet with; (fig) meet with. **T~en** nt -s,- meeting. **T~er** m -s,- hit; (Los) winner. **T~punkt** m meeting-place

treiben† vt drive; (sich befassen mit) do; carry on <Gewerbe>; indulge in <Luxus>; get up to <Unfug>; **Handel t~** trade ● vi (sein) drift; (schwimmen) float ● vi (haben) (Bot) sprout. **T~** nt -s activity

Treib|haus nt hothouse. **T~hauseffekt** m greenhouse effect. **T~holz** nt driftwood. **T~riemen** m transmission belt. **T~sand** m quicksand. **T~stoff** m fuel

trenn|bar a separable. **t~en** vt separate/(abmachen) detach (von from); divide, split <Wort>; **sich t~en** separate; (auseinander gehen) part; **sich t~en von** leave; (fortgeben) part with. **T~ung** f -, -en separation; (Silben-) division. **T~ungsstrich** m hyphen. **T~wand** f partition

trepp|ab adv downstairs. **t~auf** adv upstairs

Treppe f -, -n stairs pl; (Außen-) steps pl. **T~ngeländer** nt banisters pl

Tresor m -s, -e safe

Tresse f -, -n braid

Treteimer m pedal bin

treten† vi (sein/haben) step; (versehentlich) tread; (ausschlagen) kick (nach at); **in Verbindung t~** get in touch ● vt tread; (mit Füßen) kick

treu a faithful; (fest) loyal. **T~e** f - faithfulness; loyalty; (eheliche)

fidelity. **T~ekarte** f loyalty card. **T~händer** m -s,- trustee. **t~los** a disloyal; (untreu) unfaithful

Tribüne f -, -n platform; (Zuschauer-) stand

Trichter m -s,- funnel; (Bomben-) crater

Trick m -s, -s trick. **T~film** m cartoon. **t~reich** a clever

Trieb m -[e]s, -e drive, urge; (Instinkt) instinct; (Bot) shoot. **T~verbrecher** m sex offender. **T~werk** nt (Aviat) engine; (Uhr-) mechanism

triefen† vi (haben) drip; (nass sein) be dripping (von/vor + dat with)

Trigonometrie f - trigonometry

Trikot¹ /tri'ko:/ m -s (Tex) jersey

Trikot² nt -s, -s (Sport) jersey; (Fußball-) shirt

Trimester nt -s,- term

Trimm-dich nt -s keep-fit

trimmen vt trim; tune <Motor>; **sich t~** keep fit

trink|en† vt/i (haben) drink. **T~er(in)** m -s,- (f -, -nen) alcoholic. **T~geld** nt tip

trist a dreary

Tritt m -[e]s, -e step; (Fuß-) kick. **T~brett** nt step

Triumph m -s, -e triumph. **t~ieren** vi (haben) rejoice

trocken a dry. **T~haube** f drier. **T~heit** f -, -en dryness; (Dürre) drought. **t~legen** vt sep change <Baby>; drain <Sumpf>. **T~milch** f powdered milk

trockn|en vt/i (sein) dry. **T~er** m -s,- drier

Trödel m -s 🔲 junk. **t~n** vi (haben) dawdle

Trödler m -s,- 🔲 slowcoach; (Händler) junk-dealer

Trog m -[e]s,̈-e trough

Trommel f -, -n drum. **T~fell** nt ear-drum. **t~n** vi (haben) drum

Trommler m -s,- drummer

T

Trompete f -, -n trumpet. **T~r** m -s,- trumpeter

Tropen pl tropics

Tropf m -[e]s, -e (Med) drip

tröpfeln vt/i (sein/haben) drip

tropfen vt/i (sein/haben) drip. **T~** m -s,- drop; (fallend) drip. **t~weise** adv drop by drop

Trophäe /tro'fɛːə/ f -, -n trophy

tropisch a tropical

Trost m -[e]s consolation, comfort

tröst|en vt console, comfort; **sich t~en** console oneself. **t~lich** a comforting

trost|los a desolate; (elend) wretched; (reizlos) dreary. **T~preis** m consolation prize

Trott m -s amble; (fig) routine

Trottel m -s,- 🆋 idiot

Trottoir /trɔ'toaːɐ/ nt -s, -s pavement

trotz prep (+ gen) despite, in spite of. **T~** m -es defiance. **t~dem** adv nevertheless. **t~ig** a defiant; stubborn

trübe a dull; <Licht> dim; <Flüssigkeit> cloudy; (fig) gloomy

Trubel m -s bustle

trüben vt dull; make cloudy <Flüssigkeit>; (fig) spoil; strain <Verhältnis> **sich t~** <Flüssigkeit:> become cloudy; <Himmel:> cloud over; <Augen:> dim

Trüb|sal f - misery. **T~sinn** m melancholy. **t~sinnig** a melancholy

trügen† vt deceive ● vi (haben) be deceptive

Trugschluss m fallacy

Truhe f -, -n chest

Trümmer pl rubble sg; (T~teile) wreckage sg, (fig) ruins

Trumpf m -[e]s,¨e trump [card]. **t~en** vi (haben) play trumps

Trunk m -[e]s drink. **T~enheit** f - drunkenness; **T~enheit am Steuer** drink-driving

Trupp m -s, -s group; (Mil) squad. **T~e** f -, -n (Mil) unit; (Theat) troupe; **T~en** troops

Truthahn m turkey

Tschech|e m -n, -n, **T~in** f -, -nen Czech. **t~isch** a Czech. **T~oslowakei (die)** - Czechoslovakia

tschüs, tschüss int bye, cheerio

Tuba f -, -ben (Mus) tuba

Tube f -, -n tube

Tuberkulose f - tuberculosis

Tuch nt -[e]s,¨er cloth; (Hals-, Kopf-) scarf; (Schulter-) shawl

tüchtig a competent; (reichlich, beträchtlich) good; (groß) big ● adv competently; (ausreichend) well

Tück|e f -, - malice. **t~isch** a malicious; (gefährlich) treacherous

Tugend f -,en virtue. **t~haft** a virtuous

Tülle f -, -n spout

Tulpe f -, -n tulip

Tümmler m -s,- porpoise

Tumor m -s, -en /-'moːrən/ tumour

Tümpel m -[e]s,- pond

Tumult m -[e]s, -e commotion; (Aufruhr) riot

tun† vt do; take <Schritt, Blick>; work <Wunder>; (bringen) put (in + acc into); **sich tun** happen; **jdm etwas tun** hurt s.o.; **das tut nichts** it doesn't matter ● vi (haben) act (als ob as if); **er tut nur so** he's just pretending; **jdm/etw gut tun** do s.o./sth. good; **zu tun haben** have things/work to do; **[es] zu tun haben mit** have to deal with. **Tun** nt -s actions pl

Tünche f -, -n whitewash; (fig) veneer. **t~n** vt whitewash

Tunesien /-iən/ nt -s Tunisia

Tunfisch m = Thunfisch

Tunnel m -s,- tunnel

tupf|en vt dab ● vi (haben) **t~en an/auf** (+ acc) touch. **T~en** m -s,-

spot. **T~er** *m* **-s,-** spot; (*Med*) swab

Tür *f* **-, -en** door

Turban *m* **-s, -e** turban

Turbine *f* **-, -n** turbine

Türk|e *m* **-n, -n** Turk. **T~ei (die)** - Turkey. **T~in** *f* **-, -nen** Turk

türkis *inv a* turquoise

türkisch *a* Turkish

Turm *m* **-[e]s,̈e** tower; (*Schach*) rook, castle

Türm|chen *nt* **-s,-** turret. **t~en** *vt* pile [up]; **sich t~en** pile up

Turmspitze *f* spire

turn|en *vi* (*haben*) do gymnastics. **T~en** *nt* **-s** gymnastics *sg*; (*Sch*) physical education, ⚅ gym. **T~er(in)** *m* **-s,-** (*f* -, **-nen**) gymnast. **T~halle** *f* gymnasium

Turnier *nt* **-s, -e** tournament; (*Reit-*) show

Turnschuhe *mpl* gym shoes; trainers

Türschwelle *f* doorstep, threshold

Tusche *f* **-, -n** [drawing] ink

tuscheln *vt/i* (*haben*) whisper

Tüte *f* **-, -n** bag; (*Comm*) packet; (*Eis-*) cornet; **in die T~ blasen** ⚅ be breathalysed

TÜV *m* **- ≈** MOT [test]

Typ *m* **-s, -en** type; (⚅ *Kerl*) bloke. **T~e** *f* **-, -n** type

Typhus *m* - typhoid

typisch *a* typical (**für** of)

Typus *m* **-, Typen** type

Tyrann *m* **-en, -en** tyrant. **T~ei** *f* - tyranny. **t~isch** *a* tyrannical. **t~isieren** *vt* tyrannize

U-Bahn *f* underground

übel *a* bad; (*hässlich*) nasty; **mir ist ü~** I feel sick; **jdm etw ü~ nehmen** hold sth against s.o. **Ü~keit** *f* - nausea

üben *vt/i* (*haben*) practise

über *prep* (+ *dat/acc*) over; (*höher als*) above; (*betreffend*) about; <*Buch, Vortrag*> on; <*Scheck, Rechnung*> for; (*quer ü~*) across; **ü~ Köln fahren** go via Cologne; **ü~ Ostern** over Easter; **die Woche ü~** during the week; **Fehler ü~ Fehler** mistake after mistake ● *adv* **ü~ und ü~** all over; **jdm ü~ sein** be better/(*stärker*) stronger than s.o. ● *a* ⚅ **ü~ sein** be left over; **etw ü~ sein** be fed up with sth

überall *adv* everywhere

überanstrengen *vt insep* overtax; strain <*Augen*>

überarbeiten *vt insep* revise; **sich ü~en** overwork

überbieten† *vt insep* outbid; (*übertreffen*) surpass

Überblick *m* overall view; (*Abriss*) summary

überblicken *vt insep* overlook; (*abschätzen*) assess

überbringen† *vt insep* deliver

überbrücken *vt insep* (*fig*) bridge

überdies *adv* moreover

überdimensional *a* oversized

Überdosis *f* overdose

überdrüssig *a* **ü~ sein/werden** be/grow tired (*gen* of)

übereignen *vt insep* transfer

übereilt *a* over-hasty

übereinander *adv* one on top of/ above the other; <*sprechen*> about each other

überein|kommen† *vi sep* (sein) agree. **Ü~kunft** *f* - agreement.

ü~stimmen *vi sep* (haben) agree; <Zahlen:> tally; <Ansichten:> coincide; <Farben:> match. **Ü~stimmung** *f* agreement

überfahren† *vt insep* run over

Überfahrt *f* crossing

Überfall *m* attack; (Bank-) raid

überfallen† *vt insep* attack; raid <Bank>; (bestürmen) bombard (mit with)

Überfluss *m* abundance; (Wohlstand) affluence

überflüssig *a* superfluous

überfordern *vt insep* overtax

überführ|en *vt insep* transfer; (Jur) convict (gen of). **Ü~ung** *f* transfer; (Straße) flyover; (Fußgänger-) foot-bridge

überfüllt *a* overcrowded

Übergabe *f* handing over; transfer

Übergang *m* crossing; (Wechsel) transition

übergeben† *vt insep* hand over; (übereignen) transfer; **sich ü~** be sick

übergehen† *vt insep* (fig) pass over; (nicht beachten) ignore; (auslassen) leave out

Übergewicht *nt* excess weight; (fig) predominance; **Ü~ haben** be overweight

über|greifen† *vi sep* (haben) spread (auf + acc to). **Ü~griff** *m* infringement

über|groß *a* outsize; (übertrieben) exaggerated. **Ü~größe** *f* outsize

überhand *adv* **ü~ nehmen** increase alarmingly

überhäufen *vt insep* inundate (mit with)

überhaupt *adv* (im Allgemeinen) altogether; (eigentlich) anyway; (überdies) besides; **ü~ nicht/ nichts** not/nothing at all

überheblich *a* arrogant. **Ü~keit** *f* - arrogance

überhol|en *vt insep* overtake; (reparieren) overhaul. **ü~t** *a* out-dated. **Ü~ung** *f* -, -en overhaul. **Ü~verbot** *nt* 'Ü~verbot' 'no overtaking'

überhören *vt insep* fail to hear; (nicht beachten) ignore

überirdisch *a* supernatural

überkochen *vi sep* (sein) boil over

überlassen† *vt insep* **jdm etw ü~** leave sth to s.o.; (geben) let s.o. have sth; **sich** (dat) **selbst ü~ sein** be left to one's own devices

Überlauf *m* overflow

überlaufen† *vi sep* (sein) overflow; (Mil, Pol) defect

Überläufer *m* defector

überleben *vt/i insep* (haben) survive. **Ü~de(r)** *m/f* survivor

überlegen[1] *vt sep* put over

überlegen[2] *v insep* ● *vt* [sich dat] ü~ think over, consider; **es sich** (dat) **anders ü~** change one's mind ● *vi* (haben) think, reflect

überlegen[3] *a* superior. **Ü~heit** *f* - superiority

Überlegung *f* -, -en reflection

überliefer|n *vt insep* hand down. **Ü~ung** *f* tradition

überlisten *vt insep* outwit

Übermacht *f* superiority

übermäßig *a* excessive

Übermensch *m* superman. **ü~lich** *a* superhuman

übermitteln *vt insep* convey; (senden) transmit

übermorgen *adv* the day after tomorrow

übermüdet *a* overtired

Über|mut *m* high spirits *pl*. **ü~mütig** *a* high-spirited

übernächst|e(r,s) *a* next ... but one; **ü~es Jahr** the year after next

übernacht|en *vi insep* (haben) stay overnight. **Ü~ung** *f* -, -en overnight stay; **Ü~ung und Frühstück** bed and breakfast

Übernahme f - taking over; (*Comm*) take-over

übernatürlich a supernatural

übernehmen† vt insep take over; (*annehmen*) take on; **sich ü~** overdo things; (*finanziell*) over-reach oneself

überqueren vt insep cross

überrasch|en vt insep surprise. **ü~end** a surprising; (*unerwartet*) unexpected. **Ü~ung** f -, -en surprise

überreden vt insep persuade

Überreste mpl remains

Überschall- pref supersonic

überschätzen vt insep overestimate

Überschlag m rough estimate; (*Sport*) somersault

überschlagen[1]† vt sep cross <*Beine*>

überschlagen[2]† vt insep estimate roughly; (*auslassen*) skip; **sich ü~** somersault; <*Ereignisse:*> happen fast ● a tepid

überschneiden† (sich) vr insep intersect, cross; (*zusammenfallen*) overlap

überschreiten† vt insep cross; (*fig*) exceed

Überschrift f heading; (*Zeitungs-*) headline

Über|schuss m surplus. **ü~schüssig** a surplus

überschwemm|en vt insep flood; (*fig*) inundate. **Ü~ung** f -, -en flood

Übersee in/nach **Ü~** overseas; **aus/von Ü~** from overseas. **Ü~dampfer** m ocean liner. **ü~isch** a overseas

übersehen† vt insep look out over; (*abschätzen*) assess; (*nicht sehen*) overlook, miss; (*ignorieren*) ignore

übersenden† vt insep send

übersetzen[1] vi sep (haben/sein) cross [over]

übersetz|en[2] vt insep translate. **Ü~er(in)** m -s,- (f -, -nen) translator. **Ü~ung** f -, -en translation

Übersicht f overall view; (*Abriss*) summary; (*Tabelle*) table. **ü~lich** a clear

Übersiedlung f move

überspielen vt insep (*fig*) cover up; **auf Band ü~** tape

überstehen† vt insep come through; get over <*Krankheit*>; (*überleben*) survive

übersteigen† vt insep climb [over]; (*fig*) exceed

überstimmen vt insep outvote

Überstunden fpl overtime sg; **Ü~ machen** work overtime

überstürz|en vt insep rush; **sich ü~en** <*Ereignisse:*> happen fast. **ü~t** a hasty

übertrag|bar a transferable; (*Med*) infectious. **ü~en**† vt insep transfer; (*übergeben*) assign (*dat* to); (*Techn, Med*) transmit; (*Radio, TV*) broadcast; (*übersetzen*) translate; (*anwenden*) apply (*auf* + *acc* to) ● a transferred, figurative. **Ü~ung** f -, -en transfer; transmission; broadcast; translation, application

übertreffen† vt insep surpass; (*übersteigen*) exceed; **sich selbst ü~** excel oneself

übertreib|en† vt insep exaggerate; (*zu weit treiben*) overdo. **Ü~ung** f -, -en exaggeration

übertreten[1]† vi sep (sein) step over the line; (*Pol*) go over/ (*Relig*) convert (**zu** to)

übertret|en[2]† vt insep infringe; break <*Gesetz*>. **Ü~ung** f -, -en infringement; breach

übertrieben a exaggerated

übervölkert a overpopulated

überwachen vt insep supervise; (*kontrollieren*) monitor;

(*bespitzeln*) keep under surveillance

überwältigen *vt insep* overpower; (*fig*) overwhelm

überweis|en† *vt insep* transfer; refer <*Patienten*>. **Ü~ung** *f* transfer; (*ärztliche*) referral

überwiegen† *v insep* ● *vi* (*haben*) predominate, ● *vt* outweigh

überwind|en† *vt insep* overcome; **sich ü~en** force oneself

Über|zahl *f* majority. **ü~zählig** *a* spare

überzeug|en *vt insep* convince; **sich [selbst] ü~en** satisfy oneself. **ü~end** *a* convincing. **Ü~ung** *f* -, -en conviction

überziehen¹† *vt sep* put on

überziehen²† *vt insep* cover; overdraw <*Konto*>

Überzug *m* cover; (*Schicht*) coating

üblich *a* usual; (*gebräuchlich*) customary

U-Boot *nt* submarine

übrig *a* remaining; (*andere*) other; **alles Ü~e** [all] the rest; **im Ü~en** besides; (*ansonsten*) apart from that; **ü~ sein** *od* **bleiben** be left [over]; **etw ü~ lassen** leave sth [over]; **uns blieb nichts anderes ü~** we had no choice

Übung *f* -, -en exercise; (*Üben*) practice; **außer** *od* **aus der Ü~** out of practice

Ufer *nt* -s,- shore; (*Fluss-*) bank

Uhr *f* -, -en clock; (*Armband-*) watch; (*Zähler*) meter; **um ein U~** at one o'clock; **wie viel U~ ist es?** what's the time? **U~macher** *m* -s,- watch and clockmaker. **U~werk** *nt* clock/watch mechanism. **U~zeiger** *m* [clock-/watch-]hand. **U~zeit** *f* time

Uhu *m* -s, -s eagle owl

UKW *abbr* (*Ultrakurzwelle*) VHF

ulkig *a* funny; (*seltsam*) odd

Ulme *f* -, -n elm

Ultimatum *nt* -s, -ten ultimatum

Ultra|kurzwelle *f* very high frequency. **U~leichtflugzeug** *nt* microlight [aircraft]

Ultraschall *m* ultrasound

ultraviolett *a* ultraviolet

um *prep* (+ *acc*) [a]round; (*Uhrzeit*) at; <*bitten*> for; <*streiten*> over; <*sich sorgen*> about; <*betrügen*> out of; (*bei Angabe einer Differenz*) by; **um [… herum]** around, [round] about; **Tag um Tag** day after day; **um seinetwillen** for his sake ● *adv* (*ungefähr*) around, about; **um sein** 🛈 be over; <*Zeit*> be up ● *conj* **um zu** to; (*Absicht*) [in order] to; **zu müde, um zu …** too tired to …

umarm|en *vt insep* embrace, hug. **U~ung** *f* -, -en embrace, hug

Umbau *m* rebuilding; conversion (**zu** into). **u~en** *vt sep* rebuild; convert (**zu** into)

Umbildung *f* reorganization; (*Pol*) reshuffle

umbinden† *vt sep* put on

umblättern *v sep* ● *vt* turn [over] ● *vi* (*haben*) turn the page

umbringen† *vt sep* kill; **sich u~** kill oneself

umbuchen *v sep* ● *vt* change; (*Comm*) transfer ● *vi* (*haben*) change one's booking

umdrehen *v sep* ● *vt* turn round/ (*wenden*) over; turn <*Schlüssel*>; (*umkrempeln*) turn inside out; **sich u~** turn round; (*im Liegen*) turn over ● *vi* (*haben/sein*) turn back

Umdrehung *f* turn; (*Motor-*) revolution

umeinander *adv* around each other; **sich u~ sorgen** worry about each other

umfahren¹† *vt sep* run over

umfahren²† *vt insep* go round; bypass <*Ort*>

umfallen† *vi sep* (*sein*) fall over; <*Person:*> fall down

Umfang m girth; (Geom) circumference; (Größe) size

umfangreich a extensive; (dick) big

umfassen vt insep consist of, comprise; (umgeben) surround. **u~d** a comprehensive

Umfrage f survey, poll

umfüllen vt sep transfer

umfunktionieren vt sep convert

Umgang m [social] contact; (Umgehen) dealing (**mit** with)

Umgangssprache f colloquial language

umgeb|en vt/i insep (haben) surround ● a **u~en von** surrounded by. **U~ung** f -, -en surroundings pl

umgehen† vt insep avoid; (nicht beachten) evade; <Straße:> bypass

umgehend a immediate

Umgehungsstraße f bypass

umgekehrt a inverse; <Reihenfolge> reverse; **es war u~** it was the other way round

umgraben† vt sep dig [over]

Umhang m cloak

umhauen† vt sep knock down; (fällen) chop down

umhören (sich) vr sep ask around

Umkehr f - turning back. **u~en** v sep ● vi (sein) turn back ● vt turn round; turn inside out <Tasche>; (fig) reverse

umkippen v sep ● vt tip over; (versehentlich) knock over ● vi (sein) fall over; <Boot:> capsize

Umkleide|kabine f changing-cubicle. **u~n (sich)** vr sep change. **U~raum** m changing-room

umknicken v sep ● vt bend; (falten) fold ● vi (sein) bend; (mit dem Fuß) go over on one's ankle

umkommen† vi sep (sein) perish

Umkreis m surroundings pl; **im U~ von** within a radius of

umkreisen vt insep circle; (Astr) revolve around; <Satellit:> orbit

umkrempeln vt sep turn up; (von innen nach außen) turn inside out; (ändern) change radically

Umlauf m circulation; (Astr) revolution. **U~bahn** f orbit

Umlaut m umlaut

umlegen vt sep lay or put down; flatten <Getreide>; turn down <Kragen>; put on <Schal>; throw <Hebel>; (verlegen) transfer; (🗐 töten) kill

umleit|en vt sep divert. **U~ung** f diversion

umliegend a surrounding

umpflanzen vt sep transplant

umranden vt insep edge

umräumen vt sep rearrange

umrechn|en vt sep convert. **U~ung** f conversion

umreißen† vt insep outline

Umriss m outline

umrühren vt/i sep (haben) stir

ums pron = **um das**

Umsatz m (Comm) turnover

umschalten vt/i sep (haben) switch over; **auf Rot u~** <Ampel:> change to red

Umschau f **U~ halten nach** look out for

Umschlag m cover; (Schutz-) jacket; (Brief-) envelope; (Med) compress; (Hosen-) turn-up. **u~en†** v sep ● vt turn up; turn over <Seite>; (fällen) chop down ● vi (sein) topple over; <Wetter:> change; <Wind:> veer

umschließen† vt insep enclose

umschreiben vt insep define; (anders ausdrücken) paraphrase

umschulen vt sep retrain; (Sch) transfer to another school

Umschwung m (fig) change; (Pol) U-turn

umsehen† (sich) vr sep look round; (zurück) look back; **sich u~ nach** look for

U

umsein* vi sep (sein) um sein, s. um

umseitig a & adv overleaf

umsetzen vt sep move; (umpflanzen) transplant; (Comm) sell

umsied|eln v sep ● vt resettle ● vi (sein) move. **U~lung** f resettlement

umso conj ~ **besser/mehr** all the better/more; **je mehr, ~ besser** the more the better

umsonst adv in vain; (grundlos) without reason; (gratis) free

Umstand m circumstance; (Tatsache) fact; (Aufwand) fuss; (Mühe) trouble; **unter U~en** possibly; **jdm U~e machen** put s.o. to trouble; **in andern U~en** pregnant

umständlich a laborious; (kompliziert) involved

Umstands|kleid nt maternity dress. **U~wort** nt (pl **-wörter**) adverb

Umstehende pl bystanders

umsteigen† vi sep (sein) change

umstellen¹ vt insep surround

umstell|en² vt sep rearrange; transpose <Wörter>; (anders einstellen) reset; (Techn) convert; (ändern) change; **sich u~en** adjust. **U~ung** f rearrangement; transposition; resetting; conversion; change; adjustment

umstritten a controversial; (ungeklärt) disputed

umstülpen vt sep turn upside down; (von innen nach außen) turn inside out

Um|sturz m coup. **u~stürzen** v sep ● vt overturn; (Pol) overthrow ● vi (sein) fall over

umtaufen vt sep rename

Umtausch m exchange. **u~en** vt sep change; exchange (**gegen** for)

umwechseln vt sep change

Umweg m detour; **auf U~en** (fig) in a roundabout way

Umwelt f environment. **u~freundlich** a environmentally friendly. **U~schutz** m protection of the environment

umwerfen† vt sep knock over; (fig) upset <Plan>

umziehen† v sep ● vi (sein) move ● vt change; **sich u~** change

umzingeln vt insep surround

Umzug m move; (Prozession) procession

unabänderlich a irrevocable; <Tatsache> unalterable

unabhängig a independent; **u~ davon, ob** irrespective of whether. **U~keit** f - independence

unablässig a incessant

unabsehbar a incalculable

unabsichtlich a unintentional

unachtsam a careless

unangebracht a inappropriate

unangenehm a unpleasant; (peinlich) embarrassing

Unannehmlichkeiten fpl trouble sg

unansehnlich a shabby

unanständig a indecent

unappetitlich a unappetizing

Unart f -, **-en** bad habit. **u~ig** a naughty

unauffällig a inconspicuous; unobtrusive

unaufgefordert adv without being asked

unauf|haltsam a inexorable. **u~hörlich** a incessant

unaufmerksam a inattentive

unaufrichtig a insincere

unausbleiblich a inevitable

unausstehlich a insufferable

unbarmherzig a merciless

unbeabsichtigt a unintentional

unbedenklich a harmless ● adv without hesitation

unbedeutend a insignificant; (geringfügig) slight

unbedingt a absolute; **nicht u~** not necessarily

unbefriedig|end *a* unsatisfactory.
u~t *a* dissatisfied
unbefugt *a* unauthorized ●*adv*
without authorization
unbegreiflich *a*
incomprehensible
unbegrenzt *a* unlimited ●*adv*
indefinitely
unbegründet *a* unfounded
Unbehagen *nt* unease;
(*körperlich*) discomfort
unbekannt *a* unknown; (*nicht
vertraut*) unfamiliar. **U~e(r)** *m/f*
stranger
unbekümmert *a* unconcerned;
(*unbeschwert*) carefree
unbeliebt *a* unpopular. **U~heit** *f*
unpopularity
unbemannt *a* unmanned
unbemerkt *a* & *adv* unnoticed
unbenutzt *a* unused
unbequem *a* uncomfortable;
(*lästig*) awkward
unberechenbar *a* unpredictable
unberechtigt *a* unjustified;
(*unbefugt*) unauthorized
unberührt *a* untouched; (*fig*)
virgin; <*Landschaft*> unspoilt
unbescheiden *a* presumptuous
unbeschrankt *a* unguarded
unbeschränkt *a* unlimited ●*adv*
without limit
unbeschwert *a* carefree
unbesiegt *a* undefeated
unbespielt *a* blank
unbeständig *a* inconsistent;
<*Wetter*> unsettled
unbestechlich *a* incorruptible
unbestimmt *a* indefinite: <*Alter*>
indeterminate; (*ungewiss*)
uncertain; (*unklar*) vague
unbestritten *a* undisputed ●*adv*
indisputably
unbeteiligt *a* indifferent; **u~ an**
(+ *dat*) not involved in
unbetont *a* unstressed
unbewacht *a* unguarded
unbewaffnet *a* unarmed

unbeweglich *a* & *adv* motionless,
still
unbewohnt *a* uninhabited
unbewusst *a* unconscious
unbezahlbar *a* priceless
unbrauchbar *a* useless
und *conj* and; **und so weiter** and so
on; **nach und nach** bit by bit
Undank *m* ingratitude. **u~bar** *a*
ungrateful; (*nicht lohnend*)
thankless. **U~barkeit** *f*
ingratitude
undeutlich *a* indistinct; vague
undicht *a* leaking; **u~e Stelle** leak
Unding *nt* absurdity
undiplomatisch *a* undiplomatic
unduldsam *a* intolerant
undurch|dringlich *a*
impenetrable; <*Miene*>
inscrutable. **u~führbar** *a*
impracticable
undurch|lässig *a* impermeable.
u~sichtig *a* opaque; (*fig*)
doubtful
uneben *a* uneven. **U~heit** *f* -, **-en**
unevenness; (*Buckel*) bump
unecht *a* false; **u~er Schmuck**
imitation jewellery
unehelich *a* illegitimate
uneinig *a* (*fig*) divided; [**sich
** (*dat*)] **u~ sein** disagree
uneins *a* **u~ sein** be at odds
unempfindlich *a* insensitive
(**gegen** to); (*widerstandsfähig*)
tough; (*Med*) immune
unendlich *a* infinite; (*endlos*)
endless. **U~keit** *f* - infinity
unentbehrlich *a* indispensable
unentgeltlich *a* free, <*Arbeit*>
unpaid ●*adv* free of charge
unentschieden *a* undecided;
(*Sport*) drawn; **u~ spielen** draw.
U~ *nt* **-s,-** draw
unentschlossen *a* indecisive;
(*unentschieden*) undecided
unentwegt *a* persistent;
(*unaufhörlich*) incessant
unerfahren *a* inexperienced.
U~heit *f* - inexperience

unerfreulich *a* unpleasant
unerhört *a* enormous; (*empörend*)
outrageous
unerklärlich *a* inexplicable
unerlässlich *a* essential
unerlaubt *a* unauthorized ● *adv*
without permission
unerschwinglich *a* prohibitive
unersetzlich *a* irreplaceable;
<*Verlust*> irreparable
unerträglich *a* unbearable
unerwartet *a* unexpected
unerwünscht *a* unwanted;
<*Besuch*> unwelcome
unfähig *a* incompetent; **u∼, etw zu
tun** incapable of doing sth; (*nicht
in der Lage*) unable to do sth.
U∼keit *f* incompetence; inability
(**zu** to)
unfair *a* unfair
Unfall *m* accident. **U∼flucht** *f*
failure to stop after an accident.
U∼station *f* casualty department
unfassbar *a* incomprehensible
Unfehlbarkeit *f* - infallibility
unfolgsam *a* disobedient
unförmig *a* shapeless
unfreiwillig *a* involuntary;
(*unbeabsichtigt*) unintentional
unfreundlich *a* unfriendly;
(*unangenehm*) unpleasant.
U∼keit *f* unfriendliness;
unpleasantness
Unfriede[n] *m* discord
unfruchtbar *a* infertile; (*fig*)
unproductive. **U∼keit** *f* infertility
Unfug *m* **-s** mischief; (*Unsinn*)
nonsense
Ungar|(in) *m* **-n, -n** (*f* **-, -nen**)
Hungarian. **u∼isch** *a* Hungarian.
U∼n *nt* **-s** Hungary
ungeachtet *prep* (+ *gen*) in spite
of; **dessen u∼** notwithstanding
[this]. **ungebraucht** *a* unused.
ungedeckt *a* uncovered; (*Sport*)
unmarked; <*Tisch*> unlaid
Ungeduld *f* impatience. **u∼ig** *a*
impatient
ungeeignet *a* unsuitable

ungefähr *a* approximate, rough
ungefährlich *a* harmless
ungeheuer *a* enormous. **U∼** *nt*
-s,- monster
ungehorsam *a* disobedient. **U∼**
m disobedience
ungeklärt *a* unsolved; <*Frage*>
unsettled; <*Ursache*> unknown
ungelegen *a* inconvenient
ungelernt *a* unskilled
ungemütlich *a* uncomfortable;
(*unangenehm*) unpleasant
ungenau *a* inaccurate; vague.
U∼igkeit *f* **-, -en** inaccuracy
ungeniert /'ʊnʒeniːɐt/ *a*
uninhibited ● *adv* openly
ungenießbar *a* inedible;
<*Getränk*> undrinkable
ungenügend *a* inadequate; (*Sch*)
unsatisfactory. **ungepflegt** *a*
neglected; <*Person*> unkempt.
ungerade *a* <*Zahl*> odd
ungerecht *a* unjust. **U∼igkeit** *f*
-, -en injustice
ungern *adv* reluctantly
ungesalzen *a* unsalted
Ungeschick|lichkeit *f*
clumsiness. **u∼t** *a* clumsy
ungeschminkt *a* without make-
up; <*Wahrheit*> unvarnished.
ungesetzlich *a* illegal. **ungestört**
a undisturbed. **ungesund** *a*
unhealthy. **ungesüßt** *a*
unsweetened. **ungetrübt** *a*
perfect
Ungetüm *nt* **-s, -e** monster
ungewiss *a* uncertain; **im
Ungewissen sein/lassen** be/leave
in the dark. **U∼heit** *f* uncertainty
ungewöhnlich *a* unusual.
ungewohnt *a* unaccustomed;
(*nicht vertraut*) unfamiliar
Ungeziefer *nt* **-s** vermin
ungezogen *a* naughty
ungezwungen *a* informal;
(*natürlich*) natural
ungläubig *a* incredulous
unglaublich *a* incredible,
unbelievable

ungleich a unequal; (*verschieden*) different. **U~heit** f - inequality. **u~mäßig** a uneven

Unglück nt -s, -e misfortune; (*Pech*) bad luck; (*Missgeschick*) mishap; (*Unfall*) accident. **u~lich** a unhappy; (*ungünstig*) unfortunate. **u~licherweise** adv unfortunately

ungültig a invalid; (*Jur*) void

ungünstig a unfavourable; (*unpassend*) inconvenient

Unheil nt -s disaster; **U~ anrichten** cause havoc

unheilbar a incurable

unheimlich a eerie; (*gruselig*) creepy; (🔲 *groß*) terrific ● adv eerily; (🔲 *sehr*) terribly

unhöflich a rude. **U~keit** f rudeness

unhygienisch a unhygienic

Uni f -, -s 🔲 university

uni /yˈniː/ inv a plain

Uniform f -, -en uniform

uninteressant a uninteresting

Union f -, -en union

universell a universal

Universität f -, -en university

Universum nt -s universe

unkenntlich a unrecognizable

unklar a unclear; (*ungewiss*) uncertain; (*vage*) vague; **im U~en sein** be in the dark

unkompliziert a uncomplicated

Unkosten pl expenses

Unkraut nt weed; (*coll*) weeds pl; **U~ jäten** weed. **U~vertilgungsmittel** nt weed-killer

unlängst adv recently

unlauter a dishonest; (*unfair*) unfair

unleserlich a illegible

unleugbar a undeniable

unlogisch a illogical

Unmenge f enormous amount/ (*Anzahl*) number

Unmensch m 🔲 brute. **u~lich** a inhuman

unmerklich a imperceptible

unmittelbar a immediate; (*direkt*) direct

unmöbliert a unfurnished

unmodern a old-fashioned

unmöglich a impossible. **U~keit** f - impossibility

Unmoral f immorality. **u~isch** a immoral

unmündig a under-age

Unmut m displeasure

unnatürlich a unnatural

unnormal a abnormal

unnötig a unnecessary

unord|entlich a untidy; (*nachlässig*) sloppy. **U~nung** f disorder; (*Durcheinander*) muddle

unorthodox a unorthodox ● adv in an unorthodox manner

unparteiisch a impartial

unpassend a inappropriate; <*Moment*> inopportune

unpersönlich a impersonal

unpraktisch a impractical

unpünktlich a unpunctual ● adv late

unrealistisch a unrealistic

unrecht a wrong ● n **jdm u~ tun** do s.o. an injustice. **U~** nt wrong; **zu U~** wrongly; **U~ haben** be wrong; **jdm U~ geben** disagree with s.o. **u~mäßig** a unlawful

unregelmäßig a irregular

unreif a unripe; (*fig*) immature

unrein a impure; <*Luft*> polluted; <*Haut*> bad; **ins U~e schreiben** make a rough draft of

unrentabel a unprofitable

Unruh|e f -, -n restlessness; (*Erregung*) agitation; (*Besorgnis*) anxiety; **U~en** (*Pol*) unrest sg. **u~ig** a restless; (*laut*) noisy; (*besorgt*) anxious

uns pron (acc/dat of **wir**) us; (*refl*) ourselves; (*einander*) each other

unsauber a dirty; (*nachlässig*) sloppy

unschädlich a harmless

unscharf *a* blurred
unschätzbar *a* inestimable
unscheinbar *a* inconspicuous
unschlagbar *a* unbeatable
unschlüssig *a* undecided
Unschuld *f* - innocence;
(*Jungfräulichkeit*) virginity. **u~ig**
a innocent
unselbstständig, unselbständig *a*
dependent ● *adv* **u~ denken** not
think for oneself
unser *poss pron* our. **u~e(r,s)**
poss pron ours. **u~erseits** *adv* for
our part. **u~twegen** *adv* for our
sake; (*wegen uns*) because of us,
on our account
unsicher *a* unsafe; (*ungewiss*)
uncertain; (*nicht zuverlässig*)
unreliable; <*Schritte, Hand*>
unsteady; <*Person*> insecure
● *adv* unsteadily. **U~heit** *f*
uncertainty; unreliability;
insecurity
unsichtbar *a* invisible
Unsinn *m* nonsense. **u~ig** *a*
nonsensical, absurd
Unsitt|e *f* bad habit. **u~lich** *a*
indecent
unsportlich *a* not sporty; (*unfair*)
unsporting
uns|re(r,s) *poss pron* = **unsere(r,s)**.
u~rige *poss pron* **der/die/das**
u~rige ours
unsterblich *a* immortal. **U~keit** *f*
immortality
Unsumme *f* vast sum
unsympathisch *a* unpleasant; **er**
ist mir u~ I don't like him
untätig *a* idle
untauglich *a* unsuitable; (*Mil*)
unfit
unten *adv* at the bottom; (*auf der*
Unterseite) underneath; (*eine*
Treppe tiefer) downstairs; (*im*
Text) below; **hier/da u~** down
here/there; **nach u~**
down[wards]; (*die Treppe*
hinunter) downstairs; **siehe u~**
see below

unter *prep* (+ *dat/acc*) under;
(*niedriger als*) below; (*inmitten,*
zwischen) among; **u~ anderem**
among other things; **u~ der**
Woche during the week; **u~ sich**
by themselves
Unter|arm *m* forearm.
U~bewusstsein *nt* subconscious
unterbieten† *vt insep* undercut;
beat <*Rekord*>
unterbinden† *vt insep* stop
unterbrech|en† *vt insep*
interrupt; break <*Reise*>. **U~ung**
f -, -en interruption, break
unterbringen† *vt sep* put;
(*beherbergen*) put up
unterdessen *adv* in the
meantime
Unterdrückung *f* - suppression;
oppression
untere(r,s) *a* lower
untereinander *adv* one below the
other; (*miteinander*) among
ourselves/yourselves/themselves
unterernähr|t *a* undernourished.
U~ung *f* malnutrition
Unterführung *f* underpass;
(*Fußgänger-*) subway
Untergang *m* (*Astr*) setting;
(*Naut*) sinking; (*Zugrundegehen*)
disappearance; (*der Welt*) end
Untergebene(r) *m/f* subordinate
untergehen† *vi sep* (*sein*) (*Astr*)
set; (*versinken*) go under;
<*Schiff:*> go down, sink;
(*zugrunde gehen*) disappear;
<*Welt:*> come to an end
Untergeschoss *nt* basement
Untergrund *m* foundation;
(*Hintergrund*) background.
U~bahn *f* underground [railway]
unterhaken *vt sep* **jdn u~** take
s.o.'s arm; **untergehakt** arm in arm
unterhalb *adv & prep* (+ *gen*)
below
Unterhalt *m* maintenance
unterhalt|en† *vt insep* maintain;
(*ernähren*) support; (*betreiben*)
run; (*erheitern*) entertain; **sich**

u~en talk; (*sich vergnügen*) enjoy oneself. **U~ung** *f* **-, -en** maintenance; (*Gespräch*) conversation; (*Zeitvertreib*) entertainment

Unter|haus *nt* (*Pol*) lower house; (*in UK*) House of Commons. **U~hemd** *nt* vest. **U~hose** *f* underpants *pl*. **u~irdisch** *a & adv* underground

Unterkiefer *m* lower jaw

unterkommen† *vi sep* (*sein*) find accommodation; (*eine Stellung finden*) get a job

Unterkunft *f* **-, -künfte** accommodation

Unterlage *f* pad; **U~n** papers

Unterlass *m* **ohne U~** incessantly

Unterlassung *f* **-, -en** omission

unterlegen *a* inferior; (*Sport*) losing; **zahlenmäßig u~** outnumbered (*dat* by). **U~e(r)** *m/f* loser

Unterleib *m* abdomen

unterliegen† *vi insep* (*sein*) lose (*dat* to); (*unterworfen sein*) be subject (*dat* to)

Unterlippe *f* lower lip

Untermiete *f* **zur U~ wohnen** be a lodger. **U~r(in)** *m(f)* lodger

unternehm|en† *vt insep* undertake; take <*Schritte*>; **etw/ nichts u~en** do sth/nothing. **U~en** *nt* **-s,-** undertaking, enterprise; (*Betrieb*) concern. **U~er** *m* **-s,-** employer; (*Bau-*) contractor; (*Industrieller*) industrialist. **u~ungslustig** *a* enterprising

Unteroffizier *m* non-commissioned officer

unterordnen *vt sep* subordinate

Unterredung *f* **-, -en** talk

Unterricht *m* **-[e]s** teaching; (*Privat-*) tuition; (*U~sstunden*) lessons *pl*

unterrichten *vt/i insep* (*haben*) teach; (*informieren*) inform; **sich u~** inform oneself

Unterrock *m* slip

untersagen *vt insep* forbid

Untersatz *m* mat; (*mit Füßen*) stand; (*Gläser-*) coaster

unterscheid|en† *vt/i insep* (*haben*) distinguish; (*auseinander halten*) tell apart; **sich u~en** differ. **U~ung** *f* **-, -en** distinction

Unterschied *m* **-[e]s, -e** difference; (*Unterscheidung*) distinction; **im U~ zu ihm** unlike him. **u~lich** *a* different; (*wechselnd*) varying

unterschlag|en† *vt insep* embezzle; (*verheimlichen*) suppress. **U~ung** *f* **-, -en** embezzlement; suppression

Unterschlupf *m* **-[e]s** shelter; (*Versteck*) hiding-place

unterschreiben† *vt/i insep* (*haben*) sign

Unter|schrift *f* signature; (*Bild-*) caption. **U~seeboot** *nt* submarine

Unterstand *m* shelter

unterste(r,s) *a* lowest, bottom

unterstehen† *v insep* ● *vi* (*haben*) be answerable (*dat* to); (*unterliegen*) be subject (*dat* to)

unterstellen¹ *vt sep* put underneath; (*abstellen*) store; **sich u~** shelter

unterstellen² *vt insep* place under the control (*dat* of); (*annehmen*) assume; (*fälschlich zuschreiben*) impute (*dat* to)

unterstreichen† *vt insep* underline

unterstütz|en *vt insep* support; (*helfen*) aid. **U~ung** *f* **-, -en** support; (*finanziell*) aid; (*regelmäßiger Betrag*) allowance; (*Arbeitslosen-*) benefit

untersuch|en *vt insep* examine; (*Jur*) investigate; (*prüfen*) test; (*überprüfen*) check; (*durchsuchen*) search. **U~ung** *f* **-, -en** examination; investigation; test; check; search. **U~ungshaft** *f* detention on remand

Untertan m -s & -en, -en subject
Untertasse f saucer
Unterteil nt bottom (part)
Untertitel m subtitle
untervermieten vt/i insep (haben) sublet
Unterwäsche f underwear
unterwegs adv on the way; (außer Haus) out; (verreist) away
Unterwelt f underworld
unterzeichnen vt insep sign
unterziehen† vt insep etw einer Untersuchung/Überprüfung u~ examine/ check sth; **sich einer Operation/Prüfung u~** have an operation/take a test
Untier nt monster
untragbar a intolerable
untrennbar a inseparable
untreu a disloyal; (in der Ehe) unfaithful. **U~e** f disloyalty; infidelity
untröstlich a inconsolable
unübersehbar a obvious; (groß) immense
ununterbrochen a incessant
unveränderlich a invariable; (gleichbleibend) unchanging
unverändert a unchanged
unverantwortlich a irresponsible
unverbesserlich a incorrigible
unverbindlich a non-committal; (Comm) not binding ● adv without obligation
unverdaulich a indigestible
unver|gesslich a unforgettable. **u~gleichlich** a incomparable. **u~heiratet** a unmarried. **u~käuflich** a not for sale; <Muster> free
unverkennbar a unmistakable
unverletzt a unhurt
unvermeidlich a inevitable
unver|mindert a & adv undiminished. **u~mutet** a unexpected
Unver|nunft f folly. **u~nünftig** a foolish

unverschämt a insolent; (Ⅱ ungeheuer) outrageous. **U~heit** f -, -en insolence
unver|sehens adv suddenly. **u~sehrt** a unhurt; (unbeschädigt) intact
unverständlich a incomprehensible; (undeutlich) indistinct
unverträglich a incompatible; <Person> quarrelsome; (unbekömmlich) indigestible
unver|wundbar a invulnerable. **u~wüstlich** a indestructible; <Person, Humor> irrepressible; <Gesundheit> robust. **u~zeihlich** a unforgivable
unverzüglich a immediate
unvollendet a unfinished
unvollkommen a imperfect; (unvollständig) incomplete
unvollständig a incomplete
unvor|bereitet a unprepared. **u~hergesehen** a unforeseen
unvorsichtig a careless
unvorstellbar a unimaginable
unvorteilhaft a unfavourable; (nicht hübsch) unattractive
unwahr a untrue. **U~heit** f -, -en untruth. **u~scheinlich** a unlikely; (unglaublich) improbable; (Ⅱ groß) incredible
unweit adv & prep (+ gen) not far
unwesentlich a unimportant
Unwetter nt -s,- storm
unwichtig a unimportant
unwider|legbar a irrefutable. **u~stehlich** a irresistible
Unwill|e m displeasure. **u~ig** a angry; (widerwillig) reluctant
unwirklich a unreal
unwirksam a ineffective
unwirtschaftlich a uneconomic
unwissen|d a ignorant. **U~heit** f - ignorance
unwohl a unwell; (unbehaglich) uneasy
unwürdig a unworthy (gen of)

Unzahl f vast number. **unzählig** a innumerable, countless

unzerbrechlich a unbreakable

unzerstörbar a indestructible

unzertrennlich a inseparable

Unzucht f sexual offence; **gewerbsmäßige U~** prostitution

unzüchtig a indecent; <*Schriften*> obscene

unzufrieden a dissatisfied; (*innerlich*) discontented. **U~heit** f dissatisfaction

unzulässig a inadmissible

unzurechnungsfähig a insane. **U~keit** f insanity

unzusammenhängend a incoherent

unzutreffend a inapplicable; (*falsch*) incorrect

unzuverlässig a unreliable

unzweifelhaft a undoubted

üppig a luxuriant; (*überreichlich*) lavish

uralt a ancient

Uran nt -s uranium

Uraufführung f first performance

Urenkel m great-grandson; (*pl*) great-grandchildren

Urgroß|mutter f great-grandmother. **U~vater** m great-grandfather

Urheber m -s,- originator; (*Verfasser*) author. **U~recht** nt copyright

Urin m -s, -e urine

Urkunde f -, -n certificate; (*Dokument*) document

Urlaub m -s holiday; (*Mil, Admin*) leave; **auf U~** on holiday/leave; **U~ haben** be on holiday/leave. **U~er(in)** m -s,- (f -, -nen) holiday-maker. **U~sort** m holiday resort

Urne f -, -n urn; (*Wahl-*) ballot-box

Ursache f cause; (*Grund*) reason; **keine U~!** don't mention it!

Ursprung m origin

ursprünglich a original; (*anfänglich*) initial; (*natürlich*) natural

Urteil nt -s, -e judgement; (*Meinung*) opinion; (*U~sspruch*) verdict; (*Strafe*) sentence. **u~en** vi (*haben*) judge

Urwald m primeval forest; (*tropischer*) jungle

Urzeit f primeval times pl

USA pl USA sg

usw. abbr (**und so weiter**) etc.

utopisch a Utopian

Vakuum /'va:kuʊm/ nt -s vacuum. **v~verpackt** a vacuum-packed

Vanille /va'nɪljə/ f - vanilla

variieren vt/i (*haben*) vary

Vase /'va:zə/ f -, -n vase

Vater m -s,- father. **V~land** nt fatherland

väterlich a paternal; (*fürsorglich*) fatherly. **v~erseits** adv on one's/the father's side

Vater|schaft f - fatherhood; (*Jur*) paternity. **V~unser** nt -s,- Lord's Prayer

v. Chr. abbr (**vor Christus**) BC

Vegetar|ier(in) /vege'ta:riɐ, -jərɪn/ m(f) -s,- (f -, -nen) vegetarian. **v~isch** a vegetarian

Veilchen nt -s, -n violet

Vene /'ve:nə/ f -, -n vein

Venedig /ve'ne:dɪç/ nt -s Venice

Ventil /vɛn'ti:l/ nt -s, -e valve. **V~ator** m -s, -en /-'to:rən/ fan

verabred|en vt arrange; **sich [mit jdm] v~en** arrange to meet [s.o.]. **V~ung** f -, -en arrangement; (*Treffen*) appointment

verabschieden vt say goodbye to; (aus dem Dienst) retire; pass <Gesetz>; **sich v~** say goodbye

verachten vt despise

Verachtung f - contempt

verallgemeinern vt/i (haben) generalize

veränder|lich a changeable; (Math) variable. **v~n** vt change; **sich v~n** change; (beruflich) change one's job. **V~ung** f change

verängstigt a frightened, scared

verankern vt anchor

veranlag|t a künstlerisch/musikalisch **v~t sein** have an artistic/a musical bent; **praktisch v~t** practically minded. **V~ung** f -, -en disposition; (Neigung) tendency; (künstlerisch) bent

veranlassen vt (reg) arrange for; (einleiten) institute; **jdn v~** prompt s.o. (zu to)

veranschlagen vt (reg) estimate

veranstalt|en vt organize; hold, give <Party>; make <Lärm>. **V~er** m -s,- organizer. **V~ung** f -, -en event

verantwort|lich a responsible; **v~lich machen** hold responsible. **V~ung** f - responsibility. **v~ungsbewusst** a responsible. **v~ungslos** a irresponsible. **v~ungsvoll** a responsible

verarbeiten vt use; (Techn) process; (verdauen & fig) digest

verärgern vt annoy

verausgaben (sich) vr spend all one's money

veräußern vt sell

Verb /verp/ nt -s, -en verb

Verband m -[e]s,ː̈e association; (Mil) unit; (Med) bandage; (Wund-) dressing. **V~szeug** nt first-aid kit

verbann|en vt exile; (fig) banish. **V~ung** f - exile

verbergen† vt hide; **sich v~** hide

verbesser|n vt improve; (berichtigen) correct. **V~ung** f -, -en improvement; correction

verbeug|en (sich) vr bow. **V~ung** f bow

verbeulen vt dent

verbiegen† vt bend

verbieten† vt forbid; (Admin) prohibit, ban

verbillig|en vt reduce [in price]. **v~t** a reduced

verbinden† vt connect (mit to); (zusammenfügen) join; (verknüpfen) combine; (in Verbindung bringen) associate; (Med) bandage; dress <Wunde>. **jdm verbunden sein** (fig) be obliged to s.o.

verbindlich a friendly; (bindend) binding

Verbindung f connection; (Verknüpfung) combination; (Kontakt) contact; (Vereinigung) association; chemiche **V~** chemical compound; **in V~ stehen/sich in V~ setzen** be/get in touch

verbissen a grim

verbitter|n vt make bitter. **v~t** a bitter. **V~ung** f - bitterness

verblassen vi (sein) fade

Verbleib m -s whereabouts pl

verbleit a <Benzin> leaded

verblüff|en vt amaze, astound. **V~ung** f - amazement

verblühen vi (sein) wither, fade

verbluten vi (sein) bleed to death

verborgen vt lend

Verbot nt -[e]s, -e ban. **v~en** a forbidden; (Admin) prohibited

Verbrauch m -[e]s consumption. **v~en** vt use; consume <Lebensmittel>; (erschöpfen) use up. **V~er** m -s,- consumer

Verbrechen nt -s,- crime

Verbrecher m -s,- criminal

verbreit|en vt spread. **v~et** a widespread. **V~ung** f - spread; (Verbreiten) spreading

verbrenn|en *vt/i (sein)* burn; cremate *<Leiche>*. **V~ung** *f* -, **-en** burning; cremation; *(Wunde)* burn

verbringen† *vt* spend

verbrühen *vt* scald

verbuchen *vt* enter

verbünd|en (sich) *vr* form an alliance. **V~ete(r)** *m/f* ally

verbürgen *vt* guarantee; **sich v~ für** vouch for

Verdacht *m* -[e]s suspicion; **in** *or* **im V~ haben** suspect

verdächtig *a* suspicious. **v~en** *vt* suspect *(gen* of). **V~te(r)** *m/f* suspect

verdamm|en *vt* condemn; *(Relig)* damn. **v~t** *a & adv* 🗙 damned; **v~t!** damn!

verdampfen *vt/i (sein)* evaporate

verdanken *vt* owe *(dat* to)

verdau|en *vt* digest. **v~lich** *a* digestible. **V~ung** *f* - digestion

Verdeck *nt* -[e]s, **-e** hood; *(Oberdeck)* top deck

verderb|en† *vi (sein)* spoil; *<Lebensmittel:>* go bad ● *vt* spoil; **ich habe mir den Magen verdorben** I have an upset stomach. **V~en** *nt* -s ruin. **v~lich** *a* perishable; *(schädlich)* pernicious

verdien|en *vt/i (haben)* earn; *(fig)* deserve. **V~er** *m* -s,- wage-earner

Verdienst¹ *m* -[e]s earnings *pl*

Verdienst² *nt* -[e]s, **-e** merit

verdient *a* well-deserved

verdoppeln *vt* double

verdorben *a* spoilt, ruined; *<Magen>* upset; *(moralisch)* corrupt; *(verkommen)* depraved

verdreh|en *vt* twist; roll *<Augen>*; *(fig)* distort. **v~t** *a* 🗊 crazy

verdreifachen *vt* treble, triple

verdrücken *vt* crumple; (🗊 *essen)* polish off; **sich v~** 🗊 slip away

Verdruss *m* -es annoyance

verdünnen *vt* dilute; **sich v~** taper off

verdunst|en *vi (sein)* evaporate. **V~ung** *f* - evaporation

verdursten *vi (sein)* die of thirst

veredeln *vt* refine; *(Hort)* graft

verehr|en *vt* revere; *(Relig)* worship; *(bewundern)* admire; *(schenken)* give. **V~er(in)** *m* -s,- (*f* -, -nen) admirer. **V~ung** *f* - veneration; worship; admiration

vereidigen *vt* swear in

Verein *m* -s, **-e** society; *(Sport-)* club

vereinbar *a* compatible. **v~en** *vt* arrange. **V~ung** *f* -, **-en** agreement

vereinfachen *vt* simplify

vereinheitlichen *vt* standardize

vereinig|en *vt* unite; merge *<Firmen>*; **wieder v~en** reunite; reunify *<Land>*; **sich v~en** unite; **V~te Staaten [von Amerika]** United States *sg* [of America]. **V~ung** *f* -, **-en** union; *(Organisation)* organization

vereinzelt *a* isolated ● *adv* occasionally

vereist *a* frozen; *<Straße>* icy

vereitert *a* septic

verenden *vi (sein)* die

vereng|en *vt* restrict; **sich v~** narrow; *<Pupille:>* contract

vererb|en *vt* leave *(dat* to); *(Biol & fig)* pass on *(dat* to). **V~ung** *f* - heredity

verfahren† *vi (sein)* proceed; **v~ mit** deal with ● *vr* **sich v~** lose one's way ● *a* muddled. **V~** *nt* -s,- procedure; *(Techn)* process; *(Jur)* proceedings *pl*

Verfall *m* decay; *(eines Gebäudes)* dilapidation; *(körperlich & fig)* decline; *(Ablauf)* expiry. **v~en**† *vi (sein)* decay; *<Person, Sitten:>* decline; *(ablaufen)* expire; **v~en in** (+ *acc*) lapse into; **v~en auf** (+ *acc*) hit on *<Idee>*

verfärben (sich) *vr* change colour; *<Stoff:>* discolour

verfass|en vt write; (Jur) draw up; (entwerfen) draft. **V~er** m -s,- author. **V~ung** f (Pol) constitution; (Zustand) state

verfaulen vi (sein) rot, decay

verfechten† vt advocate

verfehlen vt miss

verfeinde|n (sich) vr become enemies; **v~t sein** be enemies

verfeinern vt refine; (verbessern) improve

verfilmen vt film

verfluch|en vt curse. **v~t** a & adv 🗊 damned; **v~t!** damn!

verfolg|en vt pursue; (folgen) follow; (bedrängen) pester; (Pol) persecute; **strafrechtlich v~en** prosecute. **V~er** m -s,- pursuer. **V~ung** f - pursuit; persecution

verfrüht a premature

verfügbar a available

verfüg|en vt order; (Jur) decree ● vi (haben) **v~en über** (+ acc) have at one's disposal. **V~ung** f -, -en order; (Jur) decree; **jdm zur V~ung stehen** be at s.o.'s disposal

verführ|en vt seduce; tempt. **V~ung** f seduction; temptation

vergangen a past; (letzte) last. **V~heit** f - past; (Gram) past tense

vergänglich a transitory

vergas|en vt gas. **V~er** m -s,- carburettor

vergeb|en† vt award (an + dat to); (weggeben) give away; (verzeihen) forgive. **v~lich** a futile, vain ● adv in vain. **V~ung** f - forgiveness

vergehen† vi (sein) pass; **sich v~** violate (**gegen etw** sth). **V~** nt -s,- offence

vergelt|en† vt repay. **V~ung** f - retaliation; (Rache) revenge

vergessen† vt forget; (liegen lassen) leave behind

vergesslich a forgetful. **V~keit** f - forgetfulness

vergeuden vt waste, squander

vergewaltig|en vt rape. **V~ung** f -, -en rape

vergießen† vt spill; shed <Tränen, Blut>

vergift|en vt poison. **V~ung** f -, -en poisoning

Vergissmeinnicht nt -[e]s, -[e] forget-me-not

vergittert a barred

verglasen vt glaze

Vergleich m -[e]s, -e comparison; (Jur) settlement. **v~bar** a comparable. **v~en†** vt compare (**mit** with/to)

vergnüg|en (sich) vr enjoy oneself. **V~en** nt -s,- pleasure; (Spaß) fun; **viel V~en!** have a good time! **v~t** a cheerful; (zufrieden) happy. **V~ungen** fpl entertainments

vergolden vt gild; (plattieren) gold-plate

vergraben† vt bury

vergriffen a out of print

vergrößer|n vt enlarge; <Linse:> magnify; (vermehren) increase; (erweitern) extend; expand <Geschäft>; **sich v~n** grow bigger; <Firma:> expand; (zunehmen) increase. **V~ung** f -, -en magnification; increase; expansion; (Phot) enlargement. **V~ungsglas** nt magnifying glass

vergüt|en† vt pay for; **jdm etw v~en** reimburse s.o. for sth. **V~ung** f -, -en remuneration; (Erstattung) reimbursement

verhaft|en vt arrest. **V~ung** f -, -en arrest

verhalten† (sich) vr behave; (handeln) act; (beschaffen sein) be. **V~** nt -s behaviour, conduct

Verhältnis nt -ses, -se relationship; (Liebes-) affair; (Math) ratio; **V~se** circumstances; conditions. **v~mäßig** adv comparatively, relatively

verhand|eln vt discuss; (*Jur*) try ● vi (*haben*) negotiate. **V~lung** f (*Jur*) trial; **V~lungen** negotiations

Verhängnis nt -ses fate, doom

verhärten vt/i (*sein*) harden

verhasst a hated

verhätscheln vt spoil

verhauen† vt 🗉 beat; make a mess of <*Prüfung*>

verheilen vi (*sein*) heal

verheimlichen vt keep secret

verheirat|en (sich) vr get married (**mit** to); **sich wieder v~en** remarry. **v~et** a married

verhelfen† vi (*haben*) jdm zu etw **v~** help s.o. get sth

verherrlichen vt glorify

verhexen vt bewitch

verhinder|n vt prevent; **v~t sein** be unable to come

Verhör nt -s, -e interrogation; **ins V~ nehmen** interrogate. **v~en** vt interrogate; **sich v~en** mishear

verhungern vi (*sein*) starve

verhüt|en vt prevent. **V~ung** f - prevention. **V~ungsmittel** nt contraceptive

verirren (sich) vr get lost

verjagen vt chase away

verjüngen vt rejuvenate

verkalkt a 🗉 senile

verkalkulieren (sich) vr miscalculate

Verkauf m sale; **zum V~** for sale. **v~en** vt sell; **zu v~en** for sale

Verkäufer(in) m(f) seller; (*im Geschäft*) shop assistant

Verkehr m -s traffic; (*Kontakt*) contact; (*Geschlechts-*) intercourse; **aus dem V~ ziehen** take out of circulation. **v~en** vi (*haben*) operate; <*Bus, Zug:*> run; (*Umgang haben*) associate, mix (**mit** with); (*Gast sein*) visit (**bei jdm** s.o.)

Verkehrs|ampel f traffic lights pl. **V~unfall** m road accident. **V~verein** m tourist office. **V~zeichen** nt traffic sign

verkehrt a wrong; **v~ herum** adv the wrong way round; (*links*) inside out

verklagen vt sue (**auf** + acc for)

verkleid|en vt disguise; (*Techn*) line; **sich v~en** disguise oneself; (*für Kostümfest*) dress up. **V~ung** f -, -en disguise; (*Kostüm*) fancy dress; (*Techn*) lining

verkleiner|n vt reduce [in size]. **V~ung** f - reduction

verknittern vt/i (*sein*) crumple

verknüpfen vt knot together

verkommen† vi (*sein*) be neglected; (*sittlich*) go to the bad; (*verfallen*) decay; <*Haus:*> fall into disrepair; <*Gegend:*> become run-down; <*Lebensmittel:*> go bad ● a neglected; (*sittlich*) depraved; <*Haus*> dilapidated; <*Gegend*> run-down

verkörpern vt embody, personify

verkraften vt cope with

verkrampft a (*fig*) tense

verkriechen† (sich) vr hide

verkrümmt a crooked, bent

verkrüppelt a crippled; <*Glied*> deformed

verkühl|en (sich) vr catch a chill. **V~ung** f -, -en chill

verkümmern vi (*sein*) waste/ <*Pflanze:*> wither away

verkünden vt announce; pronounce <*Urteil*>

verkürzen vt shorten; (*verringern*) reduce; (*abbrechen*) cut short; while away <*Zeit*>

Verlag m -[e]s, -e publishing firm

verlangen vt ask for; (*fordern*) demand; (*berechnen*) charge. **V~** nt -s desire; (*Bitte*) request

verlänger|n vt extend; lengthen <*Kleid*>; (*zeitlich*) prolong; renew <*Pass, Vertrag*>; (*Culin*) thin down. **V~ung** f -, -en extension; renewal. **V~ungsschnur** f extension cable

verlassen† vt leave; (*im Stich lassen*) desert; **sich v~ auf** (+ acc)

rely *or* depend on ● *a* deserted.
V~heit *f* - desolation
verlässlich *a* reliable
Verlauf *m* course; **im V~** (+ *gen*)
in the course of. **v~en**† *vi* (*sein*)
run; (*ablaufen*) go; **gut v~en** go
[off] well ● *vr* **sich v~en** lose
one's way
verlegen *vt* move; (*verschieben*)
postpone; (*vor-*) bring forward;
(*verlieren*) mislay; (*versperren*)
block; (*legen*) lay <*Teppich,
Rohre*>; (*veröffentlichen*) publish;
sich v~ auf (+ *acc*) take up
<*Beruf*>; resort to <*Bitten*> ● *a*
embarrassed. **V~heit** *f* -
embarrassment
Verleger *m* -s,- publisher
verleihen† *vt* lend; (*gegen
Gebühr*) hire out; (*überreichen*)
award, confer; (*fig*) give
verlernen *vt* forget
verletz|en *vt* injure; (*kränken*)
hurt; (*verstoßen gegen*) infringe;
violate <*Grenze*>. **v~end** *a*
hurtful, wounding. **V~te(r)** *m*/*f*
injured person; (*bei Unfall*)
casualty. **V~ung** *f* -, -en (*Verstoß*)
infringement; violation
verleugnen *vt* deny; disown
<*Freund*>
verleumd|en *vt* slander;
(*schriftlich*) libel. **v~erisch** *a*
slanderous; libellous. **V~ung** *f* -,
-en slander; (*schriftlich*) libel
verlieben (sich) *vr* fall in love (in
+ *acc* with); **verliebt sein** be in
love (**in** + *acc* with)
verlier|en† *vt* lose; shed <*Laub*>
● *vi* (*haben*) lose (**an etw** *dat* sth).
V~er *m* -s,- loser
verlob|en (sich) *vr* get engaged
(**mit** to); **v~t sein** be engaged.
V~te *f* fiancée. **V~te(r)** *m* fiancé.
V~ung *f* -, -en engagement.
verlock|en *vt* tempt. **V~ung** *f*
-, -en temptation
verloren *a* lost; **v~ gehen** get lost

verlos|en *vt* raffle. **V~ung** *f* -, -en
raffle; (*Ziehung*) draw
Verlust *m* -[e]s, -e loss
vermachen *vt* leave, bequeath
Vermächtnis *nt* -ses, -se legacy
vermähl|en (sich) *vr* marry.
V~ung *f* -, -en marriage
vermehren *vt* increase; propagate
<*Pflanzen*>; **sich v~** increase;
(*sich fortpflanzen*) breed
vermeiden† *vt* avoid
Vermerk *m* -[e]s, -e note. **v~en**
note [down]
vermessen† *vt* measure; survey
<*Gelände*> ● *a* presumptuous
vermiet|en *vt* let, rent [out]; hire
out <*Boot, Auto*>; **zu v~en** to let;
<*Boot:*> for hire. **V~er** *m*
landlord. **V~erin** *f* landlady
vermindern *vt* reduce
vermischen *vt* mix
vermissen *vt* miss
vermisst *a* missing
vermitteln *vi* (*haben*) mediate
● *vt* arrange; (*beschaffen*) find;
place <*Arbeitskräfte*>
Vermittl|er *m* -s,- agent;
(*Schlichter*) mediator. **V~ung** *f*
-, -en arrangement; (*Agentur*)
agency; (*Teleph*) exchange;
(*Schlichtung*) mediation
Vermögen *nt* -s,- fortune. **v~d** *a*
wealthy
vermut|en *vt* suspect; (*glauben*)
presume. **v~lich** *a* probable
● *adv* presumably. **V~ung** *f* -, -en
supposition; (*Verdacht*) suspicion
vernachlässigen *vt* neglect
vernehm|en† *vt* hear; (*verhören*)
question; (*Jur*) examine. **V~ung** *f*
-, -en questioning
verneigen (sich) *vr* bow
vernein|en *vt* answer in the
negative; (*ablehnen*) reject.
v~end *a* negative. **V~ung** *f* -, -en
negative answer
vernicht|en *vt* destroy; (*ausrotten*)
exterminate. **V~ung** *f* -
destruction; extermination

Vernunft f - reason

vernünftig a reasonable, sensible

veröffentlich|en vt publish. **V~ung** f -, -en publication

verordn|en vt prescribe (dat for). **V~ung** f -, -en prescription; (Verfügung) decree

verpachten vt lease [out]

verpack|en vt pack; (einwickeln) wrap. **V~ung** f packaging; wrapping

verpassen vt miss; (🔟 geben) give

verpfänden vt pawn

verpflanzen vt transplant

verpfleg|en vt feed: **sich selbst v~en** cater for oneself. **V~ung** f - board; (Essen) food; **Unterkunft und V~ung** board and lodging

verpflicht|en vt oblige; (einstellen) engage; (Sport) sign; **sich v~en** undertake/(versprechen) promise (zu to); (vertraglich) sign a contract. **V~ung** f -, -en obligation, commitment

verprügeln vt beat up, thrash

Verputz m -es plaster. **v~en** vt plaster

Verrat m -[e]s betrayal, treachery. **v~en**† vt betray; give away <Geheimnis>

Verräter m -s,- traitor

verrech|nen vt settle; clear <Scheck>; **sich v~nen** make a mistake; (fig) miscalculate. **V~nungsscheck** m crossed cheque

verreisen vi (sein) go away; **verreist sein** be away

verrenken vt dislocate

verrichten vt perform, do

verriegeln vt bolt

verringer|n vt reduce; **sich v~n** decrease. **V~ung** f - reduction; decrease

verrost|en vi (sein) rust. **v~et** a rusty

verrückt a crazy, mad. **V~e(r)** m/f lunatic, **V~heit** f -, -en madness; (Torheit) folly

verrühren vt mix

verrunzelt a wrinkled

verrutschen vi (sein) slip

Vers /fɛrs/ m -es, -e verse

versag|en vi (haben) fail ● vt **sich etw v~en** deny oneself sth. **V~en** nt -s,- failure. **V~er** m -s,- failure

versalzen† vt put too much salt in/on; (fig) spoil

versamm|eln vt assemble. **V~lung** f assembly, meeting

Versand m -[e]s dispatch. **V~haus** nt mail-order firm

versäumen vt miss; lose <Zeit>; (unterlassen) neglect; **[es] v~, etw zu tun** fail to do sth

verschärfen vt intensify; tighten <Kontrolle>; increase <Tempo>; aggravate <Lage>; **sich v~** intensify; increase; <Lage:> worsen

verschätzen (sich) vr **sich v~ in** (+ dat) misjudge

verschenken vt give away

verscheuchen vt shoo/(jagen) chase away

verschicken vt send; (Comm) dispatch

verschieb|en† vt move; (aufschieben) put off, postpone; **sich v~en** move, shift; (verrutschen) slip; (zeitlich) be postponed. **V~ung** f shift; postponement

verschieden a different; **v~e** pl different; (mehrere) various; **V~es** some things; (dieses und jenes) various things; **das ist v~** it varies ● adv differently; **v~ groß** of different sizes. **v~artig** a diverse

verschimmel|n vi (sein) go mouldy. **v~t** a mouldy

verschlafen† vi (haben) oversleep ● vt sleep through

<Tag>; **sich v~** oversleep ● *a* sleepy

verschlagen† *vt* lose *<Seite>*; **jdm die Sprache/den Atem v~** leave s.o. speechless/take s.o.'s breath away ● *a* sly

verschlechter|n *vt* make worse; **sich v~n** get worse, deteriorate. **V~ung** *f* -, **-en** deterioration

Verschleiß *m* **-es** wear and tear

verschleppen *vt* carry off; *(entführen)* abduct; spread *<Seuche>*; neglect *<Krankheit>*; *(hinausziehen)* delay

verschleudern *vt* sell at a loss

verschließen† *vt* close; *(abschließen)* lock; *(einschließen)* lock up

verschlimmer|n *vt* make worse; aggravate *<Lage>*; **sich v~n** get worse, deteriorate. **V~ung** *f* -, **-en** deterioration

verschlossen *a* reserved. **V~heit** *f* - reserve

verschlucken *vt* swallow; **sich v~** choke (**an** + *dat* on)

Verschluss *m* **-es,-̈e** fastener, clasp; *(Koffer-)* catch; *(Flaschen-)* top; *(luftdicht)* seal; *(Phot)* shutter

verschlüsselt *a* coded

verschmelzen† *vt/i (sein)* fuse

verschmerzen *vt* get over

verschmutz|en *vt* soil; pollute *<Luft>* ● *vi (sein)* get dirty. **V~ung** *f* - pollution

verschneit *a* snow-covered

verschnörkelt *a* ornate

verschnüren *vt* tie up

verschollen *a* missing

verschonen *vt* spare

verschossen *a* faded

verschränken *vt* cross

verschreiben† *vt* prescribe; **sich v~** make a slip of the pen

verschulden *vt* be to blame for. **V~** *nt* **-s** fault

verschuldet *a* **v~ sein** be in debt

verschütten *vt* spill; *(begraben)* bury

verschweigen† *vt* conceal, hide

verschwend|en *vt* waste. **V~ung** *f* - extravagance; *(Vergeudung)* waste

verschwiegen *a* discreet

verschwinden† *vi (sein)* disappear; **[mal] v~** 🚽 spend a penny

verschwommen *a* blurred

verschwör|en (sich) *vr* conspire **V~ung** *f* -, **-en** conspiracy

versehen† *vt* perform; hold *<Posten>*; keep *<Haushalt>*; **v~ mit** provide with; **sich v~** make a mistake. **V~** *nt* **-s,-** oversight; *(Fehler)* slip; **aus V~** by mistake. **v~tlich** *adv* by mistake

Versehrte(r) *m* disabled person

versengen *vt* singe; *(stärker)* scorch

versenken *vt* sink

versessen *a* keen (**auf** + *acc* on)

versetz|en *vt* move; transfer *<Person>*; *(Sch)* move up; *(verpfänden)* pawn; *(verkaufen)* sell; *(vermischen)* blend; **jdn v~en** (🚽 *warten lassen*) stand s.o. up; **jdm in Angst/Erstaunen v~en** frighten/astonish s.o.; **sich in jds Lage v~en** put oneself in s.o.'s place. **V~ung** *f* -, **-en** move; transfer; *(Sch)* move to a higher class

verseuchen *vt* contaminate

versicher|n *vt* insure; *(bekräftigen)* affirm; **jdm v~n** assure s.o (**dass** that). **V~ung** *f* -, **-en** insurance; assurance

versiegeln *vt* seal

versiert /vɛrˈʒiːɐt/ *a* experienced

versilbert *a* silver-plated

Versmaß /ˈfɛrs-/ *nt* metre

versöhn|en *vt* reconcile; **sich v~en** become reconciled. **V~ung** *f* -, **-en** reconciliation

versorg|en *vt* provide, supply (**mit** with); provide for *<Familie>*;

(*betreuen*) look after. **V~ung** *f* - provision, supply; (*Betreuung*) care

verspät|en (sich) *vr* be late. **v~et** *a* late; *<Zug>* delayed; *<Dank>* belated. **V~ung** *f* - lateness; **V~ung haben** be late

versperren *vt* block; bar *<Weg>*

verspiel|en *vt* gamble away. **v~t** *a* playful

verspotten *vt* mock, ridicule

versprech|en† *vt* promise; **sich v~en** make a slip of the tongue; **sich** (*dat*) **viel v~en von** have high hopes of; **ein viel v~ender Anfang** a promising start. **V~en** *nt* **-s,-** promise. **V~ungen** *fpl* promises

verstaatlich|en *vt* nationalize. **V~ung** *f* - nationalization

Verstand *m* **-[e]s** mind; (*Vernunft*) reason; **den V~ verlieren** go out of one's mind

verständig *a* sensible; (*klug*) intelligent. **v~en** *vt* notify, inform; **sich v~en** communicate; (*sich verständlich machen*) make oneself understood. **V~ung** *f* - notification; communication; (*Einigung*) agreement

verständlich *a* comprehensible; (*deutlich*) clear; (*begrifflich*) understandable; **sich v~ machen** make oneself understood. **v~erweise** *adv* understandably

Verständnis *nt* **-ses** understanding

verstärk|en *vt* strengthen, reinforce; (*steigern*) intensify, increase; amplify *<Ton>*. **V~er** *m* **-s,-** amplifier. **V~ung** *f* reinforcement; increase; amplification; (*Truppen*) reinforcements *pl*

verstaubt *a* dusty

verstauchen *vt* sprain

Versteck *nt* **-[e]s, -e** hiding-place; **V~ spielen** play hide-and-seek. **v~en** *vt* hide; **sich v~en** hide

verstehen† *vt* understand; (*können*) know; **falsch v~** misunderstand; **sich v~en** understand one another; (*auskommen*) get on

versteiger|n *vt* auction. **V~ung** *f* auction

versteinert *a* fossilized

verstell|en *vt* adjust; (*versperren*) block; (*verändern*) disguise; **sich v~en** pretend. **V~ung** *f* - pretence

versteuern *vt* pay tax on

verstimm|t *a* disgruntled; *<Magen>* upset; (*Mus*) out of tune. **V~ung** *f* - ill humour; (*Magen-*) upset

verstockt *a* stubborn

verstopf|en *vt* plug; (*versperren*) block; **v~t** blocked; *<Person>* constipated. **V~ung** *f* **-, -en** blockage; (*Med*) constipation

verstorben *a* late, deceased. **V~e(r)** *m/f* deceased

verstört *a* bewildered

Verstoß *m* infringement. **v~en†** *vt* disown ● *vi* (*haben*) **v~en gegen** contravene, infringe

verstreuen *vt* scatter

verstümmeln *vt* mutilate; garble *<Text>*

Versuch *m* **-[e]s, -e** attempt; (*Experiment*) experiment. **v~en** *vt/i* (*haben*) try; **v~t sein** be tempted (**zu** to). **V~ung** *f* **-, -en** temptation

vertagen *vt* adjourn; (*aufschieben*) postpone; **sich v~** adjourn

vertauschen *vt* exchange; (*verwechseln*) mix up

verteidig|en *vt* defend. **V~er** *m* **-s,-** defender; (*Jur*) defence counsel. **V~ung** *f* **-, -en** defence

verteil|en *vt* distribute; (*zuteilen*) allocate; (*ausgeben*) hand out; (*verstreichen*) spread. **V~ung** *f* - distribution; allocation

vertief|en vt deepen; **v∼t sein in** (+ acc) be engrossed in. **V∼ung** f -, -en hollow, depression

vertikal /verti'ka:l/ a vertical

vertilgen vt exterminate; kill [off] <Unkraut>

vertippen (sich) vr make a typing mistake

vertonen vt set to music

Vertrag m -[e]s,∸e contract; (Pol) treaty

vertragen† vt tolerate, stand; take <Kritik, Spaß>; **sich v∼** get on

vertraglich a contractual

verträglich a good-natured; (bekömmlich) digestible

vertrauen vi (haben) trust (jdm/ etw s.o./sth; auf + acc in). **V∼** nt -s trust, confidence (zu in); **im V∼** in confidence. **v∼swürdig** a trustworthy

vertraulich a confidential; (intim) familiar

vertraut a intimate; (bekannt) familiar. **V∼heit** f - intimacy; familiarity

vertreib|en† vt drive away; drive out <Feind>; (Comm) sell; **sich** (dat) **die Zeit v∼en** pass the time. **V∼ung** f -, -en expulsion

vertret|en† vt represent; (einspringen für) stand in or deputize for; (verfechten) support; hold <Meinung>; **sich** (dat) **den Fuß v∼en** twist one's ankle. **V∼er** m -s,- representative; deputy; (Arzt-) locum; (Verfechter) supporter. **V∼ung** f -, -en representation; (Person) deputy; (eines Arztes) locum; (Handels-) agency

Vertrieb m -[e]s (Comm) sale

vertrocknen vi (sein) dry up

verüben vt commit

verunglücken vi (sein) be involved in an accident; (🛈 missglücken) go wrong; **tödlich v∼** be killed in an accident

verunreinigen vt pollute; (verseuchen) contaminate

verursachen vt cause

verurteil|en vt condemn; (Jur) convict (wegen of); sentence (**zum Tode** to death). **V∼ung** f - condemnation; (Jur) conviction

vervielfachen vt multiply

vervielfältigen vt duplicate

vervollständigen vt complete

verwählen (sich) vr misdial

verwahren vt keep; (verstauen) put away

verwahrlost a neglected; <Haus> dilapidated

Verwahrung f - keeping; **in V∼ nehmen** take into safe keeping

verwaist a orphaned

verwalt|en vt administer; (leiten) manage; govern <Land>. **V∼er** m -s,- administrator; manager. **V∼ung** f -, -en administration; management; government

verwand|eln vt transform, change (**in** + acc into) **sich v∼eln** change, turn (**in** + acc into). **V∼lung** f transformation

verwandt a related (**mit** to). **V∼e(r)** m/f relative. **V∼schaft** f - relationship; (Menschen) relatives pl

verwarn|en vt warn, caution. **V∼ung** f warning, caution

verwechs|eln vt mix up, confuse; (halten für) mistake (**mit** for). **V∼lung** f -, -en mix-up

verweiger|n vt/i (haben) refuse (jdm etw s.o sth). **V∼ung** f refusal

Verweis m -es, -e reference (**auf** + acc to); (Tadel) reprimand; **v∼en†** vt refer (**auf/an** + acc to); (tadeln) reprimand; **von der Schule v∼en** expel

verwelken vi (sein) wilt

verwend|en† vt use; spend <Zeit, Mühe>. **V∼ung** f use

verwerten vt utilize, use

verwesen vi (sein) decompose

verwick|eln vt involve (in + acc in); **sich v~eln** get tangled up. **v~elt** a complicated
verwildert a wild; *<Garten>* overgrown; *<Aussehen>* unkempt
verwinden† vt (fig) get over
verwirklichen vt realize
verwirr|en vt tangle up; (fig) confuse; **sich v~en** get tangled; (fig) become confused. **v~t** a confused. **V~ung** f - confusion
verwischen vt smudge
verwittert a weathered
verwitwet a widowed
verwöhn|en vt spoil. **v~t** a spoilt
verworren a confused
verwund|bar a vulnerable. **v~en** vt wound
verwunder|lich a surprising. **v~n** vt surprise; **sich v~n** be surprised. **V~ung** f - surprise
Verwund|ete(r) m wounded soldier; **die V~eten** the wounded pl. **V~ung** f -, -en wound
verwüst|en vt devastate, ravage. **V~ung** f -, -en devastation
verzählen (sich) vr miscount
verzaubern vt bewitch; (fig) enchant; **v~ in** (+ acc) turn into
Verzehr m -s consumption. **v~en** vt eat
verzeih|en† vt forgive; **v~en Sie!** excuse me! **V~ung** f - forgiveness; **um V~ung bitten** apologize; **V~ung!** sorry! (bei Frage) excuse me!
Verzicht m -[e]s renunciation (auf + acc of). **v~en** vi (haben) do without; **v~en auf** (+ acc) give up; renounce *<Recht, Erbe>*
verziehen† vt pull out of shape; (verwöhnen) spoil; **sich v~** lose shape; *<Holz:>* warp; *<Gesicht:>* twist; (verschwinden) disappear; *<Nebel:>* disperse; *<Gewitter:>* pass ● vi (sein) move [away]
verzier|en vt decorate. **V~ung** f -, -en decoration
verzinsen vt pay interest on

verzöger|n (verlangsam~
V~ung f -, -e
verzollen vt p
Sie etwas zu v~
anything to de
verzweifel|n vi
v~elt a despera
despair; (Ratlosig~
desperation
verzweigen (sich) vr branch [out]
Veto /'ve:to/ nt -s, -s veto
Vetter m -s, -n cousin
vgl. abbr (vergleiche) cf.
Viadukt /via'dʊkt/ nt -[e]s, -e viaduct
Video /'vi:deo/ nt -s, -s video. **V~kassette** f video cassette. **V~recorder** /-rəkɔrdɐ/ m -s,- video recorder. **~spiel** nt video game
Vieh nt -[e]s livestock; (Rinder) cattle pl; (🔲 Tier) creature
viel pron a great deal/🔲 a lot of; (pl) many, 🔲 a lot of; (substantivisch) **v~[es]** much, 🔲 a lot; **nicht/so/wie/zu v~** not/so/how/too much/ (pl) many; **v~e** pl many; **das v~e Geld** all that money ● adv much, 🔲 a lot; **v~ mehr/weniger** much more/less; **v~ zu groß/klein** much or far too big/small; **so v~ wie möglich** as much as possible
viel|deutig a ambiguous. **v~fach** a multiple ● adv many times; (🔲 oft) frequently. **V~falt** f - diversity, [great] variety
vielleicht adv perhaps, maybe; (🔲 wirklich) really
vielmals adv very much
vielmehr adv rather; (im Gegenteil) on the contrary
vielseitig a varied; *<Person>* versatile. **V~keit** f - versatility
vielversprechend* a viel versprechend, s. versprechen
vier inv a, **V~** f -, -en four; (Sch) ≈ fair. **V~eck** nt -[e]s, -e oblong,

V

…; (*Quadrat*) square. …kig *a* oblong, rectangular; …quare. V~**linge** *mpl* quadruplets
viertel /'fɪrtəl/ *inv a* quarter; **um v~ neun** at [a] quarter past eight; **um drei v~ neun** at [a] quarter to nine. **V~** *nt* **-s,-** quarter; (*Wein*) quarter litre; **V~ vor/nach sechs** [a] quarter to/past six. **V~finale** *nt* quarter-final. **V~jahr** *nt* three months *pl*; (*Comm*) quarter. **v~jährlich** *a & adv* quarterly. **V~stunde** *f* quarter of an hour
vier|zehn /'fɪr-/ *inv a* fourteen. **v~zehnte(r,s)** *a* fourteenth. **v~zig** *inv a* forty. **v~zigste(r,s)** *a* fortieth
Villa /'vɪla/ *f* **-, -len** villa
violett /vio'lɛt/ *a* violet
Vio|line /vio'li:nə/ *f* **-, -n** violin. **V~linschlüssel** *m* treble clef
Virus /'vi:rʊs/ *nt* **-, -ren** virus
Visier /vi'zi:ɐ̯/ *nt* **-s, -e** visor
Visite /vi'zi:tə/ *f* **-, -n** round; **V~ machen** do one's round
Visum /'vi:zʊm/ *nt* **-s, -sa** visa
Vitamin /vita'mi:n/ *nt* **-s, -e** vitamin
Vitrine /vi'tri:nə/ *f* **-, -n** display cabinet/(*im Museum*) case
Vizepräsident /'fi:tsə-/ *m* vice president
Vogel *m* **-s, ̈** bird; **einen V~ haben** 🄸 have a screw loose. **V~scheuche** *f* **-, -n** scarecrow
Vokabeln /vo'ka:bəln/ *fpl* vocabulary *sg*
Vokal /vo'ka:l/ *m* **-s, -e** vowel
Volant /vo'lã:/ *m* **-s, -s** flounce
Volk *nt* **-[e]s, ̈er** people *sg*; (*Bevölkerung*) people *pl*
Völker|kunde *f* ethnology. **V~mord** *m* genocide. **V~recht** *nt* international law
Volks|abstimmung *f* plebiscite. **V~fest** *nt* public festival. **V~hochschule** *f* adult education classes *pl*/(*Gebäude*) centre. **V~lied** *nt* folk-song. **V~tanz** *m* folk-dance. **v~tümlich** *a* popular. **V~wirt** *m* economist. **V~wirtschaft** *f* economics *sg*. **V~zählung** *f* [national] census
voll *a* full (**von** *od* **mit** of); <*Haar*> thick; <*Erfolg, Ernst*> complete; <*Wahrheit*> whole; **v~ machen** fill up; **v~ tanken** fill up with petrol ● *adv* (*ganz*) completely; <*arbeiten*> full-time; <*auszahlen*> in full; **v~ und ganz** completely
Vollblut *nt* thoroughbred
vollende|n *vt insep* complete. **v~t** *a* perfect
Vollendung *f* completion; (*Vollkommenheit*) perfection
voller *inv a* full of
Volleyball /'vɔli-/ *m* volleyball
vollführen *vt insep* perform
vollfüllen *vt sep* fill up
Vollgas *nt* **V~ geben** put one's foot down; **mit V~** flat out
völlig *a* complete
volljährig *a* **v~ sein** (*Jur*) be of age. **V~keit** *f* - (*Jur*) majority
Vollkaskoversicherung *f* fully comprehensive insurance
vollkommen *a* perfect; (*völlig*) complete
Voll|kornbrot *nt* wholemeal bread. **V~macht** *f* **-, -en** authority; (*Jur*) power of attorney. **V~mond** *m* full moon. **V~pension** *f* full board
vollständig *a* complete
vollstrecken *vt insep* execute; carry out <*Urteil*>
volltanken* *vi sep* (*haben*) **voll tanken**, *s.* **voll**
Volltreffer *m* direct hit
vollzählig *a* complete
vollziehen† *vt insep* carry out; perform <*Handlung*>; consummate <*Ehe*>; **sich v~** take place
Volt /vɔlt/ *nt* **-[s],-** volt
Volumen /vo'lu:mən/ *nt* **-s,-** volume
vom *prep* = **von dem**

von

● *preposition (+ dative)*

! Note that **von dem** can become **vom**

····▶ *(räumlich)* from; *(nach Richtungen)* of. **von hier an** from here on[ward]. **von Wien aus** [starting] from Vienna. **nördlich/ südlich von Mannheim** [to the] north/south of Mannheim. **rechts/links von mir** to the right/ left of me; on my right/left

····▶ *(zeitlich)* from. **von jetzt an** from now on. **von heute/morgen an** [as] from today/tomorrow; starting today/tomorrow

····▶ *(zur Angabe des Urhebers, der Ursache; nach Passiv)* by. **der Roman ist von Fontane** the novel is by Fontane. **sie hat ein Kind von ihm.** she has a child by him. **er ist vom Blitz erschlagen worden** he was killed by lightning

····▶ *(anstelle eines Genitivs; Zugehörigkeit, Beschaffenheit, Menge etc.)* of. **ein Stück von dem Kuchen** a piece of the cake. **einer von euch** one of you. **eine Fahrt von drei Stunden** a drive of three hours; a three-hour drive. **das Brot von gestern** yesterday's bread. **ein Tal von erstaunlicher Schönheit** a valley of extraordinary beauty

····▶ *(betreffend)* about. **handeln/ wissen/erzählen** *od* **reden von ...** be/know/talk about .... **eine Geschichte von zwei Elefanten** a story about *or* of two elephants

voneinander *adv* from each other; *<abhängig>* on each other

vonseiten *prep* (+ *gen*) on the part of

vonstatten *adv* **v~ gehen** take place

vor *prep* (+ *dat/acc*) in front of; *(zeitlich, Reihenfolge)* before; (+ *dat*) *(bei der Uhrzeit)* to; *<warnen, sich fürchten>* of; *<schützen, davonlaufen>* from; *<Respekt haben>* for; **vor Angst zittern** tremble with fear; **vor drei Tagen** three days ago; **vor allen Dingen** above all ● *adv* forward; **vor und zurück** backwards and forwards

Vorabend *m* eve

voran *adv* at the front; *(voraus)* ahead; *(vorwärts)* forward. **v~gehen†** *vi sep* (*sein*) lead the way; *(Fortschritte machen)* make progress. **v~kommen†** *vi sep* (*sein*) make progress, *(fig)* get on

Vor|anschlag *m* estimate. **V~anzeige** *f* advance notice. **V~arbeiter** *m* foreman

voraus *adv* ahead (*dat* of); *(vorn)* at the front; *(vorwärts)* forward ● **im Voraus** in advance. **v~bezahlen** *vt sep* pay in advance. **v~gehen†** *vi sep* (*sein*) go on ahead; **jdm/etw v~gehen** precede s.o./sth. **V~sage** *f* -, -n prediction. **v~sagen** *vt sep* predict

voraussetz|en *vt sep* take for granted; *(erfordern)* require; **vorausgesetzt, dass** provided that. **V~ung** *f* -, -en assumption; *(Erfordernis)* prerequisite

voraussichtlich ● anticipated, expected ● *adv* probably

Vorbehalt *m* -[e]s, -e reservation

vorbei *adv* past (**an** jdm/etw s.o./ sth); *(zu Ende)* over. **v~fahren†** *vi sep* (*sein*) drive/go past. **v~gehen†** *vi sep* (*sein*) go past; *(verfehlen)* miss; *(vergehen)* pass; (**I** *besuchen*) drop in (**bei** on)

vorbereit|en *vt sep* prepare; prepare for *<Reise>*; **sich v~en** prepare [oneself] (**auf** + *acc* for). **V~ung** *f* -, -en preparation

vorbestellen *vt sep* order/(*im Theater, Hotel*) book in advance

vorbestraft *a* v~ sein have a [criminal] record
Vorbeugung *f* - prevention
Vorbild *nt* model. **v~lich** *a* exemplary, model ● *adv* in an exemplary manner
vorbringen† *vt sep* put forward; offer <*Entschuldigung*>
vordatieren† *vt sep* post-date
Vorder|bein *nt* foreleg. **v~e(r,s)** *a* front. **V~grund** *m* foreground. **V~rad** *nt* front wheel. **V~seite** *f* front; (*einer Münze*) obverse. **v~ste(r,s)** *a* front, first. **V~teil** *nt* front
vor|drängeln (sich) *vr sep* 🔟 jump the queue. **v~drängen (sich)** *vr sep* push forward.
v~dringen† *vi sep* (*sein*) advance
voreilig *a* rash
voreingenommen *a* biased, prejudiced. **V~heit** *f* - bias
vorenthalten† *vt sep* withhold
vorerst *adv* for the time being
Vorfahr *m* -en, -en ancestor
Vorfahrt *f* right of way; '**V~ beachten**' 'give way'. **V~sstraße** *f* ≈ major road
Vorfall *m* incident. **v~en†** *vi sep* (*sein*) happen
vorfinden† *vt sep* find
Vorfreude *f* [happy] anticipation
vorführ|en *vt sep* present, show; (*demonstrieren*) demonstrate; (*aufführen*) perform. **V~ung** *f* presentation; demonstration; performance
Vor|gabe *f* (*Sport*) handicap. **V~gang** *m* occurrence; (*Techn*) process. **V~gänger(in)** *m* -s,- (*f* -, -nen) predecessor
vorgehen† *vi sep* (*sein*) go forward; (*voraus-*) go on ahead; <*Uhr:*> be fast; (*wichtig sein*) take precedence; (*verfahren*) act, proceed; (*geschehen*) happen, go on. **V~** *nt* -s action
vor|geschichtlich *a* prehistoric. **V~geschmack** *m* foretaste.

V~gesetzte(r) *m/f* superior.
v~gestern *adv* the day before yesterday; **v~gestern Abend** the evening before last
vorhaben† *vt sep* propose, intend (zu to); **etw v~** have sth planned. **V~** *nt* -s,- plan
Vorhand *f* (*Sport*) forehand
vorhanden *a* existing; **v~ sein** exist; be available
Vorhang *m* curtain
Vorhängeschloss *nt* padlock
vorher *adv* before[hand]
vorhergehend *a* previous
vorherrschend *a* predominant
Vorher|sage *f* -, -n prediction: (*Wetter-*) forecast. **v~sagen** *vt sep* predict; forecast <*Wetter*>.
v~sehen† *vt sep* foresee
vorhin *adv* just now
vorige(r,s) *a* last, previous
Vor|kehrungen *fpl* precautions.
V~kenntnisse *fpl* previous knowledge *sg*
vorkommen† *vi sep* (*sein*) happen; (*vorhanden sein*) occur; (*nach vorn kommen*) come forward; (*hervorkommen*) come out; (*zu sehen sein*) show; **jdm bekannt v~** seem familiar to s.o.
Vorkriegszeit *f* pre-war period
vorlad|en† *vt sep* (*Jur*) summons. **V~ung** *f* summons
Vorlage *f* model; (*Muster*) pattern; (*Gesetzes-*) bill
vorlassen† *vt sep* admit; **jdn v~** 🔟 let s.o. pass; (*den Vortritt lassen*) let s.o. go first
Vor|lauf *m* (*Sport*) heat. **V~läufer** *m* forerunner. **v~läufig** *a* provisional; (*zunächst*) for the time being. **V~laut** *a* forward. **V~leben** *nt* past
vorleg|en *vt sep* put on <*Kette*>; (*unterbreiten*) present; (*vorzeigen*) show. **V~er** *m* -s,- mat; (*Bett-*) rug
vorles|en† *vt sep* read [out]; **jdm v~en** read to s.o. **V~ung** *f* lecture

vorletzt|e(r,s) *a* last ... but one;
v~es Jahr the year before last

Vorliebe *f* preference

vorliegen† *vt sep* (*haben*) be
present/(*verfügbar*) available;
(*bestehen*) exist, be

vorlügen† *vt sep* lie (*dat* to)

vormachen *vt sep* put up; put on
<*Kette*>; push <*Riegel*>; (*zeigen*)
demonstrate; **jdm etwas v~** (⚠
täuschen) kid s.o.

Vormacht *f* supremacy

vormals *adv* formerly

vormerken *vt sep* make a note of;
(*reservieren*) reserve

Vormittag *m* morning; **gestern/
heute V~** yesterday/this morning.
v~s *adv* in the morning

Vormund *m* -[e]s, -munde &
-münder guardian

vorn *adv* at the front; **nach v~** to
the front; **von v~** from the front/
(*vom Anfang*) beginning; **von v~
anfangen** start afresh

Vorname *m* first name

vorne *adv* = **vorn**

vornehm *a* distinguished; smart

vornehmen† *vt sep* carry out; **sich**
(*dat*) **v~, etw zu tun** plan to do sth

vornherein *adv* **von v~herein** from
the start

Vor|ort *m* suburb. **V~rang** *m*
priority, precedence (**vor** + *dat*
over). **V~rat** *m* -[e]s, -̈e supply,
stock (**an** + *dat* of). **v~rätig** *a*
available; **v~rätig haben** have in
stock. **V~ratskammer** *f* larder.
V~recht *nt* privilege. **V~richtung**
f device

Vorrunde *f* qualifying round

vorsagen *vt/i sep* (*haben*) recite;
jdm v~ tell s.o. the answer

Vor|satz *m* resolution. **v~sätzlich**
a deliberate; (*Jur*) premeditated

Vorschau *f* preview; (*Film-*)
trailer

Vorschein *m* **zum V~kommen**
appear

Vorschlag *m* suggestion,
proposal. **v~en†** *vt sep* suggest,
propose

vorschnell *a* rash

vorschreiben† *vt sep* lay down;
dictate (*dat* to); **vorgeschriebene
Dosis** prescribed dose

Vorschrift *f* regulation;
(*Anweisung*) instruction; **jdm
V~en machen** tell s.o. what to do.
v~smäßig *a* correct

Vorschule *f* nursery school

Vorschuss *m* advance

vorseh|en† *v sep* ● *vt* intend
(**für/als** for/as); (*planen*) plan; **sich
v~en** be careful (**vor** + *dat* of)
● *vi* (*haben*) peep out. **V~ung** *f* -
providence

Vorsicht *f* - care; (*bei Gefahr*)
caution; **V~!** careful! (*auf Schild*)
'caution'. **v~ig** *a* careful;
cautious. **V~smaßnahme** *f*
precaution

Vorsilbe *f* prefix

Vorsitz *m* chairmanship; **den V~
führen** be in the chair. **V~ende(r)**
m/f chairman

Vorsorge *f* **V~ treffen** take
precautions; make provisions (**für**
for). **v~n** *vi sep* (*haben*) provide
(**für** for)

Vorspeise *f* starter

Vorspiel *nt* prelude. **v~en** *v sep*
● *vt* perform/ (*Mus*) play (*dat*
for) ● *vi* (*haben*) audition

vorsprechen† *v sep* ● *vt* recite;
(*zum Nachsagen*) say (*dat* to) ● *vi*
(*haben*) (*Theat*) audition; **bei jdm
v~** call on s.o.

Vor|sprung *m* projection; (*Fels-*)
ledge; (*Vorteil*) lead (**vor** + *dat*
over). **V~stadt** *f* suburb.
V~stand *m* board [of directors];
(*Vereins-*) committee; (*Partei-*)
executive

vorsteh|en† *vi sep* (*haben*)
project, protrude; **einer Abteilung
v~en** be in charge of a
department. **V~er** *m* -s,- head

vorstell|en vt sep put forward <Bein, Uhr>; (darstellen) represent; (bekanntmachen) introduce; **sich v~en** introduce oneself; (als Bewerber) go for an interview; **sich** (dat) **etw v~en** imagine sth. **V~ung** f introduction; (bei Bewerbung) interview; (Aufführung) performance; (Idee) idea; (Phantasie) imagination. **V~ungsgespräch** nt interview

Vorstoß m advance

Vorstrafe f previous conviction

Vortag m day before

vortäuschen vt sep feign, fake

Vorteil m advantage. **v~haft** a advantageous; flattering

Vortrag m **-[e]s,-̈e** talk; (wissenschaftlich) lecture. **v~en†** vt sep perform; (aufsagen) recite; (singen) sing; (darlegen) present (dat to)

vortrefflich a excellent

Vortritt m precedence; **jdm den V~ lassen** let s.o. go first

vorüber adv **v~ sein** be over; **an etw** (dat) **v~** past sth. **v~gehend** a temporary

Vor|urteil nt prejudice. **V~verkauf** m advance booking

vorverlegen vt sep bring forward

Vor|wahl[nummer] f dialling code. **V~wand** m **-[e]s,-̈e** pretext; (Ausrede) excuse

vorwärts adv forward[s]; **v~ kommen** make progress; (fig) get on or ahead

vorwegnehmen† vt sep anticipate

vorweisen† vt sep show

vorwiegend adv predominantly

Vorwort nt (pl **-worte**) preface

Vorwurf m reproach; **jdm Vorwürfe machen** reproach s.o. **v~svoll** a reproachful

Vorzeichen nt sign; (fig) omen

vorzeigen vt sep show

vorzeitig a premature

vorziehen† vt sep pull forward; draw <Vorhang>; (lieber mögen) prefer; favour

Vor|zimmer nt ante-room; (Büro) outer office. **V~zug** m preference; (gute Eigenschaft) merit, virtue; (Vorteil) advantage

vorzüglich a excellent

vulgär /vʊlˈgɛːɐ̯/ a vulgar ● adv in a vulgar way

Vulkan /vʊlˈkaːn/ m **-s, -e** volcano

Ww

Waage f **-, -n** scales pl; (Astr) Libra. **w~recht** a horizontal

Wabe f **-, -n** honeycomb

wach a awake; (aufgeweckt) alert; **w~ werden** wake up

Wach|e f **-, -n** guard; (Posten) sentry; (Dienst) guard duty; (Naut) watch; (Polizei-) station. **W~e halten** keep watch. **W~hund** m guard-dog

Wacholder m **-s** juniper

Wachposten m sentry

Wachs nt **-es** wax

wachsam a vigilant. **W~keit** f - vigilance

wachsen†¹ vi (sein) grow

wachs|en² vt (reg) wax. **W~figur** f waxwork

Wachstum nt **-s** growth

Wächter m **-s,-** guard; (Park-) keeper; (Parkplatz-) attendant

Wacht|meister m [police] constable. **W~posten** m sentry

wackel|ig a wobbly; <Stuhl> rickety; <Person> shaky. **W~kontakt** m loose connection. **w~n** vi (haben) wobble; (zittern) shake

Wade f -, -n (*Anat*) calf
Waffe f -, -n weapon; **W~n** arms
Waffel f -, -n waffle; (*Eis-*) wafer
Waffen|ruhe f cease-fire.
  W~schein m firearms licence.
  W~stillstand m armistice
Wagemut m daring
wagen vt risk; **es w~**, **etw zu tun**
  dare [to] do sth; **sich w~** (*gehen*)
  venture
Wagen m -s,- cart; (*Eisenbahn-*)
  carriage, coach; (*Güter-*) wagon;
  (*Kinder-*) pram; (*Auto*) car.
  W~heber m -s,- jack
Waggon /va'gõ:/ m -s, -s wagon
Wahl f -, -en choice; (*Pol, Admin*)
  election; (*geheime*) ballot; **zweite**
  W~ (*Comm*) seconds pl
wähl|en vt/i (*haben*) choose; (*Pol,
  Admin*) elect; (*stimmen*) vote;
  (*Teleph*) dial. **W~er(in)** m -s,-
  (f -, -nen) voter. **w~erisch** a
  choosy, fussy
Wahl|fach nt optional subject.
  w~frei a optional. **W~kampf** m
  election campaign. **W~kreis** m
  constituency. **W~lokal** nt
  polling-station. **w~los** a
  indiscriminate
Wahl|spruch m motto. **W~urne** f
  ballot-box
Wahn m -[e]s delusion; (*Manie*)
  mania
Wahnsinn m madness. **w~ig** a
  mad, insane; (🄵 *unsinnig*) crazy;
  (🄵 *groß*) terrible; **w~ig werden** go
  mad ● adv 🄵 terribly. **W~ige(r)**
  m/f maniac
wahr a true; (*echt*) real; **du**
  kommst doch, nicht w~? you are
  coming, aren't you?
während prep (+ gen) during
  ● conj while; (*wohingegen*)
  whereas
Wahrheit f -, -en truth.
  w~sgemäß a truthful
wahrnehm|en† vt sep notice;
  (*nutzen*) take advantage of;
  exploit <*Vorteil*>; look after

<*Interessen*>. **W~ung** f -, -en
  perception
Wahrsagerin f -, -nen fortune
  teller
wahrscheinlich a probable.
  W~keit f - probability
Währung f -, -en currency
Wahrzeichen nt symbol
Waise f -, -n orphan. **W~nhaus** nt
  orphanage. **W~nkind** nt orphan
Wal m -[e]s, -e whale
Wald m -[e]s, -er wood; (*groß*)
  forest. **w~ig** a wooded
Walis|er m -s,- Welshman.
  w~isch a Welsh
Wall m -[e]s, -e mound
Wallfahr|er(in) m(f) pilgrim. **W~t**
  f pilgrimage
Walnuss f walnut
Walze f -, -n roller. **w~n** vt roll
Walzer m -s,- waltz
Wand f -, -e wall; (*Trenn-*)
  partition; (*Seite*) side; (*Fels-*) face
Wandel m -s change
Wander|er m -s,-, **W~in** f -, -nen
  hiker, rambler. **w~n** vi (*sein*)
  hike, ramble; (*ziehen*) travel;
  (*gemächlich gehen*) wander;
  (*ziellos*) roam. **W~schaft** f -
  travels pl. **W~ung** f -, -en hike,
  ramble. **W~weg** m footpath
Wandlung f -, -en change,
  transformation
Wand|malerei f mural. **W~tafel** f
  blackboard. **W~teppich** m
  tapestry
Wange f -, -n cheek
wann adv when
Wanne f -, -n tub
Wanze f -, -n bug
Wappen nt -s,- coat of arms.
  W~kunde f heraldry
war, wäre s. **sein**[1]
Ware f -, -n article; (*Comm*)
  commodity; (*coll*) merchandise;
  W~n goods. **W~nhaus** nt
  department store. **W~nprobe** f
  sample. **W~nzeichen** nt
  trademark

warm a warm; <*Mahlzeit*> hot;
w~ machen heat ● adv warmly;
w~ essen have a hot meal
Wärm|e f - warmth; (*Phys*) heat;
10 Grad W~e 10 degrees above
zero. **w~en** vt warm; heat
<*Essen, Wasser*>. **W~flasche** f
hot-water bottle
Warn|blinkanlage f hazard
[warning] lights pl. **w~en** vt/i
(*haben*) warn (**vor** + dat of).
W~ung f -, **-en** warning
Warteliste f waiting list
warten vi (*haben*) wait (**auf** + acc
for) ● vt service
Wärter(in) m -s,- (f -, -nen) keeper;
(*Museums-*) attendant;
(*Gefängnis-*) warder; (*Kranken-*)
orderly
Warte|raum, W~saal m
waiting-room. **W~zimmer** nt
(*Med*) waiting-room
Wartung f - (*Techn*) service
warum adv why
Warze f -, **-n** wart
was pron what ● rel pron that;
alles, was ich brauche all [that] I
need ● indef pron (🛈 *etwas*)
something; (*fragend, verneint*)
anything; **so was Ärgerliches!**
what a nuisance! ● adv 🛈
(*warum*) why; (*wie*) how
wasch|bar a washable.
W~becken nt wash-basin
Wäsche f - washing; (*Unter-*)
underwear
waschecht a colour-fast
Wäscheklammer f clothes-peg
waschen† vt wash; **sich w~** have
a wash; **W~ und Legen** shampoo
and set ● vi (*haben*) do the
washing
Wäscherei f -, **-en** laundry
Wäsche|schleuder f spin-drier.
W~trockner m tumble-drier
Wasch|küche f laundry-room.
W~lappen m face-flannel.
W~maschine f washing
machine. **W~mittel** nt detergent.

W~pulver nt washing-powder.
W~zettel m blurb
Wasser nt -s water. **W~ball** m
beach-ball; (*Spiel*) water polo.
w~dicht a watertight;
<*Kleidung*> waterproof. **W~fall** m
waterfall. **W~farbe** f water-
colour. **W~hahn** m tap. **W~kraft**
f water-power. **W~kraftwerk** nt
hydroelectric power-station.
W~leitung f water-main; **aus der
W~leitung** from the tap.
W~mann m (*Astr*) Aquarius
wässern vt soak; (*begießen*) water
● vi (*haben*) water
Wasser|ski nt -s water-skiing.
W~stoff m hydrogen. **W~straße**
f waterway. **W~waage** f spirit-
level
wässrig a watery
watscheln vi (*sein*) waddle
Watt nt -s,- (*Phys*) watt
Watt|e f - cotton wool. **w~iert** a
padded; (*gesteppt*) quilted
WC /veːˈtseː/ nt -s, -s WC
web|en vt/i (*haben*) weave. **W~er**
m -s,- weaver
Web|seite /ˈvɛp-/ f web page.
W~site /-sait/ f -, -s website
Webstuhl m loom
Wechsel m -s,- change; (*Tausch*)
exchange; (*Comm*) bill of
exchange. **W~geld** nt change.
w~haft a changeable. **W~jahre**
npl menopause sg. **W~kurs** m
exchange rate. **w~n** vt change;
(*tauschen*) exchange ● vi (*haben*)
change; vary. **w~nd** a changing;
varying. **W~strom** m alternating
current. **W~stube** f bureau de
change
weck|en vt wake [up]; (*fig*)
awaken ● vi (*haben*) <*Wecker:*>
go off. **W~er** m -s,- alarm [clock]
wedeln vi (*haben*) wave; **mit dem
Schwanz w~** wag its tail
weder conj **w~ ... noch** neither ...
nor

Weg *m* -[e]s, -e way; (*Fuß*-) path; (*Fahr*-) track; (*Gang*) errand; **sich auf den Weg machen** set off

weg *adv* away, off; (*verschwunden*) gone; **weg sein** be away; (*gegangen/verschwunden*) have gone; **Hände weg!** hands off!

wegen *prep* (+ *gen*) because of; (*um … willen*) for the sake of

weg|fahren† *vi sep* (*sein*) go away; (*abfahren*) leave. **W~fahrsperre** *f* immobilizer. **w~fallen**† *vi sep* (*sein*) be dropped/(*ausgelassen*) omitted; (*entfallen*) no longer apply. **w~geben**† *vt sep* give away. **w~gehen**† *vi sep* (*sein*) leave, go away; (*ausgehen*) go out. **w~kommen**† *vi sep* (*sein*) get away; (*verloren gehen*) disappear; **schlecht w~kommen** 🛈 get a raw deal. **w~lassen**† *vt sep* let go; (*auslassen*) omit. **w~laufen**† *vi sep* (*sein*) run away. **w~räumen** *vt sep* put away; (*entfernen*) clear away. **w~schicken** *vt sep* send away; (*abschicken*) send off. **w~tun**† *vt sep* put away; (*wegwerfen*) throw away

Wegweiser *m* -s,- signpost

weg|werfen† *vt sep* throw away. **w~ziehen**† *v sep* ● *vt* pull away ● *vi* (*sein*) move away

weh *a* sore; **weh tun** hurt; <*Kopf, Rücken:*> ache; **jdm weh tun** hurt s.o.

wehe *int* alas; **w~ [dir/euch]!** (*drohend*) don't you dare!

wehen *vi* (*haben*) blow; (*flattern*) flutter ● *vt* blow

Wehen *fpl* contractions

Wehr[1] *nt* -[e]s, -e weir

Wehr[2] *f* sich zur **W~ setzen** resist. **W~dienst** *m* military service. **W~dienstverweigerer** *m* -s,- conscientious objector

wehren (sich) *vr* resist; (*gegen Anschuldigung*) protest; (*sich sträuben*) refuse

wehr|los *a* defenceless. **W~macht** *f* armed forces *pl.* **W~pflicht** *f* conscription

Weib *nt* -[e]s, -er woman; (*Ehe*-) wife. **W~chen** *nt* -s,- (*Zool*) female. **w~lich** *a* feminine; (*Biol*) female

weich *a* soft; (*gar*) done

Weiche *f* -, -n (*Rail*) points *pl*

Weich|heit *f* - softness. **w~lich** *a* soft; <*Charakter*> weak. **W~spüler** *m* -s,- (*Tex*) conditioner. **W~tier** *nt* mollusc

Weide[1] *f* -, -n (*Bot*) willow

Weide[2] *f* -, -n pasture. **w~n** *vt/i* (*haben*) graze

weiger|n (sich) *vr* refuse. **W~ung** *f* -, -en refusal

Weihe *f* -, -n consecration; (*Priester*-) ordination. **w~n** *vt* consecrate; (*zum Priester*) ordain

Weiher *m* -s,- pond

Weihnacht|en *nt* -s & *pl* Christmas. **w~lich** *a* Christmassy. **W~sbaum** *m* Christmas tree. **W~slied** *nt* Christmas carol. **W~smann** *m* (*pl* -männer) Father Christmas. **W~stag** *m* **erster/zweiter W~stag** Christmas Day/Boxing Day

Weih|rauch *m* incense. **W~wasser** *nt* holy water

weil *conj* because; (*da*) since

Weile *f* - while

Wein *m* -[e]s, -e wine; (*Bot*) vines *pl*; (*Trauben*) grapes *pl.* **W~bau** *m* wine-growing. **W~berg** *m* vineyard. **W~brand** *m* -[e]s brandy

weinen *vt/i* (*haben*) cry, weep

Wein|glas *nt* wineglass. **W~karte** *f* wine-list. **W~lese** *f* grape harvest. **W~liste** *f* wine-list. **W~probe** *f* wine-tasting. **W~rebe** *f*, **W~stock** *m* vine. **W~stube** *f* wine-bar. **W~traube** *f* bunch of grapes; (*W~beere*) grape

weise *a* wise

Weise f -, -n way; (*Melodie*) tune
Weisheit f -, -en wisdom.
W~szahn m wisdom tooth
weiß a, **W~** nt -,- white
weissag|en vt/i insep (*haben*)
prophesy. **W~ung** f -, -en
prophecy
Weiß|brot nt white bread. **W~e(r)**
m/f white man/woman. **w~en** vt
whitewash. **W~wein** m white
wine
Weisung f -, -en instruction;
(*Befehl*) order
weit a wide; (*ausgedehnt*)
extensive; (*lang*) long ● adv
widely; <*offen, öffnen*> wide;
(*lang*) far; von **w~em** from a
distance; **bei w~em** by far; **w~**
und breit far and wide; **ist es noch**
w~? is it much further? **so w~**
wie möglich as far as possible; **ich**
bin so w~ I'm ready; **w~**
verbreitet widespread; **w~**
reichende Folgen far-reaching
consequences
Weite f -, -n expanse; (*Entfernung*)
distance; (*Größe*) width. **w~n** vt
widen; stretch <*Schuhe*>
weiter a further ● adv further;
(*außerdem*) in addition;
(*anschließend*) then; **etw w~ tun**
go on doing sth; **w~ nichts/**
niemand nothing/no one else; **und**
so w~ and so on
weiter|e(r,s) a further; **ohne w~es**
just like that; (*leicht*) easily
weiter|erzählen vt sep go on
with; (*w~sagen*) repeat.
w~fahren† vi sep (*sein*) go on.
w~geben† vt sep pass on. **w~hin**
adv (*immer noch*) still; (*in*
Zukunft) in future; (*außerdem*)
furthermore; **etw w~hin tun** go on
doing sth. **w~machen** vi sep
(*haben*) carry on
weit|gehend a extensive ● adv to
a large extent. **w~sichtig** a
long-sighted; (*fig*) far-sighted.
W~sprung m long jump.

w~verbreitet* a **w~ verbreitet**, s.
weit
Weizen m -s wheat
welch inv pron what; **w~ ein(e)**
what a. **w~e(r,s)** pron which; **um**
w~e Zeit? at what time? ● rel
pron which; (*Person*) who ● indef
pron some; (*fragend*) any; **was für**
w~e? what sort of?
Wellblech nt corrugated iron
Well|e f -, -n wave; (*Techn*) shaft.
W~enlänge f wavelength.
W~enlinie f wavy line.
W~enreiten nt surfing.
W~ensittich m -s, -e budgerigar.
w~ig a wavy
Welt f -, -en world; **auf der W~** in
the world; **auf die** od **zur W~**
kommen be born. **W~all** nt
universe. **w~berühmt** a world-
famous. **w~fremd** a unworldly.
W~kugel f globe. **w~lich** a
worldly; (*nicht geistlich*) secular
Weltmeister|(in) m(f) world
champion. **W~schaft** f world
championship
Weltraum m space. **W~fahrer** m
astronaut
Weltrekord m world record
wem pron (*dat of* **wer**) to whom
wen pron (*acc of* **wer**) whom
Wende f -, -n change. **W~kreis** m
(*Geog*) tropic
Wendeltreppe f spiral staircase
wenden¹ vt (*reg*) turn ● vi
(*haben*) turn [round]
wenden²† (& *reg*) vt turn; **sich w~**
turn; **sich an jdn w~** turn/
(*schriftlich*) write to s.o.
Wend|epunkt m (*fig*) turning-
point. **W~ung** f -, -en turn;
(*Biegung*) bend; (*Veränderung*)
change
wenig pron little; (*pl*) few; **so/zu**
w~ so/too little/(*pl*) few; **w~e** pl
few ● adv little; (*kaum*) not
much; **so w~ wie möglich** as little
as possible. **w~er** pron less; (*pl*)
fewer; **immer w~er** less and less

● *adv & conj* less. **w~ste(r,s)**
least; **am w~sten** least [of all].
w~stens *adv* at least

wenn *conj* if; (*sobald*) when;
immer w~ whenever; **w~ nicht** *od*
außer w~ unless; **w~ auch** even
though

wer *pron* who; (⊞ *jemand*)
someone; (*fragend*) anyone

Werbe|agentur *f* advertising
agency. **w~n†** *vt* recruit; attract
<*Kunden, Besucher*> ● *vi* (*haben*)
w~n für advertise; canvass for
<*Partei*>. **W~spot** /-sp-/ *m*
-s, -s commercial

Werbung *f* - advertising

----

werden†
● *intransitive verb* (*sein*)
••••▷ (+ *adjective*) become; get;
(*allmählich*) grow. **müde/alt/**
länger werden become *or* get/
grow tired/old/longer. **taub/**
blind/wahnsinnig werden go
deaf/blind/mad. **blass werden**
become *or* turn pale. **krank**
werden become *or* fall ill. **es wird**
warm/dunkel it is getting warm/
dark. **mir wurde schlecht** I began
to feel sick
••••▷ (+ *noun*) become. **Arzt/Lehrer/**
Mutter werden become a doctor/
teacher/mother. **er will Lehrer**
werden he wants to be a teacher.
was ist aus ihm geworden? what
has become of him?
••••▷ **werden zu** become; turn into.
das Erlebnis wurde zu einem
Albtraum the experience became
or turned into a nightmare. **zu**
Eis werden turn into ice
● *auxiliary verb*
••••▷ (*Zukunft*) will; shall. **er wird**
bald hier sein he will *or* he'll
soon be here. **wir werden sehen**
we shall see. **es wird bald regnen**
it's going to rain soon
••••▷ (*Konjunktiv*) **würde(n)** would.
ich würde es kaufen, wenn … I

would buy it if …. **würden Sie so**
nett sein? would you be so kind?
••••▷ (*beim Passiv; pp* **worden**) be.
geliebt/geboren werden be loved/
born. **du wirst gerufen** you are
being called. **er wurde gebeten** he
was asked. **es wurde gemunkelt** it
was rumoured. **mir wurde gesagt,**
dass … I was told that …. **das**
Haus ist soeben/1995 renoviert
worden the house has just been
renovated/was renovated in
1995

----

werfen† *vt* throw; cast <*Blick,*
Schatten>; **sich w~** <*Holz:*> warp

Werft *f* -, **-en** shipyard

Werk *nt* **-[e]s, -e** work; (*Fabrik*)
works *sg*, factory; (*Trieb-*)
mechanism. **W~en** *nt* **-s** (*Sch*)
handicraft. **W~statt** *f* -,**¨-en**
workshop; (*Auto-*) garage.
W~tag *m* weekday. **w~tags** *adv*
on weekdays. **w~tätig** *a*
working

Werkzeug *nt* tool; (*coll*) tools *pl*.
W~leiste *f* toolbar

Wermut *m* **-s** vermouth

wert *a* **viel w~** worth a lot; **nichts**
w~ sein be worthless; **jds w~ sein**
be worthy of s.o. **W~** *m* **-[e]s, -e**
value; (*Nenn-*) denomination; **im**
W~ von worth. **w~en** *vt* rate

Wert|gegenstand *m* object of
value. **w~los** *a* worthless.
W~minderung *f* depreciation.
W~papier *nt* (*Comm*) security.
W~sachen *fpl* valuables. **w~voll**
a valuable

Wesen *nt* **-s,-** nature; (*Lebe-*)
being; (*Mensch*) creature

wesentlich *a* essential;
(*grundlegend*) fundamental ● *adv*
considerably, much

weshalb *adv* why

Wespe *f* -, **-n** wasp

wessen *pron* (*gen of* **wer**) whose

westdeutsch *a* West German

Weste *f* -, **-n** waistcoat

Westen m -s west

Western m -[s],- western

Westfale m -n -n Westphalia

Westindien nt West Indies pl

west|lich a western; <Richtung> westerly ● adv & prep (+ gen) **w~lich [von] der Stadt** [to the] west of the town. **w~wärts** adv westwards

weswegen adv why

Wettbewerb m -s, -e competition

Wette f -, -n bet; **um die W~ laufen** race (**mit jdm** s.o.)

wetten vt/i (haben) bet (**auf** + acc on); **mit jdm w~** have a bet with s.o.

Wetter nt -s,- weather; (Un-) storm. **W~bericht** m weather report. **W~vorhersage** f weather forecast. **W~warte** f -, -n meteorological station

Wett|kampf m contest. **W~kämpfer(in)** m(f) competitor. **W~lauf** m race. **W~rennen** nt race. **W~streit** m contest

Whisky m -s whisky

wichtig a important; **w~ nehmen** take seriously. **W~keit** f - importance

Wicke f -, -n sweet pea

Wickel m -s,- compress

wickeln vt wind; (ein-) wrap; (bandagieren) bandage; **ein Kind frisch w~** change a baby

Widder m -s,- ram; (Astr) Aries

wider prep (+ acc) contrary to; **w~ Willen** against one's will

widerlegen vt insep refute

wider|lich a repulsive. **W~rede** f contradiction; **keine W~rede!** don't argue!

widerrufen† vt/i insep (haben) retract; revoke <Befehl>

Widersacher m -s,- adversary

widersetzen (sich) vr insep resist (**jdm/etw** s.o./sth)

widerspiegeln vt sep reflect

widersprechen† vi insep (haben) contradict (**jdm/etw** s.o./sth)

Wider|spruch m contradiction; (Protest) protest. **w~sprüchlich** a contradictory. **w~spruchslos** adv without protest

Widerstand m resistance; **W~ leisten** resist. **w~sfähig** a resistant; (Bot) hardy

widerstehen† vi insep (haben) resist (**jdm/etw** s.o./sth); (anwidern) be repugnant (**jdm** to s.o.)

Widerstreben nt -s reluctance

widerwärtig a disagreeable

Widerwill|e m aversion, repugnance. **w~ig** a reluctant

widm|en vt dedicate (dat to); (verwenden) devote (dat to); **sich w~en** (+ dat) devote oneself to. **W~ung** f -, -en dedication

wie adv how; **wie viel** how much/ (pl) many; **um wie viel Uhr?** at what time? **wie viele?** how many? **wie ist Ihr Name?** what is your name? **wie ist das Wetter?** what is the weather like? ● conj as; (gleich wie) like; (sowie) as well as; (als) when, as; **so gut wie** good as; **nichts wie** nothing but

wieder adv again; **jdn/etw w~ erkennen** recognize s.o./sth; **etw w~ verwenden/verwerten** reuse/ recycle sth; **etw w~ gutmachen** make up for <Schaden>; redress <Unrecht>; (bezahlen) pay for sth

Wiederaufbau m reconstruction

wieder|bekommen† vt sep get back. **W~belebung** f - resuscitation. **w~bringen†** vt sep bring back. **w~erkennen*** vt sep **w~ erkennen**, s. **wieder**. **w~geben†** vt sep give back, return; (darstellen) portray; (ausdrücken, übersetzen) render; (zitieren) quote. **W~geburt** f reincarnation

Wiedergutmachung f - reparation; (*Entschädigung*) compensation

wiederherstellen vt sep reestablish; restore <*Gebäude*>; restore to health <*Kranke*>

wiederhol|en vt insep repeat; (*Sch*) revise; **sich w~en** recur; <*Person:*> repeat oneself. **w~t** a repeated. **W~ung** f -, -en repetition; (*Sch*) revision

Wieder|hören nt **auf W~hören!** goodbye! **W~käuer** m -s,- ruminant. **W~kehr** f - return; (*W~holung*) recurrence. **w~kommen**† vi sep (sein) come back

wiedersehen* vt sep **wieder sehen**, s. **sehen**. **W~** nt -s,- reunion; **auf W~!** goodbye!

wiedervereinig|en* vt sep **wieder vereinigen**, s. **vereinigen**. **W~ung** f reunification

wieder|verwenden* vt sep **w~ verwenden**, s. **wieder**. **w~verwerten*** vt sep **w~ verwerten**, s. **wieder**

Wiege f -, -n cradle

wiegen¹† vt/i (haben) weigh

wiegen² vt (reg) rock. **W~lied** nt lullaby

wiehern vi (haben) neigh

Wien nt -s Vienna. **W~er** a Viennese ● m -s,- Viennese ● f -,- ≈ frankfurter. **w~erisch** a Viennese

Wiese f -, -n meadow

Wiesel nt -s,- weasel

wieso adv why

wieviel* pron **wie viel**, s. **wie**. **w~te(r,s)** a which; **der W~te ist heute?** what is the date today?

wieweit adv how far

wild a wild; <*Stamm*> savage; **w~er Streik** wildcat strike; **w~ wachsen** grow wild. **W~** nt -[e]s game; (*Rot-*) deer; (*Culin*) venison. **W~e(r)** m/f savage

Wilder|er m -s,- poacher. **w~n** vt/i (haben) poach

Wild|heger, W~hüter m -s,- gamekeeper. **W~leder** nt suede. **W~nis** f - wilderness. **W~schwein** nt wild boar. **W~westfilm** m western

Wille m -ns will

Willenskraft f will-power

willig a willing

willkommen a welcome; **w~ heißen** welcome. **W~** nt -s welcome

wimmeln vi (haben) swarm

wimmern vi (haben) whimper

Wimpel m -s,- pennant

Wimper f -, -n [eye]lash; **W~ntusche** f mascara

Wind m -[e]s, -e wind

Winde f -, -n (*Techn*) winch

Windel f -, -n nappy

winden† vt wind; make <*Kranz*>; **in die Höhe w~** winch up; **sich w~** wind; (*sich krümmen*) writhe

Wind|hund m greyhound. **w~ig** a windy. **W~mühle** f windmill. **W~park** m wind farm. **W~pocken** fpl chickenpox sg. **W~schutzscheibe** f windscreen. **W~stille** f calm. **W~stoß** m gust of wind. **W~surfen** nt windsurfing

Windung f -, -en bend; (*Spirale*) spiral

Winkel m -s,- angle; (*Ecke*) corner. **W~messer** m -s,- protractor

winken vi (haben) wave

Winter m -s,- winter. **w~lich** a wintry; (*Winter-*) winter ... **W~schlaf** m hibernation; **W~sport** m winter sports pl

Winzer m -s,- winegrower

winzig a tiny, minute

Wipfel m -s,- [tree-]top

Wippe f -, -n see-saw

wir pron we; **wir sind es** it's us

Wirbel m -s,- eddy; (*Drehung*) whirl; (*Trommel-*) roll; (*Anat*)

vertebra; (*Haar-*) crown; (*Aufsehen*) fuss. **w~n** vt/i (*sein/haben*) whirl. **W~säule** f spine. **W~sturm** m cyclone. **W~tier** nt vertebrate. **W~wind** m whirlwind

wird s. **werden**

wirken vi (*haben*) have an effect (**auf** + acc on); (*zur Geltung kommen*) be effective; (*tätig sein*) work; (*scheinen*) seem ● vt (*Tex*) knit

wirklich a real. **W~keit** f -, **-en** reality

wirksam a effective

Wirkung f -, **-en** effect. **w~slos** a ineffective. **w~svoll** a effective

wirr a tangled; <*Haar*> tousled; (*verwirrt, verworren*) confused

Wirt m -[e]s, **-e** landlord. **W~in** f -, **-nen** landlady

Wirtschaft f -, **-en** economy; (*Gast-*) restaurant; (*Kneipe*) pub. **w~en** vi (*haben*) manage one's finances. **w~lich** a economic; (*sparsam*) economical. **W~sgeld** nt housekeeping [money]. **W~sprüfer** m auditor

Wirtshaus nt inn; (*Kneipe*) pub

wischen vt/i (*haben*) wipe; wash <*Fußboden*>

wissen† vt/i (*haben*) know; **weißt du noch?** do you remember? **nichts w~ wollen von** not want anything to do with. **W~** nt **-s** knowledge; **meines W~s** to my knowledge

Wissenschaft f -, **-en** science. **W~ler** m -s,- academic; (*Natur-*) scientist. **w~lich** a academic; scientific

wissenswert a worth knowing

witter|n vt scent; (*ahnen*) sense. **W~ung** f - scent; (*Wetter*) weather

Witwe f -, **-n** widow. **W~r** m -s,- widower

Witz m **-es, -e** joke; (*Geist*) wit. **W~bold** m -[e]s, **-e** joker. **w~ig** a funny; witty

wo adv where; (*als*) when; (*irgendwo*) somewhere; **wo immer** wherever ● conj seeing that; (*obwohl*) although; (*wenn*) if

woanders adv somewhere else

wobei adv how; (*relativ*) during the course of which

Woche f -, **-n** week. **W~nende** nt weekend. **W~nkarte** f weekly ticket. **w~nlang** adv for weeks. **W~ntag** m day of the week; (*Werktag*) weekday. **w~ntags** adv on weekdays

wöchentlich a & adv weekly

Wodka m -s vodka

wofür adv what ... for; (*relativ*) for which

Woge f -, **-n** wave

woher adv where from; **woher weißt du das?** how do you know that? **wohin** adv where [to]; **wohin gehst du?** where are you going?

wohl adv well; (*vermutlich*) probably; (*etwa*) about; (*zwar*) perhaps; **w~ kaum** hardly; **sich w~ fühlen** feel well/(*behaglich*) comfortable; **jdm w~ tun** do s.o. good. **W~** nt -[e]s welfare, well-being; **zum W~** (+ gen) for the good of; **zum W~!** cheers!

Wohl|befinden nt well-being. **W~behagen** nt feeling of well-being. **W~ergehen** nt -s welfare. **w~erzogen** a well brought-up

Wohlfahrt f - welfare. **W~sstaat** m Welfare State

wohl|habend a prosperous, well-to-do. **w~ig** a comfortable. **w~schmeckend** a tasty

Wohlstand m prosperity. **W~sgesellschaft** f affluent society

Wohltat f [act of] kindness; (*Annehmlichkeit*) treat; (*Genuss*) bliss

Wohltät|er m benefactor. **w~ig** a charitable

wohl|tuend *a* agreeable. **w~tun*** *vi sep* (*haben*) **w~ tun**, *s.* **wohl**

Wohlwollen *nt* -s goodwill; (*Gunst*) favour. **w~d** *a* benevolent

Wohn|block *m* block of flats. **w~en** *vi* (*haben*) live; (*vorübergehend*) stay. **W~gegend** *f* residential area. **w~haft** *a* resident. **W~haus** *nt* house. **W~heim** *nt* hostel; (*Alten-*) home. **w~lich** *a* comfortable. **W~mobil** *nt* -s, -e camper. **W~ort** *m* place of residence. **W~sitz** *m* place of residence

Wohnung *f* -, -en flat; (*Unterkunft*) accommodation. **W~snot** *f* housing shortage

Wohn|wagen *m* caravan. **W~zimmer** *nt* living-room

wölb|en *vt* curve; arch <*Rücken*>. **W~ung** *f* -, -en curve; (*Archit*) vault

Wolf *m* -[e]s,⸚e wolf; (*Fleisch-*) mincer; (*Reiß-*) shredder

Wolk|e *f* -, -n cloud. **W~enbruch** *m* cloudburst. **W~enkratzer** *m* skyscraper. **w~enlos** *a* cloudless. **w~ig** *a* cloudy

Woll|decke *f* blanket. **W~e** *f* -, -n wool

wollen†¹

● *auxiliary verb*

····> (*den Wunsch haben*) want to. **ich will nach Hause gehen** I want to go home. **ich wollte Sie fragen, ob ...** I wanted to ask you if ...

····> (*im Begriff sein*) be about to. **wir wollten gerade gehen** we were just about to go

····> (*sich in der gewünschten Weise verhalten*) **will nicht** refuses to. **der Motor will nicht anspringen** the engine won't *or* refuses to start

● *intransitive verb*

····> want to. **ob du willst oder nicht** whether you want to or not. **ganz wie du willst** just as you like

····> (⚄ *irgendwohin zu gehen wünschen*) **ich will nach Hause** I want to go home. **zu wem wollen Sie?** who[m] do you want to see?

····> (⚄ *funktionieren*) **will nicht** won't go. **meine Beine wollen nicht mehr** my legs are giving up ⚄

● *transitive verb*

····> want; (*beabsichtigen*) intend. **er will nicht, dass du ihm hilfst** he does not want you to help him. **das habe ich nicht gewollt** I never intended *or* meant that to happen

wollen² *a* woollen. **w~ig** *a* woolly. **W~sachen** *fpl* woollens.

womit *adv* what ... with; (*relativ*) with which. **wonach** *adv* what ... after/<*suchen*> for/<*riechen*> of; (*relativ*) after/for/of which

woran *adv* what ... on/<*denken, sterben*> of; (*relativ*) on/of which; **woran hast du ihn erkannt?** how did you recognize him? **worauf** *adv* what ... on/<*warten*> for; (*relativ*) on/for which; (*woraufhin*) whereupon. **woraus** *adv* what ... from; (*relativ*) from which

Wort *nt* -[e]s,⸚er & -e word; **jdm ins W~ fallen** interrupt s.o.

Wörterbuch *nt* dictionary

Wort|führer *m* spokesman. **w~getreu** *a* & *adv* word-for-word. **w~karg** *a* taciturn. **W~laut** *m* wording

wörtlich *a* literal; (*wortgetreu*) word-for-word

wort|los *a* silent ● *adv* without a word. **W~schatz** *m* vocabulary. **W~spiel** *nt* pun, play on words

worüber *adv* what ... over/<*lachen, sprechen*> about; (*relativ*) over/

about which. **worum** *adv* what …
round/<*bitten, kämpfen*> for;
(*relativ*) round/for which; **worum
geht es?** what is it about? **wovon**
adv what … from/<*sprechen*>
about; (*relativ*) from/about which.
wovor *adv* what … in front of;
<*sich fürchten*> what … of;
(*relativ*) in front of which; of
which. **wozu** *adv* what … to/
<*brauchen, benutzen*> for; (*relativ*)
to/for which; **wozu?** what for?

Wrack *nt* -s, -s wreck
wringen† *vt* wring
Wucher|preis *m* extortionate
price. **W~ung** *f* -, -en growth
Wuchs *m* -es growth; (*Gestalt*)
stature
Wucht *f* - force
wühlen *vi* (*haben*) rummage; (*in
der Erde*) burrow ● *vt* dig
Wulst *m* -[e]s,-̈e bulge; (*Fett*-) roll
wund *a* sore; **w~ reiben** chafe;
sich w~ liegen get bedsores.
W~brand *m* gangrene
Wunde *f* -, -n wound
Wunder *nt* -s,- wonder, marvel;
(*übernatürliches*) miracle; **kein
W~!** no wonder! **w~bar** *a*
miraculous; (*herrlich*) wonderful.
W~kind *nt* infant prodigy. **w~n**
vt surprise; **sich w~n** be
surprised (*über* + *acc* at).
w~schön *a* beautiful
Wundstarrkrampf *m* tetanus
Wunsch *m* -[e]s,-̈e wish;
(*Verlangen*) desire; (*Bitte*)
request
wünschen *vt* want; **sich** (*dat*) **etw
w~** want sth; (*bitten um*) ask for
sth; **jdm Glück/gute Nacht w~** wish
s.o. luck/good night; **Sie w~?** can
I help you? **w~swert** *a* desirable
Wunschkonzert *nt* musical
request programme
wurde, würde *s.* **werden**
Würde *f* -, -n dignity; (*Ehrenrang*)
honour. **w~los** *a* undignified.

W~nträger *m* dignitary. **w~voll** *a*
dignified ● *adv* with dignity
würdig *a* dignified; (*wert*) worthy
Wurf *m* -[e]s,-̈e throw; (*Junge*)
litter
Würfel *m* -s,- cube; (*Spiel*-) dice;
(*Zucker*-) lump. **w~n** *vi* (*haben*)
throw the dice; **w~n um** play dice
for ● *vt* throw; (*in Würfel
schneiden*) dice. **W~zucker** *m*
cube sugar
würgen *vt* choke ● *vi* (*haben*)
retch; choke (**an** + *dat* on)
Wurm *m* -[e]s,-̈er worm; (*Made*)
maggot. **w~en** *vi* (*haben*) **jdn
w~en** ☐ rankle [with s.o.]
Wurst *f* -,-̈e sausage; **das ist mir
W~** ☐ I couldn't care less
Würze *f* -, -n spice; (*Aroma*)
aroma
Wurzel *f* -, -n root; **W~n schlagen**
take root. **w~n** *vi* (*haben*) root
würz|en *vt* season. **w~ig** *a* tasty;
(*aromatisch*) aromatic; (*pikant*)
spicy
wüst *a* chaotic; (*wirr*) tangled;
(*öde*) desolate; (*wild*) wild;
(*schlimm*) terrible
Wüste *f* -, -n desert
Wut *f* - rage, fury. **W~anfall** *m* fit
of rage
wüten *vi* (*haben*) rage. **w~d** *a*
furious; **w~d machen** infuriate

x /ıks/ *inv a* (*Math*) x; ☐
umpteen. **X-Beine** *ntpl* knock-
knees. **x-beinig, X-beinig** *a*
knock-kneed. **x-beliebig** *a* ☐ any.
x-mal *adv* ☐ umpteen times

Yoga /'jo:ga/ *m & nt* **-[s]** yoga

Zack|e *f* **-**, **-n** point; (*Berg-*) peak; (*Gabel-*) prong. **z~ig** *a* jagged; (*gezackt*) serrated

zaghaft *a* timid; (*zögernd*) tentative

zäh *a* tough; (*hartnäckig*) tenacious. **z~flüssig** *a* viscous; <*Verkehr*> slow-moving. **Z~igkeit** *f* **-** toughness; tenacity

Zahl *f* **-**, **-en** number; (*Ziffer, Betrag*) figure

zahlen *vt/i* (*haben*) pay; (*bezahlen*) pay for; **bitte z~!** the bill please!

zählen *vi* (*haben*) count; **z~ zu** (*fig*) be one/(*pl*) some of ● *vt* count; **z~ zu** add to; (*fig*) count among

zahlenmäßig *a* numerical

Zähler *m* **-s**, **-** meter

Zahl|grenze *f* fare-stage. **Z~karte** *f* paying-in slip. **z~los** *a* countless. **z~reich** *a* numerous; <*Anzahl, Gruppe*> large ● *adv* in large numbers. **Z~ung** *f* **-**, **-en** payment; **in Z~ung nehmen** take in part-exchange

Zählung *f* **-**, **-en** count

Zahlwort *nt* (*pl* **-wörter**) numeral

zahm *a* tame

zähmen *vt* tame; (*fig*) restrain

Zahn *m* **-[e]s**, **̈e** tooth; (*am Zahnrad*) cog. **Z~arzt** *m*, **Z~ärztin** *f* dentist. **Z~belag** *m* plaque. **Z~bürste** *f* toothbrush. **Z~fleisch** *nt* gums *pl*. **z~los** *a* toothless. **Z~pasta** *f* **-**, **-en** toothpaste. **Z~rad** *nt* cog-wheel. **Z~schmelz** *m* enamel. **Z~schmerzen** *mpl* toothache *sg*. **Z~spange** *f* brace. **Z~stein** *m* tartar. **Z~stocher** *m* **-s**, **-** toothpick

Zange *f* **-**, **-n** pliers *pl*; (*Kneif-*) pincers *pl*; (*Kohlen-, Zucker-*) tongs *pl*; (*Geburts-*) forceps *pl*

Zank *m* **-[e]s** squabble. **z~en** *vr* **sich z~en** squabble

Zäpfchen *nt* **-s**, **-** (*Anat*) uvula; (*Med*) suppository

zapfen *vt* tap, draw. **Z~streich** *m* (*Mil*) tattoo

Zapf|hahn *m* tap. **Z~säule** *f* petrol-pump

zappeln *vi* (*haben*) wriggle; <*Kind:*> fidget

zart *a* delicate; (*weich, zärtlich*) tender; (*sanft*) gentle. **Z~gefühl** *nt* tact

zärtlich *a* tender; (*liebevoll*) loving. **Z~keit** *f* **-**, **-en** tenderness; (*Liebkosung*) caress

Zauber *m* **-s** magic; (*Bann*) spell. **Z~er** *m* **-s**, **-** magician. **z~haft** *a* enchanting. **Z~künstler** *m* conjuror. **z~n** *vi* (*haben*) do magic; (*Zaubertricks ausführen*) do conjuring tricks ● *vt* produce as if by magic. **Z~stab** *m* magic wand. **Z~trick** *m* conjuring trick

Zaum *m* **-[e]s**,**Zäume** bridle

Zaun *m* **-[e]s**,**Zäune** fence

z.B. *abbr* (**zum Beispiel**) e.g.

Zebra *nt* **-s**, **-s** zebra. **Z~streifen** *m* zebra crossing

Zeche *f* **-**, **-n** bill; (*Bergwerk*) pit

zechen *vi* (*haben*) Ⓣ drink

Zeder *f* **-**, **-n** cedar

Zeh *m* **-[e]s**, **-en** toe. **Z~e** *f* **-**, **-n** toe; (*Knoblauch-*) clove

Z

zehn *inv a*, Z~ *f* -, -en ten.
z~te(r,s) *a* tenth. Z~tel *nt* -s,-
tenth
Zeichen *nt* -s,- sign; (*Signal*)
signal. **Z~setzung** *f* -
punctuation. **Z~trickfilm** *m*
cartoon
zeichn|en *vt/i* (*haben*) draw;
(*kenn-*) mark; (*unter-*) sign.
Z~ung *f* -, -en drawing
Zeige|finger *m* index finger. **z~n**
vt show; **sich z~n** appear; (*sich
herausstellen*) become clear ● *vi*
(*haben*) point (**auf** + *acc* to). **Z~r**
m -s,- pointer; (*Uhr-*) hand
Zeile *f* -, -n line; (*Reihe*) row
Zeit *f* -, -en time; **sich** (*dat*) **Z~
lassen** take one's time; **es hat Z~**
there's's no hurry; **mit der Z~** in
time; **in nächster Z~** in the near
future; **zur Z~** (*rechtzeitig*) in
time; *(derzeit) s.* **zurzeit; eine Z~
lang** for a time *or* while
Zeit|alter *nt* age, era. **z~gemäß** *a*
modern, up-to-date. **Z~genosse**
m, **Z~genossin** *f* contemporary.
z~genössisch *a* contemporary.
z~ig *a & adv* early
zeitlich *a* <*Dauer*> in time;
<*Folge*> chronological. ● *adv* **z~
begrenzt** for a limited time
zeit|los *a* timeless. **Z~lupe** *f* slow
motion. **Z~punkt** *m* time.
z~raubend *a* time-consuming.
Z~raum *m* period. **Z~schrift** *f*
magazine, periodical.
Zeitung *f* -, -en newspaper.
Z~spapier *nt* newspaper
Zeit|verschwendung *f* waste of
time. **Z~vertreib** *m* pastime.
z~weise *adv* at times. **Z~wort** *nt*
(*pl* -wörter) verb. **Z~zünder** *m*
time fuse
Zelle *f* -, -n cell; (*Telefon-*) box
Zelt *nt* -[e]s, -e tent; (*Fest-*)
marquee. **z~en** *vi* (*haben*) camp.
Z~en *nt* -s camping. **Z~plane** *f*
tarpaulin. **Z~platz** *m* campsite
Zement *m* -[e]s cement

zen|sieren *vt* (*Sch*) mark; censor
<*Presse, Film*>. **Z~sur** *f* -, -en
(*Sch*) mark; (*Presse-*) censorship
Zentimeter *m & nt* centimetre.
Z~maß *nt* tape-measure
Zentner *m* -s,- [metric]
hundredweight (*50 kg*)
zentral *a* central. **Z~e** *f* -, -n
central office; (*Partei-*)
headquarters *pl*; (*Teleph*)
exchange. **Z~heizung** *f* central
heating
Zentrum *nt* -s, -tren centre
zerbrech|en† *vt/i* (*sein*) break.
z~lich *a* fragile
zerdrücken *vt* crush
Zeremonie *f* -, -n ceremony
Zerfall *m* disintegration; (*Verfall*)
decay. **z~en†** *vi* (*sein*)
disintegrate; (*verfallen*) decay
zergehen† *vi* (*sein*) melt; (*sich
auflösen*) dissolve
zerkleinern *vt* chop/(*schneiden*)
cut up; (*mahlen*) grind
zerknüllen *vt* crumple [up]
zerkratzen *vt* scratch
zerlassen† *vt* melt
zerlegen *vt* take to pieces,
dismantle; (*zerschneiden*) cut up;
(*tranchieren*) carve
zerlumpt *a* ragged
zermalmen *vt* crush
zermürben *vt* (*fig*) wear down
zerplatzen *vi* (*sein*) burst
zerquetschen *vt* squash; crush
Zerrbild *nt* caricature
zerreißen† *vt* tear; (*in Stücke*)
tear up; break <*Faden, Seil*> ● *vi*
(*sein*) tear; break
zerren *vt* drag; pull <*Muskel*> ● *vi*
(*haben*) pull (**an** + *dat* at)
zerrissen *a* torn
zerrütten *vt* ruin, wreck; shatter
<*Nerven*>
zerschlagen† *vt* smash; smash
up <*Möbel*>; **sich z~** (*fig*) fall
through; <*Hoffnung:*> be dashed
zerschmettern *vt/i* (*sein*) smash

zerschneiden† vt cut; (in Stücke) cut up
zersplittern vi (sein) splinter; <Glas:> shatter ● vt shatter
zerspringen† vi (sein) shatter; (bersten) burst
Zerstäuber m -s,- atomizer
zerstör|en vt destroy; (zunichte machen) wreck. **Z~er** m -s,- destroyer. **Z~ung** f destruction
zerstreu|en vt scatter; disperse <Menge>; dispel <Zweifel>; **sich z~en** disperse; (sich unterhalten) amuse oneself. **z~t** a absent-minded
Zertifikat nt -[e]s, -e certificate
zertrümmern vt smash [up]; wreck <Gebäude, Stadt>
Zettel m -s,- piece of paper; (Notiz) note; (Bekanntmachung) notice
Zeug nt -s ⓘ stuff; (Sachen) things pl; (Ausrüstung) gear; **dummes Z~** nonsense
Zeuge m -n, -n witness. **z~n** vi (haben) testify; **z~n von** (fig) show ● vt father. **Z~naussage** f testimony. **Z~nstand** m witness box
Zeugin f -, -nen witness
Zeugnis nt -ses, -se certificate; (Sch) report; (Referenz) reference; (fig: Beweis) evidence
Zickzack m -[e]s, -e zigzag
Ziege f -, -n goat
Ziegel m -s,- brick; (Dach-) tile. **Z~stein** m brick
ziehen† vt pull; (sanfter; zücken; zeichnen) draw; (heraus-) pull out; extract <Zahn>; raise <Hut>; put on <Bremse>; move <Schachfigur>; (dehnen) stretch; make <Grimasse, Scheitel>; (züchten) breed; grow <Rosen>; **nach sich z~** (fig) entail ● vr **sich z~** (sich erstrecken) run; (sich verziehen) warp ● vi (haben) pull (an + dat on/at); <Tee, Ofen:> draw; (Culin) simmer; **es zieht**

there is a draught; **solche Filme z~ nicht mehr** films like that are no longer popular ● vi (sein) (um-) move (nach to); <Menge:> march; <Vögel:> migrate; <Wolken, Nebel:> drift
Ziehharmonika f accordion
Ziehung f -, -en draw
Ziel nt -[e]s, -e destination; (Sport) finish; (Z~scheibe & Mil) target; (Zweck) aim, goal. **z~bewusst** a purposeful. **z~en** vi (haben) aim (auf + acc at). **z~los** a aimless. **Z~scheibe** f target
ziemlich a ⓘ fair ● adv rather, fairly
Zier|de f -, -n ornament. **z~en** vt adorn
zierlich a dainty
Ziffer f -, -n figure, digit; (Zahlzeichen) numeral. **Z~blatt** nt dial
Zigarette f -, -n cigarette
Zigarre f -, -n cigar
Zigeuner(in) m -s,- (f -, -nen) gypsy
Zimmer nt -s,- room. **Z~mädchen** nt chambermaid. **Z~mann** m (pl -leute) carpenter. **Z~nachweis** m accommodation bureau. **Z~pflanze** f house plant
Zimt m -[e]s cinnamon
Zink nt -s zinc
Zinn m -s tin; (Gefäße) pewter
Zins|en mpl interest sg; (im Voraus) tragen earn interest. **Z~eszins** m -es, -en compound interest. **Z~fuß, Z~satz** m interest rate
Zipfel m -s,- corner; (Spitze) point
zirka adv about
Zirkel m -s,- [pair of] compasses pl; (Gruppe) circle
Zirkulation /-'tsio:n/ f - circulation. **z~ieren** vi (sein) circulate
Zirkus m -, -se circus
zirpen vi (haben) chirp
zischen vi (haben) hiss; <Fett:> sizzle ● vt hiss

Z

Zit|at nt -[e]s, -e quotation.
z~ieren vt/i (haben) quote
Zitr|onat nt -[e]s candied lemon-
peel. **Z~one** f -, -n lemon
zittern vi (haben) tremble; (vor
Kälte) shiver; (beben) shake
zittrig a shaky
Zitze f -, -n teat
zivil a civilian; <Ehe, Recht> civil.
Z~ nt -s civilian clothes pl.
Z~dienst m community service
Zivili|sation /-'tsio:n/ f -, -en
civilization. **z~sieren** vt civilize.
z~siert a civilized ● adv in a
civilized manner
Zivilist m -en, -en civilian
zögern vi (haben) hesitate. **Z~** nt
-s hesitation. **z~d** a hesitant
Zoll¹ m -[e]s,- inch
Zoll² m -[e]s,¨e [customs] duty;
(Behörde) customs pl.
Z~abfertigung f customs
clearance. **Z~beamte(r)** m
customs officer. **z~frei** a & adv
duty-free. **Z~kontrolle** f customs
check
Zone f -, -n zone
Zoo m -s, -s zoo
zoologisch a zoological
Zopf m -[e]s,¨e plait
Zorn m -[e]s anger. **z~ig** a angry

zu
● preposition (+ dative)
! Note that **zu dem** can become
zum and **zu der zur**
····➤ (Richtung) to; (bei Beruf) into.
wir gehen zur Schule we are
going to school. **ich muss zum
Arzt** I must go to the doctor's. **zu
... hin** towards. **er geht zum
Theater/Militär** he is going into
the theatre/army
····➤ (zusammen mit) with. **zu dem
Käse gab es Wein** there was wine
with the cheese. **zu etw passen**
go with sth
····➤ (räumlich; zeitlich) at. **zu
Hause** at home. **zu ihren Füßen** at

her feet. **zu Ostern** at Easter. **zur
Zeit** (+ gen) at the time of
····➤ (preislich) at; for. **zum halben
Preis** at half price. **das Stück zu
zwei Euro** at or for two euros
each. **eine Marke zu 60 Cent** a
60-cent stamp
····➤ (Zweck, Anlass) for. **zu dieser
Zweck** for this purpose. **zum
Spaß** for fun. **zum Lesen** for
reading. **zum Geburtstag bekam
ich ...** for my birthday I got ....
zum ersten Mal for the first time
····➤ (Art und Weise) **zu meinem
Erstaunen/Entsetzen** to my
surprise/horror. **zu Fuß/Pferde**
on foot/horseback. **zu Dutzenden**
by the dozen. **wir waren zu dritt/
viert** there were three/four of us
····➤ (Zahlenverhältnis) to. **es steht
5 zu 3** the score is 5–3
····➤ (Ziel, Ergebnis) into. **zu etw
werden** turn into sth
····➤ (gegenüber) to; towards.
freundlich/hässlich zu jdm sein be
friendly/nasty to s.o.
····➤ (über) on; about. **sich zu etw
äußern** to comment on sth
● adverb
····➤ (allzu) too. **zu groß/viel/weit**
too big/much/far
····➤ (Richtung) towards. **nach dem
Fluss zu** towards the river
····➤ (geschlossen) closed; (an
Schalter, Hahn) off. **zu sein** be
closed. **Augen zu!** close your
eyes! **Tür zu!** shut the door!
● conjunction
····➤ to. **etwas zu essen** something
to eat. **nicht zu glauben**
unbelievable. **zu erörternde
Probleme** problems to be
discussed

zualler|erst adv first of all.
z~letzt adv last of all
Zubehör nt -s accessories pl

zubereit|en vt sep prepare.
Z~ung f - preparation; (in Rezept) method

zubinden† vt sep tie [up]

zubring|en† vt sep spend. **Z~er** m
-s,- access road; (Bus) shuttle

Zucchini /tsuˈkiːni/ pl courgettes

Zucht f -, **-en** breeding;
(Pflanzen-) cultivation; (Art,
Rasse) breed; (von Pflanzen)
strain; (Z~farm) farm; (Pferde-)
stud

zücht|en vt breed; cultivate, grow
<Rosen>. **Z~er** m **-s,-** breeder;
grower

Zuchthaus nt prison

Züchtung f -, **-en** breeding;
(Pflanzen-) cultivation; (Art,
Rasse) breed; (von Pflanzen)
strain

zucken vi (haben) twitch; (sich
z~d bewegen) jerk; <Blitz:> flash;
<Flamme:> flicker ● vt die
Achseln z~ shrug one's shoulders

Zucker m **-s** sugar. **Z~dose** f
sugar basin. **Z~guss** m icing.
z~krank a diabetic. **Z~krankheit**
f diabetes. **z~n** vt sugar. **Z~rohr**
nt sugar cane. **Z~rübe** f sugar
beet. **Z~watte** f candyfloss

zudecken vt sep cover up; (im
Bett) tuck up; cover <Topf>

zudem adv moreover

zudrehen vt sep turn off

zueinander adv to one another;
z~ passen go together; **z~ halten**
(fig) stick together

zuerkennen† vt sep award (dat
to)

zuerst adv first; (anfangs) at first

zufahr|en† vi sep (sein) drive towards.
(+ acc) drive towards. **Z~t** f
access; (Einfahrt) drive

Zufall m chance;
(Zusammentreffen) coincidence;
durch Z~ by chance/coincidence.
z~en† vi sep (sein) close, shut;
jdm z~en <Aufgabe:> fall/<Erbe:>
go to s.o.

zufällig a chance, accidental
● adv by chance

Zuflucht f refuge; (Schutz) shelter

zufolge prep (+ dat) according to

zufrieden a contented;
(befriedigt) satisfied; **sich z~**
geben be satisfied; **jdn z~ lassen**
leave s.o. in peace; **jdn z~ stellen**
satisfy s.o.; **z~ stellend**
satisfactory. **Z~heit** f -
contentment; satisfaction

zufrieren† vi sep (sein) freeze
over

zufügen vt sep inflict (dat on); do
<Unrecht> (dat to)

Zufuhr f - supply

Zug m **-[e]s,¨e** train; (Kolonne)
column; (Um-) procession; (Mil)
platoon; (Vogelschar) flock;
(Ziehen, Zugkraft) pull;
(Wandern, Ziehen) migration;
(Schluck, Luft-) draught; (Atem-)
breath; (beim Rauchen) puff;
(Schach-) move; (beim
Schwimmen, Rudern) stroke;
(Gesichts-) feature; (Wesens-)
trait

Zugabe f (Geschenk) [free] gift;
(Mus) encore

Zugang m access

zugänglich a accessible;
<Mensch:> approachable

Zugbrücke f drawbridge

zugeben† vt sep add; (gestehen)
admit; (erlauben) allow

zugehen† vi sep (sein) close; **jdm**
z~ be sent to s.o.; **z~ auf** (+ acc)
go towards; **dem Ende z~** draw to
a close; <Vorräte:> run low; **auf**
der Party ging es lebhaft zu the
party was pretty lively

Zugehörigkeit f - membership

Zügel m **-s,-** rein

zugelassen a registered

zügel|los a unrestrained. **z~n** vt
rein in; (fig) curb

Zuge|ständnis nt concession.
z~stehen† vt sep grant

zügig a quick

Z

Zugkraft f pull; (fig) attraction
zugleich adv at the same time
Zugluft f draught
zugreifen† vi sep (haben) grab it/them; (bei Tisch) help oneself; (bei Angebot) jump at it; (helfen) lend a hand
zugrunde adv z~ richten destroy; z~ gehen be destroyed; (sterben) die; z~ liegen form the basis (dat of)
zugunsten prep (+ gen) in favour of; <Sammlung> in aid of
zugute adv jdm/etw z~ kommen benefit s.o./sth
Zugvogel m migratory bird
zuhalten† v sep ● vt keep closed; (bedecken) cover; sich (dat) die Nase z~ hold one's nose
Zuhälter m -s,- pimp
zuhause adv = zu Hause, s. Haus. Z~ nt -s,- home
zuhör|en vi sep (haben) listen (dat to). Z~er(in) m(f) listener
zujubeln vi sep (haben) jdm z~ cheer s.o.
zukleben vt sep seal
zuknöpfen vt sep button up
zukommen† vi sep (sein) z~ auf (+ acc) come towards; (sich nähern) approach; z~ lassen send (jdm s.o.); devote <Pflege> (dat to); jdm z~ be s.o.'s right
Zukunft f - future. **zukünftig** a future ● adv in future
zulächeln vi sep (haben) smile (dat at)
zulangen vi sep (haben) help oneself
zulassen† vt sep allow, permit; (teilnehmen lassen) admit; (Admin) license, register; (geschlossen lassen) leave closed; leave unopened <Brief>
zulässig a permissible
Zulassung f -, -en admission; registration; (Lizenz) licence
zuleide adv jdm etwas z~ tun hurt s.o.

zuletzt adv last; (schließlich) in the end
zuliebe adv jdm/etw z~ for the sake of s.o./sth
zum prep = zu dem; zum Spaß for fun; etw zum Lesen sth to read
zumachen v sep ● vt close, shut; do up <Jacke>; seal <Umschlag>; turn off <Hahn>; (stilllegen) close down ● vi (haben) close, shut; (stillgelegt werden) close down
zumal adv especially ● conj especially since
zumindest adv at least
zumutbar a reasonable
zumute adv mir ist nicht danach z~ I don't feel like it
zumut|en vt sep jdm etw z~en ask or expect sth of s.o.; sich (dat) zu viel z~en overdo things. Z~ung f - imposition
zunächst adv first [of all]; (anfangs) at first; (vorläufig) for the moment ● prep (+ dat) nearest to
Zunahme f -, -n increase
Zuname m surname
zünd|en vt/i (haben) ignite. Z~er m -s,- detonator, fuse. Z~holz nt match. Z~kerze f sparking-plug. Z~schlüssel m ignition key. Z~schnur f fuse. Z~ung f -, -en ignition
zunehmen† vi sep (haben) increase (an + dat in); <Mond:> wax; (an Gewicht) put on weight. z~d a increasing
Zuneigung f - affection
Zunft f -,-̈e guild
Zunge f -, -n tongue. Z~nbrecher m tongue-twister
zunutze a sich (dat) etw z~ machen make use of sth; (ausnutzen) take advantage of sth
zuoberst adv right at the top
zuordnen vt sep assign (dat to)
zupfen vt/i (haben) pluck (an + dat at); pull out <Unkraut>

zur *prep* = **zu der; zur Schule** to school; **zur Zeit** at present

zurate *adv* **z~ ziehen** consult

zurechnungsfähig *a* of sound mind

zurecht|finden† **(sich)** *vr sep* find one's way. **z~kommen**† *vi sep* (*sein*) cope (**mit** with); (*rechtzeitig kommen*) be in time. **z~legen** *vt sep* put out ready; **sich** (*dat*) **eine Ausrede z~legen** have an excuse all ready. **z~machen** *vt sep* get ready. **Z~weisung** *f* reprimand

zureden *vi sep* (*haben*) **jdm z~** try to persuade s.o.

zurichten *vt sep* prepare; (*beschädigen*) damage; (*verletzen*) injure

zuriegeln *vt sep* bolt

zurück *adv* back; **Berlin, hin und z~** return to Berlin.

z~bekommen† *vt sep* get back. **z~bleiben**† *vi sep* (*sein*) stay behind; (*nicht mithalten*) lag behind. **z~bringen**† *vt sep* bring back; (*wieder hinbringen*) take back. **z~erstatten** *vt sep* refund. **z~fahren**† *v sep* ● *vt* drive back ● *vi* (*sein*) return, go back; (*im Auto*) drive back; (*z~weichen*) recoil. **z~finden**† *vi sep* (*haben*) find one's way back. **z~führen** *v sep* ● *vt* take back; (*fig*) attribute (**auf** + *acc* to) ● *vi* (*haben*) lead back. **z~geben**† *vt sep* give back, return. **z~geblieben** *a* retarded. **z~gehen**† *vi sep* (*sein*) go back, return; (*abnehmen*) go down; **z~gehen auf** (+ *acc*) (*fig*) go back to

zurückgezogen *a* secluded. **Z~heit** *f* - seclusion

zurückhalt|en† *vt sep* hold back; (*abhalten*) stop; **sich z~en** restrain oneself. **z~end** *a* reserved. **Z~ung** *f* - reserve

zurück|kehren *vi sep* (*sein*) return. **z~kommen**† *vi sep* (*sein*) come back, return; (*ankommen*) get back. **z~lassen**† *vt sep* leave behind; (*z~kehren lassen*) allow back. **z~legen** *vt sep* put back; (*reservieren*) keep; (*sparen*) put by; cover <*Strecke*>. **z~liegen**† *vi sep* (*haben*) be in the past; (*Sport*) be behind; **das liegt lange zurück** that was long ago. **z~melden (sich)** *vr sep* report back. **z~schicken** *vt sep* send back. **z~schlagen**† *v sep* ● *vi* (*haben*) hit back ● *vt* hit back; (*umschlagen*) turn back. **z~schrecken**† *vi sep* (*sein*) shrink back, recoil; (*fig*) shrink (**vor** + *dat* from). **z~stellen** *vt sep* put back; (*reservieren*) keep; (*fig*) put aside; (*aufschieben*) postpone. **z~stoßen**† *v sep* ● *vt* push back ● *vi* (*sein*) reverse, back. **z~treten**† *vi sep* (*sein*) step back; (*vom Amt*) resign; (*verzichten*) withdraw. **z~weisen**† *vt sep* turn away; (*fig*) reject. **z~zahlen** *vt sep* pay back. **z~ziehen**† *vt sep* draw back; (*fig*) withdraw; **sich z~ziehen** withdraw; (*vom Beruf*) retire

Zuruf *m* shout. **z~en**† *vt sep* shout (*dat* to)

zurzeit *adv* at present

Zusage *f* -, -n acceptance; (*Versprechen*) promise. **z~n** *v sep* ● *vt* promise ● *vi* (*haben*) accept

zusammen *adv* together; (*insgesamt*) altogether; **z~ sein** be together. **Z~arbeit** *f* co-operation. **z~arbeiten** *vi sep* (*haben*) co-operate. **z~bauen** *vt sep* assemble. **z~bleiben**† *vi sep* (*sein*) stay together. **z~brechen**† *vi sep* (*sein*) collapse. **Z~bruch** *m* collapse; (*Nerven- & fig*) breakdown. **z~fallen**† *vi sep* (*sein*) collapse; (*zeitlich*) coincide. **z~fassen** *vt sep* summarize, sum up. **Z~fassung** *f* summary.

Z

z~**fügen** vt sep fit together.
z~**gehören** vi sep (haben) belong
together; (z~passen) go together.
z~**gesetzt** a (Gram) compound.
z~**halten†** v sep ● vt hold
together; (beisammenhalten) keep
together ● vi (haben) (fig) stick
together. Z~**hang** m connection;
(Kontext) context. z~**hanglos** a
incoherent. z~**klappen** v sep ● vt
fold up ● vi (sein) collapse.
z~**kommen†** vi sep (sein) meet;
(sich sammeln) accumulate.
Z~**kunft** f -,-̈e meeting. z~**laufen†**
vi sep (sein) gather;
<Flüssigkeit:> collect; <Linien:>
converge. z~**leben** vi sep (haben)
live together. z~**legen** v sep ● vt
put together; (z~falten) fold up;
(vereinigen) amalgamate; pool
<Geld> ● vi (haben) club
together. z~**nehmen†** vt sep
gather up; summon up <Mut>;
collect <Gedanken>; **sich**
z~nehmen pull oneself together.
z~**passen** vi sep (haben) go
together, match. Z~**prall** m
collision. z~**rechnen** vt sep add
up. z~**schlagen†** vt sep smash
up; (prügeln) beat up.
z~**schließen† (sich)** vr sep join
together; <Firmen:> merge.
Z~**schluss** m union; (Comm)
merger
Zusammensein nt -s get-together
zusammensetz|en vt sep put
together; (Techn) assemble; **sich**
z~en sit [down] together;
(bestehen) be made up (aus
from). Z~**ung** f -, -en
composition; (Techn) assembly;
(Wort) compound
zusammen|stellen vt sep put
together; (gestalten) compile.
Z~**stoß** m collision; (fig) clash.
z~**treffen†** vi sep (sein) meet;
(zeitlich) coincide. z~**zählen** vt
sep add up. z~**ziehen†** v sep ● vt
draw together; (addieren) add up;

(konzentrieren) mass; **sich**
z~**ziehen** contract; <Gewitter:>
gather ● vi (sein) move in
together; move in (**mit** with)
Zusatz m addition; (Jur) rider;
(Lebensmittel-) additive.
zusätzlich a additional ● adv in
addition
zuschau|en vi sep (haben) watch.
Z~**er(in)** m -s,- (f -, -nen)
spectator; (TV) viewer
Zuschlag m surcharge; (D-Zug-)
supplement. z~**pflichtig** a <Zug>
for which a supplement is
payable
zuschließen† v sep ● vt lock ● vi
(haben) lock up
zuschneiden† vt sep cut out; cut
to size <Holz>
zuschreiben† vt sep attribute (da
to); **jdm die Schuld z~** blame s.o.
Zuschrift f letter; (auf Annonce)
reply
zuschulden adv **sich** (dat) **etwas**
z~ **kommen lassen** do wrong
Zuschuss m contribution;
(staatlich) subsidy
zusehends adv visibly
zusein* vi sep (sein) **zu sein**, s. **zu**
zusenden† vt sep send (dat to)
zusetzen v sep ● vt add;
(einbüßen) lose
zusicher|n vt sep promise. Z~**ung**
f promise.
zuspielen vt sep (Sport) pass
zuspitzen (sich) vr sep (fig)
become critical
Zustand m condition, state
zustande adv z~ **bringen/kommen**
bring/come about
zuständig a competent;
(verantwortlich) responsible
zustehen† vi sep (haben) **jdm z~**
be s.o.'s right; <Urlaub:> be due
to s.o.
zusteigen† vi sep (sein) get on;
noch jemand zugestiegen? tickets
please; (im Bus) any more fares
please?

zustell|en vt sep block; (bringen) deliver. **Z~ung** f delivery

zusteuern v sep ● vi (sein) head (auf + acc for) ● vt contribute

zustimm|en vi sep (haben) agree; (billigen) approve (dat of). **Z~ung** f consent; approval

zustoßen† vi sep (sein) happen (dat to)

Zustrom m influx

Zutat f (Culin) ingredient

zuteil|en vt sep allocate; assign <Aufgabe>. **Z~ung** f allocation

zutiefst adv deeply

zutragen† vt sep carry/(fig) report (dat to); **sich z~** happen

zutrau|en vt sep jdm etw z~ believe s.o. capable of sth. **Z~en** nt -s confidence

zutreffen† vi sep (haben) be correct; **z~ auf** (+ acc) apply to

Zutritt m admittance

zuunterst adv right at the bottom

zuverlässig a reliable. **Z~keit** f - reliability

Zuversicht f - confidence. **z~lich** a confident

zuviel* pron & adv zu viel, s. viel

zuvor adv before; (erst) first

zuvorkommen† vi sep (sein) (+ dat) anticipate. **z~d** a obliging

Zuwachs m -es increase

zuwege adv z~ bringen achieve

zuweilen adv now and then

zuweisen† vt sep assign

Zuwendung f donation; (Fürsorge) care

zuwenig* pron & adv zu wenig, s. wenig

zuwerfen† vt sep slam <Tür>; jdm etw z~ throw s.o. sth

zuwider adv jdm z~ sein be repugnant to s.o. ● prep (+ dat) contrary to

zuzahlen vt sep pay extra

zuziehen† v sep ● vt pull tight; draw <Vorhänge>; (hinzu-) call in; **sich** (dat) **etw z~** contract <Krankheit>; sustain

<Verletzung>; incur <Zorn> ● vi (sein) move into the area

zuzüglich prep (+ gen) plus

Zwang m -[e]s,-̈e compulsion; (Gewalt) force; (Verpflichtung) obligation

zwängen vt squeeze

zwanglos a informal. **Z~igkeit** f - informality

Zwangsjacke f straitjacket

zwanzig inv a twenty. **z~ste(r,s)** a twentieth

zwar adv admittedly

Zweck m -[e]s, -e purpose; (Sinn) point. **z~los** a pointless. **z~mäßig** a suitable; (praktisch) functional

zwei inv a, **Z~** f -, -en two; (Sch) ≈ B. **Z~bettzimmer** nt twin-bedded room

zweideutig a ambiguous

zweierlei inv a two kinds of ● pron two things. **z~fach** a double

Zweifel m -s,- doubt. **z~haft** a doubtful; (fragwürdig) dubious. **z~los** adv undoubtedly. **z~n** vi (haben) doubt (**an etw** dat sth)

Zweig m -[e]s, -e branch. **Z~stelle** f branch [office]

Zweikampf m duel. **z~mal** adv twice. **z~reihig** a <Anzug> double-breasted. **z~sprachig** a bilingual

zweit adv zu z~ in twos; wir waren zu z~ there were two of us. **z~beste(r,s)** a second-best. **z~e(r,s)** a second

zweitens adv secondly

Zwerchfell nt diaphragm

Zwerg m -[e]s, -e dwarf

Zwickel m -s,- gusset

zwicken vt/i (haben) pinch

Zwieback m -[e]s,-̈e rusk

Zwiebel f -, -n onion; (Blumen-)bulb

Zwielicht nt half-light; (Dämmerlicht) twilight. **z~ig** a shady

Z

Zwiespalt *m* conflict
Zwilling *m* -s, -e twin; Z~e (*Astr*) Gemini
zwingen† *vt* force; sich z~ force oneself. z~d *a* compelling
Zwinger *m* -s,- run; (*Zucht-*) kennels *pl*
zwinkern *vi* (*haben*) blink; (*als Zeichen*) wink
Zwirn *m* -[e]s button thread
zwischen *prep* (+ *dat/acc*) between; (*unter*) among[st]. Z~bemerkung *f* interjection. z~durch *adv* in between; (*in der Z~zeit*) in the meantime. Z~fall *m* incident. Z~landung *f*

stopover. Z~raum *m* gap, space. Z~wand *f* partition. Z~zeit *f* in der Z~zeit in the meantime
Zwist *m* -[e]s, -e discord; (*Streit*) feud
zwitschern *vi* (*haben*) chirp
zwo *inv a* two
zwölf *inv a* twelve. z~te(r,s) *a* twelfth
Zylind|er *m* -s,- cylinder; (*Hut*) top hat. z~risch *a* cylindrical
Zyn|iker *m* -s,- cynic. z~isch *a* cynical. Z~ismus *m* - cynicism
Zypern *nt* -s Cyprus
Zypresse *f* -, -n cypress
Zyste /'tsʏstə/ *f* -, -n cyst

Test yourself with word games

This section contains a number of word games which will help you to use your dictionary more effectively and to build up your knowledge of German vocabulary and usage an entertaining way. You will find answers to all puzzles and games at the end of the section.

1 Join Up the Nouns

These German nouns are all made up of two separate words, but they have split apart. Draw a line between two pieces of paper that make up a noun. Watch out: one of the first words goes with two of the second words!

When you've made all the German words, do the same for the English translations and match them up with the German.

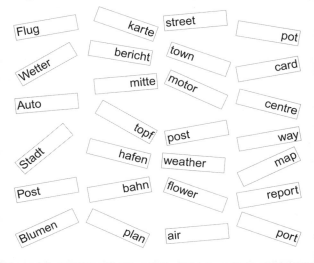

2 Wordsearch

Fifteen German words are hidden among the letters in the grid. Can you find them all? Watch out: six of the words read downwards, while all the others read across.

To help you, here are the English meanings of the German words. You can tick them off as you find the German.

ace	rough
almost	save
also	speak
better	ten
daughter	under
opera	village
powder	wide
quay	

M	W	N	B	U	N	T	E	R	V
Z	E	H	N	C	X	Z	L	K	J
H	I	G	F	P	U	L	V	E	R
D	T	O	C	H	T	E	R	S	A
D	S	P	R	E	C	H	E	N	P
O	B	E	S	S	E	R	A	O	I
R	U	R	K	U	F	A	S	T	A
F	Y	T	A	R	E	W	S	Q	U
Z	X	C	I	V	B	R	A	U	C
N	R	E	T	T	E	N	M	L	H

3 Odd Meaning Out

One word can have several different meanings. In the
following exercise, only two of the three English translations
given for each German word are correct. Use the dictionary to
spot the odd one out, and then look up the right German
translation for it:

fordern	demand	**Pilz**	mushroom
	challenge		fungus
	convince		beer

Schnee	snow	**schwer**	swift
	icing		difficult
	beaten egg-white		heavy

patent	obvious	**gerade**	straight
	resourceful		grand
	clever		even

Haken	tick	**drehen**	turn
	hake		shoot
	hook		catch

Brause	bruise	**Strom**	power
	fizzy drink		storm
	shower		stream

neben	next to	**Blase**	blanket
	apart from		blister
	foggy		bladder

4 Troubleshooting

Our computer has developed some annoying little problems.
Can you help put them right?

First, when we type any three-letter word beginning with d,
the computer shows three d's on the screen! The problem
words are all highlighted in our "Recipe of the Week".
Can you correct them in the box above each word?

Ddd Rezept ddd Woche

Für ddd Kuchenteig ddd Butter in Stückchen schneiden und

mit ddd Mehl vermischen. Ddd Gemisch mit ddd Honig und

ddd Milch zu einem festen Teig verarbeiten. Ddd Äpfel

waschen, halbieren und in ddd Pfanne mit ddd Butter, ddd

Zimt und ddd Zitronensaft aufkochen lassen. Ddd Teig in

ddd Form geben und mit ddd Obst belegen. Ddd Kuchen in

ddd Backofen schieben und 35 Minuten backen.

5 Crossword

If you need to, you can use the dictionary to solve this crossword. Just translate the clues into German, and write the translations in capital letters.

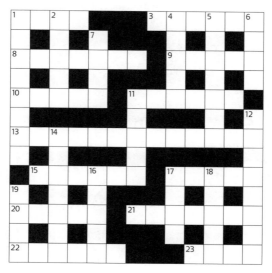

Across

1 mature (4)
3 journeys (6)
8 advertisement, small ad (7)
9 pale (adjective) (5)
10 to hurry (5)
11 few (6)
13 a (male) industrialist (13)
15 to catch (6)
17 (male) Russian (5)
20 price or prize (5)
21 bags or pockets (7)
22 saddle (noun) (6)
23 stove (4)

Down

1 (female) rider (8)
2 island (5)
4 heiress (5)
5 asparagus (7)
6 nest (4)
7 crane (machine) (4)
11 goods, or (they) were (5)
12 to appoint (8)
14 dialect (7)
16 alley (5)
17 pink (4)
18 sheep (5)
19 epic (noun) (4)

6 Curly Words

One word is missing in each of the curly lists. Which day, month, capital city, and number are missing?

Can you write out the four lists in the right order?

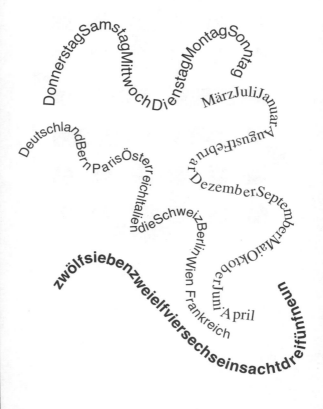

7 Sporting Links

Can you match each piece of sporting equipment to the right sport?
Can you translate the sports into German?

das Seil	**archery**
die Zielscheibe	**tennis**
der Schlittschuh	**skittles**
der Tennisschläger	**surfing**
der Kegel	**mountaineering**
der Ski	**football**
der Federball	**swimming**
das Segel	**golf**
die Kugel	**skating**
der Fußball	**riding**
die Flosse	**cycling**
der Zügel	**gymnastics**
das Sprungbrett	**skiing**
das Fahrrad	**fencing**
der Golfschläger	**diving**
die Turnschuhe	**shot-put**
das Florett	**sailing**
das Surfbrett	**badminton**

Answers

1

Flughafen	airport
Wetterbericht	weather report
Autobahn	motorway
Stadtmitte	town centre
Stadtplan	street map
Postkarte	postcard
Blumentopf	flowerpot

2

Ass	ace	rau	rough
fast	almost	retten	save
auch	also	sprechen	speak
besser	better	zehn	ten
Tochter	daughter	unter	under
Oper	opera	Dorf	village
Pulver	powder	weit	wide
Kai	quay		

3

convince	überzeugen
icing	Zuckerguss
obvious	offensichtlich
hake	Seehecht
bruise	blauer Fleck
foggy	neblig
beer	Bier
swift	schnell
grand	großartig
catch	fangen
storm	Sturm
blanket	Decke

4

Das Rezept *der* Woche

Für *den* Kuchenteig *die* Butter in Stückchen schneiden und mit *dem* Mehl vermischen. *Das* Gemisch mit *dem* Honig und *der* Milch zu einem festen Teig verarbeiten. *Die* Äpfel waschen, halbieren und in *der* Pfanne mit *der* Butter, *dem* Zimt und *dem* Zitronensaft aufkochen lassen. *Den* Teig in *die* Form geben und mit *dem* Obst belegen. *Den* Kuchen in *den* Backofen schieben und 35 Minuten backen.

5

R	E	I	F			R	E	I	S	E	N

(crossword grid)

R E I F ■ ■ R E I S E N
E ■ N ■ K ■ R ■ P ■ E
I N S E R A T ■ B L A S S
T ■ E ■ A ■ ■ I ■ R ■ T
E I L E N ■ W E N I G E ■
R ■ ■ A ■ ■ E ■ E ■ R
I N D U S T R I E L L E R
N ■ I ■ E ■ ■ ■ ■ L ■ N
■ F A N G E N ■ R U S S E
E ■ L ■ A ■ ■ O ■ C ■ N
L ■ A ■ S ■ T A S C H E N
P ■ K ■ S ■ A ■ A ■ ■ E
O ■ ■ ■ ■ ■ ■ ■ ■ ■ ■ ■
S A T T E L ■ ■ O F E N

6

Freitag; Sonntag, Montag, Dienstag, Mittwoch, Donnerstag, Freitag,
  Samstag;
November; Januar, Februar, März, April, Mai, Juni, Juli, August,
  September, Oktober, November, Dezember;
Rom; Deutschland/Berlin, Österreich/Wien, die Schweiz/Bern,
  Frankreich/Paris, Italien/Rom;
zehn; eins, zwei, drei, vier, fünf, sechs, sieben, acht, neun, zehn, elf, zwölf.

7

das Fahrrad	bicycle	cycling	das Radfahren
der Federball	shuttlecock	badminton	der Federball
das Florett	foil	fencing	das Fechten
die Flosse	flipper	swimming	das Schwimmen
der Fußball	football	football	der Fußball
der Golfschläger	golf-club	golf	das Golf
der Kegel	skittle	skittles	das Kegeln
die Kugel	shot	shot-put	das Kugelstoßen
der Schlittschuh	ice-skate	skating	das Eislaufen
das Segel	sail	sailing	der Segelsport
das Seil	rope	mountaineering	das Bergsteigen
der Ski	ski	skiing	das Skilaufen
das Sprungbrett	springboard	diving	das Kunstspringen
das Surfbrett	surfboard	surfing	das Surfen
der Tennisschläger	tennis-racket	tennis	das Tennis
die Turnschuhe	gym shoes	gymnastics	das Turnen
die Zielscheibe	target	archery	das Bogenschießen
der Zügel	rein	riding	das Reiten

Calendar of traditions, festivals, and holidays in German-speaking countries

January
1 8 15 22 29
2 9 16 23 30
3 10 17 24 31
4 11 18 25
5 12 19 26
6 13 20 27
7 14 21 28

February
1 8 15 22
2 9 16 23
3 10 17 24
4 11 18 25
5 12 19 26
6 13 20 27
7 **14** 21 28

March
1 8 15 22 29
2 9 16 23 30
3 10 17 24 31
4 11 18 25
5 12 19 26
6 13 20 27
7 14 21 28

April
1 8 15 22 29
2 9 16 23 30
3 10 17 24 31
4 11 18 25
5 12 19 26
6 13 20 27
7 14 21 28

May
1 8 15 22 29
2 9 16 23 30
3 10 17 24 31
4 11 18 25
5 12 19 26
6 13 20 27
7 14 21 28

June
1 8 15 22 29
2 9 16 23 30
3 10 17 24
4 11 18 25
5 12 19 26
6 13 20 27
7 14 21 28

July
1 8 15 22 29
2 9 16 23 30
3 10 17 24 31
4 11 18 25
5 12 19 26
6 13 20 27
7 14 21 28

August
1 8 15 22 29
2 9 16 23 30
3 10 17 24 31
4 11 18 25
5 12 19 26
6 13 20 27
7 14 21 28

September
1 8 15 22 29
2 9 16 23 30
3 10 17 24
4 11 18 25
5 12 19 26
6 13 20 27
7 14 21 28

October
1 8 15 22 29
2 9 16 23 30
3 10 17 24 **31**
4 11 18 25
5 12 19 **26**
6 13 20 27
7 14 21 28

November
1 8 15 22 29
2 9 16 23 30
3 10 17 24
4 **11** 18 25
5 12 19 26
6 13 20 27
7 14 21 28

December
1 8 15 22 29
2 9 16 23 30
3 10 17 **24** **31**
4 11 18 **25**
5 12 19 **26**
6 13 20 27
7 14 21 28

1 January

Neujahr New Year's Day is always a public holiday and tends to be a quiet day when people are recovering from the *Silvester* celebrations.

6 January

Heilige Drei Könige Epiphany or Twelfth Night is a public holiday in Austria and some parts of southern Germany. In some areas, children dressed up as the Three Kings go from house to house to bless the homes for the coming year and collect money for charity. This is also traditionally the day when the Christmas tree is taken down.

2 February

Mariä Lichtmess Candlemas is celebrated in the Catholic church but is not a public holiday.

1 April

Erster April April Fool's Day is the time to make an April fool of your family and friends (*jdn. in den April schicken*) or to play an April fool trick (*Aprilscherz*).

1 May

Erster Mai May Day is a public holiday in Germany, Austria, and Switzerland. It is celebrated by trade unions as *Labour Day*, often with rallies and demonstrations. Many people simply use the day for a family outing or picnic, and in rural areas maypoles are put up in the villages.

3 October

Tag der deutschen Einheit Germany's national holiday, the *Day of German Unity* commemorates German reunification on 3 October 1990.

26 October

Nationalfeiertag Austria's national holiday.

31 October

Reformationstag Reformation Day is a public holiday in some mainly Protestant parts of Germany and commemorates the Reformation.

1 November

Allerheiligen All Saints' Day is a public holiday in Catholic parts of Germany and Austria.

2 November

Allerseelen All Souls' Day is the day when Catholics remember their dead by visiting the cemeteries to pray and place wreaths, flowers, and lighted candles on the graves. This is often done on 1 November as *Allerseelen* is not a public holiday.

11 November

Martinstag St Martin's day is not a public holiday, but in Catholic areas the charitable Saint is commemorated with processions where children carry lanterns and sing songs. Traditional food includes the *Martinsgans* (roast goose) and *Martinsbrezel* (a kind of soft pretzel).

6 December

Nikolaustag On the eve of St Nicholas' Day, children put out their boots in the hope of finding presents and fruit, nuts, and sweets in the morning. The Saint may also turn up in person, looking much like Santa Claus or Father Christmas.

24 December

Heiligabend Christmas Eve is not a public holiday but many firms and shops close early for the Christmas period. This is the day when traditionally the Christmas tree is put up and decorated. Christmas presents are given in the evening, and many people attend midnight mass.

25 December

Erster Weihnachtstag Christmas Day is a public holiday in Germany, Austria, and Switzerland. It tends to be a quiet day for family get-togethers, often with a traditional lunch of goose or carp.

26 December

Zweiter Weihnachtstag Boxing Day is a public holiday in Germany, Austria, and Switzerland. In Austria and Switzerland it is called *Stephanstag* (St Stephen's day).

31 December

Silvester New Year's Eve is not a bank holiday, but firms and shops tend to close early. A party, or at least a meal with friends, is a must for *Silvester* evening. At midnight, the new year is toasted in Sekt (German sparkling wine), and everybody goes outside to admire the fireworks.

Movable feasts

Rosenmontag The day before Shrove Tuesday is not an official public holiday but many people, especially in the Rhineland, get the day off work or school to take part in the *Karneval* celebrations, which involve masked balls, fancy-dress parties, and parades. The street parades in Düsseldorf, Cologne, Mainz, and other cities are attended by thousands of revellers and shown live on television.

Faschingsdienstag Shrove Tuesday is the final day of *Fasching* (Carnival) in Southern Germany, with processions and fancy dress parties similar to Rosenmontag in the Northwest. In the far south, ancient customs to drive out the winter with bells and drums survive. The pre-Lent carnival in and around the Rhineland is called Karneval. Almost every town has its own carnival prince and princess, and organizes a street parade with decorated floats, which is watched by thousands of revellers in fancy dress.

Aschermittwoch Ash Wednesday marks the end of the carnival season and the beginning of Lent. This day is celebrated in the Catholic Church but is not a public holiday.

Karfreitag Good Friday is a public holiday and generally a very quiet day. Catholics traditionally eat fish on this day.

Ostern Easter traditions include hiding Easter eggs (often dyed hardboiled eggs, or the chocolate variety) in the garden for the children. The *Osterhase* (Easter bunny) is supposed to have brought them. Ostermontag (Easter Monday) is also a public holiday.

Weißer Sonntag (Sunday after Easter) In the Catholic Church, first communion is traditionally taken on this Sunday.

Muttertag (second Sunday in May) On Mothers' Day, children of all ages give their mothers small gifts, cards, or flowers.

Christi Himmelfahrt (40 days after Easter) Ascension day is a public holiday in Germany, Austria, and Switzerland. This day is also Fathers' day when fathers traditionally go out on daytrips or pub crawls.

Pfingsten (seventh Sunday after Easter) As *Pfingstmontag* (Whit Monday) is also a public holiday in Germany, Austria, and Switzerland, Whitsun is a popular time to have a long weekend away.

Fronleichnam (second Thursday after Whitsun) Corpus Christi is a public holiday in Austria and in parts of Germany and Switzerland. In Catholic areas, processions and open-air masses are held.

Buß- und Bettag (third Wednesday in November, 11 days before the first Advent Sunday) This 'day of repentance and prayer' is a public holiday only in some parts of Germany.

Volkstrauertag (second Sunday before the beginning of Advent) In Germany, this is a national day of mourning to commemorate the dead of both world wars, and the victims of the Nazis.

Totensonntag (last Sunday before the beginning of Advent) Protestants remember their dead on this day.

Advent The four weeks leading up to Christmas, beginning with the 1. Adventssonntag (first Sunday in Advent) in late November or early December, still have a special significance in Germany, even for non-religious people. An Advent wreath with four candles is present in almost every German household during this time, and on each Sunday of Advent one more candle is lit.

A–Z of German life and culture

Abendbrot, Abendessen

For most Germans, MITTAGESSEN is still the main meal of the day. *Abendbrot* or *Abendessen* normally consists of bread, cheese, meats, perhaps a salad, and a hot drink. It is eaten by the whole family at about 6 or 7 p.m. *Abendessen* can also refer to a cooked meal, especially for people who are out at work all day.

Abitur

This is the final exam taken by pupils at a GYMNASIUM, usually when they are about 19. The result is based on continuous assessment during the last two years before the *Abitur*, plus examinations in four subjects. The *Abitur* is the obligatory qualification for university entrance.

Ampel-Koalition

A term describing any coalition between the SPD (the party colour is red), the FDP (yellow), and the Green Party. This type of coalition has become increasingly common in local government over the last ten years, with some LÄNDER ruled in this way.

AOK - Allgemeine Ortskrankenkasse

The largest health insurance organization in Germany. Foreign visitors to Germany who need medical assistance can get the necessary forms at the local *AOK* office.

Arbeitsamt

The local employment office to be found in every German town. It provides career guidance, helps the unemployed find new jobs, and processes all claims for ARBEITSLOSENGELD and related benefits. Unemployed people have to report to the *Arbeitsamt* once every three months to prove they are still looking for work.

Arbeitslosengeld

This is the benefit paid to all unemployed people who are looking for a new job and have already made a minimum contribution to the ARBEITSLOSENVERSICHERUNG. The benefit is a proportion of the person's previous pay, and is higher for people supporting children. After one year, it is reduced and called *Arbeitslosenhilfe*.

Arbeitslosenversicherung

This is the compulsory state-run insurance against unemployment. All *Arbeiter* and *Angestellte* have to pay into this scheme and in return are entitled to ARBEITSLOSENGELD and related benefits. This area has been subject to wide-ranging reforms in recent years.

ARD

An umbrella organization for the regional broadcasting stations of the various German LÄNDER, financed by licence fees plus a certain amount of advertising. The *ARD* broadcasts DAS ERSTE.

Autobahn

Germany's motorway network is very extensive and not subject to a general speed limit, other than a recommended limit of about 80 mph. Many motorways have only two lanes. To ease congestion, lorries are not allowed to use the *Autobahn* on Sundays.

BAföG - Bundesausbildungsförderungsgesetz

The grant which about a quarter of German students receive from the state. Whether they are entitled to *BAföG*, and how much they get, depends on the students'

and their parents' financial circumstances. Half of the money is given in the form of a loan which has to be repaid later.

Bayern

Bayern (Bavaria), Germany's largest and southernmost LAND, is known for its beautiful scenery (the Alps and their foothills, as well as forests, rivers, and lakes, picturesque towns and villages), its excellent beer and food, and its lively cosmopolitan capital München (Munich). The Bavarians are said to be warm and hospitable, but also fiercely independent and very conservative.

Beamte

This term covers civil servants and other officials, but also occupations like teachers and lecturers. *Beamte* are legally obliged to support the democratic system in Germany and are not allowed to go on strike. In return, they enjoy many privileges, such as total job security, private health insurance, and exemption from social security contributions.

Berlin

After WIEDERVEREINIGUNG, Berlin took over from Bonn as

the capital of Germany, but the German government did not start moving there until 1998. This vibrant city in the heart of Europe lies on the river Spree. It has about 3.5 million inhabitants and is a major cultural and industrial centre.

Berufsausbildung
▶ LEHRE.

Berufsschule
A college for young people who are doing a LEHRE. They attend *Berufsschule* 2 days a week (or sometimes in blocks of several weeks) to continue their general education and receive formal training in their chosen type of job.

Biergarten
A rustic open-air pub which is traditional in Bavaria but can now be found throughout Germany. It is usually set up for the summer in the yard of a pub or restaurant. A *Biergarten* is the best place to enjoy a beer and a simple meal on a summer's day.

Bild Zeitung
Germany's largest-selling daily newspaper, *Bild* is a typical tabloid with huge headlines, lots of photos, scandal stories, gossip, and nude models. It is known for its right-wing views. *Bild* sells about 4.5 million copies every

day, almost eight times more than any other newspaper in Germany. Its Sunday edition is called *Bild am Sonntag*.

Bodensee
This is the German name for Lake Constance, Germany's biggest lake, bordered by Germany, Switzerland, and Austria. The river Rhine flows through it. This popular recreation area enjoys a particularly mild climate, especially on the three islands Lindau, Mainau, and Reichenau.

Bonn
Bonn was the capital of the Federal Republic of Germany from 1949 until BERLIN was made the capital of a reunified Germany and it remains home to a number of government institutions. This relatively small, quiet city of about 300,000 inhabitants enjoys a picturesque location on the river Rhine.

Bund
This term refers to the federal state as the top level of government, as opposed to the individual LÄNDER which make up the Federal Republic. *Bund* and *Länder* have different responsibilities, with the *Bund* in charge of foreign policy, defence,

transport, health, employment, etc.

Bundesbank

Properly called the *Deutsche Bundesbank*, Germany's central bank is located in Frankfurt/Main. With the introduction of the Euro in 1999, some of its functions have passed to the European Central Bank (also in Frankfurt).

Bundeskanzler

The Chancellor is the head of government in Germany and Austria. The German chancellor is normally elected for 4 years by the MPs in the BUNDESTAG after being proposed by the BUNDESPRÄSIDENT. He chooses the ministers and decides on government policies.

Bundesland

▶ LAND.

Bundespräsident

The President is the head of state in Germany and Austria. The German president is elected for 5 years by the MPs and delegates from the LÄNDER. He (so far there have not been any women) acts mainly as a figurehead, representing Germany abroad, and does not get involved in party politics, although he often takes a moral lead in major issues like the reform of the education system.

Bundesrat

This is the upper house of the German parliamentary system, where the LÄNDER are represented. The *Bundesrat* members are appointed by the Länder governments. It has to approve laws affecting the *Länder*, and also any changes to the GRUNDGESETZ. Sometimes the opposition parties actually hold a majority in the *Bundesrat*, which allows them to influence German legislation.

Bundestag

The lower house of the German parliament, which is elected every four years by the German people. The *Bundestag* is responsible for federal legislation, the federal budget, and electing the BUNDESKANZLER. Half of the MPs are elected directly and half by proportional representation, in a complicated voting system where each voter has two votes.

Bundeswehr

This is the name for the German armed forces, which come under the control of the defence minister. The

Bundeswehr consists of professional soldiers and conscripts serving their WEHRDIENST. Until 1994, the GRUNDGESETZ did not allow German forces to be deployed abroad, but they now take part in certain operations, notably UN peacekeeping missions.

Bündnis 90/Die Grünen
This party came into being in 1993 as the result of a merger of the West German Green party and civil rights movements of the former GDR. It is the third largest force in the German parliament, committed to environmental and social issues.

CDU - Christlich-Demokratische Union
One of the main German political parties. It was founded in 1945 and is committed to Christian and conservative values. The *CDU* is not active in Bavaria.
▶ CSU.

Christkind
Traditionally, it is *Das Christkind* (the Christ Child) who brings Christmas presents to children on Christmas Eve. The concept of *der Weihnachtsmann* (Father Christmas) is relatively new in Germany.

CSU - Christlich-Soziale Union
The Bavarian sister party of the CDU. It was founded in 1946 and has enjoyed an absolute majority in Bavaria for over 30 years. Politically, it stands to the right of the *CDU*.

Das Erste
Also called ERSTES PROGRAMM, this is the first German public TV channel, broadcast by ARD. Programming includes news, information, films, and entertainment. There is a limited amount of advertising, which is concentrated in 'blocks' at certain times of day and not after 8 p.m.

Der Spiegel
One of Germany's best-selling weekly news and current affairs magazines, *Der Spiegel* was founded in 1947 and is published in Hamburg. It has a liberal to left-wing outlook and has become synonymous with investigative journalism in Germany, as it has brought to light a number of major scandals in German business and politics over the years.

Deutsche Post
The previously state-run German postal system has undergone wide-ranging reforms in recent years which effectively removed the *Deutsche Post* monopoly in

2002. The number of post offices has been reduced, but small post office agencies can now be found in shops, newsagents, and petrol stations. German letter boxes are yellow. Postal charges are relatively high, but the service is very reliable.

Deutsche Telekom

The previously state-run German telecommunications service has undergone extensive reforms and gradual privatization and is now a public limited company. Since 1998 when the market was opened up to competition, *Deutsche Telekom* has ceased to have a monopoly.

Deutsche Welle

The German equivalent of the BBC World Service, this radio station is financed and controlled by the German government and broadcasts programmes on German politics, business, arts, and culture, aimed at listeners abroad.

Die Republikaner

This ultra right-wing party was founded in 1983 and quickly became notorious for its xenophobic and nationalistic aims. After some success in the early 90s it now has very little support and is not represented in the BUNDESTAG.

Die Welt

A national daily newspaper which was founded in 1946 and is published in Hamburg. It has a large business section and is considered to be right-wing in its views.

Die Zeit

Germany's 'heaviest' weekly newspaper is published in Hamburg and is considered essential reading for academics and intellectuals. Former BUNDESKANZLER Helmut Schmidt is a joint editor. The paper offers in-depth analysis of current issues in politics, society, culture, and the arts.

Drittes Programm

One of the eight regional television channels run by the ARD and focussing on regional affairs and educational programmes.

Duales System

This is a waste disposal and recycling system which was introduced in Germany in 1993 and is operated by the private company *DSD*. All packaging materials marked with the GRÜNER PUNKT symbol are collected separately, and sorted into plastics, glass, paper, and metal for recycling. Non-recyclable and compostable waste is still collected by the local refuse collection service.

Eigenheim
The level of home ownership in Germany is rising but still far lower than in Britain. Many people happily live in rented flats or houses, but most dream of buying or building their *Eigenheim* (own home) one day and save up towards it through the system of BAUSPAREN. German houses tend to be large and solidly built, usually with cellars, and are therefore relatively expensive. First-time buyers are usually middle-aged and expect to stay in their home for the rest of their lives.

Einwohnermeldeamt
Anybody who moves to Germany or relocates within Germany is legally obliged to register their address with the *Einwohnermeldeamt* within a week.

Entwerter
When travelling on buses and trams in Germany it is important to remember that you have to cancel (*entwerten*) your ticket in one of the *Entwerter* machines located inside the bus or tram. Your ticket, even if you have just bought it from the driver, is not valid without the stamp from the *Entwerter*.

Erste, Das
▶ DAS ERSTE.

Eurocheque
The Eurocheque is the standard cheque issued by banks in Germany. It is backed up by the *Eurochequekarte* which can also be used at cash machines and for payments in shops. Although plastic cards have become more popular in Germany, many people (and shops and restaurants) still prefer cash.

Fachhochschule
This type of university provides shorter, more vocational and practically-based courses than those available at a HOCHSCHULE.

Fahrschule
Learner drivers in Germany have to take lessons from a qualified driving instructor at a *Fahrschule* (driving school) in a specially adapted car with dual controls. It is quite common to have 20 or 30 driving lessons before sitting the driving test, as there is no other way of getting driving practice on the road.

FDP - Freie Demokratische Partei
The German Liberal party, which was founded in 1948. This relatively small party tends to gain only 5 to 10% of the vote at general elections,

but it has held the balance of power in various coalition governments both with the SPD and the CDU/CSU. It supports a free-market economy and the freedom of the individual.

Focus

A relatively new weekly news and current affairs magazine published in Munich. It was set up in 1993 and is aimed at a centre-right readership, especially businesspeople and professionals. *Focus* has become a serious competitor of DER SPIEGEL, with shorter, easier-to-read articles and a more modern presentation.

Frankfurter Allgemeine Zeitung (FAZ)

One of Germany's most serious and widely respected daily newspapers. It was founded in 1945 and is published in Frankfurt/Main. It tends to have a centre-left to liberal outlook.

Frühstück

Breakfast in Germany typically consists of strong coffee, slices of bread or fresh rolls with butter, jam, honey, sliced cheese and meat, and maybe a boiled egg. For working people and schoolchildren, who have little time for breakfast first thing in the morning, a *zweites Frühstück* is common at around 10 a.m.

Gastarbeiter

The term used for foreign workers from southern European countries, mainly Turkey, former Yugoslavia, and Italy, many of whom came to Germany in the 60s and 70s. Despite the time that they have lived in Germany and the fact that their children have grown up there, integration is still a widely discussed issue.

Gemeinde

The lowest level of local government, run by a local council chaired by the *Bürgermeister* (mayor). *Gemeinden* have their own budget, with income from local taxes. They pass local legislation and administer local affairs.

Gesamthochschule

A type of university established in some LÄNDER following reforms in the 60s and combining HOCHSCHULE and FACHHOCHSCHULE under one roof, thereby offering greater flexibility and a wider choice of subjects to the student.

Gesamtschule

A comprehensive secondary school introduced in the 70s and designed to replace the

traditional division into
GYMNASIUM, REALSCHULE, and
HAUPTSCHULE. Pupils are
taught different subjects
at their own level and may
take any of the school-leaving
exams, including the ABITUR.

Goethe-Institut

An organization for
promoting German language
and culture abroad. It is based
in Munich and runs about 140
institutes in over 70 countries,
offering German language
classes, cultural events such
as exhibitions, films and
seminars, and a library of
German books and magazines
and other documentation,
which is open to the public.

Grundgesetz

The written German
constitution which came into
force in May 1949. It lays down
the basic rights of German
citizens, the relationship
between BUND and LÄNDER,
and the legal framework of the
German state.

Grundschule

The primary school which all
German children attend for
four years from the age of 6
(some children do not start
until they are 7). Lessons are
intense but pupils only attend
school for about 4 hours a day.
At the end of the *Grundschule*,
teachers and parents decide

together which type of
secondary school the child
should attend.

Grüner Punkt

A symbol used to mark
packaging materials which
can be recycled. Any
packaging carrying this logo
is collected separately under
the DUALES SYSTEM recycling
scheme. Manufacturers have
to buy a licence from the
recycling company *DSD* to
entitle them to use this
symbol.

Gymnasium

The secondary school which
prepares pupils for the
ABITUR. The *Gymnasium* is
attended after the
GRUNDSCHULE by the most
academically-inclined pupils.
They spend nine years at this
school, and during the last
three years, they have some
choice as to which subjects
they study.
▶ SCHULE.

Hauptschule

The secondary school which
prepares pupils for the
HAUPTSCHULABSCHLUSS
(school-leaving certificate).
The *Hauptschule* aims to give
the least academically-
inclined children a sound
educational grounding.
Pupils stay at the *Hauptschule*
for 5 or 6 years after the

GRUNDSCHULE. ▶ SCHULE, LEHRE.

Hochschule

German *Hochschulen* (universities) do not charge fees, and anybody who has passed the ABITUR is entitled to go to university (except for some subjects which have a NUMERUS CLAUSUS). They tend to be very large and impersonal institutions. Students may receive a BAFÖG grant and often take more than the minimum 8 semesters (4 years) to complete their course.

ICE - Intercityexpresszug

This high-speed train runs at two-hour intervals on a number of main routes in Germany, offering shorter journey times and better facilities than ordinary trains. A futuristic new *ICE* station has been built at Frankfurt airport.

Internet

A wealth of useful information on German politics, culture, and so on can be obtained on the Internet, which is very popular in Germany. All the main German newspapers have web sites (e.g. http://www.focus.de), as do the television channels (e.g. http://www.ard.de) and

organizations like the *Goethe-Institut* (http://goethe.de). In addition, many German towns and cities have web sites (e.g. http://www.berlin.de).

Kaffee

This refers not only to coffee as a drink but also to the small meal taken at about 4 in the afternoon, consisting of coffee and cakes or biscuits. It is often a social occasion as it is common to invite family or friends for *Kaffee und Kuchen* (rather than for lunch or dinner), especially on birthdays and other family occasions.

Kanton

The name for the individual autonomous states that make up Switzerland. There are 26 *Kantone*, with the largest having just over 1 million inhabitants. Each *Kanton* has its own government and its own constitution.

Kindergarten

Every German pre-school child has the right to attend *Kindergarten* (nursery or play school) between the ages of 3 and 6. Kindergarten concentrates on play, crafts, singing etc., and aims to foster the child's social and emotional development. There is no formal teaching at all, this being reserved for the

GRUNDSCHULE.

Kindertagesstätte

Often called *Kita* for short, this is a day nursery intended for the children of working parents. The age range is usually from babies to 6, although some *Kitas* also offer after-school care for older children.

Krankenkasse

There are many different health insurance organizations in Germany with the AOK being the largest. Contributions are high, due to the high standard (and cost) of health care in Germany. The *Krankenkassen* issue their members with plastic cards which entitle them to treatment by the doctor of their choice.

Ladenschlusszeit

The strict regulations governing shop closing times in Germany were relaxed in 1996. Shops are allowed to stay open until 8 p.m. on weekdays and 4 p.m. on Saturdays, and bakeries may open for 3 hours on Sundays. However, the actual opening times vary, depending on the location and size of the shop.

Land

Germany is a federal republic consisting of 16 member states called *Länder* or *Bundesländer*. Five so-called neue *Bundesländer* were added after reunification in 1990. The Land has a degree of autonomy and is responsible for all educational and cultural affairs, the police, the environment, and local government. Austria is a federal state consisting of 9 *Länder*, and the Swiss equivalent is a KANTON.

Landtag

The parliament of a LAND, which is elected every 4 to 5 years using a similar mixed system of voting as for the BUNDESTAG elections.

Lehre

This type of apprenticeship is still the normal way to learn a trade or train for a practical career in Germany. A *Hauptschulabschluss* is the minimum requirement, although many young people with a *Realschulabschluss* or even *Lehre* opt to train in this way. A Lehre takes about 2 to 3 years and involves practial training by a MEISTER(IN) backed up by lessons at a BERUFSSCHULE, with an exam at the end.

Love Parade

A festival of techno music and dance which takes place in Berlin every summer, with about 1 million mainly young people attending. Originally a celebration of youth culture, it has become a major tourist attraction.

Markt

Weekly markets are still held in most German cities and towns, usually laid out very attractively in the picturesque market squares. Fresh fruit and vegetables, flowers, eggs, cheese and other dairy products, bread, meat and fish are available directly from the producer. Many Germans still buy most of their provisions *auf dem Markt*.

Meister(in)

A master craftsman or craftswoman who has completed rigorous training in his/her trade or vocation and has passed a final exam after several years' experience in a job. A *Meister(in)* is allowed to set up in business and train young people who are doing their LEHRE.

Mittagessen

This is a cooked meal eaten in the middle of the day and is the main meal of the day for most Germans. Schoolchildren come home from school in time for *Mittagessen* and most large companies have canteens where hot meals are served at lunchtime. On a Sunday, *Mittagessen* might consist of a starter like a clear broth, followed by a roast with gravy, boiled potatoes and vegetables, and a dessert.

Namenstag

This day is celebrated by many Germans, especially Catholics, in the same way as a birthday. It is the day dedicated to the saint whose name the person carries so, for example, someone called Martin would celebrate their *Namenstag* on *Martinstag* (November 11).

Numerus clausus

The *Numerus clausus* system is used to limit the number of students studying certain oversubscribed subjects such as medicine at German universities. It means that only those students who have achieved a minimum average mark in their ABITUR are admitted.

Orientierungsstufe

The name given to the first two years at a HAUPTSCHULE, a REALSCHULE, or a GYMNASIUM. During this time pupils can find out if they are suited to the type of school they are attending, and at the end of the two years they may transfer to a different school.

Ossi

A colloquial and sometimes derogatory term for someone from East Germany, as opposed to a WESSI (someone from West Germany).

Polterabend

This is Germany's answer to stag and hen nights. The *Polterabend* usually takes place a few days before the wedding and takes the form of a large party for the family and friends of both bride and groom. Traditionally, the guests smash some crockery, as this is supposed to bring luck to the couple.

Post

▶ DEUTSCHE POST

Premiere

Germany's main Pay-TV channel was introduced in 1991 and can be received via satellite or cable. *Premiere* subscribers can watch the latest feature films, sports events, cultural programmes, and documentaries uninterrupted by advertising.

Realschule

The secondary school which prepares pupils for the *Realschulabschluss* (school-leaving certificate). This type of school is in between HAUPTSCHULE and GYMNASIUM, catering for less academic children who will probably train for a practical career. Pupils stay at the *Realschule* for 6 years after the GRUNDSCHULE. ▶ SCHULE, LEHRE.

Rechtschreibreform

After much controversy, a reform aiming to simplify the strict rules governing German spelling and punctuation was finally implemented in 1998. The old spelling is still acceptable for a transitional period until 2005, but most newspapers and some new books already use the new spelling.

Reichstag

This historic building in the centre of Berlin became the seat of the BUNDESTAG in 1999. The refurbishment of the *Reichstag* included the addition of a glass cupola, with a walkway open to visitors, which provides a spectacular viewing platform and addition to the Berlin skyline.

Republikaner

▶ DIE REPUBLIKANER

RTL

Germany's largest privately-owned television channel is the market leader in commercial television. It broadcasts films, sport, news, and entertainment and regularly achieves the highest viewing figures.

SAT 1

Germany's second largest privately-owned television channel broadcasts films, news, sport, and entertainment. It was the first commercial channel in the country.

3SAT

This satellite TV channel is run jointly by ARD, ZDF, and Swiss and Austrian TV.

Schule

German children do not start school until they are 6, and they are not allowed to leave school until they are at least 15. All children attend the GRUNDSCHULE for four years (six in Berlin) and either a HAUPTSCHULE, REALSCHULE, GYMNASIUM, or GESAMTSCHULE, depending on their ability. Some students stay at school until they are over 20 due to the system of "SITZEN BLEIBEN".

Schultag - 1. Schultag

The first day at school is a big event for a German child, involving a ceremony at school and sometimes at church. The child is given a *Schultüte*, a large cardboard cone containing pens, small gifts, and sweets, to mark this special occasion.

Schützenfest

An annual festival celebrated in most towns, involving a shooting competition, parade, and fair. The winners of the shooting competition are crowned *Schützenkönig* and *Schützenkönigin* for the year.

Schwarzwald

This is the German name for the Black Forest, a mountainous area in south-western Germany and a popular holiday destination for Germans and foreign tourists alike. The name refers to the large coniferous forests in the area.

sitzen bleiben

If German pupils fail more than one subject in their end-of-year school report, they have to repeat the year. This is colloquially referred to as *sitzen bleiben*, and it means that some pupils do not manage to sit their ABITUR until they are 20.

Skat

A popular card game for three players playing with 32 German cards. Keen players meet regularly for a game or even join a *Skat* club.

Sozialabgaben

This term refers to the contributions every German taxpayer has to make towards the four main state insurance schemes: pension, health, nursing care, and unemployment. Altogether this amounts to over 40% of gross income, with employee and employer paying half each.

SPD - Sozialdemokratische Partei Deutschlands

One of the main German political parties and the party with the biggest membership. Re-formed after the war in 1945, it is a workers' party supporting social democratic values.

Spiegel

▶ DER SPIEGEL.

Stammtisch

A large table reserved for regulars in most German pubs. The word is also used to refer to the group of people who meet around this table for a drink and lively discussion.

Stasi - Staatssicherheitsdienst

The secret service in the former GDR. With the help of an extensive network of informers, the *Stasi* built up personal files on over 6 million people, that is one third of the population. It was disbanded a year before re-unification.

▶ IM.

Süddeutsche Zeitung

This respected daily national newspaper was founded in 1945 and is published in Munich. It has a liberal outlook and is read mainly in southern Germany.

Volkshochschule (VHS)

A local adult education centre that can be found in every German town. The *VHS* offers low-cost daytime and evening classes in a wide range of subjects, including crafts, languages, music, and exercise.

Waldorfschule

An increasingly popular type of private school originally founded by the Austrian anthroposophist Rudolf Steiner in the 1920s. The main aim of these schools is to develop pupils' creative and cognitive abilities through music, art, and crafts.

Wehrdienst

Compulsory military service for young men in Germany (10 months), Switzerland (3 months), and Austria (6 months). Young Germans are generally called up when they are 19, although there are certain exemptions. Conscientious objectors may apply to do ZIVILDIENST instead.

Weihnachtsmarkt
During the weeks of Advent, these Christmas markets take place in most German towns, selling Christmas decorations, handmade toys and crib figures, traditional Christmas biscuits, and mulled wine to sustain the shoppers.

Weinstube
A cosy wine bar which offers a wide choice of wines and usually also serves a few dishes which are considered to go well with wine. A *Weinstube* tends to be more upmarket than an ordinary pub, or else fairly rustic, especially in wine-growing areas.

Welt
▶ DIE WELT

Wende
This word can refer to any major political or social change or turning point, but it is used especially to refer to the collapse of Communism in 1989, which was symbolized by the fall of the Berlin wall and eventually led to the WIEDERVEREINIGUNG in 1990.

Wessi
A colloquial and sometimes derogatory term for someone from West Germany, as opposed to an OSSI. The expression *Besserwessi*, a pun

on *Besserwisser* ('know-all') is used by East Germans to describe a *Wessi* who thinks he knows it all.

Westdeutsche Allgemeine Zeitung (WAZ)
Germany's highest-circulation serious national paper. It was founded in 1948 and is published in Essen, catering mainly for the densely populated Ruhr area.

Wiedervereinigung
This is the German word for the reunification of Germany which officially took place on 3 October 1990, when the former GDR was incorporated into the Federal Republic. The huge financial and social costs of reunification are still being felt throughout Germany.

ZDF - Zweites Deutsches Fernsehen
The second German public TV channel which was founded in 1961 and broadcasts the *Zweites Programm* with entertainment, news, information, and a limited amount of advertising.

Zeit
▶ DIE ZEIT.

Zivildienst
Community service which recognized conscientious

objectors in Germany and
Austria can choose to carry
out instead of WEHRDIENST. It
lasts 3 months longer than
Wehrdienst (2 months longer
in Austria) and usually
involves caring for children,
the elderly, the disabled, or the
sick.

Letter-writing in German

Holiday postcard

- Beginnings (informal): *'Lieber'* here because it's a man; if it's a woman, use e.g. *Liebe Elke*.

  To two people, repeat *'Liebe(r)'*: *Lieber Hans*, *liebe Elke*.

  To a family: *Liebe Schmidts*, *Liebe Familie Schmidt*, or just *Liebe Leute*.

- Address: Note that the title (*Herrn, Frau, Fräulein*) stands on the line above the name. *Herr* always has an n on the end in addresses.

  The house number comes after the street name.

  The postcode comes before the place, and if you're writing from outside the country put a D- for Germany, A- for Austria or CH- for Switzerland in front of it.

Heidelberg, den 6. 8. 2001

Lieber Hans!

Einen schönen Gruß aus Alt-Heidelberg! Wir sind erst zwei Tage hier, aber schon sehr angetan von der Stadt und Umgebung, trotz der vielen Touristen. Wir waren gestern abend in einem Konzert im Schlosshof, eine wunderbare Stimmung! Morgen machen wir eine Bootsfahrt, dann geht's am Donnerstag wieder nach Hause. Hoffentlich ist deine Mutter inzwischen wieder gesund.

Bis bald

Max und Sophie

Herrn

Hans Matthäus

Brucknerstr. 26

91052 Erlangen

- Endings (informal): *Herzlich* or *Herzlichst*, *Herzliche Grüße*; more affectionately: *Alles Liebe*; *Bis bald* = See you soon .

Christmas and New Year wishes

On a card:

Frohe Weihnachten und viel Glück im neuen Jahr

A bit more formal: Ein gesegnetes Weihnachtsfest und die besten Wünsche zum neuen Jahr

A bit less formal: Fröhliche Weihnachten und einen guten Rutsch ins neue Jahr

In a letter:

- On most personal letters German speakers don't put their address at the top, but just the name of the place and the date

Würzburg, den 20.12.2001

Liebe Karin, lieber Ferdinand,

euch und euren Kindern wünschen wir von Herzen frohe Weihnachten und ein glückliches neues Jahr. Wir hoffen, es geht euch allen gut, und dass wir uns bald mal wieder sehen werden. Es kommt uns so vor, als hätten wir uns eine Ewigkeit nicht gesehen.

Das vergangene Jahr war für uns sehr ereignisreich. Thomas hatte im Sommer einen Unfall mit dem Fahrrad, und brach sich den Arm und das Schlüsselbein. Sabine hat das Abitur gerade noch bestanden und ist jetzt an der Uni in Erlangen, studiert Sport. Der arme Michael ist im Oktober arbeitslos geworden und sucht immer noch nach einer Stelle.

Ihr müsst unbedingt vorbeikommen, wenn ihr das nächste Mal in der Gegend seid. Ruft doch einfach ein paar Tage vorher an, damit wir etwas ausmachen können.

Mit herzlichen Grüßen

Eure Gabi und Michael

Invitation (informal)

Hamm, den 22.4.2001

Liebe Jennie,

.... wäre es möglich, dass du 1 in den Sommerferien zu uns kommst? Katrin und Gottfried würden sich riesig freuen (ich und mein Mann natürlich auch). Wir planen eine Reise zum Bodensee Ende Juli/Anfang August, du 1 könntest gerne mitfahren. Es ist wirklich sehr schön dort unten. Wir werden wahrscheinlich zelten – hoffentlich hast du 1 nichts dagegen!

Schreib bald, ob das für dich 1 in Frage kommt.

Herzliche Grüße

Monika Pfortner

■ Beginning: if you put a comma after the name on the first line (which is usual), the letter proper should start with a small letter.

1 *du, dich, dein* etc.: although many people still write these with a capital in letters, this is not necessary. But the formal *Sie, Ihnen, Ihr* must always have a capital.

Invitation (formal)

Invitations to parties are usually by word of mouth, while for weddings, announcements rather than invitations are usually sent out:

Irene Brinkmann   Stefan Hopf

Wir heiraten am Samstag, den 20. April
2001, um 14 Uhr in der Pfarrkirche
Landsberg.

Goethestraße 12   Ulrichsweg 4

Landsberg   Altötting

Accepting an invitation

> *Edinburgh, den 2.5.2001*
>
> *Liebe Frau Pfortner,*
>
> *recht herzlichen Dank für Ihre liebe Einladung. Da ich noch keine festen Pläne für die Sommerferien habe, möchte ich sie sehr gerne annehmen. Allerdings darf ich nicht mehr als vier bis fünf Tage weg sein, da es meiner Mutter nicht sehr gut geht. Sie **1** müssen mir sagen, was ich mitbringen soll (außer Edinburgh Rock!). Ist es sehr warm am Bodensee? Kann man im See schwimmen?*
>
> *Natürlich habe ich nichts gegen Zelten. Auch hier in Schottland bei Wind und Regen macht es mir Spaß!*
>
> *Ich freue mich auf ein baldiges Wiedersehen.*
>
> *Herzliche Grüße*
>
> *Jennie Stewart*

1 Since this is a letter from a younger person writing to the mother of a friend, she uses the formal *Sie* form and possessive *Ihr* (always with capitals), and writes to her as "*Frau Pfortner*". On the other hand it was quite natural for Frau Pfortner to use the *du* form to her.

Enquiry to a tourist office

■ The subject of the letter is centred.

■ A simple business-style letter. The recipient's address is on the left and the sender's on the right, with the date below.

Verkehrsverein Heidelberg e.V.
Friedrich-Ebert-Anlage 2
69117 Heidelberg

Silvia Sommer
Tannenweg 23
48149 Münster

24. April 2001

Hotels und Pensionen in Heidelberg

Sehr geehrte Damen und Herren,

würden Sie mir bitte freundlicherweise eine Liste der Hotels und Pensionen (der mittleren Kategorie) am Ort zusenden?

Ich möchte bitte auch Informationen über Busfahrten zu den Sehenswürdigkeiten der Umgebung in der zweiten Augusthälfte haben.

Mit freundlichen Grüßen

Silvia Sommer

■ This is the standard formula for starting a business letter addressed to a firm or organization, and not to a particular person.

■ "*Mit freundlichen Grüßen*" is the standard ending for a formal or business letter; another possibility is "*Mit besten Grüßen*".

Booking a hotel room

Hotel Goldener Pflug
Ortsstraße 7
69235 Steinbach

Tobias Schwarz
Gartenstr. 19
76530 Baden-
Baden

16. Juli 2001

Sehr geehrte Damen und Herren,

Ich wurde durch die Broschüre "Hotels und Pensionen im Naturpark Odenwald (Ausgabe 2000)" auf ihr Hotel aufmerksam.

Ich möchte für mich und meine Frau für die Zeit vom 2. bis 11. August (neun Nächte) ein ruhiges Doppelzimmer mit Dusche reservieren, sowie ein Einzelzimmer für unseren Sohn.

Falls Sie für diese Zeit etwas Passendes haben, informieren Sie mich doch bitte über den Preis und darüber, ob Sie eine Anzahlung wünschen.

Mit freundlichen Grüßen

Tobias Schwarz

Booking a campsite

■ For a business letter to a particular person, use "*Sehr geehrte(r)*"
and the name. (If this letter were to a man, it would start "*Sehr
geehrter Herr Sattler*").

**Camilla Stumpf
Saalgasse 10
60311 Frankfurt**

Camping am See
Frau Bettina Sattler
Auweg 6-10
87654 Waldenkirchen   Frankfurt, den 16.04.2001

Sehr geehrte Frau Sattler,

Ihr Campingplatz wurde mir von Herrn Stephan Seidel
empfohlen, der schon mehrmals bei Ihnen war. **1** Ich würde nun
gerne vom 18. bis 25. Juli mit zwei Freunden eine Woche bei Ihnen
verbringen. Könnten Sie uns bitte einen Zeltplatz **2** möglichst
in unmittelbarer Nähe des Sees **3** reservieren?

Würden Sie mir freundlicherweise mitteilen, ob Sie meine
Reservierung annehmen können und ob Sie eine Anzahlung
wünschen?

Außerdem wäre ich Ihnen dankbar für eine kurze
Wegbeschreibung von der Autobahn.

Mit vielem Dank im Voraus und freundlichen Grüßen

Camilla Stumpf

---

1 Or if you have found the campsite in a guide, say e.g.: "*Ich habe Ihre
Anschrift dem ADAC-Campingführer 2000 entnommen*".

2 Or if you have a caravan: "*einen Stellplatz für einen Wohnwagen*".

3 Alternatives: "*in schattiger/geschützter Lage*".

Cancelling a reservation

Herrn
Hans Knauer
Gasthaus Sonnenblick
Hauptstr. 6
D-94066 Bad Füssing
Germany   Aberdeen, den 2.6.2001

Sehr geehrter Herr Knauer,

leider muss ich meine Reservierung für die Woche vom 7. bis 13. August **1** rückgängig machen. Wegen unvorhergesehener Umstände **2** muss ich auf meinen Urlaub verzichten.

Es tut mir aufrichtig Leid, dass ich so spät abbestellen muss, und hoffe, dass Sie deswegen keine Unannehmlichkeiten haben.

Mit freundlichen Grüßen

Robert McDonald

1 Or: "*für die Zeit vom 7. bis 20. August*" etc.
2 Or more precisely: "*Durch den überraschenden Tod meines Vaters/die Krankheit meines Mannes*" etc.

Sending an e-mail

The illustration shows a typical interface for sending e-mail.

English–German Dictionary

a

vor einem Vokal **an**

● *indefinite article*

····▸ ein (*m*), eine (*f*), ein (*nt*). **a problem** ein Problem. **an apple** ein Apfel. **a cat** eine Katze. **have you got a pencil?** hast du einen Bleistift? **I gave it to a beggar** ich gab es einem Bettler

❗ There are some cases where a is not translated, such as when talking about people's professions or nationalities: **she is a lawyer** sie ist Rechsanwältin. **he's an Italian** er ist Italiener

····▸ (*with 'not'*) kein (*m*), keine (*f*), kein (*nt*), keine (*pl*). **that's not a problem/not a good idea** das ist kein Problem/keine gute Idee. **there was not a chance that** ... es bestand keine Möglichkeit, dass .... **she did not say a word** sie sagte kein Wort. **I didn't tell a soul** ich habe es keinem Menschen gesagt

····▸ (*per; each*) pro. **£300 a week** 300 Pfund pro Woche. **30 miles an hour** 30 Meilen pro Stunde. (*in prices*) **it costs 90p a pound** es kostet 90 Pence das Pfund.

aback *adv* **be taken** ∼ verblüfft sein

abandon *vt* verlassen; (*give up*) aufgeben

abate *vi* nachlassen

abattoir *n* Schlachthof *m*

abb|ey *n* Abtei *f*. ∼**ot** *n* Abt *m*

abbreviat|e *vt* abkürzen. ∼**ion** *n* Abkürzung *f*

abdicat|e *vi* abdanken. ∼**ion** *n* Abdankung *f*

abdom|en *n* Unterleib *m*. ∼**inal** *a* Unterleibs-

abduct *vt* entführen. ∼**ion** *n* Entführung *f*

aberration *n* Abweichung *f*; (*mental*) Verwirrung *f*

abeyance *n* **in** ∼ [zeitweilig] außer Kraft

abhor *vt* (*pt/pp* abhorred) verabscheuen. ∼**rent** *a* abscheulich

abid|e *vt* (*pt/pp* abided) (*tolerate*) aushalten; ausstehen <*person*>

ability *n* Fähigkeit *f*; (*talent*) Begabung *f*

abject *a* erbärmlich; (*humble*) demütig

ablaze *a* in Flammen

able *a* (**-r, -st**) fähig; **be** ∼ **to do sth** etw tun können. ∼**-bodied** *a* körperlich gesund

ably *adv* gekonnt

abnormal *a* anormal; (*Med*) abnorm. ∼**ity** *n* Abnormität *f*. ∼**ly** *adv* ungewöhnlich

aboard *adv & prep* an Bord (+ *gen*)

abol|ish *vt* abschaffen. ∼**ition** *n* Abschaffung *f*

abominable *a*, **-bly** *adv* abscheulich

aborigines *npl* Ureinwohner *pl*

abort *vt* abtreiben. ∼**ion** *n* Abtreibung *f*. ∼**ive** *a* <*attempt*> vergeblich

about *adv* umher, herum; (*approximately*) ungefähr; **be** ∼ (*in circulation*) umgehen; (*in existence*) vorhanden sein; **be** ∼ **to do sth** im Begriff sein, etw zu tun; **there was no one** ∼ es war kein Mensch da; **run/play** ∼ herumlaufen/-spielen ●*prep* um (+ *acc*) [... herum]; (*concerning*)

über (+ *acc*); **what is it ~?** worum
geht es? <*book*:> wovon handelt
es? **I know nothing ~** it ich weiß
nichts davon; **talk/know ~**
reden/wissen von
about: **~-face** *n*, **-turn** *n*
Kehrtwendung *f*
above *adv* oben ● *prep* über (+
dat/acc); **~ all** vor allem
above: **~-board** *a* legal. **~-
mentioned** *a* oben erwähnt
abrasive *a* Scheuer-; <*remark*>
verletzend ● *n* Scheuermittel *nt*;
(*Techn*) Schleifmittel *nt*
abreast *adv* nebeneinander; **keep
~ of** Schritt halten mit
abridge *vt* kürzen
abroad *adv* im Ausland; **go ~** ins
Ausland fahren
abrupt *a*, **-ly** *adv* abrupt; (*sudden*)
plötzlich; (*curt*) schroff
abscess *n* Abszess *m*
absence *n* Abwesenheit *f*
absent *a* abwesend; **be ~** fehlen
absentee *n* Abwesende(r) *m/f*
absent-minded *a*, **-ly** *adv*
geistesabwesend; (*forgetful*)
zerstreut
absolute *a*, **-ly** *adv* absolut
absorb *vt* absorbieren,
aufsaugen; **~ed in** vertieft in (+
acc). **~ent** *a* saugfähig
absorption *n* Absorption *f*
abstain *vi* sich enthalten (**from**
gen)
abstemious *a* enthaltsam
abstention *n* (*Pol*)
[Stimm]enthaltung *f*
abstract *a* abstrakt ● *n*
(*summary*) Abriss *m*
absurd *a*, **-ly** *adv* absurd. **~ity** *n*
Absurdität *f*
abundan|ce *n* Fülle *f* (**of** an +
dat). **~t** *a* reichlich
abuse[1] *vt* missbrauchen; (*insult*)
beschimpfen
abus|e[2] *n* Missbrauch *m*; (*insults*)
Beschimpfungen *pl*. **~ive** *a*
ausfallend

abysmal *a* 🆒 katastrophal
abyss *n* Abgrund *m*
academic *a*, **-ally** *adv* akademisch
academy *n* Akademie *f*
accelerat|e *vt/i* beschleunigen.
~ion *n* Beschleunigung *f*. **~or** *n*
(*Auto*) Gaspedal *nt*
accent *n* Akzent *m*
accept *vt* annehmen; (*fig*)
akzeptieren ● *vi* zusagen. **~able**
a annehmbar. **~ance** *n*
Annahme *f*; (*of invitation*) Zusage
f
access *n* Zugang *m*. **~ible** *a*
zugänglich
accessor|y *n* (*Jur*)
Mitschuldige(r) *m/f*. **~ies** *pl*
(*fashion*) Accessoires *pl*; (*Techn*)
Zubehör *nt*
accident *n* Unfall *m*; (*chance*)
Zufall *m*; **by ~** zufällig;
(*unintentionally*) versehentlich.
~al *a*, **-ly** *adv* zufällig;
(*unintentional*) versehentlich
acclaim *vt* feiern (**as** als)
acclimatize *vt* **become ~d** sich
akklimatisieren
accommodat|e *vt* unterbringen.
~ing *a* entgegenkommend. **~ion**
n (*rooms*) Unterkunft *f*
accompan|iment *n* Begleitung *f*.
~ist *n* (*Mus*) Begleiter(in) *m(f)*
accompany *vt* (*pt/pp* **-ied**)
begleiten
accomplice *n* Komplize/-zin *m/f*
accomplish *vt* erfüllen <*task*>;
(*achieve*) erreichen. **~ed** *a* fähig.
~ment *n* Fertigkeit *f*;
(*achievement*) Leistung *f*
accord *n* **of one's own ~** aus
eigenem Antrieb. **~ance** *n* **in
~ance with** entsprechend (+ *dat*)
according *adv* **~ to** nach (+ *dat*).
~ly *adv* entsprechend
accordion *n* Akkordeon *nt*
account *n* Konto *nt*; (*bill*)
Rechnung *f*; (*description*)
Darstellung *f*; (*report*) Bericht *m*;
~s *pl* (*Comm*) Bücher *pl*; **on ~ of**

wegen (+ *gen*); **on no ~** auf
keinen Fall; **take into ~** in
Betracht ziehen, berücksichtigen
● *vi* **~ for** Rechenschaft ablegen
für; (*explain*) erklären

accountant *n* Buchhalter(in)
m(f); (*chartered*)
Wirtschaftsprüfer *m*

accumulat|e *vt* ansammeln,
anhäufen ● *vi* sich ansammeln,
sich anhäufen. **~ion** *n*
Ansammlung *f*, Anhäufung *f*

accura|cy *n* Genauigkeit *f*. **~te** *a*,
-ly *adv* genau

accusation *n* Anklage *f*

accusative *a & n* **~ [case]** (*Gram*)
Akkusativ *m*

accuse *vt* (*Jur*) anklagen (**of** *gen*);
~ s.o. of doing sth jdn
beschuldigen, etw getan zu
haben

accustom *vt* gewöhnen (**to** an +
dat); **grow** or **get ~ed to** sich
gewöhnen an (+ *acc*). **~ed** *a*
gewohnt

ace *n* (*Cards, Sport*) Ass *nt*

ache *n* Schmerzen *pl* ● *vi* weh
tun, schmerzen

achieve *vt* leisten; (*gain*) erzielen;
(*reach*) erreichen. **~ment** *n* (*feat*)
Leistung *f*

acid *a* sauer; (*fig*) beißend ● *n*
Säure *f*. **~ity** *n* Säure *f*. **~ rain** *n*
saurer Regen *m*

acknowledge *vt* anerkennen;
(*admit*) zugeben; erwidern
<*greeting*>; **~ receipt of** den
Empfang bestätigen (+ *gen*).
~ment *n* Anerkennung *f*; (*of
letter*) Empfangsbestätigung *f*

acne *n* Akne *f*

acorn *n* Eichel *f*

acoustic *a*, **-ally** *adv* akustisch.
~s *npl* Akustik *f*

acquaint *vt* **be ~ed with** kennen;
vertraut sein mit <*fact*>. **~ance** *n*
(*person*) Bekannte(r) *m/f*; **make
s.o.'s ~ance** jdn kennen lernen

acquire *vt* erwerben

acquisit|ion *n* Erwerb *m*; (*thing*)
Erwerbung *f*. **~ive** *a* habgierig

acquit *vt* (*pt/pp* **acquitted**)
freisprechen

acre *n* ≈ Morgen *m*

acrimonious *a* bitter

acrobat *n* Akrobat(in) *m(f)*. **~ic** *a*
akrobatisch

across *adv* hinüber/herüber;
(*wide*) breit; (*not lengthwise*)
quer; (*in crossword*) waagerecht;
come ~ sth auf etw (*acc*) stoßen;
go ~ hinübergehen; **bring ~**
herüberbringen ● *prep* über (+
acc); (*on the other side of*) auf der
anderen Seite (+ *gen*)

act *n* Tat *f*; (*action*) Handlung *f*;
(*law*) Gesetz *nt*; (*Theat*) Akt *m*;
(*item*) Nummer *f* ● *vi* handeln;
(*behave*) sich verhalten; (*Theat*)
spielen; (*pretend*) sich verstellen;
~ as fungieren als ● *vt* spielen
<*role*>. **~ing** *a* (*deputy*)
stellvertretend ● *n* (*Theat*)
Schauspielerei *f*

action *n* Handlung *f*; (*deed*) Tat *f*;
(*Mil*) Einsatz *m*; (*Jur*) Klage *f*;
(*effect*) Wirkung *f*; (*Techn*)
Mechanismus *m*; **out of ~**
<*machine:*> außer Betrieb; **take ~**
handeln; **killed in ~** gefallen

activate *vt* betätigen

activ|e *a*, **-ly** *adv* aktiv; **on ~e
service** im Einsatz. **~ity** *n*
Aktivität *f*

act|or *n* Schauspieler *m*. **~ress** *n*
Schauspielerin *f*

actual *a*, **-ly** *adv* eigentlich; (*real*)
tatsächlich

acupuncture *n* Akupunktur *f*

acute *a* scharf; <*angle*> spitz;
<*illness*> akut. **~ly** *adv* sehr

ad *n* 🗊 = **advertisement**

AD *abbr* (**Anno Domini**) n.Chr.

adamant *a* **be ~ that** darauf
bestehen, dass

adapt *vt* anpassen; bearbeiten
<*play*> ● *vi* sich anpassen. **~able**
a anpassungsfähig

adaptation n (*Theat*) Bearbeitung f

add vt hinzufügen; (*Math*) addieren ● vi zusammenzählen, addieren; ~ **to** hinzufügen zu; (*fig: increase*) steigern; (*compound*) verschlimmern. ~ **up** vt zusammenzählen <*figures*> ● vi zusammenzählen, addieren

adder n Kreuzotter f

addict n Süchtige(r) m/f

addict|ed a süchtig; ~**ed to drugs** drogensüchtig. ~**ion** n Sucht f

addition n Hinzufügung f; (*Math*) Addition f; (*thing added*) Ergänzung f; **in** ~ zusätzlich. ~**al** a, **-ly** adv zusätzlich

additive n Zusatz m

address n Adresse f, Anschrift f; (*speech*) Ansprache f ● vt adressieren (**to** an + acc); (*speak to*) anreden <*person*>; sprechen vor (+ dat) <*meeting*>. ~**ee** n Empfänger m

adequate a, **-ly** adv ausreichend

adhere vi kleben/(*fig*) festhalten (**to** an + dat)

adhesive a klebend ● n Klebstoff m

adjacent a angrenzend

adjective n Adjektiv nt

adjoin vt angrenzen an (+ acc). ~**ing** a angrenzend

adjourn vt vertagen (**until** auf + acc) ● vi sich vertagen. ~**ment** n Vertagung f

adjudicate vi (*in competition*) Preisrichter sein

adjust vt einstellen; (*alter*) verstellen ● vi sich anpassen (**to** dat). ~**able** a verstellbar. ~**ment** n Einstellung f; Anpassung f

ad lib adv aus dem Stegreif ● vi (*pt/pp* **ad libbed**) Ⅰ improvisieren

administer vt verwalten; verabreichen <*medicine*>

administration n Verwaltung f; (*Pol*) Regierung f

admirable a bewundernswert

admiral n Admiral m

admiration n Bewunderung f

admire vt bewundern. ~**r** n Verehrer(in) m(f)

admission n Eingeständnis nt; (*entry*) Eintritt m

admit vt (*pt/pp* **admitted**) (*let in*) hereinlassen; (*acknowledge*) zugeben; ~ **to sth** etw zugeben. ~**tance** n Eintritt m. ~**tedly** adv zugegebenermaßen

admonish vt ermahnen

adolescen|ce n Jugend f, Pubertät f. ~**t** a Jugend-; <*boy, girl*> halbwüchsig ● n Jugendliche(r) m/f

adopt vt adoptieren; ergreifen <*measure*>; (*Pol*) annehmen <*candidate*>. ~**ion** n Adoption f

ador|able a bezaubernd. ~**ation** n Anbetung f

adore vt (*worship*) anbeten; (Ⅰ *like*) lieben

adorn vt schmücken. ~**ment** n Schmuck m

Adriatic a & n ~ **[Sea]** Adria f

adrift a **be** ~ treiben

adroit a, **-ly** adv gewandt, geschickt

adulation n Schwärmerei f

adult n Erwachsene(r) m/f

adulterate vt verfälschen; panschen <*wine*>

adultery n Ehebruch m

advance n Fortschritt m; (*Mil*) Vorrücken nt; (*payment*) Vorschuss m; **in** ~ im Voraus ● vi vorankommen; (*Mil*) vorrücken; (*make progress*) Fortschritte machen ● vt fördern <*cause*>; vorbringen <*idea*>; vorschießen <*money*>. ~**d** a fortgeschritten; (*progressive*) fortschrittlich. ~**ment** n Förderung f; (*promotion*) Beförderung f

advantage n Vorteil m; **take** ~ **of** ausnutzen. ~**ous** a vorteilhaft

A

adventur|e n Abenteuer nt. **~er** n Abenteurer m. **~ous** a abenteuerlich; <person> abenteuerlustig

adverb n Adverb nt

adverse a ungünstig

advert n 🔢 = advertisement

advertise vt Reklame machen für; (by small ad) inserieren ● vi Reklame machen; inserieren

advertisement n Anzeige f; (publicity) Reklame f; (small ad) Inserat nt

advertis|er n Inserent m. **~ing** n Werbung f

advice n Rat m

advisable a ratsam

advis|e vt raten (s.o. jdm); (counsel) beraten; (inform) benachrichtigen; **~e s.o. against sth** jdm von etw abraten ● vi raten. **~er** n Berater(in) m(f). **~ory** a beratend

advocate[1] n (supporter) Befürworter m

advocate[2] vt befürworten

aerial a Luft- ● n Antenne f

aerobics n Aerobic nt

aero|drome n Flugplatz m. **~plane** n Flugzeug nt

aerosol n Spraydose f

aesthetic a ästhetisch

affair n Angelegenheit f, Sache f; (scandal) Affäre f; [love-]~ [Liebes]verhältnis nt

affect vt sich auswirken auf (+ acc); (concern) betreffen; (move) rühren; (pretend) vortäuschen. **~ation** n Affektiertheit f. **~ed** a affektiert

affection n Liebe f. **~ate** a, **-ly** adv liebevoll

affirm vt behaupten

affirmative a bejahend ● n Bejahung f

afflict vt **be ~ed with** behaftet sein mit. **~ion** n Leiden nt

affluen|ce n Reichtum m. **~t** a wohlhabend. **~t society** n Wohlstandsgesellschaft f

afford vt **be able to ~ sth** sich (dat) etw leisten können. **~able** a erschwinglich

affront n Beleidigung f ● vt beleidigen

afloat a **be ~** <ship:> flott sein; **keep ~** <person:> sich über Wasser halten

afraid a **be ~** Angst haben (of vor + dat); **I'm ~ not** leider nicht; **I'm ~ so** [ja] leider

Africa n Afrika nt. **~n** a afrikanisch ● n Afrikaner(in) m(f)

after adv danach ● prep nach (+ dat); **~ that** danach; **~ all** schließlich; **the day ~ tomorrow** übermorgen; **be ~** aus sein auf (+ acc) ● conj nachdem

after: **~-effect** n Nachwirkung f. **~math** n Auswirkungen pl. **~noon** n Nachmittag m; **good ~noon!** guten Tag! **~-sales service** n Kundendienst m. **~shave** n Rasierwasser nt. **~thought** n nachträglicher Einfall m. **~wards** adv nachher

again adv wieder; (once more) noch einmal; **~ and ~** immer wieder

against prep gegen (+ acc)

age n Alter nt; (era) Zeitalter nt; **~s** 🔢 ewig; **under ~** minderjährig; **of ~** volljährig; **two years of ~** zwei Jahre alt ● vt (pres p ageing) ● vi altern; (mature) reifen

aged[1] a **~ two** zwei Jahre alt

aged[2] a betagt ● n **the ~** pl die Alten

ageless a ewig jung

agency n Agentur f; (office) Büro nt

agenda n Tagesordnung f

agent n Agent(in) m(f); (Comm) Vertreter(in) m(f); (substance) Mittel nt

aggravat|e vt verschlimmern; (☐ annoy) ärgern. **~ion** n ☐ Ärger m

aggregate a gesamt ● n Gesamtzahl f; (sum) Gesamtsumme f

aggress|ion n Aggression f. **~ive** a, **-ly** adv aggressiv. **~or** n Angreifer(in) m(f)

aggro n ☐ Ärger m

aghast a entsetzt

agil|e a flink, behände; <mind> wendig. **~ity** n Flinkheit f, Behändigkeit f

agitat|e vt bewegen; (shake) schütteln ● vi (fig) **~** for agitieren für. **~ed** a, **-ly** adv erregt. **~ion** n Erregung f; (Pol) Agitation f

ago adv vor (+ dat); **a long time ~** vor langer Zeit; **how long ~ is it?** wie lange ist es her?

agony n Qual f; **be in ~** furchtbare Schmerzen haben

agree vt vereinbaren; (admit) zugeben; **~ to do sth** sich bereit erklären, etw zu tun ● vi <people, figures:> übereinstimmen; (reach agreement) sich einigen; (get on) gut miteinander auskommen; (consent) einwilligen (**to** in + acc); **~ with s.o.** jdm zustimmen; <food:> jdm bekommen; **~ with sth** (approve of) mit etw einverstanden sein

agreeable a angenehm

agreed a vereinbart

agreement n Übereinstimmung f; (consent) Einwilligung f; (contract) Abkommen nt; **reach ~** sich einigen

agricultur|al a landwirtschaftlich. **~e** n Landwirtschaft f

aground a gestrandet; **run ~** <ship:> stranden

ahead adv **straight ~** geradeaus; **be ~ of s.o./sth** vor jdm/etw sein; (fig) voraus sein; **go on ~** vorgehen; **get ~** vorankommen; **go ~!** ☐ bitte! **look/plan ~** vorausblicken/-planen

aid n Hilfe f; (financial) Unterstützung f; **in ~ of** zugunsten (+ gen) ● vt helfen (+ dat)

Aids n Aids nt

aim n Ziel nt; **take ~** zielen ● vt richten (**at** auf + acc); ● vi zielen (**at** auf + acc); **~ to do sth** beabsichtigen, etw zu tun. **~less** a, **-ly** adv ziellos

air n Luft f; (expression) Miene f; (appearance) Anschein m; **be on the ~** <programme:> gesendet werden; <person:> auf Sendung sein; **by ~** auf dem Luftweg; (airmail) mit Luftpost ● vt lüften; vorbringen <views>

air: **~ bag** n (Auto) Airbag m. **~-conditioned** a klimatisiert. **~-conditioning** n Klimaanlage f. **~craft** n Flugzeug nt. **~field** n Flugplatz m. **~ force** n Luftwaffe f. **~ freshener** n Raumspray nt. **~gun** n Luftgewehr nt. **~ hostess** n Stewardess f. **~ letter** n Aerogramm nt. **~line** n Fluggesellschaft f. **~mail** n Luftpost f. **~man** n Flieger m. **~plane** n (Amer) Flugzeug nt. **~port** n Flughafen m. **~ rage** n ausfälliges Fluggastverhalten. **~-raid** n Luftangriff m. **~-raid shelter** n Luftschutzbunker m. **~ship** n Luftschiff nt. **~ ticket** n Flugschein m. **~tight** a luftdicht. **~-traffic controller** n Fluglotse m

airy a (**-ier, -iest**) luftig; <manner> nonchalant

aisle n Gang m

ajar a angelehnt

alarm n Alarm m; (device) Alarmanlage f; (clock) Wecker m; (fear) Unruhe f ● vt erschrecken

alas *int* ach!
album *n* Album *nt*
alcohol *n* Alkohol *m*. ~**ic** *a* alkoholisch ● *n* Alkoholiker(in) *m(f)*. ~**ism** *n* Alkoholismus *m*
alert *a* aufmerksam ● *n* Alarm *m*
algebra *n* Algebra *f*
Algeria *n* Algerien *nt*
alias *n* Deckname *m* ● *adv* alias
alibi *n* Alibi *nt*
alien *a* fremd ● *n* Ausländer(in) *m(f)*
alienate *vt* entfremden
alight[1] *vi* aussteigen (**from** aus)
alight[2] *a* be ~ brennen; **set** ~ anzünden
align *vt* ausrichten
alike *a & adv* ähnlich; (*same*) gleich; **look** ~ sich (*dat*) ähnlich sehen
alive *a* lebendig; **be** ~ leben; **be** ~ **with** wimmeln von

all
● *adjective*
····➤ (*plural*) alle. **all [the] children** alle Kinder. **all our children** alle unsere Kinder. **all the books** alle Bücher
····➤ (*singular = whole*) ganz. **all the wine** der ganze Wein. **all the town** die ganze Stadt. **all my money** mein ganzes Geld; all mein Geld. **all day** den ganzen Tag. **all Germany** ganz Deutschland
● *pronoun*
····➤ (*plural = all persons/things*) alle. **all are welcome** alle sind willkommen. **they all came** sie sind alle gekommen. **are we all here?** sind wir alle da? **the best pupils of all** die besten Schüler (von allen). **the most beautiful of all** der/die/das schönste von allen
····➤ (*singular = everything*) alles. **that is all** das ist alles. **all that I possess** alles, was ich besitze

····➤ **all of** ganz; (*with plural*) alle. **all of the money** das ganze Geld. **all of the paintings** alle Gemälde. **all of you/them** Sie/sie alle
····➤ (*in phrases*) **all in all** alles in allem. **in all** insgesamt. **most of all** am meisten. **once and for all** ein für alle Mal. **not at all** gar nicht
● *adverb*
····➤ (*completely*) ganz. **she was all alone** sie war ganz allein. **I was all dirty** ich war ganz schmutzig
····➤ (*in scores*) **four all** vier zu vier
····➤ **all right** (*things*) in Ordnung. **is everything all right?** ist alles in Ordnung? **is that all right for you?** passt das Ihnen? **I'm all right** mir geht es gut. **did you get home all right?** sind Sie gut nach Hause gekommen? **is it all right to go in?** kann ich reingehen? **yes, all right** ja, gut. **work out all right** gut gehen; klappen 🔲
····➤ (*in phrases*) **all but** (*almost*) fast. **all at once** auf einmal. **all the better** umso besser. **all the same** (*nevertheless*) trotzdem

allege *vt* behaupten
allegiance *n* Treue *f*
allerg|ic *a* allergisch (**to** gegen). ~**y** *n* Allergie *f*
alleviate *vt* lindern
alley *n* Gasse *f*; (*for bowling*) Bahn *f*
alliance *n* Verbindung *f*; (*Pol*) Bündnis *nt*
allied *a* alliiert
alligator *n* Alligator *m*
allocat|e *vt* zuteilen; (*share out*) verteilen. ~**ion** *n* Zuteilung *f*
allot *vt* (*pt/pp* allotted) zuteilen (**s.o.** jdm)
allow *vt* erlauben; (*give*) geben; (*grant*) gewähren; (*reckon*) rechnen; (*agree, admit*) zugeben; ~ **for** berücksichtigen; ~ **s.o. to**

do sth jdm erlauben, etw zu tun; **be ~ed to do sth** etw tun dürfen

allowance n [finanzielle] Unterstützung f; **make ~s for** berücksichtigen

alloy n Legierung f

allude vi anspielen (**to** auf + acc)

allusion n Anspielung f

ally¹ n Verbündete(r) m/f; **the Allies** pl die Alliierten

ally² vt (pt/pp -ied) verbinden; **~ oneself with** sich verbünden mit

almighty a allmächtig; (**Ⅰ** big) Riesen-. ●n **the A~** der Allmächtige

almond n (Bot) Mandel f

almost adv fast, beinahe

alone a & adv allein; **leave me ~** lass mich in Ruhe; **leave that ~!** lass die Finger davon! **let ~** ganz zu schweigen von

along prep entlang (+ acc); **~ the river** den Fluss entlang ●adv **~ with** zusammen mit; **all ~** die ganze Zeit; **come ~** komm doch; **I'll bring it ~** ich bringe es mit

alongside adv daneben ●prep neben (+ dat)

aloud adv laut

alphabet n Alphabet nt. ~**ical** a, -**ly** adv alphabetisch

alpine a alpin; **A ~** Alpen-

Alps npl Alpen pl

already adv schon

Alsace n Elsass nt

Alsatian n (dog) [deutscher] Schäferhund m

also adv auch

altar n Altar m

alter vt ändern ●vi sich verändern. ~**ation** n Änderung f

alternate¹ vi [sich] abwechseln ●vt abwechseln

alternate² a, -**ly** adv abwechselnd; **on ~ days** jeden zweiten Tag

alternative a andere(r,s); **~ medicine** Alternativmedizin f ●n Alternative f. ~**ly** adv oder aber

although conj obgleich, obwohl

altitude n Höhe f

altogether adv insgesamt; (on the whole) alles in allem

aluminium n, (Amer) **aluminum** n Aluminium nt

always adv immer

am see **be**

a.m. abbr (ante meridiem) vormittags

amass vt anhäufen

amateur n Amateur m ●attrib Amateur-; (Theat) Laien-. ~**ish** a laienhaft

amaze vt erstaunen. ~**d** a erstaunt. ~**ment** n Erstaunen nt

amazing a, -**ly** adv erstaunlich

ambassador n Botschafter m

amber n Bernstein m ●a (colour) gelb

ambigu|ity n Zweideutigkeit f. ~**ous** a -**ly** adv zweideutig

ambiti|on n Ehrgeiz m; (aim) Ambition f. ~**ous** a ehrgeizig

amble vi schlendern

ambulance n Krankenwagen m. **~ man** n Sanitäter m

ambush n Hinterhalt m ●vt aus dem Hinterhalt überfallen

amen int amen

amend vt ändern. ~**ment** n Änderung f

amenities npl Einrichtungen pl

America n Amerika nt. ~**n** a amerikanisch ●n Amerikaner(in) m(f). ~**nism** n Amerikanismus m

amiable a nett

amicable a, -**bly** adv freundschaftlich; <agreement> gütlich

amid[st] prep inmitten (+ gen)

ammonia n Ammoniak nt

ammunition n Munition f

amnesty n Amnestie f

among[st] prep unter (+ dat/acc); **~ yourselves** untereinander

amoral a amoralisch

amorous a zärtlich

amount n Menge f; (sum of money) Betrag m; (total) Gesamtsumme f ● vi **- to** sich belaufen auf (+ acc); (fig) hinauslaufen auf (+ acc)
amphibi|an n Amphibie f. ∼**ous** a amphibisch
amphitheatre n Amphitheater nt
ample a (-r, -st), **-ly** adv reichlich; (large) füllig
amplif|ier n Verstärker m. ∼**y** vt (pt/pp -ied) weiter ausführen; verstärken <sound>
amputat|e vt amputieren. ∼**ion** n Amputation f
amuse vt amüsieren, belustigen; (entertain) unterhalten. ∼**ment** n Belustigung f; Unterhaltung f
amusing a amüsant
an see **a**
anaem|ia n Blutarmut f, Anämie f. ∼**ic** a blutarm
anaesthetic n Narkosemittel nt, Betäubungsmittel nt; **under [an]** ∼ in Narkose
anaesthetist n Narkosearzt m
analogy n Analogie f
analyse vt analysieren
analysis n Analyse f
analyst n Chemiker(in) m(f); (Psych) Analytiker m
analytical a analytisch
anarch|ist n Anarchist m. ∼**y** n Anarchie f
anatom|ical a, **-ly** adv anatomisch. ∼**y** n Anatomie f
ancest|or n Vorfahr m. ∼**ry** n Abstammung f
anchor n Anker m ● vi ankern ● vt verankern
ancient a alt
and conj und; ∼ **so on** und so weiter; **six hundred** ∼ **two** sechshundertzwei; **more** ∼ **more** immer mehr; **nice** ∼ **warm** schön warm
anecdote n Anekdote f
angel n Engel m. ∼**ic** a engelhaft

anger n Zorn m ● vt zornig machen
angle n Winkel m; (fig) Standpunkt m; **at an** ∼ schräg
angler n Angler m
Anglican a anglikanisch ● n Anglikaner(in) m(f)
Anglo-Saxon a angelsächsisch ● n Angelsächsisch nt
angry a (-ier, -iest), **-ily** adv zornig; **be** ∼ **with** böse sein auf (+ acc)
anguish n Qual f
angular a eckig; <features> kantig
animal n Tier nt ● a tierisch
animat|e vt beleben. ∼**ed** a lebhaft
animosity n Feindseligkeit f
ankle n [Fuß]knöchel m
annex[e] n Nebengebäude nt; (extension) Anbau m
annihilate vt vernichten
anniversary n Jahrestag m
annotate vt kommentieren
announce vt bekannt geben; (over loudspeaker) durchsagen; (at reception) ankündigen; (Radio, TV) ansagen; (in newspaper) anzeigen. ∼**ment** n Bekanntgabe f, Bekanntmachung f; Durchsage f; Ansage f; Anzeige f. ∼**r** n Ansager(in) m(f)
annoy vt ärgern; (pester) belästigen; **get** ∼**ed** sich ärgern. ∼**ance** n Ärger m. ∼**ing** a ärgerlich
annual a, **-ly** adv jährlich ● n (book) Jahresalbum nt
anonymous a, **-ly** adv anonym
anorak n Anorak m
anorexi|a n Magersucht f. ∼**c** a **be** ∼**c** an Magersucht leiden
another a & pron ein anderer/ eine andere/ein anderes; (additional) noch ein(e); (one more) noch einer/eine/eins; ∼ **time** ein andermal; **one** ∼ einander
answer n Antwort f; (solution) Lösung f ● vt antworten (**s.o.** jdm); beantworten <question,

letter>; ~ **the door/telephone** an
die Tür/ans Telefon gehen ●*vi*
antworten; (*Teleph*) sich melden;
~ **back** eine freche Antwort
geben. ~**ing machine** *n* (*Teleph*)
Anrufbeantworter *m*

ant *n* Ameise *f*

antagonis|m *n* Antagonismus *m*.
~**tic** *a* feindselig

Antarctic *n* Antarktis *f*

antelope *n* Antilope *f*

antenatal *a* ~ **care**
Schwangerschaftsfürsorge *f*

antenna *n* Fühler *m*; (*Amer:
aerial*) Antenne *f*

anthem *n* Hymne *f*

anthology *n* Anthologie *f*

anthrax *n* Milzbrand *m*, Anthrax
m

anthropology *n* Anthropologie *f*

antibiotic *n* Antibiotikum *nt*

anticipat|e *vt* vorhersehen;
(*forestall*) zuvorkommen (+ *dat*);
(*expect*) erwarten. ~**ion** *n*
Erwartung *f*

anticlimax *n* Enttäuschung *f*

anticlockwise *a & adv* gegen den
Uhrzeigersinn

antics *npl* Mätzchen *pl*

antidote *n* Gegengift *nt*

antifreeze *n* Frostschutzmittel *nt*

antipathy *n* Abneigung *f*,
Antipathie *f*

antiquated *a* veraltet

antique *a* antik ●*n* Antiquität *f*.
~ **dealer** *n* Antiquitätenhändler
m

antiquity *n* Altertum *nt*

antiseptic *a* antiseptisch ●*n*
Antiseptikum *nt*

antisocial *a* asozial; ⚅ ungesellig

antlers *npl* Geweih *nt*

anus *n* After *m*

anvil *n* Amboss *m*

anxiety *n* Sorge *f*

anxious *a*, -**ly** *adv* ängstlich;
(*worried*) besorgt; **be** ~ **to do sth**
etw gerne machen wollen

any *a* irgendein(e); *pl*
irgendwelche; (*every*) jede(r,s); *pl*
alle; (*after negative*) kein(e); *pl*
keine; ~ **colour/number you like**
eine beliebige Farbe/Zahl; **have
you** ~ **wine/apples?** haben Sie
Wein/Äpfel? ●*pron*
[irgend]einer/eine/eins; *pl*
[irgend]welche; (*some*)
welche(r,s); *pl* welche; (*all*) alle
pl; (*negative*) keiner/keine/keins;
pl keine; **I don't want** ~ **of it** ich
will nichts davon; **there aren't** ~
es gibt keine ●*adv* noch; ~
quicker/slower noch schneller/
langsamer; **is it** ~ **better?** geht es
etwas besser? **I can't eat** ~ **more**
ich kann nichts mehr essen

anybody *pron* [irgend]jemand;
(*after negative*) niemand; ~ **can
do that** das kann jeder

anyhow *adv* jedenfalls;
(*nevertheless*) trotzdem; (*badly*)
irgendwie

anyone *pron* = **anybody**

anything *pron* [irgend]etwas;
(*after negative*) nichts;
(*everything*) alles

anyway *adv* jedenfalls; (*in any
case*) sowieso

anywhere *adv* irgendwo; (*after
negative*) nirgendwo; <*be, live*>
überall; <*go*> überallhin

apart *adv* auseinander; **live** ~
getrennt leben; ~ **from**
abgesehen von

apartment *n* Zimmer *nt*; (*flat*)
Wohnung *f*

ape *n* [Menschen]affe *m* ●*vt*
nachäffen

aperitif *n* Aperitif *m*

apologetic *a*, -**ally** *adv*
entschuldigend; **be** ~ sich
entschuldigen

apologize *vi* sich entschuldigen
(**to** bei)

apology *n* Entschuldigung *f*

apostle *n* Apostel *m*

apostrophe *n* Apostroph *m*

appal vt (pt/pp **appalled**)
entsetzen. ~**ling** a entsetzlich
apparatus n Apparatur f; (Sport)
Geräte pl; (single piece) Gerät nt
apparent a offenbar; (seeming)
scheinbar. ~**ly** adv offenbar,
anscheinend
appeal n Appell m, Aufruf m;
(request) Bitte f; (attraction) Reiz
m; (Jur) Berufung f ● vi
appellieren (**to** an + acc); (ask)
bitten (**for** um); (be attractive)
zusagen (**to** dat); (Jur) Berufung
einlegen. ~**ing** a ansprechend
appear vi erscheinen; (seem)
scheinen; (Theat) auftreten.
~**ance** n Erscheinen nt; (look)
Aussehen nt; **to all** ~**ances** allem
Anschein nach
appendicitis n
Blinddarmentzündung f
appendix n (pl **-ices**) (of book)
Anhang m ● (pl **-es**) (Anat)
Blinddarm m
appetite n Appetit m
appetizing a appetitlich
applau|d vt/i Beifall klatschen (+
dat). ~**se** n Beifall m
apple n Apfel m
appliance n Gerät nt
applicable a anwendbar (**to** auf +
acc); (on form) **not** ~ nicht
zutreffend
applicant n Bewerber(in) m(f)
application n Anwendung f;
(request) Antrag m; (for job)
Bewerbung f; (diligence) Fleiß m
applied a angewandt
apply vt (pt/pp **-ied**) auftragen
<paint>; anwenden <force, rule>
● vi zutreffen (**to** auf + acc); ~ **for**
beantragen; sich bewerben um
<job>
appoint vt ernennen; (fix)
festlegen. ~**ment** n Ernennung f;
(meeting) Verabredung f; (at
doctor's, hairdresser's) Termin m;
(job) Posten m; **make an** ~**ment**
sich anmelden

appreciable a merklich;
(considerable) beträchtlich
appreciat|e vt zu schätzen
wissen; (be grateful for) dankbar
sein für; (enjoy) schätzen;
(understand) verstehen ● vi
(increase in value) im Wert
steigen. ~**ion** n (gratitude)
Dankbarkeit f. ~**ive** a dankbar
apprehens|ion n Festnahme f;
(fear) Angst f. ~**ive** a ängstlich
apprentice n Lehrling m. ~**ship** n
Lehre f
approach n Näherkommen nt; (of
time) Nahen nt; (access) Zugang
m; (road) Zufahrt f ● vi sich
nähern; <time:> nahen ● vt sich
nähern (+ dat); (with request)
herantreten an (+ acc); (set
about) sich heranmachen an (+
acc). ~**able** a zugänglich
appropriate a angebracht,
angemessen
approval n Billigung f; **on** ~ zur
Ansicht
approv|e vt billigen ● vi ~**e of**
sth/s.o. mit etw/jdm
einverstanden sein. ~**ing** a, **-ly**
adv anerkennend
approximate a, **-ly** adv ungefähr
approximation n Schätzung f
apricot n Aprikose f
April n April m; **make an** ~ **fool of**
in den April schicken
apron n Schürze f
apt a, **-ly** adv passend; **be** ~ **to do**
sth dazu neigen, etw zu tun
aqualung n Tauchgerät nt
aquarium n Aquarium nt
aquatic a Wasser-
Arab a arabisch ● n Araber(in)
m(f). ~**ian** a arabisch
Arabic a arabisch
arbitrary a, **-ily** adv willkürlich
arbitrat|e vi schlichten. ~**ion** n
Schlichtung f
arc n Bogen m
arcade n Laubengang m; (shops)
Einkaufspassage f

arch n Bogen m; (of foot)
Gewölbe nt ● vt ~ its back <cat:>
einen Buckel machen
archaeological a archäologisch
archaeolog|ist n Archäologe m/
-login f. ~y n Archäologie f
archaic a veraltet
archbishop n Erzbischof m
archer n Bogenschütze m. ~y n
Bogenschießen nt
architect n Architekt(in) m(f).
~ural a, -ly adv architektonisch
architecture n Architektur f
archives npl Archiv nt
archway n Torbogen m
Arctic a arktisch ● n the ~ die
Arktis
ardent a, -ly adv leidenschaftlich
ardour n Leidenschaft f
arduous a mühsam
are see be
area n (surface) Fläche f; (Geom)
Flächeninhalt m; (region)
Gegend f; (fig) Gebiet nt
arena n Arena f
Argentina n Argentinien nt
Argentin|e, ~ian a argentinisch
argue vi streiten (about über +
acc); <two people:> sich streiten;
(debate) diskutieren; don't ~!
keine Widerrede! ● vt (debate)
diskutieren; (reason) ~ that
argumentieren, dass
argument n Streit m,
Auseinandersetzung f;
(reasoning) Argument nt; have an
~ sich streiten. ~ative a
streitlustig
aria n Arie f
arise vi (pt arose, pp arisen) sich
ergeben (from aus)
aristocracy n Aristokratie f
aristocrat n Aristokrat(in) m(f).
~ic a aristokratisch
arithmetic n Rechnen nt
arm n Arm m; (of chair)
Armlehne f; ~s pl (weapons)
Waffen pl; (Heraldry) Wappen nt
● vt bewaffnen

armament n Bewaffnung f; ~s pl
Waffen pl
armchair n Sessel m
armed a bewaffnet; ~ forces
Streitkräfte pl
armour n Rüstung f. ~ed a
Panzer-
armpit n Achselhöhle f
army n Heer nt; (specific) Armee
f; join the ~ zum Militär gehen
aroma n Aroma nt, Duft m. ~tic a
aromatisch
arose see arise
around adv [all] ~ rings herum;
he's not ~ er ist nicht da; travel ~
herumreisen ● prep um (+ acc)
... herum; (approximately) gegen
arouse vt aufwecken; (excite)
erregen
arrange vt arrangieren; anordnen
<furniture, books>; (settle)
abmachen. ~ment n Anordnung
f; (agreement) Vereinbarung f; (of
flowers) Gesteck nt; make ~ments
Vorkehrungen treffen
arrest n Verhaftung f; under ~
verhaftet ● vt verhaften
arrival n Ankunft f; new ~s pl
Neuankömmlinge pl
arrive vi ankommen; ~ at (fig)
gelangen zu
arrogan|ce n Arroganz f. ~t a, -ly
adv arrogant
arrow n Pfeil m
arse n (vulg) Arsch m
arson n Brandstiftung f. ~ist n
Brandstifter m
art n Kunst f; work of ~
Kunstwerk nt; ~s and crafts pl
Kunstgewerbe nt; A~s pl (Univ)
Geisteswissenschaften pl
artery n Schlagader f, Arterie f
art gallery n Kunstgalerie f
arthritis n Arthritis f
artichoke n Artischocke f
article n Artikel m; (object)
Gegenstand m; ~ of clothing
Kleidungsstück nt
artificial a, -ly adv künstlich

artillery *n* Artillerie *f*

artist *n* Künstler(in) *m(f)*

artiste *n* (*Theat*) Artist(in) *m(f)*

artistic *a*, **-ally** *adv* künstlerisch

as *conj* (*because*) da; (*when*) als; (*while*) während ● *prep* als; **as a child/foreigner** als Kind/Ausländer ● *adv* **as well** auch; **as soon as** sobald; **as much as** so viel wie; **as quick as you** so schnell wie du; **as you know** wie Sie wissen; **as far as I'm concerned** was mich betrifft

asbestos *n* Asbest *m*

ascend *vi* [auf]steigen ● *vt* besteigen <*throne*>

ascent *n* Aufstieg *m*

ascertain *vt* ermitteln

ash¹ *n* (*tree*) Esche *f*

ash² *n* Asche *f*

ashamed *a* beschämt; **be ~** sich schämen (**of** über + *acc*)

ashore *adv* an Land

ashtray *n* Aschenbecher *m*

Asia *n* Asien *nt*. **~n** *a* asiatisch ● *n* Asiat(in) *m(f)*. **~tic** *a* asiatisch

aside *adv* beiseite

ask *vt/i* fragen; stellen <*question*>; (*invite*) einladen; **~ for** bitten um; verlangen <*s.o.*>; **~ after** sich erkundigen nach; **~ s.o. in** jdn hereinbitten; **~ s.o. to do sth** jdn bitten, etw zu tun

asleep *a* **be ~** schlafen; **fall ~** einschlafen

asparagus *n* Spargel *m*

aspect *n* Aspekt *m*

asphalt *n* Asphalt *m*

aspire *vi* **~ to** streben nach

ass *n* Esel *m*

assail *vt* bestürmen. **~ant** *n* Angreifer(in) *m(f)*

assassin *n* Mörder(in) *m(f)*. **~ate** *vt* ermorden. **~ation** *n* [politischer] Mord *m*

assault *n* (*Mil*) Angriff *m*; (*Jur*) Körperverletzung *f* ● *vt* [tätlich] angreifen

assemble *vi* sich versammeln ● *vt* versammeln; (*Techn*) montieren

assembly *n* Versammlung *f*; (*Sch*) Andacht *f*; (*Techn*) Montage *f*. **~ line** *n* Fließband *nt*

assent *n* Zustimmung *f*

assert *vt* behaupten; **~ oneself** sich durchsetzen. **~ion** *n* Behauptung *f*

assess *vt* bewerten; (*fig & for tax purposes*) einschätzen: schätzen <*value*>. **~ment** *n* Einschätzung *f*; (*of tax*) Steuerbescheid *m*

asset *n* Vorteil *m*; **~s** *pl* (*money*) Vermögen *nt*; (*Comm*) Aktiva *pl*

assign *vt* zuweisen (**to** *dat*). **~ment** *n* (*task*) Aufgabe *f*

assist *vt/i* helfen (+ *dat*). **~ance** *n* Hilfe *f*. **~ant** *a* Hilfs- ● *n* Assistent(in) *m(f)*; (*in shop*) Verkäufer(in) *m(f)*

associat|e¹ *vt* verbinden; (*Psych*) assoziieren ● *vi* **~ with** verkehren mit. **~ion** *n* Verband *m*

associate² *a* assoziiert ● *n* Kollege *m*/-gin *f*

assort|ed *a* gemischt. **~ment** *n* Mischung *f*

assum|e *vt* annehmen; übernehmen <*office*>; **~ing that** angenommen, dass

assumption *n* Annahme *f*; **on the ~** in der Annahme (**that** dass)

assurance *n* Versicherung *f*; (*confidence*) Selbstsicherheit *f*

assure *vt* versichern (**s.o.** jdm); **I ~ you [of that]** das versichere ich Ihnen. **~d** *a* sicher

asterisk *n* Sternchen *nt*

asthma *n* Asthma *nt*

astonish *vt* erstaunen. **~ing** *a* erstaunlich. **~ment** *n* Erstaunen *nt*

astray *adv* **go ~** verloren gehen; <*person:*> sich verlaufen

astride *adv* rittlings ● *prep* rittlings auf (+ *dat/acc*)

astrolog|er n Astrologe m/-gin f.
~**y** n Astrologie f
astronaut n Astronaut(in) m(f)
astronom|er n Astronom m.
~**ical** a astronomisch. ~**y** n
Astronomie f
astute a scharfsinnig
asylum n Asyl nt; [**lunatic**] ~
Irrenanstalt f. ~-**seeker** n
Asylant m

at

● *preposition*

····➤ (*expressing place*) an (+ *dat*).
at the station am Bahnhof. **at the
end** am Ende. **at the corner** an
der Ecke. **at the same place** an
der gleichen Stelle

····➤ (*at s.o.'s house or shop*) bei (+
dat). **at Lisa's** bei Lisa. **at my
uncle's** bei meinem Onkel. **at the
baker's/butcher's** beim Bäcker/
Fleischer

····➤ (*inside a building*) in (+ *dat*).
at the theatre/supermarket im
Theater/Supermarkt. **we spent
the night at a hotel** wir
übernachteten in einem Hotel.
he is still at the office er ist noch
im Büro

····➤ (*expressing time*) (*with clock
time*) um; (*with main festivals*)
zu. **at six o'clock** um sechs Uhr.
at midnight um Mitternacht. **at
midday** um zwölf Uhr mittags. **at
Christmas/Easter** zu
Weihnachten/Ostern

····➤ (*expressing age*) mit. **at [the
age of] forty** mit vierzig; im Alter
von vierzig

····➤ (*expressing price*) zu. **at £2.50
[each]** zu *od* für [je] 2,50 Pfund

····➤ (*expressing speed*) mit. **at 30
m.p.h.** mit dreißig Meilen pro
Stunde

····➤ (*in phrases*) **good/bad at
languages** gut/schlecht in
Sprachen. **two at a time** zwei auf
einmal. **at that** (*at that point*)

dabei; (*at that provocation*)
daraufhin; (*moreover*) noch
dazu

ate *see* **eat**
atheist n Atheist(in) m(f)
athlet|e n Athlet(in) m(f). ~**ic** a
sportlich. ~**ics** n Leichtathletik f
Atlantic a & n **the** ~ [**Ocean**] der
Atlantik
atlas n Atlas m
atmosphere n Atmosphäre f
atom n Atom nt. ~ **bomb** n
Atombombe f
atomic a Atom-
atrocious a abscheulich
atrocity n Gräueltat f
attach vt befestigen (**to** an + *dat*);
beimessen <*importance*> (**to** + *dat*);
be ~**ed to** (*fig*) hängen an (+ *dat*)
attack n Angriff m; (*Med*) Anfall
m ● vt/i angreifen
attain vt erreichen. ~**able** a
erreichbar
attempt n Versuch m ● vt
versuchen
attend vt anwesend sein bei; (*go
regularly to*) besuchen; (*take part
in*) teilnehmen an (+ *dat*);
(*accompany*) begleiten; <*doctor:*>
behandeln ● vi anwesend sein;
(*pay attention*) aufpassen; ~ **to**
sich kümmern um; (*in shop*)
bedienen. ~**ance** n Anwesenheit
f; (*number*) Besucherzahl f. ~**ant**
n Wärter(in) m(f); (*in car park*)
Wächter m
attention n Aufmerksamkeit f; ~!
(*Mil*) stillgestanden! **pay** ~
aufpassen; **pay** ~ **to** beachten,
achten auf (+ *acc*)
attentive a, -**ly** adv aufmerksam
attic n Dachboden m
attitude n Haltung f
attorney n (*Amer: lawyer*)
Rechtsanwalt m; **power of** ~
Vollmacht f
attract vt anziehen; erregen
<*attention*>; ~ **s.o.'s attention** jds

Aufmerksamkeit auf sich (acc)
lenken. ~**ion** n Anziehungskraft
f; (charm) Reiz m; (thing)
Attraktion f. ~**ive** a, -**ly** adv
attraktiv
attribute vt zuschreiben (to dat)
aubergine n Aubergine f
auburn a kastanienbraun
auction n Auktion f,
Versteigerung f ● vt versteigern.
~**eer** n Auktionator m
audaci|ous a, -**ly** adv verwegen.
~**ty** n Verwegenheit f;
(impudence) Dreistigkeit f
audible a, -**bly** adv hörbar
audience n Publikum nt; (Theat,
TV) Zuschauer pl; (Radio)
Zuhörer pl; (meeting) Audienz f
audit n Bücherrevision f ● vt
(Comm) prüfen
audition n (Theat) Vorsprechen
nt; (Mus) Vorspielen nt; (for
singer) Vorsingen nt ● vi
vorsprechen; vorspielen;
vorsingen
auditor n Buchprüfer m
auditorium n Zuschauerraum m
August n August m
aunt n Tante f
au pair n ~ **[girl]** Au-pair-
Mädchen nt
aura n Fluidum nt
auspicious a günstig; <occasion>
freudig
auster|e a streng; (simple)
nüchtern. ~**ity** n Strenge f;
(hardship) Entbehrung f
Australia n Australien nt. ~**n** a
australisch ● n Australier(in)
m(f)
Austria n Österreich nt ~**n** a
österreichisch ● n
Österreicher(in) m(f)
authentic a echt, authentisch.
~**ate** vt beglaubigen. ~**ity** n
Echtheit f
author n Schriftsteller m, Autor
m; (of document) Verfasser m
authoritarian a autoritär

authoritative a maßgebend
authority n Autorität f; (public)
Behörde f; **in** ~ verantwortlich
authorization n Ermächtigung f
authorize vt ermächtigen <s.o.>;
genehmigen <sth>
autobiography n Autobiographie
f
autograph n Autogramm nt
automatic a, -**ally** adv
automatisch
automation n Automation f
automobile n Auto nt
autonom|ous a autonom. ~**y** n
Autonomie f
autumn n Herbst m. ~**al** a
herbstlich
auxiliary a Hilfs- ● n Helfer(in)
m(f), Hilfskraft f
avail n to no ~ vergeblich
available a verfügbar;
(obtainable) erhältlich
avalanche n Lawine f
avenge vt rächen
avenue n Allee f
average a Durchschnitts-,
durchschnittlich ● n
Durchschnitt m; **on** ~ im
Durchschnitt, durchschnittlich
● vt durchschnittlich schaffen
averse a not be ~**e** to sth etw
(dat) nicht abgeneigt sein
avert vt abwenden
aviary n Vogelhaus nt
aviation n Luftfahrt f
avocado n Avocado f
avoid vt vermeiden; ~ **s.o.**
aus dem Weg gehen. ~**able** a
vermeidbar. ~**ance** n
Vermeidung f
await vt warten auf (+ acc)
awake a wach; **wide** ~ hellwach
● vi (pt awoke, pp awoken)
erwachen
awaken vt wecken ● vi erwachen.
~**ing** n Erwachen nt
award n Auszeichnung f; (prize)
Preis m ● vt zuerkennen (to s.o.
dat); verleihen <prize>

aware a become ~ gewahr werden (of gen); be ~ that wissen, dass. ~ness n Bewusstsein nt

away adv weg, fort; (absent) abwesend; (Sport) ~ vier Kilometer entfernt; **play** ~ (Sport) auswärts spielen. ~ **game** n Auswärtsspiel nt

awful a, **-ly** adv furchtbar

awkward a schwierig; (clumsy) ungeschickt; (embarrassing) peinlich; (inconvenient) ungünstig. ~**ly** adv ungeschickt; (embarrassedly) verlegen

awning n Markise f

awoke(n) see **awake**

axe n Axt f ● vt (pres p **axing**) streichen

axle n (Techn) Achse f

B n (Mus) H nt

baboon n Pavian m

baby n Baby nt; (Amer 🔢) Schätzchen nt

baby: ~**ish** a kindisch. ~-**sit** vi babysitten. ~-**sitter** n Babysitter m

bachelor n Junggeselle m

back n Rücken m; (reverse) Rückseite f; (of chair) Rückenlehne f; (Sport) Verteidiger m; at/(Auto) **in the** ~ hinten; **on the** ~ auf der Rückseite; ~ **to front** verkehrt ● a Hinter- ● adv zurück; ~ **here/ there** hier/da hinten; ~ **at home** zu Hause; **go/pay** ~ zurückgehen/-zahlen ● vt (support) unterstützen; (with

money) finanzieren; (Auto) zurücksetzen; (Betting) [Geld] setzen auf (+ acc); (cover the back of) mit einer Verstärkung versehen ● vi (Auto) zurücksetzen. ~ **down** vi klein beigeben. ~ **in** vi rückwärts hineinfahren. ~ **out** vi rückwärts hinaus-/herausfahren; (fig) aussteigen (of aus). ~ **up** vt unterstützen; (confirm) bestätigen ● vi (Auto) zurücksetzen

back: ~**ache** n Rückenschmerzen pl. ~**biting** n gehässiges Gerede nt. ~**bone** n Rückgrat nt. ~**date** vt rückdatieren; ~**dated to** rückwirkend von. ~ **door** n Hintertür f

backer n Geldgeber m

back: ~**fire** vi (Auto) fehlzünden; (fig) fehlschlagen. ~**ground** n Hintergrund m; **family** ~**ground** Familienverhältnisse pl. ~**hand** n (Sport) Rückhand f. ~**handed** a <compliment> zweifelhaft

backing n (support) Unterstützung f; (material) Verstärkung f

back: ~**lash** n (fig) Gegenschlag m. ~**log** n Rückstand m (of an + dat). ~**pack** n Rucksack m. ~ **seat** n Rücksitz m. ~**side** n 🔢 Hintern m. ~**stroke** n Rückenschwimmen nt. ~-**up** n Unterstützung f; (Amer: traffic jam) Stau m

backward a zurückgeblieben; <country> rückständig ● adv rückwärts. ~**s** rückwärts; ~**s and forwards** hin und her

back yard n Hinterhof m; **not in my** ~ **yard** 🔢 nicht vor meiner Haustür

bacon n [Schinken]speck m

bacteria npl Bakterien pl

bad a (**worse, worst**) schlecht; (serious) schwer, schlimm; (naughty) unartig; ~ **language**

gemeine Ausdrucksweise *f*; **feel** ~ sich schlecht fühlen; (*feel guilty*) ein schlechtes Gewissen haben

badge *n* Abzeichen *nt*

badger *n* Dachs *m* ● *vt* plagen

badly *adv* schlecht; (*seriously*) schwer; ~ **off** schlecht gestellt; ~ **behaved** unerzogen; **want** ~ sich (*dat*) sehnsüchtig wünschen; **need** ~ dringend brauchen

bad-mannered *a* mit schlechten Manieren

badminton *n* Federball *m*

bad-tempered *a* schlecht gelaunt

baffle *vt* verblüffen

bag *n* Tasche *f*; (*of paper*) Tüte *f*; (*pouch*) Beutel *m*; ~**s of** T jede Menge ● *vt* (T *reserve*) in Beschlag nehmen

baggage *n* [Reise]gepäck *nt*

baggy *a* <*clothes*> ausgebeult

bagpipes *npl* Dudelsack *m*

bail *n* Kaution *f*; **on** ~ gegen Kaution ● *vt* ~ **s.o. out** jdn gegen Kaution freibekommen; (*fig*) jdm aus der Patsche helfen

bait *n* Köder *m* ● *vt* mit einem Köder versehen; (*fig: torment*) reizen

bake *vt/i* backen

baker *n* Bäcker *m*; ~**'s [shop]** Bäckerei *f*. ~**y** *n* Bäckerei *f*

baking *n* Backen *nt*. ~**-powder** *n* Backpulver *nt*

balance *n* (*equilibrium*) Gleichgewicht *nt*, Balance *f*; (*scales*) Waage *f*; (*Comm*) Saldo *m*; (*outstanding sum*) Restbetrag *m*; **[bank]** ~ Kontostand *m*; **in the** ~ (*fig*) in der Schwebe ● *vt* ausgleichen; (*equalize*) balancieren; (*Comm*) abschließen <*books*> ● *vi* balancieren; (*fig & Comm*) sich ausgleichen. ~**d** *a* ausgewogen

balcony *n* Balkon *m*

bald *a* (**-er, -est**) kahl; <*person*> kahlköpfig

gemeine Ausdrucksweise *f*; Kahlköpfigkeit *f*

ball[1] *n* Ball *m*; (*Billiards, Croquet*) Kugel *f*; (*of yarn*) Knäuel *m & nt*; **on the** ~ T auf Draht

ball[2] *n* (*dance*) Ball *m*

ball-bearing *n* Kugellager *nt*

ballerina *n* Ballerina *f*

ballet *m* Ballett *nt*. ~ **dancer** *n* Balletttänzer(in) *m(f)*

balloon *n* Luftballon *m*; (*Aviat*) Ballon *m*

ballot *n* [geheime] Wahl *f*; (*on issue*) [geheime] Abstimmung *f*. ~**-box** *n* Wahlurne *f*. ~**-paper** *n* Stimmzettel *m*

ball: ~**point [pen]** *n* Kugelschreiber *m*. ~**room** *n* Ballsaal *m*

balm *n* Balsam *m*

balmy *a* (**-ier, -iest**) *a* sanft

Baltic *a & n* **the** ~ **[Sea]** die Ostsee

bamboo *n* Bambus *m*

ban *n* Verbot *nt* ● *vt* (*pt/pp* **banned**) verbieten

banal *a* banal. ~**ity** *n* Banalität *f*

banana *n* Banane *f*

band *n* Band *nt*; (*stripe*) Streifen *m*; (*group*) Schar *f*; (*Mus*) Kapelle *f*

bandage *n* Verband *m*; (*for support*) Bandage *f* ● *vt* verbinden; bandagieren <*limb*>

b. & b. *abbr of* **bed and breakfast**

bandit *n* Bandit *m*

band: ~**stand** *n* Musikpavillon *m*. ~**wagon** *n* **jump on the** ~**wagon** (*fig*) sich einer erfolgreichen Sache anschließen

bang *n* (*noise*) Knall *m*; (*blow*) Schlag *m* ● *adv* **go** ~ knallen ● *int* bums! peng! ● *vt* knallen; (*shut noisily*) zuknallen; (*strike*) schlagen auf (+ *acc*); ~ **one's head** sich (*dat*) den Kopf stoßen (**on** an + *acc*) ● *vi* schlagen; <*door:*> zuknallen

banger n (*firework*) Knallfrosch m; (🔲 *sausage*) Wurst f; **old ~** (🔲 *car*) Klapperkiste f

bangle n Armreifen m

banish vt verbannen

banisters npl [Treppen]geländer nt

banjo n Banjo nt

bank¹ n (*of river*) Ufer nt; (*slope*) Hang m ● vi (*Aviat*) in die Kurve gehen

bank² n Bank f ● **~ on** vt sich verlassen auf (+ *acc*)

bank account n Bankkonto nt

banker ~ n Bankier m

bank: ~ holiday n gesetzlicher Feiertag m. **~ing** n Bankwesen nt. **~note** n Banknote f

bankrupt a bankrott; **go ~** Bankrott machen ● n Bankrotteur m ● vt Bankrott machen. **~cy** n Bankrott m

banner n Banner nt; (*carried by demonstrators*) Transparent nt, Spruchband nt

banquet n Bankett nt

baptism n Taufe f

baptize vt taufen

bar n Stange f; (*of cage*) [Gitter]stab m; (*of gold*) Barren m; (*of chocolate*) Tafel f; (*of soap*) Stück nt; (*long*) Riegel m; (*café*) Bar f; (*counter*) Theke f; (*Mus*) Takt m; (*fig: obstacle*) Hindernis nt; **parallel ~s** (*Sport*) Barren m; **behind ~s** 🔲 hinter Gittern ● vt (*pt/pp* **barred**) versperren <*way, door*>; ausschließen <*person*>

barbar|ic a barbarisch. **~ity** n Barbarei f. **~ous** a barbarisch

barbecue n Grill m; (*party*) Grillfest nt ● vt [im Freien] grillen

barbed a **~ wire** Stacheldraht m

barber n [Herren]friseur m

bar code n Strichkode m

bare a (-**r**, -**st**) nackt, bloß; <*tree*> kahl; (*empty*) leer; (*mere*) bloß

bare: ~back adv ohne Sattel. **~faced** a schamlos. **~foot** adv barfuß. **~headed** a mit unbedecktem Kopf

barely adv kaum

bargain n (*agreement*) Geschäft nt; (*good buy*) Gelegenheitskauf m; **into the ~** noch dazu; **make a ~** sich einigen ● vi handeln; (*haggle*) feilschen; **~ for** (*expect*) rechnen mit

barge n Lastkahn m; (*towed*) Schleppkahn m ● vi **~ in** 🔲 hereinplatzen

baritone n Bariton m

bark¹ n (*of tree*) Rinde f

bark² n Bellen nt ● vi bellen

barley n Gerste f

bar: ~maid n Schankmädchen nt. **~man** Barmann m

barmy a 🔲 verrückt

barn n Scheune f

barometer n Barometer nt

baron n Baron m. **~ess** n Baronin f

barracks npl Kaserne f

barrage n (*in river*) Wehr nt; (*Mil*) Sperrfeuer nt; (*fig*) Hagel m

barrel n Fass nt; (*of gun*) Lauf m; (*of cannon*) Rohr nt. **~-organ** n Drehorgel f

barren a unfruchtbar; <*landscape*> öde

barricade n Barrikade f ● vt verbarrikadieren

barrier n Barriere f; (*across road*) Schranke f; (*Rail*) Sperre f; (*fig*) Hindernis nt

barrow n Karre f, Karren m

base n (*fig*) Basis f; (*Mil*) Stützpunkt m ● vt stützen (**on** auf + *acc*); **be ~d on** basieren auf (+ *dat*)

base: ~ball n Baseball m. **~less** a unbegründet. **~ment** n Kellergeschoss nt

bash n Schlag m; **have a ~!** 🔲 probier es mal! ● vt hauen

basic *a* Grund-; (*fundamental*)
grundlegend; (*essential*)
wesentlich; (*unadorned*) einfach;
the ~s das Wesentliche. **~ally**
adv grundsätzlich
basin *n* Becken *nt*; (*for washing*)
Waschbecken *nt*; (*for food*)
Schüssel *f*
basis *n* (*pl* **-ses**) Basis *f*
bask *vi* sich sonnen
basket *n* Korb *m*. **~ball** *n*
Basketball *m*
Basle *n* Basel *nt*
bass *a* Bass-; **~ voice** Bassstimme
f ● *n* Bass *m*; (*person*) Bassist *m*
bassoon *n* Fagott *nt*
bastard *n* ⊠ Schuft *m*
bat¹ *n* Schläger *m*; **off one's own ~**
⊡ auf eigene Faust ● *vt* (*pt/pp*
batted) schlagen; **not ~ an eyelid**
(*fig*) nicht mit der Wimper
zucken
bat² *n* (*Zool*) Fledermaus *f*
batch *n* (*of people*) Gruppe *f*; (*of
papers*) Stoß *m*; (*of goods*)
Sendung *f*; (*of bread*) Schub *m*
bath *n* (*pl* **-s**) Bad *nt*; (*tub*)
Badewanne *f*; **~s** *pl* Badeanstalt
f; **have a ~** baden
bathe *n* Bad *nt* ● *vt/i* baden. **~r** *n*
Badende(r) *m/f*
bathing *n* Baden *nt*. **~-cap** *n*
Bademütze *f*. **~-costume** *n*
Badeanzug *m*
bath: **~-mat** *n* Badematte *f*.
~room *n* Badezimmer *nt*. **~-
towel** *n* Badetuch *nt*
battalion *n* Bataillon *nt*
batter *n* (*Culin*) flüssiger Teig *m*
● *vt* schlagen. **~ed** *a* <*car*>
verbeult; <*wife*> misshandelt
battery *n* Batterie *f*
battle *n* Schlacht *f*; (*fig*) Kampf *m*
● *vi* (*fig*) kämpfen (**for** um)
battle: **~field** *n* Schlachtfeld *nt*.
~ship *n* Schlachtschiff *nt*
batty *a* ⊡ verrückt
Bavaria *n* Bayern *nt*. **~n** *a*
bayrisch ● *n* Bayer(in) *m(f)*

bawl *vt/i* brüllen
bay¹ *n* (*Geog*) Bucht *f*; (*Archit*)
Erker *m*
bay² *n* (*Bot*) [echter] Lorbeer *m*.
~-leaf *n* Lorbeerblatt *nt*
bayonet *n* Bajonett *nt*
bay window *n* Erkerfenster *nt*
bazaar *n* Basar *m*
BC *abbr* (**before Christ**) v. Chr.

be

(*pres* **am, are, is,** *pl* **are**; *pt*
was, *pl* **were**; *pp* **been**)
● *intransitive verb*
····▸ (*expressing identity, nature,
state, age etc.*) sein. **he is a
teacher** er ist Lehrer. **she is
French** sie ist Französin. **he is
very nice** er ist nett. **I am tall**
ich bin groß. **you are thirty** du
bist dreißig. **it was very cold** es
war sehr kalt
····▸ (*expressing general position*)
sein; (*lie*) liegen; (*stand*) stehen.
where is the bank? wo ist die
Bank? **the book is on the table**
das Buch liegt auf dem Tisch.
the vase is on the shelf die Vase
steht auf dem Brett
····▸ (*feel*) **I am cold/hot** mir ist
kalt/heiß. **I am ill** ich bin krank. **I
am well** mir geht es gut. **how are
you?** wie geht es Ihnen?
····▸ (*date*) **it is the 5th today** heute
haben wir den Fünften
····▸ (*go, come, stay*) sein. **I have
been to Vienna** ich bin in Wien
gewesen. **have you ever been to
London?** bist du schon einmal in
London gewesen? **has the
postman been?** war der
Briefträger schon da? **I've been
here for an hour** ich bin seit einer
Stunde hier
····▸ (*origin*) **where are you from?**
woher stammen *od* kommen
Sie? **she is from Australia** sie
stammt *od* ist aus Australien

····➤ (*cost*) kosten. **how much are the eggs?** was kosten die Eier?

····➤ (*in calculations*) **two threes are six** zweimal drei ist *od* sind sechs

····➤ (*exist*) **there is/are** es gibt (+ *acc*). **there's no fish left** es gibt keinen Fisch mehr

● *auxiliary verb*

····➤ (*forming continuous tenses: not translated*) **I'm working** ich arbeite. **I'm leaving tomorrow** ich reise morgen [ab]. **they were singing** sie sangen. **they will be coming on Tuesday** sie kommen am Dienstag

····➤ (*forming passive*) werden. **the child was found** das Kind wurde gefunden. **German is spoken here** hier wird Deutsch gesprochen; hier spricht man Deutsch

····➤ (*expressing arrangement, obligation, destiny*) sollen. **I am to go/inform you** ich soll gehen/Sie unterrichten. **they were to fly today** sie sollten heute fliegen. **you are to do that immediately** das sollst du sofort machen. **you are not to ...** (*prohibition*) du darfst nicht .... **they were never to meet again** (*destiny*) sie sollten sich nie wieder treffen

····➤ (*in short answers*) **Are you disappointed? — Yes I am** Bist du enttäuscht? — Ja. (*negating previous statement*) **Aren't you coming? — Yes I am!** Kommst du nicht? — Doch!

····➤ (*in tag questions*) **isn't it? wasn't she? aren't they?** *etc.* nicht wahr. **it's a beautiful house, isn't it?** das Haus ist sehr schön, nicht wahr?

beach n Strand m

bead n Perle f

beak n Schnabel m

beam n Balken m; (*of light*) Strahl m ● vi strahlen. ~**ing** a [freude]strahlend

bean n Bohne f

bear[1] n Bär m

bear[2] vt/i (*pt* bore, *pp* borne) tragen; (*endure*) ertragen; gebären <child>; ~ **right** sich rechts halten. ~**able** a erträglich

beard n Bart m. ~**ed** a bärtig

bearer n Träger m; (*of news, cheque*) Überbringer m; (*of passport*) Inhaber(in) m(f)

bearing n Haltung f; (*Techn*) Lager nt; **get one's** ~**s** sich orientieren

beast n Tier nt; (🛈 *person*) Biest nt

beastly a (-ier, -iest) 🛈 scheußlich; <person> gemein

beat n Schlag m; (*of policeman*) Runde f; (*rhythm*) Takt m ● vt/i (*pt* beat, *pp* beaten) schlagen; (*thrash*) verprügeln; klopfen <carpet>; (*hammer*) hämmern (**on** an + *acc*); ~ **it!** 🛈 hau ab! **it** ~**s me** 🛈 das begreife ich nicht. ~ **up** vt zusammenschlagen

beat|en a **off the** ~**en track** abseits. ~**ing** n Prügel pl

beauti|ful a, -**ly** adv schön. ~**fy** vt (*pt/pp* -ied) verschönern

beauty n Schönheit f. ~ **parlour** n Kosmetiksalon m. ~ **spot** n Schönheitsfleck m; (*place*) landschaftlich besonders reizvolles Fleckchen nt.

beaver n Biber m

became *see* **become**

because *conj* weil ● *adv* ~ **of** wegen (+ *gen*)

becom|e vt/i (*pt* became, *pp* become) werden. ~**ing** a <clothes> kleidsam

bed n Bett nt; (*layer*) Schicht f; (*of flowers*) Beet nt; **in** ~ im Bett; **to** ~ ins *od* zu Bett gehen; ~ **and breakfast** Zimmer mit Frühstück.

~**clothes** npl, ~**ding** n Bettzeug nt. ~**room** n Schlafzimmer nt

bedside n at his ~ an seinem Bett. ~ **lamp** n Nachttischlampe f. ~ **table** n Nachttisch m

bed: ~**sitter** n, ~**-sitting-room** n Wohnschlafzimmer nt. ~**spread** n Tagesdecke f. ~**time** n at ~**time** vor dem Schlafengehen

bee n Biene f

beech n Buche f

beef n Rindfleisch nt. ~**burger** n Hamburger m

bee: ~**hive** n Bienenstock m. ~**line** n make a ~**-line for** 🗓 zusteuern auf (+ acc)

been see **be**

beer n Bier nt

beet n (Amer: beetroot) Rote Bete f; [sugar] ~ Zuckerrübe f

beetle n Käfer m

beetroot n Rote Bete f

before prep vor (+ dat/acc); **the day** ~ **yesterday** vorgestern; ~ **long** bald ● adv vorher; (already) schon; **never** ~ noch nie; ~ **that** davor ● conj (time) ehe, bevor. ~**hand** adv vorher, im Voraus

beg v (pt/pp **begged**) ● vi betteln ● vt (entreat) anflehen; (ask) bitten (**for** um)

began see **begin**

beggar n Bettler(in) m(f); 🗓 Kerl m

begin vt/i (pt **began**, pp **begun**, pres p **beginning**) anfangen, beginnen; **to** ~ **with** anfangs. ~**ner** n Anfänger(in) m(f). ~**ning** n Anfang m, Beginn m

begun see **begin**

behalf n on ~ **of** im Namen von; **on my** ~ meinetwegen

behave vi sich verhalten; ~ **oneself** sich benehmen

behaviour n Verhalten nt; **good/ bad** ~ gutes/schlechtes Benehmen nt

behind prep hinter (+ dat/acc); **be** ~ **sth** hinter etw (dat) stecken

● adv hinten; (late) im Rückstand; **a long way** ~ weit zurück ● n 🗓 Hintern m. ~**hand** adv im Rückstand

beige a beige

being n Dasein nt; **living** ~ Lebewesen nt; **come into** ~ entstehen

belated a, **-ly** adv verspätet

belfry n Glockenstube f; (tower) Glockenturm m

Belgian a belgisch ● n Belgier(in) m(f)

Belgium n Belgien nt

belief n Glaube m

believable a glaubhaft

believe vt/i glauben (**s.o.** jdm; **in** an + acc). ~**r** n (Relig) Gläubige(r) m/f

belittle vt herabsetzen

bell n Glocke f; (on door) Klingel f

bellow vt/i brüllen

belly n Bauch m

belong vi gehören (**to** dat); (be member) angehören (**to** dat). ~**ings** npl Sachen pl

beloved a geliebt ● n Geliebte(r) m/f

below prep unter (+ dat/acc) ● adv unten; (Naut) unter Deck

belt n Gürtel m; (area) Zone f; (Techn) [Treib]riemen m ● vi (🗓 rush) rasen ● vt (🗓 hit) hauen

bench n Bank f; (work-) Werkbank f

bend n Biegung f; (in road) Kurve f; **round the** ~ 🗓 verrückt ● v (pt/pp **bent**) ● vt biegen; beugen <arm, leg> ● vi sich bücken; <thing:> sich biegen; <road:> eine Biegung machen. ~ **down** vi sich bücken. ~ **over** vi sich vornüberbeugen

beneath prep unter (+ dat/acc); ~ **him** (fig) unter seiner Würde ● adv darunter

benefactor n Wohltäter(in) m(f)

beneficial a nützlich

benefit n Vorteil m; (allowance) Unterstützung f; (insurance) Leistung f; **sickness ~** Krankengeld nt ●v (pt/pp -fited, pres p -fiting) ●vt nützen (+ dat) ●vi profitieren (from von)

benevolen|ce n Wohlwollen nt. **~t** a, **-ly** adv wohlwollend

bent see **bend** ●a <person> gebeugt; (distorted) verbogen; (⚠ dishonest) korrupt; **be ~ on doing sth** darauf erpicht sein, etw zu tun ●n Hang m, Neigung f (for zu); **artistic ~** künstlerische Ader f

bequeath vt vermachen (to dat)

bereave|d n **the ~d** pl die Hinterbliebenen

beret n Baskenmütze f

Berne n Bern nt

berry n Beere f

berth n (on ship) [Schlaf]koje f; (ship's anchorage) Liegeplatz m; **give a wide ~ to** ⚠ einen großen Bogen machen um

beside prep neben (+ dat/acc); **~ oneself** außer sich (dat)

besides prep außer (+ dat) ●adv außerdem

besiege vt belagern

best a & n best(r,s); **the ~** der/die/das Beste; **at ~** bestenfalls; **all the ~!** alles Gute! **do one's ~** sein Bestes tun; **the ~ part of a year** fast ein Jahr; **to the ~ of my knowledge** so viel ich weiß; **make the ~ of it** das Beste daraus machen ●adv am besten; **as ~ I could** so gut ich konnte. **~ man** n ≈ Trauzeuge m. **~seller** n Bestseller m

bet n Wette f ●v (pt/pp bet or betted) ●vt **~ s.o. £5** mit jdm um £5 wetten ●vi wetten; **~ on** [Geld] setzen auf (+ acc)

betray vt verraten. **~al** n Verrat m

better a besser; **get ~** sich bessern; (after illness) sich erholen ●adv besser; **~ off** besser dran; **~ not** lieber nicht; **all the ~** umso besser; **the sooner the ~** je eher, desto besser; **think ~ of it** sich eines Besseren besinnen; **you'd ~ stay** du bleibst am besten hier ●vt verbessern; (do better than) übertreffen; **~ oneself** sich verbessern

between prep zwischen (+ dat/acc); **~ you and me** unter uns; **~ us** (together) zusammen ●adv **[in] ~** dazwischen

beware vi sich in Acht nehmen (of vor + dat); **~ of the dog!** Vorsicht, bissiger Hund!

bewilder vt verwirren. **~ment** n Verwirrung f

bewitch vt verzaubern; (fig) bezaubern

beyond prep über (+ acc) … hinaus; (further) weiter als; **~ reach** außer Reichweite; **~ doubt** ohne jeden Zweifel; **it's ~ me** ⚠ das geht über meinen Horizont ●adv darüber hinaus

bias n Voreingenommenheit f; (preference) Vorliebe f; (Jur) Befangenheit f ●vt (pt/pp biased) (influence) beeinflussen. **~ed** a voreingenommen; (Jur) befangen

bib n Lätzchen nt

Bible n Bibel f

biblical a biblisch

bibliography n Bibliographie f

bicycle n Fahrrad nt ●vi mit dem Rad fahren

bid n Gebot nt; (attempt) Versuch m ●vt/i (pt/pp bid, pres p bidding) bieten (for auf + acc); (Cards) reizen

bidder n Bieter(in) m(f)

bide vt **~ one's time** den richtigen Moment abwarten

big a (bigger, biggest) groß ●adv **talk ~** ⚠ angeben

bigam|ist n Bigamist m. **~y** n Bigamie f

big-headed a ⚠ eingebildet

B

bigot n Eiferer m. ~**ed** a engstirnig
bigwig n 🄣 hohes Tier nt
bike n 🄣 [Fahr]rad nt
bikini n Bikini m
bile n Galle f
bilingual a zweisprachig
bill¹ n Rechnung f; (poster) Plakat nt; (Pol) Gesetzentwurf m; (Amer: note) Banknote f; ~ **of exchange** Wechsel m ● vt eine Rechnung schicken (+ dat)
bill² n (beak) Schnabel m
billfold n (Amer) Brieftasche f
billiards n Billard nt
billion n (thousand million) Milliarde f; (million million) Billion f
bin n Mülleimer m; (for bread) Kasten m
bind vt (pt/pp bound) binden (**to** an + acc); (bandage) verbinden; (Jur) verpflichten; (cover the edge of) einfassen. ~**ing** a verbindlich ● n Einband m; (braid) Borte f; (on ski) Bindung f
binge n 🄣 **go on the** ~ eine Sauftour machen
binoculars npl **[pair of]** ~ Fernglas nt
bio|chemistry n Biochemie f. ~**degradable** a biologisch abbaubar
biograph|er n Biograph(in) m(f). ~**y** n Biographie f
biological a biologisch
biolog|ist n Biologe m. ~**y** n Biologie f
bioterrorism n Bioterrorismus m
birch n Birke f; (whip) Rute f
bird n Vogel m; (🄣 girl) Mädchen nt; **kill two** ~**s with one stone** zwei Fliegen mit einer Klappe schlagen
Biro (P) n Kugelschreiber m
birth n Geburt f
birth: ~ **certificate** n Geburtsurkunde f. ~**-control** n

Geburtenregelung f. ~**day** n Geburtstag m. ~**-rate** n Geburtenziffer f
biscuit n Keks m
bishop n Bischof m
bit¹ n Stückchen nt; (for horse) Gebiss nt; (Techn) Bohreinsatz m; **a** ~ ein bisschen; ~ **by** ~ nach und nach; **a** ~ **of bread** ein bisschen Brot; **do one's** ~ sein Teil tun
bit² see **bite**
bitch n Hündin f; 🄧 Luder nt. ~**y** a gehässig
bit|e n Biss m; **[insect]** ~ Stich m; (mouthful) Bissen m ● vt/i (pt **bit**, pp **bitten**) beißen; <insect:> stechen; kauen <one's nails>. ~**ing** a beißend
bitten see **bite**
bitter a, **-ly** adv bitter; ~**ly cold** bitterkalt ● n bitteres Bier nt. ~**ness** n Bitterkeit f
bitty a zusammengestoppelt
bizarre a bizarr
black a (**-er, -est**) schwarz; **be** ~**and blue** grün und blau sein ● n Schwarz nt; (person) Schwarze(r) m/f ● vt schwärzen; boykottieren <goods>
black: ~**berry** n Brombeere f. ~**bird** n Amsel f. ~**board** n (Sch) [Wand]tafel f. ~**currant** n schwarze Johannisbeere f
blacken vt/i schwärzen
black: ~ **eye** n blaues Auge nt. **B**~ **Forest** n Schwarzwald m. ~ **ice** n Glatteis nt. ~**list** vt auf die schwarze Liste setzen. ~**mail** n Erpressung f ● vt erpressen. ~**mailer** n Erpresser(in) m(f). ~ **market** n schwarzer Markt m. ~**-out** n **have a** ~**-out** (Med) das Bewusstsein verlieren. ~ **pudding** n Blutwurst f
bladder n (Anat) Blase f
blade n Klinge f; (of grass) Halm m

blame n Schuld f ● vt die Schuld geben (+ dat); **no one is to ~** keiner ist schuld daran. **~less** a schuldlos

bland a (-er, -est) mild

blank a leer; <look> ausdruckslos ● n Lücke f; (cartridge) Platzpatrone f. **~ cheque** n Blankoscheck m

blanket n Decke f; **wet ~** ☐ Spielverderber(in) m(f)

blare vt/i schmettern

blasé a blasiert

blast n (gust) Luftstoß m; (sound) Schmettern nt; (of horn) Tuten nt ● vt sprengen ● int ▣ verdammt. **~ed** a ▣ verdammt

blast-off n (of missile) Start m

blatant a offensichtlich

blaze n Feuer nt ● vi brennen

blazer n Blazer m

bleach n Bleichmittel nt ● vt/i bleichen

bleak a (-er, -est) öde; (fig) trostlos

bleary-eyed a mit trüben/(on waking up) verschlafenen Augen

bleat vi blöken

bleed v (pt/pp bled) ● vi bluten ● vt entlüften <radiator>

bleep n Piepton m ● vi piepsen ● vt mit dem Piepser rufen. **~er** n Piepser m

blemish n Makel m

blend n Mischung f ● vt mischen ● vi sich vermischen

bless vt segnen. **~ed** a heilig; ▣ verflixt. **~ing** n Segen m

blew see **blow²**

blight n (Bot) Brand m

blind a blind; <corner> unübersichtlich; **~ man/woman** Blinde(r) m/f ● n [roller] ~ Rouleau nt ● vt blenden

blind: **~ alley** n Sackgasse f. **~fold** a & adv mit verbundenen Augen ● n Augenbinde f ● vt die Augen verbinden (+ dat). **~ly** adv blindlings. **~ness** n Blindheit f

blink vi blinzeln; <light:> blinken

bliss n Glückseligkeit f. **~ful** a glücklich

blister n (Med) Blase f

blitz n ☐ Großaktion f

blizzard n Schneesturm m

bloated a aufgedunsen

blob n Klecks m

block n Block m; (of wood) Klotz m; (of flats) [Wohn]block m ● vt blockieren. **~ up** vt zustopfen

blockade n Blockade f ● vt blockieren

blockage n Verstopfung f

block: **~head** n ☐ Dummkopf m. **~ letters** npl Blockschrift f

bloke n ☐ Kerl m

blonde a blond ● n Blondine f

blood n Blut nt

blood: **~-curdling** a markerschütternd. **~ donor** n Blutspender m; **~ group** n Blutgruppe f. **~hound** n Bluthund m. **~-poisoning** n Blutvergiftung f. **~ pressure** n Blutdruck m. **~shed** n Blutvergießen nt. **~shot** a blutunterlaufen. **~ sports** npl Jagdsport m. **~-stained** a blutbefleckt. **~ test** n Blutprobe f. **~thirsty** a blutdürstig. **~vessel** n Blutgefäß nt

bloody a (-ier, -iest) blutig; ▣ verdammt. **~-minded** a ▣ stur

bloom n Blüte f ● vi blühen

blossom n Blüte f ● vi blühen

blot n [Tinten]klecks m; (fig) Fleck m ● **out** vt (fig) auslöschen

blotch n Fleck m. **~y** a fleckig

blotting-paper n Löschpapier nt

blouse n Bluse f

blow¹ n Schlag m

blow² v (pt blew, pp blown) ● vt blasen; (fam; squander) verpulvern; **~ one's nose** sich (dat) die Nase putzen ● vi blasen; <fuse:> durchbrennen. **~ away** vt wegblasen ● vi

wegfliegen. ~ **down** vt umwehen
● vi umfallen. ~ **out** vt
(extinguish) ausblasen. ~ **over** vi
umfallen; (fig: die down)
vorübergehen. ~ **up** vt (inflate)
aufblasen; (enlarge) vergrößern;
(shatter by explosion) sprengen
● vi explodieren

blowlamp n Lötlampe f

blown see **blow²**

blowtorch n (Amer) Lötlampe f

blowy a windig

blue a (-r, -st) blau; **feel ~**
deprimiert sein ● n Blau nt; **have
the ~s** deprimiert sein; **out of the
~** aus heiterem Himmel

blue: ~**bell** n Sternhyazinthe f.
~**berry** n Heidelbeere f. ~**bottle**
n Schmeißfliege f. ~ **film** n
Pornofilm m. ~**print** n (fig)
Entwurf m

bluff n Bluff m ● vi bluffen

blunder n Schnitzer m ● vi einen
Schnitzer machen

blunt a stumpf; <person>
geradeheraus. ~**ly** adv
unverblümt, geradeheraus

blur n **it's all a ~** alles ist
verschwommen ● vt (pt/pp
blurred) verschwommen machen;
~**red** verschwommen

blush n Erröten nt ● vi erröten

bluster n Großtuerei f. ~**y** a
windig

boar n Eber m

board n Brett nt; (for notices)
schwarzes Brett nt; (committee)
Ausschuss m; (of directors)
Vorstand m; **on ~** an Bord; **full ~**
Vollpension f; ~ **and lodging**
Unterkunft und Verpflegung pl
● vt einsteigen in (+ acc); (Naut,
Aviat) besteigen ● vi an Bord
gehen. ~ **up** vt mit Brettern
verschlagen

boarder n Pensionsgast m; (Sch)
Internatsschüler(in) m(f)

board: ~-**game** n Brettspiel nt.
~**ing-house** n Pension f. ~**ing-
school** n Internat nt

boast vt sich rühmen (+ gen) ● vi
prahlen (**about** mit). ~**ful** a, -**ly**
adv prahlerisch

boat n Boot nt; (ship) Schiff nt

bob vi (pt/pp bobbed) ~ **up and
down** sich auf und ab bewegen

bob-sleigh n Bob m

bodily a körperlich ● adv
(forcibly) mit Gewalt

body n Körper m; (corpse) Leiche
f; (corporation) Körperschaft f.
~**guard** n Leibwächter m. ~**work**
n (Auto) Karosserie f

bog n Sumpf m

bogus a falsch

boil¹ n Furunkel m

boil² n **bring/come to the ~** zum
Kochen bringen/kommen ● vt/i
kochen; ~**ed potatoes**
Salzkartoffeln pl. ~ **down** vi (fig)
hinauslaufen (**to** auf + acc). ~
over vi überkochen

boiler n Heizkessel m

boiling point n Siedepunkt m

boisterous a übermütig

bold a (-er, -est), -**ly** adv kühn;
(Typ) fett. ~**ness** n Kühnheit f

bolster n Nackenrolle f ● vt ~ **up**
Mut machen (+ dat)

bolt n Riegel m; (Techn) Bolzen m
● vt schrauben (**to** an + acc);
verriegeln <door>;
hinunterschlingen <food> ● vi
abhauen; <horse:> durchgehen

bomb n Bombe f ● vt
bombardieren

bombard vt beschießen; (fig)
bombardieren

bombastic a bombastisch

bomber n (Aviat) Bomber m;
(person) Bombenleger(in) m(f)

bond n (fig) Band nt; (Comm)
Obligation f

bone n Knochen m; (of fish)
Gräte f ● vt von den Knochen

lösen <*meat*>; entgräten <*fish*>.
~-dry a knochentrocken
bonfire n Gartenfeuer nt;
(*celebratory*) Freudenfeuer nt
bonus n Prämie f; (*gratuity*)
Gratifikation f; (*fig*) Plus nt
bony a (**-ier, -iest**) knochig; <*fish*>
grätig
boo int buh! ● vt ausbuhen ● vi
buhen
boob n (Ⅰ *mistake*) Schnitzer m
book n Buch nt; (*of tickets*) Heft
nt; **keep the ~s** (*Comm*) die
Bücher führen ● vt/i buchen;
(*reserve*) [vor]bestellen; (*for
offence*) aufschreiben
book: **~case** n Bücherregal nt.
~-ends npl Buchstützen pl.
~ing-office n Fahrkartenschalter
m. **~keeping** n Buchführung f.
~let n Broschüre f. **~maker** n
Buchmacher m. **~mark** n
Lesezeichen nt. **~seller** n
Buchhändler(in) m(f). **~shop** n
Buchhandlung f. **~stall** n
Bücherstand m
boom n (*Comm*) Hochkonjunktur
f; (*upturn*) Aufschwung m ● vi
dröhnen; (*fig*) blühen
boon n Segen m
boost n Auftrieb m ● vt Auftrieb
geben (+ *dat*)
boot n Stiefel m; (*Auto*)
Kofferraum m
booth n Bude f; (*cubicle*) Kabine f
booty n Beute f
booze n Ⅰ Alkohol m ● vi Ⅰ
saufen
border n Rand m; (*frontier*)
Grenze f; (*in garden*) Rabatte f
● vi ~ **on** grenzen an (+ *acc*).
~line case n Grenzfall m
bore¹ see **bear²**
bor|e² n (*of gun*) Kaliber nt;
(*person*) langweiliger Mensch m;
(*thing*) langweilige Sache f ● vt
langweilen; **be ~ed** sich
langweilen. **~edom** n Langeweile
f. **~ing** a langweilig

born pp **be ~** geboren werden ● a
geboren
borne see **bear²**
borrow vt [sich (*dat*)] borgen od
leihen (**from** von)
bosom n Busen m
boss n Ⅰ Chef m ● vt
herumkommandieren. **~y** a
herrschsüchtig
botanical a botanisch
botan|ist n Botaniker(in) m(f). **~y**
n Botanik f
both a & pron beide; **~[of] the
children** beide Kinder; **~ of them**
beide [von ihnen] ● adv **~ men
and women** sowohl Männer als
auch Frauen
bother n Mühe f; (*minor trouble*)
Ärger m ● int Ⅰ verflixt! ● vt
belästigen; (*disturb*) stören ● vi
sich kümmern (**about** um)
bottle n Flasche f ● vt auf
Flaschen abfüllen; (*preserve*)
einmachen
bottle: **~-neck** n (*fig*) Engpass m.
~-opener n Flaschenöffner m
bottom a unterste(r,s) ● n (*of
container*) Boden m; (*of river*)
Grund m; (*of page, hill*) Fuß m;
(*buttocks*) Hintern m; **at the ~**
unten; **get to the ~ of sth** (*fig*)
hinter etw (*acc*) kommen
bought see **buy**
bounce vi [auf]springen;
<*cheque:*> Ⅰ nicht gedeckt sein
● vt aufspringen lassen <*ball*>
bouncer n Ⅰ Rausschmeißer m
bound¹ n Sprung m ● vi springen
bound² see **bind** ● a ~ **for** <*ship*>
mit Kurs auf (+ *acc*); **be ~ to do
sth** etw bestimmt machen;
(*obliged*) verpflichtet sein, etw zu
machen
boundary n Grenze f
bounds npl (*fig*) Grenzen pl; **out
of ~** verboten
bouquet n [Blumen]strauß m; (*of
wine*) Bukett nt
bourgeois a (*pej*) spießbürgerlich

bout n (Med) Anfall m; (Sport) Kampf m

bow¹ n (weapon & Mus) Bogen m; (knot) Schleife f

bow² n Verbeugung f ● vi sich verbeugen ● vt neigen <head>

bow³ n (Naut) Bug m

bowel n Darm m. ~s pl Eingeweide pl

bowl¹ n Schüssel f; (shallow) Schale f

bowl² n (ball) Kugel f ● vt/i werfen. ~ **over** vt umwerfen

bowler n (Sport) Werfer m

bowling n Kegeln nt. ~**-alley** n Kegelbahn f

bowls n Bowlsspiel nt

bow-tie n Fliege f

box¹ n Schachtel f; (wooden) Kiste f; (cardboard) Karton m; (Theat) Loge f

box² vt/i (Sport) boxen

box|er n Boxer m. ~**ing** n Boxen nt. **B~ing Day** n zweiter Weihnachtstag m

box: ~**-office** n (Theat) Kasse f. ~**-room** n Abstellraum m

boy n Junge m

boycott n Boykott m ● vt boykottieren

boy: ~**friend** n Freund m. ~**ish** a jungenhaft

bra n BH m

brace n Strebe f, Stütze f; (dental) Zahnspange f; ~**s** npl Hosenträger mpl

bracelet n Armband nt

bracing a stärkend

bracket n Konsole f; (group) Gruppe f; (Typ) round/square ~s runde/eckige Klammern ● vt einklammern

brag vi (pt/pp bragged) prahlen (about mit)

braille n Blindenschrift f

brain n Gehirn nt; ~**s** (fig) Intelligenz f

brain: ~**less** a dumm. ~**wash** vt einer Gehirnwäsche unterziehen. ~**wave** n Geistesblitz m

brainy a (-ier, -iest) klug

brake n Bremse f ● vt/i bremsen. ~**-light** n Bremslicht nt

bramble n Brombeerstrauch m

branch n Ast m; (fig) Zweig m; (Comm) Zweigstelle f; (shop) Filiale f ● vi sich gabeln

brand n Marke f ● vt (fig) brandmarken als

brandish vt schwingen

brand-new a nagelneu

brandy n Weinbrand m

brash a nassforsch

brass n Messing nt; (Mus) Blech nt; **top** ~ Ⓘ hohe Tiere pl. ~ **band** n Blaskapelle f

brassy a (-ier, -iest) Ⓘ ordinär

brat n (pej) Balg nt

bravado n Forschheit f

brave a (-r, -st), -ly adv tapfer ● vt die Stirn bieten (+ dat). ~**ry** n Tapferkeit f

bravo int bravo!

brawl n Schlägerei f

brawn n (Culin) Sülze f

brawny a muskulös

bray vi iahen

brazen a unverschämt

Brazil n Brasilien nt. ~**ian** a brasilianisch. ~ **nut** n Paranuss f

breach n Bruch m; (Mil & fig) Bresche f; ~ **of contract** Vertragsbruch m

bread n Brot nt; **slice of** ~ **and butter** Butterbrot nt. ~**crumbs** npl Brotkrümel pl; (Culin) Paniermehl nt

breadth n Breite f

break n Bruch m; (interval) Pause f; (interruption) Unterbrechung f; (Ⓘ chance) Chance f ● v (pt broke, pp broken) ● vt brechen; (smash) zerbrechen; (damage) kaputtmachen Ⓘ; (interrupt) unterbrechen; ~ **one's arm** sich (dat) den Arm brechen ● vi

brechen; <*day:*> anbrechen;
<*storm:*> losbrechen; <*thing:*>
kaputtgehen **ⓣ**; <*rope, thread:*>
reißen; <*news:*> bekannt werden;
his voice is ~ing er ist im
Stimmbruch. ~ **away** *vi* sich
losreißen/(*fig*) sich absetzen
(**from** von). ~ **down** *vi*
zusammenbrechen; (*Techn*) eine
Panne haben; <*negotiations:*>
scheitern ● *vt* aufbrechen
<*door:*>; aufgliedern <*figures*>. ~
in *vi* einbrechen. ~ **off** *vt/i*
abbrechen; lösen <*engagement*>.
~ **out** *vi* ausbrechen. ~ **up** *vt*
zerbrechen ● *vi* <*crowd:*> sich
zerstreuen; <*marriage, couple:*>
auseinander gehen; (*Sch*) Ferien
bekommen
break|able *a* zerbrechlich. ~**age**
n Bruch *m*. ~**down** *n* (*Techn*)
Panne *f*; (*Med*) Zusammenbruch
m; (*of figures*) Aufgliederung *f*.
~**er** *n* (*wave*) Brecher *m*
breakfast *n* Frühstück *nt*
break: ~**through** *n* Durchbruch
m. ~**water** *n* Buhne *f*
breast *n* Brust *f*. ~**bone** *n*
Brustbein *nt*. ~-**feed** *vt* stillen.
~-**stroke** *n* Brustschwimmen *nt*
breath *n* Atem *m*; **out of** ~ außer
Atem; **under one's** ~ vor sich
(*acc*) hin
breathe *vt/i* atmen. ~ **in** *vt/i*
einatmen. ~ **out** *vt/i* ausatmen
breathing *n* Atmen *nt*
breath: : ~**less** *a* atemlos. ~-
taking *a* atemberaubend
bred *see* **breed**
breed *n* Rasse *f* ● *v* (*pt/pp* **bred**)
● *vt* züchten; (*give rise to*)
erzeugen ● *vi* sich vermehren.
~**er** *n* Züchter *m*. ~**ing** *n* Zucht *f*;
(*fig*) [gute] Lebensart *f*
breez|e *n* Lüftchen *nt*; (*Naut*)
Brise *f*. ~**y** *a* windig
brevity *n* Kürze *f*

brew *n* Gebräu *nt* ● *vt* brauen;
kochen <*tea*>. ~**er** *n* Brauer *m*.
~**ery** *n* Brauerei *f*
bribe *n* (*money*) Bestechungsgeld
nt ● *vt* bestechen. ~**ry** *n*
Bestechung *f*
brick *n* Ziegelstein *m*, Backstein
m
bricklayer *n* Maurer *m*
bridal *a* Braut-
bride *n* Braut *f*. ~**groom** *n*
Bräutigam *m*. ~**smaid** *n*
Brautjungfer *f*
bridge[1] *n* Brücke *f*; (*of nose*)
Nasenrücken *m*; (*of spectacles*)
Steg *m*
bridge[2] *n* (*Cards*) Bridge *nt*
bridle *n* Zaum *m*
brief[1] *a* (**-er, -est**) kurz; **be** ~
<*person:*> sich kurz fassen
brief[2] *n* Instruktionen *pl*; (*Jur:
case*) Mandat *nt*. ~**case** *n*
Aktentasche *f*
brief|ing *n* Informationsgespräch
nt. ~**ly** *adv* kurz. ~**ness** *n* Kürze
f
briefs *npl* Slip *m*
brigade *n* Brigade *f*
bright *a* (**-er, -est**), **-ly** *adv* hell;
<*day*> heiter; ~ **red** hellrot
bright|en *v* ~**en** [**up**] ● *vt*
aufheitern ● *vi* sich aufheitern.
~**ness** *n* Helligkeit *f*
brilliance *n* Glanz *m*; (*of person*)
Genialität *f*
brilliant *a*, **-ly** *adv* glänzend;
<*person*> genial
brim *n* Rand *m*; (*of hat*) Krempe *f*
bring *vt* (*pt/pp* **brought**) bringen;
~ **them with you** bring sie mit; **I
can't** ~ **myself to do it** ich bringe
es nicht fertig. ~ **about** *vt*
verursachen. ~ **along** *vt*
mitbringen. ~ **back** *vt*
zurückbringen. ~ **down** *vt*
herunterbringen; senken <*price*>.
~ **off** *vt* vollbringen. ~ **on** *vt*
(*cause*) verursachen. ~ **out** *vt*
herausbringen. ~ **round** *vt*

B

vorbeibringen; (*persuade*) überreden; wieder zum Bewusstsein bringen <*unconscious person*>. ~ **up** *vt* heraufbringen; (*vomit*) erbrechen; aufziehen <*children*>

brink *n* Rand *m*

brisk *a* (-er, -est,), -ly *adv* lebhaft; (*quick*) schnell

bristle *n* Borste *f*

Brit|ain *n* Großbritannien *nt*. ~**ish** *a* britisch; **the** ~**ish** die Briten *pl*. ~**on** *n* Brite *m*/Britin *f*

brittle *a* brüchig, spröde

broad *a* (-er, -est) breit; <*hint*> deutlich; **in** ~ **daylight** am helllichten Tag. ~ **beans** *npl* dicke Bohnen *pl*

broadcast *n* Sendung *f* ● *vt/i* (*pt/pp* -cast) senden. ~**er** *n* Rundfunk- und Fernsehpersönlichkeit *f*. ~**ing** *n* Funk und Fernsehen *pl*

broaden *vt* verbreitern; (*fig*) erweitern ● *vi* sich verbreitern

broadly *adv* breit; ~ **speaking** allgemein gesagt

broadminded *a* tolerant

broccoli *n inv* Brokkoli *pl*

brochure *n* Broschüre *f*

broke *see* **break** ● *a* 🔟 pleite

broken *see* **break** ● *a* zerbrochen, 🔟 kaputt. ~**-hearted** *a* untröstlich

broker *n* Makler *m*

bronchitis *n* Bronchitis *f*

bronze *n* Bronze *f*

brooch *n* Brosche *f*

brood *vi* (*fig*) grübeln

broom *n* Besen *m*; (*Bot*) Ginster *m*

broth *n* Brühe *f*

brothel *n* Bordell *nt*

brother *n* Bruder *m*

brother: ~**-in-law** *n* (*pl* **-s-in-law**) Schwager *m*. ~**ly** *a* brüderlich

brought *see* **bring**

brow *n* Augenbraue *f*; (*forehead*) Stirn *f*; (*of hill*) [Berg]kuppe *f*

brown *a* (-er, -est) braun; ~ **paper** Packpapier *nt* ● *n* Braun *nt* ● *vt* bräunen ● *vi* braun werden

browse *vi* (*read*) schmökern; (*in shop*) sich umsehen. ~**r** *n* (*Computing*) Browser *m*

bruise *n* blauer Fleck *m* ● *vt* beschädigen <*fruit*>; ~ **one's arm** sich (*dat*) den Arm quetschen

brunette *n* Brünette *f*

brush *n* Bürste *f*; (*with handle*) Handfeger *m*; (*for paint, pastry*) Pinsel *m*; (*bushes*) Unterholz *nt*; (*fig: conflict*) Zusammenstoß *m* ● *vt* bürsten; putzen <*teeth*>; ~ **against** streifen [gegen]; ~ **aside** (*fig*) abtun. ~ **off** *vt* abbürsten. ~ **up** *vt/i* (*fig*) ~ **up** [**on**] auffrischen

brusque *a*, -ly *adv* brüsk

Brussels *n* Brüssel *nt*. ~ **sprouts** *npl* Rosenkohl *m*

brutal *a*, -ly *adv* brutal. ~**ity** *n* Brutalität *f*

brute *n* Unmensch *m*. ~ **force** *n* rohe Gewalt *f*

BSE *abbr* (**bovine spongiform encephalopathy**) BSE *f*

bubble *n* [Luft]blase *f* ● *vi* sprudeln

buck[1] *n* (*deer & Gym*) Bock *m*; (*rabbit*) Rammler *m* ● *vi* <*horse:*> bocken

buck[2] *n* (*Amer* 🔟) Dollar *m*

buck[3] *n* **pass the** ~ die Verantwortung abschieben

bucket *n* Eimer *m*

buckle *n* Schnalle *f* ● *vt* zuschnallen ● *vi* sich verbiegen

bud *n* Knospe *f*

buddy *n* 🔟 Freund *m*

budge *vt* bewegen ● *vi* sich [von der Stelle] rühren

budget *n* Budget *nt*; (*Pol*) Haushaltsplan *m*; (*money available*) Etat *m* ● *vi* (*pt/pp* budgeted) ~ **for sth** etw einkalkulieren

buff *a* (*colour*) sandfarben ● *n*
Sandfarbe *f*; 🎬 Fan *m* ● *vt*
polieren
buffalo *n* (*inv or pl* -es) Büffel *m*
buffer *n* (*Rail*) Puffer *m*
buffet[1] *n* Büfett *nt*; (*on station*)
Imbissstube *f*
buffet[2] *vt* (*pt/pp* **buffeted**) hin und
her werfen
bug *n* Wanze *f*; (🎬 *virus*) Bazillus
m; (🎬 *device*) Abhörgerät *nt*, 🎬
Wanze *f* ● *vt* (*pt/pp* **bugged**) 🎬
verwanzen <*room*>; abhören
<*telephone*>; (*Amer: annoy*)
ärgern
bugle *n* Signalhorn
build *n* (*of person*) Körperbau *m*
● *vt/i* (*pt/pp* **built**) bauen. ~ **on** *vt*
anbauen (**to** an + *acc*). ~ **up** *vt*
aufbauen ● *vi* zunehmen
builder *n* Bauunternehmer *m*
building *n* Gebäude *nt*. ~ **site** *n*
Baustelle *f*. ~ **society** *n*
Bausparkasse *f*
built *see* **build**. ~-**in** *a* eingebaut.
~-**in cupboard** *n* Einbauschrank
m. ~-**up area** *n* bebautes Gebiet
nt; (*Auto*) geschlossene Ortschaft
f
bulb *n* [Blumen]zwiebel *f*; (*Electr*)
[Glüh]birne *f*
bulbous *a* bauchig
Bulgaria *n* Bulgarien *nt*
bulg|e *n* Ausbauchung *f* ● *vi* sich
ausbauchen. ~**ing** *a* prall; <*eyes*>
hervorquellend
bulk *n* Masse *f*; (*greater part*)
Hauptteil *m*. ~**y** *a* sperrig; (*large*)
massig
bull *n* Bulle *m*, Stier *m*
bulldog *n* Bulldogge *f*
bulldozer *n* Planierraupe *f*
bullet *n* Kugel *f*
bulletin *n* Bulletin *nt*
bullet-proof *a* kugelsicher
bullfight *n* Stierkampf *m*. ~**er** *n*
Stierkämpfer *m*
bullfinch *n* Dompfaff *m*
bullock *n* Ochse *m*

bull: ~**ring** *n* Stierkampfarena *f*.
~**'s-eye** *n* **score a** ~**'s-eye** ins
Schwarze treffen
bully *n* Tyrann *m* ● *vt*
tyrannisieren
bum *n* 🔲 Hintern *m*
bumble-bee *n* Hummel *f*
bump *n* Bums *m*; (*swelling*) Beule
f; (*in road*) holperige Stelle *f* ● *vt*
stoßen; ~ **into** stoßen gegen;
(*meet*) zufällig treffen. ~ **off** *vt* 🎬
um die Ecke bringen
bumper *a* Rekord- ● *n* (*Auto*)
Stoßstange *f*
bumpy *a* holperig
bun *n* Milchbrötchen *nt*; (*hair*)
[Haar]knoten *m*
bunch *n* (*of flowers*) Strauß *m*; (*of
radishes, keys*) Bund *m*; ~ (*of
people*) Gruppe *f*; ~ **of grapes**
[ganze] Weintraube *f*
bundle *n* Bündel *nt* ● *vt* ~ [**up**]
bündeln
bungalow *n* Bungalow *m*
bungle *vt* verpfuschen
bunk *n* [Schlaf]koje *f*. ~-**beds** *npl*
Etagenbett *nt*
bunker *n* Bunker *m*
bunny *n* 🎬 Kaninchen *nt*
buoy *n* Boje *f*
buoyan|cy *n* Auftrieb *m*. ~**t** *a* **be**
~**t** schwimmen
burden *n* Last *f*
bureau *n* (*pl* -**x** *or* -**s**) (*desk*)
Sekretär *m*; (*office*) Büro *nt*
bureaucracy *n* Bürokratie *f*
bureaucratic *a* bürokratisch
burger *n* Hamburger *m*
burglar *n* Einbrecher *m*. ~ **alarm**
n Alarmanlage *f*
burglary *n* Einbruch *m*
burgle *vt* einbrechen in (+ *acc*);
they have been ~**d** bei ihnen ist
eingebrochen worden
burial *n* Begräbnis *nt*
burly *a* (-**ier**, -**iest**) stämmig
Burm|a *n* Birma *nt*. ~**ese** *a*
birmanisch

burn n Verbrennung f; (on skin) Brandwunde f; (on material) Brandstelle f ● v (pt/pp **burnt** or **burned**) ● vt verbrennen ● vi brennen; <food:> anbrennen. ~ **down** vt/i niederbrennen

burnt see burn

burp vi 🗓 aufstoßen

burrow n Bau m ● vi wühlen

burst n Bruch m; (surge) Ausbruch m ● v (pt/pp **burst**) ● vt platzen machen ● vi platzen; <bud:> aufgehen; ~ **into tears** in Tränen ausbrechen

bury vt (pt/pp **-ied**) begraben; (hide) vergraben

bus n [Auto]bus m

bush n Strauch m; (land) Busch m. ~**y** a (**-ier, -iest**) buschig

busily adv eifrig

business n Angelegenheit f; (Comm) Geschäft nt; **on** ~ geschäftlich; **he has no** ~ er hat kein Recht (**to** zu); **mind one's own** ~ sich um die seinen Angelegenheiten kümmern; **that's none of your** ~ das geht Sie nichts an. ~**-like** a geschäftsmäßig. ~**man** n Geschäftsmann m

bus-stop n Bushaltestelle f

bust¹ n Büste f

bust² a 🗓 kaputt; **go** ~ Pleite gehen ● v (pt/pp **busted** or **bust**) 🗓 ● vt kaputtmachen ● vi kaputtgehen

busy a (**-ier, -iest**) beschäftigt; <day> voll; <street> belebt; (with traffic) stark befahren; (Amer Teleph) besetzt; **be** ~ zu tun haben ● vt ~ **oneself** sich beschäftigen (**with** mit)

but conj aber; (after negative) sondern ● prep außer (+ dat); ~ **for** (without) ohne (+ acc); **the last** ~ **one** der/die/das vorletzte; **the next** ~ **one** der/die/das übernächste ● adv nur

butcher n Fleischer m, Metzger m; ~'s [**shop**] Fleischerei f, Metzgerei f ● vt [ab]schlachten

butler n Butler m

butt n (of gun) [Gewehr]kolben m; (fig: target) Zielscheibe f; (of cigarette) Stummel m; (for water) Regentonne f ● vi ~ **in** unterbrechen

butter n Butter f ● vt mit Butter bestreichen. ~ **up** vt 🗓 schmeicheln (+ dat)

butter: ~**cup** a Butterblume f, Hahnenfuß m. ~**fly** n Schmetterling m

buttocks npl Gesäß nt

button n Knopf m ● vt ~ [**up**] zuknöpfen. ~**hole** n Knopfloch nt

buy n Kauf m ● vt (pt/pp **bought**) kaufen. ~**er** n Käufer(in) m(f)

buzz n Summen m ● vi summen

buzzer n Summer m

by prep (close to) bei (+ dat); (next to) neben (+ dat/acc); (past) an (+ dat) ... vorbei; (to the extent of) um (+ acc); (at the latest) bis; (by means of) durch; **by Mozart/Dickens** von Mozart/Dickens; ~ **oneself** allein; ~ **the sea** am Meer; ~ **car/bus** mit dem Auto/Bus; ~ **sea** mit dem Schiff; ~ **day/night** bei Tag/Nacht; ~ **the hour** pro Stunde; ~ **the metre** meterweise; **six metres** ~ **four** sechs mal vier Meter; **win** ~ **a length** mit einer Länge Vorsprung gewinnen; **miss the train** ~ **a minute** den Zug um eine Minute verpassen ● adv ~ **and large** im Großen und Ganzen; **put** ~ beiseite legen; **go/pass** ~ vorbeigehen

bye int 🗓 tschüs

by: ~**-election** n Nachwahl f. ~**pass** n Umgehungsstraße f; (Med) Bypass m ● vt umfahren. ~**-product** n Nebenprodukt m. ~**stander** n Zuschauer(in) m(f)

cab n Taxi nt; (of lorry, train) Führerhaus nt
cabaret n Kabarett nt
cabbage n Kohl m
cabin n Kabine f; (hut) Hütte f
cabinet n Schrank m; **[display]** ∼ Vitrine f; **C∼** (Pol) Kabinett nt
cable n Kabel nt; (rope) Tau nt. ∼ **railway** n Seilbahn f. ∼ **television** n Kabelfernsehen nt
cackle vi gackern
cactus n (pl **-ti** or **-tuses**) Kaktus m
cadet n Kadett m
cadge vt/i ⊞ schnorren
Caesarean a & n ∼ **[section]** Kaiserschnitt m
café n Café nt
cafeteria n Selbstbedienungsrestaurant nt
cage n Käfig m
cagey a ⊞ **be** ∼ mit der Sprache nicht herauswollen
cake n Kuchen m; (of soap) Stück nt. ∼**d** a verkrustet (**with** mit)
calculat|e vt berechnen; (estimate) kalkulieren. ∼**ing** a (fig) berechnend. ∼**ion** n Rechnung f, Kalkulation f. ∼**or** n Rechner m
calendar n Kalender m
calf¹ n (pl **calves**) Kalb nt
calf² n (pl **calves**) (Anat) Wade f
calibre n Kaliber nt
call n Ruf m; (Teleph) Anruf m; (visit) Besuch m ●vt rufen; (Teleph) anrufen; (wake) wecken; ausrufen <strike>; (name) nennen; **be** ∼**ed** heißen ●vi rufen; ∼ **[in** or **round]** vorbeikommen. ∼ **back** vt zurückrufen ●vi noch einmal

vorbeikommen. ∼ **for** vt rufen nach; (demand) verlangen; (fetch) abholen. ∼ **off** vt zurückrufen <dog>; (cancel) absagen. ∼ **on** vt bitten (**for** um); (appeal to) appellieren an (+ acc); (visit) besuchen. ∼ **out** vt rufen; aufrufen <names> ●vi rufen. ∼ **up** vt (Mil) einberufen; (Teleph) anrufen
call: ∼-box n Telefonzelle f. ∼**er** n Besucher m; (Teleph) Anrufer m. ∼**ing** n Berufung f. ∼-**up** n (Mil) Einberufung f
calm a (-**er**, -**est**), -**ly** adv ruhig ●n Ruhe f ∼ **[down]** beruhigen ●vi ∼ **down** sich beruhigen. ∼**ness** n Ruhe f; (of sea) Stille f
calorie n Kalorie f
calves npl see **calf¹** & ²
camcorder n Camcorder m
came see **come**
camel n Kamel nt
camera n Kamera f
camouflage n Tarnung f ●vt tarnen
camp n Lager nt ●vi campen; (Mil) kampieren
campaign n Feldzug m; (Comm, Pol) Kampagne f ●vi (Pol) im Wahlkampf arbeiten
camp: ∼-bed n Feldbett nt. ∼**er** n Camper m; (Auto) Wohnmobil nt. ∼**ing** n Camping nt. ∼**site** n Campingplatz m
can¹ n (for petrol) Kanister m; (tin) Dose f, Büchse f; **a** ∼ **of beer** eine Dose Bier

can²
    pres **can**, pt **could**
● auxiliary verb
····▸ (be able to) können. **I can't** or **cannot go** ich kann nicht gehen. **she couldn't** or **could not go** (was unable to) sie konnte nicht gehen; (would not be able to) sie könnte nicht gehen. **he could go if he had time** er könnte gehen,

wenn er Zeit hätte. **if I could go**
wenn ich gehen könnte. **that
cannot be true** das kann nicht
stimmen

····▸ (*know how to*) können. **can
you swim?** können Sie
schwimmen? **she can drive** sie
kann Auto fahren

····▸ (*be allowed to*) dürfen. **you
can't smoke here** hier dürfen Sie
nicht rauchen. **can I go?** kann od
darf ich gehen?

····▸ (*in requests*) können. **can I
have a glass of water, please?**
kann ich ein Glas Wasser
haben, bitte? **could you ring me
tomorrow?** könnten Sie mich
morgen anrufen?

····▸ **could** (*expressing possibility*)
könnte. **that could be so** das
könnte od kann sein. **I could
have killed him** ich hätte ihn
umbringen können

Canad|a *n* Kanada *nt*. **~ian** *a*
kanadisch ● *n* Kanadier(in) *m(f)*
canal *n* Kanal *m*
canary *n* Kanarienvogel *m*
cancel *vt/i* (*pt/pp* **cancelled**)
absagen, abbestellen
<*newspaper*>; (*Computing*)
abbrechen; **be ~led** ausfallen.
~lation *n* Absage *f*
cancer *n*, & (*Astr*) **C~** Krebs *m*.
~ous *a* krebsig
candid *a*, **-ly** *adv* offen
candidate *n* Kandidat(in) *m(f)*
candle *n* Kerze *f*. **~stick** *n*
Kerzenständer *m*, Leuchter *m*
candy *n* (*Amer*) Süßigkeiten *pl*;
[piece of] ~ Bonbon *m*
cane *n* Rohr *nt*; (*stick*) Stock *m*
● *vt* mit dem Stock züchtigen
canine *a* Hunde-. ~ **tooth** *n*
Eckzahn *m*
cannabis *n* Haschisch *nt*
canned *a* Dosen-, Büchsen-
cannibal *n* Kannibale *m*. **~ism** *n*
Kannibalismus *m*

cannon *n inv* Kanone *f*
cannot *see* **can²**
canoe *n* Paddelboot *nt*; (*Sport*)
Kanu *m*
can-opener *n* Dosenöffner *m*
can't = **cannot**. *See* **can²**
canteen *n* Kantine *f*
canter *n* Kanter *m* ● *vi* kantern
canvas *n* Segeltuch *nt*; (*Art*)
Leinwand *f*; (*painting*) Gemälde
nt
canvass *vi* um Stimmen werben
canyon *n* Cañon *m*
cap *n* Kappe *f*, Mütze *f*; (*nurse's*)
Haube *f*; (*top, lid*) Verschluss *m*
capability *n* Fähigkeit *f*
capable *a*, **-bly** *adv* fähig; **be ~ of
doing sth** fähig sein, etw zu tun
capacity *n* Fassungsvermögen *nt*;
(*ability*) Fähigkeit *f*; **in my ~ as** in
meiner Eigenschaft als
cape¹ *n* (*cloak*) Cape *nt*
cape² *n* (*Geog*) Kap *nt*
capital *a* <*letter*> groß ● *n* (*town*)
Hauptstadt *f*; (*money*) Kapital *nt*;
(*letter*) Großbuchstabe *m*
capital|ism *n* Kapitalismus *m*.
~ist *a* kapitalistisch ● *n*
Kapitalist *m*. ~ **letter** *n*
Großbuchstabe *m*. ~ **punishment**
n Todesstrafe *f*
capsize *vi* kentern ● *vt* zum
Kentern bringen
captain *n* Kapitän *m*; (*Mil*)
Hauptmann *m* ● *vt* anführen
<*team*>
caption *n* Überschrift *f*; (*of
illustration*) Bildtext *m*
captivate *vt* bezaubern
captiv|e *a* **hold/take ~e** gefangen
halten/nehmen ● *n* Gefangene(r)
m/f. **~ity** *n* Gefangenschaft *f*
capture *n* Gefangennahme *f* ● *vt*
gefangen nehmen; [ein]fangen
<*animal*>; (*Mil*) einnehmen
<*town*>
car *n* Auto *nt*, Wagen *m*; **by ~** mit
dem Auto od Wagen
caramel *n* Karamell *m*

carat n Karat nt
caravan n Wohnwagen m; (procession) Karawane f
carbon n Kohlenstoff m; (paper) Kohlepapier nt; (copy) Durchschlag m
carbon: ~ **copy** n Durchschlag m. ~ **paper** n Kohlepapier nt
carburettor n Vergaser m
carcass n Kadaver m
card n Karte f
cardboard n Pappe f, Karton m. ~ **box** n Pappschachtel f; (large) [Papp]karton m
card-game n Kartenspiel nt
cardigan n Strickjacke f
cardinal a Kardinal- ●n (Relig) Kardinal m
card index n Kartei f
care n Sorgfalt f; (caution) Vorsicht f; (protection) Obhut f; (looking after) Pflege f; (worry) Sorge f; ~ **of** (on letter abbr **c/o**) bei; **take** ~ vorsichtig sein; **take into** ~ in Pflege nehmen; **take** ~ **of** sich kümmern um ●vi ~ **for** (like) mögen; (look after) betreuen; **I don't** ~ das ist mir gleich
career n Laufbahn f; (profession) Beruf m ●vi rasen
care: ~**free** a sorglos. ~**ful** a, -**ly** adv sorgfältig; (cautious) vorsichtig. ~**less** a, -**ly** adv nachlässig. ~**lessness** n Nachlässigkeit f
caretaker n Hausmeister m
car ferry n Autofähre f
cargo n (pl -**es**) Ladung f
Caribbean n **the** ~ die Karibik
caricature n Karikatur f ●vt karikieren
caring a <parent> liebevoll; <profession, attitude> sozial
carnation n Nelke f
carnival n Karneval m
carol n [Christmas] ~ Weihnachtslied nt
carp[1] n inv Karpfen m

carp[2] vi nörgeln
car park n Parkplatz m; (multistorey) Parkhaus nt; (underground) Tiefgarage f
carpent|er n Zimmermann m; (joiner) Tischler m. ~**ry** n Tischlerei f
carpet n Teppich m
carriage n Kutsche f; (Rail) Wagen m; (of goods) Beförderung f; (cost) Frachtkosten pl; (bearing) Haltung f
carrier n Träger(in) m(f); (Comm) Spediteur m; ~ **[-bag]** Tragetasche f
carrot n Möhre f, Karotte f
carry vt/i (pt/pp -**ied**) tragen; **be carried away** I hingerissen sein. ~ **off** vt wegtragen; gewinnen <prize>. ~ **on** vi weitermachen; ~ **on with** I eine Affäre haben mit ●vt führen; (continue) fortführen. ~ **out** vt hinaus-/heraustragen; (perform) ausführen
cart n Karren m; **put the** ~ **before the horse** das Pferd beim Schwanz aufzäumen ●vt karren; (I carry) schleppen
carton n [Papp]karton m; (for drink) Tüte f; (of cream, yoghurt) Becher m
cartoon n Karikatur f; (joke) Witzzeichnung f; (strip) Comic Strips pl; (film) Zeichentrickfilm m. ~**ist** n Karikaturist m
cartridge n Patrone f; (for film) Kassette f
carve vt schnitzen; (in stone) hauen; (Culin) aufschneiden
carving n Schnitzerei f. ~**-knife** n Tranchiermesser n
car wash n Autowäsche f; (place) Autowaschanlage f
case[1] n Fall m; **in any** ~ auf jeden Fall; **just in** ~ für alle Fälle; **in** ~ **he comes** falls er kommt

case² n Kasten m; (crate) Kiste f; (for spectacles) Etui nt; (suitcase) Koffer m; (for display) Vitrine f

cash n Bargeld nt; **pay [in] ~** [in] bar bezahlen; **~ on delivery** per Nachnahme ● vt einlösen <cheque>. **~ desk** n Kasse f

cashier n Kassierer(in) m(f)

cash: ~point [machine] n Geldautomat m. **~ register** n Registrierkasse f

cassette n Kassette f. **~ recorder** n Kassettenrecorder m

cast n (mould) Form f; (model) Abguss m; (Theat) Besetzung f; **[plaster] ~** (Med) Gipsverband m ● vt (pt/pp cast) (throw) werfen; (shed) abwerfen; abgeben <vote>; gießen <metal>; (Theat) besetzen <role>. **~ off** vi (Naut) ablegen

castle n Schloss nt; (fortified) Burg f; (Chess) Turm m

cast-offs npl abgelegte Kleidung f

castor n (wheel) [Lauf]rolle f

castor sugar n Streuzucker m

casual a, **-ly** adv (chance) zufällig; (offhand) lässig; (informal) zwanglos; (not permanent) Gelegenheits-; **~ wear** Freizeitbekleidung f

casualty n [Todes]opfer nt; (injured person) Verletzte(r) m/f; **~ [department]** Unfallstation f

cat n Katze f

catalogue n Katalog m ● vt katalogisieren

catapult n Katapult nt ● vt katapultieren

cataract n (Med) grauer Star m

catarrh n Katarrh m

catastroph|e n Katastrophe f. **~ic** a katastrophal

catch n (of fish) Fang m; (fastener) Verschluss m; (on door) Klinke f; (☐ snag) Haken m ☐ ● v (pt/pp caught) ● vt fangen; (be in time for) erreichen; (travel by) fahren mit;

bekommen <illness>; **~ a cold** sich erkälten; **~ sight of** erblicken; **~ s.o. stealing** jdn beim Stehlen erwischen; **~ one's finger in the door** sich (dat) den Finger in der Tür [ein]klemmen ● vi (burn) anbrennen; (get stuck) klemmen. **~ on** vi ☐ (understand) kapieren; (become popular) sich durchsetzen. **~ up** vt einholen ● vi aufholen. **~ up with** einholen <s.o.>; nachholen <work>

catching a ansteckend

catch: ~-phrase n, **~word** n Schlagwort nt

catchy a (-ier, -iest) einprägsam

categor|ical a, **-ly** adv kategorisch. **~y** n Kategorie f

cater vi **~ for** beköstigen; <firm:> das Essen liefern für <party>; (fig) eingestellt sein auf (+ acc)

caterpillar n Raupe f

cathedral n Dom m, Kathedrale f

Catholic a katholisch ● n Katholik(in) m(f)

cattle npl Vieh nt

catty a (-ier, -iest) boshaft

caught see catch

cauliflower n Blumenkohl m

cause n Ursache f; (reason) Grund m; **good ~** gute Sache f ● vt verursachen; **~ s.o. to do sth** jdn veranlassen, etw zu tun

caution n Vorsicht f; (warning) Verwarnung f ● vt (Jur) verwarnen

cautious a, **-ly** adv vorsichtig

cavalry n Kavallerie f

cave n Höhle f ● vi **~ in** einstürzen

cavern n Höhle f

caviare n Kaviar m

cavity n Hohlraum m; (in tooth) Loch nt

CCTV abbr (closed-circuit television) CCTV nt; (surveillance) Videoüberwachung f

CD abbr (compact disc) CD f; **~-ROM** CD-ROM f

cease vt/i aufhören. ∼**-fire** n
Waffenruhe f. ∼**less** a, **-ly** adv
unaufhörlich
cedar n Zeder f
ceiling n [Zimmer]decke f; (fig)
oberste Grenze f
celebrat|e vt/i feiern. ∼**ed** a
berühmt (**for** wegen). ∼**ion** n
Feier f
celebrity n Berühmtheit f
celery n [Stangen]sellerie m & f
cell n Zelle f
cellar n Keller m
cellist n Cellist(in) m(f)
cello n Cello nt
Celsius a Celsius
Celt n Kelte m/ Keltin f. ∼**ic** a
keltisch
cement n Zement m; (adhesive)
Kitt m
cemetery n Friedhof m
censor n Zensor m ● vt
zensieren. ∼**ship** n Zensur f
census n Volkszählung f
cent n Cent m
centenary n, (Amer) **centennial** n
Hundertjahrfeier f
center n (Amer) = **centre**
centi|grade a Celsius. ∼**metre** n
Zentimeter m & nt
central a, **-ly** adv zentral. ∼
heating n Zentralheizung f. ∼**ize**
vt zentralisieren
centre n Zentrum nt; (middle)
Mitte f ● v (pt/pp **centred**) ● vt
zentrieren. ∼**-forward** n
Mittelstürmer m
century n Jahrhundert nt
ceramic a Keramik-
cereal n Getreide nt; (breakfast
food) Frühstücksflocken pl
ceremon|ial a, **-ly** adv
zeremoniell, feierlich ● n
Zeremoniell nt. ∼**ious** a, **-ly** adv
formell
ceremony n Zeremonie f, Feier f
certain a sicher; (not named)
gewiss; **for** ∼ mit Bestimmtheit;
make ∼ (check) sich vergewissern

(**that** dass); (ensure) dafür sorgen
(**that** dass); **he is** ∼ **to win** er wird
ganz bestimmt siegen. ∼**ly** adv
bestimmt, sicher; ∼**ly not!** auf
keinen Fall! ∼**ty** n Sicherheit f,
Gewissheit f; **it's a** ∼**ty** es ist
sicher
certificate n Bescheinigung f;
(Jur) Urkunde f; (Sch) Zeugnis n‹
certify vt (pt/pp **-ied**)
bescheinigen; (declare insane) für
geisteskrank erklären
cf. abbr (compare) vgl.
chafe vt wund reiben
chaffinch n Buchfink m
chain n Kette f ● vt ketten (**to an**
+ acc). ∼ **up** vt anketten
chain: ∼ **reaction** n
Kettenreaktion f. ∼**-smoker** n
Kettenraucher m. ∼ **store** n
Kettenladen m
chair n Stuhl m; (Univ) Lehrstuhl
m; (Adm) Vorsitzende(r) m/f. ∼**-
lift** n Sessellift m. ∼**man** n
Vorsitzende(r) m/f
chalet n Chalet nt
chalk n Kreide f
challeng|e n Herausforderung f;
(Mil) Anruf m ● vt
herausfordern; (Mil) anrufen;
(fig) anfechten <statement>. ∼**er**
n Herausforderer m. ∼**ing** a
herausfordernd; (demanding)
anspruchsvoll
chamber n Kammer f; **C∼ of
Commerce** Handelskammer f. ∼
music n Kammermusik f
chamber music n Kammermusik
f
chamois n ∼**[-leather]** Ledertuch
nt
champagne n Champagner m
champion n (Sport) Meister(in)
m(f); (of cause) Verfechter m ● vt
sich einsetzen für. ∼**ship** n
(Sport) Meisterschaft f
chance n Zufall m; (prospect)
Chancen pl; (likelihood) Aussicht
f; (opportunity) Gelegenheit f; **by**

~ zufällig; **take a ~** ein Risiko
eingehen; **give s.o. a ~** jdm eine
Chance geben ● *attrib* zufällig
● *vt* **~ it** es riskieren

chancellor *n* Kanzler *m*; (*Univ*)
Rektor *m*

chancy *a* riskant

change *n* Veränderung *f*;
(*alteration*) Änderung *f*; (*money*)
Wechselgeld *nt*; **for a ~** zur
Abwechslung ● *vt* wechseln;
(*alter*) ändern; (*exchange*)
umtauschen (**for** gegen);
(*transform*) verwandeln; trocken
legen <*baby*>; **~ one's clothes**
sich umziehen; **~ trains**
umsteigen ● *vi* sich verändern;
(**~** *clothes*) sich umziehen; (**~**
trains) umsteigen; **all ~!** alles
aussteigen!

changeable *a* wechselhaft

changing-room *n* Umkleideraum
m

channel *n* Rinne *f*; (*Radio, TV*)
Kanal *m*; (*fig*) Weg *m*; **the
[English] C~** der Ärmelkanal; **the
C~ Islands** die Kanalinseln

chant *vt* singen; <*demonstrators:*>
skandieren

chao|s *n* Chaos *nt*. **~tic** *a*
chaotisch

chap *n* 🛈 Kerl *m*

chapel *n* Kapelle *f*

chaplain *n* Geistliche(r) *m*

chapped *a* <*skin*> aufgesprungen

chapter *n* Kapitel *nt*

character *n* Charakter *m*; (*in
novel, play*) Gestalt *f*; (*Typ*)
Schriftzeichen *nt*; **out of ~**
uncharakteristisch; **quite a ~** 🛈
ein Original

characteristic *a*, **-ally** *adv*
charakteristisch (**of** für) ● *n*
Merkmal *nt*

characterize *vt* charakterisieren

charge *n* (*price*) Gebühr *f*;
(*Electr*) Ladung *f*; (*attack*) Angriff
m; (*Jur*) Anklage *f*; **free of ~**
kostenlos; **be in ~** verantwortlich

sein (**of** für); **take ~** die Aufsicht
übernehmen (**of** über + *acc*) ● *vt*
berechnen <*fee*>; (*Electr*) laden;
(*attack*) angreifen; (*Jur*) anklagen
(**with** *gen*); **~ s.o. for sth** jdm etw
berechnen

charitable *a* wohltätig; (*kind*)
wohlwollend

charity *n* Nächstenliebe *f*;
(*organization*) wohltätige
Einrichtung *f*; **for ~** für
Wohltätigkeitszwecke

charm *n* Reiz *m*; (*of person*)
Charme *f*; (*object*) Amulett *nt*
● *vt* bezaubern. **~ing** *a*, **-ly** *adv*
reizend; <*person, smile*>
charmant

chart *n* Karte *f*; (*table*) Tabelle *f*

charter *n* **~ [flight]** Charterflug *m*
● *vt* chartern; **~ed accountant**
Wirtschaftsprüfer(in) *m(f)*

chase *n* Verfolgungsjagd *f* ● *vt*
jagen, verfolgen. **~ away** *or* **off** *vt*
wegjagen

chassis *n* (*pl* **chassis**) Chassis *nt*

chaste *a* keusch

chat *n* Plauderei *f*; **have a ~ with**
plaudern mit ● *vi* (*pt/pp* **chatted**)
plaudern. **~ show** *n* Talkshow *f*

chatter *n* Geschwätz *nt* ● *vi*
schwatzen; <*child:*> plappern;
<*teeth:*> klappern. **~box** *n* 🛈
Plappermaul *nt*

chatty *a* (**-ier, -iest**) geschwätzig

chauffeur *n* Chauffeur *m*

cheap *a & adv* (**-er, -est**), **-ly** *adv*
billig. **~en** *vt* entwürdigen

cheat *n* Betrüger(in) *m(f)*; (*at
games*) Mogler *m* ● *vt* betrügen
● *vi* (*at games*) mogeln 🛈

check¹ *a* (*squared*) kariert ● *n*
Karo *nt*

check² *n* Überprüfung *f*;
(*inspection*) Kontrolle *f*; (*Chess*)
Schach *nt*; (*Amer: bill*) Rechnung
f; (*Amer: cheque*) Scheck *m*;
(*Amer: tick*) Haken *m*; **keep a ~
on** kontrollieren ● *vt*
[über]prüfen; (*inspect*)

kontrollieren; (*restrain*) hemmen;
(*stop*) aufhalten ● *vi* [go and] ~
nachsehen. ~ in *vi* sich
anmelden; (*Aviat*) einchecken
● *vt* abfertigen; einchecken. ~
out *vi* sich abmelden. ~ up *vi*
prüfen, kontrollieren; ~ up on
überprüfen
checked *a* kariert
check: ~-out *n* Kasse *f.* ~room *n*
(*Amer*) Garderobe *f.* ~-up *n*
(*Med*) [Kontroll]untersuchung *f*
cheek *n* Backe *f;* (*impudence*)
Frechheit *f.* ~y *a*, -ily *adv* frech
cheer *n* Beifallsruf *m;* **three ~s**
ein dreifaches Hoch (**for** auf +
acc); ~s! prost! (*goodbye*) tschüs!
● *vt* zujubeln (+ *dat*) ● *vi* jubeln.
~ up *vi* aufmuntern; aufheitern
● *vi* munterer werden. ~ful *a*, -ly
adv fröhlich. ~fulness *n*
Fröhlichkeit *f*
cheerio *int* 🔲 tschüs!
cheese *n* Käse *m.* ~cake *n*
Käsekuchen *m*
chef *n* Koch *m*
chemical *a*, -ly *adv* chemisch ● *n*
Chemikalie *f*
chemist *n* (*pharmacist*)
Apotheker(in) *m(f);* (*scientist*)
Chemiker(in) *m(f);* ~'s [shop]
Drogerie *f;* (*dispensing*)
Apotheke *f.* ~ry *n* Chemie *f*
cheque *n* Scheck *m.* ~-book *n*
Scheckbuch *nt.* ~ card *n*
Scheckkarte *f*
cherish *vt* lieben; (*fig*) hegen
cherry *n* Kirsche *f* ● *attrib*
Kirsch-
chess *n* Schach *nt*
chess: ~board *n* Schachbrett *nt.*
~-man *n* Schachfigur *f*
chest *n* Brust *f;* (*box*) Truhe *f*
chestnut *n* Esskastanie *f*, Marone
f; (*horse-*) [Ross]kastanie *f*
chest of drawers *n* Kommode *f*
chew *vt* kauen. ~ing-gum *n*
Kaugummi *m*
chick *n* Küken *nt*

chicken *n* Huhn *nt* ● *attrib*
Hühner- ● *a* 🔲 feige
chief *a* Haupt- ● *n* Chef *m;* (*of
tribe*) Häuptling *m.* ~ly *adv*
hauptsächlich
child *n* (*pl* ~ren) Kind *nt*
child: ~birth *n* Geburt *f.* ~hood *n*
Kindheit *f.* ~ish *a* kindisch.
~less *a* kinderlos. ~like *a*
kindlich. ~-minder *n*
Tagesmutter *f*
children *npl see* **child**
Chile *n* Chile *nt*
chill *n* Kälte *f;* (*illness*) Erkältung
f ● *vt* kühlen
chilly *a* kühl; **I felt ~** mich
fröstelte [es]
chime *vi* läuten; <*clock:*>
schlagen
chimney *n* Schornstein *m.* ~-pot
n Schornsteinaufsatz *m.* ~-
sweep *n* Schornsteinfeger *m*
chin *n* Kinn *nt*
china *n* Porzellan *nt*
Chin|a *n* China *nt.* ~ese *a*
chinesisch ● *n* (*Lang*) Chinesisch
nt; **the** ~ese *pl* die Chinesen
chink[1] *n* (*slit*) Ritze *f*
chink[2] *n* Geklirr *nt* ● *vi* klirren;
<*coins:*> klimpern
chip *n* (*fragment*) Span *m;* (*in
china, paintwork*) angeschlagene
Stelle *f;* (*Computing, Gambling*)
Chip *m;* ~s *pl* (*Culin*) Pommes
frites *pl;* (*Amer: crisps*) Chips *pl*
● *vt* (*pt/pp* chipped) (*damage*)
anschlagen. ~ped *a*
angeschlagen
chirp *vi* zwitschern; <*cricket:*>
zirpen. ~y *a* 🔲 munter
chit *n* Zettel *m*
chocolate *n* Schokolade *f;* (*sweet*)
Praline *f*
choice *n* Wahl *f;* (*variety*)
Auswahl *f* ● *a* auserlesen
choir *n* Chor *m.* ~boy *n*
Chorknabe *m*
choke *n* (*Auto*) Choke *m* ● *vt*
würgen; (*to death*) erwürgen ● *vi*

sich verschlucken; **~ on** [fast] ersticken an (+ *dat*)
choose *vt/i* (*pt* **chose**, *pp* **chosen**) wählen; (*select*) sich (*dat*) aussuchen; **~ to do/go** [freiwillig] tun/gehen; **as you ~** wie Sie wollen
choos[e]y *a* Ⓘ wählerisch
chop *n* (*blow*) Hieb *m*; (*Culin*) Kotelett *nt* ● *vt* (*pt/pp* **chopped**) hacken. **~ down** *vt* abhacken; fällen <*tree*>. **~ off** *vt* abhacken
chop|per *n* Beil *nt*; Ⓘ (*helicopter*) Hubschrauber *m*. **~py** *a* kabbelig
chopsticks *npl* Essstäbchen *pl*
choral *a* Chor-
chord *n* (*Mus*) Akkord *m*
chore *n* lästige Pflicht *f*; [**household**] **~s** Hausarbeit *f*
chorus *n* Chor *m*; (*of song*) Refrain *m*
chose, chosen *see* **choose**
Christ *n* Christus *m*
christen *vt* taufen
Christian *a* christlich ● *n* Christ(in) *m(f)*. **~ity** *n* Christentum *nt*. **~ name** *n* Vorname *m*
Christmas *n* Weihnachten *nt*. **~ card** *n* Weihnachtskarte *f*. **~ Day** *n* erster Weihnachtstag *m*. **~ Eve** *n* Heiligabend *m*. **~ tree** *n* Weihnachtsbaum *m*
chrome *n*, **chromium** *n* Chrom *nt*
chronic *a* chronisch
chronicle *n* Chronik *f*
chrysanthemum *n* Chrysantheme *f*
chubby *a* (**-ier, -iest**) mollig
chuck *vt* Ⓘ schmeißen. **~ out** *vt* Ⓘ rausschmeißen
chuckle *vi* in sich (*acc*) hineinlachen
chum *n* Freund(in) *m(f)*
chunk *n* Stück *nt*
church *n* Kirche *f*. **~yard** *n* Friedhof *m*
churn *vt* **~ out** am laufenden Band produzieren

cider *n* ≈ Apfelwein *m*
cigar *n* Zigarre *f*
cigarette *n* Zigarette *f*
cine-camera *n* Filmkamera *f*
cinema *n* Kino *nt*
cinnamon *n* Zimt *m*
circle *n* Kreis *m*; (*Theat*) Rang *m* ● *vt* umkreisen ● *vi* kreisen
circuit *n* Runde *f*; (*racetrack*) Rennbahn *f*; (*Electr*) Stromkreis *m*. **~ous** *a* **~ route** Umweg *m*
circular *a* kreisförmig ● *n* Rundschreiben *nt*. **~ saw** *n* Kreissäge *f*. **~ tour** *n* Rundfahrt *f*
circulat|e *vt* in Umlauf setzen ● *vi* zirkulieren. **~ion** *n* Kreislauf *m*; (*of newspaper*) Auflage *f*
circumference *n* Umfang *m*
circumstance *n* Umstand *m*; **~s** *pl* Umstände *pl*; (*financial*) Verhältnisse *pl*
circus *n* Zirkus *m*
cistern *n* (*tank*) Wasserbehälter *m*; (*of WC*) Spülkasten *m*
cite *vt* zitieren
citizen *n* Bürger(in) *m(f)*. **~ship** *n* Staatsangehörigkeit *f*
citrus *n* **~ [fruit]** Zitrusfrucht *f*
city *n* [Groß]stadt *f*
civic *a* Bürger-
civil *a* bürgerlich; <*aviation, defence*> zivil; (*polite*) höflich. **~ engineering** *n* Hoch- und Tiefbau *m*
civilian *a* Zivil-; **in ~ clothes** in Zivil ● *n* Zivilist *m*
civiliz|ation *n* Zivilisation *f*. **~e** *vt* zivilisieren
civil: ~servant *n* Beamte(r) *m*/ Beamtin *f*. **C~ Service** *n* Staatsdienst *m*
claim *n* Anspruch *m*; (*application*) Antrag *m*; (*demand*) Forderung *f*; (*assertion*) Behauptung *f* ● *vt* beanspruchen; (*apply for*) beantragen; (*demand*) fordern; (*assert*) behaupten; (*collect*) abholen
clam *n* Klaffmuschel *f*

clamber vi klettern
clammy a (-ier, -iest) feucht
clamour n Geschrei nt ● vi ~ for schreien nach
clamp n Klammer f; [wheel] ~ Parkkralle f ● vt [ein]spannen ● vi 🛈 ~ down on vorgehen gegen
clan n Clan m
clang n Schmettern nt. ~er n 🛈 Schnitzer m
clank vi klirren
clap n give s.o. a ~ jdm Beifall klatschen; ~ of thunder Donnerschlag m ● vt/i (pt/pp clapped) Beifall klatschen (+ dat); ~ one's hands [in die Hände] klatschen
clari|fication n Klärung f. ~fy vt/i (pt/pp -ied) klären
clarinet n Klarinette f
clarity n Klarheit f
clash n Geklirr nt; (fig) Konflikt m ● vi klirren; <colours:> sich beißen; <events:> ungünstig zusammenfallen
clasp n Verschluss m ● vt ergreifen; (hold) halten
class n Klasse f; travel first/second ~ erster/zweiter Klasse reisen ● vt einordnen
classic a klassisch ● n Klassiker m. ~al a klassisch
classi|fication n Klassifikation f. ~fy vt (pt/pp -ied) klassifizieren
classroom n Klassenzimmer nt
classy a (-ier, -iest) 🛈 schick
clatter n Geklapper nt ● vi klappern
clause n Klausel f; (Gram) Satzteil m
claw n Kralle f; (of bird of prey & Techn) Klaue f; (of crab, lobster) Schere f ● vt kratzen
clay n Lehm m; (pottery) Ton m
clean a (-er, -est) sauber ● adv glatt ● vt sauber machen; putzen <shoes, windows>; ~ one's teeth sich (dat) die Zähne putzen; have

sth ~ed etw reinigen lassen. ~ up vt sauber machen
cleaner n Putzfrau f; (substance) Reinigungsmittel nt; [dry] ~'s chemische Reinigung f
cleanliness n Sauberkeit f
cleanse vt reinigen
clear a (-er, -est), -ly adv klar; (obvious) eindeutig; (distinct) deutlich; <conscience> rein; (without obstacles) frei; make sth ~ etw klarmachen (to dat) ● adv stand ~ zurücktreten; keep ~ of aus dem Wege gehen (+ dat) ● vt räumen; abräumen <table>; (acquit) freisprechen; (authorize) genehmigen; (jump over) überspringen; ~ one's throat sich räuspern ● vi <fog:> sich auflösen. ~ away vt wegräumen. ~ off vi 🛈 abhauen. ~ out vt ausräumen ● vi 🛈 abhauen. ~ up vt (tidy) aufräumen; (solve) aufklären ● vi <weather:> sich aufklären
clearance n Räumung f; (authorization) Genehmigung f; (customs) [Zoll]abfertigung f; (Techn) Spielraum m. ~ sale Räumungsverkauf m
clench vt ~ one's fist die Faust ballen; ~ one's teeth die Zähne zusammenbeißen
clergy npl Geistlichkeit f. ~man n Geistliche(r) m
clerk n Büroangestellte(r) m/f; (Amer: shop assistant) Verkäufer(in) m(f)
clever a (-er, -est), -ly adv klug; (skilful) geschickt
cliché n Klischee nt
click vi klicken
client n Kunde m/ Kundin f; (Jur) Klient(in) m(f)
cliff n Kliff nt
climate n Klima nt
climax n Höhepunkt m
climb n Aufstieg m ● vt besteigen <mountain>; steigen auf (+ acc)

<ladder, tree> ● vi klettern; (rise)
steigen; <road:> ansteigen. ~
down vi hinunter-/
herunterklettern; (from ladder,
tree) heruntersteigen

:limber n Bergsteiger m; (plant)
Kletterpflanze f

:ling vi (pt/pp **clung**) sich
klammern (**to** an + acc); (stick)
haften (**to** an + dat). ~ **film** n
Sichtfolie f mit Hafteffekt

:linic n Klinik f. ~**al** a, -**ly** adv
klinisch

:link vi klirren

:lip[1] n Klammer f; (jewellery)
Klipp m ● vt (pt/pp **clipped**)
anklammern (**to** an + acc)

:lip[2] n (extract) Ausschnitt m ● vt
schneiden; knipsen <ticket>.
~**ping** n (extract) Ausschnitt m

:loak n Umhang m. ~**room** n
Garderobe f; (toilet) Toilette f

:lobber n 🛈 Zeug nt ● vt (🛈 hit,
defeat) schlagen

:lock n Uhr f; (🛈 speedometer)
Tacho m ● vi ~ **in/out** stechen

:lock: ~**wise** a & adv im
Uhrzeigersinn. ~**work** n
Uhrwerk nt; (of toy)
Aufziehmechanismus m; **like**
~**work** 🛈 wie am Schnürchen

:lod n Klumpen m

:log vt/i (pt/pp **clogged**) ~ **[up]**
verstopfen

:loister n Kreuzgang m

:lone n Klon m ● vt klonen

:lose[1] a (-**r**, -**st**) nah[e] (**to** dat);
<friend> eng; <weather> schwül;
have a ~ shave 🛈 mit knapper
Not davonkommen ● adv nahe
● n (street) Sackgasse f

:lose[2] n Ende nt; **draw to a ~** sich
dem Ende nähern ● vt
zumachen, schließen; (bring to
an end) beenden; sperren <road>
● vi sich schließen; <shop:>
schließen, zumachen; (end)
enden. ~ **down** vt schließen;
stilllegen <factory> ● vi

schließen; <factory:> stillgelegt
werden

closely adv eng, nah[e]; (with
attention) genau

closet n (Amer) Schrank m

close-up n Nahaufnahme f

closure n Schließung f; (of
factory) Stilllegung f; (of road)
Sperrung f

clot n [Blut]gerinnsel nt; (🛈 idiot)
Trottel m

cloth n Tuch nt

clothe vt kleiden

clothes npl Kleider pl. ~-**line** n
Wäscheleine f

clothing n Kleidung f

cloud n Wolke f ● vi ~ **over** sich
bewölken

cloudy a (-**ier**, -**iest**) wolkig,
bewölkt; <liquid> trübe

clout n 🛈 Schlag m; (influence)
Einfluss m

clove n [Gewürz]nelke f; ~ **of
garlic** Knoblauchzehe f

clover n Klee m. ~ **leaf** n
Kleeblatt nt

clown n Clown m ● vi ~ **[about]**
herumalbern

club n Klub m; (weapon) Keule f;
(Sport) Schläger m; ~**s** pl (Cards)
Kreuz nt, Treff nt

clue n Anhaltspunkt m; (in
crossword) Frage f; **I haven't a ~**
🛈 ich habe keine Ahnung

clump n Gruppe f

clumsiness n Ungeschicklichkeit
f

clumsy a (-**ier**, -**iest**), -**ily** adv
ungeschickt; (unwieldy) unförmig

clung see **cling**

clutch n Griff m; (Auto)
Kupplung f; **be in s.o.'s ~es** 🛈 in
jds Klauen sein ● vt festhalten;
(grab) ergreifen ● vi ~ **at** greifen
nach

clutter n Kram m ● vt ~ **[up]**
vollstopfen

c/o abbr (**care of**) bei

coach n [Reise]bus m; (Rail) Wagen m; (horse-drawn) Kutsche f; (Sport) Trainer m ● vt Nachhilfestunden geben (+ dat); (Sport) trainieren

coal n Kohle f

coalition n Koalition f

coal-mine n Kohlenbergwerk nt

coarse a (-r, -st), **-ly** adv grob

coast n Küste f ● vi (freewheel) im Freilauf fahren; (Auto) im Leerlauf fahren. ~**er** n (mat) Untersatz m

coast: ~**guard** n Küstenwache f. ~**line** n Küste f

coat n Mantel m; (of animal) Fell nt; (of paint) Anstrich m; ~ **of arms** Wappen nt ● vt überziehen; (with paint) streichen. ~**hanger** n Kleiderbügel m. ~**hook** n Kleiderhaken m

coating n Überzug m, Schicht f; (of paint) Anstrich m

coax vt gut zureden (+ dat)

cobble¹ n Kopfstein m; ~**s** pl Kopfsteinpflaster nt

cobble² vt flicken. ~**r** n Schuster m

cobweb n Spinnengewebe nt

cock n Hahn m; (any male bird) Männchen nt ● vt <animal:> ~ **its ears** die Ohren spitzen; ~ **the gun** den Hahn spannen

cockerel n [junger] Hahn m

cockney n (dialect) Cockney nt; (person) Cockney m

cock: ~**pit** n (Aviat) Cockpit nt. ~**roach** n Küchenschabe f. ~**tail** n Cocktail m. ~-**up** n ⊠ **make a** ~-**up** Mist bauen (**of** bei)

cocky a (-ier, -iest) 🄸 eingebildet

cocoa n Kakao m

coconut n Kokosnuß f

cod n inv Kabeljau m

COD abbr (cash on delivery) per Nachnahme

coddle vt verhätscheln

code n Kode m; (Computing) Code m; (set of rules) Kodex m. ~**d** a verschlüsselt

coerce vt zwingen. ~**ion** n Zwang m

coffee n Kaffee m

coffee: ~-**grinder** n Kaffeemühle f. ~-**pot** n Kaffeekanne f. ~-**tabl** n Couchtisch m

coffin n Sarg m

cogent a überzeugend

coherent a zusammenhängend; (comprehensible) verständlich

coil n Rolle f; (Electr) Spule f; (one ring) Windung f ● vt ~[**up**] zusammenrollen

coin n Münze f ● vt prägen

coincide vi zusammenfallen; (agree) übereinstimmen

coinciden|ce n Zufall m. ~**tal** a, **-ly** adv zufällig

coke n Koks m

Coke (P) n (drink) Cola f

cold a (-er, -est) kalt; **I am** or **feel** ~ mir ist kalt ● n Kälte f; (Med) Erkältung f

cold: ~-**blooded** a kaltblütig. ~-**hearted** a kaltherzig. ~**ly** adv (fig) kalt, kühl. ~**ness** n Kälte f

collaborat|e vi zusammenarbeiten (**with** mit); ~ **on sth** mitarbeiten bei etw. ~**ion** n Zusammenarbeit f, Mitarbeit f (with enemy) Kollaboration f. ~**o** n Mitarbeiter(in) m(f); Kollaborateur m

collaps|e n Zusammenbruch m; Einsturz m ● vi zusammenbrechen; <roof, building> einstürzen. ~**ible** a zusammenklappbar

collar n Kragen m; (for animal) Halsband nt. ~-**bone** n Schlüsselbein nt

colleague n Kollege m/Kollegin.

collect vt sammeln; (fetch) abholen; einsammeln <tickets>; einziehen <taxes> ● vi sich

C

[an]sammeln ● *adv* call ~ (*Amer*) ein R-Gespräch führen
collection *n* Sammlung *f*; (*in church*) Kollekte *f*; (*of post*) Leerung *f*; (*designer's*) Kollektion *f*
collector *n* Sammler(in) *m(f)*
college *n* College *nt*
collide *vi* zusammenstoßen
colliery *n* Kohlengrube *f*
collision *n* Zusammenstoß *m*
colloquial *a*, **-ly** *adv* umgangssprachlich
Cologne *n* Köln *nt*
colon *n* Doppelpunkt
colonel *n* Oberst *m*
colonial *a* Kolonial-
colony *n* Kolonie *f*
colossal *a* riesig
colour *n* Farbe *f*; (*complexion*) Gesichtsfarbe *f*; (*race*) Hautfarbe *f*; off ~ 🛈 nicht ganz auf der Höhe ● *vt* färben; ~ **[in]** ausmalen
colour: ~**-blind** *a* farbenblind. ~**ed** *a* farbig ● *n* (*person*) Farbige(r) *m/f*. ~**-fast** *a* farbecht. ~ **film** *n* Farbfilm *m*. ~**ful** *a* farbenfroh. ~**less** *a* farblos. ~ **photo[graph]** *n* Farbaufnahme *f*. ~ **television** *n* Farbfernsehen *nt*
column *n* Säule *f*; (*of soldiers, figures*) Kolonne *f*; (*Typ*) Spalte *f*; (*Journ*) Kolumne *f*
comb *n* Kamm *m* ● *vt* kämmen; (*search*) absuchen; ~ **one's hair** sich (*dat*) [die Haare] kämmen
combat *n* Kampf *m*
combination *n* Kombination *f*
combine[1] *vt* verbinden ● *vi* sich verbinden; <*people:*> sich zusammenschließen
combine[2] *n* (*Comm*) Konzern *m*
combustion *n* Verbrennung *f*
come *vi* (*pt* **came**, *pp* **come**) kommen; (*reach*) reichen (**to** an + *acc*); **that** ~ **s to £10** das macht £10; ~ **into money** zu Geld kommen; ~ **true** wahr werden; ~

in two sizes in zwei Größen erhältlich sein; **the years to** ~ die kommenden Jahre; **how** ~? 🛈 wie das? ~ **about** *vi* geschehen. ~ **across** *vi* herüberkommen; 🛈 klar werden ● *vt* stoßen auf (+ *acc*). ~ **apart** *vi* sich auseinander nehmen lassen; (*accidentally*) auseinander gehen. ~ **away** *vi* weggehen; <*thing:*> abgehen. ~ **back** *vi* zurückkommen. ~ **by** *vi* vorbeikommen ● *vt* (*obtain*) bekommen. ~ **in** *vi* hereinkommen. ~ **off** *vi* abgehen; (*take place*) stattfinden; (*succeed*) klappen 🛈. ~ **out** *vi* herauskommen; <*book:*> erscheinen; <*stain:*> herausgehen. ~ **round** *vi* vorbeikommen; (*after fainting*) [wieder] zu sich kommen; (*change one's mind*) sich umstimmen lassen. ~ **to** *vi* [wieder] zu sich kommen. ~ **up** *vi* heraufkommen; <*plant:*> aufgehen; (*reach*) reichen (**to** bis); ~ **up with** sich (*dat*) einfallen lassen
come-back *n* Comeback *nt*
comedian *n* Komiker *m*
come-down *n* Rückschritt *m*
comedy *n* Komödie *f*
comet *n* Komet *m*
comfort *n* Bequemlichkeit *f*; (*consolation*) Trost *m* ● *vt* trösten
comfortable *a*, **-bly** *adv* bequem
comfort station *n* (*Amer*) öffentliche Toilette *f*
comfy *a* 🛈 bequem
comic *a* komisch ● *n* Komiker *m*; (*periodical*) Comic-Heft *nt*
coming *a* kommend ● *n* Kommen *nt*
comma *n* Komma *nt*
command *n* Befehl *m*; (*Mil*) Kommando *nt*; (*mastery*) Beherrschung *f* ● *vt* befehlen (+ *dat*); kommandieren <*army*>

command|er n Befehlshaber m.
~**ing officer** n Befehlshaber m

commemorat|e vt gedenken (+
gen). ~**ion** n Gedenken nt

commence vt/i anfangen,
beginnen

commend vt loben; (recommend)
empfehlen (**to** dat)

comment n Bemerkung f; **no** ~!
kein Kommentar! ● vi sich
äußern (**on** zu); ~ **on** (Journ)
kommentieren

commentary n Kommentar m;
[**running**] ~ (Radio, TV)
Reportage f

commentator n Kommentator m;
(Sport) Reporter m

commerce n Handel m

commercial a, -**ly** adv
kommerziell ● n (Radio, TV)
Werbespot m

commission n (order for work)
Auftrag m; (body of people)
Kommission f; (payment)
Provision f; (Mil)
[Offiziers]patent nt; **out of** ~
außer Betrieb ● vt beauftragen
<s.o.>; in Auftrag geben <thing>;
(Mil) zum Offizier ernennen

commit vt (pt/pp **committed**)
begehen; (entrust) anvertrauen
(**to** dat); (consign) einweisen (**to**
in + acc); ~ **oneself** sich
festlegen; (involve oneself) sich
engagieren. ~**ment** n
Verpflichtung f; (involvement)
Engagement nt. ~**ted** a engagiert

committee n Ausschuss m,
Komitee nt

common a (-**er**, -**est**) gemeinsam;
(frequent) häufig; (ordinary)
gewöhnlich; (vulgar) ordinär ● n
Gemeindeland nt; **have in** ~
gemeinsam haben; **House of C**~**s**
Unterhaus nt

common: ~**ly** adv allgemein. **C**~
Market n Gemeinsamer Markt m.
~**place** a häufig. ~**-room** n

Aufenthaltsraum m. ~ **sense** n
gesunder Menschenverstand m

commotion n Tumult m

communal a gemeinschaftlich

communicate vt mitteilen (**to**
dat); übertragen <disease> ● vi
sich verständigen

communication n Verständigung
f; (contact) Verbindung f;
(message) Mitteilung f; ~**s** pl
(technology) Nachrichtenwesen
nt

communicative a mitteilsam

Communion n [**Holy**] ~ das
[heilige] Abendmahl; (Roman
Catholic) die [heilige]
Kommunion

communis|m n Kommunismus m.
~**t** a kommunistisch ● n
Kommunist(in) m(f)

community n Gemeinschaft f;
local ~ Gemeinde f

commute vi pendeln. ~**r** n
Pendler(in) m(f)

compact a kompakt

companion n Begleiter(in) m(f).
~**ship** n Gesellschaft f

company n Gesellschaft f; (firm)
Firma f; (Mil) Kompanie f; (🄸
guests) Besuch m. ~ **car** n
Firmenwagen m

comparable a vergleichbar

comparative a vergleichend;
(relative) relativ ● n (Gram)
Komparativ m. ~**ly** adv
verhältnismäßig

compare vt vergleichen (**with/to**
mit) ● vi sich vergleichen lassen

comparison n Vergleich m

compartment n Fach nt; (Rail)
Abteil nt

compass n Kompass m

compassion n Mitleid nt. ~**ate** a
mitfühlend

compatible a vereinbar; <drugs>
verträglich; (Techn) kompatibel;
be ~ <people:> [gut] zueinander
passen

compatriot n Landsmann m /-männin f

compel vt (pt/pp **compelled**) zwingen

compensat|e vt entschädigen. ~**ion** n Entschädigung f; (fig) Ausgleich m

compete vi konkurrieren; (take part) teilnehmen (**in** an + dat)

competen|ce n Fähigkeit f. ~**t** a fähig

competition n Konkurrenz f; (contest) Wettbewerb m; (in newspaper) Preisausschreiben nt

competitive a (Comm) konkurrenzfähig

competitor n Teilnehmer m; (Comm) Konkurrent m

compile vt zusammenstellen

complacen|cy n Selbstzufriedenheit f. ~**t** a, -**ly** adv selbstzufrieden

complain vi klagen (**about/of** über + acc); (formally) sich beschweren. ~**t** n Klage f; (formal) Beschwerde f; (Med) Leiden nt

complement[1] n Ergänzung f; **full ~** volle Anzahl f

complement[2] vt ergänzen

complete a vollständig; (finished) fertig; (utter) völlig ● vt vervollständigen; (finish) abschließen; (fill in) ausfüllen. ~**ly** adv völlig

completion n Vervollständigung f; (end) Abschluss m

complex a komplex ● n Komplex m

complexion n Teint m; (colour) Gesichtsfarbe f

complexity n Komplexität f

complicat|e vt komplizieren. ~**ed** a kompliziert. ~**ion** n Komplikation f

compliment n Kompliment nt; ~**s** pl Grüße pl ● vt ein Kompliment machen (+ dat).

~**ary** a schmeichelhaft; (given free) Frei-

comply vi (pt/pp -**ied**) ~ **with** nachkommen (+ dat)

compose vt verfassen; (Mus) komponieren; **be ~d of** sich zusammensetzen aus. ~**r** n Komponist m

composition n Komposition f; (essay) Aufsatz m

compost n Kompost m

composure n Fassung f

compound a zusammengesetzt; <fracture> kompliziert ● n (Chem) Verbindung f; (Gram) Kompositum nt

comprehen|d vt begreifen, verstehen. ~**sible** a, -**bly** adv verständlich. ~**sion** n Verständnis nt

comprehensive a & n umfassend; ~ [**school**] Gesamtschule f. ~ **insurance** n (Auto) Vollkaskoversicherung f

compress vt zusammenpressen; ~**ed air** Druckluft f

comprise vt umfassen, bestehen aus

compromise n Kompromiss m ● vt kompromittieren <person> ● vi einen Kompromiss schließen

compuls|ion n Zwang m. ~**ive** a zwanghaft. ~**ory** a obligatorisch

comput|er n Computer m. ~**er game** n Computerspiel. ~**erize** vt computerisieren <data>; auf Computer umstellen <firm>. ~-**literate** a mit Computern vertraut. ~**ing** n Computertechnik f

comrade n Kamerad m; (Pol) Genosse m/Genossin f

con[1] see **pro**

con[2] n 🄵 Schwindel m ● vt (pt/pp **conned**) 🄵 beschwindeln

concave a konkav

conceal vt verstecken; (keep secret) verheimlichen

concede vt zugeben; (give up)
aufgeben

conceit n Einbildung f. ~ed a
eingebildet

conceivable a denkbar

conceive vt (Biol) empfangen;
(fig) sich (dat) ausdenken ● vi
schwanger werden

concentrat|e vt konzentrieren
● vi sich konzentrieren. ~ion n
Konzentration f

concern n Angelegenheit f;
(worry) Sorge f; (Comm)
Unternehmen nt ● vt (be about,
affect) betreffen; (worry)
kümmern; **be ~ed about** besorgt
sein um; **~ oneself with** sich
beschäftigen mit; **as far as I am
~ed** was mich angeht od betrifft.
~ing prep bezüglich (+ gen)

concert n Konzert nt

concerto n Konzert nt

concession n Zugeständnis nt;
(Comm) Konzession f; (reduction)
Ermäßigung f

concise a, -ly adv kurz

conclude vt/i schließen

conclusion n Schluss m; **in ~**
abschließend, zum Schluss

conclusive a schlüssig

concoct vt zusammenstellen;
(fig) fabrizieren. ~ion n
Zusammenstellung f; (drink)
Gebräu nt

concrete a konkret ● n Beton
m ● vt betonieren

concurrently adv gleichzeitig

concussion n
Gehirnerschütterung f

condemn vt verurteilen; (declare
unfit) für untauglich erklären.
~ation n Verurteilung f

condensation n Kondensation f

condense vt zusammenfassen

condescend vi sich herablassen
(to zu). ~ing a, -ly adv
herablassend

condition n Bedingung f; (state)
Zustand m; ~s pl Verhältnisse

pl; **on ~ that** unter der
Bedingung, dass ● vt (Psych)
konditionieren. ~al a bedingt
● n (Gram) Konditional m. ~er n
Pflegespülung f; (for fabrics)
Weichspüler m

condolences npl Beileid nt

condom n Kondom nt

condominium n (Amer) ≈
Eigentumswohnung f

conduct[1] n Verhalten nt; (Sch)
Betragen nt

conduct[2] vt führen; (Phys) leiten
(Mus) dirigieren. ~or n Dirigent
m; (of bus) Schaffner m; (Phys)
Leiter m

cone n Kegel m; (Bot) Zapfen m;
(for ice-cream) [Eis]tüte f; (Auto)
Leitkegel m

confectioner n Konditor m. ~y n
Süßwaren pl

conference n Konferenz f

confess vt/i gestehen; (Relig)
beichten. ~ion n Geständnis nt;
(Relig) Beichte f

confetti n Konfetti nt

confide vt anvertrauen ● vi **~ in**
s.o. sich jdm anvertrauen

confidence n (trust) Vertrauen
nt; (self-assurance)
Selbstvertrauen nt; (secret)
Geheimnis nt; **in ~** im Vertrauen
~ trick n Schwindel m

confident a, -ly adv
zuversichtlich; (self-assured)
selbstsicher

confidential a, -ly adv vertraulich

confine vt beschränken (to auf +
acc). ~d a (narrow) eng

confirm vt bestätigen; (Relig)
konfirmieren; (Roman Catholic)
firmen. ~ation n Bestätigung f;
Konfirmation f; Firmung f

confiscat|e vt beschlagnahmen.
~ion n Beschlagnahme f

conflict[1] n Konflikt m

conflict[2] vi im Widerspruch
stehen (with zu). ~ing a
widersprüchlich

conform vi <*person:*> sich anpassen; <*thing:*> entsprechen (**to** *dat*). **∼ist** n Konformist m

confounded a 🄸 verflixt

confront vt konfrontieren. **∼ation** n Konfrontation f

confus|e vt verwirren; (*mistake for*) verwechseln (**with** mit). **∼ing** a verwirrend. **∼ion** n Verwirrung f; (*muddle*) Durcheinander nt

congenial a angenehm

congest|ed a verstopft; (*with people*) überfüllt. **∼ion** n Verstopfung f; Überfüllung f

congratulat|e vt gratulieren (+ dat) (**on** zu). **∼ions** npl Glückwünsche pl; **∼ions!** [ich] gratuliere!

congregation n (*Relig*) Gemeinde f

congress n Kongress m. **∼man** n Kongressabgeordnete(r) m

conical a kegelförmig

conifer n Nadelbaum m

conjecture n Mutmaßung f

conjunction n Konjunktion f; **in ∼ with** zusammen mit

conjur|e vi zaubern ● vt **∼e up** heraufbeschwören. **∼or** n Zauberkünstler m

conk vi **∼ out** 🄸 <*machine:*> kaputtgehen

conker n 🄸 Kastanie f

con-man n 🄸 Schwindler m

connect vt verbinden (**to** mit); (*Electr*) anschließen (**to** an + *acc*); **be ∼ed with** zu tun haben mit; (*be related to*) verwandt sein mit ● vi verbunden sein; <*train:*> Anschluss haben (**with** an + *acc*)

connection n Verbindung f; (*Rail, Electr*) Anschluss m; **in ∼ with** in Zusammenhang mit. **∼s** npl Beziehungen pl

connoisseur n Kenner m

conquer vt erobern; (*fig*) besiegen. **∼or** n Eroberer m

conquest n Eroberung f

conscience n Gewissen nt

conscientious a, **-ly** adv gewissenhaft

conscious a, **-ly** adv bewusst; [**fully**] **∼** bei [vollem] Bewusstsein; **be/become ∼ of sth** sich (*dat*) etw (*gen*) bewusst sein/werden. **∼ness** n Bewusstsein nt

conscript n Einberufene(r) m

consecrat|e vt weihen; einweihen <*church*>. **∼ion** n Weihe f; Einweihung f

consecutive a aufeinanderfolgend. **-ly** adv fortlaufend

consent n Einwilligung f, Zustimmung f ● vi einwilligen (**to** in + *acc*), zustimmen (**to** dat)

consequen|ce n Folge f. **∼t** a daraus folgend. **∼tly** adv folglich

conservation n Erhaltung f, Bewahrung f. **∼ist** n Umweltschützer m

conservative a konservativ; <*estimate*> vorsichtig. **C∼** (*Pol*) a konservativ ● n Konservative(r) m/f

conservatory n Wintergarten m

conserve vt erhalten, bewahren; sparen <*energy*>

consider vt erwägen; (*think over*) sich (*dat*) überlegen; (*take into account*) berücksichtigen; (*regard as*) betrachten als; **∼ doing sth** erwägen, etw zu tun. **∼able** a, **-bly** adv erheblich

consider|ate a, **-ly** adv rücksichtsvoll. **∼ation** n Erwägung f; (*thoughtfulness*) Rücksicht f; (*payment*) Entgelt nt; **take into ∼ation** berücksichtigen. **∼ing** prep wenn man bedenkt (**that** dass)

consist vi **∼ of** bestehen aus

consisten|cy n Konsequenz f; (*density*) Konsistenz f. **∼t** a konsequent; (*unchanging*) gleichbleibend. **∼tly** adv konsequent; (*constantly*) ständig

consolation n Trost m. ~ **prize** n Trostpreis m

console vt trösten

consonant n Konsonant m

conspicuous a auffällig

conspiracy n Verschwörung f

constable n Polizist m

constant a, **-ly** adv beständig; (continuous) ständig

constipat|ed a verstopft. ~**ion** n Verstopfung f

constituency n Wahlkreis m

constitut|e vt bilden. ~**ion** n (Pol) Verfassung f; (of person) Konstitution f

constraint n Zwang m; (restriction) Beschränkung f; (strained manner) Gezwungenheit f

construct vt bauen. ~**ion** n Bau m; (Gram) Konstruktion f; (interpretation) Deutung f; **under** ~**ion** im Bau

consul n Konsul m. ~**ate** n Konsulat nt

consult vt [um Rat] fragen; konsultieren <doctor>; nachschlagen in (+ dat) <book>. ~**ant** n Berater m; (Med) Chefarzt m. ~**ation** n Beratung f; (Med) Konsultation f

consume vt verzehren; (use) verbrauchen. ~**r** n Verbraucher m

consumption n Konsum m; (use) Verbrauch m

contact n Kontakt m; (person) Kontaktperson f ● vt sich in Verbindung setzen mit. ~ **lenses** npl Kontaktlinsen pl

contagious a direkt übertragbar

contain vt enthalten; (control) beherrschen. ~**er** n Behälter m; (Comm) Container m

contaminat|e vt verseuchen. ~**ion** n Verseuchung f

contemplat|e vt betrachten; (meditate) nachdenken über (+

acc). ~**ion** n Betrachtung f; Nachdenken nt

contemporary a zeitgenössisch ● n Zeitgenosse m/ -genossin f

contempt n Verachtung f; **beneath** ~ verabscheuungswürdig. ~**ible** a verachtenswert. ~**uous** a, **-ly** adv verächtlich

content¹ n & **contents** pl Inhalt n

content² a zufrieden ● n **to one's heart's** ~ nach Herzenslust ● vt ~ **oneself** sich begnügen (**with** mit). ~**ed** a, **-ly** adv zufrieden

contentment n Zufriedenheit f

contest n Kampf m; (competition) Wettbewerb m. ~**ant** n Teilnehmer m

context n Zusammenhang m

continent n Kontinent m

continental a Kontinental-. ~ **breakfast** n kleines Frühstück nt ~ **quilt** n Daunendecke f

continual a, **-ly** adv dauernd

continuation n Fortsetzung f

continue vt fortsetzen; ~ **doing** o **to do sth** fortfahren, etw zu tun; **to be** ~**d** Fortsetzung folgt ● vi weitergehen; (doing sth) weitermachen; (speaking) fortfahren; <weather:> anhalten

continuity n Kontinuität f

continuous a, **-ly** adv anhaltend, ununterbrochen

contort vt verzerren. ~**ion** n Verzerrung f

contour n Kontur f; (line) Höhenlinie f

contracep|tion n Empfängnisverhütung f. ~**tive** n Empfängnisverhütungsmittel nt

contract¹ n Vertrag m

contract² vi sich zusammenziehen. ~**or** n Unternehmer m

contradict vt widersprechen (+ dat). ~**ion** n Widerspruch m. ~**ory** a widersprüchlich

contralto n Alt m; (singer) Altistin f

contraption n⚡ Apparat m
contrary a & adv
entgegengesetzt; ~ **to** entgegen
(+ dat) ● n Gegenteil nt; **on the** ~
im Gegenteil
contrast[1] n Kontrast m
contrast[2] vt gegenüberstellen
(**with** dat) ● vi einen Kontrast
bilden (**with** zu). ~**ing** a
gegensätzlich; <colour> Kontrast-
contribut|e vt/i beitragen;
beisteuern <money>; (donate)
spenden. ~**ion** n Beitrag m;
(donation) Spende f. ~**or** n
Beitragende(r) m/f
contrivance n Vorrichtung f
control n Kontrolle f; (mastery)
Beherrschung f; (Techn) Regler
m; ~**s** pl (of car, plane)
Steuerung f; **get out of** ~ außer
Kontrolle geraten ● vt (pt/pp
controlled) kontrollieren;
(restrain) unter Kontrolle halten;
~ **oneself** sich beherrschen
controvers|ial a umstritten. ~**y** n
Kontroverse f
convalesce vi sich erholen.
~**nce** n Erholung f
convalescent a ~ **home** n
Erholungsheim nt
convenience n Bequemlichkeit f;
[**public**] ~ öffentliche Toilette f;
with all modern ~**s** mit allem
Komfort
convenient a, **-ly** adv günstig; **be**
~ **for s.o.** jdm gelegen sein, jdm
passen; **if it is** ~ [**for you**] wenn es
Ihnen passt
convent n [Nonnen]kloster nt
convention n (custom) Brauch m,
Sitte f. ~**al** a, **-ly** adv
konventionell
converge vi zusammenlaufen
conversation n Gespräch nt;
(Sch) Konversation f
conversion n Umbau m; (Relig)
Bekehrung f; (calculation)
Umrechnung f

convert[1] n Bekehrte(r) m/f,
Konvertit m
convert[2] vt bekehren <person>;
(change) umwandeln (**into** in +
acc); umbauen <building>;
(calculate) umrechnen; (Techn)
umstellen. ~**ible** a verwandelbar
● n (Auto) Kabrio[lett] nt
convex a konvex
convey vt befördern; vermitteln
<idea, message>. ~**or belt** n
Förderband nt
convict[1] n Sträfling m
convict[2] vt verurteilen (**of**
wegen). ~**ion** n Verurteilung f;
(belief) Überzeugung f; **previous**
~**ion** Vorstrafe f
convinc|e vt überzeugen. ~**ing** a,
-ly adv überzeugend
convoy n Konvoi m
convulse vt **be** ~**ed** sich
krümmen (**with** vor + dat)
coo vi gurren
cook n Koch m/ Köchin f ● vt/i
kochen; **is it** ~**ed?** ist es gar? ~
the books ⚡ die Bilanz frisieren.
~**book** n (Amer) Kochbuch nt
cooker n [Koch]herd m; (apple)
Kochapfel m. ~**y** n Kochen nt.
~**y book** n Kochbuch nt
cookie n (Amer) Keks m
cool a (-er, -est), **-ly** adv kühl ● n
Kühle f ● vt kühlen ● vi
abkühlen. ~**-box** n Kühlbox f.
~**ness** n Kühle f
coop vt ~ **up** einsperren
co-operat|e vi
zusammenarbeiten. ~**ion** n
Kooperation f
co-operative a hilfsbereit ● n
Genossenschaft f
cop n ⚡ Polizist m
cope vi ⚡ zurechtkommen; ~
with fertig werden mit
copious a reichlich
copper[1] n Kupfer nt ● a kupfern
copper[2] n ⚡ Polizist m
copper beech n Blutbuche f
coppice n, **copse** n Gehölz nt

copy n Kopie f; (book) Exemplar nt ● vt (pt/pp -ied) kopieren; (imitate) nachahmen; (Sch) abschreiben

copy: ~right n Copyright nt. ~writer n Texter m

coral n Koralle f

cord n Schnur f; (fabric) Cordsamt m; ~s pl Cordhose f

cordial a, -ly adv herzlich ● n Fruchtsirup m

cordon n Kordon m ● vt ~ off absperren

corduroy n Cordsamt m

core n Kern m; (of apple, pear) Kerngehäuse nt

cork n Kork m; (for bottle) Korken m. ~screw n Korkenzieher m

corn¹ n Korn nt; (Amer: maize) Mais m

corn² n (Med) Hühnerauge nt

corned beef n Cornedbeef nt

corner n Ecke f; (bend) Kurve f; (football) Eckball m ● vt (fig) in die Enge treiben; (Comm) monopolisieren <market>. ~stone n Eckstein m

cornet n (Mus) Kornett nt; (for ice-cream) [Eis]tüte f

corn: ~flour n, (Amer) ~starch n Stärkemehl nt

corny a 🔲 abgedroschen

coronation n Krönung f

coroner n Beamte(r) m, der verdächtige Todesfälle untersucht

corporal n (Mil) Stabsunteroffizier m

corps n (pl corps) Korps nt

corpse n Leiche f

correct a, -ly adv richtig; (proper) korrekt ● vt verbessern; (Sch, Typ) korrigieren. ~ion n Verbesserung f; (Typ) Korrektur f

correspond vi entsprechen (to dat); <two things:> sich entsprechen; (write)

korrespondieren. ~ence n Briefwechsel m; (Comm) Korrespondenz f. ~ent n Korrespondent(in) m(f). ~ing a, -ly adv entsprechend

corridor n Gang m; (Pol, Aviat) Korridor m

corro|de vt zerfressen ● vi rosten. ~sion n Korrosion f

corrugated a gewellt. ~ iron n Wellblech nt

corrupt a korrupt ● vt korrumpieren; (spoil) verderben. ~ion n Korruption f

corset n & -s pl Korsett nt

Corsica n Korsika nt

cosh n Totschläger m

cosmetic a kosmetisch ● n ~s pl Kosmetika pl

cosset vt verhätscheln

cost n Kosten pl; ~s pl (Jur) Kosten; **at all** ~s um jeden Preis ● vt (pt/pp cost) kosten; **it** ~ **me £20** es hat mich £20 gekostet ● vt (pt/pp costed) ~ [out] die Kosten kalkulieren für

costly a (-ier, -iest) teuer

cost: ~ **of living** n Lebenshaltungskosten pl. ~ **price** n Selbstkostenpreis m

costume n Kostüm nt; (national) Tracht f. ~ **jewellery** n Modeschmuck m

cosy a (-ier, -iest) gemütlich ● n (tea-, egg-) Wärmer m

cot n Kinderbett nt; (Amer: camp bed) Feldbett nt

cottage n Häuschen nt. ~ **chees** n Hüttenkäse m

cotton n Baumwolle f; (thread) Nähgarn nt ● a baumwollen ● vi ~ **on** on 🔲 kapieren

cotton wool n Watte f

couch n Liege f

couchette n (Rail) Liegeplatz m

cough n Husten m ● vi husten. ~ **up** vt/i husten; (🔲 pay) blechen

cough mixture n Hustensaft m

could see can²

council n Rat m; (Admin)
Stadtverwaltung f; (rural)
Gemeindeverwaltung f. **~ house**
n ≈ Sozialwohnung f
councillor n Ratsmitglied nt
council tax n Gemeindesteuer f
count¹ n Graf m
count² n Zählung f; **keep ~**
zählen ● vt/i zählen. **~ on** vt
rechnen auf (+ acc)
counter¹ n (in shop) Ladentisch
m; (in bank) Schalter m; (in café)
Theke f; (Games) Spielmarke f
counter² a Gegen- ● vt/i kontern
counteract vt entgegenwirken (+
dat)
counterfeit a gefälscht
counterfoil n Kontrollabschnitt m
counterpart n Gegenstück nt
counter-productive a **be ~** das
Gegenteil bewirken
countersign vt gegenzeichnen
countess n Gräfin f
countless a unzählig
country n Land nt; (native land)
Heimat f; (countryside)
Landschaft f; **in the ~** auf dem
Lande. **~man** n [fellow] ~man
Landsmann m. **~side** n
Landschaft f
county n Grafschaft f
coup n (Pol) Staatsstreich m
couple n Paar nt; **a ~ of** (two)
zwei ● vt verbinden
coupon n Kupon m; (voucher)
Gutschein m; (entry form) Schein
m
courage n Mut m. **~ous** a, **-ly** adv
mutig
courgettes npl Zucchini pl
courier n Bote m; (diplomatic)
Kurier m; (for tourists)
Reiseleiter(in) m(f)
course n (Naut, Sch) Kurs m;
(Culin) Gang m; (for golf) Platz
m; **~ of treatment** (Med) Kur f; **of
~** natürlich, selbstverständlich;
in the ~ of im Lauf[e] (+ gen)

court n Hof m; (Sport) Platz m;
(Jur) Gericht nt
courteous a, **-ly** adv höflich
courtesy n Höflichkeit f
court: ~ martial n (pl ~s martial)
Militärgericht nt. **~yard** n Hof m
cousin n Vetter m, Cousin m;
(female) Kusine f
cove n kleine Bucht f
cover n Decke f; (of cushion)
Bezug m; (of umbrella) Hülle f;
(of typewriter) Haube f; (of book,
lid) Deckel m; (of magazine)
Umschlag m; (protection)
Deckung f, Schutz m; **take ~**
Deckung nehmen; **under separate
~** mit getrennter Post ● vt
bedecken; beziehen <cushion>;
decken <costs, needs>;
zurücklegen <distance>; (Journ)
berichten über (+ acc); (insure)
versichern. **~ up** vt zudecken;
(fig) vertuschen
coverage n (Journ)
Berichterstattung f (**of** über +
acc)
cover: ~ing n Decke f; (for floor)
Belag m. **~-up** n Vertuschung f
cow n Kuh f
coward n Feigling m. **~ice** n
Feigheit f. **~ly** a feige
cowboy n Cowboy m; □
unsolider Handwerker m
cowshed n Kuhstall m
cox n, **coxswain** n Steuermann m
coy a (**-er, -est**) gespielt
schüchtern
crab n Krabbe f
crack n Riss m; (in china, glass)
Sprung m; (noise) Knall m; (□
joke) Witz m; (□ attempt)
Versuch m ● a □ erstklassig ● vt
knacken <nut, code>; einen
Sprung machen in (+ acc)
<china, glass>; □ reißen <joke>;
□ lösen <problem> ● vi <china,
glass:> springen; <whip:>

knallen. ~ **down** vi 🇮 durchgreifen

cracked a gesprungen; <rib> angebrochen; (🇮 crazy) verrückt

cracker n (biscuit) Kräcker m; (firework) Knallkörper m; [Christmas] ~ Knallbonbon m. ~**s** a be ~s 🇮 einen Knacks haben

crackle vi knistern

cradle n Wiege f

craft n Handwerk nt; (technique) Fertigkeit f. ~**sman** n Handwerker m

crafty a (-ier, -iest) -ily adv gerissen

crag n Felszacken m

cram v (pt/pp crammed) ● vt hineinstopfen (**into** in + acc); vollstopfen (**with** mit) ● vi (for exams) pauken

cramp n Krampf m. ~**ed** a eng

cranberry n (Culin) Preiselbeere f

crane n Kran m; (bird) Kranich m

crank n 🇮 Exzentriker m

crankshaft n Kurbelwelle f

crash n (noise) Krach m; (Auto) Zusammenstoß m; (Aviat) Absturz m ● vi krachen (**into** gegen); <cars:> zusammenstoßen; <plane:> abstürzen ● vt einen Unfall haben mit <car>

crash: ~**-helmet** n Sturzhelm m. ~**-landing** n Bruchlandung f

crate n Kiste f

crater n Krater m

crawl n (Swimming) Kraul nt; do the ~ kraulen; **at a** ~ im Kriechtempo ● vi kriechen; <baby:> krabbeln; ~ **with** wimmeln von

crayon n Wachsstift m; (pencil) Buntstift m

craze n Mode f

crazy a (-ier, -iest) verrückt; be ~ **about** verrückt sein nach

creak vi knarren

cream n Sahne f; (Cosmetic, Med, Culin) Creme f ● a (colour)

cremefarben ● vt (Culin) cremig rühren. ~**y** a sahnig; (smooth) cremig

crease n Falte f; (unwanted) Knitterfalte f ● vt falten; (accidentally) zerknittern ● vi knittern

creat|e vt schaffen. ~**ion** n Schöpfung f. ~**ive** a schöpferisch. ~**or** n Schöpfer m

creature n Geschöpf nt

crèche n Kinderkrippe f

credibility n Glaubwürdigkeit f

credible a glaubwürdig

credit n Kredit m; (honour) Ehre f ● vt glauben; ~ **s.o. with sth** (Comm) jdm etw gutschreiben; (fig) jdm etw zuschreiben. ~**able** a lobenswert

credit: ~ **card** n Kreditkarte f. ~**or** n Gläubiger m

creep vi (pt/pp crept) schleichen ● n 🇮 fieser Kerl m; **it gives me the** ~**s** es ist mir unheimlich. ~**er** n Kletterpflanze f. ~**y** a gruselig

cremat|e vt einäschern. ~**ion** n Einäscherung f

crêpe n Krepp m. ~ **paper** n Krepppapier nt

crept see creep

crescent n Halbmond m

cress n Kresse f

crest n Kamm m; (coat of arms) Wappen nt

crew n Besatzung f; (gang) Bande f. ~ **cut** n Bürstenschnitt m

crib[1] n Krippe f

crib[2] vt/i (pt/pp cribbed) 🇮 abschreiben

cricket n Kricket nt. ~**er** n Kricketspieler m

crime n Verbrechen nt; (rate) Kriminalität f

criminal a kriminell, verbrecherisch; <law, court> Straf- ● n Verbrecher m

crimson a purpurrot

crinkle vt/i knittern

cripple n Krüppel m ● vt zum Krüppel machen; (fig) lahmlegen. ~**d** a verkrüppelt

crisis n (pl -ses) Krise f

crisp a (-er, -est) knusprig. ~**bread** n Knäckebrot nt. ~**s** npl Chips pl

criss-cross a schräg gekreuzt

criterion n (pl -ria) Kriterium nt

critic n Kritiker m. ~**al** a kritisch. ~**ally** adv kritisch; ~**ally ill** schwer krank

criticism n Kritik f

criticize vt kritisieren

croak vi krächzen; <frog:> quaken

crockery n Geschirr nt

crocodile n Krokodil nt

crocus n (pl -es) Krokus m

crony n Kumpel m

crook n (stick) Stab m; (🔳 criminal) Schwindler m, Gauner m

crooked a schief; (bent) krumm; (🔳 dishonest) unehrlich

crop n Feldfrucht f; (harvest) Ernte f ● v (pt/pp cropped) ● vt stutzen ● vi ~ **up** 🔳 zur Sprache kommen; (occur) dazwischenkommen

croquet n Krocket nt

cross a, -**ly** adv (annoyed) böse (with auf + acc); **talk at** ~ **purposes** aneinander vorbeireden ● n Kreuz nt; (Bot, Zool) Kreuzung f ● vt kreuzen <cheque, animals>; überqueren <road>; ~ **oneself** sich bekreuzigen; ~ **one's arms** die Arme verschränken; ~ **one's legs** die Beine übereinander schlagen; **keep one's fingers** ~**ed for s.o.** jdm die Daumen drücken; **it** ~**ed my mind** es fiel mir ein ● vi (go across) hinübergehen/-fahren; <lines:> sich kreuzen. ~ **out** vt durchstreichen

cross: ~**-country** n (Sport) Crosslauf m. ~**-eyed** a schielend; **be** ~**-eyed** schielen. ~**fire** n Kreuzfeuer nt. ~**ing** n Übergang m; (sea journey) Überfahrt f. ~**roads** n [Straßen]kreuzung f. ~**section** n Querschnitt m. ~**wise** adv quer. ~**word** n ~**word [puzzle]** Kreuzworträtsel nt

crotchety a griesgrämig

crouch vi kauern

crow n Krähe f; **as the** ~ **flies** Luftlinie

crowd n [Menschen]menge f ● vi sich drängen. ~**ed** a [gedrängt] voll

crown n Krone f ● vt krönen; überkronen <tooth>

crucial a höchst wichtig; (decisive) entscheidend (**to** für)

crude a (-r, -st) primitiv; (raw) roh

cruel a (crueller, cruellest), -**ly** adv grausam (**to** gegen). ~**ty** n Grausamkeit f

cruis|e n Kreuzfahrt f ● vi kreuzen; <car:> fahren. ~**er** n (Mil) Kreuzer m; (motor boat) Kajütboot nt

crumb n Krümel m

crumble vt/i krümeln; (collapse) einstürzen

crumple vt zerknittern ● vi knittern

crunch n 🔳 **when it comes to the** ~ wenn es [wirklich] drauf ankommt ● vt mampfen ● vi knirschen

crusade n Kreuzzug m; (fig) Kampagne f. ~**r** n Kreuzfahrer m; (fig) Kämpfer m

crush n (crowd) Gedränge nt ● vt zerquetschen; zerknittern <clothes>; (fig: subdue) niederschlagen

crust n Kruste f

crutch n Krücke f

cry n Ruf m; (shout) Schrei m; **a far** ~ **from** (fig) weit entfernt von ● vi (pt/pp cried) (weep) weinen; <baby:> schreien; (call) rufen

crypt n Krypta f. ~**ic** a rätselhaft

crystal n Kristall m; (glass) Kristall nt
cub n (Zool) Junge(s) nt
Cuba n Kuba nt
cubby-hole n Fach nt
cub|e n Würfel m. ~**ic** a Kubik-
cubicle n Kabine f
cuckoo n Kuckuck m. ~ **clock** n Kuckucksuhr f
cucumber n Gurke f
cuddl|e vt herzen ● vi ~**e up to** sich kuscheln an (+ acc). ~**y** a kuschelig
cue[1] n Stichwort nt
cue[2] n (Billiards) Queue nt
cuff n Manschette f; (Amer: turn-up) [Hosen]aufschlag m; (blow) Klaps m; **off the** ~ 🄸 aus dem Stegreif. ~**-link** n Manschettenknopf m
cul-de-sac n Sackgasse f
culinary a kulinarisch
culprit n Täter m
cult n Kult m
cultivate vt anbauen <crop>; bebauen <land>
cultural a kulturell
culture n Kultur f. ~**d** a kultiviert
cumbersome a hinderlich; (unwieldy) unhandlich
cunning a listig ● n List f
cup n Tasse f; (prize) Pokal m
cupboard n Schrank m
Cup Final n Pokalendspiel nt
curable a heilbar
curate n Vikar m; (Roman Catholic) Kaplan m
curb vt zügeln
curdle vi gerinnen
cure n [Heil]mittel nt ● vt heilen; (salt) pökeln; (smoke) räuchern; gerben <skin>
curiosity n Neugier f; (object) Kuriosität f
curious a, **-ly** adv neugierig; (strange) merkwürdig, seltsam
curl n Locke f ● vt locken ● vi sich locken
curly a (**-ier, -iest**) lockig

currant n (dried) Korinthe f
currency n Geläufigkeit f; (money) Währung f; **foreign** ~ Devisen pl
current a augenblicklich, gegenwärtig; (in general use) geläufig, gebräuchlich ● n Strömung f; (Electr) Strom m. ~ **affairs** or **events** npl Aktuelle(s) nt. ~**ly** adv zurzeit
curriculum n Lehrplan m. ~ **vitae** n Lebenslauf m
curry n Curry nt & m; (meal) Currygericht nt
curse n Fluch m ● vt verfluchen ● vi fluchen
cursor n Cursor m
cursory a flüchtig
curt a, **-ly** adv barsch
curtain n Vorhang m
curtsy n Knicks m ● vi (pt/pp -ied) knicksen
curve n Kurve f ● vi einen Bogen machen; ~ **to the right/left** nach rechts/links biegen. ~**d** a gebogen
cushion n Kissen nt ● vt dämpfen; (protect) beschützen
custard n Vanillesoße f
custom n Brauch m; (habit) Gewohnheit f; (Comm) Kundschaft f. ~**ary** a üblich; (habitual) gewohnt. ~**er** n Kunde m/Kundin f
customs npl Zoll m. ~ **officer** n Zollbeamte(r) m
cut n Schnitt m; (Med) Schnittwunde f; (reduction) Kürzung f; (in price) Senkung f; ~ **[of meat]** [Fleisch]stück nt ● vt/i (pt/pp **cut**, pres p **cutting**) schneiden; (mow) mähen; abheben <cards>; (reduce) kürzen; senken <price>; ~ **one's finger** sich in den Finger schneiden; ~ **s.o.'s hair** jdm die Haare schneiden; ~ **short** abkürzen. ~ **back** vt zurückschneiden; (fig)

einschränken, kürzen. **~ down** vt
fällen; (fig) einschränken. **~ off**
vt abschneiden; (disconnect)
abstellen; **be ~ off** (Teleph)
unterbrochen werden. **~ out** vt
ausschneiden; (delete) streichen;
be ~ out for 🔢 geeignet sein zu.
~ up vt zerschneiden; (slice)
aufschneiden
cut-back n Kürzung f
cute a (-r, -st) 🔢 niedlich
cut glass n Kristall nt
cutlery n Besteck nt
cutlet n Kotelett nt
cut-price a verbilligt
cutting a <remark> bissig ● n
(from newspaper) Ausschnitt m;
(of plant) Ableger m
CV abbr of curriculum vitae
cyberspace n Cyberspace m
cycl|e n Zyklus m; (bicycle)
[Fahr]rad nt ● vi mit dem Rad
fahren. **~ing** n Radfahren nt.
~ist n Radfahrer(in) m(f)
cylind|er n Zylinder m. **~rical** a
zylindrisch
cynic n Zyniker m. **~al** a, **-ly** adv
zynisch. **~ism** n Zynismus m
Cyprus n Zypern nt
Czech a tschechisch; **~ Republic**
Tschechische Republik f ● n
Tscheche m/ Tschechin f

dab n Tupfer m; (of butter) Klecks
m
dabble vi **~ in sth** (fig) sich
nebenbei mit etw befassen
dachshund n Dackel m
dad[dy] n 🔢 Vati m

D

daddy-long-legs n [Kohl]schnake
f; (Amer: spider) Weberknecht m
daffodil n Osterglocke f, gelbe
Narzisse f
daft a (-er, -est) dumm
dagger n Dolch m
dahlia n Dahlie f
daily a & adv täglich
dainty a (-ier, -iest) zierlich
dairy n Molkerei f; (shop)
Milchgeschäft nt. **~ products** pl
Milchprodukte pl
daisy n Gänseblümchen nt
dam n [Stau]damm m ● vt (pt/pp
dammed) eindämmen
damage n Schaden m (to an +
dat); **~s** pl (Jur) Schadenersatz m
● vt beschädigen; (fig)
beeinträchtigen
damn a, int & adv 🔢 verdammt
● n **I don't care** or **give a ~** 🔢 ich
schere mich einen Dreck darum
● vt verdammen. **~ation** n
Verdammnis f
damp a (-er, -est) feucht ● n
Feuchtigkeit f
damp|en vt anfeuchten; (fig)
dämpfen. **~ness** n Feuchtigkeit f
dance n Tanz m; (function)
Tanzveranstaltung f ● vt/i
tanzen. **~ music** n Tanzmusik f
dancer n Tänzer(in) m(f)
dandelion n Löwenzahn m
dandruff n Schuppen pl
Dane n Däne m/Dänin f
danger n Gefahr f; **in/out of ~** in/
außer Gefahr. **~ous** a, **-ly** adv
gefährlich; **~ously ill** schwer
erkrankt
dangle vi baumeln ● vt baumeln
lassen
Danish a dänisch
Danube n Donau f
dare vt/i (challenge)
herausfordern (to zu); **~ [to] do
sth** [es] wagen, etw zu tun.
~devil n Draufgänger m
daring a verwegen ● n
Verwegenheit f

dark *a* (-er, -est) dunkel; ~ **blue**/
brown dunkelblau/ -braun; ~
horse (*fig*) stilles Wasser *nt* ● *n*
Dunkelheit *f*; **after** ~ nach
Einbruch der Dunkelheit; **in the**
~ im Dunkeln

dark|en *vt* verdunkeln ● *vi*
dunkler werden. ~**ness** *n*
Dunkelheit *f*

dark-room *n* Dunkelkammer *f*

darling *a* allerliebst ● *n* Liebling
m

darn *vt* stopfen

dart *n* Pfeil *m*; ~**s** *sg* (*game*)
[Wurf]pfeil *m* ● *vi* flitzen

dash *n* (*Typ*) Gedankenstrich *m*; **a**
~ **of milk** ein Schuss Milch ● *vi*
rennen ● *vt* schleudern. ~ **off** *vi*
losstürzen ● *vt* (*write quickly*)
hinwerfen

dashboard *n* Armaturenbrett *nt*

data *npl & sg* Daten *pl*. ~
processing *n* Datenverarbeitung
f

date¹ *n* (*fruit*) Dattel *f*

date² *n* Datum *nt*; ⓘ
Verabredung *f*; **to** ~ bis heute;
out of ~ überholt; (*expired*)
ungültig; **be up to** ~ auf dem
Laufenden sein ● *vt/i* datieren;
(*Amer* ⓘ: *go out with*) ausgehen
mit

dated *a* altmodisch

dative *a & n* (*Gram*) ~ [**case**]
Dativ *m*

daub *vt* beschmieren (**with** mit);
schmieren <*paint*>

daughter *n* Tochter *f*. ~**-in-law** *n*
(*pl* ~**s-in-law**) Schwiegertochter *f*

dawdle *vi* trödeln

dawn *n* Morgendämmerung *f*; **at**
~ bei Tagesanbruch ● *vi*
anbrechen; **it** ~**ed on me** (*fig*) es
ging mir auf

day *n* Tag *m*; ~ **by** ~ Tag für Tag;
~ **after** ~ Tag um Tag; **these** ~**s**
heutzutage; **in those** ~**s** zu der
Zeit

day: ~**-dream** *n* Tagtraum *m* ● *vi*
[mit offenen Augen] träumen.
~**light** *n* Tageslicht *nt*. ~**time** *n* **in**
the ~**time** am Tage

daze *n* **in a** ~ wie benommen. ~**d**
a benommen

dazzle *vt* blenden

dead *a* tot; <*flower*> verwelkt;
(*numb*) taub; ~ **body** Leiche *f*; ~
centre genau in der Mitte ● *adv*
~ **tired** todmüde; ~ **slow** sehr
langsam ● *n* **the** ~ *pl* die Toten

deaden *vt* dämpfen <*sound*>;
betäuben <*pain*>

dead: ~ **end** *n* Sackgasse *f*. ~
heat *n* totes Rennen *nt*. ~**line** *n*
[letzter] Termin *m*

deadly *a* (-ier, -iest) tödlich; (⬛
dreary) sterbenslangweilig

deaf *a* (-er, -est) taub; ~ **and dumb**
taubstumm

deaf|en *vt* betäuben;
(*permanently*) taub machen.
~**ening** *a* ohrenbetäubend.
~**ness** *n* Taubheit *f*

deal *n* (*transaction*) Geschäft *nt*;
whose ~? (*Cards*) wer gibt? **a**
good *or* **great** ~ eine Menge; **get a**
raw ~ ⬛ schlecht wegkommen
● *v* (*pt/pp* **dealt**) ● *vt* (*Cards*)
geben; ~ **out** austeilen ● *vi* ~ **in**
handeln mit; ~ **with** zu tun haben
mit; (*handle*) sich befassen mit;
(*cope with*) fertig werden mit; (*be*
about) handeln von; **that's been**
dealt with das ist schon erledigt

dealer *n* Händler *m*

dean *n* Dekan *m*

dear *a* (-er, -est) lieb; (*expensive*)
teuer; (*in letter*) liebe(r,s)/
(*formal*) sehr geehrte(r,s) ● *n*
Liebe(r) *m/f* ● *int* oh ~! oje! ~**ly**
adv <*love*> sehr; <*pay*> teuer

death *n* Tod *m*; **three** ~**s** drei
Todesfälle. ~ **certificate** *n*
Sterbeurkunde *f*

deathly *a* ~ **silence** Totenstille *f*
● *adv* ~ **pale** totenblass

death: ~ **penalty** n Todesstrafe f.
~-**trap** n Todesfalle f
debatable a strittig
debate n Debatte f ● vt/i
debattieren
debauchery n Ausschweifung f
debit n ~ **[side]** Soll nt ● vt (pt/pp
debited) belasten; abbuchen
<sum>
debris n Trümmer pl
debt n Schuld f; **in** ~ verschuldet.
~ **or** n Schuldner m
debut n Debüt nt
decade n Jahrzehnt nt
decaden|ce n Dekadenz f. ~**t** a
dekadent
decaffeinated a koffeinfrei
decay n Verfall m; (rot)
Verwesung f; (of tooth)
Zahnfäule f ● vi verfallen; (rot)
verwesen; <tooth:> schlecht
werden
deceased a verstorben ● n **the**
~**d** der/die Verstorbene
deceit n Täuschung f. ~**ful** a, -**ly**
adv unaufrichtig
deceive vt täuschen; (be
unfaithful to) betrügen
December n Dezember m
decency n Anstand m
decent a, -**ly** adv anständig
decept|ion n Täuschung f; (fraud)
Betrug m. ~**ive** a, -**ly** adv
täuschend
decide vt entscheiden ● vi sich
entscheiden (**on** für)
decided a, -**ly** adv entschieden
decimal a Dezimal- ● n
Dezimalzahl f. ~ **point** n Komma
nt
decipher vt entziffern
decision n Entscheidung f;
(firmness) Entschlossenheit f
decisive a ausschlaggebend;
(firm) entschlossen
deck[1] vt schmücken
deck[2] n (Naut) Deck nt; **on** ~ an
Deck; ~ **of cards** (Amer)

[Karten]spiel nt. ~-**chair** n
Liegestuhl m
declaration n Erklärung f
declare vt erklären; angeben
<goods>; **anything to** ~? etwas zu
verzollen?
decline n Rückgang m; (in health)
Verfall m ● vt ablehnen; (Gram)
deklinieren ● vi ablehnen; (fall)
sinken; (decrease) nachlassen
decommission vt stilllegen;
außer Dienst stellen <Schiff>
décor n Ausstattung f
decorat|e vt (adorn) schmücken;
verzieren <cake>; (paint)
streichen; (wallpaper) tapezieren;
(award medal to) einen Orden
verleihen (+ dat). ~**ion** n
Verzierung f; (medal) Orden m;
~**ions** pl Schmuck m. ~**ive** a
dekorativ. ~**or** n **painter and** ~**or**
Maler und Tapezierer m
decoy n Lockvogel m
decrease[1] n Verringerung f; (in
number) Rückgang m
decrease[2] vt verringern;
herabsetzen <price> ● vi sich
verringern; <price:> sinken
decrepit a altersschwach
dedicat|e vt widmen; (Relig)
weihen. ~**ed** a hingebungsvoll;
<person> aufopfernd. ~**ion** n
Hingabe f; (in book) Widmung f
deduce vt folgern (**from** aus)
deduct vt abziehen
deduction n Abzug m;
(conclusion) Folgerung f
deed n Tat f; (Jur) Urkunde f
deep a (-er, -est), -**ly** adv tief; **go**
off the ~ **end** 🆃 auf die Palme
gehen ● adv tief
deepen vt vertiefen
deep-freeze n Gefriertruhe f;
(upright) Gefrierschrank m
deer n inv Hirsch m; (roe) Reh nt
deface vt beschädigen
default n **win by** ~ (Sport)
kampflos gewinnen

defeat n Niederlage f; (defeating) Besiegung f; (rejection) Ablehnung f ● vt besiegen; ablehnen <motion>; (frustrate) vereiteln

defect n Fehler m; (Techn) Defekt m. ~ive a fehlerhaft; (Techn) defekt

defence n Verteidigung f. ~less a wehrlos

defend vt verteidigen; (justify) rechtfertigen. ~ant n (Jur) Beklagte(r) m/f; (in criminal court) Angeklagte(r) m/f

defensive a defensiv

defer vt (pt/pp deferred) (postpone) aufschieben

deferen|ce n Ehrerbietung f. ~tial a, -ly adv ehrerbietig

defian|ce n Trotz m; in ~ce of zum Trotz (+ dat). ~t a, -ly adv aufsässig

deficien|cy n Mangel m. ~t a mangelhaft

deficit n Defizit nt

define vt bestimmen; definieren <word>

definite a, -ly adv bestimmt; (certain) sicher

definition n Definition f; (Phot, TV) Schärfe f

definitive a endgültig; (authoritative) maßgeblich

deflat|e vt die Luft auslassen aus. ~ion n (Comm) Deflation f

deflect vt ablenken

deform|ed a missgebildet. ~ity n Missbildung f

defraud vt betrügen (of um)

defray vt bestreiten

defrost vt entfrosten; abtauen <fridge>; auftauen <food>

deft a (-er, -est), -ly adv geschickt. ~ness n Geschicklichkeit f

defuse vt entschärfen

defy vt (pt/pp -ied) trotzen (+ dat); widerstehen (+ dat) <attempt>

degrading a entwürdigend

degree n Grad m; (Univ) akademischer Grad m; **20** ~s 20 Grad

de-ice vt enteisen

deity n Gottheit f

dejected a, -ly adv niedergeschlagen

delay n Verzögerung f; (of train, aircraft) Verspätung f; without ~ unverzüglich ● vt aufhalten; (postpone) aufschieben ● vi zögern

delegate[1] n Delegierte(r) m/f

delegat|e[2] vt delegieren. ~ion n Delegation f

delet|e vt streichen. ~ion n Streichung f

deliberate a, -ly adv absichtlich; (slow) bedächtig

delicacy n Feinheit f; Zartheit f; (food) Delikatesse f

delicate a fein; <fabric, health> zart; <situation> heikel; <mechanism> empfindlich

delicatessen n Delikatessengeschäft nt

delicious a köstlich

delight n Freude f ● vt entzücken ● vi ~ in sich erfreuen an (+ dat). ~ed a hocherfreut; be ~ed sich sehr freuen. ~ful a reizend

delinquent a straffällig ● n Straffällige(r) m/f

deli|rious a be ~rious im Delirium sein. ~rium n Delirium nt

deliver vt liefern; zustellen <post, newspaper>; halten <speech>; überbringen <message>; versetzen <blow>; (set free) befreien; ~ a baby ein Kind zur Welt bringen. ~y n Lieferung f; (of post) Zustellung f; (Med) Entbindung f; cash on ~y per Nachnahme

delta n Delta nt

deluge n Flut f; (heavy rain) schwerer Guss m

delusion n Täuschung f

de luxe a Luxus-

demand n Forderung f; (Comm) Nachfrage f; **in ~** gefragt; **on ~** auf Verlangen ● vt verlangen, fordern (**of/from** von). **~ing** a anspruchsvoll

demented a verrückt

demister n (Auto) Defroster m

demo n (pl **~s**) 🄸 Demonstration f

democracy n Demokratie f

democrat n Demokrat m. **~ic** a, **-ally** adv demokratisch

demo|lish vt abbrechen; (destroy) zerstören. **~lition** n Abbruch m

demon n Dämon m

demonstrat|e vt beweisen; vorführen <appliance> ● vi (Pol) demonstrieren. **~ion** n Vorführung f; (Pol) Demonstration f

demonstrator n Vorführer m; (Pol) Demonstrant m

demoralize vt demoralisieren

demote vt degradieren

demure a, **-ly** adv sittsam

den n Höhle f; (room) Bude f

denial n Leugnen nt; official **~** Dementi nt

denim n Jeansstoff m; **~s** pl Jeans pl

Denmark n Dänemark nt

denounce vt denunzieren; (condemn) verurteilen

dens|e a (-r, -st), **-ly** adv dicht; (🄸 stupid) blöd[e]. **~ity** n Dichte f

dent n Delle f, Beule f ● vt einbeulen; **~ed** verbeult

dental a Zahn-; <treatment> zahnärztlich. **~ floss** n Zahnseide f. **~ surgeon** n Zahnarzt m

dentist n Zahnarzt m/-ärztin f. **~ry** n Zahnmedizin f

denture n Zahnprothese f; **~s** pl künstliches Gebiss nt

deny vt (pt/pp **-ied**) leugnen; (officially) dementieren; **~ s.o. sth** jdm etw verweigern

deodorant n Deodorant nt

depart vi abfahren; (Aviat) abfliegen; (go away) weggehen/-fahren; (deviate) abweichen (**from** von)

department n Abteilung f; (Pol) Ministerium nt. **~ store** n Kaufhaus nt

departure n Abfahrt f; (Aviat) Abflug m; (from rule) Abweichung f

depend vi abhängen (**on** von); (rely) sich verlassen (**on** auf + acc); **it all ~s** das kommt darauf an. **~able** a zuverlässig. **~ant** n Abhängige(r) m/f. **~ence** n Abhängigkeit f. **~ent** a abhängig (**on** von)

depict vt darstellen

deplor|able a bedauerlich. **~e** vt bedauern

deploy vt (Mil) einsetzen

depopulate vt entvölkern

deport vt deportieren, ausweisen. **~ation** n Ausweisung f

depose vt absetzen

deposit n Anzahlung f; (against damage) Kaution f; (on bottle) Pfand nt; (sediment) Bodensatz m; (Geol) Ablagerung f ● vt (pt/pp **deposited**) legen; (for safety) deponieren; (Geol) ablagern. **~ account** n Sparkonto nt

depot n Depot nt; (Amer: railway station) Bahnhof m

deprave vt verderben. **~d** a verkommen

depreciat|e vi an Wert verlieren. **~ion** n Wertminderung f; (Comm) Abschreibung f

depress vt deprimieren; (press down) herunterdrücken. **~ed** a deprimiert. **~ing** a deprimierend. **~ion** n Vertiefung f; (Med) Depression f; (Meteorol) Tief nt

deprivation n Entbehrung f

deprive vt **~ s.o. of sth** jdm etw entziehen. **~d** a benachteiligt

D

depth n Tiefe f; **in** ~ gründlich; **in the ~s of winter** im tiefsten Winter

deputize vi ~ **for** vertreten

deputy n Stellvertreter m ● attrib stellvertretend

derail vt **be** ~ed entgleisen. ~**ment** n Entgleisung f

derelict a verfallen; (abandoned) verlassen

derisory a höhnisch; <offer> lächerlich

derivation n Ableitung f

derivative a abgeleitet ● n Ableitung f

derive vt/i (obtain) gewinnen (from aus); **be** ~**d from** <word:> hergeleitet sein aus

derogatory a abfällig

derv n Diesel[kraftstoff] m

descend vt/i hinunter-/ heruntergehen; <vehicle, lift:> hinunter-/herunterfahren; **be** ~e**d from** abstammen von. ~**ant** n Nachkomme m

descent n Abstieg m; (lineage) Abstammung f

describe vt beschreiben

descrip|tion n Beschreibung f; (sort) Art f. ~**tive** a beschreibend; (vivid) anschaulich

desecrate vt entweihen

desert¹ n Wüste f. ~ **island** verlassene Insel f

desert² vt verlassen ● vt desertieren. ~e**d** a verlassen. ~**er** n (Mil) Deserteur m. ~**ion** n Fahnenflucht f

deserv|e vt verdienen. ~**edly** adv verdientermaßen. ~**ing** a verdienstvoll

design n Entwurf m; (pattern) Muster nt; (construction) Konstruktion f; (aim) Absicht f ● vt entwerfen; (construct) konstruieren; **be** ~ed **for** bestimmt sein für

designer n Designer m; (Techn) Konstrukteur m; (Theat) Bühnenbildner m

desirable a wünschenswert; (sexually) begehrenswert

desire n Wunsch m; (longing) Verlangen nt (**for** nach); (sexual) Begierde f ● vt [sich (dat)] wünschen; (sexually) begehren

desk n Schreibtisch m; (Sch) Pult nt

desolat|e a trostlos. ~**ion** n Trostlosigkeit f

despair n Verzweiflung f; **in** ~ verzweifelt ● vi verzweifeln

desperat|e a, -ly adv verzweifelt; (urgent) dringend; **be** ~**e for** dringend brauchen. ~**ion** n Verzweiflung f

despicable a verachtenswert

despise vt verachten

despite prep trotz (+ gen)

despondent a niedergeschlagen

dessert n Dessert nt, Nachtisch m. ~ **spoon** n Dessertlöffel m

destination n [Reise]ziel nt; (of goods) Bestimmungsort m

destiny n Schicksal nt

destitute a völlig mittellos

destroy vt zerstören; (totally) vernichten. ~**er** n (Naut) Zerstörer m

destruc|tion n Zerstörung f; Vernichtung f. -**tive** a zerstörerisch; (fig) destruktiv

detach vt abnehmen; (tear off) abtrennen. ~**able** a abnehmbar. ~e**d** a ~**ed house** Einzelhaus nt

detail n Einzelheit f, Detail nt; **in** ~ ausführlich ● vt einzeln aufführen. ~e**d** a ausführlich

detain vt aufhalten; <police:> in Haft behalten; (take into custody) in Haft nehmen

detect vt entdecken; (perceive) wahrnehmen. ~**ion** n Entdeckung f

detective n Detektiv m. ~ **story** n Detektivroman m

D

detention n Haft f; (Sch) Nachsitzen nt
deter vt (pt/pp **deterred**) abschrecken; (prevent) abhalten
detergent n Waschmittel nt
deteriorat|e vi sich verschlechtern. ~**ion** n Verschlechterung f
determination n Entschlossenheit f
determine vt bestimmen. ~**d** a entschlossen
deterrent n Abschreckungsmittel nt
detest vt verabscheuen. ~**able** a abscheulich
detonate vt zünden
detour n Umweg m
detract vi ~ **from** beeinträchtigen
detriment n **to the** ~ **(of)** zum Schaden (+ gen). ~**al** a schädlich (**to** dat)
deuce n (Tennis) Einstand m
devaluation n Abwertung f
devalue vt abwerten <currency>
devastat|e vt verwüsten. ~**ing** a verheerend. ~**ion** n Verwüstung f
develop vt entwickeln; bekommen <illness>; erschließen <area> ● vi sich entwickeln (**into** zu). ~**er** n [**property**] ~**er** Bodenspekulant m
development n Entwicklung f
deviat|e vi abweichen. ~**ion** n Abweichung f
device n Gerät nt; (fig) Mittel nt
devil n Teufel m. ~**ish** a teuflisch
devious a verschlagen
devise vt sich (dat) ausdenken
devot|e vt widmen (**to** dat). ~**ed** a, **-ly** adv ergeben; <care> liebevoll; **be** ~**ed to s.o.** sehr an jdm hängen
devotion n Hingabe f
devour vt verschlingen
devout a fromm
dew n Tau m
dexterity n Geschicklichkeit f

diabet|es n Zuckerkrankheit f. ~**ic** n Diabetiker(in) m(f)
diabolical a teuflisch
diagnose vt diagnostizieren
diagnosis n (pl **-oses**) Diagnose f
diagonal a, **-ly** adv diagonal ● n Diagonale f
diagram n Diagramm nt
dial n (of clock) Zifferblatt nt; (Techn) Skala f; (Teleph) Wählscheibe f ● vt/i (pt/pp **dialled**) (Teleph) wählen; ~ **direct** durchwählen
dialect n Dialekt m
dialling: ~ **code** n Vorwahlnummer f. ~ **tone** n Amtszeichen nt
dialogue n Dialog m
diameter n Durchmesser m
diamond n Diamant m; (cut) Brillant m; (shape) Raute f; ~**s** pl (Cards) Karo nt
diaper n (Amer) Windel f
diarrhoea n Durchfall m
diary n Tagebuch nt; (for appointments) [Termin]kalender m
dice n inv Würfel m
dictat|e vt/i diktieren. ~**ion** n Diktat nt
dictator n Diktator m. ~**ial** a diktatorisch. ~**ship** n Diktatur f
dictionary n Wörterbuch nt
did see **do**
didn't = **did not**
die[1] n (Techn) Prägestempel m; (metal mould) Gussform f
die[2] vi (pres p **dying**) sterben (**of** an + dat); <plant, animal:> eingehen; <flower:> verwelken; **be dying to do sth** [!] darauf brennen, etw zu tun; **be dying for sth** [!] sich nach etw sehnen. ~ **down** vi nachlassen; <fire:> herunterbrennen. ~ **out** vi aussterben
diesel n Diesel m. ~ **engine** n Dieselmotor m

diet n Kost f; (restricted) Diät f; (for slimming) Schlankheitskur f; **be on a ~** Diät leben; eine Schlankheitskur machen ● vi diät leben; eine Schlankheitskur machen

differ vi sich unterscheiden; (disagree) verschiedener Meinung sein

differen|ce n Unterschied m; (disagreement) Meinungsverschiedenheit f. **~t** a andere(r,s); (various) verschiedene; **be ~t** anders sein (from als)

differential a Differenzial- ● n Unterschied m; (Techn) Differenzial nt

differentiate vt/i unterscheiden (**between** zwischen + dat)

differently adv anders

difficult a schwierig, schwer. **~y** n Schwierigkeit f

diffiden|ce n Zaghaftigkeit f. **~t** a zaghaft

dig n (poke) Stoß m; (remark) spitze Bemerkung f; (Archaeol) Ausgrabung f ● vt/i (pt/pp dug, pres p digging) graben; umbraben <garden>. **~ out** vt ausgraben. **~ up** vt ausgraben; umbraben <garden>; aufreißen <street>

digest vt verdauen. **~ible** a verdaulich. **~ion** n Verdauung f

digit n Ziffer f; (finger) Finger m; (toe) Zehe f

digital a Digital-; **~ camera** Digitalkamera f; **~ television** Digitalfernsehen nt

dignified a würdevoll

dignity n Würde f

dilapidated a baufällig

dilemma n Dilemma nt

diligen|ce n Fleiß m. **~t** a, **-ly** adv fleißig

dilute vt verdünnen

dim a (dimmer, dimmest). **-ly** adv (weak) schwach; (dark) trüb[e]; (indistinct) undeutlich; (🄸 stupid)

dumm, 🄸 doof ● v (pt/pp dimmed) ● vt dämpfen

dime n (Amer) Zehncentstück nt

dimension n Dimension f; **~s** pl Maße pl

diminutive a winzig ● n Verkleinerungsform f

dimple n Grübchen nt

din n Krach m, Getöse nt

dine vi speisen. **~r** n Speisende(r) m/f; (Amer: restaurant) Esslokal nt

dinghy n Dinghi nt; (inflatable) Schlauchboot nt

dingy a (-ier, -iest) trübe

dining: ~-car n Speisewagen m. **~-room** n Esszimmer nt. **~-table** n Esstisch m

dinner n Abendessen nt; (at midday) Mittagessen nt; (formal) Essen nt. **~-jacket** n Smoking m

dinosaur n Dinosaurier m

diocese n Diözese f

dip n (in ground) Senke f; (Culin) Dip m ● v (pt/pp dipped) vt [ein]tauchen; **~ one's headlights** (Auto) [die Scheinwerfer] abblenden ● vi sich senken

diploma n Diplom nt

diplomacy n Diplomatie f

diplomat n Diplomat m. **~ic** a, **-ally** adv diplomatisch

dip-stick n (Auto) Ölmessstab m

dire a (-r, -st) bitter; <consequences> furchtbar

direct a & adv direkt ● vt (aim) richten (**at** auf / (fig) an + acc); (control) leiten; (order) anweisen; **~ a film/play** bei einem Film/ Theaterstück Regie führen

direction n Richtung f; (control) Leitung f; (of play, film) Regie f; **~s** pl Anweisungen pl; **~s for use** Gebrauchsanweisung f

directly adv direkt; (at once) sofort

director n (Comm) Direktor m; (of play, film) Regisseur m

directory n Verzeichnis nt; (Teleph) Telefonbuch nt

dirt n Schmutz m; (soil) Erde f; ~ **cheap** ⊞ spottbillig

dirty a (-ier, -iest) schmutzig

dis|ability n Behinderung f. ~**abled** a [körper]behindert

disadvantage n Nachteil m; **at a** ~ im Nachteil. ~**d** a benachteiligt

disagree vi nicht übereinstimmen (with mit); **I** ~ ich bin anderer Meinung; **oysters** ~ **with me** Austern bekommen mir nicht

disagreeable a unangenehm

disagreement n Meinungsverschiedenheit f

disappear vi verschwinden. ~**ance** n Verschwinden nt

disappoint vt enttäuschen. ~**ment** n Enttäuschung f

disapproval n Missbilligung f

disapprove vi dagegen sein; ~ **of** missbilligen

disarm vt entwaffnen ● vi (Mil) abrüsten. ~**ament** n Abrüstung f. ~**ing** a entwaffnend

disast|er n Katastrophe f; (accident) Unglück nt. ~**rous** a katastrophal

disbelief n Ungläubigkeit f; **in** ~ ungläubig

disc n Scheibe f; (record) [Schall]platte f; (CD) CD f

discard vt ablegen; (throw away) wegwerfen

discerning a anspruchsvoll

discharge[1] n Ausstoßen nt; (Naut, Electr) Entladung f; (dismissal) Entlassung f; (Jur) Freispruch m; (Med) Ausfluss m

discharge[2] vt ausstoßen; (Naut, Electr) entladen; (dismiss) entlassen; (Jur) freisprechen <accused>

disciplinary a disziplinarisch

discipline n Disziplin f ● vt Disziplin beibringen (+ dat); (punish) bestrafen

disc jockey n Diskjockey m

disclaim vt abstreiten. ~**er** n Verzichterklärung f

disclos|e vt enthüllen. ~**ure** n Enthüllung f

disco n ⊞ Disko f

discolour vt verfärben ● vi sich verfärben

discomfort n Beschwerden pl; (fig) Unbehagen nt

disconnect vt trennen; (Electr) ausschalten; (cut supply) abstellen

discontent n Unzufriedenheit f. ~**ed** a unzufrieden

discontinue vt einstellen; (Comm) nicht mehr herstellen

discord n Zwietracht f; (Mus & fig) Missklang m

discothèque n Diskothek f

discount n Rabatt m

discourage vt entmutigen; (dissuade) abraten (+ dat)

discourteous a, **-ly** adv unhöflich

discover vt entdecken. ~**y** n Entdeckung f

discreet a, **-ly** adv diskret

discretion n Diskretion f; (judgement) Ermessen nt

discriminat|e vi unterscheiden (between zwischen + dat); ~**e against** diskriminieren. ~**ing** a anspruchsvoll. ~**ion** n Diskriminierung f

discus n Diskus m

discuss vt besprechen; (examine critically) diskutieren. ~**ion** n Besprechung f; Diskussion f

disdain n Verachtung f

disease n Krankheit f

disembark vi an Land gehen

disenchant vt ernüchtern

disengage vt losmachen

disentangle vt entwirren

disfigure vt entstellen

disgrace n Schande f; in ~
Ungnade ● vt Schande machen
(+ dat). ~ful a schändlich
disgruntled a verstimmt
disguise n Verkleidung f; in ~
verkleidet ● vt verkleiden;
verstellen <voice>
disgust n Ekel m; in ~ empört
● vt anekeln; (appal) empören.
~ing a eklig; (appalling)
abscheulich
dish n Schüssel f; (shallow)
Schale f; (small) Schälchen nt;
(food) Gericht nt. ~ out vt
austeilen. ~ up vt auftragen
dishcloth n Spültuch nt
dishearten vt entmutigen
dishonest a -ly adv unehrlich. ~y
n Unehrlichkeit f
dishonour n Schande f. ~able a,
-bly adv unehrenhaft
dishwasher n
Geschirrspülmaschine f
disillusion vt ernüchtern. ~ment
n Ernüchterung f
disinfect vt desinfizieren. ~ant n
Desinfektionsmittel nt
disinherit vt enterben
disintegrate vi zerfallen
disjointed a
unzusammenhängend
disk n = disc
dislike n Abneigung f ● vt nicht
mögen
dislocate vt ausrenken
dislodge vt entfernen
disloyal a, -ly adv illoyal. ~ty n
Illoyalität f
dismal a trüb[e]; <person>
trübselig
dismantle vt auseinander
nehmen; (take down) abbauen
dismay n Bestürzung f. ~ed a
bestürzt
dismiss vt entlassen; (reject)
zurückweisen. ~al n Entlassung
f; Zurückweisung f
disobedien|ce n Ungehorsam m.
~t a ungehorsam

disobey vt/i nicht gehorchen (+
dat); nicht befolgen <rule>
disorder n Unordnung f; (Med)
Störung f. ~ly a unordentlich
disorganized a unorganisiert
disown vt verleugnen
disparaging a, -ly adv abschätzig
dispassionate a, -ly adv gelassen;
(impartial) unparteiisch
dispatch n (Comm) Versand m;
(Mil) Nachricht f; (report) Bericht
m ● vt [ab]senden; (kill) töten
dispel vt (pt/pp dispelled)
vertreiben
dispensary n Apotheke f
dispense vt austeilen; ~ with
verzichten auf (+ acc). ~r n
(device) Automat m
disperse vt zerstreuen ● vi sich
zerstreuen
dispirited a entmutigt
display n Ausstellung f; (Comm)
Auslage f; (performance)
Vorführung f ● vt zeigen;
ausstellen <goods>
displease vt missfallen (+ dat)
displeasure n Missfallen nt
disposable a Wegwerf-;
<income> verfügbar
disposal n Beseitigung f; be at
s.o.'s ~ jdm zur Verfügung
stehen
dispose vi ~ of beseitigen; (deal
with) erledigen
disposition n Veranlagung f;
(nature) Wesensart f
disproportionate a, -ly adv
unverhältnismäßig
disprove vt widerlegen
dispute n Disput m; (quarrel)
Streit m ● vt bestreiten
disqualification n
Disqualifikation f
disqualify vt disqualifizieren; ~
s.o. from driving jdm den
Führerschein entziehen
disregard vt nicht beachten
disrepair n fall into ~ verfallen
disreputable a verrufen

disrepute *n* Verruf *m*
disrespect *n* Respektlosigkeit *f*.
~**ful** *a*, **-ly** *adv* respektlos
disrupt *vt* stören. ~**ion** *n* Störung *f*
dissatisfaction *n*
Unzufriedenheit *f*
dissatisfied *a* unzufrieden
dissect *vt* zergliedern; (*Med*)
sezieren. ~**ion** *n* Zergliederung *f*;
(*Med*) Sektion *f*
dissent *n* Nichtübereinstimmung
f ● *vi* nicht übereinstimmen
dissident *n* Dissident *m*
dissimilar *a* unähnlich (**to** *dat*)
dissociate *vt* ~ **oneself** sich
distanzieren (**from** von)
dissolute *a* zügellos; <*life*>
ausschweifend
dissolve *vt* auflösen ● *vi* sich
auflösen
dissuade *vt* abbringen (**from** von)
distance *n* Entfernung *f*; **long/
short** ~ lange/kurze Strecke *f*; **in
the/from a** ~ in/aus der Ferne
distant *a* fern; (*aloof*) kühl;
<*relative*> entfernt
distasteful *a* unangenehm
distil *vt* (*pt/pp* **distilled**) brennen;
(*Chem*) destillieren. ~**lery** *n*
Brennerei *f*
distinct *a* deutlich; (*different*)
verschieden. ~**ion** *n* Unterschied
m; (*Sch*) Auszeichnung *f*. ~**ive** *a*
kennzeichnend; (*unmistakable*)
unverwechselbar. ~**ly** *adv*
deutlich
distinguish *vt/i* unterscheiden;
(*make out*) erkennen; ~ **oneself**
sich auszeichnen. ~**ed** *a*
angesehen; <*appearance*>
distinguiert
distort *vt* verzerren; (*fig*)
verdrehen. ~**ion** *n* Verzerrung *f*;
(*fig*) Verdrehung *f*
distract *vt* ablenken. ~**ion** *n*
Ablenkung *f*; (*despair*)
Verzweiflung *f*
distraught *a* [völlig] aufgelöst

distress *n* Kummer *m*; (*pain*)
Schmerz *m*; (*poverty, danger*) Not
f ● *vt* Kummer/Schmerz bereiten
(+ *dat*); (*sadden*) bekümmern;
(*shock*) erschüttern. ~**ing** *a*
schmerzlich; (*shocking*)
erschütternd
distribut|e *vt* verteilen; (*Comm*)
vertreiben. ~**ion** *n* Verteilung *f*;
Vertrieb *m*. ~**or** *n* Verteiler *m*
district *n* Gegend *f*; (*Admin*)
Bezirk *m*
distrust *n* Misstrauen *nt* ● *vt*
misstrauen (+ *dat*). ~**ful** *a*
misstrauisch
disturb *vt* stören; (*perturb*)
beunruhigen; (*touch*) anrühren.
~**ance** *n* Unruhe *f*; (*interruption*)
Störung *f*. ~**ed** *a* beunruhigt;
[**mentally**] ~**ed** geistig gestört.
~**ing** *a* beunruhigend
disused *a* stillgelegt; (*empty*) leer
ditch *n* Graben *m* ● *vt* (🄸
abandon) fallen lassen <*plan*>
dither *vi* zaudern
ditto *n* dito; 🄸 ebenfalls
dive *n* [Kopf]sprung *m*; (*Aviat*)
Sturzflug *m*; (🄸 *place*) Spelunke
f ● *vi* einen Kopfsprung machen;
(*when in water*) tauchen; (*Aviat*)
einen Sturzflug machen; (🄸
rush) stürzen
diver *n* Taucher *m*; (*Sport*)
[Kunst]springer *m*
diverse *a* verschieden
diversify *vt/i* (*pt/pp* **-ied**)
variieren; (*Comm*) diversifizieren
diversion *n* Umleitung *f*;
(*distraction*) Ablenkung *f*
diversity *n* Vielfalt *f*
divert *vt* umleiten; ablenken
<*attention*>; (*entertain*)
unterhalten
divide *vt* teilen; (*separate*)
trennen; (*Math*) dividieren (**by**
durch) ● *vi* sich teilen
dividend *n* Dividende *f*
divine *a* göttlich

D

diving n (Sport) Kunstspringen nt. **~-board** n Sprungbrett nt
divinity n Göttlichkeit f; (subject) Theologie f
division n Teilung f; (separation) Trennung f; (Math, Mil) Division f; (Parl) Hammelsprung m; (line) Trennlinie f; (group) Abteilung f
divorce n Scheidung f ● vt sich scheiden lassen von. **~d** a geschieden; **get ~d** sich scheiden lassen
DIY abbr of **do-it-yourself**
dizziness n Schwindel m
dizzy a (-ier, -iest) schwindlig; **I feel ~** mir ist schwindlig

do
    3 sg pres tense **does**; pt **did**; pp **done**
● transitive verb
····➤ (perform) machen <homework, housework, exam, handstand etc>; tun <duty, favour, something, nothing>; vorführen <trick, dance>; durchführen <test>. **what are you doing?** was tust od machst du? **what can I do for you?** was kann ich für Sie tun? **do something!** tu doch etwas! **have you nothing better to do?** hast du nichts Besseres zu tun? **do the washing-up /cleaning** abwaschen/sauber machen
····➤ (as job) **what does your father do?** was macht dein Vater?; was ist dein Vater von Beruf?
····➤ (clean) putzen; (arrange) [zurecht]machen <hair>
····➤ (cook) kochen; (roast, fry) braten. **well done** (meat) durch[gebraten]. **the potatoes aren't done yet** die Kartoffeln sind noch nicht richtig durch
····➤ (solve) lösen <problem, riddle>; machen <puzzle>
····➤ (🄸 swindle) reinlegen. **do s.o. out of sth** jdn um etw bringen

● intransitive verb
····➤ (with as or adverb) es tun; es machen. **do as they do** mach es wie sie. **he can do as he likes** er kann tun od machen, was er will. **you did well** du hast es gut gemacht
····➤ (get on) vorankommen; (in exams) abschneiden. **do well/ badly at school** gut/schlecht in der Schule sein. **how are you doing?** wie geht's dir? **how do you do?** (formal) guten Tag!
····➤ **will do** (serve purpose) es tun; (suffice) [aus]reichen; (be suitable) gehen. **that won't do** das geht nicht. **that will do!** jetzt aber genug!
● auxiliary verb
····➤ (in questions) **do you know him?** kennst du ihn? **what does he want?** was will er?
····➤ (in negation) **I don't** or **do not wish to take part** ich will nicht teilnehmen. **don't be so noisy!** seid [doch] nicht so laut!
····➤ (as verb substitute) **you mustn't act as he does** du darfst nicht so wie er handeln. **come in, do!** komm doch herein!
····➤ (in tag questions) **don't you, doesn't he** etc. nicht wahr. **you went to Paris, didn't you?** du warst in Paris, nicht wahr?
····➤ (in short questions) **Does he live in London? — Yes, he does** Wohnt er in London? — Ja [, stimmt]
····➤ (for special emphasis) **I do love Greece** Griechenland gefällt mir wirklich gut
····➤ (for inversion) **little did he know that ...** er hatte keine Ahnung, dass ...
● noun
    pl **do's** or **dos**
····➤ (🄸 celebration) Feier f
● phrasal verbs
    ● **do away with** vt abschaffen.

● **do for** vt ⊡: **do for s.o.** jdn fertig machen ⊡; **be done for** erledigt sein. ● **do in** vt (⊠ *kill*) kaltmachen ⊠. ● **do up** vt (*fasten*) zumachen; binden <*shoe-lace, bow-tie*>; (*wrap*) einpacken; (*renovate*) renovieren. ● **do with** vt: **I could do with ...** ich brauche .... ● **do without** vt: **do without sth** auf etw (*acc*) verzichten; vi darauf verzichten

docile a fügsam

dock¹ n (*Jur*) Anklagebank f

dock² n Dock nt ● vi anlegen. **~er** n Hafenarbeiter m. **~yard** n Werft f

doctor n Arzt m/ Ärztin f; (*Univ*) Doktor m ● vt kastrieren; (*spay*) sterilisieren

doctrine n Lehre f

document n Dokument nt. **~ary** a Dokumentar- ● n Dokumentarbericht m; (*film*) Dokumentarfilm m

dodge n ⊡ Trick m, Kniff m ● vt/i ausweichen (+ *dat*)

dodgy a (**-ier, -iest**) ⊡ (*awkward*) kniffelig; (*dubious*) zweifelhaft

doe n Ricke f; (*rabbit*) [Kaninchen]weibchen nt

does see do

doesn't = does not

dog n Hund m

dog: **~-biscuit** n Hundekuchen m. **~-collar** n Hundehalsband nt; (*Relig* ⊡) Kragen m eines Geistlichen. **~-eared** a **be ~-eared** Eselsohren haben

dogged a, **-ly** adv beharrlich

dogma n Dogma nt. **~tic** a dogmatisch

do-it-yourself n Heimwerken nt. **~ shop** n Heimwerkerladen m

doldrums npl **be in the ~** niedergeschlagen sein; <*business:*> daniederliegen

dole n ⊡ Stempelgeld nt; **be on the ~** arbeitslos sein ● vt **~ out** austeilen

doll n Puppe f ● vt ⊡ **~ oneself up** sich herausputzen

dollar n Dollar m

dolphin n Delphin m

domain n Gebiet nt

dome n Kuppel f

domestic a häuslich; (*Pol*) Innen-; (*Comm*) Binnen-. **~ animal** n Haustier nt. **~ flight** n Inlandflug m

dominant a vorherrschend

dominat|e vt beherrschen ● vi dominieren. **~ion** n Vorherrschaft f

domineering a herrschsüchtig

domino n (pl **-es**) Dominostein m; **~es** sg (*game*) Domino nt

donat|e vt spenden. **~ion** n Spende f

done see do

donkey n Esel m; **~'s years** ⊡ eine Ewigkeit. **~-work** n Routinearbeit f

donor n Spender(in) m(f)

don't = do not

doom n Schicksal nt; (*ruin*) Verhängnis nt

door n Tür f; **out of ~s** im Freien

door: **~man** n Portier m. **~mat** n [Fuß]abtreter m. **~step** n Türschwelle f; **on the ~step** vor der Tür. **~way** n Türöffnung f

dope n ⊡ Drogen pl; (⊡ *information*) Informationen pl; (⊡ *idiot*) Trottel m ● vt betäuben; (*Sport*) dopen

dormant a ruhend

dormitory n Schlafsaal m

dormouse n Haselmaus f

dosage n Dosierung f

dose n Dosis f

dot n Punkt m; **on the ~** pünktlich. **~-com** n Dot-com-Firma f

dote vi **~ on** vernarrt sein in (+ *acc*)

dotted a ~ **line** punktierte Linie f; **be** ~ **with** bestreut sein mit

dotty a (**-ier, -iest**) ⊞ verdreht

double a & adv doppelt; <bed, chin> Doppel-; <flower> gefüllt ● n das Doppelte; (person) Doppelgänger m; ~**s** pl (Tennis) Doppel nt; ● vt verdoppeln; (fold) falten ● vi sich verdoppeln. ~ **up** vi sich krümmen (**with** vor + dat)

double: ~**-bass** n Kontrabass m. ~**-breasted** a zweireihig. ~**-click** vt/i doppelklicken (**on** auf + acc). ~**-cross** vt ein Doppelspiel treiben mit. ~**-decker** n Doppeldecker m. ~ **glazing** n Doppelverglasung f. ~ **room** n Doppelzimmer nt

doubly adv doppelt

doubt n Zweifel m ● vt bezweifeln. ~**ful** a, **-ly** adv zweifelhaft; (disbelieving) skeptisch. ~**less** adv zweifellos

dough n [fester] Teig m; (⊞ money) Pinke f. ~**nut** n Berliner [Pfannkuchen] m

dove n Taube f

down¹ n (feathers) Daunen pl

down² adv unten; (with movement) nach unten; **go** ~ hinuntergehen; **come** ~ herunterkommen; ~ **there** da unten; **£50** ~ £50 Anzahlung; ~**!** (to dog) Platz! ~ **with ...!** nieder mit ...! ● prep ~ **the road/stairs** die Straße/Treppe hinunter; ~ **the river** den Fluss abwärts ● vt ⊞ (drink) runterkippen; ~ **tools** die Arbeit niederlegen

down: ~**cast** a niedergeschlagen. ~**fall** n Sturz m; (ruin) Ruin m. ~**-hearted** a entmutigt. ~**hill** adv bergab. ~ **payment** n Anzahlung f. ~**pour** n Platzregen m. ~**right** a & adv ausgesprochen. ~**size** vt verschlanken ● vi abspecken. ~**stairs** adv unten; <go> nach unten ●a im Erdgeschoss. ~**stream** adv stromabwärts. ~

to-earth a sachlich. ~**town** adv (Amer) im Stadtzentrum. ~**ward** a nach unten; <slope> abfallend ● adv ~[**s**] abwärts, nach unten

doze n Nickerchen nt ● vi dösen. ~ **off** vi einnicken

dozen n Dutzend nt

Dr abbr of **doctor**

draft¹ n Entwurf m; (Comm) Tratte f; (Amer Mil) Einberufung f ● vt entwerfen; (Amer Mil) einberufen

draft² n (Amer) = **draught**

drag n **in** ~ ⊞ <man> als Frau gekleidet ● vt (pt/pp **dragged**) schleppen; absuchen <river>. ~ **on** vi sich in die Länge ziehen

dragon n Drache m. ~**fly** n Libelle f

drain n Abfluss m; (underground) Kanal m; **the** ~**s** die Kanalisation ● vt entwässern <land>; ablassen <liquid>; das Wasser ablassen aus <tank>; abgießen <vegetables>; austrinken <glass> ● vi ~ [**away**] ablaufen

drain|age n Kanalisation f; (of land) Dränage f. ~**ing board** n Abtropfbrett nt. ~**-pipe** n Abflussrohr nt

drake n Enterich m

drama n Drama nt

dramatic a, **-ally** adv dramatisch

dramat|ist n Dramatiker m. ~**ize** vt für die Bühne bearbeiten; (fig) dramatisieren

drank see **drink**

drape n (Amer) Vorhang m ● vt drapieren

drastic a, **-ally** adv drastisch

draught n [Luft]zug m; ~**s** sg (game) Damespiel nt; **there is a** ~ es zieht

draught beer n Bier nt vom Fass

draughty a zugig

draw n Attraktion f; (Sport) Unentschieden nt; (in lottery) Ziehung f ● v (pt **drew**, pp **drawn**) ● vt ziehen; (attract) anziehen;

zeichnen <picture>; abheben <money>; ~ **the curtains** die Vorhänge zuziehen/ (back) aufziehen ● vi (Sport) unentschieden spielen. ~ **back** vt zurückziehen ● vi (recoil) zurückweichen. ~ **in** vt einziehen ● vi einfahren. ~ **out** vt herausziehen; abheben <money> ● vi ausfahren. ~ **up** vt aufsetzen <document>; herrücken <chair> ● vi [an]halten

draw: ~**back** n Nachteil m. ~**bridge** n Zugbrücke f

drawer n Schublade f

drawing n Zeichnung f

drawing: ~**-board** n Reißbrett nt. ~**-pin** n Reißzwecke f

drawl n schleppende Aussprache f

drawn see **draw**

dread n Furcht f (of vor + dat) ● vt fürchten. ~**ful** a, **-fully** adv fürchterlich

dream n Traum m ● vt/i (pt/pp **dreamt** or **dreamed**) träumen (about/of von)

dreary a (**-ier, -iest**) trüb[e]; (boring) langweilig

dregs npl Bodensatz m

drench vt durchnässen

dress n Kleid nt; (clothing) Kleidung f ● vt anziehen; (Med) verbinden; ~ **oneself, get** ~**ed** sich anziehen ● vi sich anziehen. ~ **up** vi sich schön anziehen; (in disguise) sich verkleiden (**as** als)

dress: ~ **circle** n (Theat) erster Rang m. ~**er** n (furniture) Anrichte f; (Amer: dressing-table) Frisiertisch m

dressing n (Culin) Soße f; (Med) Verband m

dressing: ~**-gown** n Morgenmantel m. ~**-room** n Ankleidezimmer nt; (Theat) [Künstler]garderobe f. ~**-table** n Frisiertisch m

dress: ~**maker** n Schneiderin f. ~ **rehearsal** n Generalprobe f

drew see **draw**

dried a getrocknet. ~ **fruit** Dörrobst nt

drier n Trockner m

drift n Abtrift f; (of snow) Schneewehe f; (meaning) Sinn m ● vi treiben; (off course) abtreiben; <snow:> Wehen bilden; (fig) <person:> sich treiben lassen

drill n Bohrer m; (Mil) Drill m ● vt/i bohren (**for** nach); (Mil) drillen

drily adv trocken

drink n Getränk nt; (alcoholic) Drink m; (alcohol) Alkohol m ● vt/i (pt **drank**, pp **drunk**) trinken. ~ **up** vt/i austrinken

drink|able a trinkbar. ~**er** n Trinker m

drinking-water n Trinkwasser nt

drip n Tropfen nt; (drop) Tropfen m; (Med) Tropf m; (🔢 person) Niete f ● vi (pt/pp **dripped**) tropfen

drive n [Auto]fahrt f; (entrance) Einfahrt f; (energy) Elan m; (Psych) Trieb m; (Pol) Aktion f; (Sport) Treibschlag m; (Techn) Antrieb m ● v (pt **drove**, pp **driven**) ● vt treiben; fahren <car>; (Sport: hit) schlagen; (Techn) antreiben; ~ **s.o. mad** 🔢 jdn verrückt machen; **what are you driving at?** 🔢 worauf willst du hinaus? ● vi fahren. ~ **away** vt vertreiben ● vi abfahren. ~ **off** vt vertreiben ● vi abfahren. ~ **on** vi weiterfahren. ~ **up** vi vorfahren

drivel n 🔢 Quatsch m

driven see **drive**

driver n Fahrer(in) m(f); (of train) Lokführer m

driving: ~ **lesson** n Fahrstunde f. ~ **licence** n Führerschein m. ~ **school** n Fahrschule f. ~ **test** n Fahrprüfung f

drizzle n Nieselregen m ● vi nieseln

drone n (sound) Brummen nt
droop vi herabhängen
drop n Tropfen m; (fall) Fall m; (in price, temperature) Rückgang m ● v (pt/pp **dropped**) ● vt fallen lassen; abwerfen <bomb>; (omit) auslassen; (give up) aufgeben ● vi fallen; (fall lower) sinken; <wind:> nachlassen. ~ **in** vi vorbeikommen. ~ **off** vt absetzen <person> ● vi abfallen; (fall asleep) einschlafen. ~ **out** vi herausfallen; (give up) aufgeben
drought n Dürre f
drove see **drive**
drown vi ertrinken ● vt ertränken; übertönen <noise>; **be** ~**ed** ertrinken
drowsy a schläfrig
drudgery n Plackerei f
drug n Droge f ● vt (pt/pp **drugged**) betäuben
drug: ~ **addict** n Drogenabhängige(r) m/f. ~**store** n (Amer) Drogerie f; (dispensing) Apotheke f
drum n Trommel f; (for oil) Tonne f ● v (pt/pp **drummed**) ● vi trommeln ● vt ~**sth into s.o.** Ⓘ jdm etw einbläuen. ~**mer** n Trommler m; (in pop-group) Schlagzeuger m. ~**stick** n Trommelschlegel m
drunk see **drink** ● a betrunken; **get** ~ sich betrinken ● n Betrunkene(r) m
drunk|ard n Trinker m. ~**en** a betrunken
dry a (**drier, driest**) trocken ● vt/i trocknen. ~ **up** vt/i austrocknen
dry: ~-**clean** vt chemisch reinigen. ~-**cleaner's** n (shop) chemische Reinigung f. ~**ness** n Trockenheit f
dual a doppelt
dual carriageway n ≈ Schnellstraße f
dubious a zweifelhaft
duchess n Herzogin f

duck n Ente f ● vt (in water) untertauchen ● vi sich ducken
duct n Rohr nt; (Anat) Gang m
dud a Ⓘ nutzlos; <coin> falsch; <cheque> ungedeckt; (forged) gefälscht
due a angemessen; **be** ~ fällig sein; <baby:> erwartet werden; <train:> planmäßig ankommen; ~ **to** (owing to) wegen (+ gen); **be** ~ **to** zurückzuführen sein auf (+ acc) ● adv ~ **west** genau westlich
duel n Duell nt
duet n Duo nt; (vocal) Duett nt
dug see **dig**
duke n Herzog m
dull a (**-er, -est**) (overcast, not bright) trüb[e]; (not shiny) matt; <sound> dumpf; (boring) langweilig; (stupid) schwerfällig
duly adv ordnungsgemäß
dumb a (**-er, -est**) stumm. ~ **down** vt/i verflachen
dummy n (tailor's) [Schneider]puppe f; (for baby) Schnuller m; (Comm) Attrappe f
dump n Abfallhaufen m; (for refuse) Müllhalde f, Deponie f; (Ⓘ town) Kaff nt; **be down in the** ~**s** Ⓘ deprimiert sein ● vt abladen
dumpling n Kloß m
dunce n Dummkopf m
dune n Düne f
dung n Mist m
dungarees npl Latzhose f
dungeon n Verlies nt
dunk vt eintunken
duo n Paar nt; (Mus) Duo nt
dupe n Betrogene(r) m/f ● vt betrügen
duplicate¹ n Doppel nt; **in** ~ in doppelter Ausfertigung f
duplicate² vt kopieren; (do twice) zweimal machen
durable a haltbar
duration n Dauer f
during prep während (+ gen)
dusk n [Abend]dämmerung f

dust n Staub m ● vt abstauben;
(sprinkle) bestäuben (with mit)
dust: ~**bin** n Mülltonne f. ~**cart**
n Müllwagen m. ~**er** n Staubtuch
nt. ~**jacket** n Schutzumschlag
m. ~**man** n Müllmann m. ~**pan** n
Kehrschaufel f
dusty a (-ier, -iest) staubig
Dutch a holländisch ● n (Lang)
Holländisch nt; **the** ~ pl die
Holländer. ~**man** n Holländer m
dutiful a, **-ly** adv pflichtbewusst
duty n Pflicht f; (task) Aufgabe f;
(tax) Zoll m; **be on** ~ Dienst
haben. ~**free** a zollfrei
duvet n Steppdecke f
DVD abbr (digital versatile disc)
DVD f
dwarf n (pl -s or dwarves) Zwerg
m
dwell vi (pt/pp dwelt); ~ **on** (fig)
verweilen bei. ~**ing** n Wohnung f
dwindle vi abnehmen, schwinden
dye n Farbstoff m ● vt (pres p
dyeing) färben
dying see die²
dynamic a dynamisch
dynamite n Dynamit nt
dyslex|ia n Legasthenie f. ~**ic** a
legasthenisch; **be** ~**ic**
Legastheniker sein

each a & pron jede(r,s); (per) je;
~ **other** einander; **£1** ~ £1 pro
Person; (for thing) pro Stück
eager a, **-ly** adv eifrig; **be** ~ **to do
sth** etw gerne machen wollen.
~**ness** n Eifer m
eagle n Adler m

ear n Ohr nt. ~**ache** n
Ohrenschmerzen pl. ~**drum** n
Trommelfell nt
earl n Graf m
early a & adv (-ier, -iest) früh;
<reply> baldig; **be** ~ früh dran
sein
earn vt verdienen
earnest a, **-ly** adv ernsthaft ● n **in**
~ im Ernst
earnings npl Verdienst m
ear: ~**phones** npl Kopfhörer pl.
~**ring** n Ohrring m; (clip-on)
Ohrklips m. ~**shot** n **within/out of**
~**shot** in/außer Hörweite
earth n Erde f; (of fox) Bau m ● vt
(Electr) erden
earthenware n Tonwaren pl
earthly a irdisch; **be no** ~ **use** ❗
völlig nutzlos sein
earthquake n Erdbeben nt
earthy a erdig; (coarse) derb
ease n Leichtigkeit f ● vt
erleichtern; lindern <pain> ● vi
<pain:> nachlassen; <situation:>
sich entspannen
easily adv leicht, mit Leichtigkeit
east n Osten m; **to the** ~ **of** östlich
von ● a Ost-, ost- ● adv nach
Osten
Easter n Ostern nt ● attrib Oster-.
~ **egg** n Osterei nt
east|erly a östlich. ~**ern** a östlich.
~**ward[s]** adv nach Osten
easy a (-ier, -iest) leicht; **take it** ~
❗ sich schonen; **go** ~ **with** ❗
sparsam umgehen mit
easy: ~ **chair** n Sessel m. ~**going**
a gelassen
eat vt/i (pt ate, pp eaten) essen;
<animal:> fressen. ~ **up** vt
aufessen
eatable a genießbar
eau-de-Cologne n Kölnisch
Wasser nt
eaves npl Dachüberhang m.
~**drop** vi (pt/pp ~ **dropped**)
[heimlich] lauschen

ebb n (tide) Ebbe f ● vi
zurückgehen; (fig) verebben
ebony n Ebenholz nt
EC abbr (European Community) EG
f
eccentric a exzentrisch ● n
Exzentriker m
ecclesiastical a kirchlich
echo n (pl -es) Echo nt, Widerhall
m ● v (pt/pp **echoed**, pres p
echoing) ● vi widerhallen (**with**
von)
eclipse n (Astr) Finsternis f
ecolog|ical a ökologisch. ~**y** n
Ökologie f
e-commerce n E-Commerce m
economic a wirtschaftlich. ~**al** a
sparsam. ~**ally** adv
wirtschaftlich; (thriftily) sparsam.
~**s** n Volkswirtschaft f
economist n Volkswirt m; (Univ)
Wirtschaftswissenschaftler m
economize vi sparen (**on** an +
dat)
economy n Wirtschaft f; (thrift)
Sparsamkeit f
ecstasy n Ekstase f
ecstatic a, **-ally** adv ekstatisch
eddy n Wirbel m
edge n Rand m; (of table, lawn)
Kante f; (of knife) Schneide f; **on**
~ 🔲 nervös ● vt einfassen. ~
forward vi sich nach vorn
schieben
edgy a 🔲 nervös
edible a essbar
edifice n [großes] Gebäude nt
edit vt (pt/pp **edited**) redigieren;
herausgeben <anthology,
dictionary>; schneiden <film,
tape>
edition n Ausgabe f; (impression)
Auflage f
editor n Redakteur m; (of
anthology, dictionary)
Herausgeber m; (of newspaper)
Chefredakteur m; (of film)
Cutter(in) m(f)

editorial a redaktionell,
Redaktions- ● n (Journ)
Leitartikel m
educate vt erziehen. ~**d** a
gebildet
education n Erziehung f;
(culture) Bildung f. ~**al** a
pädagogisch; <visit> kulturell
eel n Aal m
eerie a (-ier, -iest) unheimlich
effect n Wirkung f, Effekt m; **take**
~ in Kraft treten
effective a, **-ly** adv wirksam,
effektiv; (striking) wirkungsvoll,
effektvoll; (actual) tatsächlich.
~**ness** n Wirksamkeit f
effeminate a unmännlich
effervescent a sprudelnd
efficiency n Tüchtigkeit f; (of
machine, organization)
Leistungsfähigkeit f
efficient a tüchtig; <machine,
organization> leistungsfähig;
<method> rationell. ~**ly** adv gut;
<function> rationell
effort n Anstrengung f; **make an** ~
sich (dat) Mühe geben. ~**less** a,
-ly adv mühelos
e.g. abbr z.B.
egalitarian a egalitär
egg n Ei nt. ~**cup** n Eierbecher
m. ~**shell** n Eierschale f
ego n Ich nt. ~**ism** n Egoismus m.
~**ist** n Egoist m. ~**tism** n
Ichbezogenheit f. ~**tist** n
ichbezogener Mensch m
Egypt n Ägypten nt. ~**ian** a
ägyptisch ● n Ägypter(in) m(f)
eiderdown n (quilt) Daunendecke
f
eigh|t a acht ● n Acht f; (boat)
Achter m. ~**teen** a achtzehn.
~**teenth** a achtzehnte(r,s)
eighth a achte(r,s) ● n Achtel nt
eightieth a achtzigste(r,s)
eighty a achtzig
either a & pron ~ **[of them]** einer
von [den] beiden; (both) beide;
on ~ **side** auf beiden Seiten

● *adv* **I don't** ~ ich auch nicht
● *conj* ~ ... **or** entweder ... oder
eject *vt* hinauswerfen
elaborate *a*, **-ly** *adv* kunstvoll; *(fig)* kompliziert
elapse *vi* vergehen
elastic *a* elastisch. ~ **band** *n* Gummiband *nt*
elasticity *n* Elastizität *f*
elated *a* überglücklich
elbow *n* Ellbogen *m*
elder[1] *n* Holunder *m*
eld|er[2] *a* ältere(r,s) ● *n* **the** ~**er** der/die Ältere. ~**erly** *a* alt. ~**est** *a* älteste(r,s) ● *n* **the** ~**est** der/die Älteste
elect *vt* wählen. ~**ion** *n* Wahl *f*
elector *n* Wähler(in) *m(f)*. ~ **ate** *n* Wählerschaft *f*
electric *a*, **-ally** *adv* elektrisch
electrical *a* elektrisch; ~ **engineering** Elektrotechnik *f*
electric: ~ **blanket** *n* Heizdecke *f*. ~ **fire** *n* elektrischer Heizofen *m*
electrician *n* Elektriker *m*
electricity *n* Elektrizität *f*; *(supply)* Strom *m*
electrify *vt (pt/pp -ied)* elektrifizieren. ~**ing** *a (fig)* elektrisierend
electrocute *vt* durch einen elektrischen Schlag töten
electrode *n* Elektrode *f*
electronic *a* elektronisch. ~**s** *n* Elektronik *f*
elegance *n* Eleganz *f*
elegant *a*, **-ly** *adv* elegant
elegy *n* Elegie *f*
element *n* Element *nt*. ~**ary** *a* elementar
elephant *n* Elefant *m*
elevat|e *vt* heben; *(fig)* erheben. ~**ion** *n* Erhebung *f*
elevator *n (Amer)* Aufzug *m*, Fahrstuhl *m*
eleven *a* elf ● *n* Elf *f*. ~**th** *a* elfte(r,s); **at the** ~**th hour** ⚠ in letzter Minute
eligible *a* berechtigt

eliminate *vt* ausschalten
élite *n* Elite *f*
elm *n* Ulme *f*
elocution *n* Sprecherziehung *f*
elope *vi* durchbrennen ⚠
eloquen|ce *n* Beredsamkeit *f*. ~**t** *a*, ~**ly** *adv* beredt
else *adv* sonst; **nothing** ~ sonst nichts; **or** ~ oder; *(otherwise)* sonst; **someone/somewhere** ~ jemand/irgendwo anders; **anyone** ~ jeder andere; *(as question)* sonst noch jemand? **anything** ~ alles andere; *(as question)* sonst noch etwas? ~**where** *adv* woanders
elucidate *vt* erläutern
elusive *a* **be** ~ schwer zu fassen sein
emaciated *a* abgezehrt
e-mail *n* E-Mail *f* ● *vt* per E-Mail übermitteln <*Ergebnisse, Datei usw.*>; **s.o.** jdm eine E-Mail schicken ● ~ **address** *n* E-Mail-Adresse *f*. ~ **message** *n* E-Mail *f*
emancipat|ed *a* emanzipiert. ~**ion** *n* Emanzipation *f*; *(of slaves)* Freilassung *f*
embankment *n* Böschung *f*; *(of railway)* Bahndamm *m*
embark *vi* sich einschiffen. ~**ation** *n* Einschiffung *f*
embarrass *vt* in Verlegenheit bringen. ~**ed** *a* verlegen. ~**ing** *a* peinlich. ~**ment** *n* Verlegenheit *f*
embassy *n* Botschaft *f*
embellish *vt* verzieren; *(fig)* ausschmücken
embezzle *vt* unterschlagen. ~**ment** *n* Unterschlagung *f*
emblem *n* Emblem *nt*
embodiment *n* Verkörperung *f*
embody *vt (pt/pp -ied)* verkörpern; *(include)* enthalten
embrace *n* Umarmung *f* ● *vt* umarmen; *(fig)* umfassen ● *vi* sich umarmen

embroider vt besticken; sticken
<design> ● vi sticken. ~y n
Stickerei f
embryo n Embryo m
emerald n Smaragd m
emer|ge vi auftauchen (**from** aus);
(become known) sich
herausstellen; (come into being)
entstehen. ~**gence** n Auftauchen
nt; Entstehung f
emergency n Notfall m. ~ **exit** n
Notausgang m
emigrant n Auswanderer m
emigrat|e vi auswandern. ~**ion** n
Auswanderung f
eminent a, **-ly** adv eminent
emission n Ausstrahlung f; (of
pollutant) Emission f
emit vt (pt/pp **emitted**) ausstrahlen
<light, heat>; ausstoßen <smoke,
fumes, cry>
emotion n Gefühl nt. ~**al** a
emotional; **become** ~**al** sich
erregen
empathy n Einfühlungsvermögen
nt
emperor n Kaiser m
emphasis n Betonung f
emphasize vt betonen
emphatic a, **-ally** adv
nachdrücklich
empire n Reich nt
employ vt beschäftigen; (appoint)
einstellen; (fig) anwenden. ~**ee** n
Beschäftigte(r) m/f; (in contrast
to employer) Arbeitnehmer m.
~**er** n Arbeitgeber m. ~**ment** n
Beschäftigung f; (work) Arbeit f.
~**ment agency** n
Stellenvermittlung f
empress n Kaiserin f
emptiness n Leere f
empty a leer ● vt leeren;
ausleeren <container> ● vi sich
leeren
emulsion n Emulsion f
enable vt ~ **s.o. to** es jdm möglich
machen, zu
enact vt (Theat) aufführen

enamel n Email nt; (on teeth)
Zahnschmelz m; (paint) Lack m
enchant vt bezaubern. ~**ing** a
bezaubernd. ~**ment** n Zauber m
encircle vt einkreisen
enclos|e vt einschließen; (in
letter) beilegen (**with** dat). ~**ure** n
(at zoo) Gehege nt; (in letter)
Anlage f
encore n Zugabe f ● int bravo!
encounter n Begegnung f ● vt
begegnen (+ dat); (fig) stoßen auf
(+ acc)
encourag|e vt ermutigen;
(promote) fördern. ~**ement** n
Ermutigung f. ~**ing** a ermutigend
encroach vi ~ **on** eindringen in
(+ acc) <land>
encyclopaed|ia n Enzyklopädie f,
Lexikon nt. ~**ic** a enzyklopädisch
end n Ende nt; (purpose) Zweck
m; **in the** ~ schließlich; **at the** ~ **of**
May Ende Mai; **on** ~ hochkant;
for days on ~ tagelang; **make** ~**s**
meet 🔢 [gerade] auskommen; **no**
~ **of** 🔢 unheimlich viel(e) ● vt
beenden ● vi enden; ~ **up in** (🔢
arrive at) landen in (+ dat)
endanger vt gefährden
endeavour n Bemühung f ● vi
sich bemühen (**to** zu)
ending n Schluss m, Ende nt;
(Gram) Endung f
endless a, **-ly** adv endlos
endorse vt (Comm) indossieren;
(confirm) bestätigen. ~**ment** n
(Comm) Indossament nt; (fig)
Bestätigung f; (on driving licence)
Strafvermerk m
endow vt stiften; **be** ~**ed with** (fig)
haben
endurance n
Durchhaltevermögen nt; **beyond**
~ unerträglich
endure vt ertragen
enemy n Feind m ● attrib
feindlich
energetic a tatkräftig; **be** ~ voller
Energie sein

energy n Energie f
enforce vt durchsetzen. ~d a unfreiwillig
engage vt einstellen <staff>; (Theat) engagieren; (Auto) einlegen <gear> ● vi sich beteiligen (**in** an + dat); (Techn) ineinandergreifen. ~d a besetzt; <person> beschäftigt; (to be married) verlobt; **get** ~d sich verloben (**to** mit). ~ment n Verlobung f; (appointment) Verabredung f; (Mil) Gefecht nt
engaging a einnehmend
engine n Motor m; (Naut) Maschine f; (Rail) Lokomotive f; (of jet plane) Triebwerk nt. ~-driver n Lokomotivführer m
engineer n Ingenieur m; (service, installation) Techniker m; (Naut) Maschinist m; (Amer) Lokomotivführer m. ~ing n [mechanical] ~ing Maschinenbau m
England n England nt
English a englisch; **the** ~ **Channel** der Ärmelkanal ● n (Lang) Englisch nt; **in** ~ auf Englisch; **into** ~ ins Englische; **the** ~ pl die Engländer. ~man n Engländer m. ~woman n Engländerin f
engrave vt eingravieren. ~ing n Stich m
enhance vt verschönern; (fig) steigern
enigma n Rätsel nt. ~tic a rätselhaft
enjoy vt genießen; ~ **oneself** sich amüsieren; ~ **cooking** gern kochen; **I** ~**ed it** es hat mir gut gefallen; <food:> geschmeckt. ~able a angenehm, nett. ~ment n Vergnügen nt
enlarge vt vergrößern. ~ment n Vergrößerung f
enlist vt (Mil) einziehen; ~ **s.o.'s help** jdn zur Hilfe heranziehen ● vi (Mil) sich melden
enliven vt beleben

enmity n Feindschaft f
enormity n Ungeheuerlichkeit f
enormous a, **-ly** adv riesig
enough a, adv & n genug; **be** ~ reichen; **funnily** ~ komischerweise
enquir|e vi sich erkundigen (**about** nach). ~y n Erkundigung f; (investigation) Untersuchung f
enrage vt wütend machen
enrich vt bereichern
enrol v (pt/pp **-rolled**) ● vt einschreiben ● vi sich einschreiben
ensemble n (clothing & Mus) Ensemble nt
enslave vt versklaven
ensue vi folgen; (result) sich ergeben (**from** aus)
ensure vt sicherstellen; ~ **that** dafür sorgen, dass
entail vt erforderlich machen; **what does it** ~? was ist damit verbunden?
entangle vt **get** ~d sich verfangen (**in** in + dat)
enter vt eintreten/ <vehicle:> einfahren in (+ acc); einreisen in (+ acc) <country>; (register) eintragen; sich anmelden zu <competition> ● vi eintreten; <vehicle:> einfahren; (Theat) auftreten; (register as competitor) sich anmelden; (take part) sich beteiligen (**in** an + dat)
enterpris|e n Unternehmen nt; (quality) Unternehmungsgeist m. ~ing a unternehmend
entertain vt unterhalten; (invite) einladen; (to meal) bewirten <guest> ● vi unterhalten; (have guests) Gäste haben. ~er n Unterhalter m. ~ment n Unterhaltung f
enthral vt (pt/pp **enthralled**) **be** ~**led** gefesselt sein (**by** von)
enthuse vi ~ **over** schwärmen von

enthusias|m n Begeisterung f. ∼t n Enthusiast m. ∼tic a, -ally adv begeistert

entice vt locken. ∼ment n Anreiz m

entire a ganz. ∼ly adv ganz, völlig. ∼ty n in its ∼ty in seiner Gesamtheit

entitle vt berechtigen; ∼d ... mit dem Titel ...; be ∼d to sth das Recht auf etw (acc) haben. ∼ment n Berechtigung f; (claim) Anspruch m (to auf + acc)

entrance[1] n Eintritt m; (Theat) Auftritt m; (way in) Eingang m; (for vehicle) Einfahrt f. ∼ fee n Eintrittsgebühr f

entrant n Teilnehmer(in) m(f)

entreat vt anflehen (for um)

entrust vt ∼ s.o. with sth, ∼ sth to s.o. jdm etw anvertrauen

entry n Eintritt m; (into country) Einreise f; (on list) Eintrag m; no ∼ Zutritt/ (Auto) Einfahrt verboten

envelop vt (pt/pp enveloped) einhüllen

envelope n [Brief]umschlag m

enviable a beneidenswert

envious a, -ly adv neidisch (of auf + acc)

environment n Umwelt f

environmental a Umwelt-. ∼ist n Umweltschützer m. ∼ly adv ∼ly friendly umweltfreundlich

envisage vt sich (dat) vorstellen

envoy n Gesandte(r) m

envy n Neid m ● vt (pt/pp -ied) ∼ s.o. sth jdn um etw beneiden

epic a episch ● n Epos nt

epidemic n Epidemie f

epilep|sy n Epilepsie f. ∼tic a epileptisch ● n Epileptiker(in) m(f)

epilogue n Epilog m

episode n Episode f; (instalment) Folge f

epitome n Inbegriff m

epoch n Epoche f. ∼-making a epochemachend

equal a gleich (to dat); be ∼ to a task einer Aufgabe gewachsen sein ● n Gleichgestellte(r) m/f ● vt (pt/pp equalled) gleichen (+ dat); (fig) gleichkommen (+ dat). ∼ity n Gleichheit f

equalize vt/i ausgleichen

equally adv gleich; <divide> gleichmäßig; (just as) genauso

equat|e vt gleichsetzen (with mit). ∼ion n (Math) Gleichung f

equator n Äquator m

equestrian a Reit-

equilibrium n Gleichgewicht nt

equinox n Tagundnachtgleiche f

equip vt (pt/pp equipped) ausrüsten; (furnish) ausstatten. ∼ment n Ausrüstung f; Ausstattung f

equity n Gerechtigkeit f

equivalent a gleichwertig; (corresponding) entsprechend ● n Äquivalent nt; (value) Gegenwert m; (counterpart) Gegenstück nt

era n Ära f, Zeitalter nt

eradicate vt ausrotten

erase vt ausradieren; (from tape) löschen

erect a aufrecht ● vt errichten. ∼ion n Errichtung f; (building) Bau m; (Biol) Erektion f

ero|de vt <water:> auswaschen; <acid:> angreifen. ∼sion n Erosion f

erotic a erotisch

errand n Botengang m

erratic a unregelmäßig; <person> unberechenbar

erroneous a falsch; <belief, assumption> irrig

error n Irrtum m; (mistake) Fehler m; in ∼ irrtümlicherweise

erupt vi ausbrechen. ∼ion n Ausbruch m

escalat|e vt/i eskalieren. ∼or n Rolltreppe f

escape n Flucht f; (from prison) Ausbruch m; **have a narrow ~** gerade noch davonkommen ● vi flüchten; <prisoner:> ausbrechen; entkommen (**from** aus; **from s.o.** jdm); <gas:> entweichen

escapism n Eskapismus m

escort[1] n (of person) Begleiter m; (Mil) Eskorte f

escort[2] vt begleiten; (Mil) eskortieren

Eskimo n Eskimo m

esoteric a esoterisch

especially adv besonders

espionage n Spionage f

essay n Aufsatz m

essence n Wesen nt; (Chem, Culin) Essenz f

essential a wesentlich; (indispensable) unentbehrlich ● n **the ~s** das Wesentliche; (items) das Nötigste. **~ly** adv im Wesentlichen

establish vt gründen; (form) bilden; (prove) beweisen

estate n Gut nt; (possessions) Besitz m; (after death) Nachlass m; (housing) [Wohn]siedlung f. **~ agent** n Immobilienmakler m. **~ car** n Kombi[wagen] m

esteem n Achtung f ● vt hochschätzen

estimate[1] n Schätzung f; (Comm) [Kosten]voranschlag m; **at a rough ~** grob geschätzt

estimat|e[2] vt schätzen. **~ion** n Einschätzung f

estuary n Mündung f

etc. abbr (et cetera) und so weiter, usw.

eternal a, **-ly** adv ewig

eternity n Ewigkeit f

ethic|al a ethisch; (morally correct) moralisch einwandfrei. **~s** n Ethik f

Ethiopia n Äthiopien nt

ethnic a ethnisch. **~ cleansing** n ethnische Säuberung

etiquette n Etikette f

EU abbr (European Union) EU f

eulogy n Lobrede f

euphemis|m n Euphemismus m. **~tic** a, **-ally** adv verhüllend

euro n Euro m. **E~cheque** n Euroscheck m. **E~land** n Euroland nt

Europe n Europa nt

European a europäisch; **~ Union** Europäische Union f ● n Europäer(in) m(f)

eurosceptic n Euroskeptiker(in) m(f)

evacuat|e vt evakuieren; räumen <building, area>. **~ion** n Evakuierung f; Räumung f

evade vt sich entziehen (+ dat); hinterziehen <taxes>

evaluate vt einschätzen

evange|lical a evangelisch. **~list** n Evangelist m

evaporat|e vi verdunsten. **~ion** n Verdampfung f

evasion n Ausweichen nt; **tax ~** Steuerhinterziehung f

evasive a, **-ly** adv ausweichend; **be ~** ausweichen

even a (level) eben; (same, equal) gleich; (regular) gleichmäßig; <number> gerade; **get ~ with** 🅸 es jdm heimzahlen ● adv sogar, selbst; **~ so** trotzdem; **not ~** nicht einmal ● vt **~ the score** ausgleichen

evening n Abend m; **this ~** heute Abend; **in the ~** abends, am Abend. **~ class** n Abendkurs m

evenly adv gleichmäßig

event n Ereignis nt; (function) Veranstaltung f; (Sport) Wettbewerb m. **~ful** a ereignisreich

eventual a **his ~ success** der Erfolg, der ihm schließlich zuteil wurde. **~ly** adv schließlich

ever adv je[mals]; **not ~** nie; **for ~** für immer; **hardly ~** fast nie; **~ since** seitdem

evergreen n immergrüner Strauch m/ (tree) Baum m

everlasting a ewig

every a jede(r,s); ~ **one** jede(r,s) Einzelne; ~ **other day** jeden zweiten Tag

every: ~**body** pron jeder[mann]; alle pl. ~**day** a alltäglich. ~ **one** pron jeder[mann]; alle pl. ~**thing** pron alles. ~**where** adv überall

evict vt [aus der Wohnung] hinauswiesen. ~**ion** n Ausweisung f

eviden|ce n Beweise pl; (Jur) Beweismaterial nt; (testimony) Aussage f; **give** ~**ce** aussagen. ~**t** a, -ly adv offensichtlich

evil a böse ● n Böse nt

evoke vt heraufbeschwören

evolution n Evolution f

evolve vt entwickeln ● vi sich entwickeln

ewe n Schaf nt

exact a, -ly adv genau; **not** ~**ly** nicht gerade. ~**ness** n Genauigkeit f

exaggerat|e vt/i übertreiben. ~**ion** n Übertreibung f

exam n 🅸 Prüfung f

examination n Untersuchung f; (Sch) Prüfung f

examine vt untersuchen; (Sch) prüfen

example n Beispiel nt (**of** für); **for** ~ zum Beispiel; **make an** ~ **of** ein Exempel statuieren an (+ dat)

exasperat|e vt zur Verzweiflung treiben. ~**ion** n Verzweiflung f

excavat|e vt ausschachten; (Archaeol) ausgraben. ~**ion** n Ausgrabung f

exceed vt übersteigen. ~**ingly** adv äußerst

excel v (pt/pp **excelled**) vi sich auszeichnen ● vt ~ **oneself** sich selbst übertreffen

excellen|ce n Vorzüglichkeit f. ~**t** a, -ly adv ausgezeichnet, vorzüglich

except prep außer (+ dat); ~ **for** abgesehen von ● vt ausnehmen

exception n Ausnahme f. ~**al** a, -ly adv außergewöhnlich

excerpt n Auszug m

excess n Übermaß nt (**of** an + dat); (surplus) Überschuss m; ~**es** pl Exzesse pl

excessive a, -ly adv übermäßig

exchange n Austausch m; (Teleph) Fernsprechamt nt; (Comm) [Geld]wechsel m; **in** ~ dafür ● vt austauschen (**for** gegen); tauschen <places>. ~ **rate** n Wechselkurs m

excitable a [leicht] erregbar

excit|e vt aufregen; (cause) erregen. ~**ed** a, -ly adv aufgeregt; **get** ~**ed** sich aufregen. ~**ement** n Aufregung f; Erregung f. ~**ing** a aufregend; <story> spannend

exclaim vt/i ausrufen

exclamation n Ausruf m. ~ **mark** n, (Amer) ~ **point** n Ausrufezeichen nt

exclu|de vt ausschließen. ~**ding** prep ausschließlich (+ gen). ~**sion** n Ausschluss m

exclusive a, -ly adv ausschließlich; (select) exklusiv

excrement n Kot m

excrete vt ausscheiden

excruciating a grässlich

excursion n Ausflug m

excusable a entschuldbar

excuse[1] n Entschuldigung f; (pretext) Ausrede f

excuse[2] vt entschuldigen; ~ **me!** Entschuldigung!

ex-directory a **be** ~ nicht im Telefonbuch stehen

execute vt ausführen; (put to death) hinrichten

execution n Ausführung f; Hinrichtung f

executive a leitend ● n leitende(r) Angestellte(r) m/f; (Pol) Exekutive f

exemplary a beispielhaft

exemplify vt (pt/pp **-ied**) veranschaulichen

exempt a befreit ● vt befreien (**from** von). **~ion** n Befreiung f

exercise n Übung f; **physical ~** körperliche Bewegung f ● vt (use) ausüben; bewegen <horse> ● vi sich bewegen. **~ book** n [Schul]heft nt

exert vt ausüben; **~ oneself** sich anstrengen. **~ion** n Anstrengung f

exhale vt/i ausatmen

exhaust n (Auto) Auspuff m; (fumes) Abgase pl ● vt erschöpfen. **~ed** a erschöpft. **~ing** a anstrengend. **~ion** n Erschöpfung f. **~ive** a (fig) erschöpfend

exhibit n Ausstellungsstück nt; (Jur) Beweisstück nt ● vt ausstellen

exhibition n Ausstellung f; (Univ) Stipendium nt. **~ist** n Exhibitionist(in) m(f)

exhibitor n Aussteller m

exhilarat|ing a berauschend. **~ion** n Hochgefühl nt

exhume vt exhumieren

exile n Exil nt; (person) im Exil Lebende(r) m/f ● vt ins Exil schicken

exist vi bestehen, existieren. **~ence** n Existenz f; **be in ~ence** existieren

exit n Ausgang m; (Auto) Ausfahrt f; (Theat) Abgang m

exorbitant a übermäßig hoch

exotic a exotisch

expand vt ausdehnen; (explain better) weiter ausführen ● vi sich ausdehnen; (Comm) expandieren

expans|e n Weite f. **~ion** n Ausdehnung f; (Techn, Pol, Comm) Expansion f

expect vt erwarten; (suppose) annehmen; **I ~ so** wahrscheinlich

expectan|cy n Erwartung f. **~t** a, **-ly** adv erwartungsvoll; **~t mother** werdende Mutter f

expectation n Erwartung f

expedient a zweckdienlich

expedite vt beschleunigen

expedition n Expedition f

expel vt (pt/pp **expelled**) ausweisen (**from** aus); (from school) von der Schule verweisen

expenditure n Ausgaben pl

expense n Kosten pl; **business ~s** pl Spesen pl; **at my ~** auf meine Kosten

expensive a, **-ly** adv teuer

experience n Erfahrung f; (event) Erlebnis nt ● vt erleben. **~d** a erfahren

experiment n Versuch m, Experiment nt ● vi experimentieren. **~al** a experimentell

expert a, **-ly** adv fachmännisch ● n Fachmann m, Experte m

expertise n Sachkenntnis f

expire vi ablaufen

expiry n Ablauf m

explain vt erklären

explana|tion n Erklärung f. **~tory** a erklärend

explicit a, **-ly** adv deutlich

explode vi explodieren ● vt zur Explosion bringen

exploit¹ n [Helden]tat f

exploit² vt ausbeuten. **~ation** n Ausbeutung f

exploration n Erforschung f

explore vt erforschen. **~r** n Forschungsreisende(r) m

explos|ion n Explosion f. **~ive** a explosiv ● n Sprengstoff m

export¹ n Export m, Ausfuhr f

export² vt exportieren, ausführen. **~er** n Exporteur m

expos|e vt freilegen; (to danger) aussetzen (**to** dat); (reveal) aufdecken; (Phot) belichten. **~ure** n Aussetzung f; (Med) Unterkühlung f; (Phot)

Belichtung f; **24 ~ures** 24 Aufnahmen

express adv <send> per Eilpost ● n (train) Schnellzug m ● vt ausdrücken; **~ oneself** sich ausdrücken. **~ion** n Ausdruck m. **~ive** a ausdrucksvoll. **~ly** adv ausdrücklich

expulsion n Ausweisung f; (Sch) Verweisung f von der Schule

exquisite a erlesen

extend vt verlängern; (stretch out) ausstrecken; (enlarge) vergrößern ● vi sich ausdehnen; <table:> sich ausziehen lassen

extension n Verlängerung f; (to house) Anbau m; (Teleph) Nebenanschluss m

extensive a weit; (fig) umfassend. **~ly** adv viel

extent n Ausdehnung f; (scope) Ausmaß nt, Umfang m; **to a certain ~** in gewissem Maße

exterior a äußere(r,s) ● n **the ~** das Äußere

exterminat|e vt ausrotten. **~ion** n Ausrottung f

external a äußere(r,s); **for ~ use only** (Med) nur äußerlich. **~ly** adv äußerlich

extinct a ausgestorben; <volcano> erloschen. **~ion** n Aussterben nt

extinguish vt löschen. **~er** n Feuerlöscher m

extort vt erpressen. **~ion** n Erpressung f

extortionate a übermäßig hoch

extra a zusätzlich ● adv extra; (especially) besonders ● n (Theat) Statist(in) m(f); **~s** pl Nebenkosten pl; (Auto) Extras pl

extract[1] n Auszug m

extract[2] vt herausziehen; ziehen <tooth>

extraordinary a, **-ily** adv außerordentlich; (strange) seltsam

extravagan|ce n Verschwendung f; **an ~ce** ein Luxus m. **~t** a verschwenderisch

extrem|e a äußerste(r,s); (fig) extrem ● n Extrem nt; **in the ~e** im höchsten Grade. **~ely** adv äußerst. **~ist** n Extremist m

extricate vt befreien

extrovert n extravertierter Mensch m

exuberant a überglücklich

exude vt absondern; (fig) ausstrahlen

exult vi frohlocken

eye n Auge nt; (of needle) Öhr nt; (for hook) Öse f; **keep an ~ on** aufpassen auf (+ acc) ● vt (pt/pp eyed, pres p ey[e]ing) ansehen

eye: ~ brow n Augenbraue f. **~lash** n Wimper f. **~lid** n Augenlid nt. **~-shadow** n Lidschatten m. **~sight** n Sehkraft f. **~sore** n 🔲 Schandfleck m. **~witness** n Augenzeuge m

fable n Fabel f

fabric n Stoff m

fabrication n Erfindung f

fabulous a 🔲 phantastisch

façade n Fassade f

face n Gesicht nt; (surface) Fläche f; (of clock) Zifferblatt nt; **pull ~s** Gesichter schneiden; **in the ~ of** angesichts (+ gen); **on the ~ of it** allem Anschein nach ● vt/i gegenüberstehen (+ dat); **~ north** <house:> nach Norden liegen; **~ the fact that** sich damit abfinden, dass

face: ~**-flannel** n Waschlappen m. ~**less** a anonym. ~**-lift** n Gesichtsstraffung f
facet n Facette f; (fig) Aspekt m
facetious a, **-ly** adv spöttisch
facial a Gesichts-
facile a oberflächlich
facilitate vt erleichtern
facility n Leichtigkeit f; (skill) Gewandtheit f; ~**ies** pl Einrichtungen pl
facsimile n Faksimile nt
fact n Tatsache f; **in** ~ tatsächlich; (actually) eigentlich
faction n Gruppe f
factor n Faktor m
factory n Fabrik f
factual a, **-ly** adv sachlich
faculty n Fähigkeit f; (Univ) Fakultät f
fad n Fimmel m
fade vi verblassen; <material:> verbleichen; <sound:> abklingen; <flower:> verwelken
fag n (chore) Plage f; (⑤ cigarette) Zigarette f
fail n **without** ~ unbedingt ●vi <attempt:> scheitern; (grow weak) nachlassen; (break down) versagen; (in exam) durchfallen; ~ **to do sth** etw nicht tun ●vt nicht bestehen <exam>; durchfallen lassen <candidate>; (disappoint) enttäuschen
failing n Fehler m
failure n Misserfolg m; (breakdown) Versagen nt; (person) Versager m
faint a (-er, -est), **-ly** adv schwach; **I feel** ~ mir ist schwach ●n Ohnmacht f ●vi ohnmächtig werden. ~**ness** n Schwäche f
fair[1] n Jahrmarkt m; (Comm) Messe f
fair[2] a (-er, -est) <hair> blond; <skin> hell; <weather> heiter; (just) gerecht, fair; (quite good) ziemlich gut; (Sch) genügend; **a** ~ **amount** ziemlich viel ●adv **play**

~ **fair sein.** ~**ly** adv gerecht; (rather) ziemlich. ~**ness** n Blondheit f; Helle f; Gerechtigkeit f; (Sport) Fairness f
fairy n Elfe f; **good/wicked** ~ gute/böse Fee f. ~ **story,** ~**-tale** n Märchen nt
faith n Glaube m; (trust) Vertrauen nt (**in** zu)
faithful a, **-ly** adv treu; (exact) genau; **Yours** ~**ly** Hochachtungsvoll. ~**ness** n Treue f; Genauigkeit f
fake a falsch ●n Fälschung f; (person) Schwindler m ●vt fälschen; (pretend) vortäuschen
falcon n Falke m
fall n Fall m; (heavy) Sturz m; (in prices) Fallen nt; (Amer: autumn) Herbst m; **have a** ~ fallen ●vi (pt **fell,** pp **fallen**) fallen; (heavily) stürzen; <night:> anbrechen; ~**in love** sich verlieben; ~ **back on** zurückgreifen auf (+ acc); ~ **for s.o.** ⑤ sich in jdn verlieben; ~ **for sth** ⑤ auf etw (acc) hereinfallen. ~ **about** vi (with laughter) sich [vor Lachen] kringeln. ~ **down** vi umfallen; <thing:> herunterfallen; <building:> einstürzen. ~ **in** vi hineinfallen; (collapse) einfallen; (Mil) antreten; ~ **in with** sich anschließen (+ dat). ~ **off** vi herunterfallen; (diminish) abnehmen. ~ **out** vi herausfallen; <hair:> ausfallen; (quarrel) sich überwerfen. ~ **over** vi hinfallen. ~ **through** vi durchfallen; <plan:> ins Wasser fallen
fallacy n Irrtum m
fallible a fehlbar
fall-out n [radioaktiver] Niederschlag m
false a falsch; (artificial) künstlich. ~**hood** n Unwahrheit f. ~**ly** adv falsch

F

false teeth npl [künstliches] Gebiss nt

falsify vt (pt/pp **-ied**) fälschen

falter vi zögern

fame n Ruhm m.

familiar a vertraut; (known) bekannt; **too ~** familiär. **~ity** n Vertrautheit f. **~ize** vt vertraut machen (**with** mit)

family n Familie f

family: ~ doctor n Hausarzt m. **~ life** n Familienleben nt. **~ planning** n Familienplanung f. **~ tree** n Stammbaum m

famine n Hungersnot f

famished a sehr hungrig

famous a berühmt

fan[1] n Fächer m; (Techn) Ventilator m

fan[2] n (admirer) Fan m

fanatic n Fanatiker m. **~al** a, **-ly** adv fanatisch. **~ism** n Fanatismus m

fanciful a phantastisch; (imaginative) phantasiereich

fancy n Phantasie f; **I have taken a real ~ to him** er hat es mir angetan ●a ausgefallen ●vt (believe) meinen; (imagine) sich (dat) einbilden; (囗 want) Lust haben (+ acc); **~ that!** stell dir vor! (really) tatsächlich! **~ dress** n Kostüm nt

fanfare n Fanfare f

fang n Fangzahn m

fan heater n Heizlüfter m

fantas|ize vi fantasieren. **~tic** a fantastisch. **~y** n Fantasie f

far adv weit; (much) viel; **by ~** bei weitem; **~ away** weit weg; **as ~ as I know** soviel ich weiß; **as ~ as the church** bis zur Kirche ●a **at the ~ end** am anderen Ende; **the F~ East** der Ferne Osten

farc|e n Farce f. **~ical** a lächerlich

fare n Fahrpreis m; (money) Fahrgeld nt; (food) Kost f; **air ~** Flugpreis m

farewell int (liter) lebe wohl! ●n Lebewohl nt

far-fetched a weit hergeholt

farm n Bauernhof m ●vi Landwirtschaft betreiben ●vt bewirtschaften <land>. **~er** n Landwirt m

farm: ~house n Bauernhaus nt. **~ing** n Landwirtschaft f. **~yard** n Hof m

far: ~-reaching a weit reichend. **~-sighted** a (fig) umsichtig; (Amer: long-sighted) weitsichtig

farther adv weiter; **~ off** weiter entfernt

fascinat|e vt faszinieren. **~ing** a faszinierend. **~ion** n Faszination f

fascis|m n Faschismus m. **~t** n Faschist m ●a faschistisch

fashion n Mode f; (manner) Art f. **~able** a, **-bly** adv modisch

fast a & adv (**-er, -est**) schnell; (firm) fest; <colour> waschecht; **be ~** <clock:> vorgehen; **be ~ asleep** fest schlafen

fasten vt zumachen; (fix) befestigen (**to an** + dat). **~er** n, **~ing** n Verschluss m

fastidious a wählerisch; (particular) penibel

fat a (**fatter, fattest**) dick; <meat> fett ●n Fett nt

fatal a tödlich; <error> verhängnisvoll. **~ity** n Todesopfer nt. **~ly** adv tödlich

fate n Schicksal nt. **~ful** a verhängnisvoll

fat-head n 囗 Dummkopf m

father n Vater m; **F ~ Christmas** der Weihnachtsmann ●vt zeugen

father: ~hood n Vaterschaft f. **~-in-law** n (pl **~s-in-law**) Schwiegervater m. **~ly** a väterlich

fathom n (Naut) Faden m ●vt verstehen

fatigue n Ermüdung f

fatten vt mästen <*animal*>
fatty a fett; <*foods*> fetthaltig
fatuous a, **-ly** adv albern
fault n Fehler m; (*Techn*) Defekt m; (*Geol*) Verwerfung f; **at ~** im Unrecht; **find ~ with** etwas auszusetzen haben an (+ *dat*); **it's your ~** du bist schuld. **~less** a, **-ly** adv fehlerfrei
faulty a fehlerhaft
favour n Gunst f; **I am in ~** ich bin dafür; **do s.o. a ~** jdm einen Gefallen tun ● vt begünstigen; (*prefer*) bevorzugen. **~able** a, **-bly** adv günstig; <*reply*> positiv
favourite a Lieblings- ● n Liebling m; (*Sport*) Favorit(in) m(f). **~ism** n Bevorzugung f
fawn a rehbraun ● n Hirschkalb nt
fax n Fax nt ● vt faxen (**s.o.** jdm). **~ machine** n Faxgerät nt
fear n Furcht f, Angst f (**of** vor + *dat*) ● vt/i fürchten
fear|ful a besorgt; (*awful*) furchtbar. **~less** a, **-ly** adv furchtlos
feas|ibility n Durchführbarkeit f. **~ible** a durchführbar; (*possible*) möglich
feast n Festmahl nt; (*Relig*) Fest nt ● vi **~ [on]** schmausen
feat n Leistung f
feather n Feder f
feature n Gesichtszug m; (*quality*) Merkmal nt; (*Journ*) Feature nt ● vt darstellen
February n Februar m
fed ● a **be ~ up** 🆑 die Nase voll haben (**with** von)
federal a Bundes-
federation n Föderation f
fee n Gebühr f; (*professional*) Honorar nt
feeble a (**-r, -st**), **-bly** adv schwach
feed n Futter nt; (*for baby*) Essen nt ● v (*pt/pp* **fed**) ● vt füttern; (*support*) ernähren; (*into machine*) eingeben; speisen

<*computer*> ● vi sich ernähren (**on** von)
feedback n Feedback nt
feel v (*pt/pp* **felt**) ● vt fühlen; (*experience*) empfinden; (*think*) meinen ● vi sich fühlen; **~ soft/hard** sich weich/hart anfühlen; **I ~ hot/ill** mir ist heiß/schlecht; **~ing** n Gefühl nt; **no hard ~ings** nichts für ungut
feet *see* **foot**
feline a Katzen-; (*catlike*) katzenartig
fell[1] vt fällen
fell[2] *see* **fall**
fellow n (🆑 *man*) Kerl m
fellow: ~-countryman n Landsmann m. **~ men** pl Mitmenschen pl
felt[1] *see* **feel**
felt[2] n Filz m. **~-[tipped] pen** n Filzstift m
female a weiblich ● nt Weibchen nt; (*pej: woman*) Weib nt
femin|ine a weiblich ● n (*Gram*) Femininum nt. **~inity** n Weiblichkeit f. **~ist** a feministisch ● n Feminist(in) m(f)
fenc|e n Zaun m; (🆑 *person*) Hehler m ● vi (*Sport*) fechten ● vt **~e in** einzäunen. **~er** n Fechter m. **~ing** n Zaun m; (*Sport*) Fechten nt
fender n Kaminvorsetzer m; (*Naut*) Fender m; (*Amer: wing*) Kotflügel m
ferment vi gären ● vt gären lassen
fern n Farn m
feroc|ious a wild. **~ity** n Wildheit f
ferry n Fähre f
fertil|e a fruchtbar. **~ity** n Fruchtbarkeit f
fertilize vt befruchten; düngen <*land*>. **~r** n Dünger m
fervent a leidenschaftlich
fervour n Leidenschaft f

festival n Fest nt; (Mus, Theat) Festspiele pl
festiv|e a festlich. **∼ities** npl Feierlichkeiten pl
festoon vt behängen (**with** mit)
fetch vt holen; (collect) abholen; (be sold for) einbringen
fetching a anziehend
fête n Fest nt ● vt feiern
feud n Fehde f
feudal a Feudal-
fever n Fieber nt. **∼ish** a fiebrig; (fig) fieberhaft
few a (-er, -est) wenige; **every ∼ days** alle paar Tage ● n **a ∼** ein paar; **quite a ∼** ziemlich viele
fiancé n Verlobte(r) m. **fiancée** n Verlobte f
fiasco n Fiasko nt
fib n kleine Lüge
fibre n Faser f
fiction n Erfindung f; **[works of] ∼** Erzählungsliteratur f. **∼al** a erfunden
fictitious a [frei] erfunden
fiddle n Ⓕ Geige f; (cheating) Schwindel m ● vi herumspielen (**with** mit) ● vt Ⓕ frisieren <accounts>
fiddly a knifflig
fidelity n Treue f
fidget vi zappeln. **∼y** a zappelig
field n Feld nt; (meadow) Wiese f; (subject) Gebiet nt
field: ∼ events npl Sprung- und Wurfdisziplinen pl. **F∼ Marshal** n Feldmarschall m
fiendish a teuflisch
fierce a (-r, -st), **-ly** adv wild; (fig) heftig. **∼ness** n Wildheit f; (fig) Heftigkeit f
fiery a (-ier, -iest) feurig
fifteen a fünfzehn ● n Fünfzehn f. **∼th** a fünfzehnte(r,s)
fifth a fünfte(r,s)
fiftieth a fünfzigste(r,s)
fifty a fünfzig
fig n Feige f

fight n Kampf m; (brawl) Schlägerei f; (between children, dogs) Rauferei f ● v (pt/pp **fought**) ● vt kämpfen gegen; (fig) bekämpfen ● vi kämpfen; (brawl) sich schlagen; <children, dogs:> sich raufen. **∼er** n Kämpfer m; (Aviat) Jagdflugzeug nt. **∼ing** n Kampf m
figurative a, **-ly** adv bildlich, übertragen
figure n (digit) Ziffer f; (number) Zahl f; (sum) Summe f; (carving, sculpture, woman's) Figur f; (form) Gestalt f; (illustration) Abbildung f. **good at ∼s** gut im Rechnen ● vi (appear) erscheinen ● vt (Amer: think) glauben
filch vt Ⓕ klauen
file¹ n Akte f; (for documents) [Akten]ordner m ● vt ablegen <documents>; (Jur) einreichen
file² n (line) Reihe f; **in single ∼** im Gänsemarsch
file³ n (Techn) Feile f ● vt feilen
fill n **eat one's ∼** sich satt essen ● vt füllen; plombieren <tooth> ● vi sich füllen. **∼ in** vt ausfüllen <form>. **∼ out** vt ausfüllen <form>. **∼ up** vi sich füllen ● vt vollfüllen; (Auto) volltanken; ausfüllen <form>
fillet n Filet nt ● vt (pt/pp **filleted**) entgräten
filling n Füllung f; (of tooth) Plombe f. **∼ station** n Tankstelle f
filly n junge Stute f
film n Film m ● vt/i filmen; verfilmen <book>. **∼ star** n Filmstar m
filter n Filter m ● vt filtern
filth n Dreck m. **∼y** a (-ier, -iest) dreckig
fin n Flosse f
final a letzte(r,s); (conclusive) endgültig ● n (Sport) Endspiel nt; **∼s** pl (Univ) Abschlussprüfung f

finale n Finale nt

final|ist n Finalist(in) m(f)

final|ize vt endgültig festlegen. ~**ly** adv schließlich

finance n Finanz f ● vt finanzieren

financial a, **-ly** adv finanziell

find n Fund m ● vt (pt/pp **found**) finden; (establish) feststellen; **go and ~** holen; **try to ~** suchen. ~ **out** vt herausfinden; (learn) erfahren ● vi (enquire) sich erkundigen

fine[1] n Geldstrafe f ● vt zu einer Geldstrafe verurteilen

fine[2] a (**-r, -st**), **-ly** adv fein; <weather> schön; **he's ~** es geht ihm gut ● adv gut; **cut it ~** 🗊 sich (dat) wenig Zeit lassen

finesse n Gewandtheit f

finger n Finger m ● vt anfassen

finger: ~**nail** n Fingernagel m. ~**print** n Fingerabdruck m. ~**tip** n Fingerspitze f

finicky a knifflig; (choosy) wählerisch

finish n Schluss m; (Sport) Finish nt; (line) Ziel nt; (of product) Ausführung f ● vt beenden; (use up) aufbrauchen; ~ **one's drink** austrinken; ~ **reading** zu Ende lesen ● vi fertig werden; <performance:> zu Ende sein; <runner:> durchs Ziel gehen

Finland n Finnland nt

Finn n Finne m/ Finnin f. ~**ish** a finnisch

fir n Tanne f

fire n Feuer nt; (forest, house) Brand m; **be on ~** brennen; **catch ~** Feuer fangen; **set ~ to** anzünden; <arsonist:> in Brand stecken; **under ~** unter Beschuss ● vt brennen <pottery>; abfeuern <shot>; schießen mit <gun>; (🗊 dismiss) feuern ● vi schießen (**at** auf + acc); <engine:> anspringen

fire: ~ **alarm** n Feuermelder m. ~ **brigade** n Feuerwehr f. ~**-engine**

n Löschfahrzeug nt. ~ **extinguisher** n Feuerlöscher m. ~**man** n Feuerwehrmann m. ~**place** n Kamin m. ~**side** n **by** or **at the ~side** am Kamin. ~ **station** n Feuerwache f. ~**wood** n Brennholz nt. ~**work** n Feuerwerkskörper m; ~**works** pl (display) Feuerwerk nt

firm[1] n Firma f

firm[2] a (**-er, -est**), **-ly** adv fest; (resolute) entschlossen; (strict) streng

first a & n erste(r,s); **at ~** zuerst; **at ~ sight** auf den ersten Blick; **from the ~** von Anfang an ● adv zuerst; (firstly) erstens

first: ~ **aid** n erste Hilfe. ~**-aid kit** n Verbandkasten m. ~**-class** a erstklassig; (Rail) erster Klasse ● adv <travel> erster Klasse. ~ **floor** n erster Stock; (Amer: ground floor) Erdgeschoss nt. ~**ly** adv erstens. ~**name** n Vorname m. ~**-rate** a erstklassig

fish n Fisch m ● vt/i fischen; (with rod) angeln

fish: ~**bone** n Gräte f. ~**erman** n Fischer m. ~ **finger** n Fischstäbchen nt

fishing n Fischerei f. ~ **boat** n Fischerboot nt. ~**-rod** n Angel[rute] f

fish: ~**monger** n Fischhändler m. ~**y** a Fisch-; (🗊 suspicious) verdächtig

fission n (Phys) Spaltung f

fist n Faust f

fit[1] n (attack) Anfall m

fit[2] a (**fitter, fittest**) (suitable) geeignet; (healthy) gesund; (Sport) fit; ~ **to eat** essbar

fit[3] n (of clothes) Sitz m; **be a good ~** gut passen ● v (pt/pp **fitted**) ● vi (be the right size) passen ● vt anbringen (**to** an + dat); (install) einbauen; ~ **with** versehen mit. ~ **in** vi hineinpassen; (adapt) sich

einfügen (**with** in + *acc*) ● *vt*
(*accommodate*) unterbringen

fit|ness *n* Eignung *f*; **[physical]**
~**ness** Gesundheit *f*; (*Sport*)
Fitness *f*. ~**ted** *a* eingebaut;
<*garment*> tailliert

fitted: ~ **carpet** *n* Teppichboden
m. ~ **kitchen** *n* Einbauküche *f*. ~
sheet *n* Spannlaken *nt*

fitting *a* passend ● *n* (*of clothes*)
Anprobe *f*; (*of shoes*) Weite *f*;
(*Techn*) Zubehörteil *nt*; ~**s** *pl*
Zubehör *nt*

five *a* fünf ● *n* Fünf *f*. ~**r** *n*
Fünfpfundschein *m*

fix *n* (✕ *drugs*) Fix *m*; **be in a** ~ ⚠
in der Klemme sitzen ● *vt*
befestigen (**to** an + *dat*);
(*arrange*) festlegen; (*repair*)
reparieren; (*Phot*) fixieren; ~ **a**
meal Essen machen

fixed *a* fest

fixture *n* (*Sport*) Veranstaltung *f*;
~**s and fittings** zu einer Wohnung
gehörende Einrichtungen *pl*

fizz *vi* sprudeln

fizzle *vi* ~ **out** verpuffen

fizzy *a* sprudelnd. ~ **drink** *n*
Brause[limonade] *f*

flabbergasted *a* **be** ~ platt sein
⚠

flabby *a* schlaff

flag *n* Fahne *f*; (*Naut*) Flagge *f*

flag-pole *n* Fahnenstange *f*

flagrant *a* flagrant

flagstone *n* [Pflaster]platte *f*

flair *n* Begabung *f*

flake *n* Flocke *f* ● *vi* ~ **[off]**
abblättern

flamboyant *a* extravagant

flame *n* Flamme *f*

flan *n* **[fruit]** ~ Obsttorte *f*

flank *n* Flanke *f*

flannel *n* Flanell *m*; (*for washing*)
Waschlappen *m*

flap *n* Klappe *f*; **in a** ~ ⚠
aufgeregt ● *v* (*pt/pp* **flapped**) *vi*
flattern; ⚠ sich aufregen ● *vt* ~

its wings mit den Flügeln
schlagen

flare *n* Leuchtsignal *nt*. ● *vi* ~ **up**
auflodern; (⚠ *get angry*)
aufbrausen

flash *n* Blitz *m*; **in a** ~ ⚠ im Nu
● *vi* blitzen; (*repeatedly*) blinken;
~ **past** vorbeirasen

flash: ~**back** *n* Rückblende *f*. ~**e**
n (*Auto*) Blinker *m*. ~**light** *n*
(*Phot*) Blitzlicht *nt*; (*Amer: torch*)
Taschenlampe *f*. ~**y** *a* auffällig

flask *n* Flasche *f*

flat *a* (**flatter, flattest**) flach;
<*surface*> eben; <*refusal*> glatt;
<*beer*> schal; <*battery*>
verbraucht/ (*Auto*) leer; <*tyre*>
platt; (*Mus*) **A** ~ As *nt*; **B** ~ B *nt*
● *n* Wohnung *f*; (⚠ *puncture*)
Reifenpanne *f*

flat: ~**ly** *adv* <*refuse*> glatt. ~
rate *n* Einheitspreis *m*

flatten *vt* platt drücken

flatter *vt* schmeicheln (+ *dat*). ~**y**
n Schmeichelei *f*

flat tyre *n* Reifenpanne *f*

flaunt *vt* prunken mit

flautist *n* Flötist(in) *m(f)*

flavour *n* Geschmack *m* ● *vt*
abschmecken. ~**ing** *n* Aroma *nt*

flaw *n* Fehler *m*. ~**less** *a* tadellos;
<*complexion*> makellos

flea *n* Floh *m*

fleck *n* Tupfen *m*

fled *see* **flee**

flee *v* (*pt/pp* **fled**) ● *vi* fliehen
(**from** vor + *dat*) ● *vt* flüchten aus

fleece *n* Vlies *nt* ● *vt* ⚠
schröpfen

fleet *n* Flotte *f*; (*of cars*)
Wagenpark *m*

fleeting *a* flüchtig

Flemish *a* flämisch

flesh *n* Fleisch *nt*

flew *see* **fly²**

flex¹ *vt* anspannen <*muscle*>

flex² *n* (*Electr*) Schnur *f*

flexib|ility n Biegsamkeit f; (fig)
Flexibilität f. ~**le** a biegsam; (fig)
flexibel

flick vt schnippen

flicker vi flackern

flier n = flyer

flight¹ n (fleeing) Flucht f

flight² n (flying) Flug m; ~ **of
stairs** Treppe f

flight recorder n Flugschreiber m

flimsy a (-ier, -iest) dünn;
<excuse> fadenscheinig

flinch vi zurückzucken

fling vt (pt/pp flung) schleudern

flint n Feuerstein m

flip vt/i schnippen; ~ **through**
durchblättern

flippant a, **-ly** adv leichtfertig

flirt n kokette Frau f ● vi flirten

flirtat|ion n Flirt m. ~**ious** a
kokett

flit vi (pt/pp flitted) flattern

float n Schwimmer m; (in
procession) Festwagen m;
(money) Wechselgeld nt ● vi
<thing:> schwimmen; <person:>
sich treiben lassen; (in air)
schweben

flock n Herde f; (of birds)
Schwarm m ● vi strömen

flog vt (pt/pp flogged)
auspeitschen; (🔲 sell)
verkloppen

flood n Überschwemmung f; (fig)
Flut f ● vt überschwemmen

floodlight n Flutlicht nt ● vt (pt/
pp floodlit) anstrahlen

floor n Fußboden m; (storey)
Stock m

floor: ~ **board** n Dielenbrett nt.
~**-polish** n Bohnerwachs nt. ~
show n Kabarettvorstellung f

flop n (🔲 failure) Reinfall m;
(Theat) Durchfall m ● vi (pt/pp
flopped) (🔲 fail) durchfallen

floppy a schlapp. ~ **disc** n
Diskette f

floral a Blumen-

florid a <complexion> gerötet;
<style> blumig

florist n Blumenhändler(in) m(f)

flounder vi zappeln

flour n Mehl nt

flourish n große Geste f; (scroll)
Schnörkel m ● vi gedeihen; (fig)
blühen ● vt schwenken

flout vt missachten

flow n Fluss m; (of traffic, blood)
Strom m ● vi fließen

flower n Blume f ● vi blühen

flower: ~**bed** n Blumenbeet nt.
~**pot** n Blumentopf m. ~**y** a
blumig

flown see fly²

flu n 🔲 Grippe f

fluctuat|e vi schwanken. ~**ion** n
Schwankung f

fluent a, **-ly** adv fließend

fluff n Fusseln pl; (down) Flaum
m. ~**y** a (-ier, -iest) flauschig

fluid a flüssig, (fig) veränderlich
● n Flüssigkeit f

fluke n [glücklicher] Zufall m

flung see fling

fluorescent a fluoreszierend

fluoride n Fluor nt

flush n (blush) Erröten nt ● vi rot
werden ● vt spülen ● a in einer
Ebene (with mit); (🔲 affluent) gut
bei Kasse

flustered a nervös

flute n Flöte f

flutter n Flattern nt ● vi flattern

fly¹ n (pl flies) Fliege f

fly² v (pt flew, pp flown) ● vi
fliegen; <flag:> wehen; (rush)
sausen ● vt fliegen; führen
<flag>

fly³ n & **flies** pl (on trousers)
Hosenschlitz m

flyer n Flieger(in) m(f); (leaflet)
Flugblatt nt

foal n Fohlen nt

foam n Schaum m; (synthetic)
Schaumstoff m ● vi schäumen

fob vt (pt/pp **fobbed**) ~ sth off etw andrehen (**on s.o.** jdm); ~ **s.o. off** jdn abspeisen (**with** mit)

focal n Brenn-

focus n Brennpunkt m; **in** ~ scharf eingestellt ● v (pt/pp **focused** or **focussed**) ● vt einstellen (**on** auf + acc) ● vi (fig) sich konzentrieren (**on** auf + acc)

fog n Nebel m

foggy a (**foggier, foggiest**) neblig

fog-horn n Nebelhorn nt

foible n Eigenart f

foil[1] n Folie f; (Culin) Alufolie f

foil[2] vt (thwart) vereiteln

foil[3] n (Fencing) Florett nt

fold n Falte f; (in paper) Kniff m ● vt falten; ~ **one's arms** die Arme verschränken ● vi sich falten lassen; (fail) eingehen. ~ **up** vt zusammenfalten; zusammenklappen <chair> ● vi sich zusammenfalten/-klappen lassen; ⊞ <business:> eingehen

fold|er n Mappe f. ~**ing** a Klapp-

foliage n Blätter pl; (of tree) Laub nt

folk npl Leute pl

folk: ~-**dance** n Volkstanz m. ~-**song** n Volkslied nt

follow vt/i folgen (+ dat); (pursue) verfolgen; (in vehicle) nachfahren (+ dat). ~ **up** vt nachgehen (+ dat)

follow|er n Anhänger(in) m(f). ~**ing** a folgend ● n Folgende(s) nt; (supporters) Anhängerschaft f ● prep im Anschluss an (+ acc)

folly n Torheit f

fond a (-er, -est), -**ly** adv liebevoll; **be** ~ gern haben; gern essen <food>

fondle vt liebkosen

fondness n Liebe f (**for** zu)

food n Essen nt; (for animals) Futter nt; (groceries) Lebensmittel pl. ~ **poisoning** n Lebensmittelvergiftung f

food poisoning n Lebensmittelvergiftung f

fool[1] n (Culin) Fruchtcreme f

fool[2] n Narr m; **make a** ~ **of oneself** sich lächerlich machen ● vt hereinlegen ● vi ~ **around** herumalbern

fool|hardy a tollkühn. ~**ish** a, -**ly** adv dumm. ~**ishness** n Dummheit f. ~**proof** a narrensicher

foot n (pl **feet**) Fuß m; (measure) Fuß m (30,48 cm); (of bed) Fußende nt; **on** ~ zu Fuß; **on one's feet** auf den Beinen; **put one's** ~ **in it** ⊞ ins Fettnäpfchen treten

foot: ~-**and-mouth [disease]** n Maul-und Klauenseuche f. ~**ball** n Fußball m. ~**baller** n Fußballspieler m. ~**ball pools** npl Fußballtoto nt. ~-**bridge** n Fußgängerbrücke f. ~**hills** npl Vorgebirge nt. ~**hold** n Halt m. ~**ing** n Halt m. ~**lights** npl Rampenlicht nt. ~**note** n Fußnote f. ~**path** n Fußweg m. ~**print** n Fußabdruck m. ~**step** n Schritt m; **follow in s.o.'s** ~**steps** (fig) in jds Fußstapfen treten. ~**wear** n Schuhwerk nt

for

● preposition

····> (on behalf of; in place of; in favour of) für (+ acc). **I did it for you** ich habe es für dich gemacht. **I work for him/for a bank** ich arbeite für ihn/für eine Bank. **be for doing sth** dafür sein, etw zu tun. **cheque/bill for £5** Scheck/Rechnung über 5 Pfund. **for nothing** umsonst.

····> (expressing reason) wegen (+ gen); (with emotion) aus. **famous for these wines** berühmt wegen dieser Weine od für diese Weine. **he was sentenced to death for murder** er wurde wegen

Mordes zum Tode verurteilt. **were it not for you/your help** ohne dich/deine Hilfe. **for fear/love of** aus Angst vor (+ *dat*)/aus Liebe zu (+ *dat*)

····➤ (*expressing purpose*) (*with action, meal*) zu (+ *dat*); (*with object*) für (+ *acc*). **it's for washing the car** es ist zum Autowaschen. **we met for a discussion** wir trafen uns zu einer Besprechung. **for pleasure** zum Vergnügen. **meat for lunch** Fleisch zum Mittagessen. **what is that for?** wofür *od* wozu ist das? **a dish for nuts** eine Schale für Nüsse

····➤ (*expressing direction*) nach (+ *dat*); (*less precise*) in Richtung. **the train for Oxford** der Zug nach Oxford. **they were heading** *or* **making for London** sie fuhren in Richtung London

····➤ (*expressing time*) (*completed process*) … lang; (*continuing process*) seit (+ *dat*). **I lived here for two years** ich habe zwei Jahre [lang] hier gewohnt. **I have been living here for two years** ich wohne hier seit zwei Jahren. **we are staying for a week** wir werden eine Woche bleiben

····➤ (*expressing difficulty, impossibility, embarrassment etc.*) + *dat*. **it's impossible/ inconvenient for her** es ist ihr unmöglich/ungelegen. **it was embarrassing for our teacher** unserem Lehrer war es peinlich

● *conjunction*

····➤ denn. **he's not coming for he has no money** er kommt nicht mit, denn er hat kein Geld

forbade *see* **forbid**

forbid *vt* (*pt* **forbade**, *pp* **forbidden**) verbieten (**s.o.** jdm). **~ding** *a* bedrohlich; (*stern*) streng

force *n* Kraft *f*; (*of blow*) Wucht *f*; (*violence*) Gewalt *f*; **in ~** gültig; (*in large numbers*) in großer Zahl; **come into ~** in Kraft treten; **the ~s** *pl* die Streitkräfte *pl* ● *vt* zwingen; (*break open*) aufbrechen

forced *a* gezwungen; **~ landing** Notlandung *f*

force: ~-feed *vt* (*pt/pp* **-fed**) zwangsernähren. **~ful** *a*, **-ly** *adv* energisch

forceps *n inv* Zange *f*

forcible *a* gewaltsam

ford *n* Furt *f* ● *vt* durchwaten; (*in vehicle*) durchfahren

fore *a* vordere(r,s)

fore: ~arm *n* Unterarm *m*. **~cast** *n* Voraussage *f*; (*for weather*) Vorhersage *f* ● *vt* (*pt/pp* **~cast**) voraussagen, vorhersagen. **~finger** *n* Zeigefinger *m*. **~gone** *a* **be a ~gone conclusion** von vornherein feststehen. **~ground** *n* Vordergrund *m*. **~head** *n* Stirn *f*. **~hand** *n* Vorhand *f*

foreign *a* ausländisch; <*country*> fremd; **he is ~** er ist Ausländer. **~ currency** *n* Devisen *pl*. **~er** *n* Ausländer(in) *m(f)*. **~ language** *n* Fremdsprache *f*

Foreign: ~ Office *n* ≈ Außenministerium *nt*. **~ Secretary** *n* ≈ Außenminister *m*

fore: ~leg *n* Vorderbein *nt*. **~man** *n* Vorarbeiter *m*. **~most** *a* führend ● *adv* **first and ~most** zuallererst. **~name** *n* Vorname *m*. **~runner** *n* Vorläufer *m*

foresee *vt* (*pt* **-saw**, *pp* **-seen**) voraussehen, vorhersehen. **~able** *a* **in the ~able future** in absehbarer Zeit

foresight *n* Weitblick *m*

forest *n* Wald *m*. **~er** *n* Förster *m*

forestry *n* Forstwirtschaft *f*

foretaste *n* Vorgeschmack *m*

forever *adv* für immer

forewarn *vt* vorher warnen

foreword n Vorwort nt
forfeit n (in game) Pfand nt ● vt verwirken
forgave see **forgive**
forge n Schmiede f ● vt schmieden; (counterfeit) fälschen. **~r** n Fälscher m. **~ry** n Fälschung f
forget vt/i (pt **-got**, pp **-gotten**) vergessen; verlernen <language, skill>. **~ful** a vergesslich. **~fulness** n Vergesslichkeit f. **~me-not** n Vergissmeinnicht nt
forgive vt (pt **-gave**, pp **-given**) **~ s.o. for sth** jdm etw vergeben od verzeihen
forgot(ten) see **forget**
fork n Gabel f; (in road) Gabelung f ● vi <road:> sich gabeln; **~ right** rechts abzweigen
fork-lift truck n Gabelstapler m
forlorn a verlassen; <hope> schwach
form n Form f; (document) Formular nt; (bench) Bank f; (Sch) Klasse f ● vt formen (**into** zu); (create) bilden ● vi sich bilden; <idea:> Gestalt annehmen
formal a, **-ly** adv formell, förmlich. **~ity** n Förmlichkeit f; (requirement) Formalität f
format n Format nt ● vt formatieren
formation n Formation f
former a ehemalig; **the ~** der/die/das Erstere. **~ly** adv früher
formidable a gewaltig
formula n (pl **-ae** or **-s**) Formel f
formulate vt formulieren
forsake vt (pt **-sook**, pp **-saken**) verlassen
fort n (Mil) Fort nt
forth adv **back and ~** hin und her; **and so ~** und so weiter
forth: **~coming** a bevorstehend; (◨ communicative) mitteilsam. **~right** a direkt
fortieth a vierzigste(r,s)

fortification n Befestigung f
fortify vt (pt/pp **-ied**) befestigen; (fig) stärken
fortnight n vierzehn Tage pl. **~ly** a vierzehntäglich ● adv alle vierzehn Tage
fortress n Festung f
fortunate a glücklich; **be ~** Glück haben. **~ly** adv glüklicherweise
fortune n Glück nt; (money) Vermögen nt. **~-teller** n Wahrsagerin f
forty a vierzig
forward adv vorwärts; (to the front) nach vorn ● a Vorwärts-; (presumptuous) anmaßend ● n (Sport) Stürmer m ● vt nachsenden <letter>. **~s** adv vorwärts
fossil n Fossil nt
foster vt fördern; in Pflege nehmen <child>. **~-child** n Pflegekind nt. **~-mother** n Pflegemutter f
fought see **fight**
foul a (**-er**, **-est**) widerlich; <language> unflätig; **~ play** (Jur) Mord m ● n (Sport) Foul nt ● vt verschmutzen; (obstruct) blockieren; (Sport) foulen
found[1] see **find**
found[2] vt gründen
foundation n (basis) Gundlage f; (charitable) Stiftung f; **~s** pl Fundament nt
founder n Gründer(in) m(f)
foundry n Gießerei f
fountain n Brunnen m
four a vier ● n Vier f
four: **~teen** a vierzehn ● n Vierzehn f. **~teenth** a vierzehnte(r,s)
fourth a vierte(r,s)
fowl n Geflügel nt
fox n Fuchs m ● vt (puzzle) verblüffen
foyer n Foyer nt; (in hotel) Empfangshalle f

raction n Bruchteil m; (Math) Bruch m

racture n Bruch m ● vt/i brechen

ragile a zerbrechlich

ragment n Bruchstück nt, Fragment nt

ragran|ce n Duft m. ~**t** a duftend

rail a (**-er, -est**) gebrechlich

rame n Rahmen m; (of spectacles) Gestell nt; (Anat) Körperbau m ● vt einrahmen; (fig) formulieren; 🗷 ein Verbrechen anhängen (+ dat). ~**work** n Gerüst nt; (fig) Gerippe nt

ranc n (French, Belgian) Franc m; (Swiss) Franken m

rance n Frankreich nt

ranchise n (Pol) Wahlrecht nt; (Comm) Franchise nt

rank a, **-ly** adv offen

rankfurter n Frankfurter f

rantic a, **-ally** adv verzweifelt; außer sich (dat) (**with** vor)

raternal a brüderlich

raud n Betrug m; (person) Betrüger(in) m(f)

ray vi ausfransen

reak n Missbildung f; (person) Missgeburt f ● a anormal

reckle n Sommersprosse f

ree a (**freer, freest**) frei; <ticket, copy, time> Frei-; (lavish) freigebig; ~ **[of charge]** kostenlos; **set** ~ freilassen; (rescue) befreien ● vt (pt/pp **freed**) freilassen; (rescue) befreien; (disentangle) freibekommen

free: ~**dom** n Freiheit f. ~**hold** n [freier] Grundbesitz m. ~**lance** a & adv freiberuflich. ~**ly** adv frei; (voluntarily) freiwillig; (generously) großzügig. **F~mason** n Freimaurer m. ~**range** a ~ **range eggs** Landeier pl. ~ **sample** n Gratisprobe f. ~**style** n Freistil m. ~**way** n (Amer) Autobahn f

freez|e vt (pt **froze**, pp **frozen**) einfrieren; stoppen <wages> ● vi **it's** ~**ing** es friert. ~**er** n Gefriertruhe f; (upright) Gefrierschrank m. ~**ing** a eiskalt ● n below ~**ing** unter Null

freight n Fracht f. ~**er** n Frachter m. ~ **train** n Güterzug m

French a französisch ● n (Lang) Französisch nt; **the** ~ pl die Franzosen

French: ~ **beans** npl grüne Bohnen pl. ~ **bread** n Stangenbrot nt. ~ **fries** npl Pommes frites pl. ~**man** n Franzose m. ~ **window** n Terrassentür f. ~**woman** n Französin f

frenzy n Raserei f

frequency n Häufigkeit f; (Phys) Frequenz f

frequent¹ a, **-ly** adv häufig

frequent² vt regelmäßig besuchen

fresh a (**-er, -est**), **-ly** adv frisch; (new) neu; (cheeky) frech

freshness n Frische f

freshwater a Süßwasser-

fret vi (pt/pp **fretted**) sich grämen. ~**ful** a weinerlich

fretsaw n Laubsäge f

friction n Reibung f; (fig) Reibereien pl

Friday n Freitag m

fridge n Kühlschrank m

fried see **fry²** ● a gebraten; ~ **egg** Spiegelei nt

friend n Freund(in) m(f). ~**liness** n Freundlichkeit f. ~**ly** a (**-ier, -iest**) freundlich; ~**ly with** befreundet mit. ~**ship** n Freundschaft f

fright n Schreck m

frighten vt Angst machen (+ dat); (startle) erschrecken; **be** ~**ed** Angst haben (**of** vor + dat). ~**ing** a Angst erregend

frightful a, **-ly** adv schrecklich

frigid a frostig; (Psych) frigide. ~**ity** n Frostigkeit f; Frigidität f

F

frill n Rüsche f; (paper) Manschette f. ~**y** a rüschenbesetzt

fringe n Fransen pl; (of hair) Pony m; (fig: edge) Rand m

frisk vi herumspringen ● vt (search) durchsuchen

frisky a (-ier, -iest) lebhaft

fritter vt ~ **[away]** verplempern ⊞

frivol|ity n Frivolität f. ~**ous** a, -ly adv frivol, leichtfertig

fro see to

frock n Kleid nt

frog n Frosch m. ~**man** n Froschmann m

frolic vi (pt/pp frolicked) herumtollen

from prep (+ dat); (out of) aus (+ dat); (according to) nach (+ dat); ~ **Monday** ab Montag; ~ **that day** seit dem Tag

front n Vorderseite f; (fig) Fassade f; (of garment) Vorderteil nt; (sea~) Strandpromenade f; (Mil, Pol, Meteorol) Front f; **in** ~ **of** vor; **in** or **at the** ~ vorne; **to the** ~ nach vorne ● a vordere(r,s); <page, row> erste(r,s); <tooth, wheel> Vorder-

front: ~ **door** n Haustür f. ~ **garden** n Vorgarten m

frontier n Grenze f

frost n Frost m; (hoar-~) Raureif m; **ten degrees of** ~ zehn Grad Kälte. ~**bite** n Erfrierung f. ~**bitten** a erfroren

frost|ed a ~ed glass Mattglas nt. ~**ing** n (Amer Culin) Zuckerguss m. ~**y** a, -ily adv frostig

froth n Schaum m ● vi schäumen. ~**y** a schaumig

frown n Stirnrunzeln nt ● vi die Stirn runzeln

froze see freeze

frozen see freeze ● a gefroren; (Culin) tiefgekühlt; **I'm** ~ ⊞ mir ist eiskalt. ~ **food** n Tiefkühlkost f

frugal a, -ly adv sparsam; <meal> frugal

fruit n Frucht f; (collectively) Obst nt. ~ **cake** n englischer [Tee]kuchen m

fruitful a fruchtbar

fruit: ~ **juice** n Obstsaft m. ~**less** a, -ly adv fruchtlos. ~ **salad** n Obstsalat m

fruity a fruchtig

frustrat|e vt vereiteln; (Psych) frustrieren. ~**ion** n Frustration f

fry vt/i (pt/pp fried) [in der Pfanne] braten. ~**ing-pan** n Bratpfanne f

fuel n Brennstoff m; (for car) Kraftstoff m; (for aircraft) Treibstoff m

fugitive n Flüchtling m

fulfil vt (pt/pp -filled) erfüllen. ~**ment** n Erfüllung f

full a & adv (-er, -est) voll; (detailed) ausführlich; <skirt> weit; ~ **of** voll von (+ dat), voller (+ gen); **at** ~ **speed** in voller Fahrt ● n **in** ~ vollständig

full: ~ **moon** n Vollmond m. ~-**scale** a <model> in Originalgröße; <rescue, alert> großangelegt. ~ **stop** n Punkt m. ~-**time** a ganztägig ● adv ganztags

fully adv völlig; (in detail) ausführlich

fumble vi herumfummeln (with an + dat)

fume vi vor Wut schäumen

fumes npl Dämpfe pl; (from car) Abgase pl

fun n Spaß m; **for** ~ aus od zum Spaß; **make** ~ **of** sich lustig machen über (+ acc); **have** ~! vie Spaß!

function n Funktion f; (event) Veranstaltung f ● vi funktionieren; (serve) dienen (as als). ~**al** a zweckmäßig

fund n Fonds m; (fig) Vorrat m; **~s** pl Geldmittel pl ● vt finanzieren

fundamental a grundlegend; (essential) wesentlich

funeral n Beerdigung f; (cremation) Feuerbestattung f

funeral: ~ march n Trauermarsch m. **~ service** n Trauergottesdienst m

funfair n Jahrmarkt m

fungus n (pl -gi) Pilz m

funnel n Trichter m; (on ship, train) Schornstein m

funnily adv komisch; **~ enough** komischerweise

funny a (-ier, -iest) komisch

fur n Fell nt; (for clothing) Pelz m; (in kettle) Kesselstein m. **~ coat** n Pelzmantel m

furious a, **-ly** adv wütend (**with** auf + acc)

furnace n (Techn) Ofen m

furnish vt einrichten; (supply) liefern. **~ed** a **~ed room** möbliertes Zimmer nt. **~ings** npl Einrichtungsgegenstände pl

furniture n Möbel pl

further a weitere(r,s); **at the ~ end** am anderen Ende; **until ~ notice** bis auf weiteres ● adv weiter; **~ off** weiter entfernt ● vt fördern

furthest a am weitesten entfernt ● adv am weitesten

fury n Wut f

fuse[1] n (of bomb) Zünder m; (cord) Zündschnur f

fuse[2] n (Electr) Sicherung f ● vt/i verschmelzen; **the lights have ~d** die Sicherung [für das Licht] ist durchgebrannt. **~-box** n Sicherungskasten m

fuselage n (Aviat) Rumpf m

fuss n Getue nt; **make a ~ of** verwöhnen; (caress) liebkosen ● vi Umstände machen

fussy a (-ier, -iest) wählerisch; (particular) penibel

futile a zwecklos. **~ity** n Zwecklosigkeit f

future a zukünftig ● n Zukunft f; (Gram) [erstes] Futur nt

futuristic a futuristisch

fuzzy a (-ier, -iest) <hair> kraus; (blurred) verschwommen

gabble vi schnell reden

gable n Giebel m

gadget n [kleines] Gerät nt

Gaelic n Gälisch nt

gag n Knebel m; (joke) Witz m; (Theat) Gag m ● vt (pt/pp **gagged**) knebeln

gaiety n Fröhlichkeit f

gaily adv fröhlich

gain n Gewinn m; (increase) Zunahme f ● vt gewinnen; (obtain) erlangen; **~ weight** zunehmen ● vi <clock:> vorgehen

gait n Gang m

gala n Fest nt ● attrib Gala-

galaxy n Galaxie f; **the G~** die Milchstraße

gale n Sturm m

gallant a, **-ly** adv tapfer; (chivalrous) galant. **~ry** n Tapferkeit f

gall-bladder n Gallenblase f

gallery n Galerie f

galley n (ship's kitchen) Kombüse f; **~ [proof]** [Druck]fahne f

gallon n Gallone f (= 4,5 l; Amer = 3,785 l)

gallop n Galopp m ● vi galoppieren

gallows n Galgen m

galore adv in Hülle und Fülle

gamble n (risk) Risiko nt ● vi
[um Geld] spielen; ~ **on** (rely)
sich verlassen auf (+ acc). ~**r** n
Spieler(in) m(f)

game n Spiel nt; (animals, birds)
Wild nt; ~**s** (Sch) Sport m ● a
(brave) tapfer; (willing) bereit (**for**
zu). ~**keeper** n Wildhüter m. ~**s**
console n Spielkonsole f

gammon n [geräucherter]
Schinken m

gang n Bande f; (of workmen)
Kolonne f

gangling a schlaksig

gangrene n Wundbrand m

gangster n Gangster m

gangway n Gang m; (Naut, Aviat)
Gangway f

gaol n Gefängnis nt ● vt ins
Gefängnis sperren. ~**er** n
Gefängniswärter m

gap n Lücke f; (interval) Pause f;
(difference) Unterschied m

gap|e vi gaffen; ~**e at** anstarren.
~**ing** a klaffend

garage n Garage f; (for repairs)
Werkstatt f; (for petrol)
Tankstelle f

garbage n Müll m. ~ **can** n
(Amer) Mülleimer m

garbled a verworren

garden n Garten m; [**public**] ~**s**
pl [öffentliche] Anlagen pl ● vi
im Garten arbeiten. ~**er** n
Gärtner(in) m(f). ~**ing** n
Gartenarbeit f

gargle n (liquid) Gurgelwasser nt
● vi gurgeln

garish a grell

garland n Girlande f

garlic n Knoblauch m

garment n Kleidungsstück nt

garnish n Garnierung f ● vt
garnieren

garrison n Garnison f

garter n Strumpfband nt; (Amer:
suspender) Strumpfhalter m

gas n Gas nt; (Amer 🛈: petrol)
Benzin nt ● v (pt/pp **gassed**) ● vt

vergasen ● vi 🛈 schwatzen. ~
cooker n Gasherd m. ~ **fire** n
Gasofen m

gash n Schnitt m; (wound)
klaffende Wunde f

gasket n (Techn) Dichtung f

gas: ~ **mask** n Gasmaske f. ~-
meter n Gaszähler m

gasoline n (Amer) Benzin nt

gasp vi keuchen; (in surprise)
hörbar die Luft einziehen

gas station n (Amer) Tankstelle f

gastric a Magen-

gastronomy n Gastronomie f

gate n Tor nt; (to field) Gatter nt;
(barrier) Schranke f; (at airport)
Flugsteig m

gate: ~**crasher** n ungeladener
Gast m. ~**way** n Tor nt

gather vt sammeln; (pick) pflücken;
(conclude) folgern (**from** aus) ● vi
sich versammeln; <storm:> sich
zusammenziehen. ~**ing** n family
~**ing** Familientreffen nt

gaudy a (-ier, -iest) knallig

gauge n Stärke f; (Rail)
Spurweite f; (device)
Messinstrument nt

gaunt a hager

gauze n Gaze f

gave see **give**

gay a (-er, -est) fröhlich; 🛈
homosexuell, 🛈 schwul

gaze n [langer] Blick m ● vi
sehen; ~ **at** ansehen

GB abbr of **Great Britain**

gear n Ausrüstung f; (Techn)
Getriebe nt; (Auto) Gang m;
change ~ schalten

gear: ~**box** n (Auto) Getriebe nt.
~-**lever** n, (Amer) ~-**shift** n
Schalthebel m

geese see **goose**

gel n Gel nt

gelatine n Gelatine f

gem n Juwel nt

gender n (Gram) Geschlecht nt

gene n Gen nt

genealogy n Genealogie f

general a allgemein ● n General
m; **in** ∼ im Allgemeinen. ∼
election n allgemeine Wahlen pl
generaliz|ation n
Verallgemeinerung f. ∼**e** vi
verallgemeinern
generally adv im Allgemeinen
general practitioner n
praktischer Arzt m
generate vt erzeugen
generation n Generation f
generator n Generator m
generosity n Großzügigkeit f
generous a, -ly adv großzügig
genetic a, ∼**ally** adv genetisch.
∼**ally modified** gentechnisch
verändert; genmanipuliert. ∼
engineering n Gentechnologie f
Geneva n Genf nt
genial a, -ly adv freundlich
genitals pl [äußere]
Geschlechtsteile pl
genitive a & n ∼ **[case]** Genitiv m
genius n (pl -uses) Genie nt;
(quality) Genialität f
genome n Genom nt
genre n Gattung f, Genre nt
gent n Ⓣ Herr m; **the** ∼**s** sg die
Herrentoilette f
genteel a vornehm
gentle a (-r, -st) sanft
gentleman n Herr m; (well-
mannered) Gentleman m
gent|leness n Sanftheit f. ∼**ly** adv
sanft
genuine a echt; (sincere)
aufrichtig. ∼**ly** adv (honestly)
ehrlich
geograph|ical a, -ly adv
geographisch. ∼**y** n Geographie
f, Erdkunde f
geological a, -ly adv geologisch
geolog|ist n Geologe m/-gin f. ∼**y**
n Geologie f
geometr|ic(al) a geometrisch. ∼**y**
n Geometrie f
geranium n Geranie f
geriatric a geriatrisch ● n
geriatrischer Patient m

germ n Keim m; ∼**s** pl Ⓣ Bazillen
pl
German a deutsch ● n (person)
Deutsche(r) m/f; (Lang) Deutsch
nt; **in** ∼ auf Deutsch; **into** ∼ ins
Deutsche
Germanic a germanisch
Germany n Deutschland nt
germinate vi keimen
gesticulate vi gestikulieren
gesture n Geste f

get v

G

pt **got**, pp **got** (Amer also
gotten), pres p **getting**
● transitive verb
····▸ (obtain, receive) bekommen,
Ⓣ kriegen; (procure) besorgen;
(buy) kaufen; (fetch) holen. **get a
job/taxi for s.o.** jdm einen Job
verschaffen/ein Taxi besorgen. **I
must get some bread** ich muss
Brot holen. **get permission** die
Erlaubnis erhalten. **I couldn't get
her on the phone** ich konnte sie
nicht telefonisch erreichen
····▸ (prepare) machen <meal>. **he
got the breakfast** er machte das
Frühstück
····▸ (cause) **get s.o. to do sth** jdn
dazu bringen, etw zu tun. **get
one's hair cut** sich (dat) die
Haare schneiden lassen. **get
one's hands dirty** sich (dat) die
Hände schmutzig machen
····▸ **get the bus/train** (travel by)
den Bus/Zug nehmen; (be in
time for, catch) den Bus/Zug
erreichen
····▸ **have got** (Ⓣ have) haben. **I've
got a cold** ich habe eine
Erkältung
····▸ **have got to do sth** etw tun
müssen. **I've got to hurry** ich
muss mich beeilen
····▸ (Ⓣ understand) kapieren Ⓣ. **I
don't get it** ich kapiere nicht
● intransitive verb

·····▶ (*become*) werden. **get older** älter werden. **the weather got worse** wurde das Wetter schlechter. **get to** kommen zu/ nach <*town*>; (*reach*) erreichen. **get dressed** sich anziehen. **get married** heiraten.

● *phrasal verbs*
● **get about** vi (*move*) sich bewegen; (*travel*) herumkommen; (*spread*) sich verbreiten. ● **get at** vt (*have access*) herankommen an (+ acc); (Ⅰ *criticize*) anmachen Ⅰ. (*mean*) **what are you getting at?** worauf willst du hinaus? ● **get away** vi (*leave*) wegkommen; (*escape*) entkommen. ● **get back** vi zurückkommen; vt (*recover*) zurückbekommen; **get one's own back** sich revanchieren. ● **get by** vi vorbeikommen; (*manage*) sein Auskommen haben. ● **get down** vi herunterkommen; **get down to** sich [heran]machen an (+ acc); vt (*depress*) deprimieren. ● **get in** vi (*into bus*) einsteigen; vt (*fetch*) hereinholen. ● **get off** vi (*dismount*) absteigen; (*from bus*) aussteigen; (*leave*) wegkommen; (*Jur*) freigesprochen werden; vt (*remove*) abbekommen. ● **get on** vi (*mount*) aufsteigen; (*to bus*) einsteigen; (*be on good terms*) gut auskommen (**with** mit + dat); (*make progress*) Fortschritte machen; **how are you getting on?** wie geht's? ● **get out** vi herauskommen; (*of car*) aussteigen; **get out of** (*avoid doing*) sich drücken um; vt (*take out*) herausholen; herausbekommen <*cork, stain*>. ● **get over** vi hinübersteigen; vt (*fig*) hinwegkommen über (+ acc).

● **get round** vi herumkommen; **I never get round to it** ich komme nie dazu; vt herumkriegen; (*avoid*) umgehen. ● **get through** vi durchkommen. ● **get up** vi aufstehen.

get: ∼**away** n Flucht f. ∼**-up** n Aufmachung f
ghastly a (-ier, -iest) grässlich; (*pale*) blass
gherkin n Essiggurke f
ghost n Geist m, Gespenst nt. ∼**ly** a geisterhaft
ghoulish a makaber
giant n Riese m ● a riesig
gibberish n Kauderwelsch nt
giblets npl Geflügelklein nt
giddiness n Schwindel m
giddy a (-ier, -iest) schwindlig
gift n Geschenk nt; (*to charity*) Gabe f; (*talent*) Begabung f. ∼**ed** a begabt
gigantic a riesig, riesengroß
giggle n Kichern nt ● vi kichern
gild vt vergolden
gilt a vergoldet ● n Vergoldung f. ∼**-edged** a (Comm) mündelsicher
gimmick n Trick m
gin n Gin m
ginger a rotblond; <*cat*> rot ● n Ingwer m. ∼**bread** n Pfefferkuchen m
gingerly adv vorsichtig
gipsy n = gypsy
giraffe n Giraffe f
girder n (Techn) Träger m
girl n Mädchen nt; (*young woman*) junge Frau f. ∼**friend** n Freundin f. ∼**ish** a, **-ly** adv mädchenhaft
gist n the ∼ das Wesentliche
give n Elastizität f ● v (pt gave, pp given) ● vt geben/(*as present*) schenken (**to** dat); (*donate*) spenden; <*lecture*> halten; <*one's name*> angeben ● vi geben; (*yield*) nachgeben. ∼ **away** vt verschenken; (*betray*) verraten; (*distribute*) verteilen. ∼ **back** vt

zurückgeben. ~ **in** vt einreichen ● vi (*yield*) nachgeben. ~ **off** vt abgeben. ~ **up** vt/i aufgeben; ~ **oneself up** sich stellen. ~ **way** vi nachgeben; (*Auto*) die Vorfahrt beachten

glacier n Gletscher m

glad a froh (**of** über + acc)

gladly adv gern[e]

glamorous a glanzvoll; <*film star*> glamourös

glamour n [betörender] Glanz m

glance n [flüchtiger] Blick m ● vi ~ **at** einen Blick werfen auf (+ acc). ~ **up** vi aufblicken

gland n Drüse f

glare n grelles Licht nt; (*look*) ärgerlicher Blick m ● vi ~ **at** böse ansehen

glaring a grell; <*mistake*> krass

glass n Glas nt; (*mirror*) Spiegel m; ~es pl (*spectacles*) Brille f. ~**y** a glasig

glaze n Glasur f

gleam n Schein m ● vi glänzen

glib a, **-ly** adv (*pej*) gewandt

glid|e vi gleiten; (*through the air*) schweben. ~**er** n Segelflugzeug nt. ~**ing** n Segelfliegen nt

glimmer n Glimmen nt ● vi glimmen

glimpse vt flüchtig sehen

glint n Blitzen nt ● vi blitzen

glisten vi glitzern

glitter vi glitzern

global a, **-ly** adv global

globaliz|e vt globalisieren. ~**ation** n Globalisierung f

globe n Kugel f; (*map*) Globus m

gloom n Düsterkeit f; (*fig*) Pessimismus m

gloomy a (**-ier, -iest**), **-ily** adv düster; (*fig*) pessimistisch

glorify vt (*pt/pp* **-ied**) verherrlichen

glorious a herrlich; <*deed, hero*> glorreich

glory n Ruhm m; (*splendour*) Pracht f ● vi ~ **in** genießen

gloss n Glanz m ● a Glanz- ● vi ~ **over** beschönigen

glossary n Glossar nt

glossy a (**-ier, -iest**) glänzend

glove n Handschuh m

glow n Glut f; (*of candle*) Schein m ● vi glühen; <*candle:*> scheinen. ~**ing** a glühend; <*account*> begeistert

glucose n Traubenzucker m, Glukose f

glue n Klebstoff m ● vt (*pres p* **gluing**) kleben (**to** an + acc)

glum a (**glummer, glummest**), **-ly** adv niedergeschlagen

glut n Überfluss m (**of** an + dat)

glutton n Vielfraß m

GM abbr (**genetically modified**); ~ **crops/food** gentechnisch veränderte Feldfrüchte/ Nahrungsmittel

gnash vt ~ **one's teeth** mit den Zähnen knirschen

gnat n Mücke f

gnaw vt/i nagen (**at** an + dat)

go
  3 sg pres tense **goes**; pt **went**; pp **gone**
● *intransitive verb*
···▶ gehen; (*in vehicle*) fahren. **go by air** fliegen. **where are you going?** wo gehst du hin? **I'm going to France** ich fahre nach Frankreich. **go to the doctor's/ dentist's** zum Arzt/Zahnarzt gehen. **go to the theatre/cinema** ins Theater/Kino gehen. **I must go to Paris/to the doctor's** ich muss nach Paris/zum Arzt. **go shopping** einkaufen gehen. **go swimming** schwimmen gehen. **go to see s.o.** jdn besuchen [gehen]
···▶ (*leave*) weggehen; (*on journey*) abfahren. **I must go now** ich muss jetzt gehen. **we're going on Friday** wir fahren am Freitag
···▶ (*work, function*) <*engine, clock*> gehen

····▸ *(become)* werden. **go deaf** taub werden. **go mad** verrückt werden. **he went red** er wurde rot

····▸ *(pass)* <*time*> vergehen

····▸ *(disappear)* weggehen; <*coat, hat, stain*> verschwinden. **my headache/my coat/the stain has gone** mein Kopfweh/mein Mantel/der Fleck ist weg

····▸ *(turn out, progress)* gehen; verlaufen. **everything's going very well** alles geht *od* verläuft sehr gut. **how did the party go?** wie war die Party? **go smoothly/according to plan** reibungslos/planmäßig verlaufen

····▸ *(match)* zusammenpassen. **the two colours don't go [together]** die beiden Farben passen nicht zusammen

····▸ *(cease to function)* kaputtgehen; <*fuse*> durchbrennen. **his memory is going** sein Gedächtnis lässt nach

● *auxiliary verb*

····▸ **be going to** werden + *inf.* **it's going to rain** es wird regnen. **I'm not going to** ich werde es nicht tun

● *noun*

pl **goes**

····▸ *(turn)* **it's your go** du bist jetzt an der Reihe *od* dran

····▸ *(attempt)* Versuch. **have a go at doing sth** Versuch, etw zu tun. **have another go!** versuch's noch mal!

····▸ *(energy, drive)* Energie

····▸ *(in phrases)* **on the go** auf Trab. **make a go of sth** das Beste aus etw machen

● *phrasal verbs*

● **go across** *vi* hinübergehen/-fahren; *vt* überqueren. ● **go after** *vt* *(pursue)* jagen. ● **go away** *vi* weggehen/-fahren; *(on holiday or business)* verreisen. ● **go back** *vi* zurückgehen/-fahren. ● **go back on** *vt* nicht

go by *vi* vorbeigehen/-fahren; <*time*> vergehen. ● **go down** *vi* hinuntergehen/-fahren; <*sun, ship*> untergehen; <*prices*> fallen; <*temperature, swelling*> zurückgehen. ● **go for** *vt* holen; (Ⅰ *attack*) losgehen auf (+ *acc*). ● **go in** *vi* hineingehen/-fahren; ● **go in for** *vt* teilnehmen an (+ *dat*) <*competition*>; *(take up)* sich verlegen auf (+ *acc*). ● **go off** *vi* weggehen/-fahren; <*alarm clock*> klingeln; <*alarm, gun, bomb*> losgehen; <*light*> ausgehen; *(go bad)* schlecht werden; **go off well** gut verlaufen; *vt*: **go off sth** von etw abkommen. ● **go on** *vi* weitergehen/-fahren; <*light*> angehen; *(continue)* weitermachen; *(talking)* fortfahren; *(happen)* vorgehen. ● **go on at** *vt* Ⅰ herumnörgeln an (+ *dat*). ● **go out** *vi* *(from home)* ausgehen; *(leave)* hinausgehen/-fahren; <*fire, light*> ausgehen; **go out to work/for a meal** arbeiten/essen gehen; **go out with s.o.** (Ⅰ *date s.o.*) mit jdm gehen Ⅰ. ● **go over** *vi* hinübergehen/-fahren; *vt* *(rehearse)* durchgehen. ● **go round** *vi* herumgehen/-fahren; *(visit)* vorbeigehen; *(turn)* sich drehen; *(be enough)* reichen. ● **go through** *vi* durchgehen/-fahren; *vt* *(suffer)* durchmachen; *(rehearse)* durchgehen; <*bags*> durchsuchen. ● **go through with** *vt* zu Ende machen. ● **go under** *vi* untergehen/-fahren; *(fail)* scheitern. ● **go up** *vi* hinaufgehen/-fahren; <*lift*> hochfahren; <*prices*> steigen. ● **go without** *vt*: **go without sth** auf etw (*acc*) verzichten; *vi* darauf verzichten

go-ahead a fortschrittlich; (*enterprising*) unternehmend ●n (*fig*) grünes Licht nt

goal n Ziel nt; (*sport*) Tor nt. **∼keeper** n Torwart m. **∼-post** n Torpfosten m

goat n Ziege f

gobble vt hinunterschlingen

God, god n Gott m

god: ∼child n Patenkind nt. **∼-daughter** n Patentochter f. **∼dess** n Göttin f. **∼father** n Pate m. **∼mother** n Patin f. **∼parents** npl Paten pl. **∼send** n Segen m. **∼son** n Patensohn m

goggles npl Schutzbrille f

going a <*price, rate*> gängig; <*concern*> gut gehend ●n **it is hard ∼** es ist schwierig

gold n Gold nt ●a golden

golden a golden. **∼ wedding** n goldene Hochzeit f

gold: ∼fish n inv Goldfisch m. **∼-mine** n Goldgrube f. **∼-plated** a vergoldet. **∼smith** n Goldschmied m

golf n Golf nt

golf: ∼-club n Golfklub m; (*implement*) Golfschläger m. **∼-course** n Golfplatz m. **∼er** m Golfspieler(in) m(f)

gone see **go**

good a (**better, best**) gut; (*well-behaved*) brav, artig; **∼ at** gut in (+ *dat*); **a ∼ deal** ziemlich viel; **∼ morning/evening** guten Morgen/Abend ●n **for ∼** für immer; **do ∼** Gutes tun; **do s.o. ∼** jdm gut tun; **it's no ∼** es ist nutzlos; (*hopeless*) da ist nichts zu machen

goodbye int auf Wiedersehen; (*Teleph, Radio*) auf Wiederhören

good: G∼ Friday n Karfreitag m. **∼-looking** a gut aussehend. **∼-natured** a gutmütig

goodness n Güte f; **thank ∼!** Gott sei Dank!

goods npl Waren pl. **∼ train** n Güterzug m

goodwill n Wohlwollen nt; (*Comm*) Goodwill m

gooey a 🗓 klebrig

goose n (pl **geese**) Gans f

gooseberry n Stachelbeere f

goose: ∼-flesh n, **∼-pimples** npl Gänsehaut f

gorge n (*Geog*) Schlucht f ●vt **∼ oneself** sich vollessen

gorgeous a prachtvoll; 🗓 herrlich

gorilla n Gorilla m

gormless a 🗓 doof

gorse n Stechginster m

gory a (**-ier, -iest**) blutig; <*story*> blutrünstig

gosh int 🗓 Mensch!

gospel n Evangelium nt

gossip n Klatsch m; (*person*) Klatschbase f ●vi klatschen

got see **get**; **have ∼** haben; **have ∼ to** müssen; **have ∼ to do sth** etw tun müssen

Gothic a gotisch

gotten see **get**

goulash n Gulasch nt

gourmet n Feinschmecker m

govern vt/i regieren; (*determine*) bestimmen

government n Regierung f

governor n Gouverneur m; (*on board*) Vorstandsmitglied nt; (*of prison*) Direktor m; (🗓 *boss*) Chef m

gown n [elegantes] Kleid nt; (*Univ, Jur*) Talar m

GP abbr of **general practitioner**

grab vt (*pt/pp* **grabbed**) ergreifen; **∼ [hold of]** packen

grace n Anmut f; (*before meal*) Tischgebet nt; **three days' ∼** drei Tage Frist. **∼ful** a, **-ly** adv anmutig

gracious a gnädig; (*elegant*) vornehm

grade n Stufe f; (*Comm*) Güteklasse f; (*Sch*) Note f; (*Amer, Sch: class*) Klasse f; (*Amer*) = **gradient** ●vt einstufen; (*Comm*)

sortieren. ~ **crossing** n (Amer)
Bahnübergang m

gradient n Steigung f;
(downward) Gefälle nt

gradual a, **-ly** adv allmählich

graduate n Akademiker(in) m(f)

graffiti npl Graffiti pl

graft n (Bot) Pfropfreis nt; (Med)
Transplantat nt; (🗉 hard work)
Plackerei f

grain n (sand, salt, rice) Korn nt;
(cereals) Getreide nt; (in wood)
Maserung f

gram n Gramm nt

grammar n Grammatik f. ~
school n ≈ Gymnasium nt

grammatical a, **-ly** adv
grammatisch

grand a (-er, -est) großartig

grandad n 🗉 Opa m

grandchild n Enkelkind nt

granddaughter n Enkelin f

grandeur n Pracht f

grandfather n Großvater m. ~
clock n Standuhr f

grandiose a grandios

grand: ~**mother** n Großmutter f.
~**parents** npl Großeltern pl. ~
piano n Flügel m. ~**son** n Enkel
m. ~**stand** n Tribüne f

granite n Granit m

granny n 🗉 Oma f

grant n Subvention f; (Univ)
Studienbeihilfe f ● vt gewähren;
(admit) zugeben; **take sth for** ~**ed**
etw als selbstverständlich
hinnehmen

grape n [Wein]traube f; **bunch of**
~**s** [ganze] Weintraube f

grapefruit n invar Grapefruit f

graph n grafische Darstellung f

graphic a, **-ally** adv grafisch;
(vivid) anschaulich

graph paper n Millimeterpapier
nt

grapple vi ringen

grasp n Griff m ● vt ergreifen;
(understand) begreifen. ~**ing** a
habgierig

grass n Gras nt; (lawn) Rasen m.
~**hopper** n Heuschrecke f

grassy a grasig

grate[1] n Feuerrost m; (hearth)
Kamin m

grate[2] vt (Culin) reiben

grateful a, **-ly** adv dankbar (**to**
dat)

grater n (Culin) Reibe f

gratify vt (pt/pp **-ied**) befriedigen.
~**ing** a erfreulich

gratis adv gratis

gratitude n Dankbarkeit f

gratuitous a (uncalled for)
überflüssig

grave[1] a (-r, -st), **-ly** adv ernst; ~**ly**
ill schwer krank

grave[2] n Grab nt. ~**-digger** n
Totengräber m

gravel n Kies m

grave: ~**stone** n Grabstein m.
~**yard** n Friedhof m

gravity n Ernst m; (force)
Schwerkraft f

gravy n [Braten]soße f

gray a (Amer) = grey

graze[1] vi <animal:> weiden

graze[2] n Schürfwunde f ● vt
<car> streifen; <knee>
aufschürfen

grease n Fett nt; (lubricant)
Schmierfett nt ● vt einfetten;
(lubricate) schmieren

greasy a (-ier, -iest) fettig

great a (-er, -est) groß; (🗉
marvellous) großartig

great: ~**-aunt** n Großtante f. **G~**
Britain n Großbritannien nt. ~**-**
grandchildren npl Urenkel pl.
~**-grandfather** n Urgroßvater m.
~**-grandmother** n Urgroßmutter f

great|ly adv sehr. ~**ness** n Größe
f

great-uncle n Großonkel m

Greece n Griechenland nt

greed n [Hab]gier f

greedy a (-ier, -iest), **-ily** adv gierig

Greek a griechisch ● n Grieche
m/Griechin f; (Lang) Griechisch

nt

green a (-er, -est) grün; (fig) unerfahren ●n Grün nt; (grass) Wiese f; ~s pl Kohl m; **the G~s** pl (Pol) die Grünen pl

greenery n Grün nt

green: ~**fly** n Blattlaus f. ~**grocer** n Obst- und Gemüsehändler m. ~**house** n Gewächshaus nt

Greenland n Grönland nt

greet vt grüßen; (welcome) begrüßen. ~**ing** n Gruß m; (welcome) Begrüßung f

grew see **grow**

grey a (-er, -est) grau ●n Grau nt ●vi grau werden. ~**hound** n Windhund m

grid n Gitter nt

grief n Trauer f

grievance n Beschwerde f

grieve vi trauern (for um)

grill n Gitter nt; (Culin) Grill m; **mixed** ~ Gemischtes nt vom Grill ●vt/i grillen; (interrogate) [streng] verhören

grille n Gitter nt

grim a (grimmer, grimmest), -ly adv ernst; <determination> verbissen

grimace n Grimasse f ●vi Grimassen schneiden

grime n Schmutz m

grimy a (-ier, -iest) schmutzig

grin n Grinsen nt ●vi (pt/pp grinned) grinsen

grind n (🄸 hard work) Plackerei f ●vt (pt/pp ground) mahlen; (smooth, sharpen) schleifen; (Amer: mince) durchdrehen

grip n Griff m; (bag) Reisetasche f ●vt (pt/pp gripped) ergreifen; (hold) festhalten

gripping a fesselnd

grisly a (-ier, -iest) grausig

gristle n Knorpel m

grit n [grober] Sand m; (for roads) Streugut nt; (courage) Mut m ●vt (pt/pp gritted) streuen <road>

groan n Stöhnen nt ●vi stöhnen

grocer n Lebensmittelhändler m; ~'s [shop] Lebensmittelgeschäft nt. ~**ies** npl Lebensmittel pl

groin n (Anat) Leiste f

groom n Bräutigam m; (for horse) Pferdepfleger(in) m(f) ●vt striegeln <horse>

groove n Rille f

grope vi tasten (for nach)

gross a (-er, -est) fett; (coarse) derb; (glaring) grob; (Comm) brutto; <salary, weight> Brutto-. ~**ly** adv (very) sehr

grotesque a, -ly adv grotesk

ground[1] see **grind**

ground[2] n Boden m; (terrain) Gelände nt; (reason) Grund m; (Amer, Electr) Erde f; ~s pl (park) Anlagen pl; (of coffee) Satz m

ground: ~ **floor** n Erdgeschoss nt. ~**ing** n Grundlage f. ~**less** a grundlos. ~**sheet** n Bodenplane f. ~**work** n Vorarbeiten pl

group n Gruppe f ●vt gruppieren ●vi sich gruppieren

grouse vi 🄸 meckern

grovel vi (pt/pp grovelled) kriechen

grow v (pt grew, pp grown) ●vi wachsen; (become) werden; (increase) zunehmen ●vt anbauen. ~ **up** vi aufwachsen; <town:> entstehen

growl n Knurren nt ●vi knurren

grown see **grow**. ~-**up** a erwachsen ●n Erwachsene(r) m/f

growth n Wachstum nt; (increase) Zunahme f; (Med) Gewächs nt

grub n (larva) Made f; (fam: food) Essen nt

grubby a (-ier, -iest) schmuddelig

grudge n Groll m ●vt ~e s.o. sth jdm etw missgönnen. ~**ing** a, -**ly** adv widerwillig

gruelling a strapaziös

gruesome a grausig

gruff a, -**ly** adv barsch

G

grumble vi schimpfen (**at** mit)

grumpy a (**-ier, -iest**) griesgrämig

grunt n Grunzen nt ● vi grunzen

guarantee n Garantie f; (document) Garantieschein m ● vt garantieren; garantieren für <quality, success>

guard n Wache f; (security) Wächter m; (on train) ≈ Zugführer m; (Techn) Schutz m; **be on** ∼ Wache stehen; **on one's** ∼ auf der Hut ● vt bewachen; (protect) schützen ● vi ∼ **against** sich hüten vor (+ dat). ∼**-dog** n Wachhund m

guarded a vorsichtig

guardian n Vormund m

guess n Vermutung f ● vt erraten ● vi raten; (Amer: believe) glauben. ∼**work** n Vermutung f

guest n Gast m. ∼**-house** n Pension f

guidance n Führung f, Leitung f; (advice) Beratung f

guide n Führer(in) m(f); (book) Führer m; [**Girl**] **G**∼ Pfadfinderin f ● vt führen, leiten. ∼**book** n Führer m

guided a ∼ **tour** Führung f

guide: ∼**-dog** n Blindenhund m. ∼**lines** npl Richtlinien pl

guilt n Schuld f. ∼**ily** adv schuldbewusst

guilty a (**-ier, -iest**) a schuldig (of gen); <look> schuldbewusst; <conscience> schlecht

guinea-pig n Meerschweinchen nt; (person) Versuchskaninchen nt

guitar n Gitarre f. ∼**ist** n Gitarrist(in) m(f)

gulf n (Geog) Golf m; (fig) Kluft f

gull n Möwe f

gullible a leichtgläubig

gully n Schlucht f; (drain) Rinne f

gulp n Schluck m ● vi schlucken ● vt ∼ **down** hinunterschlucken

gum¹ n & **-s** pl (Anat) Zahnfleisch nt

gum² n Gummi[harz] nt; (glue) Klebstoff m; (chewing gum) Kaugummi m

gummed see **gum**² ● a <label> gummiert

gun n Schusswaffe f; (pistol) Pistole f; (rifle) Gewehr nt; (cannon) Geschütz nt

gun: ∼**fire** n Geschützfeuer nt. ∼**man** bewaffneter Bandit m

gunner n Artillerist m

gunpowder n Schießpulver nt

gurgle vi gluckern; (of baby) glucksen

gush vi strömen; (enthuse) schwärmen (**over** von)

gust n (of wind) Windstoß m; (Naut) Bö f

gusto n **with** ∼ mit Schwung

gusty a böig

gut n Darm m; ∼**s** pl Eingeweide pl; (**I** courage) Schneid m ● vt (pt/pp **gutted**) (Culin) ausnehmen; ∼**ted by fire** ausgebrannt

gutter n Rinnstein m; (fig) Gosse f; (on roof) Dachrinne f

guy n **I** Kerl m

guzzle vt/i schlingen; (drink) schlürfen

gym n **I** Turnhalle f; (gymnastics) Turnen nt

gymnasium n Turnhalle f

gymnast n Turner(in) m(f). ∼**ics** n Turnen nt

gym shoes pl Turnschuhe pl

gynaecolog|ist n Frauenarzt m /-ärztin f. ∼**y** n Gynäkologie f

gypsy n Zigeuner(in) m(f)

habit n Gewohnheit f; (Relig: costume) Ordenstracht f; **be in the ~** die Angewohnheit haben (**of** zu)

habitat n Habitat nt

habitation n **unfit for human ~** für Wohnzwecke ungeeignet

habitual a gewohnt; (inveterate) gewohnheitsmäßig. **~ly** adv gewohnheitsmäßig; (constantly) ständig

hack¹ n (writer) Schreiberling m; (hired horse) Mietpferd nt

hack² vt hacken; **~ to pieces** zerhacken

hackneyed a abgedroschen

hacksaw n Metallsäge f

had see **have**

haddock n inv Schellfisch m

haggard a abgehärmt

haggle vi feilschen (**over** um)

hail¹ vt begrüßen; herbeirufen <taxi> ●vi **~ from** kommen aus

hail² n Hagel m ●vi hageln. **~stone** n Hagelkorn nt

hair n Haar nt; **wash one's ~** sich (dat) die Haare waschen

hair: ~brush n Haarbürste f. **~cut** n Haarschnitt m; **have a ~cut** sich (dat) die Haare schneiden lassen. **~-do** n 🔲 Frisur f. **~dresser** n Friseur m/ Friseuse f. **~-drier** n Haartrockner m; (hand-held) Föhn m. **~pin** n Haarnadel f. **~pin bend** n Haarnadelkurve f. **~-raising** a haarsträubend. **~-style** n Frisur f

hairy a (-ier, -iest) behaart; (excessively) haarig; (fam; frightening) brenzlig

hake n inv Seehecht m

half n (pl **halves**) Hälfte f; **cut in ~** halbieren; **one and a ~** eineinhalb, anderthalb; **~ a dozen** ein halbes Dutzend; **~ an hour** eine halbe Stunde ●a & adv halb; **~ past two** halb drei; **[at] ~ price** zum halben Preis

half: ~-hearted a lustlos. **~-term** n schulfreie Tage nach dem halben Trimester. **~-timbered** a Fachwerk-. **~-time** n (Sport) Halbzeit f. **~-way** a **the ~-way mark/stage** die Hälfte ●adv auf halbem Weg

halibut n inv Heilbutt m

hall n Halle f; (room) Saal m; (Sch) Aula f; (entrance) Flur m; (mansion) Gutshaus nt; **~ of residence** (Univ) Studentenheim nt

hallmark n [Feingehalts]stempel m; (fig) Kennzeichen nt (**of** für)

hallo int [guten] Tag! 🔲 hallo!

hallucination n Halluzination f

halo n (pl **-es**) Heiligenschein m; (Astr) Hof m

halt n Halt m; **come to a ~** stehen bleiben; <traffic:> zum Stillstand kommen ●vi Halt machen; **~!** halt! **~ing** a, adv **-ly** zögernd

halve vt halbieren; (reduce) um die Hälfte reduzieren

ham n Schinken m

hamburger n Hamburger m

hammer n Hammer m ●vt/i hämmern (**at** an + acc)

hammock n Hängematte f

hamper vt behindern

hamster n Hamster m

hand n Hand f; (of clock) Zeiger m; (writing) Handschrift f; (worker) Arbeiter(in) m(f); (Cards) Blatt nt; **on the one/other ~** einer-/andererseits; **out of ~** außer Kontrolle; (summarily) kurzerhand; **in ~** unter Kontrolle; (available) verfügbar; **give s.o. a ~** jdm behilflich sein ●vt reichen (**to** dat). **~ in** vt

abgeben. ~ **out** vt austeilen. ~
over vt überreichen

hand: ~**bag** n Handtasche f.
~**book** n Handbuch nt. ~**brake** n
Handbremse f. ~**cuffs** npl
Handschellen pl. ~**ful** n
Handvoll f; **be [quite] a** ~**ful** 🛈
nicht leicht zu haben sein

handicap n Behinderung f; (Sport
& fig) Handikap nt. ~**ped** a
mentally/physically ~**ped** geistig/
körperlich behindert

handkerchief n (pl ~**s** & **-chieves**)
Taschentuch nt

handle n Griff m; (of door) Klinke
f; (of cup) Henkel m; (of broom)
Stiel m ● vt handhaben; (treat)
umgehen mit; (touch) anfassen.
~**bars** npl Lenkstange f

hand: ~**made** a handgemacht. ~**s-
free kit** n Freisprecheinrichtung
f. ~**shake** n Händedruck m

handsome a gut aussehend;
(generous) großzügig; (large)
beträchtlich

hand: ~**writing** n Handschrift f.
~**written** a handgeschrieben

handy a (-ier, -iest) handlich;
<person> geschickt; **have/keep** ~
griffbereit haben/halten

hang vt/i (pt/pp hung) hängen; ~
wallpaper tapezieren ● vt (pt/pp
hanged) hängen <criminal> ● n
get the ~ **of it** 🛈 den Dreh
herauskriegen. ~ **about** vi sich
herumdrücken. ~ **on** vi sich
festhalten (**to** an + dat); (🛈 wait)
warten. ~ **out** vi heraushängen;
(🛈 live) wohnen ● vt draußen
aufhängen <washing>. ~ **up** vt/i
aufhängen

hangar n Flugzeughalle f

hanger n [Kleider]bügel m

hang: ~**-glider** n Drachenflieger
m. ~**-gliding** n Drachenfliegen nt.
~**man** n Henker m. ~**over** n 🛈
Kater m 🛈. ~**-up** n 🛈 Komplex
m

hanker vi ~ **after sth** sich (dat)
etw wünschen

hanky n 🛈 Taschentuch nt

haphazard a, **-ly** adv planlos

happen vi geschehen, passieren; **I**
~**ed to be there** ich war zufällig
da; **what has** ~**ed to him?** was ist
mit ihm los? (become of) was ist
aus ihm geworden? ~**ing** n
Ereignis nt

happi|ly adv glücklich;
(fortunately) glücklicherweise.
~**ness** n Glück nt

happy a (-ier, -iest) glücklich. ~**-
go-lucky** a sorglos

harass vt schikanieren. ~**ed** a
abgehetzt. ~**ment** n Schikane f;
(sexual) Belästigung f

harbour n Hafen m

hard a (-er, -est) hart; (difficult)
schwer; ~ **of hearing** schwerhörig
● adv hart; <work> schwer;
<pull> kräftig; <rain, snow> stark;
be ~ **up** 🛈 knapp bei Kasse sein;
be ~ **done by** 🛈 ungerecht
behandelt werden

hard: ~**back** n gebundene
Ausgabe f. ~**board** n
Hartfaserplatte f. ~**-boiled** a hart
gekocht

harden vi hart werden

hard-hearted a hartherzig

hard|ly adv kaum; ~**ly ever** kaum
[jemals]. ~**ness** n Härte f. ~**ship**
n Not f

hard: ~ **shoulder** n (Auto)
Randstreifen m. ~**ware** n
Haushaltswaren pl; (Computing)
Hardware f. ~**-wearing** a
strapazierfähig. ~**-working** a
fleißig

hardy a (-ier, -iest) abgehärtet;
<plant> winterhart

hare n Hase m

harm n Schaden m; **it won't do any**
~ es kann nichts schaden ● vt ~
s.o. jdm etwas antun. ~**ful** a
schädlich. ~**less** a harmlos

harmonious *a*, **-ly** *adv* harmonisch

harmon|ize *vi* (*fig*) harmonieren. **~y** *n* Harmonie *f*

harness *n* Geschirr *nt*; (*of parachute*) Gurtwerk *nt* ● *vt* anschirren <*horse*>; (*use*) nutzbar machen

harp *n* Harfe *f*. **~ist** *n* Harfenist(in) *m(f)*

harrowing *a* grauenhaft

harsh *a* (**-er, -est**), **-ly** *adv* hart; <*voice*> rau; <*light*> grell. **~ness** *n* Härte *f*; Rauheit *f*

harvest *n* Ernte *f* ● *vt* ernten

has *see* **have**

hassle *n* 🔟 Ärger *m* ● *vt* schikanieren

haste *n* Eile *f*

hasten *vi* sich beeilen (**to** zu); (*go quickly*) eilen ● *vt* beschleunigen

hasty *a* (**-ier, -iest**), **-ily** *adv* hastig; <*decision*> voreilig

hat *n* Hut *m*; (*knitted*) Mütze *f*

hatch[1] *n* (*for food*) Durchreiche *f*; (*Naut*) Luke *f*

hatch[2] *vi* **~[out]** ausschlüpfen ● *vt* ausbrüten

hatchback *n* (*Auto*) Modell *nt* mit Hecktür

hate *n* Hass *m* ● *vt* hassen. **~ful** *a* abscheulich

hatred *n* Hass *m*

haughty *a* (**-ier, -iest**), **-ily** *adv* hochmütig

haul *n* (*loot*) Beute *f* ● *vt/i* ziehen (**on** an + *dat*)

haunt *n* Lieblingsaufenthalt *m* ● *vt* umgehen in (+ *dat*); **this house is ~ed** in diesem Haus spukt es

have
3 sg pres tense **has**; pt and pp **had**
● *transitive verb*
····▶ (*possess*) haben. **he has [got] a car** er hat ein Auto. **she has [got] a brother** sie hat einen Bruder.

we have [got] five minutes wir haben fünf Minuten

····▶ (*eat*) essen; (*drink*) trinken; (*smoke*) rauchen. **have a cup of tea** eine Tasse Tee trinken. **have a pizza** eine Pizza essen. **have a cigarette** eine Zigarette rauchen. **have breakfast/dinner/lunch** frühstücken/zu Abend essen/zu Mittag essen

····▶ (*take esp. in shop, restaurant*) nehmen. **I'll have the soup/the red dress** ich nehme die Suppe/das rote Kleid. **have a cigarette!** nehmen Sie eine Zigarette!

····▶ (*get, receive*) bekommen. **I had a letter from her** ich bekam einen Brief von ihr. **have a baby** ein Baby bekommen

····▶ (*suffer*) haben <*illness, pain, disappointment*>; erleiden <*shock*>

····▶ (*organize*) **have a party** eine Party veranstalten. **they had a meeting** sie hielten eine Versammlung ab

····▶ (*take part in*) **have a game of football** Fußball spielen. **have a swim** schwimmen

····▶ (*as guest*) **have s.o. to stay** jdn zu Besuch haben

····▶ **have had it** 🔟 <*thing*> ausgedient haben; <*person*> geliefert sein. **you've had it now** jetzt ist es aus

····▶ **have sth done** etw machen lassen. **we had the house painted** wir haben das Haus malen lassen. **have a dress made** sich (*dat*) ein Kleid machen lassen. **have a tooth out** sich (*dat*) einen Zahn ziehen lassen. **have one's hair cut** sich (*dat*) die Haare schneiden lassen

····▶ **have to do sth** etw tun müssen. **I have to go now** ich muss jetzt gehen

● *auxiliary verb*

·····▸ (*forming perfect and past perfect tenses*) haben; (*with verbs of motion and some others*) sein. **I have seen him** ich habe ihn gesehen. **he has never been there** er ist nie da gewesen. **I had gone** ich war gegangen. **if I had known …** wenn ich gewusst hätte …

·····▸ (*in tag questions*) nicht wahr. **you've met her, haven't you?** du kennst sie, nicht wahr?

·····▸ (*in short answers*) **Have you seen the film? — Yes, I have** Hast du den Film gesehen? — Ja [, stimmt]

● ● **have on** vt (*be wearing*) anhaben; (*dupe*) anführen

havoc n Verwüstung f
hawk n Falke m
hawthorn n Hagedorn m
hay n Heu nt. ~ **fever** n Heuschnupfen m. ~**stack** n Heuschober m
hazard n Gefahr f; (*risk*) Risiko nt ● vt riskieren. ~**ous** a gefährlich; (*risky*) riskant
haze n Dunst m
hazel n Haselbusch m. ~**nut** n Haselnuss f
hazy a (-ier, -iest) dunstig; (*fig*) unklar
he pron er
head n Kopf m; (*chief*) Oberhaupt nt; (*of firm*) Chef(in) m(f); (*of school*) Schulleiter(in) m(f); (*on beer*) Schaumkrone f; (*of bed*) Kopfende nt; ~ **first** kopfüber ● vt anführen; (*Sport*) köpfen <*ball*> ● vi ~ **for** zusteuern auf (+ acc). ~**ache** n Kopfschmerzen pl
head|er n Kopfball m; (*dive*) Kopfsprung m. ~**ing** n Überschrift f
head: ~**lamp**, ~**light** n (*Auto*) Scheinwerfer m. ~**line** n Schlagzeile f. ~**long** adv kopfüber. ~**master** n Schulleiter

m. ~**mistress** n Schulleiterin f. ~**on** a & adv frontal. ~**phones** npl Kopfhörer m. ~**quarters** npl Hauptquartier nt; (*Pol*) Zentrale f. ~**rest** n Kopfstütze f. ~**room** r lichte Höhe f. ~**scarf** n Kopftuch nt. ~**strong** a eigenwillig. ~**way** n **make** ~**way** Fortschritte machen. ~**word** n Stichwort nt
heady a berauschend
heal vt/i heilen
health n Gesundheit f
health: ~ **farm** n Schönheitsfarm f. ~ **foods** npl Reformkost f. ~-**food shop** n Reformhaus nt. ~ **insurance** n Krankenversicherung f
healthy a (-ier, -iest), -**ily** adv gesund
heap n Haufen m; ~**s** [] jede Menge ● vt ~ **[up]** häufen
hear vt/i (*pt/pp heard*) hören; ~,~! hört, hört! **he would not ~ o'** it er ließ es nicht zu
hearing n Gehör nt; (*Jur*) Verhandlung f. ~-**aid** n Hörgerät nt
hearse n Leichenwagen m
heart n Herz nt; (*courage*) Mut m; ~**s** pl (*Cards*) Herz nt; **by** ~ auswendig
heart: ~**ache** n Kummer m. ~**attack** n Herzanfall m. ~**beat** n Herzschlag m. ~-**breaking** a herzzerreißend. ~-**broken** a untröstlich. ~**burn** n Sodbrennen nt. ~**en** vt ermutigen. ~**felt** a herzlich[st]
hearth n Herd m; (*fireplace*) Kamin m
heart|ily adv herzlich; <*eat*> viel. ~**less** a, -**ly** adv herzlos. ~**y** a herzlich; <*meal*> groß; <*person*> burschikos
heat n Hitze f; (*Sport*) Vorlauf m ● vt heiß machen; heizen <*room*>. ~**ed** a geheizt; <*swimming pool*> beheizt;

<discussion> hitzig. **~er** *n*
Heizgerät *nt*; *(Auto)* Heizanlage *f*
heath *n* Heide *f*
heathen *a* heidnisch ● *n* Heide
m/Heidin *f*
heather *n* Heidekraut *nt*
heating *n* Heizung *f*
heat wave *n* Hitzewelle *f*
heave *vt/i* ziehen; *(lift)* heben; *(Ⅰ*
throw) schmeißen
heaven *n* Himmel *m*. **~ly** *a*
himmlisch
heavy *a* (**-ier, -iest**), **-ily** *adv*
schwer; *<traffic, rain>* stark.
~weight *n* Schwergewicht *nt*
heckle *vt* [durch Zwischenrufe]
unterbrechen. **~r** *n*
Zwischenrufer *m*
hectic *a* hektisch
hedge *n* Hecke *f*. **~hog** *n* Igel *m*
heed *vt* beachten
heel¹ *n* Ferse *f*; *(of shoe)* Absatz
m; **down at ~** heruntergekommen
heel² *vi* **~ over** *(Naut)* sich auf die
Seite legen
hefty *a* (**-ier, -iest**) kräftig; *(heavy)*
schwer
height *n* Höhe *f*; *(of person)*
Größe *f*. **~en** *vt* *(fig)* steigern
heir *n* Erbe *m*. **~ess** *n* Erbin *f*.
~loom *n* Erbstück *nt*
held *see* **hold**²
helicopter *n* Hubschrauber *m*
hell *n* Hölle *f*; **go to ~!** ⚠ **geh zum**
Teufel! ● *int* verdammt!
hello *int* [guten] Tag! Ⅰ hallo!
helm *n* [Steuer]ruder *nt*
helmet *n* Helm *m*
help *n* Hilfe *f*; *(employees)*
Hilfskräfte *pl*; **that's no ~** das
nützt nichts ● *vt/i* helfen (**s.o.**
jdm); **~ oneself to sth** sich *(dat)*
etw nehmen; **~ yourself** *(at table)*
greif zu; **I could not ~ laughing** ich
musste lachen; **it cannot be ~ed**
es lässt sich nicht ändern; **I can't**
~ it ich kann nichts dafür
help|er *n* Helfer(in) *m(f)*. **~ful** *a*,
-ly *adv* hilfsbereit; *<advice>*

nützlich. **~ing** *n* Portion *f*. **~less**
a, **-ly** *adv* hilflos
hem *n* Saum *m* ● *vt* *(pt/pp*
hemmed) säumen; **~ in**
umzingeln
hemisphere *n* Hemisphäre *f*
hem-line *n* Rocklänge *f*
hen *n* Henne *f*; *(any female bird)*
Weibchen *nt*
hence *adv* daher; **five years ~** in
fünf Jahren. **~forth** *adv* von nun
an
henpecked *a* **~ husband**
Pantoffelheld *m*
her *a* ihr ● *pron* *(acc)* sie; *(dat)*
ihr
herald *vt* verkünden. **~ry** *n*
Wappenkunde *f*
herb *n* Kraut *nt*
herbaceous *a* **~ border**
Staudenrabatte *f*
herd *n* Herde *f*. **~ together** *vt*
zusammentreiben
here *adv* hier; *(to this place)*
hierher; **in ~** hier drinnen;
come/bring ~ herkommen/
herbringen
hereditary *a* erblich
here|sy *n* Ketzerei *f*. **~tic** *n*
Ketzer(in) *m(f)*
herewith *adv* *(Comm)* beiliegend
heritage *n* Erbe *nt*
hero *n* *(pl* **-es**) Held *m*
heroic *a*, **-ally** *adv* heldenhaft
heroin *n* Heroin *nt*
hero|ine *n* Heldin *f*. **~ism** *n*
Heldentum *nt*
heron *n* Reiher *m*
herring *n* Hering *m*
hers *poss pron* ihre(r), ihrs; **a**
friend of ~ ein Freund von ihr;
that is ~ das gehört ihr
herself *pron* selbst; *(refl)* sich; **by**
~ allein
hesitant *a*, **-ly** *adv* zögernd
hesitat|e *vi* zögern. **~ion** *n*
Zögern *nt*; **without ~ion** ohne zu
zögern
hexagonal *a* sechseckig

H

heyday n Glanzzeit f

hi int he! (hallo) Tag!

hiatus n (pl -tuses) Lücke f

hibernat|e vi Winterschlaf halten.
~ion n Winterschlaf m

hiccup n Hick m; (🔟 hitch) Panne
f; **have the ~s** den Schluckauf
haben ●vi hick machen

hid, hidden see hide²

hide v (pt hid, pp hidden) ●vt
verstecken; (keep secret)
verheimlichen ●vi sich
verstecken

hideous a, **-ly** adv hässlich;
(horrible) grässlich

hide-out n Versteck nt

hiding¹ n 🔟 **give s.o. a ~** jdn
verdreschen

hiding² n **go into ~** untertauchen

hierarchy n Hierarchie f

high a (-er, -est) hoch; attrib
hohe(r,s); <meat> angegangen;
<wind> stark; (on drugs) high; **it's
~ time** es ist höchste Zeit ●adv
hoch; **~ and low** überall ●n Hoch
nt; (temperature)
Höchsttemperatur f

high: **~brow** a intellektuell.
~chair n Kinderhochstuhl m. **~-
handed** a selbstherrlich. **~-
heeled** a hochhackig. **~ jump** n
Hochsprung m

highlight n (fig) Höhepunkt m;
~s pl (in hair) helle Strähnen pl
●vt (emphasize) hervorheben

highly adv hoch; **speak ~ of**
loben; **think ~ of** sehr schätzen.
~-strung a nervös

Highness n Hoheit f

high: **~ season** n Hochsaison f. **~
street** n Hauptstraße f. **~ tide** n
Hochwasser nt. **~way** n public
~way öffentliche Straße f

hijack vt entführen. **~er** n
Entführer m

hike n Wanderung f ●vi
wandern. **~r** n Wanderer m

hilarious a sehr komisch

hill n Berg m; (mound) Hügel m;
(slope) Hang m

hill: **~side** n Hang m. **~y** a
hügelig

him pron (acc) ihn; (dat) ihm.
~self pron selbst; (refl) sich; **by
~self** allein

hind a Hinter-

hind|er vt hindern. **~rance** n
Hindernis nt

hindsight n **with ~** rückblickend

Hindu n Hindu m ●a Hindu-.
~ism n Hinduismus m

hinge n Scharnier nt; (on door)
Angel f

hint n Wink m, Andeutung f;
(advice) Hinweis m; (trace) Spur
f ●vi **~ at** anspielen auf (+ acc)

hip n Hüfte f

hip pocket n Gesäßtasche f

hippopotamus n (pl -muses or
-mi) Nilpferd nt

hire vt mieten <car>; leihen
<suit>; einstellen <person>;
~[out] vermieten; verleihen

his a sein ●poss pron seine(r),
seins; **a friend of ~** ein Freund
von ihm; **that is ~** das gehört ihm

hiss n Zischen nt ●vt/i zischen

historian n Historiker(in) m(f)

historic a historisch. **~al** a, **-ly**
adv geschichtlich, historisch

history n Geschichte f

hit n (blow) Schlag m; (🔟 success)
Erfolg m; **direct ~** Volltreffer m
●vt/i (pt/pp hit, pres p hitting)
schlagen; (knock against, collide
with, affect) treffen; **~ the target**
das Ziel treffen; **~ on** (fig)
kommen auf (+ acc); **~ it off** gut
auskommen (with mit); **~ one's
head on sth** sich (dat) den Kopf
an etw (dat) stoßen

hitch n Problem nt; **technical ~**
Panne f ●vt festmachen (**to** an +
dat); **~ up** hochziehen. **~-hike** vi
🔟 trampen. **~-hiker** n
Anhalter(in) m(f)

hive n Bienenstock m

hoard n Hort m ● vt horten, hamstern

hoarding n Bauzaun m; (with advertisements) Reklamewand f

hoar-frost n Raureif m

hoarse a (-r, -st), **-ly** adv heiser. **~ness** Heiserkeit f

hoax n übler Scherz m; (false alarm) blinder Alarm m

hobble vi humpeln

hobby n Hobby nt. **~-horse** n (fig) Lieblingsthema nt

hockey n Hockey nt

hoe n Hacke f ● vt (pres p **hoeing**) hacken

hog vt (pt/pp **hogged**) 🗉 mit Beschlag belegen

hoist n Lastenaufzug m ● vt hochziehen; hissen <flag>

hold¹ n (Naut) Laderaum m

hold² n Halt m; (Sport) Griff m; (fig: influence) Einfluss m; **get ~ of** fassen; (🗉 contact) erreichen ● v (pt/pp **held**) ● vt halten; <container:> fassen; (believe) meinen; (possess) haben; anhalten <breath> ● vi <rope:> halten; <weather:> sich halten. **~ back** vt zurückhalten ● vi zögern. **~ on** vi (wait) warten; (on telephone) am Apparat bleiben; **~ on to** (keep) behalten; (cling to) sich festhalten an (+ dat). **~ out** vt hinhalten ● vi (resist) aushalten. **~ up** vt hochhalten; (delay) aufhalten; (rob) überfallen

hold|all n Reisetasche f. **~er** n Inhaber(in) m(f); (container) Halter m. **~-up** n Verzögerung f; (attack) Überfall m

hole n Loch nt

holiday n Urlaub m; (Sch) Ferien pl; (public) Feiertag m; (day off) freier Tag m; **go on ~** in Urlaub fahren

holiness n Heiligkeit f

Holland n Holland nt

hollow a hohl; <promise> leer ● n Vertiefung f; (in ground) Mulde f. **~ out** vt aushöhlen

holly n Stechpalme f

holster n Pistolentasche f

holy a (-ier, -est) heilig. **H~ Ghost** or **Spirit** n Heiliger Geist m

homage n Huldigung f; **pay ~ to** huldigen (+ dat)

home n Zuhause nt (house) Haus nt; (institution) Heim nt; (native land) Heimat f ● adv **at ~** zu Hause; **come/go ~** nach Hause kommen/gehen

home: ~ address n Heimatanschrift f. **~ game** n Heimspiel nt. **~land** n Heimatland nt. **~less** a obdachlos

homely a (-ier, -iest) a gemütlich; (Amer: ugly) unscheinbar

home: ~-made a selbst gemacht. **H~ Office** n Innenministerium nt. **~ page** n Homepage f. **H~ Secretary** Innenminister m. **~sick** a **be ~sick** Heimweh haben (**for** nach). **~sickness** n Heimweh nt. **~ town** n Heimatstadt f. **~work** n (Sch) Hausaufgaben pl

homosexual a homosexuell ● n Homosexuelle(r) m/f

honest a, **-ly** adv ehrlich. **~y** n Ehrlichkeit f

honey n Honig m; (🗉 darling) Schatz m

honey: ~comb n Honigwabe f. **~moon** n Flitterwochen pl; (journey) Hochzeitsreise f

honorary a ehrenamtlich; <member, doctorate> Ehren-

honour n Ehre f ● vt ehren; honorieren <cheque>. **~able** a, **-bly** adv ehrenhaft

hood n Kapuze f; (of car, pram) [Klapp]verdeck nt; (over cooker) Abzugshaube f; (Auto, Amer) Kühlerhaube f

hoof n (pl **~s** or **hooves**) Huf m

hook n Haken m ● vt festhaken (**to** an + acc)
hook|ed a ~**ed nose** Hakennase f; ~**ed on** Ⓣ abhängig von; (keen on) besessen von. ~**er** n (Amer ✖) Nutte f
hookey n **play** ~ (Amer Ⓣ) schwänzen
hooligan n Rowdy m. ~**ism** n Rowdytum nt
hooray int & n = **hurrah**
hoot n Ruf m; ~**s of laughter** schallendes Gelächter nt ● vi <owl:> rufen; <car:> hupen; (jeer) johlen. ~**er** n (of factory) Sirene f; (Auto) Hupe f
hoover n H~ (P) Staubsauger m ● vt/i [staub]saugen
hop¹ n, & ~**s** pl Hopfen m
hop² vi (pt/pp hopped) hüpfen; ~ **it!** Ⓣ hau ab!
hope n Hoffnung f; (prospect) Aussicht f (**of** auf + acc) ● vt/i hoffen (**for** auf + acc); **I** ~ **so** hoffentlich
hope|ful a hoffnungsvoll; **be** ~**ful that** hoffen, dass. ~**fully** adv hoffnungsvoll; (it is hoped) hoffentlich. ~**less** a, **-ly** adv hoffnungslos; (useless) nutzlos; (incompetent) untauglich
horde n Horde f
horizon n Horizont m
horizontal a, **-ly** adv horizontal. ~ **bar** n Reck nt
horn n Horn nt; (Auto) Hupe f
hornet n Hornisse f
horoscope n Horoskop nt
horrible a, **-bly** adv schrecklich
horrid a grässlich
horrific a entsetzlich
horrify vt (pt/pp -ied) entsetzen
horror n Entsetzen nt
hors-d'œuvre n Vorspeise f
horse n Pferd nt
horse: ~**back** n **on** ~**back** zu Pferde. ~**man** n Reiter m. ~**power** n Pferdestärke f. ~**racing** n Pferderennen nt.

~**radish** n Meerrettich m. ~**shoe** n Hufeisen nt
horticulture n Gartenbau m
hose n (pipe) Schlauch m ● vt ~ **down** abspritzen
hosiery n Strumpfwaren pl
hospitable a, **-bly** adv gastfreundlich
hospital n Krankenhaus nt
hospitality n Gastfreundschaft f
host n Gastgeber m
hostage n Geisel f
hostel n [Wohn]heim nt
hostess n Gastgeberin f
hostile a feindlich; (unfriendly) feindselig
hostilit|y n Feindschaft f; ~**ies** pl Feindseligkeiten pl
hot a (hotter, hottest) heiß; <meal> warm; (spicy) scharf; **I am** or **feel** ~ mir ist heiß
hotel n Hotel nt
hot: ~**head** n Hitzkopf m. ~**house** n Treibhaus nt. ~**ly** adv (fig) heiß, heftig. ~**plate** n Tellerwärmer m; (of cooker) Kochplatte f. ~ **tap** n Warmwasserhahn m. ~-**tempered** a jähzornig. ~-**water bottle** n Wärmflasche f
hound n Jagdhund m ● vt (fig) verfolgen
hour n Stunde f. ~**ly** a & adv stündlich
house¹ n Haus nt; **at my** ~ bei mir
house² vt unterbringen
house: ~**breaking** n Einbruch m. ~**hold** n Haushalt m. ~**holder** n Hausinhaber(in) m(f). ~**keeper** n Haushälterin f. ~**keeping** n Hauswirtschaft f; (money) Haushaltsgeld nt. ~-**plant** n Zimmerpflanze f. ~-**trained** a stubenrein. ~-**warming** n **have a** ~-**warming party** Einstand feiern. ~**wife** n Hausfrau f. ~**work** n Hausarbeit f
housing n Wohnungen pl; (Techn) Gehäuse nt

hovel *n* elende Hütte *f*
hover *vi* schweben. **~craft** *n* Luftkissenfahrzeug *nt*
how *adv* wie; **~ do you do?** guten Tag!; **and ~!** und ob!
however *adv* (*in question*) wie; (*nevertheless*) jedoch, aber; **~ small** wie klein es auch sein mag
howl *n* Heulen *nt* ●*vi* heulen; <*baby:*> brüllen
hub *n* Nabe *f*
huddle *vi* **~ together** sich zusammendrängen
huff *n* **in a ~** beleidigt
hug *n* Umarmung *f* ●*vt* (*pt/pp* **hugged**) umarmen
huge *a*, **-ly** *adv* riesig
hull *n* (*Naut*) Rumpf *m*
hullo *int* = **hallo**
hum *n* Summen *nt*; Brummen *nt* ●*vt/i* (*pt/pp* **hummed**) summen; <*motor:*> brummen
human *a* menschlich ●*n* Mensch *m*. **~ being** *n* Mensch *m*
humane *a*, **-ly** *adv* human
humanitarian *a* humanitär
humanity *n* Menschheit *f*
humble *a* (**-r**, **-st**), **-bly** *adv* demütig ●*vt* demütigen
humdrum *a* eintönig
humid *a* feucht. **~ity** *n* Feuchtigkeit *f*
humiliat|e *vt* demütigen. **~ion** *n* Demütigung *f*
humility *n* Demut *f*
humorous *a*, **-ly** *adv* humorvoll; <*story*> humoristisch
humour *n* Humor *m*; (*mood*) Laune *f*; **have a sense of ~** Humor haben
hump *n* Buckel *m*; (*of camel*) Höcker *m* ●*vt* schleppen
hunch *n* (*idea*) Ahnung *f*
hunchback *n* Bucklige(r) *m/f*
hundred *a* **one/a ~** [ein]hundert ●*n* Hundert *nt*; (*written figure*) Hundert *f*. **~th** *a* hundertste(r,s) ●*n* Hundertstel *nt*. **~weight** *n* ≈ Zentner *m*

hung *see* **hang**
Hungarian *a* ungarisch ●*n* Ungar(in) *m(f)*
Hungary *n* Ungarn *nt*
hunger *n* Hunger *m*. **~-strike** *n* Hungerstreik *m*
hungry *a* (**-ier**, **-iest**), **-ily** *adv* hungrig; **be ~** Hunger haben
hunt *n* Jagd *f*; (*for criminal*) Fahndung *f* ●*vt/i* jagen; fahnden nach <*criminal*>; **~ for** suchen. **~er** *n* Jäger *m*; (*horse*) Jagdpferd *nt*. **~ing** *n* Jagd *f*
hurdle *n* (*Sport & fig*) Hürde *f*
hurl *vt* schleudern
hurrah, **hurray** *int* hurra! ●*n* Hurra *nt*
hurricane *n* Orkan *m*
hurried *a*, **-ly** *adv* eilig; (*superficial*) flüchtig
hurry *n* Eile *f*; **be in a ~** es eilig haben ●*vi* (*pt/pp* **-ied**) sich beeilen; (*go quickly*) eilen. **~ up** *vi* sich beeilen ●*vt* antreiben
hurt *n* Schmerz *m* ●*vt/i* (*pt/pp* **hurt**) weh tun (+ *dat*); (*injure*) verletzen; (*offend*) kränken
hurtle *vi* **~ along** rasen
husband *n* [Ehe]mann *m*
hush *n* Stille *f* ●*vt* **~ up** vertuschen. **~ed** *a* gedämpft
husky *a* (**-ier**, **-iest**) heiser; (*burly*) stämmig
hustle *vt* drängen ●*n* Gedränge *nt*
hut *n* Hütte *f*
hutch *n* [Kaninchen]stall *m*
hybrid *a* hybrid ●*n* Hybride *f*
hydraulic *a*, **-ally** *adv* hydraulisch
hydroelectric *a* hydroelektrisch
hydrogen *n* Wasserstoff *m*
hygien|e *n* Hygiene *f*. **~ic** *a*, **-ally** *adv* hygienisch
hymn *n* Kirchenlied *nt*. **~-book** *n* Gesangbuch *nt*
hyphen *n* Bindestrich *m*. **~ate** *vt* mit Bindestrich schreiben
hypno|sis *n* Hypnose *f*. **~tic** *a* hypnotisch

H

hypno|tism n Hypnotik f. **~tist** n Hypnotiseur m. **~tize** vt hypnotisieren

hypochondriac n Hypochonder m

hypocrisy n Heuchelei f

hypocrite n Heuchler(in) m(f)

hypodermic a & n ~ **[syringe]** Injektionsspritze f

hypothe|sis n Hypothese f. **~tical** a, **-ly** adv hypothetisch

hyster|ia n Hysterie f. **~ical** a, **-ly** adv hysterisch. **~ics** npl hysterischer Anfall m

I pron ich

ice n Eis nt ● vt mit Zuckerguss überziehen <cake>

ice: **~berg** n Eisberg m. **~box** n (Amer) Kühlschrank m. **~-cream** n [Speise]eis nt. **~-cube** n Eiswürfel m

Iceland n Island nt

ice: **~lolly** n Eis nt am Stiel. **~ rink** n Eisbahn f

icicle n Eiszapfen m

icing n Zuckerguss m. **~ sugar** n Puderzucker m

icon n Ikone f

icy a (-ier, -iest), **-ily** adv eisig; <road> vereist

idea n Idee f; (conception) Vorstellung f; **I have no ~!** ich habe keine Ahnung!

ideal a ideal ● n Ideal nt. **~ism** n Idealismus m. **~ist** n Idealist(in) m(f). **~istic** a idealistisch. **~ize** vt idealisieren. **~ly** adv ideal; (in ideal circumstances) idealerweise

identical a identisch; <twins> eineiig

identi|fication n Identifizierung f; (proof of identity) Ausweispapiere pl. **~fy** vt (pt/pp -ied) identifizieren

identity n Identität f. **~ card** n [Personal]ausweis m

idiom n [feste] Redewendung f. **~atic** a, **-ally** adv idiomatisch

idiosyncrasy n Eigenart f

idiot n Idiot m. **~ic** a idiotisch

idle a (-r, -st), **-ly** adv untätig; (lazy) faul; (empty) leer; <machine> nicht in Betrieb ● vi faulenzen; <engine:> leer laufen. **~ness** n Untätigkeit f; Faulheit f

idol n Idol nt. **~ize** vt vergöttern

idyllic a idyllisch

i.e. abbr (id est) d.h.

if conj wenn; (whether) ob; **as if** als ob

ignition n (Auto) Zündung f. **~ key** n Zündschlüssel m

ignoramus n Ignorant m

ignoran|ce n Unwissenheit f. **~t** a unwissend

ignore vt ignorieren

ill a krank; (bad) schlecht; **feel ~ at ease** sich unbehaglich fühlen ● adv schlecht

illegal a, **-ly** adv illegal

illegible a, **-bly** adv unleserlich

illegitimate a unehelich; <claim> unberechtigt

illicit a, **-ly** adv illegal

illiterate a **be ~te** nicht lesen und schreiben können

illness n Krankheit f

illogical a, **-ly** adv unlogisch

ill-treat vt misshandeln. **~ment** n Misshandlung f

illuminat|e vt beleuchten. **~ion** n Beleuchtung f

illusion n Illusion f; **be under the ~ that** sich (dat) einbilden, dass

illustrat|e vt illustrieren. **~ion** n Illustration f

illustrious a berühmt

image *n* Bild *nt*; (*statue*) Standbild *nt*; (*exact likeness*) Ebenbild *nt*; [public] ~ Image *nt*

imagin|able *a* vorstellbar. ~**ary** *a* eingebildet

imagination *n* Fantasie *f*; (*fancy*) Einbildung *f*. ~**ive** *a*, **-ly** *adv* fantasievoll; (*full of ideas*) einfallsreich

imagine *vt* sich (*dat*) vorstellen; (*wrongly*) sich (*dat*) einbilden

imbecile *n* Schwachsinnige(r) *m/f*; (*pej*) Idiot *m*

imitat|e *vt* nachahmen, imitieren. ~**ion** *n* Nachahmung *f*, Imitation *f*

immaculate *a*, **-ly** *adv* tadellos; (*Relig*) unbefleckt

immature *a* unreif

immediate *a* sofortig; (*nearest*) nächste(r,s). ~**ly** *adv* sofort; ~**ly next to** unmittelbar neben ● *conj* sobald

immemorial *a* **from time** ~ seit Urzeiten

immense *a*, **-ly** *adv* riesig; ⚠ enorm

immerse *vt* untertauchen

immigrant *n* Einwanderer *m*

immigration *n* Einwanderung *f*

imminent *a* **be** ~ unmittelbar bevorstehen

immobil|e *a* unbeweglich. ~**ize** *vt* (*fig*) lähmen; (*Med*) ruhig stellen. ~**izer** *n* (*Auto*) Wegfahrsperre *f*

immodest *a* unbescheiden

immoral *a*, **-ly** *adv* unmoralisch. ~**ity** *n* Unmoral *f*

immortal *a* unsterblich. ~**ity** *n* Unsterblichkeit *f*. ~**ize** *vt* verewigen

immune *a* immun (**to/from** gegen)

immunity *n* Immunität *f*

imp *n* Kobold *m*

impact *n* Aufprall *m*; (*collision*) Zusammenprall *m*; (*of bomb*) Einschlag *m*; (*fig*) Auswirkung *f*

impair *vt* beeinträchtigen

impart *vt* übermitteln (**to** *dat*); vermitteln <*knowledge*>

impartial *a* unparteiisch. ~**ity** *n* Unparteilichkeit *f*

impassable *a* unpassierbar

impassioned *a* leidenschaftlich

impassive *a*, **-ly** *adv* unbeweglich

impatien|ce *n* Ungeduld *f*. ~**t** *a*, **-ly** *adv* ungeduldig

impeccable *a*, **-bly** *adv* tadellos

impede *vt* behindern

impediment *n* Hindernis *nt*; (*in speech*) Sprachfehler *m*

impel *vt* (*pt/pp* **impelled**) treiben

impending *a* bevorstehend

impenetrable *a* undurchdringlich

imperative *a* **be** ~ dringend notwendig sein ● *n* (*Gram*) Imperativ *m*

imperceptible *a* nicht wahrnehmbar

imperfect *a* unvollkommen; (*faulty*) fehlerhaft ● *n* (*Gram*) Imperfekt *nt*. ~**ion** *n* Unvollkommenheit *f*; (*fault*) Fehler *m*

imperial *a* kaiserlich. ~**ism** *n* Imperialismus *m*

impersonal *a* unpersönlich

impersonat|e *vt* sich ausgeben als; (*Theat*) nachahmen, imitieren. ~**or** *n* Imitator *m*

impertinen|ce *n* Frechheit *f*. ~**t** *a* frech

imperturbable *a* unerschütterlich

impetuous *a*, **-ly** *adv* ungestüm

impetus *n* Schwung *m*

implacable *a* unerbittlich

implant *vt* einpflanzen

implement[1] *n* Gerät *nt*

implement[2] *vt* ausführen

implication *n* Verwicklung *f*; ~**s** *pl* Auswirkungen *pl*; **by** ~ implizit

implicit *a*, **-ly** *adv* unausgesprochen; (*absolute*) unbedingt

implore *vt* anflehen

imply *vt* (*pt/pp* -ied) andeuten; **what are you ~ing?** was wollen Sie damit sagen?

impolite *a*, **-ly** *adv* unhöflich

import[1] *n* Import *m*, Einfuhr *f*

import[2] *vt* importieren, einführen

importan|ce *n* Wichtigkeit *f*. **~t** *a* wichtig

importer *n* Importeur *m*

impos|e *vt* auferlegen (**on** *dat*) ● *vi* sich aufdrängen (**on** *dat*). **~ing** *a* eindrucksvoll

impossibility *n* Unmöglichkeit *f*

impossible *a*, **-bly** *adv* unmöglich

impostor *n* Betrüger(in) *m(f)*

impoten|ce *n* Machtlosigkeit *f*; (*Med*) Impotenz *f*. **~t** *a* machtlos; (*Med*) impotent

impoverished *a* verarmt

impracticable *a* undurchführbar

impractical *a* unpraktisch

imprecise *a* ungenau

impress *vt* beeindrucken; **~ sth [up]on s.o.** jdm etw einprägen

impression *n* Eindruck *m*; (*imitation*) Nachahmung *f*; (*edition*) Auflage *f*. **~ism** *n* Impressionismus *m*

impressive *a* eindrucksvoll

imprison *vt* gefangen halten; (*put in prison*) ins Gefängnis sperren

improbable *a* unwahrscheinlich

impromptu *a* improvisiert ● *adv* aus dem Stegreif

improper *a*, **-ly** *adv* inkorrekt; (*indecent*) unanständig

impropriety *n* Unkorrektheit *f*

improve *vt* verbessern; verschönern <*appearance*> ● *vi* sich bessern; **~ [up]on** übertreffen. **~ment** *n* Verbesserung *f*; (*in health*) Besserung *f*

improvise *vt/i* improvisieren

imprudent *a* unklug

impuden|ce *n* Frechheit *f*. **~t** *a*, **-ly** *adv* frech

impuls|e *n* Impuls *m*; **on [an] ~e** impulsiv. **~ive** *a*, **-ly** *adv* impulsiv

impur|e *a* unrein. **~ity** *n* Unreinheit *f*

in *prep* in (+ *dat*/(*into*) + *acc*); **sit in the garden** im Garten sitzen; **go in the garden** in den Garten gehen; **in May** im Mai; **in 1992** [im Jahre] 1992; **in this heat** bei dieser Hitze; **in the evening** am Abend; **in the sky** am Himmel; **in the world** auf der Welt; **in the street** auf der Straße; **deaf in one ear** auf einem Ohr taub; **in the army** beim Militär; **in English/German** auf Englisch/Deutsch; **in ink/pencil** mit Tinte/Bleistift; **in a soft/loud voice** mit leiser/lauter Stimme; **in doing this, he …** indem er das tut/tat, … er ● *adv* (*at home*) zu Hause; (*indoors*) drinnen; **he's not in yet** er ist noch nicht da; **all in** alles inbegriffen; (🗓) *exhausted*) kaputt; **day in, day out** tagaus, tagein; **have it in for s.o.** 🗓 es auf jdn abgesehen haben; **send/go in** hineinschicken/ -gehen; **come/bring in** hereinkommen/-bringen ● *a* (🗓 *in fashion*) in ● *n* **the ins and outs** alle Einzelheiten *pl*

inability *n* Unfähigkeit *f*

inaccessible *a* unzugänglich

inaccura|cy *n* Ungenauigkeit *f*. **~te** *a*, **-ly** *adv* ungenau

inac|tive *a* untätig. **~tivity** *n* Untätigkeit *f*

inadequate *a*, **-ly** *adv* unzulänglich

inadmissible *a* unzulässig

inadvertently *adv* versehentlich

inadvisable *a* nicht ratsam

inane *a*, **-ly** *adv* albern

inanimate *a* unbelebt

inapplicable *a* nicht zutreffend

inappropriate *a* unangebracht

inarticulate *a* undeutlich; **be ~** sich nicht gut ausdrücken können

inattentive *a* unaufmerksam

inaudible *a*, **-bly** *adv* unhörbar

inaugural a Antritts-
inauspicious a ungünstig
inborn a angeboren
inbred a angeboren
incalculable a nicht
berechenbar; (*fig*) unabsehbar
incapable a unfähig; **be ~ of**
doing sth nicht fähig sein, etw zu
tun
incapacitate vt unfähig machen
incarnation n Inkarnation f
incendiary a & n ~ **[bomb]**
Brandbombe f
incense[1] n Weihrauch m
incense[2] vt wütend machen
incentive n Anreiz m
incessant a, **-ly** adv unaufhörlich
incest n Inzest m, Blutschande f
inch n Zoll m ● vi ~ **forward** sich
ganz langsam vorwärts schieben
incident n Zwischenfall m
incidental a nebensächlich;
<*remark*> beiläufig; <*expenses*>
Neben-. **~ly** adv übrigens
incinerate vt verbrennen
incision n Einschnitt m
incisive a scharfsinnig
incite vt aufhetzen. **~ment** n
Aufhetzung f
inclement a rau
inclination n Neigung f
incline vt neigen; **be ~d to do sth**
dazu neigen, etw zu tun ● vi sich
neigen
inclu|de vt einschließen; (*contain*)
enthalten; (*incorporate*)
aufnehmen (**in** in + *acc*). **~ding**
prep einschließlich (+ *gen*).
~sion n Aufnahme f
inclusive a Inklusiv-; ~ **of**
einschließlich (+ *gen*)
incognito adv inkognito
incoherent a, **-ly** adv
zusammenhanglos;
(*incomprehensible*)
unverständlich
income n Einkommen nt. ~ **tax** n
Einkommensteuer f

incoming a ankommend; <*mail,
call*> eingehend
incomparable a unvergleichlich
incompatible a unvereinbar; **be**
~ <*people:*> nicht zueinander
passen
incompeten|ce n Unfähigkeit f.
~t a unfähig
incomplete a unvollständig
incomprehensible a
unverständlich
inconceivable a undenkbar
inconclusive a nicht schlüssig
incongruous a unpassend
inconsiderate a rücksichtslos
inconsistent a, **-ly** adv
widersprüchlich; (*illogical*)
inkonsequent; **be ~** <*things:*>
nicht übereinstimmen
inconsolable a untröstlich
inconspicuous a unauffällig
incontinen|ce n Inkontinenz f.
~t a inkontinent
inconvenien|ce n
Unannehmlichkeit f; (*drawback*)
Nachteil m. **~t** a, **-ly** adv
ungünstig; **be ~t for s.o.** jdm
nicht passen
incorporate vt aufnehmen;
(*contain*) enthalten
incorrect a, **-ly** adv inkorrekt
incorrigible a unverbesserlich
incorruptible a unbestechlich
increase[1] n Zunahme f; (*rise*)
Erhöhung f; **be on the ~**
zunehmen
increas|e[2] vt vergrößern; (*raise*)
erhöhen ● vi zunehmen; (*rise*)
sich erhöhen. **~ing** a, **-ly** adv
zunehmend
incredible a, **-bly** adv unglaublich
incredulous a ungläubig
incriminate vt (*Jur*) belasten
incur vt (*pt/pp* **incurred**) sich (*dat*)
zuziehen; machen <*debts*>
incurable a, **-bly** adv unheilbar
indebted a verpflichtet (**to** *dat*)
indecent a, **-ly** adv unanständig

indecision n Unentschlossenheit f

indecisive a ergebnislos; <*person*> unentschlossen

indeed adv in der Tat, tatsächlich; **very much** ~ sehr

indefatigable a unermüdlich

indefinite a unbestimmt. ~**ly** adv unbegrenzt; <*postpone*> auf unbestimmte Zeit

indent vt (*Typ*) einrücken. ~**ation** n Einrückung f; (*notch*) Kerbe f

independen|ce n Unabhängigkeit f; (*self-reliance*) Selbstständigkeit f. ~**t** a, -**ly** adv unabhängig; selbstständig

indescribable a, -**bly** adv unbeschreiblich

indestructible a unzerstörbar

indeterminate a unbestimmt

index n Register nt

index: ~ **card** n Karteikarte f. ~ **finger** n Zeigefinger m. ~-**linked** a <*pension*> dynamisch

India n Indien nt. ~**n** a indisch; (*American*) indianisch ● n Inder(in) m(f); (*American*) Indianer(in) m(f)

Indian summer n Nachsommer m

indicat|e vt zeigen; (*point at*) zeigen auf (+ *acc*); (*hint*) andeuten; (*register*) anzeigen ● vi <*car:*> blinken. ~**ion** n Anzeichen nt

indicative n (*Gram*) Indikativ m

indicator n (*Auto*) Blinker m

indifferen|ce n Gleichgültigkeit f. ~**t** a, -**ly** adv gleichgültig; (*not good*) mittelmäßig

indigest|ible a unverdaulich; (*difficult to digest*) schwer verdaulich. ~**ion** n Magenverstimmung f

indigna|nt a, -**ly** adv entrüstet, empört. ~**tion** n Entrüstung f, Empörung f

indignity n Demütigung f

indirect a, -**ly** adv indirekt

indiscreet a indiskret

indiscretion n Indiskretion f

indispensable a unentbehrlich

indisposed a indisponiert

indisputable a, -**bly** adv unbestreitbar

indistinct a, -**ly** adv undeutlich

indistinguishable a be ~ nicht zu unterscheiden sein

individual a, -**ly** adv individuell; (*single*) einzeln ● n Individuum nt. ~**ity** n Individualität f

indivisible a unteilbar

indoctrinate vt indoktrinieren

indolen|ce n Faulheit f. ~**t** a faul

indomitable a unbeugsam

indoor a Innen-; <*clothes*> Haus-; <*plant*> Zimmer-; (*Sport*) Hallen-. ~**s** adv im Haus, drinnen; **go** ~**s** ins Haus gehen

indulge vt frönen (+ *dat*); verwöhnen <*child*> ● vi ~ **in** frönen (+ *dat*). ~**nce** n Nachgiebigkeit f; (*leniency*) Nachsicht f. ~**nt** a [zu] nachgiebig; nachsichtig

industrial a Industrie-. ~**ist** n Industrielle(r) m

industr|ious a, -**ly** adv fleißig. ~**y** n Industrie f; (*zeal*) Fleiß m

inebriated a betrunken

inedible a nicht essbar

ineffective a, -**ly** adv unwirksam; <*person*> untauglich

inefficient a unfähig; <*organization*> nicht leistungsfähig; <*method*> nicht rationell

ineligible a nicht berechtigt

inept a ungeschickt

inequality n Ungleichheit f

inertia n Trägheit f

inescapable a unvermeidlich

inestimable a unschätzbar

inevitab|le a unvermeidlich. ~**ly** adv zwangsläufig

inexact a ungenau

inexcusable a unverzeihlich

inexhaustible a unerschöpflich

inexpensive a, -**ly** adv preiswert

inexperience n Unerfahrenheit f.
∼**d** a unerfahren
inexplicable a unerklärlich
infallible a unfehlbar
infamous a niederträchtig;
(notorious) berüchtigt
infan|cy n frühe Kindheit f; (fig)
Anfangsstadium nt. ∼**t** n
Kleinkind nt. ∼**tile** a kindisch
infantry n Infanterie f
infatuated a vernarrt (with in +
acc)
infect vt anstecken, infizieren;
become ∼**ed** <wound:> sich
infizieren. ∼**ion** n Infektion f.
∼**ious** a ansteckend
inferior a minderwertig; (in rank)
untergeordnet ● n
Untergebene(r) m/f
inferiority n Minderwertigkeit f.
∼ **complex** n
Minderwertigkeitskomplex m
infern|al a höllisch. ∼**o** n
flammendes Inferno nt
infertile a unfruchtbar
infest vt be ∼**ed with** befallen sein
von; <place> verseucht sein mit
infidelity n Untreue f
infighting n (fig) interne
Machtkämpfe pl
infinite a, **-ly** adv unendlich
infinitive n (Gram) Infinitiv m
infinity n Unendlichkeit f
inflame vt entzünden. ∼**d** a
entzündet
inflammable a feuergefährlich
inflammation n Entzündung f
inflammatory a aufrührerisch
inflat|e vt aufblasen; (with pump)
aufpumpen. ∼**ion** n Inflation f.
∼**ionary** a inflationär
inflexible a starr; <person>
unbeugsam
inflict vt zufügen (on dat);
versetzen <blow> (on dat)
influen|ce n Einfluss m ● vt
beeinflussen. ∼**tial** a
einflussreich
influenza n Grippe f

inform vt benachrichtigen;
(officially) informieren; ∼ **s.o. of
sth** jdm etw mitteilen; **keep s.o.**
∼**ed** jdn auf dem Laufenden
halten ● vi ∼ **against**
denunzieren
informal a, **-ly** adv zwanglos;
(unofficial) inoffiziell. ∼**ity** n
Zwanglosigkeit f
informant n Gewährsmann m
informat|ion n Auskunft f; **a piece
of** ∼**ion** eine Auskunft. ∼**ive** a
aufschlussreich; (instructive)
lehrreich
informer n Spitzel m; (Pol)
Denunziant m
infra-red a infrarot
infrequent a, **-ly** adv selten
infringe vt/i ∼ **[on]** verstoßen
gegen. ∼**ment** n Verstoß m
infuriat|e vt wütend machen.
∼**ing** a ärgerlich
ingenious a erfinderisch; <thing>
raffiniert
ingenuity n Geschicklichkeit f
ingrained a eingefleischt; **be** ∼
<dirt:> tief sitzen
ingratiate vt ∼ **oneself** sich
einschmeicheln (with bei)
ingratitude n Undankbarkeit f
ingredient n (Culin) Zutat f
ingrowing a <nail> eingewachsen
inhabit vt bewohnen. ∼**ant** n
Einwohner(in) m(f)
inhale vt/i einatmen; (Med &
when smoking) inhalieren
inherent a natürlich
inherit vt erben. ∼**ance** n
Erbschaft f, Erbe nt
inhibit|ed a gehemmt. ∼**ion** n
Hemmung f
inhospitable a ungastlich
inhuman a unmenschlich
inimitable a unnachahmlich
initial a anfänglich, Anfangs- ● n
Anfangsbuchstabe m; **my** ∼**s**
meine Initialen. ∼**ly** adv anfangs,
am Anfang

initiat|e vt einführen. ~**ion** n
Einführung f
initiative n Initiative f
inject vt einspritzen, injizieren.
~**ion** n Spritze f, Injektion f
injur|e vt verletzen. ~**y** n
Verletzung f
injustice n Ungerechtigkeit f; **do
s.o. an** ~ jdm unrecht tun
ink n Tinte f
inlaid a eingelegt
inland a Binnen- ●adv
landeinwärts
in-laws npl 🄸 Schwiegereltern pl
inlay n Einlegearbeit f
inlet n schmale Bucht f; (Techn)
Zuleitung f
inmate n Insasse m
inn n Gasthaus nt
innate a angeboren
inner a innere(r,s). ~**most** a
innerste(r,s)
innocen|ce n Unschuld f. ~**t** a
unschuldig. ~**tly** adv in aller
Unschuld
innocuous a harmlos
innovat|ion n Neuerung f. ~**ive** a
innovativ. ~**or** n Neuerer m
innumerable a unzählig
inoculat|e vt impfen. ~**ion** n
Impfung f
inoffensive a harmlos
inoperable a nicht operierbar
inopportune a unpassend
inorganic a anorganisch
in-patient n [stationär
behandelter]
Krankenhauspatient m
input n Input m & nt
inquest n gerichtliche
Untersuchung f der
Todesursache
inquir|e vi sich erkundigen (**about**
nach); ~**e into** untersuchen ●vt
sich erkundigen nach. ~**y** n
Erkundigung f; (investigation)
Untersuchung f
inquisitive a, **-ly** adv neugierig

insane a geisteskrank; (fig)
wahnsinnig
insanitary a unhygienisch
insanity n Geisteskrankheit f
insatiable a unersättlich
inscription n Inschrift f
inscrutable a unergründlich;
<expression> undurchdringlich
insect n Insekt nt. ~**icide** n
Insektenvertilgungsmittel nt
insecur|e a nicht sicher; (fig)
unsicher. ~**ity** n Unsicherheit f
insensitive a gefühllos; ~ **to**
unempfindlich gegen
inseparable a untrennbar;
(people) unzertrennlich
insert¹ n Einsatz m
insert² vt einfügen, einsetzen;
einstecken <key>; einwerfen
<coin>. ~**ion** n (insert) Einsatz m;
(in text) Einfügung f
inside n Innenseite f; (of house)
Innere(s) nt ●attrib Innen-
●adv innen; (indoors) drinnen;
go ~ hineingehen; **come** ~
hereinkommen; ~ **out** links
[herum]; **know sth** ~ **out** etw in-
und auswendig kennen ●prep ~
[of] in (+ dat/ (into) + acc)
insight n Einblick m (**into** in +
acc); (understanding) Einsicht f
insignificant a unbedeutend
insincere a unaufrichtig
insinuat|e vt andeuten. ~**ion** n
Andeutung f
insipid a fade
insist vi darauf bestehen; ~ **on**
bestehen auf (+ dat) ●vt ~ **that**
darauf bestehen, dass. ~**ence** n
Bestehen nt. ~**ent** a, **-ly** adv
beharrlich; **be** ~**ent** darauf
bestehen
insole n Einlegesohle f
insolen|ce n Unverschämtheit f.
~**t** a, **-ly** adv unverschämt
insoluble a unlöslich; (fig)
unlösbar
insolvent a zahlungsunfähig
insomnia n Schlaflosigkeit f

inspect vt inspizieren; (test) prüfen; kontrollieren <ticket>. ~ion n Inspektion f. ~or n Inspektor m; (of tickets) Kontrolleur m

inspiration n Inspiration f

inspire vt inspirieren

instability n Unbeständigkeit f; (of person) Labilität f

install vt installieren. ~ation n Installation f

instalment n (Comm) Rate f; (of serial) Fortsetzung f; (Radio, TV) Folge f

instance n Fall m; (example) Beispiel nt; in the first ~ zunächst; for ~ zum Beispiel

instant a sofortig; (Culin) Instant- ● n Augenblick m, Moment m. ~aneous a unverzüglich, unmittelbar

instant coffee n Pulverkaffee m

instantly adv sofort

instead adv statt dessen; ~ of statt (+ gen), anstelle von; ~ of me an meiner Stelle; ~ of going anstatt zu gehen

instep n Spann m, Rist m

instigat|e vt anstiften; einleiten <proceedings>. ~ion n Anstiftung f; at his ~ion auf seine Veranlassung

instil vt (pt/pp instilled) einprägen (into s.o.) jdm

instinct n Instinkt m. ~ive a, -ly adv instinktiv

institut|e n Institut nt. ~ion n Institution f; (home) Anstalt f

instruct vt unterrichten; (order) anweisen. ~ion n Unterricht m; Anweisung f; ~ions pl for use Gebrauchsanweisung f; ~ive a lehrreich. ~or n Lehrer(in) m(f); (Mil) Ausbilder m

instrument n Instrument nt. ~al a Instrumental-

insubordi|nate a ungehorsam. ~nation n Ungehorsam m; (Mil) Insubordination f

insufficient a, -ly adv nicht genügend

insulat|e vt isolieren. ~ing tape n Isolierband nt. ~ion n Isolierung f

insult¹ n Beleidigung f

insult² vt beleidigen

insur|ance n Versicherung f. ~e vt versichern

intact a unbeschädigt; (complete) vollständig

intake n Aufnahme f

intangible a nicht greifbar

integral a wesentlich

integrat|e vt integrieren ● vi sich integrieren. ~ion n Integration f

integrity n Integrität f

intellect n Intellekt m. ~ual a intellektuell

intelligen|ce n Intelligenz f; (Mil) Nachrichtendienst m; (information) Meldungen pl. ~t a, -ly adv intelligent

intelligible a verständlich

intend vt beabsichtigen; be ~ed for bestimmt sein für

intense a intensiv; <pain> stark. ~ly adv äußerst; <study> intensiv

intensify v (pt/pp -ied) ● vt intensivieren ● vi zunehmen

intensity n Intensität f

intensive a, -ly adv intensiv; be in ~ care auf der Intensivstation sein

intent a, -ly adv aufmerksam; ~ on (absorbed in) vertieft in (+ acc) ● n Absicht f

intention n Absicht f. ~al a, -ly adv absichtlich

interacti|on n Wechselwirkung f. ~ve a interaktiv

intercede vi Fürsprache einlegen (on behalf of für)

intercept vt abfangen

interchange n Austausch m; (Auto) Autobahnkreuz nt

intercom n [Gegen]sprechanlage f

intercourse n (sexual) Geschlechtsverkehr m

interest n Interesse nt; (Comm) Zinsen pl ● vt interessieren; be ~ed sich interessieren (in für). ~ing a interessant. ~ rate n Zinssatz m

interfere vi sich einmischen. ~nce n Einmischung f; (Radio, TV) Störung f

interim a Zwischen-; (temporary) vorläufig

interior a innere(r,s), Innen- ● n Innere(s) nt

interject vt einwerfen. ~ion n Interjektion f; (remark) Einwurf m

interlude n Pause f; (performance) Zwischenspiel nt

intermarry vi untereinander heiraten; <different groups:> Mischehen schließen

intermediary n Vermittler(in) m(f)

intermediate a Zwischen-

interminable a endlos [lang]

intermittent a in Abständen auftretend

internal a innere(r,s); <matter, dispute> intern. ~ly adv innerlich; <deal with> intern

international a, -ly adv international ● n Länderspiel nt; (player) Nationalspieler(in) m(f)

Internet n Internet nt; on the ~ im Internet

internment n Internierung f

interplay n Wechselspiel nt

interpolate vt einwerfen

interpret vt interpretieren; auslegen <text>; deuten <dream>; (translate) dolmetschen ● vi dolmetschen. ~ation n Interpretation f. ~er n Dolmetscher(in) m(f)

interrogat|e vt verhören. ~ion n Verhör nt

interrogative a & n ~ [pronoun] Interrogativpronomen nt

interrupt vt/i unterbrechen; don't ~! red nicht dazwischen! ~ion n Unterbrechung f

intersect vi sich kreuzen; (Geom) sich schneiden. ~ion n Kreuzung f

interspersed a ~ with durchsetzt mit

intertwine vi sich ineinanderschlingen

interval n Abstand m; (Theat) Pause f; (Mus) Intervall nt; at hourly ~s alle Stunde; bright ~s pl Aufheiterungen pl

interven|e vi eingreifen; (occur) dazwischenkommen. ~tion n Eingreifen nt; (Mil, Pol) Intervention f

interview n (Journ) Interview nt; (for job) Vorstellungsgespräch nt ● vt interviewen; ein Vorstellungsgespräch führen mit ~er n Interviewer(in) m(f)

intimacy n Vertrautheit f; (sexual) Intimität f

intimate a, -ly adv vertraut; <friend> eng; (sexually) intim

intimidat|e vt einschüchtern. ~ion n Einschüchterung f

into prep in (+ acc); be ~ ⚠ sich auskennen mit; 7 ~ 21 21 [geteilt] durch 7

intolerable a unerträglich

intoleran|ce n Intoleranz f. ~t a intolerant

intonation n Tonfall m

intoxicat|ed a betrunken; (fig) berauscht. ~ion n Rausch m

intransigent a unnachgiebig

intransitive a, -ly adv intransitiv

intrepid a kühn, unerschrocken

intricate a kompliziert

intrigu|e n Intrige f ● vt faszinieren. ~ing a faszinierend

intrinsic a ~ value Eigenwert m

introduce vt vorstellen; (bring in, insert) einführen

introduct|ion n Einführung f; *(to person)* Vorstellung f; *(to book)* Einleitung f. **~ory** a einleitend
introvert n introvertierter Mensch m
intru|de vi stören. **~der** n Eindringling m. **~sion** n Störung f
intuit|ion n Intuition f. **~ive** a, **-ly** adv intuitiv
inundate vt überschwemmen
invade vt einfallen in (+ acc). **~r** n Angreifer m
invalid[1] n Kranke(r) m/f
invalid[2] a ungültig
invaluable a unschätzbar; <person> unersetzlich
invariab|le a unveränderlich. **~ly** adv immer
invasion n Invasion f
invent vt erfinden. **~ion** n Erfindung f. **~ive** a erfinderisch. **~or** n Erfinder m
inventory n Bestandsliste f
invert vt umkehren. **~ed commas** npl Anführungszeichen pl
invest vt investieren, anlegen; **~ in** (I buy) sich (dat) zulegen
investigat|e vt untersuchen. **~ion** n Untersuchung f
invest|ment n Anlage f; **be a good ~ment** (fig) sich bezahlt machen. **~or** n Kapitalanleger m
invidious a unerfreulich; *(unfair)* ungerecht
invincible a unbesiegbar
inviolable a unantastbar
invisible a unsichtbar
invitation n Einladung f
invit|e vt einladen. **~ing** a einladend
invoice n Rechnung f ● vt **~ s.o.** jdm eine Rechnung schicken
involuntary a, **-ily** adv unwillkürlich
involve vt beteiligen; *(affect)* betreffen; *(implicate)* verwickeln; *(entail)* mit sich bringen; *(mean)* bedeuten; **be ~d in** beteiligt sein

an (+ dat); *(implicated)* verwickelt sein in (+ acc); **get ~d with s.o.** sich mit jdm einlassen. **~d** a kompliziert
invulnerable a unverwundbar; <position> unangreifbar
inward a innere(r,s). **~s** adv nach innen
iodine n Jod nt
IOU abbr Schuldschein m
Iran n der Iran
Iraq n der Irak
irascible a aufbrausend
irate a wütend
Ireland n Irland nt
iris n (Anat) Regenbogenhaut f, Iris f; (Bot) Schwertlilie f
Irish a irisch ● n **the ~** pl die Iren. **~man** n Ire m. **~woman** n Irin f
iron a Eisen-; *(fig)* eisern ● n Eisen nt; *(appliance)* Bügeleisen nt ● vt/i bügeln
ironic[al] a ironisch
ironing n Bügeln nt; *(articles)* Bügelwäsche f. **~-board** n Bügelbrett nt
ironmonger n **~'s [shop]** Haushaltswarengeschäft nt
irony n Ironie f
irrational a irrational
irreconcilable a unversöhnlich
irrefutable a unwiderlegbar
irregular a, **-ly** adv unregelmäßig; *(against rules)* regelwidrig. **~ity** n Unregelmäßigkeit f; Regelwidrigkeit f
irrelevant a irrelevant
irreparable a nicht wieder gutzumachen
irreplaceable a unersetzlich
irrepressible a unverwüstlich; **be ~** <person:> nicht unterzukriegen sein
irresistible a unwiderstehlich
irresolute a unentschlossen
irrespective a **~ of** ungeachtet (+ gen)

irresponsible *a*, **-bly** *adv* unverantwortlich; <*person*> verantwortungslos

irreverent *a*, **-ly** *adv* respektlos

irrevocable *a*, **-bly** *adv* unwiderruflich

irrigat|e *vt* bewässern. ~**ion** *n* Bewässerung *f*

irritable *a* reizbar

irritant *n* Reizstoff *m*

irritat|e *vt* irritieren; (*Med*) reizen. ~**ion** *n* Ärger *m*; (*Med*) Reizung *f*

is *see* be

Islam *n* der Islam. ~**ic** *a* islamisch

island *n* Insel *f*. ~**er** *n* Inselbewohner(in) *m(f)*

isolat|e *vt* isolieren. ~**ed** *a* (*remote*) abgelegen; (*single*) einzeln. ~**ion** *n* Isoliertheit *f*; (*Med*) Isolierung *f*

Israel *n* Israel *nt*. ~**i** *a* israelisch ● *n* Israeli *m/f*

issue *n* Frage *f*; (*outcome*) Ergebnis *nt*; (*of magazine, stamps*) Ausgabe *f*; (*offspring*) Nachkommen *pl* ● *vt* ausgeben; ausstellen <*passport*>; erteilen <*order*>; herausgeben <*book*>; **be** ~**d with sth** etw erhalten

it
● *pronoun*
····▸ (*as subject*) er (*m*), sie (*f*), es (*nt*); (*in impersonal sentence*) es. **where is the spoon? it's on the table** wo ist der Löffel? Er liegt auf dem Tisch. **it was very kind of you** es war sehr nett von Ihnen. **it's five o'clock** es ist fünf Uhr

····▸ (*as direct object*) ihn (*m*), sie (*f*), es (*nt*). **that's my pencil — give it to me** das ist mein Bleistift — gib ihn mir.

····▸ (*as dative object*) ihm (*m*), ihr (*f*), ihm (*nt*). **he found a track and followed it** er fand eine Spur und folgte ihr.

····▸ (*after prepositions*)

❗ Combinations such as *with it*, *from it*, *to it* are translated by the prepositions with the prefix **da-** (**damit, davon, dazu**). Prepositions beginning with a vowel insert an 'r' (**daran, darauf, darüber**). **I can't do anything with it** ich kann nichts damit anfangen. **don't lean on it!** lehn dich nicht daran!

····▸ (*the person in question*) es. **it's me** ich bin's. **is it you, Dad?** bist du es, Vater? **who is it?** wer ist da?

Italian *a* italienisch ● *n* Italiener(in) *m(f)*; (*Lang*) Italienisch *nt*

italics *npl* Kursivschrift *f*; **in** ~**s** kursiv

Italy *n* Italien *nt*

itch *n* Juckreiz *m*; **I have an** ~ es juckt mich ● *vi* jucken; **I'm** ~**ing** 🔲 es juckt mich (**to** zu). ~**y** *a* **be** ~**y** jucken

item *n* Gegenstand *m*; (*Comm*) Artikel *m*; (*on agenda*) Punkt *m*; (*on invoice*) Posten *m*; (*act*) Nummer *f*

itinerary *n* [Reise]route *f*

its *poss pron* sein; (*f*) ihr

it's = **it is**, **it has**

itself *pron* selbst; (*refl*) sich; **by** ~ von selbst; (*alone*) allein

ivory *n* Elfenbein *nt* ● *attrib* Elfenbein-

ivy *n* Efeu *m*

jab *n* Stoß *m*; (🔲 *injection*) Spritze *f* ● *vt* (*pt/pp* **jabbed**) stoßen

jabber vi plappern

jack n (Auto) Wagenheber m; (Cards) Bube m ● vt ~ up (Auto) aufbocken

jacket n Jacke f; (of book) Schutzumschlag m

jackpot n hit the ~ das große Los ziehen

jade n Jade m

jagged a zackig

jail = gaol

jam[1] n Marmelade f

jam[2] n Gedränge nt; (Auto) Stau m; (fam. difficulty) Klemme f ● v (pt/pp jammed) ● vt klemmen (in in + acc); stören <broadcast> ● vi klemmen

Jamaica n Jamaika nt

jangle vi klimpern ● vt klimpern mit

January n Januar m

Japan n Japan nt. ~ese a japanisch ● n Japaner(in) m(f); (Lang) Japanisch nt

jar n Glas nt; (earthenware) Topf m

jargon n Jargon m

jaunt n Ausflug m

jaunty a (-ier, -iest) -ily adv keck

javelin n Speer m

jaw n Kiefer m

jazz n Jazz m. ~y a knallig

jealous a, -ly adv eifersüchtig (of auf + acc). ~y n Eifersucht f

jeans npl Jeans pl

jeer vi johlen; ~ at verhöhnen

jelly n Gelee nt; (dessert) Götterspeise f. ~fish n Qualle f

jeopar|dize vt gefährden. ~dy n in ~dy gefährdet

jerk n Ruck m ● vt stoßen; (pull) reißen ● vi rucken; <limb, muscle:> zucken. ~ily adv ruckweise. ~y a ruckartig

jersey n Pullover m; (Sport) Trikot nt; (fabric) Jersey m

jest n in ~ im Spaß

jet n (of water) [Wasser]strahl m; (nozzle) Düse f; (plane) Düsenflugzeug nt

jet: ~-black a pechschwarz. ~-propelled a mit Düsenantrieb

jetty n Landesteg m; (breakwater) Buhne f

Jew n Jude m /Jüdin f

jewel n Edelstein m; (fig) Juwel nt. ~ler n Juwelier m; ~ler's [shop] Juweliergeschäft nt. ~lery n Schmuck m

Jew|ess n Jüdin f. ~ish a jüdisch

jib vi (pt/pp jibbed) (fig) sich sträuben (at gegen)

jigsaw n ~ [puzzle] Puzzlespiel nt

jilt vt sitzen lassen

jingle n (rhyme) Verschen nt ● vi klimpern

jinx n 🄸 it's got a ~ on it es ist verhext

jittery a 🄸 nervös

job n Aufgabe f; (post) Stelle f, 🄸 Job m; be a ~ 🄸 nicht leicht sein; it's a good ~ that es ist [nur] gut, dass. ~less a arbeitslos

jockey n Jockei m

jocular a, -ly adv spaßhaft

jog n Stoß m ● v (pt/pp jogged) ● vt anstoßen; ~ s.o.'s memory jds Gedächtnis nachhelfen ● vi (Sport) joggen. ~ging n Jogging nt

john n (Amer 🄸) Klo nt

join n Nahtstelle f ● vt verbinden (to mit); sich anschließen (+ dat) <person>; (become member of) beitreten (+ dat); eintreten in (+ acc) <firm>; sich treffen. ~ in vi mitmachen. ~ up vi (Mil) Soldat werden ● vt zusammenfügen

joint a, -ly adv gemeinsam ● n Gelenk nt; (in wood, brickwork) Fuge f; (Culin) Braten m; (🄸 bar) Lokal nt

jok|e n Scherz m; (funny story) Witz m; (trick) Streich m ● vi scherzen. ~er n Witzbold m;

J

(*Cards*) Joker *m*. ~**ing** *n* ~**ing apart** Spaß beiseite. ~**ingly** *adv* im Spaß

jolly *a* (**-ier, -iest**) lustig ● *adv* 🔲 sehr

jolt *n* Ruck *m* ● *vt* einen Ruck versetzen (+ *dat*) ● *vi* holpern

Jordan *n* Jordanien *nt*

jostle *vt* anrempeln

jot *vt* (*pt/pp* **jotted**) ~ **[down]** sich (*dat*) notieren

journal *n* Zeitschrift *f*; (*diary*) Tagebuch *nt*. ~**ese** *n* Zeitungsjargon *m*. ~**ism** *n* Journalismus *m*. ~**ist** *n* Journalist(in) *m(f)*

journey *n* Reise *f*

jovial *a* lustig

joy *n* Freude *f*. ~**ful** *a*, **-ly** *adv* freudig, froh. ~**ride** *n* 🔲 Spritztour *f* [im gestohlenen Auto]

jubil|ant *a* überglücklich. ~**ation** *n* Jubel *m*

jubilee *n* Jubiläum *nt*

judder *vi* rucken

judge *n* Richter *m*; (*of competition*) Preisrichter *m* ● *vt* beurteilen; (*estimate*) [ein]schätzen ● *vi* urteilen (**by** nach). ~**ment** *n* Beurteilung *f*; (*Jur*) Urteil *nt*; (*fig*) Urteilsvermögen *nt*

judic|ial *a* gerichtlich. ~**ious** *a* klug

jug *n* Kanne *f*; (*small*) Kännchen *nt*; (*for water, wine*) Krug *m*

juggle *vi* jonglieren. ~**r** *n* Jongleur *m*

juice *n* Saft *m*

juicy *a* (**-ier, -iest**) saftig; 🔲 <*story*> pikant

juke-box *n* Musikbox *f*

July *n* Juli *m*

jumble *n* Durcheinander *nt* ● *vt* ~ **[up]** durcheinander bringen. ~ **sale** *n* [Wohltätigkeits]basar *m*

jump *n* Sprung *m*; (*in prices*) Anstieg *m*; (*in horse racing*) Hindernis *nt* ● *vi* springen; (*start*) zusammenzucken; **make s.o.** ~ jdn erschrecken; ~ **at** (*fig*) sofort zugreifen bei <*offer*>; ~ **to conclusions** voreilige Schlüsse ziehen ● *vt* überspringen. ~ **up** *vi* aufspringen

jumper *n* Pullover *m*, Pulli *m*

jumpy *a* nervös

junction *n* Kreuzung *f*; (*Rail*) Knotenpunkt *m*

June *n* Juni *m*

jungle *n* Dschungel *m*

junior *a* jünger; (*in rank*) untergeordnet; (*Sport*) Junioren- ● *n* Junior *m*

junk *n* Gerümpel *nt*, Trödel *m*

junkie *n* 🗴 Fixer *m*

junk-shop *n* Trödelladen *m*

jurisdiction *n* Gerichtsbarkeit *f*

jury *n* **the** ~ die Geschworenen *pl*; (*for competition*) die Jury

just *a* gerecht ● *adv* gerade; (*only*) nur; (*simply*) einfach; (*exactly*) genau; ~ **as tall** ebenso groß; **I'm** ~ **going** ich gehe schon

justice *n* Gerechtigkeit *f*; **do** ~ **to** gerecht werden (+ *dat*)

justifiab|le *a* berechtigt. ~**ly** *adv* berechtigterweise

justi|fication *n* Rechtfertigung *f*. ~**fy** *vt* (*pt/pp* **-ied**) rechtfertigen

justly *adv* zu Recht

jut *vi* (*pt/pp* **jutted**) ~ **out** vorstehen

juvenile *a* jugendlich; (*childish*) kindisch ● *n* Jugendliche(r) *m/f*. ~ **delinquency** *n* Jugendkriminalität *f*

kangaroo n Känguru nt
kebab n Spießchen nt
keel n Kiel m ●vi ~ **over**
umkippen; (*Naut*) kentern
keen a (**-er, -est**) (*sharp*) scharf;
(*intense*) groß; (*eager*) eifrig,
begeistert; ~ **on** 🛈 erpicht auf (+
acc); ~ **on s.o.** von jdm sehr
angetan; **be** ~ **to do sth** gerne
machen wollen. ~**ly** adv tief.
~**ness** n Eifer m, Begeisterung f
keep n (*maintenance*) Unterhalt
m; (*of castle*) Bergfried m; **for** ~**s**
für immer ●v (*pt/pp* **kept**) ●vt
behalten; (*store*) aufbewahren;
(*not throw away*) aufheben;
(*support*) unterhalten; (*detain*)
aufhalten; freihalten <*seat*>;
halten <*promise, animals*>;
führen, haben <*shop*>; einhalten
<*law, rules*>; ~ **s.o. waiting** jdn
warten lassen; ~ **sth to oneself**
etw nicht weitersagen ●vi
(*remain*) bleiben; <*food:*> sich
halten; ~ **left/right** sich links/
rechts halten; ~ **on doing sth** etw
dauernd machen; ~ **in with** sich
gut stellen mit. ~ **up** vi Schritt
halten ●vt (*continue*)
weitermachen
keep|er n Wärter(in) m(f). ~**ing** n
be in ~**ing with** passen zu
kennel n Hundehütte f; ~**s** pl
(*boarding*) Hundepension f;
(*breeding*) Zwinger m
Kenya n Kenia nt
kept see **keep**
kerb n Bordstein m
kernel n Kern m
ketchup n Ketchup m

kettle n [Wasser]kessel m; **put the**
~ **on** Wasser aufsetzen
key n Schlüssel m; (*Mus*) Tonart
f; (*of piano, typewriter*) Taste f
●vt ~ **in** eintasten
key: ~**board** n Tastatur f; (*Mus*)
Klaviatur f. ~**hole** n
Schlüsselloch nt. ~**-ring** n
Schlüsselring m
khaki a khakifarben ●n Khaki nt
kick n [Fuß]tritt m; **for** ~**s** 🛈 zum
Spaß ●vt treten; ~ **the bucket** 🛈
abkratzen ●vi <*animal*>
ausschlagen
kid n (🛈 *child*) Kind nt ●vt (*pt/pp*
kidded) 🛈 ~ **s.o.** jdm etwas
vormachen
kidnap vt (*pt/pp* **-napped**)
entführen. ~**per** n Entführer m.
~**ping** n Entführung f
kidney n Niere f
kill vt töten; 🛈 totschlagen
<*time*>: ~ **two birds with one stone**
zwei Fliegen mit einer Klappe
schlagen. ~**er** n Mörder(in) m(f).
~**ing** n Tötung f; (*murder*) Mord
m
killjoy n Spielverderber m
kilo n Kilo nt
kilo:: ~**gram** n Kilogramm nt.
~**metre** n Kilometer m. ~**watt** n
Kilowatt nt
kilt n Schottenrock m
kind¹ n Art f; (*brand, type*) Sorte f;
what ~ **of car?** was für ein Auto?
~ **of** 🛈 irgendwie
kind² a (**-er, -est**) nett; ~ **to animals**
gut zu Tieren
kind|ly a (**-ier, -iest**) nett ●adv
netterweise; (*if you please*)
gefälligst. ~**ness** n Güte f;
(*favour*) Gefallen m
king n König m; (*Draughts*) Dame
f. ~**dom** n Königreich nt; (*fig &
Relig*) Reich nt
king: ~**fisher** n Eisvogel m. ~**-
sized** a extragroß
kink n Knick m. ~**y** a 🛈 pervers
kiosk n Kiosk m

K

kip n have a ~ 🔵 pennen ●vi
(pt/pp kipped) 🔵 pennen
kipper n Räucherhering m
kiss n Kuss m ●vt/i küssen
kit n Ausrüstung f; (tools)
Werkzeug nt; (construction ~)
Bausatz m ●vt (pt/pp kitted) ~out
ausrüsten
kitchen nt; Küche f ●attrib
Küchen-. ~ette n Kochnische f
kitchen: ~garden n
Gemüsegarten m. ~sink n
Spülbecken nt
kite n Drachen m
kitten n Kätzchen nt
kitty n (money) [gemeinsame]
Kasse f
knack n Trick m, Dreh m
knead vt kneten
knee n Knie nt. ~cap n
Kniescheibe f
kneel vi (pt/pp knelt) knien; ~
[down] sich [nieder]knien
knelt see **kneel**
knew see **know**
knickers npl Schlüpfer m
knife n (pl knives) Messer nt ●vt
einen Messerstich versetzen (+
dat)
knight n Ritter m; (Chess)
Springer m ●vt adeln
knit vt/i (pt/pp knitted) stricken; ~
one's brow die Stirn runzeln.
~ting n Stricken nt; (work)
Strickzeug nt. ~ting-needle n
Stricknadel f. ~wear n
Strickwaren pl
knives npl see **knife**
knob n Knopf m; (on door) Knauf
m; (small lump) Beule f. ~bly a
knorrig; (bony) knochig
knock n Klopfen nt; (blow) Schlag
m; there was a ~ es klopfte ●vt
anstoßen; (🔵 criticize)
heruntermachen; ~ a hole in sth
ein Loch in etw (acc) schlagen; ~
one's head sich (dat) den Kopf
stoßen (on an + dat) ●vi klopfen.
~ about vt schlagen ●vi 🔵

herumkommen. ~ down vt
herunterwerfen; (with fist)
niederschlagen; (in car)
anfahren; (demolish) abreißen;
(🔵 reduce) herabsetzen. ~ off vt
herunterwerfen; (🔵 steal)
klauen; (🔵 complete quickly)
hinhauen ●vi (🔵 cease work)
Feierabend machen. ~ out vt
ausschlagen; (make unconscious)
bewusstlos schlagen; (Boxing)
k.o. schlagen. ~ over vt
umwerfen; (in car) anfahren
knock: ~-down a ~-down prices
Schleuderpreise pl. ~er n
Türklopfer m. ~-out n (Boxing)
K.o. m
knot n Knoten m ●vt (pt/pp
knotted) knoten
know vt/i (pt knew, pp known)
wissen; kennen <person>;
können <language>; get to ~
kennen lernen ●n in the ~ 🔵 im
Bild
know: ~-all n 🔵 Alleswisser m.
~-how n 🔵 [Sach]kenntnis f.
~ing a wissend. ~ingly adv
wissend; (intentionally)
wissentlich
knowledge n Kenntnis f (of von/
gen); (general) Wissen nt;
(specialized) Kenntnisse pl.
~able a be ~able viel wissen
knuckle n [Finger]knöchel m;
(Culin) Hachse f
kosher a koscher
kudos n 🔵 Prestige nt

lab n 🔵 Labor nt

label n Etikett nt ● vt (pt/pp labelled) etikettieren

laboratory n Labor nt

laborious a, **-ly** adv mühsam

labour n Arbeit f; (workers) Arbeitskräfte pl; (Med) Wehen pl; **L~** (Pol) die Labourpartei ● attrib Labour- ● vi arbeiten ● vt (fig) sich lange auslassen über (+ acc). **~er** n Arbeiter m

labour-saving a arbeitssparend

lace n Spitze f; (of shoe) Schnürsenkel m ● vt schnüren

lack n Mangel m (of an + dat) ● vt **I ~ the time** mir fehlt die Zeit ● vi be **~ing** fehlen

laconic a, **-ally** adv lakonisch

lacquer n Lack m; (for hair) [Haar]spray m

lad n Junge m

ladder n Leiter f; (in fabric) Laufmasche f

ladle n [Schöpf]kelle f ● vt schöpfen

lady n Dame f; (title) Lady f

lady: **~bird** n, (Amer) **~bug** n Marienkäfer m. **~like** a damenhaft

lag¹ vi (pt/pp lagged) **~ behind** zurückbleiben; (fig) nachhinken

lag² vt (pt/pp lagged) umwickeln <pipes>

lager n Lagerbier nt

laid see **lay³**

lain see **lie²**

lake n See m

lamb n Lamm nt

lame a (**-r, -st**) lahm

lament n Klage f; (song) Klagelied nt ● vt beklagen ● vi klagen

laminated a laminiert

lamp n Lampe f; (in street) Laterne f. **~ post** n Laternenpfahl m. **~shade** n Lampenschirm m

lance vt (Med) aufschneiden

land n Land nt; **plot of ~** Grundstück nt ● vt/i landen; **~ s.o. with sth** 🛈 jdm etw aufhalsen

landing n Landung f; (top of stairs) Treppenflur m. **~-stage** n Landesteg m

land: **~lady** n Wirtin f. **~lord** n Wirt m; (of land) Grundbesitzer m; (of building) Hausbesitzer m. **~mark** n Erkennungszeichen nt; (fig) Meilenstein m. **~owner** n Grundbesitzer m. **~scape** n Landschaft f. **~slide** n Erdrutsch m

lane n kleine Landstraße f; (Auto) Spur f; (Sport) Bahn f; '**get in ~**' (Auto) 'bitte einordnen'

language n Sprache f; (speech, style) Ausdrucksweise f

languid a, **-ly** adv träge

languish vi schmachten

lanky a (**-ier, -iest**) schlaksig

lantern n Laterne f

lap¹ n Schoß m

lap² n (Sport) Runde f; (of journey) Etappe f ● vi (pt/pp lapped) plätschern (against gegen)

lap³ vt (pt/pp lapped) **~ up** aufschlecken

lapel n Revers nt

lapse n Fehler m; (moral) Fehltritt m; (of time) Zeitspanne f ● vi (expire) erlöschen; **~ into** verfallen in (+ acc)

lard n [Schweine]schmalz nt

larder n Speisekammer f

large a (**-r, -st**) & adv groß; **by and ~** im Großen und Ganzen; **at ~** auf freiem Fuß. **~ly** adv großenteils

lark¹ n (bird) Lerche f

lark² n (joke) Jux m ● vi **~ about** herumalbern

laryngitis n Kehlkopfentzündung f

larynx n Kehlkopf m

laser n Laser m

lash n Peitschenhieb m; (eyelash) Wimper f ● vt peitschen; (tie) festbinden (**to** an + acc). ~ **out** vi um sich schlagen; (spend) viel Geld ausgeben (**on** für)

lass n Mädchen nt

lasso n Lasso nt

last a & n letzte(r,s); ~ **night** heute od gestern Nacht; (evening) gestern Abend; **at** ~ endlich; **for the** ~ **time** zum letzten Mal; **the** ~ **but one** der/die/das vorletzte ● adv zuletzt; (last time) das letzte Mal; **he/she went** ~ er/sie ging als Letzter/Letzte ● vi dauern; <weather:> sich halten; <relationship:> halten. ~ing a dauerhaft. ~ly adv schließlich, zum Schluss

latch n [einfache] Klinke f

late a & adv (**-r, -st**) spät; (delayed) verspätet; (deceased) verstorben; **the** ~st **news** die neuesten Nachrichten; **stay up** ~ bis spät aufbleiben; **arrive** ~ zu spät ankommen; **I am** ~ ich komme zu spät od habe mich verspätet; **the train is** ~ der Zug hat Verspätung. ~comer n Zuspätkommende(r) m/f. ~ly adv in letzter Zeit. ~ness n Zuspätkommen nt; (delay) Verspätung f

later a & adv später; ~ **on** nachher

lateral a seitlich

lather n [Seifen]schaum m

Latin a lateinisch ● n Latein nt. ~ **America** n Lateinamerika nt

latitude n (Geog) Breite f; (fig) Freiheit f

latter a & n **the** ~ der/die/das Letztere

Latvia n Lettland nt

laudable a lobenswert

laugh n Lachen nt; **with a** ~ lachend ● vi lachen (**at/about** über + acc); ~ **at s.o.** (mock) jdn auslachen. ~able a lachhaft, lächerlich

laughter n Gelächter nt

launch¹ n (boat) Barkasse f

launch² n Stapellauf m; (of rocket) Abschuss m; (of product) Lancierung f ● vt vom Stapel lassen <ship>; zu Wasser lassen <lifeboat>; abschießen <rocket>; starten <attack>; (Comm) lancieren <product>

laund(e)rette n Münzwäscherei f

laundry n Wäscherei f; (clothes) Wäsche f

laurel n Lorbeer m

lava n Lava f

lavatory n Toilette f

lavender n Lavendel m

lavish a, **-ly** adv großzügig; (wasteful) verschwenderisch ● vt ~ **sth on s.o.** jdn mit etw überschütten

law n Gesetz nt; (system) Recht nt; **study** ~ Jura studieren; ~ **and order** Recht und Ordnung

law: ~-**abiding** a gesetzestreu. ~ **court** n Gerichtshof m. ~ful a rechtmäßig. ~less a gesetzlos

lawn n Rasen m. ~-**mower** n Rasenmäher m

lawyer n Rechtsanwalt m /-anwältin f

lax a lax, locker

laxative n Abführmittel nt

laxity n Laxheit f

lay¹ see **lie**²

lay² vt (pt/pp **laid**) legen; decken <table>; ~ **a trap** eine Falle stellen; ~ **down** vt hinlegen; festlegen <rules, conditions>. ~ **off** vt entlassen <workers> ● vi (🄸 stop) aufhören. ~ **out** vt hinlegen; aufbahren <corpse>; anlegen <garden>; (Typ) gestalten

lay-by n Parkbucht f

layer n Schicht f

lay: ~**man** n Laie m. ~**out** n Anordnung f; (design) Gestaltung f; (Typ) Layout nt

laze vi ~**[about]** faulenzen

laziness n Faulheit f

lazy a (-ier, -iest) faul. ~**-bones** n Faulenzer m

lead[1] n Blei nt; (of pencil) [Bleistift]mine f

lead[2] n Führung f; (leash) Leine f; (flex) Schnur f; (clue) Hinweis m, Spur f; (Theat) Hauptrolle f; (distance ahead) Vorsprung m; **be in the** ~ in Führung liegen ● vt/i (pt/pp led) führen; leiten <team>; (induce) bringen; (at cards) ausspielen; ~ **the way** vorangehen; ~ **up to sth** (fig) etw (dat) vorangehen

leader n Führer m; (of expedition, group) Leiter(in) m(f); (of orchestra) Konzertmeister m; (in newspaper) Leitartikel m. ~**ship** n Führung f; Leitung f

leading a führend; ~ **lady** Hauptdarstellerin f

leaf n (pl **leaves**) Blatt nt ● vi ~ **through** sth etw durchblättern. ~**let** n Merkblatt nt; (advertising) Reklameblatt nt; (political) Flugblatt nt

league n Liga f

leak n (hole) undichte Stelle f; (Naut) Leck nt; (of gas) Gasausfluss m ● vi undicht sein; <ship:> leck sein, lecken; <liquid:> auslaufen; <gas:> ausströmen ● vt auslaufen lassen; ~ **sth to s.o.** (fig) jdm etw zuspielen. ~**y** a undicht; (Naut) leck

lean[1] a (-er, -est) mager

lean[2] v (pt/pp **leaned** or **leant**) ● vt lehnen (**against/on** an + acc) ● vi <person> sich lehnen (**against/on** an + acc); (not be straight) sich neigen; **be** ~**ing against** lehnen an (+ dat). ~ **back** vi sich zurücklehnen. ~ **forward** vi sich

vorbeugen. ~ **out** vi sich hinauslehnen. ~ **over** vi sich vorbeugen

leaning a schief ● n Neigung f

leap n Sprung m ● vi (pt/pp **leapt** or **leaped**) springen; **he leapt at it** ❗ er griff sofort zu. ~ **year** n Schaltjahr nt

learn vt/i (pt/pp **learnt** or **learned**) lernen; (hear) erfahren; ~ **to swim** schwimmen lernen

learn|ed a gelehrt. ~**er** n Anfänger m; ~**er [driver]** Fahrschüler(in) m(f). ~**ing** n Gelehrsamkeit f

lease n Pacht f; (contract) Mietvertrag m ● vt pachten

leash n Leine f

least a geringste(r,s) ● n **the** ~ das wenigste; **at** ~ wenigstens, mindestens; **not in the** ~ nicht im Geringsten ● adv am wenigsten

leather n Leder nt

leave n Erlaubnis f; (holiday) Urlaub m; **on** ~ auf Urlaub; **take one's** ~ sich verabschieden ● v (pt/pp **left**) ● vt lassen; (go out of, abandon) verlassen; (forget) liegen lassen; (bequeath) vermachen (**to** dat); ~ **it to me!** überlassen Sie es mir! **there is nothing left** es ist nichts mehr übrig ● vi [weg]gehen/-fahren; <train, bus:> abfahren. ~ **behind** vt zurücklassen; (forget) liegen lassen. ~ **out** vt liegen lassen; (leave outside) draußen lassen; (omit) auslassen

leaves see **leaf**

Lebanon n Libanon m

lecherous a lüstern

lecture n Vortrag m; (Univ) Vorlesung f; (reproof) Strafpredigt f ● vi einen Vortrag/eine Vorlesung halten (**on** über + acc) ● vt ~ **s.o.** jdm eine Strafpredigt halten. ~**r** n Vortragende(r) m/f; (Univ) Dozent(in) m(f)

L

led see lead²

ledge n Leiste f; (shelf, of window) Sims m; (in rock) Vorsprung m

ledger n Hauptbuch nt

leech n Blutegel m

leek n Stange f Porree; ∼s pl Porree m

left¹ see leave

left² a linke(r,s) ●adv links; <go> nach links ●n linke Seite f; on the ∼ links; from/to the ∼ von/ nach links; the ∼ (Pol) die Linke

left: ∼-handed a linkshändig. ∼-luggage [office] n Gepäckaufbewahrung f. ∼overs npl Reste pl. ∼-wing a (Pol) linke(r,s)

leg n Bein nt; (Culin) Keule f; (of journey) Etappe f

legacy n Vermächtnis nt, Erbschaft f

legal a, -ly adv gesetzlich; <matters> rechtlich; <department, position> Rechts-; be ∼ [gesetzlich] erlaubt sein

legality n Legalität f

legend n Legende f. ∼ary a legendär

legible a, -bly adv leserlich

legion n Legion f

legislat|e vi Gesetze erlassen. ∼ion n Gesetzgebung f; (laws) Gesetze pl

legislative a gesetzgebend

legitimate a rechtmäßig; (justifiable) berechtigt

leisure n Freizeit f; at your ∼ wenn Sie Zeit haben. ∼ly a gemächlich

lemon n Zitrone f. ∼ade n Zitronenlimonade f

lend vt (pt/pp lent) leihen (s.o. sth jdm etw)

length n Länge f; (piece) Stück nt; (of wallpaper) Bahn f; (of time) Dauer f

length|en vt länger machen ●vi länger werden. ∼ways adv der Länge nach

lengthy a (-ier, -iest) langwierig

lenien|t a, -ly adv nachsichtig

lens n Linse f; (Phot) Objektiv nt; (of spectacles) Glas nt

lent see lend

Lent n Fastenzeit f

lentil n (Bot) Linse f

leopard n Leopard m

leotard n Trikot nt

lesbian a lesbisch ●n Lesbierin f

less a, adv, n & prep weniger; ∼ and ∼ immer weniger

lessen vt verringern ●vi nachlassen; <value:> abnehmen

lesser a geringere(r,s)

lesson n Stunde f; (in textbook) Lektion f; (Relig) Lesung f; teach s.o. a ∼ (fig) jdm eine Lehre erteilen

lest conj (liter) damit ... nicht

let vt (pt/pp let, pres p letting) lassen; (rent) vermieten; ∼ alone (not to mention) geschweige denn; ∼ us go gehen wir; ∼ me know sagen Sie mir Bescheid; ∼ oneself in for sth Ⓘ sich (dat) etw einbrocken. ∼ down vt hinunter-/herunterlassen; (lengthen) länger machen; ∼ s.o. down Ⓘ jdm im Stich lassen; (disappoint) jdn enttäuschen. ∼ in vt hereinlassen. ∼ off vt abfeuern <gun>; hochgehen lassen <firework, bomb>; (emit) ausstoßen; (excuse from) befreien von; (not punish) frei ausgehen lassen. ∼ out vt hinaus-/herauslassen; (make larger) auslassen. ∼ through vt durchlassen. ∼ up vi Ⓘ nachlassen

let-down n Enttäuschung f, Ⓘ Reinfall m

lethal a tödlich

letharg|ic a lethargisch. ∼y n Lethargie f

letter n Brief m; (of alphabet) Buchstabe m. **~-box** n Briefkasten m. **~head** n Briefkopf m. **~ing** n Beschriftung f

lettuce n [Kopf]salat m

let-up n ☐ Nachlassen nt

level a eben; (horizontal) waagerecht; (in height) auf gleicher Höhe; <spoonful> gestrichen; **one's ~ best** sein Möglichstes ● n Höhe f; (fig) Ebene f, Niveau nt; (stage) Stufe f; **on the ~** ☐ ehrlich ● vt (pt/pp levelled) einebnen

level crossing n Bahnübergang m

lever n Hebel m ● vt **~ up** mit einem Hebel anheben. **~age** n Hebelkraft f

lewd a (-er, -est) anstößig

liabilit|y n Haftung f; **~ies** pl Verbindlichkeiten pl

liable a haftbar; **be ~ to do sth** etw leicht tun können

liaise vi ☐ Verbindungsperson sein

liaison n Verbindung f; (affair) Verhältnis nt

liar n Lügner(in) m(f)

libel n Verleumdung f ● vt (pt/pp libelled) verleumden. **~lous** a verleumderisch

liberal a, -ly adv tolerant; (generous) großzügig. **L~** a (Pol) liberal ● n Liberale(r) m/f

liberat|e vt befreien. **~ed** a <woman> emanzipiert. **~ion** n Befreiung f. **~or** n Befreier m

liberty n Freiheit f; **take liberties** sich (dat) Freiheiten erlauben

librarian n Bibliothekar(in) m(f)

library n Bibliothek f

Libya n Libyen nt

lice see **louse**

licence n Genehmigung f; (Comm) Lizenz f; (for TV) ≈ Fernsehgebühr f; (for driving) Führerschein m; (for alcohol) Schankkonzession f

license vt eine Genehmigung/ (Comm) Lizenz erteilen (+ dat); **be ~d** <car:> zugelassen sein; <restaurant:> Schankkonzession haben. **~-plate** n (Amer) Nummernschild nt

lick n Lecken nt; **a ~ of paint** ein bisschen Farbe ● vt lecken; (☐ defeat) schlagen

lid n Deckel m; (of eye) Lid nt

lie¹ n Lüge f; **tell a ~** lügen ● vi (pt/pp lied, pres p lying) lügen; **~ to** belügen

lie² vi (pt lay, pp lain, pres p lying) liegen; **here ~s ...** hier ruht ... **~ down** vi sich hinlegen

lie-in n **have a ~** [sich] ausschlafen

lieu n **in ~ of** statt (+ gen)

lieutenant n Oberleutnant m

life n (pl lives) Leben nt; **lose one's ~** ums Leben kommen

life: ~-boat n Rettungsboot nt. **~-guard** n Lebensretter m. **~-jacket** n Schwimmweste f. **~less** a leblos. **~like** a naturgetreu. **~long** a lebenslang. **~ preserver** n (Amer) Rettungsring m. **~-size(d)** a ... in Lebensgröße. **~time** n Leben nt; **in s.o.'s ~time** zu jds Lebzeiten; **the chance of a ~time** eine einmalige Gelegenheit

lift n Aufzug m, Lift m; **give s.o. a ~** jdn mitnehmen; **get a ~** mitgenommen werden ● vt heben; aufheben <restrictions> ● vi <fog:> sich lichten. **~ up** vt hochheben

light¹ a (-er, -est) (not dark) hell; **~ blue** hellblau ● n Licht nt; (lamp) Lampe f; **have you [got] a ~?** haben Sie Feuer? ● vt (pt/pp lit or lighted) anzünden <fire, cigarette>; (illuminate) beleuchten. **~ up** vi <face:> sich erhellen

light² a (-er, -est) (not heavy)
leicht; ~ sentence milde Strafe f
●adv travel ~ mit wenig Gepäck
reisen
light-bulb n Glühbirne f
lighten¹ vt heller machen
lighten² vt leichter machen <load>
lighter n Feuerzeug nt
light: ~-hearted a unbekümmert.
~house n Leuchtturm m. ~ing n
Beleuchtung f. ~ly adv leicht; get
off ~ly glimpflich davonkommen
lightning n Blitz m
lightweight a leicht ●n (Boxing)
Leichtgewicht nt
like¹ a ähnlich; (same) gleich
●prep wie; (similar to) ähnlich
(+ dat); ~ this so; what's he ~?
wie ist er denn? ●conj (🔲) as)
wie; (Amer: as if) als ob
like² vt mögen; I should/would ~
ich möchte; I ~ the car das Auto
gefällt mir; ~ dancing/singing
gern tanzen/singen ●n ~s and
dislikes pl Vorlieben und
Abneigungen pl
like|able a sympathisch. ~lihood
n Wahrscheinlichkeit f. ~ly a
(-ier, -iest) & adv wahrscheinlich;
not ~ly! 🔲 auf gar keinen Fall!
like-minded a gleich gesinnt
liken vt vergleichen (to mit)
like|ness n Ähnlichkeit f. ~wise
adv ebenso
liking n Vorliebe f; is it to your ~?
gefällt es Ihnen?
lilac n Flieder m
lily n Lilie f
limb n Glied nt
lime n (fruit) Limone f; (tree)
Linde f. ~light n be in the ~light
im Rampenlicht stehen
limit n Grenze f; (limitation)
Beschränkung f; that's the ~! 🔲
das ist doch die Höhe! ●vt
beschränken (to auf + acc).
~ation n Beschränkung f; ~ed a
beschränkt. ~ed company
Gesellschaft f mit beschränkter

Haftung
limousine n Limousine f
limp¹ n Hinken nt ●vi hinken
limp² a (-er -est), -ly adv schlaff
limpid a klar
line¹ n Linie f; (length of rope,
cord) Leine f; (Teleph) Leitung f;
(of writing) Zeile f; (row) Reihe f;
(wrinkle) Falte f; (of business)
Branche f; (Amer: queue)
Schlange f; in ~ with gemäß (+
dat) ●vt säumen <street>
line² vt füttern <garment>;
(Techn) auskleiden
lined¹ a (wrinkled) faltig; <paper>
liniert
lined² a <garment> gefüttert
line dancing n Linedance-
Tanzen nt
linen n Leinen nt; (articles)
Wäsche f
liner n Passagierschiff nt
linesman n Linienrichter m
linger vi [zurück]bleiben
lingerie n Damenunterwäsche f
linguist n Sprachkundige(r) m/f
linguistic a, -ally adv sprachlich
lining n (of garment) Futter nt;
(Techn) Auskleidung f
link n (of chain) Glied nt (fig)
Verbindung f ●vt verbinden; ~
arms sich unterhaken
links n or npl Golfplatz m
lint n Verbandstoff m
lion n Löwe m; ~'s share (fig)
Löwenanteil m. ~ess n Löwin f
lip n Lippe f; (edge) Rand m; (of
jug) Schnabel m
lip: ~-reading n Lippenlesen nt.
~-service n pay ~-service ein
Lippenbekenntnis ablegen (to
zu). ~stick n Lippenstift m
liqueur n Likör m
liquid n Flüssigkeit f ●a flüssig
liquidation n Liquidation f
liquidize vt [im Mixer] pürieren.
~r n Mixer m
liquor n Alkohol m. ~ store n
(Amer) Spirituosengeschäft nt

lisp n Lispeln nt ●vt/i lispeln
list¹ n Liste f; ●vt aufführen
list² vi <ship:> Schlagseite haben
listen vi zuhören (**to** dat); ~ **to the radio** Radio hören. ~**er** n Zuhörer(in) m(f); (Radio) Hörer(in) m(f)
listless a, **-ly** adv lustlos
lit see **light¹**
literacy n Lese- und Schreibfertigkeit f
literal a wörtlich. ~**ly** adv buchstäblich
literary a literarisch
literate a **be ~** lesen und schreiben können
literature n Literatur f; Ⓘ Informationsmaterial nt
lithe a geschmeidig
Lithuania n Litauen nt
litre n Liter m & nt
litter n Abfall m; (Zool) Wurf m. ~**-bin** n Abfalleimer m
little a klein; (not much) wenig ●adv & n wenig; **a ~** ein bisschen/wenig; ~ **by** ~ nach und nach
live¹ a lebendig; <ammunition> scharf; ~ **broadcast** Live-Sendung f; **be ~** (Electr) unter Strom stehen
live² vi leben; (reside) wohnen. ~ **on** vt leben von; (eat) sich ernähren von ●vi weiterleben
liveli|hood n Lebensunterhalt m. ~**ness** n Lebendigkeit f
lively a (**-ier**, **-iest**) lebhaft, lebendig
liver n Leber f
lives see **life**
livid a Ⓘ wütend
living a lebend ●n **earn one's ~** seinen Lebensunterhalt verdienen. ~**-room** n Wohnzimmer nt
lizard n Eidechse f
load n Last f; (quantity) Ladung f; (Electr) Belastung f; ~**s of** Ⓘ jede Menge ●vt laden <goods, gun>;

beladen <vehicle>; ~ **a camera** einen Film in eine Kamera einlegen. ~**ed** a beladen; (Ⓘ rich) steinreich
loaf n (pl **loaves**) Brot nt
loan n Leihgabe f; (money) Darlehen nt; **on ~** geliehen ●vt leihen (**to** dat)
loath a **be ~ to do sth** etw ungern tun
loath|e vt verabscheuen. ~**ing** n Abscheu m
loaves see **loaf¹**
lobby n Foyer nt; (anteroom) Vorraum m; (Pol) Lobby f
lobster n Hummer m
local a hiesig; <time, traffic> Orts-; ~ **anaesthetic** örtliche Betäubung; **I'm not ~** ich bin nicht von hier ●n Hiesige(r) m/f; (Ⓘ public house) Stammkneipe f. ~ **call** n (Teleph) Ortsgespräch nt
locality n Gegend f
locally adv am Ort
locat|e vt ausfindig machen; **be ~ed** sich befinden. ~**ion** n Lage f; **filmed on ~ion** als Außenaufnahme gedreht
lock¹ n (hair) Strähne f
lock² n (on door) Schloss nt; (on canal) Schleuse f ●vt abschließen ●vi sich abschließen lassen. ~ **in** vt einschließen. ~ **out** vt ausschließen. ~ **up** vt abschließen; einsperren <person>
locker n Schließfach nt; (Mil) Spind m
lock: ~**-out** n Aussperrung f. ~**smith** n Schlosser m
locomotive n Lokomotive f
locum n Vertreter(in) m(f)
locust n Heuschrecke f
lodge n (porter's) Pförtnerhaus nt ●vt (submit) einreichen; (deposit) deponieren ●vi zur Untermiete wohnen (**with** bei);

L

(*become fixed*) stecken bleiben.
~r *n* Untermieter(in) *m(f)*

lodging *n* Unterkunft *f;* ~s *npl* möbliertes Zimmer *nt*

loft *n* Dachboden *m*

lofty *a* (**-ier, -iest**) hoch

log *n* Baumstamm *m;* (*for fire*) [Holz]scheit *nt;* **sleep like a ~** 🔲 wie ein Murmeltier schlafen ● *vi* ~ **off** sich abmelden; ~ **on** sich anmelden

loggerheads *npl* **be at ~** 🔲 sich in den Haaren liegen

logic *n* Logik *f.* ~al *a,* **-ly** *adv* logisch

logo *n* Symbol *nt,* Logo *nt*

loiter *vi* herumlungern

loll *vi* sich lümmeln

loll|ipop *n* Lutscher *m.* ~y *n* Lutscher *m;* (🔲 *money*) Moneten *pl*

London *n* London *nt* ● *attrib* Londoner. ~er *n* Londoner(in) *m(f)*

lone *a* einzeln. ~liness *n* Einsamkeit *f*

lonely *a* (**-ier, -iest**) einsam

lone|r *n* Einzelgänger *m.* ~some *a* einsam

long[1] *a* (**-er, -est**) lang; <*journey*> weit; **a ~ time** lange; **a ~ way** weit; **in the ~ run** auf lange Sicht; (*in the end*) letzten Endes ● *adv* lange; **all day ~** den ganzen Tag; **not ~ ago** vor kurzem; **before ~** bald; **no ~er** nicht mehr; **as** *or* **so ~as** solange; **so ~!** 🔲 tschüs!

long[2] *vi* ~ **for** sich sehnen nach

long-distance *a* Fern-; (*Sport*) Langstrecken-

longing *a,* **-ly** *adv* sehnsüchtig ● *n* Sehnsucht *f*

longitude *n* (*Geog*) Länge *f*

long: ~ **jump** *n* Weitsprung *m.* ~-**lived** *a* langlebig. ~-**range** *a* (*Mil, Aviat*) Langstrecken-; <*forecast*> langfristig. ~-**sighted** *a* weitsichtig. ~-**sleeved** *a* langärmelig. ~-**suffering** *a*

langmütig. ~-**term** *a* langfristig. ~ **wave** *n* Langwelle. ~-**winded** *a* langatmig

loo *n* 🔲 Klo *nt*

look *n* Blick *m;* (*appearance*) Aussehen *nt;* [**good**] ~s *pl* [gutes] Aussehen *nt;* **have a ~ at** sich (*dat*) ansehen; **go and have a ~** sieh mal nach ● *vi* sehen; (*search*) nachsehen; (*seem*) aussehen; **don't ~** sieh nicht hin; ~ **here!** hören Sie mal! ~ **at** ansehen; ~ **for** suchen; ~ **forward to** sich freuen auf (+ *acc*); ~ **in on** vorbeischauen bei; ~ **into** (*examine*) nachgehen (+ *dat*); ~ **like** aussehen wie; ~ **on to** <*room:*> gehen auf (+ *acc*). ~ **after** *vt* betreuen. ~ **down** *vi* hinuntersehen; ~ **down on s.o.** (*fig*) auf jdn herabsehen. ~ **out** *vi* hinaus-/heraussehen; (*take care*) aufpassen; ~ **out for** Ausschau halten nach; ~ **out!** Vorsicht! ~ **round** *vi* sich umsehen. ~ **up** *vi* aufblicken; ~ **up to s.o.** (*fig*) zu jdm aufsehen ● *vt* nachschlagen <*word*>

look-out *n* Wache *f;* (*prospect*) Aussicht *f;* **be on the ~ for** Ausschau halten nach

loom[1] *n* Webstuhl *m*

loom[2] *vi* auftauchen

loony *a* 🔲 verrückt

loop *n* Schlinge *f;* (*in road*) Schleife *f.* ~**hole** *n* Hintertürchen *nt;* (*in the law*) Lücke *f*

loose *a* (**-r, -st**), **-ly** *adv* lose; (*not tight enough*) locker; (*inexact*) frei; **be at a ~ end** nichts zu tun haben. ~ **change** *n* Kleingeld *nt*

loosen *vt* lockern

loot *n* Beute *f* ● *vt/i* plündern. ~**er** *n* Plünderer *m*

lop *vt* (*pt/pp* **lopped**) stutzen

lopsided *a* schief

lord n Herr m; (title) Lord m; **House of L~** s ≈ Oberhaus nt; **the L~'s Prayer** das Vaterunser

lorry n Last[kraft]wagen m

lose v (pt/pp **lost**) ● vt verlieren; (miss) verpassen ● vi verlieren; <clock:> nachgehen; **get lost** verloren gehen; <person:> sich verlaufen. **~r** n Verlierer m

loss n Verlust m; **be at a ~** nicht mehr weiter wissen

lost see **lose**. **~ property office** n Fundbüro nt

lot[1] Los nt; (at auction) Posten m; **draw ~s** losen (für um)

lot[2] n **the ~** alle; (everything) alles; **a ~ [of]** viel; (many) viele; **~s of** 🗊 eine Menge; **it has changed a ~** es hat sich sehr verändert

lotion n Lotion f

lottery n Lotterie f. **~ ticket** n Los nt

loud a (-er, -est), **-ly** adv laut; <colours:> grell ● adv **[out]** ~ laut. **~ speaker** n Lautsprecher m

lounge n Wohnzimmer nt; (in hotel) Aufenthaltsraum m. ● vi sich lümmeln

louse n (pl **lice**) Laus f

lousy a (-ier, -iest) 🗊 lausig

lout n Flegel m, Lümmel m

lovable a liebenswert

love n Liebe f; (Tennis) null; **in ~** verliebt ● vt lieben; **~ doing sth** etw sehr gerne machen. **~-affair** n Liebesverhältnis nt. **~ letter** n Liebesbrief m

lovely a (-ier, -iest) schön

lover n Liebhaber m

love: **~ song** n Liebeslied nt. **~ story** n Liebesgeschichte f

loving a, **-ly** adv liebevoll

low a (-er, -est) niedrig; <cloud, note:> tief; <voice:> leise; (depressed) niedergeschlagen ● adv niedrig; <fly, sing:> tief; <speak:> leise ● n (Meteorol) Tief nt; (fig) Tiefstand m

low: **~brow** a geistig anspruchslos. **~-cut** a <dress:> tief ausgeschnitten

lower a & adv see **low** ● vt niedriger machen; (let down) herunterlassen; (reduce) senken

low: **~-fat** a fettarm. **~lands** npl Tiefland nt. **~ tide** n Ebbe f

loyal a, **-ly** adv treu. **~ty** n Treue f. **~ty card** n Treuekarte f

lozenge n Pastille f

Ltd abbr (Limited) GmbH

lubricant n Schmiermittel nt

lubricat|e vt schmieren. **~ion** n Schmierung f

lucid a klar. **~ity** n Klarheit f

luck n Glück nt; **bad ~** Pech nt; **good ~!** viel Glück! **~ily** adv glücklicherweise, zum Glück

lucky a (-ier, -iest) glücklich; <day, number:> Glücks-; **be ~** Glück haben; <thing:> Glück bringen

lucrative a einträglich

ludicrous a lächerlich

lug vt (pt/pp **lugged**) 🗊 schleppen

luggage n Gepäck nt

luggage: **~-rack** in Gepäckablage f. **~-van** n Gepäckwagen m

lukewarm a lauwarm

lull n Pause f ● vt **~ to sleep** einschläfern

lullaby n Wiegenlied nt

lumber n Gerümpel nt; (Amer: timber) Bauholz nt ● vt **~ s.o. with sth** jdm etw aufhalsen. **~jack** n (Amer) Holzfäller m

luminous a leuchtend

lump n Klumpen m; (of sugar) Stück nt; (swelling) Beule f; (in breast) Knoten m; (tumour) Geschwulst f; **a ~ in one's throat** 🗊 ein Kloß im Hals

lump: **~ sugar** n Würfelzucker m. **~ sum** n Pauschalsumme f

lumpy a (-ier, -iest) klumpig

lunacy n Wahnsinn m

lunar a Mond-

lunatic n Wahnsinnige(r) m/f

lunch *n* Mittagessen *nt* ●*vi* zu
Mittag essen
luncheon *n* Mittagessen *nt*. ~
voucher *n* Essensbon *m*
lunch: ~-**hour** *n* Mittagspause *f*.
~-**time** *n* Mittagszeit *f*
lung *n* Lungenflügel *m*; ~**s** *pl*
Lunge *f*
lunge *vi* sich stürzen (**at** auf +
acc)
lurch¹ *n* **leave in the** ~ 🛈 im Stich
lassen
lurch² *vi* <*person:*> torkeln
lure *vt* locken
lurid *a* grell; (*sensational*)
reißerisch
lurk *vi* lauern
luscious *a* lecker, köstlich
lush *a* üppig
lust *n* Begierde *f*. ~**ful** *a* lüstern
lustre *n* Glanz *m*
lusty *a* (-**ier**, -**iest**) kräftig
luxuriant *a* üppig
luxurious *a*, -**ly** *adv* luxuriös
luxury *n* Luxus *m* ●*attrib* Luxus-
lying *see* **lie**¹, **lie**²
lynch *vt* lynchen
lyric *a* lyrisch. ~**al** *a* lyrisch;
(*enthusiastic*) schwärmerisch. ~
poetry *n* Lyrik *f*. ~**s** *npl*
[Lied]text *m*

mac *n* 🛈 Regenmantel *m*
macabre *a* makaber
macaroni *n* Makkaroni *pl*
machine *n* Maschine *f* ●*vt* (*sew*)
mit der Maschine nähen; (*Techn*)
maschinell bearbeiten. ~-**gun** *n*
Maschinengewehr *nt*
machinery *n* Maschinerie *f*

mackerel *n inv* Makrele *f*
mackintosh *n* Regenmantel *m*
mad *a* (**madder, maddest**) verrückt;
(*dog*) tollwütig; (*fam: angry*) böse
(**at** auf + *acc*)
madam *n* gnädige Frau *f*
mad cow disease *n* 🛈
Rinderwahnsinn *m*
madden *vt* (*make angry*) wütend
machen
madden *vt* (*make angry*) wütend
machen
made *see* **make**; ~ **to measure**
maßgeschneidert
mad|ly *adv* 🛈 wahnsinnig. ~**man**
n Irre(r) *m*. ~**ness** *n* Wahnsinn
m
madonna *n* Madonna *f*
magazine *n* Zeitschrift *f*; (*Mil,
Phot*) Magazin *nt*
maggot *n* Made *f*
magic *n* Zauber *m*; (*tricks*)
Zauberkunst *f* ●*a* magisch;
<*word, wand*> Zauber-. ~**al** *a*
zauberhaft
magician *n* Zauberer *m*;
(*entertainer*) Zauberkünstler *m*
magistrate *n* ≈ Friedensrichter *m*
magnet *n* Magnet *m*. ~**ic** *a*
magnetisch. ~**ism** *n*
Magnetismus *m*
magnification *n* Vergrößerung *f*
magnificen|ce *n* Großartigkeit *f*.
~**t** *a*, -**ly** *adv* großartig
magnify *vt* (*pt/pp* -**ied**)
vergrößern; (*exaggerate*)
übertreiben. ~**ing glass** *n*
Vergrößerungsglas *nt*
magnitude *n* Größe *f*;
(*importance*) Bedeutung *f*
magpie *n* Elster *f*
mahogany *n* Mahagoni *nt*
maid *n* Dienstmädchen *nt*; **old** ~
(*pej*) alte Jungfer *f*
maiden *a* <*speech, voyage*>
Jungfern-. ~ **name** *n*
Mädchenname *m*
mail *n* Post *f* ●*vt* mit der Post
schicken

mail: ~**bag** n Postsack m. ~**box** n (Amer) Briefkasten m. ~**ing list** n Postversandliste f. ~**man** n (Amer) Briefträger m. ~**order firm** n Versandhaus nt

maim vt verstümmeln

main a Haupt- ● n (water, gas, electricity) Hauptleitung f

main: ~**land** n Festland nt. ~**ly** adv hauptsächlich. ~**stay** n (fig) Stütze f. ~ **street** n Hauptstraße f

maintain vt aufrechterhalten; (keep in repair) instand halten; (support) unterhalten; (claim) behaupten

maintenance n Aufrechterhaltung f; (care) Instandhaltung f; (allowance) Unterhalt m

maize n Mais m

majestic a, **-ally** adv majestätisch

majesty n Majestät f

major a größer ● n (Mil) Major m; (Mus) Dur nt ● vi ~ **in** als Hauptfach studieren

majority n Mehrheit f; **in the** ~ in der Mehrzahl

major road n Hauptverkehrsstraße f

make n (brand) Marke f ● v (pt/ pp **made**) ● vt machen; (force) zwingen; (earn) verdienen; halten <speech>; treffen <decision>; erreichen <destination> ● vi ~ **do** vi zurechtkommen (**with** mit). ~ **for** vi zusteuern auf (+ acc). ~ **off** vi sich davonmachen (**with** mit). ~ **out** vt (distinguish) ausmachen; (write out) ausstellen; (assert) behaupten. ~ **up** vt (constitute) bilden; (invent) erfinden; (apply cosmetics) schminken; ~ **up one's mind** sich entschließen ● vi sich versöhnen; ~ **up for sth** etw wieder gutmachen; ~ **up for lost time** verlorene Zeit aufholen

make-believe n Phantasie f

maker n Hersteller m

make: ~ **shift** a behelfsmäßig ● n Notbehelf m. ~**-up** n Make-up nt

maladjusted a verhaltensgestört

male a männlich ● n Mann m; (animal) Männchen nt. ~ **nurse** n Krankenpfleger m. ~ **voice choir** n Männerchor m

malice n Bosheit f

malicious a, **-ly** adv böswillig

malign vt verleumden

malignant a bösartig

mallet n Holzhammer m

malnutrition n Unterernährung f

malpractice n Berufsvergehen nt

malt n Malz nt

maltreat vt misshandeln. ~**ment** n Misshandlung f

mammal n Säugetier nt

mammoth a riesig

man n (pl **men**) Mann m; (mankind) der Mensch; (chess) Figur f; (draughts) Stein m ● vt (pt/pp **manned**) bemannen <ship>; bedienen <pump>; besetzen <counter>

manage vt leiten; verwalten <estate>; (cope with) fertig werden mit; ~ **to do sth** es schaffen, etw zu tun ● vi zurechtkommen; ~ **on** auskommen mit. ~**able** a <tool> handlich; <person> fügsam. ~**ment** n Leitung f; **the** ~**ment** die Geschäftsleitung f

manager n Geschäftsführer m; (of bank) Direktor m; (of estate) Verwalter m; (Sport) [Chef]trainer m. ~**ess** n Geschäftsführerin f. ~**ial** a **-ial staff** Führungskräfte pl

managing a ~ **director** Generaldirektor m

mandate n Mandat nt. ~**ory** a obligatorisch

mane n Mähne f

manful a, **-ly** adv mannhaft

man: ~**handle** vt grob behandeln <person>. ~**hole** n Kanalschacht *m.* **~hood** *n* Mannesalter *nt*; (*quality*) Männlichkeit *f.* **~-hour** *n* Arbeitsstunde *f.* **~-hunt** *n* Fahndung *f*

mania *n* Manie *f.* **~c** *n* Wahnsinnige(r) *m/f*

manicure *n* Maniküre *f* ●*vt* maniküren

manifest *a*, **-ly** *adv* offensichtlich

manifesto *n* Manifest *nt*

manifold *a* mannigfaltig

manipulat|e *vt* handhaben; (*pej*) manipulieren. **~ion** *n* Manipulation *f*

mankind *n* die Menschheit

manly *a* männlich

man-made *a* künstlich. **~ fibre** *n* Kunstfaser *f*

manner *n* Weise *f*; (*kind, behaviour*) Art *f*; [**good/bad**] **~s** [gute/schlechte] Manieren *pl.* **~ism** *n* Angewohnheit *f*

manœuvrable *a* manövrierfähig

manœuvre *n* Manöver *nt* ●*vt/i* manövrieren

manor *n* Gutshof *m*; (*house*) Gutshaus *nt*

manpower *n* Arbeitskräfte *pl*

mansion *n* Villa *f*

manslaughter *n* Totschlag *m*

mantelpiece *n* Kaminsims *m & nt*

manual *a* Hand- ●*n* Handbuch *nt*

manufacture *vt* herstellen ●*n* Herstellung *f.* **~r** *n* Hersteller *m*

manure *n* Mist *m*

manuscript *n* Manuskript *nt*

many *a* viele ●*n* **a good/great ~** sehr viele

map *n* Landkarte *f*; (*of town*) Stadtplan *m*

maple *n* Ahorn *m*

mar *vt* (*pt/pp* marred) verderben

marathon *n* Marathon *m*

marble *n* Marmor *m*; (*for game*) Murmel *f*

March *n* März *m*

march *n* Marsch *m* ●*vi* marschieren ●*vt* marschieren lassen; **~ s.o. off** jdn abführen

mare *n* Stute *f*

margarine *n* Margarine *f*

margin *n* Rand *m*; (*leeway*) Spielraum *m*; (*Comm*) Spanne *f.* **~al** *a*, **-ly** *adv* geringfügig

marigold *n* Ringelblume *f*

marina *n* Jachthafen *m*

marine *a* Meeres- ●*n* Marine *f*; (*sailor*) Marineinfanterist *m*

marital *a* ehelich. **~ status** *n* Familienstand *m*

maritime *a* See-

mark¹ *n* (*former German currency*) Mark *f*

mark² *n* Fleck *m*; (*sign*) Zeichen *nt*; (*trace*) Spur *f*; (*target*) Ziel *nt*; (*Sch*) Note *f* ●*vt* markieren; (*spoil*) beschädigen; (*characterize*) kennzeichnen; (*Sch*) korrigieren; (*Sport*) decken; **~ time** (*Mil*) auf der Stelle treten; (*fig*) abwarten. **~ out** *vt* markieren

marked *a*, **~ly** *adv* deutlich; (*pronounced*) ausgeprägt

market *n* Markt *m* ●*vt* vertreiben; (*launch*) auf den Markt bringen. **~ing** *n* Marketing *nt.* **~ research** *n* Marktforschung *f*

marking *n* Markierung *f*; (*on animal*) Zeichnung *f*

marksman *n* Scharfschütze *m*

marmalade *n* Orangenmarmelade *f*

maroon *a* dunkelrot

marooned *a* (*fig*) von der Außenwelt abgeschnitten

marquee *n* Festzelt *nt*

marquetry *n* Einlegearbeit *f*

marriage *n* Ehe *f*; (*wedding*) Hochzeit *f.* **~able** *a* heiratsfähig

married *see* marry ●*a* verheiratet. **~ life** *n* Eheleben *nt*

marrow *n* (*Anat*) Mark *nt*; (*vegetable*) Kürbis *m*

marr|y vt/i (pt/pp **married**) heiraten; (unite) trauen; **get ~ied** heiraten

marsh n Sumpf m

marshal n Marschall m; (steward) Ordner m

marshy a sumpfig

martial a kriegerisch. ~ **law** n Kriegsrecht nt

martyr n Märtyrer(in) m(f). ~**dom** n Martyrium nt

marvel n Wunder nt ● vi (pt/pp **marvelled**) staunen (at über + acc). ~**lous** a, -**ly** adv wunderbar

Marxis|m n Marxismus m. ~**t** a marxistisch ● n Marxist(in) m(f)

marzipan n Marzipan nt

mascot n Maskottchen nt

masculin|e a männlich ● n (Gram) Maskulinum nt. ~**ity** n Männlichkeit f

mash n 🇬🇧, ~**ed potatoes** npl Kartoffelpüree nt

mask n Maske f ● vt maskieren

masochis|m n Masochismus m. ~**t** n Masochist m

mason n Steinmetz m. ~**ry** n Mauerwerk nt

mass[1] n (Relig) Messe f

mass[2] n Masse f ● vi sich sammeln; (Mil) sich massieren

massacre n Massaker nt ● vt niedermetzeln

massage n Massage f ● vt massieren

masseu|r n Masseur m. ~**se** n Masseuse f

massive a massiv; (huge) riesig

mass: ~ **media** npl Massenmedien pl. ~-**produce** vt in Massenproduktion herstellen. ~ **production** n Massenproduktion f

mast n Mast m

master n Herr m; (teacher) Lehrer m; (craftsman, artist) Meister m; (of ship) Kapitän m ● vt meistern; beherrschen <language>

master: ~**ly** a meisterhaft. ~-**mind** n führender Kopf m ● vt der führende Kopf sein. ~**piece** n Meisterwerk nt. ~**y** n (of subject) Beherrschung f

mat n Matte f; (on table) Untersatz m

match[1] n Wettkampf m; (in ball games) Spiel nt; (Tennis) Match nt; (marriage) Heirat f; **be a good** ~ <colours:> gut zusammenpassen; **be no** ~ **for s.o.** jdm nicht gewachsen sein ● vt (equal) gleichkommen (+ dat); (be like) passen zu; (find sth similar) etwas Passendes finden zu ● vi zusammenpassen

match[2] n Streichholz nt. ~**box** n Streichholzschachtel f

mate[1] n Kumpel m; (assistant) Gehilfe m; (Naut) Maat m; (Zool) Männchen nt; (female) Weibchen nt ● vi sich paaren

mate[2] n (Chess) Matt nt

material n Material nt; (fabric) Stoff m; **raw** ~**s** Rohstoffe pl ● a materiell

material|ism n Materialismus m. ~**istic** a materialistisch. ~**ize** vi sich verwirklichen

maternal a mütterlich

maternity n Mutterschaft f. ~ **clothes** npl Umstandskleidung f. ~ **ward** n Entbindungsstation f

mathematic|al a, -**ly** adv mathematisch. ~**ian** n Mathematiker(in) m(f)

mathematics n Mathematik f

maths n 🇬🇧 Mathe f

matinée n (Theat) Nachmittagsvorstellung f

matrimony n Ehe f

matron n (of hospital) Oberin f; (of school) Hausmutter f

matt a matt

matted a verfilzt

matter n (affair) Sache f; (Phys: substance) Materie f; **money** ~**s** Geldangelegenheiten pl; **what is**

M

the **~**? was ist los? ● *vi* wichtig
sein; **~ to s.o.** jdm etwas
ausmachen; **it doesn't ~** es macht
nichts. **~-of-fact** *a* sachlich
mattress *n* Matratze *f*
matur|e *a* reif; (*Comm*) fällig ● *vi*
reifen; <*person:*> reifer werden;
(*Comm*) fällig werden ● *vt* reifen
lassen. **~ity** *n* Reife *f*; (*Comm*)
Fälligkeit *f*
mauve *a* lila
maximum *a* maximal ● *n* (*pl* **-ima**)
Maximum *nt*. **~ speed** *n*
Höchstgeschwindigkeit *f*

may
  pres **may**, *pt* **might**
● *auxiliary verb*
····▸ (*expressing possibility*)
  können. **she may come** es kann
  sein, dass sie kommt; es ist
  möglich, dass sie kommt. **she
  might come** (*more distant
  possibility*) sie könnte kommen.
  it may/might rain es könnte
  regnen. **I may be wrong** vielleicht
  irre ich mich. **he may have
  missed his train** vielleicht hat er
  seinen Zug verpasst
····▸ (*expressing permission*)
  dürfen. **may I come in?** darf ich
  reinkommen? **you may smoke**
  Sie dürfen rauchen
····▸ (*expressing wish*) **may the best
  man win!** auf dass der Beste
  gewinnt!
····▸ (*expressing concession*) **he
  may be slow but he's accurate**
  mag *od* kann sein, dass er
  langsam ist, aber dafür ist er
  auch genau
····▸ **may/might as well** ebenso gut
  können. **we may/might as well go**
  wir könnten eigentlich
  ebensogut [auch] gehen. **we
  might as well give up** da können
  wir gleich aufgeben

May *n* Mai *m*

maybe *adv* vielleicht
May Day *n* der Erste Mai
mayonnaise *n* Mayonnaise *f*
mayor *n* Bürgermeister *m*. **~ess**
n Bürgermeisterin *f*; (*wife of
mayor*) Frau Bürgermeister *f*
maze *n* Irrgarten *m*; (*fig*)
Labyrinth *nt*
me *pron* (*acc*) mich; (*dat*) mir; **it's
~** 🔟 ich bin es
meadow *n* Wiese *f*
meagre *a* dürftig
meal *n* Mahlzeit *f*; (*food*) Essen
nt; (*grain*) Schrot *m*
mean[1] *a* (**-er, -est**) (*miserly*) geizig;
(*unkind*) gemein; (*poor*) schäbig
mean[2] *a* mittlere(r,s) ● *n*
(*average*) Durchschnitt *m*
mean[3] *vt* (*pt/pp* **meant**) heißen;
(*signify*) bedeuten; (*intend*)
beabsichtigen; **I ~ it** das ist mein
Ernst; **~ well** es gut meinen; **be
meant for** <*present:*> bestimmt
sein für; <*remark:*> gerichtet sein
an (+ *acc*)
meaning *n* Bedeutung *f*. **~ful** *a*
bedeutungsvoll. **~less** *a*
bedeutungslos
means *n* Möglichkeit *f*, Mittel *nt*;
~ of transport Verkehrsmittel *nt*;
by ~ of durch; **by all ~!** aber
natürlich! **by no ~** keineswegs
● *npl* (*resources*) [Geld]mittel *pl*
meant *see* **mean**[3]
meantime *n* **in the ~** in der
Zwischenzeit ● *adv* inzwischen
meanwhile *adv* inzwischen
measles *n* Masern *pl*
measure *n* Maß *nt*; (*action*)
Maßnahme *f* ● *vt/i* messen; **~ up
to** (*fig*) herankommen an (+ *acc*).
~d *a* gemessen. **~ment** *n* Maß *nt*
meat *n* Fleisch *nt*
mechan|ic *n* Mechaniker *m*.
~ical *a*, **-ly** *adv* mechanisch.
~ical engineering Maschinenbau
m
mechan|ism *n* Mechanismus *m*.
~ize *vt* mechanisieren

medal n Orden m; (Sport)
Medaille f

medallist n
Medaillengewinner(in) m(f)

meddle vi sich einmischen (**in** in
+ acc); (tinker) herumhantieren
(**with** an + acc)

media see **medium** ● n pl **the ~** die
Medien pl

mediat|e vi vermitteln. **~or** n
Vermittler(in) m(f)

medical a medizinisch;
<treatment> ärztlich ● n ärztliche
Untersuchung f. **~ insurance** n
Krankenversicherung f. **~
student** n Medizinstudent m

medicat|ed a medizinisch. **~ion**
n (drugs) Medikamente pl

medicinal a medizinisch; <plant>
heilkräftig

medicine n Medizin f;
(preparation) Medikament nt

medieval a mittelalterlich

mediocr|e a mittelmäßig. **~ity** n
Mittelmäßigkeit f

meditat|e vi nachdenken (**on**
über + acc). **~ion** n Meditation f

Mediterranean n Mittelmeer nt
● a Mittelmeer-

medium a mittlere(r,s); <steak>
medium; **of ~ size** von mittlerer
Größe ● n (pl **media**) Medium nt;
(means) Mittel nt

medium: **~-sized** a mittelgroß. **~
wave** n Mittelwelle f

medley n Gemisch nt; (Mus)
Potpourri m

meek a (-er, -est), **-ly** adv
sanftmütig; (unprotesting)
widerspruchslos

meet v (pt/pp **met**) ● vt treffen;
(by chance) begegnen (+ dat); (at
station) abholen; (make the
acquaintance of) kennen lernen;
stoßen auf (+ acc) <problem>;
bezahlen <bill>; erfüllen
<requirements> ● vi sich treffen;
(for the first time) sich kennen
lernen

meeting n Treffen nt; (by chance)
Begegnung f; (discussion)
Besprechung f; (of committee)
Sitzung f; (large) Versammlung f

megalomania n Größenwahnsinn
m

megaphone n Megaphon nt

melancholy a melancholisch ● n
Melancholie f

mellow a(-er, -est) <fruit>
ausgereift; <sound, person> sanft
● vi reifer werden

melodious a melodiös

melodramatic a, **-ally** adv
melodramatisch

melody n Melodie f

melon n Melone f

melt vt/i schmelzen

member n Mitglied nt; (of family)
Angehörige(r) m/f; **M~ of
Parliament** Abgeordnete(r) m/f.
~ship n Mitgliedschaft f;
(members) Mitgliederzahl f

memento n Andenken nt

memo n Mitteilung f

memoirs n pl Memoiren pl

memorable a denkwürdig

memorial n Denkmal nt. **~
service** n Gedenkfeier f

memorize vt sich (dat) einprägen

memory n Gedächtnis m; (thing
remembered) Erinnerung f; (of
computer) Speicher m; **from ~**
auswendig; **in ~ of** zur
Erinnerung an (+ acc)

men see **man**

menac|e n Drohung f; (nuisance)
Plage f ● vt bedrohen. **~ing** a,
~ly adv drohend

mend vt reparieren; (patch)
flicken; ausbessern <clothes>

menfolk n pl Männer pl

menial a niedrig

menopause n Wechseljahre pl

mental a, **-ly** adv geistig; (🔲 mad)
verrückt. **~ arithmetic** n
Kopfrechnen nt. **~ illness** n
Geisteskrankheit f

mentality n Mentalität f

M

mention n Erwähnung f ● vt
erwähnen; **don't ~ it** keine
Ursache; bitte
menu n Speisekarte f
merchandise n Ware f
merchant n Kaufmann m;
(*dealer*) Händler m. **~ navy** n
Handelsmarine f
merci|ful a barmherzig. **~fully**
adv ⚠ glücklicherweise. **~less** a,
-ly adv erbarmungslos
mercury n Quecksilber nt
mercy n Barmherzigkeit f, Gnade
f; **be at s.o.'s ~** jdm ausgeliefert
sein
mere a, **-ly** adv bloß
merest a kleinste(r,s)
merge vi zusammenlaufen;
(*Comm*) fusionieren
merger n Fusion f
meringue n Baiser nt
merit n Verdienst nt; (*advantage*)
Vorzug m; (*worth*) Wert m ● vt
verdienen
merry a (**-ier, -iest**) fröhlich
merry-go-round n Karussell nt
mesh n Masche f
mesmerized a (*fig*) [wie] gebannt
mess n Durcheinander nt;
(*trouble*) Schwierigkeiten pl;
(*something spilt*) Bescherung f ⚠;
(*Mil*) Messe f; **make a ~ of** (*botch*)
verpfuschen ● vt **~ up** in
Unordnung bringen; (*botch*)
verpfuschen ● vi **~ about**
herumalbern; (*tinker*)
herumspielen (**with** mit)
message n Nachricht f; **give s.o. a**
~ jdm etwas ausrichten
messenger n Bote m
Messrs n pl see **Mr**; (*on letter*) **~**
Smith Firma Smith
messy a (**-ier, -iest**) schmutzig;
(*untidy*) unordentlich
met see **meet**
metal n Metall nt ● a Metall-.
~lic a metallisch
metaphor n Metapher f. **~ical** a,
-ly adv metaphorisch

meteor n Meteor m. **~ic** a
kometenhaft
meteorological a Wetter-
meteorolog|ist n Meteorologe m/
-gin f. **~y** n Meteorologie f
meter[1] n Zähler m
meter[2] n (*Amer*) = metre
method n Methode f; (*Culin*)
Zubereitung f
methodical a, **-ly** adv
systematisch, methodisch
methylated a **~ spirit[s]**
Brennspiritus m
meticulous a, **-ly** adv sehr genau
metre n Meter m & n; (*rhythm*)
Versmaß nt
metric a metrisch
metropolis n Metropole f
mew n Miau nt ● vi miauen
Mexican a mexikanisch ● n
Mexikaner(in) m(f). **Mexico** n
Mexiko nt
miaow n Miau nt ● vi miauen
mice see **mouse**
micro: **~film** n Mikrofilm m.
~light [aircraft] n
Ultraleichtflugzeug nt. **~phone** n
Mikrofon nt. **~scope** n
Mikroskop nt. **~scopic** a
mikroskopisch. **~wave [oven]** n
Mikrowellenherd m
mid a **~ May** Mitte Mai; **in ~ air** in
der Luft
midday n Mittag m
middle a mittlere(r,s); **the M~**
Ages das Mittelalter; **the ~**
class[es] der Mittelstand; **the M~**
East der Nahe Osten ● n Mitte f;
in the ~ of the night mitten in der
Nacht
middle: **~-aged** a mittleren
Alters. **~-class** a bürgerlich
midge n [kleine] Mücke f
midget n Liliputaner(in) m(f)
Midlands npl **the ~** Mittelengland
n
midnight n Mitternacht f
midriff n ⚠ Taille f

midst n in the ~ of mitten in (+ dat); in our ~ unter uns
mid: ~**summer** n Hochsommer m. ~**way** adv auf halbem Wege. ~**wife** n Hebamme f. ~**winter** n Mitte f des Winters
might¹ v aux I ~ vielleicht; it ~ be true es könnte wahr sein; he asked if he ~ go er fragte, ob er gehen dürfte; you ~ have drowned du hättest ertrinken können
might² n Macht f
mighty a (-ier, -iest) mächtig
migraine n Migräne f
migrat|e vi abwandern; <birds:> ziehen. ~**ion** n Wanderung f; (of birds) Zug m
mike n 🛈 Mikrofon nt
mild a (-er, -est) mild
mild|ly adv leicht; to put it ~ly gelinde gesagt. ~**ness** n Milde f
mile n Meile f (= 1,6 km); ~**s too big** 🛈 viel zu groß
mile|age n Meilenzahl f; (of car) Meilenstand m
militant a militant
military a militärisch. ~ **service** n Wehrdienst m
milk n Milch f ● vt melken
milk: ~**man** n Milchmann m. ~**shake** n Milchmixgetränk nt. ~**tooth** n Milchzahn m
milky a (-ier, -iest) milchig. **M~ Way** n (Astr) Milchstraße f
mill n Mühle f; (factory) Fabrik f
millennium n Jahrtausend nt
milli|gram n Milligramm nt. ~**metre** n Millimeter m & nt
million n Million f; **a ~ pounds** eine Million Pfund. ~**aire** n Millionär(in) m(f)
mime n Pantomime f ● vt pantomimisch darstellen
mimic n Imitator m ● vt (pt/pp mimicked) nachahmen
mince n Hackfleisch nt ● vt (Culin) durchdrehen; **not ~ words** kein Blatt vor den Mund nehmen

mince: ~**meat** n Masse f aus Korinthen, Zitronat usw; **make ~ meat of** (fig) vernichtend schlagen. ~ **pie** n mit 'mincemeat' gefülltes Pastetchen nt
mincer n Fleischwolf m
mind n Geist m; (sanity) Verstand m; **give s.o. a piece of one's ~** jdm gehörig die Meinung sagen; **make up one's ~** sich entschließen; **be out of one's ~** nicht bei Verstand sein; **have sth in ~** etw im Sinn haben; **bear sth in ~** an etw (acc) denken; **have a good ~ to** große Lust haben, zu; **I have changed my ~** ich habe es mir anders überlegt ● vt aufpassen auf (+ acc); **I don't ~ the noise** der Lärm stört mich nicht; ~ **the step!** Achtung Stufe! ● vi (care) sich kümmern (about um); **I don't ~** mir macht es nichts aus; **never ~!** macht nichts! **do you ~ if?** haben Sie etwas dagegen, wenn? ~ **out** vi aufpassen
mindless a geistlos
mine¹ poss pron meine(r), meins; **a friend of ~** ein Freund von mir; **that is ~** das gehört mir
mine² n Bergwerk nt; (explosive) Mine f ● vt abbauen; (Mil) verminen
miner n Bergarbeiter m
mineral n Mineral nt. ~ **water** n Mineralwasser nt
minesweeper n Minenräumboot nt
mingle vi ~ **with** sich mischen unter (+ acc)
miniature a Klein- ● n Miniatur f
mini|bus n Kleinbus m. ~**cab** n Kleintaxi nt
minim|al a minimal. ~**um** n (pl -ima) Minimum nt ● a Mindest-
mining n Bergbau m
miniskirt n Minirock m
minister n Minister m; (Relig) Pastor m. ~**ial** a ministeriell

ministry n (Pol) Ministerium nt

mink n Nerz m

minor a kleiner; (less important) unbedeutend ● n Minderjährige(r) m/f; (Mus) Moll nt

minority Minderheit f

minor road n Nebenstraße f

mint[1] n Münzstätte f ● a <stamp> postfrisch; **in ~ condition** wie neu ● vt prägen

mint[2] n (herb) Minze f; (sweet) Pfefferminzbonbon m & nt

minus prep minus, weniger; (🗉 without) ohne

minute[1] n Minute f; **in a ~** (shortly) gleich; **~s** pl (of meeting) Protokoll nt

minute[2] a winzig

mirac|le n Wunder nt. **~ulous** a wunderbar

mirror n Spiegel m ● vt widerspiegeln

mirth n Heiterkeit f

misadventure n Missgeschick nt

misapprehension n Missverständnis nt; **be under a ~** sich irren

misbehav|e vi sich schlecht benehmen. **~iour** n schlechtes Benehmen nt

miscalcu|late vt falsch berechnen ● vi sich verrechnen. **~lation** n Fehlkalkulation f

miscarriage n Fehlgeburt f

miscellaneous a vermischt

mischief n Unfug m

mischievous a, **-ly** adv schelmisch; (malicious) boshaft

misconception n falsche Vorstellung f

misconduct n unkorrektes Verhalten nt; (adultery) Ehebruch m

miser n Geizhals m

miserable a, **-bly** adv unglücklich; (wretched) elend

miserly adv geizig

misery n Elend nt; (🗉 person) Miesepeter m

misfire vi fehlzünden; (go wrong) fehlschlagen

misfit n Außenseiter(in) m(f)

misfortune n Unglück nt

misgivings npl Bedenken pl

misguided a töricht

mishap n Missgeschick nt

misinform vt falsch unterrichten

misinterpret vt missdeuten

misjudge vt falsch beurteilen

mislay vt (pt/pp -laid) verlegen

mislead vt (pt/pp -led) irreführen. **~ing** a irreführend

mismanage vt schlecht verwalten. **~ment** n Misswirtschaft f

misnomer n Fehlbezeichnung f

misprint n Druckfehler m

misquote vt falsch zitieren

misrepresent vt falsch darstellen

miss n Fehltreffer m ● vt verpassen; (fail to hit or find) verfehlen; (fail to attend) versäumen; (fail to notice) übersehen; (feel the loss of) vermissen ● vi (fail to hit) nicht treffen. **~ out** vt auslassen

Miss n (pl **-es**) Fräulein nt

missile n [Wurf]geschoss nt; (Mil) Rakete f

missing a fehlend; (lost) verschwunden; (Mil) vermisst; **be ~** fehlen

mission n Auftrag m; (Mil) Einsatz m; (Relig) Mission f

missionary n Missionar(in) m(f)

misspell vt (pt/pp -spelt or -spelled) falsch schreiben

mist n Dunst m; (fog) Nebel m; (on window) Beschlag m ● vi **~ up** beschlagen

mistake n Fehler m; **by ~** aus Versehen ● vt (pt mistook, pp mistaken) **~ for** verwechseln mit

mistaken a falsch; **be ~** sich irren. **~ly** adv irrtümlicherweise

mistletoe n Mistel f

mistress n Herrin f; *(teacher)* Lehrerin f; *(lover)* Geliebte f
mistrust n Misstrauen nt ● vt misstrauen (+ dat)
misty a (-ier, -iest) dunstig; *(foggy)* neblig; *(fig)* unklar
misunderstand vt *(pt/pp -stood)* missverstehen. ~ing n Missverständnis nt
misuse¹ vt missbrauchen
misuse² n Missbrauch m
mitigating a mildernd
mix n Mischung f ● vt mischen ● vi sich mischen; ~ **with** *(associate with)* verkehren mit. ~ **up** vt mischen; *(muddle)* durcheinander bringen; *(mistake for)* verwechseln (**with** mit)
mixed a gemischt; **be** ~ **up** durcheinander sein
mixer n Mischmaschine f; *(Culin)* Küchenmaschine f
mixture n Mischung f; *(medicine)* Mixtur f; *(Culin)* Teig m
mix-up n Durcheinander nt; *(confusion)* Verwirrung f; *(mistake)* Verwechslung f
moan n Stöhnen nt ● vi stöhnen; *(complain)* jammern
mob n Horde f; *(rabble)* Pöbel m; (🔲 *gang*) Bande f ● vt *(pt/pp mobbed)* herfallen über (+ acc); belagern *<celebrity>*
mobile a beweglich ● n Mobile nt; *(telephone)* Handy nt. ~ **home** n Wohnwagen m. ~ **phone** n Handy nt
mobility n Beweglichkeit f
mock a Schein- ● vt verspotten. ~ery n Spott m
mock-up n Modell nt
mode n [Art und] Weise f; *(fashion)* Mode f
model n Modell nt; *(example)* Vorbild nt; **[fashion]** ~ Mannequin nt ● a Modell-; *(exemplary)* Muster- ● v *(pt/pp modelled)* ● vt formen, modellieren; vorführen *<clothes>*

● vi Mannequin sein; *(for artist)* Modell stehen
moderate¹ vt mäßigen
moderate² a mäßig; *<opinion>* gemäßigt. ~ly adv mäßig; *(fairly)* einigermaßen
moderation n Mäßigung f; **in** ~ mit Maß[en]
modern a modern. ~ize vt modernisieren. ~ **languages** npl neuere Sprachen pl
modest a bescheiden; *(decorous)* schamhaft. ~y n Bescheidenheit f
modif|ication n Abänderung f. ~y vt *(pt/pp -fied)* abändern
moist a (-er, -est) feucht
moisten vt befeuchten
moistur|e n Feuchtigkeit f. ~izer n Feuchtigkeitscreme f
molar n Backenzahn m
mole¹ n Leberfleck m
mole² n *(Zool)* Maulwurf m
molecule n Molekül nt
molest vt belästigen
mollify vt *(pt/pp -ied)* besänftigen
mollycoddle vt verzärteln
molten a geschmolzen
mom n *(Amer fam)* Mutti f
moment n Moment m, Augenblick m; **at the** ~ im Augenblick, augenblicklich. ~ary a vorübergehend
momentous a bedeutsam
momentum n Schwung m
monarch n Monarch(in) m(f). ~y n Monarchie f
monastery n Kloster nt
Monday n Montag m
money n Geld nt
money: ~-**box** n Sparbüchse f. ~-**lender** n Geldverleiher m. ~ **order** n Zahlungsanweisung f
mongrel n Promenadenmischung f
monitor n *(Techn)* Monitor m ● vt überwachen *<progress>*; abhören *<broadcast>*
monk n Mönch m

M

monkey *n* Affe *m*

mono *n* Mono *nt*

monogram *n* Monogramm *nt*

monologue *n* Monolog *m*

monopol|ize *vt* monopolisieren. **~y** *n* Monopol *nt*

monosyllable *n* einsilbiges Wort *nt*

monotone *n* **in a ~** mit monotoner Stimme

monoton|ous *a*, **-ly** *adv* eintönig, monoton; (*tedious*) langweilig. **~y** *n* Eintönigkeit *f*, Monotonie *f*

monster *n* Ungeheuer *nt*; (*cruel person*) Unmensch *m*

monstrosity *n* Monstrosität *f*

monstrous *a* ungeheuer; (*outrageous*) ungeheuerlich

month *n* Monat *m*. **~ly** *a & adv* monatlich ● *n* (*periodical*) Monatszeitschrift *f*

monument *n* Denkmal *nt*. **~al** *a* (*fig*) monumental

moo *n* Muh *nt* ● *vi* (*pt/pp* **mooed**) muhen

mood *n* Laune *f*; **be in a good/bad ~** gute/schlechte Laune haben

moody *a* (**-ier, -iest**) launisch

moon *n* Mond *m*; **over the ~** ☐ überglücklich

moon: ~light *n* Mondschein *m*. **~lighting** *n* ☐ ≈ Schwarzarbeit *f*. **~lit** *a* mondhell

moor[1] *n* Moor *nt*

moor[2] *vt* (*Naut*) festmachen ● *vi* anlegen

mop *n* Mopp *m*; **~ of hair** Wuschelkopf *m* ● *vt* (*pt/pp* **mopped**) wischen. **~ up** *vt* aufwischen

moped *n* Moped *nt*

moral *a*, **-ly** *adv* moralisch, sittlich; (*virtuous*) tugendhaft ● *n* Moral *f*; **~s** *pl* Moral *f*

morale *n* Moral *f*

morality *n* Sittlichkeit *f*

morbid *a* krankhaft; (*gloomy*) trübe

more *a*, *adv* & *n* mehr; (*in addition*) noch; **a few ~** noch ein paar; **any ~** noch etwas; **once ~** noch einmal; **~ or less** mehr oder weniger; **some ~ tea?** noch etwas Tee? **~ interesting** interessanter; **~ [and ~] quickly** [immer] schneller

moreover *adv* außerdem

morgue *n* Leichenschauhaus *nt*

morning *n* Morgen *m*; **in the ~** morgens, am Morgen; (*tomorrow*) morgen früh

Morocco *n* Marokko *nt*

moron *n* ☐ Idiot *m*

morose *a*, **-ly** *adv* mürrisch

morsel *n* Happen *m*

mortal *a* sterblich; (*fatal*) tödlich ● *n* Sterbliche(r) *m/f*. **~ity** *n* Sterblichkeit *f*. **~ly** *adv* tödlich

mortar *n* Mörtel *m*

mortgage *n* Hypothek *f* ● *vt* hypothekarisch belasten

mortuary *n* Leichenhalle *f*; (*public*) Leichenschauhaus *nt*; (*Amer: undertaker's*) Bestattungsinstitut *nt*

mosaic *n* Mosaik *nt*

Moscow *n* Moskau *nt*

mosque *n* Moschee *f*

mosquito *n* (*pl* **-es**) [Stech]mücke *f*, Schnake *f*; (*tropical*) Moskito *m*

moss *n* Moos *nt*. **~y** *a* moosig

most *a* der/die/das meiste; (*majority*) die meisten; **for the ~ part** zum größten Teil ● *adv* am meisten; (*very*) höchst; **the ~ interesting day** der interessanteste Tag; **~ unlikely** höchst unwahrscheinlich ● *n* das meiste; **~ of them** die meisten [von ihnen]; **at [the] ~** höchstens; **~ of the time** die meiste Zeit. **~ly** *adv* meist

MOT *n* ≈ TÜV *m*

motel *n* Motel *nt*

moth *n* Nachtfalter *m*; **[clothes-] ~** Motte *f*

mothball *n* Mottenkugel *f*

mother n Mutter f

mother: ~**hood** n Mutterschaft f.
~**in-law** n (pl ~**s-in-law**)
Schwiegermutter f. ~**land** n
Mutterland nt. ~**ly** a mütterlich.
~**of-pearl** n Perlmutter f. ~**to-
be** n werdende Mutter f

mothproof a mottenfest

motif n Motiv nt

motion n Bewegung f; (proposal)
Antrag m. ~**less** a, **-ly** adv
bewegungslos

motivat|e vt motivieren. ~**ion** n
Motivation f

motive n Motiv nt

motor n Motor m; (car) Auto nt
● a Motor-; (Anat) motorisch ● vi
[mit dem Auto] fahren

motor: ~**bike** n 🆃 Motorrad nt. ~
boat n Motorboot nt. ~ **car** n
Auto nt, Wagen m. ~**cycle** n
Motorrad nt. ~**cyclist** n
Motorradfahrer m. ~**ing** n
Autofahren nt. ~**ist** n
Autofahrer(in) m(f). ~ **vehicle** n
Kraftfahrzeug nt. ~**way** n
Autobahn f

mottled a gesprenkelt

motto n (pl **-es**) Motto nt

mould[1] n (fungus) Schimmel m

mould[2] n Form f ● vt formen (**into**
zu). ~**ing** n (Archit) Fries m

mouldy a schimmelig; (🆃
worthless) schäbig

mound n Hügel m; (of stones)
Haufen m

mount n (animal) Reittier nt; (of
jewel) Fassung f; (of photo,
picture) Passepartout nt ● vt (get
on) steigen auf (+ acc); (on
pedestal) montieren auf (+ acc);
besteigen <horse>; fassen
<jewel>; aufziehen <photo,
picture> ● vi aufsteigen;
<tension:> steigen. ~ **up** vi sich
häufen; (add up) sich anhäufen

mountain n Berg m

mountaineer n Bergsteiger(in)
m(f). ~**ing** n Bergsteigen nt

mountainous a bergig, gebirgig

mourn vt betrauern ● vi trauern
(**for** um). ~**er** n Trauernde(r) m/f.
~**ful** a, **-ly** adv trauervoll. ~**ing** n
Trauer f

mouse n (pl **mice**) Maus f. ~**trap**
n Mausefalle f

moustache n Schnurrbart m

mouth[1] vt ~ sth etw lautlos mit
den Lippen sagen

mouth[2] n Mund m; (of animal)
Maul nt; (of river) Mündung f

mouth: ~**ful** n Mundvoll m; (bite)
Bissen m. ~**-organ** n
Mundharmonika f. ~**wash** n
Mundwasser nt

movable a beweglich

move n Bewegung f; (fig) Schritt
m; (moving house) Umzug m; (in
board game) Zug m; **on the** ~
unterwegs; **get a** ~ **on** 🆃 sich
beeilen ● vt bewegen;
(emotionally) rühren; (move
along) rücken; (in board game)
ziehen; (take away) wegnehmen;
wegfahren <car>; (rearrange)
umstellen; (transfer) versetzen
<person>; verlegen <office>;
(propose) beantragen; ~ **house**
umziehen ● vi sich bewegen;
(move house) umziehen; **don't** ~**!**
stillhalten! (stop) stillstehen! ~
along vt/i weiterrücken. ~ **away**
vt/i wegrücken; (move house)
wegziehen. ~ **in** vi einziehen. ~
off vi <vehicle:> losfahren. ~ **out**
vi ausziehen. ~ **over** vt/i [zur
Seite] rücken. ~ **up** vi aufrücken

movement n Bewegung f; (Mus)
Satz m; (of clock) Uhrwerk nt

movie n (Amer) Film m; **go to the**
~**s** ins Kino gehen

moving a beweglich; (touching)
rührend

mow vt (pt **mowed**, pp **mown** or
mowed) mähen

mower n Rasenmäher m

MP abbr see **Member of Parliament**

Mr n (pl **Messrs**) Herr m

M

Mrs n Frau f
Ms n Frau f
much a, adv & n viel; **as ∼ as** so viel wie; **∼ loved** sehr geliebt
muck n Mist m; (🔲 filth) Dreck m. **∼ about** vi herumalbern; (tinker) herumspielen (**with** mit). **∼ out** vt ausmisten. **∼ up** vt 🔲 vermasseln; (make dirty) schmutzig machen
mucky a (-ier, -iest) dreckig
mud n Schlamm m
muddle n Durcheinander nt; (confusion) Verwirrung f ● vt **∼ [up]** durcheinander bringen
muddy a (-ier, -iest) schlammig; <shoes> schmutzig
mudguard n Kotflügel m; (on bicycle) Schutzblech nt
muffle vt dämpfen
muffler n Schal m; (Amer, Auto) Auspufftopf m
mug[1] n Becher m; (for beer) Bierkrug m; (🔲 face) Visage f; (🔲 simpleton) Trottel m
mug[2] vt (pt/pp mugged) überfallen. **∼ger** n Straßenräuber m. **∼ging** n Straßenraub m
muggy a (-ier, -iest) schwül
mule n Maultier nt
mulled a **∼ wine** Glühwein m
multi: **∼coloured** a vielfarbig, bunt. **∼lingual** a mehrsprachig. **∼national** a multinational
multiple a vielfach; (with pl) mehrere ● n Vielfache(s) nt
multiplication n Multiplikation f
multiply v (pt/pp -ied) ● vt multiplizieren (**by** mit) ● vi sich vermehren
multistorey a **∼ car park** Parkhaus nt
mum n 🔲 Mutti f
mumble vt/i murmeln
mummy[1] n 🔲 Mutti f
mummy[2] n (Archaeol) Mumie f
mumps n Mumps m
munch vt/i mampfen

municipal a städtisch
munitions npl Kriegsmaterial nt
mural n Wandgemälde nt
murder n Mord m ● vt ermorden. **∼er** n Mörder m. **∼ess** n Mörderin f. **∼ous** a mörderisch
murky a (-ier, -iest) düster
murmur n Murmeln nt ● vt/i murmeln
muscle n Muskel m
muscular a Muskel-; (strong) muskulös
museum n Museum nt
mushroom n [essbarer] Pilz m, esp Champignon m ● vi (fig) wie Pilze aus dem Boden schießen
mushy a breiig
music n Musik f; (written) Noten pl; **set to ∼** vertonen
musical a musikalisch ● n Musical nt. **∼ box** n Spieldose f. **∼ instrument** n Musikinstrument nt
musician n Musiker(in) m(f)
music-stand n Notenständer m
Muslim a mohammedanisch ● n Mohammedaner(in) m(f)
must v aux (nur Präsens) müssen; (with negative) dürfen ● n **a ∼** 🔲 ein Muss nt
mustard n Senf m
musty a (-ier, -iest) muffig
mute a stumm
mutilat|e vt verstümmeln. **∼ion** n Verstümmelung f
mutin|ous a meuterisch. **∼y** n Meuterei f ● vi (pt/pp -ied) meutern
mutter n Murmeln nt ● vt/i murmeln
mutton n Hammelfleisch nt
mutual a gegenseitig; (🔲 common) gemeinsam. **∼ly** adv gegenseitig
muzzle n (of animal) Schnauze f; (of firearm) Mündung f; (for dog) Maulkorb m
my a mein

myself *pron* selbst; (*refl*) mich; **by ~** allein; **I thought to ~** ich habe mir gedacht

mysterious *a*, **-ly** *adv* geheimnisvoll; (*puzzling*) mysteriös, rätselhaft

mystery *n* Geheimnis *nt*; (*puzzle*) Rätsel *nt*; **~ [story]** Krimi *m*

mysti|c[al] *a* mystisch. **~cism** *n* Mystik *f*

mystified *a* **be ~** vor einem Rätsel stehen

mystique *n* geheimnisvoller Zauber *m*

myth *n* Mythos *m*; (⚁ *untruth*) Märchen *nt*. **~ical** *a* mythisch; (*fig*) erfunden

mythology *n* Mythologie *f*

nab *vt* (*pt/pp* **nabbed**) ⚁ erwischen

nag¹ *n* (*horse*) Gaul *m*

nag² *vt/i* (*pp/pp* **nagged**) herumnörgeln (**s.o.** an jdm)

nail *n* (*Anat, Techn*) Nagel *m*; **on the ~** ⚁ sofort ● *vt* nageln (**to** an + *acc*)

nail: **~-brush** *n* Nagelbürste *f*. **~-file** *n* Nagelfeile *f*. **~ scissors** *npl* Nagelschere *f*. **~ varnish** *n* Nagellack *m*

naïve *a*, **-ly** *adv* naiv. **~ty** *n* Naivität *f*

naked *a* nackt; <*flame*> offen; **with the ~ eye** mit bloßem Auge. **~ness** *n* Nacktheit *f*

name *n* Name *m*; (*reputation*) Ruf *m*; **by ~** dem Namen nach; **by the ~ of** namens; **call s.o. ~s** ⚁ jdn beschimpfen ● *vt* nennen; (*give a name to*) einen Namen geben (+ *dat*); (*announce publicly*) den Namen bekannt geben von. **~less** *a* namenlos. **~ly** *adv* nämlich

name: **~-plate** *n* Namensschild *nt*. **~sake** *n* Namensvetter *m*/ Namensschwester *f*

nanny *n* Kindermädchen *nt*

nap *n* Nickerchen *nt*

napkin *n* Serviette *f*

nappy *n* Windel *f*

narcotic *n* (*drug*) Rauschgift *nt*

narrat|e *vt* erzählen. **~ion** *n* Erzählung *f*

narrative *n* Erzählung *f*

narrator *n* Erzähler(in) *m(f)*

narrow *a* (**-er, -est**) schmal; (*restricted*) eng; <*margin, majority*> knapp; **have a ~ escape** mit knapper Not davonkommen ● *vi* sich verengen. **~-minded** *a* engstirnig

nasal *a* nasal; (*Med & Anat*) Nasen-

nasty *a* (**-ier, -iest**) übel; (*unpleasant*) unangenehm; (*unkind*) boshaft; (*serious*) schlimm

nation *n* Nation *f*; (*people*) Volk *nt*

national *a* national; <*newspaper*> überregional; <*campaign*> landesweit ● *n* Staatsbürger(in) *m(f)*

national: **~ anthem** *n* Nationalhymne *f*. **N~ Health Service** *n* staatlicher Gesundheitsdienst *m*. **N~ Insurance** *n* Sozialversicherung *f*

nationalism *n* Nationalismus *m*

nationality *n* Staatsangehörigkeit *f*

national|ization *n* Verstaatlichung *f*. **~ize** *vt* verstaatlichen

native *a* einheimisch; (*innate*) angeboren ● *n* Eingeborene(r) *m/f*; (*local inhabitant*)

N

Einheimische(r) *m/f*; **a ~ of**
Vienna ein gebürtiger Wiener
native: ~ land *n* Heimatland *nt*.
~ language *n* Muttersprache *f*
natter *vi* 🇮 schwatzen
natural *a*, **-ly** *adv* natürlich; **~[-
coloured]** naturfarben
natural: ~ gas *n* Erdgas *nt*. **~
history** *n* Naturkunde *f*
naturalist *n* Naturforscher *m*
natural|ization *n* Einbürgerung *f*.
~ize *vt* einbürgern
nature *n* Natur *f*; (*kind*) Art *f*; **by
~** von Natur aus. **~ reserve** *n*
Naturschutzgebiet *nt*
naughty *a* (**-ier, -iest**), **-ily** *adv*
unartig; (*slightly indecent*) gewagt
nausea *n* Übelkeit *f*
nautical *a* nautisch. **~ mile** *n*
Seemeile *f*
naval *a* Marine-
nave *n* Kirchenschiff *nt*
navel *n* Nabel *m*
navigable *a* schiffbar
navigat|e *vi* navigieren ●*vt*
befahren <*river*>. **~ion** *n*
Navigation *f*
navy *n* [Kriegs]marine *f* ●*a* **~
[blue]** marineblau
near *a* (**-er, -est**) nah[e]; **the ~est
bank** die nächste Bank ●*adv*
nahe; **draw ~** sich nähern ●*prep*
nahe an (+ *dat/acc*); in der Nähe
von
near: ~by *a* nahe gelegen, nahe
liegend. **~ly** *adv* fast, beinahe;
not ~ly bei weitem nicht. **~ness**
n Nähe *f*. **~ side** *n* Beifahrerseite
f. **~-sighted** *a* (*Amer*) kurzsichtig
neat *a* (**-er, -est**), **-ly** *adv* adrett;
(*tidy*) ordentlich; (*clever*)
geschickt; (*undiluted*) pur. **~ness**
n Ordentlichkeit *f*
necessarily *adv*
notwendigerweise; **not ~** nicht
unbedingt
necessary *a* nötig, notwendig
necessit|ate *vt* notwendig
machen. **~y** *n* Notwendigkeit *f*;

work from ~y arbeiten, weil man
es nötig hat
neck *n* Hals *m*; **~ and ~** Kopf an
Kopf
necklace *n* Halskette *f*
neckline *n* Halsausschnitt *m*
née *a* **~ X** geborene X
need *n* Bedürfnis *nt*; (*misfortune*)
Not *f*; **be in ~ of** brauchen; **in case
of ~** notfalls; **if ~ be** wenn nötig;
there is a ~ for es besteht ein
Bedarf an (+ *dat*); **there is no ~
for that** das ist nicht nötig ●*vt*
brauchen; **you ~ not go** du
brauchst nicht zu gehen; **~ I
come?** muss ich kommen? **I ~ to
know** ich muss es wissen
needle *n* Nadel *f*
needless *a*, **-ly** *adv* unnötig; **~ to
say** selbstverständlich, natürlich
needlework *n* Nadelarbeit *f*
needy *a* (**-ier, -iest**) bedürftig
negation *n* Verneinung *f*
negative *a* negativ ●*n*
Verneinung *f*; (*photo*) Negativ *nt*
neglect *n* Vernachlässigung *f* ●*vt*
vernachlässigen; (*omit*)
versäumen (**to** zu). **~ed** *a*
verwahrlost. **~ful** *a* nachlässig
negligen|ce *n* Nachlässigkeit *f*.
~t *a*, **-ly** *adv* nachlässig
negligible *a* unbedeutend
negotiat|e *vt* aushandeln; (*Auto*)
nehmen <*bend*> ●*vi* verhandeln.
~ion *n* Verhandlung *f*. **~or** *n*
Unterhändler(in) *m*(*f*)
Negro *a* Neger- ●*n* (*pl* **-es**) Neger
m
neigh *vi* wiehern
neighbour *n* Nachbar(in) *m*(*f*).
~hood *n* Nachbarschaft *f*. **~ing** *a*
Nachbar-. **~ly** *a* [gut]nachbarlich
neither *a* & *pron* keine(r, s) [von
beiden] ●*adv* **~... nor** weder ...
noch ●*conj* auch nicht
neon *n* Neon *nt*
nephew *n* Neffe *m*
nepotism *n* Vetternwirtschaft *f*

nerve n Nerv m; (⚁ courage) Mut m; (⚁ impudence) Frechheit f. **~-racking** a nervenaufreibend

nervous a, **-ly** adv (afraid) ängstlich; (highly strung) nervös; (Anat, Med) Nerven-. **~ breakdown** n Nervenzusammenbruch m. **~ness** Ängstlichkeit f

nervy a (-ier, -iest) nervös; (Amer: impudent) frech

nest n Nest nt ● vi nisten

nestle vi sich schmiegen (against an + acc)

net¹ n Netz nt; (curtain) Store m

net² a netto; <salary, weight> Netto-

netball n ≈ Korbball m

Netherlands npl the **~** die Niederlande pl

nettle n Nessel f

network n Netz nt

neurolog|ist n Neurologe m/ -gin f. **~y** n Neurologie f

neur|osis n (pl -oses) Neurose f. **~otic** a neurotisch

neuter a (Gram) sächlich ● n (Gram) Neutrum nt ● vt kastrieren; (spay) sterilisieren

neutral a neutral ● n in **~** (Auto) im Leerlauf. **~ity** n Neutralität f

never adv nie, niemals; (⚁ not) nicht; **~ mind** macht nichts; **well I ~!** ja so was! **~-ending** a endlos

nevertheless adv dennoch, trotzdem

new a (-er, -est) neu

new: ~comer n Neuankömmling m. **~fangled** a (pej) neumodisch. **~-laid** a frisch gelegt

newly adv frisch. **~-weds** npl Jungverheiratete pl

new: ~ moon n Neumond m. **~ness** n Neuheit f

news n Nachricht f; (Radio, TV) Nachrichten pl; **piece of ~** Neuigkeit f

news: ~agent n Zeitungshändler m. **~ bulletin** n

Nachrichtensendung f. **~letter** n Mitteilungsblatt nt. **~paper** n Zeitung f; (material) Zeitungspapier nt. **~reader** n Nachrichtensprecher(in) m(f)

New: ~ Year's Day n Neujahr nt. **~ Year's Eve** n Silvester nt. **~ Zealand** n Neuseeland nt

next a & n nächste(r, s); **who's ~?** wer kommt als Nächster dran? **the ~ best** das nächstbeste; **~ door** nebenan; **my ~ of kin** mein nächster Verwandter; **~ to nothing** fast gar nichts; **the week after ~** übernächste Woche ● adv als Nächstes; **~ to** neben

nib n Feder f

nibble vt/i knabbern (at an + dat)

nice a (-r, -st) nett; <day, weather> schön; <food> gut; <distinction> fein. **~ly** adv nett; (well) gut

niche n Nische f; (fig) Platz m

nick n Kerbe f; (⚁ prison) Knast m; (⚁ police station) Revier nt; **in good ~** ⚁ in gutem Zustand ● vt einkerben; (steal) klauen; (⚁ arrest) schnappen

nickel n Nickel nt; (Amer) Fünfcentstück nt

nickname n Spitzname m

nicotine n Nikotin nt

niece n Nichte f

Nigeria n Nigeria nt. **~n** a nigerianisch ● n Nigerianer(in) m(f)

night n Nacht f; (evening) Abend m; **at ~** nachts

night: ~-club n Nachtklub m. **~-dress** n Nachthemd nt. **~fall** n **at ~fall** bei Einbruch der Dunkelheit. **~-gown** n, ⚁ **~ie** n Nachthemd nt

nightingale n Nachtigall f

night: ~-life n Nachtleben nt. **~ly** a nächtlich ● adv jede Nacht. **~mare** n Albtraum m. **~-time** n **at ~-time** bei Nacht

nil n null

nimble a (-r, -st), **-bly** adv flink

N

nine *a* neun ● *n* Neun *f.* ~**teen** *a* neunzehn. ~**teenth** *a* neunzehnte(r, s)

ninetieth *a* neunzigste(r, s)

ninety *a* neunzig

ninth *a* neunte(r, s)

nip *vt* kneifen; *(bite)* beißen; ~ **in the bud** *(fig)* im Keim ersticken ● *vi* (⚅ *run*) laufen

nipple *n* Brustwarze *f*; *(Amer: on bottle)* Sauger *m*

nitwit *n* ⚅ Dummkopf *m*

no *adv* nein ● *n* (*pl* **noes**) Nein *nt* ● *a* kein(e); (*pl*) keine; **in no time** [sehr] schnell; **no parking/smoking** Parken/Rauchen verboten; **no one = nobody**

nobility *n* Adel *m*

noble *a* (**-r, -st**) edel; *(aristocratic)* adlig. ~**man** *n* Adlige(r) *m*

nobody *pron* niemand, keiner ● *n* **a** ~ ein Niemand *m*

nocturnal *a* nächtlich; *<animal, bird>* Nacht-

nod *n* Nicken *nt* ● *v* (*pt/pp* **nodded**) ● *vi* nicken ● *vt* ~ **one's head** mit dem Kopf nicken

noise *n* Geräusch *nt*; *(loud)* Lärm *m.* ~**less** *a,* **-ly** *adv* geräuschlos

noisy *a* (**-ier, -iest**), **-ily** *adv* laut; *<eater>* geräuschvoll

nomad *n* Nomade *m.* ~**ic** *a* nomadisch; *<life, tribe>* Nomaden-

nominal *a,* **-ly** *adv* nominell

nominat|e *vt* nominieren, aufstellen; *(appoint)* ernennen. ~**ion** *n* Nominierung *f*; Ernennung *f*

nominative *a & n* *(Gram)* ~**[case]** Nominativ *m*

nonchalant *a,* **-ly** *adv* nonchalant; *<gesture>* lässig

nondescript *a* unbestimmbar; *<person>* unscheinbar

none *pron* keine(r)/keins; ~ **of it/ this** nichts davon ● *adv* ~ **too** nicht gerade; ~ **too soon** [um]

keine Minute zu früh; ~ **the less** dennoch

nonentity *n* Null *f*

non-existent *a* nicht vorhanden

non-fiction *n* Sachliteratur *f*

nonplussed *a* verblüfft

nonsens|e *n* Unsinn *m.* ~**ical** *a* unsinnig

non-smoker *n* Nichtraucher *m*

non-stop *adv* ununterbrochen; *<fly>* nonstop

non-swimmer *n* Nichtschwimmer *m*

non-violent *a* gewaltlos

noodles *npl* Bandnudeln *pl*

noon *n* Mittag *m*; **at** ~ um 12 Uhr mittags

noose *n* Schlinge *f*

nor *adv* noch ● *conj* auch nicht

Nordic *a* nordisch

norm *n* Norm *f*

normal *a* normal. ~**ity** *n* Normalität *f.* ~**ly** *adv* normal; *(usually)* normalerweise

north *n* Norden *m*; **to the** ~ **of** nördlich von ● *a* Nord-, nord- ● *adv* nach Norden

north: **N**~ **America** *n* Nordamerika *nt.* ~**-east** *a* Nordost- ● *n* Nordosten *m*

norther|ly *a* nördlich. ~**n** *a* nördlich. **N**~**n Ireland** *n* Nordirland *nt*

north: **N**~ **Pole** *n* Nordpol *m.* **N**~ **Sea** *n* Nordsee *f.* ~**ward[s]** *adv* nach Norden. ~**-west** *a* Nordwest- ● *n* Nordwesten *m*

Nor|way *n* Norwegen *nt.* ~**wegian** *a* norwegisch ● *n* Norweger(in) *m(f)*

nose *n* Nase *f*

nosebleed *n* Nasenbluten *nt*

nostalg|ia *n* Nostalgie *f.* ~**ic** *a* nostalgisch

nostril *n* Nasenloch *nt*

nosy *a* (**-ier, -iest**) ⚅ neugierig

not
● *adverb*

····▶ nicht. **I don't know** ich weiß
nicht. **isn't she pretty?** ist sie
nicht hübsch?

····▶ **not a** kein. **he is not a doctor**
er ist kein Arzt. **she didn't wear a
hat** sie trug keinen Hut. **there
was not a person to be seen** es
gab keinen Menschen zu sehen.
not a thing gar nichts. **not a bit**
kein bisschen

····▶ (*in elliptical phrases*) **I hope
not** ich hoffe nicht. **of course not**
natürlich nicht. **not at all**
überhaupt nicht; (*in polite reply
to thanks*) keine Ursache; gern
geschehen. **certainly not!** auf
keinen Fall! **not I** ich nicht

····▶ **not ... but ...** nicht ... sondern
.... **it was not a small town but a
big one** es war keine kleine
Stadt, sondern eine große

notab|**le** *a* bedeutend;
(*remarkable*) bemerkenswert.
∼**ly** *adv* insbesondere
notation *n* Notation *f*; (*Mus*)
Notenschrift *f*
notch *n* Kerbe *f*
note *n* (*written comment*) Notiz *f*,
Anmerkung *f*; (*short letter*)
Briefchen *nt*, Zettel *m*; (*bank* ∼)
Banknote *f*, Schein *m*; (*Mus*)
Note *f*; (*sound*) Ton *m*; (*on piano*)
Taste *f*; **half/whole** ∼ (*Amer*)
halbe/ganze Note *f*; **of** ∼ von
Bedeutung; **make a** ∼ **of** notieren
● *vt* beachten; (*notice*) bemerken
(*that* dass)
notebook *n* Notizbuch *nt*
noted *a* bekannt (**for** für)
note: ∼**paper** *n* Briefpapier *nt*.
∼**worthy** *a* beachtenswert
nothing *n, pron & adv* nichts; **for**
∼ umsonst; ∼ **but** nichts als; ∼
much nicht viel; ∼ **interesting**
nichts Interessantes
notice *n* (*on board*) Anschlag *m*,
Bekanntmachung *f*;
(*announcement*) Anzeige *f*;

(*review*) Kritik *f*; (*termination of
lease, employment*) Kündigung *f*;
give [in one's] ∼ kündigen; **give
s.o.** ∼ jdm kündigen; **take no** ∼!
ignoriere es! ● *vt* bemerken.
∼**able,** *a,* -**bly** *adv* merklich. ∼-
board *n* Anschlagbrett *nt*
noti|**fication** *n* Benachrichtigung
f. ∼**fy** *vt* (*pt/pp* -**ied**)
benachrichtigen
notion *n* Idee *f*
notorious *a* berüchtigt
notwithstanding *prep* trotz (+
gen) ● *adv* trotzdem, dennoch
nought *n* Null *f*
noun *n* Substantiv *nt*
nourish *vt* nähren. ∼**ing** *a*
nahrhaft. ∼**ment** *n* Nahrung *f*
novel *a* neu[artig] ● *n* Roman *m*.
∼**ist** *n* Romanschriftsteller(in)
m(f). ∼**ty** *n* Neuheit *f*
November *n* November *m*
novice *n* Neuling *m*; (*Relig*)
Novize *m*/Novizin *f*
now *adv & conj* jetzt; ∼ **[that]** jetzt,
wo; **just** ∼ gerade, eben; **right** ∼
sofort; ∼ **and again** hin und
wieder; **now, now!** na, na!
nowadays *adv* heutzutage
nowhere *adv* nirgendwo,
nirgends
nozzle *n* Düse *f*
nuance *n* Nuance *f*
nuclear *a* Kern-. ∼ **deterrent** *n*
nukleares Abschreckungsmittel
nt
nucleus *n* (*pl* -**lei**) Kern *m*
nude *a* nackt ● *n* (*Art*) Akt *m*; **in
the** ∼ nackt
nudge *vt* stupsen
nud|**ist** *n* Nudist *m*. ∼**ity** *n*
Nacktheit *f*
nuisance *n* Ärgernis *nt*; (*pest*)
Plage *f*; **be a** ∼ ärgerlich sein
null *a* ∼ **and void** null und nichtig
numb *a* gefühllos, taub ● *vt*
betäuben
number *n* Nummer *f*; (*amount*)
Anzahl *f*; (*Math*) Zahl *f* ● *vt*

nummerieren; (*include*) zählen
(**among** zu). **~-plate** *n*
Nummernschild *nt*
numeral *n* Ziffer *f*
numerical *a*, **-ly** *adv* numerisch;
in ~ **order** zahlenmäßig geordnet
numerous *a* zahlreich
nun *n* Nonne *f*
nurse *n* [Kranken]schwester *f*;
(*male*) Krankenpfleger *m*;
children's ~ Kindermädchen *nt*
● *vt* pflegen
nursery *n* Kinderzimmer *nt*;
(*Hort*) Gärtnerei *f*. **[day]** ~
Kindertagesstätte *f*. ~ **rhyme** *n*
Kinderreim *m*. ~ **school** *n*
Kindergarten *m*
nursing *n* Krankenpflege *f*. ~
home *n* Pflegeheim *nt*
nut *n* Nuss *f*; (*Techn*)
[Schrauben]mutter *f*; (🔢 *head*)
Birne 🔢; **be ~s** 🔢 spinnen 🔢.
~crackers *npl* Nussknacker *m*.
~meg *n* Muskat *m*
nutrient *n* Nährstoff *m*
nutrit|ion *n* Ernährung *f*. **~ious** *a*
nahrhaft
nutshell *n* Nussschale *f*; **in a** ~
(*fig*) kurz gesagt
nylon *n* Nylon *nt*

O *n* (*Teleph*) null
oak *n* Eiche *f*
OAP *abbr* (**old-age pensioner**)
Rentner(in) *m(f)*
oar *n* Ruder *nt*. **~sman** *n* Ruderer
m
oasis *n* (*pl* **oases**) Oase *f*
oath *n* Eid *m*; (*swear-word*) Fluch
m

oatmeal *n* Hafermehl *nt*
oats *npl* Hafer *m*; (*Culin*) **[rolled]**
~ Haferflocken *pl*
obedien|ce *n* Gehorsam *m*. **~t** *a*,
-ly *adv* gehorsam
obey *vt/i* gehorchen (+ *dat*);
befolgen <*instructions, rules*>
obituary *n* Nachruf *m*; (*notice*)
Todesanzeige *f*
object¹ *n* Gegenstand *m*; (*aim*)
Zweck *m*; (*intention*) Absicht *f*;
(*Gram*) Objekt *nt*; **money is no** ~
Geld spielt keine Rolle
object² *vi* Einspruch erheben (**to**
gegen); (*be against*) etwas
dagegen haben
objection *n* Einwand *m*; **have no**
~ nichts dagegen haben. **~able**
a anstößig; <*person*>
unangenehm
objectiv|e *a*, **-ly** *adv* objektiv ● *n*
Ziel *nt*. **~ity** *n* Objektivität *f*
objector *n* Gegner *m*
obligation *n* Pflicht *f*; **without** ~
unverbindlich
obligatory *a* obligatorisch; **be** ~
Vorschrift sein
oblig|e *vt* verpflichten; (*compel*)
zwingen; (*do a small service*)
einen Gefallen tun (+ *dat*). **~ing**
a entgegenkommend
oblique *a* schräg; <*angle*> schief;
(*fig*) indirekt
obliterate *vt* auslöschen
oblivion *n* Vergessenheit *f*
oblivious *a* **be** ~ sich (*dat*) nicht
bewusst sein (**of** *gen*)
oblong *a* rechteckig ● *n* Rechteck
nt
obnoxious *a* widerlich
oboe *n* Oboe *f*
obscen|e *a* obszön. **~ity** *n*
Obszönität *f*
obscur|e *a* dunkel; (*unknown*)
unbekannt ● *vt* verdecken;
(*confuse*) verwischen. **~ity** *n*
Dunkelheit *f*; Unbekanntheit *f*
observa|nce *n* (*of custom*)
Einhaltung *f*. **~nt** *a* aufmerksam.

~**tion** n Beobachtung f; (remark) Bemerkung f

observatory n Sternwarte f

observe vt beobachten; (say, notice) bemerken; (keep, celebrate) feiern; (obey) einhalten. ~**r** n Beobachter m

obsess vt be ~**ed** by besessen sein von. ~**ion** n Besessenheit f; (persistent idea) fixe Idee f. ~**ive** a, -**ly** adv zwanghaft

obsolete a veraltet

obstacle n Hindernis nt

obstina|cy n Starrsinn m. ~**te** a, -**ly** adv starrsinnig; <refusal> hartnäckig

obstruct vt blockieren; (hinder) behindern. ~**ion** n Blockierung f; Behinderung f; (obstacle) Hindernis nt. ~**ive** a be ~**ive** Schwierigkeiten bereiten

obtain vt erhalten. ~**able** a erhältlich

obtrusive a aufdringlich; <thing> auffällig

obtuse a begriffsstutzig

obvious a, -**ly** adv offensichtlich, offenbar

occasion n Gelegenheit f; (time) Mal nt; (event) Ereignis nt; (cause) Anlass m, Grund m; **on the** ~ **of** anlässlich (+ gen)

occasional a gelegentlich. ~**ly** adv gelegentlich, hin und wieder

occult a okkult

occupant n Bewohner(in) m(f); (of vehicle) Insasse m

occupation n Beschäftigung f; (job) Beruf m; (Mil) Besetzung f; (period) Besatzung f. ~**al** a Berufs-. ~**al therapy** n Beschäftigungstherapie f

occupier n Bewohner(in) m(f)

occupy vt (pt/pp occupied) besetzen <seat, (Mil) country>; einnehmen <space>; in Anspruch nehmen <time>; (live in) bewohnen; (fig) bekleiden <office>; (keep busy) beschäftigen

occur vi (pt/pp occurred) geschehen; (exist) vorkommen, auftreten; **it** ~ **red to me that** es fiel mir ein, dass. ~**rence** n Auftreten nt; (event) Ereignis nt

ocean n Ozean m

o'clock adv [at] **7** ~ [um] 7 Uhr

octagonal a achteckig

October n Oktober m

octopus n (pl -**puses**) Tintenfisch m

odd a (-er, -est) seltsam, merkwürdig; <number> ungerade; (not of set) einzeln; **forty** ~ über vierzig; ~ **jobs** Gelegenheitsarbeiten pl; **the** ~ **one out** die Ausnahme; **at** ~ **moments** zwischendurch

odd|ity n Kuriosität f. ~**ly** adv merkwürdig; ~**ly enough** merkwürdigerweise ~**ment** n (of fabric) Rest m

odds npl (chances) Chancen pl; **at** ~ uneinig; ~ **and ends** Kleinkram m

ode n Ode f

odious a widerlich

odour n Geruch m. ~**less** a geruchlos

O

....

of

● preposition

····▸ (indicating belonging, origin) von (+ dat); genitive. **the mother of twins** die Mutter von Zwillingen. **the mother of the twins** die Mutter der Zwillinge or von den Zwillingen. **the Queen of England** die Königin von England. **a friend of mine** ein Freund von mir. **a friend of the teacher's** ein Freund des Lehrers. **the brother of her father** der Bruder ihres Vaters. **the works of Shakespeare** Shakespeares Werke. **it was nice of him** es war nett von ihm

····> (*made of*) aus (+ *dat*). **a dress of cotton** ein Kleid aus Baumwolle

····> (*following number*) **five of us** fünf von uns. **the two of us** wir zwei. **there were four of us waiting** wir waren vier, die warteten

····> (*followed by number, description*) von (+ *dat*). **a girl of ten** ein Mädchen von zehn Jahren. **a distance of 50 miles** eine Entfernung von 50 Meilen. **a man of character** ein Mann von Charakter. **a woman of exceptional beauty** eine Frau von außerordentlicher Schönheit. **a person of strong views** ein Mensch mit festen Ansichten

❗ of is not translated after measures and in some other cases: **a pound of apples** ein Pfund Äpfel; **a cup of tea** eine Tasse Tee; **a glass of wine** ein Glas Wein; **the city of Chicago** die Stadt Chicago; **the fourth of January** der vierte Januar

off *prep* von (+ *dat*); ∼ **the coast** vor der Küste; **get** ∼ **the ladder/ bus** von der Leiter/aus dem Bus steigen ● *adv* weg; <*button, lid, handle*> ab; <*light*> aus; <*brake*> los; <*machine*> abgeschaltet; <*tap*> zu; (*on appliance*) 'off' 'aus'; **2 kilometres** ∼ 2 Kilometer entfernt; **a long way** ∼ weit weg; (*time*) noch lange hin; ∼ **and on** hin und wieder; **with his hat/coat** ∼ ohne Hut/Mantel; **20%** ∼ 20% Nachlass; **be** ∼ (*leave*) [weg]gehen; (*Sport*) starten; <*food:*> schlecht sein; **be well** ∼ gut dran sein; (*financially*) wohlhabend sein; **have a day** ∼ einen freien Tag haben

offal *n* (*Culin*) Innereien *pl*

offence *n* (*illegal act*) Vergehen *nt*; **give/take** ∼ Anstoß erregen/ nehmen (**at** an + *dat*)

offend *vt* beleidigen. **∼er** *n* (*Jur*) Straftäter *m*

offensive *a* anstößig; (*Mil, Sport*) offensiv ● *n* Offensive *f*

offer *n* Angebot *nt*; **on (special)** ∼ im Sonderangebot ● *vt* anbieten (**to** *dat*); leisten <*resistance*>; ∼ **to do sth** sich anbieten, etw zu tun. **∼ing** *n* Gabe *f*

offhand *a* brüsk; (*casual*) lässig

office *n* Büro *nt*; (*post*) Amt *nt*

officer *n* Offizier *m*; (*official*) Beamte(r) *m*/ Beamtin *f*; (*police*) Polizeibeamte(r) *m*/-beamtin *f*

official *a* offiziell, amtlich ● *n* Beamte(r) *m*/ Beamtin *f*; (*Sport*) Funktionär *m*. **∼ly** *adv* offiziell

officious *a*, **-ly** *adv* übereifrig

off-licence *n* Wein und Spirituosenhandlung *f*

off-load *vt* ausladen

off-putting *a* 🔟 abstoßend

offset *vt* (*pt/pp* **-set**, *pres p* **-setting**) ausgleichen

offshoot *n* Schössling *m*; (*fig*) Zweig *m*

offshore *a* Offshore-

offside *a* (*Sport*) abseits

offspring *n* Nachwuchs *m*

offstage *adv* hinter den Kulissen

off-white *a* fast weiß

often *adv* oft; **every so** ∼ von Zeit zu Zeit

oh *int* oh! ach! **oh dear!** o weh!

oil *n* Öl *nt*; (*petroleum*) Erdöl *nt* ● *vt* ölen

oil: ∼**field** *n* Ölfeld *nt*. ∼**-painting** *n* Ölgemälde *nt*. ∼ **refinery** *n* [Erd]ölraffinerie *f*. ∼**-tanker** *n* Öltanker *m*. ∼ **well** *n* Ölquelle *f*

oily *a* (**-ier, -iest**) ölig

ointment *n* Salbe *f*

OK *a & int* 🔟 in Ordnung; okay ● *adv* (*well*) gut ● *vt* (*auch* **okay**) (*pt/pp* **okayed**) genehmigen

old a (-er, -est) alt; (former)
ehemalig

old: ~ **age** n Alter nt. ~**-age
pensioner** n Rentner(in) m(f). ~
boy n ehemaliger Schüler. ~-
fashioned a altmodisch. ~ **girl**
ehemalige Schülerin f

olive n Olive f; (colour) Oliv nt ● a
olivgrün. ~ **oil** n Olivenöl nt

Olympic a olympisch ● n the ~**s**
die Olympischen Spiele pl

omelette n Omelett nt

ominous a bedrohlich

omission n Auslassung f; (failure
to do) Unterlassung f

omit vt (pt/pp omitted) auslassen;
~ **to do sth** es unterlassen, etw
zu tun

omnipotent a allmächtig

on prep auf (+ dat/(on to) + acc);
(on vertical surface) an (+ dat/(on
to) + acc); (about) über (+ acc);
on Monday [am] Montag; **on
Mondays** montags; **on the first of
May** am ersten Mai; **on arriving** als
ich ankam; **on one's finger** am
Finger; **on the right/left** rechts/
links; **on the Rhine** am Rhein; **on
the radio/television** im Radio/
Fernsehen; **on the bus/train** im
Bus/Zug; **go on the bus/train** mit
dem Bus/Zug fahren; **on me** (with
me) bei mir; **it's on me** 🔟 das
spendiere ich ● adv (further on)
weiter; (switched on) an; <brake>
angezogen; <machine>
angeschaltet; (on appliance) 'on'
'ein'; **with/without his hat/coat on**
mit/ohne Hut/Mantel; **be on**
<film:> <event:>
stattfinden; **be on at** 🔟 bedrängen
(**zu** to); **it's not on** 🔟 das geht
nicht; **on and on** immer weiter; **on
and off** hin und wieder; **and so on**
und so weiter

once adv einmal; (formerly)
früher; **at ~** sofort; (at the same
time) gleichzeitig; ~ **and for all**
ein für alle Mal ● conj wenn;
(with past tense) als

oncoming a ~ **traffic**
Gegenverkehr m

one a ein(e); (only) einzig; **not ~**
kein(e); ~ **day/evening** eines
Tages/Abends ● n Eins f ● pron
eine(r)/eins; (impersonal) man;
which ~ welche(r,s); ~ **another**
einander; ~ **by** ~ einzeln; ~
never knows man kann nie
wissen

one: ~**-parent family** n
Einelternfamilie f. ~**self** pron
selbst; (refl) sich; **by ~self** allein.
~**-sided** a einseitig. ~**-way** a
<street> Einbahn-; <ticket>
einfach

onion n Zwiebel f

on-line adv online

onlooker n Zuschauer(in) m(f)

only a einzige(r,s); **an ~ child** ein
Einzelkind nt ● adv & conj nur;
~ **just** gerade erst; (barely)
gerade noch

onset n Beginn m; (of winter)
Einsetzen nt

onward[s] adv vorwärts; **from then
~** von der Zeit an

ooze vi sickern

opaque a undurchsichtig

open a, -ly adv offen; **be ~**
<shop:> geöffnet sein; **in the ~ air**
im Freien ● n **in the ~** im Freien
● vt öffnen, aufmachen; (start,
set up) eröffnen ● vi sich öffnen;
<flower:> aufgehen; <shop:>
öffnen, aufmachen. ~ **up** vt
öffnen, aufmachen

open day n Tag m der offenen
Tür

opener n Öffner m

opening n Öffnung f; (beginning)
Eröffnung f; (job)
Einstiegsmöglichkeit f. ~ **hours**
npl Öffnungszeiten pl

open: ~**-minded** a
aufgeschlossen. ~ **sandwich** n
belegtes Brot nt

opera n Oper f. **~-house** n Opernhaus nt. **~-singer** n Opernsänger(in) m(f)

operate vt bedienen <machine, lift>; betätigen <lever, brake>; (fig: run) betreiben ● vi (Techn) funktionieren; (be in action) in Betrieb sein; (Mil & fig) operieren; **~ [on]** (Med) operieren

operatic a Opern-

operation n (see operate) Bedienung f; Betätigung f; Operation f; **in ~** (Techn) in Betrieb; **come into ~** (fig) in Kraft treten; **have an ~** (Med) operiert werden. **~al** a **be ~al** in Betrieb sein; <law:> in Kraft sein

operative a wirksam

operator n (user) Bedienungsperson f; (Teleph) Vermittlung f

operetta n Operette f

opinion n Meinung f; **in my ~** meiner Meinung nach. **~ated** a rechthaberisch

opponent n Gegner(in) m(f)

opportun|e a günstig. **~ist** n Opportunist m

opportunity n Gelegenheit f

oppos|e vt Widerstand leisten (+ dat); (argue against) sprechen gegen; **be ~ed to sth** gegen etw sein; **as ~ed to** im Gegensatz zu. **~ing** a gegnerisch

opposite a entgegengesetzt; <house, side> gegenüberliegend; **~ number** (fig) Gegenstück nt; **the ~ sex** das andere Geschlecht ● n Gegenteil nt ● adv gegenüber ● prep gegenüber (+ dat)

opposition n Widerstand m; (Pol) Opposition f

oppress vt unterdrücken. **~ion** n Unterdrücken f. **~ive** a tyrannisch; <heat> drückend

opt vi **~ for** sich entscheiden für

optical a optisch

optician n Optiker m

optimis|m n Optimismus m. **~t** n Optimist m. **~tic** a, **-ally** adv optimistisch

optimum a optimal

option n Wahl f; (Comm) Option f. **~al** a auf Wunsch erhältlich; <subject> wahlfrei

opu|lence n Prunk m. **~lent** a prunkvoll

or conj oder; (after negative) noch; **or [else]** sonst; **in a year or two** in ein bis zwei Jahren

oral a, **-ly** adv mündlich; (Med) oral ● n Mündliche(s) nt

orange n Apfelsine f, Orange f; (colour) Orange nt ● a orangefarben

oratorio n Oratorium nt

oratory n Redekunst f

orbit n Umlaufbahn f ● vt umkreisen

orchard n Obstgarten m

orches|tra n Orchester nt. **~tral** a Orchester-. **~trate** vt orchestrieren

ordeal n (fig) Qual f

order n Ordnung f; (sequence) Reihenfolge f; (condition) Zustand m; (command) Befehl m; (in restaurant) Bestellung f; (Comm) Auftrag m; (Relig, medal) Orden m; **out of ~** <machine> außer Betrieb; **in ~ that** damit; **in ~ to help** um zu helfen ● vt (put in ~) ordnen; (command) befehlen (+ dat); (Comm, in restaurant) bestellen; (prescribe) verordnen

orderly a ordentlich; (not unruly) friedlich ● n (Mil, Med) Sanitäter m

ordinary a gewöhnlich, normal

ore n Erz nt

organ n (Biol & fig) Organ nt; (Mus) Orgel f

organic a, **-ally** adv organisch; (without chemicals) biodynamisch; <crop> biologisch

angebaut; *<food>* Bio-. **~ farming**
n biologischer Anbau *m*

organism *n* Organismus *m*

organist *n* Organist *m*

organization *n* Organisation *f*

organize *vt* organisieren;
veranstalten *<event>*. **~r** *n*
Organisator *m*; Veranstalter *m*

orgy *n* Orgie *f*

Orient *n* Orient *m*. **o~al** *a*
orientalisch ● *n* Orientale *m*/
Orientalin *f*

orientation *n* Orientierung *f*

origin *n* Ursprung *m*; (*of person,
goods*) Herkunft *f*

original *a* ursprünglich; (*not
copied*) original; (*new*) originell
● *n* Original *nt*. **~ity** *n*
Originalität *f*. **~ly** *adv*
ursprünglich

originate *vi* entstehen

ornament *n* Ziergegenstand *m*;
(*decoration*) Verzierung *f*. **~al** *a*
dekorativ

ornate *a* reich verziert

ornithology *n* Vogelkunde *f*

orphan *n* Waisenkind *nt*, Waise *f*.
~age *n* Waisenhaus *nt*

orthodox *a* orthodox

ostensible *a*, **-bly** *adv* angeblich

ostentat|ion *n* Protzerei *f* 🖪.
~ious *a* protzig 🖪

osteopath *n* Osteopath *m*

ostrich *n* Strauß *m*

other *a, pron & n* andere(r,s); the
~ [one] der/die/das andere; the **~
two** die zwei anderen; no **~s**
sonst keine; any **~ questions?**
sonst noch Fragen? every **~ day**
jeden zweiten Tag; the **~ day**
neulich; the **~ evening** neulich
abends; someone/something or **~**
irgendjemand/-etwas ● *adv*
anders; **~ than him** außer ihm;
somehow/somewhere or **~**
irgendwie/irgendwo

otherwise *adv* sonst; (*differently*)
anders

ought *v aux* I/we **~ to stay** ich
sollte/wir sollten eigentlich
bleiben; he **~ not to have done it**
er hätte es nicht machen sollen

ounce *n* Unze *f* (28, 35 *g*)

our *a* unser

ours *poss pron* unsere(r,s); **a
friend of ~** ein Freund von uns;
that is ~ das gehört uns

ourselves *pron* selbst; (*refl*) uns;
by ~ allein

out *adv* (*not at home*) weg;
(*outside*) draußen; (*not alight*)
aus; (*unconscious*) bewusstlos; **be
~** *<sun:>* scheinen; *<flower>*
blühen; *<workers>* streiken;
<calculation:> nicht stimmen;
(*Sport*) aus sein; (*fig: not feasible*)
nicht infrage kommen; **~ and
about** unterwegs; **have it ~ with
s.o.** 🖪 jdn zur Rede stellen; **get
~!** 🖪 raus! **~ with it!** 🖪 heraus
damit! ● *prep* **~ of** aus (+ *dat*); **go
~ (of) the door** zur Tür
hinausgehen; **be ~ of bed/ the
room** nicht im Bett/im Zimmer
sein; **~ of breath/danger** außer
Atem/Gefahr; **~ of work**
arbeitslos; **nine ~ of ten** neun von
zehn; **be ~ of sugar** keinen
Zucker mehr haben

outboard *a* **~ motor**
Außenbordmotor *m*

outbreak *n* Ausbruch *m*

outbuilding *n* Nebengebäude *nt*

outburst *n* Ausbruch *m*

outcast *n* Ausgestoßene(r) *m/f*

outcome *n* Ergebnis *nt*

outcry *n* Aufschrei *m* [der
Entrüstung]

outdated *a* überholt

outdo *vt* (*pt* **-did**, *pp* **-done**)
übertreffen, übertrumpfen

outdoor *a* (*life, sports*) im
Freien; **~ swimming pool** Freibad
nt

outdoors *adv* draußen; **go ~** nach
draußen gehen

outer *a* äußere(r,s)

outfit n Ausstattung f; (clothes) Ensemble nt; (🅸 organization) Laden m

outgoing a ausscheidend; <mail> ausgehend; (sociable) kontaktfreudig. **~s** npl Ausgaben pl

outgrow vi (pt -grew, pp -grown) herauswachsen aus

outing n Ausflug m

outlaw n Geächtete(r) m/f ● vt ächten

outlay n Auslagen pl

outlet n Abzug m; (for water) Abfluss m; (fig) Ventil nt; (Comm) Absatzmöglichkeit f

outline n Umriss m; (summary) kurze Darstellung f ● vt umreißen

outlive vt überleben

outlook n Aussicht f; (future prospect) Aussichten pl; (attitude) Einstellung f

outmoded a überholt

outnumber vt zahlenmäßig überlegen sein (+ dat)

out-patient n ambulanter Patient m

outpost n Vorposten m

output n Leistung f; Produktion f

outrage n Gräueltat f; (fig) Skandal m; (indignation) Empörung f. **~ous** a empörend

outright[1] a völlig, total; <refusal> glatt

outright[2] adv ganz; (at once) sofort; (frankly) offen

outset n Anfang m

outside[1] a äußere(r,s); **~ wall** Außenwand f ● n Außenseite f; **from the ~** von außen; **at the ~** höchstens

outside[2] adv außen; (out of doors) draußen; **go ~** nach draußen gehen ● prep außerhalb (+ gen); (in front of) vor (+ dat/acc)

outsider n Außenseiter m

outsize a übergroß

outskirts npl Rand m

outspoken a offen; **be ~** kein Blatt vor den Mund nehmen

outstanding a hervorragend; (conspicuous) bemerkenswert; (Comm) ausstehend

outstretched a ausgestreckt

outvote vt überstimmen

outward a äußerlich; **~ journey** Hinreise f ● adv nach außen. **~ly** adv nach außen hin, äußerlich. **~s** adv nach außen

outwit vt (pt/pp -witted) überlisten

oval a oval ● n Oval nt

ovation n Ovation f

oven n Backofen m

over prep über (+ acc/dat); **~ dinner** beim Essen; **~ the phone** am Telefon; **~ the page** auf der nächsten Seite ● adv (remaining) übrig; (ended) zu Ende; **~ again** noch einmal; **~ and ~** immer wieder; **~ here/there** hier/da drüben; **all ~** (everywhere) überall; **it's all ~** es ist vorbei; **I ache all ~** mir tut alles weh

overall[1] n Kittel m; **~s** pl Overall m

overall[2] a gesamt; (general) allgemein ● adv insgesamt

overbalance vi das Gleichgewicht verlieren

overbearing a herrisch

overboard adv (Naut) über Bord

overcast a bedeckt

overcharge vt **~ s.o.** jdm zu viel berechnen ● vi zu viel verlangen

overcoat n Mantel m

overcome vt (pt -came, pp -come) überwinden; **be ~ by** überwältigt werden von

overcrowded a überfüllt

overdo vt (pt -did, pp -done) übertreiben; (cook too long) zu lange kochen; **~ it** (🅸 do too much) sich übernehmen

overdose n Überdosis f

overdraft n [Konto]überziehung f; **have an ~** sein Konto überzogen haben

overdue a überfällig
overestimate vt überschätzen
overflow¹ n Überschuss m; (outlet) Überlauf m
overflow² vi überlaufen
overgrown a <garden> überwachsen
overhang¹ n Überhang m
overhang² vt/i (pt/pp -hung) überhängen (über + acc)
overhaul¹ n Überholung f
overhaul² vt (Techn) überholen
overhead¹ adv oben
overhead² a Ober-; (ceiling) Decken-. ~s npl allgemeine Unkosten pl
overhear vt (pt/pp -heard) mit anhören <conversation>
overheat vi zu heiß werden
overjoyed a überglücklich
overland a & adv auf dem Landweg; ~ **route** Landroute f
overlap vi (pt/pp -lapped) sich überschneiden
overleaf adv umseitig
overload vt überladen
overlook vt überblicken; (fail to see, ignore) übersehen
overnight¹ adv über Nacht; **stay** ~ übernachten
overnight² a Nacht-; ~ **stay** Übernachtung f
overpass n Überführung f
overpay vt (pt/pp -paid) überbezahlen
overpopulated a übervölkert
overpower vt überwältigen. ~ing a überwältigend
overpriced a zu teuer
overrated a überbewertet
overreact vi überreagieren. ~ion n Überreaktion f
overriding a Haupt-
overrule vt ablehnen; **we were** ~d wir wurden überstimmt
overrun vt (pt -ran, pp -run, pres p -running) überrennen; überschreiten <time>; **be** ~ **with** überlaufen sein von

overseas¹ adv in Übersee; **go** ~ nach Übersee gehen
overseas² a Übersee-
oversee vt (pt -saw, pp -seen) beaufsichtigen
overshadow vt überschatten
overshoot vt (pt/pp -shot) hinausschießen über (+ acc)
oversight n Versehen nt
oversleep vi (pt/pp -slept) [sich] verschlafen
overstep vt (pt/pp -stepped) überschreiten
overt a offen
overtake vt/i (pt -took, pp -taken) überholen
overthrow vt (pt -threw, pp -thrown) (Pol) stürzen
overtime n Überstunden pl ● adv **work** ~ Überstunden machen
overtired a übermüdet
overture n (Mus) Ouvertüre f; ~s pl (fig) Annäherungsversuche pl
overturn vt umstoßen ● vi umkippen
overweight a übergewichtig; **be** ~ Übergewicht haben
overwhelm vt überwältigen. ~ing a überwältigend
overwork n Überarbeitung f ● vt überfordern ● vi sich überarbeiten
overwrought a überreizt
ow|e vt schulden/ (fig) verdanken ([to] s.o. jdm); ~**e s.o. sth** jdm etw schuldig sein. ~**ing** a schuldig sein. ~**ing to** prep wegen (+ gen)
owl n Eule f
own¹ a & pron eigen; **it's my** ~ es gehört mir; **a car of my** ~ mein eigenes Auto; **on one's** ~ allein; **get one's** ~ **back** 🛈 sich revanchieren
own² vt besitzen; **I don't** ~ **it** es gehört mir nicht. ~ **up** vi es zugeben
owner n Eigentümer(in) m(f), Besitzer(in) m(f); (of shop)

O

Inhaber(in) *m(f)*. ~**ship** *n* Besitz *m*
oxygen *n* Sauerstoff *m*
oyster *n* Auster *f*

pace *n* Schritt *m*; (*speed*) Tempo *nt*; **keep ~ with** Schritt halten mit ● *vi* ~ **up and down** auf und ab gehen. ~**maker** *n* (*Sport & Med*) Schrittmacher *m*
Pacific *a & n* **the ~ [Ocean]** der Pazifik
pacifist *n* Pazifist *m*
pacify *vt* (*pt/pp* **-ied**) beruhigen
pack *n* Packung *f*; (*Mil*) Tornister *m*; (*of cards*) [Karten]spiel *nt*; (*gang*) Bande *f*; (*of hounds*) Meute *f*; (*of wolves*) Rudel *nt*; **a ~ of lies** ein Haufen Lügen ● *vt/i* packen; einpacken *<article>*; **be ~ed** (*crowded*) [gedrängt] voll sein. **~ up** *vt* einpacken ● *vi* 🛈 *<machine:>* kaputtgehen
package *n* Paket *nt*. **~ holiday** *n* Pauschalreise *f*
packet *n* Päckchen *nt*
packing *n* Verpackung *f*
pact *n* Pakt *m*
pad *n* Polster *nt*; (*for writing*) [Schreib]block *m* ● *vt* (*pt/pp* **padded**) polstern
padding *n* Polsterung *f*; (*in written work*) Füllwerk *nt*
paddle[1] *n* Paddel *nt* ● *vt* (*row*) paddeln
paddle[2] *vi* waten
paddock *n* Koppel *f*
padlock *n* Vorhängeschloss *nt* ● *vt* mit einem Vorhängeschloss verschließen

paediatrician *n* Kinderarzt *m* /-ärztin *f*
pagan *a* heidnisch ● *n* Heide *m*/ Heidin *f*
page[1] *n* Seite *f*
page[2] *n* (*boy*) Page *m* ● *vt* ausrufen *<person>*
paid *see* **pay** ● *a* bezahlt; **put ~ to** 🛈 zunichte machen
pail *n* Eimer *m*
pain *n* Schmerz *m*; **be in ~** Schmerzen haben; **take ~s** sich (*dat*) Mühe geben; **~ in the neck** 🛈 Nervensäge *f*
pain: ~ful *a* schmerzhaft; (*fig*) schmerzlich. **~-killer** *n* schmerzstillendes Mittel *nt*. **~less** *a*, **-ly** *adv* schmerzlos
painstaking *a* sorgfältig
paint *n* Farbe *f* ● *vt/i* streichen; *<artist:>* malen. **~brush** *n* Pinsel *m*. **~er** *n* Maler *m*; (*decorator*) Anstreicher *m*. **~ing** *n* Malerei *f*; (*picture*) Gemälde *nt*
pair *n* Paar *nt*; **~ of trousers** Hose *f* ● *vi* **~ off** Paare bilden
pajamas *n pl* (*Amer*) Schlafanzug *m*
Pakistan *n* Pakistan *nt*. **~i** *a* pakistanisch ● *n* Pakistaner(in) *m(f)*
pal *n* Freund(in) *m(f)*
palace *n* Palast *m*
palatable *a* schmackhaft
palate *n* Gaumen *m*
palatial *a* palastartig
pale *a* (**-r, -st**) blass ● *vi* blass werden. **~ness** *n* Blässe *f*
Palestin|e *n* Palästina *nt*. **~ian** *a* palästinensisch ● *n* Palästinenser(in) *m(f)*
palette *n* Palette *f*
palm *n* Handfläche *f*; (*tree, symbol*) Palme *f* ● *vt* **~ sth off on s.o.** jdm etw andrehen. **P~ Sunday** *n* Palmsonntag *m*
palpable *a* tastbar; (*perceptible*) spürbar
palpitations *npl* Herzklopfen *nt*

paltry *a* (**-ier, -iest**) armselig
pamper *vt* verwöhnen
pamphlet *n* Broschüre *f*
pan *n* Pfanne *f*; (*saucepan*) Topf
m; (*of scales*) Schale *f*
panacea *n* Allheilmittel *nt*
pancake *n* Pfannkuchen *m*
panda *n* Panda *m*
pandemonium *n* Höllenlärm *m*
pane *n* [Glas]scheibe *f*
panel *n* Tafel *f*, Platte *f*; ~ **of
experts** Expertenrunde *f*; ~ **of
judges** Jury *f*. ~**ling** *n* Täfelung *f*
pang *n* ~**s of hunger**
Hungergefühl *nt*; ~**s of
conscience** Gewissensbisse *pl*
panic *n* Panik *f* ● *vi* (*pt/pp*
panicked) in Panik geraten. ~-
stricken *a* von Panik ergriffen
panoram|a *n* Panorama *nt*. ~**ic** *a*
Panorama-
pansy *n* Stiefmütterchen *nt*
pant *vi* keuchen; <*dog:*> hecheln
panther *n* Panther *m*
panties *npl* [Damen]slip *m*
pantomime *n* [zu Weihnachten
aufgeführte] Märchenvorstellung
f
pantry *n* Speisekammer *f*
pants *npl* Unterhose *f*; (*woman's*)
Schlüpfer *m*; (*trousers*) Hose *f*
pantyhose *n* (*Amer*) Strumpfhose
f
paper *n* Papier *nt*; (*newspaper*)
Zeitung *f*; (*exam* ~) Testbogen
m; (*exam*) Klausur *f*; (*treatise*)
Referat *nt*; ~**s** *pl* (*documents*)
Unterlagen *pl*; (*for identification*)
[Ausweis]papiere *pl* ● *vt*
tapezieren
paper: ~**back** *n* Taschenbuch *nt*.
~**-clip** *n* Büroklammer *f*.
~**weight** *n* Briefbeschwerer *m*.
~**work** *n* Schreibarbeit *f*
par *n* (*Golf*) Par *nt*; **on a** ~
gleichwertig (**with** *dat*)
parable *n* Gleichnis *nt*
parachut|e *n* Fallschirm *m* ● *vi*
[mit dem Fallschirm]

abspringen. ~**ist** *n*
Fallschirmspringer *m*
parade *n* Parade *f*; (*procession*)
Festzug *m* ● *vt* (*show off*) zur
Schau stellen
paradise *n* Paradies *nt*
paradox *n* Paradox *nt*. ~**ical** *a*
paradox
paraffin *n* Paraffin *nt*
paragraph *n* Absatz *m*
parallel *a* & *adv* parallel ● *n*
(*Geog*) Breitenkreis *m*; (*fig*)
Parallele *f*
paralyse *vt* lähmen; (*fig*)
lahmlegen
paralysis *n* (*pl* **-ses**) Lähmung *f*
paranoid *a* [krankhaft]
misstrauisch
parapet *n* Brüstung *f*
paraphernalia *n* Kram *m*
parasite *n* Parasit *m*,
Schmarotzer *m*
paratrooper *n* Fallschirmjäger *m*
parcel *n* Paket *nt*
parch *vt* austrocknen; **be** ~**ed**
<*person:*> einen furchtbaren
Durst haben
parchment *n* Pergament *nt*
pardon *n* Verzeihung *f*; (*Jur*)
Begnadigung *f*; ~? ① bitte? **I beg
your** ~ wie bitte? (*sorry*)
Verzeihung! ● *vt* verzeihen; (*Jur*)
begnadigen
parent *n* Elternteil *m*; ~**s** *pl*
Eltern *pl*. ~**al** *a* elterlich
parenthesis *n* (*pl* **-ses**) Klammer
f
parish *n* Gemeinde *f*. ~**ioner** *n*
Gemeindemitglied *nt*
park *n* Park *m* ● *vt/i* parken
parking *n* Parken *nt*; **'no** ~**'**
'Parken verboten'. ~**-lot** *n*
(*Amer*) Parkplatz *m*. ~**-meter** *n*
Parkuhr *f*. ~ **space** *n* Parkplatz
m
parliament *n* Parlament *nt*. ~**ary**
a parlamentarisch
parochial *a* Gemeinde-; (*fig*)
beschränkt

parody n Parodie f ● vt (pt/pp
-ied) parodieren

parole n on ~ auf Bewährung

parquet n ~ **floor** Parkett nt

parrot n Papagei m

parsley n Petersilie f

parsnip n Pastinake f

parson n Pfarrer m

part n Teil m; (Techn) Teil nt;
(area) Gegend f; (Theat) Rolle f;
(Mus) Part m; **spare** ~ Ersatzteil
nt; **for my** ~ meinerseits; **on the** ~
of vonseiten (+ gen); **take s.o.'s** ~
für jdn Partei ergreifen; **take** ~ **in**
teilnehmen an (+ dat) ● adv teils
● vt trennen; scheiteln <hair>
● vi <people:> sich trennen; ~
with sich trennen von

partial a Teil-; **be** ~ **to** mögen. **-ly**
adv teilweise

particip|ant n Teilnehmer(in)
m(f). ~**ate** vi teilnehmen (**in** an +
dat). ~**ation** n Teilnahme f

particle n Körnchen nt; (Phys)
Partikel nt; (Gram) Partikel f

particular a besondere(r,s);
(precise) genau; (fastidious)
penibel; **in** ~ besonders. ~**ly** adv
besonders. ~**s** npl nähere
Angaben pl

parting n Abschied m; (in hair)
Scheitel m

partition n Trennwand f; (Pol)
Teilung f ● vt teilen

partly adv teilweise

partner n Partner(in) m(f);
(Comm) Teilhaber m. ~**ship** n
Partnerschaft f; (Comm)
Teilhaberschaft f

partridge n Rebhuhn nt

part-time a & adv Teilzeit-; **be** or
work ~ Teilzeitarbeit machen

party n Party f, Fest nt; (group)
Gruppe f; (Pol, Jur) Partei f

pass n Ausweis m; (Geog, Sport)
Pass m; (Sch) ≈ ausreichend; **get**
a ~ bestehen ● vt vorbeigehen/
-fahren an (+ dat); (overtake)
überholen; (hand) reichen;

(Sport) abgeben, abspielen;
(approve) annehmen; (exceed)
übersteigen; bestehen <exam>;
machen <remark>; fällen
<judgement>; (Jur) verhängen
<sentence>; ~ **the time** sich (dat)
die Zeit vertreiben; ~ **one's hand**
over sth mit der Hand über etw
(acc) fahren ● vi vorbeigehen/
-fahren; (get by) vorbeikommen;
(overtake) überholen; <time:>
vergehen; (in exam) bestehen; ~
away vi sterben. ~ **down** vt
herunterreichen; (fig)
weitergeben. ~ **out** vi
ohnmächtig werden. ~ **round** vt
herumreichen. ~ **up** vt
heraufreichen; (🛙 miss)
vorübergehen lassen

passable a <road> befahrbar;
(satisfactory) passabel

passage n Durchgang m;
(corridor) Gang m; (voyage)
Überfahrt f; (in book) Passage f

passenger n Fahrgast m; (Naut,
Aviat) Passagier m; (in car)
Mitfahrer m. ~ **seat** n
Beifahrersitz m

passer-by n (pl **-s-by**) Passant(in)
m(f)

passion n Leidenschaft f. ~**ate** a,
-ly adv leidenschaftlich

passive a passiv ● n Passiv nt

pass: ~**port** n [Reise]pass m.
~**word** n Kennwort nt; (Mil)
Losung f

past a vergangene(r,s); (former)
ehemalig; **that's all** ~ das ist jetzt
vorbei ● n Vergangenheit f
● prep an (+ dat) … vorbei;
(after) nach; **at ten** ~ **two** um
zehn nach zwei ● adv vorbei; **go**
~ vorbeigehen

pasta n Nudeln pl

paste n Brei m; (adhesive)
Kleister m; (jewellery) Strass m
● vt kleistern

pastel n Pastellfarbe f; (drawing)
Pastell nt ● attrib Pastell-

pastime n Zeitvertreib m
pastry n Teig m; **cakes and ~ies** Kuchen und Gebäck
pasture n Weide f
pasty n Pastete f
pat n Klaps m; (of butter) Stückchen nt ● vt (pt/pp **patted**) tätscheln; **~ s.o. on the back** jdm auf die Schulter klopfen
patch n Flicken m; (spot) Fleck m; **not a ~ on** 🔲 gar nicht zu vergleichen mit ● vt flicken. **~ up** vt [zusammen]flicken; beilegen <quarrel>
patchy a ungleichmäßig
patent n Patent nt ● vt patentieren. **~ leather** n Lackleder nt
paternal a väterlich
path n (pl **-s**) [Fuß]weg m, Pfad m; (orbit, track) Bahn f; (fig) Weg m
pathetic a mitleiderregend; <attempt> erbärmlich
patience n Geduld f; (game) Patience f
patient a, **-ly** adv geduldig ● n Patient(in) m(f)
patio n Terrasse f
patriot n Patriot(in) m(f). **~ic** a patriotisch. **~ism** n Patriotismus m
patrol n Patrouille f ● vt/i patrouillieren [in (+ dat)]; <police:> auf Streife gehen/ fahren [in (+ dat)]. **~ car** n Streifenwagen m
patron n Gönner m; (of charity) Schirmherr m; (of the arts) Mäzen m; (customer) Kunde m/ Kundin f; (Theat) Besucher m. **~age** n Schirmherrschaft f
patroniz|e vt (fig) herablassend behandeln. **~ing** a, **-ly** adv gönnerhaft
patter n (speech) Gerede nt
pattern n Muster nt
paunch n [Schmer]bauch m
pause n Pause f ● vi innehalten

pave vt pflastern; **~ the way** den Weg bereiten (**for** dat). **~ment** n Bürgersteig m
paw n Pfote f; (of large animal) Pranke f, Tatze f
pawn[1] n (Chess) Bauer m; (fig) Schachfigur f
pawn[2] vt verpfänden. **~ broker** n Pfandleiher m
pay n Lohn m; (salary) Gehalt nt; **be in the ~ of** bezahlt werden von ● v (pt/pp **paid**) ● vt bezahlen; zahlen <money>; **~ s.o. a visit** jdm einen Besuch abstatten; **~ s.o. a compliment** jdm ein Kompliment machen ● vi zahlen; (be profitable) sich bezahlt machen; (fig) sich lohnen; **~ for** sth etw bezahlen. **~ back** vt zurückzahlen. **~ in** vt einzahlen. **~ off** vt abzahlen <debt> ● vi (fig) sich auszahlen
payable a zahlbar; **make ~ to** ausstellen auf (+ acc)
payment n Bezahlung f; (amount) Zahlung f
pea n Erbse f
peace n Frieden m; **for my ~ of mind** zu meiner eigenen Beruhigung
peace|ful a, **-ly** adv friedlich. **~maker** n Friedensstifter m
peach n Pfirsich m
peacock n Pfau m
peak n Gipfel m; (fig) Höhepunkt m. **~ed cap** n Schirmmütze f. **~ hours** npl Hauptbelastungszeit f; (for traffic) Hauptverkehrszeit f
peal n (of bells) Glockengeläut nt; **~s of laughter** schallendes Gelächter m
peanut n Erdnuss f
pear n Birne f
pearl n Perle f
peasant n Bauer m
peat n Torf m
pebble n Kieselstein m

P

peck n Schnabelhieb m; (kiss) flüchtiger Kuss m ● vt/i picken/ (nip) hacken (**at** nach)

peculiar a eigenartig, seltsam; ~ **to** eigentümlich (+ dat). ~**ity** n Eigenart f

pedal n Pedal nt ● vt fahren <bicycle> ● vi treten

pedantic a, **-ally** adv pedantisch

pedestal n Sockel m

pedestrian n Fußgänger(in) m(f) ● a (fig) prosaisch. ~ **crossing** n Fußgängerüberweg m. ~ **precinct** n Fußgängerzone f

pedigree n Stammbaum m ● attrib <animal> Rasse-

pedlar n Hausierer m

peek vi 🛈 gucken

peel n Schale f ● vt schälen; ● vi <skin:> sich schälen; <paint:> abblättern. ~**ings** npl Schalen pl

peep n kurzer Blick m ● vi gucken. ~**hole** n Guckloch nt

peer[1] vi ~ **at** forschend ansehen

peer[2] n Peer m; **his** ~**s** pl seinesgleichen

peg n (hook) Haken m; (for tent) Pflock m, Hering m; (for clothes) [Wäsche]klammer f; **off the** ~ 🛈 von der Stange

pejorative a, **-ly** adv abwertend

pelican n Pelikan m

pellet n Kügelchen nt

pelt[1] n (skin) Pelz m, Fell nt

pelt[2] vt bewerfen ● vi ~ [**down**] <rain:> [hernieder]prasseln

pelvis n (Anat) Becken nt

pen[1] n (for animals) Hürde f

pen[2] n Federhalter m; (ballpoint) Kugelschreiber m

penal a Straf-. ~**ize** vt bestrafen; (fig) benachteiligen

penalty n Strafe f; (fine) Geldstrafe f; (Sport) Strafstoß m; (Football) Elfmeter m

penance n Buße f

pence see **penny**

pencil n Bleistift m ● vt (pt/pp **pencilled**) mit Bleistift schreiben. ~**-sharpener** n Bleistiftspitzer m

pendulum n Pendel nt

penetrat|e vt durchdringen; ~**e into** eindringen in (+ acc). ~**ing** a durchdringend. ~**ion** n Durchdringen nt

penfriend n Brieffreund(in) m(f)

penguin n Pinguin m

penicillin n Penizillin nt

peninsula n Halbinsel f

penis n Penis m

penitentiary n (Amer) Gefängnis nt

pen: ~**knife** n Taschenmesser nt. ~**-name** n Pseudonym nt

penniless a mittellos

penny n (pl **pence**; single coins **pennies**) Penny m; (Amer) Centstück nt; **the** ~**'s dropped** 🛈 der Groschen ist gefallen

pension n Rente f; (of civil servant) Pension f. ~**er** n Rentner(in) m(f); Pensionär(in) m(f)

pensive a nachdenklich

pent-up a angestaut

penultimate a vorletzte(r,s)

people npl Leute pl, Menschen pl; (citizens) Bevölkerung f; **the** ~ das Volk; **English** ~ die Engländer; ~ **say** man sagt; **for four** ~ für vier Personen ● vt bevölkern

pepper n Pfeffer m; (vegetable) Paprika m

pepper: ~**mint** n Pfefferminz nt; (Bot) Pfefferminze f. ~**pot** n Pfefferstreuer m

per prep pro; ~ **cent** Prozent nt

percentage n Prozentsatz m; (part) Teil m

perceptible a wahrnehmbar

percept|ion n Wahrnehmung f. ~**ive** a feinsinnig

perch[1] n Stange f ● vi <bird:> sich niederlassen

perch[2] n inv (fish) Barsch m

percussion n Schlagzeug nt. ~ **instrument** n Schlaginstrument nt

perennial a <problem> immer wiederkehrend ● n (Bot) mehrjährige Pflanze f

perfect[1] a perfekt, vollkommen; (I utter) völlig ● n (Gram) Perfekt nt

perfect[2] vt vervollkommnen. ~**ion** n Vollkommenheit f; **to** ~**ion** perfekt

perfectly adv perfekt; (completely) vollkommen, völlig

perforated a perforiert

perform vt ausführen; erfüllen <duty>; (Theat) aufführen <play>; spielen <role> ● vi (Theat) auftreten; (Techn) laufen. ~**ance** n Aufführung f; (at theatre, cinema) Vorstellung f; (Techn, Sport) Leistung f. ~**er** n Künstler(in) m(f)

perfume n Parfüm nt; (smell) Duft m

perhaps adv vielleicht

perilous a gefährlich

perimeter n [äußere] Grenze f; (Geom) Umfang m

period n Periode f; (Sch) Stunde f; (full stop) Punkt m ● attrib <costume> zeitgenössisch; <furniture> antik. ~**ic** a, ~**ally** adv periodisch. ~**ical** n Zeitschrift f

peripher|al a nebensächlich. ~**y** n Peripherie f

perish vi <rubber:> verrotten; <food:> verderben; (liter: die) ums Leben kommen. ~**able** a leicht verderblich. ~**ing** a (I cold) eiskalt

perjur|e vt ~**e oneself** einen Meineid leisten. ~**y** n Meineid m

perk[1] n I [Sonder]vergünstigung f

perk[2] vi ~ **up** munter werden

perm n Dauerwelle f ● vt ~ **s.o.'s hair** jdm eine Dauerwelle machen

permanent a ständig; <job, address> fest. ~**ly** adv ständig; <work, live> dauernd, permanent; <employed> fest

permissible a erlaubt

permission n Erlaubnis f

permit[1] vt (pt/pp -**mitted**) erlauben (s.o. jdm)

permit[2] n Genehmigung f

perpendicular a senkrecht ● n Senkrechte f

perpetual a, ~**ly** adv ständig, dauernd

perpetuate vt bewahren; verewigen <error>

perplex vt verblüffen. ~**ed** a verblüfft

persecut|e vt verfolgen. ~**ion** n Verfolgung f

perseverance n Ausdauer f

persevere vi beharrlich weitermachen

Persia n Persien nt

Persian a persisch; <cat, carpet> Perser-

persist vi beharrlich weitermachen; (continue) anhalten; <view:> weiter bestehen; ~ **in doing sth** dabei bleiben, etw zu tun. ~**ence** n Beharrlichkeit f. ~**ent** a, ~**ly** adv beharrlich; (continuous) anhaltend

person n Person f; **in** ~ persönlich

personal a, ~**ly** adv persönlich. ~ **hygiene** n Körperpflege f

personality n Persönlichkeit f

personify vt (pt/pp -**ied**) personifizieren, verkörpern

personnel n Personal nt

perspective n Perspektive f

persp|iration n Schweiß m. ~**ire** vi schwitzen

persua|de vt überreden; (convince) überzeugen. ~**sion** n Überredung f; (powers of ~**sion**) Überredungskunst f

persuasive *a*, **-ly** *adv* beredsam; (*convincing*) überzeugend

pertinent *a* relevant (**to** für)

perturb *vt* beunruhigen

peruse *vt* lesen

pervers|e *a* eigensinnig. ~**ion** *n* Perversion *f*

pervert[1] *vt* verdrehen; verführen <*person*>

pervert[2] *n* Perverse(r) *m*

pessimis|m *n* Pessimismus *m*. ~**t** *n* Pessimist *m*. ~**tic** *a*, **-ally** *adv* pessimistisch

pest *n* Schädling *m*; (🔲 *person*) Nervensäge *f*

pester *vt* belästigen

pesticide *n* Schädlingsbekämpfungsmittel *nt*

pet *n* Haustier *nt*; (*favourite*) Liebling *m* ● *vt* (*pt/pp* **petted**) liebkosen

petal *n* Blütenblatt *nt*

peter *vi* ~ **out** allmählich aufhören

petition *n* Bittschrift *f*

pet name *n* Kosename *m*

petrified *a* vor Angst wie versteinert

petrol *n* Benzin *nt*

petroleum *n* Petroleum *nt*

petrol: ~**-pump** *n* Zapfsäule *f*. ~ **station** *n* Tankstelle *f*. ~ **tank** *n* Benzintank *m*

petticoat *n* Unterrock *m*

petty *a* (**-ier, -iest**) kleinlich. ~ **cash** *n* Portokasse *f*

petulant *a* gekränkt

pew *n* [Kirchen]bank *f*

pharmaceutical *a* pharmazeutisch

pharmac|ist *n* Apotheker(in) *m(f)*. ~**y** *n* Pharmazie *f*; (*shop*) Apotheke *f*

phase *n* Phase *f* ● *vt* ~ **in/out** allmählich einführen/abbauen

Ph.D. (*abbr of* **Doctor of Philosophy**) Dr. phil.

pheasant *n* Fasan *m*

phenomen|al *a* phänomenal. ~**on** *n* (*pl* **-na**) Phänomen *nt*

philharmonic *n* (*orchestra*) Philharmoniker *pl*

Philippines *npl* Philippinen *pl*

philistine *n* Banause *m*

philosoph|er *n* Philosoph *m*. ~**ical** *a*, **-ly** *adv* philosophisch. ~**y** *n* Philosophie *f*

phlegmatic *a* phlegmatisch

phobia *n* Phobie *f*

phone *n* Telefon *nt*; **be on the** ~ Telefon haben; (*be phoning*) telefonieren ● *vt* anrufen ● *vi* telefonieren. ~ **back** *vt/i* zurückrufen. ~ **book** *n* Telefonbuch *nt*. ~ **box** *n* Telefonzelle *f*. ~ **card** *n* Telefonkarte *f*. ~**in** *n* (*Radio*) Hörersendung *f*. ~ **number** *n* Telefonnummer *f*

phonetic *a* phonetisch. ~**s** *n* Phonetik *f*

phoney *a* (**-ier, -iest**) falsch; (*forged*) gefälscht

photo *n* Foto *nt*, Aufnahme *f*. ~**copier** *n* Fotokopiergerät *nt*. ~**copy** *n* Fotokopie *f* ● *vt* fotokopieren

photogenic *a* fotogen

photograph *n* Fotografie *f*, Aufnahme *f* ● *vt* fotografieren

photograph|er *n* Fotograf(in) *m(f)*. ~**ic** *a*, **-ally** *adv* fotografisch. ~**y** *n* Fotografie *f*

phrase *n* Redensart *f* ● *vt* formulieren. ~**-book** *n* Sprachführer *m*

physical *a*, **-ly** *adv* körperlich

physician *n* Arzt *m*/ Ärztin *f*

physic|ist *n* Physiker(in) *m(f)*. ~**s** *n* Physik *f*

physiotherap|ist *n* Physiotherapeut(in) *m(f)*. ~**y** *n* Physiotherapie *f*

physique *n* Körperbau *m*

pianist *n* Klavierspieler(in) *m(f)*; (*professional*) Pianist(in) *m(f)*

piano *n* Klavier *nt*

pick[1] n Spitzhacke f

pick[2] n Auslese f; **take one's ~** sich (dat) aussuchen ● vt/i (*pluck*) pflücken; (*select*) wählen, sich (dat) aussuchen; **~ and choose** wählerisch sein; **~ a quarrel** einen Streit anfangen; **~ holes in** [I] kritisieren; **~ at one's food** im Essen herumstochern. **~ on** vt wählen; ([I] *find fault with*) herumhacken auf (+ dat). **~ up** vt in die Hand nehmen; (*off the ground*) aufheben; hochnehmen <*baby*>; (*learn*) lernen; (*acquire*) erwerben; (*buy*) kaufen; (*Teleph*) abnehmen <*receiver*>; auffangen <*signal*>; (*collect*) abholen; aufnehmen <*passengers*>; <*police*:> aufgreifen <*criminal*>; sich holen <*illness*>; [I] aufgabeln <*girl*>; **~ oneself up** aufstehen ● vi (*improve*) sich bessern

pickaxe n Spitzhacke f

picket n Streikposten m

pickle n (*Amer: gherkin*) Essiggurke f; **~s** pl [Mixed] Pickles pl ● vt einlegen

pick: **~pocket** n Taschendieb m. **~-up** n (*truck*) Lieferwagen m

picnic n Picknick nt ● vi (*pt/pp* -nicked) picknicken

picture n Bild nt; (*film*) Film m; **as pretty as a ~** bildhübsch; **put s.o. in the ~** (*fig*) jdn ins Bild setzen ● vt (*imagine*) sich (dat) vorstellen

picturesque a malerisch

pie n Pastete f; (*fruit*) Kuchen m

piece n Stück nt; (*of set*) Teil nt; (*in game*) Stein m; (*Journ*) Artikel m; **a ~ of bread/paper** ein Stück Brot/Papier; **a ~ of news/advice** eine Nachricht/ein Rat; **take to ~s** auseinander nehmen ● vt **~ together** zusammensetzen; (*fig*) zusammenstückeln. **~meal** adv stückweise

pier n Pier m; (*pillar*) Pfeiler m

pierc|e vt durchstechen. **~ing** a durchdringend

pig n Schwein nt

pigeon n Taube f. **~-hole** n Fach nt

piggy|back n **give s.o. a ~back** jdn huckepack tragen. **~ bank** n Sparschwein nt

pigheaded a [I] starrköpfig

pigment n Pigment nt

pig: **~skin** n Schweinsleder nt. **~sty** n Schweinestall m. **~tail** n [I] Zopf m

pilchard n Sardine f

pile[1] n (*of fabric*) Flor m

pile[2] n Haufen m ● vt **~ sth on to sth** etw auf etw (acc) häufen. **~ up** vt häufen ● vi sich häufen

piles npl Hämorrhoiden pl

pile-up n Massenkarambolage f

pilgrim n Pilger(in) m(f). **~age** n Pilgerfahrt f, Wallfahrt f

pill n Pille f

pillar n Säule f. **~-box** n Briefkasten m

pillow n Kopfkissen nt. **~case** n Kopfkissenbezug m

pilot n Pilot m; (*Naut*) Lotse m ● vt fliegen <*plane*>; lotsen <*ship*>. **~-light** n Zündflamme f

pimple n Pickel m

pin n Stecknadel f; (*Techn*) Bolzen m, Stift m; (*Med*) Nagel m; **I have ~s and needles in my leg** [I] mein Bein ist eingeschlafen ● vt (*pt/pp* pinned) anstecken (**to/on** an + acc); (*sewing*) stecken; (*hold down*) festhalten

pinafore n Schürze f. **~ dress** n Kleiderrock m

pincers npl Kneifzange f; (*Zool*) Scheren pl

pinch n Kniff m; (*of salt*) Prise f; **at a ~** [I] zur Not ● vt kneifen, zwicken; (*fam: steal*) klauen; **~ one's finger** sich (dat) den Finger klemmen ● vi <*shoe*:> drücken

pine[1] n (*tree*) Kiefer f

pine[2] vi **~ for** sich sehnen nach

pineapple n Ananas f
pink a rosa
pinnacle n Gipfel m; (on roof) Turmspitze f
pin: ~**point** vt genau festlegen. ~**stripe** n Nadelstreifen m
pint n Pint nt (0,57 l, Amer: 0,47 l)
pioneer n Pionier m ● vt bahnbrechende Arbeit leisten für
pious a, -**ly** adv fromm
pip[1] n (seed) Kern m
pip[2] n (sound) Tonsignal nt
pipe n Pfeife f; (for water, gas) Rohr nt ● vt in Rohren leiten; (Culin) spritzen
pipe: ~**dream** n Luftschloss nt. ~**line** n Pipeline f; **in the** ~**line** 🅣 in Vorbereitung
piping a ~ **hot** kochend heiß
pirate n Pirat m
piss vi 🆇 pissen
pistol n Pistole f
piston n (Techn) Kolben m
pit n Grube f; (for orchestra) Orchestergraben m; (for audience) Parkett nt; (motor racing) Box f
pitch[1] n (steepness) Schräge f; (of voice) Stimmlage f; (of sound) [Ton]höhe f; (Sport) Feld nt; (of street trader) Standplatz m; (fig: degree) Grad m ● vt werfen; aufschlagen <tent> ● vi fallen
pitch[2] n (tar) Pech nt. ~-**black** a pechschwarz. ~-**dark** a stockdunkel
pitfall n (fig) Falle f
pith n (Bot) Mark nt; (of orange) weiße Haut f
pithy a (-ier, -iest) (fig) prägnant
piti|ful a bedauernswert. ~**less** a mitleidslos
pit stop n Boxenstopp m
pittance n Hungerlohn m
pity n Mitleid nt, Erbarmen nt; **[what a]** ~! [wie] schade! **take** ~ **on** sich erbarmen über (+ acc) ● vt bemitleiden

pivot n Drehzapfen m ● vi sich drehen (**on** um)
pizza n Pizza f
placard n Plakat nt
placate vt beschwichtigen
place n Platz m; (spot) Stelle f; (town, village) Ort m; (🅣 house) Haus nt; **out of** ~ fehl am Platze; **take** ~ stattfinden ● vt setzen; (upright) stellen; (flat) legen; (remember) unterbringen 🅣; ~ **an order** eine Bestellung aufgeben; **be** ~**d** (in race) sich platzieren. ~-**mat** n Set nt
placid a gelassen
plague n Pest f ● vt plagen
plaice n inv Scholle f
plain a (-er, -est) klar; (simple) einfach; (not pretty) nicht hübsch; (not patterned) einfarbig; <chocolate> zartbitter; **in** ~ **clothes** in Zivil ● adv (simply) einfach ● n Ebene f. ~**ly** adv klar, deutlich; (simply) einfach; (obviously) offensichtlich
plait n Zopf m ● vt flechten
plan n Plan m ● vt (pt/pp planned) planen; (intend) vorhaben
plane[1] n (tree) Platane f
plane[2] n Flugzeug nt; (Geom & fig) Ebene f
plane[3] n (Techn) Hobel m ● vt hobeln
planet n Planet m
plank n Brett nt; (thick) Planke f
planning n Planung f
plant n Pflanze f; (Techn) Anlage f; (factory) Werk nt ● vt pflanzen; (place in position) setzen; ~ **oneself** sich hinstellen. ~**ation** n Plantage f
plaque n [Gedenk]tafel f; (on teeth) Zahnbelag m
plaster n Verputz m; (sticking ~) Pflaster nt; **~ [of Paris]** Gips m ● vt verputzen <wall>; (cover) bedecken mit
plastic n Kunststoff m, Plastik nt ● a Kunststoff-, Plastik-; (malleable) formbar, plastisch

plastic surgery n plastische Chirurgie f

plate n Teller m; (flat sheet) Platte f; (with name, number) Schild nt; (gold and silverware) vergoldete/versilberte Ware f; (in book) Tafel f ● vt (with gold) vergolden; (with silver) versilbern

platform n Plattform f; (stage) Podium nt; (Rail) Bahnsteig m; ~ 5 Gleis 5

platinum n Platin nt

platitude n Plattitüde f

plausible a plausibel

play n Spiel nt; [Theater]stück nt; (Radio) Hörspiel nt; (TV) Fernsehspiel nt; ~ on words Wortspiel nt ● vt/i spielen; ausspielen <card>; ~ safe sichergehen. ~ down vt herunterspielen. ~ up vi 🄸 Mätzchen machen

play: ~er n Spieler(in) m(f). ~ful a, -ly adv verspielt. ~ground n Spielplatz m; (Sch) Schulhof m. ~group n Kindergarten m

playing: ~-card n Spielkarte f. ~-field n Sportplatz m

play: ~mate n Spielkamerad m. ~thing n Spielzeug nt. ~wright n Dramatiker m

plc abbr (public limited company) ≈ GmbH

plea n Bitte f; make a ~ for bitten um

plead vi flehen (for um); ~ guilty sich schuldig bekennen; ~ with s.o. jdn anflehen

pleasant a angenehm; <person> nett. ~ly adv angenehm; <say, smile> freundlich

pleas|e adv bitte ● vt gefallen (+ dat); ~e s.o. jdm eine Freude machen; ~e oneself tun, was man will. ~ed a erfreut; be ~ed with/about sth sich über etw (acc) freuen. ~ing a erfreulich

pleasure n Vergnügen nt; (joy) Freude f; with ~ gern[e]

pleat n Falte f ● vt fälteln

pledge n Versprechen nt ● vt verpfänden; versprechen

plentiful a reichlich

plenty n eine Menge; (enough) reichlich; ~ of money/people viel Geld/viele Leute

pliable a biegsam

pliers npl [Flach]zange f

plight n [Not]lage f

plinth n Sockel m

plod vi (pt/pp plodded) trotten; (work) sich abmühen

plonk n 🄸 billiger Wein m

plot n Komplott nt; (of novel) Handlung f; ~ of land Stück nt Land ● vt einzeichnen ● vi ein Komplott schmieden

plough n Pflug m ● vt/i pflügen

ploy n 🄸 Trick m

pluck n Mut m ● vt zupfen; rupfen <bird>; pflücken <flower>; ~ up courage Mut fassen

plucky a (-ier, -iest) tapfer, mutig

plug n Stöpsel m; (wood) Zapfen m; (cotton wool) Bausch m; (Electr) Stecker m; (Auto) Zündkerze f; (🄸 advertisement) Schleichwerbung f ● vt zustopfen; (🄸 advertise) Schleichwerbung machen für. ~ in vt (Electr) einstecken

plum n Pflaume f

plumage n Gefieder nt

plumb|er n Klempner m. ~ing n Wasserleitungen pl

plume n Feder f

plump a (-er, -est) mollig, rundlich ● vt ~ for wählen

plunge n Sprung m; take the ~ 🄸 den Schritt wagen ● vt/i tauchen

plural a pluralisch ● n Mehrzahl f, Plural m

plus prep plus (+ dat) ● a Plus- ● n Pluszeichen nt; (advantage) Plus nt

plush[y] a luxuriös

P

ply vt (pt/pp **plied**) ausüben
<trade>; ~ **s.o. with drink** jdm ein
Glas nach dem anderen
eingießen. ~**wood** n Sperrholz nt
p.m. adv (abbr of **post meridiem**)
nachmittags
pneumatic a pneumatisch. ~ **drill**
n Presslufthammer m
pneumonia n Lungenentzündung
f
poach vt (Culin) pochieren;
(steal) wildern. ~**er** n Wilddieb
m
pocket n Tasche f; **be out of** ~ [an
einem Geschäft] verlieren ● vt
einstecken. ~**book** n Notizbuch
nt; (wallet) Brieftasche f. ~**-
money** n Taschengeld nt
pod n Hülse f
poem n Gedicht nt
poet n Dichter(in) m(f). ~**ic** a
dichterisch
poetry n Dichtung f
poignant a ergreifend
point n Punkt m; (sharp end)
Spitze f; (meaning) Sinn m;
(purpose) Zweck m; (Electr)
Steckdose f; ~**s** pl (Rail) Weiche
f; ~ **of view** Standpunkt m; **good/
bad** ~**s** gute/schlechte Seiten;
what is the ~? wozu? **the** ~ **is** es
geht darum; **up to a** ~ bis zu
einem gewissen Grade; **be on the**
~ **of doing sth** im Begriff sein,
etw zu tun ● vt richten (**at** auf +
acc); ausfugen <brickwork> ● vi
deuten (**at/to** auf + acc); (with
finger) mit dem Finger zeigen. ~
out vt zeigen auf (+ acc); ~ **sth
out to s.o.** jdn auf etw (acc)
hinweisen
point-blank a aus nächster
Entfernung; (fig) rundweg
point|ed a spitz; <question>
gezielt. ~**less** a zwecklos, sinnlos
poise n Haltung f
poison n Gift nt ● vt vergiften.
~**ous** a giftig

poke n Stoß m ● vt stoßen;
schüren <fire>; (put) stecken
poker[1] n Schüreisen nt
poker[2] n (Cards) Poker nt
poky a (-ier, -iest) eng
Poland n Polen nt
polar a Polar-. ~**bear** n Eisbär m
Pole n Pole m/Polin f
pole[1] n Stange f
pole[2] n (Geog, Electr) Pol m
pole-vault n Stabhochsprung m
police npl Polizei f
police: ~**man** n Polizist m. ~
station n Polizeiwache f.
~**woman** n Polizistin f
policy[1] n Politik f
policy[2] n (insurance) Police f
Polish a polnisch
polish n (shine) Glanz m; (for
shoes) [Schuh]creme f; (for floor)
Bohnerwachs m; (for furniture)
Politur f; (for silver) Putzmittel
nt; (for nails) Lack m; (fig) Schliff
m ● vt polieren; bohnern <floor>.
~ **off** vt Ⅰ verputzen <food>;
erledigen <task>
polite a, **-ly** adv höflich. ~**ness** n
Höflichkeit f
politic|al a, **-ly** adv politisch. ~**ian**
n Politiker(in) m(f)
politics n Politik f
poll n Abstimmung f; (election)
Wahl f; **[opinion]** ~
[Meinungs]umfrage f
pollen n Blütenstaub m, Pollen m
polling: ~**booth** n Wahlkabine f.
~**-station** n Wahllokal nt
pollut|e vt verschmutzen. ~**ion** n
Verschmutzung f
polo n Polo nt. ~**-neck** n
Rollkragen m
polystyrene n Polystyrol nt; (for
packing) Styropor (P) nt
polythene n Polyäthylen nt. ~
bag n Plastiktüte f
pomp n Pomp m
pompous a, **-ly** adv großspurig
pond n Teich m
ponder vi nachdenken

ponderous a schwerfällig
pony n Pony nt. **~-tail** n
  Pferdeschwanz m
poodle n Pudel m
pool n [Schwimm]becken nt;
  (pond) Teich m; (of blood) Lache
  f; (common fund) [gemeinsame]
  Kasse f; **~s** pl [Fußball]toto nt
  ● vt zusammenlegen
poor a (-er, -est) arm; (not good)
  schlecht; **in ~ health** nicht
  gesund. **~ly** a **be ~ly** krank sein
  ● adv ärmlich; (badly) schlecht
pop[1] n Knall m ● v (pt/pp popped)
  ● vt (🔢 put) stecken (**in** in + acc)
  ● vi knallen; (burst) platzen. **~ in**
  vi 🔢 reinschauen. **~ out** vi 🔢
  kurz rausgehen
pop[2] n 🔢 Popmusik f, Pop m
  ● attrib Pop-
popcorn n Puffmais m
pope n Papst m
poplar n Pappel f
poppy n Mohn m
popular a beliebt, populär;
  <belief> volkstümlich. **~ity** n
  Beliebtheit f, Popularität f
populat|e vt bevölkern. **~ion** n
  Bevölkerung f
porcelain n Porzellan nt
porch n Vorbau m; (Amer)
  Veranda f
porcupine n Stachelschwein nt
pore n Pore f
pork n Schweinefleisch nt
porn n 🔢 Porno m
pornograph|ic a pornographisch.
  ~y n Pornographie f
porridge n Haferbrei m
port[1] n Hafen m; (town)
  Hafenstadt f
port[2] n (Naut) Backbord nt
port[3] n (wine) Portwein m
portable a tragbar
porter n Portier m; (for luggage)
  Gepäckträger m
porthole n Bullauge nt
portion n Portion f; (part, share)
  Teil nt

portrait n Porträt nt
portray vt darstellen. **~al** n
  Darstellung f
Portug|al n Portugal nt. **~uese** a
  portugiesisch ● n Portugiese m/
  -giesin f
pose n Pose f ● vt aufwerfen
  <problem>; stellen <question>
  ● vi posieren; (for painter)
  Modell stehen
posh a 🔢 feudal
position n Platz m; (posture)
  Haltung f; (job) Stelle f;
  (situation) Lage f, Situation f;
  (status) Stellung f ● vt platzieren;
  ~ oneself sich stellen
positive a, **-ly** adv positiv;
  (definite) eindeutig; (real)
  ausgesprochen ● n Positiv nt
possess vt besitzen. **~ion** n
  Besitz m; **~ions** pl Sachen pl
possess|ive a Possessiv-; **be ~ive
  about s.o.** zu sehr an jdm hängen
possibility n Möglichkeit f
possib|le a möglich. **~ly** adv
  möglicherweise; **not ~ly**
  unmöglich
post[1] n (pole) Pfosten m
post[2] n (place of duty) Posten m;
  (job) Stelle f
post[3] n (mail) Post f; **by ~** mit der
  Post ● vt aufgeben <letter>; (send
  by ~) mit der Post schicken;
  keep s.o. ~ed jdn auf dem
  Laufenden halten
postage n Porto nt
postal a Post-. **~ order** n ≈
  Geldanweisung f
post: ~-box n Briefkasten m.
  ~card n Postkarte f; (picture)
  Ansichtskarte f. **~code** n
  Postleitzahl f. **~-date** vt
  vordatieren
poster n Plakat nt
posterity n Nachwelt f
posthumous a, **-ly** adv postum
post: ~man n Briefträger m.
  ~mark n Poststempel m
post-mortem n Obduktion f

P

post office n Post f
postpone vt aufschieben; ~ **until** verschieben auf (+ acc). ~**ment** n Verschiebung f
postscript n Nachschrift f
posture n Haltung f
pot n Topf m; (for tea, coffee) Kanne f; ~**s of money** 🛈 eine Menge Geld
potato n (pl -**es**) Kartoffel f
potent a stark
potential a, -**ly** adv potenziell ● n Potenzial f
pot: ~**hole** n Höhle f; (in road) Schlagloch nt. ~**shot** nt take a ~**shot at** schießen auf (+ acc)
potter n Töpfer(in) m(f). ~**y** n Töpferei f; (articles) Töpferwaren pl
potty a (-**ier**, -**iest**) 🛈 verrückt ● n Töpfchen nt
pouch n Beutel m
poultry n Geflügel nt
pounce vi zuschlagen; ~ **on** sich stürzen auf (+ acc)
pound[1] n (money & 0,454 kg) Pfund nt
pound[2] vi <heart:> hämmern; (run heavily) stampfen
pour vt gießen; einschenken <drink> ● vi strömen; (with rain) gießen. ~ **out** vi ausströmen ● vt ausschütten; einschenken <drink>
pout vi einen Schmollmund machen
poverty n Armut f
powder n Pulver nt; (cosmetic) Puder m ● vt pudern
power n Macht f; (strength) Kraft f; (Electr) Strom m; (nuclear) Energie f; (Math) Potenz f. ~ **cut** n Stromsperre f. ~**ed** a betrieben (**by** mit); ~**ed by electricity** mit Elektroantrieb. ~**ful** a mächtig; (strong) stark. ~**less** a machtlos. ~**-station** n Kraftwerk nt
practicable a durchführbar, praktikabel

practical a, -**ly** adv praktisch. ~ **joke** n Streich m
practice n Praxis f; (custom) Brauch m; (habit) Gewohnheit f; (exercise) Übung f; (Sport) Training nt; **in** ~ (in reality) in der Praxis; **out of** ~ außer Übung; **put into** ~ ausführen
practise vt üben; (carry out) praktizieren; ausüben <profession> ● vi üben; <doctor:> praktizieren. ~**d** a geübt
praise n Lob nt ● vt loben. ~**worthy** a lobenswert
pram n Kinderwagen m
prank n Streich m
prawn n Garnele f, Krabbe f
pray vi beten. ~**er** n Gebet nt
preach vt/i predigen. ~**er** n Prediger m
pre-arrange vt im Voraus arrangieren
precarious a, -**ly** adv unsicher
precaution n Vorsichtsmaßnahme f
precede vt vorangehen (+ dat)
preceden|ce n Vorrang m. ~**t** n Präzedenzfall m
preceding a vorhergehend
precinct n Bereich m; (traffic-free) Fußgängerzone f; (Amer: district) Bezirk m
precious a kostbar; <style> preziös ● adv 🛈 ~ **little** recht wenig
precipice n Steilabfall m
precipitation n (Meteorol) Niederschlag m
precis|e a, -**ly** adv genau. ~**ion** n Genauigkeit f
precocious a frühreif
pre|conceived a vorgefasst. ~**conception** n vorgefasste Meinung f
predator n Raubtier nt
predecessor n Vorgänger(in) m(f)
predicat|e n (Gram) Prädikat nt. ~**ive** a, -**ly** adv prädikativ

predict vt voraussagen. ~able a voraussagbar; <person> berechenbar. ~ion n Voraussage f

predomin|ant a vorherrschend. ~antly adv hauptsächlich, überwiegend. ~ate vi vorherrschen

preen vt putzen

prefab n Ⅰ [einfaches] Fertighaus nt. ~ricated a vorgefertigt

preface n Vorwort nt

prefect n Präfekt m

prefer vt (pt/pp preferred) vorziehen; I ~ to walk ich gehe lieber zu Fuß; I ~ wine ich trinke lieber Wein

prefera|ble a be ~ble vorzuziehen sein (to dat). ~bly adv vorzugsweise

preferen|ce n Vorzug m. ~tial a bevorzugt

pregnan|cy n Schwangerschaft f. ~t a schwanger; <animal> trächtig

prehistoric a prähistorisch

prejudice n Vorurteil nt; (bias) Voreingenommenheit f ● vt einnehmen (against gegen). ~d a voreingenommen

preliminary a Vor-

prelude n Vorspiel nt

premature a vorzeitig; <birth> Früh-. ~ly adv zu früh

premeditated a vorsätzlich

premier a führend ● n (Pol) Premier[minister] m

premiere n Premiere f

premises npl Räumlichkeiten pl; on the ~ im Haus

premium n Prämie f; be at a ~ hoch im Kurs stehen

premonition n Vorahnung f

preoccupied a [in Gedanken] beschäftigt

preparation n Vorbereitung f; (substance) Präparat nt

preparatory a Vor-

prepare vt vorbereiten; anrichten <meal> ● vi sich vorbereiten (for auf + acc); ~d to bereit zu

preposition n Präposition f

preposterous a absurd

prerequisite n Voraussetzung f

Presbyterian a presbyterianisch ● n Presbyterian(in) m(f)

prescribe vt vorschreiben; (Med) verschreiben

prescription n (Med) Rezept nt

presence n Anwesenheit f, Gegenwart f; ~ of mind Geistesgegenwart f

present[1] a gegenwärtig; be ~ anwesend sein; (occur) vorkommen ● n Gegenwart f; (Gram) Präsens nt; at ~ zurzeit; for the ~ vorläufig

present[2] n (gift) Geschenk nt

present[3] vt überreichen; (show) zeigen; vorlegen <cheque>; (introduce) vorstellen; ~ s.o. with sth jdm etw überreichen. ~able a be ~able sich zeigen lassen können

presentation n Überreichung f

presently adv nachher; (Amer: now) zurzeit

preservation n Erhaltung f

preservative n Konservierungsmittel nt

preserve vt erhalten; (Culin) konservieren; (bottle) einmachen ● n (Hunting & fig) Revier nt; (jam) Konfitüre f

preside vi den Vorsitz haben (over bei)

presidency n Präsidentschaft f

president n Präsident m; (Amer: chairman) Vorsitzende(r) m/f. ~ial a Präsidenten-; <election> Präsidentschafts-

press n Presse f ● vt/i drücken; drücken auf (+ acc) <button>; pressen <flower>; (iron) bügeln; (urge) bedrängen; ~ for drängen auf (+ acc); be ~ed for time in Zeitdruck sein. ~ on vi weitergehen/-fahren; (*fig*) weitermachen

press: ~ **cutting** *n* Zeitungsausschnitt *m*. ~**ing** *a* dringend

pressure *n* Druck *m*. ~-**cooker** *n* Schnellkochtopf *m*

pressurize *vt* Druck ausüben auf (+ *acc*). ~**d** *a* Druck-

prestig|e *n* Prestige *nt*. ~**ious** *a* Prestige-

presumably *adv* vermutlich

presume *vt* vermuten

presumpt|ion *n* Vermutung *f*; (*boldness*) Anmaßung *f*. ~**uous** *a*, -**ly** *adv* anmaßend

pretence *n* Verstellung *f*; (*pretext*) Vorwand *m*

pretend *vt* (*claim*) vorgeben; ~ **that** so tun, als ob; ~ **to be** sich ausgeben als

pretentious *a* protzig

pretext *n* Vorwand *m*

pretty *a* (-**ier**, -**iest**), ~**ily** *adv* hübsch ● *adv* (🄸 *fairly*) ziemlich

prevail *vi* siegen; <*custom*:> vorherrschen; ~ **on s.o. to do sth** jdn dazu bringen, etw zu tun

prevalen|ce *n* Häufigkeit *f*. ~**t** *a* vorherrschend

prevent *vt* verhindern, verhüten; ~ **s.o. [from] doing sth** jdn daran hindern, etw zu tun. ~**ion** *n* Verhinderung *f*, Verhütung *f*. ~**ive** *a* vorbeugend

preview *n* Voraufführung *f*

previous *a* vorhergehend; ~ **to** vor (+ *dat*). ~**ly** *adv* vorher, früher

prey *n* Beute *f*; **bird of** ~ Raubvogel *m*

price *n* Preis *m* ● *vt* (*Comm*) auszeichnen. ~**less** *a* unschätzbar; (*fig*) unbezahlbar

prick *n* Stich *m* ● *vt/i* stechen

prickl|e *n* Stachel *m*; (*thorn*) Dorn *m*. ~**y** *a* stachelig; <*sensation*> stechend

pride *n* Stolz *m*; (*arrogance*) Hochmut *m* ● *vt* ~ **oneself on** stolz sein auf (+ *acc*)

priest *n* Priester *m*

prim *a* (**primmer**, **primmest**) prüde

primarily *adv* hauptsächlich, in erster Linie

primary *a* Haupt-. ~ **school** *n* Grundschule *f*

prime[1] *a* Haupt-; (*first-rate*) erstklassig

prime[2] *vt* scharf machen <*bomb*>; grundieren <*surface*>

Prime Minister *n* Premierminister(in) *m(f)*

primitive *a* primitiv

primrose *n* gelbe Schlüsselblume *f*

prince *n* Prinz *m*

princess *n* Prinzessin *f*

principal *a* Haupt- ● *n* (*Sch*) Rektor(in) *m(f)*

principally *adv* hauptsächlich

principle *n* Prinzip *nt*, Grundsatz *m*; **in/on** ~ im/aus Prinzip

print *n* Druck *m*; (*Phot*) Abzug *m*; **in** ~ gedruckt; (*available*) erhältlich; **out of** ~ vergriffen ● *vt* drucken; (*write in capitals*) in Druckschrift schreiben; (*Computing*) ausdrucken; (*Phot*) abziehen. ~**ed matter** *n* Drucksache *f*

print|er *n* Drucker *m*. ~**ing** *n* Druck *m*

printout *n* (*Computing*) Ausdruck *m*

prior *a* frühere(r,s); ~ **to** vor (+ *dat*)

priority *n* Priorität *f*, Vorrang *m*

prise *vt* ~ **open/up** aufstemmen/ hochstemmen

prison *n* Gefängnis *nt*. ~**er** *n* Gefangene(r) *m/f*

privacy *n* Privatsphäre *f*; **have no** ~ nie für sich sein

private *a*, -**ly** *adv* privat; (*confidential*) vertraulich; <*car, secretary, school*> Privat- ● *n*

(Mil) [einfacher] Soldat *m*; **in ~** privat; *(confidentially)* vertraulich
privation *n* Entbehrung *f*
privilege *n* Privileg *nt*. **~d** *a* privilegiert
prize *n* Preis *m* ● *vt* schätzen
pro *n* Ⅰ Profi *m*; **the ~s and cons** das Für und Wider
probability *n* Wahrscheinlichkeit *f*
probable *a*, **-bly** *adv* wahrscheinlich
probation *n (Jur)* Bewährung *f*
probe *n* Sonde *f*; *(fig: investigation)* Untersuchung *f*
problem *n* Problem *nt*; *(Math)* Textaufgabe *f*. **~atic** *a* problematisch
procedure *n* Verfahren *nt*
proceed *vi* gehen; *(in vehicle)* fahren; *(continue)* weitergehen/ -fahren; *(speaking)* fortfahren; *(act)* verfahren
proceedings *npl* Verfahren *nt*; *(Jur)* Prozess *m*
proceeds *npl* Erlös *m*
process *n* Prozess *m*; *(procedure)* Verfahren *nt*; **in the ~** dabei ● *vt* verarbeiten; *(Admin)* bearbeiten; *(Phot)* entwickeln
procession *n* Umzug *m*, Prozession *f*
proclaim *vt* ausrufen
proclamation *n* Proklamation *f*
procure *vt* beschaffen
prod *n* Stoß *m* ● *vt* stoßen
prodigy *n* **[infant] ~** Wunderkind *nt*
produce¹ *n* landwirtschaftliche Erzeugnisse *pl*
produce² *vt* erzeugen, produzieren; *(manufacture)* herstellen; *(bring out)* hervorholen; *(cause)* hervorrufen; inszenieren *<play>*; *(Radio, TV)* redigieren. **~r** *n* Erzeuger *m*, Produzent *m*; Hersteller *m*; *(Theat)* Regisseur

m; *(Radio, TV)* Redakteur(in) *m(f)*
product *n* Erzeugnis *nt*, Produkt *nt*. **~ion** *n* Produktion *f*; *(Theat)* Inszenierung *f*
productive *a* produktiv; *<land, talks>* fruchtbar. **~ity** *n* Produktivität *f*
profession *n* Beruf *m*. **~al** *a*, **-ly** *adv* beruflich; *(not amateur)* Berufs-; *(expert)* fachmännisch; *(Sport)* professionell ● *n* Fachmann *m*; *(Sport)* Profi *m*
professor *n* Professor *m*
proficien|cy *n* Können *nt*. **~t** *a* **be ~t in** beherrschen
profile *n* Profil *nt*; *(character study)* Porträt *nt*
profit *n* Gewinn *m*, Profit *m* ● *vi* **~ from** profitieren von. **~able** *a*, **-bly** *adv* gewinnbringend; *(fig)* nutzbringend
profound *a*, **-ly** *adv* tief
program *(Amer & Computing)* *n* Programm *nt* ● *vt* *(pt/pp* **programmed)** programmieren
programme *n* Programm *nt*; *(Radio, TV)* Sendung *f*. **~r** *n* *(Computing)* Programmierer(in) *m(f)*
progress¹ *n* Vorankommen *nt*; *(fig)* Fortschritt *m*; **in ~** im Gange; **make ~** *(fig)* Fortschritte machen
progress² *vi* vorankommen; *(fig)* fortschreiten. **~ion** *n* Folge *f*; *(development)* Entwicklung *f*
progressive *a* fortschrittlich. **~ly** *adv* zunehmend
prohibit *vt* verbieten **(s.o.** jdm). **~ive** *a* unerschwinglich
project¹ *n* Projekt *nt*; *(Sch)* Arbeit *f*
project² *vt* projizieren *<film>*; *(plan)* planen ● *vi* *(jut out)* vorstehen
projector *n* Projektor *m*
prolific *a* fruchtbar; *(fig)* produktiv

P

prologue n Prolog m
prolong vt verlängern
promenade n Promenade f ● vi spazieren gehen
prominent a vorstehend; (*important*) prominent; (*conspicuous*) auffällig
promiscuous a be ~ous häufig den Partner wechseln
promis|e n Versprechen nt ● vt/i versprechen (**s.o.** jdm). ~ing a viel versprechend
promot|e vt befördern; (*advance*) fördern; (*publicize*) Reklame machen für; be ~ed (*Sport*) aufsteigen. ~ion n Beförderung f; (*Sport*) Aufstieg m; (*Comm*) Reklame f
prompt a prompt, unverzüglich; (*punctual*) pünktlich ● adv pünktlich ● vt/i veranlassen (**to** zu); (*Theat*) soufflieren (+ dat). ~er n Souffleur m/Souffleuse f. ~ly adv prompt
prone a be or lie ~ auf dem Bauch liegen; be ~ to neigen zu
pronoun n Fürwort nt, Pronomen nt
pronounce vt aussprechen; (*declare*) erklären. ~d a ausgeprägt; (*noticeable*) deutlich. ~ment n Erklärung f
pronunciation n Aussprache f
proof n Beweis m; (*Typ*) Korrekturbogen m. ~-reader n Korrektor m
prop[1] n Stütze f ● vt (*pt/pp* propped). ~ against lehnen an (+ acc). ~ up vt stützen
prop[2] n (*Theat* 🄸) Requisit nt
propaganda n Propaganda f
propel vt (*pt/pp* propelled) [an]treiben. ~ler n Propeller m
proper a, -ly adv richtig; (*decent*) anständig
property n Eigentum nt; (*quality*) Eigenschaft f; (*Theat*) Requisit nt; (*land*) [Grund]besitz m; (*house*) Haus nt

prophecy n Prophezeiung f
prophesy vt (*pt/pp* -ied) prophezeien
prophet n Prophet m. ~ic a prophetisch
proportion n Verhältnis nt; (*share*) Teil m; ~s pl Proportionen; (*dimensions*) Maße. ~al a, -ly adv proportional
proposal n Vorschlag m; (*of marriage*) [Heirats]antrag m
propose vt vorschlagen; (*intend*) vorhaben; einbringen <*motion*> ● vi einen Heiratsantrag machen
proposition n Vorschlag m
proprietor n Inhaber(in) m(f)
propriety n Korrektheit f; (*decorum*) Anstand m
prose n Prosa f
prosecut|e vt strafrechtlich verfolgen. ~ion n strafrechtliche Verfolgung f; die ~ion die Anklage. ~or n [Public] P~or Staatsanwalt m
prospect n Aussicht f
prospect|ive a (*future*) zukünftig. ~or n Prospektor m
prospectus n Prospekt m
prosper vi gedeihen, florieren; <*person*> Erfolg haben. ~ity n Wohlstand m
prosperous a wohlhabend
prostitut|e n Prostituierte f. ~ion n Prostitution f
prostrate a ausgestreckt
protagonist n Kämpfer m; (*fig*) Protagonist m
protect vt schützen (**from** vor + dat); beschützen <*person*>. ~ion n Schutz m. ~ive a Schutz-; (*fig*) beschützend. ~or n Beschützer m
protein n Eiweiß nt
protest[1] n Protest m
protest[2] vi protestieren
Protestant a protestantisch ● n Protestant(in) m(f)
protester n Protestierende(r) m/f
prototype n Prototyp m

protrude *vi* [her]vorstehen
proud *a*, **-ly** *adv* stolz (**of** auf + *acc*)
prove *vt* beweisen ● *vi* ~ **to be** sich erweisen als
proverb *n* Sprichwort *nt*
provide *vt* zur Verfügung stellen; spenden <*shade*>; ~ **s.o. with sth** jdn mit etw versorgen *od* versehen ● *vi* ~ **for** sorgen für
provided *conj* ~ **[that]** vorausgesetzt [dass]
providen|ce *n* Vorsehung *f*. ~**tial** *a* be ~**tial** ein Glück sein
provinc|e *n* Provinz *f*; (*fig*) Bereich *m*. ~**ial** *a* provinziell
provision *n* Versorgung *f* (**of** mit); ~**s** *pl* Lebensmittel *pl*. ~**al** *a*, **-ly** *adv* vorläufig
provocat|ion *n* Provokation *f*. ~**ive** *a*, **-ly** *adv* provozierend; (*sexually*) aufreizend
provoke *vt* provozieren; (*cause*) hervorrufen
prow *n* Bug *m*
prowl *vi* herumschleichen
proximity *n* Nähe *f*
pruden|ce *n* Umsicht *f*. ~**t** *a*, **-ly** *adv* umsichtig; (*wise*) klug
prudish *a* prüde
prune[1] *n* Backpflaume *f*
prune[2] *vt* beschneiden
pry *vi* (*pt/pp* **pried**) neugierig sein
psalm *n* Psalm *m*
psychiatric *a* psychiatrisch
psychiatr|ist *n* Psychiater(in) *m(f)*. ~**y** *n* Psychiatrie *f*
psychic *a* übersinnlich
psycho|analysis *n* Psychoanalyse *f*. ~**analyst** *n* Psychoanalytiker(in) *m(f)*
psychological *a*, **-ly** *adv* psychologisch; <*illness*> psychisch
psycholog|ist *n* Psychologe *m*/ -login *f*. ~**y** *n* Psychologie *f*
P.T.O. *abbr* (**please turn over**) b.w.
pub *n* ⓘ Kneipe *f*
puberty *n* Pubertät *f*

public *a*, **-ly** *adv* öffentlich; **make** ~ publik machen ● *n* **the** ~ die Öffentlichkeit
publican *n* [Gast]wirt *m*
publication *n* Veröffentlichung *f*
public: ~ **holiday** *n* gesetzlicher Feiertag *m*. ~ **house** *n* [Gast]wirtschaft *f*
publicity *n* Publicity *f*; (*advertising*) Reklame *f*
publicize *vt* Reklame machen für
public: ~ **school** *n* Privatschule *f*; (*Amer*) staatliche Schule *f*. ~-**spirited** *a* be ~-**spirited** Gemeinsinn haben
publish *vt* veröffentlichen. ~**er** *n* Verleger(in) *m(f)*; (*firm*) Verlag *m*. ~**ing** *n* Verlagswesen *nt*
pudding *n* Pudding *m*; (*course*) Nachtisch *m*
puddle *n* Pfütze *f*
puff *n* (*of wind*) Hauch *m*; (*of smoke*) Wölkchen *nt* ● *vt* blasen, pusten; ~ **out** ausstoßen. ● *vi* keuchen; ~ **at** paffen an (+ *dat*) <*pipe*>. ~**ed** *a* (*out of breath*) aus der Puste. ~ **pastry** *n* Blätterteig *m*
pull *n* Zug *m*; (*jerk*) Ruck *m*; (ⓘ *influence*) Einfluss *m* ● *vt* ziehen; ziehen an (+ *dat*) <*rope*>; ~ **a muscle** sich (*dat*) einen Muskel zerren; ~ **oneself together** sich zusammennehmen; ~ **one's weight** tüchtig mitarbeiten; ~ **s.o.'s leg** ⓘ jdn auf den Arm nehmen. ~ **down** *vt* herunterziehen; (*demolish*) abreißen. ~ **in** *vt* hereinziehen ● *vi* (*Auto*) einscheren. ~ **off** *vt* abziehen; ⓘ schaffen. ~ **out** *vt* herausziehen ● *vi* (*Auto*) ausscheren. ~ **through** *vt* durchziehen ● *vi* (*recover*) durchkommen. ~ **up** *vt* heraufziehen; ausziehen <*plant*> ● *vi* (*Auto*) anhalten
pullover *n* Pullover *m*

pulp n Brei m; (of fruit) [Frucht]fleisch nt

pulpit n Kanzel f

pulse n Puls m

pulses npl Hülsenfrüchte pl

pummel vt (pt/pp pummelled) mit den Fäusten bearbeiten

pump n Pumpe f ● vt pumpen; ⟨⟩ aushorchen. ~ up vt (inflate) aufpumpen

pumpkin n Kürbis m

pun n Wortspiel nt

punch¹ n Faustschlag m; (device) Locher m ● vt boxen; lochen ⟨ticket⟩; stanzen ⟨hole⟩

punch² n (drink) Bowle f

punctual a, -ly adv pünktlich. ~ity n Pünktlichkeit f

punctuat|e vt mit Satzzeichen versehen. ~ion n Interpunktion f

puncture n Loch nt; (tyre) Reifenpanne f ● vt durchstechen

punish vt bestrafen. ~able a strafbar. ~ment n Strafe f

punt n (boat) Stechkahn m

puny a (-ier, -iest) mickerig

pup n = puppy

pupil n Schüler(in) m(f); (of eye) Pupille f

puppet n Puppe f; (fig) Marionette f

puppy n junger Hund m

purchase n Kauf m; (leverage) Hebelkraft f ● vt kaufen. ~r n Käufer m

pure a (-r, -st,) -ly adv rein

purge n (Pol) Säuberungsaktion f ● vt reinigen

puri|fication n Reinigung f. ~fy vt (pt/pp -ied) reinigen

puritanical a puritanisch

purity n Reinheit f

purple a [dunkel]lila

purpose n Zweck m; (intention) Absicht f; (determination) Entschlossenheit f; on ~ absichtlich. ~ful a, -ly adv entschlossen. ~ly adv absichtlich

purr vi schnurren

purse n Portemonnaie nt; (Amer: handbag) Handtasche f

pursue vt verfolgen; (fig) nachgehen (+ dat). ~r n Verfolger m

pursuit n Verfolgung f; Jagd f; (pastime) Beschäftigung f

pus n Eiter m

push n Stoß m; get the ~ ⟨⟩ hinausfliegen ● vt/i schieben; (press) drücken; (roughly) stoßen. ~ off vt hinunterstoßen ● vi (⟨⟩ leave) abhauen. ~ on vi (continue) weitergehen/-fahren; (with activity) weitermachen. ~ up vt hochschieben; hochtreiben ⟨price⟩

push: ~-button n Druckknopf m. ~-chair n [Kinder]sportwagen m

pushy a ⟨⟩ aufdringlich

puss n, **pussy** n Mieze f

put vt (pt/pp put, pres p putting) tun; (place) setzen; (upright) stellen; (flat) legen; (express) ausdrücken; (say) sagen; (estimate) schätzen (at auf + acc); ~ aside or by beiseite legen ● vi ~ to sea auslaufen ● a stay ~ dableiben. ~ away vt wegräumen. ~ back vt wieder hinsetzen/-stellen/-legen; zurückstellen ⟨clock⟩. ~ down vt hinsetzen/-stellen/-legen; (suppress) niederschlagen; (kill) töten; (write) niederschreiben; (attribute) zuschreiben (to dat). ~ forward vt vorbringen; vorstellen ⟨clock⟩. ~ in vt hineinsetzen/ -stellen/-legen; (insert) einstecken; (submit) einreichen ● vi ~ in for beantragen. ~ off vt ausmachen ⟨light⟩; (postpone) verschieben; ~ s.o. off jdn abbestellen; (disconcert) jdn aus der Fassung bringen. ~ on vt anziehen ⟨clothes, brake⟩; sich (dat) aufsetzen ⟨hat⟩; (Culin) aufsetzen; anmachen ⟨light⟩; aufführen ⟨play⟩; annehmen

<accent>; ~ **on weight** zunehmen.
~ **out** vt hinaussetzen/-stellen/
-legen; ausmachen <fire, light>;
ausstrecken <hand>; (disconcert)
aus der Fassung bringen; ~ **s.o./
oneself out** jdm/sich Umstände
machen. ~ **through** vt
durchstecken; (Teleph)
verbinden (**to** mit). ~ **up** vt
errichten <building>; aufschlagen
<tent>; aufspannen <umbrella>;
anschlagen <notice>; erhöhen
<price>; unterbringen <guest>
● vi (at hotel) absteigen in (+
dat); ~ **up with sth** sich (dat) etw
bieten lassen
putrid a faulig
putty n Kitt m
puzzl|e n Rätsel nt; (jigsaw)
Puzzlespiel nt ● vt **it ~es me** es
ist mir rätselhaft. ~**ing** a
rätselhaft
pyjamas npl Schlafanzug m
pylon n Mast m
pyramid n Pyramide f
python n Pythonschlange f

quack n Quaken nt; (doctor)
Quacksalber m ● vi quaken
quadrangle n Viereck nt; (court)
Hof m
quadruped n Vierfüßer m
quadruple a vierfach ● vt
vervierfachen ● vi sich
vervierfachen
quaint a (-er, -est) malerisch;
(odd) putzig
quake n 🔟 Erdbeben nt ● vi
beben; (with fear) zittern

qualif|ication n Qualifikation f;
(reservation) Einschränkung f.
~**ied** a qualifiziert; (trained)
ausgebildet; (limited) bedingt
qualify v (pt/pp -ied) ● vt
qualifizieren; (entitle)
berechtigen; (limit) einschränken
● vi sich qualifizieren
quality n Qualität f;
(characteristic) Eigenschaft f
qualm n Bedenken pl
quantity n Quantität f, Menge f; **in
~** in großen Mengen
quarantine n Quarantäne f
quarrel n Streit m ● vi (pt/pp
quarrelled) sich streiten. ~**some** a
streitsüchtig
quarry[1] n (prey) Beute f
quarry[2] n Steinbruch m
quart n Quart nt
quarter n Viertel nt; (of year)
Vierteljahr nt; (Amer) 25-Cent-
Stück nt; ~**s** pl Quartier nt; **at [a]
~ to six** um Viertel vor sechs ● vt
vierteln; (Mil) einquartieren (**on**
bei). ~**-final** n Viertelfinale nt
quarterly a & adv vierteljährlich
quartet n Quartett nt
quartz n Quarz m
quay n Kai m
queasy a **I feel ~** mir ist übel
queen n Königin f; (Cards, Chess)
Dame f
queer a (-er, -est) eigenartig;
(dubious) zweifelhaft; (ill)
unwohl
quell vt unterdrücken
quench vt löschen
query n Frage f; (question mark)
Fragezeichen nt ● vt (pt/pp -ied)
infrage stellen; reklamieren
<bill>
quest n Suche f (**for** nach)
question n Frage f; (for
discussion) Thema nt; **out of the
~** ausgeschlossen; **the person in
~** die fragliche Person ● vt
infrage stellen; ~ **s.o.** jdn
ausfragen; <police:> jdn

Q

verhören. ~**able** *a* zweifelhaft. ~
mark *n* Fragezeichen *nt*

questionnaire *n* Fragebogen *m*

queue *n* Schlange *f* ● *vi* ~ **[up]**
Schlange stehen, sich anstellen
(**for** nach)

quibble *vi* Haarspalterei treiben

quick *a* (-er, -est), -ly *adv* schnell;
be ~! mach schnell! ● *adv*
schnell. ~**en** *vt* beschleunigen
● *vi* sich beschleunigen

quick: ~**sand** *n* Treibsand *m*. ~-
tempered *a* aufbrausend

quid *n inv* 🛈 Pfund *nt*

quiet *a* (-er, -est), -ly *adv* still;
(*calm*) ruhig; (*soft*) leise; **keep** ~
about 🛈 nichts sagen von ● *n*
Stille *f*; Ruhe *f*

quiet|en *vt* beruhigen ● *vi* ~**en**
down ruhig werden. ~**ness** *n*
Stille *f*; Ruhe *f*

quilt *n* Steppdecke *f*. ~**ed** *a*
Stepp-

quintet *n* Quintett *nt*

quirk *n* Eigenart *f*

quit *v* (*pt/pp* quitted or quit) ● *vt*
verlassen; (*give up*) aufgeben; ~
doing sth aufhören, etw zu tun
● *vi* gehen

quite *adv* ganz; (*really*) wirklich;
~ **[so]!** genau! ~ **a few** ziemlich
viele

quits *a* quitt

quiver *vi* zittern

quiz *n* Quiz *nt* ● *vt* (*pt/pp* quizzed)
ausfragen. ~**zical** *a*, -ly *adv*
fragend

quota *n* Anteil *m*; (Comm)
Kontingent *nt*

quotation *n* Zitat *nt*; (*price*)
Kostenvoranschlag *m*; (*of shares*)
Notierung *f*. ~ **marks** *npl*
Anführungszeichen *pl*

quote *n* 🛈 = quotation; **in** ~**s** in
Anführungszeichen ● *vt/i*
zitieren

rabbi *n* Rabbiner *m*; (*title*) Rabbi
m

rabbit *n* Kaninchen *nt*

rabid *a* fanatisch; <*animal*>
tollwütig

rabies *n* Tollwut *f*

race¹ *n* Rasse *f*

race² *n* Rennen *nt*; (*fig*) Wettlauf
m ● *vi* [am Rennen] teilnehmen;
<*athlete, horse:*> laufen; (🛈 rush)
rasen ● *vt* um die Wette laufen
mit; an einem Rennen
teilnehmen lassen <*horse*>

race: ~**course** *n* Rennbahn *f*.
~**horse** *n* Rennpferd *nt*. ~**track**
n Rennbahn *f*

racial *a*, -ly *adv* rassisch;
<*discrimination*> Rassen-

racing *n* Rennsport *m*; (*horse-*)
Pferderennen *nt*. ~ **car** *n*
Rennwagen *m*. ~ **driver** *n*
Rennfahrer *m*

racis|m *n* Rassismus *m*. ~**t** *a*
rassistisch ● *n* Rassist *m*

rack¹ *n* Ständer *m*; (*for plates*)
Gestell *nt* ● *vt* ~ **one's brains** sich
(*dat*) den Kopf zerbrechen

rack² *n* **go to** ~ **and ruin** verfallen;
(*fig*) herunterkommen

racket *n* (Sport) Schläger *m*; (*din*)
Krach *m*; (*swindle*)
Schwindelgeschäft *nt*

racy *a* (-ier, -iest) schwungvoll;
(*risqué*) gewagt

radar *n* Radar *m*

radian|ce *n* Strahlen *nt*. ~**t** *a*, -ly
adv strahlend

radiat|e *vt* ausstrahlen ● *vi*
<*heat:*> ausgestrahlt werden;
<*roads:*> strahlenförmig
ausgehen. ~**ion** *n* Strahlung *f*

radiator n Heizkörper m; (Auto) Kühler m

radical a, **-ly** adv radikal ● n Radikale(r) m/f

radio n Radio nt; **by ∼** über Funk ● vt funken <message>

radio|active a radioaktiv. **∼activity** n Radioaktivität f

radish n Radieschen nt

radius n (pl **-dii**) Radius m, Halbmesser m

raffle n Tombola f

raft n Floß nt

rafter n Dachsparren m

rag n Lumpen m; (pej: newspaper) Käseblatt nt

rage n Wut f; **all the ∼** ⊞ der letzte Schrei ● vi rasen

ragged a zerlumpt; <edge> ausgefranst

raid n Überfall m; (Mil) Angriff m; (police) Razzia f ● vt überfallen; (Mil) angreifen; <police> eine Razzia durchführen in (+ dat); (break in) eindringen in (+ acc). **∼er** n Eindringling m; (of bank) Bankräuber m

rail n Schiene f; (pole) Stange f; (hand∼) Handlauf m; (Naut) Reling f; **by ∼** mit der Bahn

railings npl Geländer nt

railroad n (Amer) = **railway**

railway n [Eisen]bahn f. **∼ station** n Bahnhof m

rain n Regen m ● vi regnen

rain: **∼bow** n Regenbogen m. **∼coat** n Regenmantel m. **∼fall** n Niederschlag m

rainy a (**-ier, -iest**) regnerisch

raise n (Amer) Lohnerhöhung f ● vt erheben; (upright) aufrichten; (make higher) erhöhen; (lift) [hoch]heben; aufziehen <child, animal>; aufwerfen <question>; aufbringen <money>

raisin n Rosine f

rake n Harke f, Rechen m ● vt harken, rechen

rally n Versammlung f; (Auto) Rallye f; (Tennis) Ballwechsel m ● vt sammeln

ram n Schafbock m ● vt (pt/pp **rammed**) rammen

rambl|e n Wanderung f ● vi wandern; (in speech) irrereden. **∼er** n Wanderer m; (rose) Kletterrose f. **∼ing** a weitschweifig; <club> Wander-

ramp n Rampe f; (Aviat) Gangway f

rampage[1] n **be/go on the ∼** randalieren

rampage[2] vi randalieren

ramshackle a baufällig

ran see **run**

ranch n Ranch f

random a willkürlich; **a ∼ sample** eine Stichprobe ● n **at ∼** aufs Geratewohl; <choose> willkürlich

rang see **ring**[2]

range n Serie f, Reihe f; (Comm) Auswahl f, Angebot nt (**of** an + dat); (of mountains) Kette f; (Mus) Umfang m; (distance) Reichweite f; (for shooting) Schießplatz m; (stove) Kohlenherd m ● vi reichen; **∼ from ... to** gehen von ... bis. **∼r** n Aufseher m

rank n (row) Reihe f; (Mil) Rang m; (social position) Stand m; **the ∼ and file** die breite Masse ● vt/i einstufen; **∼ among** zählen zu

ransack vt durchwühlen; (pillage) plündern

ransom n Lösegeld nt; **hold s.o. to ∼** Lösegeld für jdn fordern

rape n Vergewaltigung f ● vt vergewaltigen

rapid a, **-ly** adv schnell. **∼ity** n Schnelligkeit f

rapist n Vergewaltiger m

raptur|e n Entzücken nt. **∼ous** a, **-ly** adv begeistert

rare[1] a (**-r, -st**), **-ly** adv selten

rare[2] a (Culin) englisch gebraten

rarefied a dünn

rarity n Seltenheit f

rascal n Schlingel m

rash[1] n (Med) Ausschlag m

rash[2] a (-er, -est), **-ly** adv voreilig

rasher n Speckscheibe f

raspberry n Himbeere f

rat n Ratte f; (🔲 person) Schuft m; **smell a ~** 🔲 Lunte riechen

rate n Rate f; (speed) Tempo nt; (of payment) Satz m; (of exchange) Kurs m; **~s** pl (taxes) ≈ Grundsteuer f; **at any ~** auf jeden Fall; **at this ~** auf diese Weise ● vt einschätzen; **~ among** zählen zu ● vi **~ as** gelten als

rather adv lieber; (fairly) ziemlich; **~!** und ob!

rating n Einschätzung f; (class) Klasse f; (sailor) [einfacher] Matrose m; **~s** pl (Radio, TV) ≈ Einschaltquote f

ratio n Verhältnis nt

ration n Ration f ● vt rationieren

rational a, **-ly** adv rational. **~ize** vt/i rationalisieren

rattle n Rasseln nt; (of windows) Klappern nt; (toy) Klapper f ● vi rasseln; klappern ● vt rasseln mit

raucous a rau

rave vi toben; **~ about** schwärmen von

raven n Rabe m

ravenous a heißhungrig

ravine n Schlucht f

raving a **~ mad** 🔲 total verrückt

ravishing a hinreißend

raw a (-er, -est) roh; (not processed) Roh-; <skin> wund; <weather> nasskalt; (inexperienced) unerfahren; **get a ~ deal** 🔲 schlecht wegkommen. **~ materials** npl Rohstoffe pl

ray n Strahl m

razor n Rasierapparat m. **~ blade** n Rasierklinge f

re prep betreffs (+ gen)

reach n Reichweite f; (of river) Strecke f; **within/out of ~** in/außer Reichweite ● vt erreichen; (arrive at) ankommen in (+ dat); (~ as far as) reichen bis zu; kommen zu <decision, conclusion>; (pass) reichen ● vi reichen (**to** bis zu); **~ for** greifen nach

react vi reagieren (**to** auf + acc)

reaction n Reaktion f. **~ary** a reaktionär

reactor n Reaktor m

read vt/i (pt/pp read) lesen; (aloud) vorlesen (**to** dat); (Univ) studieren; ablesen <meter>. **~ out** vt vorlesen

readable a lesbar

reader n Leser(in) m(f); (book) Lesebuch nt

readily adv bereitwillig; (easily) leicht

reading n Lesen nt; (Pol, Relig) Lesung f

readjust vt neu einstellen ● vi sich umstellen (**to** auf + acc)

ready a (-ier, -iest) fertig; (willing) bereit; (quick) schnell; **get ~** sich fertig machen; (prepare to) sich bereitmachen

ready: ~-made a fertig. **~-to-wear** a Konfektions-

real a wirklich; (genuine) echt; (actual) eigentlich ● adv (Amer 🔲) echt. **~ estate** n Immobilien pl

realis|m n Realismus m. **~t** n Realist m. **~tic** a, **-ally** adv realistisch

reality n Wirklichkeit f

realization n Erkenntnis f

realize vt einsehen; (become aware) gewahr werden; verwirklichen <hopes, plans>; einbringen <price>

really adv wirklich; (actually) eigentlich

realm n Reich nt

realtor n (Amer) Immobilienmakler m

reap vt ernten

reappear vi wiederkommen

rear¹ a Hinter-; (Auto) Heck- ● n the ~ der hintere Teil; from the ~ von hinten

rear² vt aufziehen ● vi ~ [up] <horse:> sich aufbäumen

rearrange vt umstellen

reason n Grund m; (good sense) Vernunft f; (ability to think) Verstand m; within ~ in vernünftigen Grenzen ● vi argumentieren; ~ with vernünftig reden mit. ~able a vernünftig; (not expensive) preiswert. ~ably adv (fairly) ziemlich

reassur|ance n Beruhigung f; Versicherung f. ~e vt beruhigen; ~e s.o. of sth jdm etw (gen) versichern

rebel¹ n Rebell m

rebel² vi (pt/pp rebelled) rebellieren. ~lion n Rebellion f. ~lious a rebellisch

rebound¹ vi abprallen

rebound² n Rückprall m

rebuild vt (pt/pp -built) wieder aufbauen

rebuke n Tadel m ● vt tadeln

recall n Erinnerung f ● vt zurückrufen; abberufen <diplomat>; (remember) sich erinnern an (+ acc)

recant vi widerrufen

recap vt/i 🔢 = recapitulate

recapitulate vt/i zusammenfassen; rekapitulieren

recapture vt wieder gefangen nehmen <person>; wieder einfangen <animal>

reced|e vi zurückgehen. ~ing a <forehead, chin> fliehend

receipt n Quittung f; (receiving) Empfang m; ~s pl (Comm) Einnahmen pl

receive vt erhalten, bekommen; empfangen <guests>. ~r n (Teleph) Hörer m; (of stolen goods) Hehler m

recent a kürzlich erfolgte(r,s). ~ly adv vor kurzem

receptacle n Behälter m

reception n Empfang m; ~ [desk] (in hotel) Rezeption f; ~ist n Empfangsdame f

receptive a aufnahmefähig; ~ to empfänglich für

recess n Nische f; (holiday) Ferien pl

recession n Rezession f

recharge vt [wieder] aufladen

recipe n Rezept nt

recipient n Empfänger m

recital n (of poetry, songs) Vortrag m; (of instrumental music) Konzert nt

recite vt aufsagen; (before audience) vortragen

reckless a, -ly adv leichtsinnig; (careless) rücksichtslos. ~ness n Leichtsinn m; (carelessness) Rücksichtslosigkeit f

reckon vt rechnen; (consider) glauben ● vi ~ on/with rechnen mit

reclaim vt zurückfordern; zurückgewinnen <land>

reclin|e vi liegen. ~ing seat n Liegesitz m

recluse n Einsiedler(in) m(f)

recognition n Erkennen nt; (acknowledgement) Anerkennung f; in ~ als Anerkennung (of gen)

recognize vt erkennen; (know again) wieder erkennen; (acknowledge) anerkennen

recoil vi zurückschnellen; (in fear) zurückschrecken

recollect vt sich erinnern an (+ acc). ~ion n Erinnerung f

recommend vt empfehlen. ~ation n Empfehlung f

recon|cile vt versöhnen; ~cile oneself to sich abfinden mit. ~ciliation n Versöhnung f

reconnaissance n (Mil) Aufklärung f

R

reconnoitre vi (pres p -tring) auf Erkundung ausgehen

reconsider vt sich (dat) noch einmal überlegen

reconstruct vt wieder aufbauen; rekonstruieren <crime>

record¹ vt aufzeichnen; (register) registrieren; (on tape) aufnehmen

record² n Aufzeichnung f; (Jur) Protokoll nt; (Mus) [Schall]platte f; (Sport) Rekord m; **~s** pl Unterlagen pl; **off the ~** inoffiziell; **have a [criminal] ~** vorbestraft sein

recorder n (Mus) Blockflöte f

recording n Aufnahme f

re-count¹ vt nachzählen

re-count² n (Pol) Nachzählung f

recover vt zurückbekommen ● vi sich erholen. **~y** n Wiedererlangung f; (of health) Erholung f

recreation n Erholung f; (hobby) Hobby nt. **~al** a Freizeit-; **be ~al** erholsam sein

recruit n (Mil) Rekrut m; **new ~** (member) neues Mitglied nt; (worker) neuer Mitarbeiter m ● vt rekrutieren; anwerben <staff>. **~ment** n Rekrutierung f; Anwerbung f

rectangle n Rechteck nt. **~ular** a rechteckig

rectify vt (pt/pp -ied) berichtigen

rector n Pfarrer m; (Univ) Rektor m. **~y** n Pfarrhaus nt

recur vi (pt/pp recurred) sich wiederholen; <illness:> wiederkehren

recurren|ce n Wiederkehr f. **~t** a wiederkehrend

recycle vt wieder verwerten

red a (redder, reddest) rot ● n Rot nt

redd|en vt röten ● vi rot werden. **~ish** a rötlich

redecorate vt renovieren; (paint) neu streichen; (wallpaper) neu tapezieren

redeem vt einlösen; (Relig) erlösen

redemption n Erlösung f

red: ~-haired a rothaarig. **~-handed** a **catch s.o. ~-handed** jdn auf frischer Tat ertappen. **~ herring** n falsche Spur f. **~-hot** a glühend heiß. **~ light** n (Auto) rote Ampel f. **~ness** n Röte f

redo vt (pt -did, pp -done) noch einmal machen

redouble vt verdoppeln

red tape n Ⓘ Bürokratie f

reduc|e vt verringern, vermindern; (in size) verkleinern; ermäßigen <costs>; herabsetzen <price, goods>; (Culin) einkochen lassen. **~tion** n Verringerung f; (in price) Ermäßigung f; (in size) Verkleinerung f

redundan|cy n Beschäftigungslosigkeit f. **~t** a überflüssig; **make ~t** entlassen; **be made ~t** beschäftigungslos werden

reed n [Schilf]rohr nt; **~s** pl Schilf nt

reef n Riff nt

reek vi riechen (of nach)

reel n Rolle f, Spule f ● vi (stagger) taumeln ● vt **~ off** (fig) herunterrasseln

refectory n Refektorium nt; (Univ) Mensa f

refer v (pt/pp referred) ● vt verweisen (to an + acc); übergeben, weiterleiten <matter> (to an + acc) ● vi **~ to** sich beziehen auf (+ acc); (mention) erwähnen; (concern) betreffen; (consult) sich wenden an (+ acc); nachschlagen in (+ dat) <book>; **are you ~ring to me?** meinen Sie mich?

referee n Schiedsrichter m; (Boxing) Ringrichter m; (for job) Referenz f ● vt/i (pt/pp refereed) Schiedsrichter/Ringrichter sein (bei)

reference n Erwähnung f; (in book) Verweis m; (for job) Referenz f; **with ~ to** in Bezug auf (+ acc); **make [a] ~ to** erwähnen. **~ book** n Nachschlagewerk nt

referendum n Volksabstimmung f

refill[1] vt nachfüllen

refill[2] n (for pen) Ersatzmine f

refine vt raffinieren. **~d** a fein, vornehm. **~ment** n Vornehmheit f; (Techn) Verfeinerung f. **~ry** n Raffinerie f

reflect vt reflektieren; <mirror:> [wider]spiegeln; **be ~ed in** sich spiegeln in (+ dat) ● vi nachdenken (**on** über + acc). **~ion** n Reflexion f; (image) Spiegelbild nt; **on ~ion** nach nochmaliger Überlegung. **~or** n Rückstrahler m

reflex n Reflex m

reflexive a reflexiv

reform n Reform f ● vt reformieren ● vi sich bessern

refrain[1] n Refrain m

refrain[2] vi **~ from doing sth** etw nicht tun

refresh vt erfrischen. **~ing** a erfrischend. **~ments** npl Erfrischungen pl

refrigerat|e vt kühlen. **~or** n Kühlschrank m

refuel vt/i (pt/pp -fuelled) auftanken

refuge n Zuflucht f; **take ~** Zuflucht nehmen

refugee n Flüchtling m

refund[1] n **get a ~** sein Geld zurückbekommen

refund[2] vt zurückerstatten

refusal n (see **refuse**[1]) Ablehnung f; Weigerung f

refuse[1] vt ablehnen; (not grant) verweigern; **~ to do sth** sich weigern, etw zu tun ● vi ablehnen; sich weigern

refuse[2] n Müll m

refute vt widerlegen

regain vt wiedergewinnen

regal a, **-ly** adv königlich

regard n (heed) Rücksicht f; (respect) Achtung f; **~s** pl Grüße pl; **with ~ to** in Bezug auf (+ acc) ● vt ansehen, betrachten (**as** als). **~ing** prep bezüglich (+ gen). **~less** adv ohne Rücksicht (**of** auf + acc)

regatta n Regatta f

regime n Regime nt

regiment n Regiment nt. **~al** a Regiments-

region n Region f; **in the ~ of** (fig) ungefähr. **~al** a, **-ly** adv regional

register n Register nt; (Sch) Anwesenheitsliste f ● vt registrieren; (report) anmelden; einschreiben <letter>; aufgeben <luggage> ● vi (report) sich anmelden

registrar n Standesbeamte(r) m

registration n Registrierung f; Anmeldung f. **~ number** n Autonummer f

registry office n Standesamt nt

regret n Bedauern nt ● vt (pt/pp regretted) bedauern. **~fully** adv mit Bedauern

regrettab|le a bedauerlich. **~ly** adv bedauerlicherweise

regular a, **-ly** adv regelmäßig; (usual) üblich ● n (in pub) Stammgast m; (in shop) Stammkunde m. **~ity** n Regelmäßigkeit f

regulat|e vt regulieren. **~ion** n (rule) Vorschrift f

rehears|al n (Theat) Probe f. **~e** vt proben

reign n Herrschaft f ● vi herrschen, regieren

rein n Zügel m

R

reindeer *n inv* Rentier *nt*
reinforce *vt* verstärken. **~ment** *n* Verstärkung *f*; **send ~ments** Verstärkung schicken
reiterate *vt* wiederholen
reject *vt* ablehnen. **~ion** *n* Ablehnung *f*
rejects *npl* (*Comm*) Ausschussware *f*
rejoic|e *vi* (*liter*) sich freuen. **~ing** *n* Freude *f*
rejoin *vt* sich wieder anschließen (+ *dat*); wieder beitreten (+ *dat*) <*club, party*>
rejuvenate *vt* verjüngen
relapse *n* Rückfall *m* ● *vi* einen Rückfall erleiden
relate *vt* (*tell*) erzählen; (*connect*) verbinden
relation *n* Beziehung *f*; (*person*) Verwandte(r) *m/f*. **~ship** *n* Beziehung *f*; (*link*) Verbindung *f*; (*blood tie*) Verwandtschaft *f*; (*affair*) Verhältnis *nt*
relative *n* Verwandte(r) *m/f* ● *a* relativ; (*Gram*) Relativ-. **~ly** *adv* relativ, verhältnismäßig
relax *vt* lockern, entspannen ● *vi* sich lockern, sich entspannen. **~ation** *n* Entspannung *f*. **~ing** *a* entspannend
relay[1] *vt* (*pt/pp* **-layed**) weitergeben; (*Radio, TV*) übertragen
relay[2] *n.* **~ [race]** *n* Staffel *f*
release *n* Freilassung *f*, Entlassung *f*; (*Techn*) Auslöser *m* ● *vt* freilassen; (*let go of*) loslassen; (*Techn*) auslösen; veröffentlichen <*information*>
relent *vi* nachgeben. **~less** *a*, **-ly** *adv* erbarmungslos; (*unceasing*) unaufhörlich
relevan|ce *n* Relevanz *f*. **~t** *a* relevant (**to** für)
reliab|ility *n* Zuverlässigkeit *f*. **~le** *a*, **-ly** *adv* zuverlässig

relian|ce *n* Abhängigkeit *f* (**on** von). **~t** *a* angewiesen (**on** auf + *acc*)
relic *n* Überbleibsel *nt*; (*Relig*) Reliquie *f*
relief *n* Erleichterung *f*; (*assistance*) Hilfe *f*; (*replacement*) Ablösung *f*; (*Art*) Relief *nt*
relieve *vt* erleichtern; (*take over from*) ablösen; **~ of** entlasten von
religion *n* Religion *f*
religious *a* religiös
relinquish *vt* loslassen; (*give up*) aufgeben
relish *n* Genuss *m*; (*Culin*) Würze *f* ● *vt* genießen
reluctan|ce *n* Widerstreben *nt*. **~t** *a* widerstrebend; **be ~t** zögern (**to** zu). **~tly** *adv* ungern, widerstrebend
rely *vi* (*pt/pp* **-ied**) **~ on** sich verlassen auf (+ *acc*); (*be dependent on*) angewiesen sein auf (+ *acc*)
remain *vi* bleiben; (*be left*) übrig bleiben. **~der** *n* Rest *m*. **~ing** *a* restlich. **~s** *npl* Reste *pl*; [*mortal*] **~s** [sterbliche] Überreste *pl*
remand *n* **on ~ in** Untersuchungshaft ● *vt* **~ in custody** in Untersuchungshaft schicken
remark *n* Bemerkung *f* ● *vt* bemerken. **~able** *a*, **-bly** *adv* bemerkenswert
remarry *vi* wieder heiraten
remedy *n* [Heil]mittel *nt* (**for** gegen); (*fig*) Abhilfe *f* ● *vt* (*pt/pp* **-ied**) abhelfen (+ *dat*); beheben <*fault*>
remember *vt* sich erinnern an (+ *acc*); **~ to do sth** daran denken, etw zu tun ● *vi* sich erinnern
remind *vt* erinnern (**of** an + *acc*). **~er** *n* Andenken *nt*; (*letter, warning*) Mahnung *f*
reminisce *vi* sich seinen Erinnerungen hingeben. **~nces**

npl Erinnerungen *pl.* ~**nt** *a* be ~**nt of** erinnern an (+ *acc*)
remnant *n* Rest *m*
remorse *n* Reue *f.* ~**ful** *a*, **-ly** *adv* reumütig. ~**less** *a*, **-ly** *adv* unerbittlich
remote *a* fern; (*isolated*) abgelegen; (*slight*) gering. ~ **control** *n* Fernsteuerung *f*; (*for TV*) Fernbedienung *f*
remotely *adv* entfernt; **not** ~ nicht im Entferntesten
removable *a* abnehmbar
removal *n* Entfernung *f*; (*from house*) Umzug *m.* ~ **van** *n* Möbelwagen *m*
remove *vt* entfernen; (*take off*) abnehmen; (*take out*) herausnehmen
render *vt* machen; erweisen <*service*>; (*translate*) wiedergeben; (*Mus*) vortragen
renegade *n* Abtrünnige(r) *m/f*
renew *vt* erneuern; verlängern <*contract*>. ~**al** *n* Erneuerung *f*; Verlängerung *f*
renounce *vt* verzichten auf (+ *acc*)
renovat|e *vt* renovieren. ~**ion** *n* Renovierung *f*
renown *n* Ruf *m.* ~**ed** *a* berühmt
rent *n* Miete *f* ● *vt* mieten; (*hire*) leihen; ~ [**out**] vermieten; verleihen. ~**al** *n* Mietgebühr *f*; Leihgebühr *f*
renunciation *n* Verzicht *m*
reopen *vt/i* wieder aufmachen
reorganize *vt* reorganisieren
rep *n* Ⅰ Vertreter *m*
repair *n* Reparatur *f*; **in good/bad** ~ in gutem/schlechtem Zustand ● *vt* reparieren
repatriate *vt* repatriieren
repay *vt* (*pt/pp* **-paid**) zurückzahlen; ~ **s.o. for sth** jdm etw zurückzahlen. ~**ment** *n* Rückzahlung *f*
repeal *n* Aufhebung *f* ● *vt* aufheben

repeat *n* Wiederholung *f* ● *vt/i* wiederholen; ~ **after me** sprechen Sie mir nach. ~**ed** *a*, **-ly** *adv* wiederholt
repel *vt* (*pt/pp* **repelled**) abwehren; (*fig*) abstoßen. ~**lent** *a* abstoßend
repent *vi* Reue zeigen. ~**ance** *n* Reue *f.* ~**ant** *a* reuig
repercussions *npl* Auswirkungen *pl*
repertoire, repertory *n* Repertoire *nt*
repetit|ion *n* Wiederholung *f.* ~**ive** *a* eintönig
replace *vt* zurücktun; (*take the place of*) ersetzen; (*exchange*) austauschen. ~**ment** *n* Ersatz *m*
replay *n* (*Sport*) Wiederholungsspiel *nt*; [**action**] ~ Wiederholung *f*
replenish *vt* auffüllen <*stocks*>; (*refill*) nachfüllen
replica *n* Nachbildung *f*
reply *n* Antwort *f* (**to** auf + *acc*) ● *vt/i* (*pt/pp* **replied**) antworten
report *n* Bericht *m*; (*Sch*) Zeugnis *nt*; (*rumour*) Gerücht *nt*; (*of gun*) Knall *m* ● *vt* berichten; (*notify*) melden; ~ **s.o. to the police** jdn anzeigen ● *vi* berichten (**on** über + *acc*); (*present oneself*) sich melden (**to** bei). ~**er** *n* Reporter(in) *m(f)*
reprehensible *a* tadelnswert
represent *vt* darstellen; (*act for*) vertreten, repräsentieren. ~**ation** *n* Darstellung *f*
representative *a* repräsentativ (**of** für) ● *n* Bevollmächtigte(r) *m(f)*; (*Comm*) Vertreter(in) *m(f)*; (*Amer, Pol*) Abgeordnete(r) *m/f*
repress *vt* unterdrücken. ~**ion** *n* Unterdrückung *f.* ~**ive** *a* repressiv
reprieve *n* Begnadigung *f*; (*fig*) Gnadenfrist *f* ● *vt* begnadigen
reprimand *n* Tadel *m* ● *vt* tadeln
reprint[1] *n* Nachdruck *m*

R

reprint² *vt* neu auflegen

reprisal *n* Vergeltungsmaßnahme *f*

reproach *n* Vorwurf *m* ● *vt* Vorwürfe *pl* machen (+ *dat*). ~**ful** *a*, **-ly** *adv* vorwurfsvoll

reproduc|e *vt* wiedergeben, reproduzieren ● *vi* sich fortpflanzen. ~**tion** *n* Reproduktion *f*; (*Biol*) Fortpflanzung *f*

reptile *n* Reptil *nt*

republic *n* Republik *f*. ~**an** *a* republikanisch ● *n* Republikaner(in) *m(f)*

repugnan|ce *n* Widerwille *m*. ~**t** *a* widerlich

repuls|ion *n* Widerwille *m*. ~**ive** *a* abstoßend, widerlich

reputable *a* ‹*firm*› von gutem Ruf; (*respectable*) anständig

reputation *n* Ruf *m*

request *n* Bitte *f* ● *vt* bitten

require *vt* (*need*) brauchen; (*demand*) erfordern; **be** ~**d to do sth** etw tun müssen. ~**ment** *n* Bedürfnis *nt*; (*condition*) Erfordernis *nt*

resale *n* Weiterverkauf *m*

rescue *n* Rettung *f* ● *vt* retten. ~**r** *n* Retter *m*

research *n* Forschung *f* ● *vt* erforschen; (*Journ*) recherchieren. ~**er** *n* Forscher *m*; (*Journ*) Rechercheur *m*

resem|blance *n* Ähnlichkeit *f*. ~**ble** *vt* ähneln (+ *dat*)

resent *vt* übel nehmen; einen Groll hegen gegen ‹*person*›. ~**ful** *a*, **-ly** *adv* verbittert. ~**ment** *n* Groll *m*

reservation *n* Reservierung *f*; (*doubt*) Vorbehalt *m*; (*enclosure*) Reservat *nt*

reserve *n* Reserve *f*; (*for animals*) Reservat *nt*; (*Sport*) Reservespieler(in) *m(f)* ● *vt* reservieren; ‹*client:*› reservieren lassen; (*keep*) aufheben; sich

(*dat*) vorbehalten ‹*right*›. ~**d** *a* reserviert

reservoir *n* Reservoir *nt*

reshuffle *n* (*Pol*) Umbildung *f* ● *vt* (*Pol*) umbilden

residence *n* Wohnsitz *m*; (*official*) Residenz *f*; (*stay*) Aufenthalt *m*

resident *a* ansässig (**in** in + *dat*); ‹*housekeeper, nurse*› im Haus wohnend ● *n* Bewohner(in) *m(f)*; (*of street*) Anwohner *m*. ~**ial** *a* Wohn-

residue *n* Rest *m*; (*Chem*) Rückstand *m*

resign *vt* ~ **oneself to** sich abfinden mit ● *vi* kündigen; (*from public office*) zurücktreten. ~**ation** *n* Resignation *f*; (*from job*) Kündigung *f*; Rücktritt *m*. ~**ed** *a*, **-ly** *adv* resigniert

resilient *a* federnd; (*fig*) widerstandsfähig

resin *n* Harz *nt*

resist *vt/i* sich widersetzen (+ *dat*), (*fig*) widerstehen (+ *dat*). ~**ance** *n* Widerstand *m*. ~**ant** *a* widerstandsfähig

resolut|e *a*, **-ly** *adv* entschlossen. ~**ion** *n* Entschlossenheit *f*; (*intention*) Vorsatz *m*; (*Pol*) Resolution *f*

resolve *n* Entschlossenheit *f*; (*decision*) Beschluss *m* ● *vt* beschließen; (*solve*) lösen

resort *n* (*place*) Urlaubsort *m*; **as a last** ~ wenn alles andere fehlschlägt ● *vi* ~ **to** (*fig*) greifen zu

resound *vi* widerhallen

resource *n* ~**s** *pl* Ressourcen *pl*. ~**ful** *a* findig

respect *n* Respekt *m*, Achtung *f* (**for** vor + *dat*); (*aspect*) Hinsicht *f*; **with** ~ **to** in Bezug auf (+ *acc*) ● *vt* respektieren, achten

respect|able *a*, **-bly** *adv* ehrbar; (*decent*) anständig; (*considerable*)

ansehnlich. **~ful** *a*, **-ly** *adv*
respektvoll

respective *a* jeweilig. **~ly** *adv*
beziehungsweise

respiration *n* Atmung *f*

respite *n* [Ruhe]pause *f*; *(delay)*
Aufschub *m*

respond *vi* antworten; *(react)*
reagieren (**to** auf + *acc*)

response *n* Antwort *f*; Reaktion *f*

responsibility *n* Verantwortung *f*;
(duty) Verpflichtung *f*

responsible *a* verantwortlich;
(trustworthy) verantwortungsvoll.
~ly *adv* verantwortungsbewusst

rest¹ *n* Ruhe *f*; *(holiday)* Erholung
f; *(interval & Mus)* Pause *f*; **have a
~** eine Pause machen; *(rest)* sich
ausruhen ●*vt* ausruhen; *(lean)*
lehnen (**on** an/auf + *acc*) ●*vi*
ruhen; *(have a rest)* sich
ausruhen

rest² *n* **the ~** der Rest; *(people)*
die Übrigen *pl* ●*vi* **it ~s with you**
es ist an Ihnen (**to** zu)

restaurant *n* Restaurant *nt*,
Gaststätte *f*

restful *a* erholsam

restive *a* unruhig

restless *a*, **-ly** *adv* unruhig

restoration *n* *(of building)*
Restaurierung *f*

restore *vt* wiederherstellen;
restaurieren <*building*>

restrain *vt* zurückhalten; **~
oneself** sich beherrschen. **~ed** *a*
zurückhaltend. **~t** *n*
Zurückhaltung *f*

restrict *vt* einschränken; **~ to**
beschränken auf (+ *acc*). **~ion** *n*
Einschränkung *f*; Beschränkung
f. **~ive** *a* einschränkend

rest room *n* *(Amer)* Toilette *f*

result *n* Ergebnis *nt*, Resultat *nt*;
(consequence) Folge *f*; **as a ~** als
Folge (**of** *gen*) ●*vi* sich ergeben
(**from** aus); **~ in** enden in (+ *dat*);
(lead to) führen zu

resume *vt* wieder aufnehmen ●*vi*
wieder beginnen

résumé *n* Zusammenfassung *f*

resumption *n* Wiederaufnahme *f*

resurrect *vt* *(fig)* wieder beleben.
~ion *n* **the R ~ion** *(Relig)* die
Auferstehung

resuscitat|e *vt* wieder beleben.
~ion *n* Wiederbelebung *f*

retail *n* Einzelhandel *m* ●*a*
Einzelhandels- ●*adv* im
Einzelhandel ●*vt* im
Einzelhandel verkaufen ●*vi* **~ at**
im Einzelhandel kosten. **~er** *n*
Einzelhändler *m*

retain *vt* behalten

retaliat|e *vi* zurückschlagen. **~ion**
n Vergeltung *f*; **in ~ion** als
Vergeltung

retarded *a* zurückgeblieben

reticen|ce *n* Zurückhaltung *f*. **~t**
a zurückhaltend

retina *n* Netzhaut *f*

retinue *n* Gefolge *nt*

retire *vi* in den Ruhestand treten;
(withdraw) sich zurückziehen.
~d *a* im Ruhestand. **~ment** *n*
Ruhestand *m*

retiring *a* zurückhaltend

retort *n* scharfe Erwiderung *f*;
(Chem) Retorte *f* ●*vt* scharf
erwidern

retrace *vt* **~ one's steps**
denselben Weg zurückgehen

retrain *vt* umschulen ●*vi*
umgeschult werden

retreat *n* Rückzug *m*; *(place)*
Zufluchtsort *m* ●*vi* sich
zurückziehen

retrial *n*
Wiederaufnahmeverfahren *nt*

retrieve *vt* zurückholen; *(from
wreckage)* bergen; *(Computing)*
wieder auffinden

retrograde *a* rückschrittlich

retrospect *n* **in ~** rückblickend.
~ive *a*, **-ly** *adv* rückwirkend;
(looking back) rückblickend

R

return n Rückkehr f; (giving back) Rückgabe f; (Comm) Ertrag m; (ticket) Rückfahrkarte f; (Aviat) Rückflugschein m; **by ~ [of post]** postwendend; **in ~** dafür; **in ~ for** für; **many happy ~s!** herzlichen Glückwunsch zum Geburtstag! ●vt zurückgehen/-fahren; (come back) zurückkommen ●vt zurückgeben; (put back) zurückstellen/-legen; (send back) zurückschicken

return ticket n Rückfahrkarte f; (Aviat) Rückflugschein m

reunion n Wiedervereinigung f; (social gathering) Treffen nt

reunite vt wieder vereinigen

reuse vt wieder verwenden

rev n (Auto 🇬🇧) Umdrehung f ●vt/i **~ [up]** den Motor auf Touren bringen

reveal vt zum Vorschein bringen; (fig) enthüllen. **~ing** a (fig) aufschlussreich

revel vi (pt/pp revelled) **~ in sth** etw genießen

revelation n Offenbarung f, Enthüllung f

revenge n Rache f; (fig & Sport) Revanche f ●vt rächen

revenue n [Staats]einnahmen pl

revere vt verehren. **~nce** n Ehrfurcht f

Reverend a the **~ X** Pfarrer X; (Catholic) Hochwürden X

reverent a, **-ly** adv ehrfürchtig

reversal n Umkehrung f

reverse a umgekehrt ●n Gegenteil nt; (back) Rückseite f; (Auto) Rückwärtsgang m ●vt umkehren; (Auto) zurücksetzen ●vi zurücksetzen

revert vi **~ to** zurückfallen an (+ acc)

review n Rückblick m (of auf + acc); (re-examination) Überprüfung f; (Mil) Truppenschau f; (of book, play) Kritik f, Rezension f ●vt

zurückblicken auf (+ acc); überprüfen <situation>; rezensieren <book, play>. **~er** n Kritiker m, Rezensent m

revis|e vt revidieren; (for exam) wiederholen. **~ion** n Revision f; (for exam) Wiederholung f

revival n Wiederbelebung f

revive vt wieder beleben; (fig) wieder aufleben lassen ●vi wieder aufleben

revolt n Aufstand m ●vi rebellieren ●vt anwidern. **~ing** a widerlich, eklig

revolution n Revolution f; (Auto) Umdrehung f. **~ary** a revolutionär. **~ize** vt revolutionieren

revolve vi sich drehen; **~ around** kreisen um

revolv|er n Revolver m. **~ing** a Dreh-

revue n Revue f; (satirical) Kabarett nt

revulsion n Abscheu m

reward n Belohnung f ●vt belohnen. **~ing** a lohnend

rewrite vt (pt rewrote, pp rewritten) noch einmal [neu] schreiben; (alter) umschreiben

rhetoric n Rhetorik f. **~al** a rhetorisch

rheumatism n Rheumatismus m, Rheuma nt

Rhine n Rhein m

rhinoceros n Nashorn nt, Rhinozeros nt

rhubarb n Rhabarber m

rhyme n Reim m ●vt reimen ●vi sich reimen

rhythm n Rhythmus m. **~ic[al]** a, **-ally** adv rhythmisch

rib n Rippe f

ribbon n Band nt; (for typewriter) Farbband nt

rice n Reis m

rich a (-er, -est), **-ly** adv reich; <food> gehaltvoll; (heavy) schwer

● n the ~ pl die Reichen; ~es pl
Reichtum m

ricochet vi abprallen

rid vt (pt/pp **rid**, pres p **ridding**)
befreien (**of** von); **get** ~ **of**
loswerden

riddance n good ~! auf
Nimmerwiedersehen!

ridden see **ride**

riddle n Rätsel nt

riddled a ~ **with** durchlöchert mit

ride n Ritt m; (in vehicle) Fahrt f;
take s.o. for a ~ ⚏ jdn reinlegen
● v (pt **rode**, pp **ridden**) ● vt reiten
<horse>; fahren mit <bicycle>
● vi reiten; (in vehicle) fahren.
~**r** n Reiter(in) m(f); (on bicycle)
Fahrer(in) m(f)

ridge n Erhebung f; (on roof)
First m; (of mountain) Grat m,
Kamm m

ridicule n Spott m ● vt
verspotten, spotten über (+ acc)

ridiculous a, **-ly** adv lächerlich

riding n Reiten m ● attrib Reit-

riff-raff n Gesindel nt

rifle n Gewehr nt ● vt plündern;
~ **through** durchwühlen

rift n Spalt m; (fig) Riss m

rig n Ölbohrturm m; (at sea)
Bohrinsel f ● vt (pt/pp **rigged**) ~
out ausrüsten; ~ **up** aufbauen

right a richtig; (not left)
rechte(r,s); **be** ~ <person:> Recht
haben; <clock:> richtig gehen; **put**
~ wieder in Ordnung bringen;
(fig) richtig stellen; **that's** ~! das
stimmt! ● adv richtig; (directly)
direkt; (completely) ganz; (not
left) rechts; <go> nach rechts; ~
away sofort ● n Recht nt; (not
left) rechte Seite f; **on the** ~
rechts; **from/to the** ~ von/nach
rechts; **be in the** ~ Recht haben;
by ~**s** eigentlich; **the R**~ (Pol) die
Rechte. ~ **angle** n rechter
Winkel m

rightful a, **-ly** adv rechtmäßig

right-handed a rechtshändig

rightly adv mit Recht

right-wing a (Pol) rechte(r,s)

rigid a starr; (strict) streng. ~**ity** n
Starrheit f; Strenge f

rigorous a, **-ly** adv streng

rigour n Strenge f

rim n Rand m; (of wheel) Felge f

rind n (on fruit) Schale f; (on
cheese) Rinde f; (on bacon)
Schwarte f

ring[1] n Ring m; (for circus)
Manege f; **stand in a** ~ im Kreis
stehen ● vt umringen

ring[2] n Klingeln nt; **give s.o. a** ~
(Teleph) jdn anrufen ● v (pt **rang**,
pp **rung**) ● vt läuten; ~ **[up]**
(Teleph) anrufen ● vi <bells:>
läuten; <telephone:> klingeln. ~
back vt/i (Teleph) zurückrufen

ring: ~**leader** n Rädelsführer m.
~ **road** n Umgehungsstraße f

rink n Eisbahn f

rinse n Spülung f; (hair colour)
Tönung f ● vt spülen

riot n Aufruhr m; ~**s** pl Unruhen
pl; **run** ~ randalieren ● vi
randalieren. ~**er** n Randalierer
m. ~**ous** a aufrührerisch;
(boisterous) wild

rip n Riss m ● vt/i (pt/pp **ripped**)
zerreißen; ~ **open** aufreißen. ~
off vt ⚏ neppen

ripe a (**-r**, **-st**) reif

ripen vi reifen ● vt reifen lassen

ripeness n Reife f

rip-off n ⚏ Nepp m

ripple n kleine Welle f

rise n Anstieg m; (fig) Aufstieg m;
(increase) Zunahme f; (in wages)
Lohnerhöhung f; (in salary)
Gehaltserhöhung f; **give** ~ **to**
Anlass geben zu ● vi (pt **rose**, pp
risen) steigen; <ground:>
ansteigen; <sun, dough:>
aufgehen; <river:> entspringen;
(get up) aufstehen; (fig)
aufsteigen (**to** zu). ~**r** n early ~**r**
Frühaufsteher m

R

rising a steigend; <sun> aufgehend
risk n Risiko nt; **at one's own ~** auf eigene Gefahr ● vt riskieren
risky a (-ier, -iest) riskant
rite n Ritus m
ritual a rituell ● n Ritual nt
rival a rivalisierend ● n Rivale m/Rivalin f. ~**ry** n Rivalität f; (Comm) Konkurrenzkampf m
river n Fluss m
rivet n Niete f ● vt [ver]nieten; ~**ed by** (fig) gefesselt von
road n Straße f; (fig) Weg m
road: ~**-map** n Straßenkarte f. ~ **safety** n Verkehrssicherheit f. ~**side** n Straßenrand m. ~**way** n Fahrbahn f. ~**-works** npl Straßenarbeiten pl. ~**worthy** a verkehrssicher
roam vi wandern
roar n Gebrüll nt; ~**s of laughter** schallendes Gelächter nt ● vi brüllen; (with laughter) schallend lachen. ~**ing** a <fire> prasselnd; **do a** ~**ing trade** 🔢 ein Bombengeschäft machen
roast a gebraten, Brat-; ~ **beef**/ **pork** Rinder-/Schweinebraten m ● n Braten m ● vt/i braten; rösten <coffee, chestnuts>
rob vt (pt/pp robbed) berauben (**of** gen); ausrauben <bank>. ~**ber** n Räuber m. ~**bery** n Raub m
robe n Robe f; (Amer: bathrobe) Bademantel m
robin n Rotkehlchen nt
robot n Roboter m
robust a robust
rock¹ n Fels m; **on the** ~**s** <ship> aufgelaufen; <marriage> kaputt; <drink> mit Eis
rock² vt/i schaukeln
rock³ n (Mus) Rock m
rockery n Steingarten m
rocket n Rakete f
rocking: ~**-chair** n Schaukelstuhl m. ~**-horse** n Schaukelpferd nt

rocky a (-ier, -iest) felsig; (unsteady) wackelig
rod n Stab m; (stick) Rute f; (for fishing) Angel[rute] f
rode see ride
rodent n Nagetier nt
rogue n Gauner m
role n Rolle f
roll n Rolle f; (bread) Brötchen nt; (list) Liste f; (of drum) Wirbel m ● vi rollen; **be** ~**ing in money** 🔢 Geld wie Heu haben ● vt rollen; walzen <lawn>; ausrollen <pastry>. ~ **over** vi sich auf die andere Seite rollen. ~ **up** vt aufrollen; hochkrempeln <sleeves> ● vi 🔢 auftauchen
roller n Rolle f; (lawn, road) Walze f; (hair) Lockenwickler m. **R~blades** (P) npl Rollerblades (P) mpl. ~ **blind** n Rollo nt. ~**coaster** n Berg-und-Talbahn f. ~**-skate** n Rollschuh m
rolling-pin n Teigrolle f
Roman a römisch ● n Römer(in) m(f)
romance n Romantik f; (love-affair) Romanze f; (book) Liebesgeschichte f
Romania n Rumänien nt. ~**n** a rumänisch ● n Rumäne m/-nin f
romantic a, **-ally** adv romantisch. ~**ism** n Romantik f
Rome n Rom nt
romp vi [herum]tollen
roof n Dach nt; (of mouth) Gaumen m ● vt ~ **[over]** überdachen. ~**-top** n Dach nt
rook n Saatkrähe f; (Chess) Turm m
room n Zimmer nt; (for functions) Saal m; (space) Platz m. ~**y** a geräumig
roost n Hühnerstange f
root¹ n Wurzel f; **take** ~ anwachsen ● vi Wurzeln schlagen. ~ **out** vt (fig) ausrotten
root² vi ~ **about** wühlen; ~ **for s.o.** 🔢 für jdn sein

rope n Seil nt; **know the ~s** 🖃 sich auskennen. **~ in** vt 🖃 einspannen

rose[1] n Rose f; (of watering-can) Brause f

rose[2] see **rise**

rostrum n Podium nt

rosy a (-ier, -iest) rosig

rot n Fäulnis f; (🖃 nonsense) Quatsch m ● vi (pt/pp **rotted**) [ver]faulen

rota n Dienstplan m

rotary a Dreh-; (Techn) Rotations-

rotat|e vt drehen ● vi sich drehen; (Techn) rotieren. **~ion** n Drehung f; **in ~ion** im Wechsel

rote n **by ~** auswendig

rotten a faul; 🖃 mies; <person> fies

rough a (-er, -est) rau; (uneven) uneben; (coarse, not gentle) grob; (brutal) roh; (turbulent) stürmisch; (approximate) ungefähr ● adv **sleep ~** im Freien übernachten ● vt **~ it** primitiv leben. **~ out** vt im Groben entwerfen

rough draft n grober Entwurf m

rough|ly adv (see **rough**) rau; grob; roh; ungefähr. **~ness** n Rauheit f

rough paper n Konzeptpapier nt

round a (-er, -est) rund ● n Runde f; (slice) Scheibe f; **do one's ~s** seine Runde machen ● prep um (+ acc); **~ the clock** rund um die Uhr ● adv **all ~** ringsherum; **ask s.o. ~** jdn einladen ● vt biegen um <corner>. **~ off** vt abrunden. **~ up** vt aufrunden; zusammentreiben <animals>; festnehmen <criminals>

roundabout a **~ route** Umweg m ● n Karussell nt; (for traffic) Kreisverkehr m

round trip n Rundreise f

rous|e vt wecken; (fig) erregen. **~ing** a mitreißend

route n Route f; (of bus) Linie f

routine a, **-ly** adv routinemäßig ● n Routine f; (Theat) Nummer f

row[1] n (line) Reihe f

row[2] vt/i rudern

row[3] n 🖃 Krach m ● vi 🖃 sich streiten

rowdy a (-ier, -iest) laut

rowing boat n Ruderboot nt

royal a, **-ly** adv königlich

royalt|y n Königtum nt; (persons) Mitglieder pl der königlichen Familie; **-ies** pl (payments) Tantiemen pl

RSI abbr (repetitive strain injury) chronisches Überlastungssyndrom nt

rub vt (pt/pp **rubbed**) reiben; (polish) polieren; **don't ~ it in** 🖃 reib es mir nicht unter die Nase. **~ off** vt abreiben ● vi abgehen. **~ out** vt ausradieren

rubber n Gummi m; (eraser) Radiergummi m. **~ band** n Gummiband nt

rubbish n Abfall m, Müll m; (🖃 nonsense) Quatsch m; (🖃 junk) Plunder m. **~ bin** n Abfalleimer m. **~ dump** n Abfallhaufen m; (official) Müllhalde f

rubble n Trümmer pl

ruby n Rubin m

rudder n [Steuer]ruder nt

rude a (-r, -st), **-ly** adv unhöflich; (improper) unanständig

rudimentary a elementar; (Biol) rudimentär

ruffian n Rüpel m

ruffle vt zerzausen

rug n Vorleger m, [kleiner] Teppich m; (blanket) Decke f

rugged a <coastline> zerklüftet

ruin n Ruine f; (fig) Ruin m ● vt ruinieren

rule n Regel f; (control) Herrschaft f; (government) Regierung f; (for measuring) Lineal nt; **as a ~** in der Regel ● vt regieren, herrschen über (+ acc); (fig) beherrschen; (decide)

R

entscheiden; ziehen <*line*> ● *vi* regieren, herrschen. ~ **out** *vt* ausschließen

ruled *a* <*paper*> liniert

ruler *n* Herrscher(in) *m(f)*; (*measure*) Lineal *nt*

ruling *a* herrschend; <*factor*> entscheidend; (*Pol*) regierend ● *n* Entscheidung *f*

rum *n* Rum *m*

rumble *n* Grollen *nt* ● *vi* grollen; <*stomach:*> knurren

rummage *vi* wühlen; ~ **through** durchwühlen

rumour *n* Gerücht *nt* ● *vt* **it is** ~**ed that** es geht das Gerücht, dass

rump *n* Hinterteil *nt*. ~ **steak** *n* Rumpsteak *nt*

run *n* Lauf *m*; (*journey*) Fahrt *f*; (*series*) Serie *f*, Reihe *f*; (*Theat*) Laufzeit *f*; (*Skiing*) Abfahrt *f*; (*enclosure*) Auslauf *m*; (*Amer: ladder*) Laufmasche *f*; ~ **of bad luck** Pechsträhne *f*; **be on the** ~ flüchtig sein; **in the long** ~ auf lange Sicht ● *v* (*pt* **ran**, *pp* **run**, *pres p* **running**) ● *vi* laufen; (*flow*) fließen; <*eyes:*> tränen; <*bus:*> verkehren; <*butter, ink:*> zerfließen; <*colours:*> [ab]färben; (*in election*) kandidieren ● *vt* laufen lassen; einlaufen lassen <*bath*>; (*manage*) führen, leiten; (*drive*) fahren; eingehen <*risk*>; (*Journ*) bringen <*article*>; ~ **one's hand over sth** mit der Hand über etw (*acc*) fahren. ~ **away** *vi* weglaufen. ~ **down** *vi* hinunter-/herunterlaufen; <*clockwork:*> ablaufen; <*stocks:*> sich verringern ● *vt* (*run over*) überfahren; (*reduce*) verringern; (🛈 *criticize*) heruntermachen. ~ **in** *vi* hinein-/hereinlaufen. ~ **off** *vi* weglaufen ● *vt* abziehen <*copies*>. ~ **out** *vi* hinaus-/herauslaufen; <*supplies, money:*> ausgehen; **I've** ~ **out of sugar** ich habe keinen Zucker mehr. ~

over *vt* überfahren. ~ **up** *vi* hinauf-/herauflaufen; (*towards*) hinlaufen ● *vt* machen <*debts*>; auflaufen lassen <*bill*>; (*sew*) schnell nähen

runaway *n* Ausreißer *m*

run-down *a* <*area*> verkommen

rung[1] *n* (*of ladder*) Sprosse *f*

rung[2] *see* **ring**[2]

runner *n* Läufer *m*; (*Bot*) Ausläufer *m*; (*on sledge*) Kufe *f*. ~ **bean** *n* Stangenbohne *f*. ~-**up** *n* Zweite(r) *m/f*

running *a* laufend; <*water*> fließend; **four times** ~ viermal nacheinander ● *n* Laufen *nt*; (*management*) Führung *f*, Leitung *f*; **be/not be in the** ~ eine/keine Chance haben

runny *a* flüssig

run: ~-**up** *n* (*Sport*) Anlauf *m*; (*to election*) Zeit *f* vor der Wahl. ~**way** *n* Start- und Landebahn *f*

rupture *n* Bruch *m* ● *vt/i* brechen

rural *a* ländlich

ruse *n* List *f*

rush[1] *n* (*Bot*) Binse *f*

rush[2] *n* Hetze *f*; **in a** ~ in Eile ● *vi* sich hetzen; (*run*) rasen; <*water:*> rauschen ● *vt* hetzen, drängen. ~-**hour** *n* Hauptverkehrszeit *f*, Stoßzeit *f*

Russia *n* Russland *nt*. ~**n** *a* russisch ● *n* Russe *m*/Russin *f*; (*Lang*) Russisch *nt*

rust *n* Rost *m* ● *vi* rosten

rustle *vi* rascheln ● *vt* rascheln mit; (*Amer*) stehlen <*cattle*>. ~ **up** *vt* 🛈 improvisieren

rustproof *a* rostfrei

rusty *a* (-**ier**, -**iest**) rostig

rut *n* Furche *f*

ruthless *a*, -**ly** *adv* rücksichtslos. ~**ness** *n* Rücksichtslosigkeit *f*

rye *n* Roggen *m*

sabbath n Sabbat m
sabotage n Sabotage f ● vt sabotieren
sachet n Beutel m; (*scented*) Kissen nt
sack n Sack m; **get the ~** 🛈 rausgeschmissen werden ● vt 🛈 rausschmeißen
sacred a heilig
sacrifice n Opfer nt ● vt opfern
sacrilege n Sakrileg nt
sad a (**sadder, saddest**) traurig; <*loss, death*> schmerzlich. **~den** vt traurig machen
saddle n Sattel m ● vt satteln; **~ s.o. with sth** 🛈 jdm etw aufhalsen
sadist n Sadist m. **~ic** a, **-ally** adv sadistisch
sad|ly adv traurig; (*unfortunately*) leider. **~ness** n Traurigkeit f
safe a (**-r, -st**) sicher; <*journey*> gut; (*not dangerous*) ungefährlich; **~ and sound** gesund und wohlbehalten ● n Safe m. **~guard** n Schutz m ● vt schützen. **~ly** adv sicher; <*arrive*> gut
safety n Sicherheit f. **~-belt** n Sicherheitsgurt m. **~-pin** n Sicherheitsnadel f. **~-valve** n [Sicherheits]ventil nt
sag vi (*pt/pp* **sagged**) durchhängen
saga n Saga f; (*fig*) Geschichte f
said *see* **say**
sail n Segel nt; (*trip*) Segelfahrt f ● vi segeln; (*on liner*) fahren; (*leave*) abfahren (**for** nach) ● vt segeln mit
sailing n Segelsport m. **~-boat** n Segelboot nt. **~-ship** n Segelschiff nt

sailor n Seemann m; (*in navy*) Matrose m
saint n Heilige(r) m/f. **~ly** a heilig
sake n **for the ~ of ...** um ... (*gen*) willen; **for my/your ~** um meinet-/deinetwillen
salad n Salat m. **~-dressing** n Salatsoße f
salary n Gehalt nt
sale n Verkauf m; (*event*) Basar m; (*at reduced prices*) Schlussverkauf m; **for ~** zu verkaufen
sales|man n Verkäufer m. **~woman** n Verkäuferin f
saliva n Speichel m
salmon n Lachs m
saloon n Salon m; (*Auto*) Limousine f; (*Amer: bar*) Wirtschaft f
salt n Salz nt ● a salzig; <*water, meat*> Salz- ● vt salzen; (*cure*) pökeln; streuen <*road*>. **~-cellar** n Salzfass nt. **~ water** n Salzwasser nt. **~y** a salzig
salute n (*Mil*) Gruß m ● vt/i (*Mil*) grüßen
salvage n (*Naut*) Bergung f ● vt bergen
salvation n Rettung f; (*Relig*) Heil nt
same a & pron **the ~** der/die/das gleiche; (*pl*) die gleichen; (*identical*) der-/die-/dasselbe; (*pl*) dieselben ● adv **the ~** gleich; **all the ~** trotzdem
sample n Probe f; (*Comm*) Muster nt ● vt probieren; kosten <*food*>
sanatorium n Sanatorium nt
sanction n Sanktion f ● vt sanktionieren
sanctuary n (*Relig*) Heiligtum nt; (*refuge*) Zuflucht f; (*for wildlife*) Tierschutzgebiet nt
sand n Sand m ● vt **~ [down]** [ab]schmirgeln
sandal n Sandale f

S

sand: ~**bank** n Sandbank f.
~**paper** n Sandpapier nt. ~-**pit** n
Sandkasten m
sandwich n; Sandwich m ● vt
~**ed between** eingeklemmt
zwischen
sandy a (-ier, -iest) sandig; <beach,
soil> Sand-; <hair> rotblond
sane a (-r, -st) geistig normal;
(sensible) vernünftig
sang see **sing**
sanitary a hygienisch; <system>
sanitär. ~ **napkin** n (Amer), ~
towel n [Damen]binde f
sanitation n Kanalisation und
Abfallbeseitigung pl
sanity n [gesunder] Verstand m
sank see **sink**
sap n (Bot) Saft m ● vt (pt/pp
sapped) schwächen
sarcas|m n Sarkasmus m. ~**tic** a,
-**ally** adv sarkastisch
sardine n Sardine f
sash n Schärpe f
sat see **sit**
satchel n Ranzen m
satellite n Satellit m. ~ **television**
n Satellitenfernsehen nt
satin n Satin m
satire n Satire f
satirical a, -**ly** adv satirisch
satir|ist n Satiriker(in) m(f)
satisfaction n Befriedigung f; to
my ~ zu meiner Zufriedenheit
satisfactory a, -**ily** adv zufrieden
stellend
satisfy vt (pp/pp -ied) befriedigen;
zufrieden stellen <customer>;
(convince) überzeugen; be ~ied
zufrieden sein. ~**ing** a
befriedigend; <meal> sättigend
saturate vt durchtränken; (Chem
& fig) sättigen
Saturday n Samstag m
sauce n Soße f; (cheek) Frechheit
f. ~**pan** n Kochtopf m
saucer n Untertasse f
saucy a (-ier, -iest) frech
Saudi Arabia n Saudi-Arabien n

sauna n Sauna f
saunter vi schlendern
sausage n Wurst f
savage a wild; (fierce) scharf;
(brutal) brutal ● n Wilde(r) m/f.
~**ry** n Brutalität f
save n (Sport) Abwehr f ● vt
retten (**from** vor + dat); (keep)
aufheben; (not waste) sparen;
(collect) sammeln; (avoid)
ersparen; (Sport) verhindern
<goal> ● vi ~ [**up**] sparen
saver n Sparer m
saving n (see save) Rettung f;
Sparen nt; Ersparnis f; ~**s** pl
(money) Ersparnisse pl
savour n Geschmack m ● vt
auskosten. ~**y** a würzig
saw[1] see **see**[1]
saw[2] n Säge f ● vt/i (pt sawed, pp
sawn or sawed) sägen
saxophone n Saxophon nt
say n Mitspracherecht nt; **have
one's** ~ seine Meinung sagen
● vt/i (pt/pp said) sagen;
sprechen <prayer>; **that is to** ~
das heißt; **that goes without** ~**ing**
das versteht sich von selbst.
~**ing** n Redensart f
scab n Schorf m; (pej)
Streikbrecher m
scaffolding n Gerüst nt
scald vt verbrühen
scale[1] n (of fish) Schuppe f
scale[2] n Skala f; (Mus) Tonleiter
f; (ratio) Maßstab m ● vt (climb)
erklettern. ~ **down** vt
verkleinern
scales npl (for weighing) Waage f
scalp n Kopfhaut f
scamper vi huschen
scan n (Med) Szintigramm nt ● v
(pt/pp scanned) ● vt absuchen;
(quickly) flüchtig ansehen; (Med)
szintigraphisch untersuchen
scandal n Skandal m; (gossip)
Skandalgeschichten pl. ~**ize** vt
schockieren. ~**ous** a skandalös

Scandinavia n Skandinavien nt.
~n a skandinavisch ● n
Skandinavier(in) m(f)

scanner n Scanner m

scanty a (-ier, -iest), **-ily** adv
spärlich; <clothing> knapp

scapegoat n Sündenbock m

scar n Narbe f

scarc|e a (-r, -st) knapp; **make
oneself ~e** 🔲 sich aus dem Staub
machen. **~ely** adv kaum. **~ity** n
Knappheit f

scare n Schreck m; (panic)
[allgemeine] Panik f ● vt Angst
machen (+ dat); **be ~d** Angst
haben (of vor + dat)

scarf n (pl **scarves**) Schal m;
(square) Tuch nt

scarlet a scharlachrot

scary a unheimlich

scathing a bissig

scatter vt verstreuen; (disperse)
zerstreuen ● vi sich zerstreuen.
~ed a verstreut; <showers>
vereinzelt

scatty a (-ier, -iest) 🔲 verrückt

scene n Szene f; (sight) Anblick
m; (place of event) Schauplatz m;
behind the ~s hinter den
Kulissen

scenery n Landschaft f; (Theat)
Szenerie f

scenic a landschaftlich schön

scent n Duft m; (trail) Fährte f;
(perfume) Parfüm nt. **~ed** a
parfümiert

sceptic|al a, **-ly** adv skeptisch.
~ism n Skepsis f

schedule n Programm nt; (of
work) Zeitplan m; (timetable)
Fahrplan m; **behind ~** im
Rückstand; **according to ~**
planmäßig ● vt planen

scheme n Programm nt; (plan)
Plan m; (plot) Komplott nt ● vi
Ränke schmieden

schizophrenic a schizophren

scholar n Gelehrte(r) m/f. **~ly** a
gelehrt. **~ship** n Gelehrtheit f;
(grant) Stipendium nt

school n Schule f; (Univ) Fakultät
f ● vt schulen

school: **~boy** n Schüler m. **~girl**
n Schülerin f. **~ing** n
Schulbildung f. **~master** n
Lehrer m. **~mistress** n Lehrerin
f. **~-teacher** n Lehrer(in) m(f)

scien|ce n Wissenschaft f. **~tific**
a wissenschaftlich. **~tist** n
Wissenschaftler m

scissors npl Schere f; **a pair of ~**
eine Schere

scoff[1] vi **~ at** spotten über (+ acc)

scoff[2] vt 🔲 verschlingen

scold vt ausschimpfen

scoop n Schaufel f; (Culin)
Portionierer m; (Journ)
Exklusivmeldung f ● vt **~ out**
aushöhlen; (remove) auslöffeln

scooter n Roller m

scope n Bereich m; (opportunity)
Möglichkeiten pl

scorch vt versengen. **~ing** a
glühend heiß

score n [Spiel]stand m;
(individual) Punktzahl f; (Mus)
Partitur f; (Cinema) Filmmusik f;
on that ~ was das betrifft ● vt
erzielen; schießen <goal>; (cut)
einritzen ● vi Punkte erzielen;
(Sport) ein Tor schießen; (keep
score) Punkte zählen. **~r** n
Punktezähler m; (of goals)
Torschütze m

scorn n Verachtung f ● vt
verachten. **~ful** a, **-ly** adv
verächtlich

Scot n Schotte m/Schottin f

Scotch a schottisch ● n (whisky)
Scotch m

Scot|land n Schottland nt. **~s,**
~tish a schottisch

scoundrel n Schurke m

scour vt (search) absuchen;
(clean) scheuern

S

scout n (Mil) Kundschafter m; **[Boy] S~** Pfadfinder m

scowl n böser Gesichtsausdruck m ● vi ein böses Gesicht machen

scram vi 🗓 abhauen

scramble n Gerangel nt ● vi klettern; **~ for** sich drängen nach. **~d egg[s]** n[pl] Rührei nt

scrap[1] n (🗓 fight) Rauferei f ● vi sich raufen

scrap[2] n Stückchen nt; (metal) Schrott m; **~s** pl Reste; **not a ~** kein bisschen ● vt (pt/pp **scrapped**) aufgeben

scrapbook n Sammelalbum nt

scrape vt schaben; (clean) abkratzen; (damage) [ver]schrammen. **~ through** vi gerade noch durchkommen. **~ together** vt zusammenkriegen

scrappy a lückenhaft

scrapyard n Schrottplatz m

scratch n Kratzer m; **start from ~** von vorne anfangen; **not be up to ~** zu wünschen übrig lassen ● vt/i kratzen; (damage) zerkratzen

scrawl n Gekrakel nt ● vt/i krakeln

scream n Schrei m ● vt/i schreien

screech n Kreischen nt ● vt/i kreischen

screen n Schirm m; (Cinema) Leinwand f; (TV) Bildschirm m ● vt schützen; (conceal) verdecken; vorführen <film>; (examine) überprüfen; (Med) untersuchen

screw n Schraube f ● vt schrauben. **~ up** vt festschrauben; (crumple) zusammenknüllen; zusammenkneifen <eyes>; (🗓 bungle) vermasseln

screwdriver n Schraubenzieher m

scribble n Gekritzel nt ● vt/i kritzeln

script n Schrift f; (of speech, play) Text m; (Radio, TV) Skript nt; (of film) Drehbuch nt

scroll n Rolle f ● vt **~ up/down** nach oben/unten rollen. **~ bar** n Rollbalken m

scrounge vt/i schnorren. **~r** n Schnorrer m

scrub vt/i (pt/pp **scrubbed**) schrubben

scruff n **by the ~ of the neck** beim Genick

scruffy a (-ier, -iest) vergammelt

scrum n Gedränge nt

scruple n Skrupel m

scrupulous a, **-ly** adv gewissenhaft

scuffle n Handgemenge nt

sculpt|or n Bildhauer(in) m(f). **~ure** n Bildhauerei f; (piece of work) Skulptur f, Plastik f

scum n Schmutzschicht f; (people) Abschaum m

scurry vi (pt/pp **-ied**) huschen

scuttle[1] vt versenken <ship>

scuttle[2] vi schnell krabbeln

sea n Meer nt, See f; **at ~** auf See; **by ~** mit dem Schiff. **~food** n Meeresfrüchte pl. **~gull** n Möwe f

seal[1] n (Zool) Seehund m

seal[2] n Siegel nt ● vt versiegeln; (fig) besiegeln. **~ off** vt abriegeln

sea-level n Meeresspiegel m

seam n Naht f; (of coal) Flöz nt

seaman n Seemann m; (sailor) Matrose m

seance n spiritistische Sitzung f

search n Suche f; (official) Durchsuchung f ● vt durchsuchen; absuchen <area> ● vi suchen (**for** nach). **~ engine** n Suchmaschine f. **~ing** a prüfend, forschend **~light** n [Such]scheinwerfer m. **~-party** n Suchmannschaft f

sea: ~sick a seekrank. **~side** n **at/to the ~side** am/ans Meer

season n Jahreszeit f; (social,

tourist, sporting) Saison f ● vt
(*flavour*) würzen. ~al a Saison-.
~ing n Gewürze pl
season ticket n Dauerkarte f
seat n Sitz m; (*place*) Sitzplatz m;
(*bottom*) Hintern m; **take a ~**
Platz nehmen ● vt setzen; (*have
seats for*) Sitzplätze bieten (+
dat); **remain ~ed** sitzen bleiben.
~-**belt** n Sicherheitsgurt m; **fasten
one's ~-belt** sich anschnallen
sea: ~**weed** n [See]tang m.
~**worthy** a seetüchtig
seclu|ded a abgelegen. ~**sion** n
Zurückgezogenheit f
second a zweite(r,s); **on ~
thoughts** nach weiterer
Überlegung ● n Sekunde f;
(*Sport*) Sekundant m; ~**s** pl
(*goods*) Waren zweiter Wahl
● adv (*in race*) an zweiter Stelle
● vt unterstützen <*proposal*>
secondary a zweitrangig; (*Phys*)
Sekundär-. ~ **school** n höhere
Schule f
second: ~-**best** a zweitbeste(r,s).
~ **class** adv <*travel, send*>
zweiter Klasse. ~-**class** a
zweitklassig
second hand n (*on clock*)
Sekundenzeiger m
second-hand a gebraucht ● adv
aus zweiter Hand
secondly adv zweitens
second-rate a zweitklassig
secrecy n Heimlichkeit f
secret a geheim; <*agent, police*>
Geheim-; <*drinker, lover*>
heimlich ● n Geheimnis nt
secretarial a Sekretärinnen-;
<*work, staff*> Sekretariats-
secretary n Sekretär(in) m(f)
secretive a geheimtuerisch
secretly adv heimlich
sect n Sekte f
section n Teil m; (*of text*)
Abschnitt m; (*of firm*) Abteilung
f; (*of organization*) Sektion f
sector n Sektor m

secular a weltlich
secure a, -**ly** adv sicher; (*firm*)
fest; (*emotionally*) geborgen ● vt
sichern; (*fasten*) festmachen;
(*obtain*) sich (*dat*) sichern
securit|y n Sicherheit f;
(*emotional*) Geborgenheit f; ~**ies**
pl Wertpapiere pl
sedan n (*Amer*) Limousine f
sedate a, -**ly** adv gesetzt
sedative a beruhigend ● n
Beruhigungsmittel nt
sediment n [Boden]satz m
seduce vt verführen
seduct|ion n Verführung f. ~**ive**
a, -**ly** adv verführerisch
see v (*pt* saw, *pp* seen) ● vt sehen;
(*understand*) einsehen; (*imagine*)
sich (*dat*) vorstellen; (*escort*)
begleiten; **go and ~** nachsehen;
(*visit*) besuchen; ~ **you later!** bis
nachher! ~**ing that** da ● vi sehen;
(*check*) nachsehen; ~ **about** sich
kümmern um. ~ **off** vt
verabschieden; (*chase away*)
vertreiben. ~ **through** vt (*fig*)
durchschauen <*person*>
seed n Samen m; (*of grape*) Kern
m; (*fig*) Saat f; (*Tennis*) gesetzter
Spieler m; **go to ~** Samen bilden;
(*fig*) herunterkommen
seedy a (-ier, -iest) schäbig;
<*area*> heruntergekommen
seek vt (*pt/pp* sought) suchen
seem vi scheinen
seen see **see¹**
seep vi sickern
seethe vi ~ **with anger** vor Wut
schäumen
see-through a durchsichtig
segment n Teil m; (*of worm*)
Segment nt; (*of orange*) Spalte f
segregat|e vt trennen. ~**ion** n
Trennung f
seize vt ergreifen; (*Jur*)
beschlagnahmen; ~ **s.o. by the
arm** jdn am Arm packen. ~ **up** vi
(*Techn*) sich festfressen
seldom adv selten

S

select a ausgewählt; (*exclusive*) exklusiv ● vt auswählen; aufstellen *<team>*. ~**ion** n Auswahl f

self n (*pl* **selves**) Ich nt

self: ~-**assurance** n Selbstsicherheit f. ~-**assured** a selbstsicher. ~-**catering** n Selbstversorgung f. ~-**centred** a egozentrisch. ~-**confidence** n Selbstbewusstsein nt, Selbstvertrauen nt. ~-**confident** a selbstbewusst. ~-**conscious** a befangen. ~-**contained** a *<flat>* abgeschlossen. ~-**control** n Selbstbeherrschung f. ~-**defence** n Selbstverteidigung f; (*Jur*) Notwehr f. ~-**employed** selbstständig. ~-**esteem** n Selbstachtung f. ~-**evident** a offensichtlich. ~-**indulgent** a maßlos. ~-**interest** n Eigennutz m

self|ish a, -**ly** adv egoistisch, selbstsüchtig. ~**less** a, -**ly** adv selbstlos

self: ~-**pity** n Selbstmitleid nt. ~-**portrait** n Selbstporträt nt. ~-**respect** n Selbstachtung f. ~-**righteous** a selbstgerecht. ~-**sacrifice** n Selbstaufopferung f. ~-**satisfied** a selbstgefällig. ~-**service** n Selbstbedienung f ● attrib Selbstbedienungs-. ~-**sufficient** a selbstständig

sell v (*pt/pp* **sold**) ● vt verkaufen; **be sold out** ausverkauft sein ● vi sich verkaufen. ~ **off** vt verkaufen

seller n Verkäufer m

Sellotape (P), n ≈ Tesafilm (P) m

sell-out n **be a** ~ ausverkauft sein; (⊞ *betrayal*) Verrat sein

selves see **self**

semester n (*Amer*) Semester nt

semi|breve n (*Mus*) ganze Note f. ~**circle** n Halbkreis m. ~**circular** a halbkreisförmig. ~**colon** n Semikolon nt. ~-**detached** a & n

~-**detached [house]** Doppelhaushälfte f. ~-**final** n Halbfinale nt

seminar n Seminar nt

senat|e n Senat m. ~**or** n Senator m

send vt/i (*pt/pp* **sent**) schicken; ~ **for** kommen lassen *<person>*; sich (*dat*) schicken lassen *<thing>*. ~-**er** n Absender m. ~-**off** n Verabschiedung f

senile a senil

senior a älter; (*in rank*) höher ● n Ältere(r) m/f; (*in rank*) Vorgesetzte(r) m/f. ~ **citizen** n Senior(in) m(f)

seniority n höheres Alter nt; (*in rank*) höherer Rang m

sensation n Sensation f; (*feeling*) Gefühl nt. ~**al** a, -**ly** adv sensationell

sense n Sinn m; (*feeling*) Gefühl nt; (*common* ~) Verstand m; **make** ~ Sinn ergeben ● vt spüren. ~**less** a, -**ly** adv sinnlos; (*unconscious*) bewusstlos

sensible a, -**bly** adv vernünftig; *<suitable>* zweckmäßig

sensitiv|e a, -**ly** adv empfindlich; (*understanding*) einfühlsam. ~**ity** n Empfindlichkeit f

sensual a sinnlich. -**ity** n Sinnlichkeit f

sensuous a sinnlich

sent see **send**

sentence n Satz m; (*Jur*) Urteil nt; (*punishment*) Strafe f ● vt verurteilen

sentiment n Gefühl nt; (*opinion*) Meinung f; (*sentimentality*) Sentimentalität f ~**al** a sentimental. ~**ality** n Sentimentalität f

sentry n Wache f

separable a trennbar

separate¹ a, -**ly** adv getrennt, separat

separat|e² vt trennen ● vi sich trennen. ~**ion** n Trennung f

September n September m
septic a vereitert
sequel n Folge f; (fig) Nachspiel nt
sequence n Reihenfolge f
serenade n Ständchen nt ● vt ~ **s.o.** jdm ein Ständchen bringen
seren|e a, **-ly** adv gelassen. ~**ity** n Gelassenheit f
sergeant n (Mil) Feldwebel m; (in police) Polizeimeister m
serial n Fortsetzungsgeschichte f; (Radio, TV) Serie f. ~**ize** vt in Fortsetzungen veröffentlichen/ (Radio, TV) senden
series n inv Serie f
serious a, **-ly** adv ernst; <illness, error> schwer. ~**ness** n Ernst m
sermon n Predigt f
servant n Diener(in) m(f)
serve n (Tennis) Aufschlag m ● vt dienen (+ dat); bedienen <customer, guest>; servieren <food>; verbüßen <sentence>; **it ~s you right!** das geschieht dir recht! ● vi dienen; (Tennis) aufschlagen
service n Dienst m; (Relig) Gottesdienst m; (in shop, restaurant) Bedienung f; (transport) Verbindung f; (maintenance) Wartung f; (set of crockery) Service nt; (Tennis) Aufschlag m; ~**s** pl Dienstleistungen pl; (on motorway) Tankstelle und Raststätte f; **in the ~s** beim Militär; **out of/in ~** <machine:> außer/in Betrieb ● vt (Techn) warten
service: ~ **area** n Tankstelle und Raststätte f. ~ **charge** n Bedienungszuschlag m. ~**man** n Soldat m. ~ **station** n Tankstelle f
serviette n Serviette f
servile a unterwürfig
session n Sitzung f

set n Satz m; (of crockery) Service nt; (of cutlery) Garnitur f; (TV, Radio) Apparat m; (Math) Menge f; (Theat) Bühnenbild nt; (Cinema) Szenenaufbau m; (of people) Kreis m ● a (ready) fertig, bereit; (rigid) fest; <book> vorgeschrieben; **be ~ on doing sth** entschlossen sein, etw zu tun ● v (pt/pp **set**, pres p **setting**) ● vt setzen; (adjust) einstellen; stellen <task, alarm clock>; festsetzen, festlegen <date, limit>; aufgeben <homework>; zusammenstellen <questions>; [ein]fassen <gem>; einrichten <bone>; legen <hair>; decken <table> ● vi <sun:> untergehen; (become hard) fest werden. ~ **back** vt zurücksetzen; (hold up) aufhalten; (☐ cost) kosten. ~ **off** vi losgehen; (in vehicle) losfahren ● vt auslösen <alarm>; explodieren lassen <bomb>. ~ **out** vi losgehen; (in vehicle) losfahren ● vt auslegen; (state) darlegen. ~ **up** vt aufbauen; (fig) gründen
settee n Sofa nt, Couch f
setting n Rahmen m; (surroundings) Umgebung f
settle vt (decide) entscheiden; (agree) regeln; (fix) festsetzen; (calm) beruhigen; (pay) bezahlen ● vi sich niederlassen; <snow, dust:> liegen bleiben; (subside) sich senken; <sediment:> sich absetzen. ~ **down** vi sich beruhigen; (permanently) sesshaft werden. ~ **up** vi abrechnen
settlement n (see settle) Entscheidung f; Regelung f; Bezahlung f; (Jur) Vergleich m; (colony) Siedlung f
settler n Siedler m
set-up n System nt
seven a sieben. ~**teen** a siebzehn. ~**teenth** a siebzehnte(r,s)

S

seventh a siebte(r,s)

seventieth a siebzigste(r,s)

seventy a siebzig

several a & pron mehrere, einige

sever|e a (-r, -st,) **-ly** adv streng; <pain> stark; <illness> schwer. ~**ity** n Strenge f; Schwere f

sew vt/i (pt **sewed**, pp **sewn** or **sewed**) nähen

sewage n Abwasser nt

sewer n Abwasserkanal m

sewing n Nähen nt; (work) Näharbeit f. ~ **machine** n Nähmaschine f

sewn see sew

sex n Geschlecht nt; (sexuality, intercourse) Sex m. ~**ist** a sexistisch

sexual a, **-ly** adv sexuell. ~ **intercourse** n Geschlechtsverkehr m

sexuality n Sexualität f

sexy a (-ier, -iest) sexy

shabby a (-ier, -iest), **-ily** adv schäbig

shack n Hütte f

shade n Schatten m; (of colour) [Farb]ton m; (for lamp) [Lampen]schirm m; (Amer: window-blind) Jalousie f ● vt beschatten

shadow n Schatten m ● vt (follow) beschatten

shady a (-ier, -iest) schattig; (🛈 disreputable) zwielichtig

shaft n Schaft m; (Techn) Welle f; (of light) Strahl m; (of lift) Schacht m

shaggy a (-ier, -iest) zottig

shake n Schütteln nt ● v (pt **shook**, pp **shaken**) ● vt schütteln; (shock) erschüttern; ~ **hands with s.o.** jdm die Hand geben ● vi wackeln; (tremble) zittern. ~ **off** vt abschütteln

shaky a (-ier, -iest) wackelig; <hand, voice> zittrig

shall v aux **we** ~ **see** wir werden sehen; **what** ~ **I do?** was soll ich machen?

shallow a (-er, -est) seicht; <dish> flach; (fig) oberflächlich

sham a unecht ● n Heuchelei f ● vt (pt/pp **shammed**) vortäuschen

shambles n Durcheinander nt

shame n Scham f; (disgrace) Schande f; **be a** ~ schade sein; **what a** ~! wie schade!

shame|ful a, **-ly** adv schändlich. ~**less** a, **-ly** adv schamlos

shampoo n Shampoo nt ● vt schamponieren

shan't = shall not

shape n Form f; (figure) Gestalt f ● vt formen (**into** zu). ~**less** a formlos; <clothing> unförmig

share n [An]teil m; (Comm) Aktie f ● vt/i teilen. ~**holder** n Aktionär(in) m(f)

shark n Hai[fisch] m

sharp a (-er, -est), **-ly** adv scharf; (pointed) spitz; (severe) heftig; (sudden) steil; (alert) clever; (unscrupulous) gerissen ● adv scharf; (Mus) zu hoch; **at six o'clock** ~ Punkt sechs Uhr ● n (Mus) Kreuz nt. ~**en** vt schärfen; [an]spitzen <pencil>

shatter vt zertrümmern; (fig) zerstören; ~**ed** <person:> erschüttert; (🛈 exhausted) kaputt ● vi zersplittern

shave n Rasur f; **have a** ~ sich rasieren ● vt rasieren ● vi sich rasieren. ~**r** n Rasierapparat m

shawl n Schultertuch nt

she pron sie

shears npl [große] Schere f

shed¹ n Schuppen m

shed² vt (pt/pp **shed**, pres p **shedding**) verlieren; vergießen <blood, tears>; ~ **light on** Licht bringen in (+ acc)

sheep n inv Schaf nt. ~**-dog** n Hütehund m

sheepish *a*, **-ly** *adv* verlegen
sheer *a* rein; (*steep*) steil;
(*transparent*) hauchdünn
sheet *n* Laken *nt*, Betttuch *nt*; (*of
paper*) Blatt *nt*; (*of glass, metal*)
Platte *f*
shelf *n* (*pl* **shelves**) Brett *nt*, Bord
nt; (*set of shelves*) Regal *nt*
shell *n* Schale *f*; (*of snail*) Haus
nt; (*of tortoise*) Panzer *m*; (*on
beach*) Muschel *f*; (*Mil*) Granate *f*
● *vt* pellen; enthülsen <*peas*>;
(*Mil*) [mit Granaten] beschießen.
~ **out** *vi* 🛈 blechen
shellfish *n inv* Schalentiere *pl*;
(*Culin*) Meeresfrüchte *pl*
shelter *n* Schutz *m*; (*air-raid* ~)
Luftschutzraum *m* ● *vt* schützen
(**from** vor + *dat*) ● *vi* sich
unterstellen. ~**ed** *a* geschützt;
<*life*> behütet
shelve *vt* auf Eis legen; (*abandon*)
aufgeben
shelving *n* (*shelves*) Regale *pl*
shepherd *n* Schäfer *m* ● *vt*
führen
sherry *n* Sherry *m*
shield *n* Schild *m*; (*for eyes*)
Schirm *m*; (*Techn & fig*) Schutz
m ● *vt* schützen (**from** vor + *dat*)
shift *n* Verschiebung *f*; (*at work*)
Schicht *f* ● *vt* rücken; (*take away*)
wegnehmen; (*rearrange*)
umstellen; schieben <*blame*> (**on
to** auf + *acc*) ● *vi* sich
verschieben; (🛈 *rush*) rasen
shifty *a* (**-ier, -iest**) (*pej*)
verschlagen
shimmer *n* Schimmer *m* ● *vi*
schimmern
shin *n* Schienbein *nt*
shine *n* Glanz *m* ● *v* (*pt/pp* **shone**)
● *vi* leuchten; (*reflect light*)
glänzen; <*sun:*> scheinen ● *vt* ~
a light on beleuchten
shingle *n* (*pebbles*) Kiesel *pl*
shiny *a* (**-ier, -iest**) glänzend
ship *n* Schiff *nt* ● *vt* (*pt/pp*
shipped) verschiffen

ship: ~**building** *n* Schiffbau *m*.
~**ment** *n* Sendung *f*. ~**per** *n*
Spediteur *m*. ~**ping** *n* Versand
m; (*traffic*) Schifffahrt *f*. ~**shape**
a & adv in Ordnung. ~**wreck** *n*
Schiffbruch *m*. ~**wrecked** *a*
schiffbrüchig. ~**yard** *n* Werft *f*
shirt *n* [Ober]hemd *nt*; (*for
woman*) Hemdbluse *f*
shit *n* (*vulg*) Scheiße *f* ● *vi* (*pt/pp*
shit) (*vulg*) scheißen
shiver *n* Schauder *m* ● *vi* zittern
shoal *n* (*fish*) Schwarm *m*
shock *n* Schock *m*; (*Electr*) Schlag
m; (*impact*) Erschütterung *f* ● *vt*
einen Schock versetzen (+ *dat*);
(*scandalize*) schockieren. ~**ing** *a*
schockierend; (🛈 *bad*)
fürchterlich
shoddy *a* (**-ier, -iest**) minderwertig
shoe *n* Schuh *m*; (*of horse*)
Hufeisen *nt* ● *vt* (*pt/pp* **shod**, *pres
p* **shoeing**) beschlagen <*horse*>
shoe: ~**horn** *n* Schuhanzieher *m*.
~**-lace** *n* Schnürsenkel *m*. ~**-
string** *n* **on a** ~**-string** 🛈 mit ganz
wenig Geld
shone *see* **shine**
shoo *vt* scheuchen ● *int* sch!
shook *see* **shake**
shoot *n* (*Bot*) Trieb *m*; (*hunt*) Jagd
f ● *v* (*pt/pp* **shot**) ● *vt* schießen;
(*kill*) erschießen; drehen <*film*>
● *vi* schießen. ~ **down** *vi*
abschießen. ~ **out** *vi* (*rush*)
herausschießen. ~ **up** *vi* (*grow*)
in die Höhe schießen/<*prices:*>
schnellen
shop *n* Laden *m*, Geschäft *nt*;
(*workshop*) Werkstatt *f*; **talk** ~ 🛈
fachsimpeln ● *vi* (*pt/pp* **shopped**,
pres p **shopping**) einkaufen; **go**
~**ping** einkaufen gehen
shop: ~ **assistant** *n*
Verkäufer(in) *m(f)*. ~**keeper** *n*
Ladenbesitzer(in) *m(f)*. ~**-lifter** *n*
Ladendieb *m*. ~**-lifting** *n*
Ladendiebstahl *m*

S

shopping n Einkaufen nt;
(articles) Einkäufe pl; **do the ~**
einkaufen. **~ bag** n
Einkaufstasche f. **~ centre** n
Einkaufszentrum nt. **~ trolley** n
Einkaufswagen m
shop-window n Schaufenster nt
shore n Strand m; (of lake) Ufer
nt
short a (-er, -est) kurz; <person>
klein; (curt) schroff; **a ~ time ago**
vor kurzem; **be ~ of ...** zu wenig
... haben; **be in ~ supply** knapp
sein ● adv kurz; (abruptly)
plötzlich; (curtly) kurz
angebunden; **in ~** kurzum; **~ of**
(except) außer; **go ~** Mangel
leiden
shortage n Mangel m (**of** an +
dat); (scarcity) Knappheit f
short: ~bread n ≈ Mürbekekse
pl. **~ circuit** n Kurzschluss m.
~coming n Fehler m. **~ cut** n
Abkürzung f
shorten vt [ab]kürzen; kürzer
machen <garment>
short: ~hand n Kurzschrift f,
Stenographie f. **~list** n engere
Auswahl f
short|ly adv in Kürze; **~ly before/**
after kurz vorher/danach. **~ness**
n Kürze f; (of person) Kleinheit f
shorts npl Shorts pl
short: ~-sighted a kurzsichtig.
~-sleeved a kurzärmelig. **~**
story n Kurzgeschichte f. **~**
tempered a aufbrausend. **~**
term a kurzfristig. **~ wave** n
Kurzwelle f
shot see shoot ● n Schuss m;
(pellets) Schrot m; (person)
Schütze m; (Phot) Aufnahme f;
(injection) Spritze f; (I attempt)
Versuch m; **like a ~** sofort.
~gun n Schrotflinte f. **~-put** n
(Sport) Kugelstoßen nt
should v aux **you ~ go** du solltest
gehen; **I ~ have seen him** ich
hätte ihn sehen sollen; **I ~ like**

ich möchte; **this ~ be enough** das
müsste eigentlich reichen; **if he ~**
be there hätte er da sein sollte
shoulder n Schulter f ● vt
schultern; (fig) auf sich (acc)
nehmen. **~-blade** n Schulterblatt
nt
shout n Schrei m ● vt/i schreien.
~ down vt niederschreien
shouting n Geschrei nt
shove n Stoß m ● vt stoßen; (I
put) tun ● vi drängeln. **~ off** vi
I abhauen
shovel n Schaufel f ● vt (pt/pp
shovelled) schaufeln
show n (display) Pracht f;
(exhibition) Ausstellung f, Schau
f; (performance) Vorstellung f;
(Theat, TV) Show f; **on ~**
ausgestellt ● v (pt showed, pp
shown). ● vt zeigen; (put on
display) ausstellen; vorführen
<film> ● vi sichtbar sein; <film:>
gezeigt werden. **~ in** vt
hereinführen. **~ off** vi I
angeben ● vt vorführen; (flaunt)
angeben mit. **~ up** vi [deutlich]
zu sehen sein; (I arrive)
auftauchen ● vt deutlich zeigen;
(I embarrass) blamieren
shower n Dusche f; (of rain)
Schauer m; **have a ~** duschen
● vt **~ with** überschütten mit ● vi
duschen
show-jumping n Springreiten nt
shown see show
show: ~-off n Angeber(in) m(f).
~room n Ausstellungsraum m
showy a protzig
shrank see shrink
shred n Fetzen m; (fig) Spur f
● vt (pt/pp shredded) zerkleinern;
(Culin) schnitzeln. **~der** n
Reißwolf m; (Culin)
Schnitzelwerk nt
shrewd a (-er, -est), **-ly** adv klug.
~ness n Klugheit f
shriek n Schrei m ● vt/i schreien
shrill a, **-y** adv schrill

shrimp n Garnele f, Krabbe f
shrink vi (pt **shrank**, pp **shrunk**) schrumpfen; <garment:> einlaufen; (draw back) zurückschrecken (**from** vor + dat)
shrivel vi (pt/pp **shrivelled**) verschrumpeln
Shrove n ~**Tuesday** Fastnachtsdienstag m
shrub n Strauch m
shrug n Achselzucken nt ● vt/i (pt/pp **shrugged**) ~ **[one's shoulders]** die Achseln zucken
shrunk see **shrink**
shudder n Schauder m ● vi schaudern; (tremble) zittern
shuffle vi schlurfen ● vt mischen <cards>
shun vt (pt/pp **shunned**) meiden
shunt vt rangieren
shut v (pt/pp **shut**, pres p **shutting**) ● vt zumachen, schließen ● vi sich schließen; <shop:> schließen, zumachen. ~ **down** vt schließen; stilllegen <factory> ● vi schließen. ~ **up** vt abschließen; (lock in) einsperren ● vi Ⓘ den Mund halten
shutter n [Fenster]laden m; (Phot) Verschluss m
shuttle n (Tex) Schiffchen nt
shuttle service n Pendelverkehr m
shy a (**-er, -est**), **-ly** adv schüchtern; (timid) scheu. ~**ness** n Schüchternheit f
siblings npl Geschwister pl
Sicily n Sizilien nt
sick a krank; <humour> makaber; **be** ~ (vomit) sich übergeben; **be** ~ **of sth** Ⓘ etw satt haben; **I feel** ~ mir ist schlecht
sick|ly a (**-ier, -iest**) kränklich. ~**ness** n Krankheit f; (vomiting) Erbrechen nt
side n Seite f; **on the** ~ (as sideline) nebenbei; ~ **by** ~ nebeneinander; (fig) Seite an Seite; **take** ~**s** Partei ergreifen

(**with** für) ● attrib Seiten- ● vi ~ **with** Partei ergreifen für
side: ~**board** n Anrichte f. ~**effect** n Nebenwirkung f. ~**lights** npl Standlicht nt. ~**line** n Nebenbeschäftigung f. ~**show** n Nebenattraktion f. ~**step** vt ausweichen (+ dat). ~**walk** n (Amer) Bürgersteig m. ~**ways** adv seitwärts
siding n Abstellgleis nt
siege n Belagerung f; (by police) Umstellung f
sieve n Sieb nt ● vt sieben
sift vt sieben; (fig) durchsehen
sigh n Seufzer m ● vi seufzen
sight n Sicht f; (faculty) Sehvermögen nt; (spectacle) Anblick m; (on gun) Visier nt; ~**s** pl Sehenswürdigkeiten pl; **at first** ~ auf den ersten Blick; **lose** ~ **of** aus dem Auge verlieren; **know by** ~ vom Sehen kennen ● vt sichten
sightseeing n **go** ~ die Sehenswürdigkeiten besichtigen
sign n Zeichen nt; (notice) Schild nt ● vt/i unterschreiben; <author, artist:> signieren. ~ **on** vi (as unemployed) sich arbeitslos melden; (Mil) sich verpflichten
signal n Signal nt ● vt/i (pt/pp **signalled**) signalisieren; ~ **to s.o.** jdm ein Signal geben
signature n Unterschrift f; (of artist) Signatur f
significan|ce n Bedeutung f. ~**t** a, **-ly** adv (important) bedeutend
signify vt (pt/pp **-ied**) bedeuten
signpost n Wegweiser m
silence n Stille f; (of person) Schweigen nt ● vt zum Schweigen bringen. ~**r** n (on gun) Schalldämpfer m; (Auto) Auspufftopf m
silent a, **-ly** adv still; (without speaking) schweigend; **remain** ~ schweigen

S

silhouette n Silhouette f; (picture) Schattenriss m ● vt be ∼d sich als Silhouette abheben

silicon n Silizium nt

silk n Seide f ● attrib Seiden-

silky a (-ier, -iest) seidig

sill n Sims m & nt

silly a (-ier, -iest) dumm, albern

silver a silbern; <coin, paper> Silber- ● n Silber nt

silver: ∼-**plated** a versilbert. ∼**ware** n Silber nt

similar a, **-ly** adv ähnlich. ∼**ity** n Ähnlichkeit f

simmer vi leise kochen, ziehen ● vt ziehen lassen

simple a (-r, -st) einfach; <person> einfältig. ∼-**minded** a einfältig

simplicity n Einfachheit f

simpli|fication n Vereinfachung f. ∼**fy** vt (pt/pp -ied) vereinfachen

simply adv einfach

simulate vt vortäuschen; (Techn) simulieren

simultaneous a, **-ly** adv gleichzeitig

sin n Sünde f ● vi (pt/pp sinned) sündigen

since

● preposition

····▸ seit (+ dat). he's been living here since 1991 er wohnt* seit 1991 hier. I had been waiting since 8 o'clock ich wartete* [schon] seit 8 Uhr. since seeing you seit ich dich gesehen habe.

● adverb

····▸ seitdem. I haven't spoken to her since seitdem habe ich mit ihr nicht gesprochen. the house has been empty ever since das Haus steht seitdem leer. he has since remarried er hat danach wieder geheiratet. long since vor langer Zeit

● conjunction

····▸ seit. since she has been living in Germany seit sie in Deutschland wohnt*. since they had been in London seit sie in London waren*. how long is it since he left? wie lange ist es her, dass er weggezogen ist? it's a year since he left es ist ein Jahr her, dass er weggezogen ist

····▸ (because) da. since she was ill, I had to do it da sie krank war, musste ich es tun

❗ *Note the different tenses in German

sincere a aufrichtig; (heartfelt) herzlich. ∼**ly** adv aufrichtig; Yours ∼**ly** Mit freundlichen Grüßen

sincerity n Aufrichtigkeit f

sinful a sündhaft

sing vt/i (pt sang, pp sung) singen

singe vt (pres p singeing) versengen

singer n Sänger(in) m(f)

single a einzeln; (one only) einzig; (unmarried) ledig; <ticket> einfach; <room, bed> Einzel- ● n (ticket) einfache Fahrkarte f; (record) Single f; ∼s pl (Tennis) Einzel nt ● vt ∼ out auswählen

single: ∼-**handed** a & adv allein. ∼ **parent** n Alleinerziehende(r) m/f

singly adv einzeln

singular a eigenartig; (Gram) im Singular ● n Singular m

sinister a finster

sink n Spülbecken nt ● v (pt sank, pp sunk) ● vi sinken ● vt versenken <ship>; senken <shaft>. ∼ in vi einsinken; (❗ be understood) kapiert werden

sinner n Sünder(in) m(f)

sip n Schlückchen nt ● vt (pt/pp sipped) in kleinen Schlucken trinken

siphon n (*bottle*) Siphon m. ~ **off** vt mit einem Saugheber ablassen

sir n mein Herr; **S~** (*title*) Sir; **Dear S~s** Sehr geehrte Herren

siren n Sirene f

sister n Schwester f; (*nurse*) Oberschwester f. ~-**in-law** n Schwägerin f

sit v (*pt/pp* **sat**, *pres p* **sitting**) ● vi sitzen; (*sit down*) sich setzen; <*committee:*> tagen ● vt setzen; machen <*exam*>. ~ **back** vi sich zurücklehnen. ~ **down** vi sich setzen. ~ **up** vi [aufrecht] sitzen; (*rise*) sich aufsetzen; (*not slouch*) gerade sitzen

site n Gelände nt; (*for camping*) Platz m; (*Archaeol*) Stätte f

sitting n Sitzung f; (*for meals*) Schub m

situat|e vt legen; **be ~ed** liegen. ~**ion** n Lage f; (*circumstances*) Situation f; (*job*) Stelle f

six a sechs. ~**teen** a sechzehn. ~**teenth** a sechzehnte(r,s)

sixth a sechste(r,s)

sixtieth a sechzigste(r,s)

sixty a sechzig

size n Größe f

sizzle vi brutzeln

skate n Schlittschuh m ● vi Schlittschuh laufen. ~**board** n Skateboard nt ● vi Skateboard fahren. ~**boarding** n Skateboardfahren nt. ~**r** n Eisläufer(in) m(f)

skating n Eislaufen nt. ~-**rink** n Eisbahn f

skeleton n Skelett nt. ~ **key** n Dietrich m

sketch n Skizze f; (*Theat*) Sketch m ● vt skizzieren

sketchy a (**-ier, -iest**), **-ily** adv skizzenhaft

ski n Ski m ● vi (*pt/pp* **skied**, *pres p* **skiing**) Ski fahren *or* laufen

skid n Schleudern nt ● vi (*pt/pp* **skidded**) schleudern

skier n Skiläufer(in) m(f)

skiing n Skilaufen nt

skilful a, **-ly** adv geschickt

skill n Geschick nt. ~**ed** a geschickt; (*trained*) ausgebildet

skim vt (*pt/pp* **skimmed**) entrahmen <*milk*>

skimp vt sparen an (+ *dat*)

skimpy a (**-ier, -iest**) knapp

skin n Haut f; (*on fruit*) Schale f ● vt (*pt/pp* **skinned**) häuten; schälen <*fruit*>

skin: ~-**deep** a oberflächlich. ~-**diving** n Sporttauchen nt

skinny a (**-ier, -iest**) dünn

skip[1] n Container m

skip[2] n Hüpfer m ● v (*pt/pp* **skipped**) vi hüpfen; (*with rope*) seilspringen ● vt überspringen

skipper n Kapitän m

skipping-rope n Sprungseil nt

skirmish n Gefecht nt

skirt n Rock m ● vt herumgehen um

skittle n Kegel m

skive vi 🅸 blaumachen

skull n Schädel m

sky n Himmel m. ~**light** n Dachluke f. ~**scraper** n Wolkenkratzer m

slab n Platte f; (*slice*) Scheibe f; (*of chocolate*) Tafel f

slack a (**-er, -est**) schlaff, locker; <*person*> nachlässig; (*Comm*) flau ● vi bummeln

slacken vi sich lockern; (*diminish*) nachlassen ● vt lockern; (*diminish*) verringern

slain see **slay**

slam v (*pt/pp* **slammed**) ● vt zuschlagen; (*put*) knallen 🅸; (🅸 *criticize*) verreißen ● vi zuschlagen

slander n Verleumdung f ● vt verleumden

slang n Slang m. ~**y** a salopp

slant n Schräge f; **on the** ~ schräg ● vt abschrägen; (*fig*) färben <*report*> ● vi sich neigen

slap n Schlag m ● vt (pt/pp
slapped) schlagen; (put) knallen
🔢 ● adv direkt
slapdash a 🔢 schludrig
slash n Schlitz m ● vt
aufschlitzen; [drastisch]
reduzieren <prices>
slat n Latte f
slate n Schiefer m ● vt 🔢
heruntermachen; verreißen
<performance>
slaughter n Schlachten nt;
(massacre) Gemetzel nt ● vt
schlachten; abschlachten <men>
Slav a slawisch ● n Slawe m/
Slawin f
slave n Sklave m/ Sklavin f ● vi
~ [away] schuften
slavery n Sklaverei f
slay vt (pt slew, pp slain)
ermorden
sledge n Schlitten m
sleek a (-er, -est) seidig; (well-fed)
wohlgenährt
sleep n Schlaf m; go to ~
einschlafen; put to ~
einschläfern ● v (pt/pp slept) ● vi
schlafen ● vt (accommodate)
Unterkunft bieten für. ~er n
Schläfer(in) m(f); (Rail)
Schlafwagen m; (on track)
Schwelle f
sleeping: ~-bag n Schlafsack m.
~-pill n Schlaftablette f
sleep: ~less a schlaflos. ~-
walking n Schlafwandeln nt
sleepy a (-ier, -iest), -ily adv
schläfrig
sleet n Schneeregen m
sleeve n Ärmel m; (for record)
Hülle f. ~less a ärmellos
sleigh n [Pferde]schlitten m
slender a schlank; (fig) gering
slept see sleep
slew see slay
slice n Scheibe f ● vt in Scheiben
schneiden
slick a clever

slid|e n Rutschbahn f; (for hair)
Spange f; (Phot) Dia nt ● v (pt/pp
slid) ● vi rutschen ● vt schieben.
~ing a gleitend; <door, seat>
Schiebe-
slight a (-er, -est), -ly adv leicht;
<importance> gering;
<acquaintance> flüchtig; (slender)
schlank; not in the ~est nicht im
Geringsten; ~ly better ein
bisschen besser ● vt kränken,
beleidigen ● n Beleidigung f
slim a (slimmer, slimmest) schlank;
<volume> schmal; (fig) gering
● vi eine Schlankheitskur
machen
slim|e n Schleim m. ~y a
schleimig
sling n (Med) Schlinge f ● vt (pt/
pp slung) 🔢 schmeißen
slip n (mistake) Fehler m, 🔢
Patzer m; (petticoat) Unterrock
m; (paper) Zettel m; give s.o. the
~ 🔢 jdm entwischen; ~ of the
tongue Versprecher m ● v (pt/pp
slipped) ● vi rutschen; (fall)
ausrutschen; (go quickly)
schlüpfen ● vt schieben; ~ s.o.'s
mind jdm entfallen. ~ away vi
sich fortschleichen. ~ up vi 🔢
einen Schnitzer machen
slipper n Hausschuh m
slippery a glitschig; <surface>
glatt
slipshod a schludrig
slip-up n 🔢 Schnitzer m
slit n Schlitz m ● vt (pt/pp slit)
aufschlitzen
slither vi rutschen
slog n [hard] ~ Schinderei f ● vi
(pt/pp slogged) schuften
slogan n Schlagwort nt;
(advertising) Werbespruch m
slop|e n Hang m; (inclination)
Neigung f ● vi sich neigen. ~ing
a schräg
sloppy a (-ier, -iest) schludrig;
(sentimental) sentimental
slosh vi 🔢 schwappen

slot n Schlitz m; (TV) Sendezeit f
● v (pt/pp **slotted**) ● vt einfügen
● vi sich einfügen (**in** in + acc)
slot-machine n Münzautomat m;
(for gambling) Spielautomat m
slouch vi sich schlecht halten
slovenly a schlampig
slow a (-er, -est), -ly adv langsam;
be ~ <clock:> nachgehen; **in** ~
motion in Zeitlupe ● adv langsam
● vt verlangsamen ● vi ~ **down**,
~ **up** langsamer werden. ~**ness**
n Langsamkeit f
sludge n Schlamm m
slug n Nacktschnecke f
sluggish a, -ly adv träge
sluice n Schleuse f
slum n Elendsviertel nt
slumber n Schlummer m ● vi
schlummern
slump n Sturz m ● vi fallen;
(crumple) zusammensacken;
<prices:> stürzen; <sales:>
zurückgehen
slung see **sling**
slur vt (pt/pp **slurred**) undeutlich
sprechen
slurp vt/i schlürfen
slush n [Schnee]matsch m; (fig)
Kitsch m
slut n Schlampe f 🔲
sly a (-er, -est), -ly adv
verschlagen ● n **on the** ~
heimlich
smack n Schlag m, Klaps m ● vt
schlagen ● adv 🔲 direkt
small a (-er, -est) klein ● adv **chop**
up ~ klein hacken ● n ~ **of the**
back Kreuz nt
small: ~ **ads** npl Kleinanzeigen
pl. ~ **change** n Kleingeld nt.
~**pox** n Pocken pl. ~ **talk** n
leichte Konversation f
smart a (-er, -est), -ly adv schick;
(clever) schlau, clever; (brisk)
flott; (Amer 🔲: cheeky) frech ● vi
brennen
smarten vt ~ **oneself up** mehr auf
sein Äußeres achten

smash n Krach m; (collision)
Zusammenstoß m; (Tennis)
Schmetterball m ● vt
zerschlagen; (strike) schlagen;
(Tennis) schmettern ● vi
zerschmettern; (crash) krachen
(**into** gegen). ~**ing** a 🔲 toll
smear n verschmierter Fleck m;
(Med) Abstrich m; (fig)
Verleumdung f ● vt schmieren;
(coat) beschmieren (**with** mit);
(fig) verleumden ● vi schmieren
smell n Geruch m; (sense)
Geruchssinn m ● v (pt/pp **smelt**
or **smelled**) ● vt riechen; (sniff)
riechen an (+ dat) ● vi riechen
(**of** nach)
smelly a (-ier, -iest) übel riechend
smelt see **smell**
smile n Lächeln nt ● vi lächeln; ~
at anlächeln
smirk vi feixen
smith n Schmied m
smock n Kittel m
smog n Smog m
smoke n Rauch m ● vt/i rauchen;
(Culin) räuchern. ~**less** a
rauchfrei; <fuel> rauchlos
smoker n Raucher m; (Rail)
Raucherabteil nt
smoking n Rauchen nt; 'no ~'
'Rauchen verboten'
smoky a (-ier, -iest) verraucht;
<taste> rauchig
smooth a (-er, -est), -ly adv glatt
● vt glätten. ~ **out** vt glatt
streichen
smother vt ersticken; (cover)
bedecken; (suppress)
unterdrücken
smoulder vi schwelen
smudge n Fleck m ● vt
verwischen ● vi schmieren
smug a (**smugger**, **smuggest**), -ly
adv selbstgefällig
smuggl|e vt schmuggeln. ~**er** n
Schmuggler m. ~**ing** n
Schmuggel m

S

snack n Imbiss m. **~-bar** n Imbissstube f

snag n Schwierigkeit f, ⚠ Haken m

snail n Schnecke f; **at a ~'s pace** im Schneckentempo

snake n Schlange f

snap n Knacken nt; (photo) Schnappschuss m ● attrib <decision> plötzlich ● v (pt/pp snapped) ● vi [entzwei]brechen; **~ at** (bite) schnappen nach; (speak sharply) [scharf] anfahren ● vt zerbrechen; (say) fauchen; (Phot) knipsen. **~ up** vt wegschnappen

snappy a (-ier, -iest) (smart) flott; **make it ~!** ein bisschen schnell!

snapshot n Schnappschuss m

snare n Schlinge f

snarl vi [mit gefletschten Zähnen] knurren

snatch n (fragment) Fetzen pl ● vt schnappen; (steal) klauen; entführen <child>; **~ sth from s.o.** jdm etw entreißen

sneak n ⚠ Petze f ● vi schleichen; (⚠ tell tales) petzen ● vt (take) mitgehen lassen ● vi **~ in/out** sich hinein-/ hinausschleichen

sneakers npl (Amer) Turnschuhe pl

sneer vi höhnisch lächeln; (mock) spotten

sneeze n Niesen nt ● vi niesen

snide a ⚠ abfällig

sniff vi schnüffeln ● vt schnüffeln an (+ dat)

snigger vi [boshaft] kichern

snip n Schnitt m ● vt/i **~ [at]** schnippeln an (+ dat)

snippet n Schnipsel m; (of information) Bruchstück n

snivel vi (pt/pp snivelled) flennen

snob n Snob m. **~bery** n Snobismus m. **~bish** a snobistisch

snoop vi ⚠ schnüffeln

snooty a ⚠ hochnäsig

snooze n Nickerchen nt ● vi dösen

snore vi schnarchen

snorkel n Schnorchel m

snort vi schnauben

snout n Schnauze f

snow n Schnee m ● vi schneien; **~ed under with** (fig) überhäuft mit

snow: ~ball n Schneeball m. **~-drift** n Schneewehe f. **~drop** n Schneeglöckchen nt. **~fall** n Schneefall m. **~flake** n Schneeflocke f. **~man** n Schneemann m. **~plough** n Schneepflug m

snub n Abfuhr f ● vt (pt/pp snubbed) brüskieren

snub-nosed a stupsnasig

snuffle vi schnüffeln

snug a (snugger, snuggest) behaglich, gemütlich

snuggle vi sich kuscheln (**up to** an + acc)

so adv so; **so am I** ich auch; **so I see** das sehe ich; **that is so** das stimmt; **so much the better** umso besser; **if so** wenn ja; **so as to** um zu; **so long!** ⚠ tschüs! ● pron **I hope so** hoffentlich; **I think so** ich glaube schon; **I'm afraid so** leider ja; **so saying/doing, he/she …** indem er/sie das sagte/tat, … ● conj (therefore) also; **so that** damit; **so what!** na und! **so you see** wie du siehst

soak vt nass machen; (steep) einweichen; (⚠ fleece) schröpfen ● vi weichen; <liquid:> sickern. **~ up** vt aufsaugen

soaking a & adv **~ [wet]** patschnass ⚠

soap n Seife f. **~ opera** n Seifenoper f. **~ powder** n Seifenpulver nt

soapy a (-ier, -iest) seifig

soar vi aufsteigen; <prices:> in die Höhe schnellen

sob n Schluchzer m ● vi (pt/pp **sobbed**) schluchzen

sober a, **-ly** adv nüchtern; (serious) ernst; <colour> gedeckt. ~ **up** vi nüchtern werden

so-called a sogenannt

soccer n ⚀ Fußball m

sociable a gesellig

social a gesellschaftlich; (Admin, Pol, Zool) sozial

socialis|m n Sozialismus m. ~**t** a sozialistisch ● n Sozialist m

socialize vi [gesellschaftlich] verkehren

socially adv gesellschaftlich; **know** ~ privat kennen

social: ~ **security** n Sozialhilfe f. ~ **worker** n Sozialarbeiter(in) m(f)

society n Gesellschaft f; (club) Verein m

sociolog|ist n Soziologe m. ~**y** n Soziologie f

sock n Socke f; (kneelength) Kniestrumpf m

socket n (of eye) Augenhöhle f; (of joint) Gelenkpfanne f; (wall plug) Steckdose f

soda n Soda nt; (Amer) Limonade f. ~ **water** n Sodawasser nt

sodden a durchnässt

sofa n Sofa nt. ~ **bed** n Schlafcouch f

soft a (-er, -est), **-ly** adv weich; (quiet) leise; (gentle) sanft; (⚀ silly) dumm. ~ **drink** n alkoholfreies Getränk nt

soften vt weich machen; (fig) mildern ● vi weich werden

soft: ~ **toy** n Stofftier nt. ~**ware** n Software f

soggy a (-ier, -iest) aufgeweicht

soil[1] n Erde f, Boden m

soil[2] vt verschmutzen

solar a Sonnen-

sold see **sell**

soldier n Soldat m ● vi ~ **on** [unbeirrbar] weitermachen

sole[1] n Sohle f

sole[2] n (fish) Seezunge f

sole[3] a einzig. ~**ly** adv einzig und allein

solemn a, **-ly** adv feierlich; (serious) ernst

solicitor n Rechtsanwalt m/-anwältin f

solid a fest; (sturdy) stabil; (not hollow, of same substance) massiv; (unanimous) einstimmig; (complete) ganz

solidarity n Solidarität f

solidify vi (pt/pp **-ied**) fest werden

solitary a einsam; (sole) einzig

solitude n Einsamkeit f

solo n Solo nt ● a Solo-; <flight> Allein- ● adv solo. ~**ist** n Solist(in) m(f)

solstice n Sonnenwende f

soluble a löslich

solution n Lösung f

solvable a lösbar

solve vt lösen

solvent n Lösungsmittel nt

sombre a dunkel; <mood> düster

some a & pron etwas; (a little) ein bisschen; (with pl noun) einige; (a few) ein paar; (certain) manche(r,s); (one or the other) [irgend]ein; ~ **day** eines Tages; I **want** ~ ich möchte etwas/ (pl) welche; **will you have** ~ **wine?** möchten Sie Wein? **do** ~ **shopping** einkaufen

some: ~**body** pron & n jemand; (emphatic) irgendjemand. ~**how** adv irgendwie. ~**one** pron & n = somebody

somersault n Purzelbaum m ⚀; (Sport) Salto m; **turn a** ~ einen Purzelbaum schlagen/einen Salto springen

something pron & adv etwas; (emphatic) irgendetwas; ~ **different** etwas anderes; ~ **like this** so etwas [wie das]

some: ~**time** adv irgendwann ● a ehemalig. ~**times** adv manchmal.

S

~**what** adv ziemlich. ~**where** adv
irgendwo; <*go*> irgendwohin
son n Sohn m
song n Lied nt. ~**bird** n Singvogel
m
son-in-law n (pl ~**s-in-law**)
Schwiegersohn m
soon adv (-er, -est) bald; (*quickly*)
schnell; **too** ~ zu früh; **as** ~ **as
possible** so bald wie möglich; ~**er
or later** früher oder später; **no** ~**er
had I arrived than ...** kaum war ich
angekommen, da ...; **I would** ~**er
stay** ich würde lieber bleiben
soot n Ruß m
sooth|e vt beruhigen; lindern
<*pain*>. ~**ing** a, **-ly** adv
beruhigend; lindernd
sophisticated a weltgewandt;
(*complex*) hoch entwickelt
sopping a & adv ~ [**wet**]
durchnässt
soppy a (-ier, -iest) 🄸 rührselig
soprano n Sopran m; (*woman*)
Sopranistin f
sordid a schmutzig
sore a (-r, -st) wund; (*painful*)
schmerzhaft; **have a** ~ **throat**
Halsschmerzen haben ● n wunde
Stelle f. ~**ly** adv sehr
sorrow n Kummer m
sorry a (-ier, -iest) (*sad*) traurig;
(*wretched*) erbärmlich; **I am** ~ es
tut mir Leid; **she is** or **feels** ~ **for
him** er tut ihr Leid; **I am** ~ **to say**
leider; ~! Entschuldigung!
sort n Art f; (*brand*) Sorte f; **he's a
good** ~ 🄸 er ist in Ordnung ● vt
sortieren. ~ **out** vt sortieren; (*fig*)
klären
sought see **seek**
soul n Seele f
sound¹ a (-er, -est) gesund;
(*sensible*) vernünftig; (*secure*)
solide; (*thorough*) gehörig ● adv
be ~ **asleep** fest schlafen
sound² n (*strait*) Meerenge f
sound³ n Laut m; (*noise*)
Geräusch nt; (*Phys*) Schall m;

(*Radio, TV*) Ton m; (*of bells,
music*) Klang m; **I don't like the** ~
of it 🄸 das hört sich nicht gut an
● vi [er]tönen; (*seem*) sich
anhören ● vt (*pronounce*)
aussprechen; schlagen <*alarm*>;
(*Med*) abhorchen <*chest*>
soundly adv solide; <*sleep*> fest;
<*defeat*> vernichtend
soundproof a schalldicht
soup n Suppe f
sour a (-er, -est) sauer; (*bad-
tempered*) griesgrämig,
verdrießlich
source n Quelle f
south n Süden m; **to the** ~ **of**
südlich von ● a Süd-, süd- ● adv
nach Süden
south: S~ **Africa** n Südafrika nt.
S~ **America** n Südamerika nt.
~**-east** n Südosten m
southerly a südlich
southern a südlich
southward[s] adv nach Süden
souvenir n Andenken nt,
Souvenir nt
Soviet a <*History*> sowjetisch; ~
Union Sowjetunion f
sow¹ n Sau f
sow² vt (pt **sowed**, pp **sown** or
sowed) säen
soya n ~ **bean** Sojabohne f
spa n Heilbad nt
space n Raum m; (*gap*) Platz m;
(*Astr*) Weltraum m ● vt ~ [**out**]
[in Abständen] verteilen
space: ~**craft** n Raumfahrzeug
nt. ~**ship** n Raumschiff nt
spacious a geräumig
spade n Spaten m; (*for child*)
Schaufel f; ~**s** pl (*Cards*) Pik nt
Spain n Spanien nt
span¹ n Spanne f; (*of arch*)
Spannweite f ● vt (pt/pp
spanned) überspannen;
umspannen <*time*>
span² see **spick**
Span|iard n Spanier(in) m(f).
~**ish** a spanisch ● n (*Lang*)

Spanisch *nt;* **the** ~**ish** *pl* die
Spanier
spank *vt* verhauen
spanner *n* Schraubenschlüssel *m*
spare *a* (*surplus*) übrig;
(*additional*) zusätzlich; <*seat,
time*> frei; <*room*> Gäste-; <*bed,
cup*> Extra- ●*n* (*part*) Ersatzteil
nt ●*vt* ersparen; (*not hurt*)
verschonen; (*do without*)
entbehren; (*afford to give*)
erübrigen. ~ **wheel** *n* Reserverad
nt
sparing *a*, **-ly** *adv* sparsam
spark *n* Funke *nt.* ~**[ing]-plug** *n*
(*Auto*) Zündkerze *f*
sparkl|e *n* Funkeln *nt* ●*vi*
funkeln. ~**ing** *a* funkelnd;
<*wine*> Schaum-
sparrow *n* Spatz *m*
sparse *a* spärlich. ~**ly** *adv*
spärlich; <*populated*> dünn
spasm *n* Anfall *m;* (*cramp*)
Krampf *m.* ~**odic** *a*, **-ally** *adv*
sporadisch
spat *see* spit²
spatter *vt* spritzen; ~ **with**
bespritzen mit
spawn *n* Laich *m* ●*vt* (*fig*)
hervorbringen
speak *v* (*pt* **spoke**, *pp* **spoken**) ●*vi*
sprechen (**to** mit) ~**ing!** (*Teleph*)
am Apparat! ●*vt* sprechen;
sagen <*truth*>. ~ **up** *vi* lauter
sprechen; ~ **up for oneself** seine
Meinung äußern
speaker *n* Sprecher(in) *m(f);* (*in
public*) Redner(in) *m(f);*
(*loudspeaker*) Lautsprecher *m*
spear *n* Speer *m* ●*vt* aufspießen
spec *n* **on** ~ 🄳 auf gut Glück
special *a* besondere(r,s), speziell.
~**ist** *n* Spezialist *m;* (*Med*)
Facharzt *m*/-ärztin *f.* ~**ity** *n*
Spezialität *f*
special|ize *vi* sich spezialisieren
(**in** auf + *acc*). ~**ly** *adv* speziell;
(*particularly*) besonders
species *n* Art *f*

specific *a* bestimmt; (*precise*)
genau; (*Phys*) spezifisch. ~**ally**
adv ausdrücklich
specification *n &* ~**s** *pl* genaue
Angaben *pl*
specify *vt* (*pt/pp* **-ied**) [genau]
angeben
specimen *n* Exemplar *nt;*
(*sample*) Probe *f;* (*of urine*)
Urinprobe *f*
speck *n* Fleck *m*
speckled *a* gesprenkelt
spectacle *n* (*show*) Schauspiel
nt; (*sight*) Anblick *m.* ~**s** *npl*
Brille *f*
spectacular *a* spektakulär
spectator *n* Zuschauer(in) *m(f)*
speculat|e *vi* spekulieren. ~**ion** *n*
Spekulation *f.* ~**or** *n* Spekulant
m
sped *see* speed
speech *n* Sprache *f;* (*address*)
Rede *f.* ~**less** *a* sprachlos
speed *n* Geschwindigkeit *f;*
(*rapidity*) Schnelligkeit *f* ●*vi*
(*pt/pp* **sped**) schnell fahren
●(*pt/pp* **speeded**) (*go too fast*) zu
schnell fahren. ~ **up** (*pt/pp*
speeded up) ●*vt/i* beschleunigen
speed: ~**boat** *n* Rennboot *nt.* ~
camera *n* Geschwindigkeits-
überwachungskamera *f.* ~**ing** *n*
Geschwindigkeitsüberschreitung
f. ~ **limit** *n* Geschwindigkeits-
beschränkung *f*
speedometer *n* Tachometer *m*
speedy *a* (**-ier, -iest**), **-ily** *adv*
schnell
spell¹ *n* Weile *f;* (*of weather*)
Periode *f*
spell² *v* (*pt/pp* **spelled** or **spelt**)
●*vt* schreiben; (*aloud*)
buchstabieren; (*fig: mean*)
bedeuten ●*vi* richtig schreiben;
(*aloud*) buchstabieren. ~ **out** *vt*
buchstabieren; (*fig*) genau
erklären

S

spell[3] n Zauber m; (words)
Zauberspruch m. ~**bound** a wie
verzaubert
spell checker n
Rechtschreibprogramm nt
spelling n (of a word)
Schreibweise f; (orthography)
Rechtschreibung f
spelt see **spell**[2]
spend vt/i (pt/pp spent) ausgeben;
verbringen <time>
spent see **spend**
sperm n Samen m
sphere n Kugel f; (fig) Sphäre f
spice n Gewürz nt; (fig) Würze f
spicy a würzig, pikant
spider n Spinne f
spik|e n Spitze f; (Bot, Zool)
Stachel m; (on shoe) Spike m. ~**y**
a stachelig
spill v (pt/pp spilt or spilled) ● vt
verschütten ● vi überlaufen
spin v (pt/pp spun, pres p
spinning) ● vt drehen; spinnen
<wool>; schleudern <washing>
● vi sich drehen
spinach n Spinat m
spindl|e n Spindel f. ~**y** a
spindeldürr
spin-drier n Wäscheschleuder f
spine n Rückgrat nt; (of book)
[Buch]rücken m; (Bot, Zool)
Stachel m. ~**less** a (fig)
rückgratlos
spin-off n Nebenprodukt nt
spinster n ledige Frau f
spiral a spiralig ● n Spirale f ● vi
(pt/pp spiralled) sich hochwinden.
~ **staircase** n Wendeltreppe f
spire n Turmspitze f
spirit n Geist m; (courage) Mut m;
~**s** pl (alcohol) Spirituosen pl; in
low ~**s** niedergedrückt. ~ **away**
vt verschwinden lassen
spirited a lebhaft; (courageous)
beherzt
spiritual a geistig; (Relig) geistlich
spit[1] n (for meat) [Brat]spieß m

spit[2] n Spucke f ● vt/i (pt/pp spat,
pres p spitting) spucken; <cat:>
fauchen; <fat:> spritzen; **it's**
~**ting with rain** es tröpfelt
spite n Boshaftigkeit f; in ~ of
trotz (+ gen) ● vt ärgern. ~**ful** a,
-**ly** adv gehässig
splash n Platschen nt; (I drop)
Schuss m; ~ **of colour** Farbfleck
m ● vt spritzen; ~ **s.o. with sth**
jdn mit etw bespritzen ● vi
spritzen. ~ **about** vi planschen
splendid a herrlich, großartig
splendour n Pracht f
splint n (Med) Schiene f
splinter n Splitter m ● vi
zersplittern
split n Spaltung f; (Pol) Bruch m;
(tear) Riss m ● v (pt/pp split, pres
p splitting) ● vt spalten; (share)
teilen; (tear) zerreißen ● vi sich
spalten; (tear) zerreißen; ~ **on
s.o.** I jdn verpfeifen. ~ **up** vt
aufteilen ● vi <couple:> sich
trennen
splutter vi prusten
spoil n ~**s** pl Beute f ● v (pt/pp
spoilt or spoiled) ● vt verderben;
verwöhnen <person> ● vi
verderben. ~**sport** n
Spielverderber m
spoke[1] n Speiche f
spoke[2], **spoken** see **speak**
spokesman n Sprecher m
sponge n Schwamm m ● vt
abwaschen ● vi ~ on
schmarotzen bei. ~-**cake** n
Biskuitkuchen m
sponsor n Sponsor m;
(godparent) Pate m/Patin f ● vt
sponsern
spontaneous a, -**ly** adv spontan
spoof n I Parodie f
spooky a (-ier, -iest) I
gespenstisch
spool n Spule f
spoon n Löffel m ● vt löffeln.
~**ful** n Löffel m
sporadic a, -**ally** adv sporadisch

sport n Sport m ● vt [stolz] tragen. ~**ing** a sportlich

sports: ~ **car** n Sportwagen m. ~ **coat** n, ~ **jacket** n Sakko m. ~**man** n Sportler m. ~**woman** n Sportlerin f

sporty a (-ier, -iest) sportlich

spot n Fleck m; (place) Stelle f (dot) Punkt m; (drop) Tropfen m; (pimple) Pickel m; ~s pl (rash) Ausschlag m; **on the** ~ auf der Stelle ● vt (pt/pp **spotted**) entdecken

spot: ~ **check** n Stichprobe f. ~**less** a makellos; (Ⅱ very clean) blitzsauber. ~**light** n Scheinwerfer m; (fig) Rampenlicht nt

spotted a gepunktet

spouse n Gatte m/Gattin f

spout n Schnabel m, Tülle f ● vi schießen (**from** aus)

sprain n Verstauchung f ● vt verstauchen

sprang see **spring²**

sprawl vi sich ausstrecken

spray¹ n (of flowers) Strauß m

spray² n Sprühnebel m; (from sea) Gischt m; (device) Spritze f; (container) Sprühdose f; (preparation) Spray nt ● vt spritzen; (with aerosol) sprühen

spread n Verbreitung f; (paste) Aufstrich m; (Ⅱ feast) Festessen nt ● v (pt/pp **spread**) ● vt ausbreiten; streichen <butter, jam>; bestreichen <bread, surface>; streuen <sand, manure>; verbreiten <news, disease>; verteilen <payments> ● vi sich ausbreiten. ~ **out** vt ausbreiten; (space out) verteilen ● vi sich verteilen

spree n Ⅱ **go on a shopping** ~ groß einkaufen gehen

sprightly a (-ier, -iest) rüstig

spring¹ n Frühling m ● attrib Frühlings-

spring² n (jump) Sprung m; (water) Quelle f; (device) Feder f; (elasticity) Elastizität f ● v (pt sprang, pp sprung) ● vi springen; (arise) entspringen (**from** dat) ● vt ~ **sth on** s.o. jdn mit etw überfallen

spring: ~-**cleaning** n Frühjahrsputz m. ~**time** n Frühling m

sprinkl|e vt sprengen; (scatter) streuen; bestreuen <surface>. ~**ing** n dünne Schicht f

sprint n Sprint m ● vi rennen; (Sport) sprinten. ~**er** n Kurzstreckenläufer(in) m(f)

sprout n Trieb m; [**Brussels**] ~s pl Rosenkohl m ● vi sprießen

sprung see **spring²**

spud n Ⅱ Kartoffel f

spun see **spin**

spur n Sporn m; (stimulus) Ansporn m; **on the** ~ **of the moment** ganz spontan ● vt (pt/pp **spurred**) ~ [**on**] (fig) anspornen

spurn vt verschmähen

spurt n (Sport) Spurt m; **put on a** ~ spurten ● vi spritzen

spy n Spion(in) m(f) ● vi spionieren; ~ **on** s.o. jdm nachspionieren. ● vt (Ⅱ see) sehen

spying n Spionage f

squabble n Zank m ● vi sich zanken

squad n Gruppe f; (Sport) Mannschaft f

squadron n (Mil) Geschwader nt

squalid a, -**ly** adv schmutzig

squall n Bö f ● vi brüllen

squalor n Schmutz m

squander vt vergeuden

square a quadratisch; <metre, mile> Quadrat-; <meal> anständig; **all** ~ Ⅱ quitt ● n Quadrat nt; (area) Platz m; (on chessboard) Feld nt ● vt (settle) klären; (Math) quadrieren

S

squash n Gedränge nt; (drink) Fruchtsaftgetränk nt; (Sport) Squash nt ● vt zerquetschen; (suppress) niederschlagen. ~y a weich

squat a gedrungen ● vi (pt/pp **squatted**) hocken; ~ **in a house** ein Haus besetzen. ~**ter** n Hausbesetzer m

squawk vi krächzen

squeak n Quieken nt; (of hinge, brakes) Quietschen nt ● vi quieken; quietschen

squeal n Kreischen nt ● vi kreischen

squeamish a empfindlich

squeeze n Druck m; (crush) Gedränge nt ● vt drücken; (to get juice) ausdrücken; (force) zwängen

squiggle n Schnörkel m

squint n Schielen nt ● vi schielen

squirm vi sich winden

squirrel n Eichhörnchen nt

squirt n Spritzer m ● vt/i spritzen

St abbr (**Saint**) St.; (**Street**) Str.

stab n Stich m; (🔲 attempt) Versuch m ● vt (pt/pp **stabbed**) stechen; (to death) erstechen

stability n Stabilität f

stable¹ a (-r, -st) stabil

stable² n Stall m; (establishment) Reitstall m

stack n Stapel m; (of chimney) Schornstein m ● vt stapeln

stadium n Stadion nt

staff n (stick & Mil) Stab m ● (& pl) (employees) Personal nt; (Sch) Lehrkräfte pl ● vt mit Personal besetzen. ~**room** n (Sch) Lehrerzimmer nt

stag n Hirsch m

stage n Bühne f; (in journey) Etappe f; (in process) Stadium nt; **by** or **in** ~**s** in Etappen ● vt aufführen; (arrange) veranstalten

stagger vi taumeln ● vt staffeln <holidays>; versetzt anordnen <seats>; **I was** ~**ed** es hat mir die Sprache verschlagen. ~**ing** a unglaublich

stagnant a stehend; (fig) stagnierend

stagnate vi (fig) stagnieren

stain n Fleck m; (for wood) Beize f ● vt färben; beizen <wood>; ~**ed glass** farbiges Glas nt. ~**less** a <steel> rostfrei

stair n Stufe f; ~**s** pl Treppe f. ~**case** n Treppe f

stake n Pfahl m; (wager) Einsatz m; (Comm) Anteil m; **be at** ~ auf dem Spiel stehen ● vt ~ **a claim to sth** Anspruch auf etw (acc) erheben

stale a (-r, -st) alt; <air> verbraucht. ~**mate** n Patt nt

stalk¹ n Stiel m, Stängel m

stall n Stand m; ~**s** pl (Theat) Parkett nt ● vi <engine:> stehen bleiben; (fig) ausweichen ● vt abwürgen <engine>

stalwart a treu ● n treuer Anhänger m

stamina n Ausdauer f

stammer n Stottern nt ● vt/i stottern

stamp n Stempel m; (postage ~) [Brief]marke f ● vt stempeln; (impress) prägen; (put postage on) frankieren ● vi stampfen. ~ **out** vt [aus]stanzen; (fig) ausmerzen

stampede n wilde Flucht f ● vi in Panik fliehen

stance n Haltung f

stand n Stand m; (rack) Ständer m; (pedestal) Sockel m; (Sport) Tribüne f; (fig) Einstellung f ● v (pt/pp **stood**) ● vi stehen; (rise) aufstehen; (be candidate) kandidieren; (stay valid) gültig bleiben; ~ **still** stillstehen; ~ **firm** (fig) festbleiben; ~ **to reason** logisch sein; ~ **in for** vertreten; ~ **for** (mean) bedeuten ● vt stellen; (withstand) standhalten (+ dat); (endure) ertragen; vertragen

\<climate\>; (put up with)
aushalten; haben \<chance\>; ~
s.o. a beer jdm ein Bier
spendieren; I can't ~ her 🗓 ich
kann sie nicht ausstehen. ~ by vi
danebenstehen; (be ready) sich
bereithalten ●vt ~ by s.o. (fig)
zu jdm stehen. ~ down vi (retire)
zurücktreten. ~ out vi
hervorstehen; (fig) herausragen.
~ up vi aufstehen; ~ up for
eintreten für; ~ up to sich
wehren gegen

standard a Normal- ●n Maßstab
m; (Techn) Norm f; (level) Niveau
nt; (flag) Standarte f; ~s pl
(morals) Prinzipien pl. ~ize vt
standardisieren; (Techn) normen
stand-in n Ersatz m
standing a (erect) stehend;
(permanent) ständig ●n Rang m;
(duration) Dauer f. ~-room n
Stehplätze pl
stand: ~-offish a distanziert.
~point n Standpunkt m. ~still n
Stillstand m; come to a ~still zum
Stillstand kommen
stank see stink
staple¹ a Grund-
staple² n Heftklammer f ●vt
heften. ~r n Heftmaschine f
star n Stern m; (asterisk)
Sternchen nt; (Theat, Sport) Star
m ●vi (pt/pp starred) die
Hauptrolle spielen
starboard n Steuerbord nt
starch n Stärke f ●vt stärken. ~y
a stärkehaltig; (fig) steif
stare n Starren nt ●vt starren; ~
at anstarren
stark a (-er, -est) scharf;
\<contrast\> krass
starling n Star m
start n Anfang m, Beginn m;
(departure) Aufbruch m; (Sport)
Start m; from the ~ von Anfang
an; for a ~ erstens ●vi anfangen,
beginnen; (set out) aufbrechen;
\<engine:\> anspringen; (Auto,

Sport) starten; (jump)
aufschrecken; to ~ with zuerst
●vt anfangen, beginnen; (cause)
verursachen; (found) gründen;
starten \<car, race\>; in Umlauf
setzen \<rumour\>. ~er n (Culin)
Vorspeise f; (Auto, Sport) Starter
m. ~ing-point n Ausgangspunkt
m
startle vt erschrecken
starvation n Verhungern nt
starve vi hungern; (to death)
verhungern ●vt verhungern
lassen
state n Zustand m; (Pol) Staat m;
~ of play Spielstand m; be in a ~
\<person:\> aufgeregt sein ●attrib
Staats-, staatlich ●vt erklären;
(specify) angeben
stately a (-ier, -iest) stattlich. ~
home n Schloss nt
statement n Erklärung f; (Jur)
Aussage f; (Banking) Auszug m
statesman n Staatsmann m
static a statisch; remain ~
unverändert bleiben
station n Bahnhof m; (police)
Wache f; (radio) Sender m;
(space, weather) Station f; (Mil)
Posten m; (status) Rang m ●vt
stationieren; (post) postieren.
~ary a stehend; be ~ary stehen
stationery n Briefpapier nt;
(writing materials) Schreibwaren
pl
station-wagon n (Amer)
Kombi[wagen] n
statistic n statistische Tatsache f.
~al a, -ly adv statistisch. ~s n &
pl Statistik f
statue n Statue f
stature n Statur f; (fig) Format nt
status n Status m, Rang m
statut|e n Statut nt. ~ory a
gesetzlich
staunch a (-er, -est), -ly adv treu
stave vt ~ off abwenden
stay n Aufenthalt m ●vi bleiben;
(reside) wohnen; ~ the night

übernachten. ~ **behind** vi
zurückbleiben. ~ **in** vi zu Hause
bleiben; (Sch) nachsitzen. ~ **up**
vi <person:> aufbleiben

steadily adv fest; (continually)
stetig

steady a (-ier, -iest) fest; (not
wobbly) stabil; <hand> ruhig;
(regular) regelmäßig;
(dependable) zuverlässig

steak n Steak nt

steal vt/i (pt **stole**, pp **stolen**)
stehlen (**from** dat). ~ **in/out** vi
sich hinein-/hinausstehlen

stealthy a heimlich

steam n Dampf m ● vt (Culin)
dämpfen, dünsten ● vi dampfen.
~ **up** vi beschlagen

steam engine n Dampfmaschine
f; (Rail) Dampflokomotive f

steamer n Dampfer m

steamy a dampfig

steel n Stahl m

steep a, -**ly** adv steil; (🛈
exorbitant) gesalzen

steeple n Kirchturm m

steer vt/i (Auto) lenken; (Naut)
steuern; ~ **clear of s.o./sth** jdm/
etw aus dem Weg gehen. ~**ing** n
(Auto) Lenkung f. ~**ing-wheel** n
Lenkrad nt

stem[1] n Stiel m; (of word) Stamm
m

stem[2] vt (pt/pp **stemmed**)
eindämmen; stillen <bleeding>

stench n Gestank m

stencil n Schablone f

step n Schritt m; (stair) Stufe f;
~**s** pl (ladder) Trittleiter f; **in** ~
im Schritt; ~ **by** ~ Schritt für
Schritt; **take** ~**s** (fig) Schritte
unternehmen ● vi (pt/pp **stepped**)
treten; ~ **in** (fig) eingreifen. ~ **up**
vt (increase) erhöhen, steigen;
verstärken <efforts>

step: ~**brother** n Stiefbruder m.
~**child** n Stiefkind nt. ~**daughter**
n Stieftochter f. ~**father** n
Stiefvater m. ~**ladder** n

Trittleiter f. ~**mother** n
Stiefmutter f. ~**sister** n
Stiefschwester f. ~**son** n
Stiefsohn m

stereo n Stereo nt; (equipment)
Stereoanlage f. ~**phonic** a
stereophon

stereotype n stereotype Figur f

steril|e a steril. ~**ize** vt
sterilisieren

sterling a Sterling-; (fig) gediegen
● n Sterling m

stern[1] a (-er, -est), -**ly** adv streng

stern[2] n (of boat) Heck nt

stew n Eintopf m; **in a** ~ 🛈
aufgeregt ● vt/i schmoren; ~**ed**
fruit Kompott nt

steward n Ordner m; (on ship,
aircraft) Steward m. ~**ess** n
Stewardess f

stick[1] n Stock m; (of chalk) Stück
nt; (of rhubarb) Stange f; (Sport)
Schläger m

stick[2] v (pt/pp **stuck**) ● vt stecken;
(stab) stechen; (glue) kleben; (🛈
put) tun; (🛈 endure) aushalten
● vi stecken; (adhere) kleben,
haften (**to** an + dat); (jam)
klemmen; ~ **at it** 🛈 dranbleiben;
~ **up for** 🛈 eintreten für; **be stuck**
nicht weiterkönnen; <vehicle:>
festsitzen, festgefahren sein;
<drawer:> klemmen; **be stuck with**
sth 🛈 etw am Hals haben. ~ **out**
vi abstehen; (project) vorstehen
● vt hinausstrecken;
herausstrecken <tongue>

sticker n Aufkleber m

sticking plaster n Heftpflaster nt

sticky a (-ier, -iest) klebrig;
(adhesive) Klebe-

stiff a (-er, -est), -**ly** adv steif;
<brush> hart; <dough> fest;
(difficult) schwierig; <penalty>
schwer; **be bored** ~ 🛈 sich zu
Tode langweilen. ~**en** vt steif
machen ● vi steif werden. ~**ness**
n Steifheit f

stifl|e vt ersticken; (fig) unterdrücken. **~ing** a be **~ing** zum Ersticken sein

still a still; *<drink>* ohne Kohlensäure; **keep ~** stillhalten; **stand ~** stillstehen ● adv noch; (emphatic) immer noch; (nevertheless) trotzdem; **~ not** immer noch nicht

stillborn a tot geboren

still life n Stilleben nt

stilted a gestelzt, geschraubt

stimulant n Anregungsmittel nt

stimulat|e vt anregen. **~ion** n Anregung f

stimulus n (pl **-li**) Reiz m

sting n Stich m; (from nettle, jellyfish) Brennen nt; (organ) Stachel m ● v (pt/pp **stung**) vt stechen ● vi brennen; *<insect:>* stechen

stingy a (**-ier, -iest**) geizig, ☐ knauserig

stink n Gestank m ● vi (pt **stank**, pp **stunk**) stinken (**of** nach)

stipulat|e vt vorschreiben. **~ion** n Bedingung f

stir n (commotion) Aufregung f ● v (pt/pp **stirred**) vt rühren ● vi sich rühren

stirrup n Steigbügel m

stitch n Stich m; (Knitting) Masche f; (pain) Seitenstechen nt; **be in ~es** ☐ sich kaputtlachen ● vt nähen

stock n Vorrat m (**of** an + dat); (in shop) [Waren]bestand m; (livestock) Vieh nt; (lineage) Abstammung f; (Finance) Wertpapiere pl; (Culin) Brühe f; (plant) Levkoje f; **in/out of ~** vorrätig/nicht vorrätig; **take ~** (fig) Bilanz ziehen ● a Standard- ● vt *<shop:>* führen; auffüllen *<shelves>*. **~ up** vi sich eindecken (**with** mit)

stock: ~broker n Börsenmakler m. **S~ Exchange** n Börse f

stocking n Strumpf m

stock: ~market n Börse f. **~taking** n (Comm) Inventur f

stocky a (**-ier, -iest**) untersetzt

stodgy a pappig [und schwer verdaulich]

stoke vt heizen

stole, stolen see **steal**

stomach n Magen m. **~ache** n Magenschmerzen pl

stone n Stein m; (weight) 6,35kg ● a steinern; *<wall, Age>* Stein- ● vt mit Steinen bewerfen; entsteinen *<fruit>*. **~-cold** a eiskalt. **~-deaf** n ☐ stocktaub

stony a steinig

stood see **stand**

stool n Hocker m

stoop n **walk with a ~** gebeugt gehen ● vi sich bücken

stop n Halt m; (break) Pause f; (for bus) Haltestelle f; (for train) Station f; (Gram) Punkt m; (on organ) Register nt; **come to a ~** stehen bleiben; **put a ~ to sth** etw unterbinden ● v (pt/pp **stopped**) ● vt anhalten, stoppen; (switch off) abstellen; (plug, block) zustopfen; (prevent) verhindern; **~ s.o. doing sth** jdn daran hindern, etw zu tun; **~ doing sth** aufhören, etw zu tun; **~ that!** hör auf damit! ● vi anhalten; (cease) aufhören; *<clock:>* stehen bleiben ● int halt!

stop: ~gap n Notlösung f. **~over** n (Aviat) Zwischenlandung f

stoppage n Unterbrechung f; (strike) Streik m

stopper n Stöpsel m

stop-watch n Stoppuhr f

storage n Aufbewahrung f; (in warehouse) Lagerung f; (Computing) Speicherung f

store n (stock) Vorrat m; (shop) Laden m; (department ~) Kaufhaus nt; (depot) Lager nt; **in ~** auf Lager; **be in ~ for s.o.** (fig) jdm bevorstehen ● vt aufbewahren; (in warehouse)

S

lagern; (*Computing*) speichern.
~-**room** n Lagerraum m
storey n Stockwerk nt
stork n Storch m
storm n Sturm m; (*with thunder*)
Gewitter nt ● vt/i stürmen. ~y a
stürmisch
story n Geschichte f; (*in
·newspaper*) Artikel m; (🛈 *lie*)
Märchen nt
stout a (-**er**, -**est**) beleibt; (*strong*)
fest
stove n Ofen m; (*for cooking*)
Herd m
stow vt verstauen. ~**away** n
blinder Passagier m
straggl|e vi hinterherhinken. ~**er**
n Nachzügler m. ~y a strähnig
straight a (-**er**, -**est**) gerade;
(*direct*) direkt; (*clear*) klar;
<*hair*> glatt; <*drink*>; pur; **be** ~
(*tidy*) in Ordnung sein ● adv
gerade; (*directly*) direkt,
geradewegs; (*clearly*) klar; ~
away sofort; ~ **on** or **ahead**
geradeaus; ~ **out** (*fig*)
geradeheraus; **sit/stand up** ~
gerade sitzen/stehen
straighten vt gerade machen;
(*put straight*) gerade richten ● vi
gerade werden; ~ [**up**] <*person:*>
sich aufrichten. ~ **out** vt gerade
biegen
straightforward a offen; (*simple*)
einfach
strain n Belastung f; ~**s** pl (*of
music*) Klänge pl ● vt belasten;
(*overexert*) überanstrengen;
(*injure*) zerren <*muscle*>; (*Culin*)
durchseihen; abgießen
<*vegetables*>. ~**ed** a <*relations*>
gespannt. ~**er** n Sieb nt
strait n Meerenge f; **in dire** ~**s** in
großen Nöten
strand¹ n (*of thread*) Faden m; (*of
hair*) Strähne f
strand² vt **be** ~**ed** festsitzen
strange a (-**r**, -**st**) fremd; (*odd*)
seltsam, merkwürdig. ~**ly** adv

seltsam, merkwürdig; ~ **enough**
seltsamerweise. ~**r** n Fremde(r)
m/f
strangle vt erwürgen; (*fig*)
unterdrücken
strap n Riemen m; (*for safety*)
Gurt m; (*to grasp in vehicle*)
Halteriemen m; (*of watch*)
Armband nt; (*shoulder* ~) Träger
m ● vt (*pt/pp* **strapped**) schnallen
strapping a stramm
strategic a, -**ally** adv strategisch
strategy n Strategie f
straw n Stroh nt; (*single piece,
drinking*) Strohhalm m; **that's the
last** ~ jetzt reicht's aber
strawberry n Erdbeere f
stray a streunend ● n
streunendes Tier nt ● vi sich
verirren; (*deviate*) abweichen
streak n Streifen m; (*in hair*)
Strähne f; (*fig: trait*) Zug m
stream n Bach m; (*flow*) Strom m;
(*current*) Strömung f; (*Sch*)
Parallelzug m ● vi strömen
streamline vt (*fig*) rationalisieren.
~**d** a stromlinienförmig
street n Straße f. ~**car** n (*Amer*)
Straßenbahn f. ~**lamp** n
Straßenlaterne f
strength n Stärke f; (*power*) Kraft
f; **on the** ~ auf Grund (+ *gen*).
~**en** vt stärken; (*reinforce*)
verstärken
strenuous a anstrengend
stress n (*emphasis*) Betonung f;
(*strain*) Belastung f; (*mental*)
Stress m ● vt betonen; (*put a
strain on*) belasten. ~**ful** a
stressig 🛈
stretch n (*of road*) Strecke f;
(*elasticity*) Elastizität f; **at a** ~
ohne Unterbrechung; **have a** ~
sich strecken ● vt strecken;
(*widen*) dehnen; (*spread*)
ausbreiten; fordern <*person*>; ~
one's legs sich (*dat*) die Beine
vertreten ● vt sich erstrecken;
(*become wider*) sich dehnen;

<person:> sich strecken. **~er** *n* Tragbahre *f*

strict *a* (-er, -est), **-ly** *adv* streng; **~ly speaking** streng genommen

stride *n* [großer] Schritt *m*; **take sth in one's ~** mit etw gut fertig werden ● *vi* (*pt* **strode**, *pp* **stridden**) [mit großen Schritten] gehen

strident *a*, **-ly** *adv* schrill; *<colour>* grell

strife *n* Streit *m*

strike *n* Streik *m*; (*Mil*) Angriff *m*; **be on ~** streiken ● *v* (*pt/pp* **struck**) ● *vt* schlagen; (*knock against, collide with*) treffen; anzünden *<match>*; stoßen auf (+ *acc*) *<oil, gold>*; abbrechen *<camp>*; (*impress*) beeindrucken; (*occur to*) einfallen (+ *dat*); **~ s.o. a blow** jdm einen Schlag versetzen ● *vi* treffen; *<lightning:>* einschlagen; *<clock:>* schlagen; (*attack*) zuschlagen; *<workers:>* streiken

striker *n* Streikende(r) *m/f*

striking *a* auffallend

string *n* Schnur *f*; (*thin*) Bindfaden *m*; (*of musical instrument, racket*) Saite *f*; (*of bow*) Sehne *f*; (*of pearls*) Kette *f*; **the ~s** (*Mus*) die Streicher *pl*; **pull ~s** 🛈 seine Beziehungen spielen lassen ● *vt* (*pt/pp* **strung**) (*thread*) aufziehen *<beads>*

stringent *a* streng

strip *n* Streifen *m* ● *v* (*pt/pp* **stripped**) ● *vt* ablösen; ausziehen *<person, clothes>*; abziehen *<bed>*; abbeizen *<wood, furniture>*; auseinander nehmen *<machine>*; (*deprive*) berauben (*of gen*); **~ sth off sth** etw von etw entfernen ● *vi* (*undress*) sich ausziehen

stripe *n* Streifen *m*. **~d** *a* gestreift

stripper *n* Stripperin *f*; (*male*) Stripper *m*

strive *vi* (*pt* **strove**, *pp* **striven**) sich bemühen (**to** zu); **~ for** streben nach

strode *see* **stride**

stroke[1] *n* Schlag *m*; (*of pen*) Strich *m*; (*Swimming*) Zug *m*; (*style*) Stil *m*; (*Med*) Schlaganfall *m*; **~ of luck** Glücksfall *m*

stroke[2] ● *vt* streicheln

stroll *n* Bummel *m* 🛈 ● *vi* bummeln 🛈. **~er** *n* (*Amer: pushchair*) [Kinder]sportwagen *m*

strong *a* (-er, -est), **-ly** *adv* stark; (*powerful, healthy*) kräftig; (*severe*) streng; (*sturdy*) stabil; (*convincing*) gut

strong: **~hold** *n* Festung *f*; (*fig*) Hochburg *f*. **~-room** *n* Tresorraum *m*

strove *see* **strive**

struck *see* **strike**

structural *a*, **-ly** *adv* baulich

structure *n* Struktur *f*; (*building*) Bau *m*

struggle *n* Kampf *m*; **with a ~** mit Mühe ● *vt* kämpfen; **~ to do sth** sich abmühen, etw zutun

strum *v* (*pt/pp* **strummed**) ● *vt* klimpern auf (+ *dat*) ● *vi* klimpern

strung *see* **string**

strut[1] *n* Strebe *f*

strut[2] *vi* (*pt/pp* **strutted**) stolzieren

stub *n* Stummel *m*; (*counterfoil*) Abschnitt *m*. **~ out** *vt* (*pt/pp* **stubbed**) ausdrücken *<cigarette>*

stubble *n* Stoppeln *pl*

stubborn *a*, **-ly** *adv* starrsinnig; *<refusal>* hartnäckig

stubby *a*, (-ier, -iest) kurz und dick

stuck *see* **stick**[2]. **~-up** *a* 🛈 hochnäsig

stud *n* Nagel *m*; (*on clothes*) Niete *f*; (*for collar*) Kragenknopf *m*; (*for ear*) Ohrstecker *m*

student *n* Student(in) *m(f)*; (*Sch*) Schüler(in) *m(f)*

S

studio n Studio nt; (for artist) Atelier nt

studious a lerneifrig; (earnest) ernsthaft

stud|y n Studie f; (room) Arbeitszimmer nt; (investigation) Untersuchung f; ~ies pl Studium nt ● v (pt/pp studied) ● vt studieren; (examine) untersuchen ● vi lernen; (at university) studieren

stuff n Stoff m; (🛈 things) Zeug nt ● vt vollstopfen; (with padding, Culin) füllen; ausstopfen <animal>; (cram) [hinein]stopfen. ~ing n Füllung f

stuffy a (-ier, -iest) stickig; (old-fashioned) spießig

stumbl|e vi stolpern; ~e across zufällig stoßen auf (+ acc). ~ing-block n Hindernis nt

stump n Stumpf m ● ~ up vt/i 🛈 blechen. ~ed a 🛈 überfragt

stun vt (pt/pp stunned) betäuben

stung see sting

stunk see stink

stunning a 🛈 toll

stunt n 🛈 Kunststück nt

stupendous a, -ly adv enorm

stupid a dumm. ~ity n Dummheit f. ~ly adv dumm; ~ly [enough] dummerweise

sturdy a (-ier, -iest) stämmig; <furniture> stabil; <shoes> fest

stutter n Stottern nt ● vt/i stottern

sty n (pl sties) Schweinestall m

style n Stil m; (fashion) Mode f; (sort) Art f; (hair~) Frisur f; in ~ in großem Stil

stylish a, -ly adv stilvoll

stylist n Friseur m/ Friseuse f. ~ic a, -ally adv stilistisch

suave a (pej) gewandt

subconscious a, -ly adv unterbewusst ● n Unterbewusstsein nt

subdivi|de vt unterteilen. ~sion n Unterteilung f

subdue vt unterwerfen. ~d a gedämpft; <person> still

subject¹ a be ~ to sth etw (dat) unterworfen sein ● n Staatsbürger(in) m(f); (of ruler) Untertan m; (theme) Thema nt; (of investigation) Gegenstand m; (Sch) Fach nt; (Gram) Subjekt nt

subject² vt unterwerfen (to dat); (expose) aussetzen (to dat)

subjective a, -ly adv subjektiv

subjunctive n Konjunktiv m

sublime a, -ly adv erhaben

submarine n Unterseeboot nt

submerge vt untertauchen; be ~d unter Wasser stehen ● vi tauchen

submission n Unterwerfung f

submit v (pt/pp -mitted, pres p -mitting) ● vt vorlegen (to dat); (hand in) einreichen ● vi sich unterwerfen (to dat)

subordinate¹ a untergeordnet ● n Untergebene(r) m/f

subordinate² vt unterordnen (to dat)

subscribe vi spenden; ~ to (fig); abonnieren <newspaper>. ~r n Spender m; Abonnent m

subscription n (to club) [Mitglieds]beitrag m; (to newspaper) Abonnement nt; by ~ mit Spenden; <buy> im Abonnement

subsequent a, -ly adv folgend; (later) später

subside vi sinken; <ground:> sich senken; <storm:> nachlassen

subsidiary a untergeordnet ● n Tochtergesellschaft f

subsid|ize vt subventionieren. ~y n Subvention f

substance n Substanz f

substandard a unzulänglich; <goods> minderwertig

substantial a solide; <meal> reichhaltig; (considerable) beträchtlich. ~ly adv solide; (essentially) im Wesentlichen

substitut|e n Ersatz m; (Sport)
Ersatzspieler(in) m(f) ● vt ~e A
for B B durch A ersetzen ● vi ~e
for s.o. jdn vertreten. ~ion n
Ersetzung f
subterranean a unterirdisch
subtitle n Untertitel m
subtle a (-r, -st), -tly adv fein; (fig)
subtil
subtract vt abziehen,
subtrahieren. ~ion n Subtraktion
f
suburb n Vorort m. ~an a
Vorort-. ~ia n die Vororte pl
subway n Unterführung f; (Amer:
railway) U-Bahn f
succeed vi Erfolg haben; <plan:>
gelingen; (follow) nachfolgen (+
dat); **I ~ed** es ist mir gelungen; **he
~ed in escaping** es gelang ihm zu
entkommen ● vt folgen (+ dat)
success n Erfolg m. ~ful a,-ly
adv erfolgreich
succession n Folge f; (series)
Serie f; (to title, office) Nachfolge
f; (to throne) Thronfolge f; **in ~**
hintereinander
successive a aufeinander
folgend
successor n Nachfolger(in) m(f)
succumb vi erliegen (to dat)

such
● adjective
····▸ (of that kind) solch. **such a
book** ein solches Buch; so ein
Buch 🔢. **such a person** ein
solcher Mensch; so ein Mensch
🔢. **such people** solche Leute.
such a thing so etwas. **no such
example** kein solches Beispiel.
there is no such thing so etwas
gibt es nicht; das gibt es gar
nicht. **there is no such person**
eine solche Person gibt es nicht.
**such writers as Goethe and
Schiller** Schriftsteller wie Goethe
und Schiller

····▸ (so great) solch; derartig. **I've
got such a headache!** ich habe
solche Kopfschmerzen! **it was
such fun!** das machte solchen
Spaß! **I got such a fright that ...**
ich bekam einen derartigen od
🔢 so einen Schrecken, dass ...
····▸ (with adjective) so. **such a big
house** ein so großes Haus. **he
has such lovely blue eyes** er hat
so schöne blaue Augen. **such a
long time** so lange
● pronoun
····▸ **as such** als solcher/solche/
solches. **the thing as such** die
Sache als solche. (strictly
speaking) **this is not a promotion
as such** dies ist im Grunde
genommen keine Beförderung
····▸ **such is: such is life** so ist das
Leben. **such is not the case** das
ist nicht der Fall
····▸ **such as** wie [zum Beispiel]

suchlike pron 🔢 dergleichen
suck vt/i saugen; lutschen
<sweet>. **~ up** vt aufsaugen ● vi
~ up to s.o. 🔢 sich bei jdm
einschmeicheln
suction n Saugwirkung f
sudden a, -ly adv plötzlich;
(abrupt) jäh ● n **all of a ~** auf
einmal
sue vt (pres p suing) verklagen
(for auf + acc) ● vi klagen
suede n Wildleder nt
suet n [Nieren]talg m
suffer vi leiden (from an + dat)
● vt erleiden; (tolerate) dulden
suffice vi genügen
sufficient a, -ly adv genug,
genügend; **be ~** genügen
suffocat|e vt/i ersticken. ~ion n
Ersticken nt
sugar n Zucker m ● vt zuckern;
(fig) versüßen. **~ basin, ~-bowl**
n Zuckerschale f. ~y a süß; (fig)
süßlich

S

suggest vt vorschlagen; (indicate, insinuate) andeuten. ~ion n Vorschlag m; Andeutung f; (trace) Spur f. ~ive a, -ly adv anzüglich

suicidal a selbstmörderisch

suicide n Selbstmord m

suit n Anzug m; (woman's) Kostüm nt; (Cards) Farbe f; (Jur) Prozess m ● vt (adapt) anpassen (to dat); (be convenient for) passen (+ dat); (go with) passen zu; <clothing:> stehen (s.o. jdm); be ~ed for geeignet sein für; ~ yourself! wie du willst!

suit|able a geeignet; (convenient) passend; (appropriate) angemessen; (for weather, activity) zweckmäßig. ~ably adv angemessen; zweckmäßig

suitcase n Koffer m

suite n Suite f; (of furniture) Garnitur f

sulk vi schmollen. ~y a schmollend

sullen a, -ly adv mürrisch

sultry a (-ier, -iest) <weather> schwül

sum n Summe f; (Sch) Rechenaufgabe f ● vt/i (pt/pp summed) ~ up zusammenfassen; (assess) einschätzen

summar|ize vt zusammenfassen. ~y n Zusammenfassung f ● a, -ily adv summarisch; <dismissal> fristlos

summer n Sommer m. ~time n Sommer m

summery a sommerlich

summit n Gipfel m. ~ conference n Gipfelkonferenz f

summon vt rufen; holen <help>; (Jur) vorladen

summons n (Jur) Vorladung f ● vt vorladen

sumptuous a, -ly adv prunkvoll; <meal> üppig

sun n Sonne f ● vt (pt/pp sunned) ~ oneself sich sonnen

sun: ~bathe vi sich sonnen. ~bed n Sonnenbank f. ~burn n Sonnenbrand m

Sunday n Sonntag m

sunflower n Sonnenblume f

sung see sing

sunglasses npl Sonnenbrille f

sunk see sink

sunny a (-ier, -iest) sonnig

sun: ~rise n Sonnenaufgang m. ~-roof n (Auto) Schiebedach nt. ~set n Sonnenuntergang m. ~shade n Sonnenschirm m. ~shine n Sonnenschein m. ~stroke n Sonnenstich m. ~-tan n [Sonnen]bräune f ● a braun [gebrannt]. ~-tan oil n Sonnenöl nt

super a ⊞ prima, toll

superb a erstklassig

superficial a, -ly adv oberflächlich

superfluous a überflüssig

superintendent n (of police) Kommissar m

superior a überlegen; (in rank) höher ● n Vorgesetzte(r) m/f. ~ity n Überlegenheit f

superlative a unübertrefflich ● n Superlativ m

supermarket n Supermarkt m

supernatural a übernatürlich

supersede vt ersetzen

superstiti|on n Aberglaube m. ~ous a, -ly adv abergläubisch

supervis|e vt beaufsichtigen; überwachen <work>. ~ion n Aufsicht f; Überwachung f. ~or n Aufseher(in) m(f)

supper n Abendessen nt

supple a geschmeidig

supplement n Ergänzung f; (addition) Zusatz m; (to fare) Zuschlag m; (book) Ergänzungsband m; (to newspaper) Beilage f ● vt ergänzen. ~ary a zusätzlich

supplier n Lieferant m

supply n Vorrat m; **supplies** pl (Mil) Nachschub m ● vt (pt/pp **-ied**) liefern; ~ **s.o. with sth** jdn mit etw versorgen
support n Stütze f; (fig) Unterstützung f ● vt stützen; (bear weight of) tragen; (keep) ernähren; (speak in favour of) befürworten; (Sport) Fan sein von. ~**er** n Anhänger(in) m(f); (Sport) Fan m
suppose vt annehmen; (presume) vermuten; (imagine) sich (dat) vorstellen; **be** ~**d to do sth** etw tun sollen; **not be** ~**d to** [!] nicht dürfen; **I** ~ **so** vermutlich. ~**dly** adv angeblich
supposition n Vermutung f
suppress vt unterdrücken. ~**ion** n Unterdrückung f
supremacy n Vorherrschaft f
supreme a höchste(r,s); <court> oberste(r,s)
sure a (-r, -st) sicher; **make** ~ sich vergewissern (of gen); (check) nachprüfen (Amer [!]) klar; ~ **enough** tatsächlich. ~**ly** adv sicher; (for emphasis) doch; (Amer: gladly) gern
surf n Brandung f ● vi surfen
surface n Oberfläche f ● vi (emerge) auftauchen
surfboard n Surfbrett nt
surfing n Surfen nt
surge n (of sea) Branden nt; (fig) Welle f ● vi branden; ~ **forward** nach vorn drängen
surgeon n Chirurg(in) m(f)
surgery n Chirurgie f; (place) Praxis f; (room) Sprechzimmer nt; (hours) Sprechstunde f; **have** ~ operiert werden
surgical a, **-ly** adv chirurgisch
surly a (-ier, -iest) mürrisch
surname n Nachname m
surpass vt übertreffen
surplus a überschüssig ● n Überschuss m (**of** an + dat)

surpris|e n Überraschung f ● vt überraschen; **be** ~**ed** sich wundern (**at** über + acc). ~**ing** a, **-ly** adv überraschend
surrender n Kapitulation f ● vi sich ergeben; (Mil) kapitulieren ● vt aufgeben
surround vt umgeben; (encircle) umzingeln; ~**ed by** umgeben von. ~**ing** a umliegend. ~**ings** npl Umgebung f
surveillance n Überwachung f; **be under** ~ überwacht werden
survey¹ n Überblick m; (poll) Umfrage f; (investigation) Untersuchung f; (of land) Vermessung f; (of house) Gutachten nt
survey² vt betrachten; vermessen <land>; begutachten <building>. ~**or** n Landvermesser m; Gutachter m
survival n Überleben nt; (of tradition) Fortbestand m
surviv|e vt überleben ● vi überleben; <tradition:> erhalten bleiben. ~**or** n Überlebende(r) m/f; **be a** ~**or** nicht unterzukriegen sein
susceptible a empfänglich/ (Med) anfällig (**to** für)
suspect¹ vt verdächtigen; (assume) vermuten; **he** ~**s** **nothing** er ahnt nichts
suspect² a verdächtig ● n Verdächtige(r) m/f
suspend vt aufhängen; (stop) [vorläufig] einstellen; (from duty) vorläufig beurlauben. ~**ders** npl (Amer: braces) Hosenträger pl
suspense n Spannung f
suspension n (Auto) Federung f. ~ **bridge** n Hängebrücke f
suspici|on n Verdacht m; (mistrust) Misstrauen nt; (trace) Spur f. ~**ous** a, **-ly** adv misstrauisch; (arousing suspicion) verdächtig

S

sustain vt tragen; (fig)
aufrechterhalten; erhalten <life>;
erleiden <injury>

sustenance n Nahrung f

swagger vi stolzieren

swallow[1] vt/i schlucken. ~ **up** vt
verschlucken; verschlingen
<resources>

swallow[2] n (bird) Schwalbe f

swam see swim

swamp n Sumpf m ● vt
überschwemmen

swan n Schwan m

swank vi 🆄 angeben

swap n 🆄 Tausch m ● vt/i (pt/pp
swapped) 🆄 tauschen (**for** gegen)

swarm n Schwarm m ● vi
schwärmen; **be** ~**ing with**
wimmeln von

swat vt (pt/pp **swatted**)
totschlagen

sway vi schwanken; (gently) sich
wiegen ● vt (influence)
beeinflussen

swear v (pt **swore**, pp **sworn**) ● vt
schwören ● vi schwören (**by** auf
+ acc); (curse) fluchen. ~-**word** n
Kraftausdruck m

sweat n Schweiß m ● vi
schwitzen

sweater n Pullover m

Swed|e n Schwede m/Schwedin f.
~**en** n Schweden nt. ~**ish** a
schwedisch

sweep n Schornsteinfeger m;
(curve) Bogen m; (movement)
ausholende Bewegung f ● v (pt/
pp **swept**) ● vt fegen, kehren ● vi
(go swiftly) rauschen; <wind:>
fegen

sweeping a ausholend;
<statement> pauschal; <changes>
weit reichend

sweet a (-er, -est) süß; **have a** ~
tooth gern Süßes mögen ● n
Bonbon m & nt; (dessert)
Nachtisch m

sweeten vt süßen

sweet: ~**heart** n Schatz m. ~**ness**
n Süße f. ~ **pea** n Wicke f. ~-
shop n Süßwarenladen m

swell n Dünung f ● v (pt **swelled**,
pp **swollen** or **swelled**) ● vi
[an]schwellen; <wood:>
aufquellen ● vt anschwellen
lassen; (increase) vergrößern.
~**ing** n Schwellung f

swelter vi schwitzen

swept see sweep

swerve vi einen Bogen machen

swift a (-er, -est), -**ly** adv schnell

swig n 🆄 Schluck m

swim n **have a** ~ schwimmen ● vi
(pt **swam**, pp **swum**) schwimmen;
my head is ~**ming** mir dreht sich
der Kopf. ~**mer** n
Schwimmer(in) m(f)

swimming n Schwimmen nt. ~-
baths npl Schwimmbad nt. ~-
pool n Schwimmbecken nt;
(private) Swimmingpool m

swimsuit n Badeanzug m

swindle n Schwindel m, Betrug m
● vt betrügen. ~**r** n Schwindler
m

swine n (pej) Schwein nt

swing n Schwung m; (shift)
Schwenk m; (seat) Schaukel f; **in
full** ~ in vollem Gange ● (pt/pp
swung) ● vi schwingen; (on
swing) schaukeln; (dangle)
baumeln; (turn) schwenken ● vt
schwingen; (influence)
beeinflussen

swipe n 🆄 Schlag m ● vt 🆄
knallen; (steal) klauen

swirl n Wirbel m ● vt/i wirbeln

Swiss a Schweizer, schweizerisch
● n Schweizer(in) m(f); **the** ~ pl
die Schweizer. ~ **roll** n
Biskuitrolle f

switch n Schalter m; (change)
Wechsel m; (Amer, Rail) Weiche
f ● vt wechseln; (exchange)
tauschen ● vi wechseln; ~ **to**
umstellen auf (+ acc). ~ **off** vt

ausschalten; abschalten
<*engine*>. ~ **on** *vt* einschalten
switchboard *n* [Telefon]zentrale
f

Switzerland *n* die Schweiz

swivel *v* (*pt/pp* **swivelled**) ●*vt*
drehen ●*vi* sich drehen

swollen *see* **swell**

swoop *n* (*by police*) Razzia *f* ●*vi*
~ **down** herabstoßen

sword *n* Schwert *nt*

swore *see* **swear**

sworn *see* **swear**

swot *n* 🔲 Streber *m* ●*vt* (*pt/pp*
swotted) 🔲 büffeln

swum *see* **swim**

swung *see* **swing**

syllable *n* Silbe *f*

syllabus *n* Lehrplan *m*; (*for
exam*) Studienplan *m*

symbol *n* Symbol *nt* (**of** für). ~**ic**
a, **-ally** *adv* symbolisch ~**ism** *n*
Symbolik *f*. ~**ize** *vt*
symbolisieren

symmetr|ical *a*, **-ly** *adv*
symmetrisch. ~**y** *n* Symmetrie *f*

sympathetic *a*, **-ally** *adv*
mitfühlend; (*likeable*)
sympathisch

sympathize *vi* mitfühlen

sympathy *n* Mitgefühl *nt*;
(*condolences*) Beileid *nt*

symphony *n* Sinfonie *f*

symptom *n* Symptom *nt*

synagogue *n* Synagoge *f*

synchronize *vt* synchronisieren

synonym *n* Synonym *nt*. ~**ous** *a*,
-ly *adv* synonym

synthesis *n* (*pl* **-ses**) Synthese *f*

synthetic *a* synthetisch

Syria *n* Syrien *nt*

syringe *n* Spritze *f*

syrup *n* Sirup *m*

system *n* System *nt*. ~**atic** *a*, **-ally**
adv systematisch

tab *n* (*projecting*) Zunge *f*; (*with
name*) Namensschild *nt*; (*loop*)
Aufhänger *m*; **pick up the** ~ 🔲
bezahlen

table *n* Tisch *m*; (*list*) Tabelle *f*; **at
[the]** ~ bei Tisch. ~**-cloth** *n*
Tischdecke *f*. ~**spoon** *n*
Servierlöffel *m*

tablet *n* Tablette *f*; (*of soap*)
Stück *nt*

table tennis *n* Tischtennis *nt*

tabloid *n* kleinformatige Zeitung
f; (*pej*) Boulevardzeitung *f*

taciturn *a* wortkarg

tack *n* (*nail*) Stift *m*; (*stitch*)
Heftstich *m*; (*Naut & fig*) Kurs *m*
●*vt* festnageln; (*sew*) heften ●*vi*
(*Naut*) kreuzen

tackle *n* Ausrüstung *f* ●*vt*
angehen <*problem*>; (*Sport*)
angreifen

tact *n* Takt *m*, Taktgefühl *nt*. ~**ful**
a, **-ly** *adv* taktvoll

tactic|al *a*, **-ly** *adv* taktisch. ~**s**
npl Taktik *f*

tactless *a*, **-ly** *adv* taktlos. ~**ness**
n Taktlosigkeit *f*

tag *n* (*label*) Schild *nt* ●*vi* (*pt/pp*
tagged) ~ **along** mitkommen

tail *n* Schwanz *m*; ~**s** *pl* (*tailcoat*)
Frack *m*; **heads or** ~**s?** Kopf oder
Zahl? ●*vt* (🔲 *follow*) beschatten
●*vi* ~ **off** zurückgehen

tail: ~**back** *n* Rückstau *m*. ~ **light**
n Rücklicht *nt*

tailor *n* Schneider *m*. ~**-made** *a*
maßgeschneidert

taint *vt* verderben

take *v* (*pt* **took**, *pp* **taken**) ●*vt*
nehmen: (*with one*) mitnehmen;
(*take to a place*) bringen; (*steal*)
stehlen; (*win*) gewinnen;

(capture) einnehmen; *(require)* brauchen; *(last)* dauern; *(teach)* geben; machen *<exam, subject, holiday, photograph>*; messen *<pulse, temperature>*; ~ **sth to the cleaner's** etw in die Reinigung bringen; **be ~n ill** krank werden; ~ **sth calmly** etw gelassen aufnehmen ● *vi <plant:>* angehen; ~ **after s.o.** jdm nachschlagen; *(in looks)* jdm ähnlich sehen; ~ **to** *(like)* mögen; *(as a habit)* sich *(dat)* angewöhnen. ~ **away** *vt* wegbringen; *(remove)* wegnehmen; *(subtract)* abziehen; **'to ~ away'** 'zum Mitnehmen'. ~ **back** *vt* zurücknehmen; *(return)* zurückbringen. ~ **down** *vt* herunternehmen; *(remove)* abnehmen; *(write down)* aufschreiben. ~ **in** *vt* hineinbringen; *(bring indoors)* hereinholen; *(to one's home)* aufnehmen; *(understand)* begreifen; *(deceive)* hereinlegen; *(make smaller)* enger machen. ~ **off** *vt* abnehmen; ablegen *<coat>*; sich *(dat)* ausziehen *<clothes>*; *(deduct)* abziehen; *(mimic)* nachmachen ● *vi (Aviat)* starten. ~ **on** *vt* annehmen; *(undertake)* übernehmen; *(engage)* einstellen; *(as opponent)* antreten gegen. ~ **out** *vt* hinausbringen; *(for pleasure)* ausgehen mit; ausführen *<dog>*; *(remove)* herausnehmen; *(withdraw)* abheben *<money>*; *(from library)* ausleihen; ~ **it out on s.o.** ⃞ seinen Ärger an jdm auslassen. ~ **over** *vt* hinüberbringen; übernehmen *<firm, control>* ● *vi* ~ **over from s.o.** jdn ablösen. ~ **up** *vt* hinaufbringen; annehmen *<offer>*; ergreifen *<profession>*; sich *(dat)* zulegen *<hobby>*; in Anspruch nehmen *<time>*; einnehmen *<space>*; aufreißen

<floorboards>; ~ **sth up with s.o.** mit jdm über etw *(acc)* sprechen
take: **~-away** *n* Essen *nt* zum Mitnehmen; *(restaurant)* Restaurant *nt* mit Straßenverkauf. **~-off** *n (Aviat)* Start *m*, Abflug *m*. **~-over** *n* Übernahme *f*
takings *npl* Einnahmen *pl*
talcum *n* ~ **[powder]** Körperpuder *m*
tale *n* Geschichte *f*
talent *n* Talent *nt*
talk *n* Gespräch *nt*; *(lecture)* Vortrag *m* ● *vi* reden, sprechen (**to/with** mit) ● *vt* reden; ~ **s.o. into sth** jdn zu etw überreden. ~ **over** *vt* besprechen
talkative *a* gesprächig
tall *a* (**-er, -est**) groß; *<building, tree>* hoch. ~ **story** *n* übertriebene Geschichte *f*
tally *vi* übereinstimmen
tame *a* (**-r, -st**), **-ly** *adv* zahm; *(dull)* lahm ⃞ ● *vt* zähmen. ~**r** *n* Dompteur *m*
tamper *vi* ~ **with** sich *(dat)* zu schaffen machen an (+ *dat*)
tampon *n* Tampon *m*
tan *a* gelbbraun ● *n* Gelbbraun *nt*; *(from sun)* Bräune *f* ● *v (pt/pp* **tanned**) ● *vt* gerben *<hide>* ● *vi* braun werden
tang *n* herber Geschmack *m*; *(smell)* herber Geruch *m*
tangible *a* greifbar
tangle *n* Gewirr *nt*; *(in hair)* Verfilzung *f* ● *vt* ~ **[up]** verheddern ● *vi* sich verheddern
tank *n* Tank *m*; *(Mil)* Panzer *m*
tanker *n* Tanker *m*; *(lorry)* Tank[last]wagen *m*
tantrum *n* Wutanfall *m*
tap *n* Hahn *m*; *(knock)* Klopfen *nt*; **on** ~ zur Verfügung ● *v (pt/pp* **tapped**) ● *vt* klopfen an (+ *acc*); anzapfen *<barrel, tree>*; erschließen *<resources>*; abhören *<telephone>* ● *vi* klopfen. ~-

dance n Stepp[tanz] m ●vi
Stepp tanzen, steppen
tape n Band nt; (adhesive)
Klebstreifen m; (for recording)
Tonband nt ●vt mit Klebstreifen
zukleben; (record) auf Band
aufnehmen
tape-measure n Bandmaß nt
taper vi sich verjüngen
tape recorder n Tonbandgerät nt
tar n Teer m ●vt (pt/pp tarred)
teeren
target n Ziel nt; (board)
[Ziel]scheibe f
tarnish vi anlaufen
tarpaulin n Plane f
tart¹ a (-er, -est) sauer
tart² n ≈ Obstkuchen m;
(individual) Törtchen nt; (✕
prostitute) Nutte f ●vt ~ oneself
up 🗓 sich auftakeln
tartan n Schottenmuster nt;
(cloth) Schottenstoff m
task n Aufgabe f; take s.o. to ~
jdm Vorhaltungen machen. ~
force n Sonderkommando nt
tassel n Quaste f
taste n Geschmack m; (sample)
Kostprobe f ●vt kosten,
probieren; schmecken <flavour>
●vi schmecken (of nach). ~ful a,
-ly adv (fig) geschmackvoll.
~less a, -ly adv geschmacklos
tasty a (-ier, -iest) lecker
tat see tit²
tatters npl in ~s in Fetzen
tattoo n Tätowierung f ●vt
tätowieren
tatty a (-ier, -iest) schäbig; <book>
zerfleddert
taught see teach
taunt n höhnische Bemerkung f
●vt verhöhnen
taut a straff
tawdry a (-ier, -iest) billig und
geschmacklos
tax n Steuer f ●vt besteuern; (fig)
strapazieren. ~able a

steuerpflichtig. ~ation n
Besteuerung f
taxi n Taxi nt ●vi (pt/pp taxied,
pres p taxiing) <aircraft:> rollen.
~ **driver** n Taxifahrer m. ~ **rank**
n Taxistand m
taxpayer n Steuerzahler m
tea n Tee m. ~-**bag** n Teebeutel
m. ~-**break** n Teepause f
teach vt/i (pt/pp taught)
unterrichten; ~ **s.o. sth** jdm etw
beibringen. ~**er** n Lehrer(in)
m(f). ~**ing** n Unterrichten nt
tea: ~-**cloth** n (for drying)
Geschirrtuch nt. ~**cup** n
Teetasse f
teak n Teakholz nt
team n Mannschaft f; (fig) Team
nt; (of animals) Gespann nt
teapot n Teekanne f
tear¹ n Riss m ●v (pt tore, pp
torn) ●vt reißen; (damage)
zerreißen; ~ **oneself away** sich
losreißen ●vi [zer]reißen; (run)
rasen. ~ **up** vt zerreißen
tear² n Träne f. ~**ful** a weinend.
~**fully** adv unter Tränen. ~**gas** n
Tränengas nt
tease vt necken
tea: ~-**set** n Teeservice nt. ~
shop n Café nt. ~**spoon** n
Teelöffel m
teat n Zitze f; (on bottle) Sauger
m
tea-towel n Geschirrtuch nt
technical a technisch;
(specialized) fachlich. ~**ity** n
technisches Detail nt; (Jur)
Formfehler m. ~**ly** adv technisch;
(strictly) streng genommen. ~
term n Fachausdruck m
technician n Techniker m
technique n Technik f
technological a, -**ly** adv
technologisch
technology n Technik f
teddy n ~ [**bear**] Teddybär m
tedious a langweilig
tedium n Langeweile f

teenage a Teenager-; ~ **boy/girl** Junge m/Mädchen nt im Teenageralter. ~**r** n Teenager m

teens npl **the** ~ die Teenagerjahre pl

teeter vi schwanken

teeth see **tooth**

teeth|e vi zahnen. ~**ing troubles** npl (fig) Anfangsschwierigkeiten pl

teetotal a abstinent. ~**ler** n Abstinenzler m

telebanking n Telebanking nt

telecommunications npl Fernmeldewesen nt

telegram n Telegramm nt

telegraph pole n Telegrafenmast m

telephone n Telefon nt; **be on the** ~ Telefon haben; (be telephoning) telefonieren ● vt anrufen ● vi telefonieren

telephone: ~ **booth** n, ~ **box** n Telefonzelle f. ~ **directory** n Telefonbuch nt. ~ **number** n Telefonnummer f

telephoto a ~ **lens** Teleobjektiv nt

telescop|e n Teleskop nt, Fernrohr nt. ~**ic** a (collapsible) ausziehbar

televise vt im Fernsehen übertragen

television n Fernsehen nt; **watch** ~ fernsehen; ~ **[set]** Fernseher m 🔲

teleworking n Telearbeit f

tell vt/i (pt/pp **told**) sagen (**s.o.** jdm); (relate) erzählen; (know) wissen; (distinguish) erkennen; ~ **the time** die Uhr lesen; **time will** ~ das wird man erst sehen; **his age is beginning to** ~ sein Alter macht sich bemerkbar. ~ **off** vt ausschimpfen

telly n 🔲 = **television**

temp n 🔲 Aushilfssekretärin f

temper n (disposition) Naturell nt; (mood) Laune f; (anger) Wut f; **lose one's** ~ wütend werden ● vt (fig) mäßigen

temperament n Temperament nt. ~**al** a temperamentvoll; (moody) launisch

temperate a gemäßigt

temperature n Temperatur f; **have** or **run a** ~ Fieber haben

temple¹ n Tempel m

temple² n (Anat) Schläfe f

tempo n Tempo nt

temporary a, **-ily** adv vorübergehend; <measure, building> provisorisch

tempt vt verleiten; (Relig) versuchen; herausfordern <fate>; (entice) [ver]locken; **be** ~**ed** versucht sein (**to** zu). ~**ation** n Versuchung f. ~**ing** a verlockend

ten a zehn

tenaci|ous a, **-ly** adv hartnäckig. ~**ty** n Hartnäckigkeit f

tenant n Mieter(in) m(f); (Comm) Pächter(in) m(f)

tend vi ~ **to do sth** dazu neigen, etw zu tun

tendency n Tendenz f; (inclination) Neigung f

tender a zart; (loving) zärtlich; (painful) empfindlich. ~**ly** adv zärtlich. ~**ness** n Zartheit f; Zärtlichkeit f

tendon n Sehne f

tenner n 🔲 Zehnpfundschein m

tennis n Tennis nt. ~-**court** n Tennisplatz m

tenor n Tenor m

tense a (**-r, -st**) gespannt ● vt anspannen <muscle>

tension n Spannung f

tent n Zelt nt

tentative a, **-ly** adv vorläufig; (hesitant) zaghaft

tenterhooks npl **be on** ~ wie auf glühenden Kohlen sitzen

tenth a zehnte(r,s) ● n Zehntel nt

tepid a lauwarm

term n Zeitraum m; (Sch) ≈ Halbjahr nt; (Univ) ≈ Semester

nt; (*expression*) Ausdruck *m*; ~**s**
pl (*conditions*) Bedingungen *pl*; **in
the short/long ~** kurz-/langfristig;
be on good/bad ~s gut/nicht gut
miteinander auskommen
terminal *a* End-; (*Med*) unheilbar
● *n* (*Aviat*) Terminal *m*; (*of bus*)
Endstation *f*; (*on battery*) Pol *m*;
(*Computing*) Terminal *nt*
terminat|e *vt* beenden; lösen
<*contract*>; unterbrechen
<*pregnancy*> ● *vi* enden
terminology *n* Terminologie *f*
terminus *n* (*pl* -ni) Endstation *f*
terrace *n* Terrasse *f*; (*houses*)
Häuserreihe *f*. ~**d house** *n*
Reihenhaus *nt*
terrain *n* Gelände *nt*
terrible *a*, -**bly** *adv* schrecklich
terrific *a* 🔲 (*excellent*) sagenhaft;
(*huge*) riesig
terri|fy *vt* (*pt/pp* -ied) Angst
machen (+ *dat*); **be ~fied** Angst
haben. ~**fying** *a* Furcht erregend
territorial *a* Territorial-
territory *n* Gebiet *nt*
terror *n* [panische] Angst *f*; (*Pol*)
Terror *m*. ~**ism** *n* Terrorismus
m. ~**ist** *n* Terrorist *m*. ~**ize** *vt*
terrorisieren
terse *a*, -**ly** *adv* kurz, knapp
test *n* Test *m*; (*Sch*) Klassenarbeit
f; **put to the ~** auf die Probe
stellen ● *vt* prüfen; (*examine*)
untersuchen (**for** auf + *acc*)
testament *n* Testament *nt*
testify *v* (*pt/pp* -ied) ● *vt*
beweisen; ~ **that** bezeugen, dass
● *vi* aussagen
testimonial *n* Zeugnis *nt*
testimony *n* Aussage *f*
test-tube *n* Reagenzglas *nt*
tether *n* **be at the end of one's ~**
am Ende seiner Kraft sein ● *vt*
anbinden
text *n* Text *m* ● *vt/i* texten.
~**book** *n* Lehrbuch *nt*
textile *a* Textil- ● *n* ~**s** *pl*
Textilien *pl*

text message *n* Textnachricht *f*
texture *n* Beschaffenheit *f*; (*Tex*)
Struktur *f*
Thai *a* thailändisch. ~**land** *n*
Thailand *nt*
Thames *n* Themse *f*
than *conj* als
thank *vt* danken (+ *dat*); ~ **you
[very much]** danke [schön]. ~**ful**
a, -**ly** *adv* dankbar. ~**less** *a*
undankbar
thanks *npl* Dank *m*; ~**!** 🔲 danke!
~ **to** dank (+ *dat or gen*)

---

that
  pl **those**
● *adjective*
····▸ der (*m*), die (*f*), das (*nt*), die
(*pl*); (*just seen or experienced*)
dieser (*m*), diese (*f*), dieses (*nt*),
diese (*pl*). **I'll never forget that day**
den Tag werde ich nie
vergessen. **I liked that house**
dieses Haus hat mir gut gefallen
● *pronoun*
····▸ der (*m*), die (*f*), das (*nt*), die
(*pl*). **that is not true** das ist nicht
wahr. **who is that in the garden?**
wer ist das [da] im Garten? **I'll
take that** ich nehme den/die/das.
I don't like those die mag ich
nicht. **is that you?** bist du es?
that is why deshalb
····▸ **like that** so. **don't be like that!**
sei doch nicht so! **a man like that**
ein solcher Mann; so ein Mann
🔲
····▸ (*after prepositions*) da ....
after that danach. **with that** damit.
apart from that außerdem
····▸ (*relative pronoun*) der (*m*),
die (*f*), das (*nt*), die (*pl*). **the book
that I'm reading** das Buch, das ich
lese. **the people that you got it
from** die Leute, von denen du es
bekommen hast. **everyone that I
know** jeder, den ich kenne
● *adverb*

T

••••▶ so. **he's not that stupid** so blöd ist er [auch wieder] nicht. **it wasn't that bad** so schlecht war es auch nicht. **a nail about that long** ein etwa so langer Nagel

••••▶ (*relative adverb*) der (*m*), die (*f*), das (*nt*), die (*pl*). **the day that I first met her** der Tag, an dem ich sie zum ersten Mal sah. **at the speed that he was going** bei der Geschwindigkeit, die er hatte

● *conjunction*

••••▶ dass. **I don't think that he'll come** ich denke nicht, dass er kommt. **we know that you're right** wir wissen, dass du Recht hast. **I'm so tired that I can hardly walk** ich bin so müde, dass ich kaum gehen kann

••••▶ so that (*purpose*) damit; (*result*) sodass. **he came earlier so that they would have more time** er kam früher, damit sie mehr Zeit hatten. **it was late, so that I had to catch the bus** es war spät, sodass ich den Bus nehmen musste

thatch *n* Strohdach *nt*. ∼**ed** *a* strohgedeckt

thaw *n* Tauwetter *nt* ●*vt/i* auftauen; **it's** ∼**ing** es taut

the *def art* der/die/das; (*pl*) die; **play** ∼ **piano/violin** Klavier/Geige spielen ●*adv* ∼ **more** ∼ **better** je mehr, desto besser; **all** ∼ **better** umso besser

theatre *n* Theater *nt*; (*Med*) Operationssaal *m*

theatrical *a* Theater-; (*showy*) theatralisch

theft *n* Diebstahl *m*

their *a* ihr

theirs *poss pron* ihre(r), ihrs; **a friend of** ∼ ein Freund von ihnen; **those are** ∼ die gehören ihnen

them *pron* (*acc*) sie; (*dat*) ihnen

theme *n* Thema *nt*

themselves *pron* selbst; (*refl*) sich; **by** ∼ allein

then *adv* dann; (*at that time in past*) damals; **by** ∼ bis dahin; **since** ∼ seitdem; **before** ∼ vorher; **from** ∼ **on** von da an; **now and** ∼ dann und wann; **there and** ∼ auf der Stelle ●*a* damalig

theology *n* Theologie *f*

theoretical *a*, **-ly** *adv* theoretisch

theory *n* Theorie *f*; **in** ∼ theoretisch

therap|ist *n* Therapeut(in) *m(f)*. ∼**y** *n* Therapie *f*

there *adv* da; (*with movement*) dahin, dorthin; **down/up** ∼ da unten/oben; ∼ **is/are** da ist/sind; (*in existence*) es gibt ●*int* ∼, ∼**!** nun, nun!

there: ∼**abouts** *adv* da [in der Nähe]; **or** ∼**abouts** (*roughly*) ungefähr. ∼**fore** *adv* deshalb, also

thermometer *n* Thermometer *nt*

Thermos (P) *n* ∼ **[flask]** Thermosflasche (P) *f*

thermostat *n* Thermostat *m*

these *see* **this**

thesis *n* (*pl* **-ses**) Dissertation *f*; (*proposition*) These *f*

they *pron* sie; ∼ **say** (*generalizing*) man sagt

thick *a* (**-er, -est**), **-ly** *adv* dick; (*dense*) dicht; <*liquid*> dickflüssig; (🄸 *stupid*) dumm ●*adv* dick ●*n* **in the** ∼ **of** mitten in (+ *dat*). ∼**en** *vt* dicker machen; eindicken <*sauce*> ●*vi* dicker werden; <*fog:*> dichter werden; <*plot:*> komplizierter werden. ∼**ness** *n* Dicke *f*; (*density*) Dichte *f*; (*of liquid*) Dickflüssigkeit *f*

thief *n* (*pl* **thieves**) Dieb(in) *m(f)*

thigh *n* Oberschenkel *m*

thimble *n* Fingerhut *m*

thin *a* (**thinner, thinnest**), **-ly** *adv* dünn ●*adv* dünn ●*v* (*pt/pp* **thinned**) ●*vt* verdünnen <*liquid*> ●*vi* sich lichten

thing n Ding nt; (subject, affair)
Sache f; ~s pl (belongings)
Sachen pl; for one ~ erstens; just
the ~! genau das Richtige! how
are ~s? wie geht's? the latest ~
🗓 der letzte Schrei
think vt/i (pt/pp **thought**) denken
(about/of an + acc); (believe)
meinen; (consider) nachdenken;
(regard as) halten für; I ~ so ich
glaube schon; what do you ~ of it?
was halten Sie davon? ~ over vt
sich (dat) überlegen. ~ up vt sich
(dat) ausdenken
third a dritte(r,s) ●n Drittel nt.
~ly adv drittens. ~-rate a
drittrangig
thirst n Durst m. ~y a, -ily adv
durstig; be ~y Durst haben
thirteen a dreizehn. ~th a
dreizehnte(r,s)
thirtieth a dreißigste(r,s)
thirty a dreißig
this a (pl **these**) diese(r,s); (pl)
diese; ~ one diese(r,s) da; I'll take
~ ich nehme diesen/diese/
dieses; ~ evening/morning heute
Abend/Morgen; these days
heutzutage ●pron (pl **these**) das,
dies[es]; (pl) die, diese; ~ and
that dies und das; ~ or that dieses
oder das da; like ~ so; ~ is Peter
das ist Peter; (Teleph) hier
[spricht] Peter; who is ~? wer ist
das? (Teleph, Amer) wer ist am
Apparat?
thistle n Distel f
thorn n Dorn m
thorough a gründlich
thoroughbred n reinrassiges Tier
nt; (horse) Rassepferd nt
thoroughly adv gründlich;
(completely) völlig; (extremely)
äußerst. ~ness n Gründlichkeit f
those see that
though conj obgleich, obwohl; as
~ als ob 🗓 doch
thought see think ●n Gedanke m;
(thinking) Denken nt. ~ful a, -ly

adv nachdenklich; (considerate)
rücksichtsvoll. ~less a, -ly adv
gedankenlos
thousand a one/a ~ [ein]tausend
●n Tausend nt. ~th a
tausendste(r,s) ●n Tausendstel
nt
thrash vt verprügeln; (defeat)
[vernichtend] schlagen
thread n Faden m; (of screw)
Gewinde nt ●vt einfädeln;
auffädeln <beads>. ~bare a
fadenscheinig
threat n Drohung f; (danger)
Bedrohung f
threaten vt drohen (+ dat); (with
weapon) bedrohen; ~ s.o. with sth
jdm etw androhen ●vi drohen.
~ing a, -ly adv drohend;
(ominous) bedrohlich
three a drei. ~fold a & adv
dreifach
thresh vt dreschen
threshold n Schwelle f
threw see throw
thrift n Sparsamkeit f. ~y a
sparsam
thrill n Erregung f; 🗓
Nervenkitzel m ●vt (excite)
erregen; be ~ed with sich sehr
freuen über (+ acc). ~er n
Thriller m. ~ing a erregend
thrive vi (pt **thrived** or **throve**, pp
thrived or **thriven**) gedeihen (on
bei); <business:> florieren
throat n Hals m; cut s.o.'s ~ jdm
die Kehle durchschneiden
throb n Pochen nt ●vi (pt/pp
throbbed) pochen; (vibrate)
vibrieren
throes npl in the ~ of (fig) mitten
in (+ dat)
throne n Thron m
throttle vt erdrosseln
through prep durch (+ acc);
(during) während (+ gen); (Amer:
up to & including) bis
einschließlich ●adv durch; wet ~
durch und durch nass; read sth ~

etw durchlesen ●*a* <*train*> durchgehend; **be** ~ (*finished*) fertig sein; (*Teleph*) durch sein

throughout *prep* ~ **the country** im ganzen Land; ~ **the night** die Nacht durch ●*adv* ganz; (*time*) die ganze Zeit

throve *see* **thrive**

throw *n* Wurf *m* ●*vt* (*pt* **threw**, *pp* **thrown**) werfen; schütten <*liquid*>; betätigen <*switch*>; abwerfen <*rider*>; (**I** *disconcert*) aus der Fassung bringen; **I** geben <*party*>; ~ **sth to s.o.** jdm etw zuwerfen. ~ **away** *vt* wegwerfen. ~ **out** *vt* hinauswerfen; (~ *away*) wegwerfen; verwerfen <*plan*>. ~ **up** *vt* hochwerfen ●*vi* sich übergeben

throw-away *a* Wegwerf-

thrush *n* Drossel *f*

thrust *n* Stoß *m*; (*Phys*) Schub *m* ●*vt* (*pt/pp* **thrust**) stoßen; (*insert*) stecken

thud *n* dumpfer Schlag *m*

thug *n* Schläger *m*

thumb *n* Daumen *m* ●*vt* ~ **a lift** **I** per Anhalter fahren. ~**tack** *n* (*Amer*) Reißzwecke *f*

thump *n* Schlag *m*; (*noise*) dumpfer Schlag *m* ●*vt* schlagen ●*vi* hämmern; <*heart*:> pochen

thunder *n* Donner *m* ●*vi* donnern. ~**clap** *n* Donnerschlag *m*. ~**storm** *n* Gewitter *nt*. ~**y** *a* gewittrig

Thursday *n* Donnerstag *m*

thus *adv* so

thwart *vt* vereiteln; ~ **s.o.** jdm einen Strich durch die Rechnung machen

tick[1] *n* on~ **I** auf Pump

tick[2] *n* (*sound*) Ticken *nt*; (*mark*) Häkchen *nt*; (**I** *instant*) Sekunde *f* ●*vi* ticken ●*vt* abhaken. ~ **off** *vt* abhaken; **I** rüffeln

ticket *n* Karte *f*; (*for bus, train*) Fahrschein *m*; (*Aviat*) Flugschein

m; (*for lottery*) Los *nt*; (*for article deposited*) Schein *m*; (*label*) Schild *nt*; (*for library*) Lesekarte *f*; (*fine*) Strafzettel *m*. ~ **collector** *n* Fahrkartenkontrolleur *m*. ~ **office** *n* Fahrkartenschalter *m*; (*for entry*) Kasse *f*

tick|**le** *n* Kitzeln *nt* ●*vt/i* kitzeln. ~**lish** *a* kitzlig

tidal *a* ~ **wave** Flutwelle *f*

tide *n* Gezeiten *pl*; (*of events*) Strom *m*; **the** ~ **is in/out** es ist Flut/Ebbe ●*vt* ~ **s.o. over** jdm über die Runden helfen

tidiness *n* Ordentlichkeit *f*

tidy *a* (**-ier, -iest**), **-ily** *adv* ordentlich ●*vt* ~ [**up**] aufräumen

tie *n* Krawatte *f*; Schlips *m*; (*cord*) Schnur *f*; (*fig: bond*) Band *nt*; (*restriction*) Bindung *f*; (*Sport*) Unentschieden *nt*; (*in competition*) Punktgleichheit *f* ●*v* (*pres p* **tying**) ●*vt* binden; machen <*knot*> ●*vi* (*Sport*) unentschieden spielen; (*have equal scores, votes*) punktgleich sein. ~ **up** *vt* festbinden; verschnüren <*parcel*>; fesseln <*person*>; **be** ~**d up** (*busy*) beschäftigt sein

tier *n* Stufe *f*; (*of cake*) Etage *f*; (*in stadium*) Rang *m*

tiger *n* Tiger *m*

tight *a* (**-er, -est**), **-ly** *adv* fest; (*taut*) straff; <*clothes*> eng; <*control*> streng; (**I** *drunk*) blau ●*adv* fest

tighten *vt* fester ziehen; straffen <*rope*>; anziehen <*screw*>; verschärfen <*control*> ●*vi* sich spannen

tightrope *n* Hochseil *nt*

tights *npl* Strumpfhose *f*

tile *n* Fliese *f*; (*on wall*) Kachel *f*; (*on roof*) [Dach]ziegel *m* ●*vt* mit Fliesen auslegen; kacheln <*wall*>; decken <*roof*>

till[1] *prep & conj* = **until**

till[2] *n* Kasse *f*

tilt n Neigung f ● vt kippen; [zur Seite] neigen <*head*> ● vi sich neigen

timber n [Nutz]holz nt

time n Zeit f; (*occasion*) Mal nt; (*rhythm*) Takt m; ~s (*Math*) mal; **at ~s** manchmal; **~ and again** immer wieder; **two at a ~** zwei auf einmal; **on ~** pünktlich; **in ~** rechtzeitig; (*eventually*) mit der Zeit; **in no ~** im Handumdrehen; **in a year's ~** in einem Jahr; **behind ~** verspätet; **behind the ~s** rückständig; **for the ~ being** vorläufig; **what is the ~?** wie spät ist es? wie viel Uhr ist es? **did you have a nice ~?** hat es dir gut gefallen? ● vt stoppen <*race*>; **be well ~d** gut abgepaßt sein

time: ~ **bomb** n Zeitbombe f. **~less** a zeitlos. **~ly** a rechtzeitig. **~-switch** n Zeitschalter m. **~table** n Fahrplan m; (*Sch*) Stundenplan m

timid a, **-ly** adv scheu; (*hesitant*) zaghaft

timing n (*Sport, Techn*) Timing nt

tin n Zinn nt; (*container*) Dose f ● vt (*pt/pp* **tinned**) in Dosen konservieren. ~ **foil** n Stanniol nt; (*Culin*) Alufolie f

tinge n Hauch m

tingle vi kribbeln

tinker vi herumbasteln (**with** an + dat)

tinkle n Klingeln nt ● vi klingeln

tinned a Dosen-

tin opener n Dosenöffner m

tinsel n Lametta nt

tint n Farbton m ● vt tönen

tiny a (**-ier, -iest**) winzig

tip¹ n Spitze f

tip² n (*money*) Trinkgeld nt; (*advice*) Rat m, ① Tipp m; (*for rubbish*) Müllhalde f ● vt (*pt/pp* **tipped**) ● vt (*tilt*) kippen; (*reward*) Trinkgeld geben (**s.o.** jdm) ● vi kippen. ~ **out** vt auskippen. ~ **over** vt/i umkippen

tipped a Filter-

tipsy a ① beschwipst

tiptoe n **on ~** auf Zehenspitzen

tiptop a ① erstklassig

tire vt/i ermüden. **~d** a müde; **be ~d of sth** etw satt haben; **~d out** [völlig] erschöpft. **~less** a, **-ly** adv unermüdlich. **~some** a lästig

tiring a ermüdend

tissue n Gewebe nt; (*handkerchief*) Papiertaschentuch nt

tit n (*bird*) Meise f

titbit n Leckerbissen m

title n Titel m

to

● *preposition*

····▸ (*destinations: most cases*) zu (+ dat). **go to work/the station** zur Arbeit/zum Bahnhof gehen. **from house to house** von Haus zu Haus. **go/come to s.o.** zu jdm gehen/kommen

····▸ (*with name of place or points of compass*) nach. **to Paris/ Germany** nach Paris/ Deutschland. **to Switzerland** in die Schweiz. **from East to West** von Osten nach Westen. **I've never been to Berlin** ich war noch nie in Berlin

····▸ (*to cinema, theatre, bed*) in (+ acc). **to bed with you!** ins Bett mit dir!

····▸ (*to wedding, party, university, the toilet*) auf (+ acc).

····▸ (*up to*) bis zu (+ dat). **to the end** bis zum Schluss. **to this day** bis heute. **5 to 6 pounds** 5 bis 6 Pfund

····▸ <*give, say, write*> + dat. **give/ say sth to s.o.** jdm etw geben/ sagen. **she wrote to him/the firm** sie hat ihm/an die Firma geschrieben

····▸ <*address, send, fasten*> an (+ acc). **she sent it to her brother** sie schickte es an ihren Bruder

T

····▶ (*in telling the time*) vor. **five to eight** fünf vor acht. **a quarter to ten** Viertel vor zehn

● *before infinitive*

····▶ (*after modal verb*) (*not translated*). **I want to go** ich will gehen. **he is learning to swim** er lernt schwimmen. **you have to** du musst [es tun]

····▶ (*after adjective*) zu. **it is easy to forget** es ist leicht zu vergessen

····▶ (*expressing purpose, result*) um … zu. **he did it to annoy me** er tat es, um mich zu ärgern. **she was too tired to go** sie war zu müde um zu gehen

● *adverb*

····▶ **be to** <*door, window*> angelehnt sein. **pull a door to** eine Tür anlehnen

····▶ **to and fro** hin und her

toad *n* Kröte *f*

toast *n* Toast *m* ● *vt* toasten <*bread*>; (*drink a ~ to*) trinken auf (+ *acc*). **~er** *n* Toaster *m*

tobacco *n* Tabak *m*. **~nist's [shop]** *n* Tabakladen *m*

toboggan *n* Schlitten *m* ● *vi* Schlitten fahren

today *n* & *adv* heute; **~ week** heute in einer Woche

toddler *n* Kleinkind *nt*

toe *n* Zeh *m*; (*of footwear*) Spitze *f* ● *vt* **~ the line** spuren. **~nail** *n* Zehennagel *m*

toffee *n* Karamell *m* & *nt*

together *adv* zusammen; (*at the same time*) gleichzeitig

toilet *n* Toilette *f*. **~ bag** *n* Kulturbeutel *m*. **~ paper** *n* Toilettenpapier *nt*

toiletries *npl* Toilettenartikel *pl*

token *n* Zeichen *nt*; (*counter*) Marke *f*; (*voucher*) Gutschein *m* ● *attrib* symbolisch

told *see* **tell** ● *a* **all ~** insgesamt

tolerable *a*, **-bly** *adv* erträglich; (*not bad*) leidlich

toleran|ce *n* Toleranz *f*. **~t** *a*, **-ly** *adv* tolerant

tolerate *vt* dulden, tolerieren; (*bear*) ertragen

toll *n* Gebühr *f*; (*for road*) Maut *f* (*Aust*); **death ~** Zahl *f* der Todesopfer

tomato *n* (*pl* **-es**) Tomate *f*

tomb *n* Grabmal *nt*

tombstone *n* Grabstein *m*

tom-cat *n* Kater *m*

tomorrow *n* & *adv* morgen; **~ morning** morgen früh; **the day after ~** übermorgen; **see you ~!** bis morgen!

ton *n* Tonne *f*; **~s of** 🔟 jede Menge

tone *n* Ton *m*; (*colour*) Farbton *m* ● *vt* **~ down** dämpfen; (*fig*) mäßigen. **~ up** *vt* kräftigen; straffen <*muscles*>

tongs *npl* Zange *f*

tongue *n* Zunge *f*; **~ in cheek** 🔟 nicht ernst

tonic *n* Tonikum *nt*; (*for hair*) Haarwasser *nt*; (*fig*) Wohltat *f*; **~ [water]** *n* Tonic *nt*

tonight *n* & *adv* heute Nacht; (*evening*) heute Abend

tonne *n* Tonne *f*

tonsil *n* (*Anat*) Mandel *f*. **~litis** *n* Mandelentzündung *f*

too *adv* zu; (*also*) auch; **~ much/ little** zu viel/zu wenig

took *see* **take**

tool *n* Werkzeug *nt*; (*for gardening*) Gerät *nt*. **~bar** *n* Werkzeugleiste *f*

tooth *n* (*pl* **teeth**) Zahn *m*

tooth:~ache *n* Zahnschmerzen *pl*. **~brush** *n* Zahnbürste *f*. **~less** *a* zahnlos. **~paste** *n* Zahnpasta *f*. **~pick** *n* Zahnstocher *m*

top¹ *n* (*toy*) Kreisel *m*

top² *n* oberer Teil *m*; (*apex*) Spitze *f*; (*summit*) Gipfel *m*; (*Sch*) Erste(r) *m/f*; (*top part or half*)

Oberteil nt; (head) Kopfende nt; (of road) oberes Ende nt; (upper surface) Oberfläche f; (lid) Deckel m; (of bottle) Verschluss m; (garment) Top nt; **at the/on ~** oben; **on ~ of** oben auf (+ dat/ acc); **on ~ of that** (besides) obendrein; **from ~ to bottom** von oben bis unten ● a oberste(r,s); (highest) höchste(r,s); (best) beste(r,s) ● vt (pt/pp **topped**) an erster Stelle stehen auf (+ dat) <list>; (exceed) übersteigen; (remove the ~ of) die Spitze abschneiden von. **~ up** vt nachfüllen, auffüllen

top: ~ hat n Zylinder[hut] m. **~-heavy** a kopflastig

topic n Thema nt. **~al** a aktuell

topple vt/i umstürzen

torch n Taschenlampe f; (flaming) Fackel f

tore see tear[1]

torment[1] n Qual f

torment[2] vt quälen

torn see tear[1] ● a zerrissen

torpedo n (pl **-es**) Torpedo m ● vt torpedieren

torrent n reißender Strom m. **~ial** a <rain> wolkenbruchartig

tortoise n Schildkröte f. **~shell** n Schildpatt m

tortuous a verschlungen; (fig) umständlich

torture n Folter f; (fig) Qual f ● vt foltern; (fig) quälen

toss vt werfen; (into the air) hochwerfen; (shake) schütteln; (unseat) abwerfen; mischen <salad>; wenden <pancake>; **~ a coin** mit einer Münze losen ● vi **~ and turn** (in bed) sich [schlaflos] im Bett wälzen

tot[1] n kleines Kind nt; (🎔 of liquor) Gläschen nt

tot[2] vt (pt/pp **totted**) **~ up** 🎔 zusammenzählen

total a gesamt; (complete) völlig, total ● n Gesamtzahl f; (sum)

Gesamtsumme f ● vt (pt/pp **totalled**); (amount to) sich belaufen auf (+ acc)

totalitarian a totalitär

totally adv völlig, total

totter vi taumeln

touch n Berührung f; (sense) Tastsinn m; (Mus) Anschlag m; (contact) Kontakt m; (trace) Spur f; (fig) Anflug m; **get/be in ~** sich in Verbindung setzen/in Verbindung stehen (**with** mit) ● vt berühren; (get hold of) anfassen; (lightly) tippen auf/an (+ acc); (brush against) streifen [gegen]; (fig: move) rühren; anrühren <food, subject>; **don't ~ that!** fass das nicht an! ● vi sich berühren; **~ on** (fig) berühren. **~ down** vi (Aviat) landen. **~ up** vt ausbessern

touch|ing a rührend. **~y** a empfindlich

tough a (-er, -est) zäh; (severe, harsh) hart; (difficult) schwierig; (durable) strapazierfähig

toughen vt härten; **~ up** abhärten

tour n Reise f, Tour f; (of building, town) Besichtigung f; (Theat, Sport) Tournee f; (of duty) Dienstzeit f ● vt fahren durch ● vi herumreisen

touris|m n Tourismus m, Fremdenverkehr m. **~t** n Tourist(in) m(f) ● attrib Touristen-. **~t office** n Fremdenverkehrsbüro nt

tournament n Turnier nt

tour operator n Reiseveranstalter m

tousle vt zerzausen

tow n **give s.o./a car a ~** jdn/ein Auto abschleppen ● vt schleppen; ziehen <trailer>

toward[s] prep zu (+ dat); (with time) gegen (+ acc); (with respect to) gegenüber (+ dat)

towel n Handtuch nt. **~ling** n (Tex) Frottee nt

T

tower n Turm m ● vi ~ **above** überragen. ~ **block** n Hochhaus nt. ~**ing** a hoch aufragend

town n Stadt f. ~ **hall** n Rathaus nt

tow-rope n Abschleppseil nt

toxic a giftig

toy n Spielzeug nt ● vi ~ **with** spielen mit; stochern in (+ dat) <food>. ~**shop** n Spielwarengeschäft nt

trace n Spur f ● vt folgen (+ dat); (find) finden; (draw) zeichnen; (with tracing-paper) durchpausen

track n Spur f; (path) [unbefestigter] Weg m; (Sport) Bahn f; (Rail) Gleis nt; **keep** ~ **of** im Auge behalten ● vt verfolgen. ~ **down** vt aufspüren; (find) finden

tracksuit n Trainingsanzug m

tractor n Traktor m

trade n Handel m; (line of business) Gewerbe nt; (business) Geschäft nt; (craft) Handwerk nt; **by** ~ von Beruf ● vt tauschen; ~ **in** (give in part exchange) in Zahlung geben ● vi handeln (**in** mit)

trade mark n Warenzeichen nt

trader n Händler m

trade: ~ **union** n Gewerkschaft f. ~ **unionist** n Gewerkschaftler(in) m(f)

trading n Handel m

tradition n Tradition f. ~**al** a, **-ly** adv traditionell

traffic n Verkehr m; (trading) Handel m

traffic: ~ **circle** n (Amer) Kreisverkehr m. ~ **jam** n [Verkehrs]stau m. ~ **lights** npl [Verkehrs]ampel f. ~ **warden** n ≈ Hilfspolizist m; (woman) Politesse f

tragedy n Tragödie f

tragic a, **-ally** adv tragisch

trail n Spur f; (path) Weg m, Pfad m ● vi schleifen; <plant:> sich ranken ● vt verfolgen, folgen (+ dat); (drag) schleifen

trailer n (Auto) Anhänger m; (Amer: caravan) Wohnwagen m; (film) Vorschau f

train n Zug m; (of dress) Schleppe f ● vt ausbilden; (Sport) trainieren; (aim) richten auf (+ acc); erziehen <child>; abrichten/(to do tricks) dressieren <animal>; ziehen <plant> ● vi eine Ausbildung machen; (Sport) trainieren. ~**ed** a ausgebildet

trainee n Auszubildende(r) m/f; (Techn) Praktikant(in) m(f)

train|er n (Sport) Trainer m; (in circus) Dompteur m; ~**ers** pl Trainingsschuhe pl. ~**ing** n Ausbildung f; (Sport) Training nt; (of animals) Dressur f

trait n Eigenschaft f

traitor n Verräter m

tram n Straßenbahn f

tramp n Landstreicher m ● vi stapfen; (walk) marschieren

trample vt/i trampeln

trance n Trance f

tranquil a ruhig. ~**lity** n Ruhe f

tranquillizer n Beruhigungsmittel nt

transaction n Transaktion f

transcend vt übersteigen

transfer[1] n (see **transfer**[2]) Übertragung f; Verlegung f; Versetzung f; Überweisung f; (Sport) Transfer m; (design) Abziehbild nt

transfer[2] v (pt/pp **transferred**) ● vt übertragen; verlegen <firm, prisoners>; versetzen <employee>; überweisen <money>; (Sport) transferieren ● vi [über]wechseln; (when travelling) umsteigen

transform vt verwandeln. ~**ation** n Verwandlung f. ~**er** n Transformator m

transfusion n Transfusion f

transistor n Transistor m
transit n Transit m; (of goods) Transport m; **in ~** <goods> auf dem Transport
transition n Übergang m. **~al** a Übergangs-
translat|e vt übersetzen. **~ion** n Übersetzung f. **~or** n Übersetzer(in) m(f)
transmission n Übertragung f
transmit vt (pt/pp **transmitted**) übertragen. **~ter** n Sender m
transparen|cy n (Phot) Dia nt. **~t** a durchsichtig
transplant¹ n Verpflanzung f, Transplantation f
transplant² vt umpflanzen; (Med) verpflanzen
transport¹ n Transport m
transport² vt transportieren. **~ation** n Transport m
transpose vt umstellen
trap n Falle f; (⊡ mouth) Klappe f; pony and **~** Einspänner m ● vt (pt/pp **trapped**) [mit einer Falle] fangen; (jam) einklemmen; **be ~ped** festsitzen; (shut in) eingeschlossen sein. **~door** n Falltür f
trash n Schund m; (rubbish) Abfall m; (nonsense) Quatsch m. **~can** n (Amer) Mülleimer m. **~y** a Schund-
trauma n Trauma nt. **~tic** a traumatisch
travel n Reisen nt ● v (pt/pp **travelled**) ● vi reisen; (go in vehicle) fahren; <light, sound:> sich fortpflanzen; (Techn) sich bewegen ● vt bereisen; fahren <distance>. **~ agency** n Reisebüro nt. **~ agent** n Reisebürokaufmann m
traveller n Reisende(r) m/f; (Comm) Vertreter m; **~s** pl (gypsies) Zigeuner pl. **~'s cheque** n Reisescheck m
trawler n Fischdampfer m

tray n Tablett nt; (for baking) [Back]blech nt; (for documents) Ablagekorb m
treacher|ous a treulos; (dangerous, deceptive) tückisch. **~y** n Verrat m
tread n Schritt m; (step) Stufe f; (of tyre) Profil nt ● v (pt **trod**, pp **trodden**) ● vi (walk) gehen; **~ on/in** treten auf/ in (+ acc) ● vt treten
treason n Verrat m
treasure n Schatz m ● vt in Ehren halten. **~r** n Kassenwart m
treasury n Schatzkammer f; **the T~** das Finanzministerium
treat n [besonderes] Vergnügen nt ● vt behandeln; **~ s.o. to sth** jdm etw spendieren
treatment n Behandlung f
treaty n Vertrag m
treble a dreifach; **~ the amount** dreimal so viel ● n (Mus) Diskant m; (voice) Sopran m ● vt verdreifachen ● vi sich verdreifachen
tree n Baum m
trek n Marsch m ● vi (pt/pp **trekked**) latschen
trellis n Gitter nt
tremble vi zittern
tremendous a, **-ly** adv gewaltig; (⊡ excellent) großartig
tremor n Zittern nt; **[earth] ~** Beben nt
trench n Graben m; (Mil) Schützengraben m
trend n Tendenz f; (fashion) Trend m. **~y** a (-ier, -iest) ⊡ modisch
trepidation n Beklommenheit f
trespass vi **~ on** unerlaubt betreten
trial n (Jur) [Gerichts]verfahren nt, Prozess m; (test) Probe f; (ordeal) Prüfung f; **be on ~** auf Probe sein; (Jur) angeklagt sein

T

(for wegen); **by ~ and error** durch
Probieren

triang|le n Dreieck nt; (Mus)
Triangel m. **~ular** a dreieckig

tribe n Stamm m

tribunal n Schiedsgericht nt

tributary n Nebenfluss m

tribute n Tribut m; **pay ~** Tribut
zollen (**to** dat)

trick n Trick m; (joke) Streich m;
(Cards) Stich m; (feat of skill)
Kunststück nt ● vt täuschen, 🔲
hereinlegen

trickle vi rinnen

trick|ster n Schwindler m. **~y** a
(-ier, -iest) a schwierig

tricycle n Dreirad nt

tried see **try**

trifl|e n Kleinigkeit f; (Culin)
Trifle nt. **~ing** a unbedeutend

trigger n Abzug m; (fig) Auslöser
m ● vt **~ [off]** auslösen

trim a (trimmer, trimmest) gepflegt
● n (cut) Nachschneiden nt;
(decoration) Verzierung f;
(condition) Zustand m ● vt
schneiden; (decorate) besetzen.
~ming n Besatz m; **~mings** pl
(accessories) Zubehör nt;
(decorations) Verzierungen pl

trio n Trio nt

trip n Reise f; (excursion) Ausflug
m ● v (pt/pp tripped) ● vt **~ s.o.
up** jdm ein Bein stellen ● vi
stolpern (**on/over** über + acc)

tripe n Kaldaunen pl; (nonsense)
Quatsch m

triple a dreifach ● vt
verdreifachen ● vi sich
verdreifachen

triplets npl Drillinge pl

triplicate n **in ~** in dreifacher
Ausfertigung

tripod n Stativ nt

tripper n Ausflügler m

trite a banal

triumph n Triumph m ● vi
triumphieren (**over** über + acc).
~ant a, **-ly** adv triumphierend

trivial a belanglos. **~ity** n
Belanglosigkeit f

trod, trodden see **tread**

trolley n (for food) Servierwagen
m; (for shopping) Einkaufswagen
m; (for luggage) Kofferkuli m;
(Amer: tram) Straßenbahn f

trombone n Posaune f

troop n Schar f; **~s** pl Truppen pl

trophy n Trophäe f; (in
competition) ≈ Pokal m

tropics npl Tropen pl. **~al** a
tropisch; <fruit> Süd-

trot n Trab m ● vi (pt/pp trotted)
traben

trouble n Ärger m; (difficulties)
Schwierigkeiten pl;
(inconvenience) Mühe f; (conflict)
Unruhe f; (Med) Beschwerden pl;
(Techn) Probleme pl; **get into ~**
Ärger bekommen; **take ~** sich
(dat) Mühe geben ● vt (disturb)
stören; (worry) beunruhigen ● vi
sich bemühen. **~-maker** n
Unruhestifter m. **~some** a
schwierig; <flies, cough> lästig

trough n Trog m

troupe n Truppe f

trousers npl Hose f

trousseau n Aussteuer f

trout n inv Forelle f

trowel n Kelle f

truant n **play ~** die Schule
schwänzen

truce n Waffenstillstand m

truck n Last[kraft]wagen m; (Rail)
Güterwagen m

trudge vi latschen

true a (-r, -st) wahr; (loyal) treu;
(genuine) echt; **come ~** in
Erfüllung gehen; **is that ~?**
stimmt das?

truly adv wirklich; (faithfully)
treu; **Yours ~** mit freundlichen
Grüßen

trump n (Cards) Trumpf m ● vt
übertrumpfen

trumpet n Trompete f. **~er** n
Trompeter m

truncheon n Schlagstock m
trunk n [Baum]stamm m; (body)
Rumpf m; (of elephant) Rüssel m;
(for travelling) [Übersee]koffer
m; (Amer: of car) Kofferraum m;
~s pl Badehose f
trust n Vertrauen nt; (group of
companies) Trust m;
(organization)
Treuhandgesellschaft f;
(charitable) Stiftung f ● vt trauen
(+ dat), vertrauen (+ dat); (hope)
hoffen ● vi vertrauen (in/to auf +
acc)
trustee n Treuhänder m
trust|ful a, **-ly** adv, **~ing** a
vertrauensvoll. **~worthy** a
vertrauenswürdig
truth n (pl **-s**) Wahrheit f. **~ful** a,
-ly adv ehrlich
try n Versuch m ● v (pt/pp tried)
● vt versuchen; (sample, taste)
probieren; (be a strain on)
anstrengen; (Jur) vor Gericht
stellen; verhandeln <case> ● vi
versuchen; (make an effort) sich
bemühen. **~ on** vt anprobieren;
aufprobieren <hat>. **~ out** vt
ausprobieren
trying a schwierig
T-shirt n T-Shirt nt
tub n Kübel m; (carton) Becher m;
(bath) Wanne f
tuba n (Mus) Tuba f
tubby a (**-ier, -iest**) rundlich
tube n Röhre f; (pipe) Rohr nt;
(flexible) Schlauch m; (of
toothpaste) Tube f; (Rail 🅸) U-
Bahn f
tuberculosis n Tuberkulose f
tubular a röhrenförmig
tuck n Saum m; (decorative) Biese
f ● vt (put) stecken. **~ in** vt
hineinstecken; **~ s.o. in** or **up** jdn
zudecken ● vi (🅸 eat) zulangen
Tuesday n Dienstag m
tuft n Büschel nt
tug n Ruck m; (Naut)
Schleppdampfer m ● v (pt/pp

tugged) ● vt ziehen ● vi zerren
(at an + dat)
tuition n Unterricht m
tulip n Tulpe f
tumble n Sturz m ● vi fallen.
~down a verfallen. **~-drier** n
Wäschetrockner m
tumbler n Glas nt
tummy n 🅸 Bauch m
tumour n Tumor m
tumult n Tumult m
tuna n Thunfisch m
tune n Melodie f; out of **~**
<instrument> verstimmt ● vt
stimmen; (Techn) einstellen. **~ in**
vt einstellen; ● vi **~ in to a station**
einen Sender einstellen. **~ up** vi
(Mus) stimmen
tuneful a melodisch
Tunisia n Tunesien nt
tunnel n Tunnel m ● vi (pt/pp
tunnelled) einen Tunnel graben
turban n Turban m
turbine n Turbine f
turbulen|ce n Turbulenz f. **~t** a
stürmisch
turf n Rasen m; (segment)
Rasenstück nt
Turk n Türke m/Türkin f
turkey n Truthahn m
Turk|ey n die Türkei. **~ish** a
türkisch; **the ~ish** die Türken
turmoil n Aufruhr m; (confusion)
Durcheinander nt
turn n (rotation) Drehung f;
(bend) Kurve f; (change of
direction) Wende f; (Theat)
Nummer f; (🅸 attack) Anfall m;
do s.o. a good ~ jdm einen guten
Dienst erweisen; **take ~s** sich
abwechseln; **in ~** der Reihe
nach; **out of ~** außer der Reihe;
it's your ~ du bist an der Reihe
● vt drehen; (~ over) wenden;
(reverse) umdrehen; (Techn)
drechseln <wood>; **~ the page**
umblättern; **~ the corner** um die
Ecke biegen ● vi sich drehen; (~
round) sich umdrehen; <car:>

wenden; <*leaves*:> sich färben:
<*weather*:> umschlagen; (*become*)
werden; ~ **right/left** nach rechts/
links abbiegen; ~ **to s.o.** sich an
jdn wenden. ~ **away** vt abweisen
● vi sich abwenden. ~ **down** vt
herunterschlagen <*collar*>;
herunterdrehen <*heat, gas*>;
leiser stellen <*sound*>; (*reject*)
ablehnen; abweisen <*person*>. ~
in vt einschlagen <*edges*> ● vi
<*car*:> einbiegen; (🛏 *go to bed*)
ins Bett gehen. ~ **off** vt zudrehen
<*tap*>; ausschalten <*light, radio*>;
abstellen <*water, gas, engine,
machine*> ● vi abbiegen. ~ **on** vt
aufdrehen <*tap*>; einschalten
<*light, radio*>; anstellen <*water,
gas, engine, machine*>. ~ **out** vt
(*expel*) vertreiben, 🛏
hinauswerfen; ausschalten
<*light*>; abdrehen <*gas*>;
(*produce*) produzieren; (*empty*)
ausleeren; [gründlich]
aufräumen <*room, cupboard*>
● vi (*go out*) hinausgehen;
(*transpire*) sich herausstellen. ~
over vt umdrehen. ~ **up** vt
hochschlagen <*collar*>;
aufdrehen <*heat, gas*>; lauter
stellen <*sound, radio*> ● vi
auftauchen
turning n Abzweigung f. ~**-point**
n Wendepunkt m
turnip n weiße Rübe f
turn: ~**-out** n (*of people*)
Beteiligung f. ~**over** n (*Comm*)
Umsatz m; (*of staff*)
Personalwechsel m. ~**pike** n
(*Amer*) gebührenpflichtige
Autobahn f. ~**table** n
Drehscheibe f; (*on record player*)
Plattenteller m. ~**-up** n
[Hosen]aufschlag m
turquoise a türkis[farben] ● n
(*gem*) Türkis m
turret n Türmchen nt
turtle n Seeschildkröte f
tusk n Stoßzahn m

tutor n [Privat]lehrer m
tuxedo n (*Amer*) Smoking m
TV abbr of **television**
tweed n Tweed m
tweezers npl Pinzette f
twelfth a zwölfter(r,s)
twelve a zwölf
twentieth a zwanzigste(r,s)
twenty a zwanzig
twice adv zweimal
twig n Zweig m
twilight n Dämmerlicht nt
twin n Zwilling m ● attrib
Zwillings-
twine n Bindfaden m
twinge n Stechen nt; ~ **of
conscience** Gewissensbisse pl
twinkle n Funkeln nt ● vi funkeln
twin town n Partnerstadt f
twirl vt/i herumwirbeln
twist n Drehung f; (*curve*) Kurve
f; (*unexpected occurrence*)
überraschende Wendung f ● vt
drehen; (*distort*) verdrehen; (🛏
swindle) beschummeln; ~ **one's
ankle** sich (*dat*) den Knöchel
verrenken ● vi sich drehen;
<*road*:> sich winden. ~**er** n 🛏
Schwindler m
twit n 🛏 Trottel m
twitch n Zucken nt ● vi zucken
twitter n Zwitschern nt ● vi
zwitschern
two a zwei
two: ~**-faced** a falsch. ~**-piece** a
zweiteilig. ~**-way** a ~**-way traffic**
Gegenverkehr m
tycoon n Magnat m
tying see **tie**
type n Art f, Sorte f; (*person*) Typ
m; (*printing*) Type f ● vt mit der
Maschine schreiben, 🛏 tippen
● vi Maschine schreiben, 🛏
tippen. ~**writer** n
Schreibmaschine f. ~**written** a
maschinegeschrieben
typical a, **-ly** adv typisch (**of** für)
typify vt (*pt/pp* **-ied**) typisch sein
für

typing n Maschineschreiben nt
typist n Schreibkraft f
tyrannical a tyrannisch
tyranny n Tyrannei f
tyrant n Tyrann m
tyre n Reifen m

ugl|iness n Hässlichkeit f. **~y** a
(-ier, -iest) hässlich; (nasty) übel
UK abbr see **United Kingdom**
ulcer n Geschwür nt
ultimate a letzte(r,s); (final)
endgültig; (fundamental)
grundlegend, eigentlich. **~ly** adv
schließlich
ultimatum n Ultimatum nt
ultraviolet a ultraviolett
umbrella n [Regen]schirm m
umpire n Schiedsrichter m ● vt/i
Schiedsrichter sein (bei)
umpteen a 🔢 zig. **~th** a 🔢
zigste(r,s)
unable a be **~** to do sth etw nicht
tun können
unabridged a ungekürzt
unaccompanied a ohne
Begleitung; <luggage>
unbegleitet
unaccountable a unerklärlich
unaccustomed a ungewohnt; be
~ to sth etw (acc) nicht gewohnt
sein
unaided a ohne fremde Hilfe
unanimous a, **-ly** adv einmütig;
<vote, decision> einstimmig
unarmed a unbewaffnet
unassuming a bescheiden
unattended a unbeaufsichtigt
unauthorized a unbefugt
unavoidable a unvermeidlich

unaware a be **~** of sth sich (dat)
etw (gen) nicht bewusst sein. **~s**
adv catch s.o. **~s** jdn überraschen
unbearable a, **-bly** adv
unerträglich
unbeat|able a unschlagbar. **~en**
a ungeschlagen; <record>
ungebrochen
unbelievable a unglaublich
unbiased a unvoreingenommen
unblock vt frei machen
unbolt vt aufriegeln
unbreakable a unzerbrechlich
unbutton vt aufknöpfen
uncalled-for a unangebracht
uncanny a unheimlich
unceasing a unaufhörlich
uncertain a (doubtful) ungewiss;
<origins> unbestimmt; be **~** nicht
sicher sein. **~ty** n Ungewissheit f
unchanged a unverändert
uncharitable a lieblos
uncle n Onkel m
uncomfortable a, **-bly** adv
unbequem; feel **~** (fig) sich nicht
wohl fühlen
uncommon a ungewöhnlich
uncompromising a
kompromisslos
unconditional a, **~ly** adv
bedingungslos
unconscious a bewusstlos;
(unintended) unbewusst; be **~** of
sth sich (dat) etw (gen) nicht
bewusst sein. **~ly** adv unbewusst
unconventional a
unkonventionell
uncooperative a nicht hilfsbereit
uncork vt entkorken
uncouth a ungehobelt
uncover vt aufdecken
undecided a unentschlossen; (not
settled) nicht entschieden
undeniable a, **-bly** adv
unbestreitbar
under prep unter (+ dat/acc); **~** it
darunter; **~** there da drunter; **~**
repair in Reparatur; **~**

U

construction im Bau; $\sim$ age minderjährig ● *adv* darunter

undercarriage *n* (*Aviat*) Fahrwerk *nt*, Fahrgestell *nt*

underclothes *npl* Unterwäsche *f*

undercover *a* geheim

undercurrent *n* Unterströmung *f*; (*fig*) Unterton *m*

underdog *n* Unterlegene(r) *m*

underdone *a* nicht gar; (*rare*) nicht durchgebraten

underestimate *vt* unterschätzen

underfed *a* unterernährt

underfoot *adv* am Boden

undergo *vt* (*pt* -**went**, *pp* -**gone**) durchmachen; sich unterziehen (+ *dat*) <*operation, treatment*>

undergraduate *n* Student(in) *m(f)*

underground¹ *adv* unter der Erde; <*mining*> unter Tage

underground² *a* unterirdisch; (*secret*) Untergrund- ● *n* (*railway*) U-Bahn *f*. $\sim$ **car park** *n* Tiefgarage *f*

undergrowth *n* Unterholz *nt*

underhand *a* hinterhältig

underlie *vt* (*pt* -**lay**, *pp* -**lain**, *pres p* -**lying**) zugrunde liegen (+ *dat*)

underline *vt* unterstreichen

underlying *a* eigentlich

undermine *vt* (*fig*) unterminieren, untergraben

underneath *prep* unter (+ *dat/acc*) ● *adv* darunter

underpants *npl* Unterhose *f*

underpass *n* Unterführung *f*

underprivileged *a* unterprivilegiert

underrate *vt* unterschätzen

undershirt *n* (*Amer*) Unterhemd *nt*

understand *vt/i* (*pt/pp* -**stood**) verstehen; **I** $\sim$ **that** … (*have heard*) ich habe gehört, dass … $\sim$**able** *a* verständlich. $\sim$**ably** *adv* verständlicherweise

understanding *a* verständnisvoll ● *n* Verständnis *nt*; (*agreement*) Vereinbarung *f*; **reach an** $\sim$ sich verständigen

understatement *n* Untertreibung *f*

undertake *vt* (*pt* -**took**, *pp* -**taken**) unternehmen; $\sim$ **to do sth** sich verpflichten, etw zu tun

undertaker *n* Leichenbestatter *m*; [**firm of**] $\sim$**s** Bestattungsinstitut *n*

undertaking *n* Unternehmen *nt*; (*promise*) Versprechen *nt*

undertone *n* (*fig*) Unterton *m*; **in an** $\sim$ mit gedämpfter Stimme

undervalue *vt* unterbewerten

underwater¹ *a* Unterwasser-

underwater² *adv* unter Wasser

underwear *n* Unterwäsche *f*

underweight *a* untergewichtig; **be** $\sim$ Untergewicht haben

underworld *n* Unterwelt *f*

undesirable *a* unerwünscht

undignified *a* würdelos

undo *vt* (*pt* -**did**, *pp* -**done**) aufmachen; (*fig*) ungeschehen machen

undone *a* offen; (*not accomplished*) unerledigt

undoubted *a* unzweifelhaft. $\sim$**ly** *adv* zweifellos

undress *vt* ausziehen; **get** $\sim$**ed** sich ausziehen ● *vi* sich ausziehen

undue *a* übermäßig

unduly *adv* übermäßig

unearth *vt* ausgraben; (*fig*) zutage bringen. $\sim$**ly** *a* unheimlich; **at an** $\sim$**ly hour** Ⅰ in aller Herrgottsfrühe

uneasy *a* unbehaglich

uneconomic *a*, -**ally** *adv* unwirtschaftlich

unemployed *a* arbeitslos ● *npl* **the** $\sim$ die Arbeitslosen

unemployment *n* Arbeitslosigkeit *f*

unending *a* endlos

unequal *a* unterschiedlich; <*struggle*> ungleich. $\sim$**ly** *adv* ungleichmäßig

unequivocal *a*, **-ly** *adv* eindeutig
unethical *a* unmoralisch; **be ~** gegen das Berufsethos verstoßen
uneven *a* uneben; (*unequal*) ungleich; (*not regular*) ungleichmäßig; <*number*> ungerade
unexpected *a*, **-ly** *adv* unerwartet
unfair *a*, **-ly** *adv* ungerecht, unfair. **~ness** *n* Ungerechtigkeit *f*
unfaithful *a* untreu
unfamiliar *a* ungewohnt; (*unknown*) unbekannt
unfasten *vt* aufmachen; (*detach*) losmachen
unfavourable *a* ungünstig
unfeeling *a* gefühllos
unfit *a* ungeeignet; (*incompetent*) unfähig; (*Sport*) nicht fit; **~ for work** arbeitsunfähig
unfold *vt* auseinander falten, entfalten; (*spread out*) ausbreiten ● *vi* sich entfalten
unforeseen *a* unvorhergesehen
unforgettable *a* unvergesslich
unforgivable *a* unverzeihlich
unfortunate *a* unglücklich; (*unfavourable*) ungünstig; (*regrettable*) bedauerlich; **be ~** <*person:*> Pech haben. **~ly** *adv* leider
unfounded *a* unbegründet
unfurl *vt* entrollen
unfurnished *a* unmöbliert
ungainly *a* unbeholfen
ungrateful *a*, **-ly** *adv* undankbar
unhappiness *n* Kummer *m*
unhappy *a* unglücklich; (*not content*) unzufrieden
unharmed *a* unverletzt
unhealthy *a* ungesund
unhurt *a* unverletzt
unification *n* Einigung *f*
uniform *a*, **-ly** *adv* einheitlich ● *n* Uniform *f*
unify *vt* (*pt/pp* **-ied**) einigen
unilateral *a*, **-ly** *adv* einseitig
unimaginable *a* unvorstellbar

unimportant *a* unwichtig
uninhabited *a* unbewohnt
unintentional *a*, **-ly** *adv* unabsichtlich
union *n* Vereinigung *f*; (*Pol*) Union *f*; (*trade ~*) Gewerkschaft *f*
unique *a* einzigartig. **~ly** *adv* einmalig
unison *n* **in ~** einstimmig
unit *n* Einheit *f*; (*Math*) Einer *m*; (*of furniture*) Teil *nt*, Element *nt*
unite *vt* vereinigen ● *vi* sich vereinigen
united *a* einig. **U~ Kingdom** *n* Vereinigtes Königreich *nt*. **U~ Nations** *n* Vereinte Nationen *pl*. **U~ States [of America]** *n* Vereinigte Staaten *pl* [von Amerika]
unity *n* Einheit *f*; (*harmony*) Einigkeit *f*
universal *a*, **-ly** *adv* allgemein
universe *n* [Welt]all *nt*, Universum *nt*
university *n* Universität *f* ● *attrib* Universitäts-
unjust *a*, **-ly** *adv* ungerecht
unkind *a*, **-ly** *adv* unfreundlich; (*harsh*) hässlich
unknown *a* unbekannt
unlawful *a*, **-ly** *adv* gesetzwidrig
unleaded *a* bleifrei
unleash *vt* (*fig*) entfesseln
unless *conj* wenn … nicht; **~ I am mistaken** wenn ich mich nicht irre
unlike *prep* im Gegensatz zu (+ *dat*)
unlikely *a* unwahrscheinlich
unlimited *a* unbegrenzt
unload *vt* entladen; ausladen <*luggage*>
unlock *vt* aufschließen
unlucky *a* unglücklich; <*day, number*> Unglücks-; **be ~** Pech haben; <*thing:*> Unglück bringen
unmarried *a* unverheiratet. **~ mother** *n* ledige Mutter *f*

unmask vt (fig) entlarven
unmistakable a, **-bly** adv unverkennbar
unnatural a, **-ly** adv unnatürlich; (not normal) nicht normal
unnecessary a, **-ily** adv unnötig
unnoticed a unbemerkt
unobtainable a nicht erhältlich
unobtrusive a, **-ly** adv unaufdringlich; <thing> unauffällig
unofficial a, **-ly** adv inoffiziell
unpack vt/i auspacken
unpaid a unbezahlt
unpleasant a, **-ly** adv unangenehm
unplug vt (pt/pp **-plugged**) den Stecker herausziehen von
unpopular a unbeliebt
unprecedented a beispiellos
unpredictable a unberechenbar
unprepared a nicht vorbereitet
unpretentious a bescheiden
unprofitable a unrentabel
unqualified a unqualifiziert; (fig: absolute) uneingeschränkt
unquestionable a unbezweifelbar; <right> unbestreitbar
unravel vt (pt/pp **-ravelled**) entwirren; (Knitting) aufziehen
unreal a unwirklich
unreasonable a unvernünftig
unrelated a unzusammenhängend; **be ~** nicht verwandt sein; <events:> nicht miteinander zusammenhängen
unreliable a unzuverlässig
unrest n Unruhen pl
unrivalled a unübertroffen
unroll vt aufrollen ● vi sich aufrollen
unruly a ungebärdig
unsafe a nicht sicher
unsatisfactory a unbefriedigend
unsavoury a unangenehm; (fig) unerfreulich
unscathed a unversehrt

unscrew vt abschrauben
unscrupulous a skrupellos
unseemly a unschicklich
unselfish a selbstlos
unsettled a ungeklärt; <weather> unbeständig; <bill> unbezahlt
unshakeable a unerschütterlich
unshaven a unrasiert
unsightly a unansehnlich
unskilled a ungelernt; <work> unqualifiziert
unsociable a ungesellig
unsophisticated a einfach
unsound a krank, nicht gesund; <building> nicht sicher; <advice> unzuverlässig; <reasoning> nicht stichhaltig
unstable a nicht stabil; (mentally) labil
unsteady a, **-ily** adv unsicher; (wobbly) wackelig
unstuck a **come ~** sich lösen; (🔢 fail) scheitern
unsuccessful a, **-ly** adv erfolglos; **be ~** keinen Erfolg haben
unsuitable a ungeeignet; (inappropriate) unpassend; (for weather, activity) unzweckmäßig
unthinkable a unvorstellbar
untidiness n Unordentlichkeit f
untidy a, **-ily** adv unordentlich
untie vt aufbinden; losbinden <person, boat, horse>
until prep bis (+ acc); **not ~** erst; **~ the evening** bis zum Abend ● conj bis; **not ~** erst wenn; (in past) erst als
untold a unermesslich
untrue a unwahr; **that's ~** das ist nicht wahr
unused¹ a unbenutzt; (not utilized) ungenutzt
unused² a **be ~ to sth** etw nicht gewohnt sein
unusual a, **-ly** adv ungewöhnlich
unveil vt enthüllen
unwanted a unerwünscht
unwelcome a unwillkommen

unwell *a* be *or* feel ∼ sich nicht wohl fühlen

unwieldy *a* sperrig

unwilling *a*, **-ly** *adv* widerwillig; **be** ∼ **to do sth** etw nicht tun wollen

unwind *v* (*pt/pp* **unwound**) ● *vt* abwickeln ● *vi* sich abwickeln; (**!** *relax*) sich entspannen

unwise *a*, **-ly** *adv* unklug

unworthy *a* unwürdig

unwrap *vt* (**-wrapped**) auswickeln; auspacken <*present*>

unwritten *a* ungeschrieben

up *adv* oben; (*with movement*) nach oben; (*not in bed*) auf; <*road*> aufgerissen; <*price*> gestiegen; **be up for sale** zu verkaufen sein; **up there** da oben; **up to** (*as far as*) bis; **time's up** die Zeit ist um; **what's up?** **!** was ist los? **what's he up to?** **!** was hat er vor? **I don't feel up to it** ich fühle mich dem nicht gewachsen; **go up** hinaufgehen; **come up** heraufkommen ● *prep* **be up on sth** [oben] auf etw (*dat*) sein; **up the mountain** oben am Berg; (*movement*) den Berg hinauf; **be up the tree** oben im Baum sein; **up the road** die Straße entlang; **up the river** stromaufwärts; **go up the stairs** die Treppe hinaufgehen

upbringing *n* Erziehung *f*

update *vt* auf den neuesten Stand bringen

upgrade *vt* aufstufen

upheaval *n* Unruhe *f*; (*Pol*) Umbruch *m*

uphill *a* (*fig*) mühsam ● *adv* bergauf

uphold *vt* (*pt/pp* **upheld**) unterstützen; bestätigen <*verdict*>

upholster *vt* polstern. ∼**y** *n* Polsterung *f*

upkeep *n* Unterhalt *m*

upmarket *a* anspruchsvoll

upon *prep* auf (+ *dat/acc*)

upper *a* obere(r,s); <*deck, jaw, lip*> Ober-; **have the** ∼ **hand** die Oberhand haben ● *n* (*of shoe*) Obermaterial *nt*

upper class *n* Oberschicht *f*

upright *a* aufrecht

uprising *n* Aufstand *m*

uproar *n* Aufruhr *m*

upset¹ *vt* (*pt/pp* **upset**, *pres p* **upsetting**) umstoßen; (*spill*) verschütten; durcheinander bringen <*plan*>; (*distress*) erschüttern; <*food:*> nicht bekommen (+ *dat*); **get** ∼ **about sth** sich über etw (*acc*) aufregen

upset² *n* Aufregung *f*; **have a stomach** ∼ einen verdorbenen Magen haben

upshot *n* Ergebnis *nt*

upside down *adv* verkehrt herum; **turn** ∼ umdrehen

upstairs¹ *adv* oben; <*go*> nach oben

upstairs² *a* im Obergeschoss

upstart *n* Emporkömmling *m*

upstream *adv* stromaufwärts

uptake *n* **slow on the** ∼ schwer von Begriff; **be quick on the** ∼ schnell begreifen

upturn *n* Aufschwung *m*

upward *a* nach oben; <*movement*> Aufwärts-; ∼ **slope** Steigung *f* ● *adv* ∼**[s]** aufwärts, nach oben

uranium *n* Uran *nt*

urban *a* städtisch

urge *n* Trieb *m*, Drang *m* ● *vt* drängen; ∼ **on** antreiben

urgen|cy *n* Dringlichkeit *f*. ∼ **t** *a*, **-ly** *adv* dringend

urine *n* Urin *m*, Harn *m*

us *pron* uns; **it's us** wir sind es

US[A] *abbr* USA *pl*

usable *a* brauchbar

usage *n* Brauch *m*; (*of word*) [Sprach]gebrauch *m*

use¹ *n* (*see* **use²**) Benutzung *f*; Verwendung *f*; Gebrauch *m*; **be (of) no** ∼ nichts nützen; **it is no** ∼

es hat keinen Zweck; **what's the**
∼? wozu?

use² *vt* benutzen <*implement,*
room, lift>; verwenden
<*ingredient, method, book,*
money>; gebrauchen <*words,*
force, brains>; **∼ [up]**
aufbrauchen

used¹ *a* gebraucht; <*towel*>
benutzt; <*car*> Gebraucht-

used² *pt* **be ∼ to sth** an etw (*acc*)
gewöhnt sein; **get ∼ to** sich
gewöhnen an (+ *acc*); **he ∼ to say**
er hat immer gesagt; **he ∼ to live**
here er hat früher hier gewohnt

useful *a* nützlich. **∼ness** *n*
Nützlichkeit *f*

useless *a* nutzlos; (*not usable*)
unbrauchbar; (*pointless*)
zwecklos

user *n* Benutzer(in) *m(f)*

usher *n* Platzanweiser *m*; (*in*
court) Gerichtsdiener *m*

usherette *n* Platzanweiserin *f*

USSR *abbr* (*History*) UdSSR *f*

usual *a* üblich. **∼ly** *adv*
gewöhnlich

utensil *n* Gerät *nt*

utility *a* Gebrauchs-

utilize *vt* nutzen

utmost *a* äußerste(r,s), größte(r,s)
● *n* **do one's ∼** sein Möglichstes
tun

utter¹ *a*, **-ly** *adv* völlig

utter² *vt* von sich geben <*sigh,*
sound>; sagen <*word*>

U-turn *n* (*fig*) Kehrtwendung *f*; '**no**
∼s' (*Auto*) 'Wenden verboten'

vacan|cy *n* (*job*) freie Stelle *f*;
(*room*) freies Zimmer *nt*; '**no**
∼cies' 'belegt'. **∼t** *a* frei; <*look*>
[gedanken]leer

vacate *vt* räumen

vacation *n* (*Univ & Amer*) Ferien
pl

vaccinat|e *vt* impfen. **∼ion** *n*
Impfung *f*

vaccine *n* Impfstoff *m*

vacuum *n* Vakuum *nt*, luftleerer
Raum *m* ● *vt* saugen. **∼ cleaner**
n Staubsauger *m*

vagina *n* (*Anat*) Scheide *f*

vague *a* (**-r, -st**), **-ly** *adv* vage;
<*outline*> verschwommen

vain *a* (**-er, -est**) eitel; <*hope,*
attempt> vergeblich; **in ∼**
vergeblich. **∼ly** *adv* vergeblich

valiant *a*, **-ly** *adv* tapfer

valid *a* gültig; <*claim*> berechtigt;
<*argument*> stichhaltig; <*reason*>
triftig. **∼ity** *n* Gültigkeit *f*

valley *n* Tal *nt*

valour *n* Tapferkeit *f*

valuable *a* wertvoll. **∼s** *npl*
Wertsachen *pl*

valuation *n* Schätzung *f*

value *n* Wert *m*; (*usefulness*)
Nutzen *m* ● *vt* schätzen. **∼ added**
tax *n* Mehrwertsteuer *f*

valve *n* Ventil *nt*; (*Anat*) Klappe *f*;
(*Electr*) Röhre *f*

van *n* Lieferwagen *m*

vandal *n* Rowdy *m*. **∼ism** *n*
mutwillige Zerstörung *f*. **∼ize** *vt*
demolieren

vanilla *n* Vanille *f*

vanish *vi* verschwinden

vanity *n* Eitelkeit *f*

vapour *n* Dampf *m*

variable a unbeständig; (*Math*) variabel; (*adjustable*) regulierbar

variant n Variante f

variation n Variation f; (*difference*) Unterschied m

varied a vielseitig; <*diet:*> abwechslungsreich

variety n Abwechslung f; (*quantity*) Vielfalt f; (*Comm*) Auswahl f; (*type*) Art f; (*Bot*) Abart f; (*Theat*) Varieté nt

various a verschieden. ∼ly adv unterschiedlich

varnish n Lack m ● vt lackieren

vary v (*pt/pp* -ied) ● vi sich ändern; (*be different*) verschieden sein ● vt [ver]ändern; (*add variety to*) abwechslungsreicher gestalten

vase n Vase f

vast a riesig; <*expanse*> weit. ∼ly adv gewaltig

vat n Bottich m

VAT abbr (**value added tax**) Mehrwertsteuer f, MwSt.

vault[1] n (*roof*) Gewölbe nt; (*in bank*) Tresor m; (*tomb*) Gruft f

vault[2] n Sprung m ● vt/i ∼ **[over]** springen über (+ acc)

VDU abbr (**visual display unit**) Bildschirmgerät nt

veal n Kalbfleisch nt ● attrib Kalbs-

veer vi sich drehen; (*Auto*) ausscheren

vegetable n Gemüse nt; ∼s pl Gemüse nt ● attrib Gemüse-; <*oil, fat*> Pflanzen-

vegetarian a vegetarisch ● n Vegetarier(in) m(f)

vegetation n Vegetation f

vehement a, -ly adv heftig

vehicle n Fahrzeug nt

veil n Schleier m ● vt verschleiern

vein n Ader f; (*mood*) Stimmung f; (*manner*) Art f

velocity n Geschwindigkeit f

velvet n Samt m

vending-machine n [Verkaufs]automat m

vendor n Verkäufer(in) m(f)

veneer n Furnier nt; (*fig*) Tünche f. ∼ed a furniert

venerable a ehrwürdig

Venetian a venezianisch. v∼ **blind** n Jalousie f

vengeance n Rache f; **with a** ∼ gewaltig

Venice n Venedig nt

venison n (*Culin*) Reh(fleisch) nt

venom n Gift nt; (*fig*) Hass m. ∼ous a giftig

vent n Öffnung f

ventilat|e vt belüften. ∼ion n Belüftung f; (*installation*) Lüftung f. ∼or n Lüftungsvorrichtung f; (*Med*) Beatmungsgerät nt

ventriloquist n Bauchredner m

venture n Unternehmung f ● vt wagen ● vi sich wagen

venue n (*for event*) Veranstaltungsort m

veranda n Veranda f

verb n Verb nt. ∼al a, -ly adv mündlich; (*Gram*) verbal

verbose a weitschweifig

verdict n Urteil nt

verge n Rand m ● vi ∼ **on** (*fig*) grenzen an (+ acc)

verify vt (*pt/pp* -ied) überprüfen; (*confirm*) bestätigen

vermin n Ungeziefer nt

vermouth n Wermut m

versatil|e a vielseitig. ∼ity n Vielseitigkeit f

verse n Strophe f; (*of Bible*) Vers m; (*poetry*) Lyrik f

version n Version f; (*translation*) Übersetzung f; (*model*) Modell nt

versus prep gegen (+ acc)

vertical a, -ly adv senkrecht ● n Senkrechte f

vertigo n (*Med*) Schwindel m

verve n Schwung m

very adv sehr; ∼ **much** sehr; (*quantity*) sehr viel; ∼ **probably** höchstwahrscheinlich; **at the** ∼

V

most allerhöchstens ● a (mere)
bloß; **the ~ first** der/die/das
allererste; **at the ~ end/beginning**
ganz am Ende/Anfang; **only a ~**
little nur ein ganz kleines
bisschen

vessel n Schiff nt; (receptacle &
Anat) Gefäß nt

vest n [Unter]hemd nt; (Amer:
waistcoat) Weste f

vestige n Spur f

vestry n Sakristei f

vet n Tierarzt m /-ärztin f ● vt
(pt/pp vetted) überprüfen

veteran n Veteran m

veterinary a tierärztlich. ~
surgeon n Tierarzt m /-ärztin f

veto n (pl -es) Veto nt

VHF abbr (very high frequency)
UKW

via prep über (+ acc)

viable a lebensfähig; (fig)
realisierbar; <firm> rentabel

viaduct n Viadukt nt

vibrat|e vi vibrieren. ~ion n
Vibrieren nt

vicar n Pfarrer m. ~age n
Pfarrhaus nt

vice¹ n Laster nt

vice² n (Techn) Schraubstock m

vice³ a Vize-; ~ **chairman**
stellvertretender Vorsitzender m

vice versa adv umgekehrt

vicinity n Umgebung f; **in the ~ of**
in der Nähe von

vicious a, **-ly** adv boshaft;
<animal> bösartig

victim n Opfer nt. ~ize vt
schikanieren

victor n Sieger m

victor|ious a siegreich. ~y n Sieg
m

video n Video nt; (recorder)
Videorecorder m ● attrib Video-

video: ~ **cassette** n
Videokassette f. ~ **game** n
Videospiel nt. ~**phone** n
Bildtelefon nt. ~ **recorder** n
Videorecorder m

Vienn|a n Wien nt. ~ese a
Wiener

view n Sicht f; (scene) Aussicht f,
Blick m; (picture, opinion)
Ansicht f; **in my ~** meiner
Ansicht nach; **in ~ of** angesichts
(+ gen); **be on ~** besichtigt
werden können ● vt sich (dat)
ansehen; besichtigen <house>;
(consider) betrachten ● vi (TV)
fernsehen. ~er n (TV)
Zuschauer(in) m(f)

view: ~**finder** n (Phot) Sucher m.
~**point** n Standpunkt m

vigilan|ce n Wachsamkeit f. ~t a,
-ly adv wachsam

vigorous a, **-ly** adv kräftig; (fig)
heftig

vigour n Kraft f; (fig) Heftigkeit f

vile a abscheulich

villa n (for holidays) Ferienhaus
nt

village n Dorf nt. ~r n
Dorfbewohner(in) m(f)

villain n Schurke m; (in story)
Bösewicht m

vindicat|e vt rechtfertigen. ~ion
n Rechtfertigung f

vindictive a nachtragend

vine n Weinrebe f

vinegar n Essig m

vineyard n Weinberg m

vintage a erlesen ● n (year)
Jahrgang m. ~ **car** n Oldtimer m

viola n (Mus) Bratsche f

violat|e vt verletzen; (break)
brechen; (disturb) stören; (defile)
schänden. ~ion n Verletzung f;
Schändung f

violen|ce n Gewalt f; (fig)
Heftigkeit f. ~t a gewalttätig;
(fig) heftig. ~**tly** adv brutal; (fig)
heftig

violet a violett ● n (flower)
Veilchen n

violin n Geige f, Violine f. ~**ist** n
Geiger(in) m(f)

VIP abbr (very important person)
Prominente(r) m/f

viper n Kreuzotter f

virgin a unberührt ● n Jungfrau f. ~**ity** n Unschuld f

viril|e a männlich. ~**ity** n Männlichkeit f

virtual a a ~ ... praktisch ein ... ~**ly** adv praktisch

virtu|e n Tugend f; (advantage) Vorteil m; **by** or **in** ~**e of** auf Grund (+ gen)

virtuoso n (pl -si) Virtuose m

virtuous a tugendhaft

virus n Virus nt

visa n Visum nt

visibility n Sichtbarkeit f; (Meteorol) Sichtweite f

visible a, **-bly** adv sichtbar

vision n Vision f; (sight) Sehkraft f; (foresight) Weitblick m

visit n Besuch m ● vt besuchen; besichtigen <town, building>. ~**or** n Besucher(in) m(f); (in hotel) Gast m; **have** ~**ors** Besuch haben

visor n Schirm m; (Auto) [Sonnen]blende f

vista n Aussicht f

visual a, **-ly** adv visuell. ~ **display unit** n Bildschirmgerät nt

visualize vt sich (dat) vorstellen

vital a unbedingt notwendig; (essential to life) lebenswichtig. ~**ity** n Vitalität f. ~**ly** adv äußerst

vitamin n Vitamin nt

vivaci|ous a, **-ly** adv lebhaft. ~**ty** n Lebhaftigkeit f

vivid a, **-ly** adv lebhaft; <description> lebendig

vocabulary n Wortschatz m; (list) Vokabelverzeichnis nt; **learn** ~ Vokabeln lernen

vocal a, **-ly** adv stimmlich; (vociferous) lautstark

vocalist n Sänger(in) m(f)

vocation n Berufung f. ~**al** a Berufs-

vociferous a lautstark

vodka n Wodka m

vogue n Mode f

voice n Stimme f ● vt zum Ausdruck bringen. ~ **mail** n Voicemail f

void a leer; (not valid) ungültig; ~ **of** ohne ● n Leere f

volatile a flüchtig; <person> sprunghaft

volcanic a vulkanisch

volcano n Vulkan m

volley n (of gunfire) Salve f; (Tennis) Volley m

volt n Volt nt. ~**age** n (Electr) Spannung f

voluble a, **-bly** adv redselig; <protest> wortreich

volume n (book) Band m; (Geom) Rauminhalt m; (amount) Ausmaß nt; (Radio, TV) Lautstärke f

voluntary a, **-ily** adv freiwillig

volunteer n Freiwillige(r) m/f ● vt anbieten; geben <information> ● vi sich freiwillig melden

vomit n Erbrochene(s) nt ● vt erbrechen ● vi sich übergeben

voracious a gefräßig; <appetite> unbändig

vot|e n Stimme f; (ballot) Abstimmung f; (right) Wahlrecht nt ● vi abstimmen; (in election) wählen. ~**er** n Wähler(in) m(f)

vouch vi ~ **for** sich verbürgen für. ~**er** n Gutschein m

vowel n Vokal m

voyage n Seereise f; (in space) Reise f, Flug m

vulgar a vulgär, ordinär. ~**ity** n Vulgarität f

vulnerable a verwundbar

vulture n Geier m

wad n Bausch m; (bundle) Bündel
nt. **~ding** n Wattierung f
waddle vi watscheln
wade vi waten
wafer n Waffel f
waffle[1] vi 🗈 schwafeln
waffle[2] n (Culin) Waffel f
waft vt/i wehen
wag v (pt/pp wagged) ● vt wedeln
mit ● vi wedeln
wage n, & **~s** pl Lohn m
wager n Wette f
wagon n Wagen m; (Rail)
Waggon m
wail n [klagender] Schrei m ● vi
heulen; (lament) klagen
waist n Taille f. **~coat** n Weste f.
~line n Taille f
wait n Wartezeit f; lie in **~** for
auflauern (+ dat) ● vi warten (for
auf + acc); (at table) servieren; **~**
on bedienen ● vt **~** one's turn
warten, bis man an der Reihe ist
waiter n Kellner m; **~!** Herr
Ober!
waiting: ~-list n Warteliste f. **~-**
room n Warteraum m; (doctor's)
Wartezimmer nt
waitress n Kellnerin f
waive vt verzichten auf (+ acc)
wake[1] n Totenwache f ● v (pt
woke, pp woken) **~** [up] ● vt
[auf]wecken ● vi aufwachen
wake[2] n (Naut) Kielwasser nt; in
the **~** of im Gefolge (+ gen)
Wales n Wales nt
walk n Spaziergang m; (gait)
Gang m; (path) Weg m; go for a **~**
spazieren gehen ● vi gehen; (not
ride) laufen, zu Fuß gehen;
(ramble) wandern; learn to **~**
laufen lernen ● vt ausführen

<dog>. **~** out vi hinausgehen;
<workers:> in den Streik treten;
~ out on s.o. jdn verlassen
walker n Spaziergänger(in) m(f);
(rambler) Wanderer m/Wanderin
f
walking n Gehen nt; (rambling)
Wandern nt. **~-stick** n
Spazierstock m
wall n Wand f; (external) Mauer f;
drive s.o. up the **~** 🗈 jdn auf die
Palme bringen ● vt **~** up
zumauern
wallet n Brieftasche f
wallflower n Goldlack m
wallop vt (pt/pp walloped) 🗈
schlagen
wallow vi sich wälzen; (fig)
schwelgen
wallpaper n Tapete f ● vt
tapezieren
walnut n Walnuss f
waltz n Walzer m ● vi Walzer
tanzen
wander vi umherwandern, 🗈
bummeln; (fig: digress)
abschweifen. **~** about vi
umherwandern
wangle vt 🗈 organisieren
want n Mangel m (of an + dat);
(hardship) Not f; (desire)
Bedürfnis nt ● vt wollen; (need)
brauchen; **[to have]** sth etw
haben wollen; **~** to do sth etw
tun wollen; I **~** you to go ich will,
dass du gehst; it **~s** painting es
müsste gestrichen werden ● vi he
doesn't **~** for anything ihm fehlt
es an nichts. **~ed** a <criminal>
gesucht
war n Krieg m; be at **~** sich im
Krieg befinden
ward n [Kranken]saal m; (unit)
Station f; (of town) Wahlbezirk
m; (child) Mündel nt ● vt **~** off
abwehren
warden n (of hostel)
Heimleiter(in) m(f); (of youth

hostel) Herbergsvater m;
(*supervisor*) Aufseher(in) m(f)
warder n Wärter(in) m(f)
wardrobe n Kleiderschrank m;
(*clothes*) Garderobe f
warehouse n Lager nt; (*building*)
Lagerhaus nt
wares npl Waren pl
war: ~**fare** n Krieg m. ~**like** a
kriegerisch
warm a (**-er**, **-est**), **-ly** adv warm;
<*welcome*> herzlich; **I am** ~ mir
ist warm ●vt wärmen. ~ **up** vt
aufwärmen ●vi warm werden;
(*Sport*) sich aufwärmen. ~-
hearted a warmherzig
warmth n Wärme f
warn vt warnen (**of** vor + dat).
~**ing** n Warnung f; (*advance
notice*) Vorwarnung f; (*caution*)
Verwarnung f
warp vt verbiegen ●vi sich
verziehen
warrant n (*for arrest*) Haftbefehl
m; (*for search*)
Durchsuchungsbefehl m ●vt
(*justify*) rechtfertigen;
(*guarantee*) garantieren
warranty n Garantie f
warrior n Krieger m
warship n Kriegsschiff nt
wart n Warze f
wartime n Kriegszeit f
wary a (**-ier**, **-iest**), **-ily** adv
vorsichtig; (*suspicious*)
misstrauisch
was see **be**
wash n Wäsche f; (*Naut*) Wellen
pl; **have a** ~ sich waschen ●vt
waschen; spülen <*dishes*>;
aufwischen <*floor*>; ~ **one's
hands** sich (dat) die Hände
waschen ●vi sich waschen. ~
out vt auswaschen; ausspülen
<*mouth*>. ~ **up** vt/i abwaschen,
spülen ●vi (*Amer*) sich waschen
washable a waschbar
wash-basin n Waschbecken nt

washer n (*Techn*) Dichtungsring
m; (*machine*) Waschmaschine f
washing n Wäsche f. ~**-machine**
n Waschmaschine f. ~**-powder** n
Waschpulver nt. ~**-up** n
Abwasch m; **do the** ~**-up**
abwaschen, spülen. ~**-up liquid** n
Spülmittel nt
wasp n Wespe f
waste n Verschwendung f;
(*rubbish*) Abfall m; ~**s** pl Öde f
●a <*product*> Abfall- ●vt
verschwenden ●vi ~ **away**
immer mehr abmagern
waste: ~**ful** a verschwenderisch.
~ **land** n Ödland nt. ~ **paper** n
Altpapier nt. ~**-paper basket** n
Papierkorb m
watch n Wache f; (*timepiece*)
[Armband]uhr f ●vt beobachten;
sich (dat) ansehen <*film, match*>;
(*keep an eye on*) achten auf (+
acc); ~ **television** fernsehen ●vi
zusehen. ~ **out** vi Ausschau
halten (**for** nach); (*be careful*)
aufpassen
watch: ~**dog** n Wachhund m.
~**ful** a, **-ly** adv wachsam. ~**man** n
Wachmann m
water n Wasser nt; ~**s** pl
Gewässer nt ●vt gießen <*garden,
plant*>; (*dilute*) verdünnen ●vi
<*eyes:*> tränen; **my mouth was**
~**ing** mir lief das Wasser im
Munde zusammen. ~ **down** vt
verwässern
water: ~**colour** n Wasserfarbe f;
(*painting*) Aquarell nt. ~**cress** n
Brunnenkresse f. ~**fall** n
Wasserfall m
watering-can n Gießkanne f
water: ~**-lily** n Seerose f. ~
logged a be ~**logged** <*ground:*>
unter Wasser stehen. ~ **polo** n
Wasserball m. ~**proof** a
wasserdicht. ~**skiing** n
Wasserskilaufen nt. ~**tight** a
wasserdicht. ~**way** n
Wasserstraße f

W

watery *a* wässrig

watt *n* Watt *nt*

wave *n* Welle *f*; (*gesture*) Handbewegung *f*; (*as greeting*) Winken *nt* ● *vt* winken mit; (*brandish*) schwingen; wellen <*hair*>; ~ **one's hand** winken ● *vi* winken (**to** *dat*); <*flag*> wehen. ~**length** *n* Wellenlänge *f*

waver *vi* schwanken

wavy *a* wellig

wax *n* Wachs *nt*; (*in ear*) Schmalz *nt* ● *vt* wachsen. ~**works** *n* Wachsfigurenkabinett *nt*

way *n* Weg *m*; (*direction*) Richtung *f*; (*respect*) Hinsicht *f*; (*manner*) Art *f*; (*method*) Art und Weise *f*; ~**s** *pl* Gewohnheiten *pl*; **on the** ~ auf dem Weg (**to** nach/zu); (*under way*) unterwegs; **a little/long** ~ ein kleines/ganzes Stück; **a long** ~ **off** weit weg; **this** ~ hierher; (*like this*) so; **which** ~ in welche Richtung; (*how*) wie; **by the** ~ übrigens; **in some** ~**s** in gewisser Hinsicht; **either** ~ so oder so; **in this** ~ auf diese Weise; **in a** ~ in gewisser Weise; **lead the** ~ vorausgehen; **make** ~ Platz machen (**for** *dat*); **'give** ~**'** (*Auto*) 'Vorfahrt beachten'; **get one's [own]** ~ seinen Willen durchsetzen ● *adv* weit; ~ **behind** weit zurück. ~ **in** *n* Eingang *m*

way out *n* Ausgang *m*; (*fig*) Ausweg *m*

WC *abbr* WC *nt*

we *pron* wir

weak *a* (**-er, -est**), **-ly** *adv* schwach; <*liquid*> dünn. ~**en** *vt* schwächen ● *vi* schwächer werden. ~**ling** *n* Schwächling *m*. ~**ness** *n* Schwäche *f*

wealth *n* Reichtum *m*; (*fig*) Fülle *f* (**of** an + *dat*). ~**y** *a* (**-ier, -iest**) reich

weapon *n* Waffe *f*

wear *n* (*clothing*) Kleidung *f*; ~ **and tear** Abnutzung *f*, Verschleiß

m ● *v* (*pt* **wore**, *pp* **worn**) ● *vt* tragen; (*damage*) abnutzen; **what shall I** ~? was soll ich anziehen? ● *vi* sich abnutzen; (*last*) halten. ~ **off** *vi* abgehen; <*effect*> nachlassen. ~ **out** *vt* abnutzen; (*exhaust*) erschöpfen ● *vi* sich abnutzen

weary *a* (**-ier, -iest**), **-ily** *adv* müde

weather *n* Wetter *nt*; **in this** ~ bei diesem Wetter; **under the** ~ 🛈 nicht ganz auf dem Posten ● *vt* abwettern <*storm*>; (*fig*) überstehen

weather: ~**-beaten** *a* verwittert; wettergegerbt <*face*>. ~ **forecast** *n* Wettervorhersage *f*

weave[1] *vi* (*pt/pp* **weaved**) sich schlängeln (**through** durch)

weave[2] *n* (*Tex*) Bindung *f* ● *vt* (*pt* **wove**, *pp* **woven**) weben. ~**r** *n* Weber *m*

web *n* Netz *nt*. **the W**~ das Web; ~**cam** *n* Webcam *f*, Webkamera *f*. ~**master** *n* Webmaster *m*. ~**page** *n* Webseite *f*. ~**site** *n* Website *f*

wed *vt/i* (*pt/pp* **wedded**) heiraten. ~**ding** *n* Hochzeit *f*

wedding: ~ **day** *n* Hochzeitstag *m*. ~ **dress** *n* Hochzeitskleid *nt*. ~**-ring** *n* Ehering *m*, Trauring *m*

wedge *n* Keil *m* ● *vt* festklemmen

Wednesday *n* Mittwoch *m*

wee *a* 🛈 klein ● *vi* Pipi machen

weed *n* & ~**s** *pl* Unkraut *nt* ● *vt/i* jäten. ~ **out** *vt* (*fig*) aussieben

weedkiller *n* Unkrautvertilgungsmittel *nt*

weedy *a* 🛈 spillerig

week *n* Woche *f*. ~**day** *n* Wochentag *m*. ~**end** *n* Wochenende *nt*

weekly *a* & *adv* wöchentlich ● *n* Wochenzeitschrift *f*

weep *vi* (*pt/pp* **wept**) weinen

weigh *vt/i* wiegen. ~ **down** *vt* (*fig*) niederdrücken. ~ **up** *vt* (*fig*) abwägen

weight n Gewicht nt; **put on/lose ∼** zunehmen/abnehmen
weight-lifting n Gewichtheben nt
weighty a (-ier, -iest) schwer; (important) gewichtig
weir n Wehr nt.
weird a (-er, -est) unheimlich; (bizarre) bizarr
welcome a willkommen; **you're ∼!** nichts zu danken! **you're ∼ to (have) it** das können Sie gerne haben ●n Willkommen nt ●vt begrüßen
weld vt schweißen. **∼er** n Schweißer m
welfare n Wohl nt; (Admin) Fürsorge f. **W∼ State** n Wohlfahrtsstaat m
well[1] n Brunnen m; (oil ∼) Quelle f
well[2] adv (better, best) gut; **as ∼** auch; **as ∼ as** (in addition) sowohl … als auch; **∼ done!** gut gemacht! ●a gesund; **he is not ∼** es geht ihm nicht gut; **get ∼ soon!** gute Besserung! ●int nun, na
well: ∼-behaved a artig. **∼-being** n Wohl nt
wellingtons npl Gummistiefel pl
well: ∼-known a bekannt. **∼-off** a wohlhabend; **be ∼-off** gut dransein. **∼-to-do** a wohlhabend
Welsh a walisisch ●n (Lang) Walisisch nt; **the ∼** pl die Waliser. **∼man** n Waliser m
went see **go**
wept see **weep**
were see **be**
west n Westen m; **to the ∼ of** westlich von ●a West-, west- ●adv nach Westen. **∼erly** a westlich. **∼ern** a westlich ●n Western m
West: ∼ Germany n Westdeutschland nt. **∼ Indian** a westindisch ●n Westinder(in) m(f). **∼ Indies** npl Westindische Inseln pl

westward[s] adv nach Westen
wet a (wetter, wettest) nass; <🄵 person> weichlich, lasch; **'∼ paint'** 'frisch gestrichen' ●vt (pt/pp wet or wetted) nass machen
whack vt 🄵 schlagen. **∼ed** a 🄵 kaputt
whale n Wal m
wharf n Kai m

---

what

● pronoun

····▸ (in questions) was. **what is it?** was ist das? **what do you want?** was wollen Sie? **what is your name?** wie heißen Sie? **what?** (🄵 say that again) wie?; was? **what is the time?** wie spät ist es? (indirect) **I didn't know what to do** ich wusste nicht, was ich machen sollte

❗ The equivalent of a preposition with **what** in English is a special word in German beginning with wo- (wor- before a vowel): **for what? what for?** = wofür? wozu? **from what?** wovon? **on what?** worauf? worüber? **under what?** worunter? **with what?** womit? etc. **what do you want the money for?** wozu willst du das Geld? **what is he talking about?** wovon redet er?

····▸ (relative pronoun) was. **do what I tell you** tu, was ich dir sage. **give me what you can** gib mir, so viel du kannst. **what little I know** das bisschen, das ich weiß. **I don't agree with what you are saying** ich stimme dem nicht zu, was Sie sagen

····▸ (in phrases) **what about me?** was ist mit mir? **what about a cup of coffee?** wie wäre es mit einer Tasse Kaffee? **what if she doesn't come?** was ist, wenn sie nicht kommt?

● *adjective*

····➤ *(asking for selection)* welcher (*m*), welche (*f*), welches (*nt*), welche (*pl*). **what book do you want?** welches Buch willst du haben? **what colour are the walls?** welche Farbe haben die Wände? **I asked him what train to take** ich habe ihn gefragt, welchen Zug ich nehmen soll

····➤ *(asking how much/many)* **what money does he have?** wie viel Geld hat er? **what time is it?** wie spät ist es? **what time does it start?** um wie viel Uhr fängt es an?

····➤ **what kind of ...?** was für [ein(e)]? **what kind of man is he?** was für ein Mensch ist er?

····➤ *(in exclamations)* was für (+ *nom*). **what a fool you are!** was für ein Dummkopf du doch bist! **what cheek/luck!** was für eine Frechheit/ein Glück! **what a huge house!** was für ein riesiges Haus! **what a lot of people!** was für viele Leute!

whatever *a* [egal] welche(r,s) ● *pron* was ... auch; ~ **is it?** was ist das bloß? ~ **he does** was er auch tut; **nothing ~** überhaupt nichts

whatsoever *pron & a* ≈ **whatever**

wheat *n* Weizen *m*

wheel *n* Rad *nt*; *(pottery)* Töpferscheibe *f*; *(steering ~)* Lenkrad *nt*; **at the ~** am Steuer ● *vt (push)* schieben ● *vi* kehrtmachen; *(circle)* kreisen

wheel: ~**barrow** *n* Schubkarre *f*. ~**chair** *n* Rollstuhl *m*. ~**clamp** *n* Parkkralle *f*

when *adv* wann; **the day ~** der Tag, an dem ● *conj* wenn; *(in the past)* als; *(although)* wo ... doch; ~ **swimming/reading** beim Schwimmen/Lesen

whenever *conj & adv* [immer] wenn; *(at whatever time)* wann immer; ~ **did it happen?** wann ist das bloß passiert?

where *adv & conj* wo; ~ **[to]** wohin; ~ **[from]** woher

whereabouts[1] *adv* wo

whereabouts[2] *n* Verbleib *m*; *(of person)* Aufenthaltsort *m*

whereas *conj* während; *(in contrast)* wohingegen

whereupon *adv* worauf[hin]

wherever *conj & adv* wo immer; *(to whatever place)* wohin immer; *(from whatever place)* woher immer; *(everywhere)* überall wo; ~ **possible** wenn irgend möglich

whether *conj* ob

which

● *adjective*

····➤ *(in questions)* welcher (*m*), welche (*f*), welches (*nt*), welche (*pl*). **which book do you need?** welches Buch brauchst du? **which one?** welcher/welche/ welches? **which ones?** welche? **which one of you did it?** wer von euch hat es getan? **which way?** *(which direction)* welche Richtung?; *(where)* wohin?; *(how)* wie?

····➤ *(relative)* **he always comes at one, at which time I'm having lunch/by which time I've finished** er kommt immer um ein Uhr; dann esse ich gerade zu Mittag/bis dahin bin ich schon fertig

● *pronoun*

····➤ *(in questions)* welcher (*m*), welche (*f*), welches (*nt*), welche (*pl*). **which is which?** welcher/ welche/welches ist welcher/ welche/welches? **which of you?** wer von euch?

····➤ *(relative)* der (*m*), die (*f*), das (*nt*), die (*pl*); *(genitive)* dessen (*m, nt*), deren (*f, pl*); *(dative)*

dem (*m, nt*), der (*f*), denen (*pl*); (*referring to a clause*) was. **the book which I gave you** das Buch, das ich dir gab. **the trial, the result of which we are expecting** der Prozess, dessen Ergebnis wir erwarten. **the house of which I was speaking** das Haus, von dem *od* wovon ich redete. **after which** wonach; nach dem. **on which** worauf; auf dem. **the shop opposite which we parked** der Laden, gegenüber dem wir parkten. **everything which I tell you** alles, was ich dir sage

whichever *a & pron* [egal] welche(r,s); ~ **it is** was es auch ist

while *n* Weile *f*; **a long** ~ lange; **be worth** ~ sich lohnen; **it's worth my** ~ es lohnt sich für mich ●*conj* während; (*as long as*) solange; (*although*) obgleich ●*vt* ~ **away** sich (*dat*) vertreiben

whilst *conj* während

whim *n* Laune *f*

whimper *vi* wimmern; <*dog:*> winseln

whine *vi* winseln

whip *n* Peitsche *f*; (*Pol*) Einpeitscher *m* ●*vt* (*pt/pp* whipped) peitschen; (*Culin*) schlagen. ~**ped cream** *n* Schlagsahne *f*

whirl *vt/i* wirbeln. ~**pool** *n* Strudel *m*. ~**-wind** *n* Wirbelwind *m*

whirr *vi* surren

whisk *n* (*Culin*) Schneebesen *m* ●*vt* (*Culin*) schlagen

whisker *n* Schnurrhaar *nt*

whisky *n* Whisky *m*

whisper *n* Flüstern *nt* ●*vt/i* flüstern

whistle *n* Pfiff *m*; (*instrument*) Pfeife *f* ●*vt/i* pfeifen

white *a* (**-r, -st**) weiß ●*n* Weiß *nt*; (*of egg*) Eiweiß *nt*; (*person*) Weiße(r) *m/f*

white: ~ **coffee** *n* Kaffee *m* mit Milch. ~**-collar worker** *n* Angestellte(r) *m*. ~ **lie** *n* Notlüge *f*

whiten *vt* weiß machen ●*vi* weiß werden

whiteness *n* Weiß *nt*

Whitsun *n* Pfingsten *nt*

whiz[z] *vi* (*pt/pp* whizzed) zischen. ~**-kid** *n* 🄵 Senkrechtstarter *m*

who *pron* wer; (*acc*) wen; (*dat*) wem ●*rel pron* der/die/das, (*pl*) die

whoever *pron* wer [immer]; ~ **he is** wer er auch ist; ~ **is it?** wer ist das bloß?

whole *a* ganz; <*truth*> voll ●*n* Ganze(s) *nt*; **as a** ~ als Ganzes; **on the** ~ im Großen und Ganzen; **the** ~ **of Germany** ganz Deutschland

whole: ~**food** *n* Vollwertkost *f*. ~**-hearted** *a* rückhaltlos. ~**meal** *a* Vollkorn-

wholesale *a* Großhandels- ●*adv* en gros; (*fig*) in Bausch und Bogen. ~**r** *n* Großhändler *m*

wholly *adv* völlig

whom *pron* wen; **to** ~ wem ●*rel pron* den/die/das, (*pl*) die; (*dat*) dem/der/dem, (*pl*) denen

whopping *a* 🄵 Riesen-

whore *n* Hure *f*

whose *pron* wessen; ~ **is that?** wem gehört das? ●*rel pron* dessen/deren/dessen, (*pl*) deren

why *adv* warum; (*for what purpose*) wozu; **that's** ~ darum

wick *n* Docht *m*

wicked *a* böse; (*mischievous*) frech, boshaft

wicker *n* Korbgeflecht *nt* ●*attrib* Korb-

wide *a* (**-r, -st**) weit; (*broad*) breit; (*fig*) groß ●*adv* weit; (*off target*) daneben; ~ **awake** hellwach; **far**

and ∼ weit und breit. ∼ly adv
weit; <known, accepted> weithin;
<differ> stark
widen vt verbreitern; (fig)
erweitern ● vi sich verbreitern
widespread a weit verbreitet
widow n Witwe f. ∼ed a
verwitwet. ∼er n Witwer m
width n Weite f; (breadth) Breite f
wield vt schwingen; ausüben
<power>
wife n (pl wives) [Ehe]frau f
wig n Perücke f
wiggle vi wackeln ● vt wackeln
mit
wild a (-er, -est), -ly adv wild;
<animal> wild lebend; <flower>
wild wachsend; (furious) wütend
● adv wild; **run** ∼ frei
herumlaufen ● n **in the** ∼ wild;
the ∼**s** pl die Wildnis f
wilderness n Wildnis f; (desert)
Wüste f
wildlife n Tierwelt f

will¹
● auxiliary verb
past **would**
····► (expressing the future)
werden. **she will arrive tomorrow**
sie wird morgen ankommen. **he
will be there by now** er wird jetzt
schon da sein
····► (expressing intention) (present
tense) **will you go?** gehst du? **I
promise I won't do it again** ich
verspreche, ich machs nicht
noch mal
····► (in requests) **will/would you
please tidy up?** würdest du bitte
aufräumen? **will you be quiet!**
willst du ruhig sein!
····► (in invitations) **will you have/
would you like some wine?** wollen
Sie/möchten Sie Wein?
····► (negative: refuse to) nicht
wollen. **they won't help me** sie
wollen mir nicht helfen. **the car**

won't start das Auto will nicht
anspringen
····► (in tag questions) nicht wahr.
you'll be back soon, won't you? du
kommst bald wieder, nicht
wahr? **you will help her, won't
you?** du hilfst ihr doch, nicht
wahr?
····► (in short answers) **Will you be
there? — Yes I will** Wirst du da
sein? — Ja

will² n Wille m; (document)
Testament nt
willing a willig; (eager)
bereitwillig; **be** ∼ bereit sein. ∼ly
adv bereitwillig; (gladly) gern.
∼ness n Bereitwilligkeit f
willow n Weide f
will-power n Willenskraft f
wilt vi welk werden, welken
wily a (-ier, -iest) listig
win n Sieg m ● v (pt/pp won; pres
p winning) ● vt gewinnen;
bekommen <scholarship> ● vi
gewinnen; (in battle) siegen. ∼
over vt auf seine Seite bringen
wince vi zusammenzucken
winch n Winde f ● vt ∼ up
hochwinden
wind¹ n Wind m; (🩺 flatulence)
Blähungen pl ● vt ∼ s.o. jdm den
Atem nehmen
wind² v (pt/pp wound) ● vt (wrap)
wickeln; (move by turning)
kurbeln; aufziehen <clock> vi
<road:> sich winden. ∼ **up** vt
aufziehen <clock>; schließen
<proceedings>
wind: ∼ **farm** n Windpark m. ∼
instrument n Blasinstrument nt.
∼**mill** n Windmühle f
window n Fenster nt; (of shop)
Schaufenster nt
window: ∼**-box** n Blumenkasten
m. ∼**-cleaner** n Fensterputzer m.
∼**-pane** n Fensterscheibe f. ∼**-
shopping** n Schaufensterbummel
m. ∼**-sill** n Fensterbrett nt

windpipe n Luftröhre f
windscreen n, (Amer) **windshield** n Windschutzscheibe f. **~-wiper** n Scheibenwischer m
wind surfing n Windsurfen nt
windy a (-ier, -iest) windig
wine n Wein m
wine: **~-bar** n Weinstube f. **~ glass** n Weinglas nt. **~-list** n Weinkarte f
winery n (Amer) Weingut nt
wine-tasting n Weinprobe f
wing n Flügel m; (Auto) Kotflügel m; **~s** pl (Theat) Kulissen pl
wink n Zwinkern nt; **not sleep a ~** kein Auge zutun ● vi zwinkern; <light:> blinken
winner n Gewinner(in) m(f); (Sport) Sieger(in) m(f)
winning a siegreich; <smile> gewinnend. **~-post** n Zielpfosten m. **~s** npl Gewinn m
wint|er n Winter m. **~ry** a winterlich
wipe n **give sth a ~** etw abwischen ● vt abwischen; aufwischen <floor>; (dry) abtrocknen. **~ out** vt (cancel) löschen; (destroy) ausrotten. **~ up** vt aufwischen
wire n Draht m
wiring n [elektrische] Leitungen pl
wisdom n Weisheit f; (prudence) Klugheit f. **~ tooth** n Weisheitszahn m
wise a (-r, -st), **-ly** adv weise; (prudent) klug
wish n Wunsch m ● vt wünschen; **~ s.o. well** jdm alles Gute wünschen; **I ~ you could stay** ich wünschte, du könntest hier bleiben ● vi sich (dat) etwas wünschen. **~ful** a **~ful thinking** Wunschdenken nt
wistful a, **-ly** adv wehmütig
wit n Geist m, Witz m; (intelligence) Verstand m; (person) geistreicher Mensch m;

be at one's ~s' end sich (dat) keinen Rat mehr wissen
witch n Hexe f. **~craft** n Hexerei f
with prep mit (+ dat); **~ fear/cold** vor Angst/Kälte; **~ it** damit; **I'm going ~ you** ich gehe mit; **take it ~ you** nimm es mit; **I haven't got it ~ me** ich habe es nicht bei mir
withdraw v (pt -drew, pp -drawn) ● vt zurückziehen; abheben <money> ● vi sich zurückziehen. **~al** n Zurückziehen nt; (of money) Abhebung f; (from drugs) Entzug m
wither vi [ver]welken
withhold vt (pt/pp -held) vorenthalten (from s.o. jdm)
within prep innerhalb (+ gen) ● adv innen
without prep ohne (+ acc); **~ my noticing it** ohne dass ich es merkte
withstand vt (pt/pp -stood) standhalten (+ dat)
witness n Zeuge m/ Zeugin f ● vt Zeuge/Zeugin sein (+ gen); bestätigen <signature>
witticism n geistreicher Ausspruch m
witty a (-ier, -iest) witzig, geistreich
wives see **wife**
wizard n Zauberer m
wizened a verhutzelt
wobb|le vi wackeln. **~ly** a wackelig
woke, woken see **wake**[1]
wolf n (pl **wolves**) Wolf m
woman n (pl **women**) Frau f. **~izer** n Schürzenjäger m
womb n Gebärmutter f
women npl see **woman**
won see **win**
wonder n Wunder nt; (surprise) Staunen nt ● vt/i sich fragen; (be surprised) sich wundern; **I ~** da frage ich mich; **I ~ whether she is**

W

ill ob sie wohl krank ist? **~ful** *a*,
-ly *adv* wunderbar
won't = will not
wood *n* Holz *nt*; (*forest*) Wald *m*;
touch ~! unberufen!
wood: ~ed *a* bewaldet. **~en** *a*
Holz-; (*fig*) hölzern. **~pecker** *n*
Specht *m*. **~wind** *n* Holzbläser
pl. **~work** *n* (*wooden parts*)
Holzteile *pl*; (*craft*) Tischlerei *f*.
~worm *n* Holzwurm *m*
wool *n* Wolle *f* ● *attrib* Woll-.
~len *a* wollen
woolly *a* (**-ier, -iest**) wollig; (*fig*)
unklar
word *n* Wort *nt*; (*news*) Nachricht
f; **by ~ of mouth** mündlich; **have a
~ with** sprechen mit; **have ~s**
einen Wortwechsel haben. **~ing**
n Wortlaut *m*. **~ processor** *n*
Textverarbeitungssystem *nt*
wore *see* **wear**
work *n* Arbeit *f*; (*Art, Literature*)
Werk *nt*; **~s** *pl* (*factory,
mechanism*) Werk *nt*; **at ~** bei der
Arbeit; **out of ~** arbeitslos ● *vi*
arbeiten; <*machine, system:*>
funktionieren; (*have effect*)
wirken; (*study*) lernen; **it won't ~**
(*fig*) es klappt nicht ● *vt* arbeiten
lassen; bedienen <*machine*>;
betätigen <*lever*>. **~ off** *vt*
abarbeiten. **~ out** *vt* ausrechnen;
(*solve*) lösen ● *vi* gut gehen, 🄸
klappen. **~ up** *vt* aufbauen; sich
(*dat*) holen <*appetite*>; **get ~ed
up** sich aufregen
workable *a* (*feasible*)
durchführbar
worker *n* Arbeiter(in) *m(f)*
working *a* berufstätig; <*day,
clothes*> Arbeits-; **be in ~ order**
funktionieren. **~ class** *n*
Arbeiterklasse *f*
work: ~man *n* Arbeiter *m*;
(*craftsman*) Handwerker *m*.
~manship *n* Arbeit *f*. **~shop** *n*
Werkstatt *f*

world *n* Welt *f*; **in the ~** auf der
Welt; **think the ~ of s.o.** große
Stücke auf jdn halten. **~ly** *a*
weltlich; <*person*> weltlich
gesinnt. **~-wide** *a & adv* weltweit
worm *n* Wurm *m*
worn *see* **wear** ● *a* abgetragen.
~-out *a* abgetragen; <*carpet*>
abgenutzt; <*person*> erschöpft
worried *a* besorgt
worry *n* Sorge *f* ● *v* (*pt/pp*
worried) ● *vt* beunruhigen;
(*bother*) stören ● *vi* sich
beunruhigen, sich (*dat*) Sorgen
machen. **~ing** *a* beunruhigend
worse *a & adv* schlechter; (*more
serious*) schlimmer ● *n*
Schlechtere(s) *nt*; Schlimmere(s)
nt
worsen *vt* verschlechtern ● *vi*
sich verschlechtern
worship *n* Anbetung *f*; (*service*)
Gottesdienst *m*. ● *vt* (*pt/pp*
-shipped) anbeten
worst *a* schlechteste(r,s); (*most
serious*) schlimmste(r,s) ● *adv*
am schlechtesten; am
schlimmsten ● *n* **the ~** das
Schlimmste
worth *n* Wert *m*; **£10's ~ of petrol**
Benzin für £10 ● *a* **be ~ £5** £5
wert sein; **be ~ it** (*fig*) sich
lohnen. **~less** *a* wertlos. **~while**
a lohnend
worthy *a* würdig
would *v aux* **I ~ do it** ich würde es
tun, ich täte es; **~ you go?**
würdest du gehen? **he said he
~n't** er sagte, er würde es nicht
tun; **what ~ you like?** was
möchten Sie?
wound¹ *n* Wunde *f* ● *vt*
verwunden
wound² *see* **wind²**
wove, woven *see* **weave²**
wrangle *n* Streit *m*
wrap *n* Umhang *m* ● *vt* (*pt/pp*
wrapped) **~ [up]** wickeln;
einpacken <*present*> ● *vi* **~ up**

warmly sich warm einpacken.
~per *n* Hülle *f*. **~ping** *n*
Verpackung *f*

wrath *n* Zorn *m*

wreath *n* (*pl* **-s**) Kranz *m*

wreck *n* Wrack *nt* ●*vt* zerstören;
zunichte machen <*plans*>;
zerrütten <*marriage*>. **~age** *n*
Wrackteile *pl*; (*fig*) Trümmer *pl*

wren *n* Zaunkönig *m*

wrench *n* Ruck *m*; (*tool*)
Schraubenschlüssel *m*; **be a ~**
(*fig*) weh tun ●*vt* reißen; **~ sth
from s.o.** jdm etw entreißen

wrestl|e *vi* ringen. **~er** *n* Ringer
m. **~ing** *n* Ringen <*hands*>

wretch *n* Kreatur *f*. **~ed** *a* elend;
(*very bad*) erbärmlich

wriggle *n* Zappeln *nt* ●*vi*
zappeln; (*move forward*) sich
schlängeln; **~ out of sth** 🛈 sich
vor etw (*dat*) drücken

wring *vt* (*pt/pp* **wrung**) wringen;
(**~ out**) auswringen; umdrehen
<*neck*>; ringen <*hands*>

wrinkle *n* Falte *f*; (*on skin*)
Runzel *f* ●*vt* kräuseln ●*vi* sich
kräuseln, sich falten. **~d** *a*
runzlig

wrist *n* Handgelenk *nt*. **~-watch** *n*
Armbanduhr *f*

write *vt/i* (*pt* **wrote**, *pp* **written**,
pres p **writing**) schreiben. **~ down**
vt aufschreiben. **~ off** *vt*
abschreiben; zu Schrott fahren
<*car*>

write-off *n* ≈ Totalschaden *m*

writer *n* Schreiber(in) *m(f)*;
(*author*) Schriftsteller(in) *m(f)*

writhe *vi* sich winden

writing *n* Schreiben *nt*;
(*handwriting*) Schrift *f*; **in ~**
schriftlich. **~-paper** *n*
Schreibpapier *nt*

written *see* **write**

wrong *a*, **-ly** *adv* falsch; (*morally*)
unrecht; (*not just*) ungerecht; **be
~** nicht stimmen; <*person:*>
Unrecht haben; **what's ~?** was ist

los? ●*adv* falsch; **go ~** <*person:*>
etwas falsch machen; <*machine:*>
kaputtgehen; <*plan:*> schief
gehen ●*n* Unrecht *nt* ●*vt*
Unrecht tun (+ *dat*). **~ful** *a*
ungerechtfertigt. **~fully** *adv*
<*accuse*> zu Unrecht

wrote *see* **write**

wrung *see* **wring**

wry *a* (**-er**, **-est**) ironisch;
<*humour*> trocken

Xmas *n* 🛈 Weihnachten *nt*

X-ray *n* (*picture*)
Röntgenaufnahme *f*; **~s** *pl*
Röntgenstrahlen *pl* ●*vt* röntgen;
durchleuchten <*luggage*>

yacht *n* Jacht *f*; (*for racing*)
Segeljacht *f*. **~ing** *n* Segeln *nt*

yank *vt* 🛈 reißen

Yank *n* 🛈 Ami *m* 🛈

yap *vi* (*pt/pp* **yapped**) <*dog:*>
kläffen

yard¹ *n* Hof *m*; (*for storage*) Lager
nt

yard² *n* Yard *nt* (= *0,91 m*)

yarn *n* Garn *nt*; (🛈 *tale*)
Geschichte *f*

yawn *n* Gähnen *nt* ●*vi* gähnen

year n Jahr nt; (of wine) Jahrgang m; **for** ~**s** jahrelang. ~**ly** a & adv jährlich

yearn vi sich sehnen (**for** nach). ~**ing** n Sehnsucht f

yeast n Hefe f

yell n Schrei m ●vi schreien

yellow a gelb ●n Gelb nt

yelp vi jaulen

yes adv ja; (contradicting) doch ●n Ja nt

yesterday n & adv gestern; ~**'s paper** die gestrige Zeitung; **the day before** ~ vorgestern

yet adv noch; (in question) schon; (nevertheless) doch; **as** ~ bisher; **not** ~ noch nicht; **the best** ~ das bisher beste ●conj doch

Yiddish n Jiddisch nt

yield n Ertrag m ● vt bringen; abwerfen <profit> ● vi nachgeben; (Amer, Auto) die Vorfahrt beachten

yoga n Yoga m

yoghurt n Joghurt m

yoke n Joch nt; (of garment) Passe f

yolk n Dotter m, Eigelb nt

you pron du; (acc) dich; (dat) dir; (pl) ihr; (acc, dat) euch; (formal) (nom & acc, sg & pl) Sie; (dat, sg & pl) Ihnen; (one) man; (acc) einen; (dat) einem; **all of** ~ ihr/ Sie alle; **I know** ~ ich kenne dich/euch/Sie; **I'll give** ~ **the money** ich gebe dir/euch/Ihnen das Geld; **it does** ~ **good** es tut einem gut; **it's bad for** ~ es ist ungesund

young a (-er, -est) jung ●npl (animals) Junge pl; **the** ~ die Jugend f. ~**ster** n Jugendliche(r) m/f; (child) Kleine(r) m/f

your a dein; (pl) euer; (formal) Ihr

yours poss pron deine(r), deins;

(pl) eure(r), euers; (formal, sg & pl) Ihre(r), Ihr[e]s; **a friend of** ~ ein Freund von dir/Ihnen/euch; **that is** ~ das gehört dir/Ihnen/ euch

yourself pron (pl -**selves**) selbst; (refl) dich; (dat) dir; (pl) euch; (formal) sich; **by** ~ allein

youth n (pl -**s**) Jugend f; (boy) Jugendliche(r) m. ~**ful** a jugendlich. ~ **hostel** n Jugendherberge f

Yugoslavia n Jugoslawien nt

zeal n Eifer m

zealous a, -**ly** adv eifrig

zebra n Zebra nt. ~ **crossing** n Zebrastreifen m

zero n Null f

zest n Begeisterung f

zigzag n Zickzack m ●vi (pt/pp -**zagged**) im Zickzack laufen/ (in vehicle) fahren

zinc n Zink nt

zip n ~ [**fastener**] Reißverschluss m ● vt ~ [**up**] den Reißverschluss zuziehen an (+ dat)

zip code n (Amer) Postleitzahl f

zipper n Reißverschluss m

zodiac n Tierkreis m

zone n Zone f

zoo n Zoo m

zoological a zoologisch

zoolog|ist n Zoologe m/gin f. ~**y** Zoologie f

zoom vi sausen. ~ **lens** n Zoomobjektiv nt

Summary of German grammar

Regular verbs

Most German verbs are regular and add the same endings to
their stem. You find the stem by taking away the **-en** (or
sometimes just **-n**) from the end of the infinitive. The
infinitive of the verb, for example **machen**, is the form you
look up in the dictionary. The stem of **machen** is **mach-**.
There are six endings for each tense, to go with the different
pronouns:

ich = *I*   du = *you*   er/sie/es = *he/she/it*
wir = *we*   ihr = *you*   sie/Sie = *they/you (polite form)*.

Present tense

For example, *I make, I am making,* or *I do make*:

infinitive	ich	du	er/sie/es	wir	ihr	sie/Sie
machen	mache	machst	macht	machen	macht	machen

Imperfect tense

For example, *I made, I was making,* or *I used to make*:

infinitive	ich	du	er/sie/es	wir	ihr	sie/Sie
machen	machte	machtest	machte	machten	machtet	machten

Future tense

For example, *I will make* or *I shall make*. This is formed by
using the present tense of **werden**, which is the equivalent of
will or *shall*, with the infinitive verb: **ich werde machen**.

infinitive	ich	du	er/sie/es	wir	ihr	sie/Sie
werden	werde	wirst	wird	werden	werdet	werden

Perfect tense

For example, *I made* or *I have made*. For most German verbs
the perfect is formed by using the present tense of **haben**,
which is the equivalent of *have*, with the past participle: **ich
habe gemacht**. Some verbs take **sein** instead of **haben**, and
these are all marked (*sein*) in the dictionary. They are mainly
verbs expressing motion and involving a change of place:

he drove to Berlin today = er ist heute nach Berlin gefahren

Or they express a change of state, and this includes verbs meaning to happen (**geschehen**, **passieren**, **vorkommen**):

he woke up = er ist aufgewacht

infinitive	ich	du	er/sie/es	wir	ihr	sie/Sie
haben	habe	hast	hat	haben	habt	haben
sein	bin	bist	ist	sind	seid	sind

Irregular verbs and other forms

Some German verbs are irregular and change their stem or add different endings. All the irregular verbs that appear in the dictionary are given in the section *German irregular verbs* on pages 601–606.

The subjunctive

This is a form of the verb that is used to express speculation, doubt, or unlikelihood. It is rarely used in English (*if I were you* instead of *if I was you* is an exceptional example), but is still used in both written and spoken German.

Present tense

infinitive	ich	du	er/sie/es	wir	ihr	sie/Sie
machen	mache	machest	mache	machen	machet	machen
sein	sei	sei(e)st	sei	seien	seid	seien

Imperfect tense

For regular verbs this is the same as the normal imperfect forms, but irregular verbs vary.

infinitive	ich	du	er/sie/es	wir	ihr	sie/Sie
machen	machte	machtest	machte	machten	machtet	machten
werden	würde	würdest	würde	würden	würdet	würden
sein	wäre	wär(e)st	wäre	wären	wär(e)t	wären

The imperfect subjunctive of werden is used with an infinitive to form the conditional tense. This tense expresses what would happen if something else occurred.

he would go = er würde gehen
I wouldn't do that = das würde ich nicht machen

Reflexive verbs

The object of a reflexive verb is the same as its subject. In German, the object is a reflexive pronoun. This is usually in the accusative (I wash = **ich wasche mich**). The reflexive pronouns of some verbs are in the dative (I imagine = **ich stelle mir vor**), and these are marked in the English–German part of the dictionary with (*dat*).

infinitive	ich	du	er/sie/es	wir	ihr	sie/Sie
sich waschen	wasche mich	wäschst dich	wäscht sich	waschen uns	wascht euch	waschen sich
sich vorstellen	stelle mir vor	stellst dir vor	stellt sich vor	stellen uns vor	stellt euch vor	stellen sich vor

The passive

In the passive form, the subject of the verb experiences the action rather than performs it: he was asked = **er wurde gefragt**. In German, the passive is formed using parts of **werden** with the past participle:

PRESENT PASSIVE	*it is done*	es wird gemacht
IMPERFECT PASSIVE	*it was done*	es wurde gemacht
FUTURE PASSIVE	*it will be done*	es wird gemacht werden
PERFECT PASSIVE	*it has been done*	es ist gemacht worden

When forming the perfect passive, note that the past participle of **werden** becomes **worden** rather than **geworden**.

Separable verbs

Separable verbs are marked in the German–English part of the dictionary with the label *sep*. In the perfect tense, the **ge-** of the past participle comes between the prefix and the verb, for example **er/sie/es hat angefangen**.

Articles

There are two articles in English, the definite article *the* and the indefinite article *a/an*. The way these are translated into German depends on the gender, number, and case of the noun with which the article goes.

There are three genders of nouns in German: masculine (**der Mann** = the man), feminine (**die Frau** = the woman), and neuter (**das Buch** = the book). There are two forms of number: singular (**der Baum** = the tree) and plural (**die Bäume** = the trees). And there are four cases, which show the part a noun plays in a sentence: nominative, accusative, genitive, and dative.

Definite article

the = der/die/das, (*plural*) = die

| | SINGULAR | | | PLURAL |
	masculine	feminine	neuter	all genders
NOMINATIVE	**der** Mann	**die** Frau	**das** Buch	**die** Bäume
ACCUSATIVE	**den** Mann	**die** Frau	**das** Buch	**die** Bäume
GENITIVE	**des** Mannes	**der** Frau	**des** Buches	**der** Bäume
DATIVE	**dem** Mann	**der** Frau	**dem** Buch	**den** Bäumen

Indefinite article

a/an = ein/eine/ein. This article can only be singular.

	masculine	feminine	neuter
NOMINATIVE	**ein** Mann	**eine** Frau	**ein** Buch
ACCUSATIVE	**einen** Mann	**eine** Frau	**ein** Buch
GENITIVE	**eines** Mannes	**einer** Frau	**eines** Buches
DATIVE	**einem** Mann	**einer** Frau	**einem** Buch

Nouns

In German, all nouns start with a capital letter: **das Buch** = the book.

Gender

There are three genders of nouns in German: masculine (**der Mann** = the man), feminine (**die Frau** = the woman), and neuter (**das Buch** = the book). These three examples are logical, with masculine for a male person, feminine for a female person, and neuter for an object. But it is not always like this with German nouns. Gender is sometimes determined by a noun's ending. For example, **das Mädchen** (= the girl) is neuter rather than feminine, simply because the ending **-chen** is always neuter.

The gender of German nouns is given in the dictionary. There are some general rules regarding the gender of groups of nouns, but individual genders must be checked by looking them up.

Masculine nouns

- male persons and animals: **der Arbeiter** = worker; **der Bär** = bear
- 'doers' and 'doing' instruments ending in -er in German: **der Gärtner** = gardener; **der Computer** = computer
- days, months, and seasons: (**der**) **Montag** = Monday

- words ending in **-ich**, **-ig**, and **-ling**: **der Honig** = honey; **der Lehrling** = apprentice
- words ending in **-ismus**, **-ist**, and **-ant**.

Feminine nouns

- female persons and animals: **die Schauspielerin** = actress; **die Henne** = hen; the feminine form of professions and animals is made by adding **-in** to the masculine (**der Schauspieler/die Schauspielerin** = actor/actress)
- nouns ending in **-ei**, **-ie**, **-ik**, **-in**, **-ion**, **-heit**, **-keit**, **-schaft**, **-tät**, **-ung**, **-ur**: **die Gärtnerei** = gardening; **die Energie** = energy
- most nouns ending in **-e**: **die Blume** = flower; note that there are many exceptions, including **der Name** = name, **der Käse** = cheese, **das Ende** = end.

Neuter nouns

- names of continents, most countries, and towns: (**das**) **Deutschland** = Germany; (**das**) **Köln** = Cologne
- nouns ending in **-chen** and **-lein** (indicating *small*): **das Mädchen**, **das Fräulein** = girl.
- most (but not all!) nouns beginning with **Ge-** or ending in **-nis**, **-tel**, or **-um**: **das Geheimnis** = secret; **das Zentrum** = centre
- infinitives of verbs used as nouns: **das Lachen** = laughter; **das Essen** = food.

Compound nouns

When two nouns are put together to make one compound noun, it takes the gender of the second noun:
der Brief + die Marke = die Briefmarke.

Plural

There are no absolutely definitive rules for the plural forms of German nouns. Plurals generally add an ending (**der Freund**, **die Freunde**), and change a vowel to an umlaut (**der Gast**, **die Gäste**; **das Haus**, **die Häuser**). Feminine words ending in **-heit**, **-keit**, and **-ung** add **-en** to make the plural (**die Abbildung**, **die Abbildungen**).

The plurals of all nouns are given in the German–English part of the dictionary.

Case

There are four cases, which show the part a noun plays in a sentence: nominative, accusative, genitive, and dative. The noun's article changes according to the case, and the ending of the noun changes in some cases:

	SINGULAR masculine	feminine	neuter
NOMINATIVE	der Mann	die Frau	das Buch
ACCUSATIVE	den Mann	die Frau	das Buch
GENITIVE	des **Mannes**	der Frau	des **Buches**
DATIVE	dem Mann	der Frau	dem Buch

	PLURAL masculine	feminine	neuter
NOMINATIVE	die Männer	die Frauen	die Bücher
ACCUSATIVE	die Männer	die Frauen	die Bücher
GENITIVE	der Männer	der Frauen	der Bücher
DATIVE	den **Männern**	den Frauen	den **Büchern**

The nominative is used for the subject of a sentence; in sentences with **sein** (to be) and **werden** (to become), the noun after the verb is in the nominative.

the dog barked = der Hund bellte
that is my car = das ist mein Wagen

The accusative is used for the direct object and after some prepositions (listed on page 597):

she has a son = sie hat einen Sohn

The genitive shows possession, and is also used after some prepositions (listed on page 597):

my husband's dog = der Hund meines Mannes

The dative is used for the indirect object. Some German verbs, such as **helfen**, take only the dative. The dative is also used after some prepositions (listed on page 596):

she gave the books to the children = sie gab den Kindern die Bücher

The following sentence combines all four cases:

der Mann gibt der Frau den Bleistift des Mädchens = *the man gives the woman the girl's pencil*
der Mann *is the subject* (*in the nominative*)
gibt *is the verb*
der Frau *is the indirect object* (*in the dative*)
den Bleistift *is the direct object* (*in the accusative*)
des Mädchens *is in the genitive* (*showing possession*).

Adjectives

An adjective is a word qualifying a noun. In German, an adjective in front of a noun adds endings that vary with the noun's gender, number, and case. Adjectives that come after a noun do not add endings.

With the definite article

Adjectives following **der/die/das** take these endings:

	SINGULAR masculine	feminine	neuter	PLURAL all genders
NOMINATIVE	der rote Hut	die rote Lampe	das rote Buch	die roten Autos
ACCUSATIVE	den roten Hut	die rote Lampe	das rote Buch	die roten Autos
GENITIVE	des roten Hutes	der roten Lampe	des roten Buches	der roten Autos
DATIVE	dem roten Hut	der roten Lampe	dem roten Buch	den roten Autos

Some German adjectives follow the pattern of the definite article, and adjectives after them change their endings in the same way as after **der/die/das**. For example, **dieser/diese/dieses** (= this):

	SINGULAR masculine	feminine	neuter	PLURAL all genders
NOMINATIVE	dieser	diese	dieses	diese
ACCUSATIVE	diesen	diese	dieses	diese
GENITIVE	dieses	dieser	dieses	dieser
DATIVE	diesem	dieser	diesem	diesen

Other common examples are:

jeder/jede/jedes = *every, each*
jener/jene/jenes = *that*
mancher/manche/manches = *many a, some*
solcher/solche/solches = *such*
welcher/welche/welches = *which*

With the indefinite article

Adjectives following **ein/eine/ein** take these endings:

	SINGULAR masculine	feminine	neuter
NOMINATIVE	ein roter Hut	eine rote Lampe	ein rotes Buch
ACCUSATIVE	einen roten Hut	eine rote Lampe	ein rotes Buch
GENITIVE	eines roten Hutes	einer roten Lampe	eines roten Buches
DATIVE	einem roten Hut	einer roten Lampe	einem roten Buch

Some German adjectives follow the pattern of the indefinite article, and adjectives after them change their endings in the same way as after **ein/eine/ein**. They are:

dein = *your*	kein = *no*
euer = *your*	mein = *my*
Ihr = *your*	sein = *his/its*
ihr = *her/their*	unser = *our*

These adjectives can also go with plural nouns: no cars = **keine Autos**. All genders take the same endings in the plural:

	PLURAL all genders
NOMINATIVE	keine roten Autos
ACCUSATIVE	keine roten Autos
GENITIVE	keiner roten Autos
DATIVE	keinen roten Autos

Without an article

Adjectives in front of a noun on their own, without an article, take the following endings:

	SINGULAR masculine	feminine	neuter	PLURAL all genders
NOMINATIVE	guter Wein	frische Milch	kaltes Bier	alte Leute
ACCUSATIVE	guten Wein	frische Milch	kaltes Bier	alte Leute
GENITIVE	guten Weins	frischer Milch	kalten Biers	alter Leute
DATIVE	gutem Wein	frischer Milch	kaltem Bier	alten Leuten

Adjectives as nouns

In German, adjectives can be used as nouns, spelt with a capital letter: **alt** = old, **ein Alter** = an old man, **eine Alte** = an old woman.

With the definite article (**der/die/das**), these nouns take the following endings:

	SINGULAR masculine	feminine	PLURAL both genders
NOMINATIVE	der Fremde	die Fremde	die Fremden
ACCUSATIVE	den Fremden	die Fremde	die Fremden
GENITIVE	des Fremden	der Fremden	der Fremden
DATIVE	dem Fremden	der Fremden	den Fremden

The feminine noun refers to a female stranger or foreigner.

With the indefinite article (**ein/eine/ein**), these nouns take the following endings:

	SINGULAR masculine	feminine	**PLURAL** both genders without an article
NOMINATIVE	ein Fremder	eine Fremde	Fremde
ACCUSATIVE	einen Fremden	eine Fremde	Fremde
GENITIVE	eines Fremden	einer Fremden	Fremder
DATIVE	einem Fremden	einer Fremden	Fremden

Comparative and superlative

In English, the comparative of the adjective *small* is *smaller*, and of *difficult* is *more difficult*. The superlatives are *smallest* and *most difficult*. In German, there is just one way to form the comparative and superlative: by adding the endings **-er** and -(e)**st**:

small, smaller, smallest = klein, kleiner, der/die/das kleinste

Many adjectives change their vowel to an umlaut in the comparative and superlative:

cold, colder, coldest = kalt, kälter, der/die/das kälteste

Some important adjectives are irregular:

big, bigger, biggest	= groß, größer, der/die/das größte
good, better, best	= gut, besser, der/die/das beste
high, higher, highest	= hoch, höher, der/die/das höchste
much, more, most	= viel, mehr, der/die/das meiste
near, nearer, nearest	= nah, näher, der/die/das nächste

Comparative and superlative adjectives take the same endings as basic adjectives:

a smaller child	= ein kleineres Kind
the coldest month	= der kälteste Monat

Adverbs

In German almost all adjectives can also be used as adverbs, describing a verb, an adjective, or another adverb.

she sings beautifully = sie singt schön

Some words, such as **auch** (= also), **fast** (= almost), **immer** (= always), and **leider** (= unfortunately) are used only as adverbs:

she is very clever = sie ist sehr klug

Comparative and superlative

The comparative is formed by adding **-er** to the basic adverb,

and the superlative by putting **am** in front of the basic adverb
and adding the ending -(e)**sten**:

clearly, more clearly, most clearly = klar, klarer, am klarsten

Some important adverbs are irregular:

soon, earlier, at the earliest = bald, früher, am frühesten
well, better, best = gut, besser, am besten
willingly, more willingly, most willingly = gern, lieber, am liebsten

Pronouns

Pronouns are words—such as *he*, *which,* and *mine* in
English—that stand instead of a noun.

Personal pronouns

These pronouns, such as he/she/it = **er/sie/es**, refer to
people or things.

	I	you	he/it	she/it	it	we	you	they	you
NOMINATIVE	ich	du	er	sie	es	wir	ihr	sie	Sie
ACCUSATIVE	mich	dich	ihn	sie	es	uns	euch	sie	Sie
DATIVE	mir	dir	ihm	ihr	ihm	uns	euch	ihnen	Ihnen
	me	*you*	*him/it*	*her/it*	*it*	*us*	*you*	*them*	*you*

The genitive form is not given, because it is so rarely used.

In German there are two forms for you, **du** and **Sie**. **Du** is less
formal and is used when speaking to someone you know well,
a child, or a family member. When speaking to a person or a
group of people you do not know very well, use the polite
form, **Sie**.

German pronouns agree in gender with the noun they refer
to. In the nominative case, *it* might be translated by **er** or **sie**,
as well as **es**:

it (the pencil) is red = er (der Bleistift) ist rot
it (the rose) is beautiful = sie (die Rose) ist schön
it (the car) is expensive = es (das Auto) ist teuer

Possessive pronouns

The possessive pronouns are:

mine = meiner/meine/mein(e)s
yours (informal singular) =
  deiner/deine/dein(e)s
his = seiner/seine/sein(e)s
hers = ihrer/ihre/ihr(e)s
its = seiner/seine/sein(e)s

ours = unserer/unsere/unser(e)s
yours (informal plural) =
  eurer/eure/eures
theirs = ihrer/ihre/ihr(e)s
yours (polite) = Ihrer, Ihre, Ihr(e)s

They all take endings like **meiner/meine/mein(e)s**, as follows:

	SINGULAR masculine	feminine	neuter	PLURAL all genders
NOMINATIVE	meiner	meine	mein(e)s	meine
ACCUSATIVE	meinen	meine	mein(e)s	meine
GENITIVE	meines	meiner	meines	meiner
DATIVE	meinem	meiner	meinem	meinen

As can be seen in the table, in the neuter form an -e- can be added (making **meines**). This applies to all the possessive pronouns, but the extra -e- is rare.

Relative pronouns

These pronouns are used to introduce and link a new clause. In English they are *who*, *which*, *that*, and *what*. In German they are **der**, **die**, or **das**, depending on the noun referred to:

	SINGULAR masculine	feminine	neuter	PLURAL all genders
NOMINATIVE	der	die	das	die
ACCUSATIVE	den	die	das	die
GENITIVE	dessen	deren	dessen	deren
DATIVE	dem	der	dem	denen

Relative pronouns can be left out in English, but never in German:

the book (that) I'm reading = das Buch, das ich lese

They agree in gender and number with the noun they refer back to:

the man who visited us = der Mann, der uns besucht hat (**der** is masculine singular)

But the case of the pronoun depends on its function in the clause it introduces:

the pencil I bought yesterday = der Bleistift, den ich gestern gekauft habe

(**den** is masculine singular, but accusative because it is the object of the clause it introduces)

Interrogative pronouns

These pronouns are used to ask questions:

who? = wer?
what? = was?
which? = welcher/welche/welches?

Wer changes as follows:

NOMINATIVE	wer?
ACCUSATIVE	wen?
GENITIVE	wessen?
DATIVE	wem?

Reflexive pronouns

The object of a reflexive verb is the same as its subject. In German, the object is a reflexive pronoun. This is usually in the accusative (I wash = **ich wasche** mich). The reflexive pronouns of some verbs are in the dative (I imagine = **ich stelle** mir **vor**).

Indefinite pronouns

These pronouns do not refer to identifiable people or objects. In German, many indefinite pronouns, such as **etwas** (= something) and **nichts** (= nothing), never change. But some do take endings:

	someone	no one
NOMINATIVE	jemand	niemand
ACCUSATIVE	jemanden	niemanden
DATIVE	jemandem	niemandem

The genitive case is rarely used.

Prepositions

Prepositions are small words like *in*, that stand in front of a noun or pronoun. In German, the noun following a preposition always has to be in one of three cases—dative, accusative, or genitive.

Prepositions can be prefixes and form separable verbs:

to walk along the street = die Straße entlanggehen
he is walking along the street = er geht die Straße entlang

In the dictionary, the case governed by a preposition is given:

mit (+ *dat*) means mit *always takes the dative case.*

The most common case used after prepositions is the dative. The following prepositions always take the dative:

aus	mit	von
außer	nach	zu
bei	seit	

Some prepositions always take the accusative:

bis   entlang   gegen   um
durch   für   ohne

Some prepositions always take the genitive:

anstatt   während
trotz   wegen

There is a group of prepositions that can take the dative or the accusative, depending on the sentence. They are:

an   in   unter
auf   neben   vor
hinter   über   zwischen

If the phrase containing one of these prepositions describes position—where something is happening—the dative case is used:

she sat in the kitchen = sie saß in der Küche

But if the phrase containing the preposition describes movement—motion towards something—the accusative follows:

she went into the kitchen = sie ging in die Küche

Some forms of the definite article are usually shortened when used with prepositions:

am (an dem); **ans** (an das); **aufs** (auf das); **beim** (bei dem); **durchs** (durch das); **fürs** (für das); **im** (in dem); **ins** (in das); **ums** (um das); **vom** (von dem); **zum** (zu dem); **zur** (zu der).

Conjunctions

Conjunctions are small words, such as *and* = **und**, which join clauses together in a sentence.

These common conjunctions link clauses together:

aber = *but*
denn = *for*
oder = *or*
sondern = *but (on the contrary)*
und = *and*

These conjunctions do not change normal word order in the two clauses:

ich gehe, und er kommt auch = *I am going, and he is coming too*

But there are many other conjunctions that send the verb to the end of the subordinate clause:

als = *when*, = *as*	dass = *that*	weil = *because*
bevor = *before*	ob = *whether*	
bis = *until*	während = *while*	
da = *since*	wenn = *when*, = *if*	

er konnte nicht in die Schule gehen, weil er krank war = *he couldn't go to school, because he was ill*

Word order

The basic rule for German word order is that the verb comes second in a sentence. The subject of the sentence usually comes before the verb:

meine Mutter fährt am Freitag nach Köln = *my mother is going to Cologne on Friday*

When the verb is made up of two parts, such as in the perfect and the future tenses, the auxiliary verb comes second in the sentence, while the past participle (in the perfect) or infinitive (in the future tense) goes to the end:

wir haben sehr lang gewartet = *we waited a very long time*
sie wird sicher bald kommen = *she is sure to turn up soon*

Past participles and infinitives go to the end in other sentences too:

ich kann dieses Lied nicht leiden = *I can't stand this song*
du musst hier bleiben = *you must stay here*

When a sentence starts with a subordinate clause, the verb stays in second place:

da ich kein Geld hatte, blieb ich zu Hause = *since I had no money, I stayed at home*

In the clause itself, the verb goes to the end:

er konnte nicht in die Schule gehen, weil er krank war

The relative pronouns **der**, **die**, and **das**, as well as a number of conjunctions, send the verb to the end of the clause:

der Junge, der hier wohnt = *the boy who lives here*

When separable verbs separate, the prefix goes to the end:

der Film fängt um acht Uhr an = *the film starts at 8 o'clock*

In questions and commands, the verb is usually first in the sentence:

kommst du heute Abend? = *are you coming this evening?*
komm schnell rein! = *come in quickly!*

When there are a number of phrases in a sentence, the usual order for the different elements is 1 time, 2 manner, 3 place:

wir fahren heute mit dem Auto nach München = *we are driving to Munich today* (*time* = heute; *manner* = mit dem Auto; *place* = nach München)

German irregular verbs

1st, 2nd, and 3rd person present are given after the infinitive, and past subjunctive after the past indicative, where there is a change of vowel or any other irregularity.

Compound verbs are only given if they do not take the same forms as the corresponding simple verb, e.g. *befehlen*, or if there is no corresponding simple verb, e.g. *bewegen*.

An asterisk (*) indicates a verb which is also conjugated regularly.

Infinitive	Past tense	Past participle
abwägen	wog (wöge) ab	abgewogen
ausbedingen	bedang (bedänge) aus	ausbedungen
backen (du bäckst, er bäckt)	buk (büke)	gebacken
befehlen (du befiehlst, er befiehlt)	befahl (beföhle, befähle)	befohlen
beginnen	begann (begänne)	begonnen
beißen (du/er beißt)	biss (bisse)	gebissen
bergen (du birgst, er birgt)	barg (bärge)	geborgen
bewegen²	bewog (bewöge)	bewogen
biegen	bog (böge)	gebogen
bieten	bot (böte)	geboten
binden	band (bände)	gebunden
bitten	bat (bäte)	gebeten
blasen (du/er bläst)	blies	geblasen
bleiben	blieb	geblieben
bleichen*	blich	geblichen
braten (du brätst, er brät)	briet	gebraten
brechen (du brichst, er bricht)	brach (bräche)	gebrochen
brennen	brannte (brennte)	gebrannt
bringen	brachte (brächte)	gebracht
denken	dachte (dächte)	gedacht
dreschen (du drischst, er drischt)	drosch (drösche)	gedroschen
dringen	drang (dränge)	gedrungen

Infinitive	Past tense	Past participle
dürfen (ich/er darf, du darfst)	durfte (dürfte)	gedurft
empfehlen (du empfiehlst, er empfiehlt)	empfahl (empföhle)	empfohlen
erlöschen (du erlischst, er erlischt)	erlosch (erlösche)	erloschen
erschrecken (du erschrickst, er erschrickt)	erschrak (erschräke)	erschrocken
erwägen	erwog (erwöge)	erwogen
essen (du/er isst)	aß (äße)	gegessen
fahren (du fährst, er fährt)	fuhr (führe)	gefahren
fallen (du fällst, er fällt)	fiel	gefallen
fangen (du fängst, er fängt)	fing	gefangen
fechten (du fichtst, er ficht)	focht (föchte)	gefochten
finden	fand (fände)	gefunden
flechten (du flichtst, er flicht)	flocht (flöchte)	geflochten
fliegen	flog (flöge)	geflogen
fliehen	floh (flöhe)	geflohen
fließen (du/er fließt)	floss (flösse)	geflossen
fressen (du/er frisst)	fraß (fräße)	gefressen
frieren	fror (fröre)	gefroren
gären*	gor (göre)	gegoren
gebären (du gebierst, sie gebiert)	gebar (gebäre)	geboren
geben (du gibst, er gibt)	gab (gäbe)	gegeben
gedeihen	gedieh	gediehen
gehen	ging	gegangen
gelingen	gelang (gelänge)	gelungen
gelten (du giltst, er gilt)	galt (gölte, gälte)	gegolten
genesen (du/er genest)	genas (genäse)	genesen
genießen (du/er genießt)	genoss (genösse)	genossen
geschehen (es geschieht)	geschah (geschähe)	geschehen
gewinnen	gewann (gewönne, gewänne)	gewonnen
gießen (du/er gießt)	goss (gösse)	gegossen
gleichen	glich	geglichen
gleiten	glitt	geglitten
glimmen	glomm (glömme)	geglommen
graben (du gräbst, er gräbt)	grub (grübe)	gegraben
greifen	griff	gegriffen

Infinitive	Past tense	Past participle
haben (du hast, er hat)	hatte (hätte)	gehabt
halten (du hältst, er hält)	hielt	gehalten
hängen[2]	hing	gehangen
hauen	haute	gehauen
heben	hob (höbe)	gehoben
heißen (du/er heißt)	hieß	geheißen
helfen (du hilfst, er hilft)	half (hülfe)	geholfen
kennen	kannte (kennte)	gekannt
klingen	klang (klänge)	geklungen
kneifen	kniff	gekniffen
kommen	kam (käme)	gekommen
können (ich/er kann, du kannst)	konnte (könnte)	gekonnt
kriechen	kroch (kröche)	gekrochen
laden (du lädst, er lädt)	lud (lüde)	geladen
lassen (du/er lässt)	ließ	gelassen
laufen (du läufst, er läuft)	lief	gelaufen
leiden	litt	gelitten
leihen	lieh	geliehen
lesen (du/er liest)	las (läse)	gelesen
liegen	lag (läge)	gelegen
lügen	log (löge)	gelogen
mahlen	mahlte	gemahlen
meiden	mied	gemieden
melken	molk (mölke)	gemolken
messen (du/er misst)	maß (mäße)	gemessen
misslingen	misslang (misslänge)	misslungen
mögen (ich/er mag, du magst)	mochte (möchte)	gemocht
müssen (ich/er muss, du musst)	musste (müsste)	gemusst
nehmen (du nimmst, er nimmt)	nahm (nähme)	genommen
nennen	nannte (nennte)	genannt
pfeifen	pfiff	gepfiffen
preisen (du/er preist)	pries	gepriesen
raten (du rätst, er rät)	riet	geraten
reiben	rieb	gerieben
reißen (du/er reißt)	riss	gerissen
reiten	ritt	geritten
rennen	rannte (rennte)	gerannt
riechen	roch (röche)	gerochen
ringen	rang (ränge)	gerungen
rinnen	rann (ränne)	geronnen

Infinitive	Past tense	Past participle
rufen	rief	gerufen
salzen* (du/er salzt)	salzte	gesalzen
saufen (du säufst, er säuft)	soff (söffe)	gesoffen
saugen*	sog (söge)	gesogen
schaffen[1]	schuf (schüfe)	geschaffen
scheiden	schied	geschieden
scheinen	schien	geschienen
scheißen (du/er scheißt)	schiss	geschissen
schelten (du schiltst, er schilt)	schalt (schölte)	gescholten
scheren[1]	schor (schöre)	geschoren
schieben	schob (schöbe)	geschoben
schießen (du/er schießt)	schoss (schösse)	geschossen
schlafen (du schläfst, er schläft)	schlief	geschlafen
schlagen (du schlägst, er schlägt)	schlug (schlüge)	geschlagen
schleichen	schlich	geschlichen
schleifen[2]	schliff	geschliffen
schließen (du/er schließt)	schloss (schlösse)	geschlossen
schlingen	schlang (schlänge)	geschlungen
schmeißen (du/er schmeißt)	schmiss (schmisse)	geschmissen
schmelzen (du/er schmilzt)	schmolz (schmölze)	geschmolzen
schneiden	schnitt	geschnitten
schrecken* (du schrickst, er schrickt)	schrak (schräke)	geschreckt
schreiben	schrieb	geschrieben
schreien	schrie	geschrie[e]n
schreiten	schritt	geschritten
schweigen	schwieg	geschwiegen
schwellen (du schwillst, er schwillt)	schwoll (schwölle)	geschwollen
schwimmen	schwamm (schwömme)	geschwommen
schwinden	schwand (schwände)	geschwunden
schwingen	schwang (schwänge)	geschwungen
schwören	schwor (schwüre)	geschworen
sehen (du siehst, er sieht)	sah (sähe)	gesehen
sein (ich bin, du bist, er ist, wir sind, ihr seid, sie sind)	war (wäre)	gewesen

Infinitive	Past tense	Past participle
senden[1]	sandte (sendete)	gesandt
sieden	sott (sötte)	gesotten
singen	sang (sänge)	gesungen
sinken	sank (sänke)	gesunken
sitzen (du/er sitzt)	saß (säße)	gesessen
sollen (ich/er soll, du sollst)	sollte	gesollt
spalten*	spaltete	gespalten
spinnen	spann (spönne, spänne)	gesponnen
sprechen (du sprichst, er spricht)	sprach (spräche)	gesprochen
sprießen (du/er sprießt)	spross (sprösse)	gesprossen
springen	sprang (spränge)	gesprungen
stechen (du stichst, er sticht)	stach (stäche)	gestochen
stehen	stand (stünde, stände)	gestanden
stehlen (du stiehlst, er stiehlt)	stahl (stähle)	gestohlen
steigen	stieg	gestiegen
sterben (du stirbst, er stirbt)	starb (stürbe)	gestorben
stinken	stank (stänke)	gestunken
stoßen (du/er stößt)	stieß	gestoßen
streichen	strich	gestrichen
streiten	stritt	gestritten
tragen (du trägst, er trägt)	trug (trüge)	getragen
treffen (du triffst, er trifft)	traf (träfe)	getroffen
treiben	trieb	getrieben
treten (du trittst, er tritt)	trat (träte)	getreten
triefen*	troff (tröffe)	getroffen
trinken	trank (tränke)	getrunken
trügen	trog (tröge)	getrogen
tun (du tust, er tut)	tat (täte)	getan
verderben (du verdirbst, er verdirbt)	verdarb (verdürbe)	verdorben
vergessen (du/er vergisst)	vergaß (vergäße)	vergessen
verlieren	verlor (verlöre)	verloren
verzeihen	verzieh	verziehen
wachsen[1] (du/er wächst)	wuchs (wüchse)	gewachsen
waschen (du wäschst, er wäscht)	wusch (wüsche)	gewaschen
wenden[2]*	wandte (wendete)	gewandt
werben (du wirbst, er wirbt)	warb (würbe)	geworben

Infinitive	Past tense	Past participle
werden (du wirst, er wird)	wurde (würde)	geworden
werfen (du wirfst, er wirft)	warf (würfe)	geworfen
wiegen[1]	wog (wöge)	gewogen
winden	wand (wände)	gewunden
wissen (ich/er weiß, du weißt)	wusste (wüsste)	gewusst
wollen (ich/er will, du willst)	wollte	gewollt
wringen	wrang (wränge)	gewrungen
ziehen	zog (zöge)	gezogen
zwingen	zwang (zwänge)	gezwungen